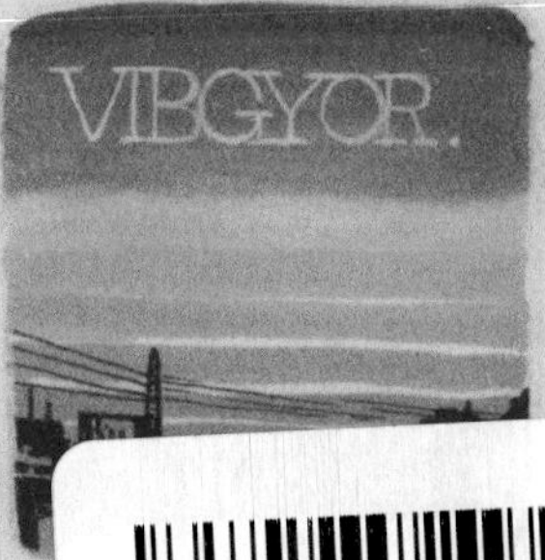
VIBGYOR.

The new workspace I moved into last year is a bit small, but at dawn, when I open the front door after work, I can see the sunrise. The sky lights up like a fiery rainbow. Lately ... been working until ... e just to catch the ... t's not that I have ... rk all night because I ... till noon every day. I ... just look at that ... se.

-Tite Kubo, 2005

Bleach is author Tite Kubo's second title. Kubo made his debut with *Zombie Powder*, a four-volume series for *Weekly Shonen Jump*. To date, *Bleach* has been translated into numerous languages and has also inspired an animated TV series that began airing in Japan in 2004. Beginning its serialization in 2001, *Bleach* is still a mainstay in the pages of *Weekly Shonen Jump*. In 2005, *Bleach* was awarded the prestigious Shogakukan Manga Award in the *shonen* (boys) category.

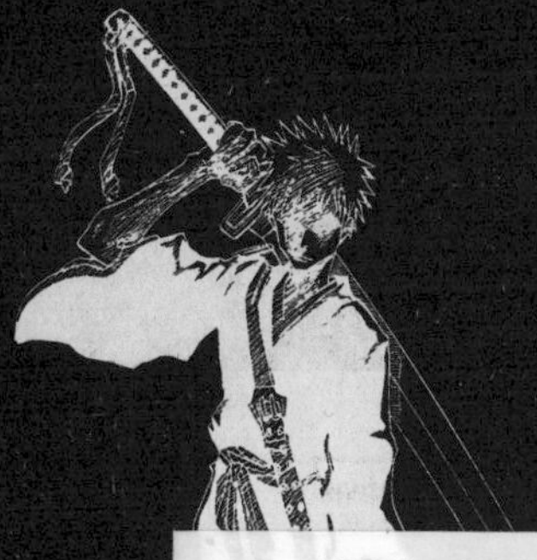

BLEACH
3-in-1 Edition

SHONEN JUMP Manga Omnibus Edition Volume 6
A compilation of the graphic novel volumes 16–18

STORY AND ART BY
TITE KUBO

English Adaptation/Lance Caselman
Translation/Joe Yamazaki
Touch-up Art & Lettering/Mark McMurray, Andy Ristaino
Design - Manga Edition/Sean Lee
Design - Omnibus Edition/Fawn Lau
Editor - Manga Edition/Yuki Takagaki
Editor - Omnibus Edition/Pancha Diaz

Published by VIZ Media, LLC
P.O. Box 77010
San Francisco, CA 94107

10 9 8 7 6 5 4 3 2
Omnibus edition first printing, September 2013
Second printing, August 2017

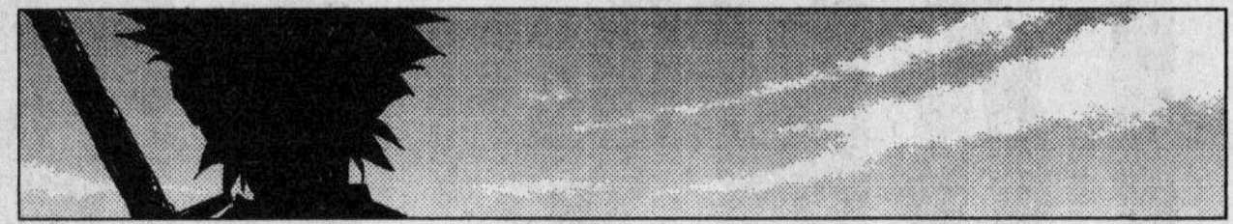

The mane of the sun pouring down
Erases the footprints on thin ice
Do not fear deception
The world already lies atop deception

BLEACH 16

NIGHT OF WIJNRUIT

Shonen Jump Manga

STARS AND

Rukia Kuchiki

Tôshirô Hitsugaya

Ichigo Kurosaki

★ plot

Ichigo and the others struggle to rescue Rukia, who awaits death in a tower of the Seireitei. But Ichigo's decisive battle with Byakuya Kuchiki is delayed while Yoruichi puts him through a crash course on achieving Bankai. Meanwhile, the murder of Captain Aizen casts a pall over the entire Seireitei. Suspecting Gin Ichimaru of the deed, Tôshirô challenges him to a duel. But when Momo suddenly appears between them, Tôshirô finds himself switching from avenger to the accused!

BLEACH ALL

浮竹十四郎
Jûshirô Ukitake

雛森桃
Momo Hinamori

Gin Ichimaru

市丸ギン

STORIES

BLEACH 16

NIGHT OF WIJNRUIT

Contents

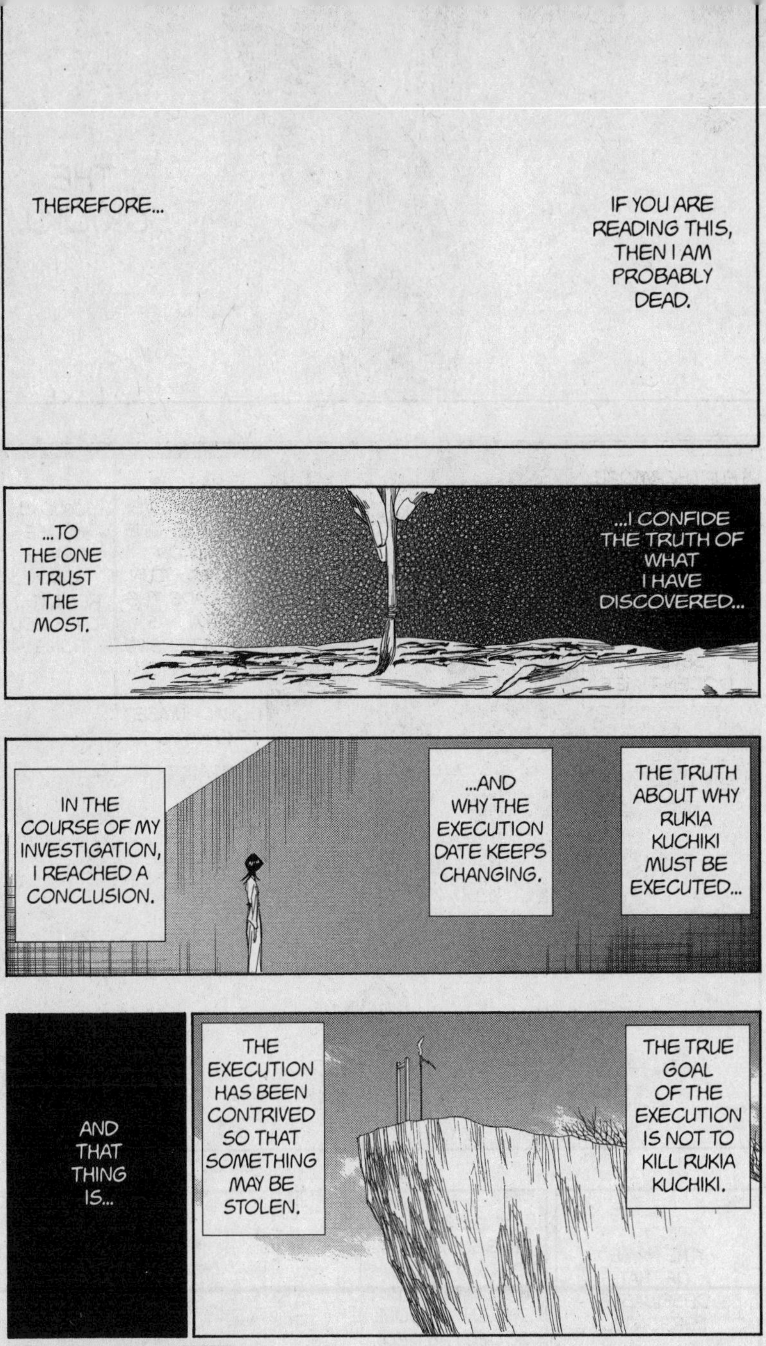
IF YOU ARE READING THIS, THEN I AM PROBABLY DEAD.
THEREFORE...
...I CONFIDE THE TRUTH OF WHAT I HAVE DISCOVERED...
...TO THE ONE I TRUST THE MOST.
THE TRUTH ABOUT WHY RUKIA KUCHIKI MUST BE EXECUTED...
...AND WHY THE EXECUTION DATE KEEPS CHANGING.
IN THE COURSE OF MY INVESTIGATION, I REACHED A CONCLUSION.
THE TRUE GOAL OF THE EXECUTION IS NOT TO KILL RUKIA KUCHIKI.
THE EXECUTION HAS BEEN CONTRIVED SO THAT SOMETHING MAY BE STOLEN.
AND THAT THING IS...

131. The True Will

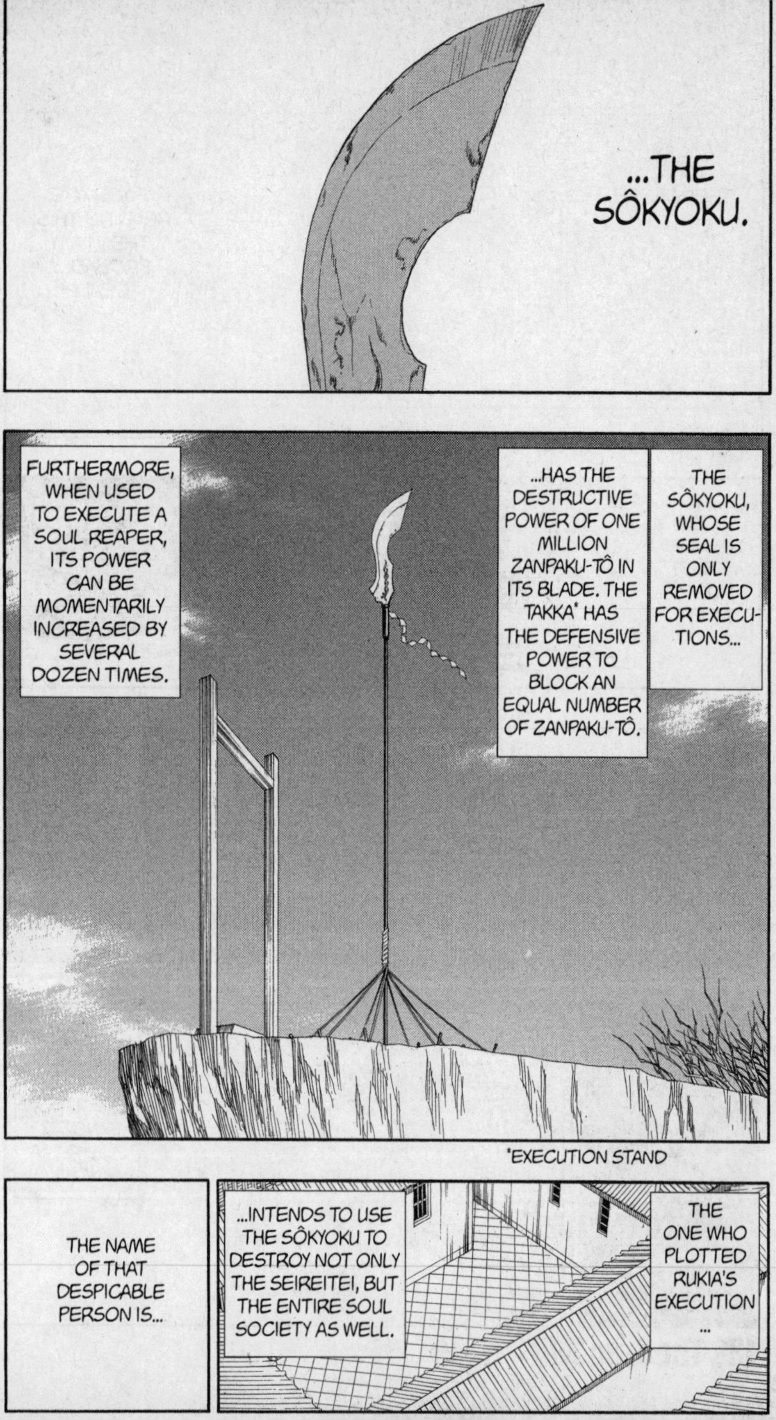
...THE SÔKYOKU.
THE SÔKYOKU, WHOSE SEAL IS ONLY REMOVED FOR EXECUTIONS...
...HAS THE DESTRUCTIVE POWER OF ONE MILLION ZANPAKU-TÔ IN ITS BLADE. THE TAKKA* HAS THE DEFENSIVE POWER TO BLOCK AN EQUAL NUMBER OF ZANPAKU-TÔ.
FURTHERMORE, WHEN USED TO EXECUTE A SOUL REAPER, ITS POWER CAN BE MOMENTARILY INCREASED BY SEVERAL DOZEN TIMES.
*EXECUTION STAND
THE ONE WHO PLOTTED RUKIA'S EXECUTION ...
...INTENDS TO USE THE SÔKYOKU TO DESTROY NOT ONLY THE SEIREITEI, BUT THE ENTIRE SOUL SOCIETY AS WELL.
THE NAME OF THAT DESPICABLE PERSON IS...

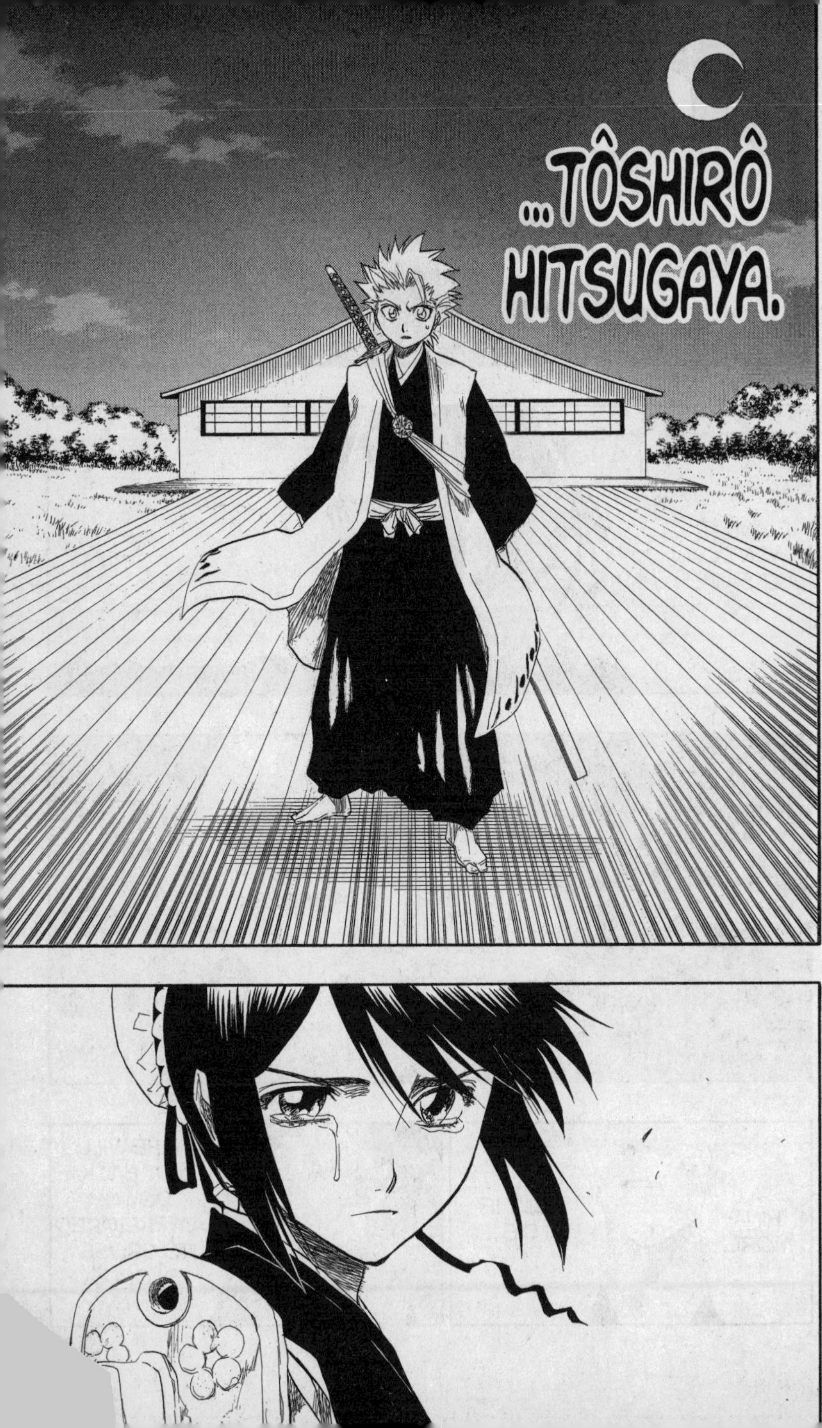
...TÔSHIRÔ HITSUGAYA.

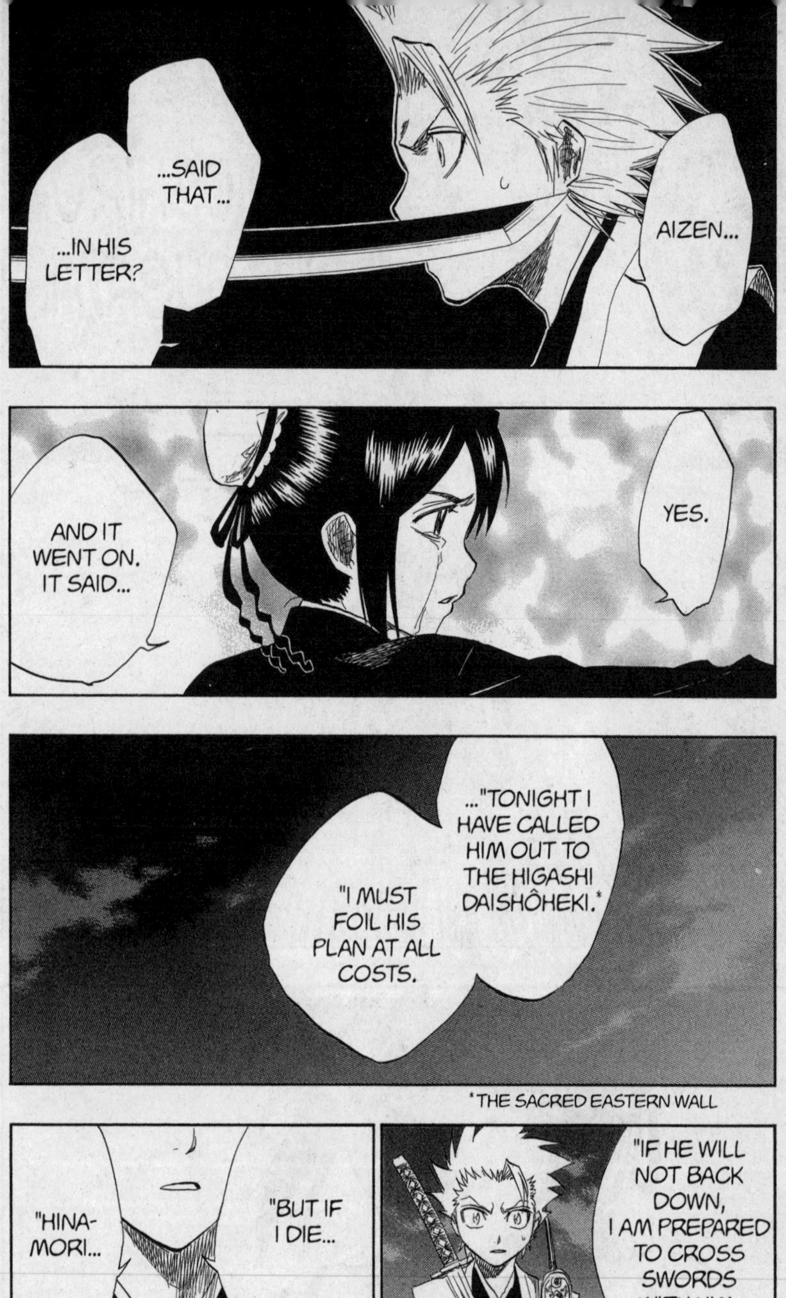
AIZEN...
...SAID THAT...
...IN HIS LETTER?
YES.
AND IT WENT ON. IT SAID...
..."TONIGHT I HAVE CALLED HIM OUT TO THE HIGASHI DAISHÔHEKI.*
"I MUST FOIL HIS PLAN AT ALL COSTS.
*THE SACRED EASTERN WALL
"IF HE WILL NOT BACK DOWN, I AM PREPARED TO CROSS SWORDS WITH HIM.
"BUT IF I DIE...
"HINAMORI...

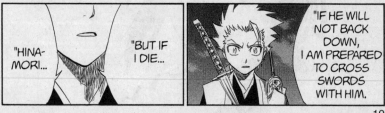

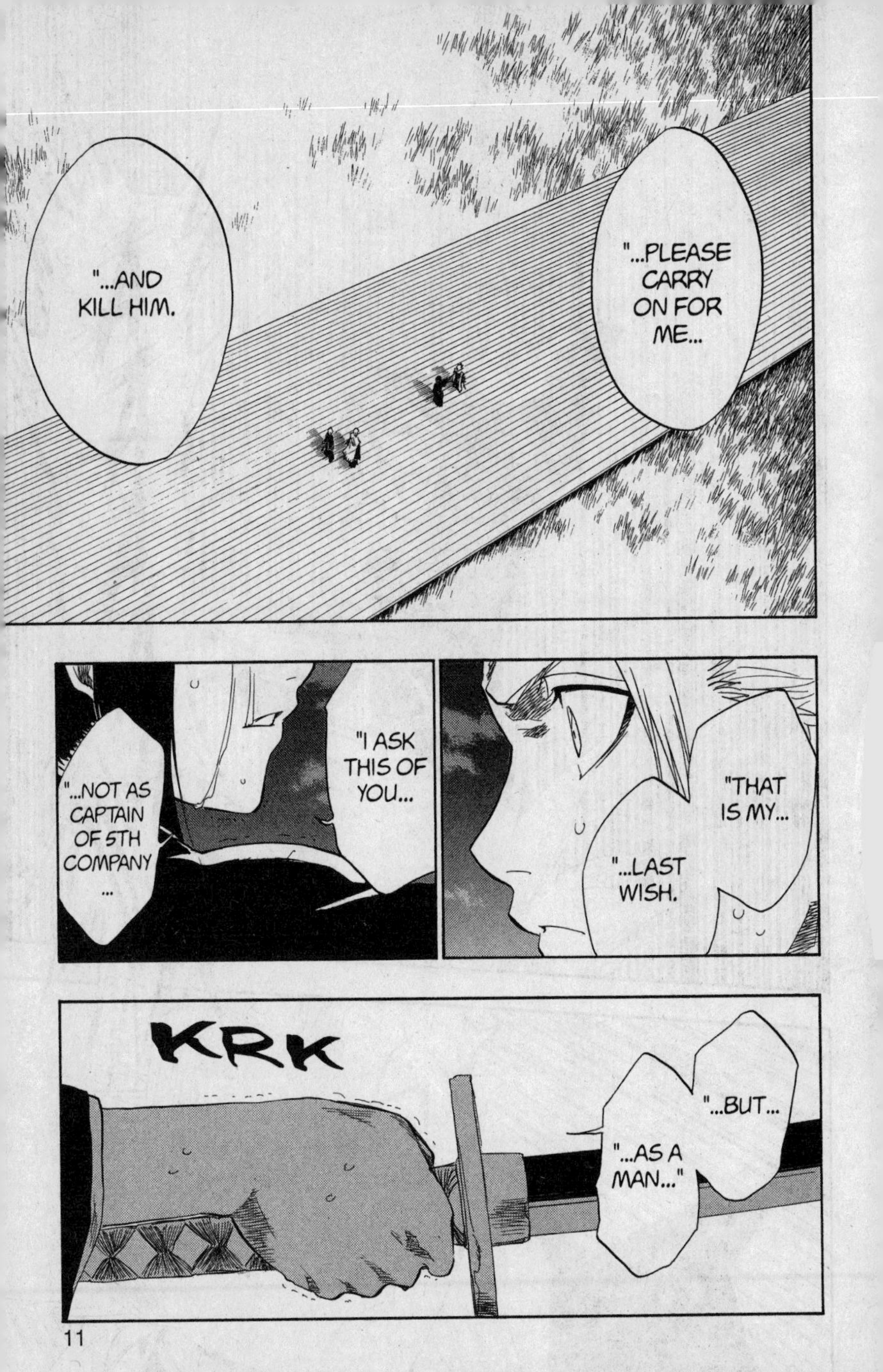
"...PLEASE CARRY ON FOR ME...
"...AND KILL HIM.
"THAT IS MY...
"...LAST WISH.
"I ASK THIS OF YOU...
"...NOT AS CAPTAIN OF 5TH COMPANY ...
"...BUT...
"...AS A MAN..."
KRK

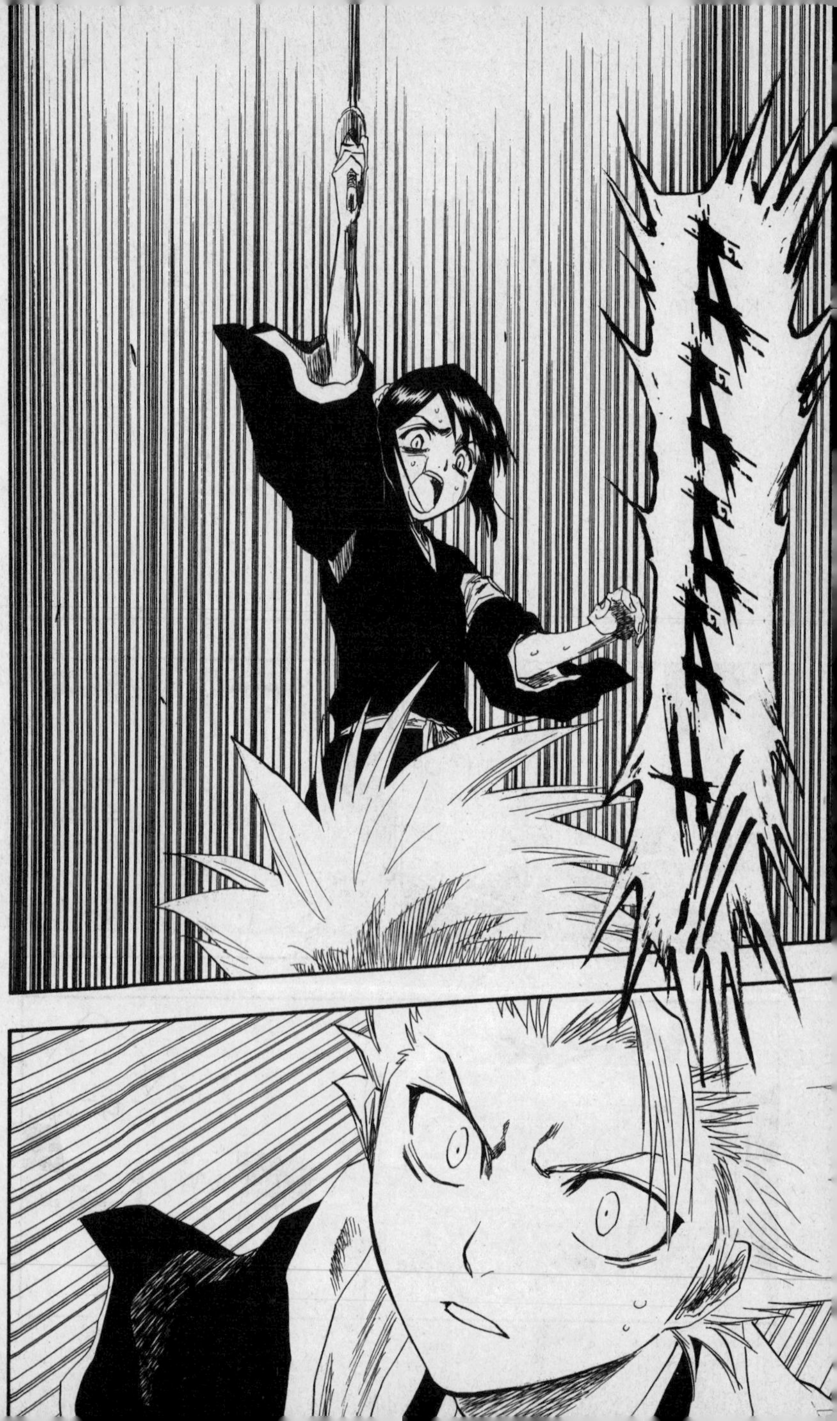
AAAAAH

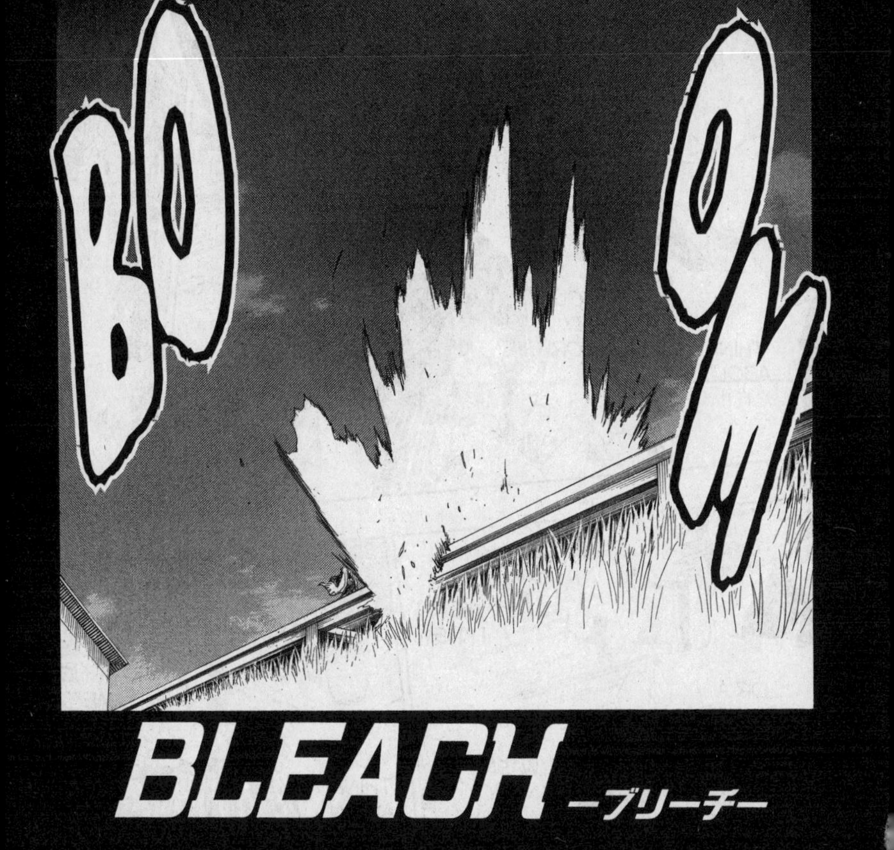
BOOM

BLEACH —ブリーチ—

131. The True Will

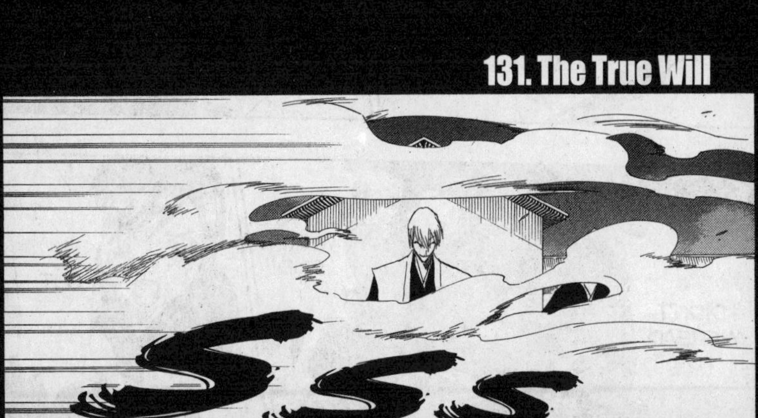
SSS

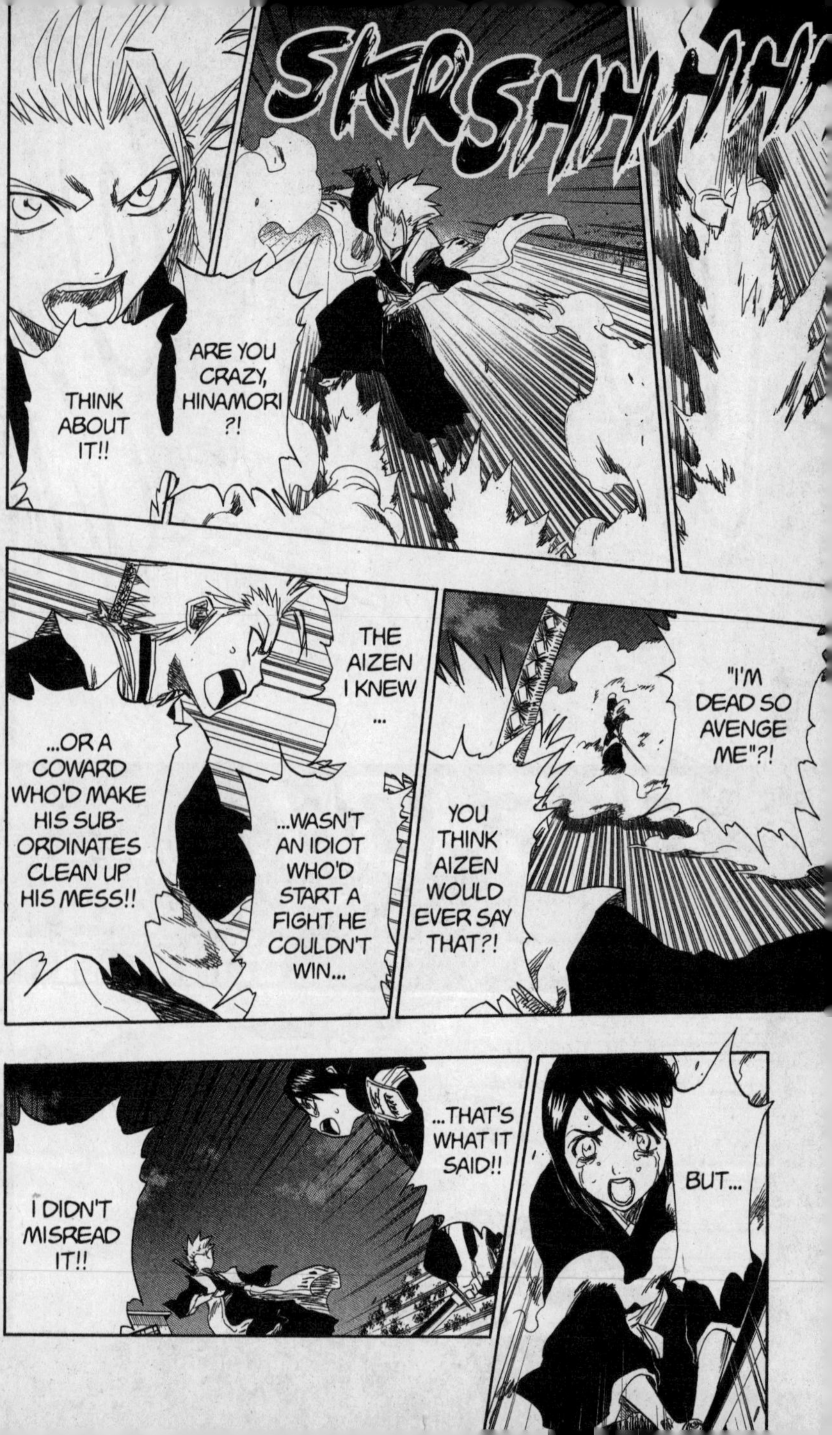
SKRSHHHHH
ARE YOU CRAZY, HINAMORI?!
THINK ABOUT IT!!
"I'M DEAD SO AVENGE ME"?!
YOU THINK AIZEN WOULD EVER SAY THAT?!
THE AIZEN I KNEW...
...WASN'T AN IDIOT WHO'D START A FIGHT HE COULDN'T WIN...
...OR A COWARD WHO'D MAKE HIS SUB-ORDINATES CLEAN UP HIS MESS!!
BUT...
...THAT'S WHAT IT SAID!!
I DIDN'T MISREAD IT!!

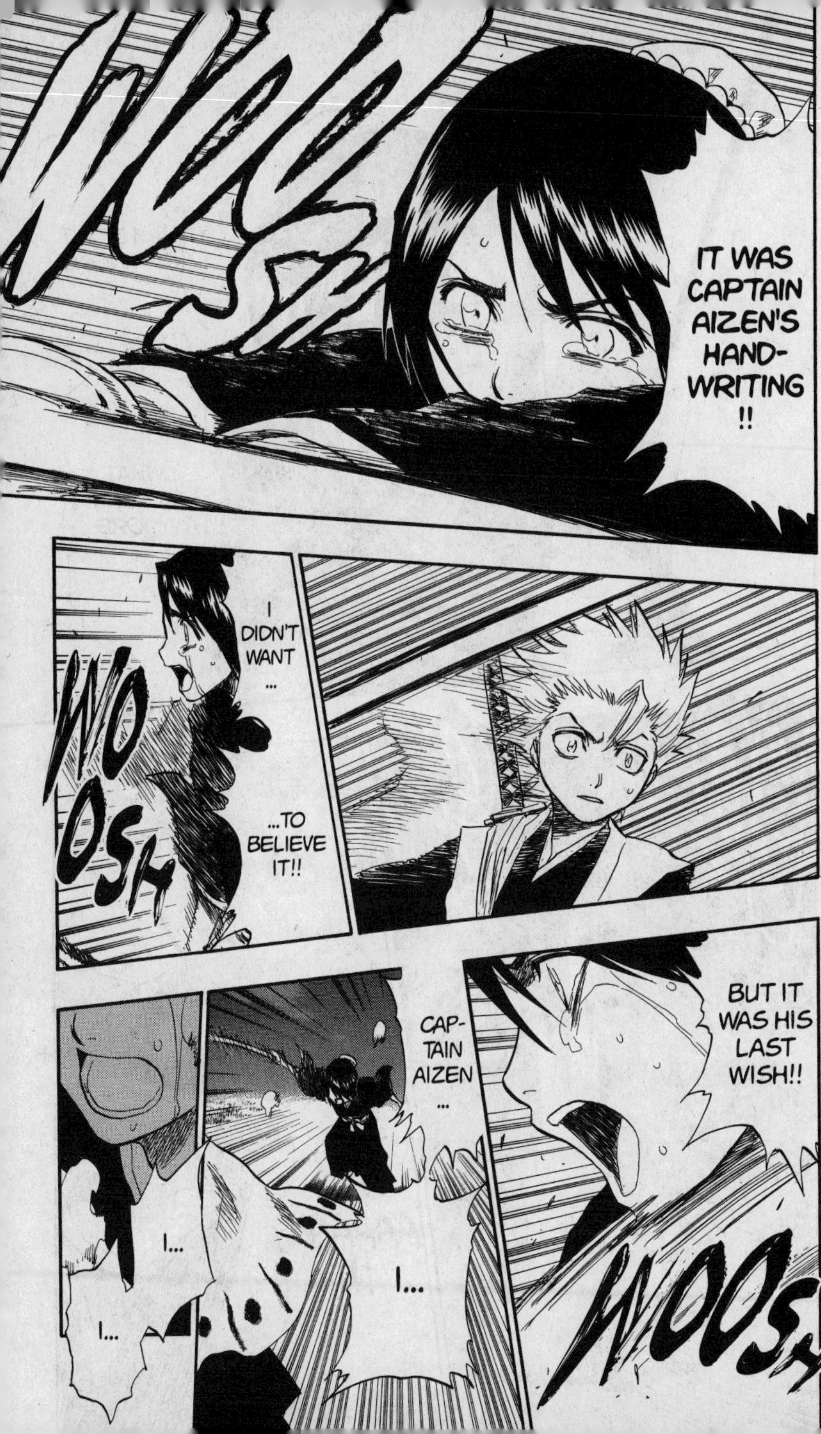
IT WAS CAPTAIN AIZEN'S HAND-WRITING !!
I DIDN'T WANT ...
...TO BELIEVE IT!!
WHOOSH
BUT IT WAS HIS LAST WISH!!
WHOOSH
CAP-TAIN AIZEN ...
I...
I...
I...

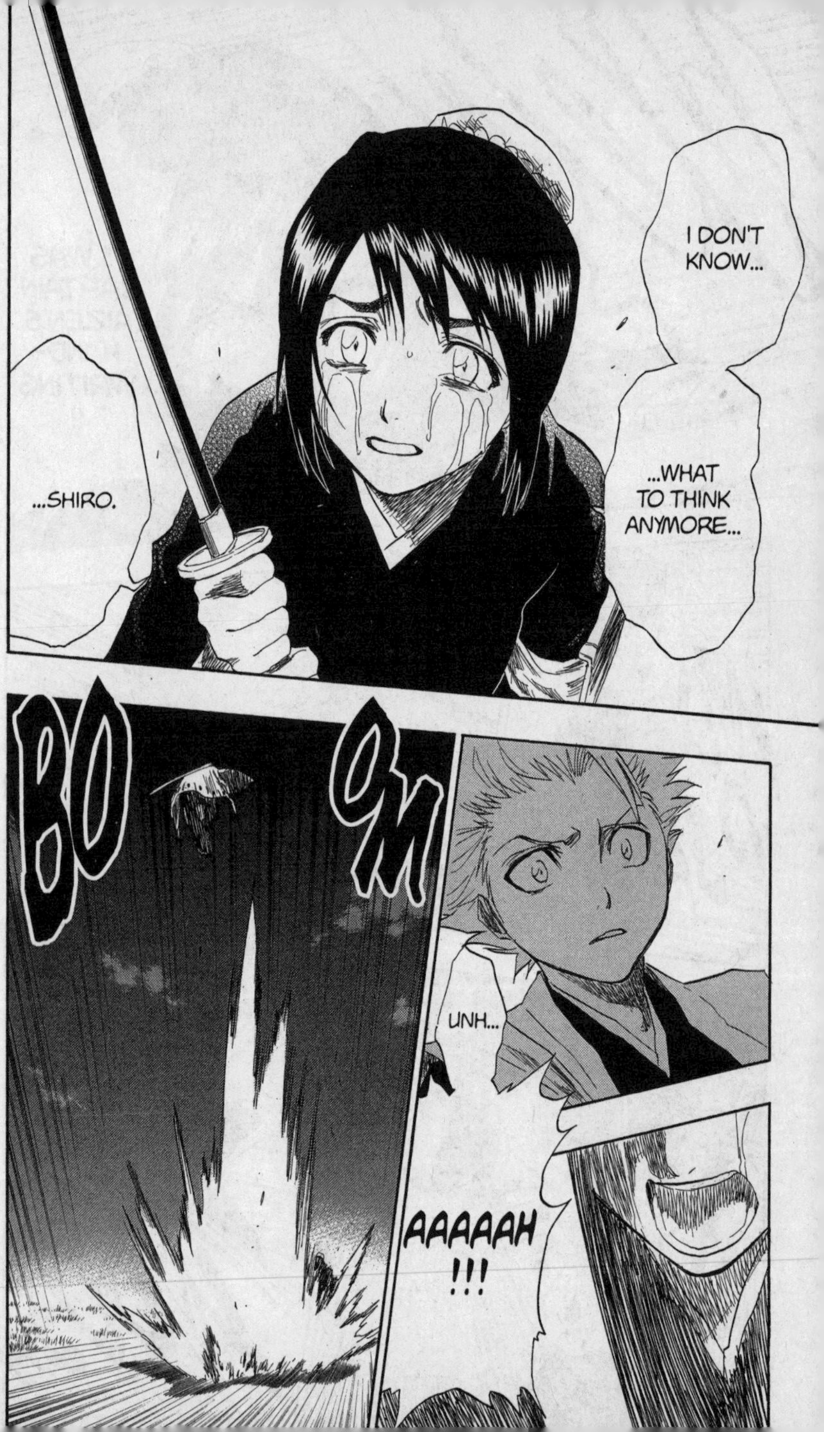
I DON'T KNOW...
...WHAT TO THINK ANYMORE...
...SHIRO.
UNH...
AAAAAH!!!
BOOM

READ THIS WAY

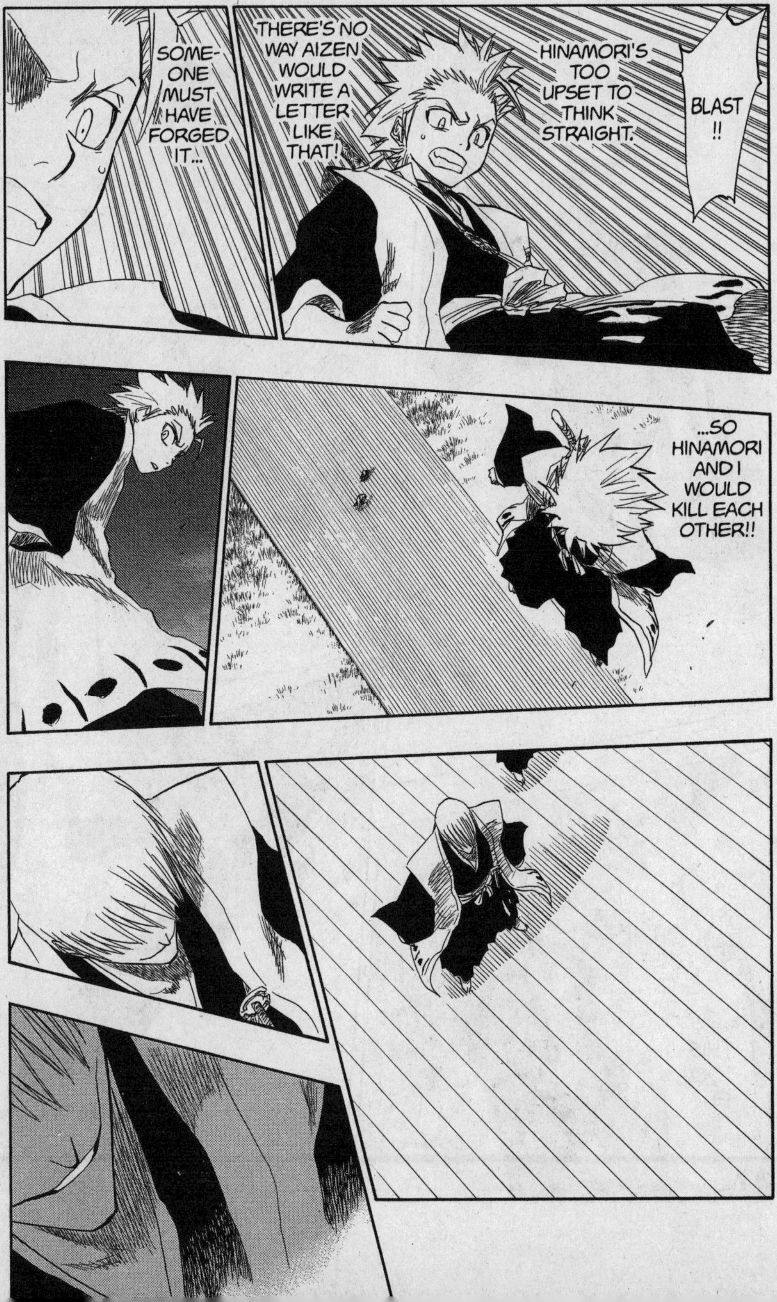
BLAST!!
HINAMORI'S TOO UPSET TO THINK STRAIGHT.
THERE'S NO WAY AIZEN WOULD WRITE A LETTER LIKE THAT!
SOME-ONE MUST HAVE FORGED IT...
...SO HINAMORI AND I WOULD KILL EACH OTHER!!

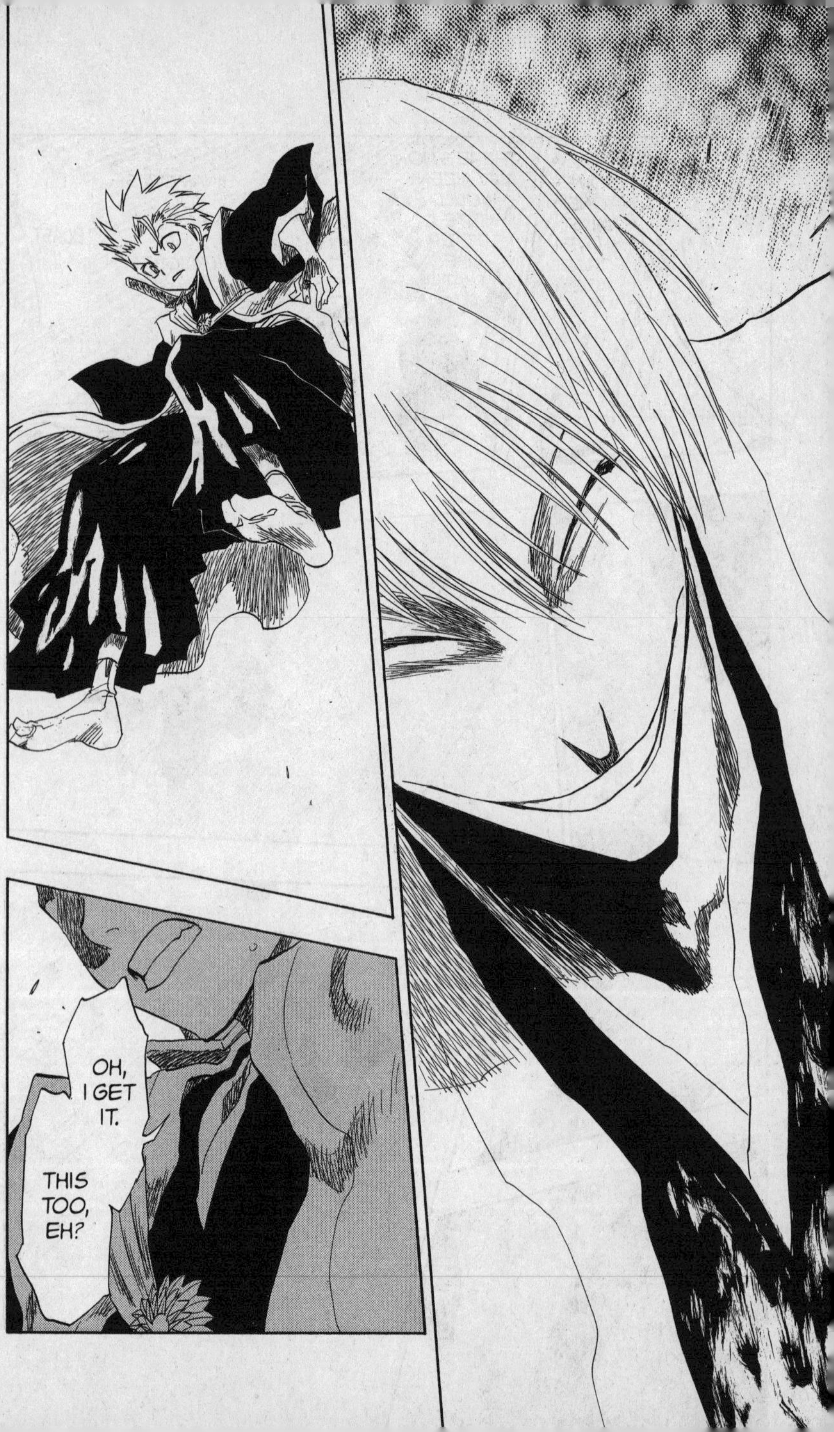
OH, I GET IT.
THIS TOO, EH?

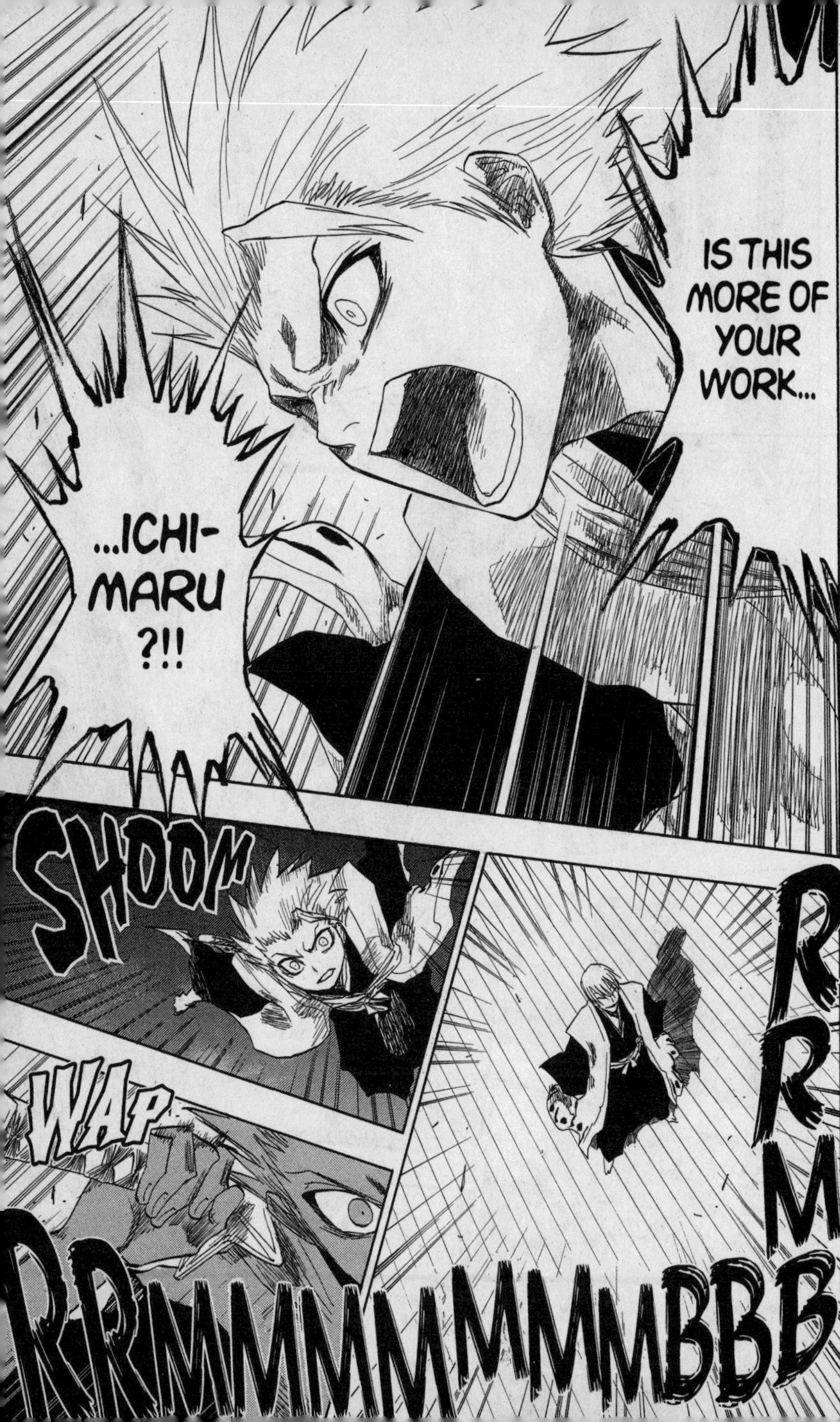
IS THIS MORE OF YOUR WORK...
...ICHI-MARU?!!
RRM
SHOOM
WAP
RRMMMMMMMMBBB

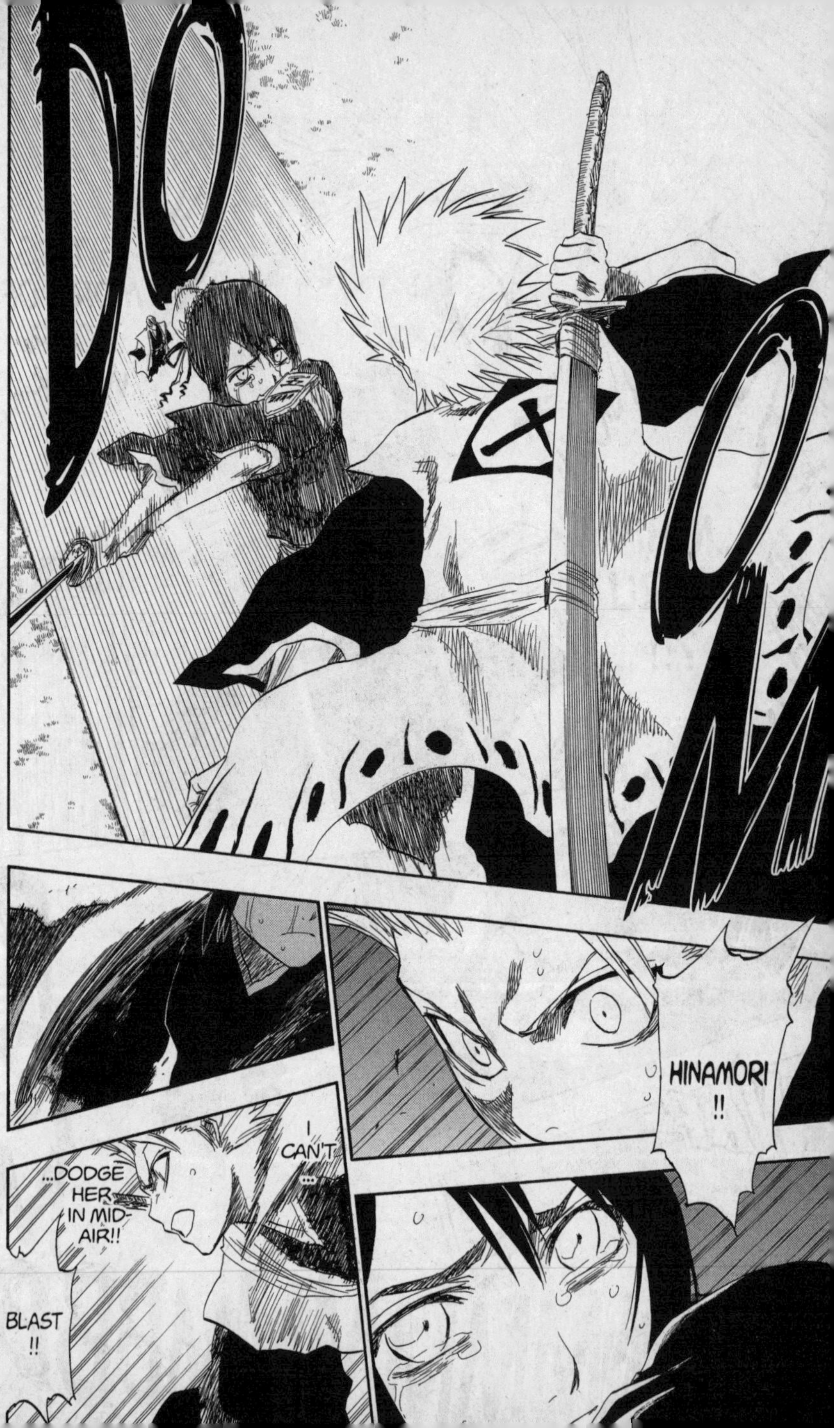
DOOM
HINAMORI !!
I CAN'T ...
...DODGE HER IN MID-AIR!!
BLAST !!

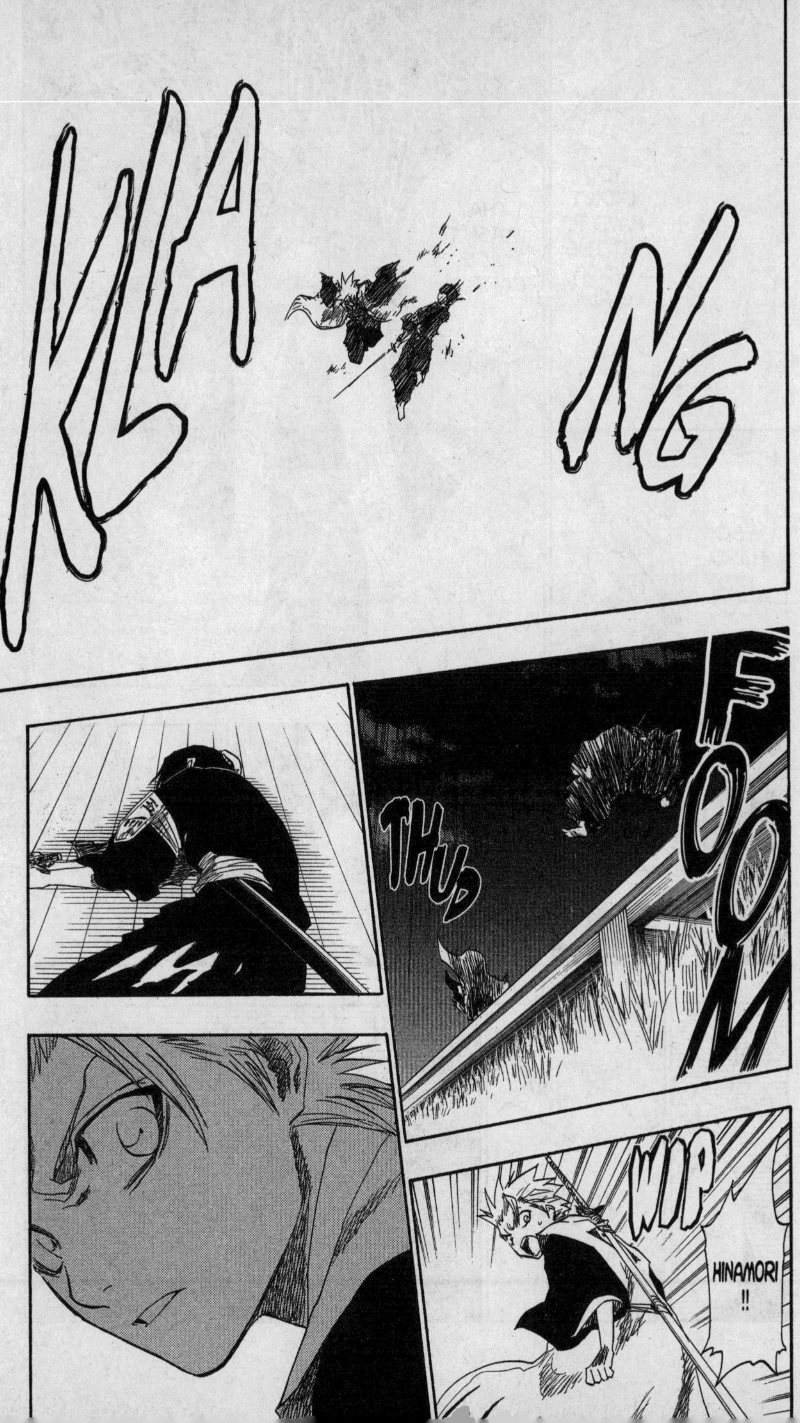
KLANG
FOOM
THUD
WIP
HINAMORI !!

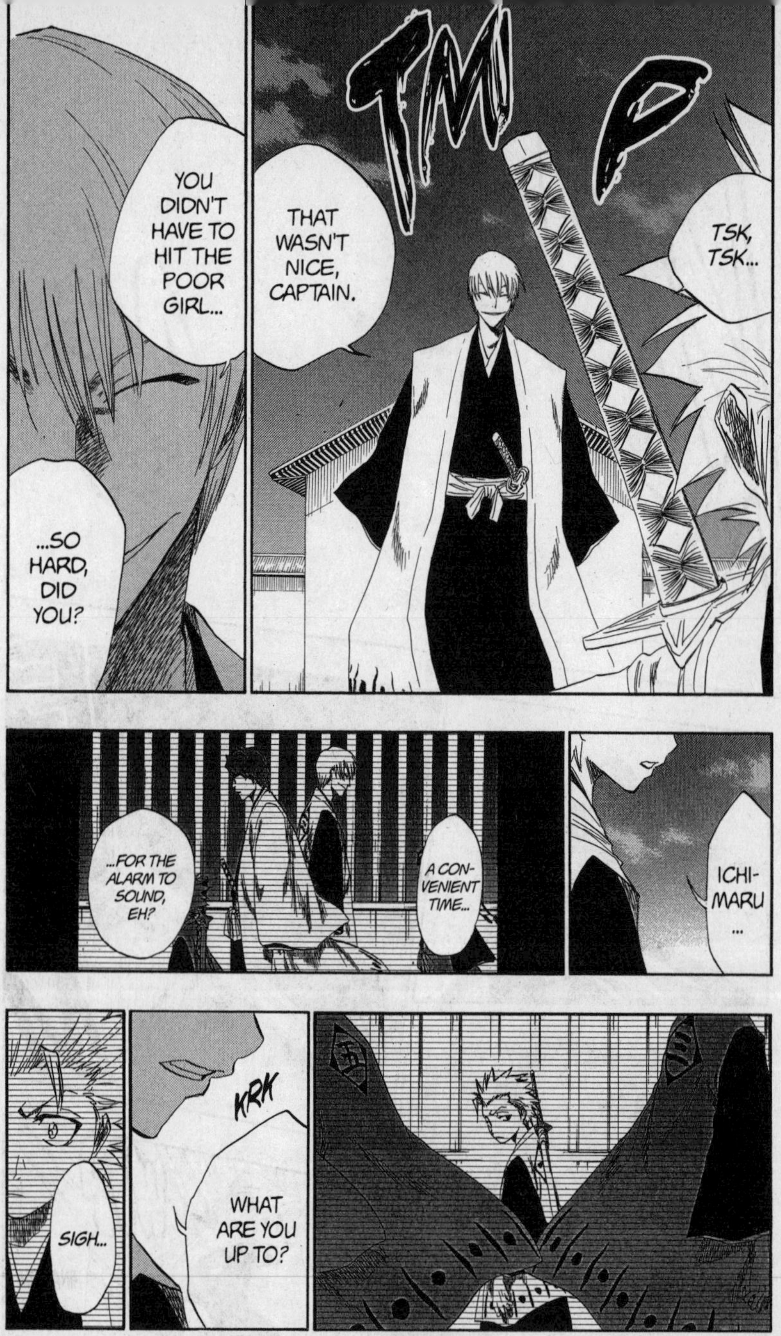
TMP
TSK, TSK...
THAT WASN'T NICE, CAPTAIN.
YOU DIDN'T HAVE TO HIT THE POOR GIRL...
...SO HARD, DID YOU?
ICHI-MARU...
A CON-VENIENT TIME...
...FOR THE ALARM TO SOUND, EH?
KRK
WHAT ARE YOU UP TO?
SIGH...

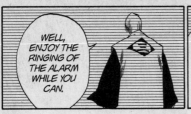

YOU NEVER CHANGE.
WELL, ENJOY THE RINGING OF THE ALARM WHILE YOU CAN.
'CAUSE...
...YOU WON'T BE HEARING IT AGAIN.
AIZEN JUST WASN'T ENOUGH FOR YOU.
YOU HAD TO MAKE...
...HINAMORI SUFFER, TOO.
SHE WAS GRIPPING HER SWORD SO HARD, SHE'S BLEEDING.
YOU'VE GONE TOO FAR.
WHY...
...I DON'T KNOW WHAT YOU'RE TALKING ABOUT.
TMP
I WARNED YOU, ICHI-MARU...

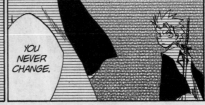

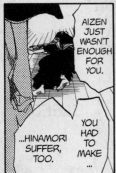

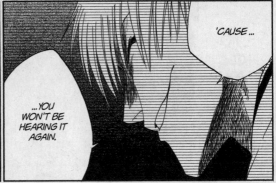

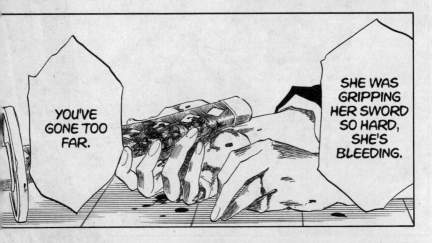

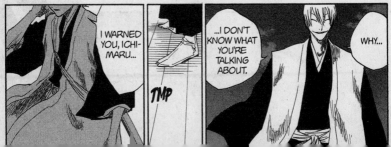

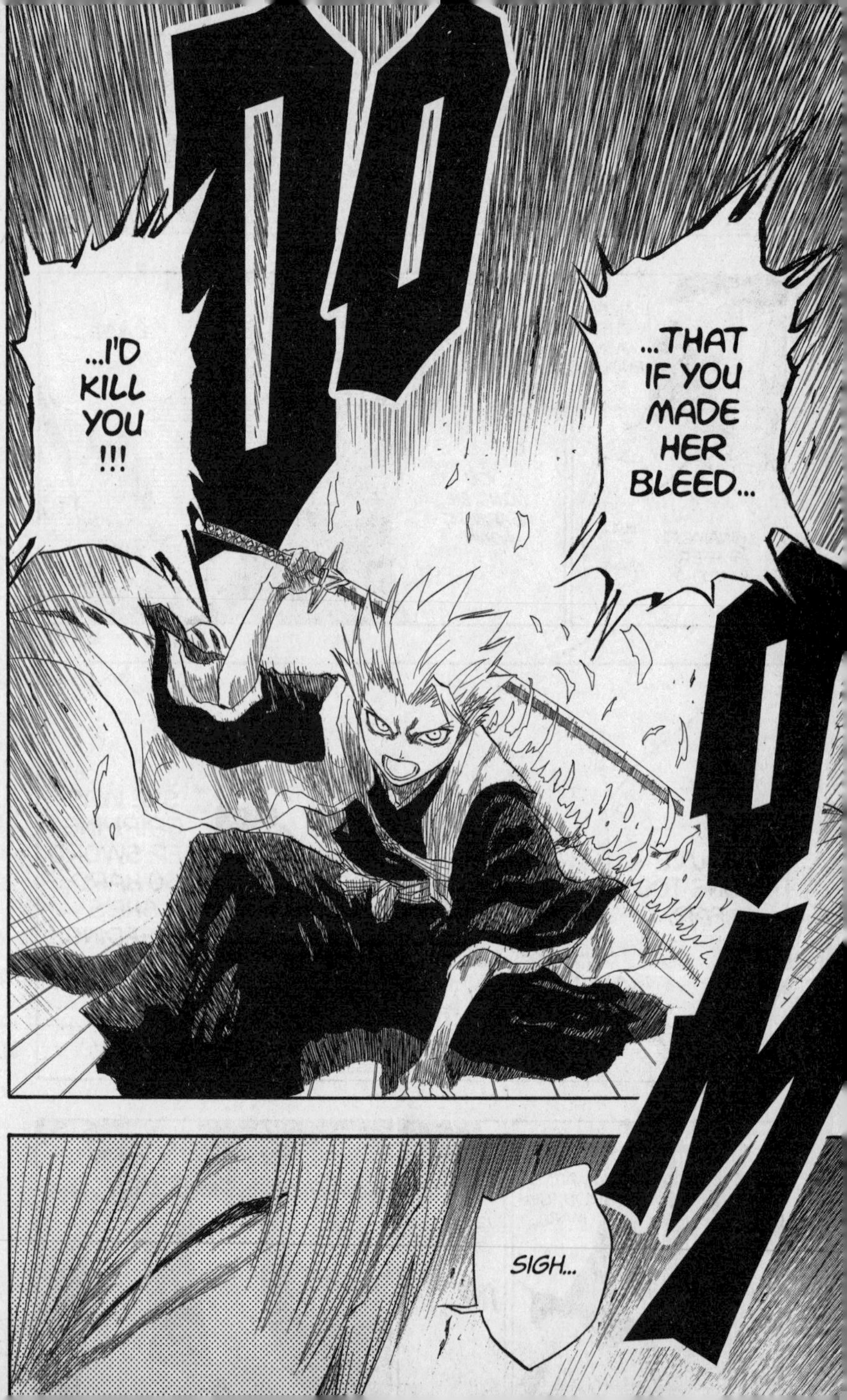
...THAT IF YOU MADE HER BLEED...
...I'D KILL YOU!!!
SIGH...

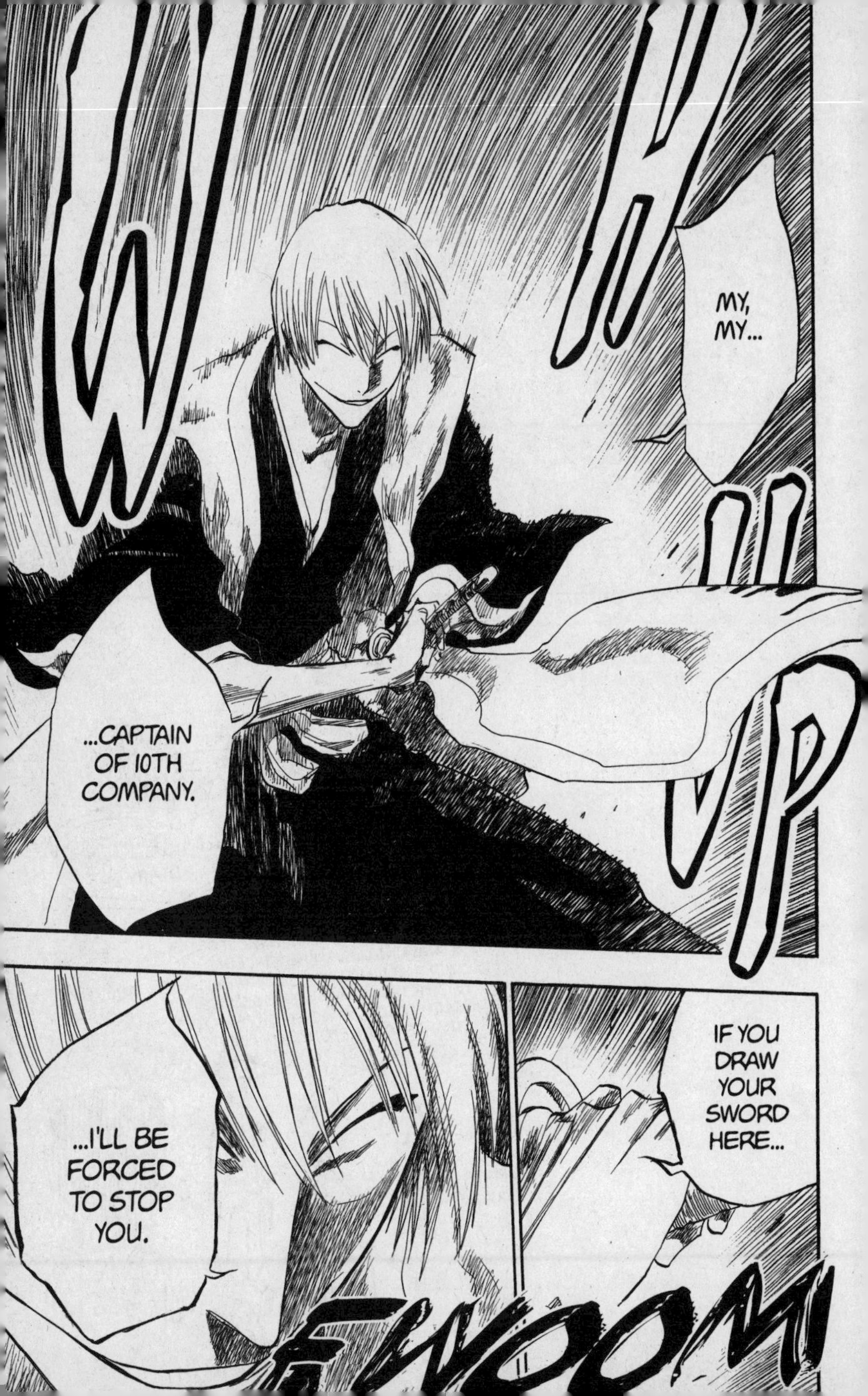
WHUP
MY, MY...
...CAPTAIN OF 10TH COMPANY.
IF YOU DRAW YOUR SWORD HERE...
...I'LL BE FORCED TO STOP YOU.
FWOOM

MEANWHILE IN THE WORLD OF THE LIVING, SERIES 4
YUZU'S Super HEARTFELT DIARY☆
SHE'S ONLY IN 5TH GRADE, BUT SHE CAN WRITE IN CURSIVE!
AUGUST 8, CLOUDY.
ICHIGO CAME HOME THIS MORNING OUT OF THE BLUE. I WAS KIND OF SURPRISED SINCE DAD HAD SAID THAT ICHIGO WOULD BE GONE ALL SUMMER. I WAS REALLY HAPPY TO SEE HIM! HE SAID HE'D LOST HIS TICKET FOR THE BULLET TRAIN AND COME HOME. HOW CUTE! ♡
WHAT SHALL WE DO TOGETHER TOMORROW? ♡

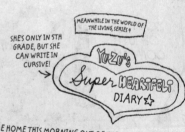

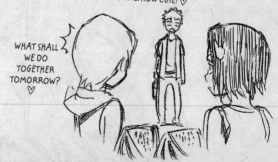

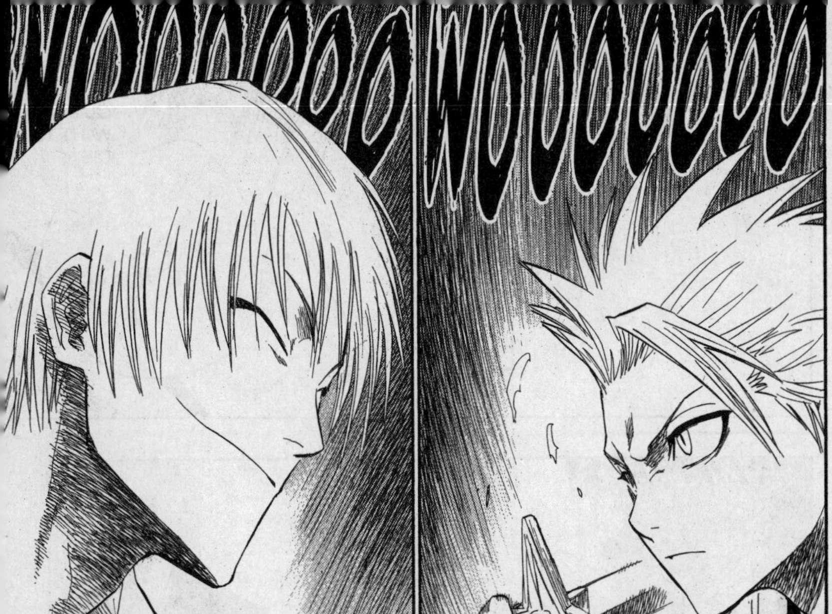
WOOOOOOO
WOOOOOOO

132. Creeping Limit

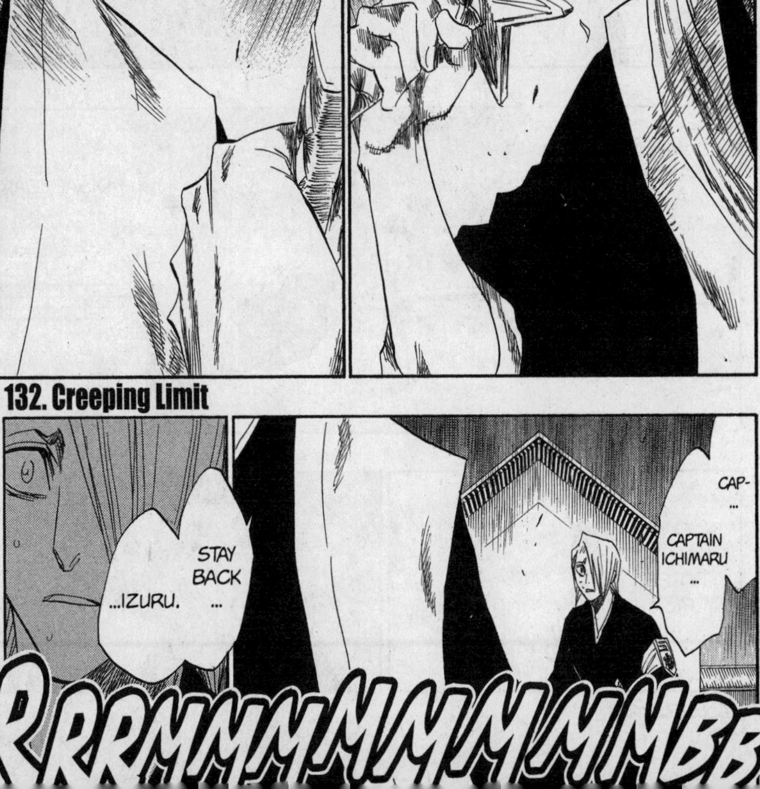
CAP-...
CAPTAIN ICHIMARU...
STAY BACK...
...IZURU.
RRRMMMMMMMMMBB

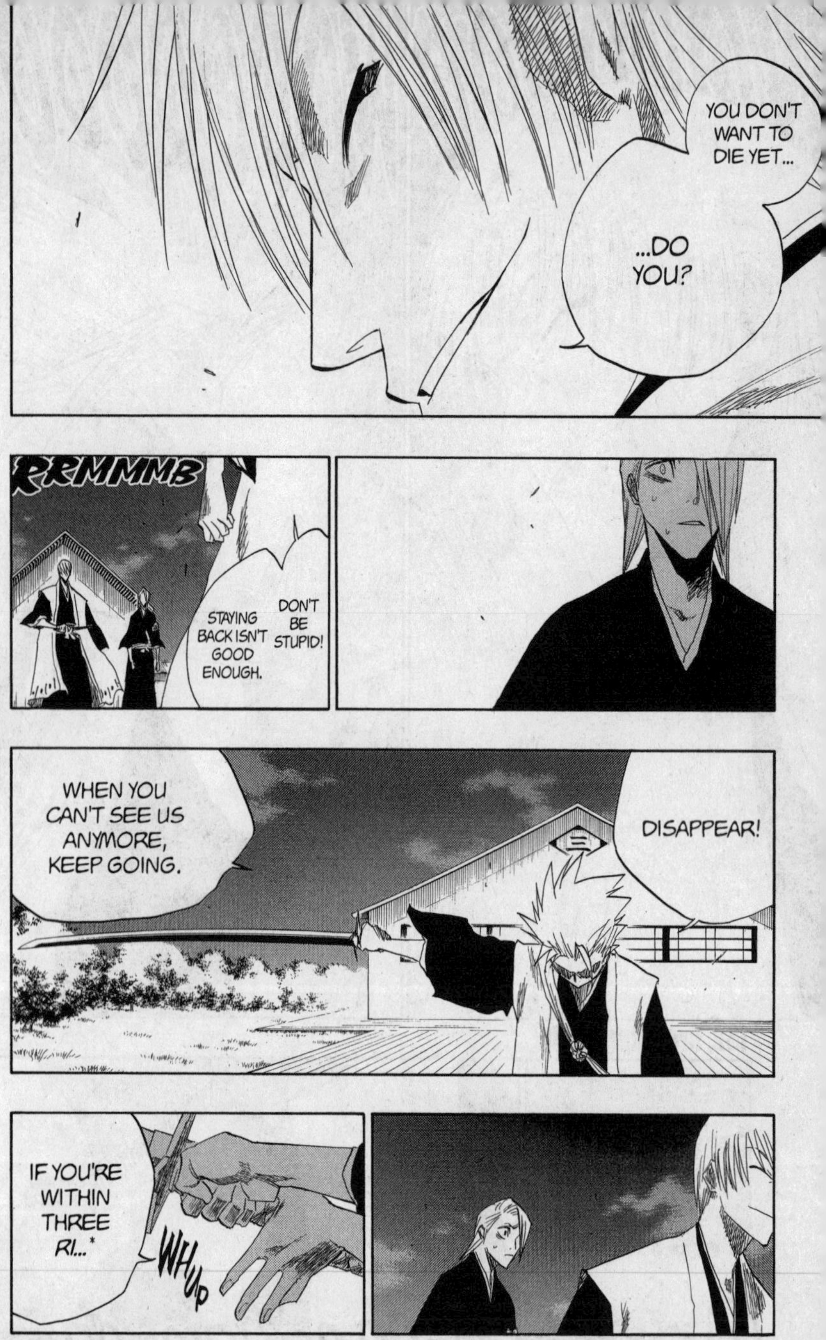
YOU DON'T WANT TO DIE YET...
...DO YOU?
RRMMMB
DON'T BE STUPID!
STAYING BACK ISN'T GOOD ENOUGH.
DISAPPEAR!
WHEN YOU CAN'T SEE US ANYMORE, KEEP GOING.
IF YOU'RE WITHIN THREE RI...*
WHUP

*About 7.3 miles

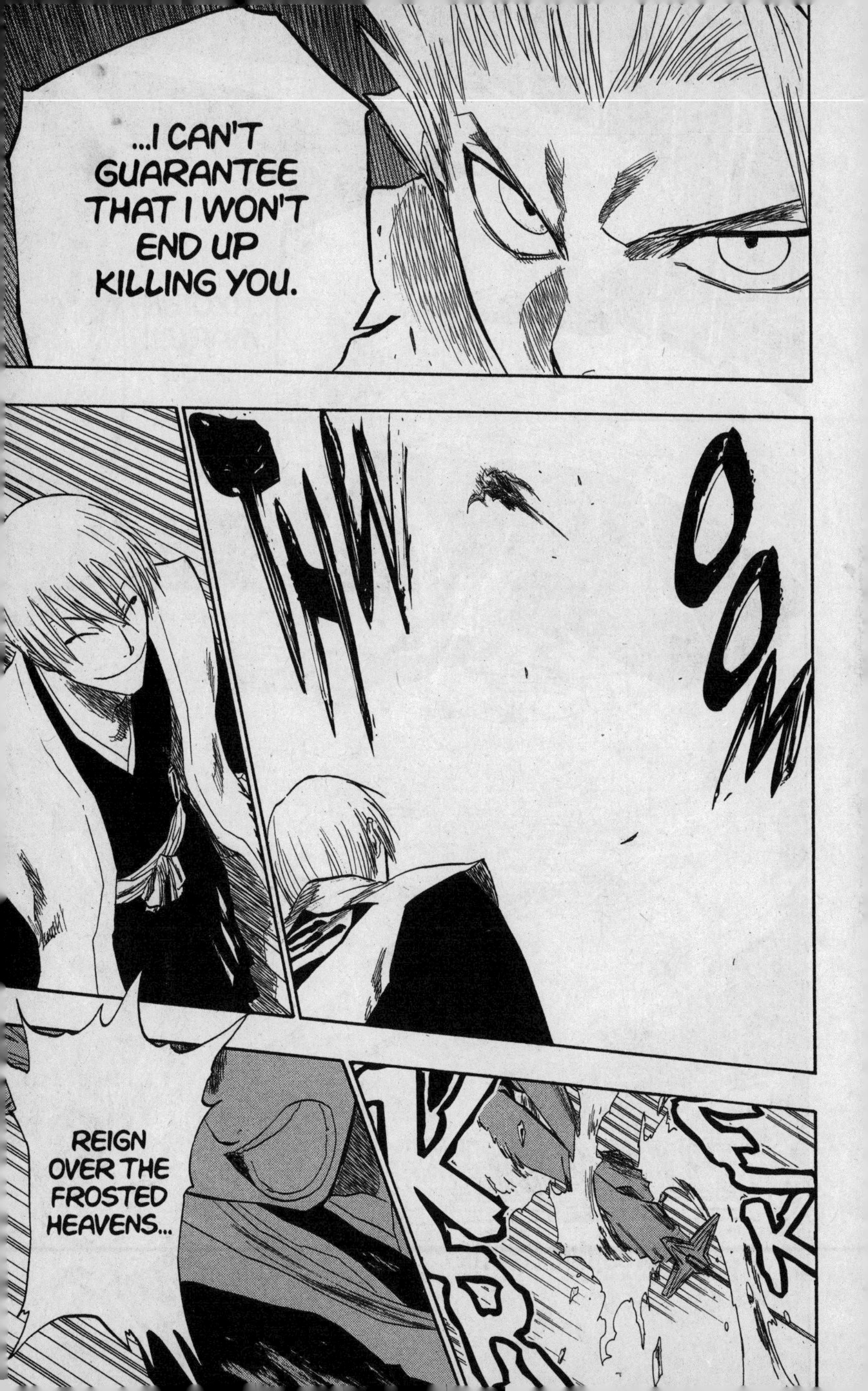
...I CAN'T GUARANTEE THAT I WON'T END UP KILLING YOU.
THWOOM
REIGN OVER THE FROSTED HEAVENS...

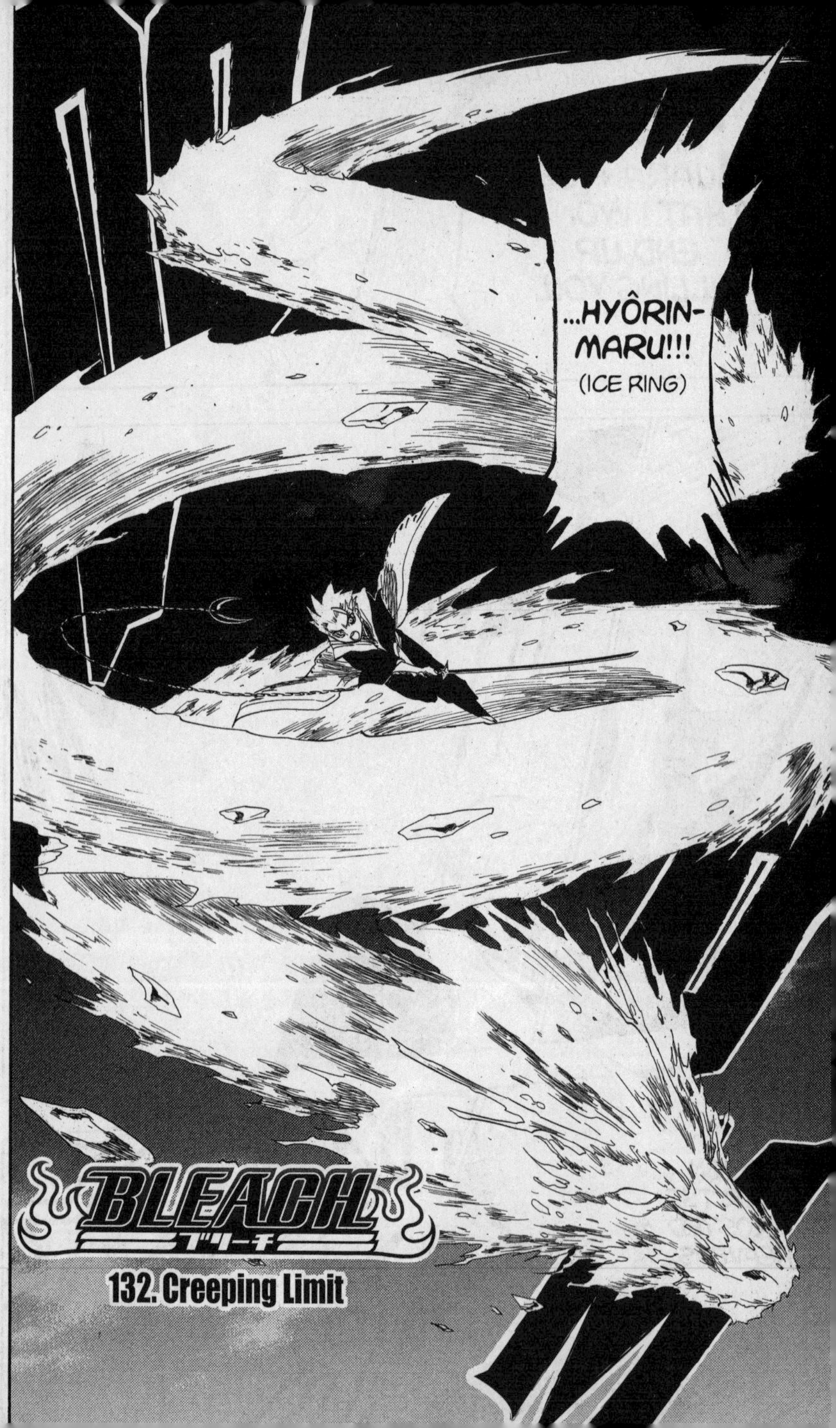
...HYÔRIN-
MARU!!!
(ICE RING)
BLEACH
ブリーチ
132. Creeping Limit

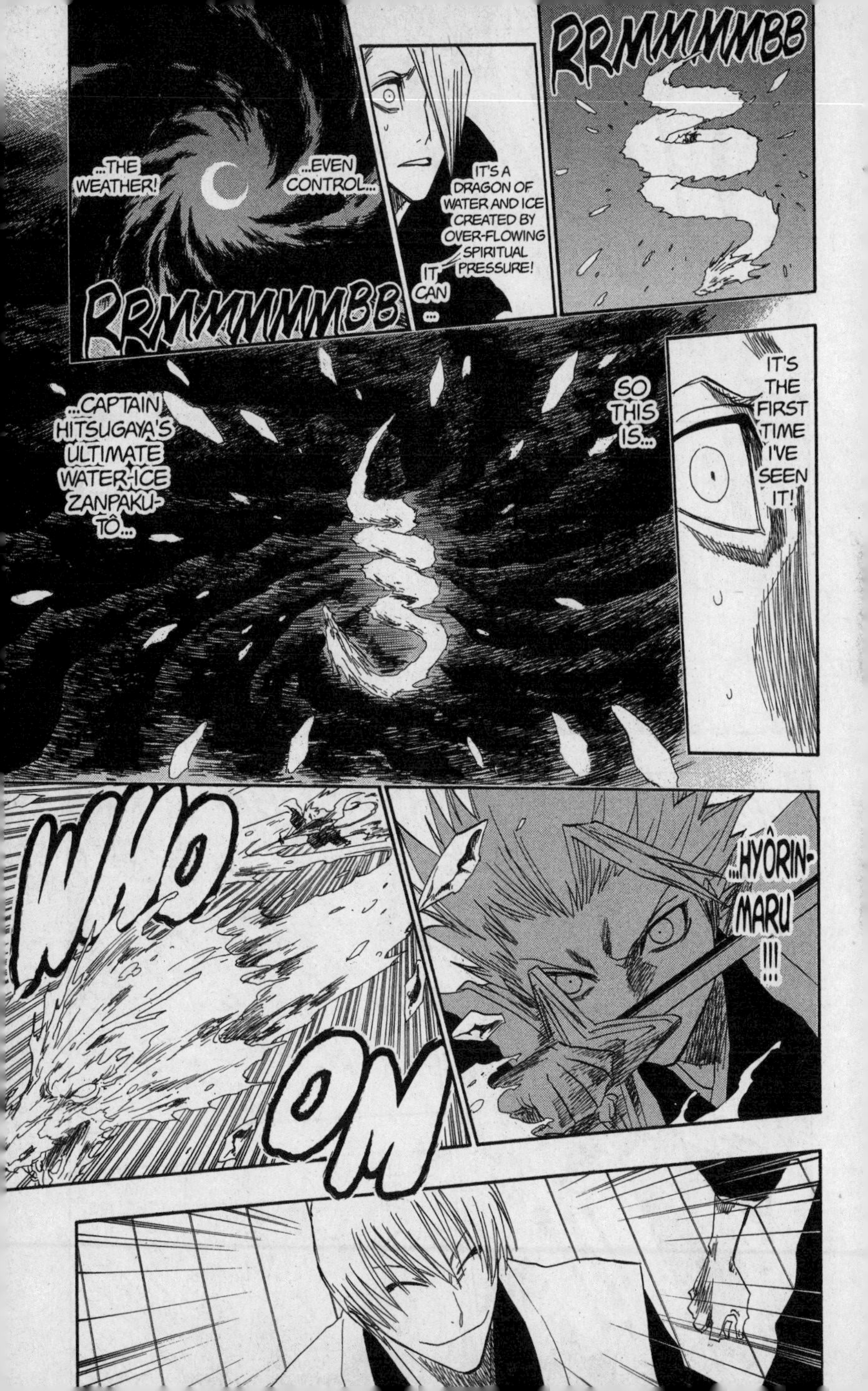
RRMMMMMBB
IT'S A DRAGON OF WATER AND ICE CREATED BY OVER-FLOWING SPIRITUAL PRESSURE!
IT CAN ...
...EVEN CONTROL...
...THE WEATHER!
RRMMMMMMBB
IT'S THE FIRST TIME I'VE SEEN IT!
SO THIS IS...
...CAPTAIN HITSUGAYA'S ULTIMATE WATER-ICE ZANPAKU-TÔ...
...HYÔRIN-MARU!!!
WHOOM

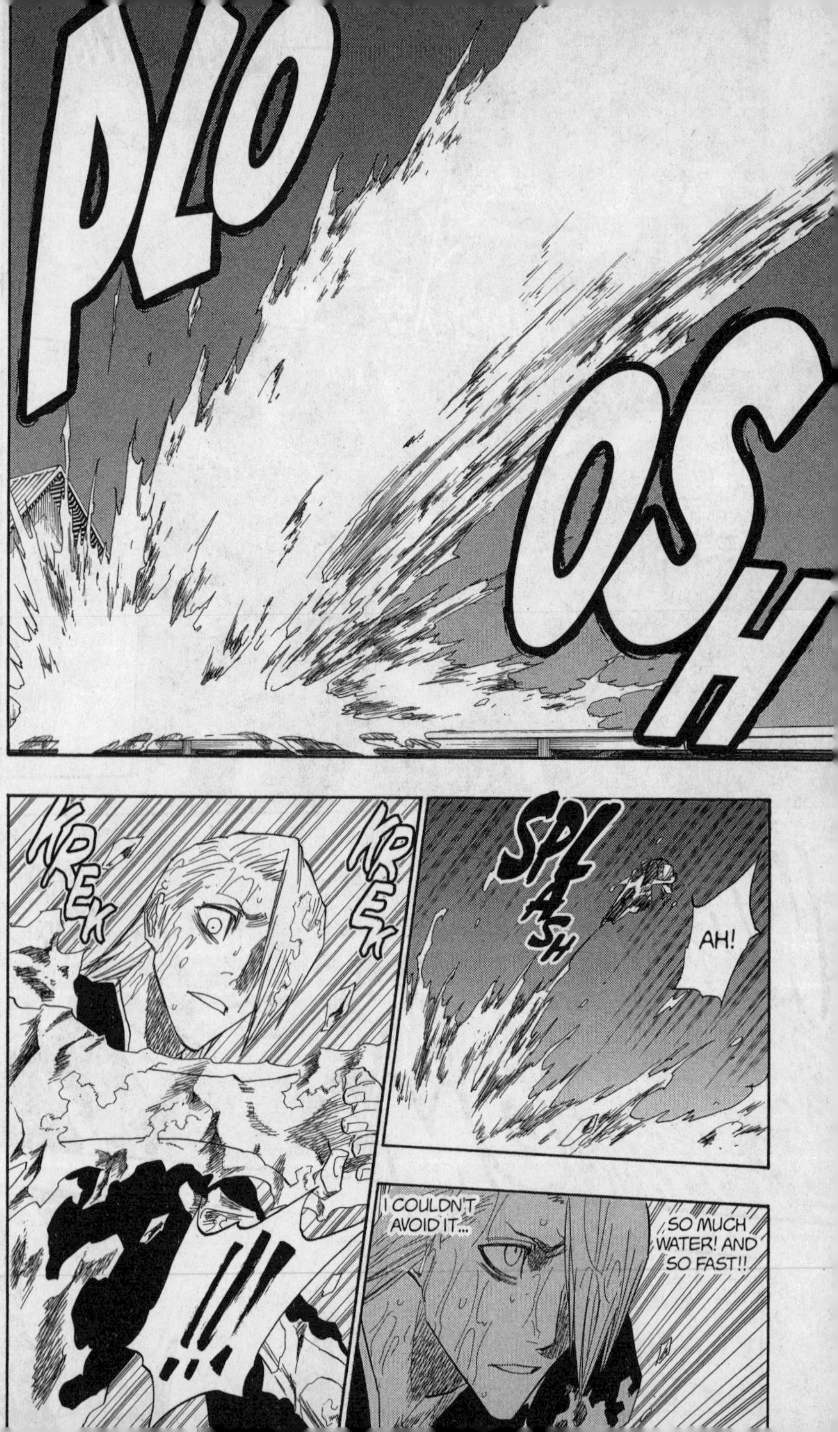
PLOOSH
SPLASH
AH!
SO MUCH WATER! AND SO FAST!!
I COULDN'T AVOID IT...
KREK
KREK
?!!

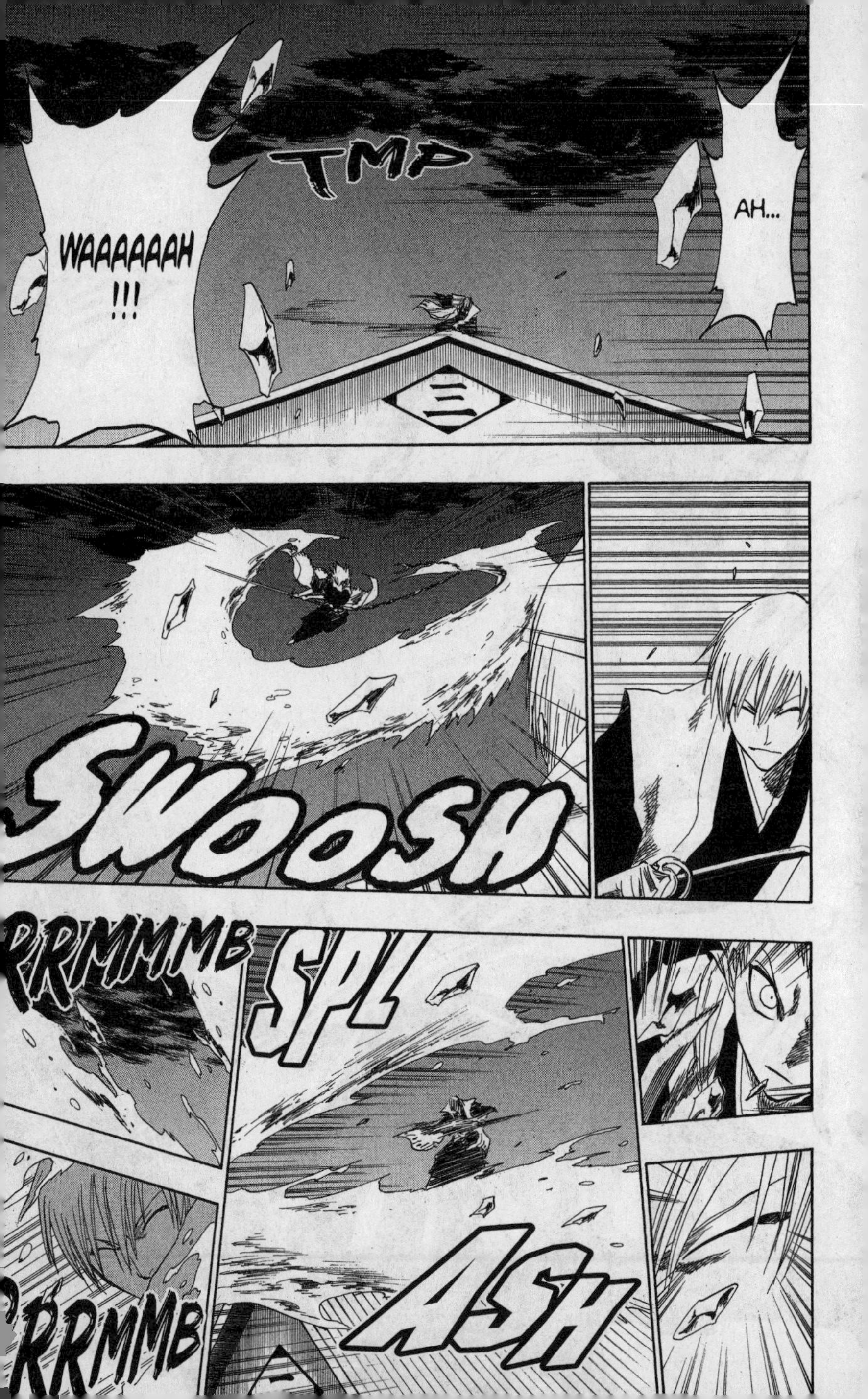
AH...
TMP
WAAAAAAH !!!
SWOOSH
SPL
ASH
RRMMMB
RRMMB

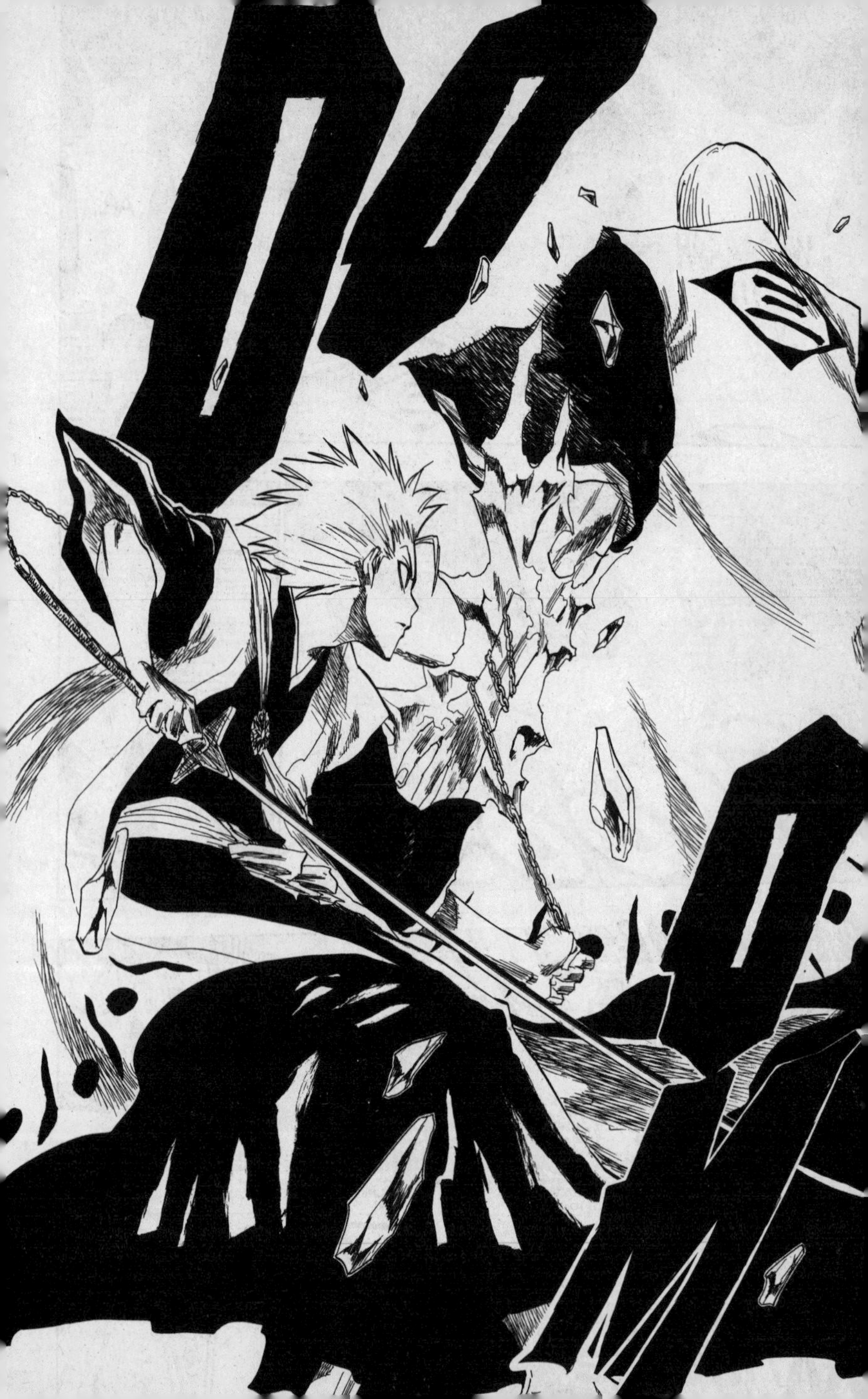

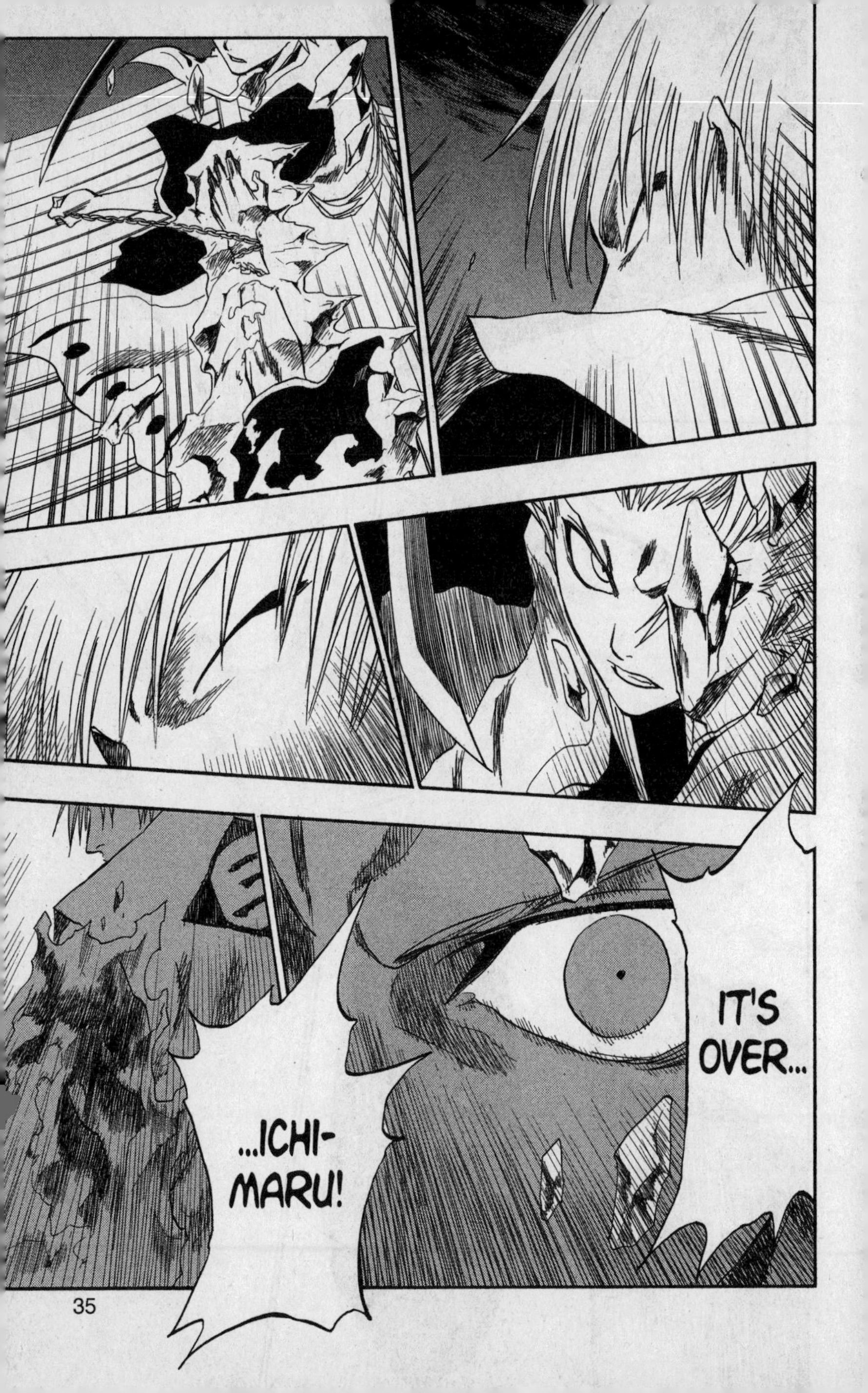
IT'S OVER...
...ICHI-MARU!

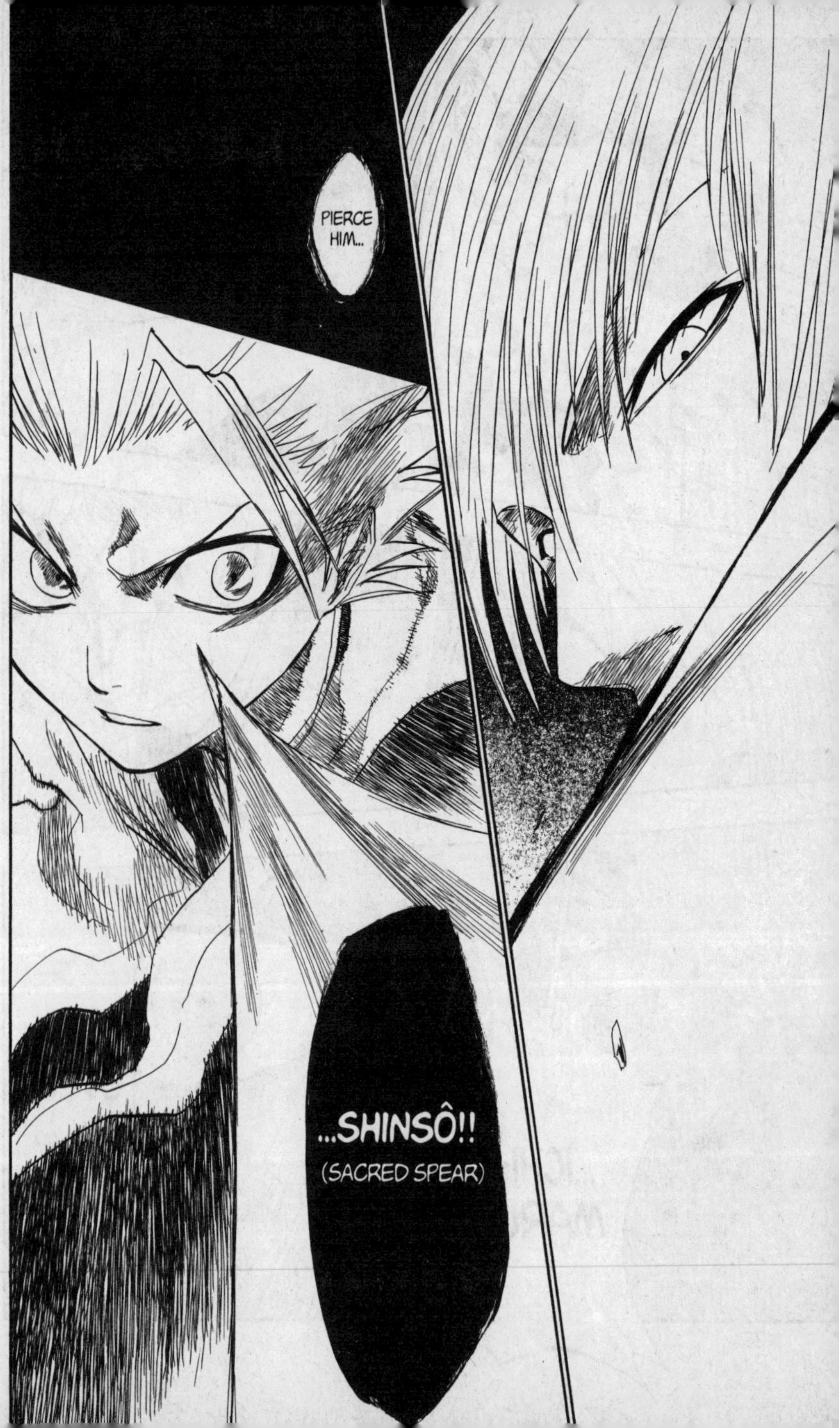
PIERCE HIM...
...SHINSÔ!!
(SACRED SPEAR)

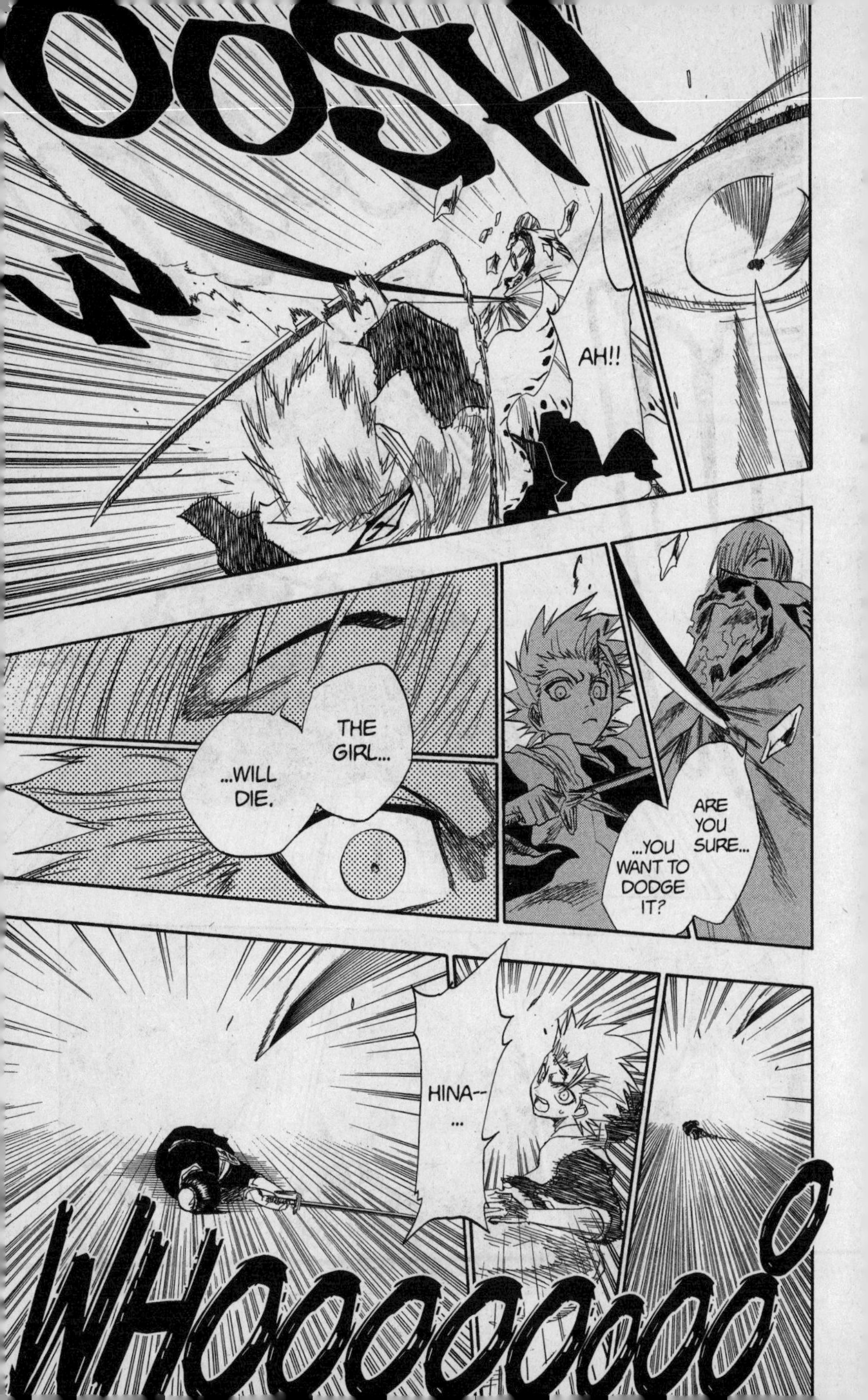
WOOSH
AH!!
ARE YOU SURE...
...YOU WANT TO DODGE IT?
THE GIRL...
...WILL DIE.
HINA-- ...
WHOOOOOOO

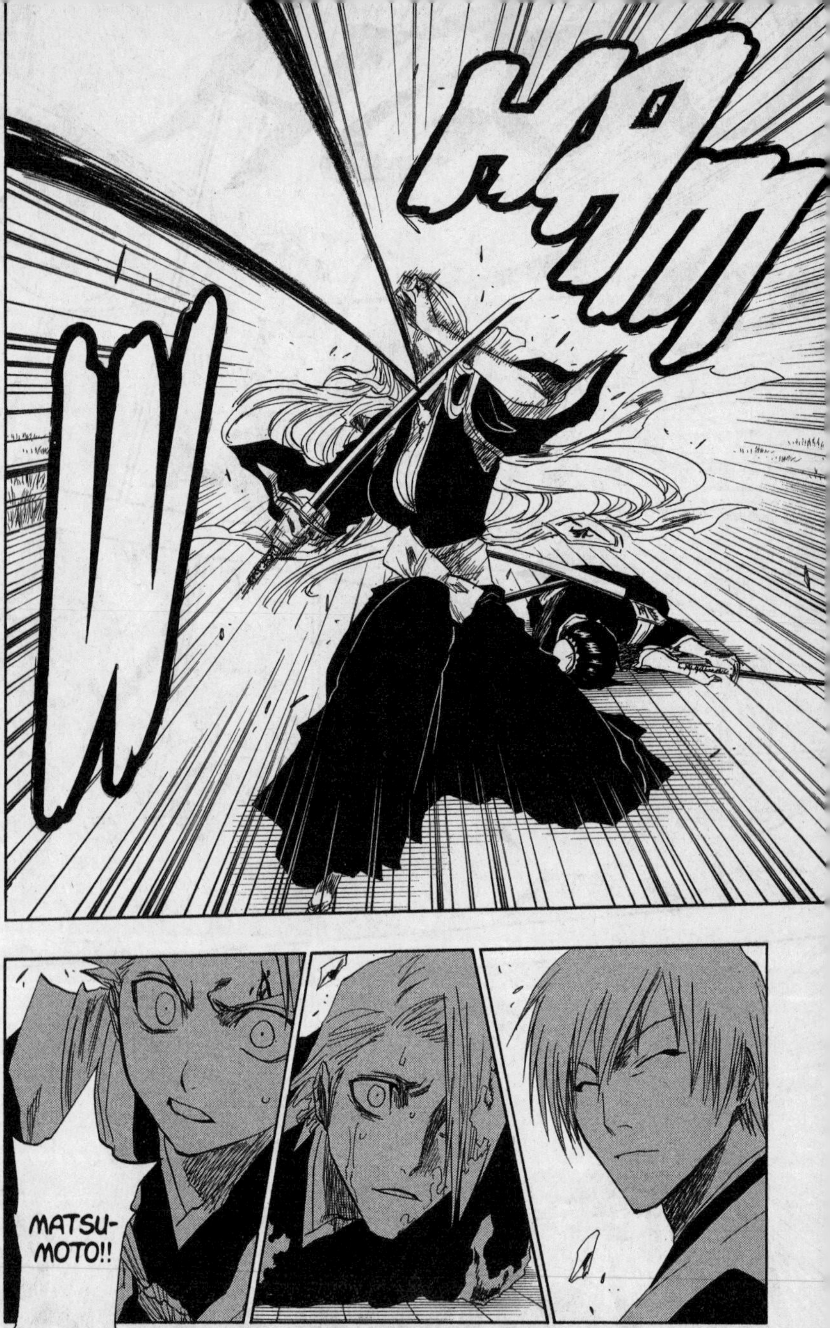
MATSU-
MOTO!!

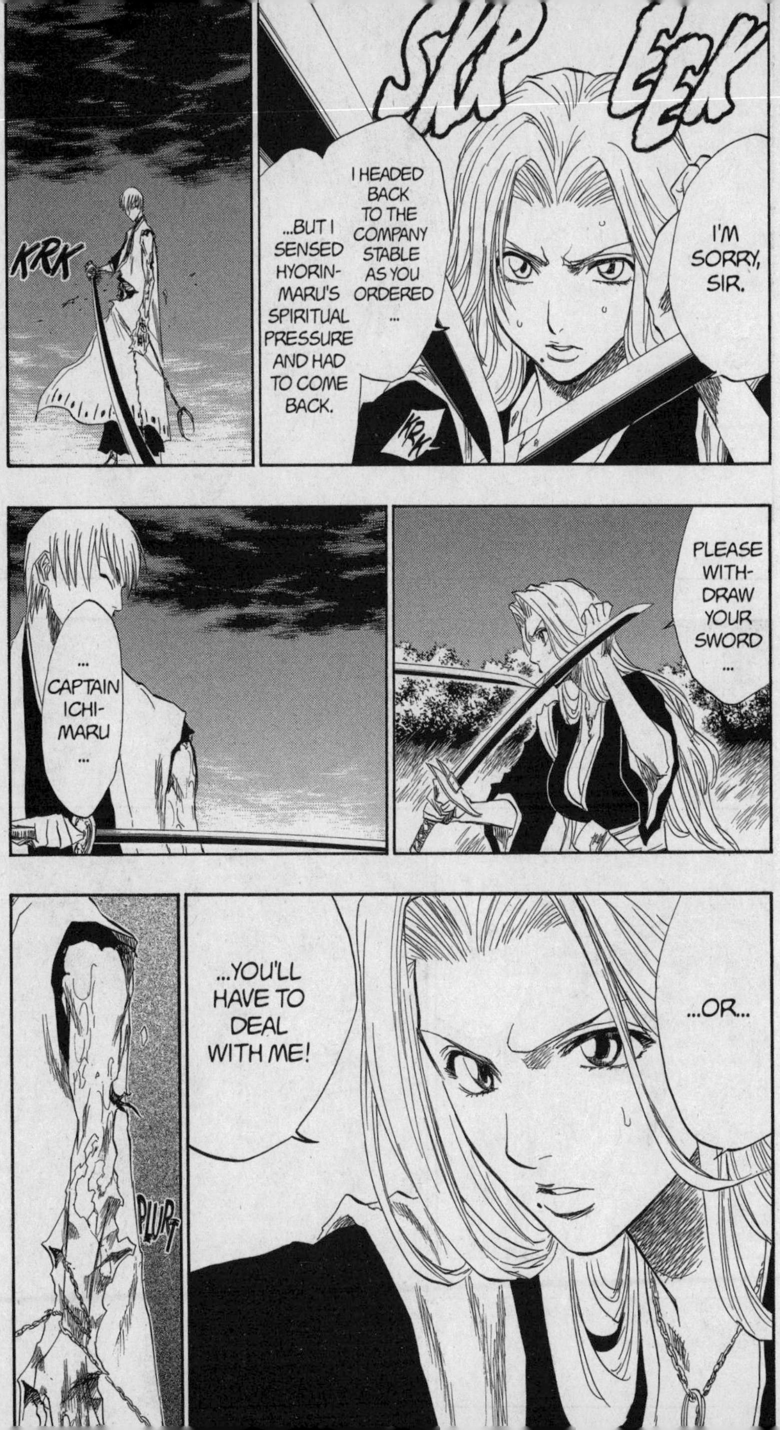
SHREEK
I'M SORRY, SIR.
I HEADED BACK TO THE COMPANY STABLE AS YOU ORDERED...
...BUT I SENSED HYORIN-MARU'S SPIRITUAL PRESSURE AND HAD TO COME BACK.
KRK
KRK
PLEASE WITH-DRAW YOUR SWORD...
...CAPTAIN ICHI-MARU...
...OR...
...YOU'LL HAVE TO DEAL WITH ME!
PLURT

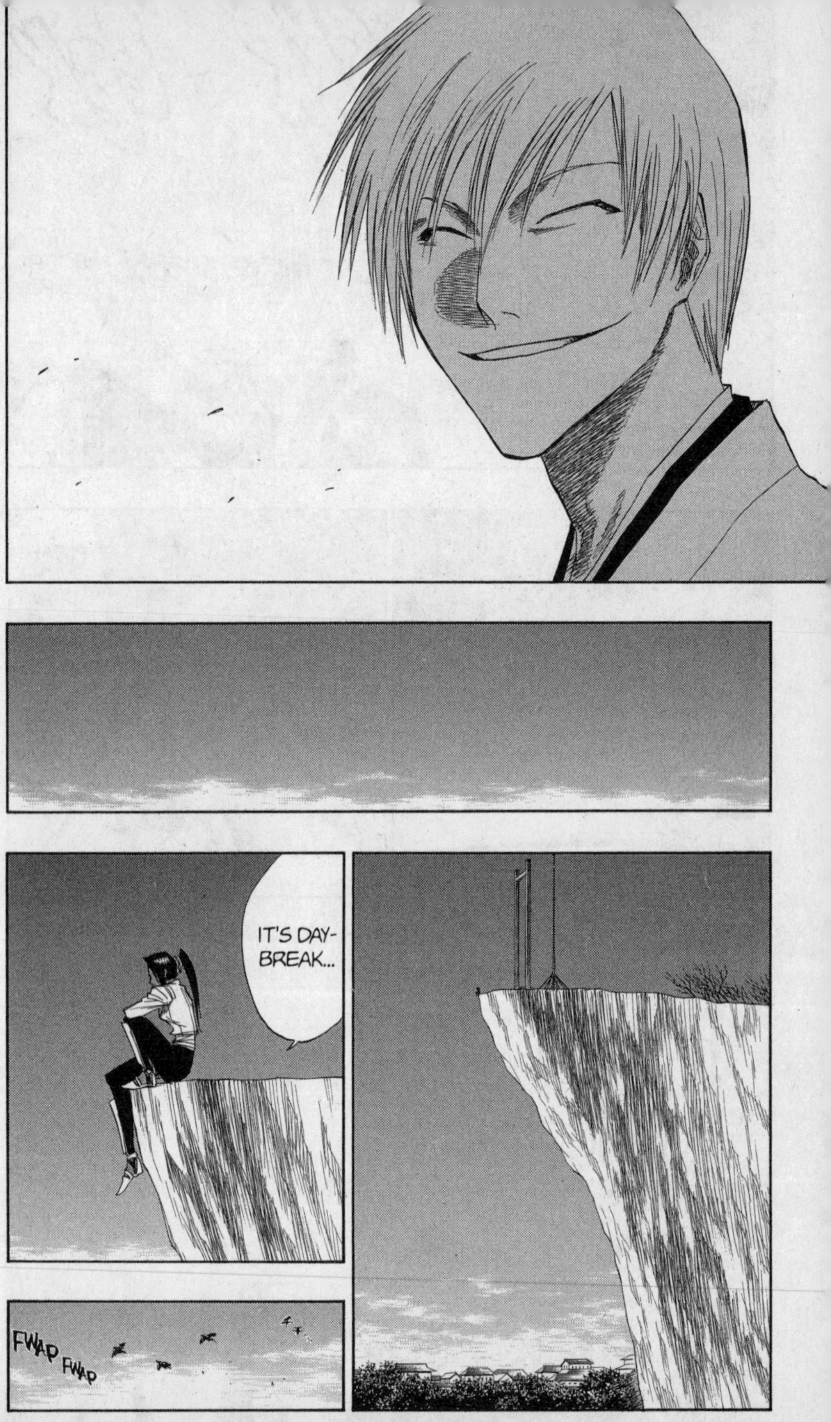
IT'S DAY-BREAK...
FWAP FWAP

READ THIS WAY

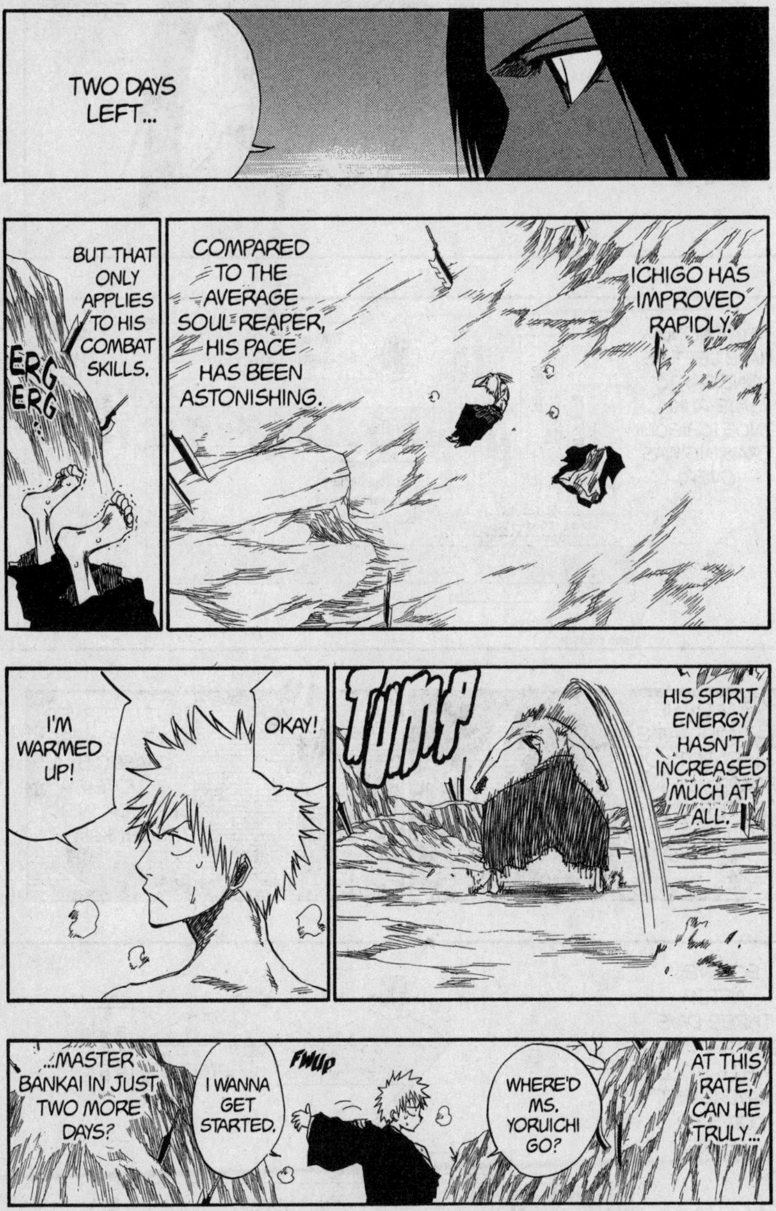
TWO DAYS LEFT...
ICHIGO HAS IMPROVED RAPIDLY.
COMPARED TO THE AVERAGE SOUL REAPER, HIS PACE HAS BEEN ASTONISHING.
BUT THAT ONLY APPLIES TO HIS COMBAT SKILLS.
ERG ERG
HIS SPIRIT ENERGY HASN'T INCREASED MUCH AT ALL.
TUMP
OKAY!
I'M WARMED UP!
AT THIS RATE, CAN HE TRULY...
WHERE'D MS. YORUICHI GO?
FWUP
I WANNA GET STARTED.
...MASTER BANKAI IN JUST TWO MORE DAYS?

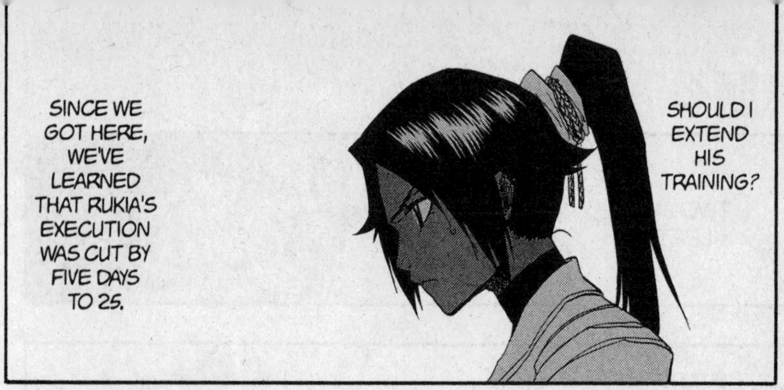
SHOULD I EXTEND HIS TRAINING?
SINCE WE GOT HERE, WE'VE LEARNED THAT RUKIA'S EXECUTION WAS CUT BY FIVE DAYS TO 25.

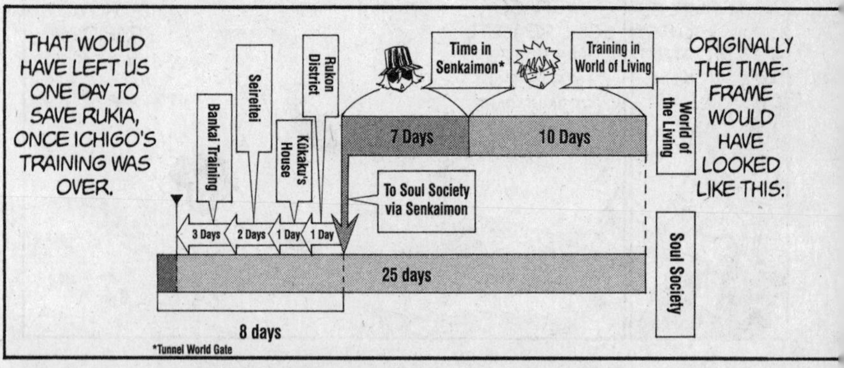
ORIGINALLY THE TIME-FRAME WOULD HAVE LOOKED LIKE THIS:
World of the Living
Training in World of Living
Time in Senkaimon*
10 Days
7 Days
Soul Society
To Soul Society via Senkaimon
Rukon District
Kûkaku's House
Seireitei
Bankai Training
1 Day
1 Day
2 Days
3 Days
25 days
8 days
THAT WOULD HAVE LEFT US ONE DAY TO SAVE RUKIA, ONCE ICHIGO'S TRAINING WAS OVER.
*Tunnel World Gate

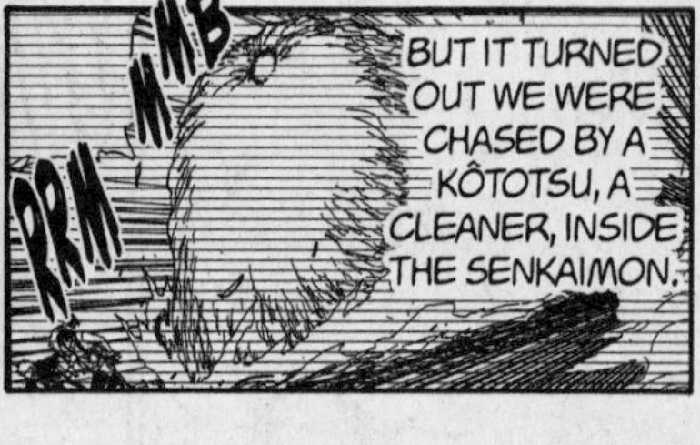
BUT IT TURNED OUT WE WERE CHASED BY A KÔTOTSU, A CLEANER, INSIDE THE SENKAIMON.
RRMMMB

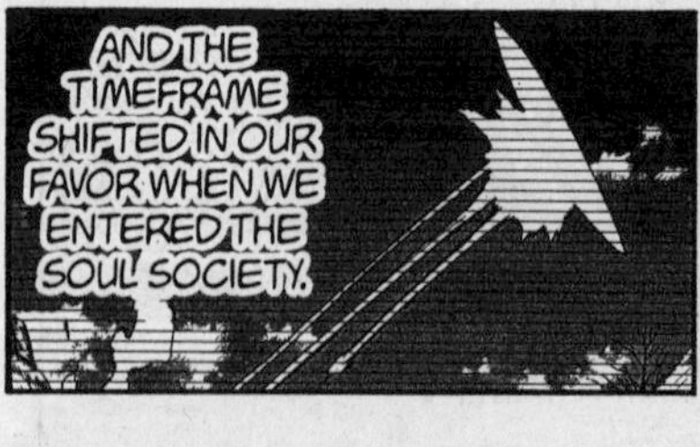
AND THE TIMEFRAME SHIFTED IN OUR FAVOR WHEN WE ENTERED THE SOUL SOCIETY.

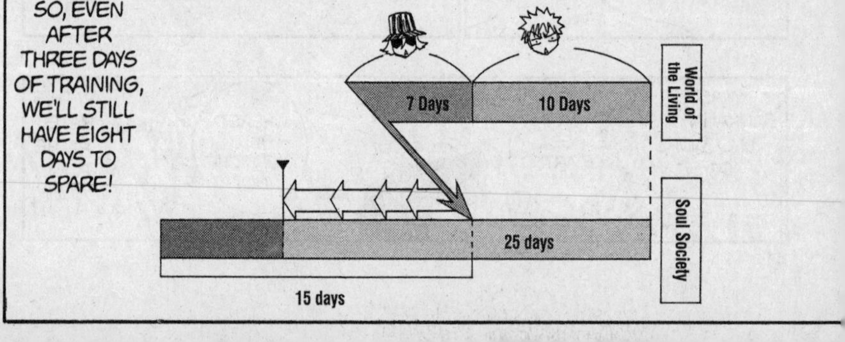
World of the Living
10 Days
7 Days
Soul Society
25 days
15 days
SO, EVEN AFTER THREE DAYS OF TRAINING, WE'LL STILL HAVE EIGHT DAYS TO SPARE!

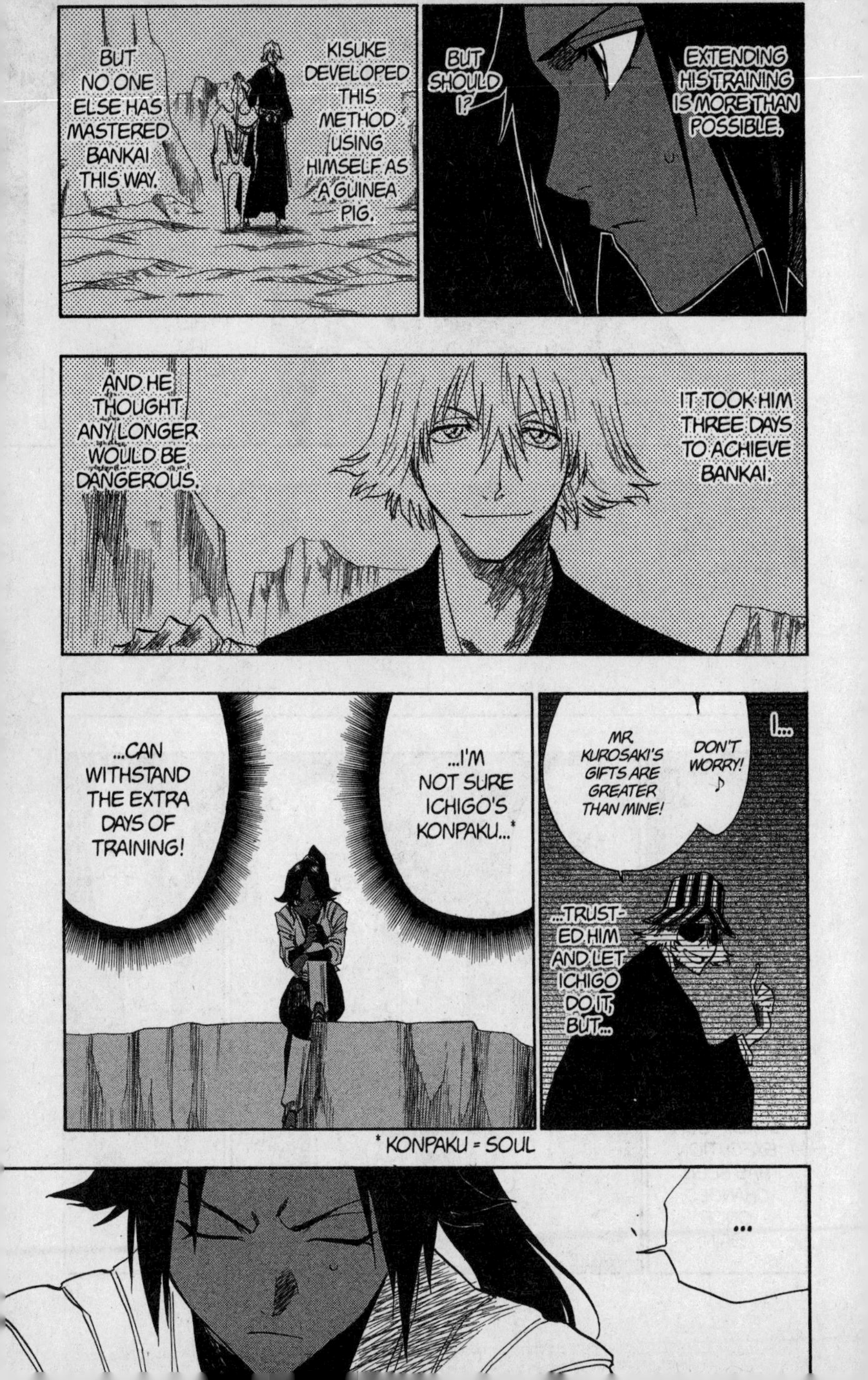
EXTENDING HIS TRAINING IS MORE THAN POSSIBLE.
BUT SHOULD I?
KISUKE DEVELOPED THIS METHOD USING HIMSELF AS A GUINEA PIG.
BUT NO ONE ELSE HAS MASTERED BANKAI THIS WAY.
IT TOOK HIM THREE DAYS TO ACHIEVE BANKAI.
AND HE THOUGHT ANY LONGER WOULD BE DANGEROUS.
I...
DON'T WORRY! ♪
MR. KUROSAKI'S GIFTS ARE GREATER THAN MINE!
...TRUSTED HIM AND LET ICHIGO DO IT, BUT...
...I'M NOT SURE ICHIGO'S KONPAKU...*
...CAN WITHSTAND THE EXTRA DAYS OF TRAINING!
...

* KONPAKU = SOUL

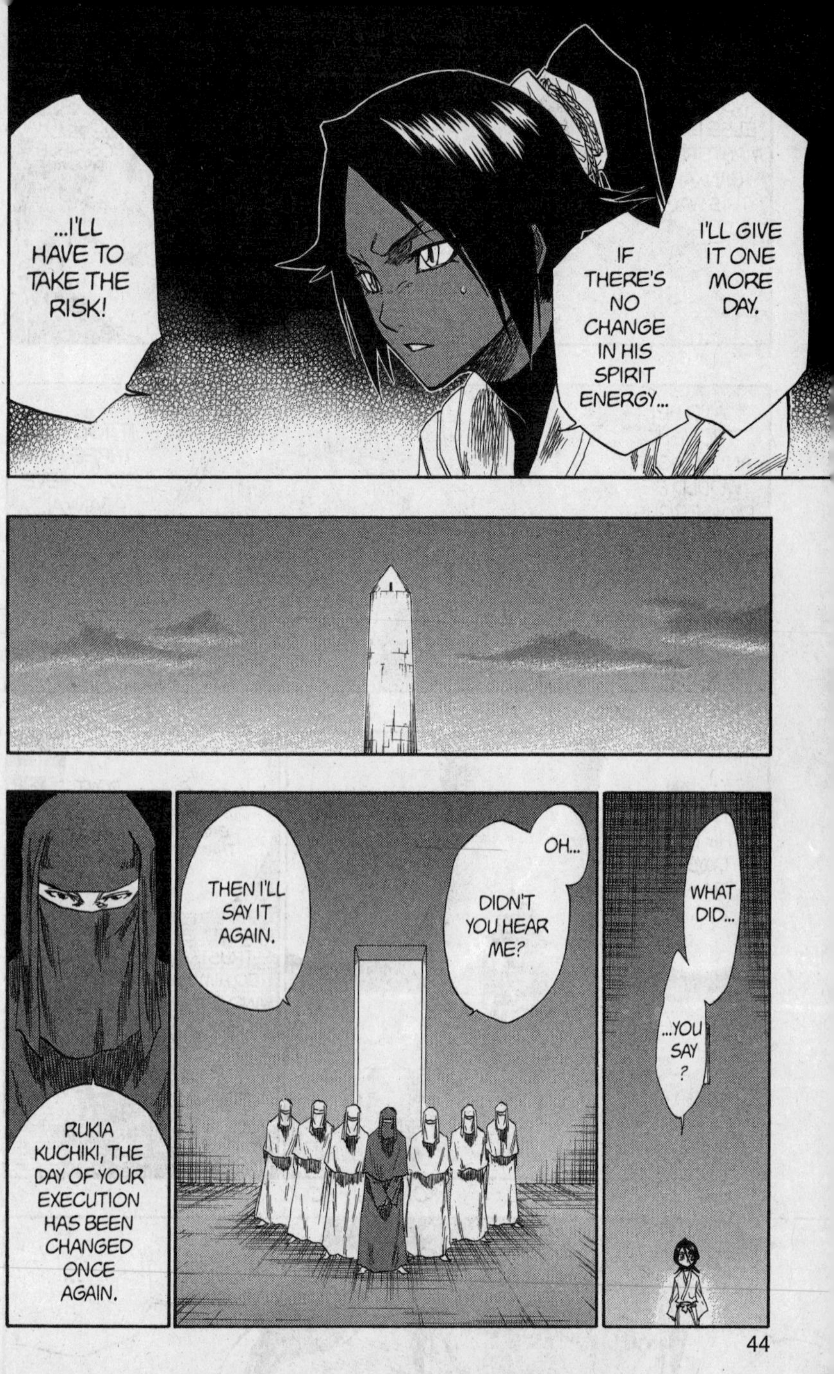
I'LL GIVE IT ONE MORE DAY.
IF THERE'S NO CHANGE IN HIS SPIRIT ENERGY...
...I'LL HAVE TO TAKE THE RISK!
WHAT DID...
...YOU SAY?
OH...
DIDN'T YOU HEAR ME?
THEN I'LL SAY IT AGAIN.
RUKIA KUCHIKI, THE DAY OF YOUR EXECUTION HAS BEEN CHANGED ONCE AGAIN.

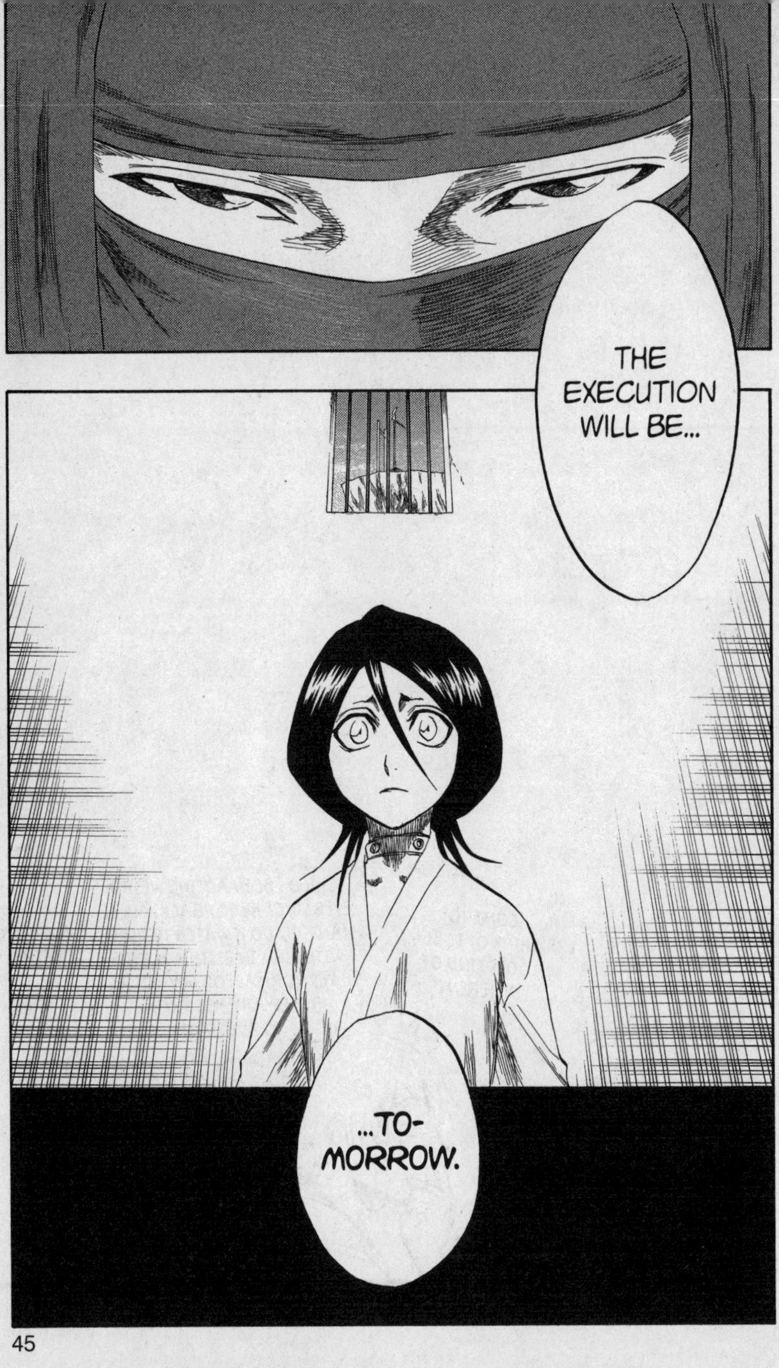
THE EXECUTION WILL BE...
...TO-MORROW.

AUGUST 9, RAINY.
ICHIGO'S BEEN ACTING WEIRD EVER SINCE HE GOT BACK. ALL HE WANTS TO DO IS WATCH TV SHOWS WITH GIRLS IN BIKINIS. MAYBE THAT'S NORMAL FOR GUYS HIS AGE, BUT IT'S LIKE HE'S TRYING TO AVOID ME.
COME TO THINK OF IT, HE LOOKS KIND OF DIFFERENT.

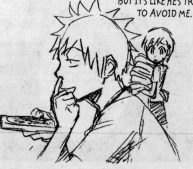

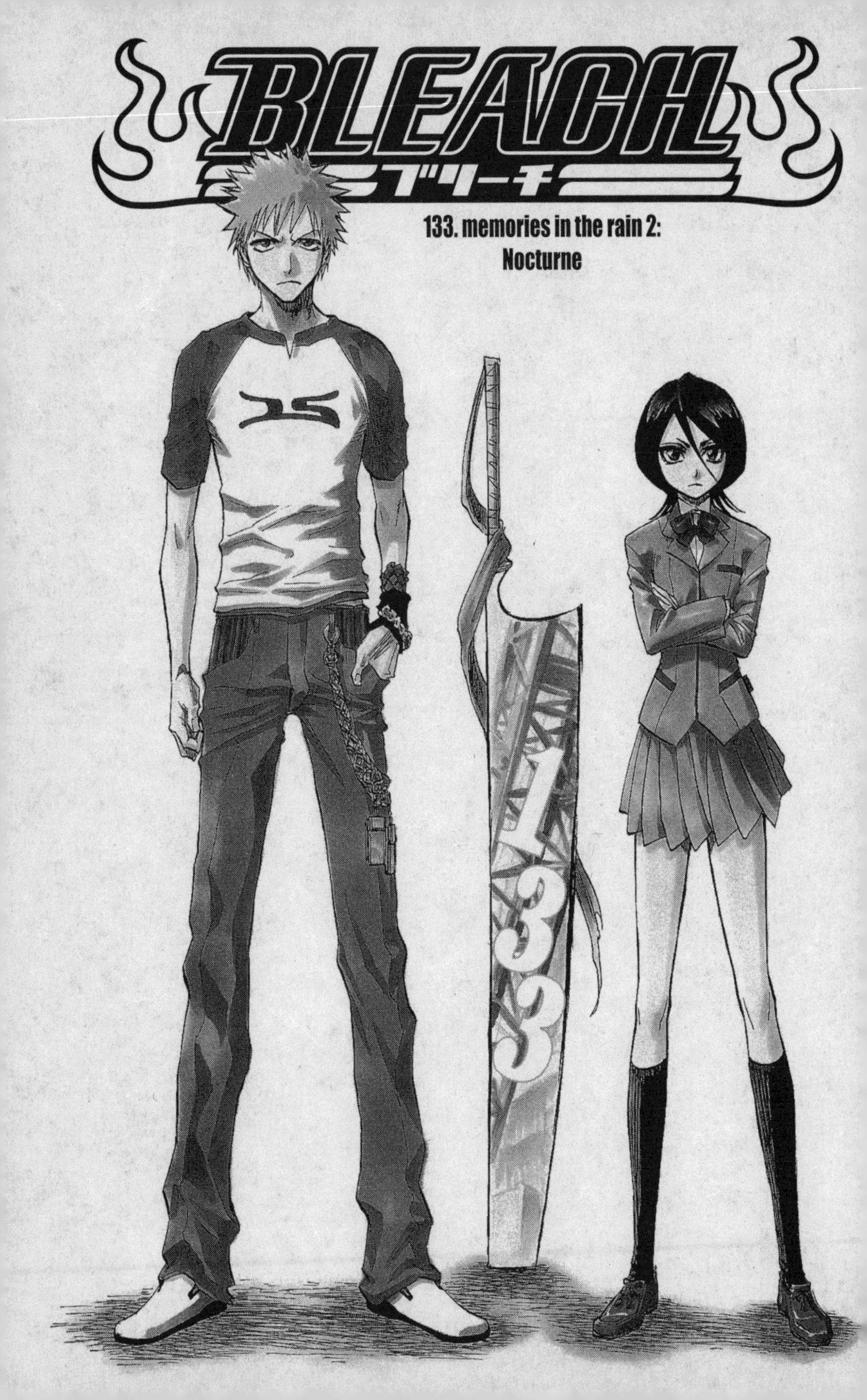
BLEACH
ブリーチ
133. memories in the rain 2:
Nocturne
133

BLEACH
ブリーチ

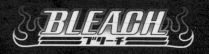

READ THIS WAY

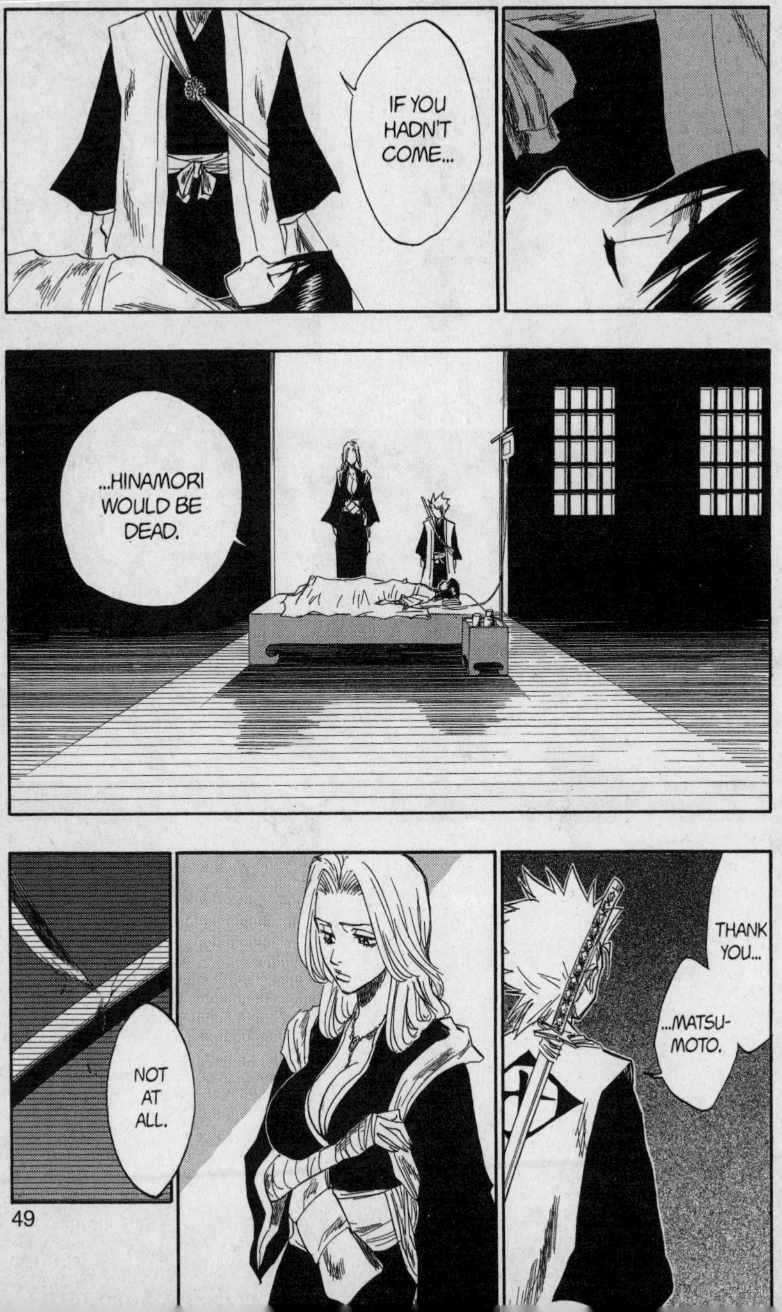
IF YOU HADN'T COME...
...HINAMORI WOULD BE DEAD.
THANK YOU...
...MATSU-MOTO.
NOT AT ALL.

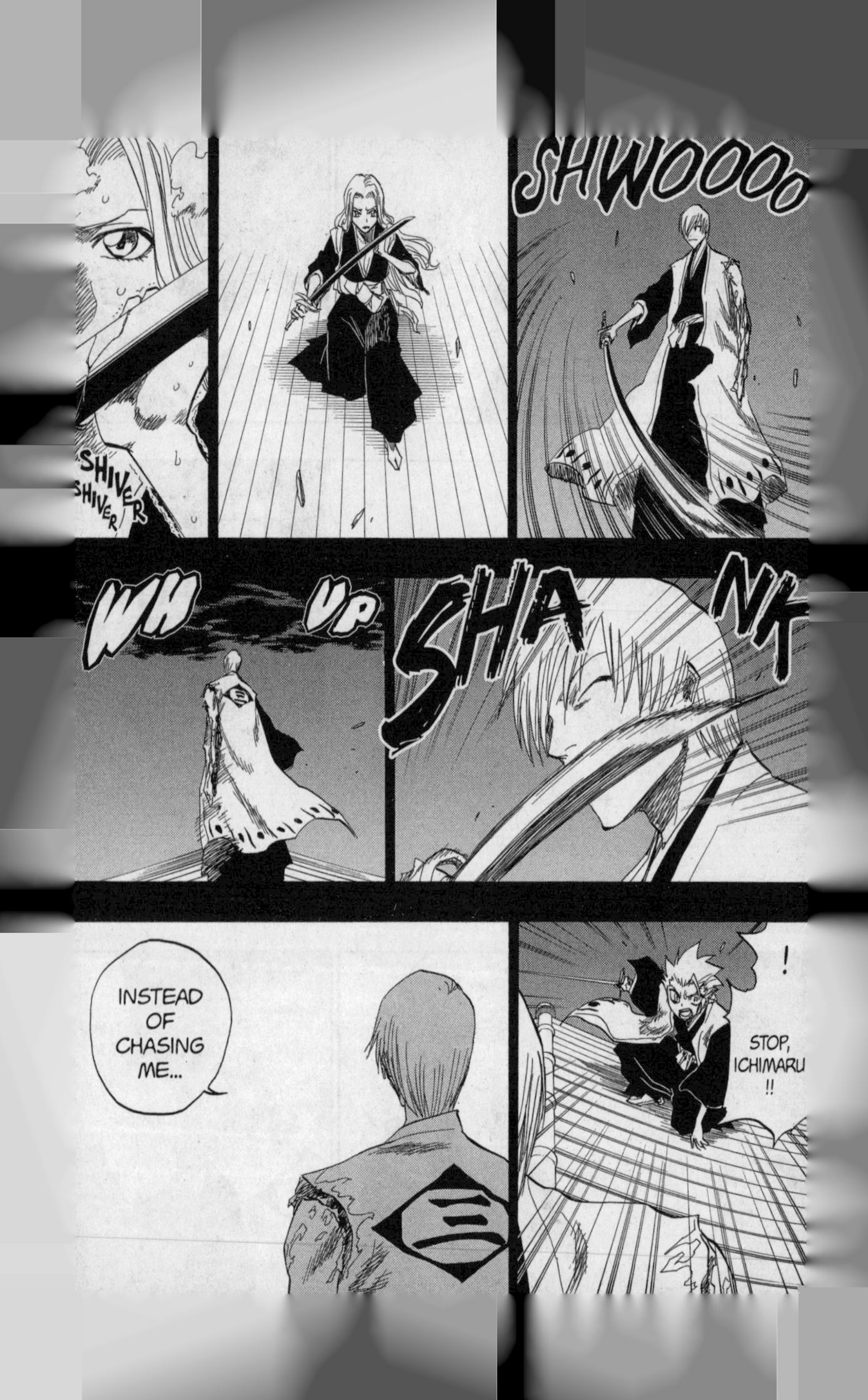
SHWOOOO
SHIVER SHIVER
SHA NK
WH UP
!
STOP, ICHIMARU!!
INSTEAD OF CHASING ME...

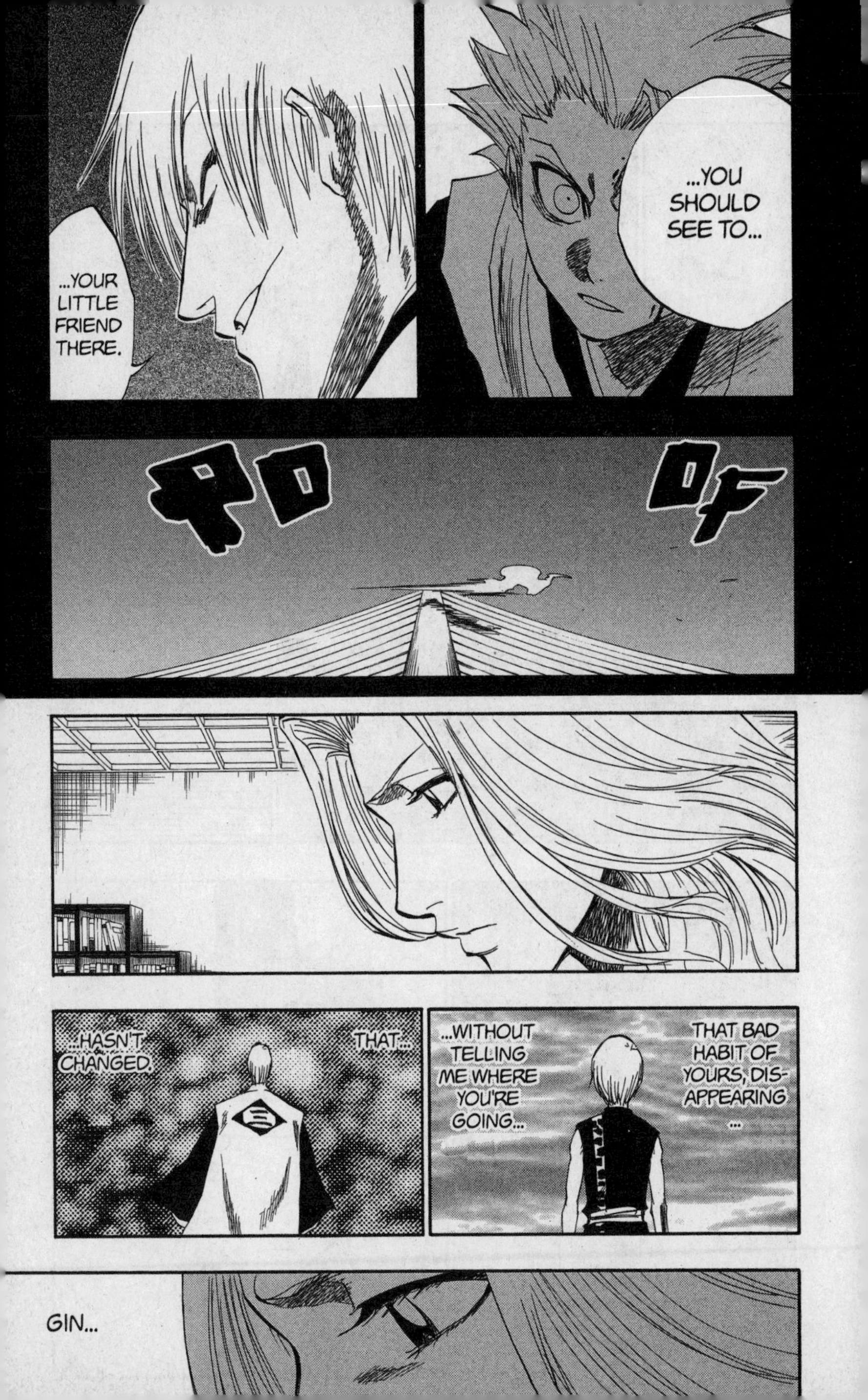
...YOU SHOULD SEE TO...
...YOUR LITTLE FRIEND THERE.
PO
OF
THAT BAD HABIT OF YOURS, DIS-APPEARING...
...WITHOUT TELLING ME WHERE YOU'RE GOING...
THAT...
...HASN'T CHANGED.
GIN...

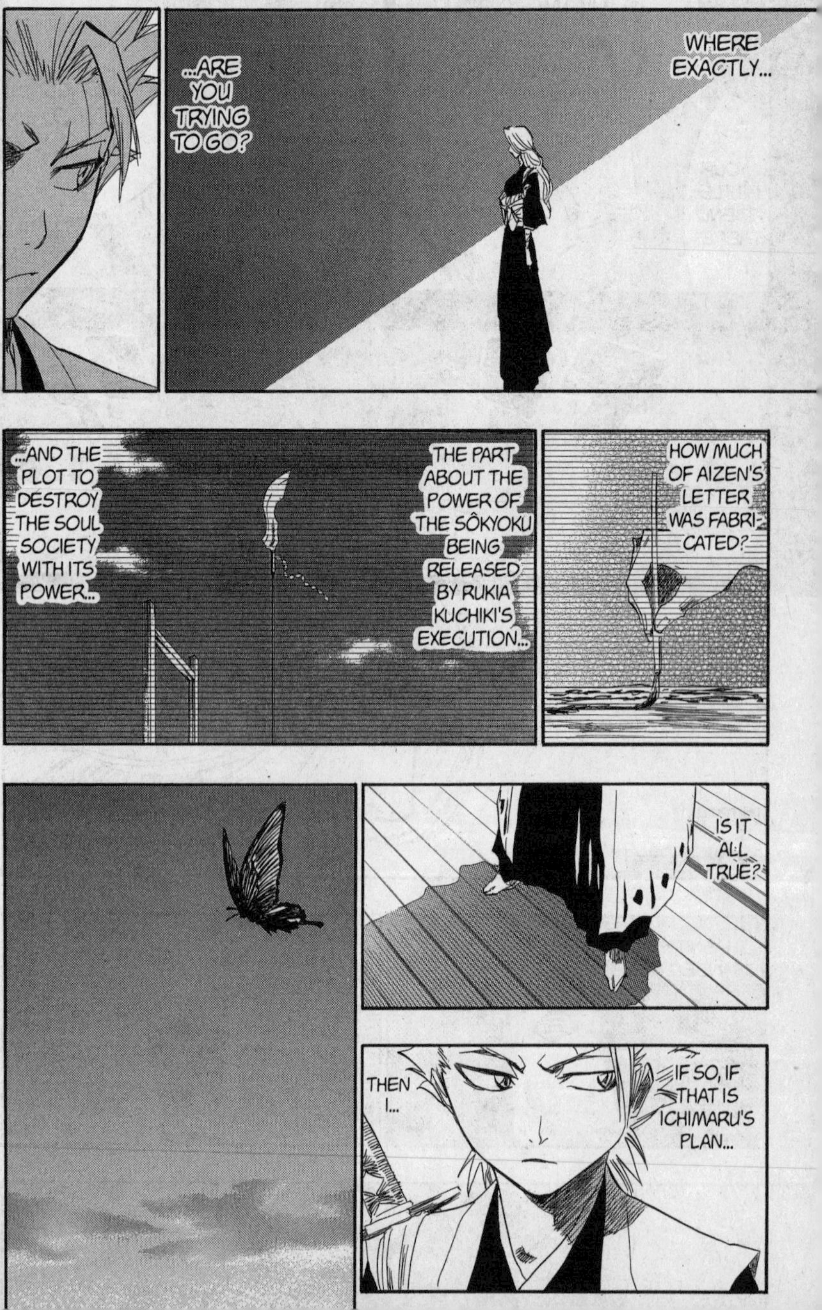
WHERE EXACTLY...
...ARE YOU TRYING TO GO?
HOW MUCH OF AIZEN'S LETTER WAS FABRICATED?
THE PART ABOUT THE POWER OF THE SÔKYOKU BEING RELEASED BY RUKIA KUCHIKI'S EXECUTION...
...AND THE PLOT TO DESTROY THE SOUL SOCIETY WITH ITS POWER...
IS IT ALL TRUE?
IF SO, IF THAT IS ICHIMARU'S PLAN...
THEN I...

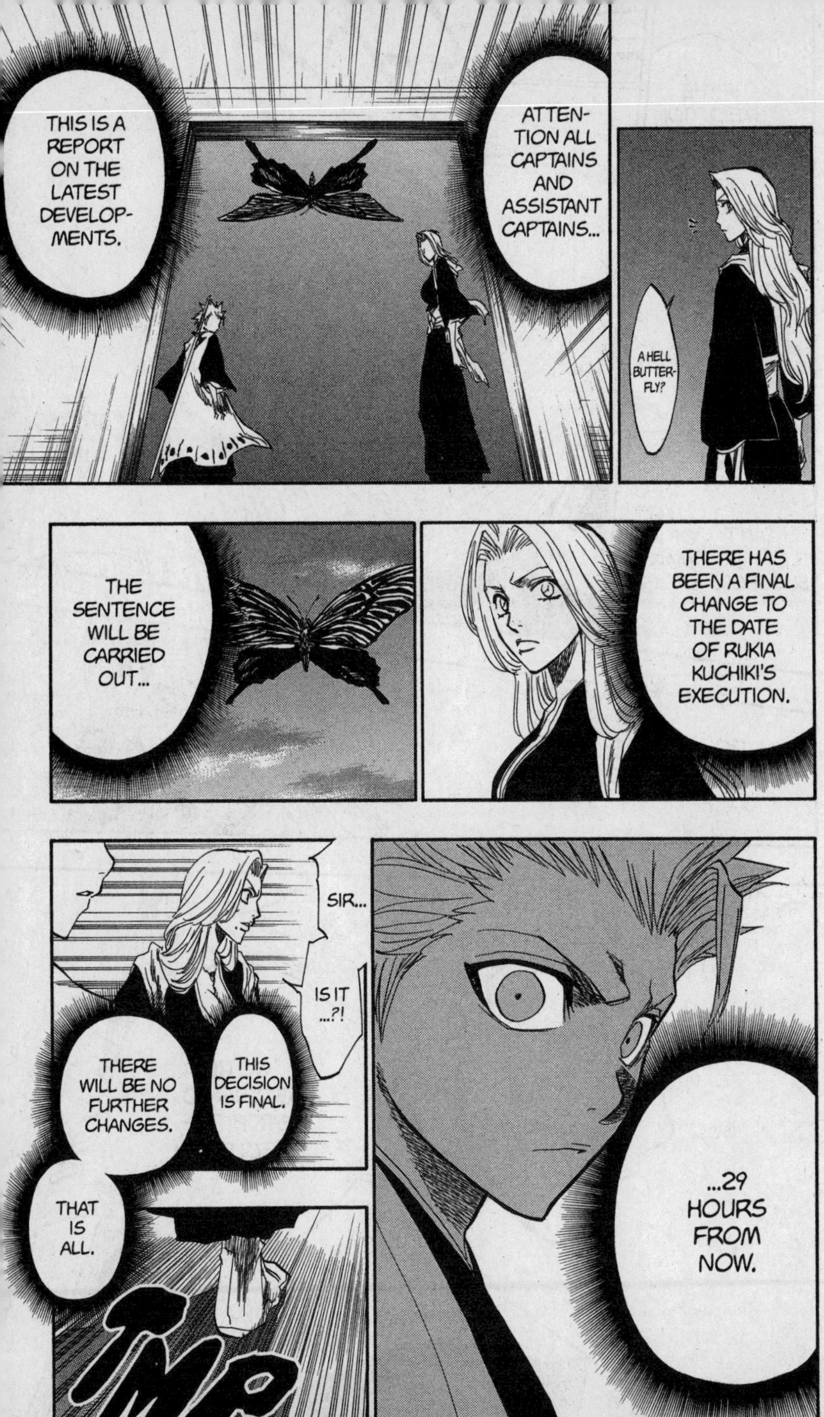
A HELL BUTTERFLY?
ATTENTION ALL CAPTAINS AND ASSISTANT CAPTAINS...
THIS IS A REPORT ON THE LATEST DEVELOPMENTS.
THERE HAS BEEN A FINAL CHANGE TO THE DATE OF RUKIA KUCHIKI'S EXECUTION.
THE SENTENCE WILL BE CARRIED OUT...
...29 HOURS FROM NOW.
SIR...
IS IT ...?!
THIS DECISION IS FINAL.
THERE WILL BE NO FURTHER CHANGES.
THAT IS ALL.
TMP

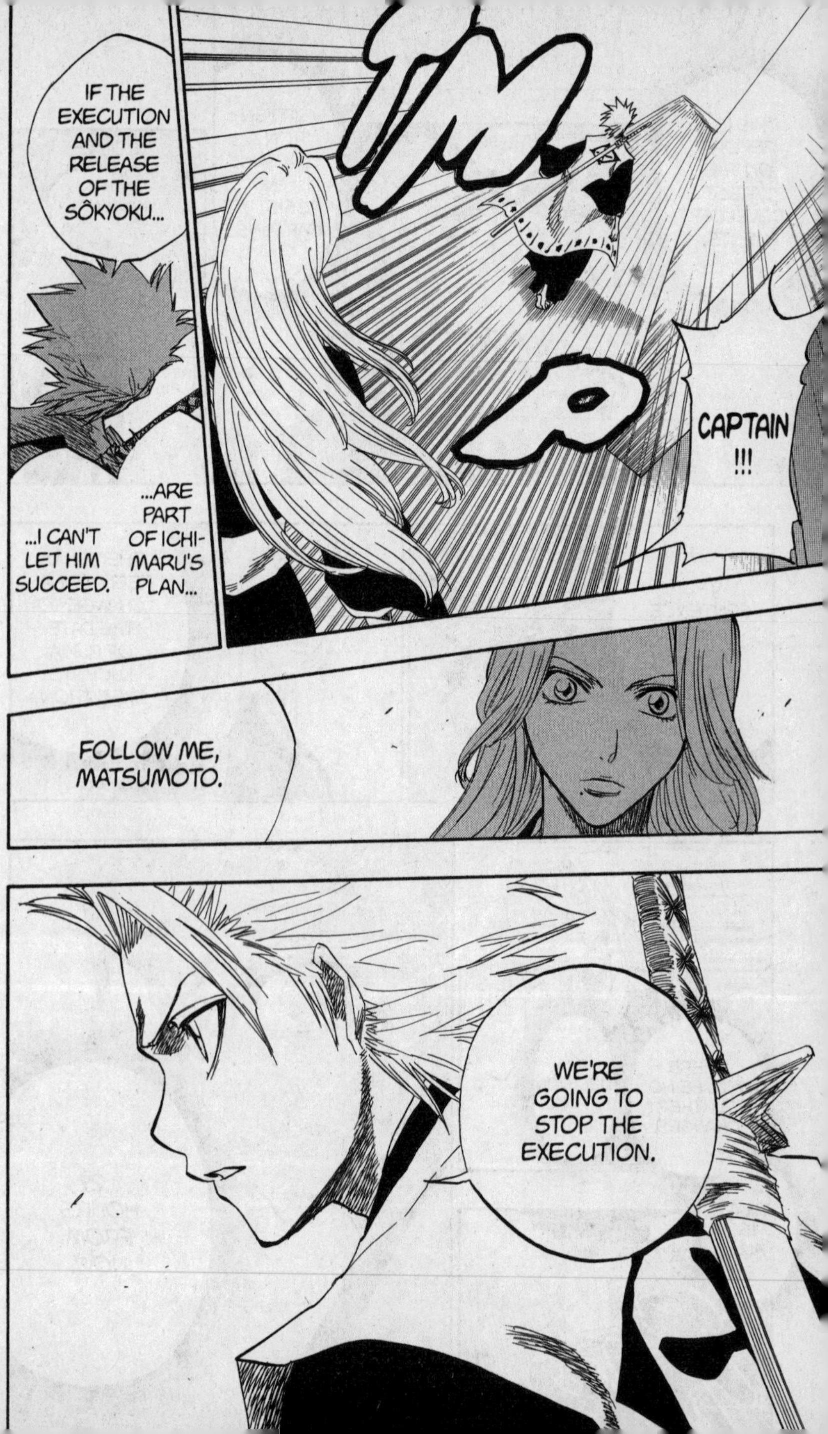
CAPTAIN !!!
IF THE EXECUTION AND THE RELEASE OF THE SÔKYOKU...
...ARE PART OF ICHI-MARU'S PLAN...
...I CAN'T LET HIM SUCCEED.
FOLLOW ME, MATSUMOTO.
WE'RE GOING TO STOP THE EXECUTION.

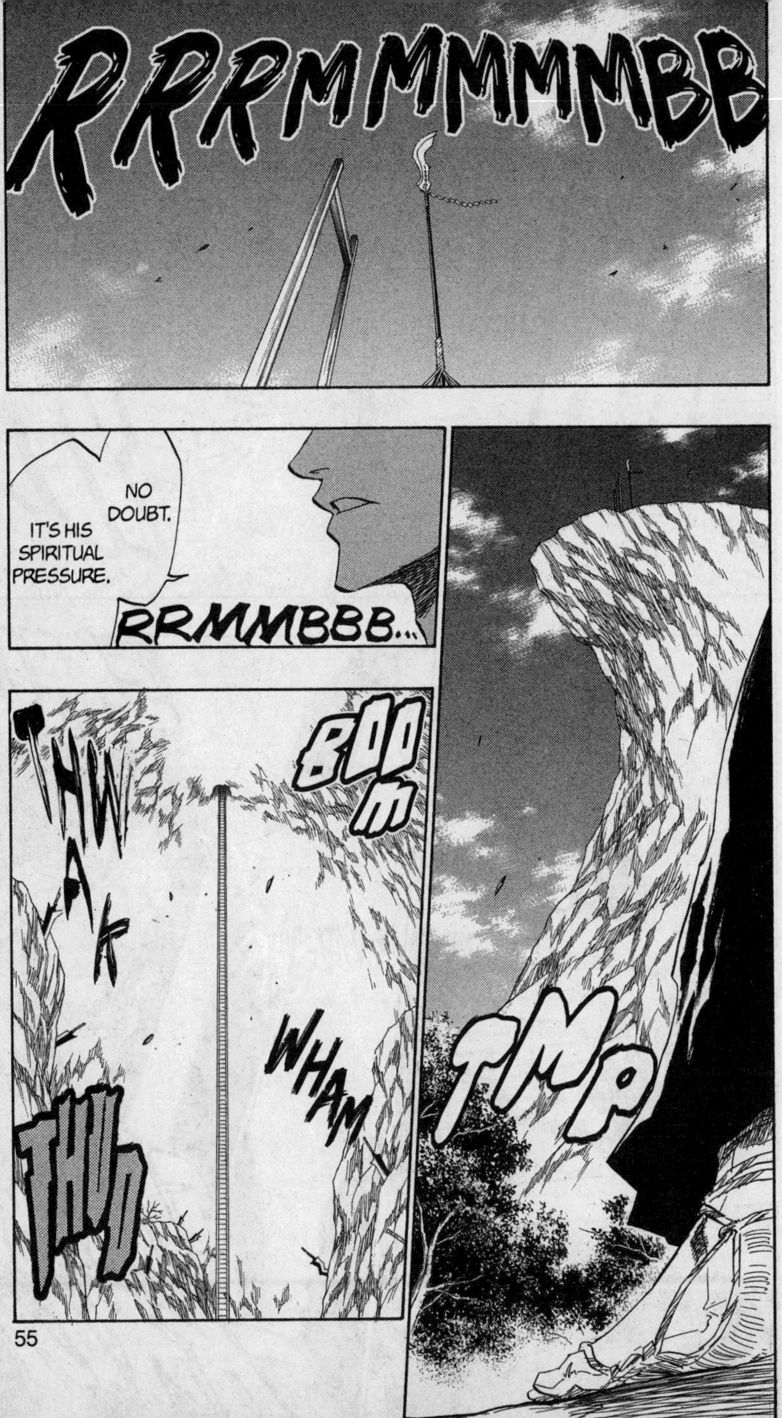
RRRMMMMMBB
TMP
NO DOUBT.
IT'S HIS SPIRITUAL PRESSURE.
RRMMBBB...
BOOM
WHAM
THWAK
THUD

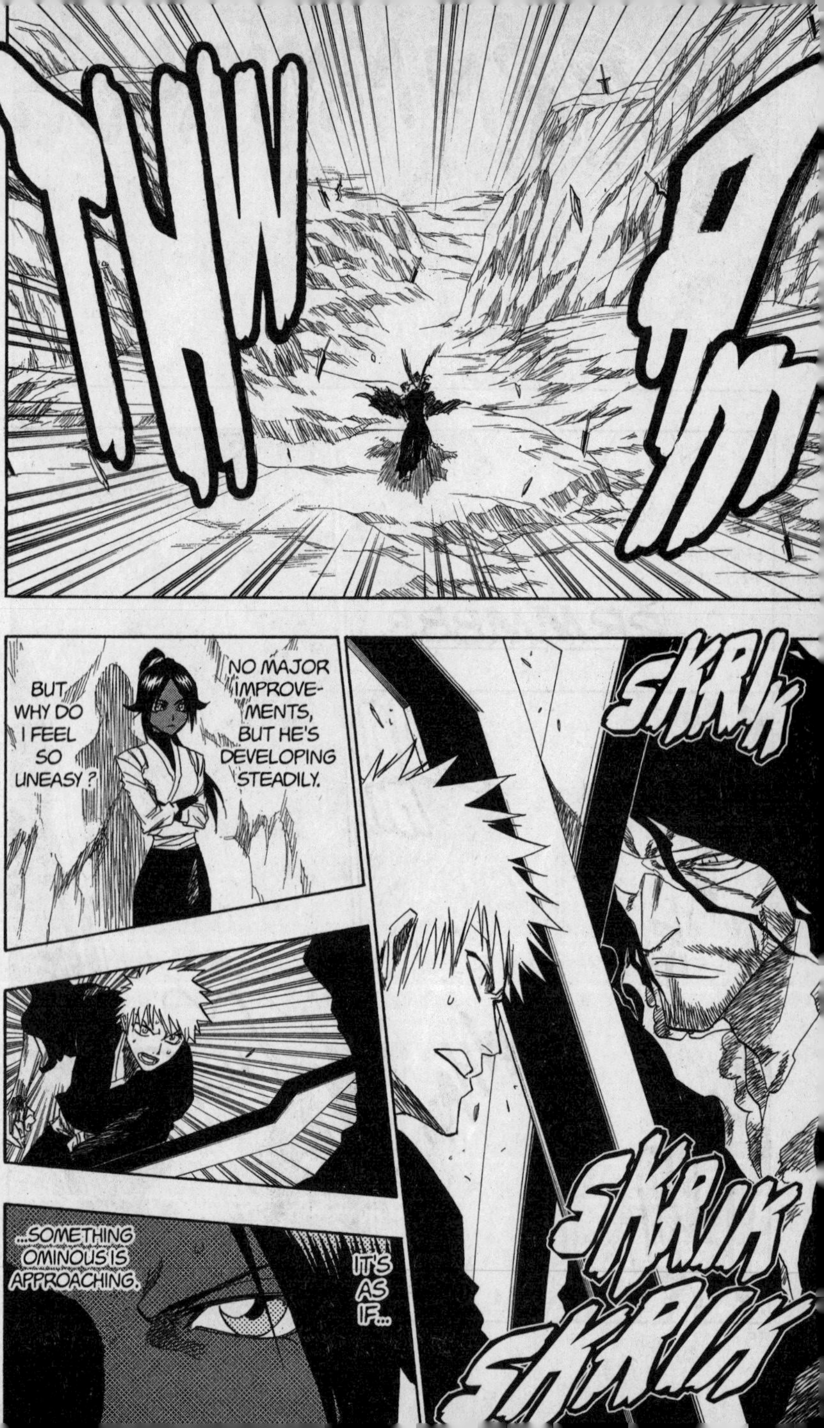
THW
SKRIK
SKRIK
SKRIK
NO MAJOR IMPROVEMENTS, BUT HE'S DEVELOPING STEADILY.
BUT WHY DO I FEEL SO UNEASY?
IT'S AS IF...
...SOMETHING OMINOUS IS APPROACHING.

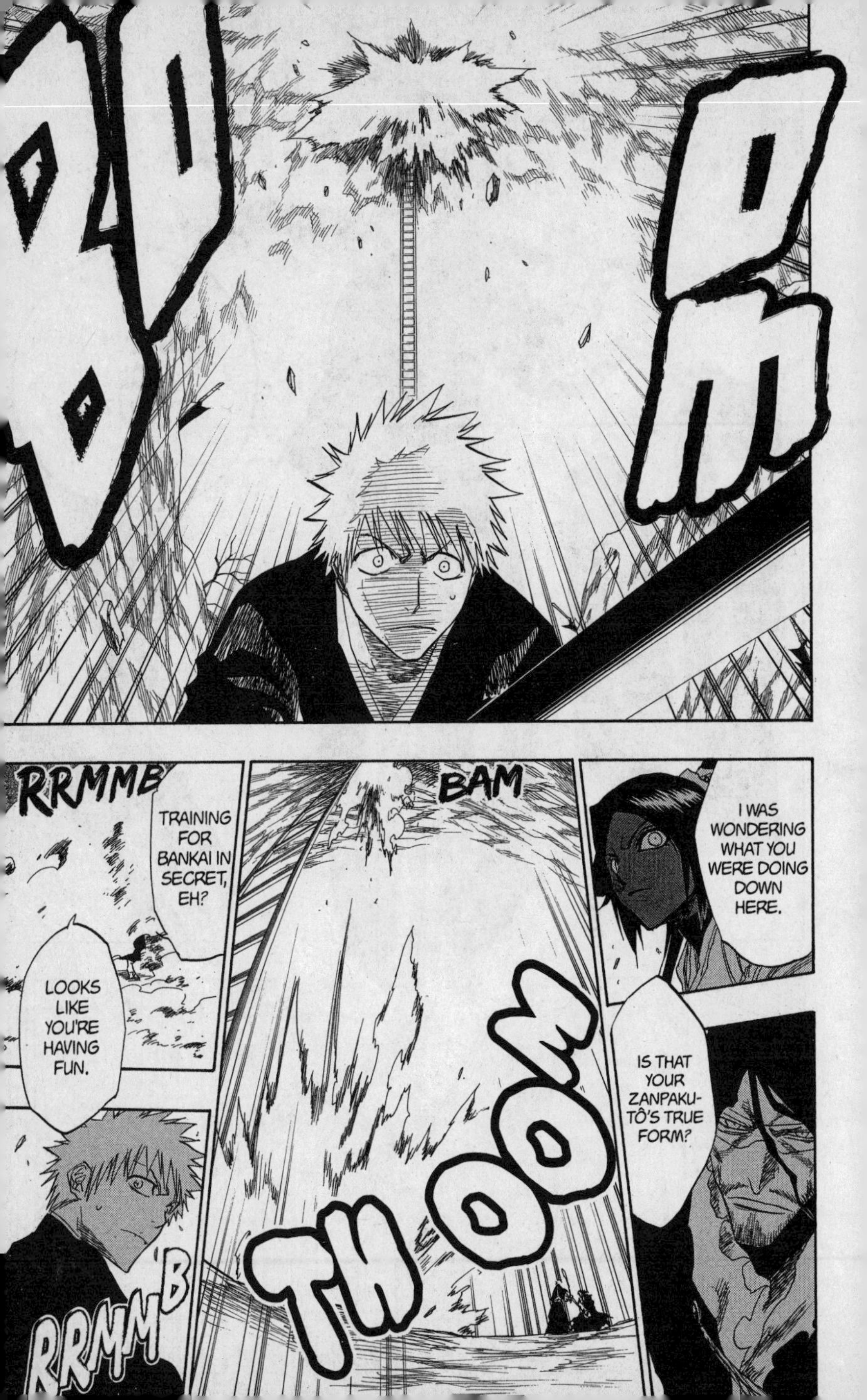
I WAS WONDERING WHAT YOU WERE DOING DOWN HERE.
IS THAT YOUR ZANPAKU-TÔ'S TRUE FORM?
BAM
THOOOM
RRMMB
TRAINING FOR BANKAI IN SECRET, EH?
LOOKS LIKE YOU'RE HAVING FUN.
RRMMB

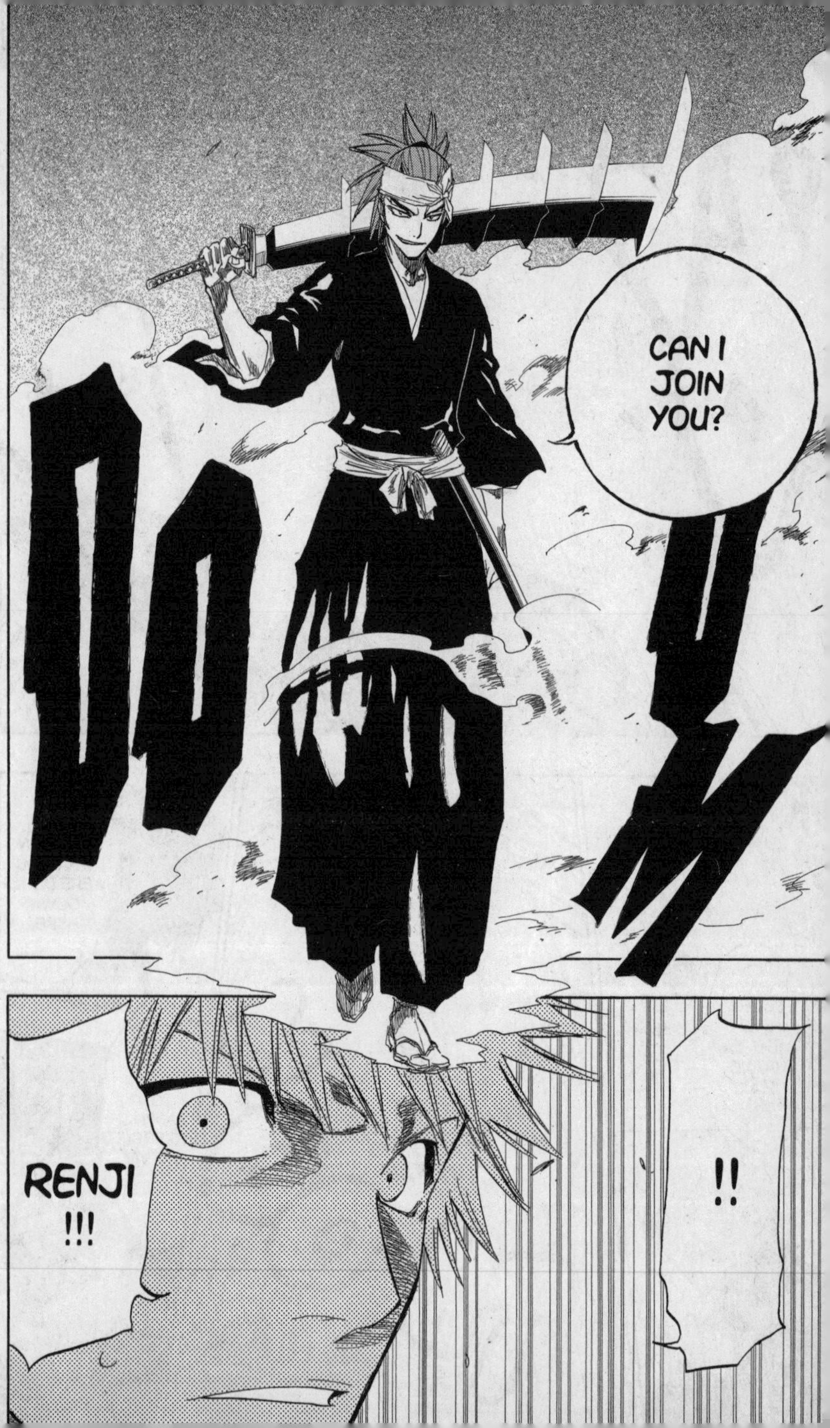
DOOM
CAN I JOIN YOU?
!!
RENJI !!!

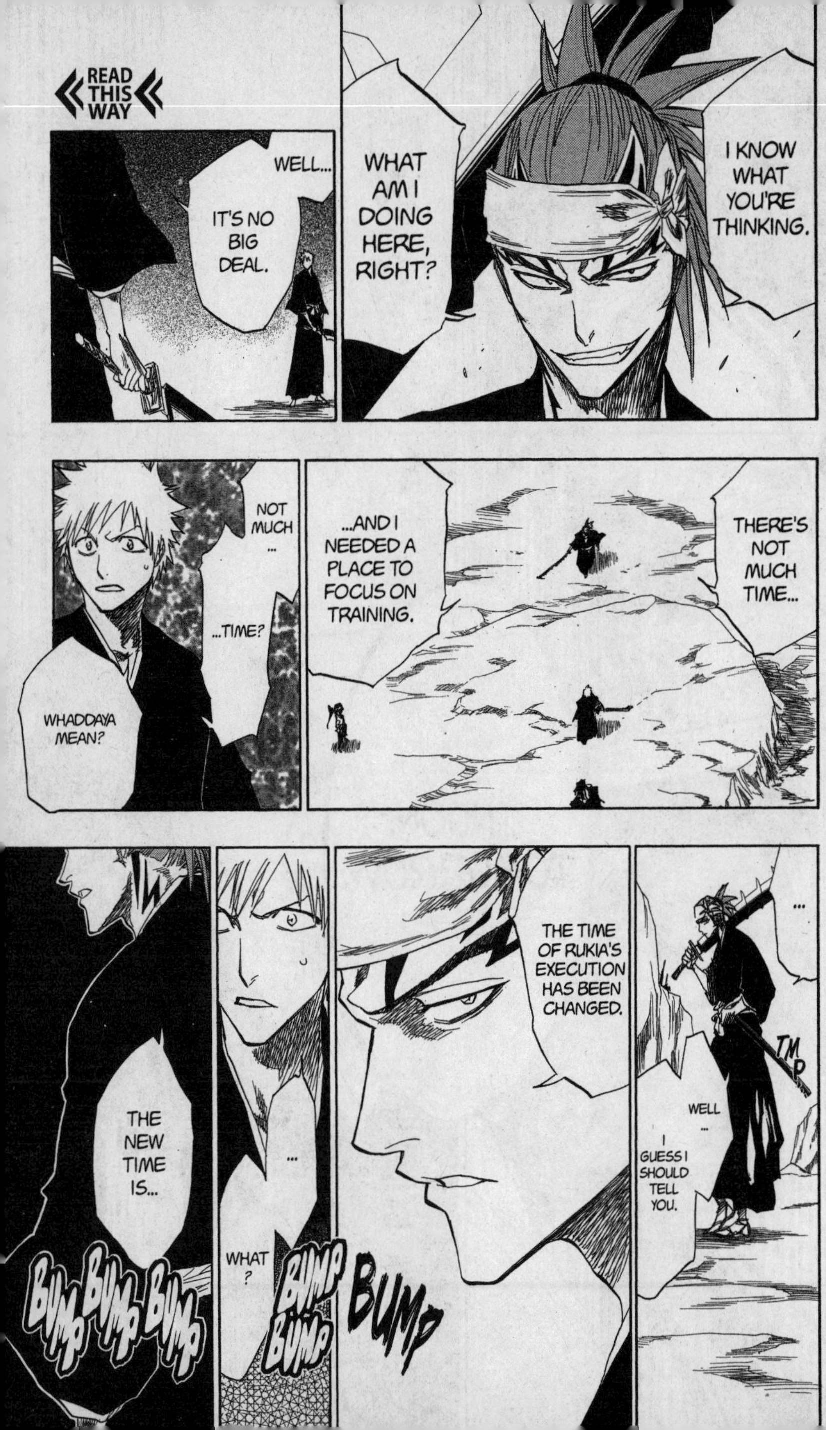
READ THIS WAY
I KNOW WHAT YOU'RE THINKING.
WHAT AM I DOING HERE, RIGHT?
WELL...
IT'S NO BIG DEAL.
THERE'S NOT MUCH TIME...
...AND I NEEDED A PLACE TO FOCUS ON TRAINING.
NOT MUCH ...
...TIME?
WHADDAYA MEAN?
...
TMP
WELL ...
I GUESS I SHOULD TELL YOU.
THE TIME OF RUKIA'S EXECUTION HAS BEEN CHANGED.
BUMP
...
WHAT ?
BUMP BUMP
THE NEW TIME IS...
BUMP BUMP BUMP

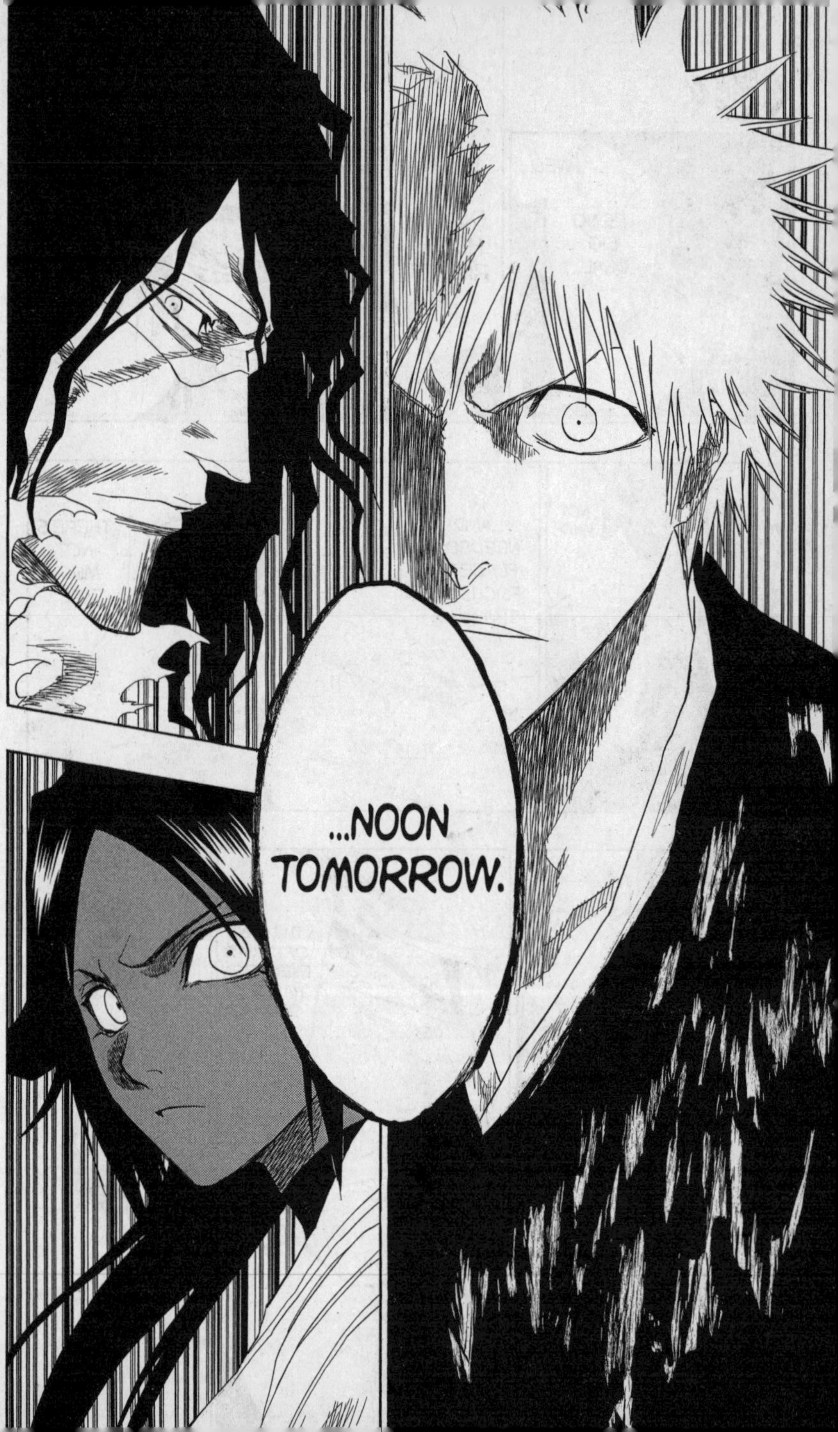
...NOON TOMORROW.

READ THIS WAY

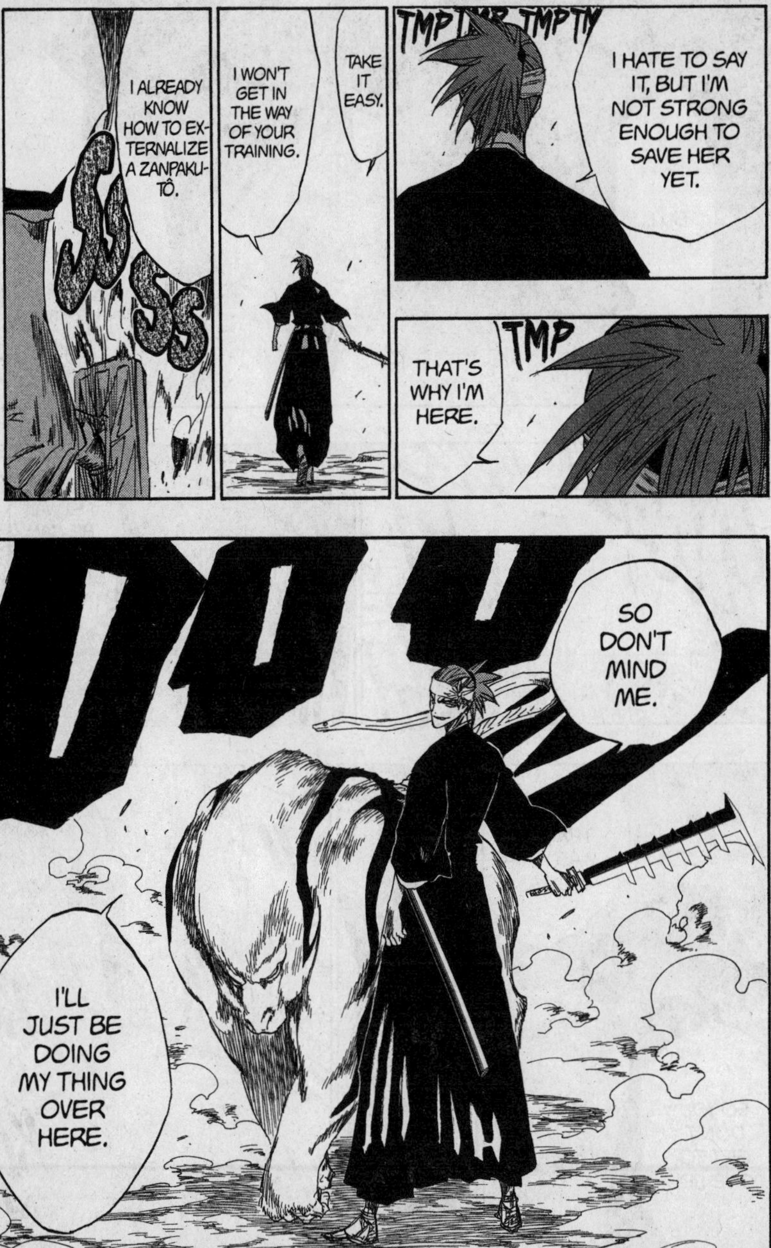
TMP TMP TMP
I HATE TO SAY IT, BUT I'M NOT STRONG ENOUGH TO SAVE HER YET.
TMP
THAT'S WHY I'M HERE.
TAKE IT EASY.
I WON'T GET IN THE WAY OF YOUR TRAINING.
I ALREADY KNOW HOW TO EX-TERNALIZE A ZANPAKU-TÔ.
SSS
SO DON'T MIND ME.
I'LL JUST BE DOING MY THING OVER HERE.

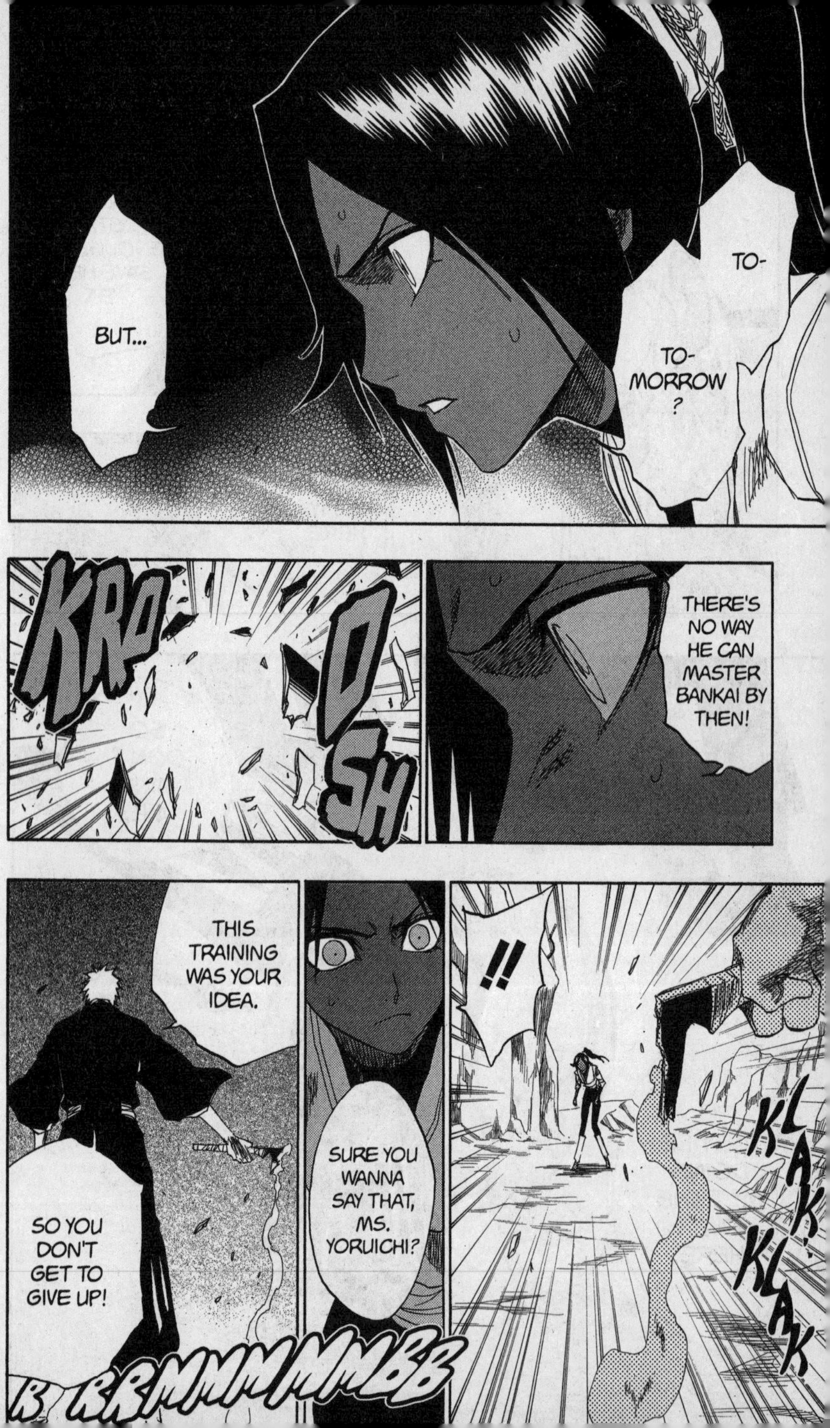
TO-
TO- MORROW ?
BUT...
THERE'S NO WAY HE CAN MASTER BANKAI BY THEN!
KRO-OSH
!!
KLAK! KLAK
SURE YOU WANNA SAY THAT, MS. YORUICHI?
THIS TRAINING WAS YOUR IDEA.
SO YOU DON'T GET TO GIVE UP!
BRRMMMMMMMBB

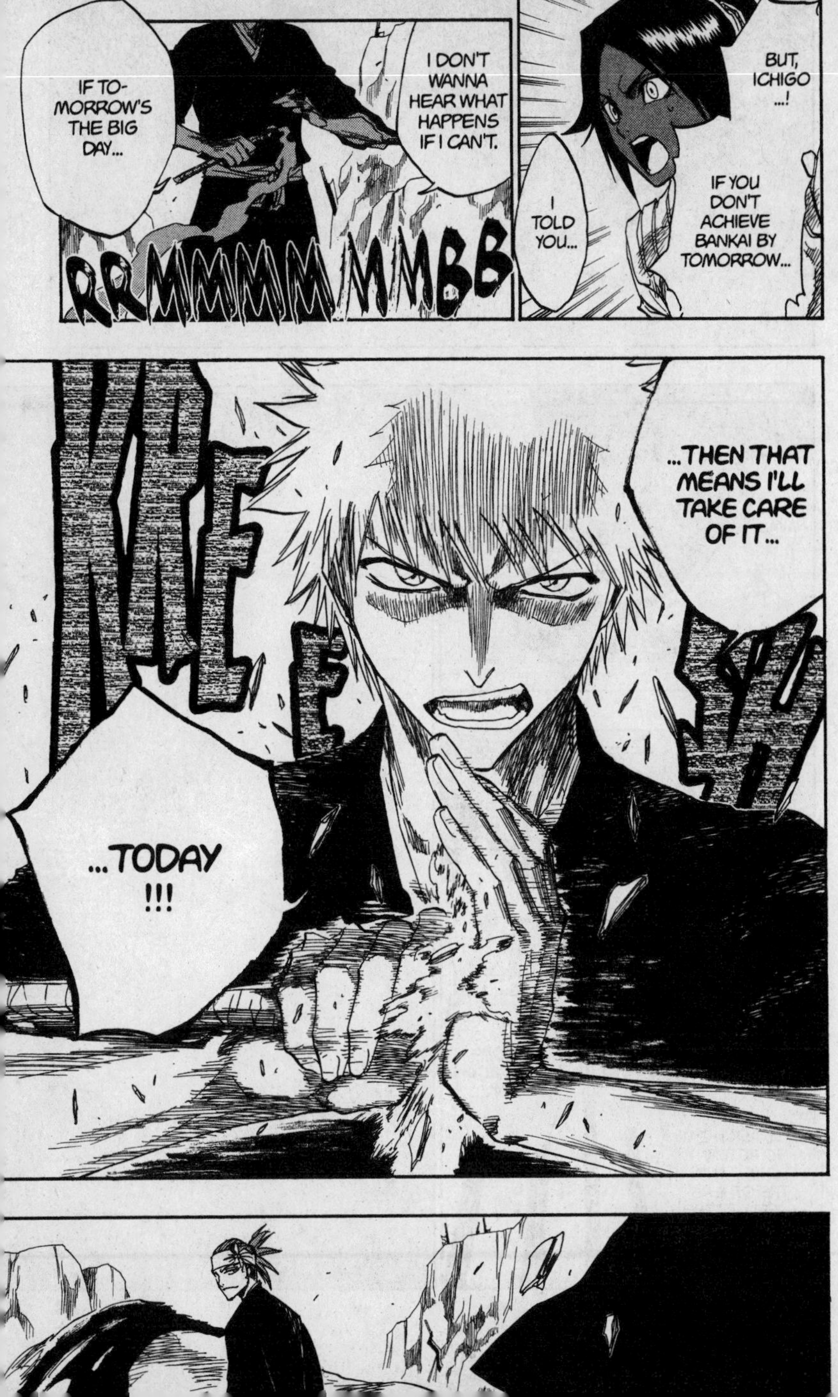
BUT, ICHIGO ...!
IF YOU DON'T ACHIEVE BANKAI BY TOMORROW...
I TOLD YOU...
I DON'T WANNA HEAR WHAT HAPPENS IF I CAN'T.
IF TO-MORROW'S THE BIG DAY...
RRMMMMMMMBB
...THEN THAT MEANS I'LL TAKE CARE OF IT...
...TODAY !!!

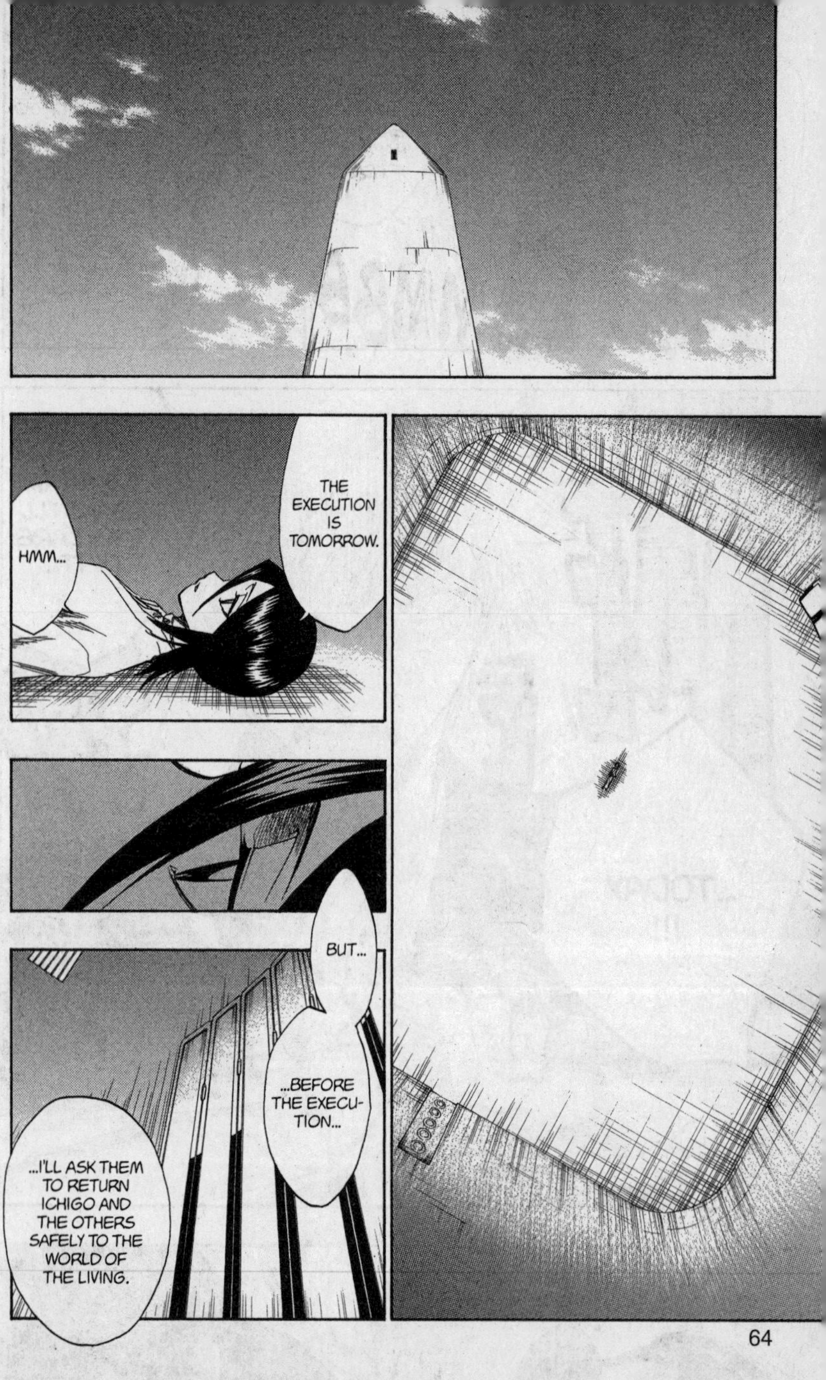
THE EXECUTION IS TOMORROW.
HMM...
BUT...
...BEFORE THE EXECU-TION...
...I'LL ASK THEM TO RETURN ICHIGO AND THE OTHERS SAFELY TO THE WORLD OF THE LIVING.

READ THIS WAY

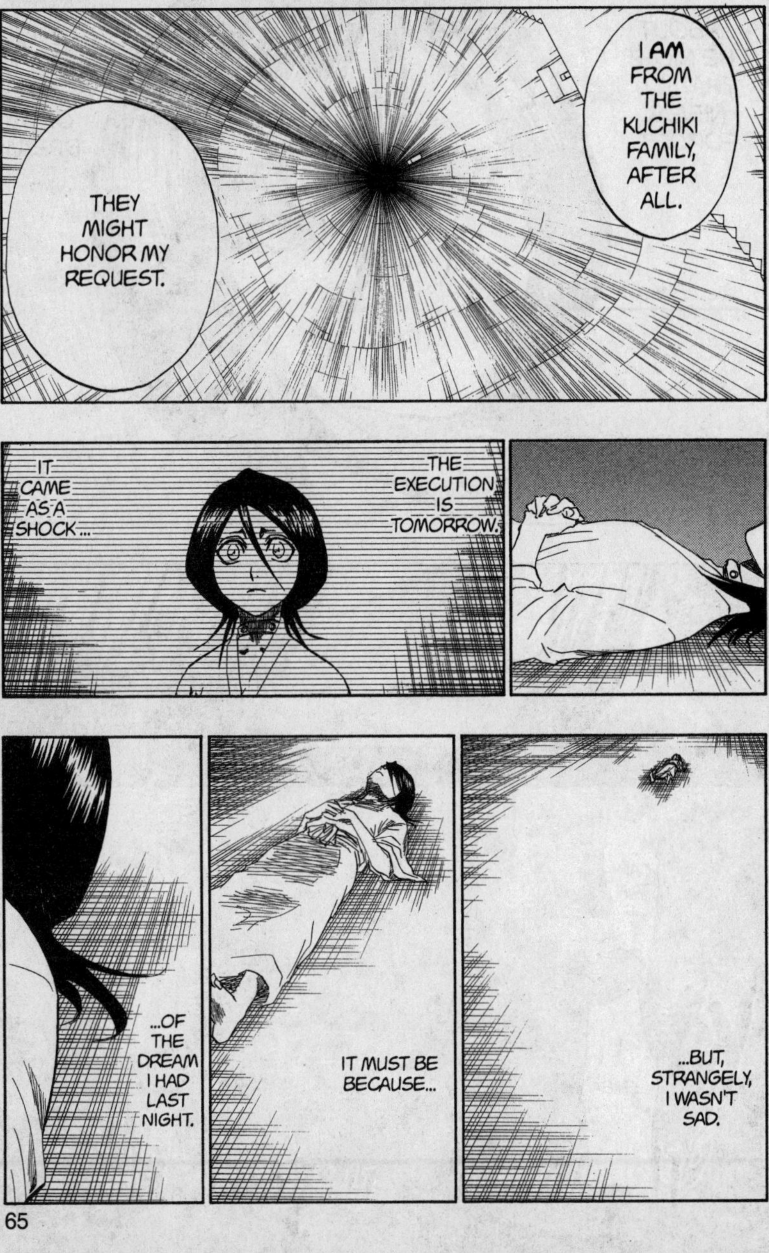
I AM FROM THE KUCHIKI FAMILY, AFTER ALL.
THEY MIGHT HONOR MY REQUEST.
THE EXECUTION IS TOMORROW.
IT CAME AS A SHOCK...
...BUT, STRANGELY, I WASN'T SAD.
IT MUST BE BECAUSE...
...OF THE DREAM I HAD LAST NIGHT.

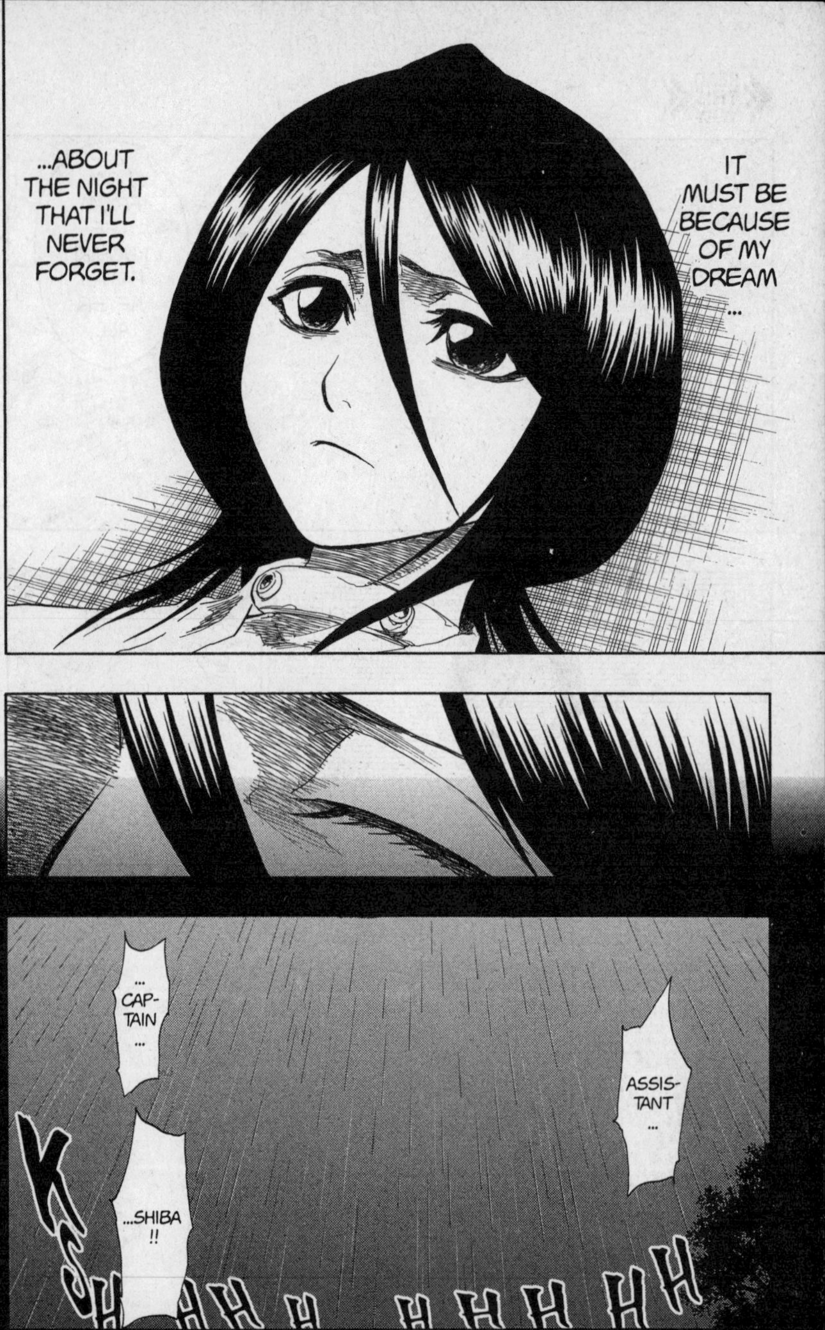
IT MUST BE BECAUSE OF MY DREAM...
...ABOUT THE NIGHT THAT I'LL NEVER FORGET.
ASSIS-TANT...
...CAP-TAIN...
...SHIBA!!
KSHHHHHHHHHHH

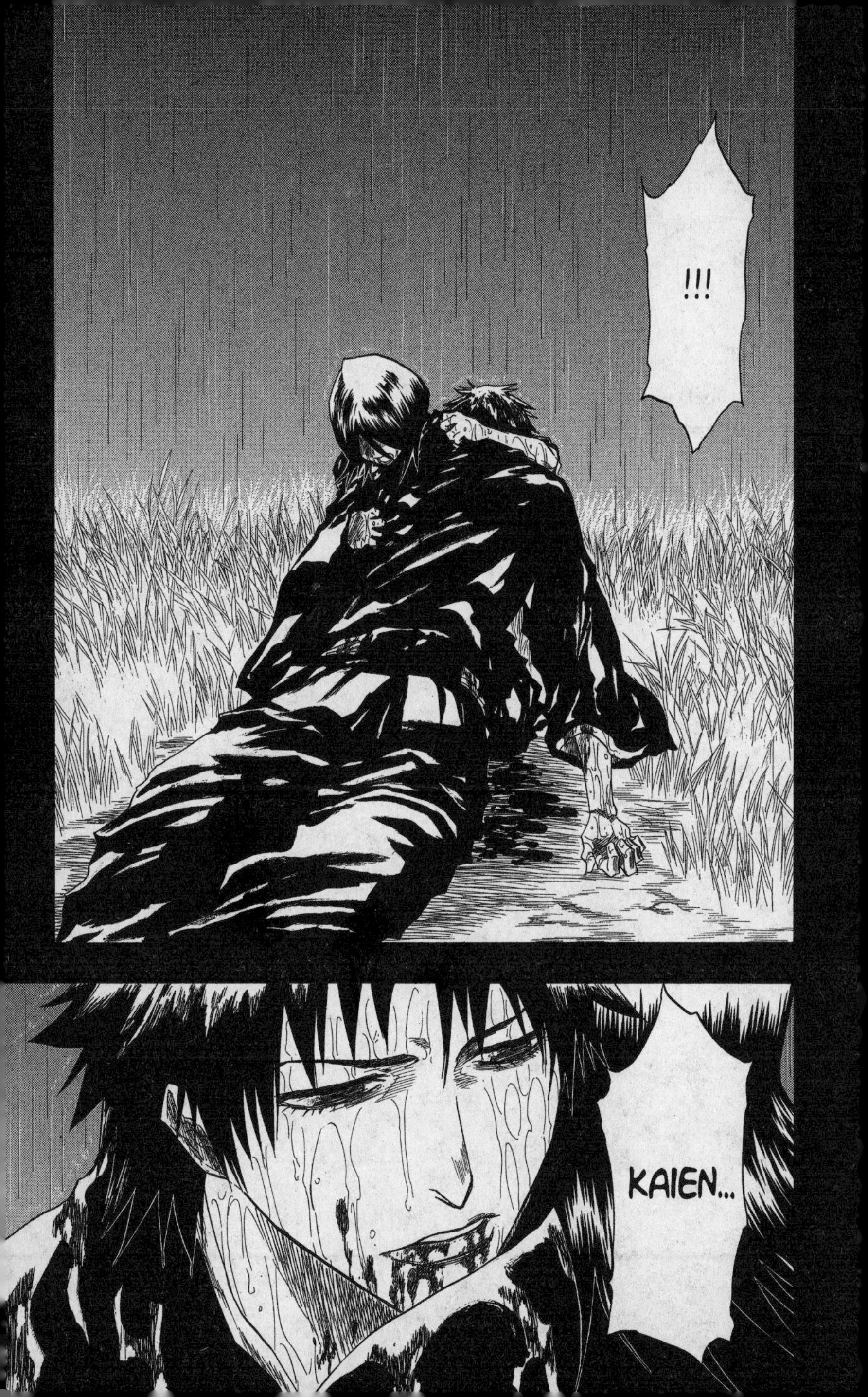
!!!
KAIEN...

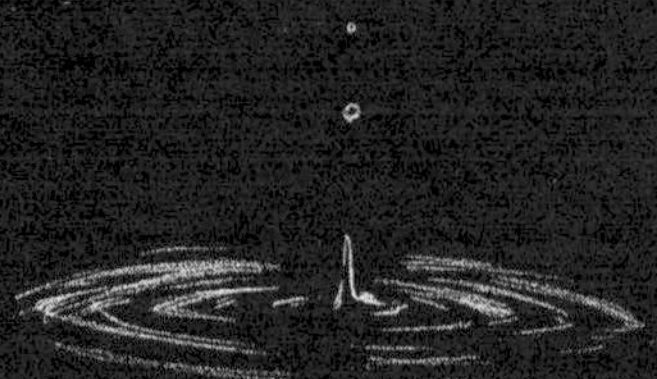

134. memories in the rain 2, op. 2: Longing for Sanctuary

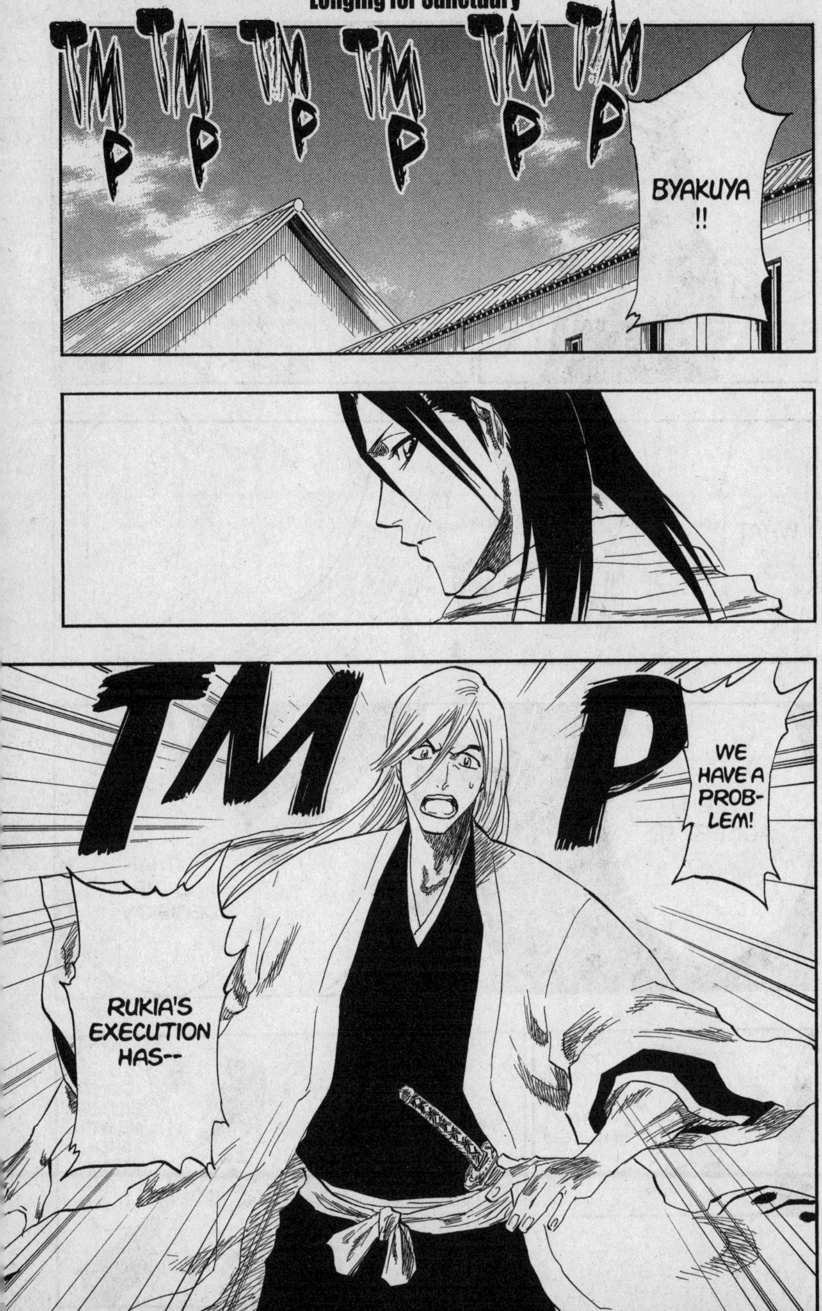
TMP TMP TMP TMP TMP TMP
BYAKUYA!!
WE HAVE A PROB-LEM!
TMP
RUKIA'S EXECUTION HAS--

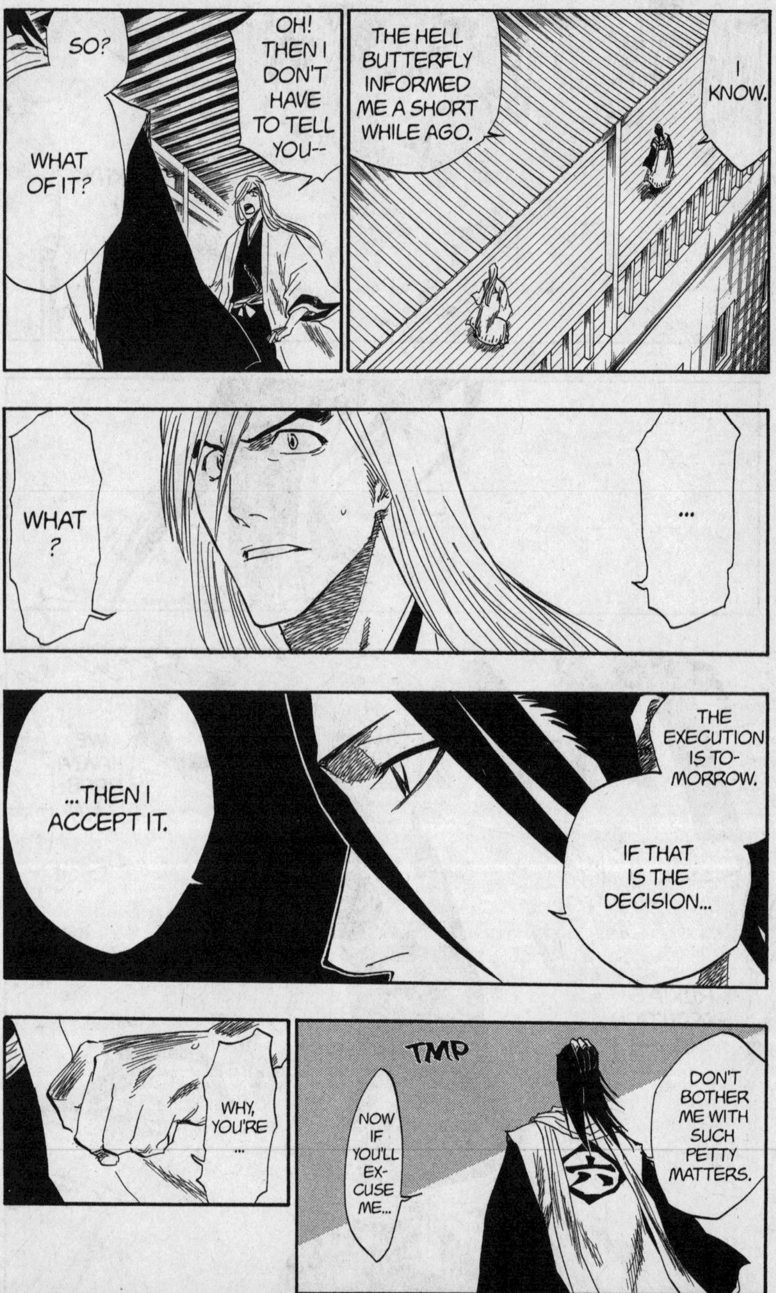
I KNOW.
THE HELL BUTTERFLY INFORMED ME A SHORT WHILE AGO.
OH! THEN I DON'T HAVE TO TELL YOU--
SO?
WHAT OF IT?
...
WHAT ?
THE EXECUTION IS TO-MORROW.
IF THAT IS THE DECISION...
...THEN I ACCEPT IT.
TMP
DON'T BOTHER ME WITH SUCH PETTY MATTERS.
NOW IF YOU'LL EX-CUSE ME...
WHY, YOU'RE ...

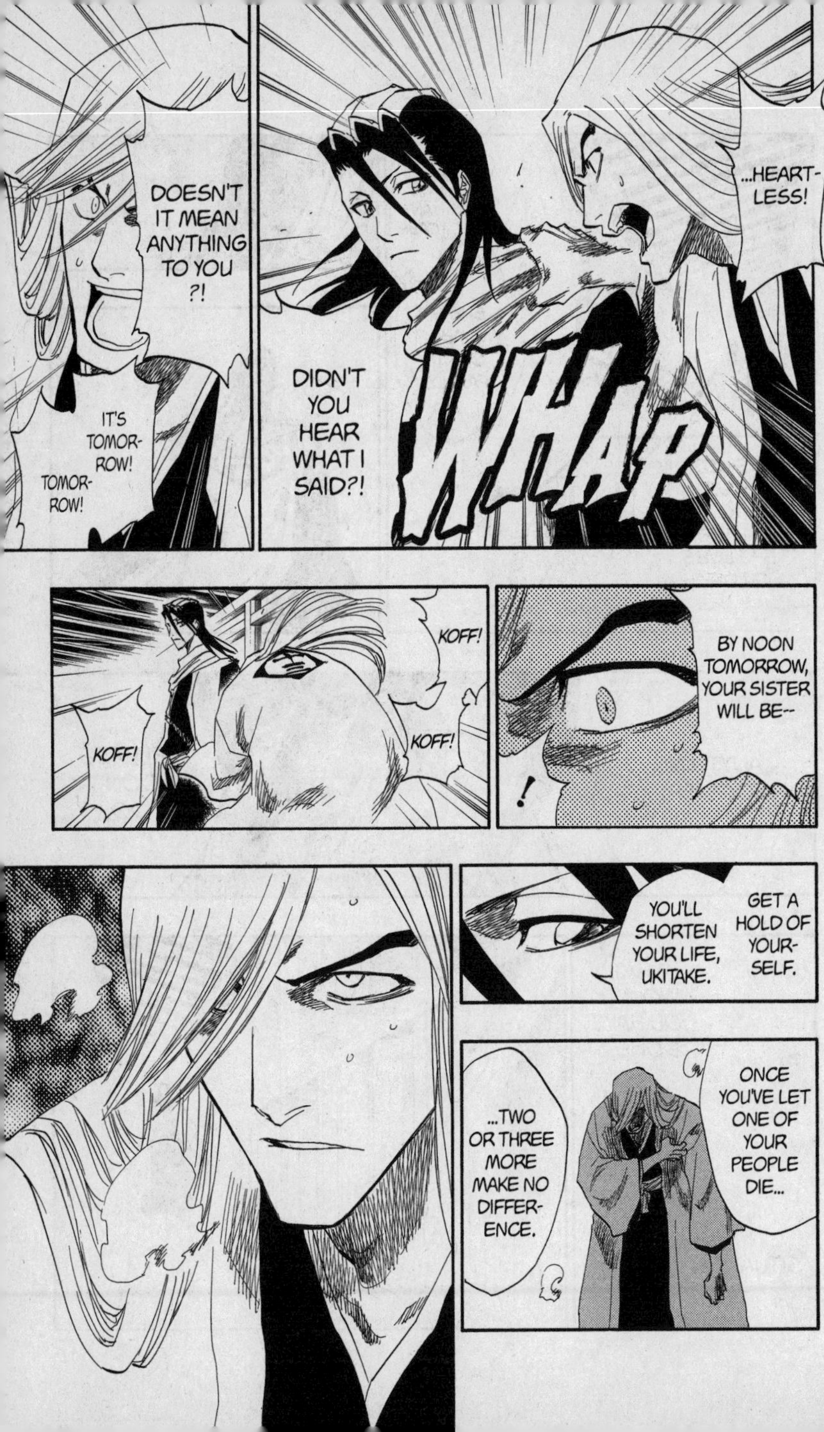
...HEART-LESS!
WHAP
DIDN'T YOU HEAR WHAT I SAID?!
DOESN'T IT MEAN ANYTHING TO YOU ?!
IT'S TOMOR-ROW!
TOMOR-ROW!
BY NOON TOMORROW, YOUR SISTER WILL BE--
!
KOFF!
KOFF!
KOFF!
GET A HOLD OF YOUR-SELF.
YOU'LL SHORTEN YOUR LIFE, UKITAKE.
ONCE YOU'VE LET ONE OF YOUR PEOPLE DIE...
...TWO OR THREE MORE MAKE NO DIFFER-ENCE.

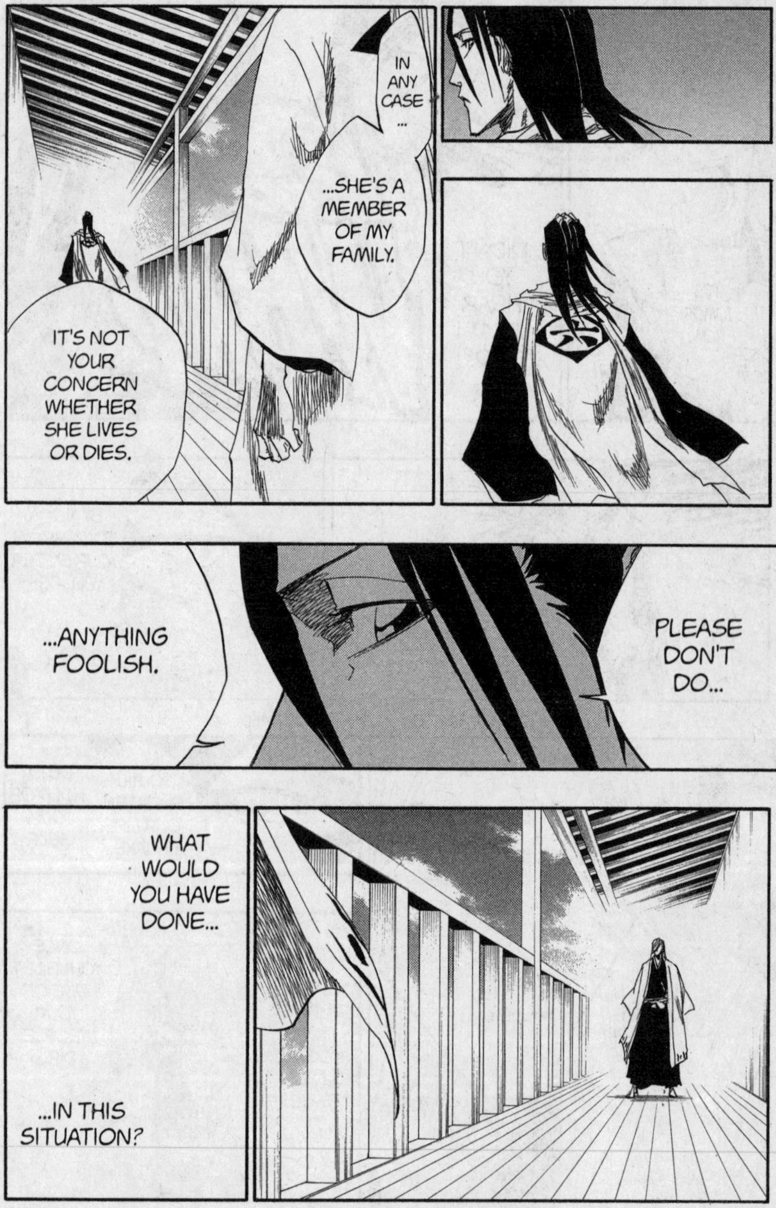
IN ANY CASE ...
...SHE'S A MEMBER OF MY FAMILY.
IT'S NOT YOUR CONCERN WHETHER SHE LIVES OR DIES.
PLEASE DON'T DO...
...ANYTHING FOOLISH.
WHAT WOULD YOU HAVE DONE...
...IN THIS SITUATION?

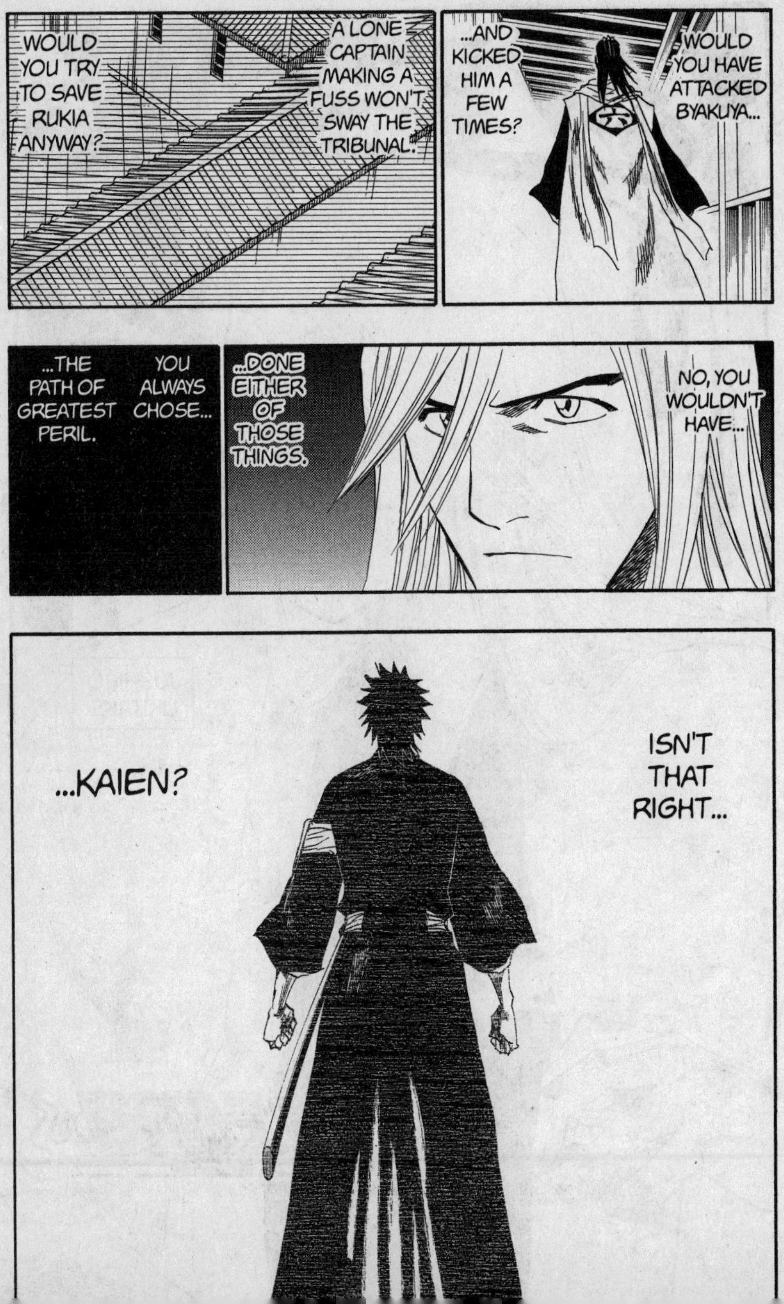
WOULD YOU HAVE ATTACKED BYAKUYA...
...AND KICKED HIM A FEW TIMES?
A LONE CAPTAIN MAKING A FUSS WON'T SWAY THE TRIBUNAL.
WOULD YOU TRY TO SAVE RUKIA ANYWAY?
NO, YOU WOULDN'T HAVE...
...DONE EITHER OF THOSE THINGS.
YOU ALWAYS CHOSE...
...THE PATH OF GREATEST PERIL.
ISN'T THAT RIGHT...
...KAIEN?

134. memories in the rain 2, op. 2: Longing for Sanctuary

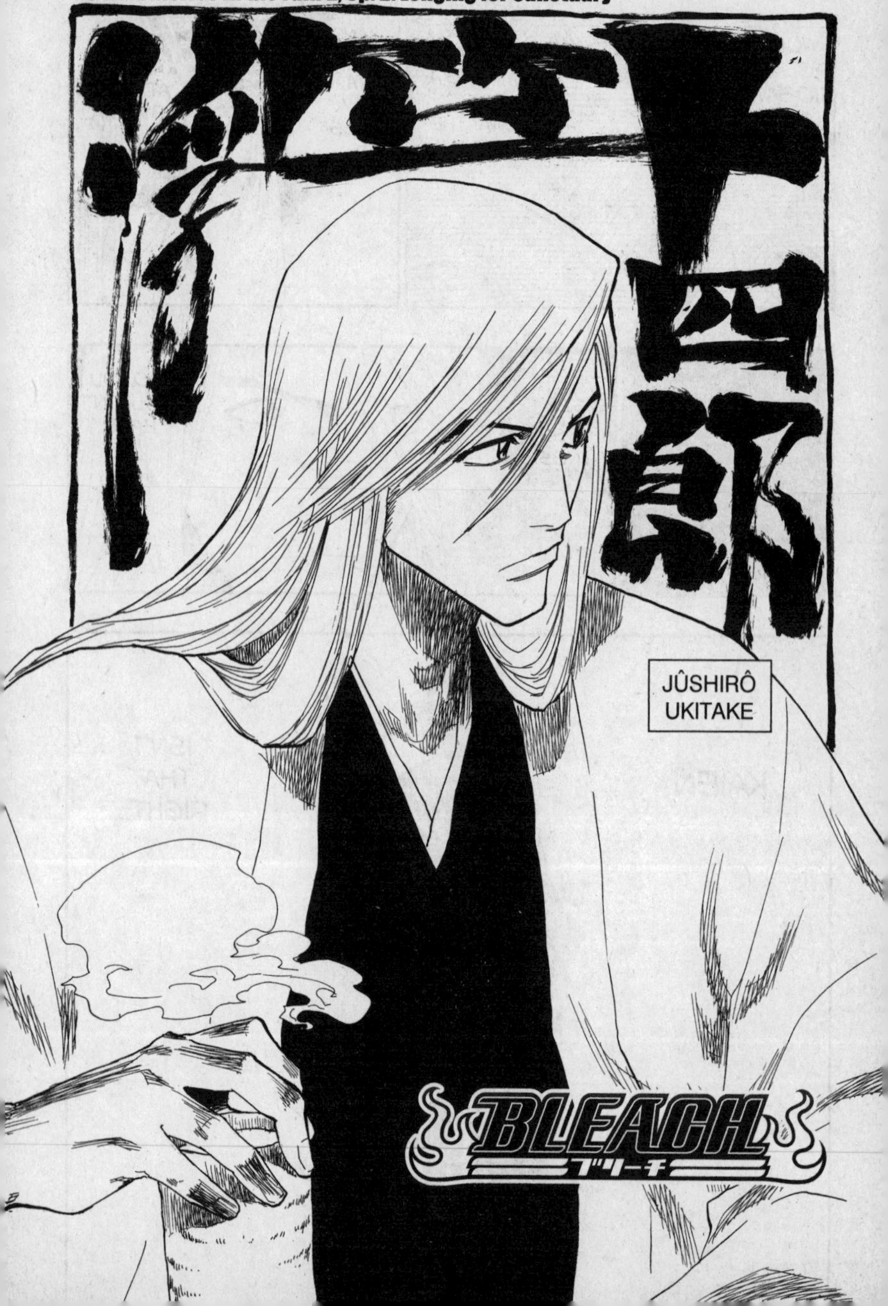
浮竹十四郎
JÛSHIRÔ UKITAKE
BLEACH
ブリーチ

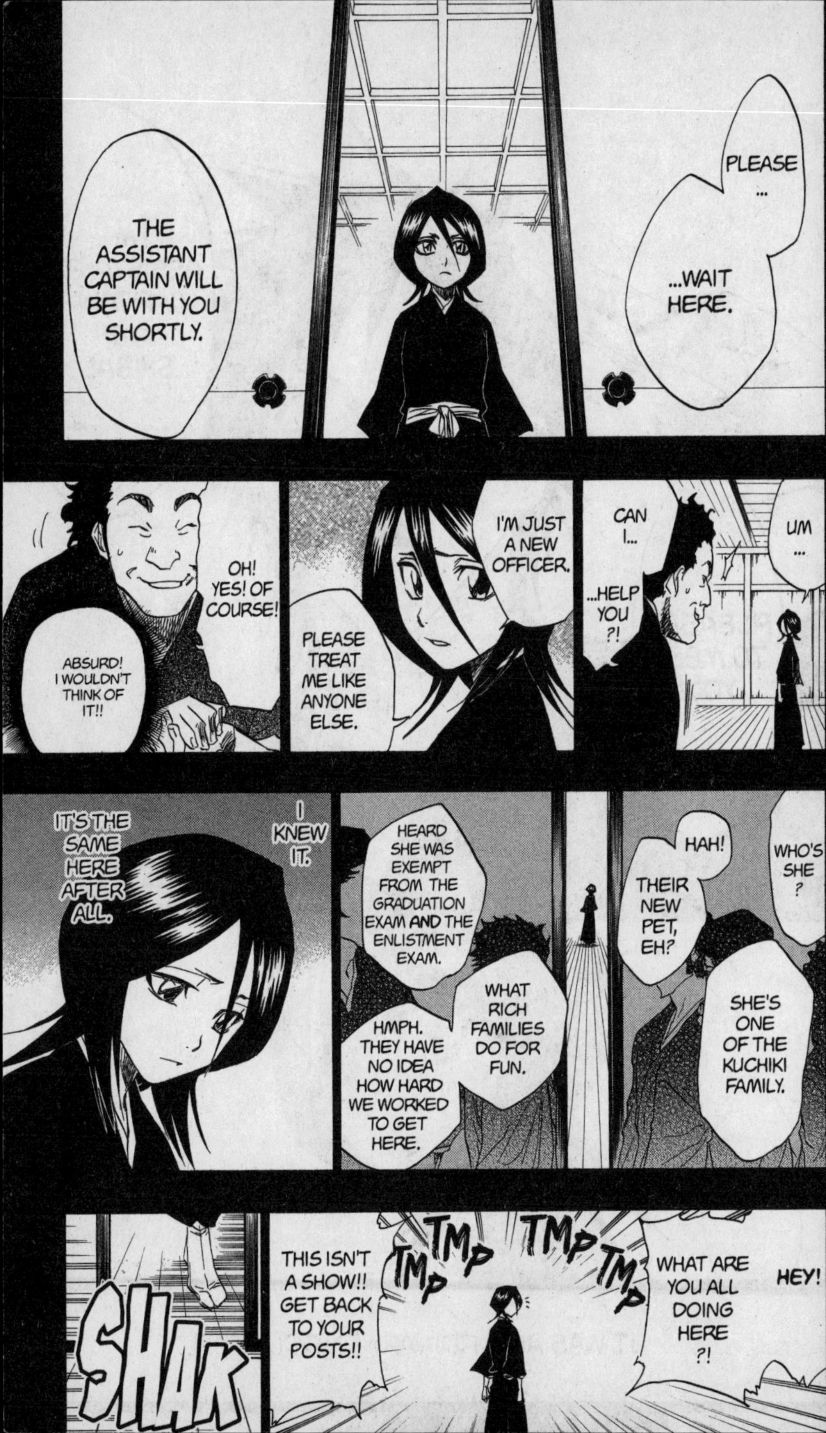
PLEASE ... ...WAIT HERE.
THE ASSISTANT CAPTAIN WILL BE WITH YOU SHORTLY.
UM ...
CAN I... ...HELP YOU ?!
I'M JUST A NEW OFFICER.
PLEASE TREAT ME LIKE ANYONE ELSE.
OH! YES! OF COURSE!
ABSURD! I WOULDN'T THINK OF IT!!
WHO'S SHE ?
HAH! THEIR NEW PET, EH?
SHE'S ONE OF THE KUCHIKI FAMILY.
HEARD SHE WAS EXEMPT FROM THE GRADUATION EXAM AND THE ENLISTMENT EXAM.
WHAT RICH FAMILIES DO FOR FUN.
HMPH. THEY HAVE NO IDEA HOW HARD WE WORKED TO GET HERE.
I KNEW IT.
IT'S THE SAME HERE AFTER ALL.
HEY!
WHAT ARE YOU ALL DOING HERE ?!
TMP TMP TMP TMP
THIS ISN'T A SHOW!! GET BACK TO YOUR POSTS!!
SHAK

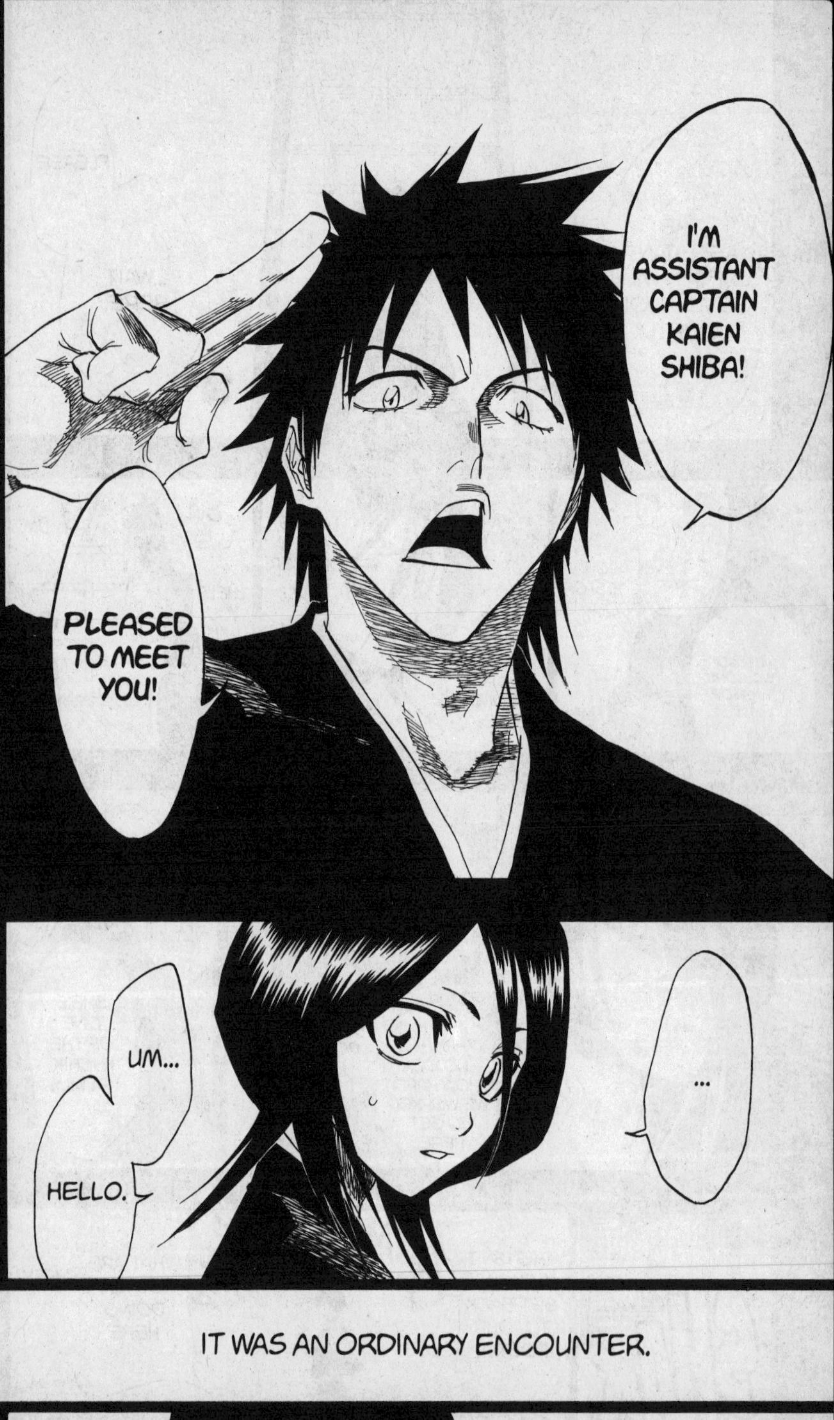
I'M ASSISTANT CAPTAIN KAIEN SHIBA!
PLEASED TO MEET YOU!
...
UM...
HELLO.
IT WAS AN ORDINARY ENCOUNTER.

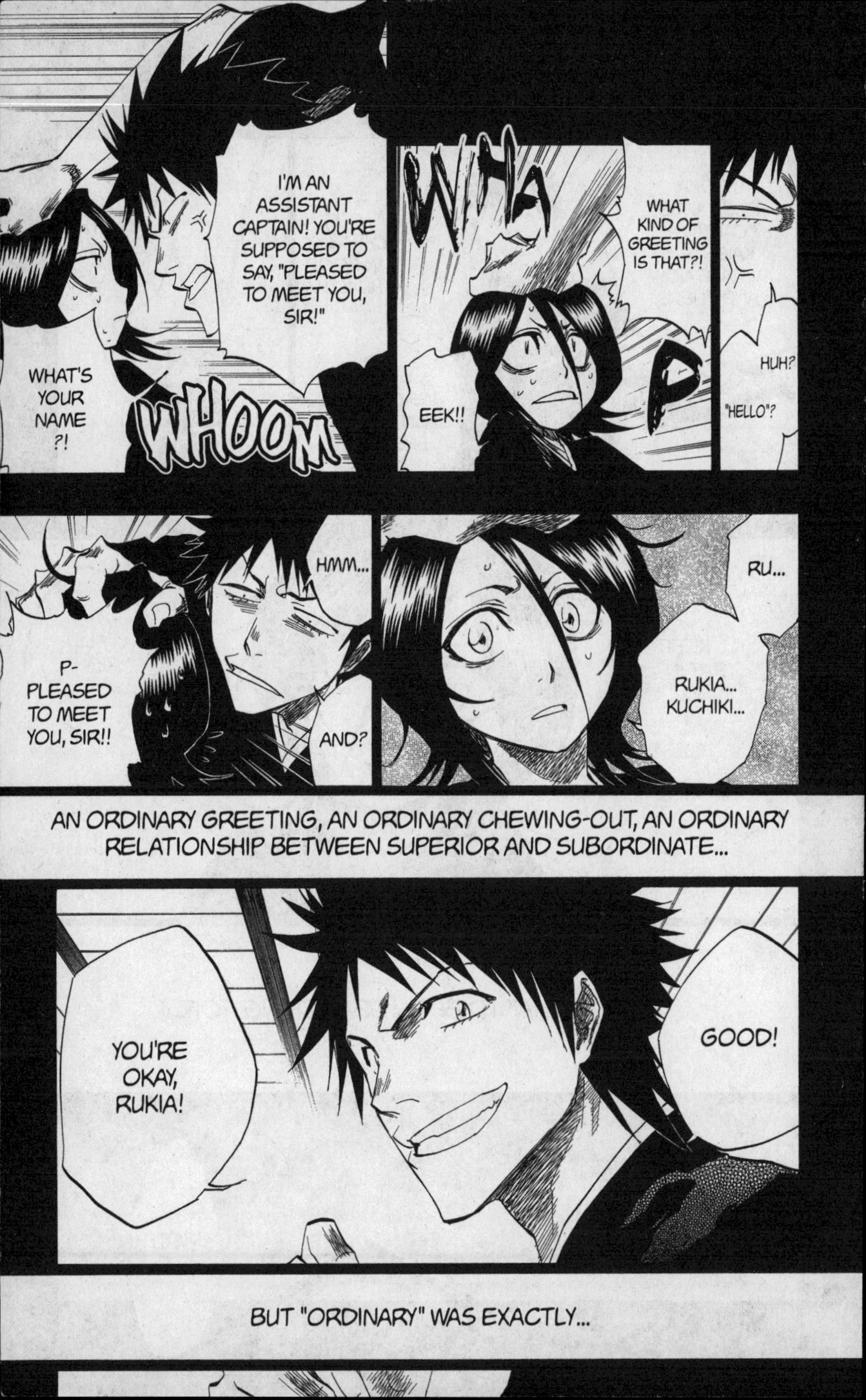
HUH?
"HELLO"?
WHAT KIND OF GREETING IS THAT?!
WHAP
EEK!!
I'M AN ASSISTANT CAPTAIN! YOU'RE SUPPOSED TO SAY, "PLEASED TO MEET YOU, SIR!"
WHOOM
WHAT'S YOUR NAME ?!
RU...
RUKIA... KUCHIKI...
HMM...
AND?
P-PLEASED TO MEET YOU, SIR!!
AN ORDINARY GREETING, AN ORDINARY CHEWING-OUT, AN ORDINARY RELATIONSHIP BETWEEN SUPERIOR AND SUBORDINATE...
GOOD!
YOU'RE OKAY, RUKIA!
BUT "ORDINARY" WAS EXACTLY...

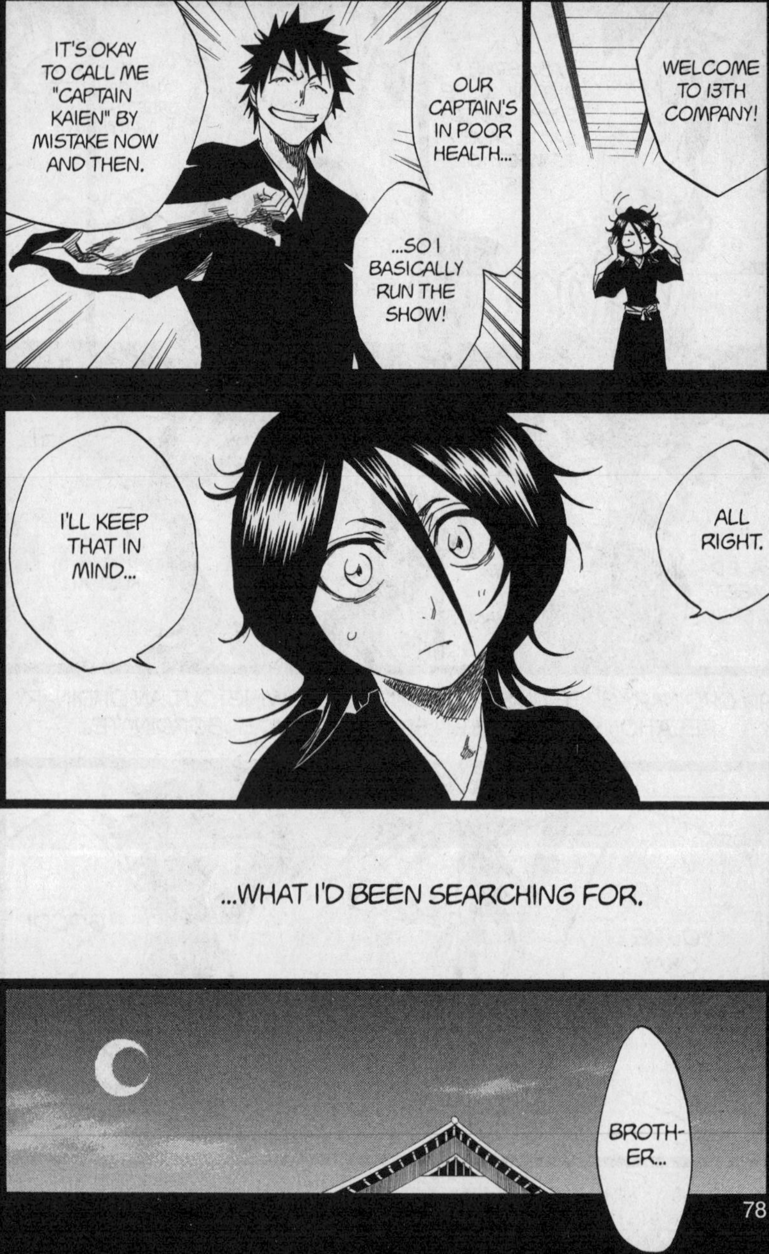
WELCOME TO 13TH COMPANY!
OUR CAPTAIN'S IN POOR HEALTH...
...SO I BASICALLY RUN THE SHOW!
IT'S OKAY TO CALL ME "CAPTAIN KAIEN" BY MISTAKE NOW AND THEN.
ALL RIGHT.
I'LL KEEP THAT IN MIND...
...WHAT I'D BEEN SEARCHING FOR.
BROTH-ER...

READ THIS WAY

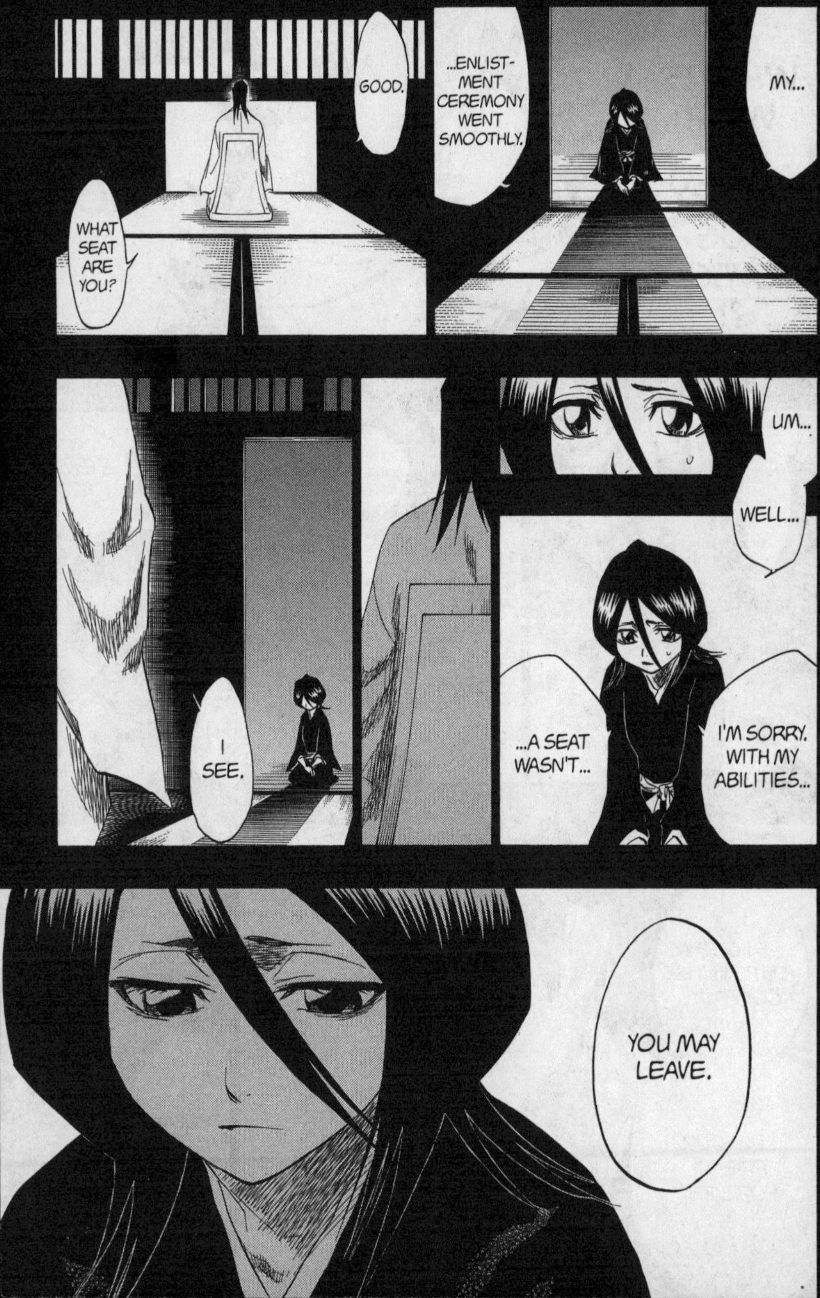

MY...
...ENLIST-MENT CEREMONY WENT SMOOTHLY.
GOOD.
WHAT SEAT ARE YOU?
UM...
WELL...
I'M SORRY. WITH MY ABILITIES...
...A SEAT WASN'T...
I SEE.
YOU MAY LEAVE.

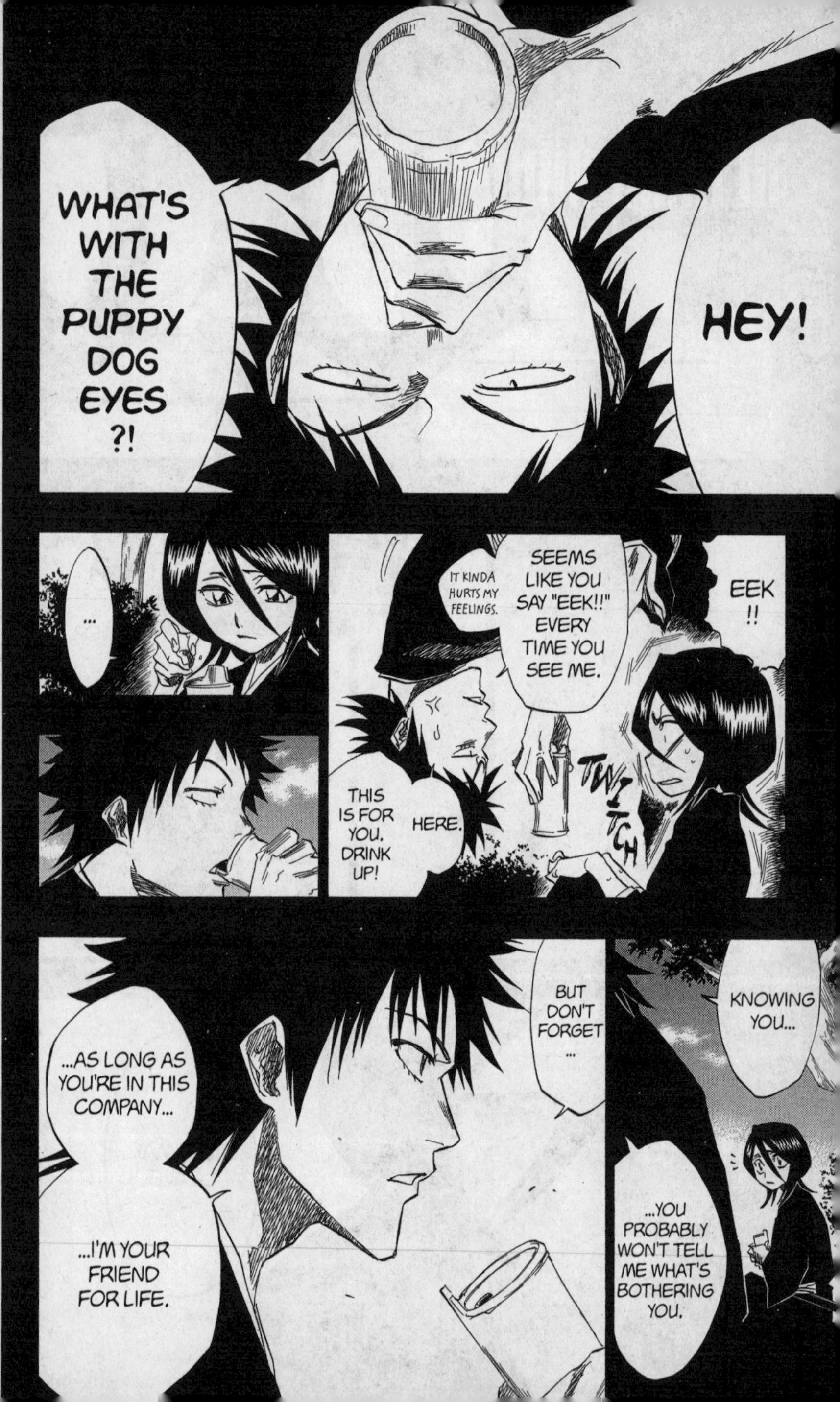
HEY!
WHAT'S WITH THE PUPPY DOG EYES ?!
EEK !!
SEEMS LIKE YOU SAY "EEK!!" EVERY TIME YOU SEE ME.
IT KINDA HURTS MY FEELINGS.
TWITCH
HERE.
THIS IS FOR YOU. DRINK UP!
...
KNOWING YOU...
...YOU PROBABLY WON'T TELL ME WHAT'S BOTHERING YOU.
BUT DON'T FORGET ...
...AS LONG AS YOU'RE IN THIS COMPANY...
...I'M YOUR FRIEND FOR LIFE.

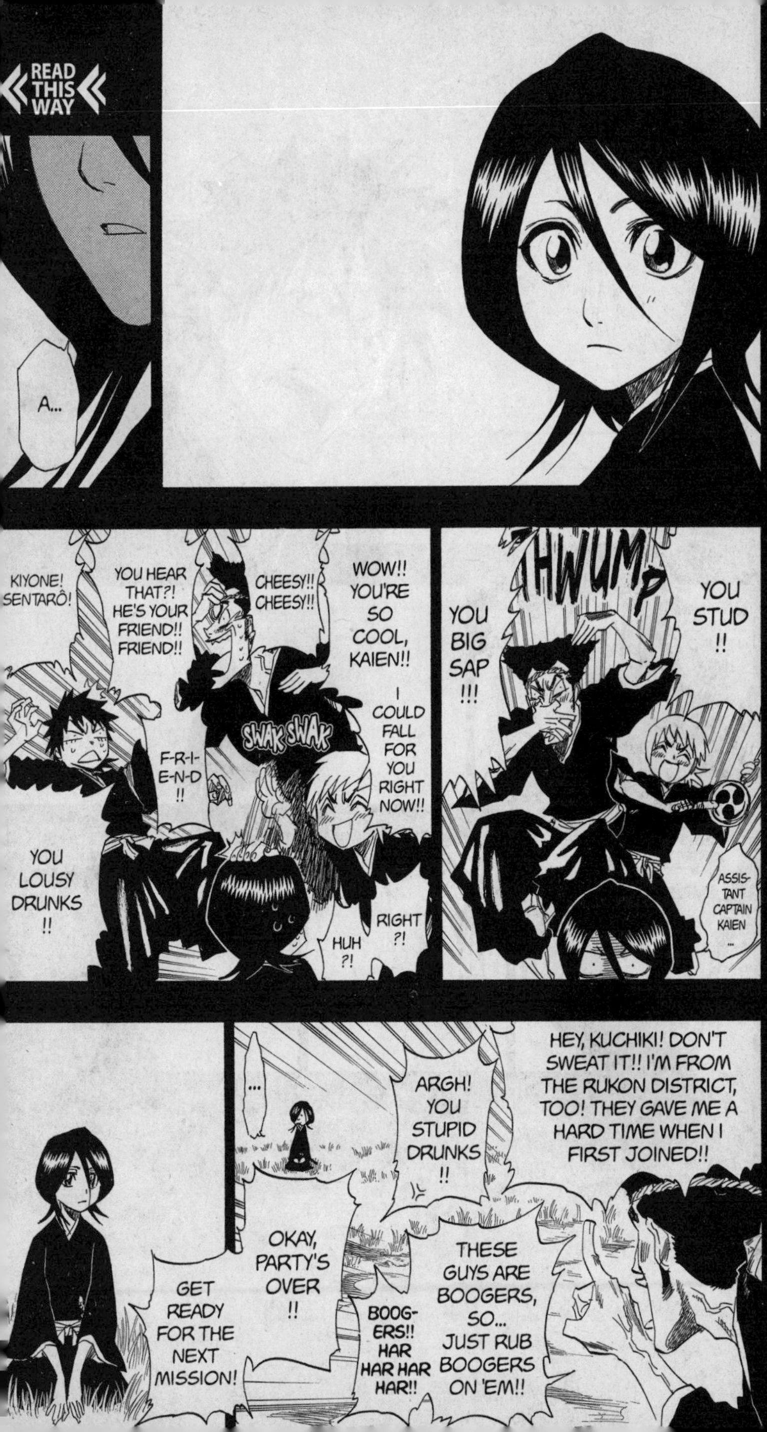
READ THIS WAY
A...
THWUMP
YOU STUD!!
YOU BIG SAP!!!
ASSISTANT CAPTAIN KAIEN...
WOW!! YOU'RE SO COOL, KAIEN!!
CHEESY!! CHEESY!!
I COULD FALL FOR YOU RIGHT NOW!!
YOU HEAR THAT?! HE'S YOUR FRIEND!! FRIEND!!
KIYONE! SENTARÔ!
SWAK SWAK
F-R-I-E-N-D!!
RIGHT?!
HUH?!
YOU LOUSY DRUNKS!!
HEY, KUCHIKI! DON'T SWEAT IT!! I'M FROM THE RUKON DISTRICT, TOO! THEY GAVE ME A HARD TIME WHEN I FIRST JOINED!!
ARGH! YOU STUPID DRUNKS!!
THESE GUYS ARE BOOGERS, SO... JUST RUB BOOGERS ON 'EM!!
BOOGERS!! HAR HAR HAR!!
OKAY, PARTY'S OVER!!
...
GET READY FOR THE NEXT MISSION!

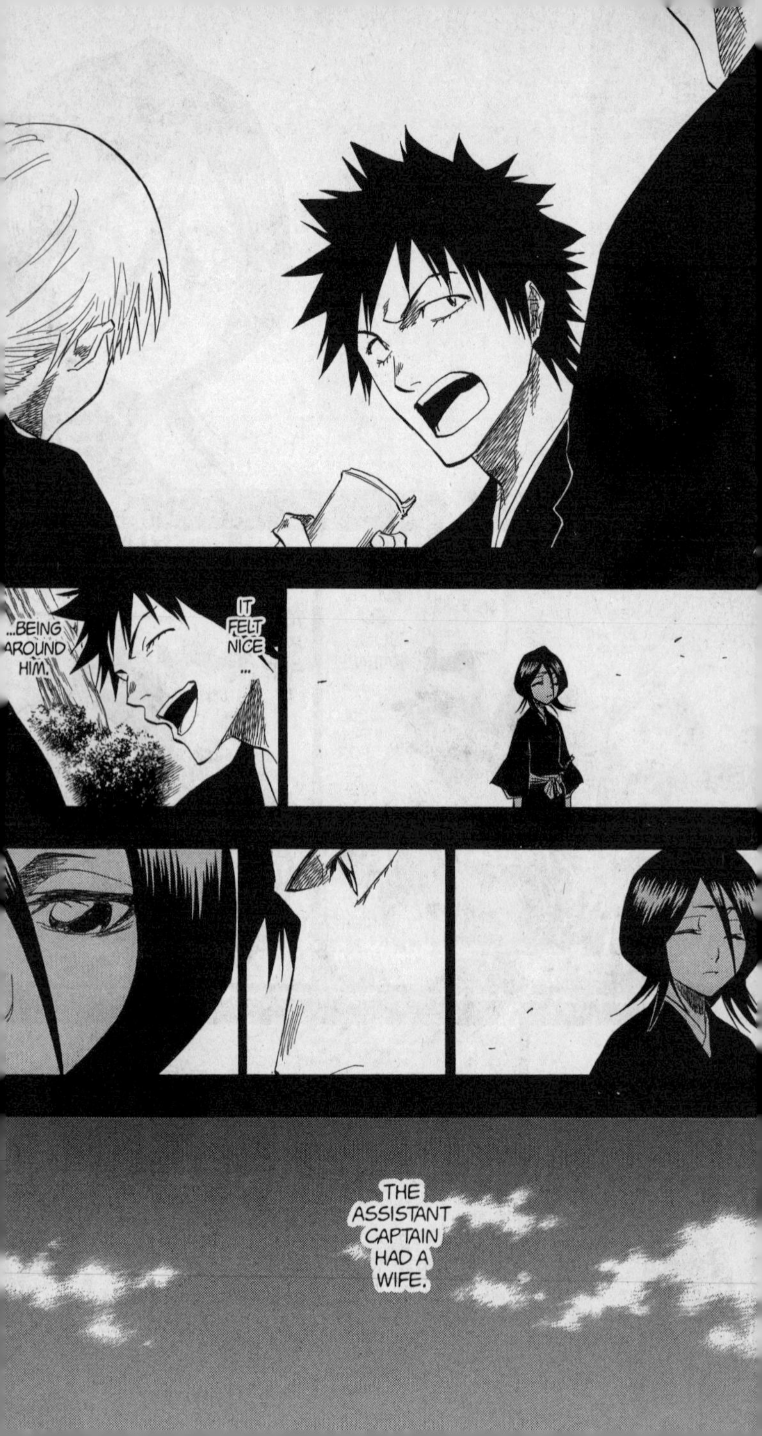
IT FELT NICE...
...BEING AROUND HIM.
THE ASSISTANT CAPTAIN HAD A WIFE.

DESPITE BEING A STRONG WOMAN WHO HAD RISEN TO THIRD SEAT...

...SHE WAS WISE AND KIND.

AND SHE WAS BEAUTIFUL.

I LOOKED UP TO HER.

I WANTED TO BE...

...JUST LIKE HER.

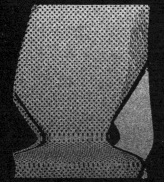

SHE WAS...

...MY IDOL.

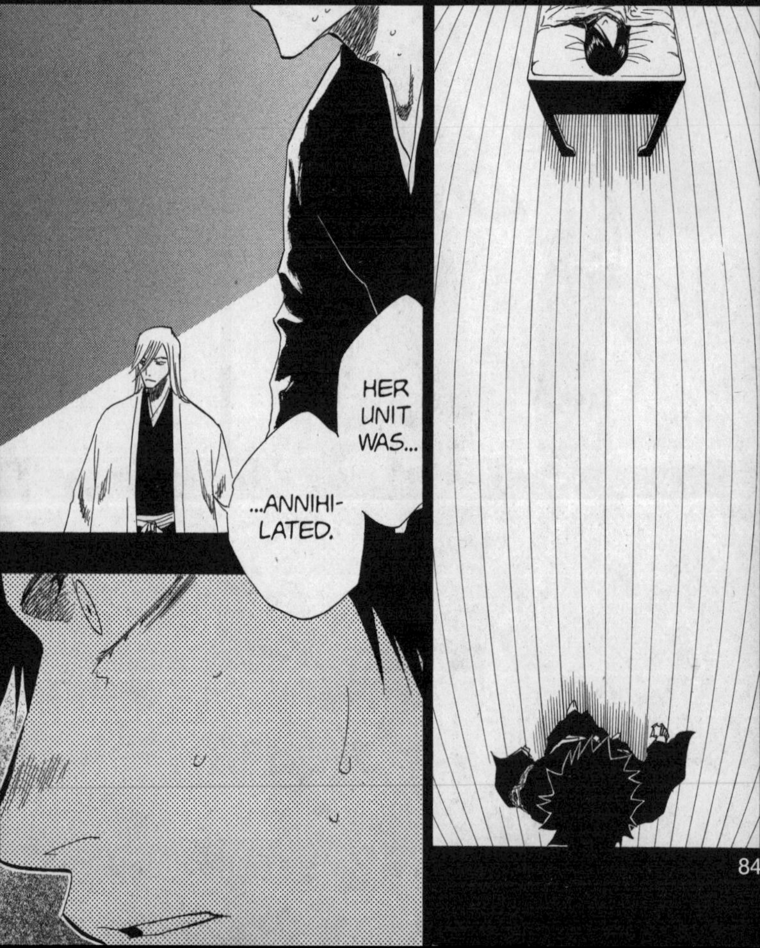
HER UNIT WAS...
...ANNIHI-LATED.

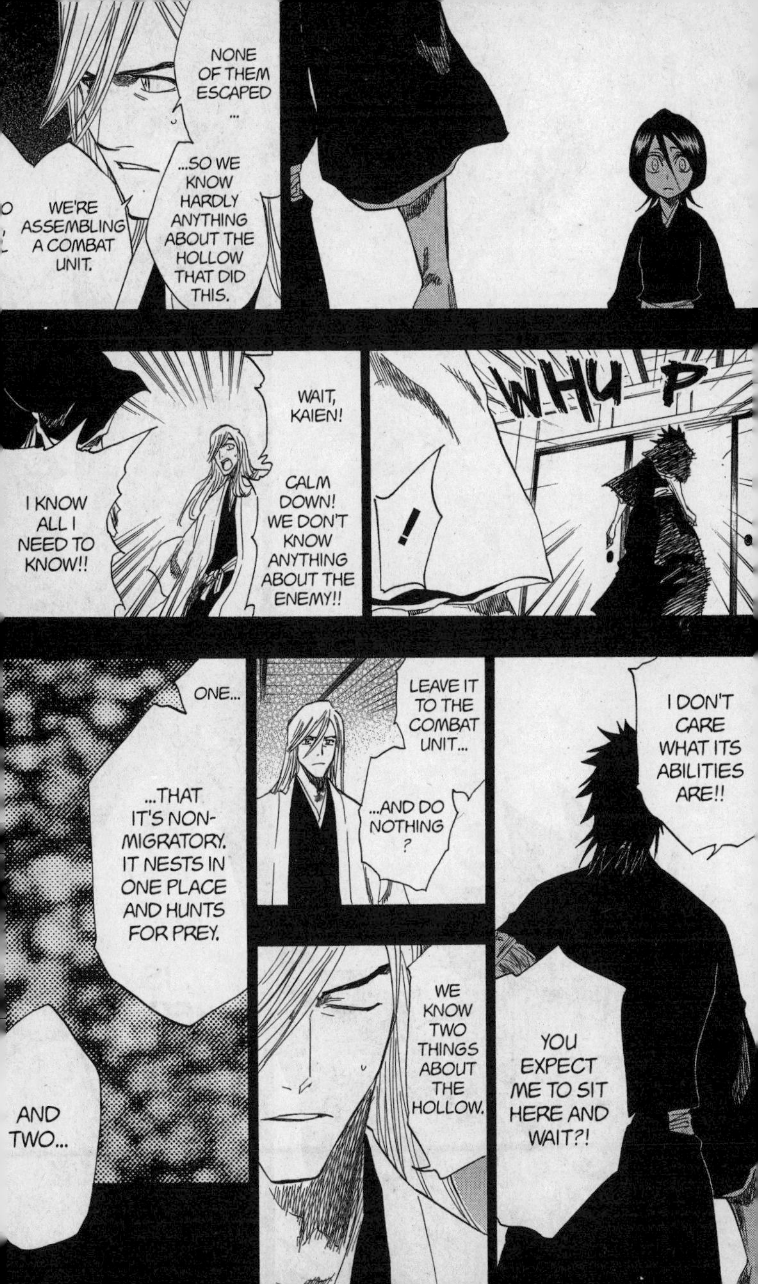
NONE OF THEM ESCAPED ...
...SO WE KNOW HARDLY ANYTHING ABOUT THE HOLLOW THAT DID THIS.
WE'RE ASSEMBLING A COMBAT UNIT.
WHUP
!
WAIT, KAIEN!
CALM DOWN! WE DON'T KNOW ANYTHING ABOUT THE ENEMY!!
I KNOW ALL I NEED TO KNOW!!
I DON'T CARE WHAT ITS ABILITIES ARE!!
YOU EXPECT ME TO SIT HERE AND WAIT?!
LEAVE IT TO THE COMBAT UNIT...
...AND DO NOTHING?
WE KNOW TWO THINGS ABOUT THE HOLLOW.
ONE...
...THAT IT'S NON-MIGRATORY. IT NESTS IN ONE PLACE AND HUNTS FOR PREY.
AND TWO...

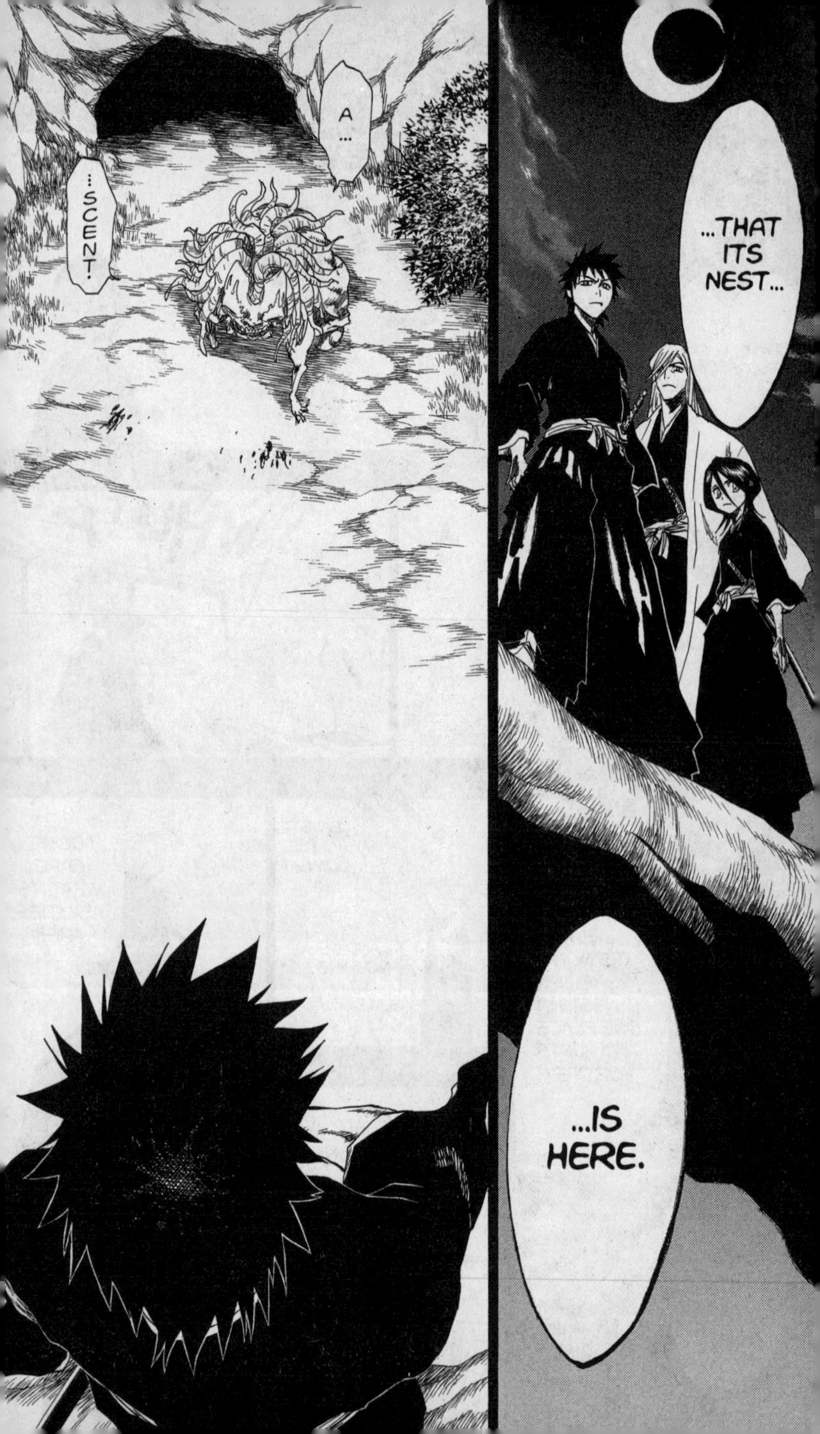
...THAT ITS NEST...
...IS HERE.
A...
...SCENT!

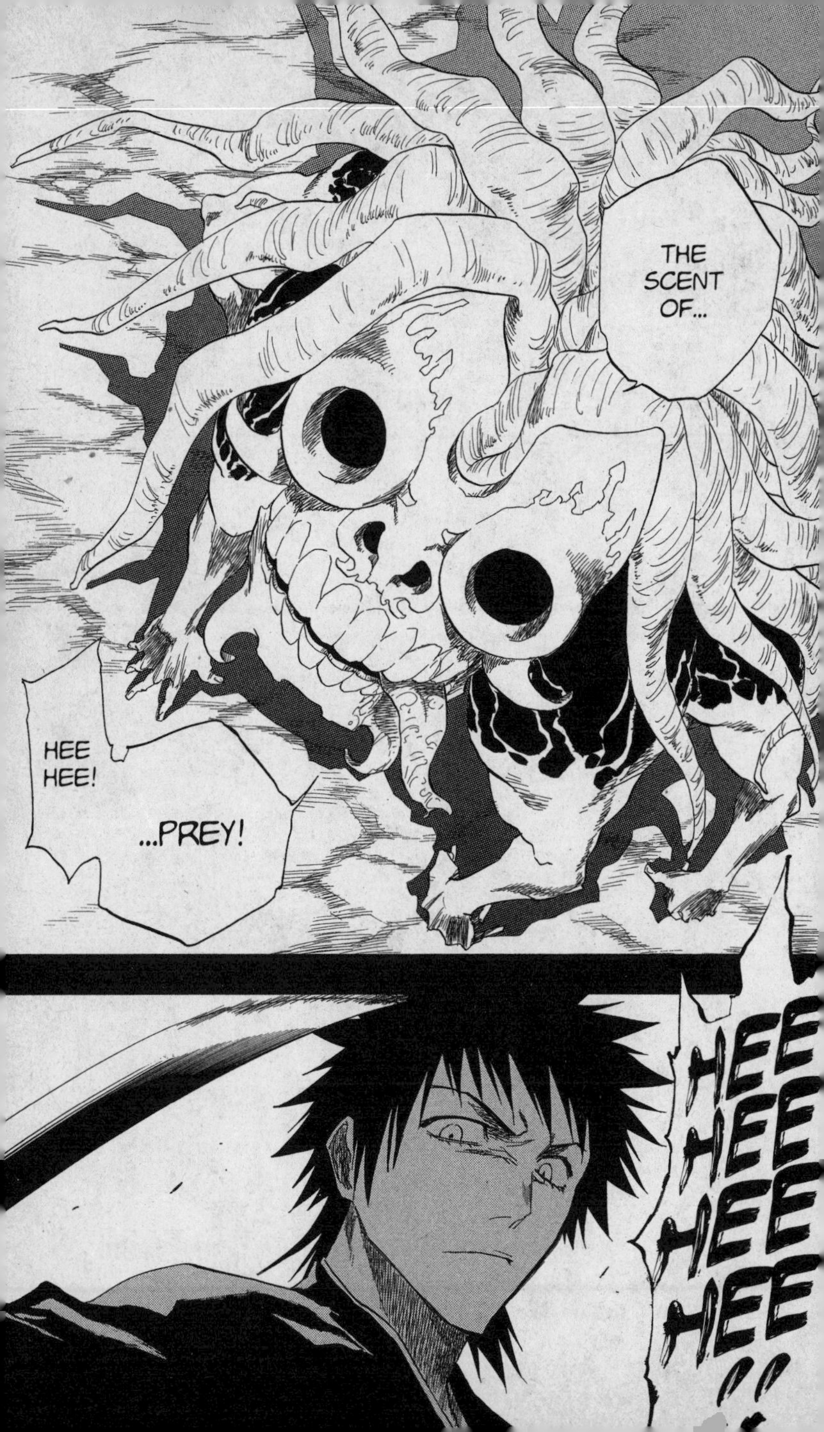
THE SCENT OF...
HEE HEE!
...PREY!
HEE HEE HEE HEE HEE!!

134. memories in the rain 2, op. 2:
Affected by the Night

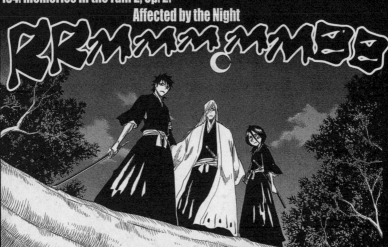

CAP-
TAIN...

TMP

KAIEN,
SIR...

I'LL GO
FIRST.

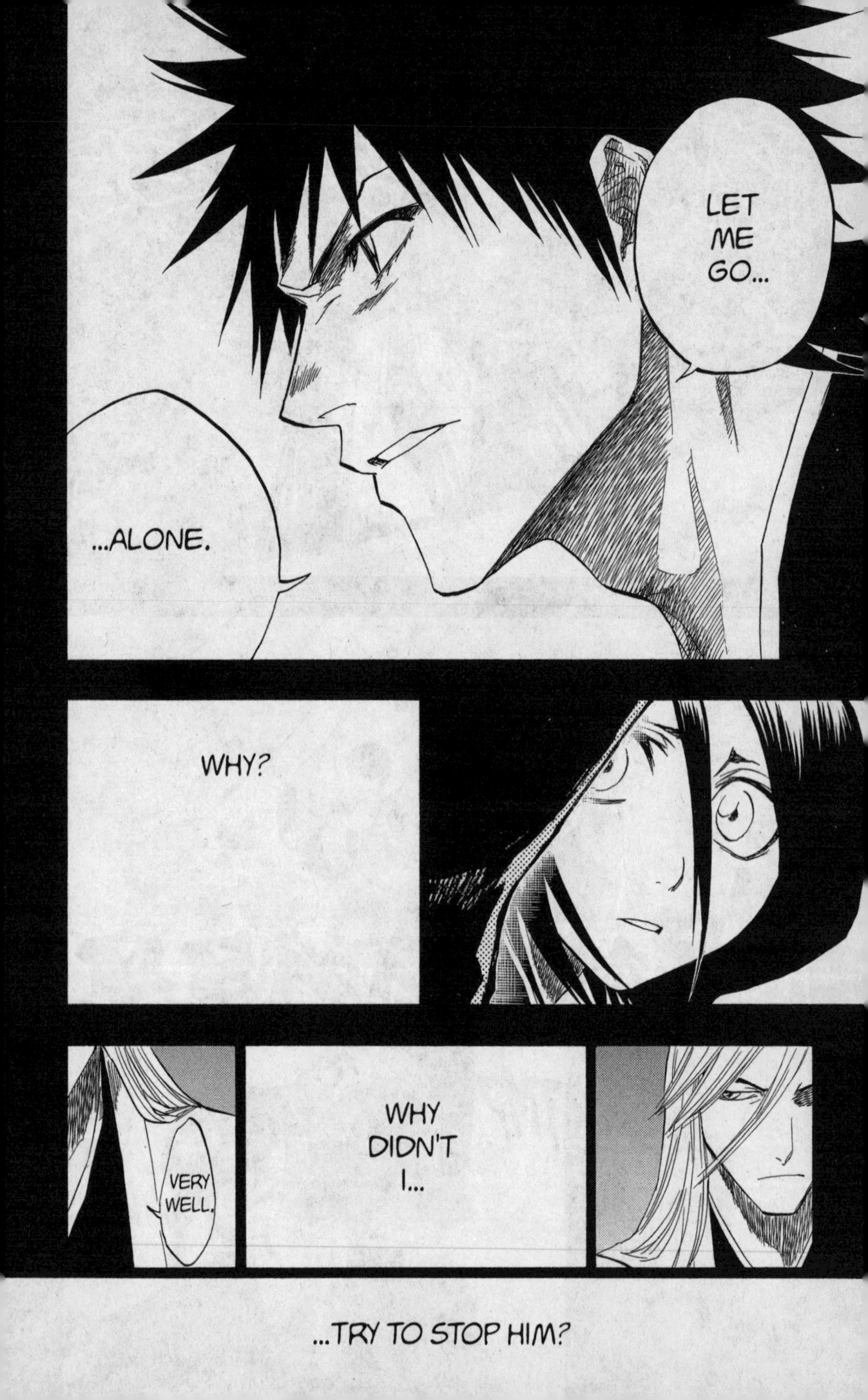
LET ME GO...
...ALONE.
WHY?
WHY DIDN'T I...
VERY WELL.
...TRY TO STOP HIM?

135. memories in the rain 2, op. 3: Affected by the Night

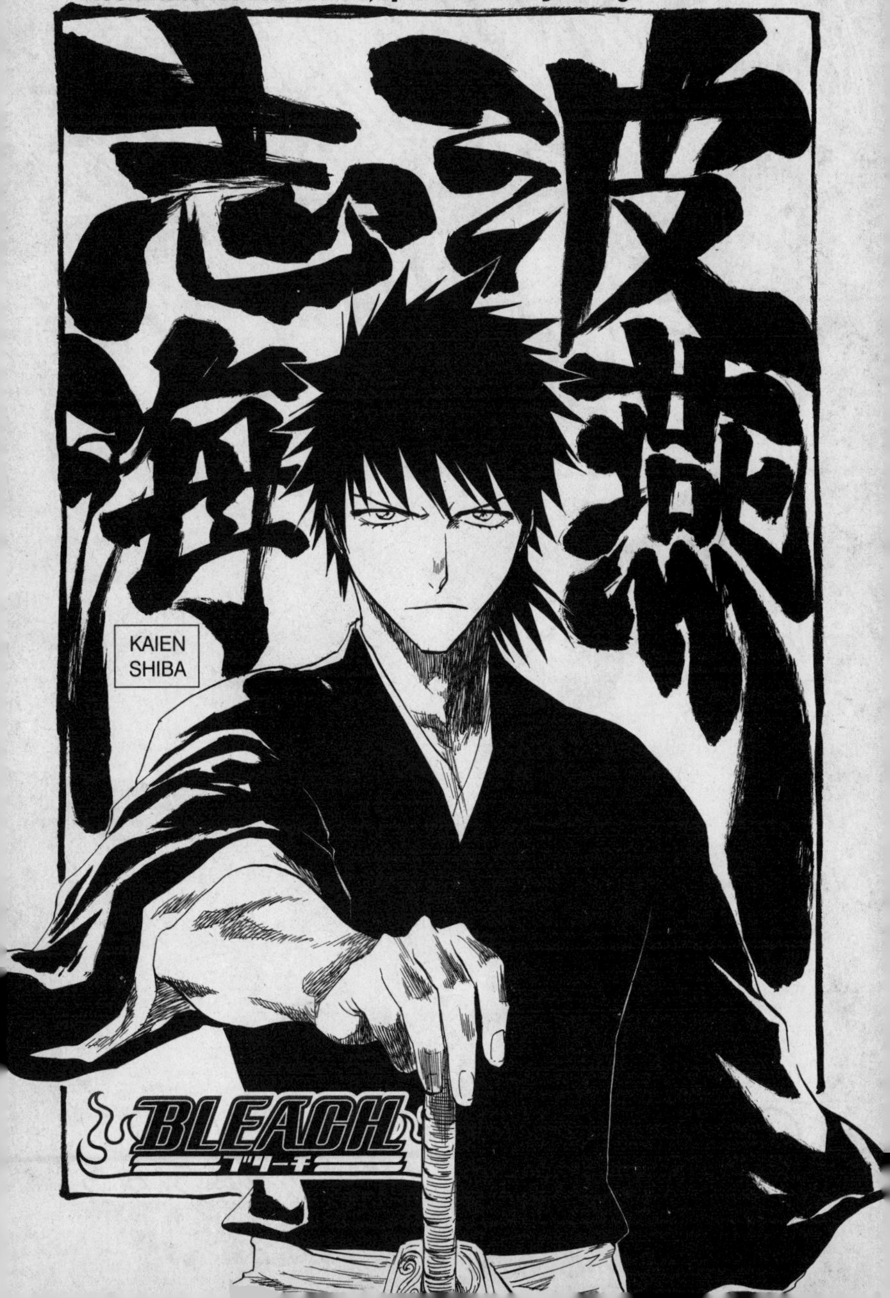
志波海燕
KAIEN SHIBA

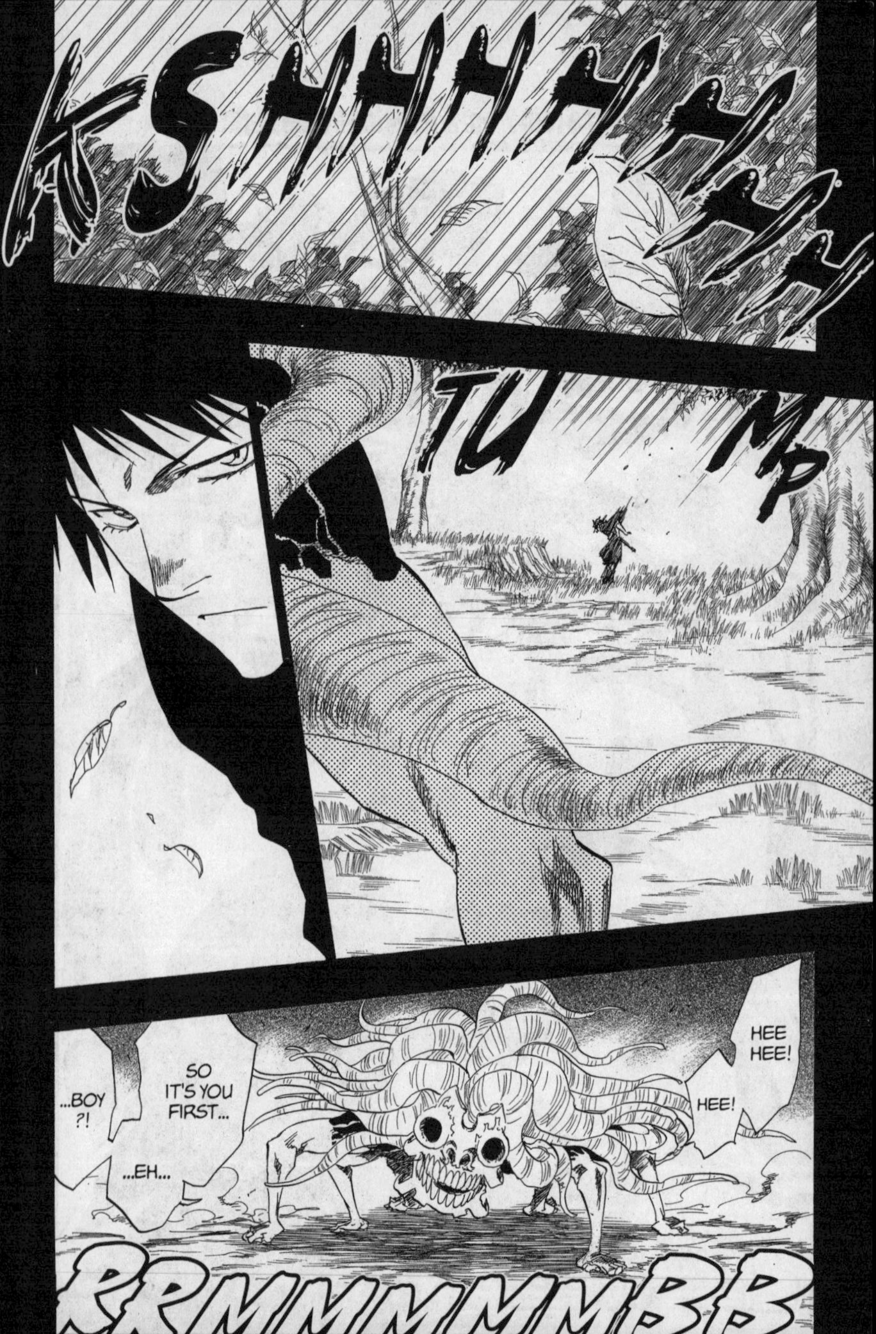
KSHHHHHHHH
TUMP
HEE HEE!
HEE!
SO IT'S YOU FIRST...
...BOY ?!
...EH...
RRMMMMMMBB

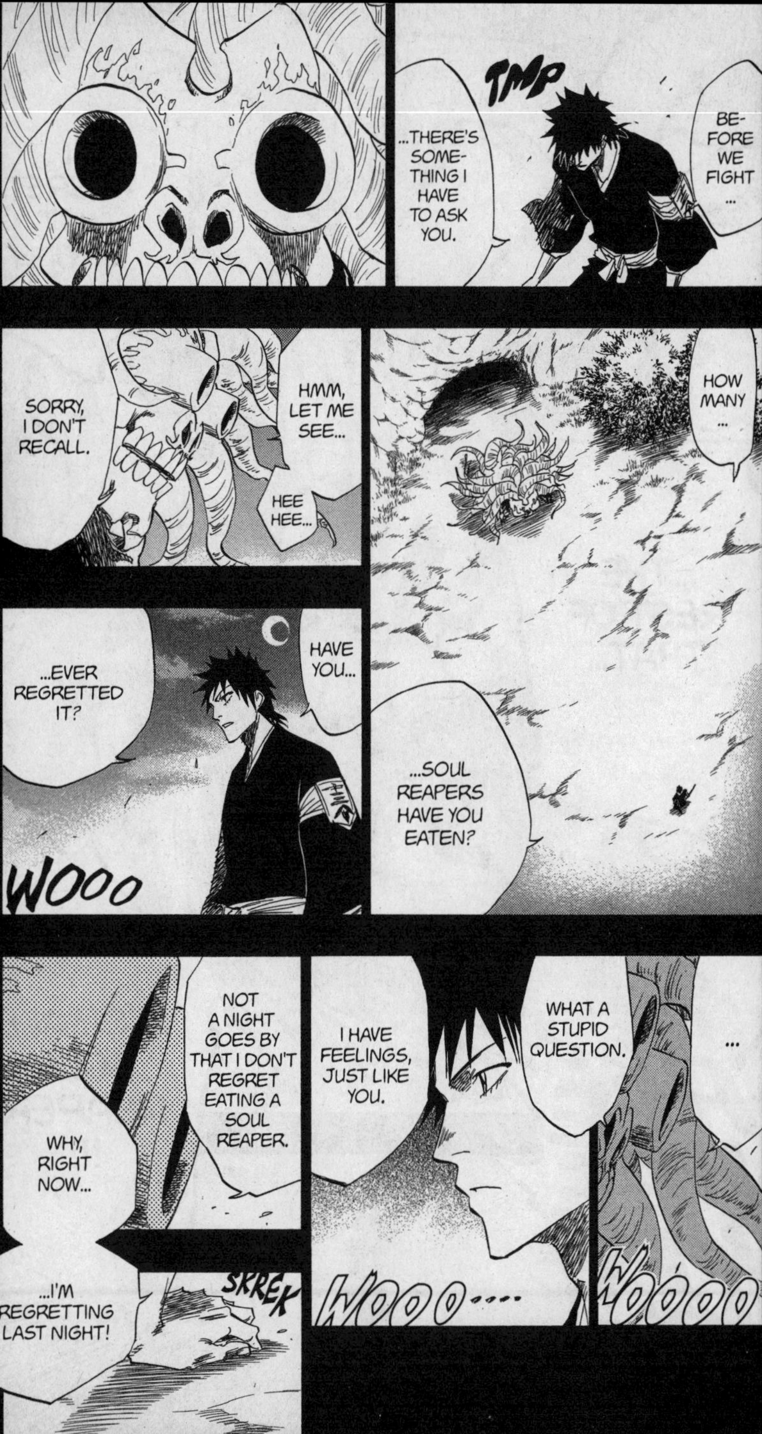
TMP
BEFORE WE FIGHT...
...THERE'S SOMETHING I HAVE TO ASK YOU.
HOW MANY...
...SOUL REAPERS HAVE YOU EATEN?
HMM, LET ME SEE...
HEE HEE...
SORRY, I DON'T RECALL.
HAVE YOU...
...EVER REGRETTED IT?
WOOO
...
WOOOO
WHAT A STUPID QUESTION.
I HAVE FEELINGS, JUST LIKE YOU.
WOOO....
NOT A NIGHT GOES BY THAT I DON'T REGRET EATING A SOUL REAPER.
WHY, RIGHT NOW...
...I'M REGRETTING LAST NIGHT!
SKREK

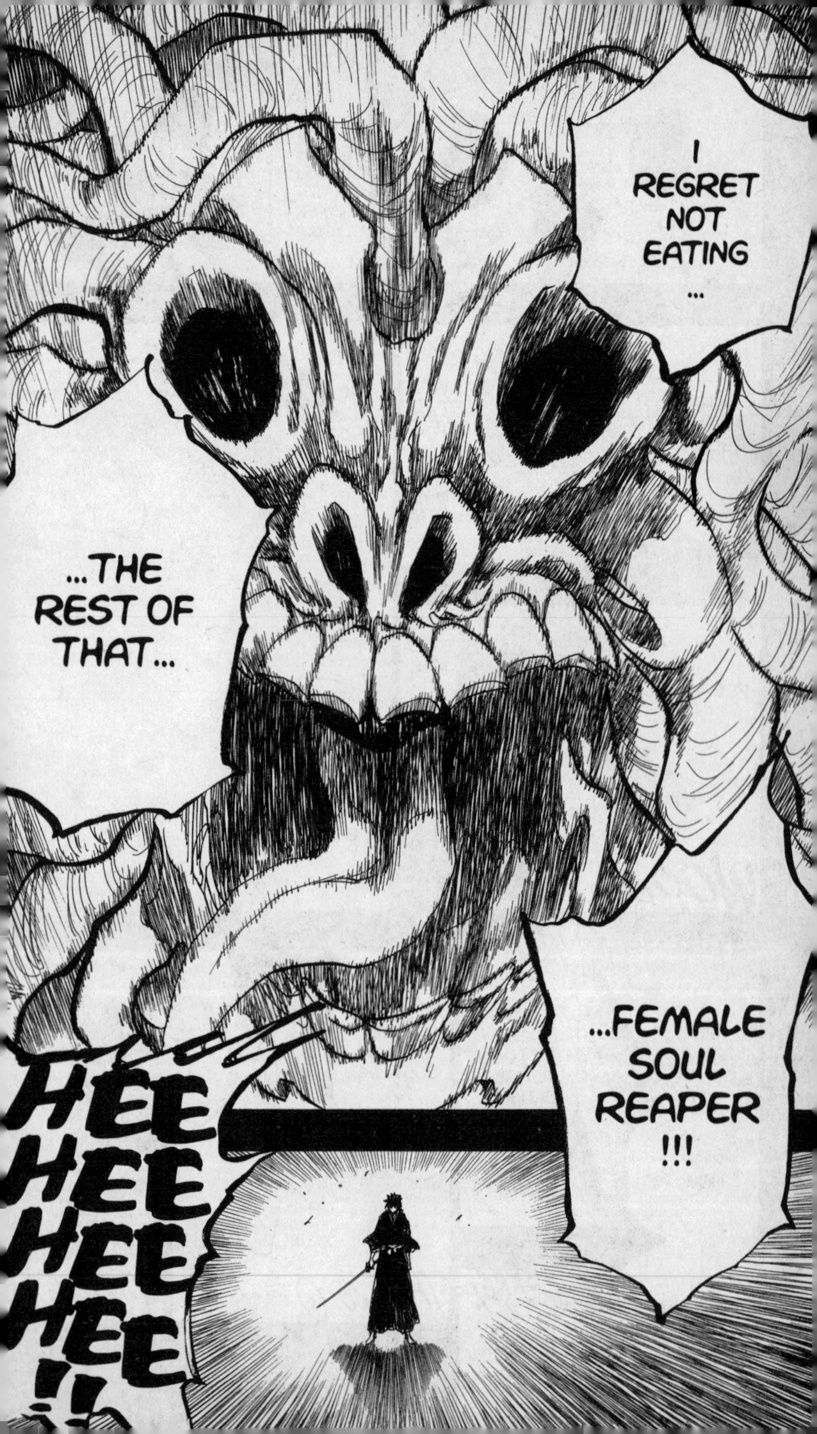
I REGRET NOT EATING ...
...THE REST OF THAT...
...FEMALE SOUL REAPER !!!
HEE HEE HEE HEE !!

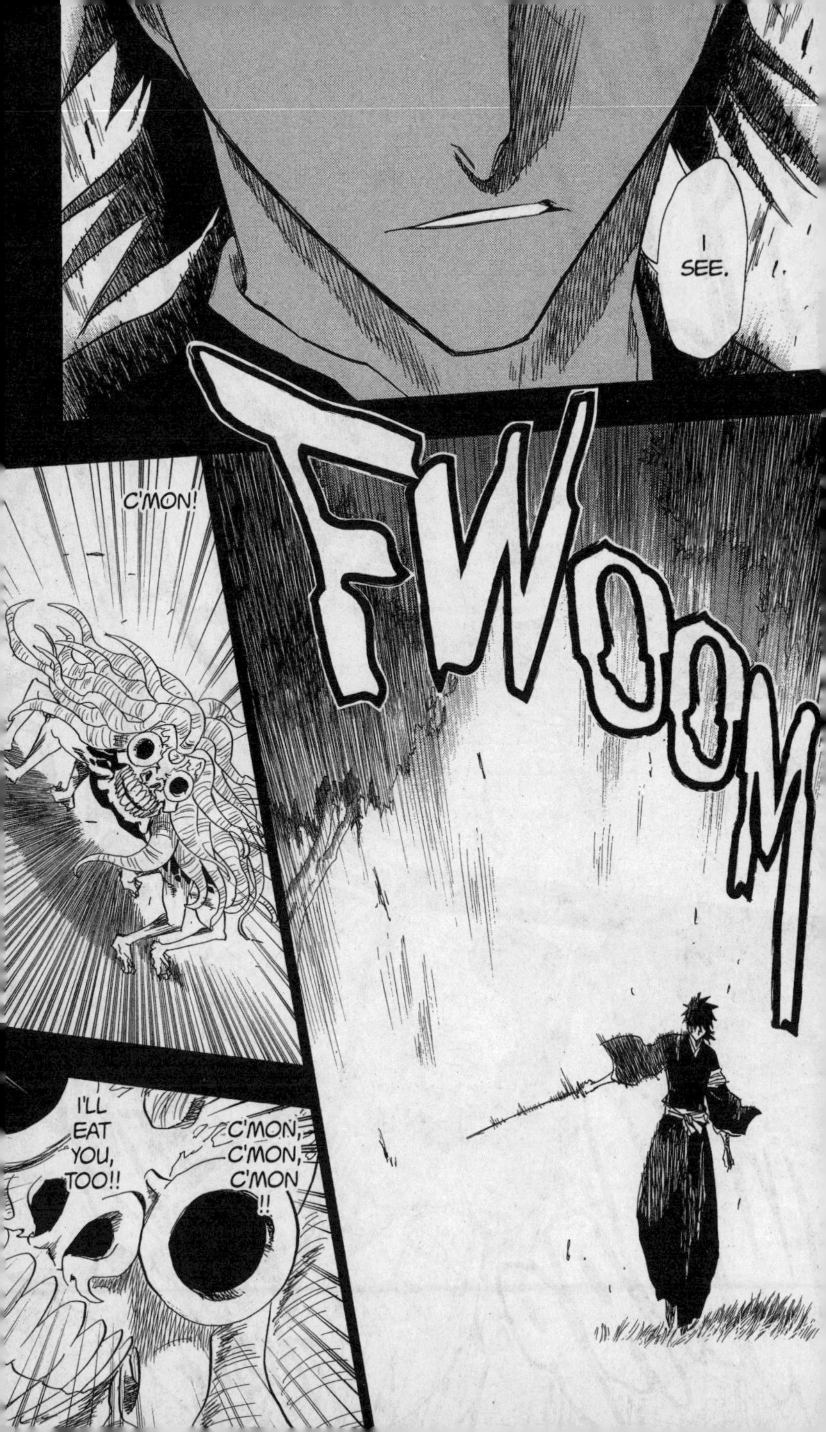
I SEE.
FWOOM
C'MON!
C'MON, C'MON, C'MON!!
I'LL EAT YOU, TOO!!

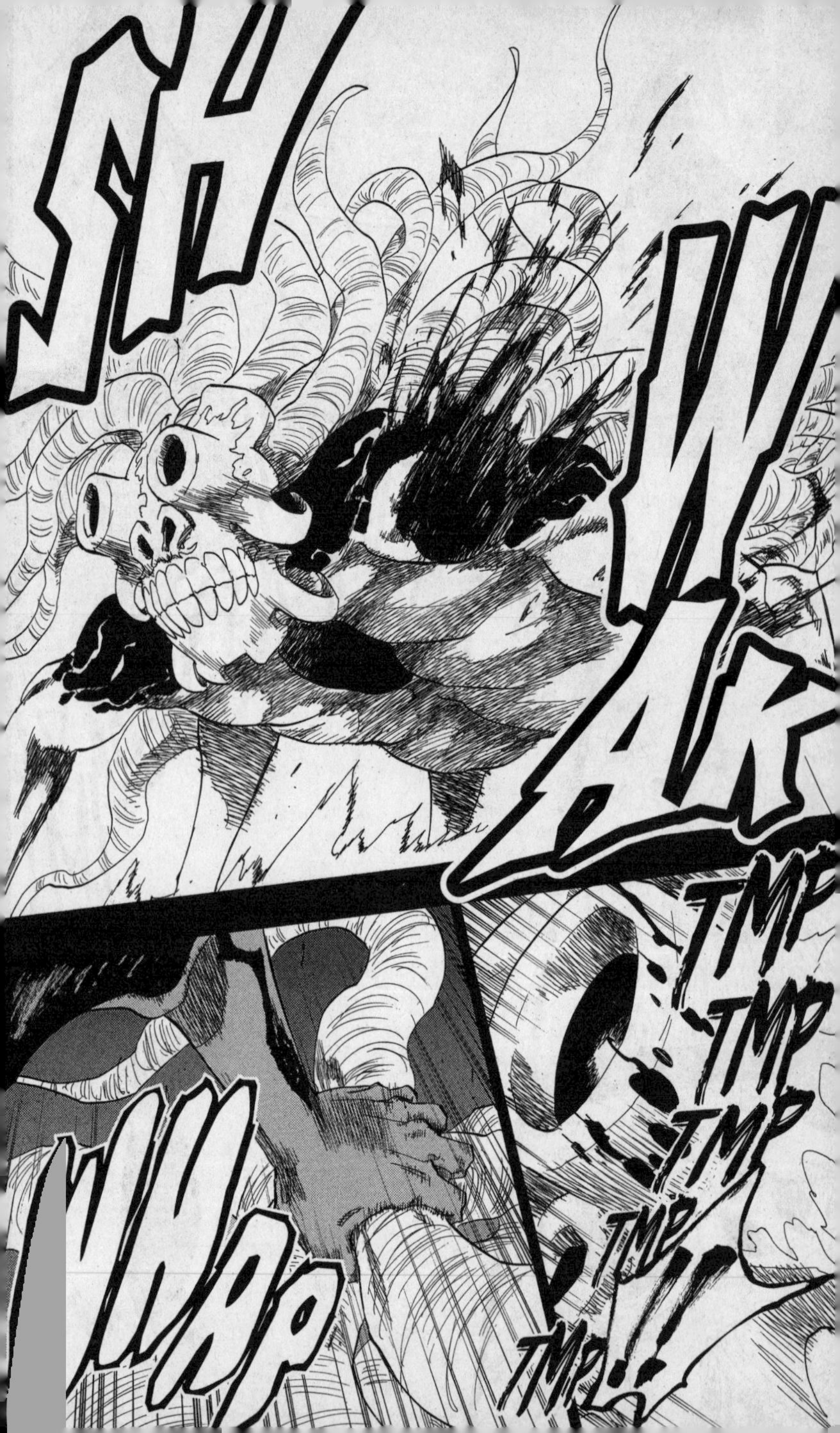
TMP
TMP
TMP
TMP
TMP
TMP!!

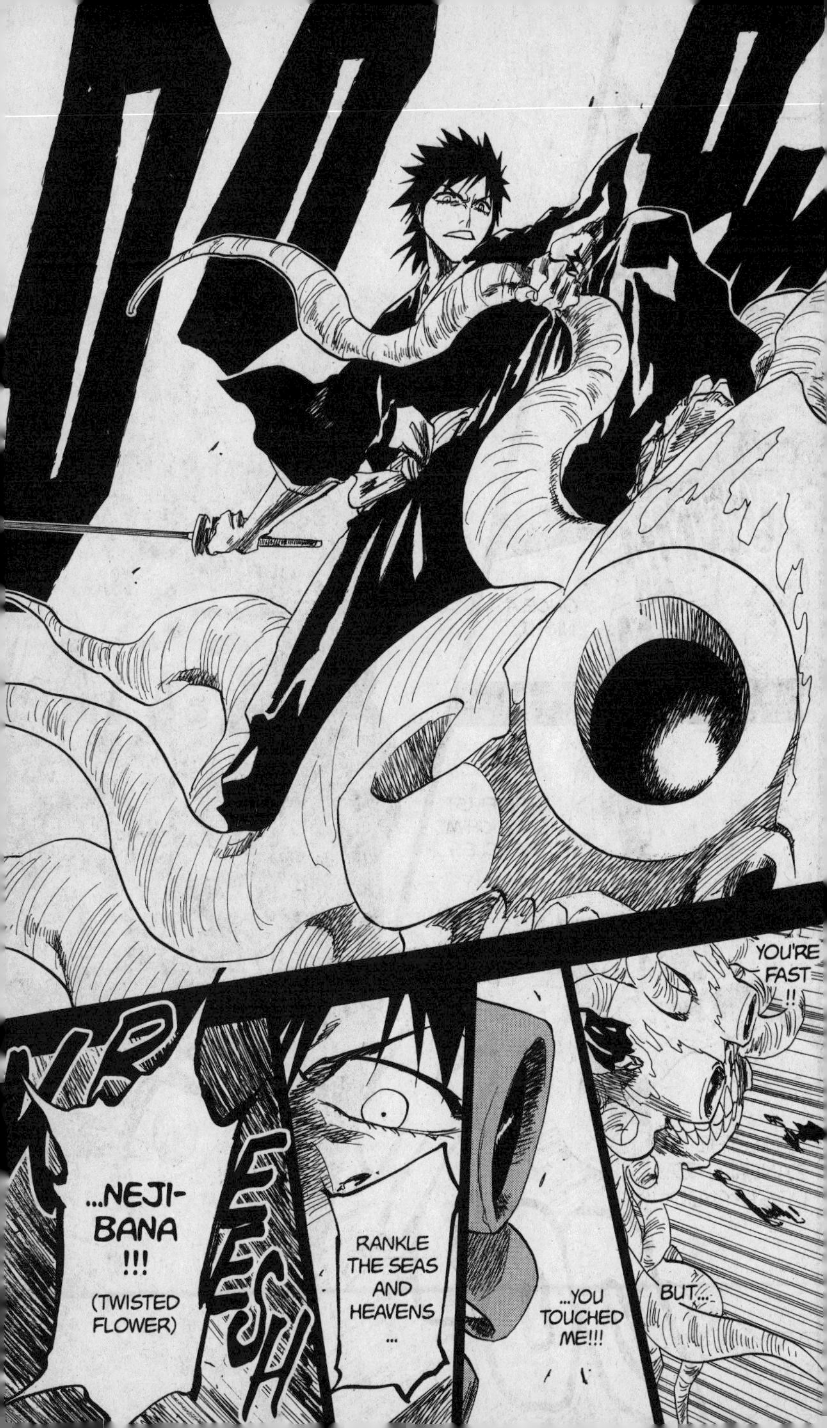
YOU'RE FAST!!
BUT...
...YOU TOUCHED ME!!!
RANKLE THE SEAS AND HEAVENS...
...NEJI-BANA!!!
(TWISTED FLOWER)

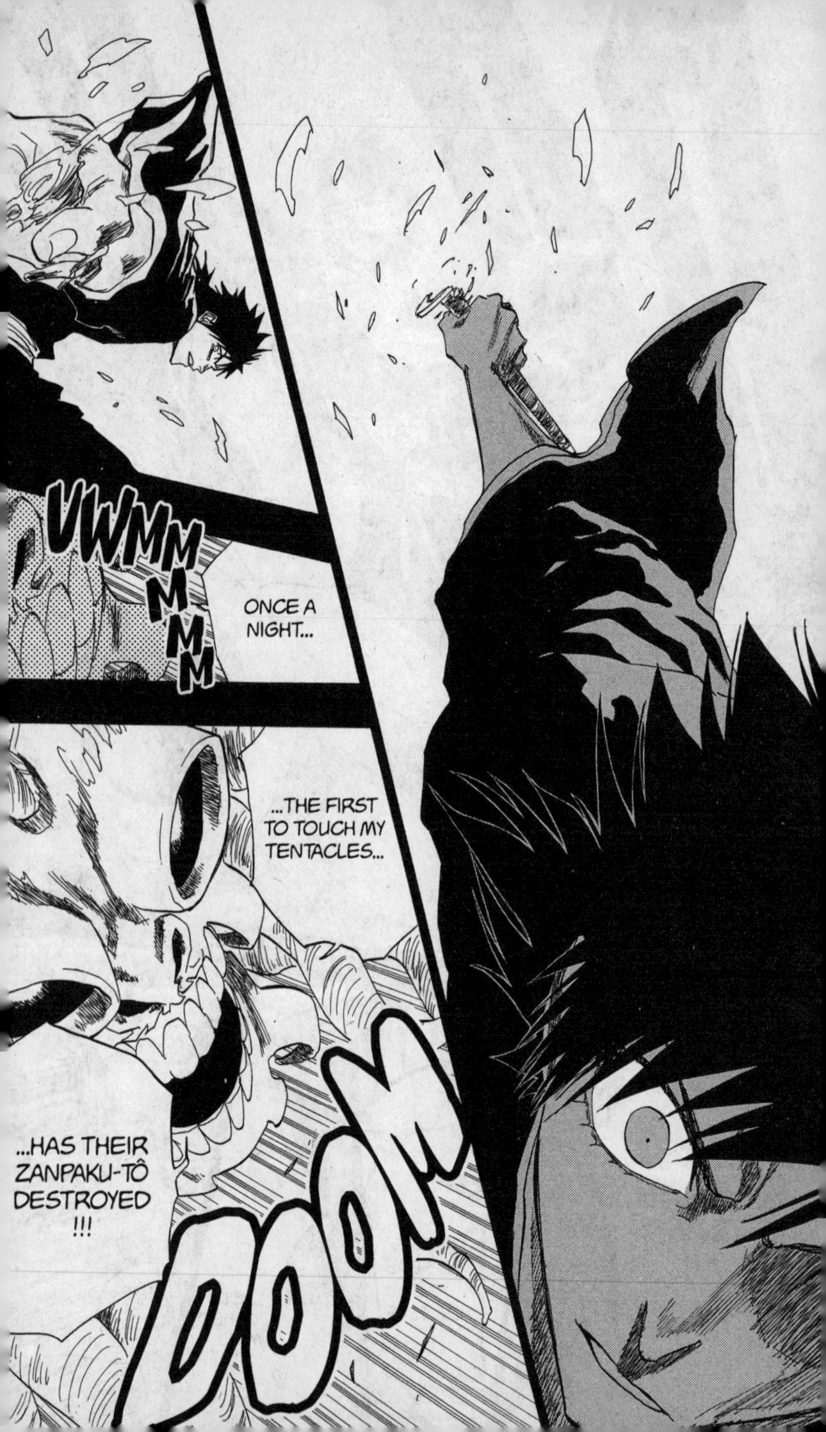
VWMMMMMMM
ONCE A NIGHT...
...THE FIRST TO TOUCH MY TENTACLES...
...HAS THEIR ZANPAKU-TÔ DESTROYED !!!
DOOM

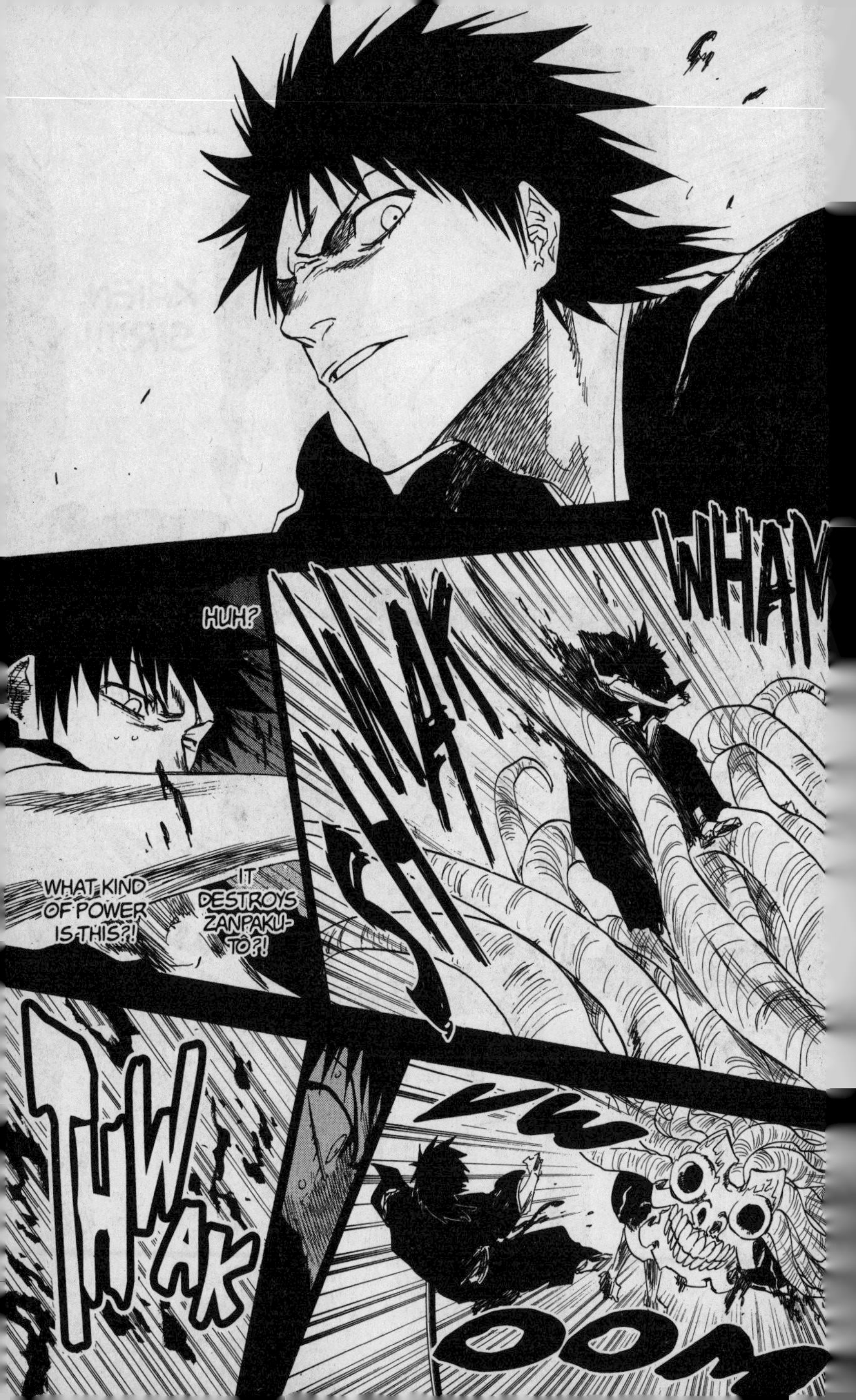
WHAM
HUH?
IT DESTROYS ZANPAKU-TÔ?!
WHAT KIND OF POWER IS THIS?!
THWAK

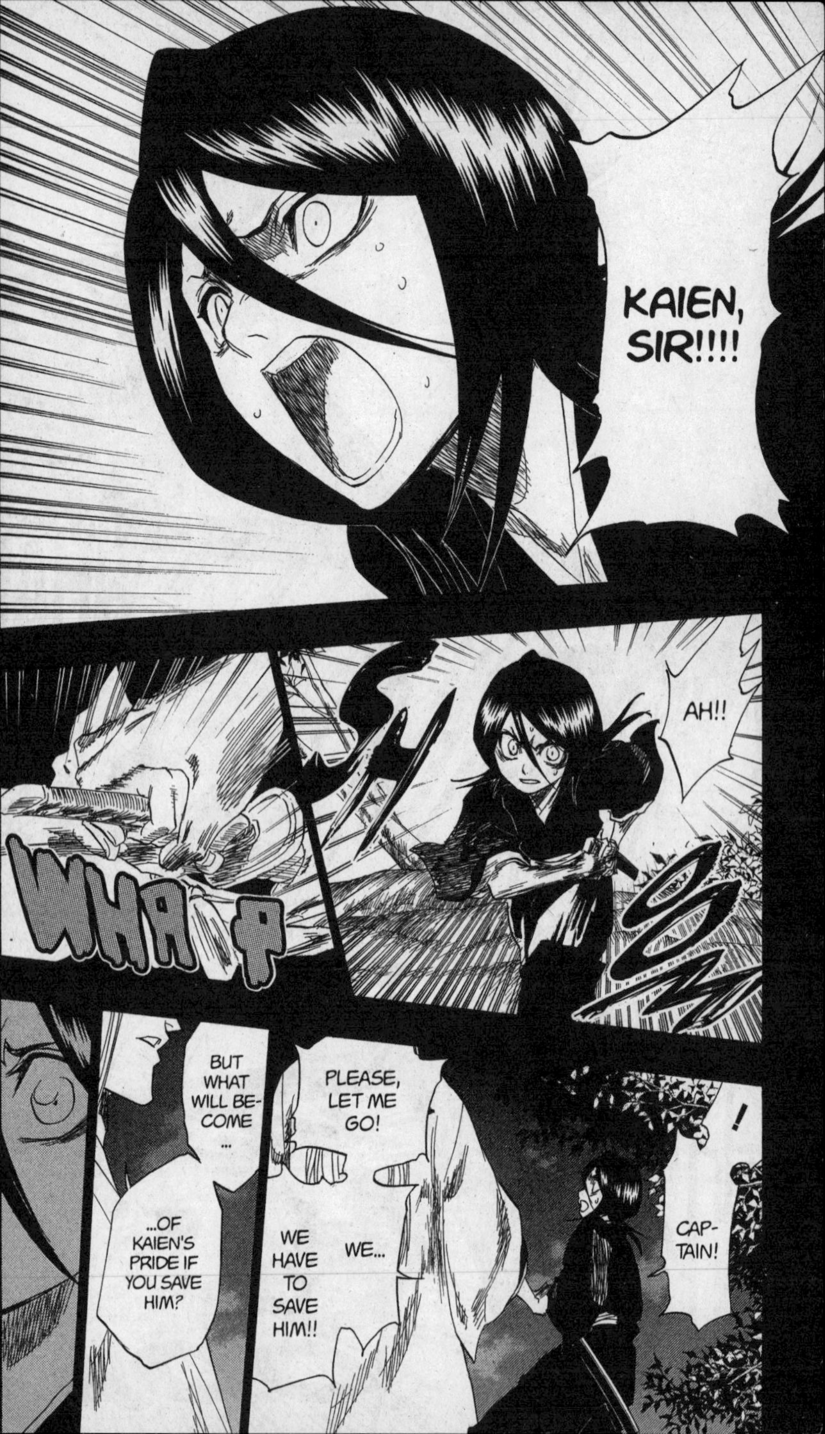
KAIEN, SIR!!!!
AH!!
WHAP
!
CAP-TAIN!
PLEASE, LET ME GO!
WE...
WE HAVE TO SAVE HIM!!
BUT WHAT WILL BE-COME ...
...OF KAIEN'S PRIDE IF YOU SAVE HIM?

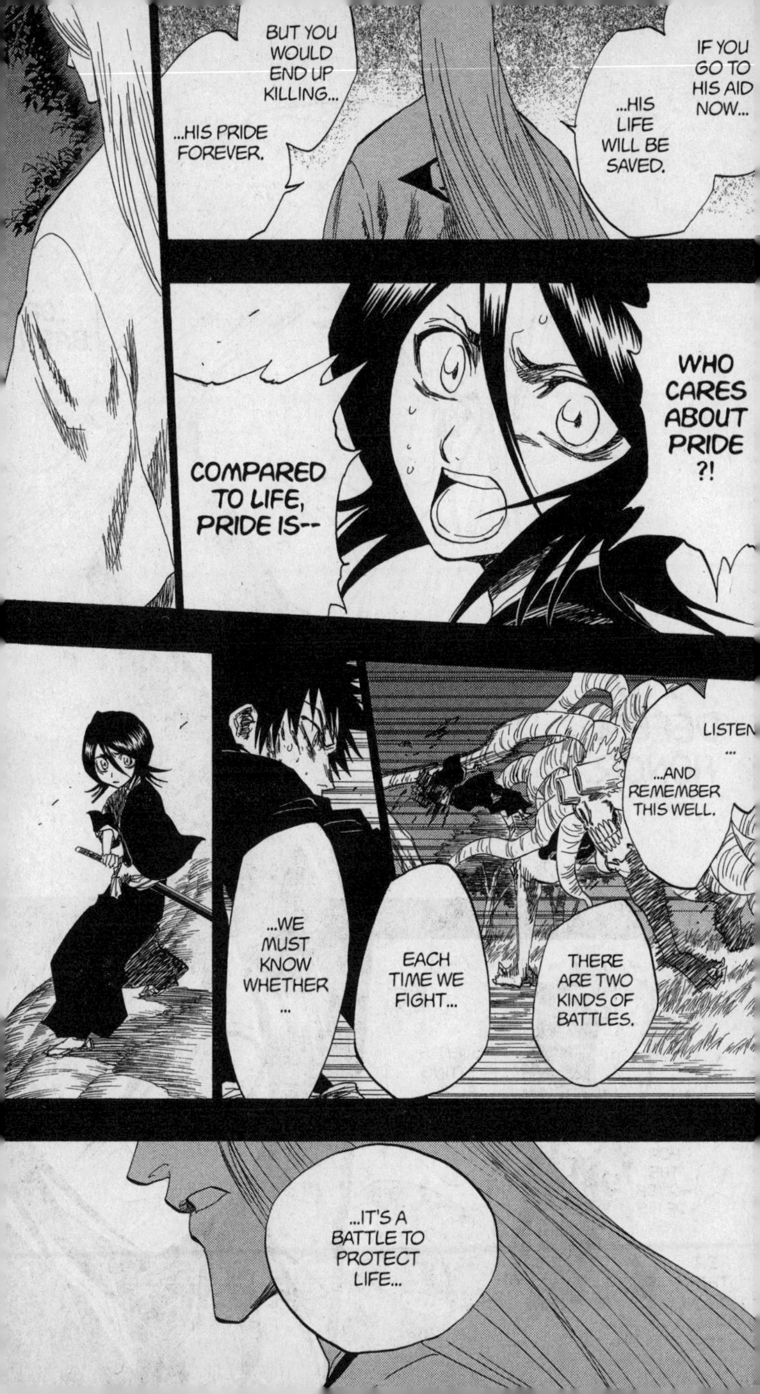
IF YOU GO TO HIS AID NOW...
...HIS LIFE WILL BE SAVED.
BUT YOU WOULD END UP KILLING...
...HIS PRIDE FOREVER.
WHO CARES ABOUT PRIDE ?!
COMPARED TO LIFE, PRIDE IS--
LISTEN ...
...AND REMEMBER THIS WELL.
THERE ARE TWO KINDS OF BATTLES.
EACH TIME WE FIGHT...
...WE MUST KNOW WHETHER ...
...IT'S A BATTLE TO PROTECT LIFE...

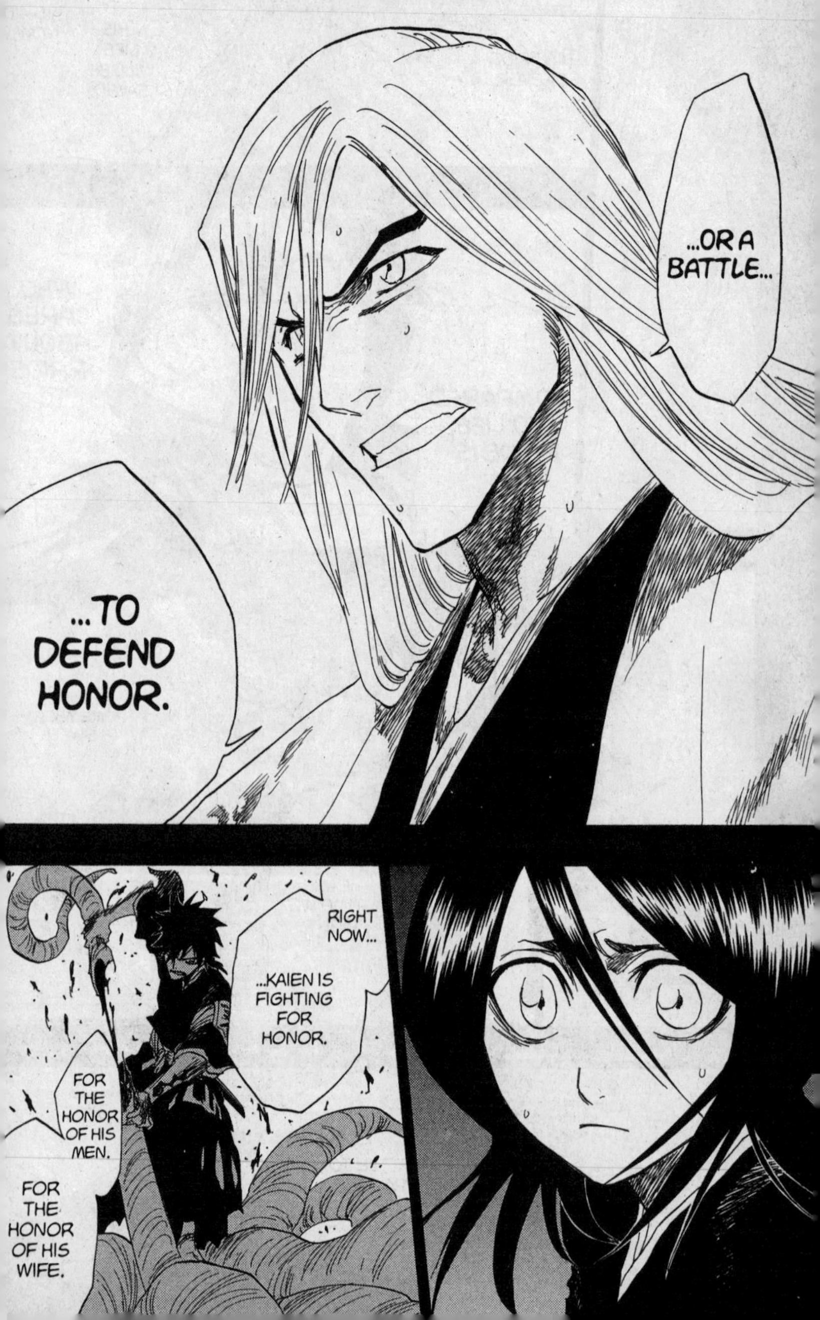
...OR A BATTLE...
...TO DEFEND HONOR.
RIGHT NOW...
...KAIEN IS FIGHTING FOR HONOR.
FOR THE HONOR OF HIS MEN.
FOR THE HONOR OF HIS WIFE.

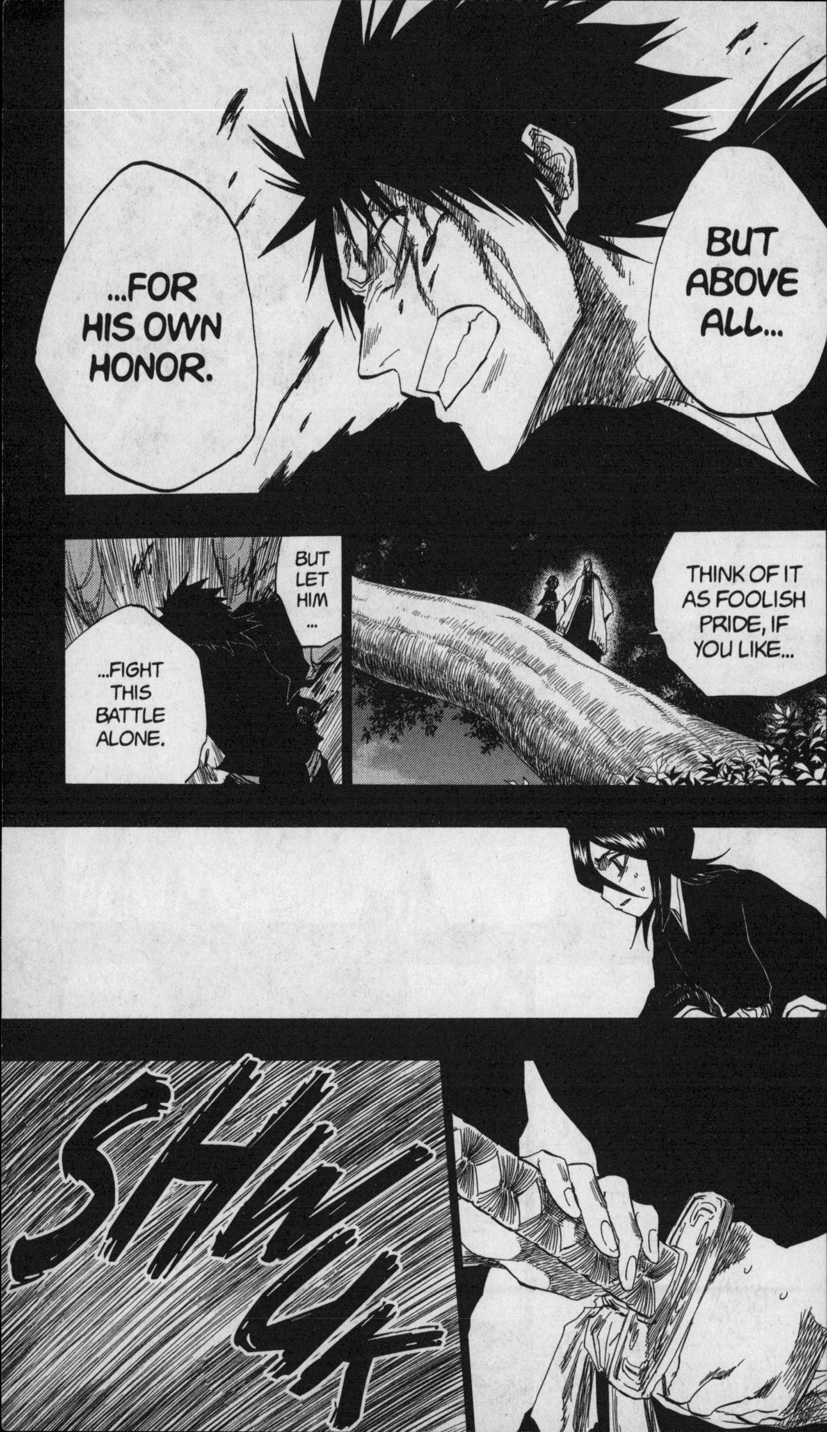
BUT ABOVE ALL...
...FOR HIS OWN HONOR.
THINK OF IT AS FOOLISH PRIDE, IF YOU LIKE...
BUT LET HIM ...
...FIGHT THIS BATTLE ALONE.
SHNK

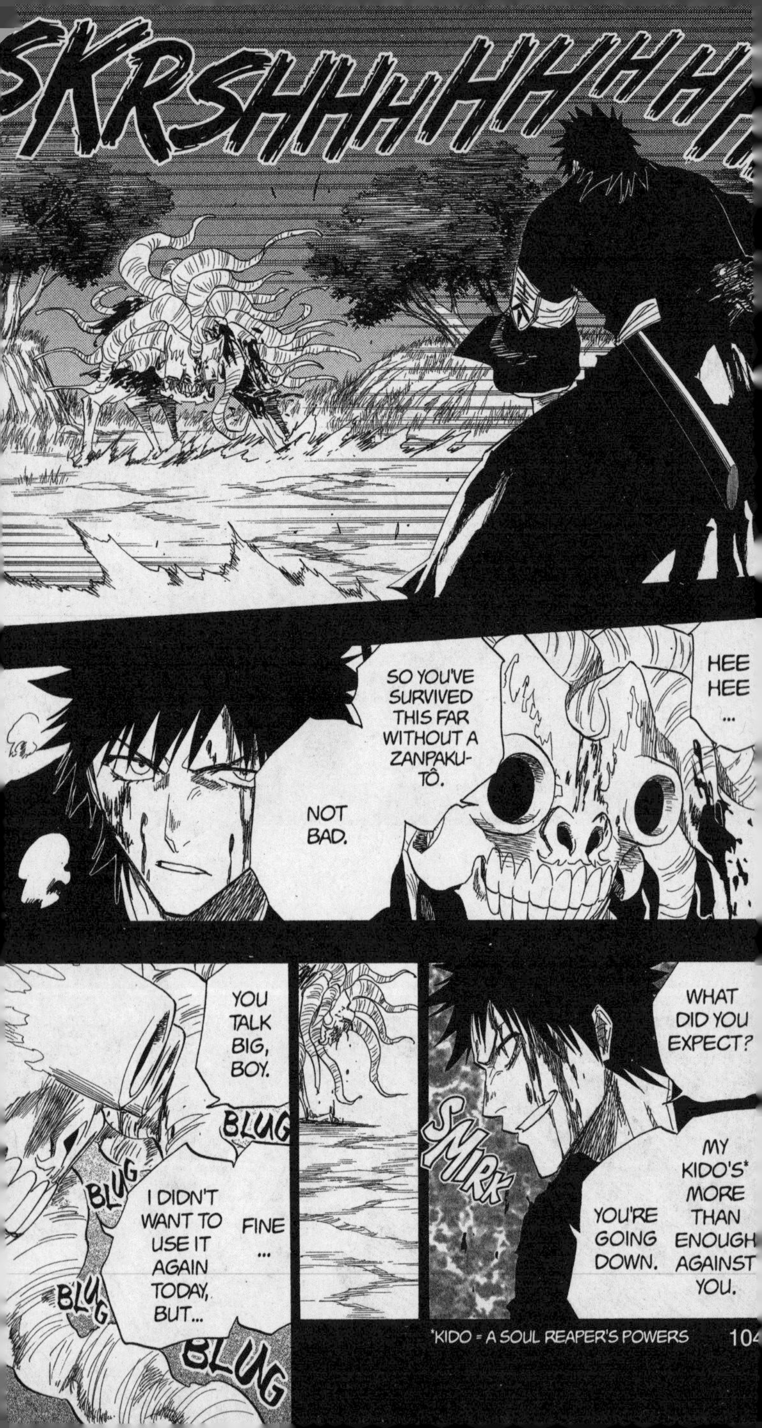
SKRSHHHHHHHH
HEE HEE ...
SO YOU'VE SURVIVED THIS FAR WITHOUT A ZANPAKU-TÔ.
NOT BAD.
WHAT DID YOU EXPECT?
SMIRK
MY KIDO'S* MORE THAN ENOUGH AGAINST YOU.
YOU'RE GOING DOWN.
YOU TALK BIG, BOY.
BLUG
FINE ...
I DIDN'T WANT TO USE IT AGAIN TODAY, BUT...
BLUG
BLUG
BLUG

*KIDO = A SOUL REAPER'S POWERS

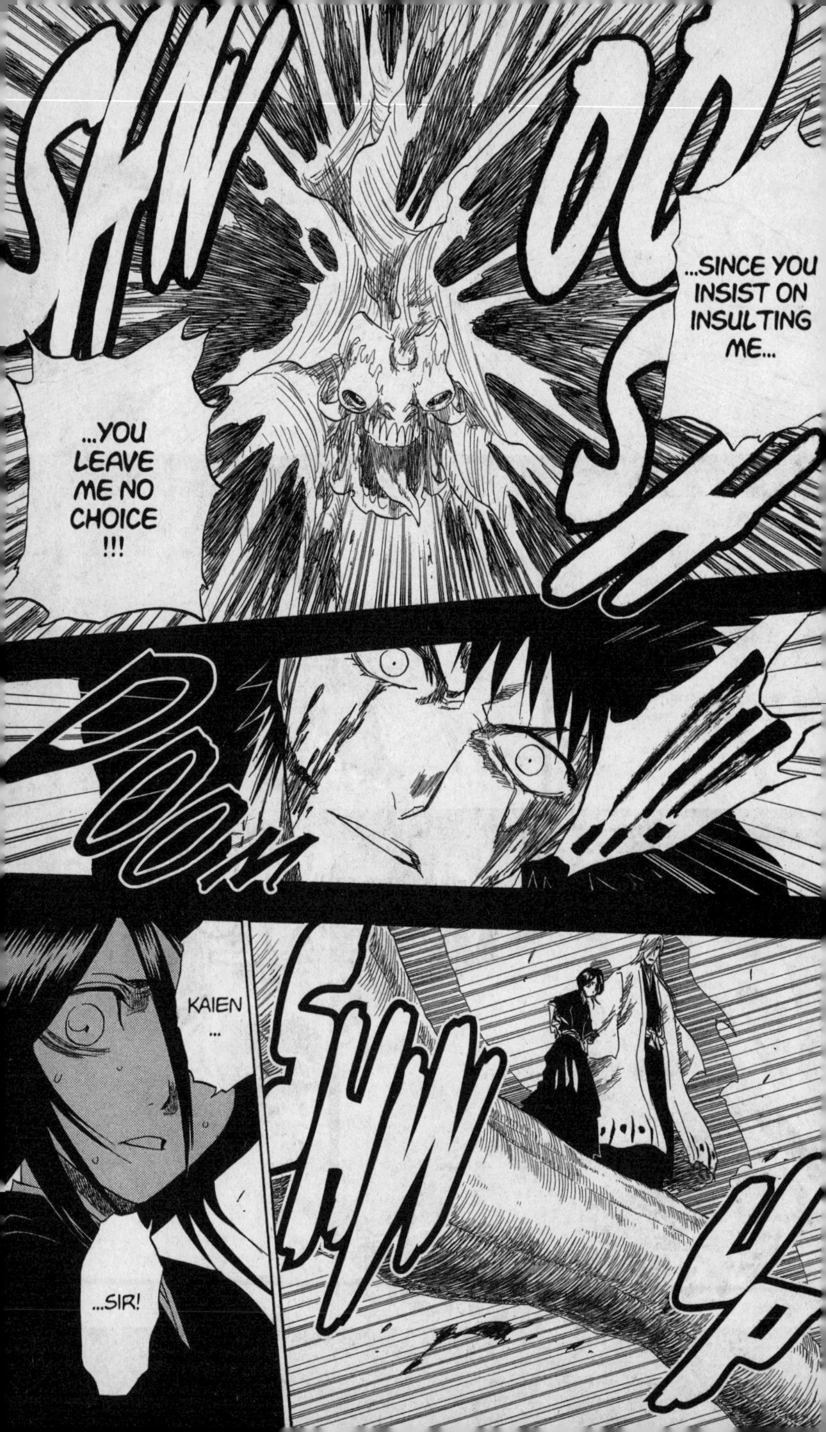
...SINCE YOU INSIST ON INSULTING ME...
...YOU LEAVE ME NO CHOICE!!!
SHWOOSH
DOOM!!
KAIEN...
...SIR!

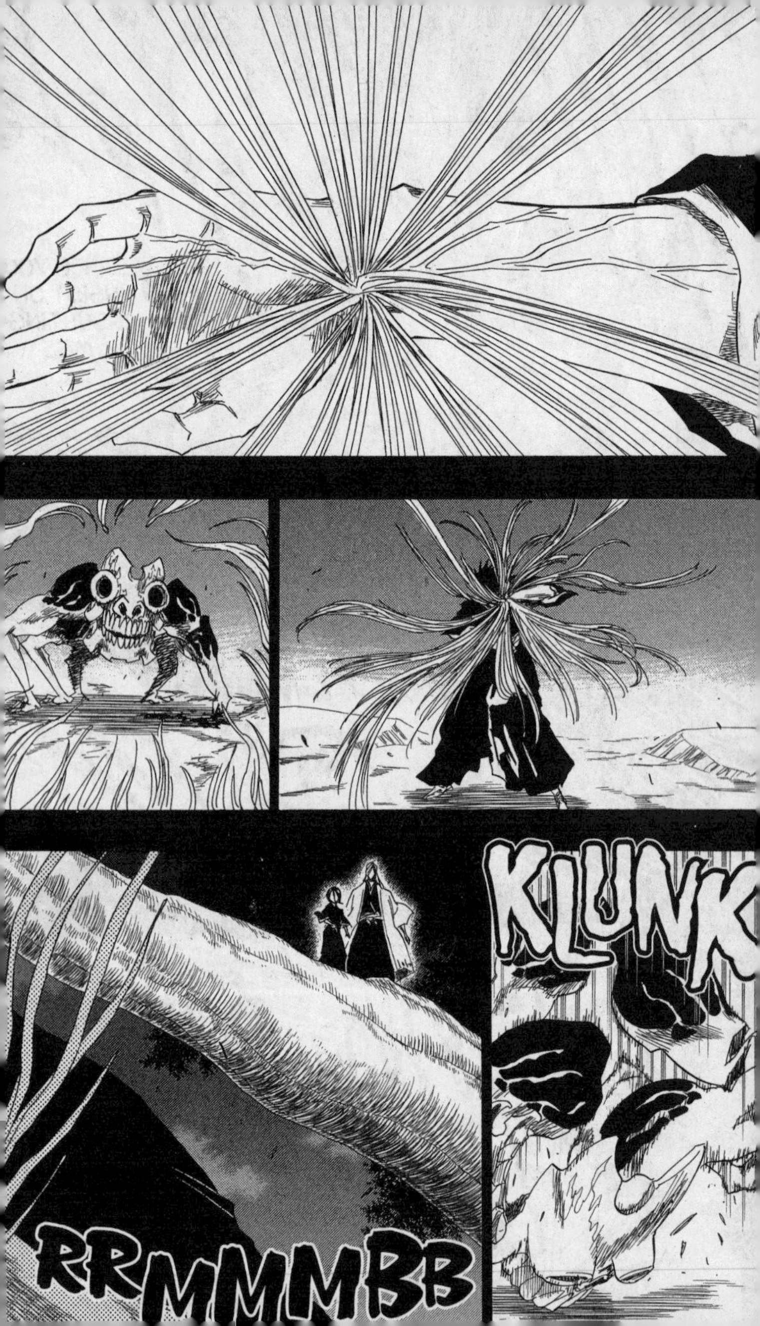
KLUNK
RRMMMBB

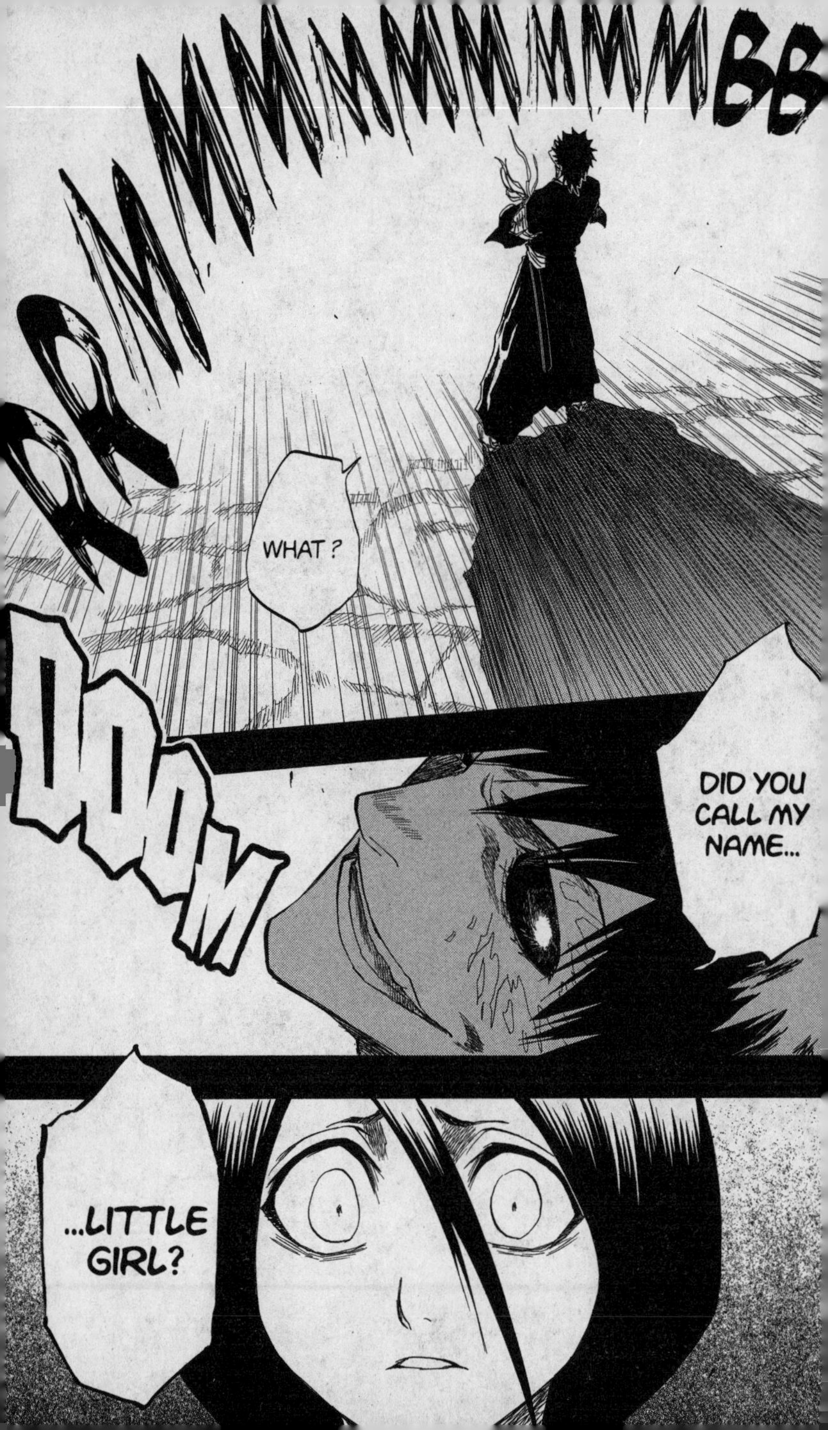
BRMMMMMMMMMBB
WHAT ?
DOOM
DID YOU CALL MY NAME...
...LITTLE GIRL?

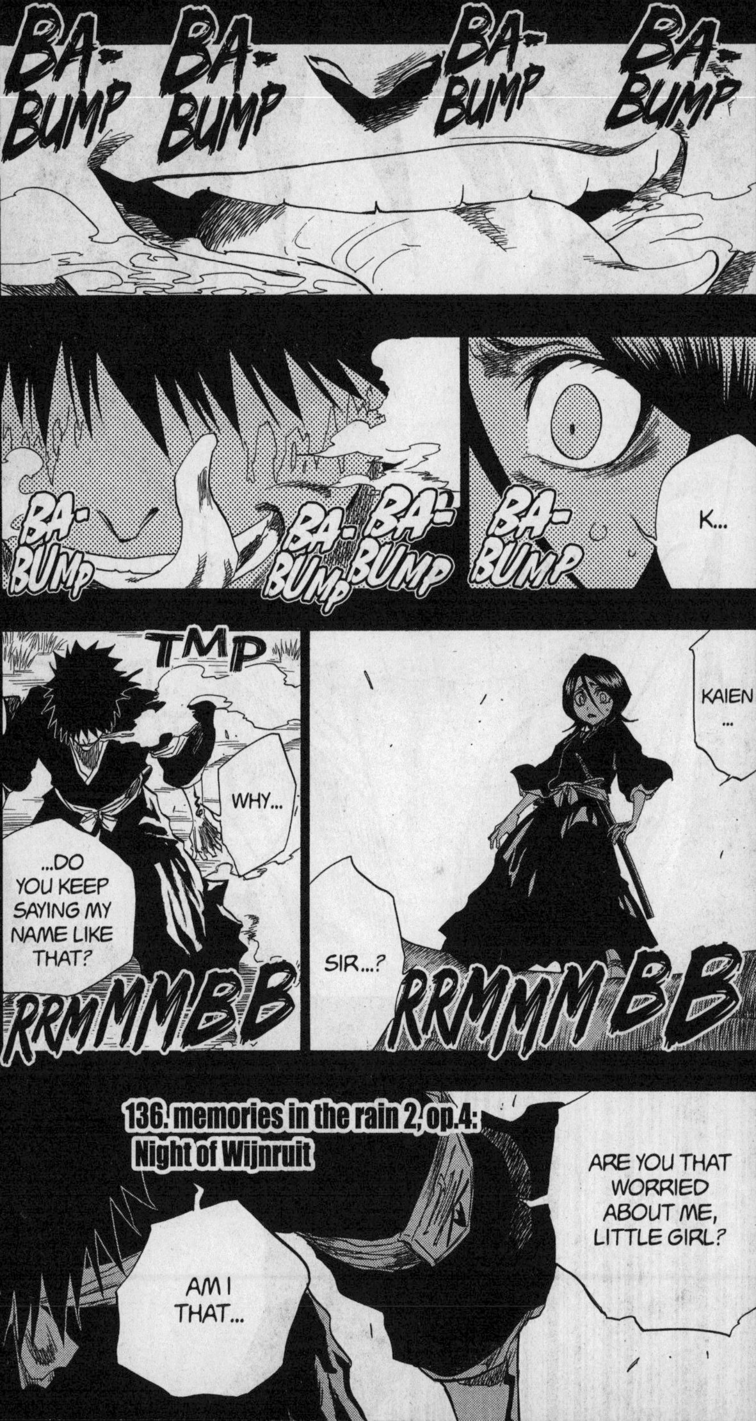
BA-BUMP
BA-BUMP
BA-BUMP
BA-BUMP
K...
BA-BUMP
BA-BUMP
BA-BUMP
BA-BUMP
KAIEN ...
SIR...?
RRMMMBB
TMP
WHY...
...DO YOU KEEP SAYING MY NAME LIKE THAT?
RRMMMBB
136. memories in the rain 2, op.4: Night of Wijnruit
ARE YOU THAT WORRIED ABOUT ME, LITTLE GIRL?
AM I THAT...

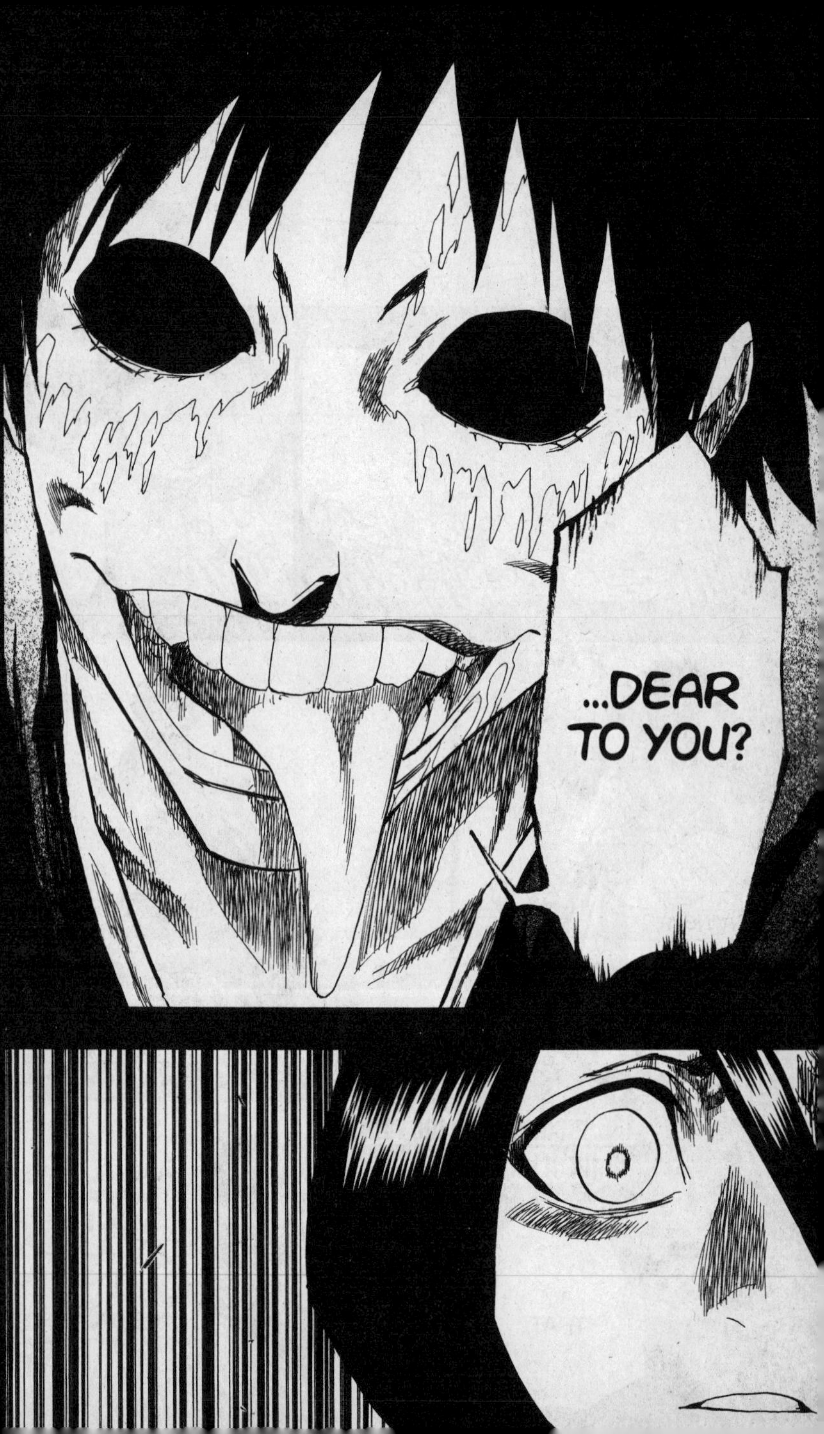
...DEAR
TO YOU?

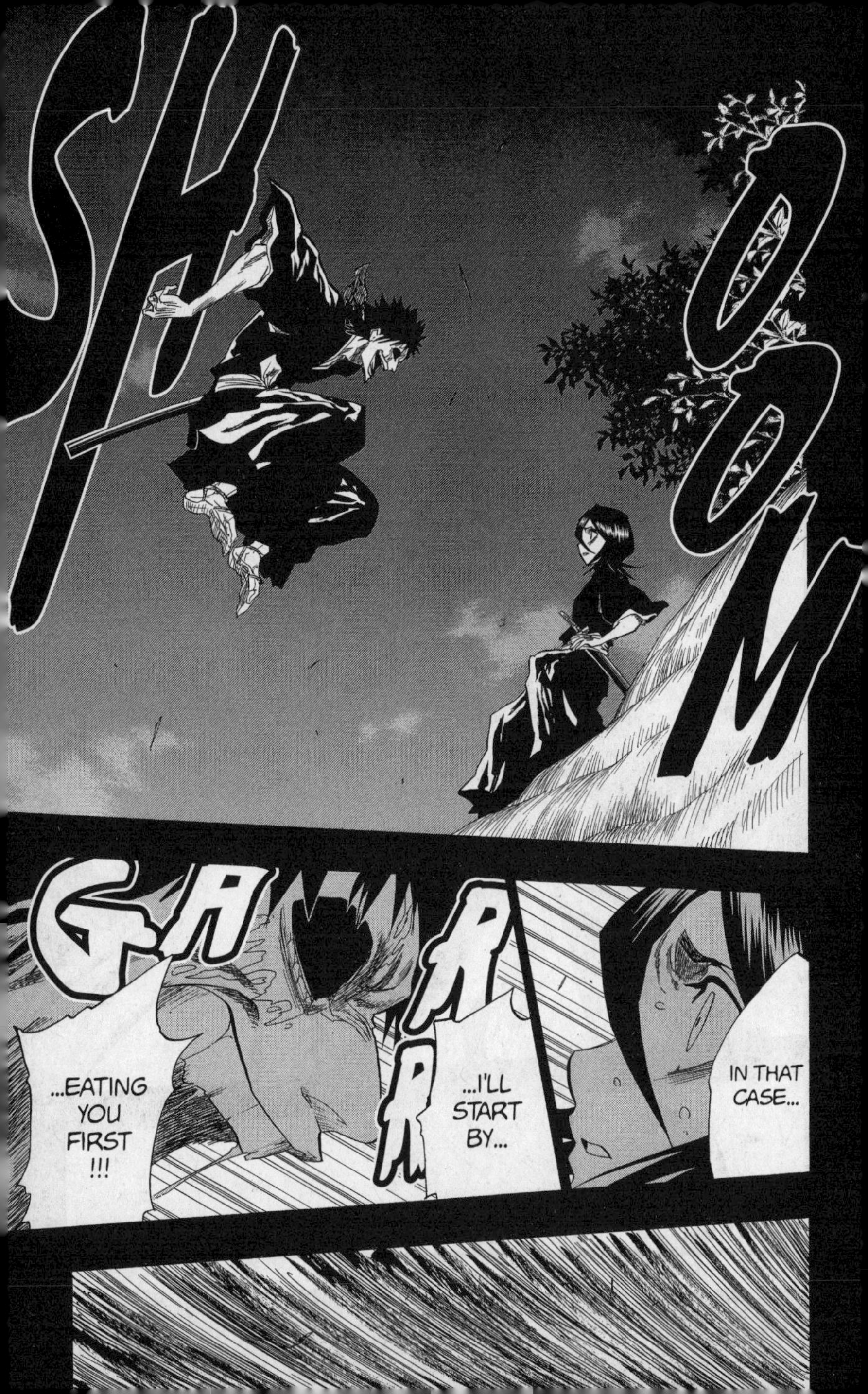
SHOOOM
IN THAT CASE...
...I'LL START BY...
GRARR
...EATING YOU FIRST !!!

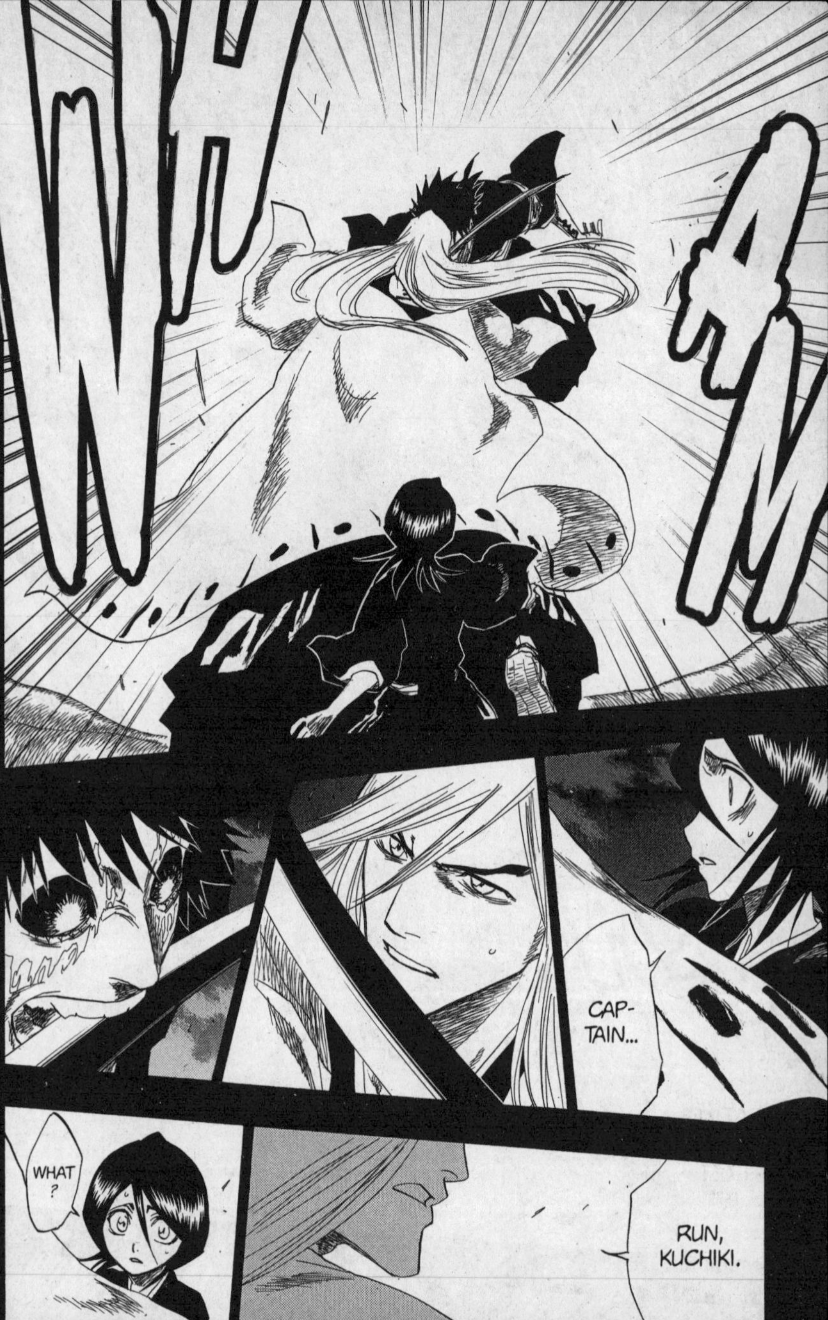
WHAM
CAP-TAIN...
RUN, KUCHIKI.
WHAT ?

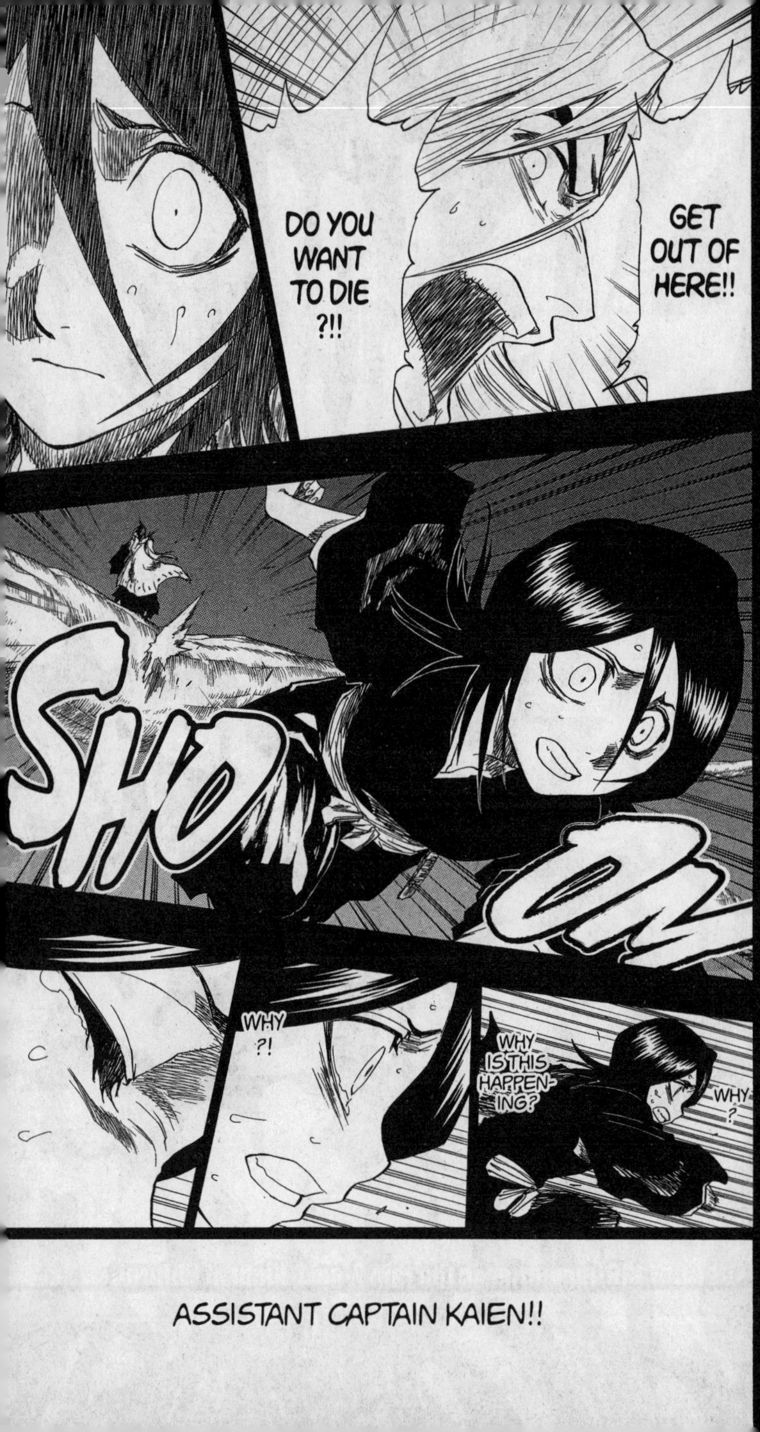
GET OUT OF HERE!!
DO YOU WANT TO DIE ?!!
SHOOM
WHY ?
WHY IS THIS HAPPEN-ING?
WHY ?!
ASSISTANT CAPTAIN KAIEN!!

136. memories in the rain 2, op.4: Night of Wijnruit

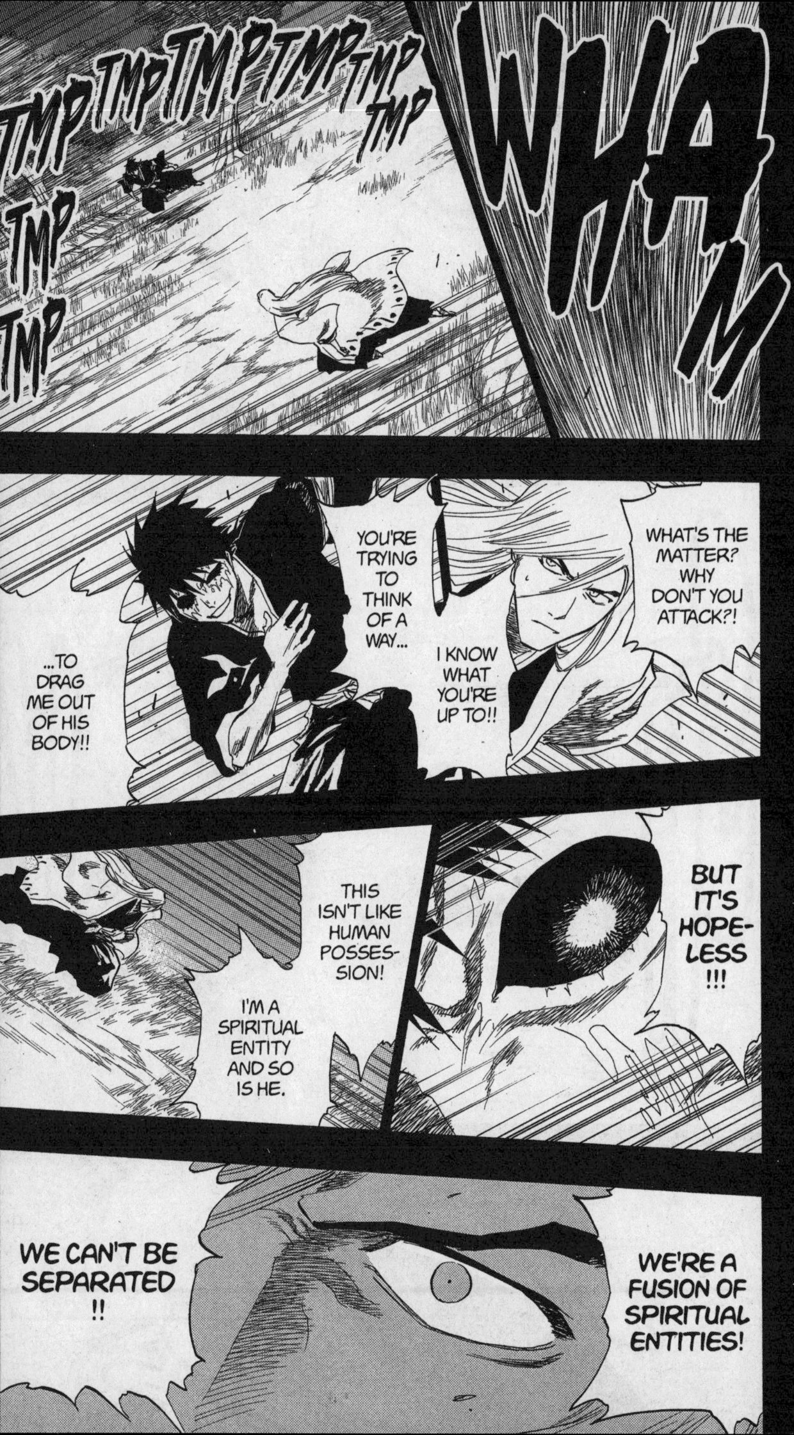
WHAM
TMP TMP TMP TMP TMP TMP TMP TMP TMP TMP
WHAT'S THE MATTER? WHY DON'T YOU ATTACK?!
I KNOW WHAT YOU'RE UP TO!!
YOU'RE TRYING TO THINK OF A WAY...
...TO DRAG ME OUT OF HIS BODY!!
BUT IT'S HOPE-LESS!!!
THIS ISN'T LIKE HUMAN POSSES-SION!
I'M A SPIRITUAL ENTITY AND SO IS HE.
WE'RE A FUSION OF SPIRITUAL ENTITIES!
WE CAN'T BE SEPARATED!!

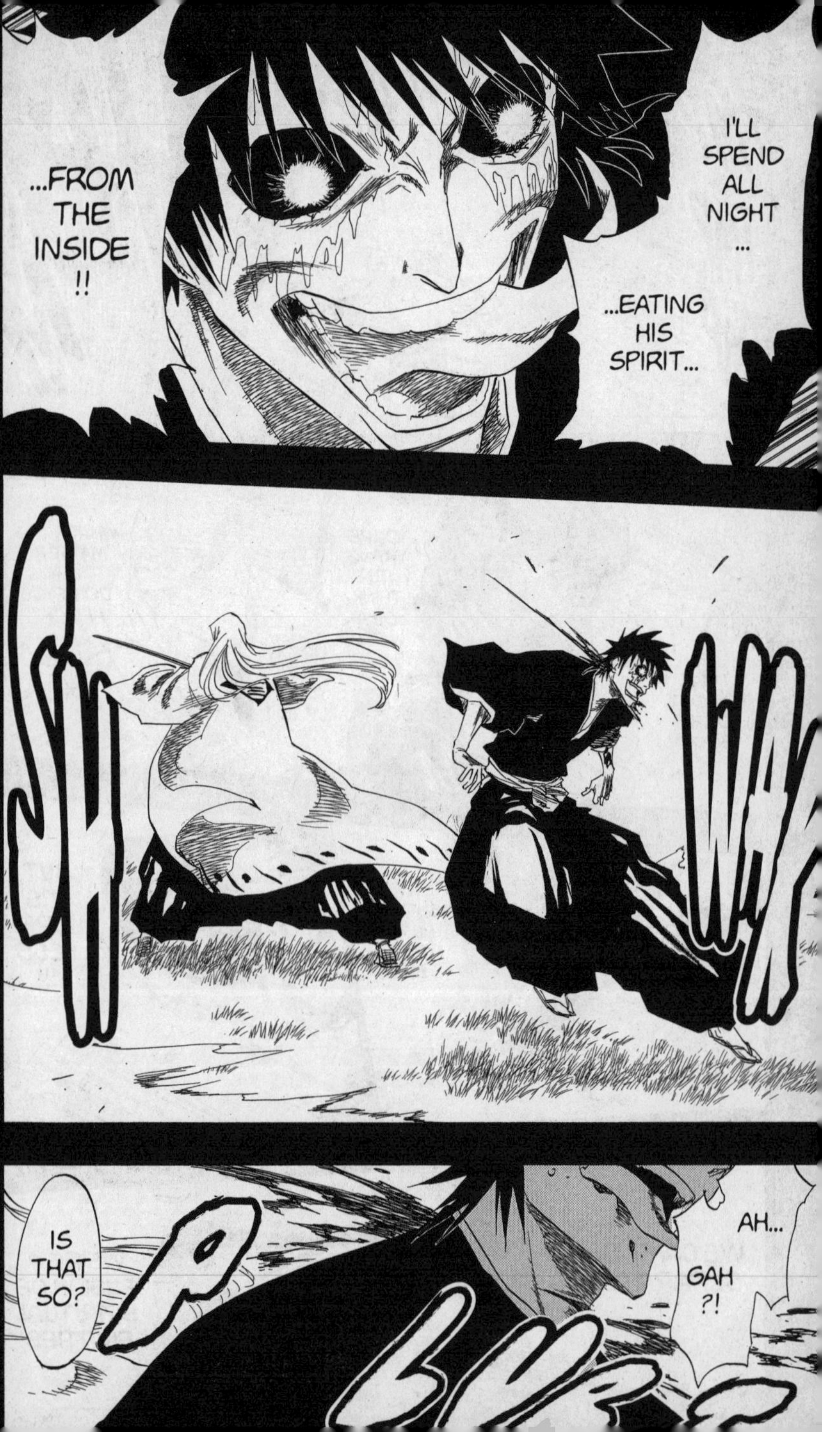
I'LL SPEND ALL NIGHT ...
...EATING HIS SPIRIT...
...FROM THE INSIDE !!
AH...
GAH ?!
IS THAT SO?

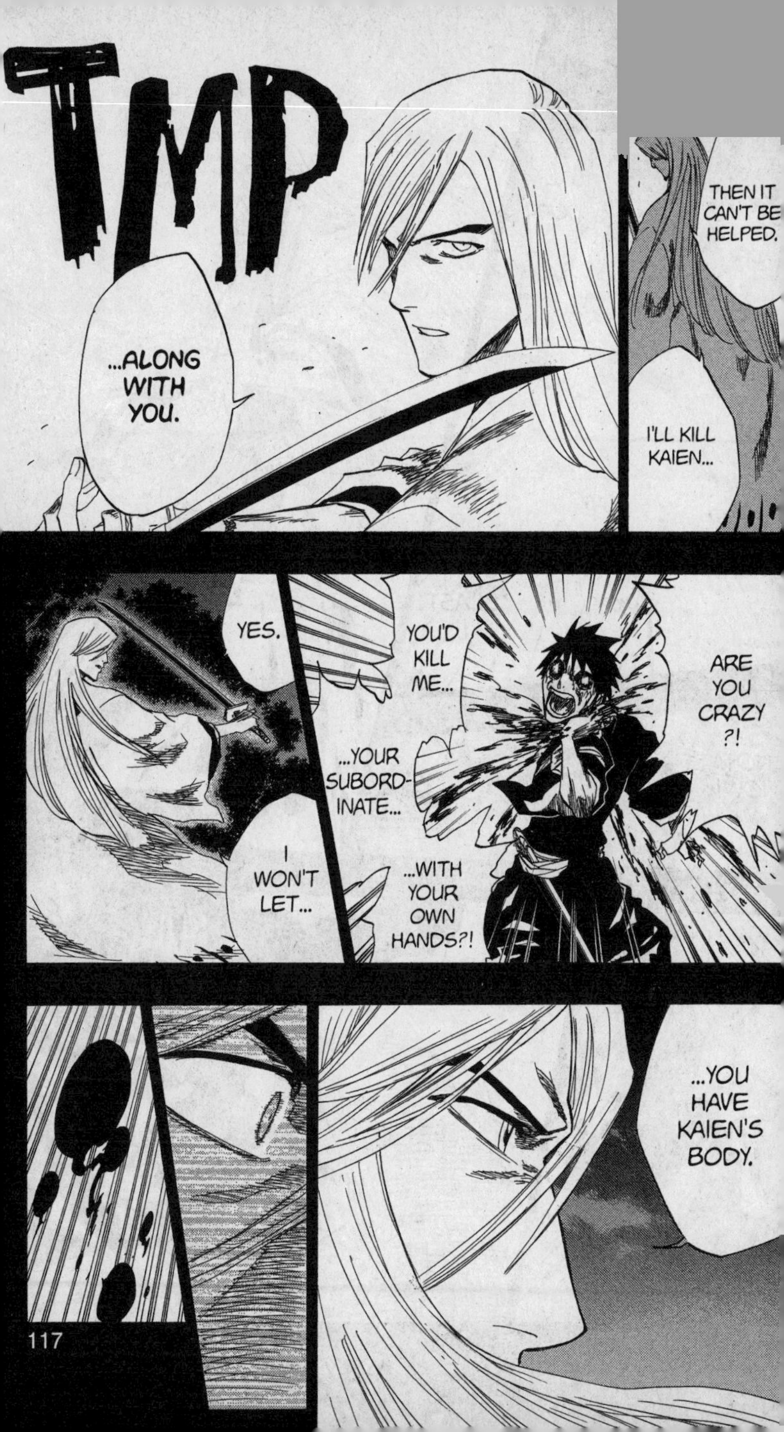
THEN IT CAN'T BE HELPED.
I'LL KILL KAIEN...
TMP
...ALONG WITH YOU.
ARE YOU CRAZY?!
YOU'D KILL ME...
...YOUR SUBORD-INATE...
...WITH YOUR OWN HANDS?!
YES.
I WON'T LET...
...YOU HAVE KAIEN'S BODY.

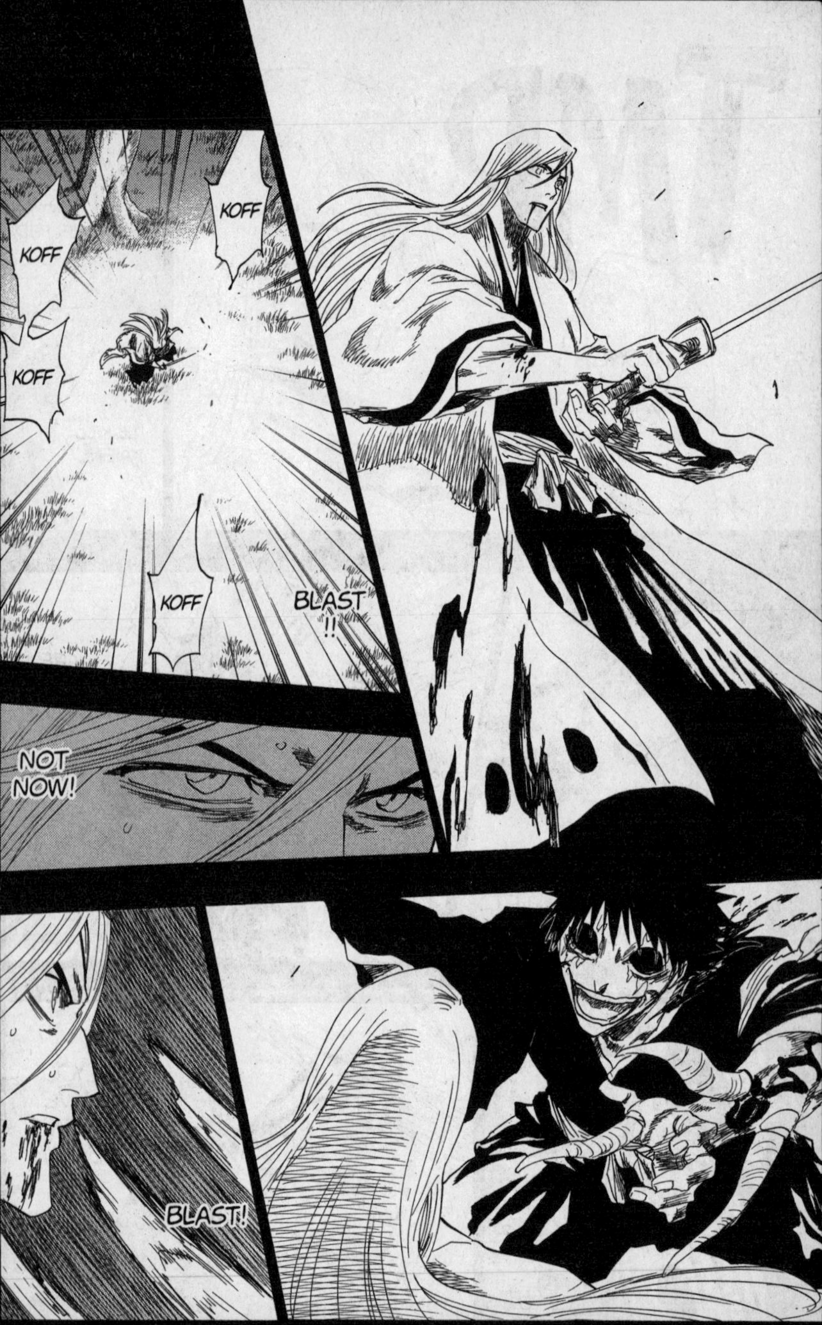
KOFF
KOFF
KOFF
BLAST !!
KOFF
NOT NOW!
BLAST!

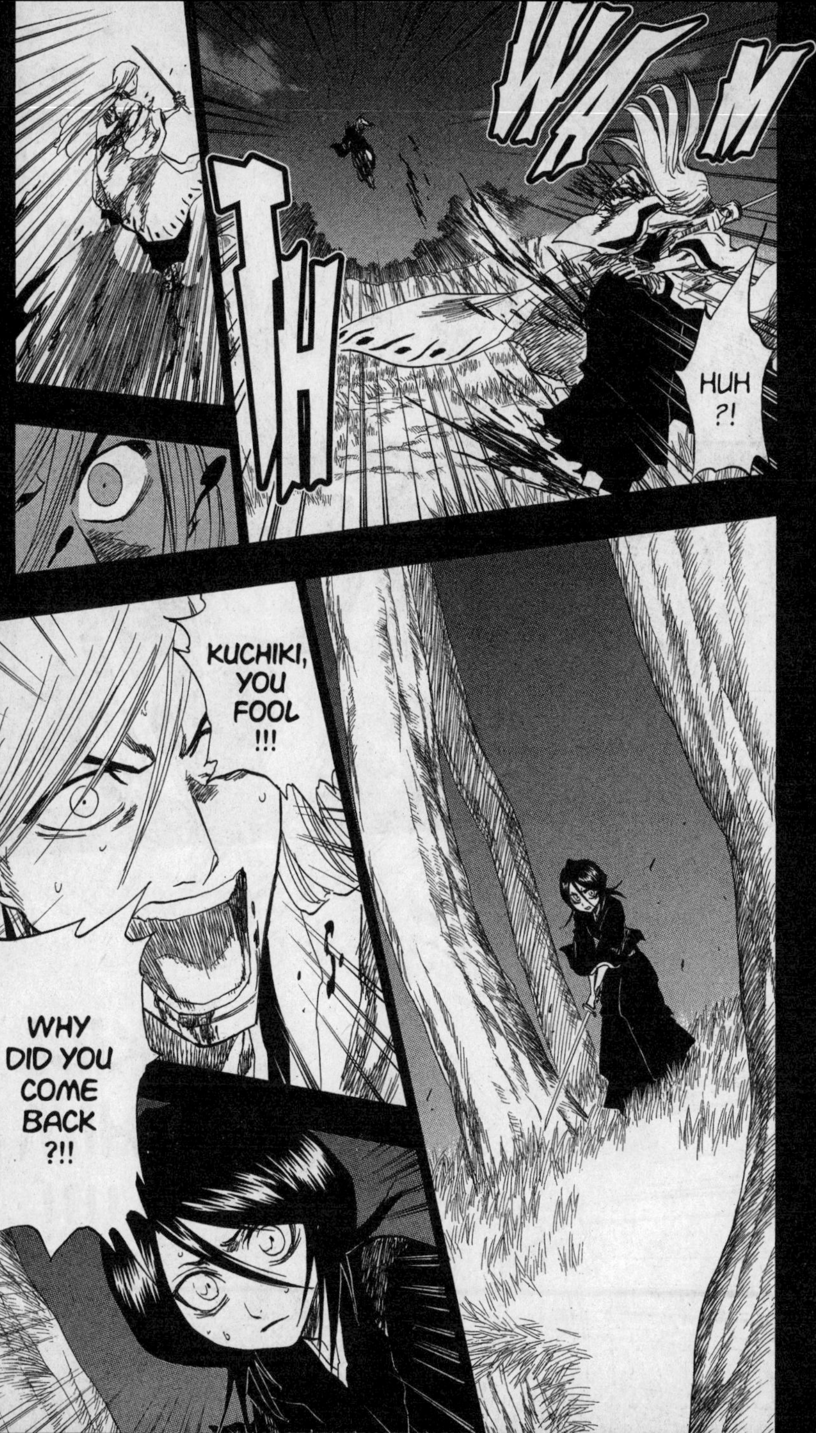
WAM
TH
HUH ?!
KUCHIKI, YOU FOOL !!!
WHY DID YOU COME BACK ?!!

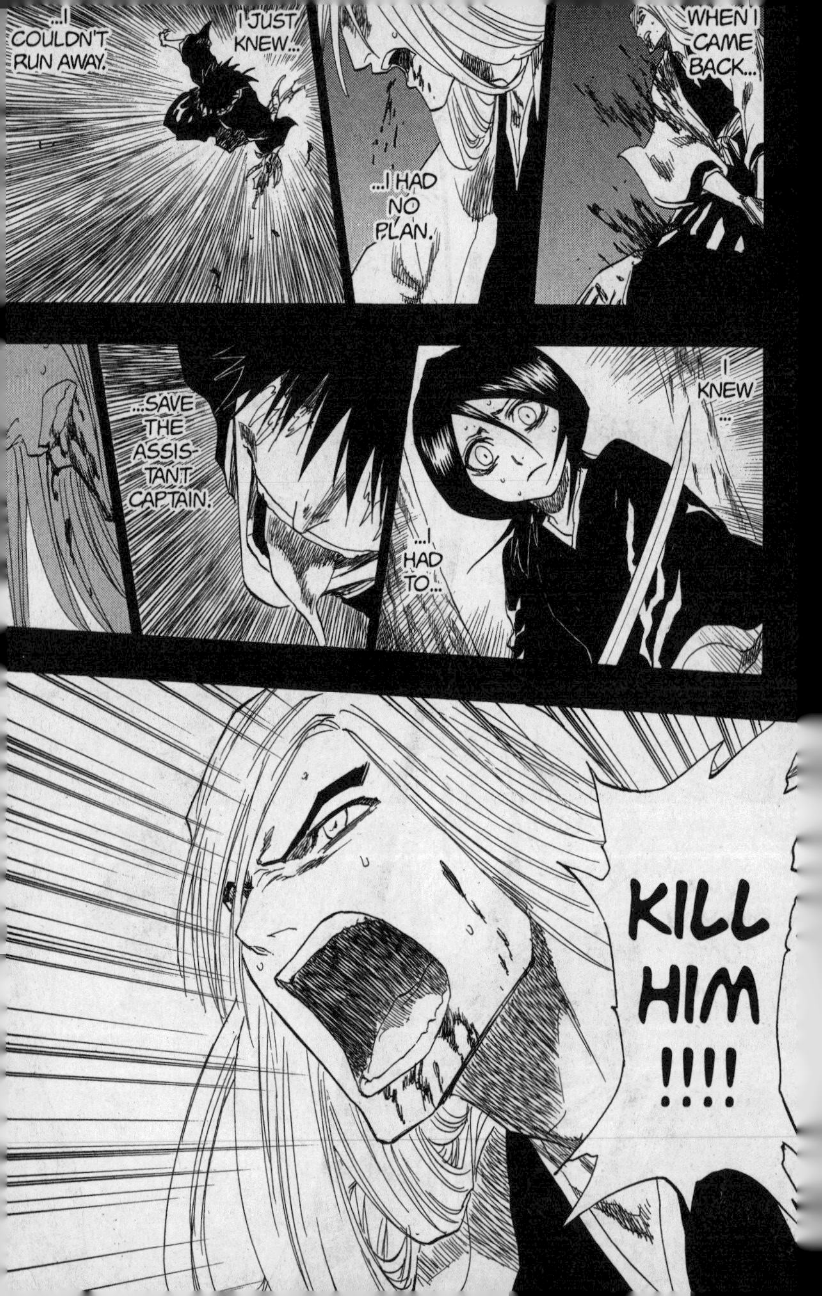
WHEN I CAME BACK...
...I HAD NO PLAN.
I JUST KNEW...
...I COULDN'T RUN AWAY.
I KNEW...
...I HAD TO...
...SAVE THE ASSISTANT CAPTAIN.
KILL HIM!!!!

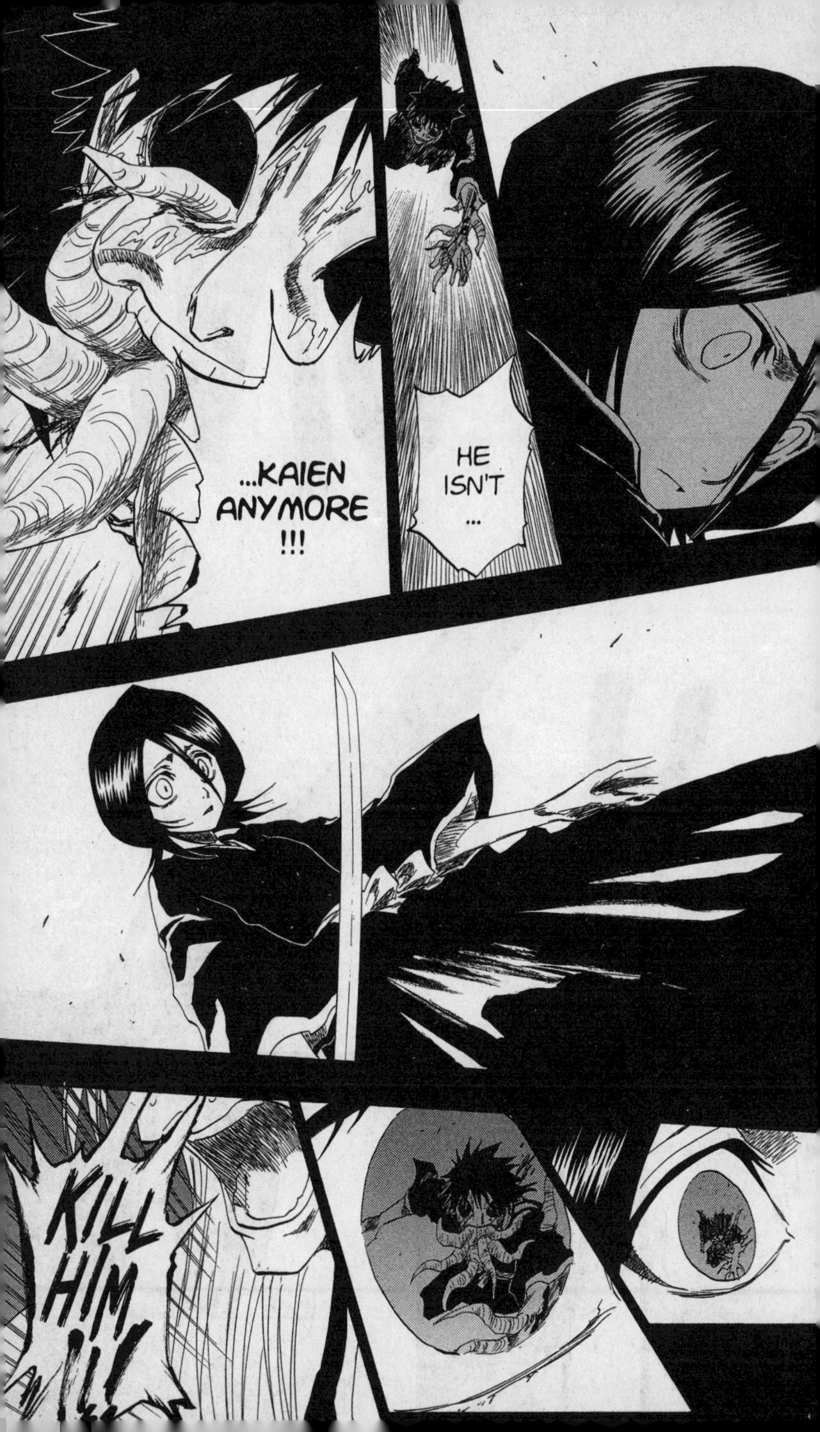
HE ISN'T ...
...KAIEN ANYMORE !!!
KILL HIM !!

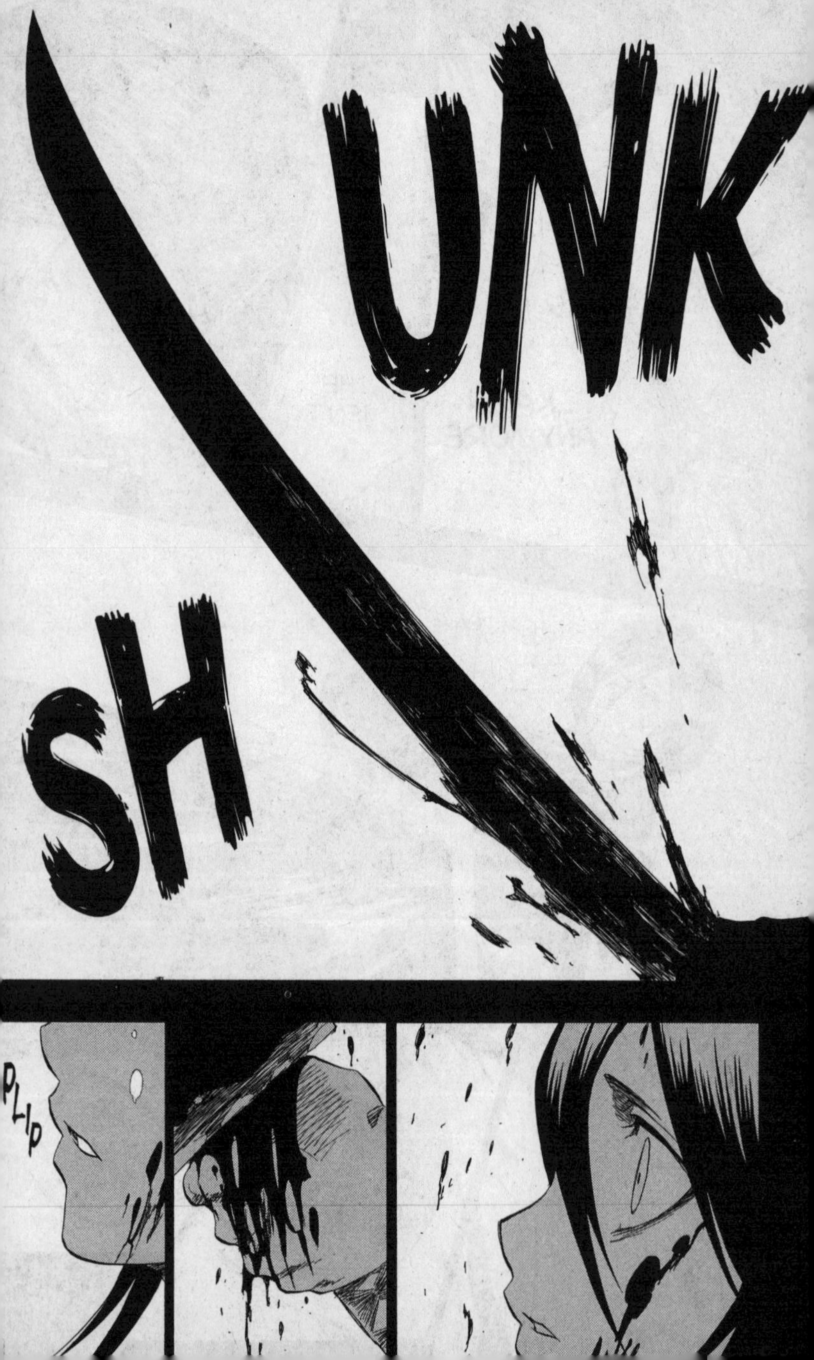
SH
UNK
PLIP

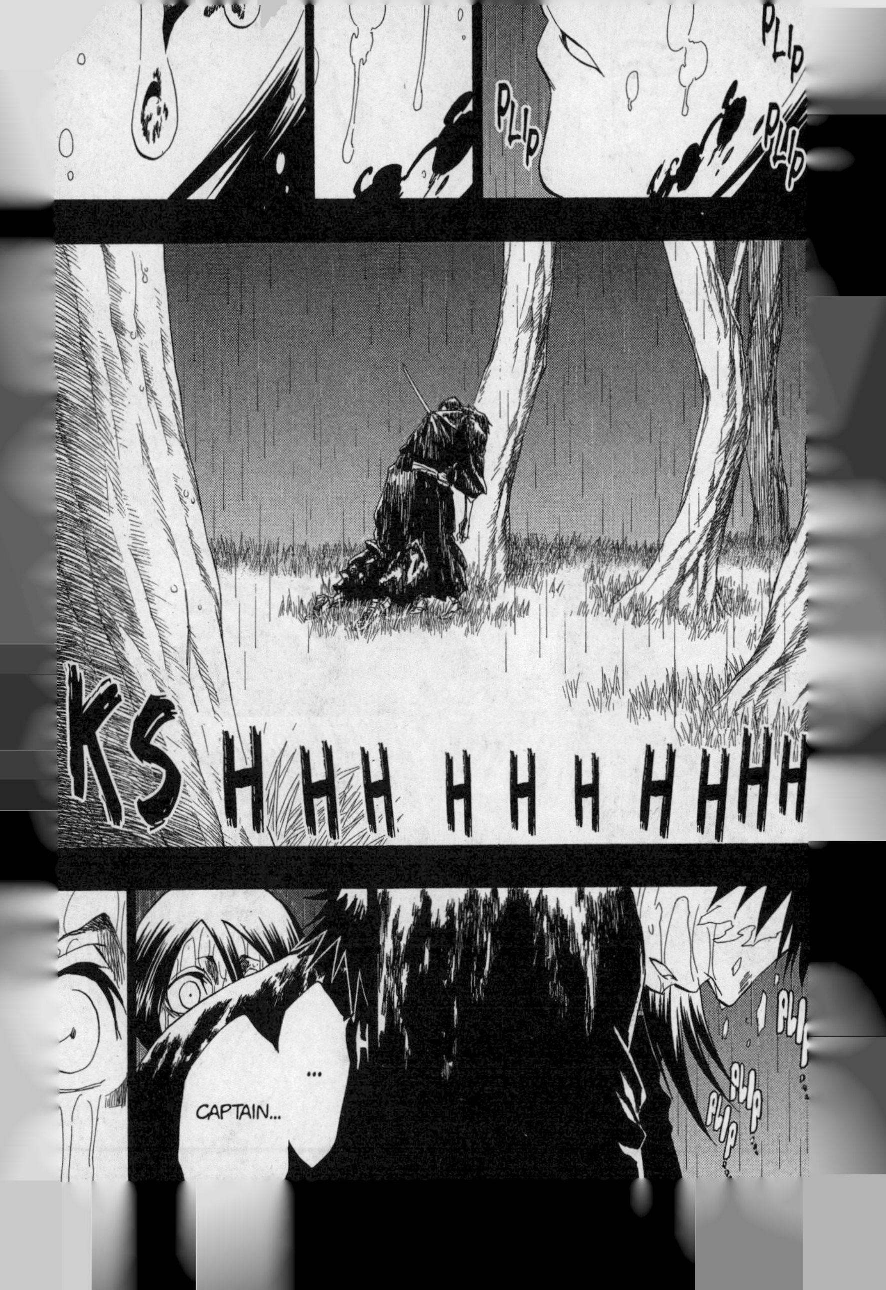
PLIP
PLIP
PLIP
KSHHHHHHHHHH
PLIP
PLIP
PLIP
...
CAPTAIN...

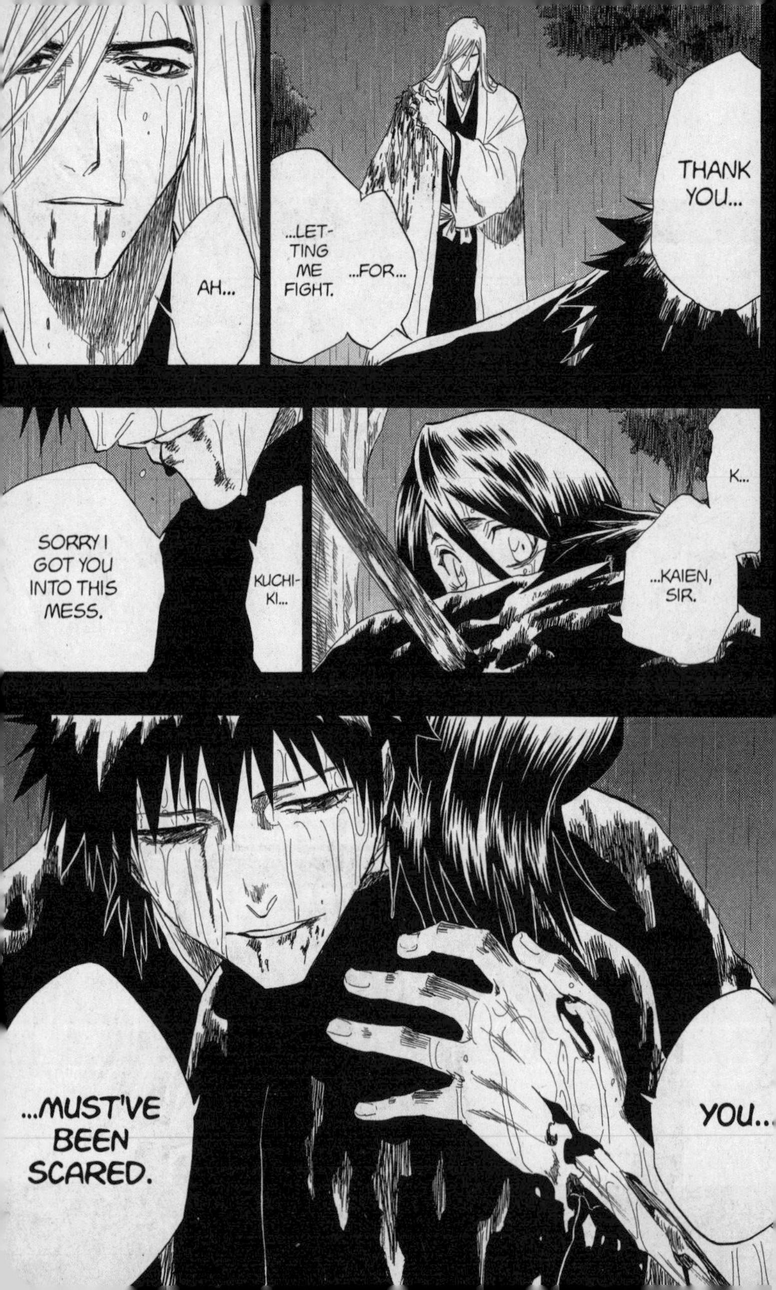
THANK YOU...
...FOR...
...LETTING ME FIGHT.
AH...
K...
...KAIEN, SIR.
KUCHIKI...
SORRY I GOT YOU INTO THIS MESS.
YOU...
...MUST'VE BEEN SCARED.

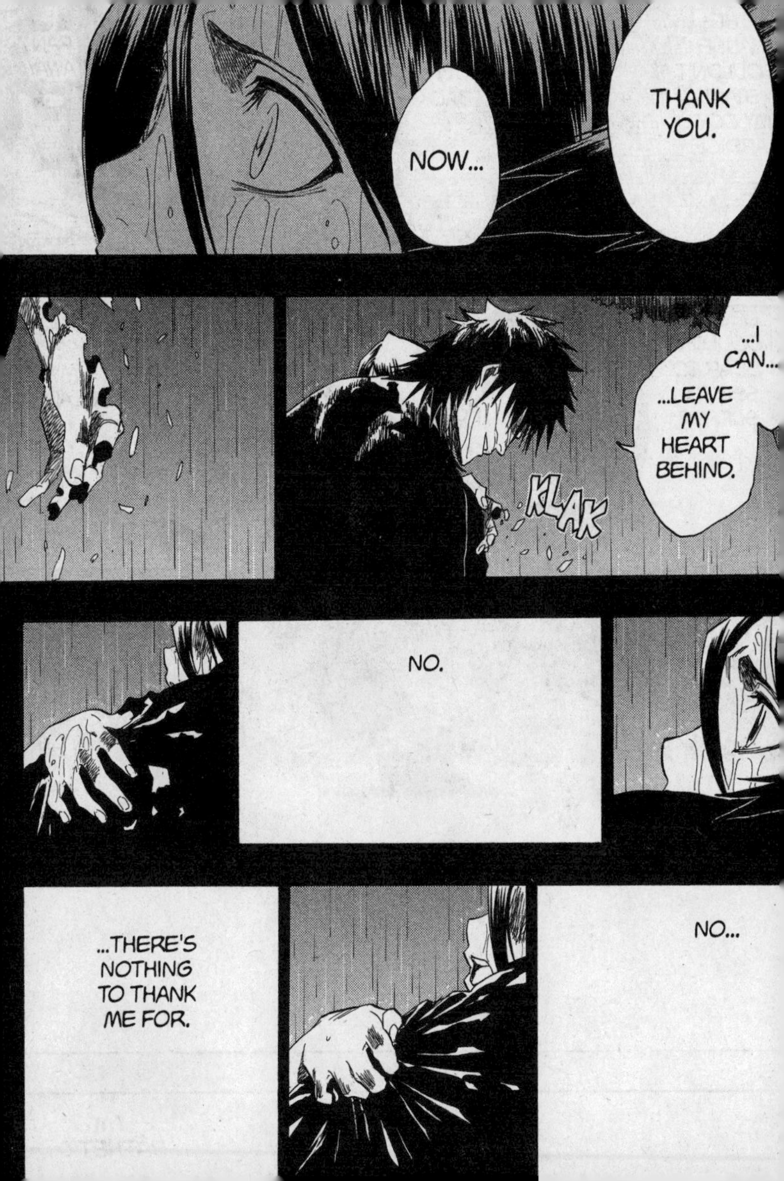
THANK YOU.
NOW...
...I CAN...
...LEAVE MY HEART BEHIND.
KLAK
NO.
NO...
...THERE'S NOTHING TO THANK ME FOR.

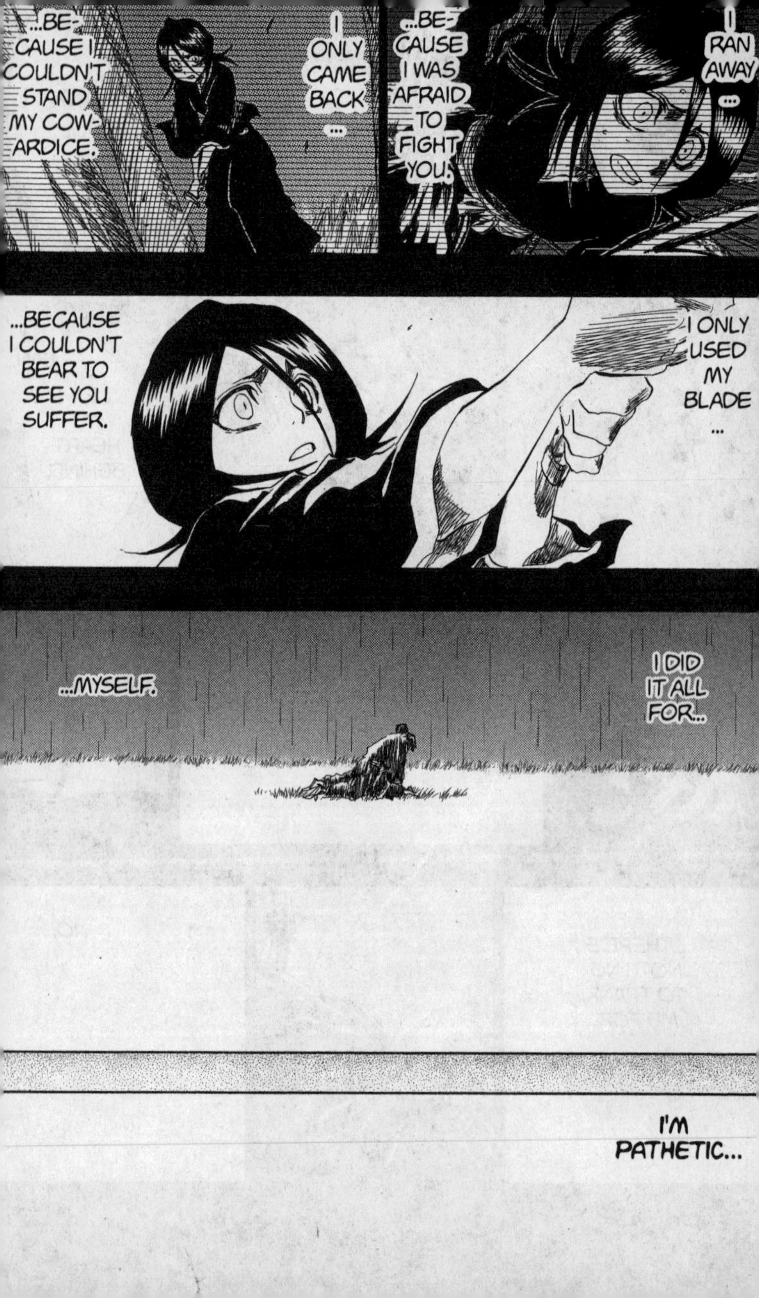
I RAN AWAY...
...BE-CAUSE I WAS AFRAID TO FIGHT YOU.
I ONLY CAME BACK...
...BE-CAUSE I COULDN'T STAND MY COW-ARDICE.
I ONLY USED MY BLADE...
...BECAUSE I COULDN'T BEAR TO SEE YOU SUFFER.
I DID IT ALL FOR...
...MYSELF.
I'M PATHETIC...

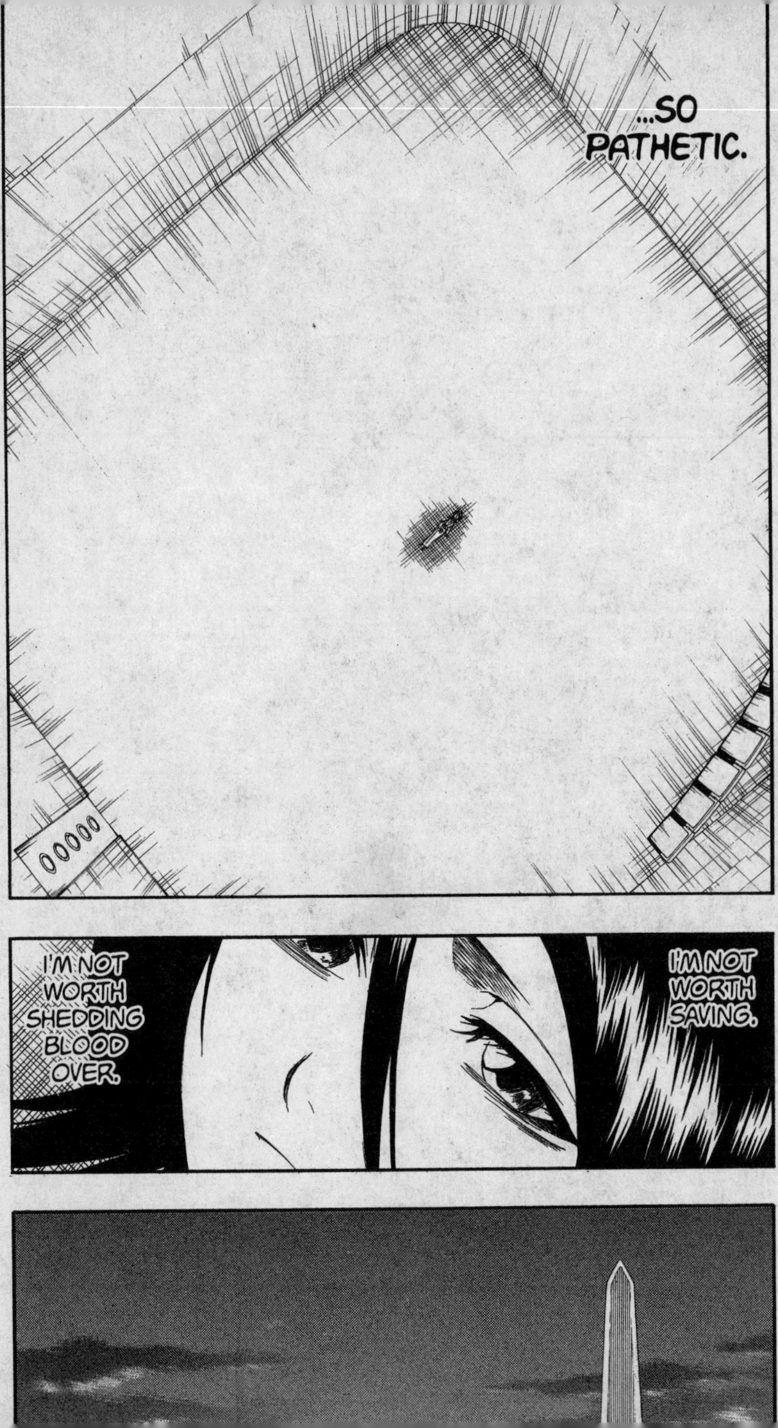
...SO PATHETIC.
I'M NOT WORTH SAVING.
I'M NOT WORTH SHEDDING BLOOD OVER.

137. Surrounding Clutch

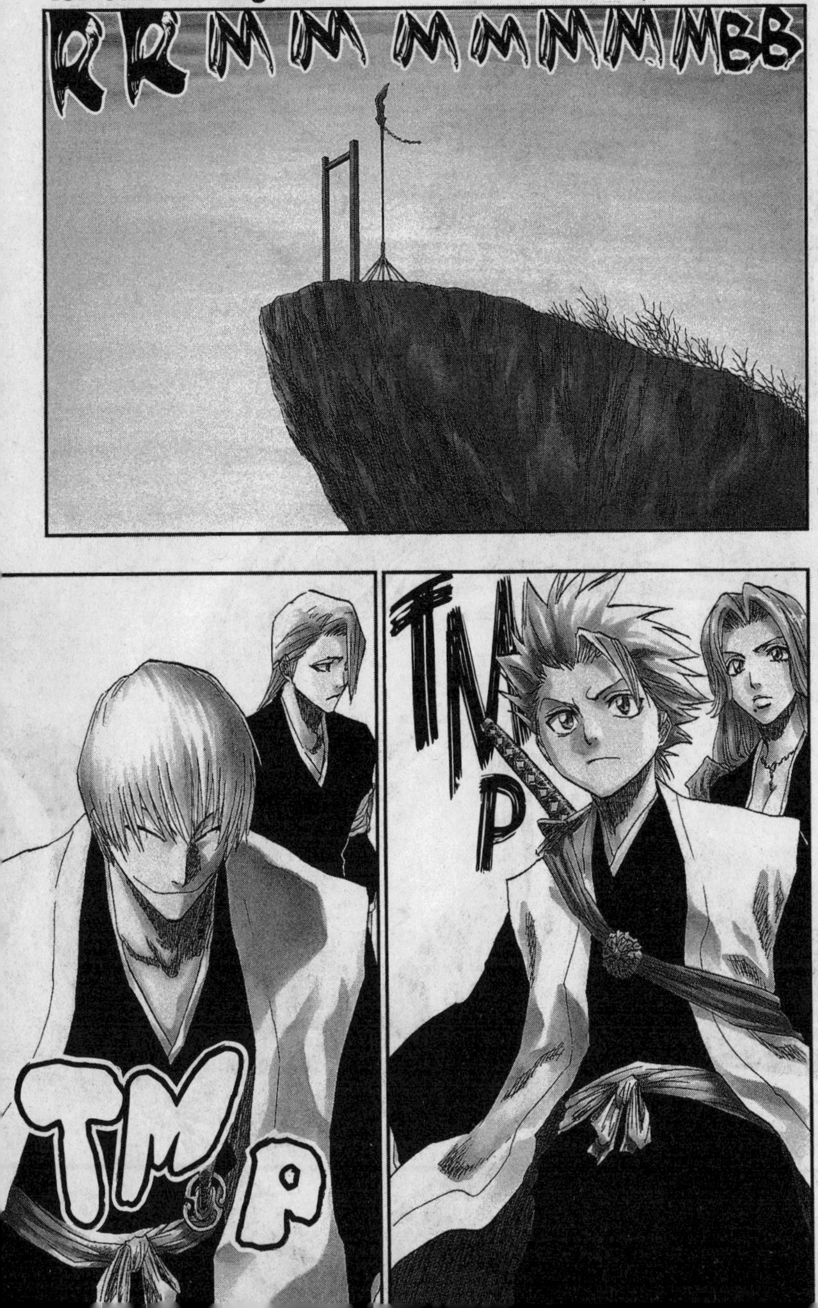
RRMM MMMMMMBB
TMP
TMP

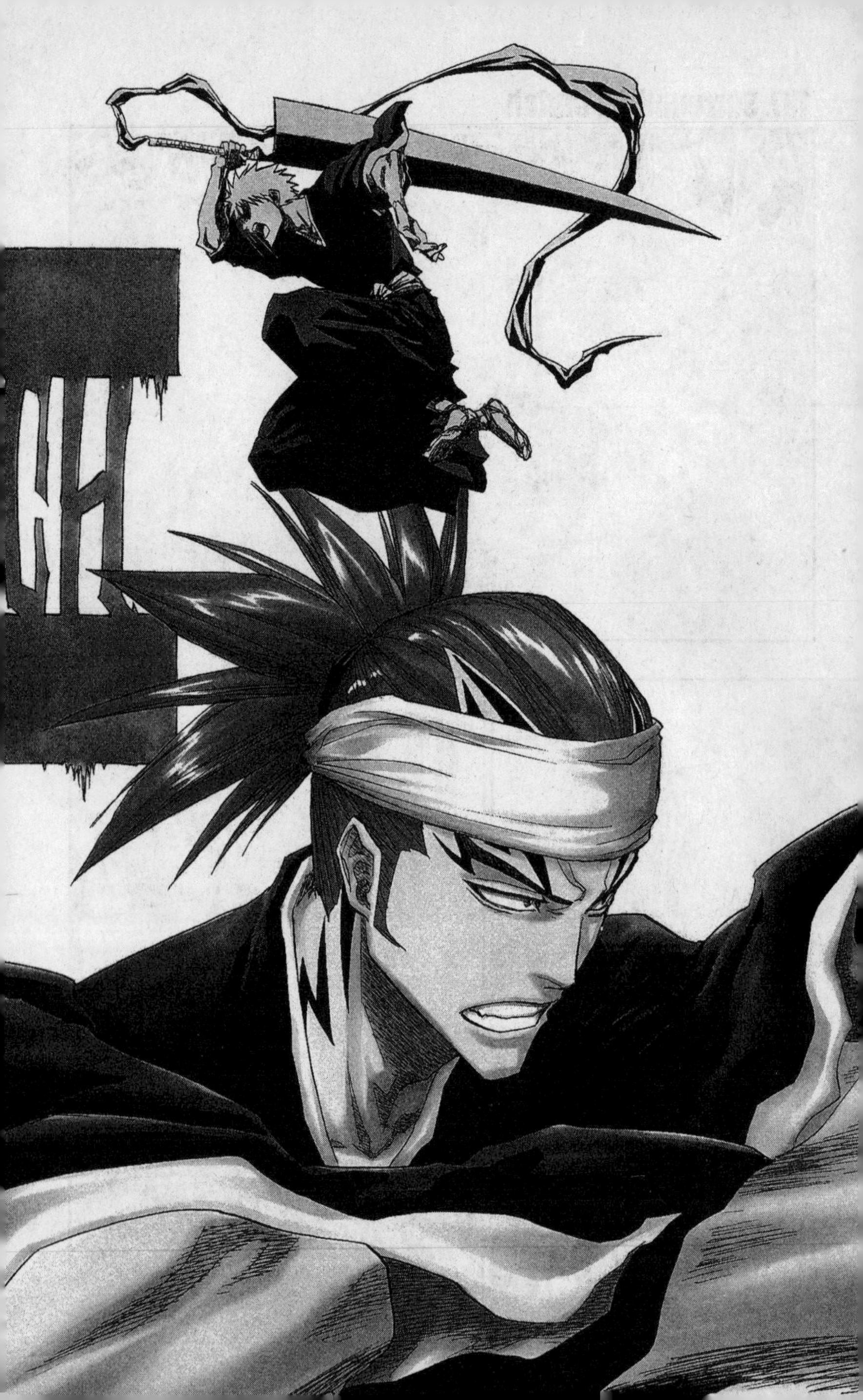

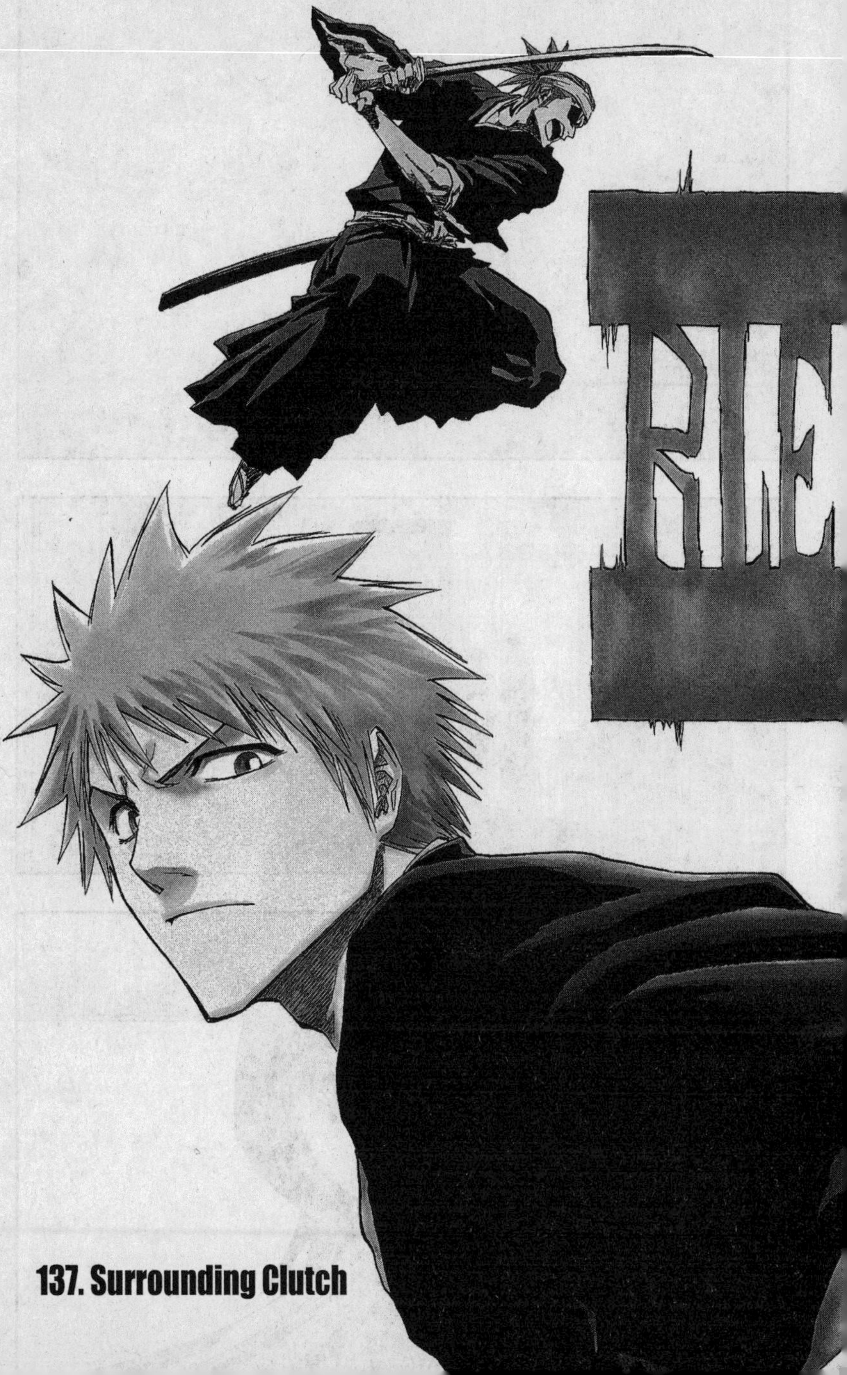

137. Surrounding Clutch

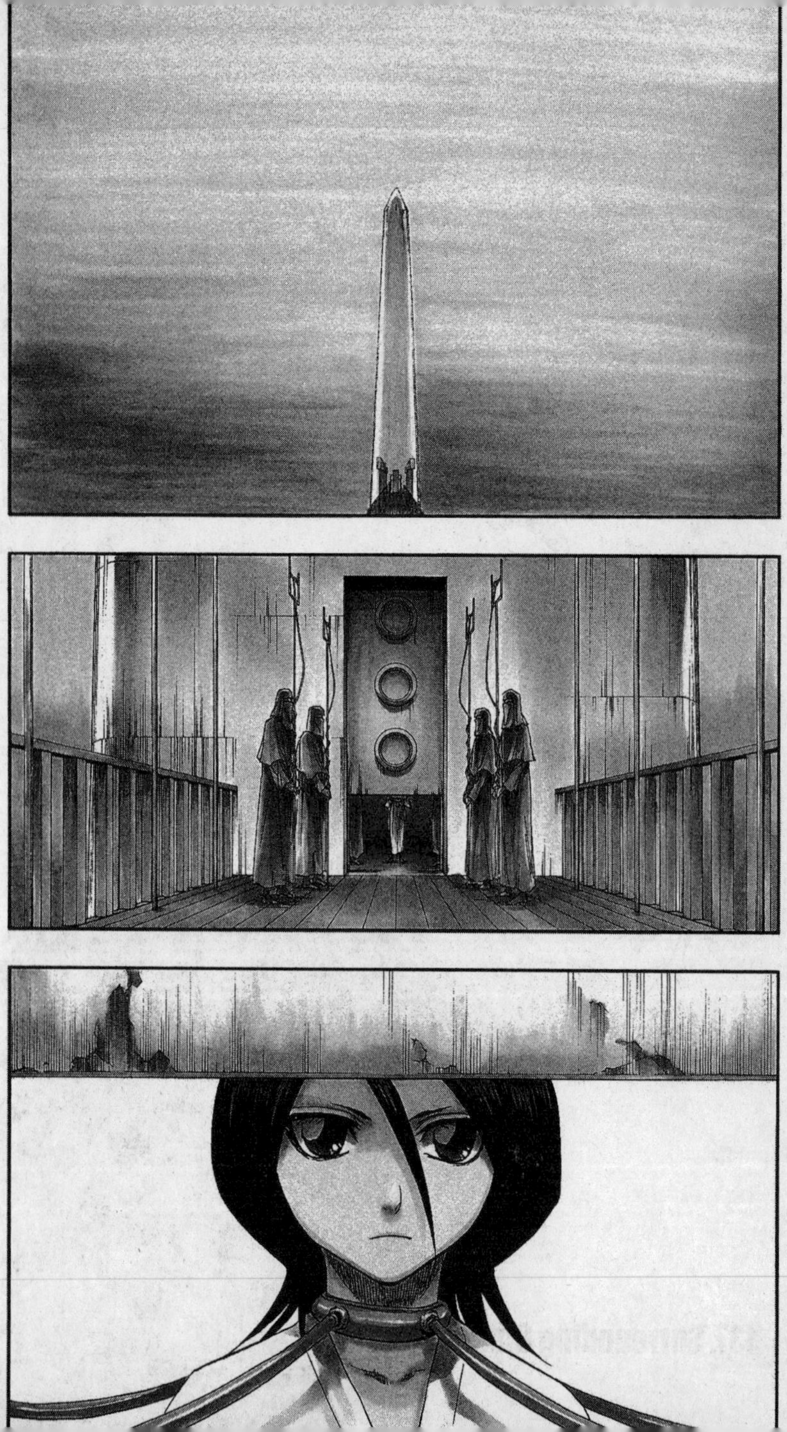

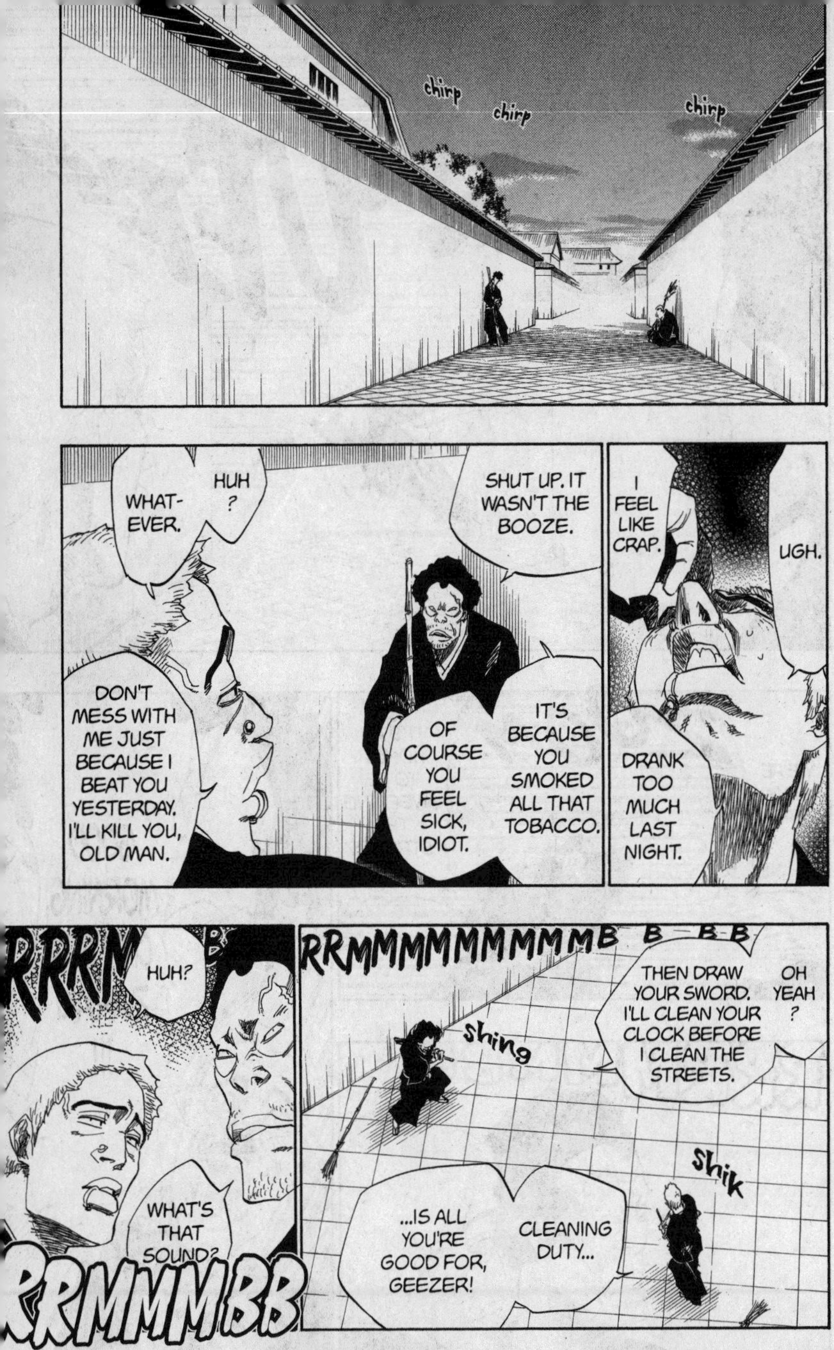
chirp
chirp
chirp
UGH.
I FEEL LIKE CRAP.
DRANK TOO MUCH LAST NIGHT.
SHUT UP. IT WASN'T THE BOOZE.
IT'S BECAUSE YOU SMOKED ALL THAT TOBACCO.
OF COURSE YOU FEEL SICK, IDIOT.
HUH? WHATEVER.
DON'T MESS WITH ME JUST BECAUSE I BEAT YOU YESTERDAY. I'LL KILL YOU, OLD MAN.
RRMMMMMMMMMMB B B-B
OH YEAH?
THEN DRAW YOUR SWORD. I'LL CLEAN YOUR CLOCK BEFORE I CLEAN THE STREETS.
Shing
Shik
CLEANING DUTY...
...IS ALL YOU'RE GOOD FOR, GEEZER!
RRRM
B
HUH?
WHAT'S THAT SOUND?
RRMMMBB

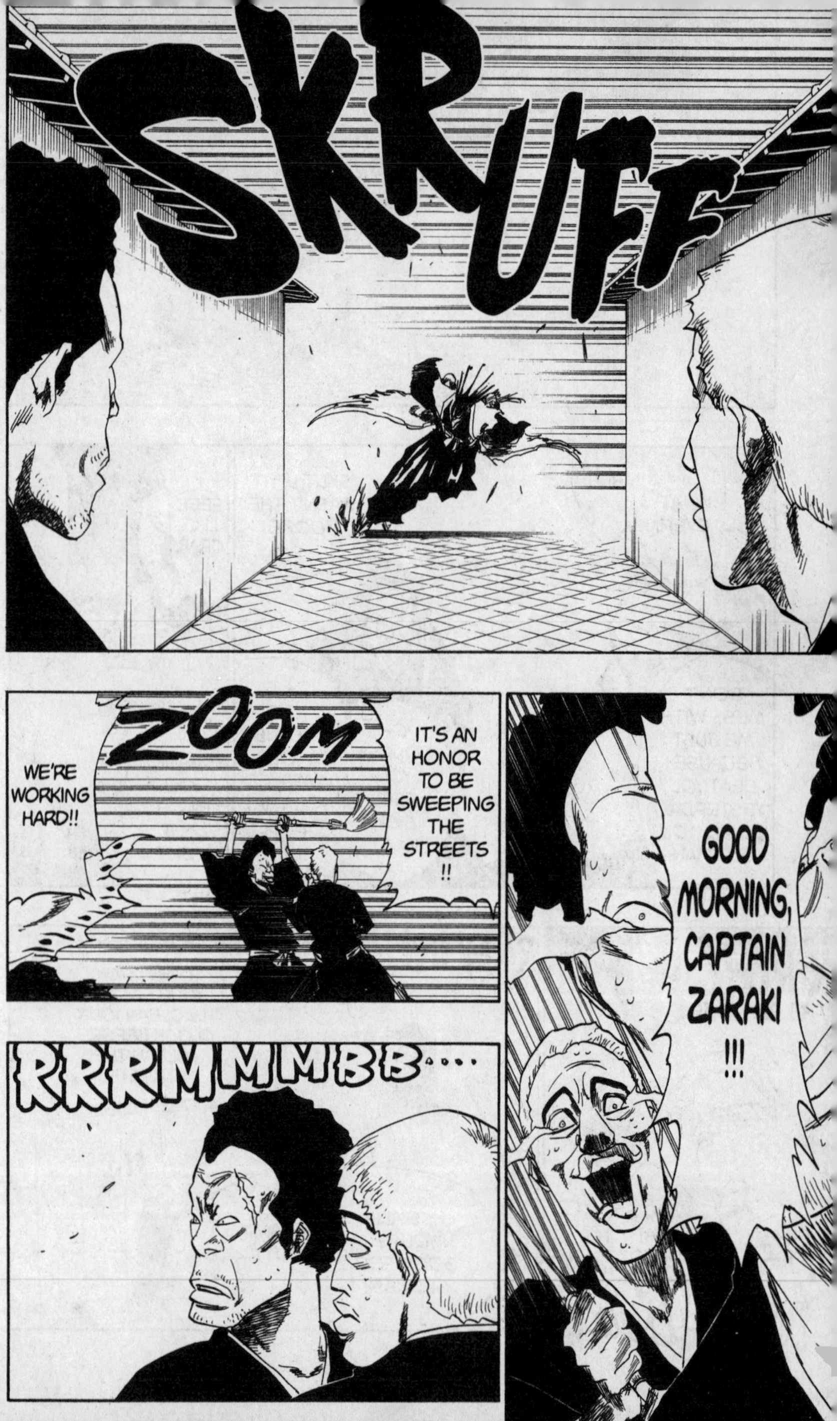
SKRUFF
GOOD MORNING, CAPTAIN ZARAKI!!!
ZOOM
IT'S AN HONOR TO BE SWEEPING THE STREETS!!
WE'RE WORKING HARD!!
RRRMMMBB...

READ THIS WAY

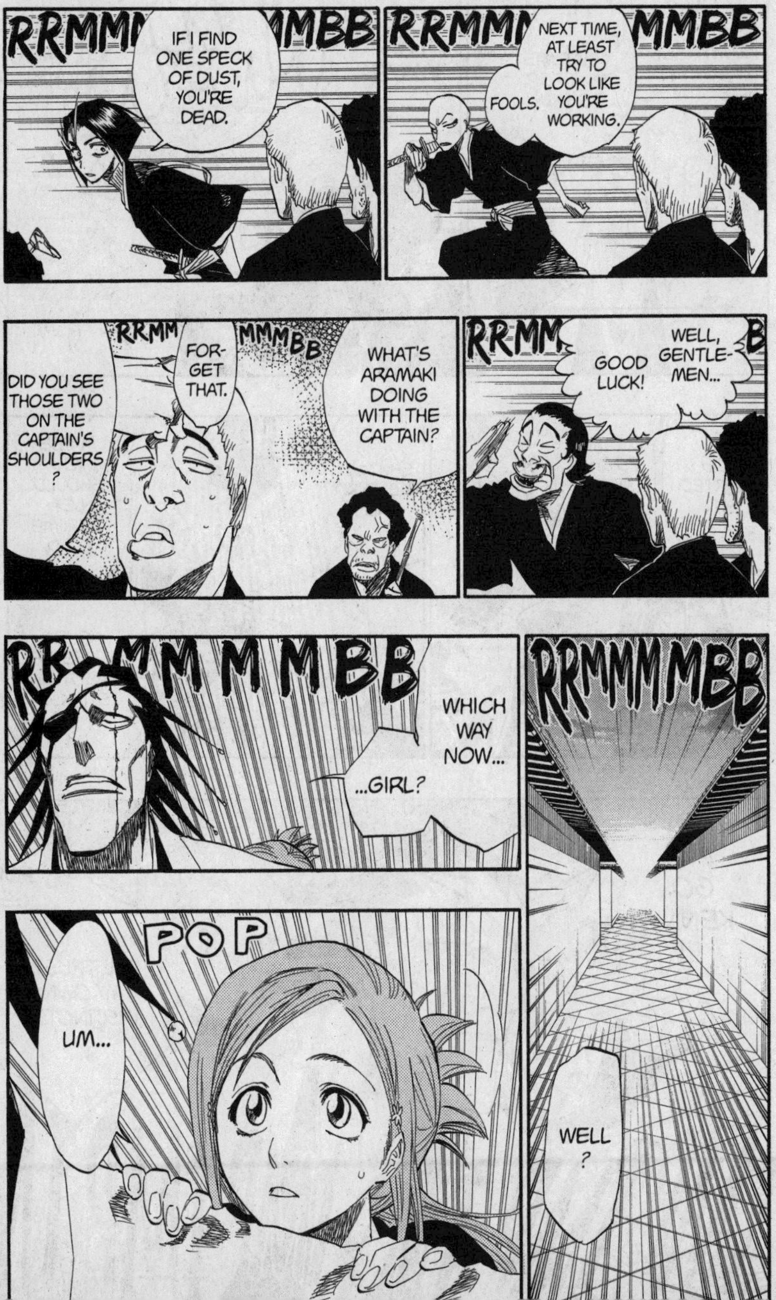
RRMMM MMBB
NEXT TIME, AT LEAST TRY TO LOOK LIKE YOU'RE WORKING.
FOOLS.
RRMMM MMBB
IF I FIND ONE SPECK OF DUST, YOU'RE DEAD.
RRMM B
WELL, GENTLE-MEN...
GOOD LUCK!
RRMM MMMBB
WHAT'S ARAMAKI DOING WITH THE CAPTAIN?
FOR-GET THAT.
DID YOU SEE THOSE TWO ON THE CAPTAIN'S SHOULDERS?
RRMMMMBB
WELL?
RR MMMMMBB
WHICH WAY NOW...
...GIRL?
POP
UM...

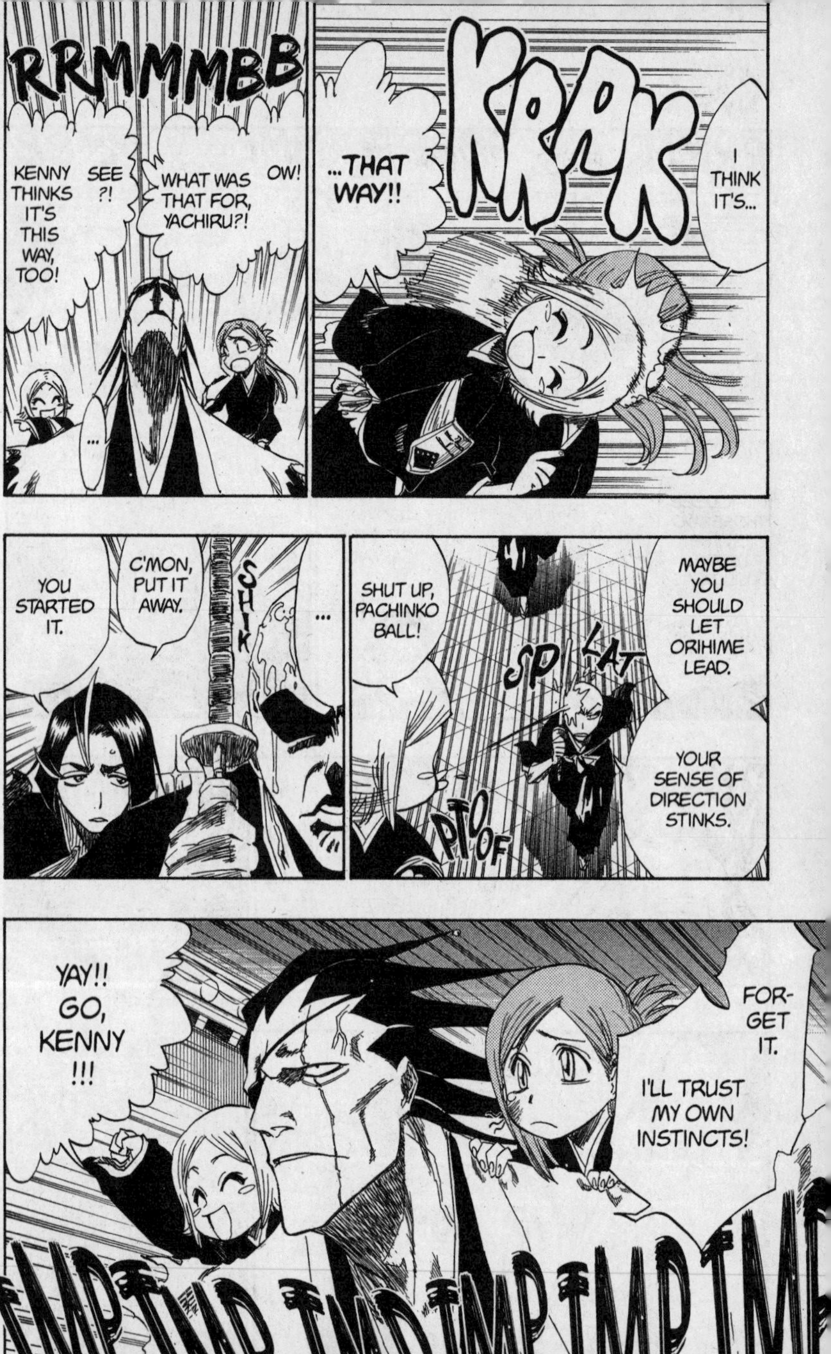
I THINK IT'S...
KRAK
...THAT WAY!!
RRMMMBB
OW!
WHAT WAS THAT FOR, YACHIRU?!
SEE?!
KENNY THINKS IT'S THIS WAY, TOO!
...
MAYBE YOU SHOULD LET ORIHIME LEAD.
YOUR SENSE OF DIRECTION STINKS.
SHUT UP, PACHINKO BALL!
SPLAT
PTOOF
...
SHIK
C'MON, PUT IT AWAY.
YOU STARTED IT.
FOR-GET IT.
I'LL TRUST MY OWN INSTINCTS!
YAY!! GO, KENNY !!!
TMP TMP TMP TMP TMP TMP

READ THIS WAY

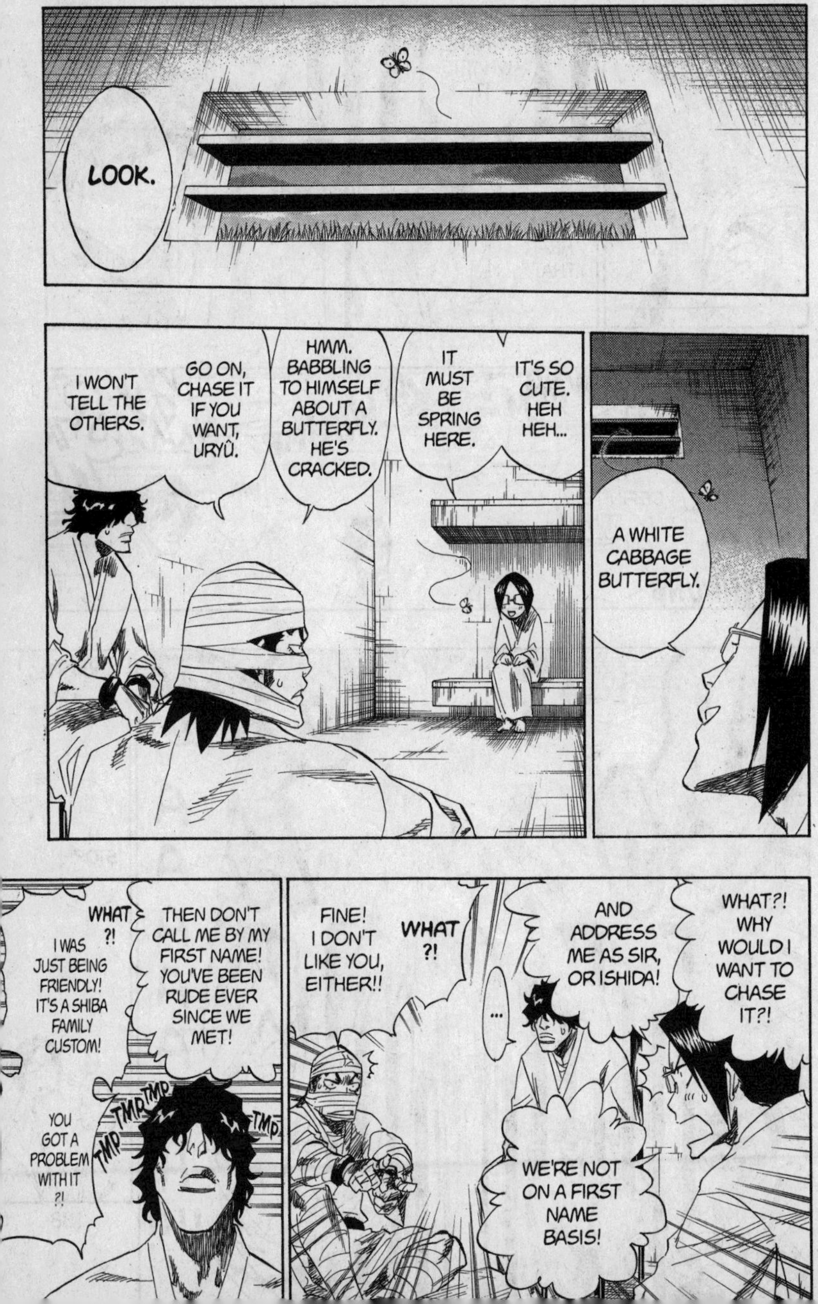
LOOK.
A WHITE CABBAGE BUTTERFLY.
IT'S SO CUTE. HEH HEH...
IT MUST BE SPRING HERE.
HMM. BABBLING TO HIMSELF ABOUT A BUTTERFLY. HE'S CRACKED.
GO ON, CHASE IT IF YOU WANT, URYÛ.
I WON'T TELL THE OTHERS.
WHAT?! WHY WOULD I WANT TO CHASE IT?!
AND ADDRESS ME AS SIR, OR ISHIDA!
...
WE'RE NOT ON A FIRST NAME BASIS!
WHAT ?!
FINE! I DON'T LIKE YOU, EITHER!!
THEN DON'T CALL ME BY MY FIRST NAME! YOU'VE BEEN RUDE EVER SINCE WE MET!
WHAT ?!
I WAS JUST BEING FRIENDLY! IT'S A SHIBA FAMILY CUSTOM!
TMP TMP TMP TMP
YOU GOT A PROBLEM WITH IT ?!

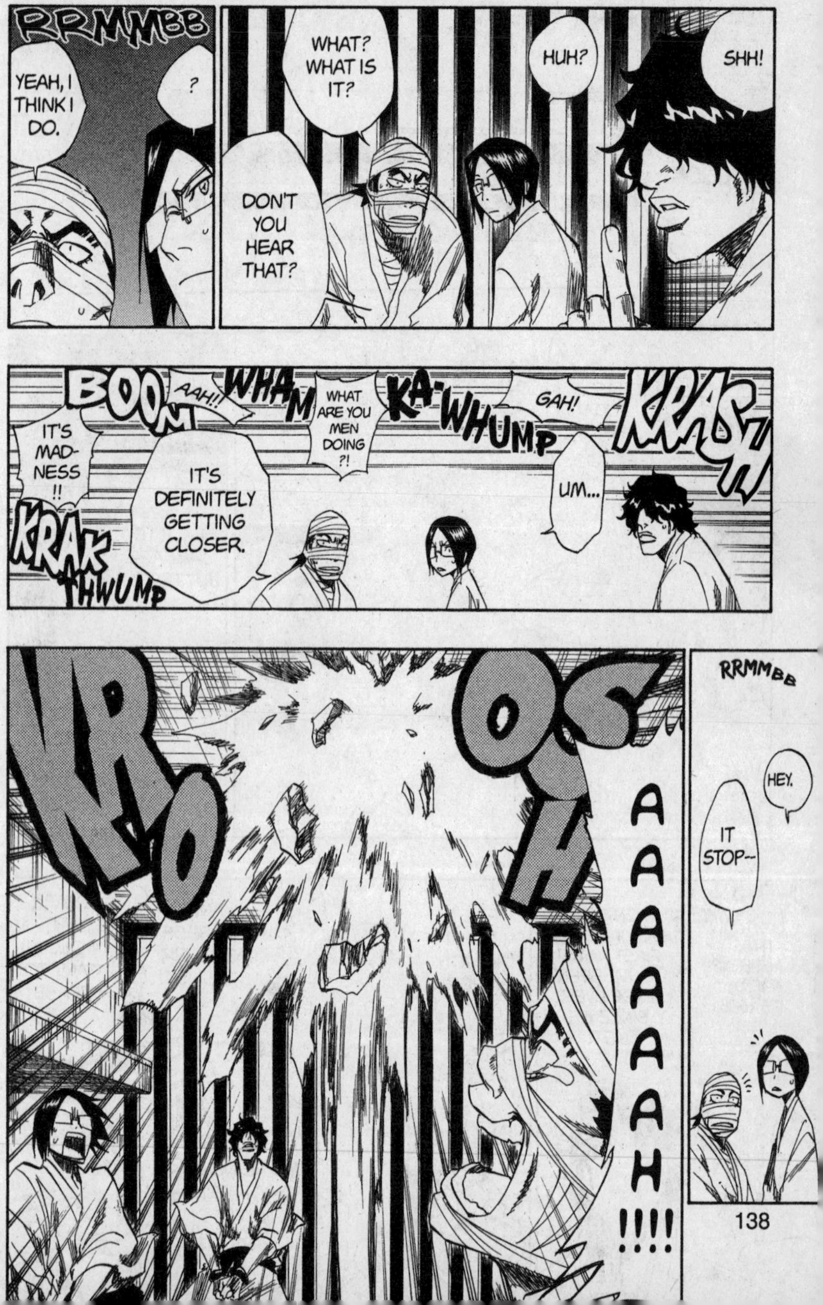
SHH!
HUH?
WHAT? WHAT IS IT?
DON'T YOU HEAR THAT?
RRMMBB
?
YEAH, I THINK I DO.
KRASH
GAH!
UM...
KA-WHUMP
WHAT ARE YOU MEN DOING?!
WHAM
AAH!!
BOOM
IT'S DEFINITELY GETTING CLOSER.
IT'S MADNESS!!
KRAK
THWUMP
RRMMBB
HEY.
IT STOP--
AAAAAAAAAH!!!!

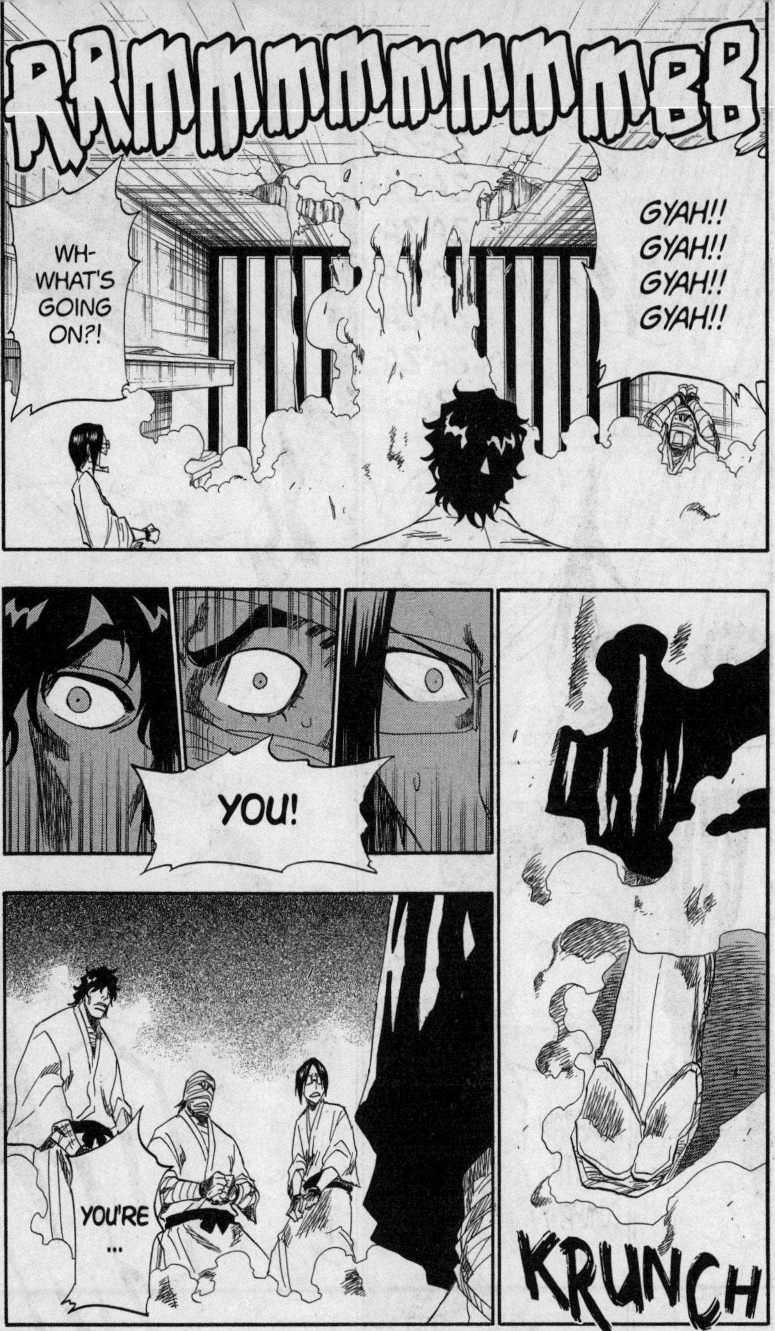
RRMMMMMMMMMMBB
GYAH!! GYAH!! GYAH!! GYAH!!
WH-WHAT'S GOING ON?!
KRUNCH
YOU!
YOU'RE ...

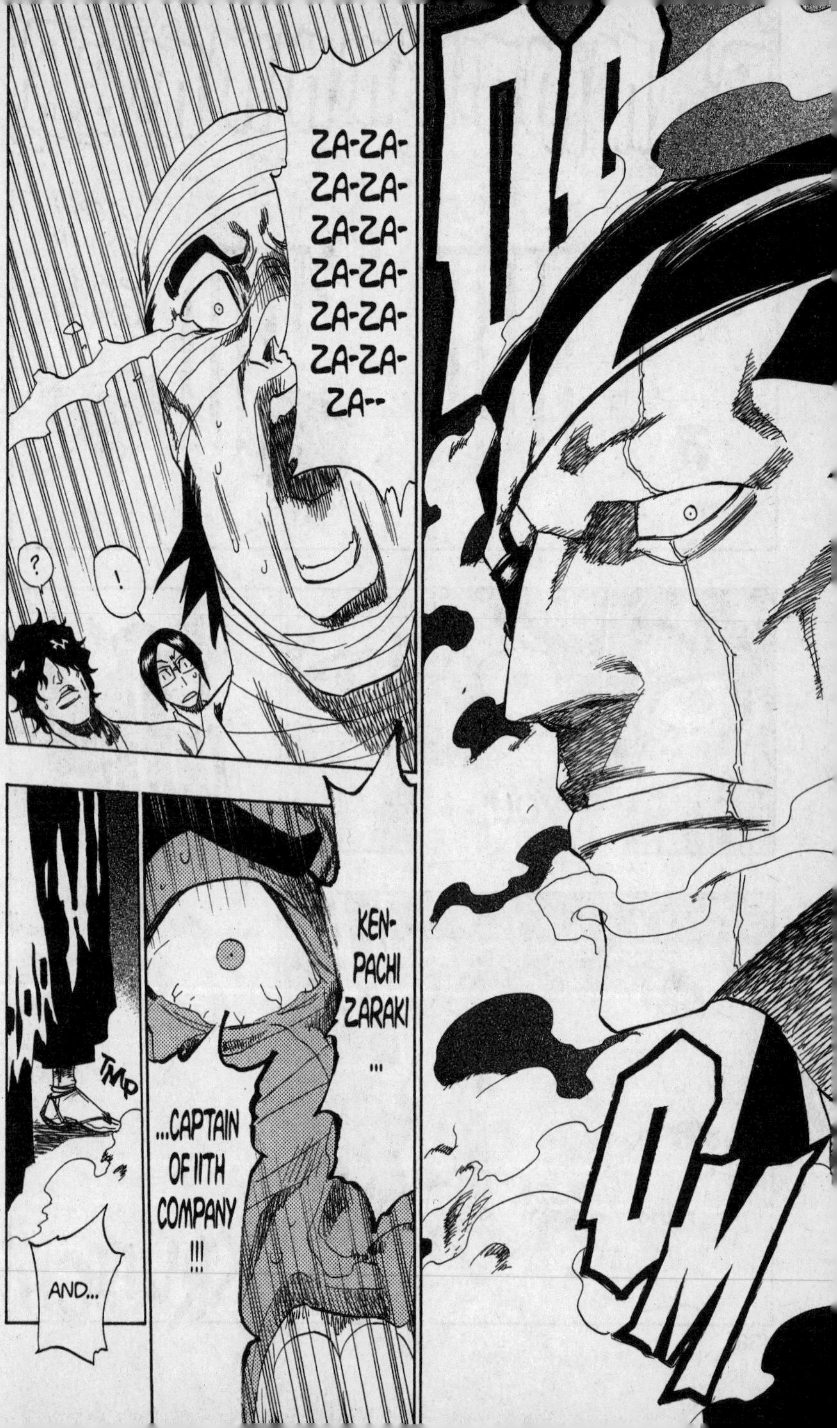
ZA-ZA-ZA-ZA-ZA-ZA-ZA-ZA-ZA-ZA-ZA-ZA-ZA--
?
!
KEN-PACHI ZARAKI...
...CAPTAIN OF 11TH COMPANY!!!
TMP
AND...

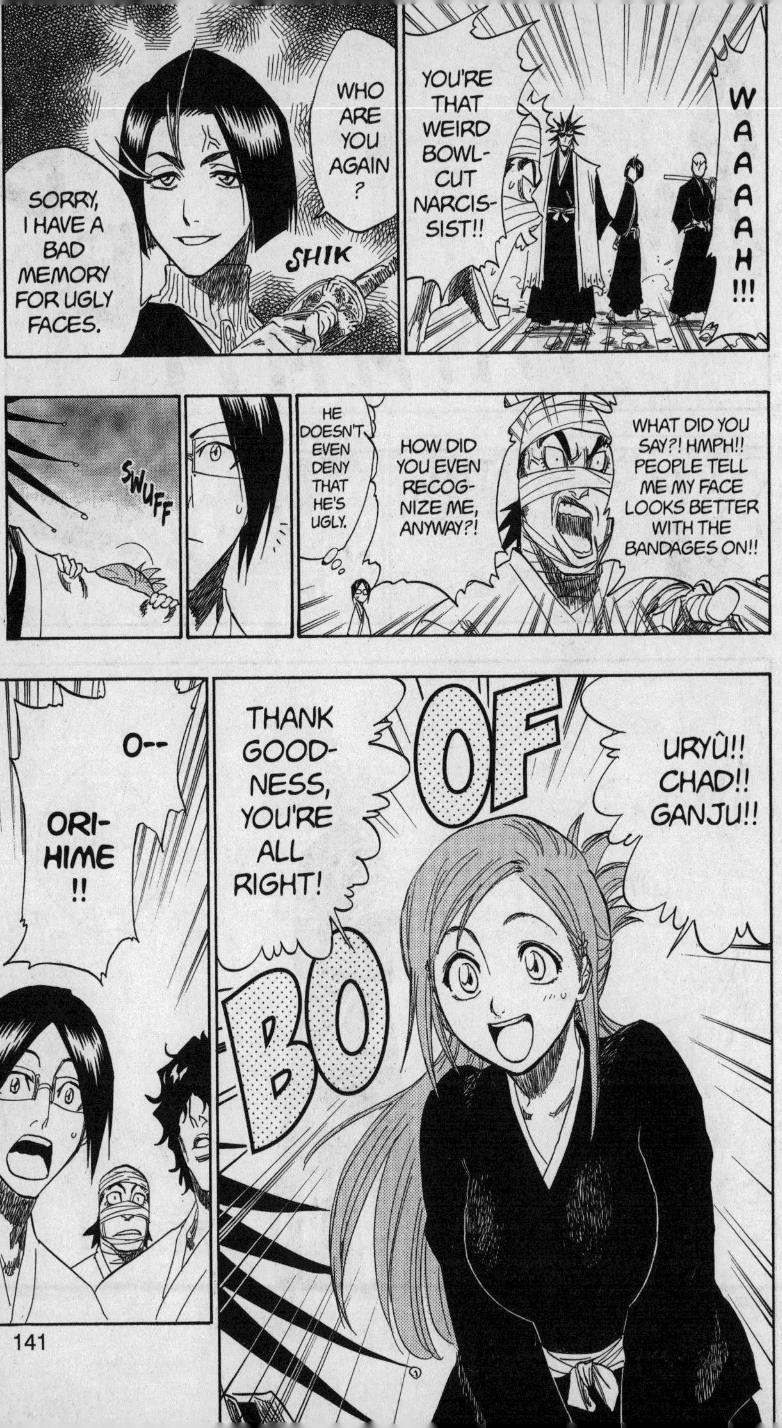
WAAAAAH!!!
YOU'RE THAT WEIRD BOWL-CUT NARCIS-SIST!!
WHO ARE YOU AGAIN?
SHIK
SORRY, I HAVE A BAD MEMORY FOR UGLY FACES.
WHAT DID YOU SAY?! HMPH!! PEOPLE TELL ME MY FACE LOOKS BETTER WITH THE BANDAGES ON!!
HOW DID YOU EVEN RECOG-NIZE ME, ANYWAY?!
HE DOESN'T EVEN DENY THAT HE'S UGLY.
SWUFF
URYÛ!! CHAD!! GANJU!!
OF
THANK GOOD-NESS, YOU'RE ALL RIGHT!
BO
O--
ORI-HIME!!

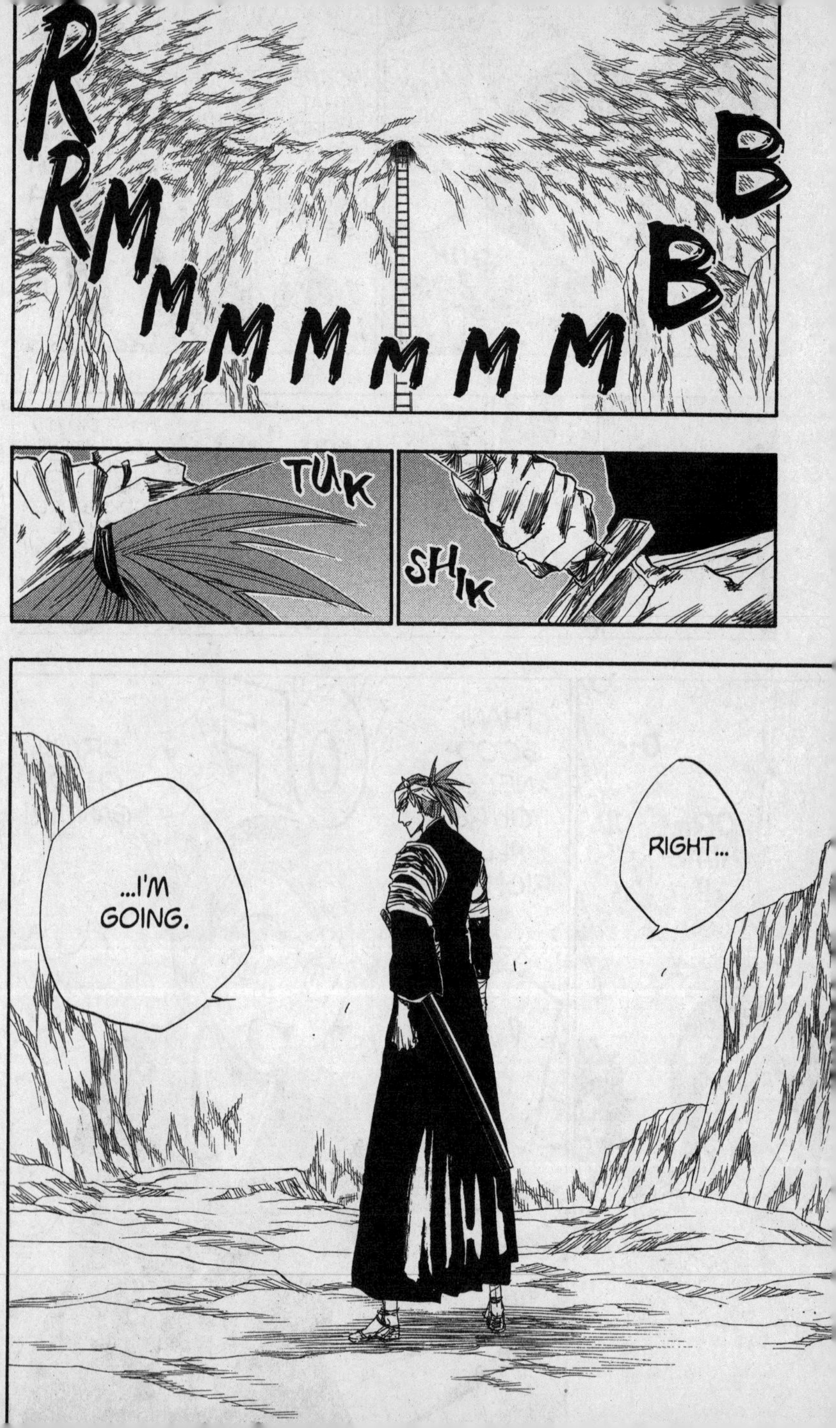
RRMMMMMMMBB
SHIK
TUK
RIGHT...
...I'M GOING.

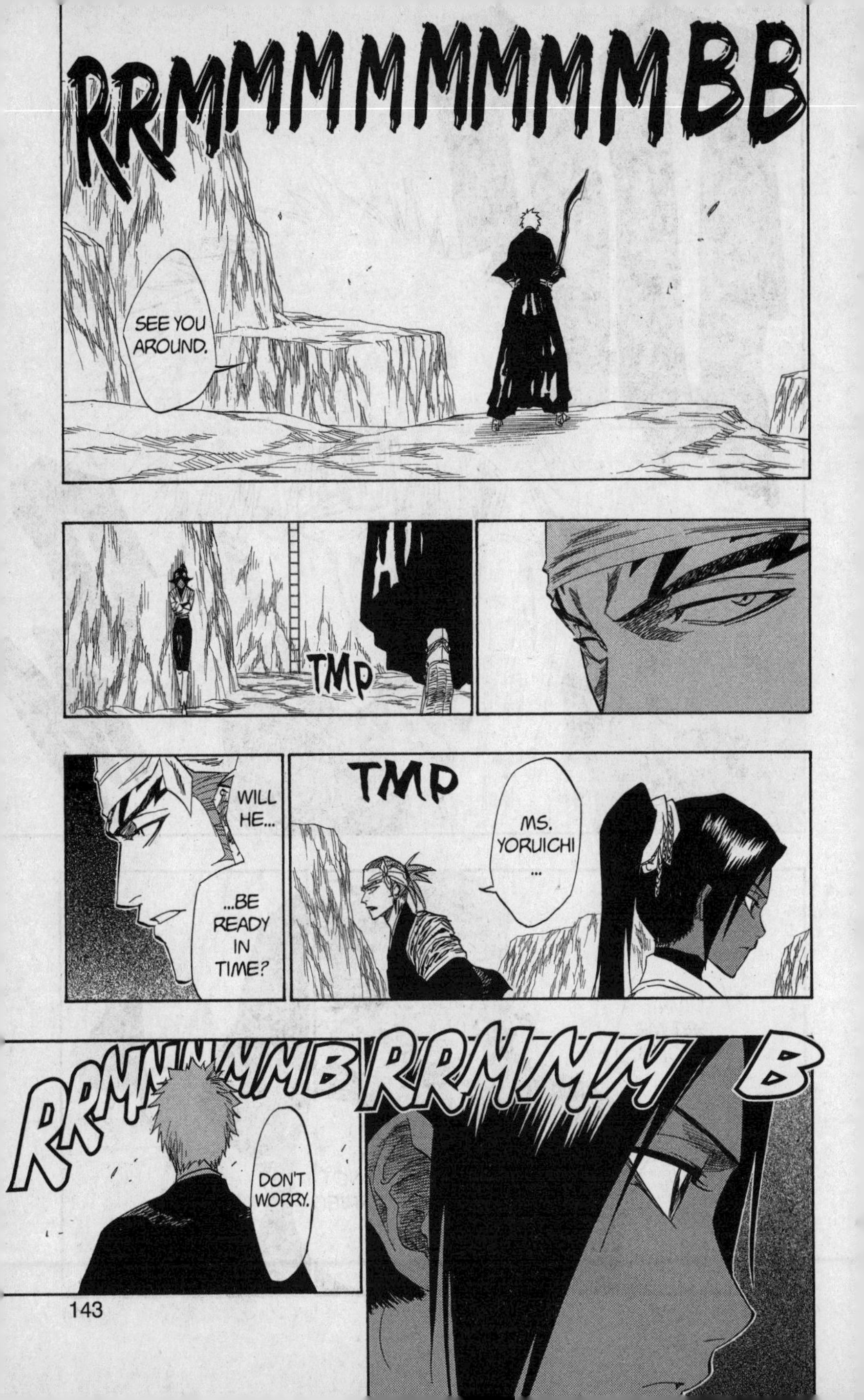
RRMMMMMMMMBB
SEE YOU AROUND.
TMP
TMP
MS. YORUICHI ...
WILL HE...
...BE READY IN TIME?
RRMNNMMB RRMMM B
DON'T WORRY.

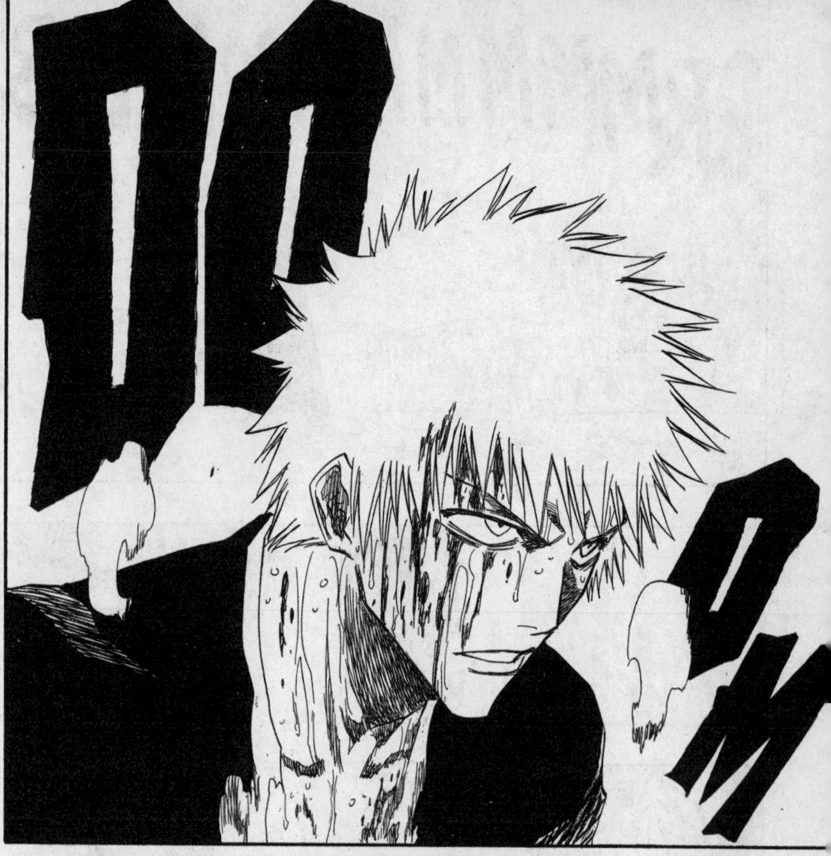
DO
OM
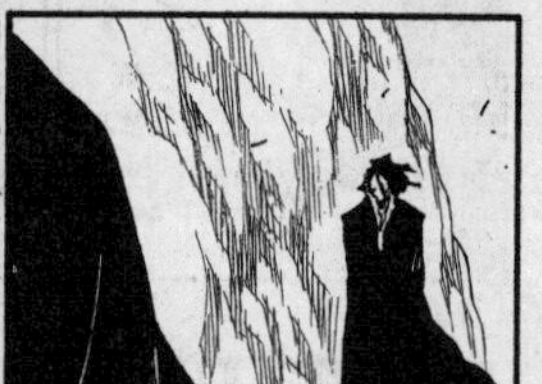
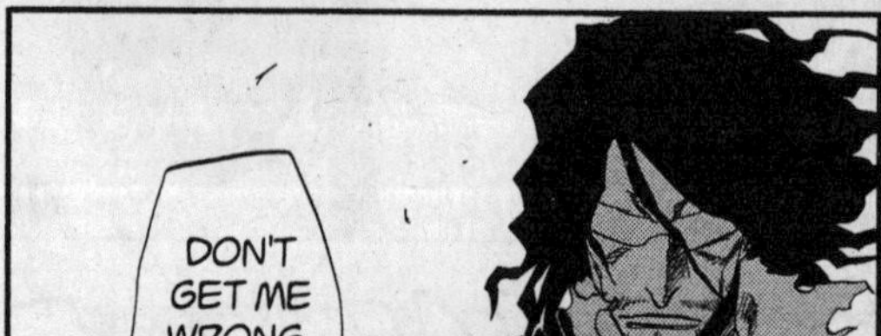
I'M NOT WORRIED.
DON'T GET ME WRONG.
I'M NOT ASKING IF HE'LL GET KILLED OR NOT.

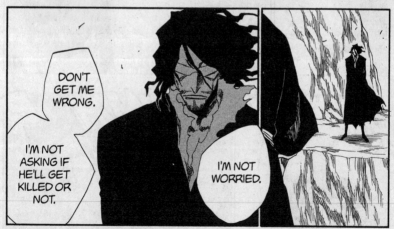

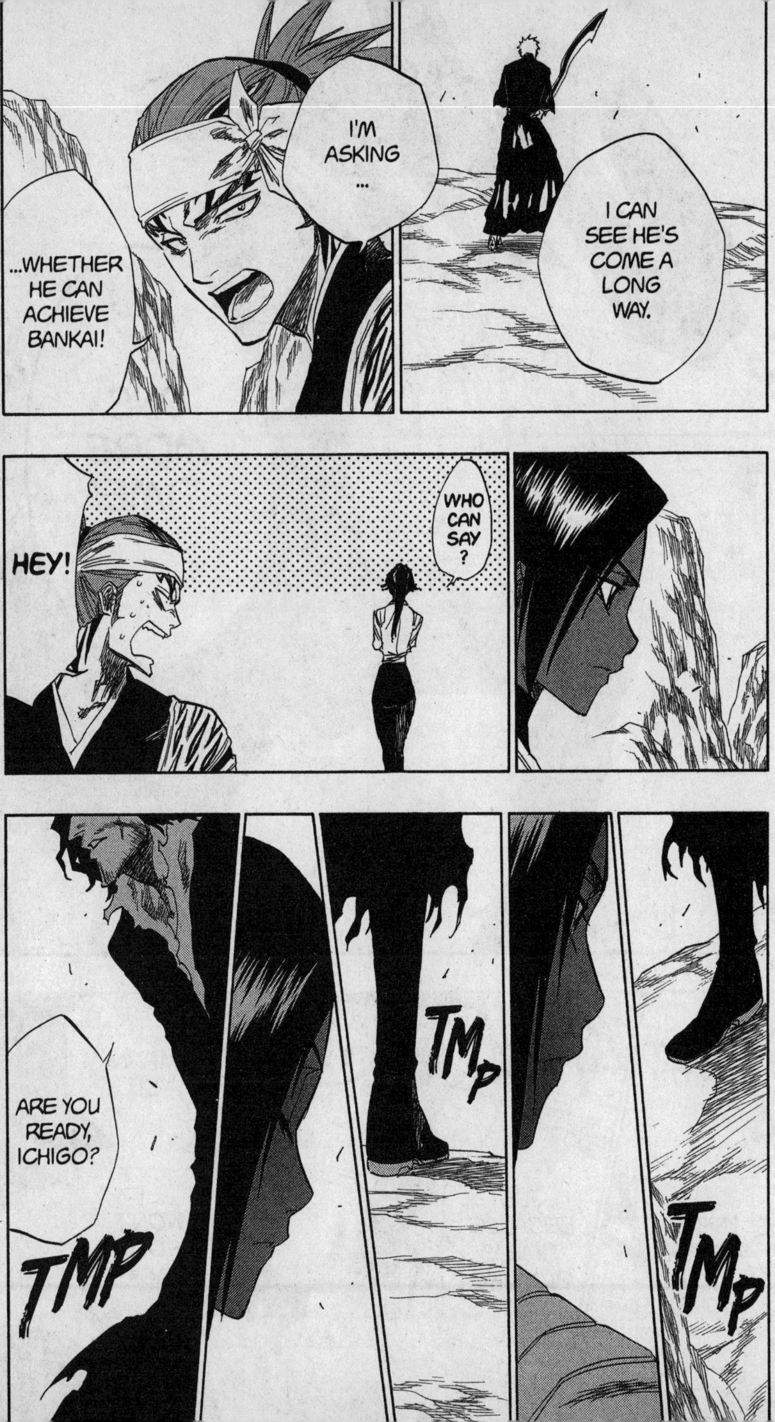
I CAN SEE HE'S COME A LONG WAY.
I'M ASKING ...
...WHETHER HE CAN ACHIEVE BANKAI!
WHO CAN SAY?
HEY!
TMp
TMp
ARE YOU READY, ICHIGO?
TMP

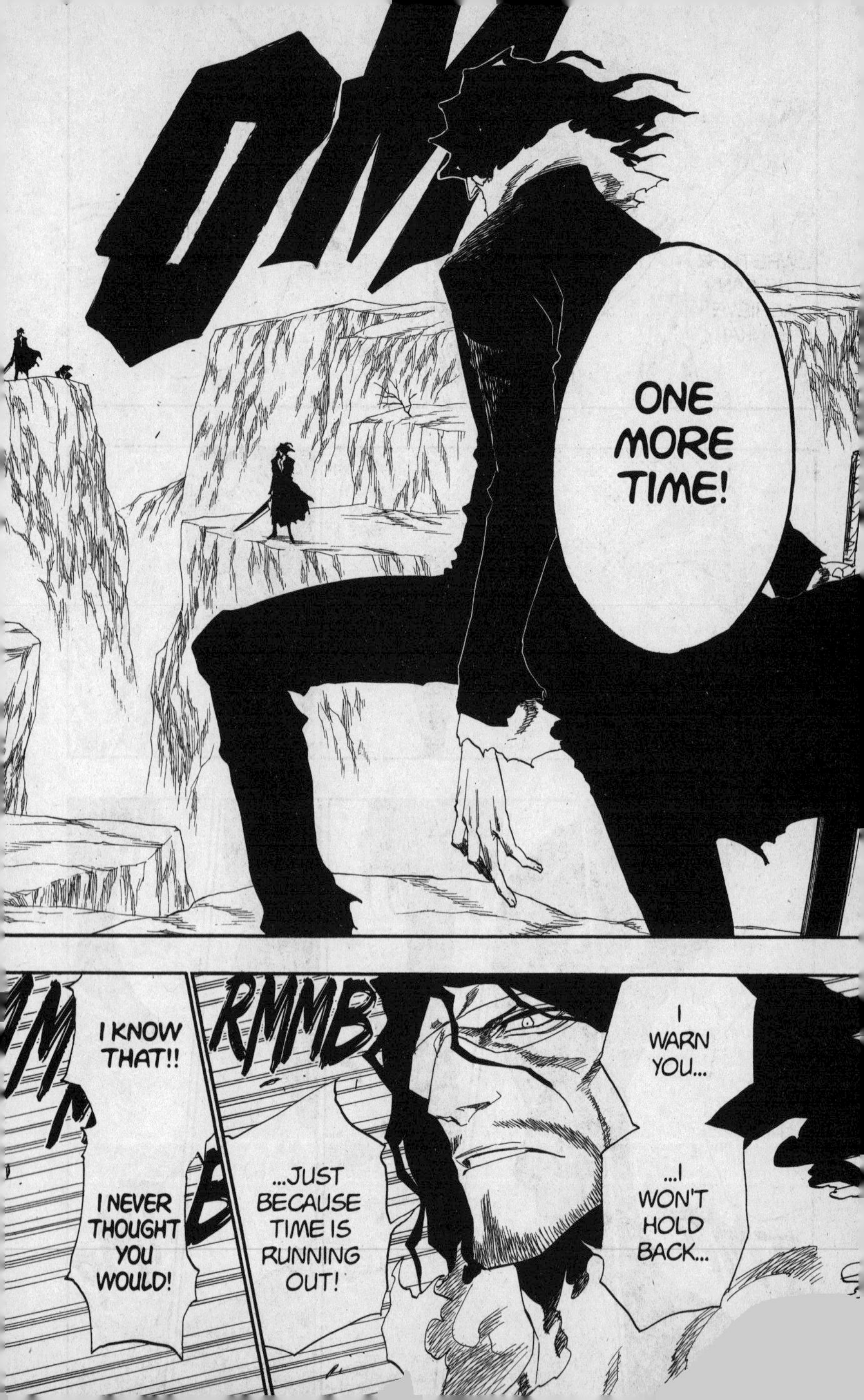
ONE MORE TIME!
I WARN YOU...
...I WON'T HOLD BACK...
RMMB
...JUST BECAUSE TIME IS RUNNING OUT!
I KNOW THAT!!
I NEVER THOUGHT YOU WOULD!

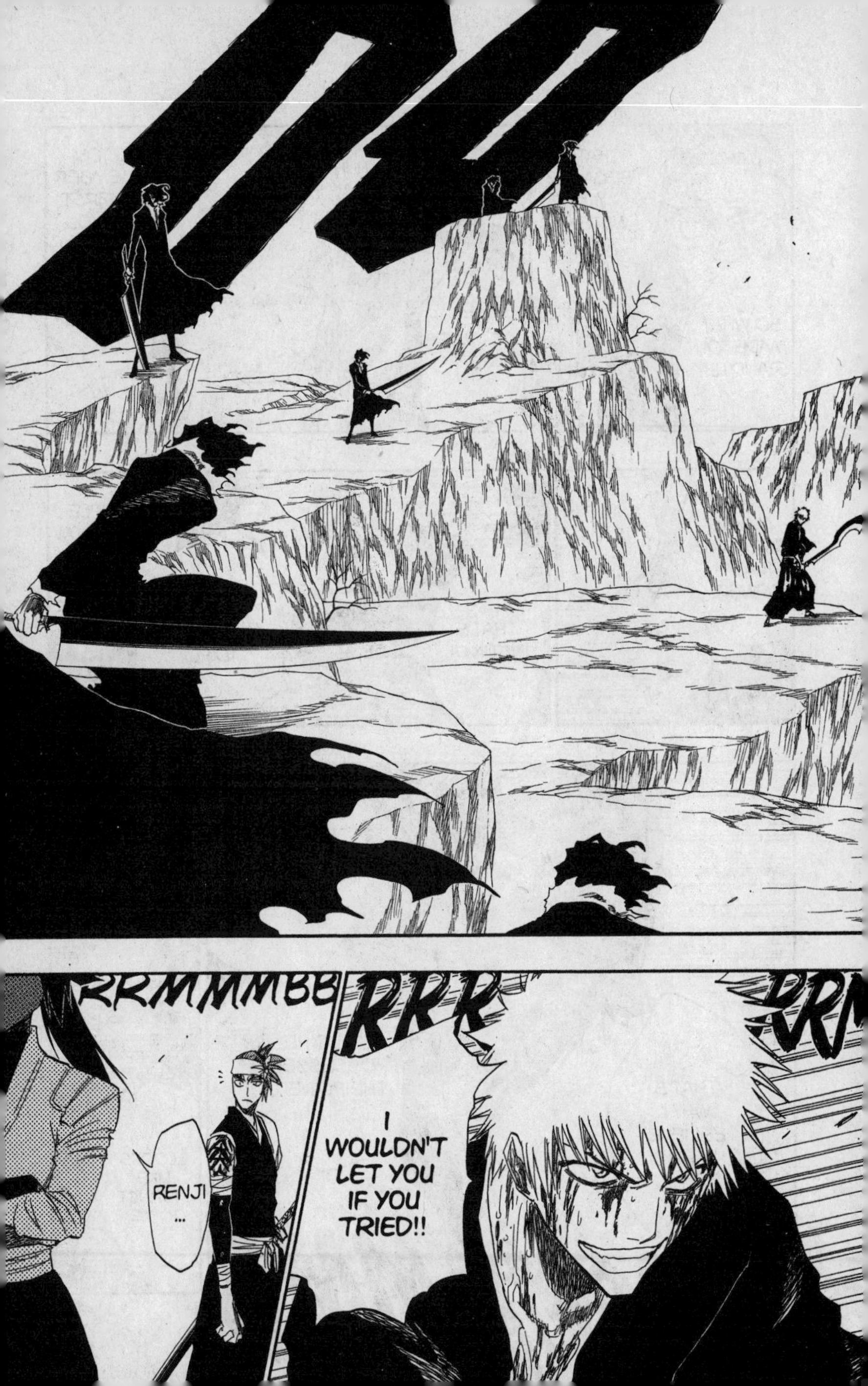
RRM
RRR
I WOULDN'T LET YOU IF YOU TRIED!!
RRMMMBB
RENJI ...

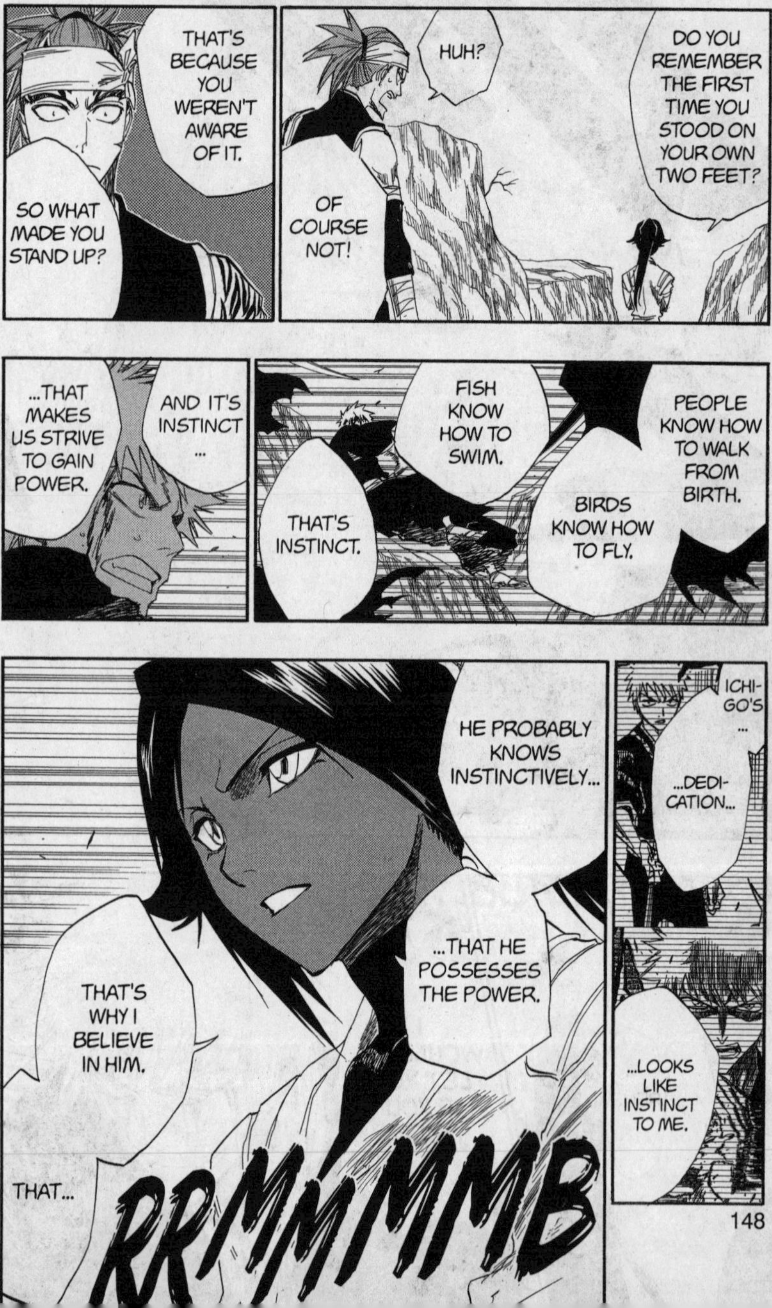
DO YOU REMEMBER THE FIRST TIME YOU STOOD ON YOUR OWN TWO FEET?
HUH?
OF COURSE NOT!
THAT'S BECAUSE YOU WEREN'T AWARE OF IT.
SO WHAT MADE YOU STAND UP?
PEOPLE KNOW HOW TO WALK FROM BIRTH.
FISH KNOW HOW TO SWIM.
BIRDS KNOW HOW TO FLY.
THAT'S INSTINCT.
AND IT'S INSTINCT ...
...THAT MAKES US STRIVE TO GAIN POWER.
ICHI-GO'S ...
...DEDI-CATION...
...LOOKS LIKE INSTINCT TO ME.
HE PROBABLY KNOWS INSTINCTIVELY...
...THAT HE POSSESSES THE POWER.
THAT'S WHY I BELIEVE IN HIM.
THAT...
RRMMMMB

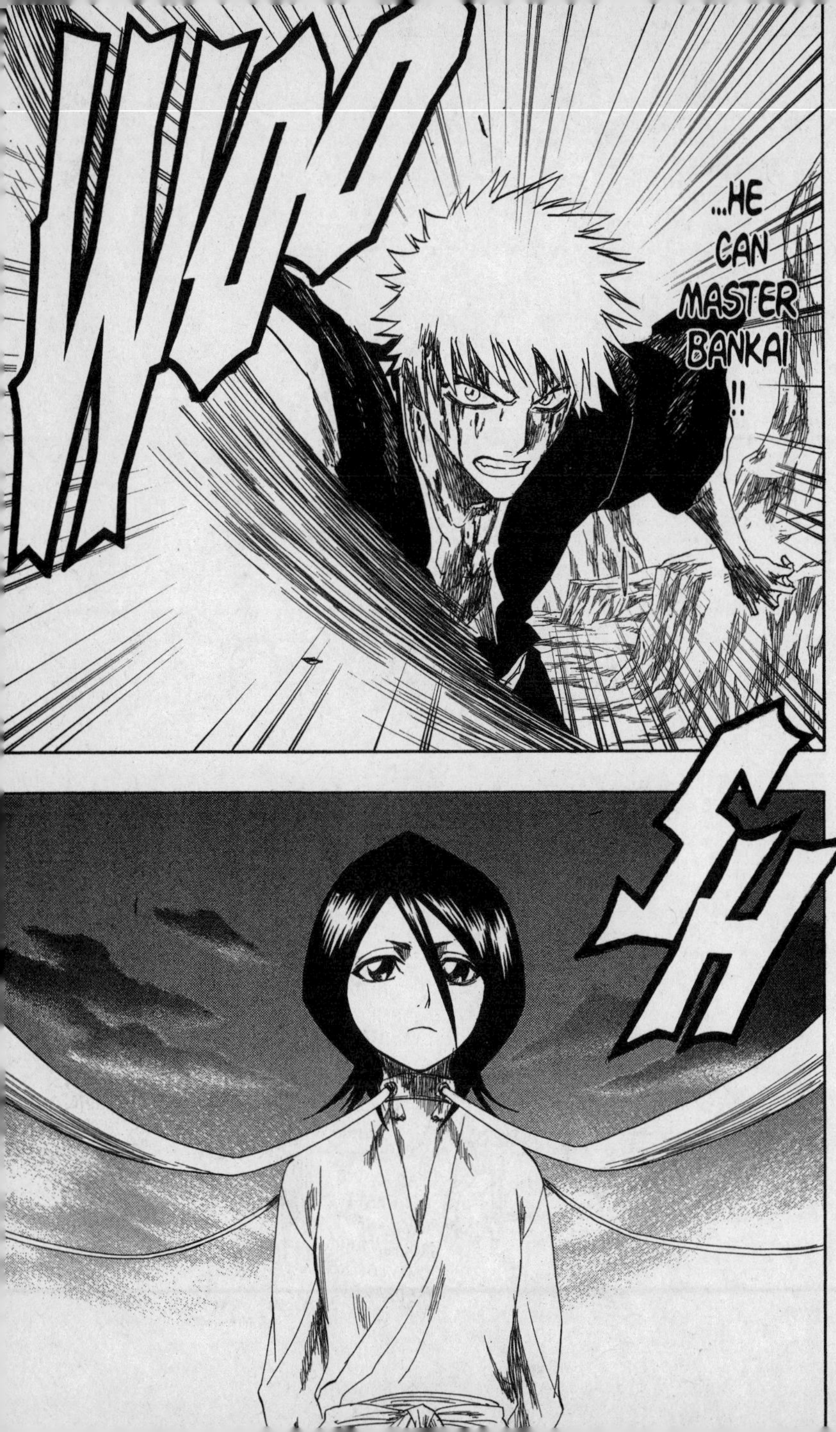
WHO
...HE CAN MASTER BANKAI !!
SH

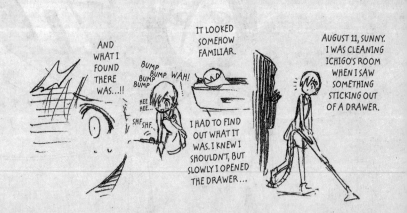

AUGUST 11, SUNNY. I WAS CLEANING ICHIGO'S ROOM WHEN I SAW SOMETHING STICKING OUT OF A DRAWER.
IT LOOKED SOMEHOW FAMILIAR.
I HAD TO FIND OUT WHAT IT WAS. I KNEW I SHOULDN'T, BUT SLOWLY I OPENED THE DRAWER...
WAH!
BUMP BUMP BUMP BUMP
HEE HEE...
SHF SHF...
AND WHAT I FOUND THERE WAS...!!

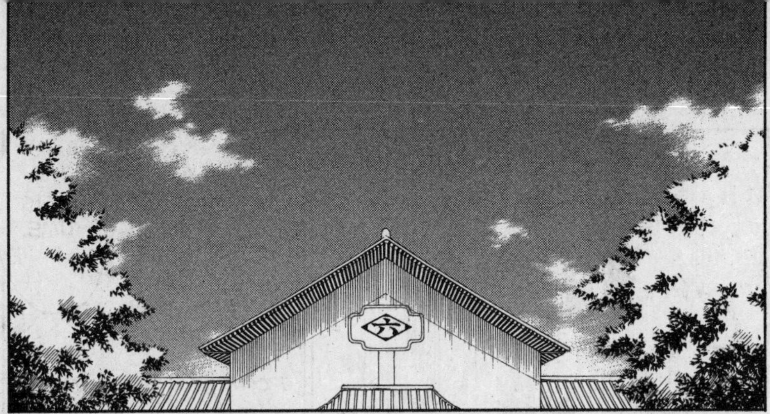

138. Private Thoughts

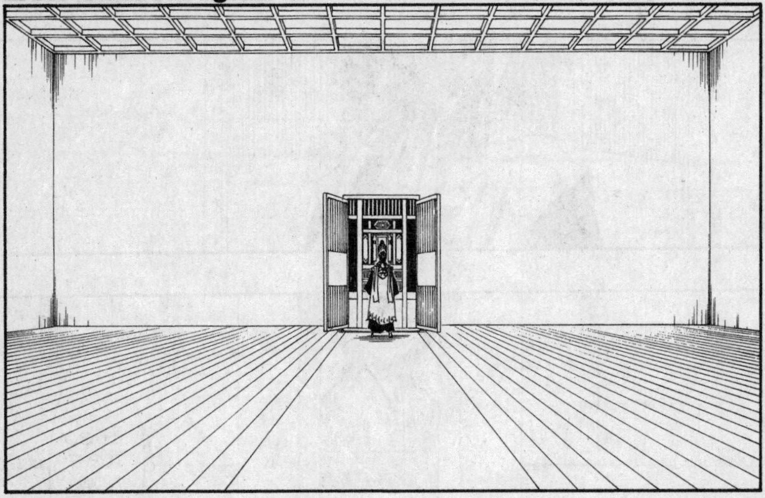

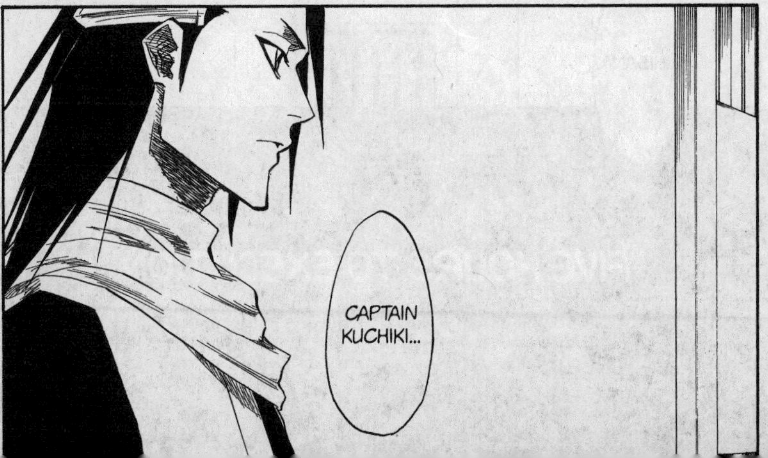
CAPTAIN KUCHIKI...

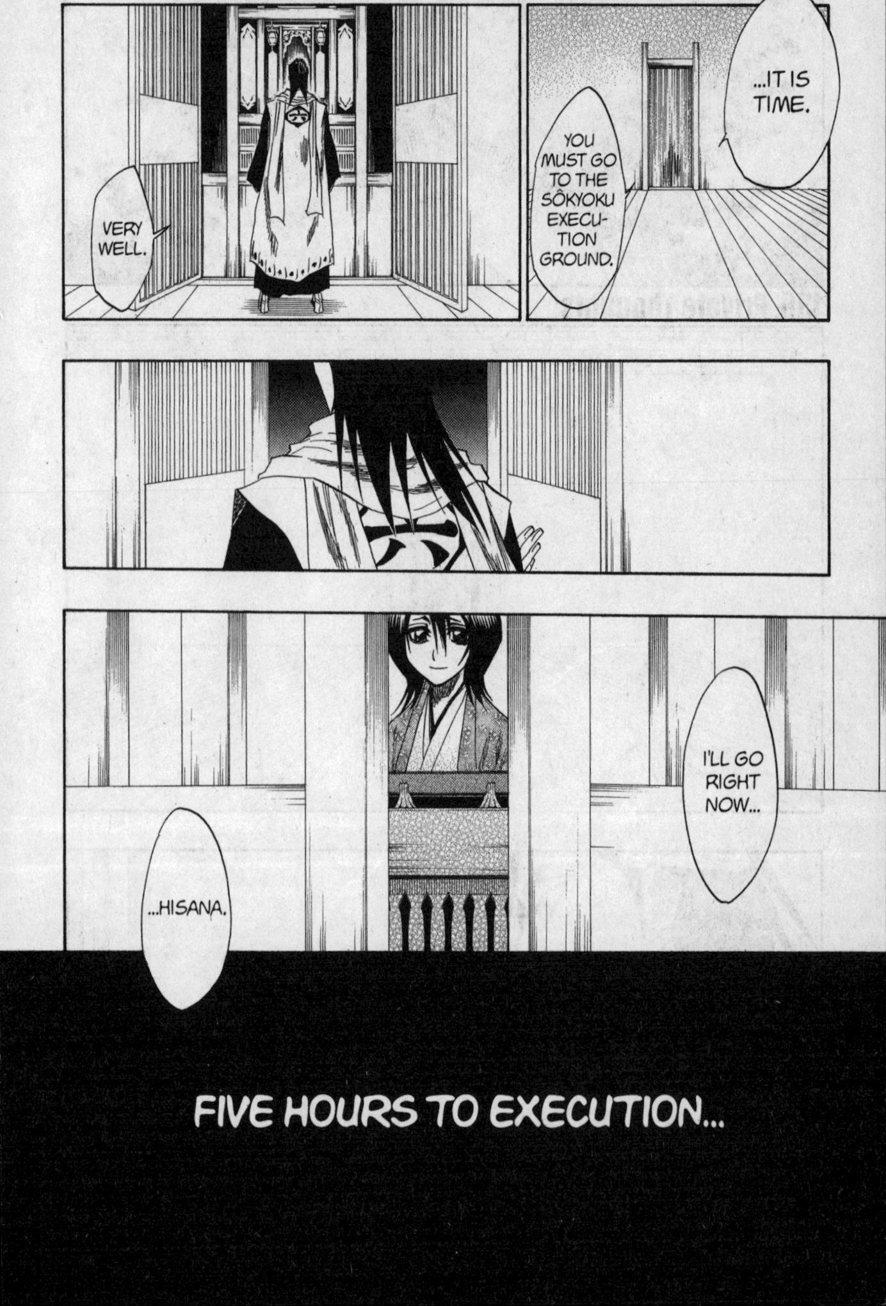
...IT IS TIME.
YOU MUST GO TO THE SÔKYOKU EXECUTION GROUND.
VERY WELL.
I'LL GO RIGHT NOW...
...HISANA.
FIVE HOURS TO EXECUTION...

138. Private Thoughts

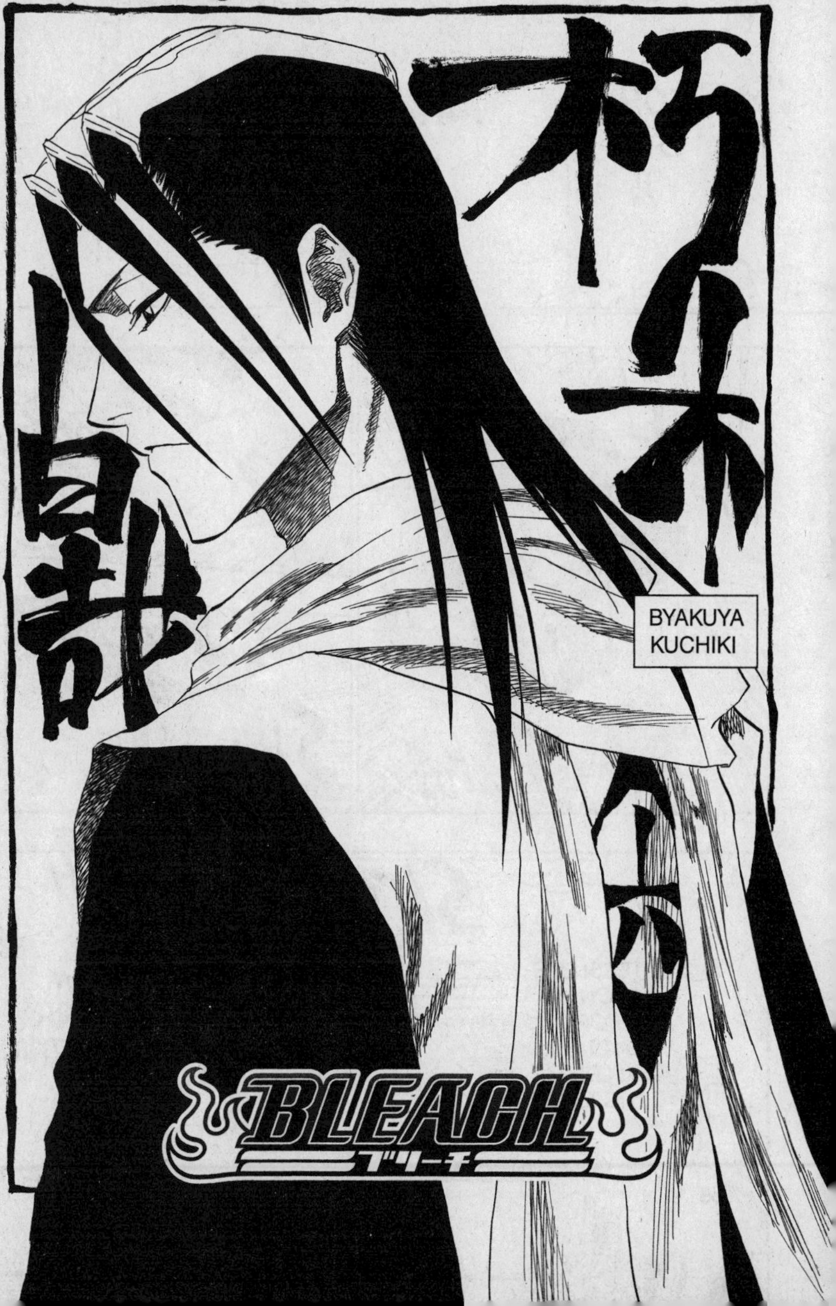
BYAKUYA
KUCHIKI
BLEACH
ブリーチ

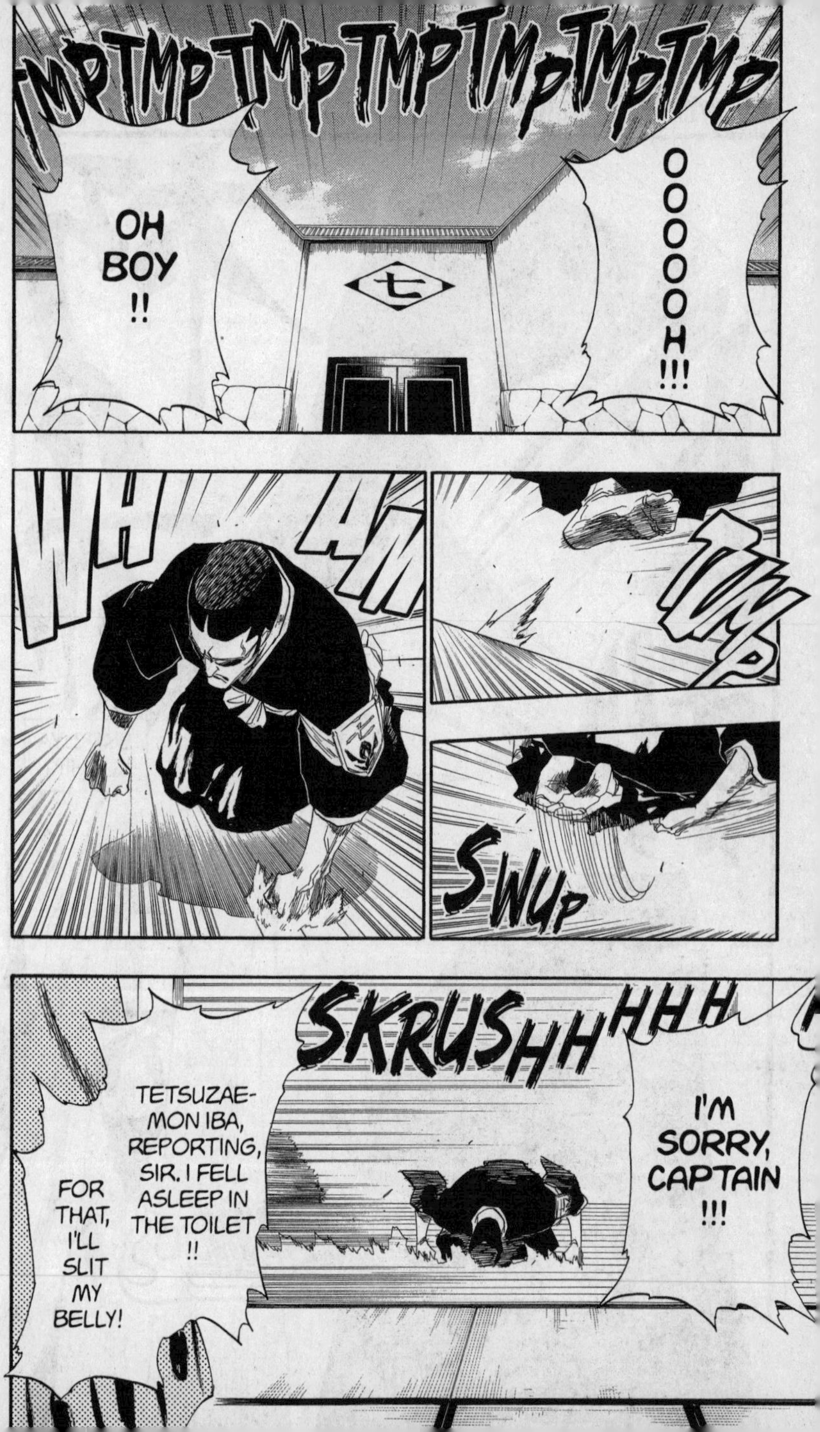
TMP TMP TMP TMP TMP TMP TMP
OOOOOOH!!!
OH BOY!!
TMP
SWUP
WHAM
SKRUSHHHHH
I'M SORRY, CAPTAIN!!!
TETSUZAE-MON IBA, REPORTING, SIR. I FELL ASLEEP IN THE TOILET!!
FOR THAT, I'LL SLIT MY BELLY!

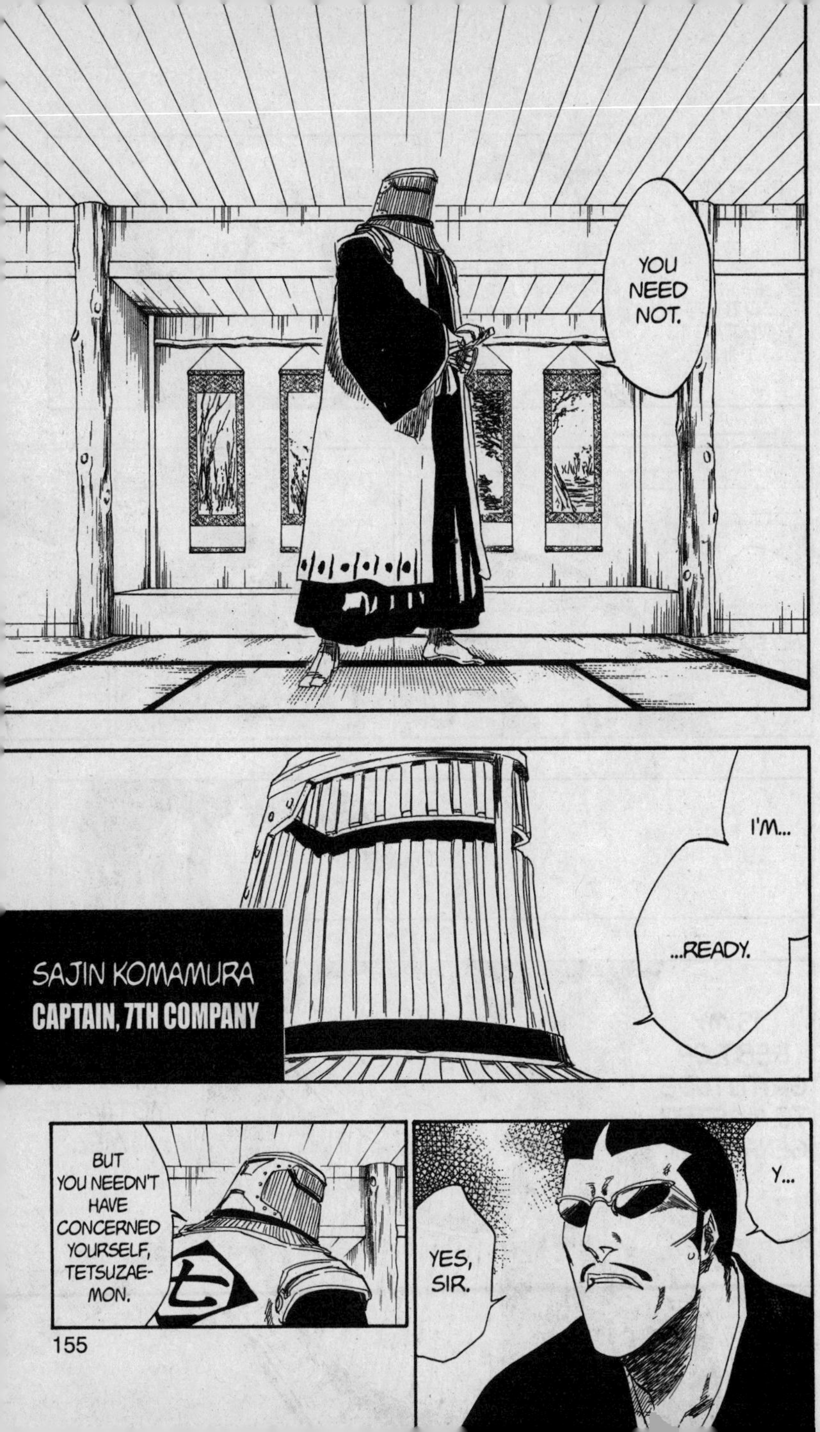
YOU NEED NOT.
I'M...
...READY.
SAJIN KOMAMURA
CAPTAIN, 7TH COMPANY
Y...
YES, SIR.
BUT YOU NEEDN'T HAVE CONCERNED YOURSELF, TETSUZAEMON.

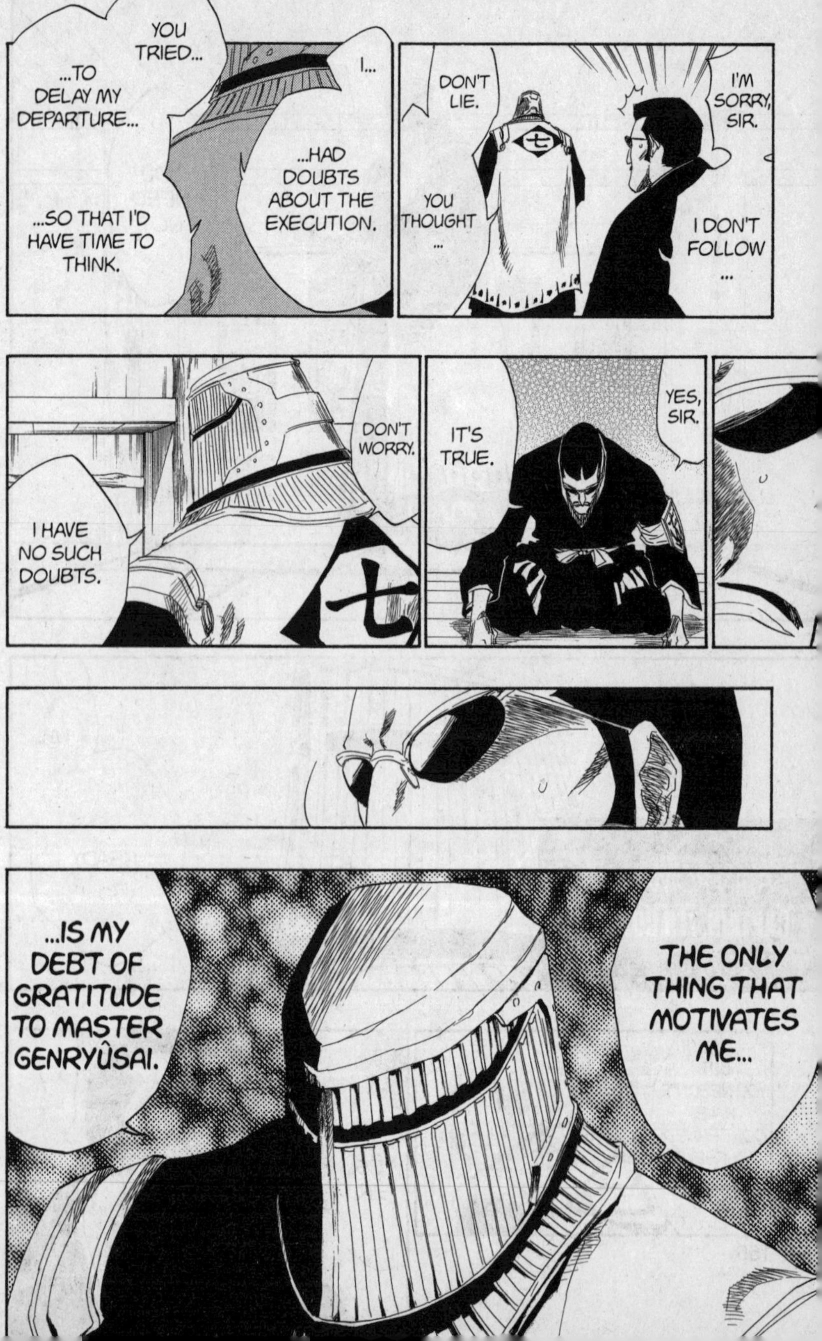
I'M SORRY, SIR.
DON'T LIE.
I DON'T FOLLOW...
YOU THOUGHT...
I...
...HAD DOUBTS ABOUT THE EXECUTION.
YOU TRIED...
...TO DELAY MY DEPARTURE...
...SO THAT I'D HAVE TIME TO THINK.
YES, SIR.
IT'S TRUE.
DON'T WORRY.
I HAVE NO SUCH DOUBTS.
THE ONLY THING THAT MOTIVATES ME...
...IS MY DEBT OF GRATITUDE TO MASTER GENRYÛSAI.

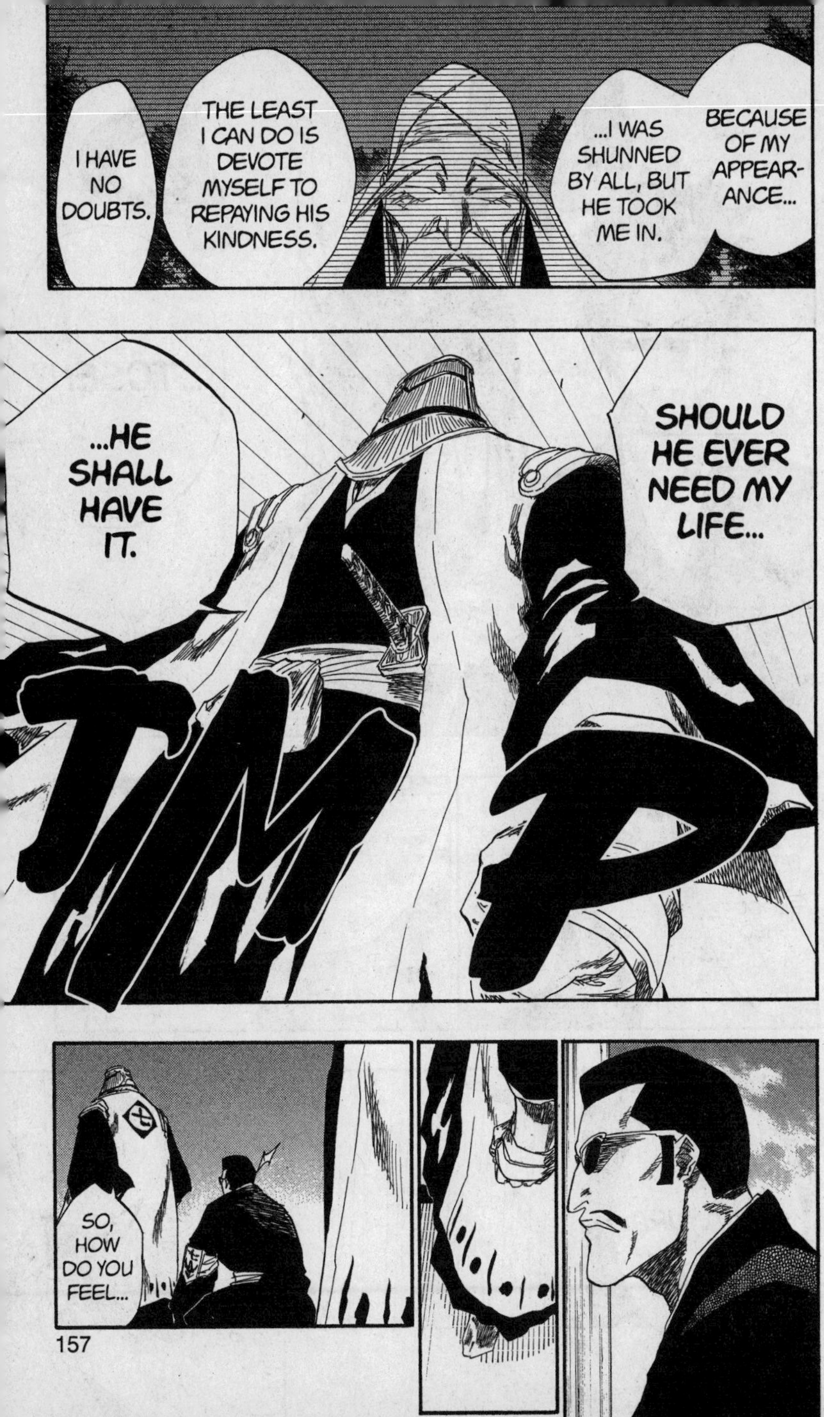
BECAUSE OF MY APPEARANCE...
...I WAS SHUNNED BY ALL, BUT HE TOOK ME IN.
THE LEAST I CAN DO IS DEVOTE MYSELF TO REPAYING HIS KINDNESS.
I HAVE NO DOUBTS.
SHOULD HE EVER NEED MY LIFE...
...HE SHALL HAVE IT.
TMP
SO, HOW DO YOU FEEL...

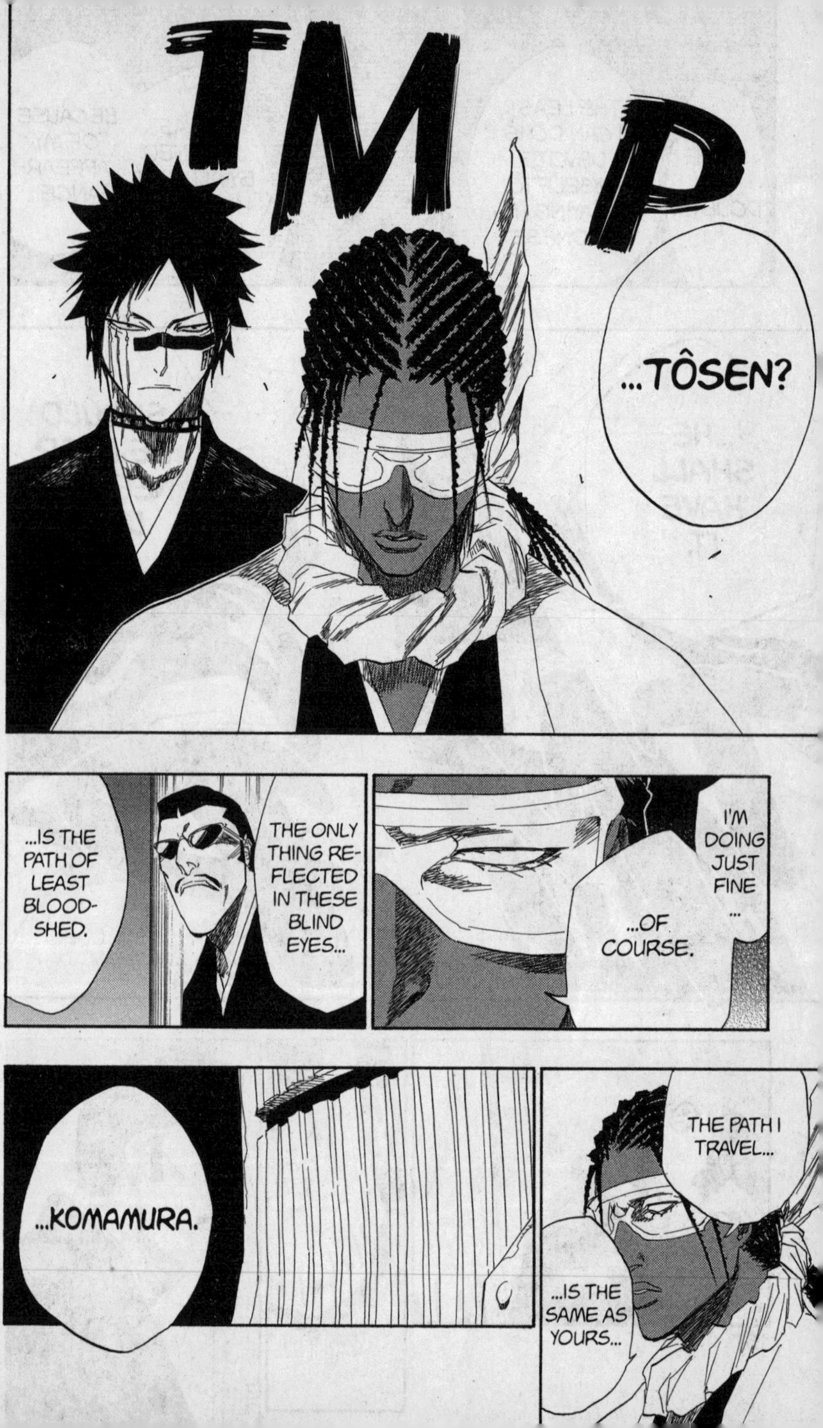
TMP
...TÔSEN?
I'M DOING JUST FINE ...
...OF COURSE.
THE ONLY THING RE-FLECTED IN THESE BLIND EYES...
...IS THE PATH OF LEAST BLOOD-SHED.
THE PATH I TRAVEL...
...IS THE SAME AS YOURS...
...KOMAMURA.

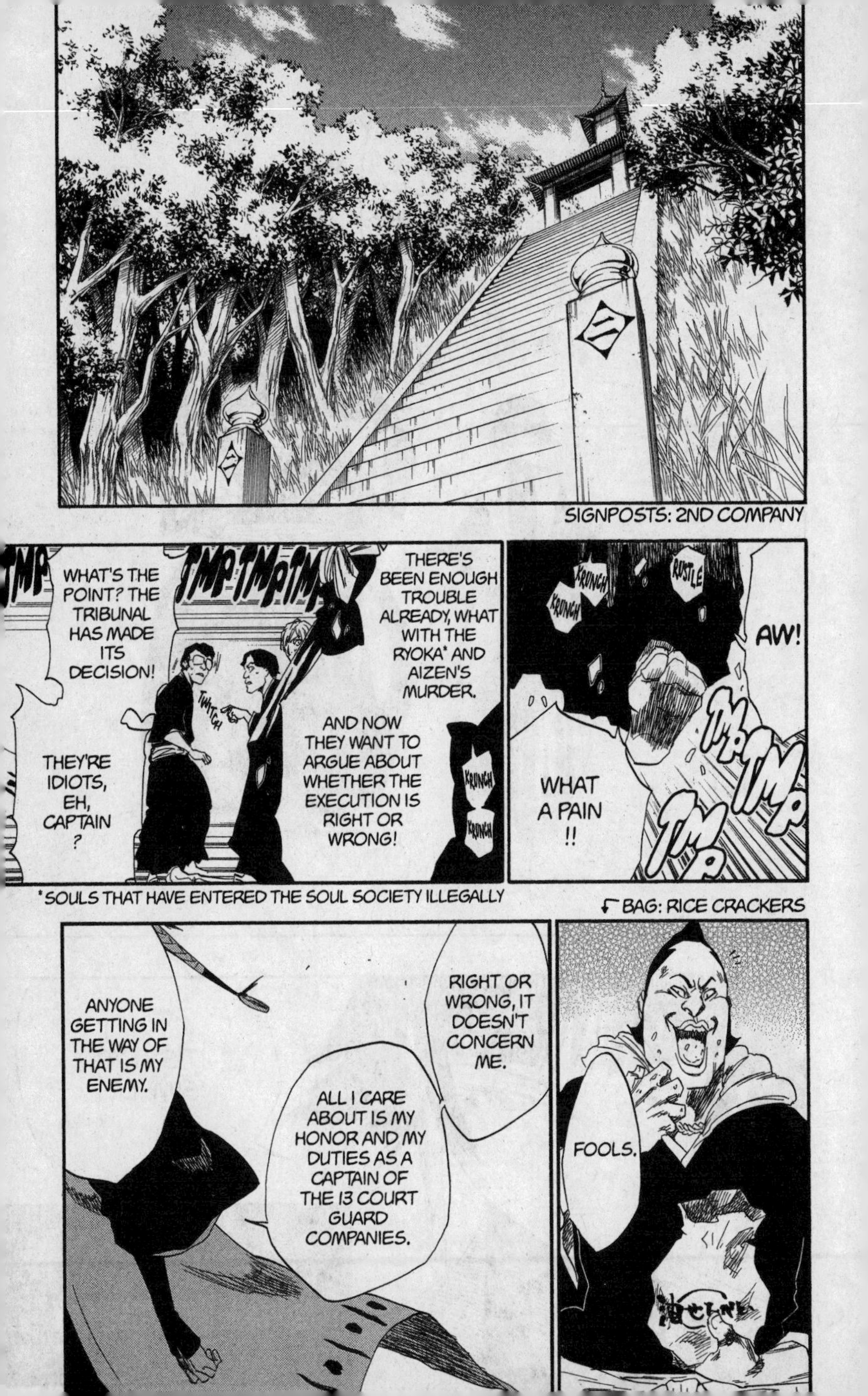
SIGNPOSTS: 2ND COMPANY
RUSTLE
KRUNCH
KRUNCH
AW!
WHAT A PAIN !!
TMP TMP TMP
THERE'S BEEN ENOUGH TROUBLE ALREADY, WHAT WITH THE RYOKA* AND AIZEN'S MURDER.
AND NOW THEY WANT TO ARGUE ABOUT WHETHER THE EXECUTION IS RIGHT OR WRONG!
KRUNCH
KRUNCH
TMP TMP TMP
WHAT'S THE POINT? THE TRIBUNAL HAS MADE ITS DECISION!
TWITCH
THEY'RE IDIOTS, EH, CAPTAIN?
TMP
*SOULS THAT HAVE ENTERED THE SOUL SOCIETY ILLEGALLY
BAG: RICE CRACKERS
FOOLS.
RIGHT OR WRONG, IT DOESN'T CONCERN ME.
ALL I CARE ABOUT IS MY HONOR AND MY DUTIES AS A CAPTAIN OF THE 13 COURT GUARD COMPANIES.
ANYONE GETTING IN THE WAY OF THAT IS MY ENEMY.

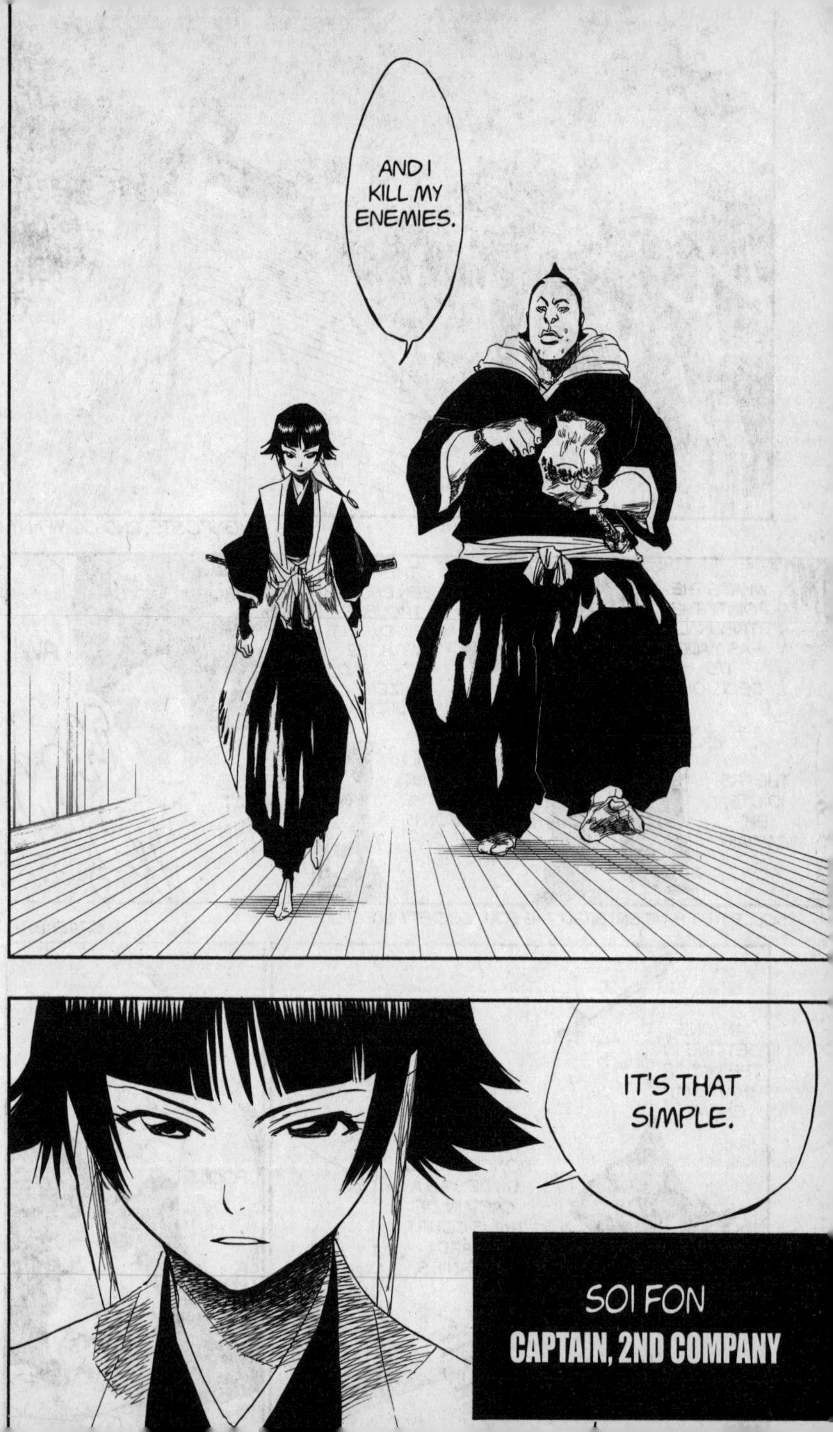
AND I KILL MY ENEMIES.
IT'S THAT SIMPLE.
SOI FON
CAPTAIN, 2ND COMPANY

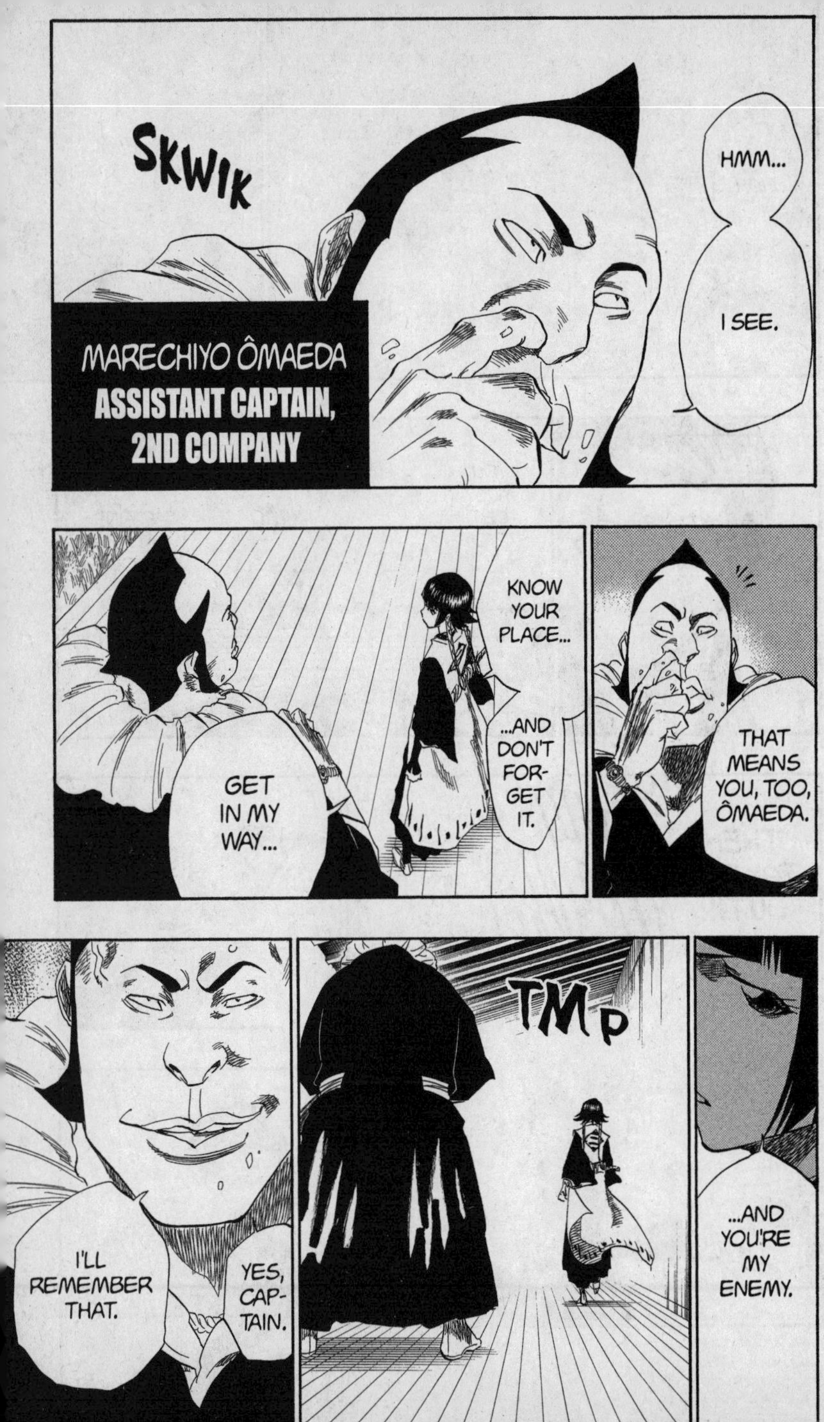
HMM...
I SEE.
SKWIK
MARECHIYO ÔMAEDA
ASSISTANT CAPTAIN, 2ND COMPANY
THAT MEANS YOU, TOO, ÔMAEDA.
KNOW YOUR PLACE...
...AND DON'T FOR-GET IT.
GET IN MY WAY...
...AND YOU'RE MY ENEMY.
TMP
YES, CAP-TAIN.
I'LL REMEMBER THAT.

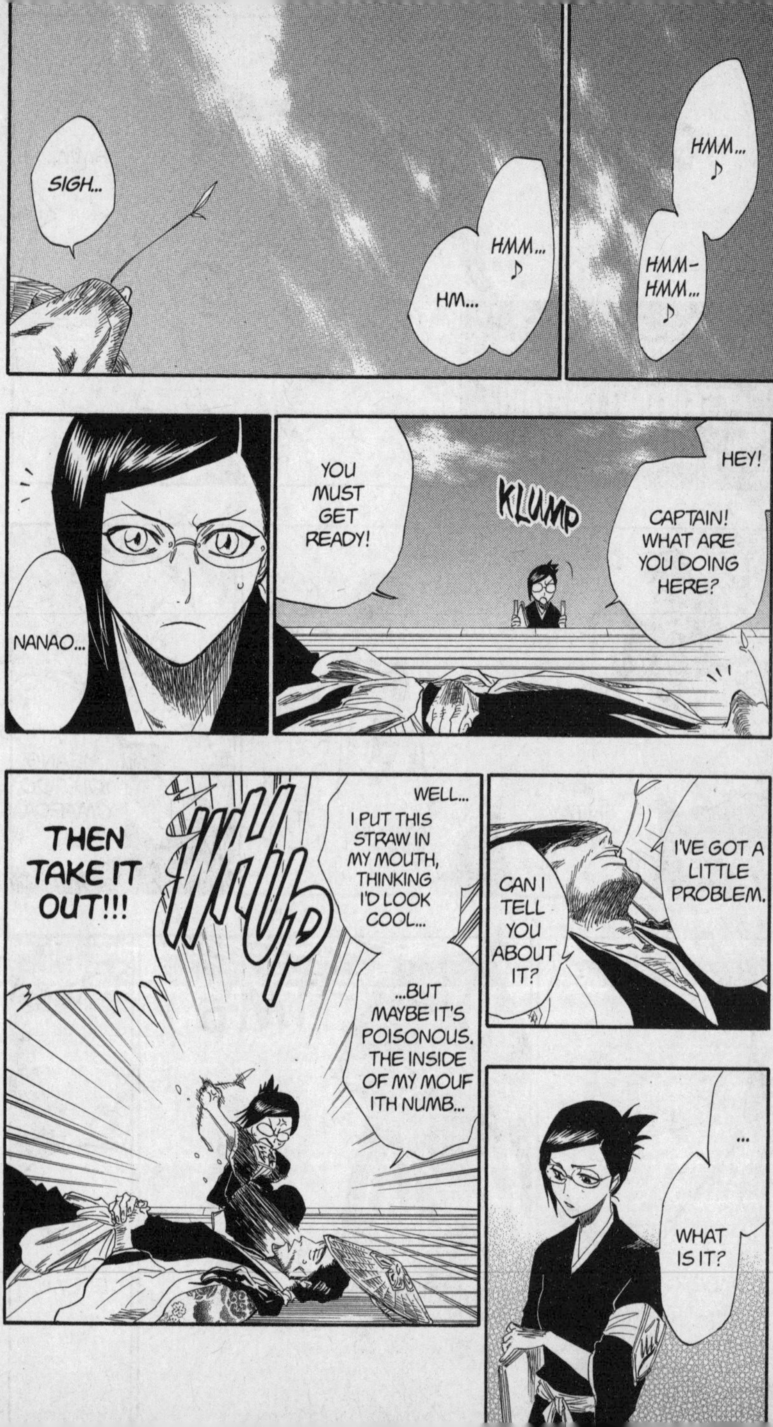
HMM... ♪
HMM-HMM... ♪
HMM... ♪
HM...
SIGH...
HEY!
CAPTAIN! WHAT ARE YOU DOING HERE?
KLUMP
YOU MUST GET READY!
NANAO...
I'VE GOT A LITTLE PROBLEM.
CAN I TELL YOU ABOUT IT?
...
WHAT IS IT?
WELL... I PUT THIS STRAW IN MY MOUTH, THINKING I'D LOOK COOL...
...BUT MAYBE IT'S POISONOUS. THE INSIDE OF MY MOUF ITH NUMB...
WHUP
THEN TAKE IT OUT!!!

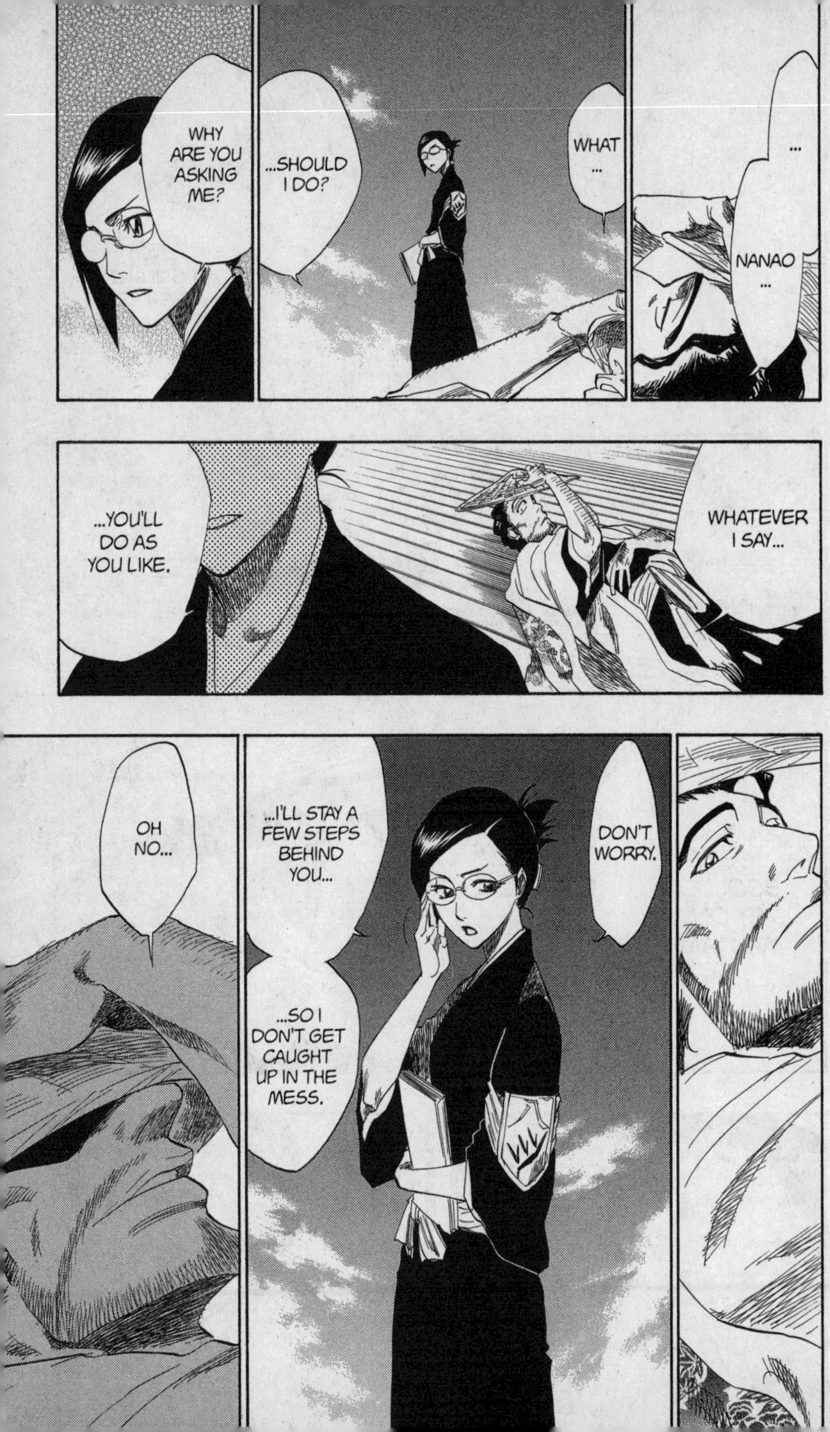
...
NANAO ...
WHAT ...
...SHOULD I DO?
WHY ARE YOU ASKING ME?
WHATEVER I SAY...
...YOU'LL DO AS YOU LIKE.
DON'T WORRY.
...I'LL STAY A FEW STEPS BEHIND YOU...
...SO I DON'T GET CAUGHT UP IN THE MESS.
OH NO...

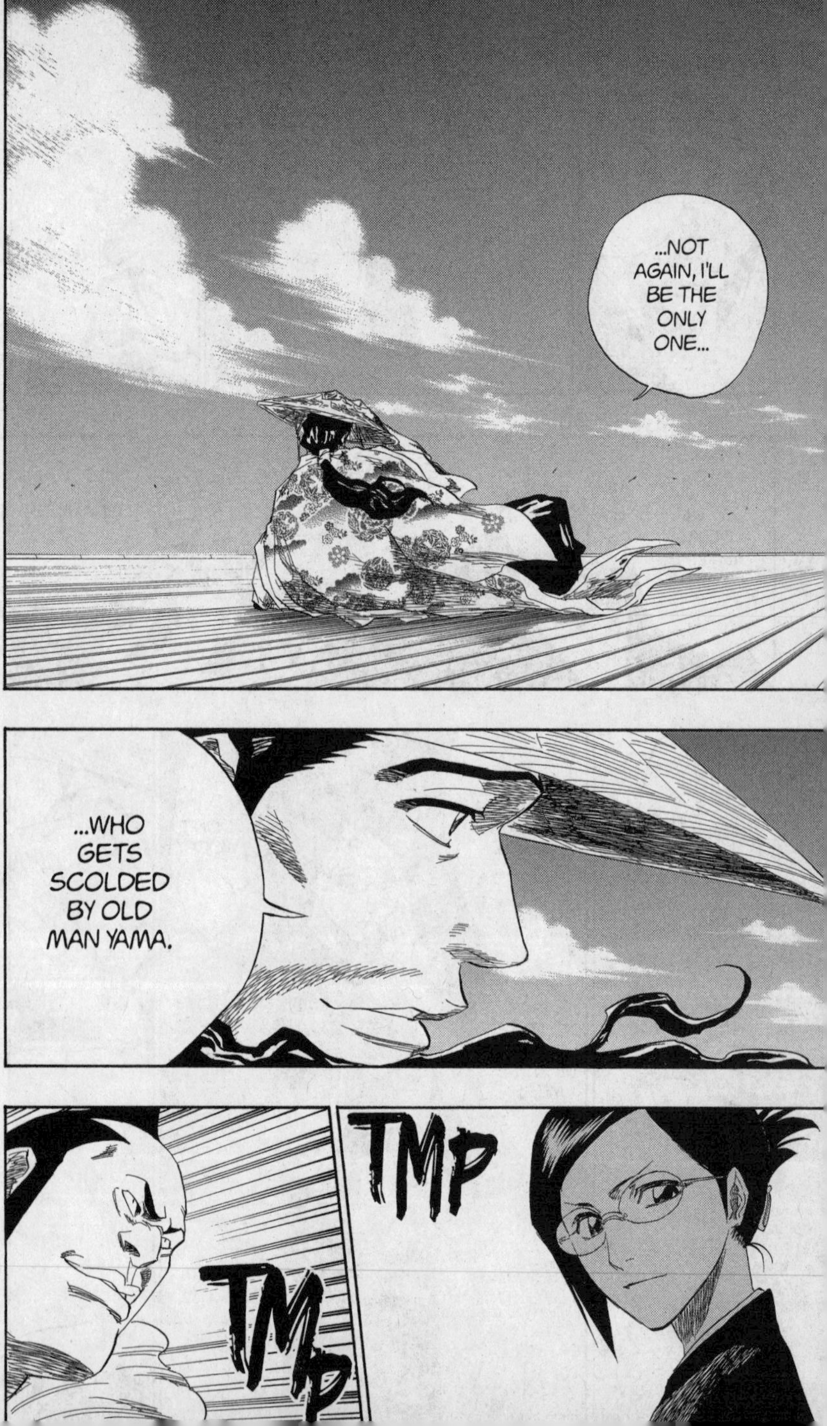
...NOT AGAIN, I'LL BE THE ONLY ONE...
...WHO GETS SCOLDED BY OLD MAN YAMA.
TMP
TMP

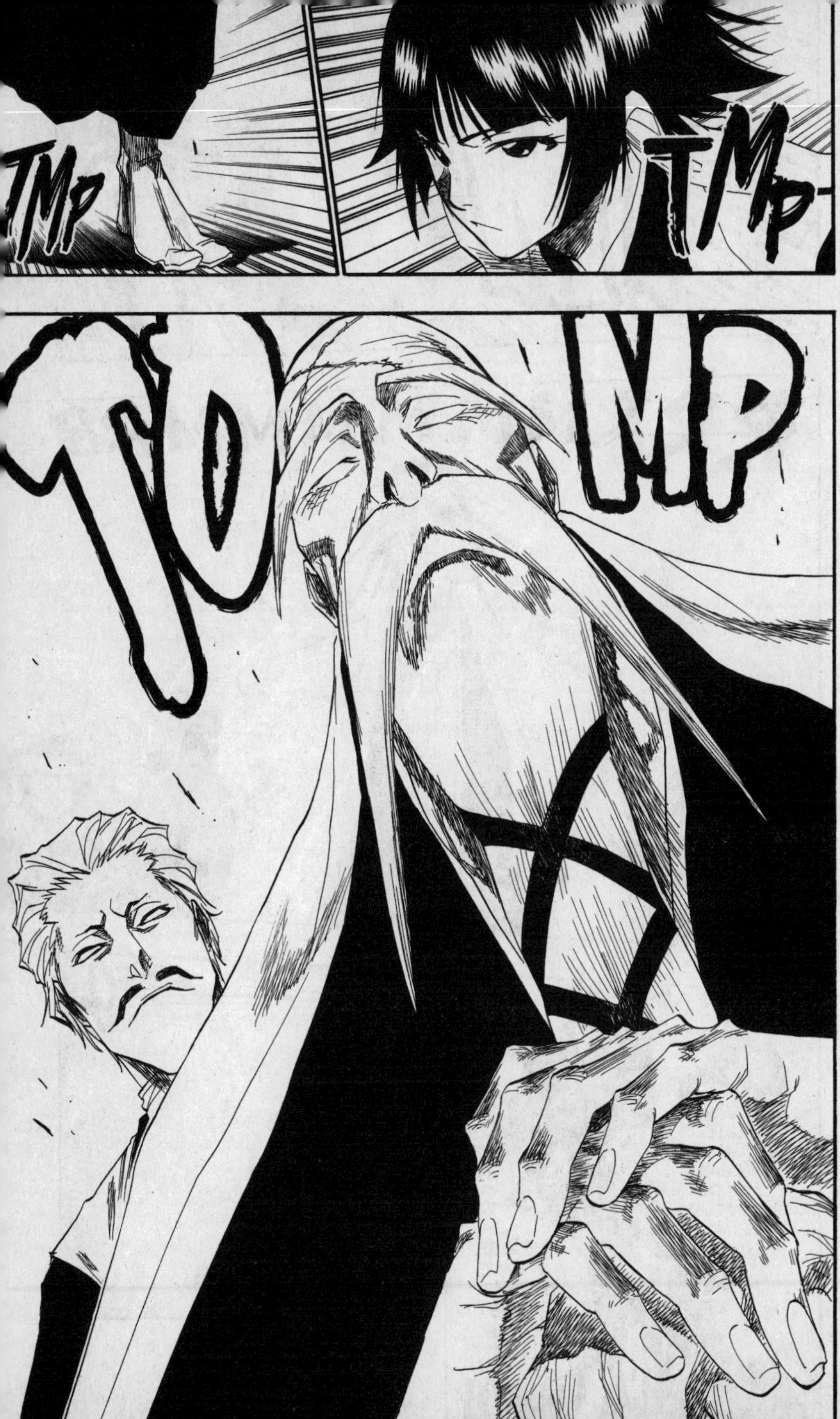
TMP
TMP
TOMP

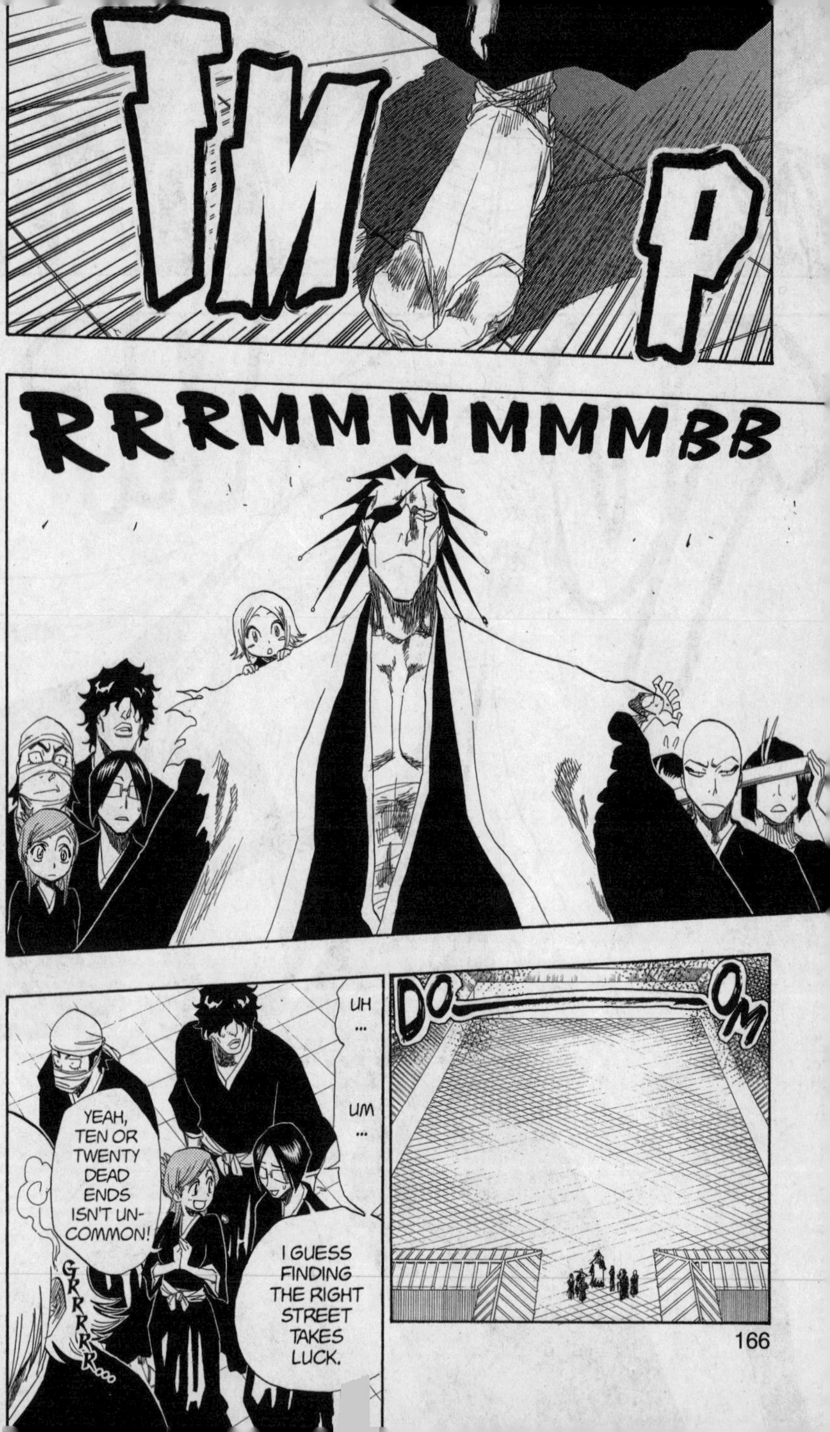

TMP
RRRMMMMMMBB
DO—OM
UH...
UM...
YEAH, TEN OR TWENTY DEAD ENDS ISN'T UN-COMMON!
I GUESS FINDING THE RIGHT STREET TAKES LUCK.
GRRRRR...

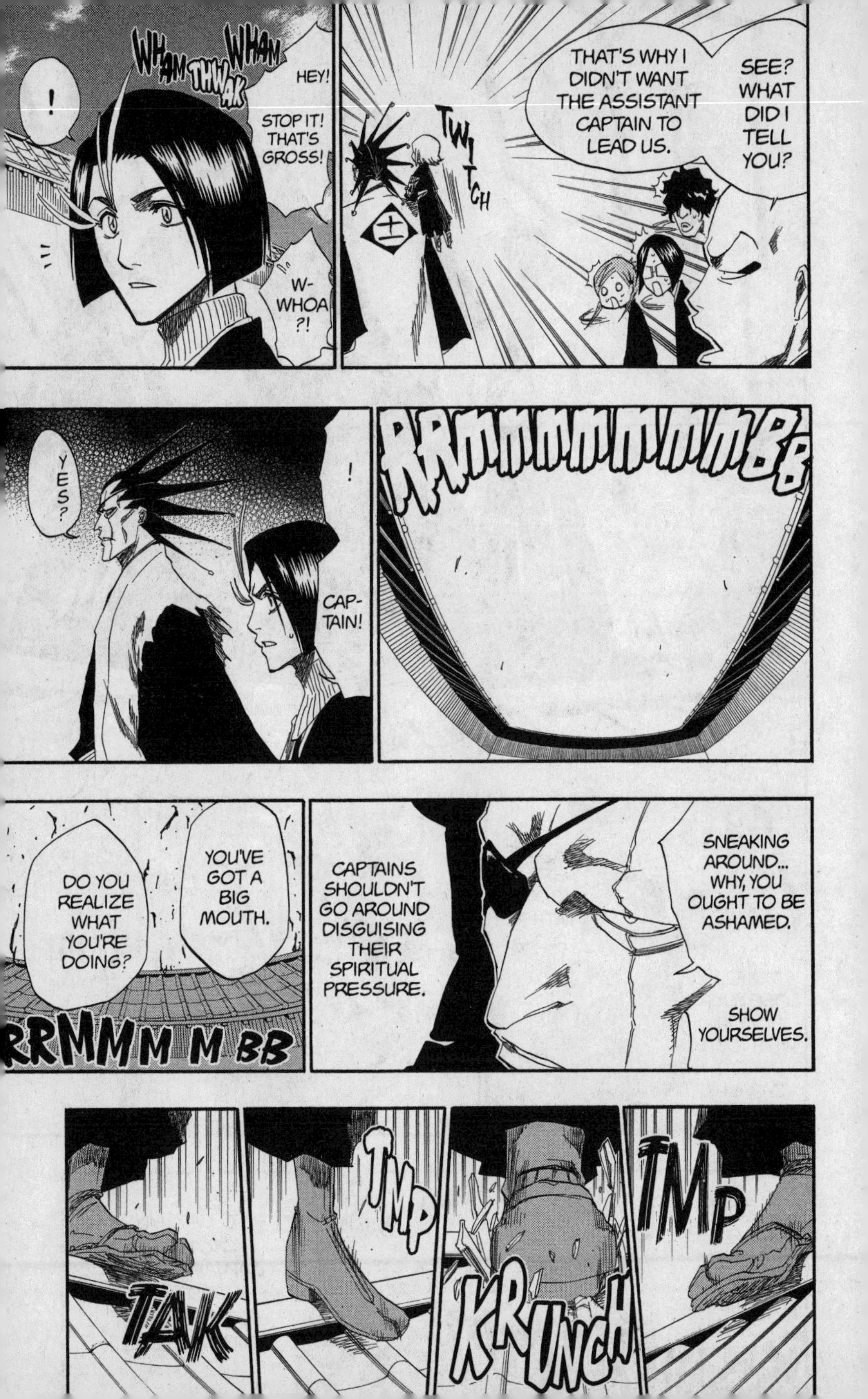
SEE? WHAT DID I TELL YOU?
THAT'S WHY I DIDN'T WANT THE ASSISTANT CAPTAIN TO LEAD US.
TWITCH
WHAM WHAM THWAK
HEY!
STOP IT! THAT'S GROSS!
!
W-WHOA?!
RRMMMMMMMMMBB
!
CAPTAIN!
YES?
SNEAKING AROUND... WHY, YOU OUGHT TO BE ASHAMED.
CAPTAINS SHOULDN'T GO AROUND DISGUISING THEIR SPIRITUAL PRESSURE.
SHOW YOURSELVES.
YOU'VE GOT A BIG MOUTH.
DO YOU REALIZE WHAT YOU'RE DOING?
RRMMMM M BB
TMP
KRUNCH
TMP
TAK

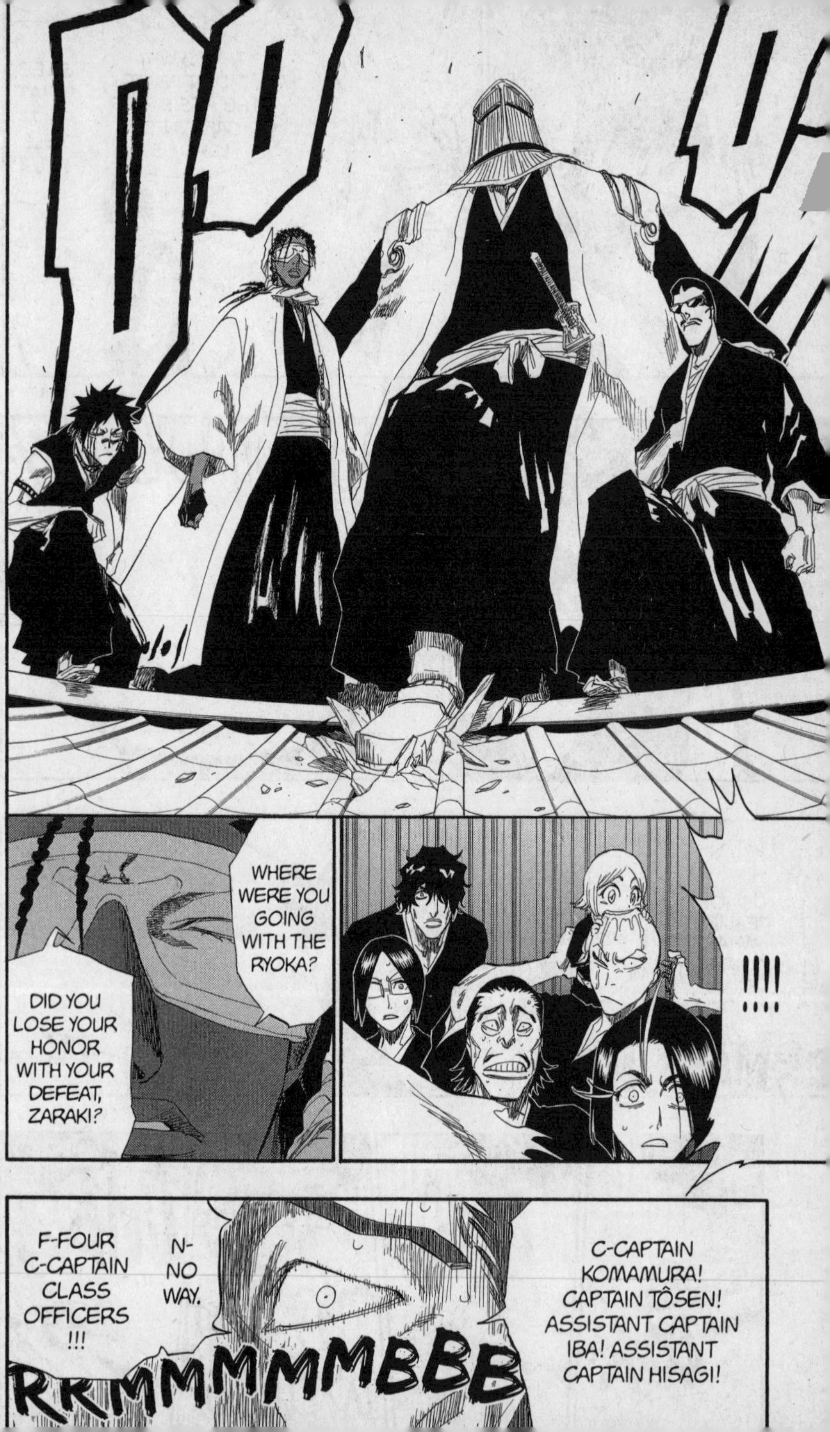
!!!!
WHERE WERE YOU GOING WITH THE RYOKA?
DID YOU LOSE YOUR HONOR WITH YOUR DEFEAT, ZARAKI?
C-CAPTAIN KOMAMURA! CAPTAIN TÔSEN! ASSISTANT CAPTAIN IBA! ASSISTANT CAPTAIN HISAGI!
N- NO WAY.
F-FOUR C-CAPTAIN CLASS OFFICERS !!!
RKMMMMMMBBB

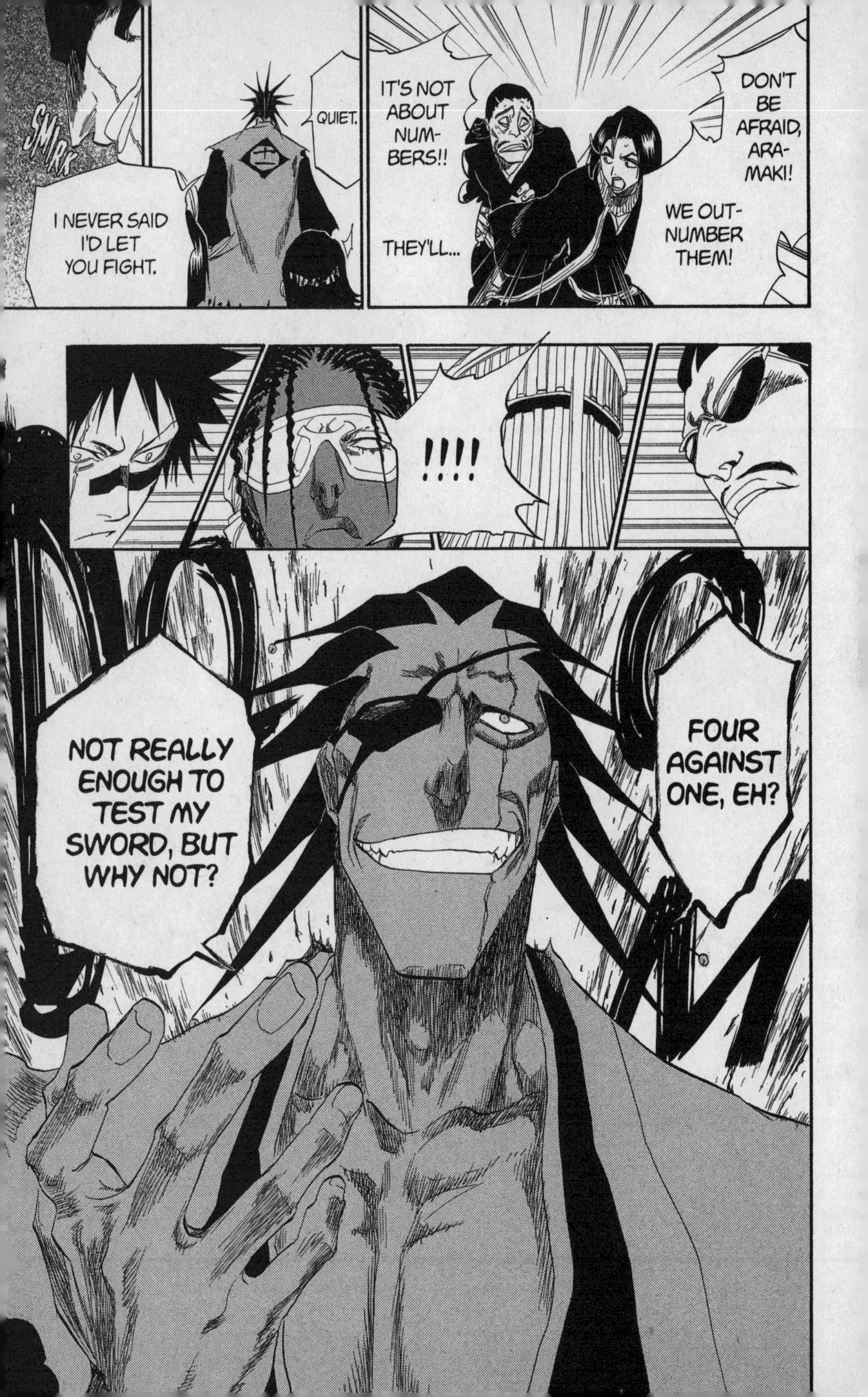
DON'T BE AFRAID, ARAMAKI!
WE OUTNUMBER THEM!
IT'S NOT ABOUT NUMBERS!!
THEY'LL...
QUIET.
SMIRK
I NEVER SAID I'D LET YOU FIGHT.
!!!!
FOUR AGAINST ONE, EH?
NOT REALLY ENOUGH TO TEST MY SWORD, BUT WHY NOT?

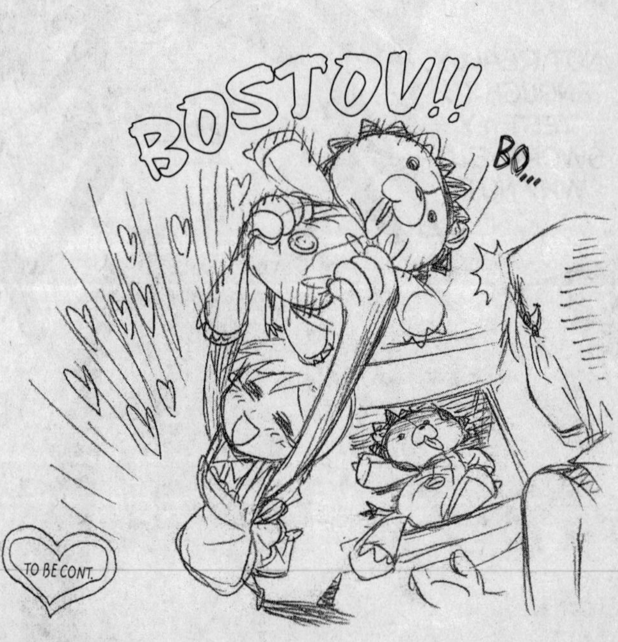
BOSTOV!!
BO...
TO BE CONT.

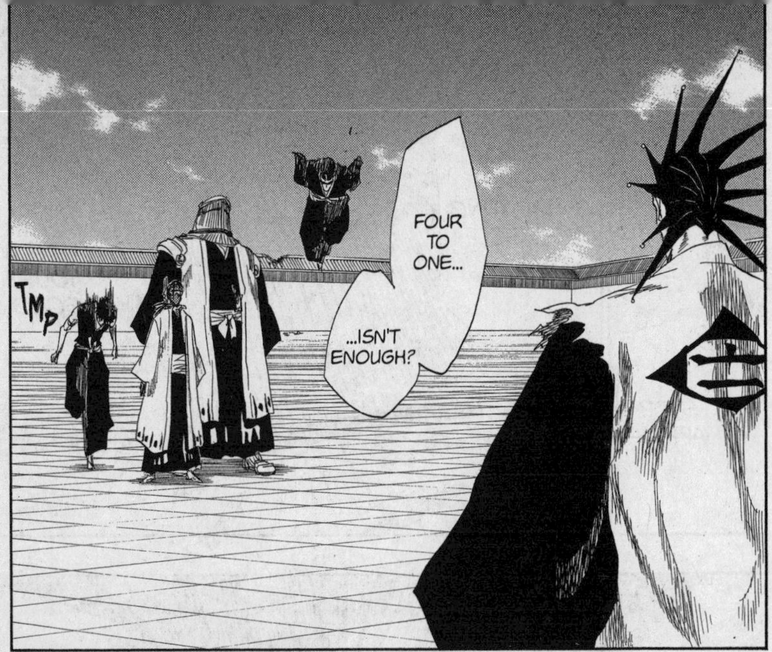
FOUR TO ONE...
...ISN'T ENOUGH?
TMP

139. Drowsy, Bloody, Crazy

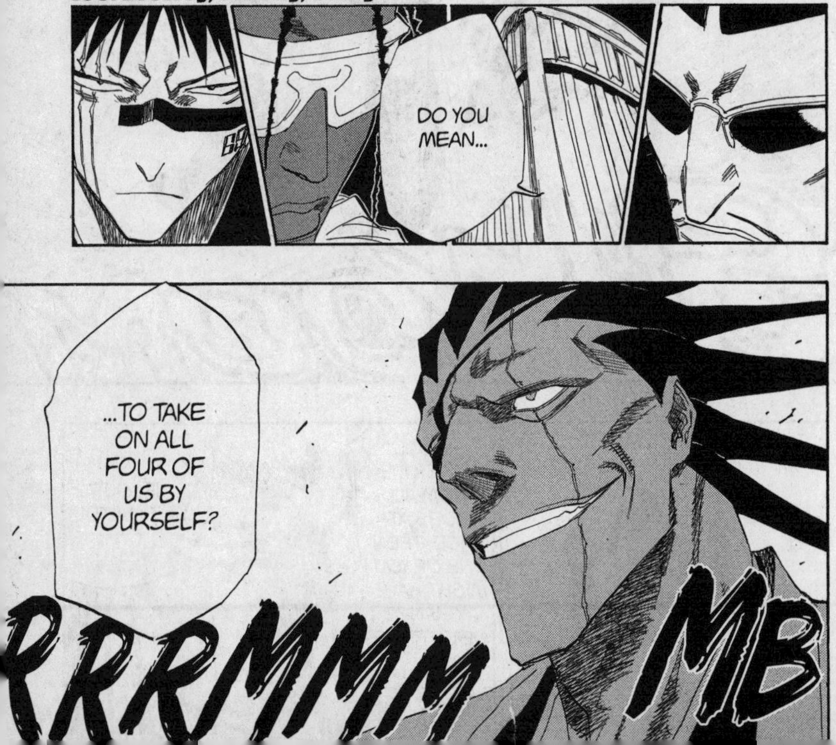
DO YOU MEAN...
...TO TAKE ON ALL FOUR OF US BY YOURSELF?
RRRMMMM MB

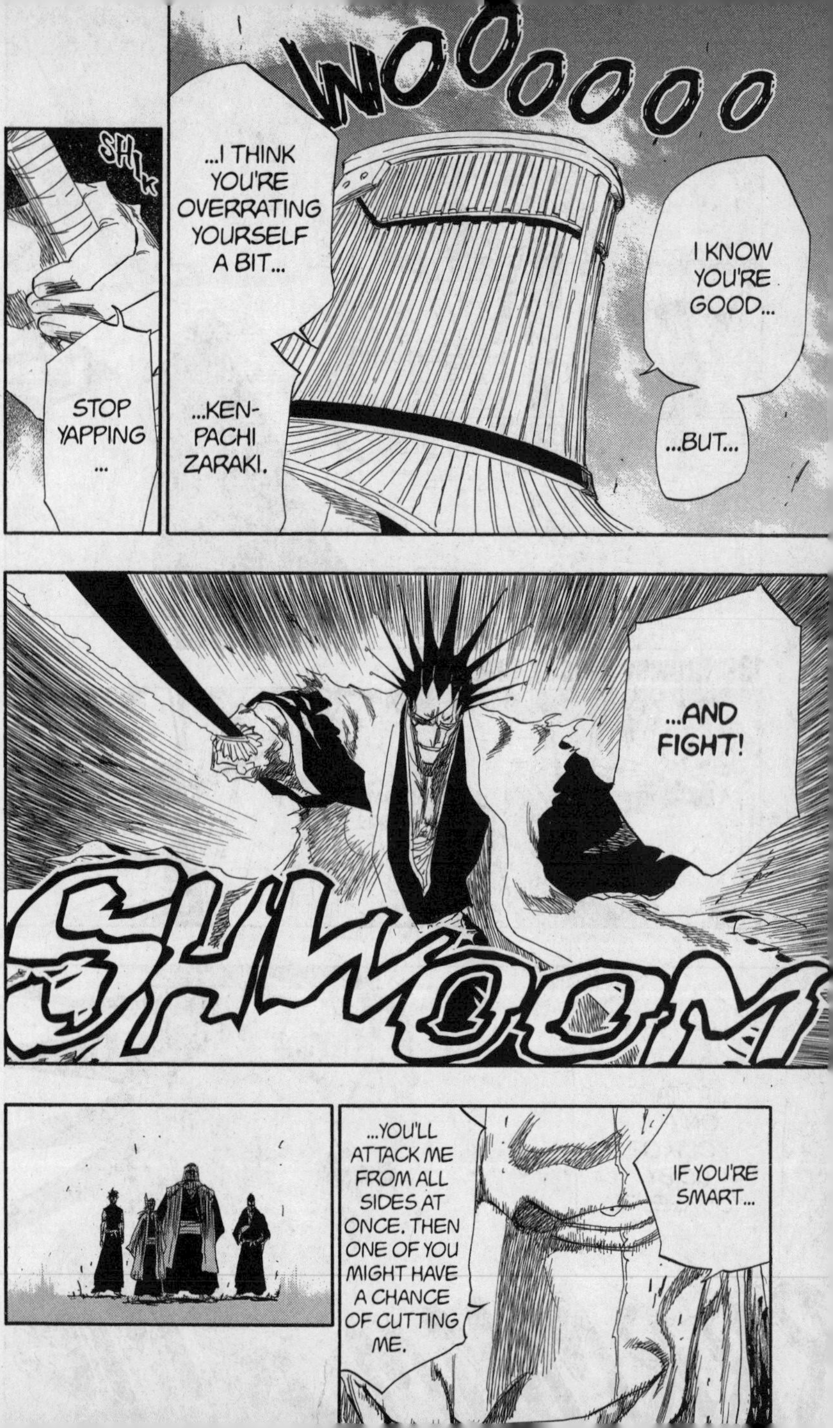
WOOOOOOO
I KNOW YOU'RE GOOD...
...BUT...
...I THINK YOU'RE OVERRATING YOURSELF A BIT...
...KEN-PACHI ZARAKI.
STOP YAPPING ...
...AND FIGHT!
SHWOOM
IF YOU'RE SMART...
...YOU'LL ATTACK ME FROM ALL SIDES AT ONCE. THEN ONE OF YOU MIGHT HAVE A CHANCE OF CUTTING ME.

READ THIS WAY

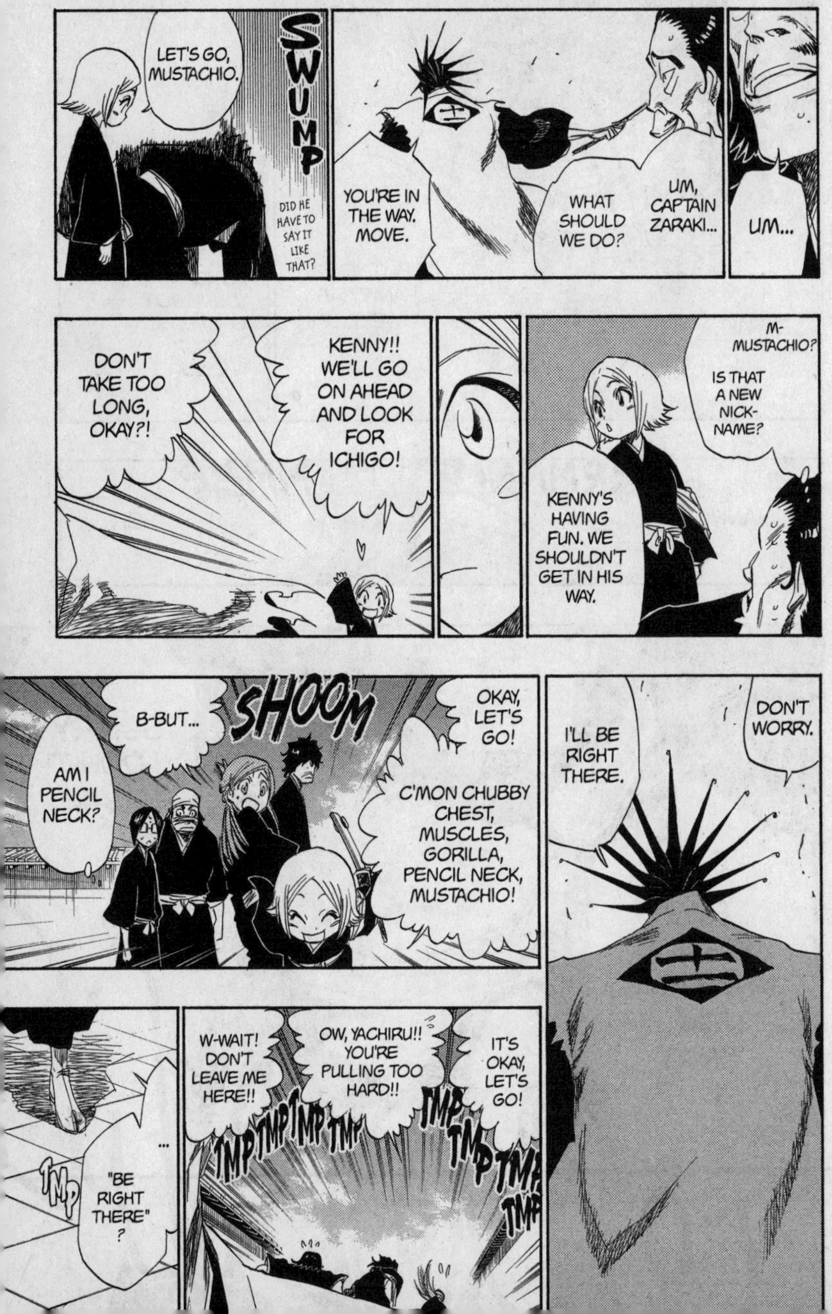
UM...
UM, CAPTAIN ZARAKI...
WHAT SHOULD WE DO?
YOU'RE IN THE WAY. MOVE.
SWUMP
LET'S GO, MUSTACHIO.
DID HE HAVE TO SAY IT LIKE THAT?
M-MUSTACHIO?
IS THAT A NEW NICK-NAME?
KENNY'S HAVING FUN. WE SHOULDN'T GET IN HIS WAY.
KENNY!! WE'LL GO ON AHEAD AND LOOK FOR ICHIGO!
DON'T TAKE TOO LONG, OKAY?!
DON'T WORRY.
I'LL BE RIGHT THERE.
OKAY, LET'S GO!
C'MON CHUBBY CHEST, MUSCLES, GORILLA, PENCIL NECK, MUSTACHIO!
SHOOM
B-BUT...
AM I PENCIL NECK?
IT'S OKAY, LET'S GO!
OW, YACHIRU!! YOU'RE PULLING TOO HARD!!
W-WAIT! DON'T LEAVE ME HERE!!
TMP TMP TMP TMP TMP TMP TMP TMP TMP TMP
...
"BE RIGHT THERE"?
TMP

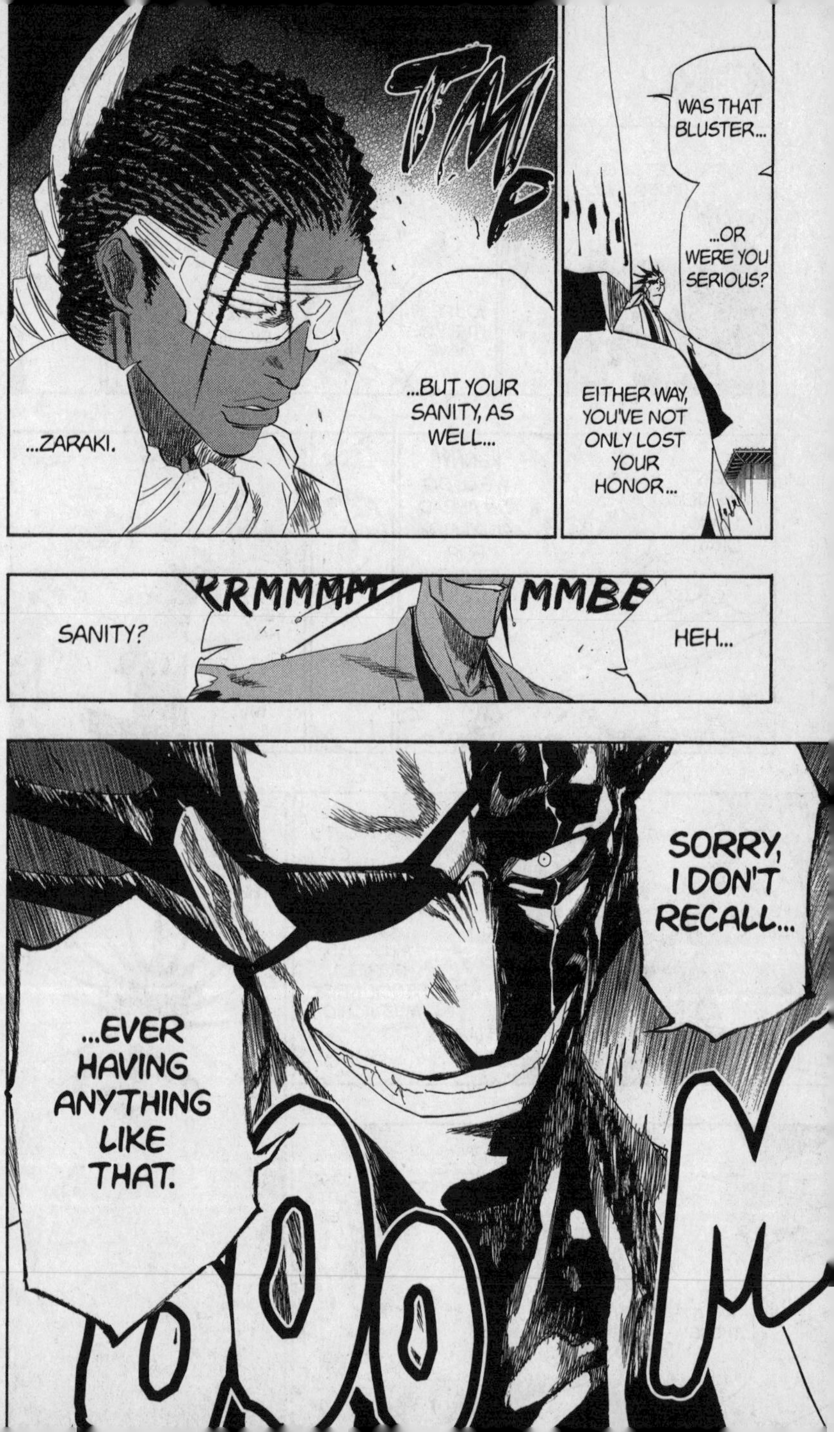
WAS THAT BLUSTER...
...OR WERE YOU SERIOUS?
EITHER WAY, YOU'VE NOT ONLY LOST YOUR HONOR...
TMP
...BUT YOUR SANITY, AS WELL...
...ZARAKI.
HEH...
MMBE
RRMMMMM
SANITY?
SORRY, I DON'T RECALL...
...EVER HAVING ANYTHING LIKE THAT.

139. Drowsy, Bloody, Crazy

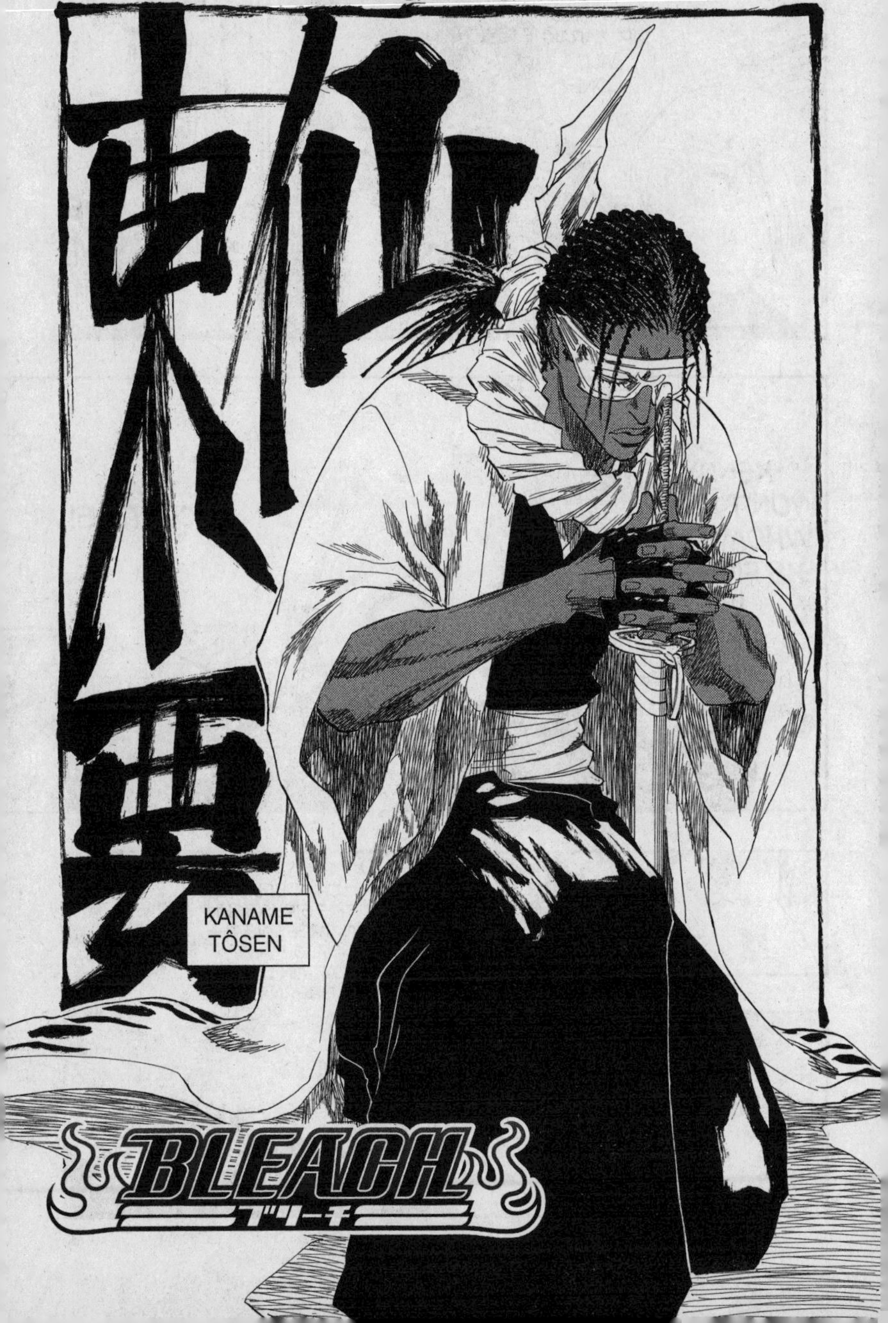
東仙要
KANAME TÔSEN
BLEACH
ブリーチ

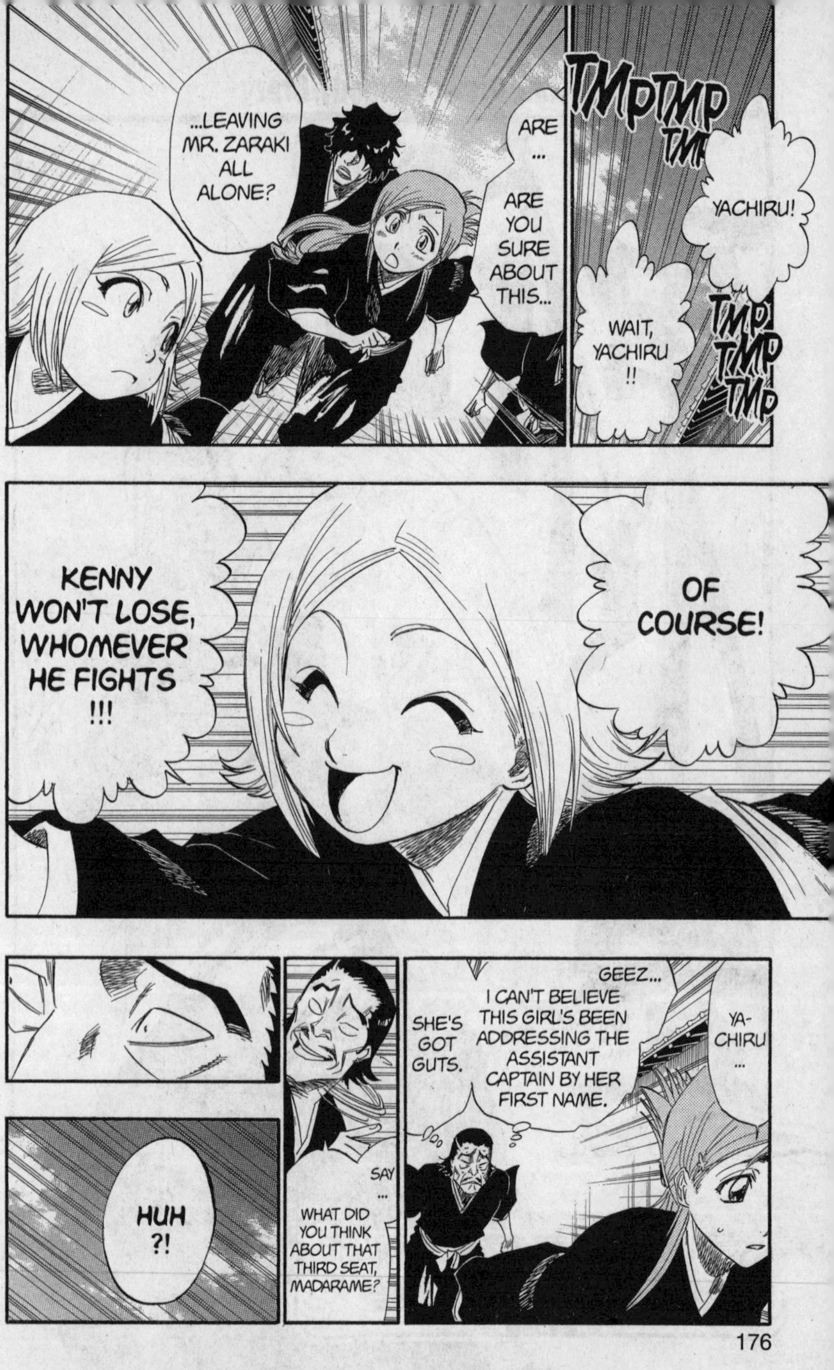
TMPTMP TMP
YACHIRU!
WAIT, YACHIRU!!
TMP TMP TMP
ARE... ARE YOU SURE ABOUT THIS...
...LEAVING MR. ZARAKI ALL ALONE?
OF COURSE!
KENNY WON'T LOSE, WHOMEVER HE FIGHTS!!!
YA-CHIRU...
GEEZ... I CAN'T BELIEVE THIS GIRL'S BEEN ADDRESSING THE ASSISTANT CAPTAIN BY HER FIRST NAME.
SHE'S GOT GUTS.
SAY... WHAT DID YOU THINK ABOUT THAT THIRD SEAT, MADARAME?
HUH?!

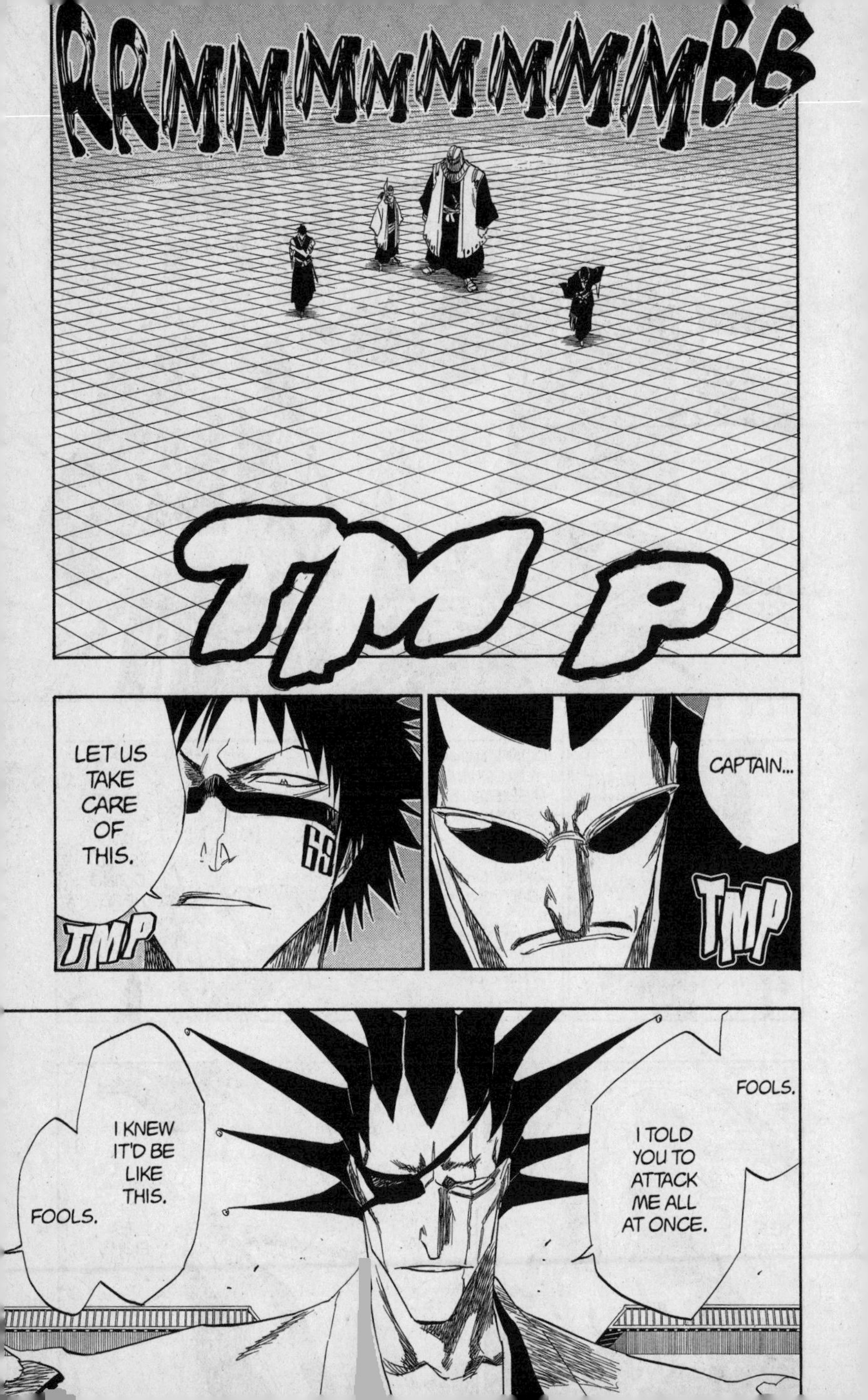
RRMMMMMMMMMBB
TMP
CAPTAIN...
TMP
LET US TAKE CARE OF THIS.
TMP
FOOLS.
I TOLD YOU TO ATTACK ME ALL AT ONCE.
I KNEW IT'D BE LIKE THIS.
FOOLS.

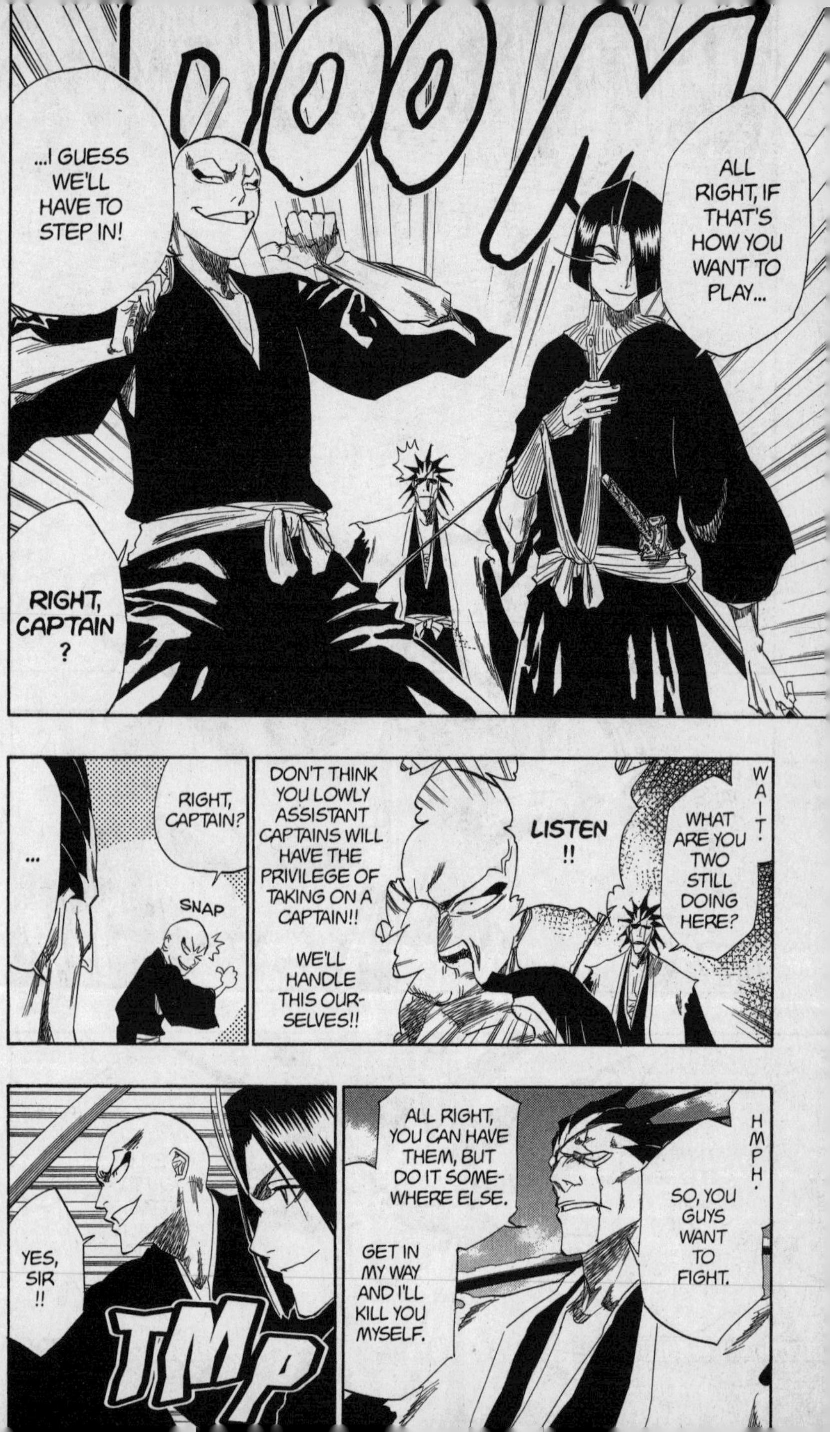
DOOM
ALL RIGHT, IF THAT'S HOW YOU WANT TO PLAY...
...I GUESS WE'LL HAVE TO STEP IN!
RIGHT, CAPTAIN ?
WAIT.
WHAT ARE YOU TWO STILL DOING HERE?
LISTEN !!
DON'T THINK YOU LOWLY ASSISTANT CAPTAINS WILL HAVE THE PRIVILEGE OF TAKING ON A CAPTAIN!!
WE'LL HANDLE THIS OUR-SELVES!!
RIGHT, CAPTAIN?
SNAP
...
HMPH.
SO, YOU GUYS WANT TO FIGHT.
ALL RIGHT, YOU CAN HAVE THEM, BUT DO IT SOME-WHERE ELSE.
GET IN MY WAY AND I'LL KILL YOU MYSELF.
YES, SIR !!
TMP

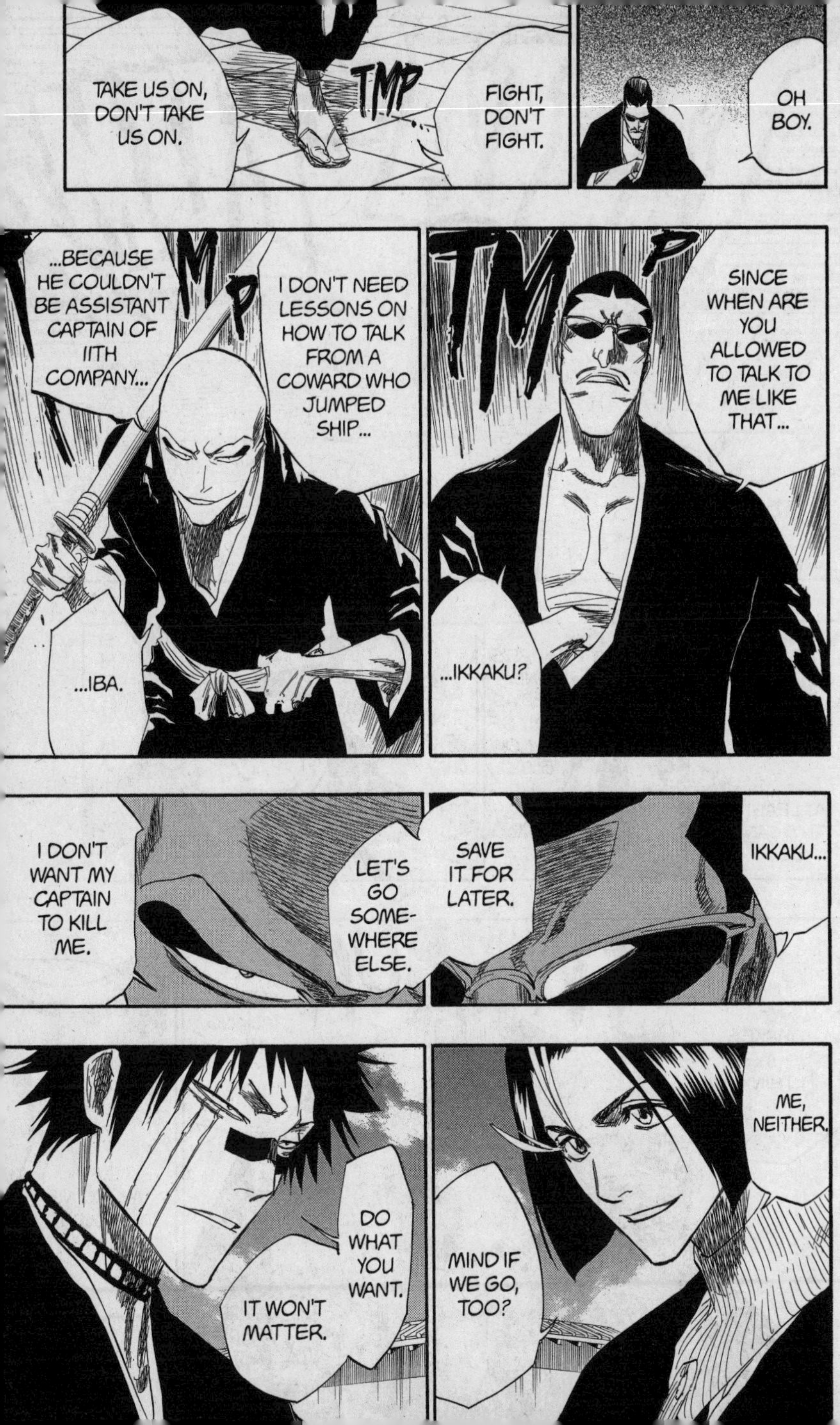
OH BOY.
FIGHT, DON'T FIGHT.
TMP
TAKE US ON, DON'T TAKE US ON.
TMP
SINCE WHEN ARE YOU ALLOWED TO TALK TO ME LIKE THAT...
...IKKAKU?
I DON'T NEED LESSONS ON HOW TO TALK FROM A COWARD WHO JUMPED SHIP...
TMP
...BECAUSE HE COULDN'T BE ASSISTANT CAPTAIN OF 11TH COMPANY...
...IBA.
IKKAKU...
SAVE IT FOR LATER.
LET'S GO SOMEWHERE ELSE.
I DON'T WANT MY CAPTAIN TO KILL ME.
ME, NEITHER.
MIND IF WE GO, TOO?
DO WHAT YOU WANT.
IT WON'T MATTER.

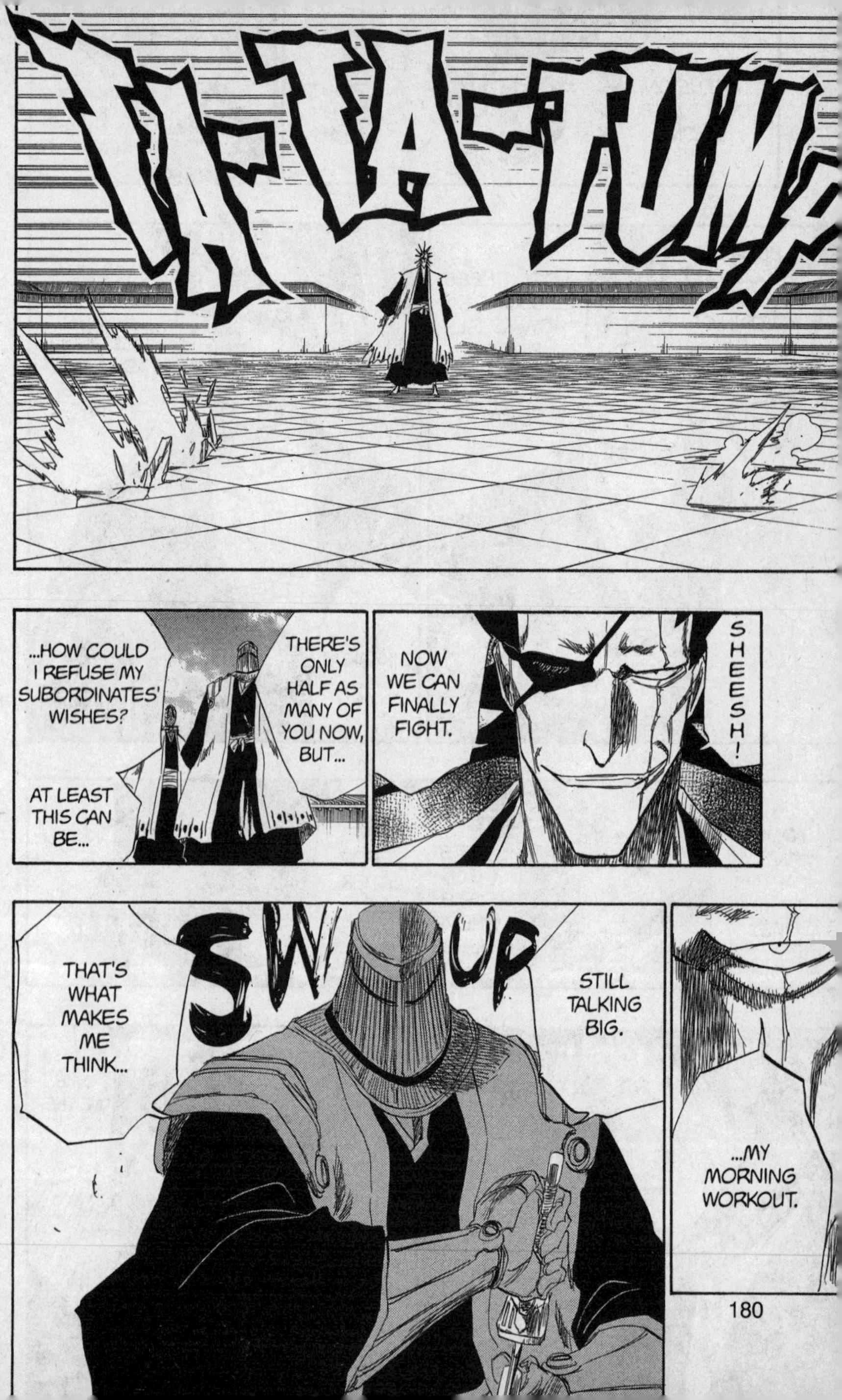
TA-TA-TUM
SHEESH!
NOW WE CAN FINALLY FIGHT.
THERE'S ONLY HALF AS MANY OF YOU NOW, BUT...
...HOW COULD I REFUSE MY SUBORDINATES' WISHES?
AT LEAST THIS CAN BE...
...MY MORNING WORKOUT.
STILL TALKING BIG.
SWUP
THAT'S WHAT MAKES ME THINK...

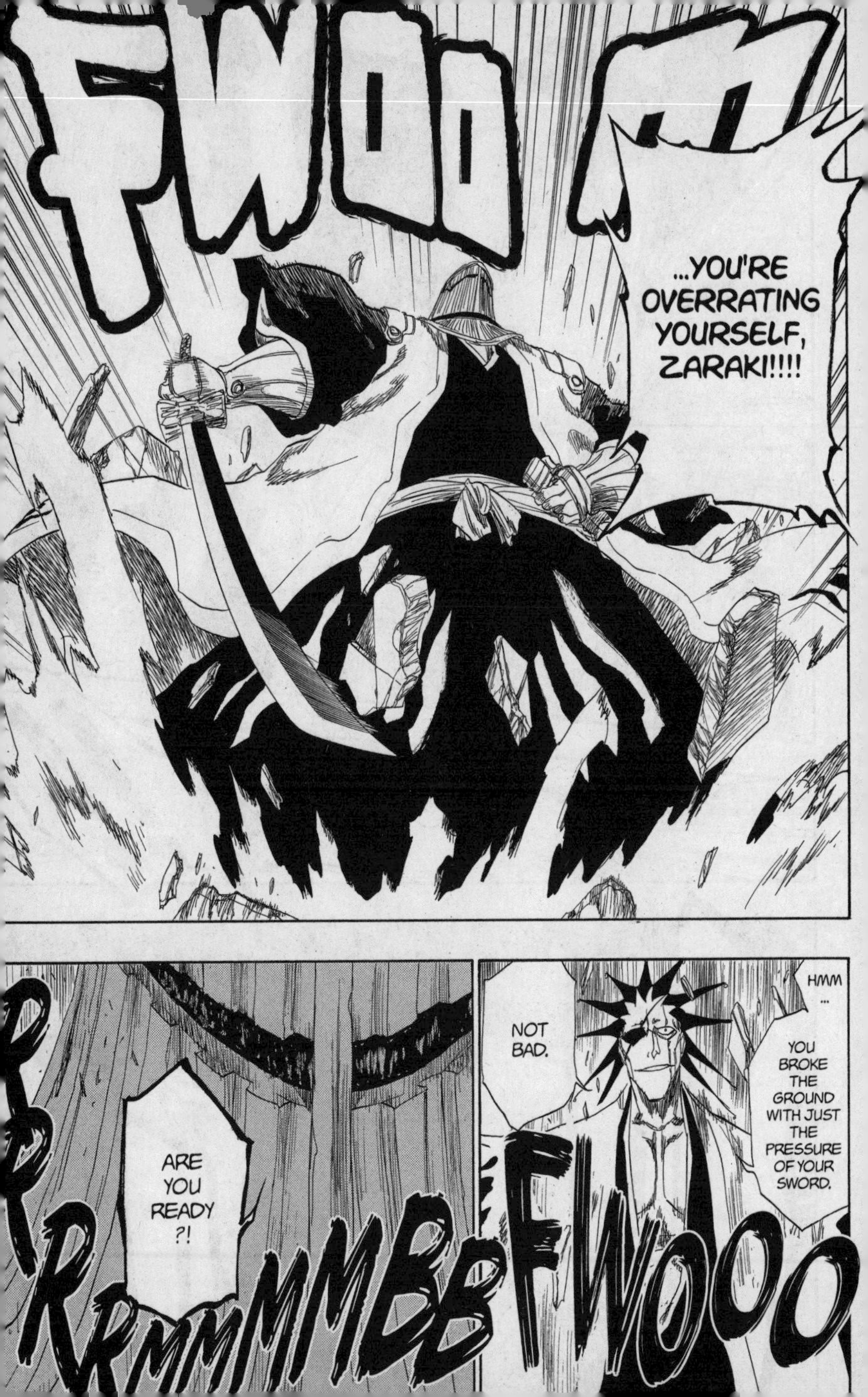
FWOO
...YOU'RE OVERRATING YOURSELF, ZARAKI!!!!!
HMM...
YOU BROKE THE GROUND WITH JUST THE PRESSURE OF YOUR SWORD.
NOT BAD.
FWOOO
ARE YOU READY ?!
RRMMMBB

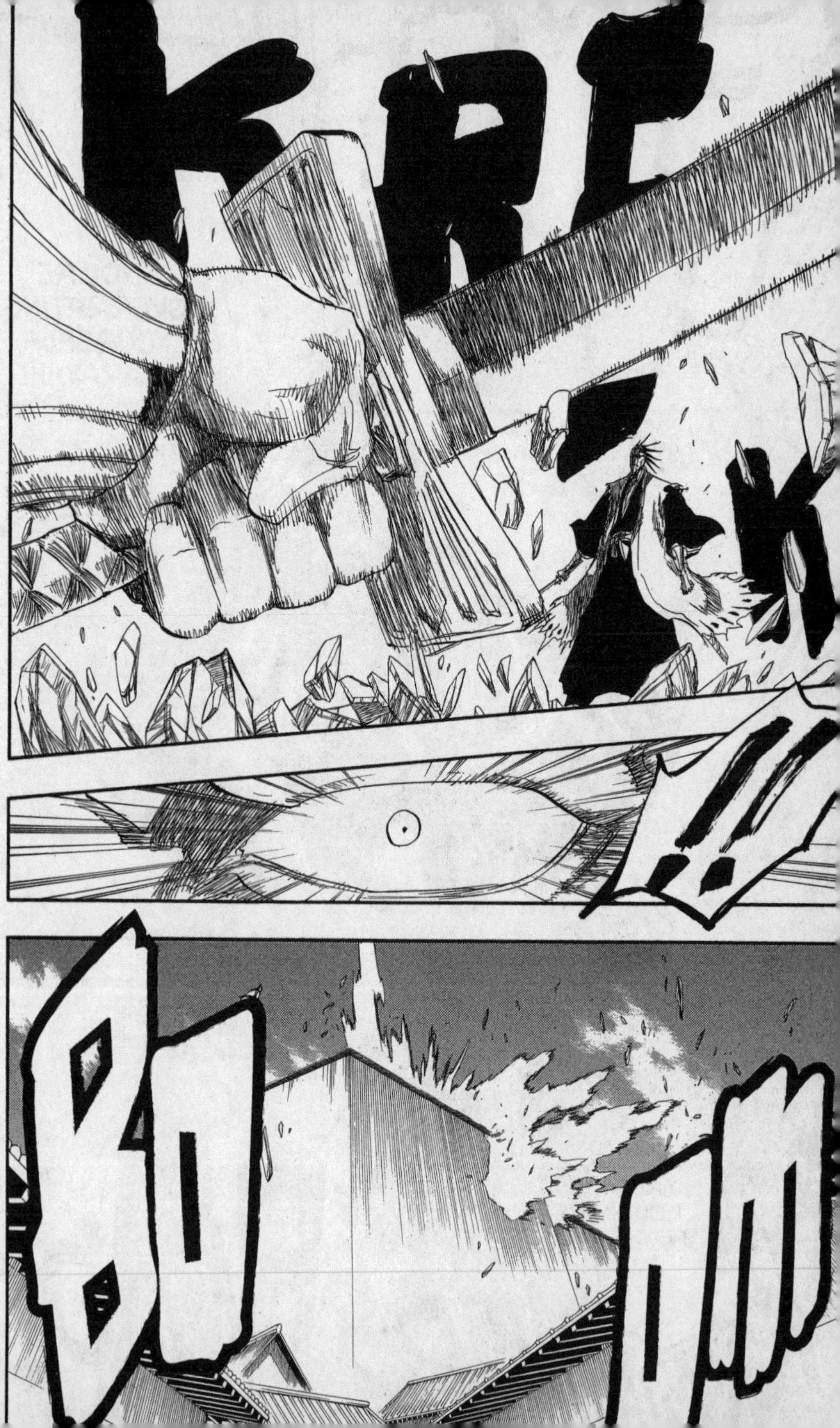
KRR
K
!!
BO

READ THIS WAY

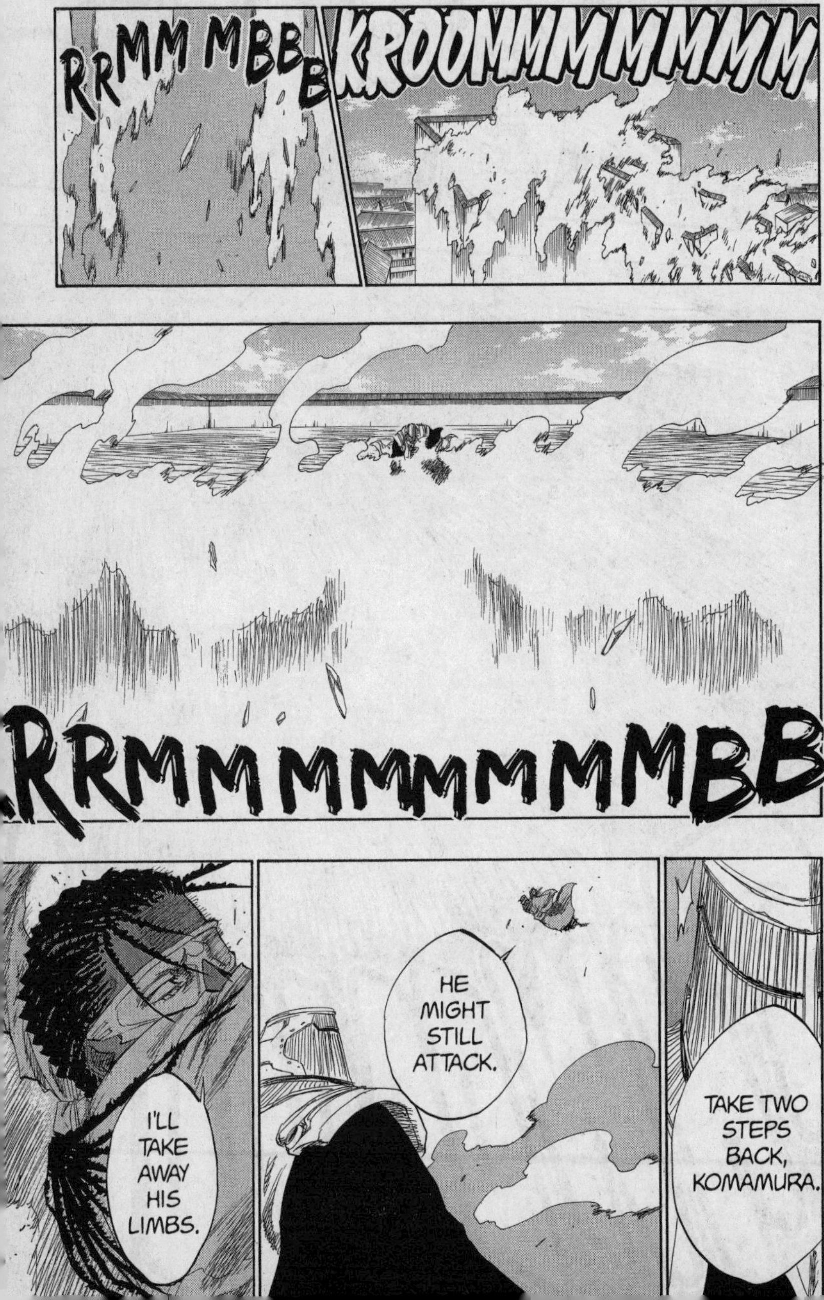
KROOMMMMMMMM
RRMM MBBB
RRMMMMMMMMMBB
TAKE TWO STEPS BACK, KOMAMURA.
HE MIGHT STILL ATTACK.
I'LL TAKE AWAY HIS LIMBS.

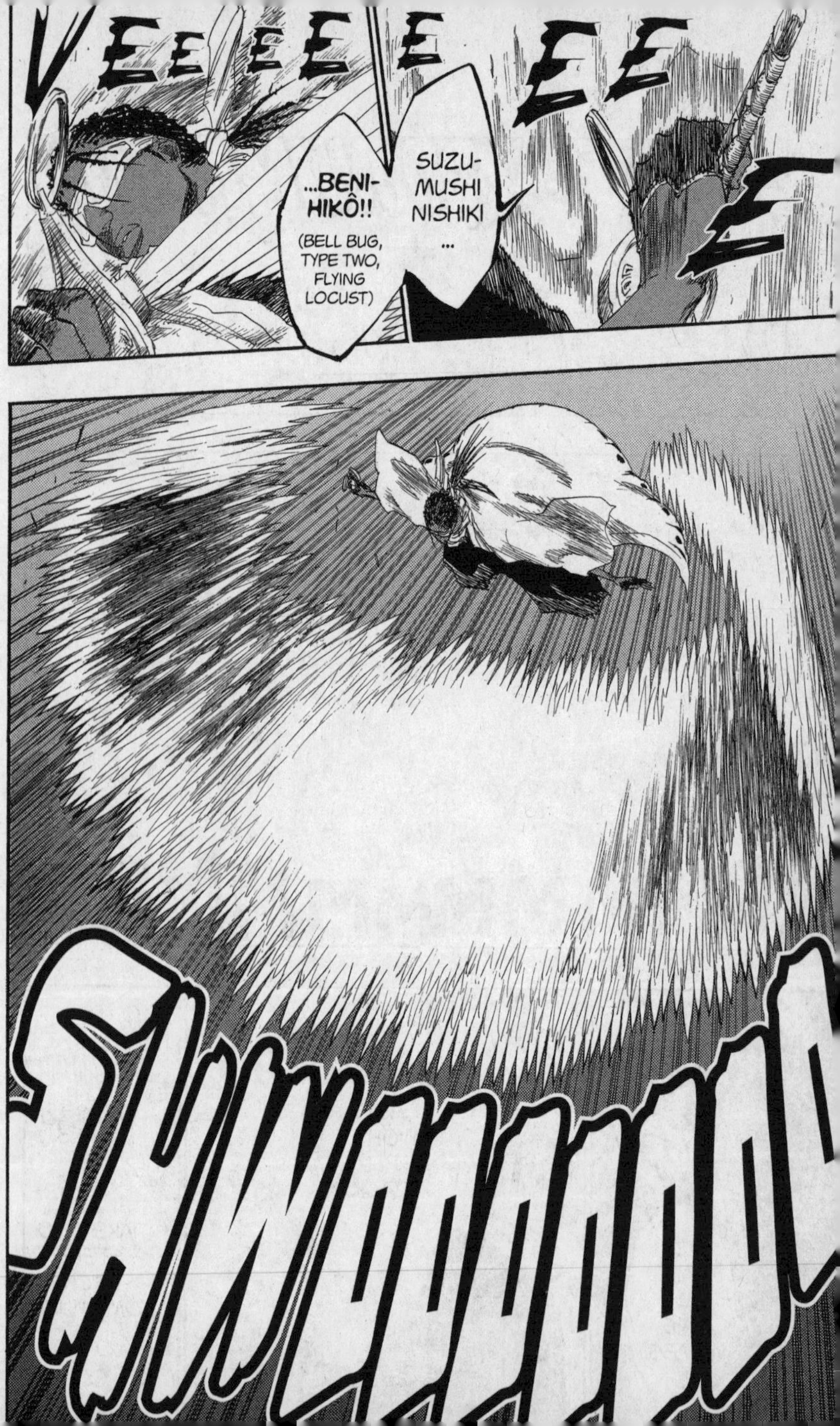
VEEEEEEEE
SUZU-MUSHI NISHIKI ...
...BENI-HIKÔ!!
(BELL BUG, TYPE TWO, FLYING LOCUST)

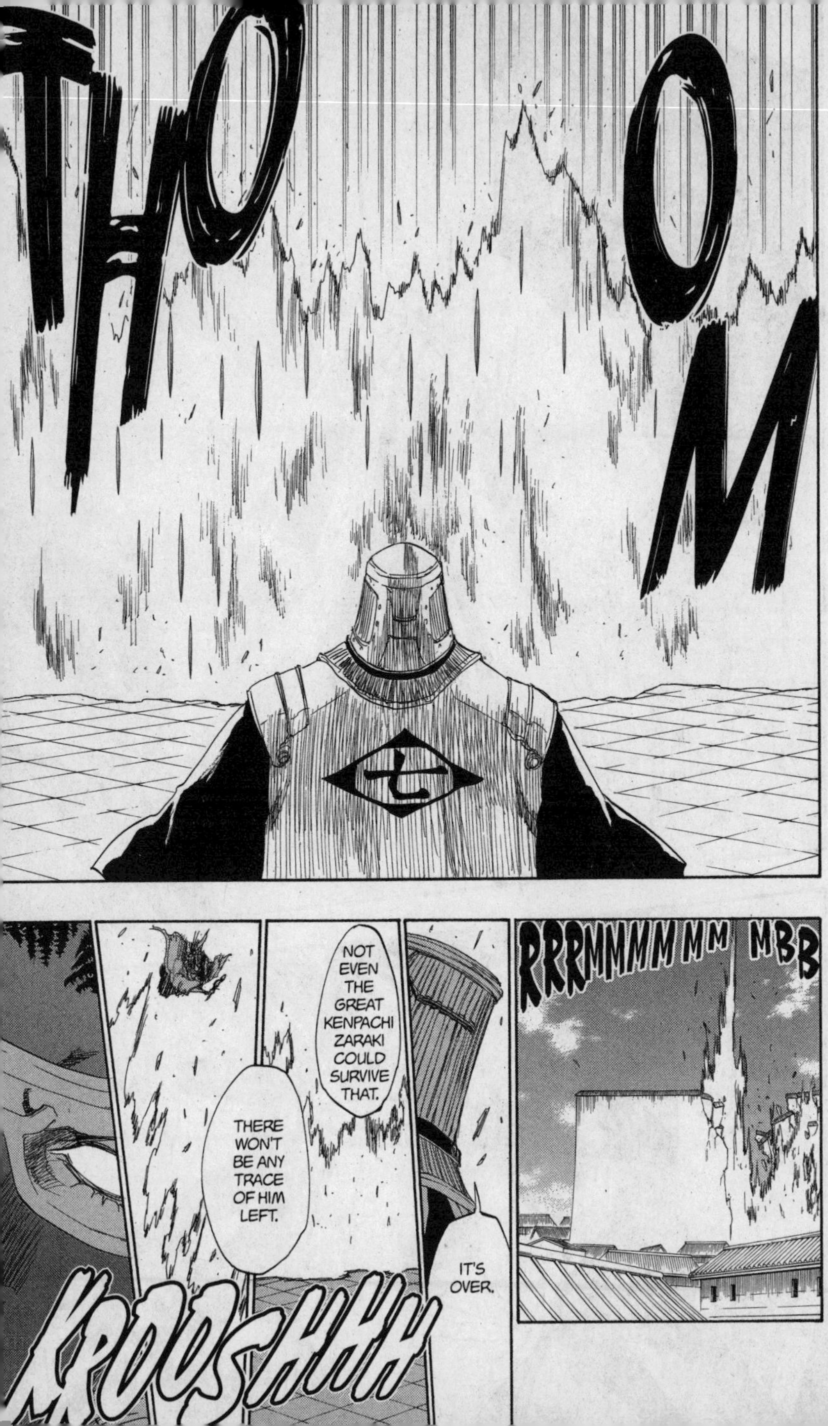
THOOM
RRRMMMMMM MM MBB
IT'S OVER.
NOT EVEN THE GREAT KENPACHI ZARAKI COULD SURVIVE THAT.
THERE WON'T BE ANY TRACE OF HIM LEFT.
KROOSHHH

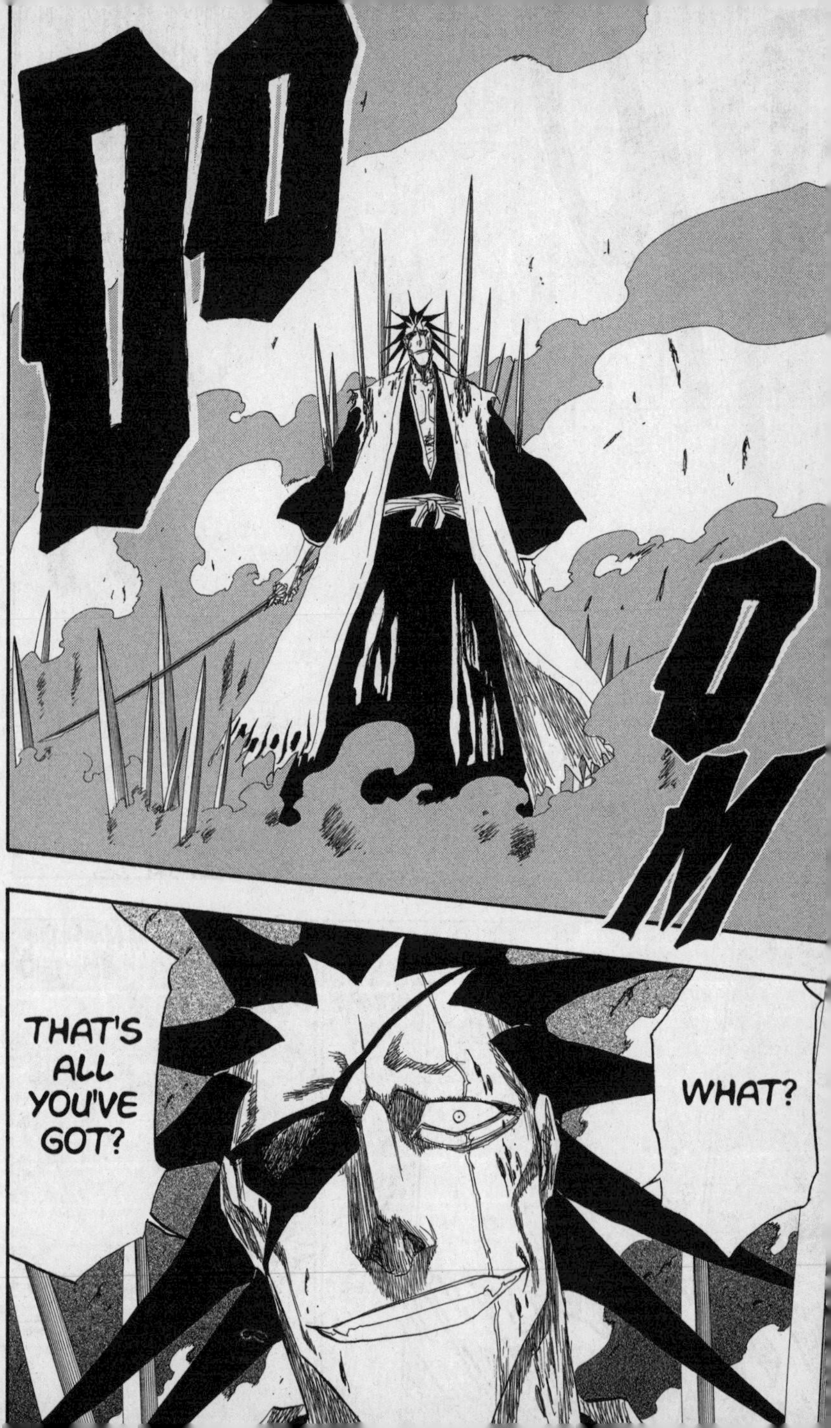
DOOM
WHAT?
THAT'S ALL YOU'VE GOT?

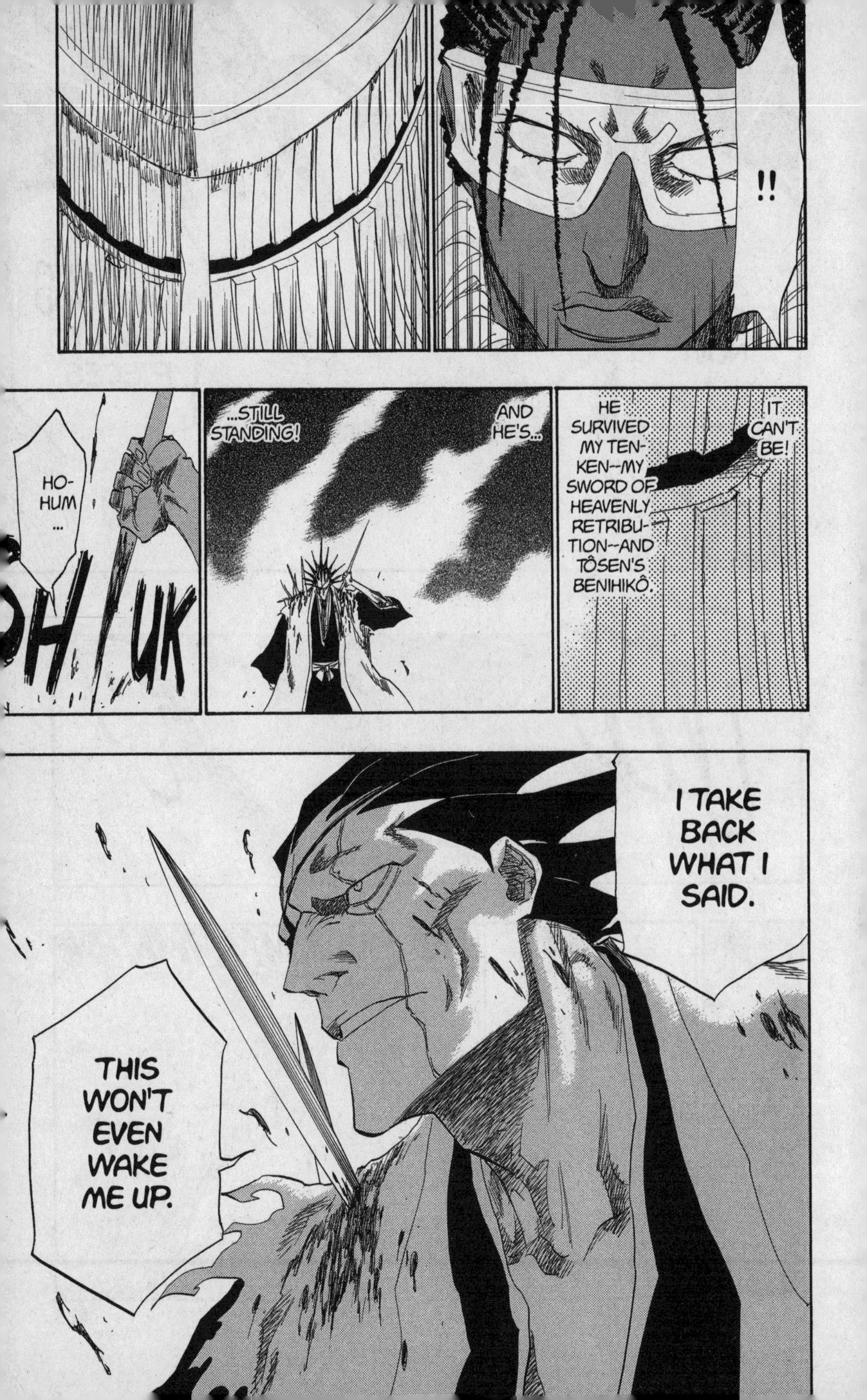
!!
IT CAN'T BE!
HE SURVIVED MY TEN-KEN--MY SWORD OF HEAVENLY RETRIBU-TION--AND TÔSEN'S BENIHIKÔ.
AND HE'S...
...STILL STANDING!
HO-HUM ...
I TAKE BACK WHAT I SAID.
THIS WON'T EVEN WAKE ME UP.

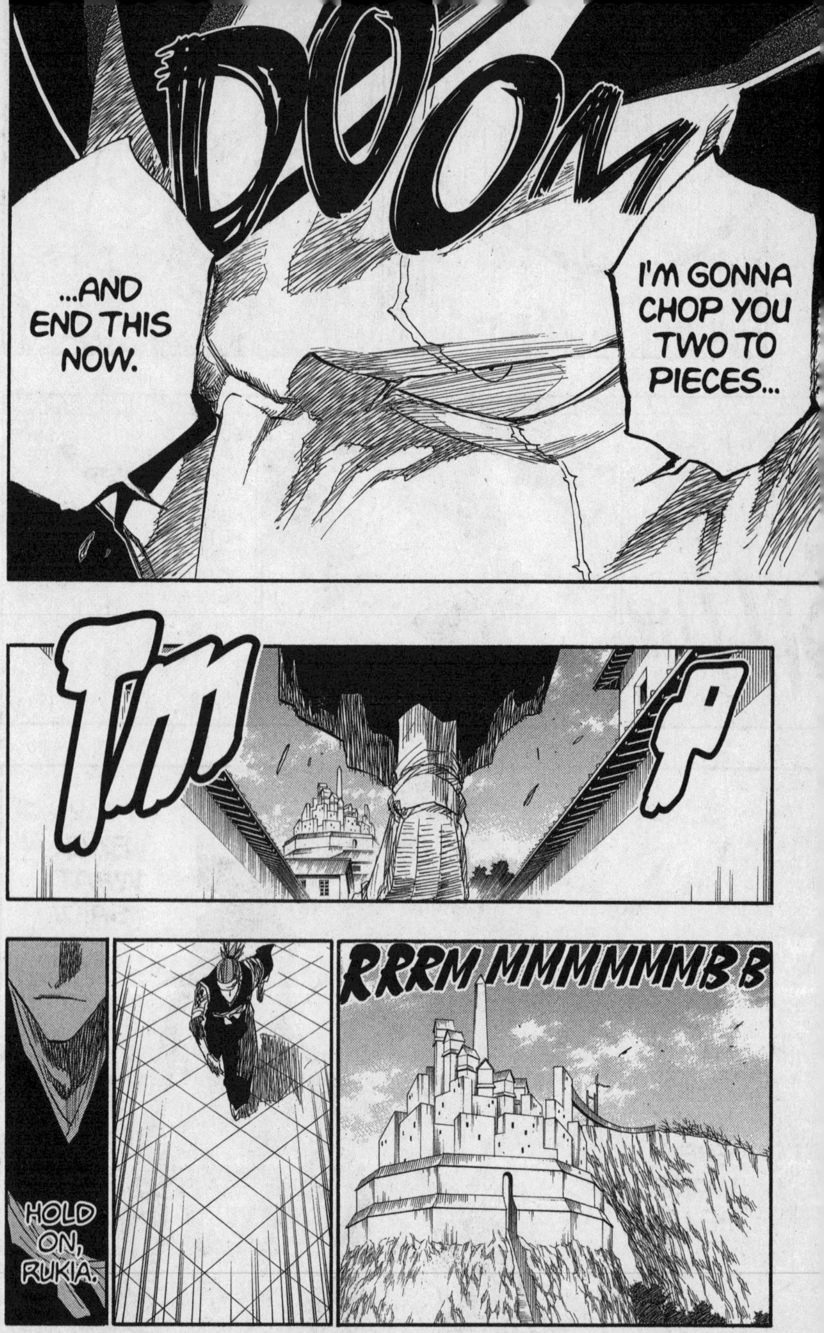
DOOOM
I'M GONNA CHOP YOU TWO TO PIECES...
...AND END THIS NOW.
TMP
RRRM MMMMMMB B
HOLD ON, RUKIA.

READ THIS WAY

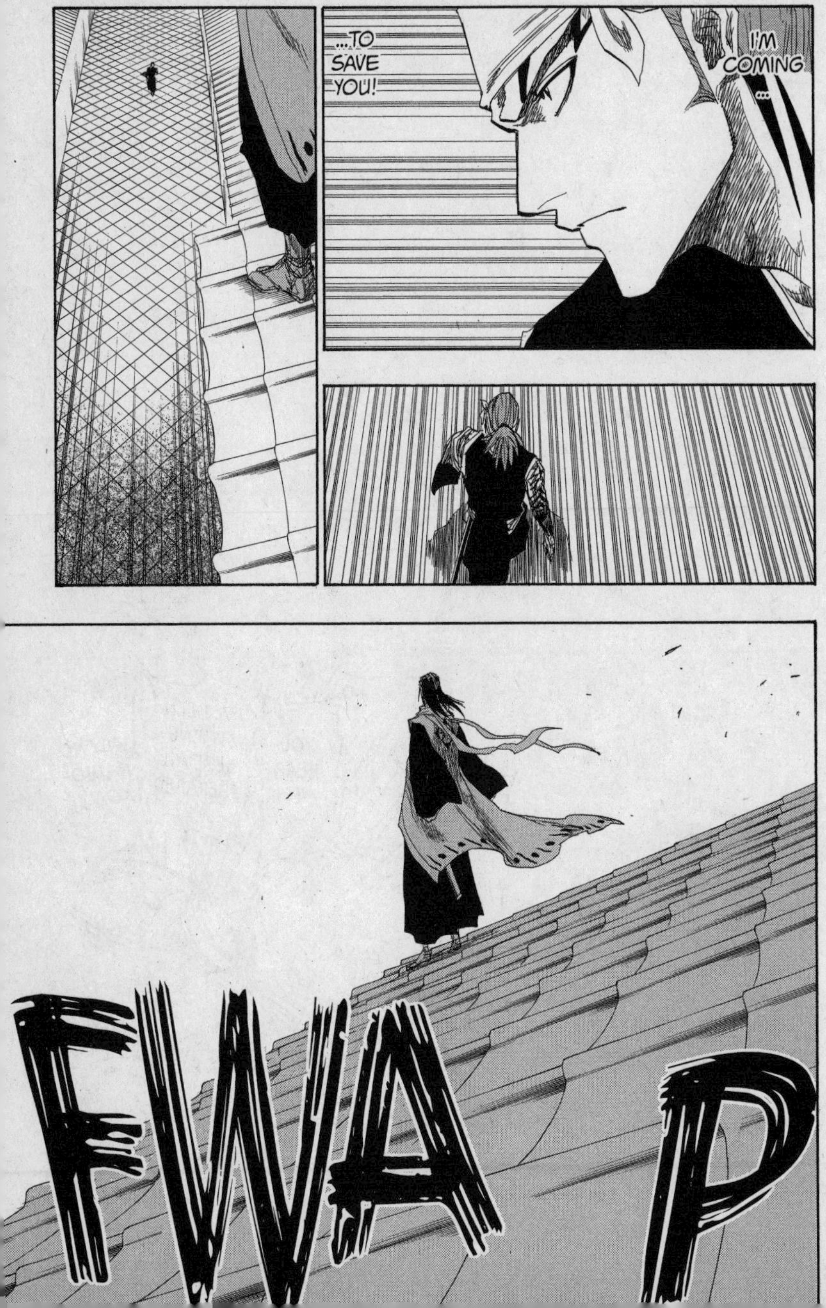
I'M COMING...
...TO SAVE YOU!
FWAP

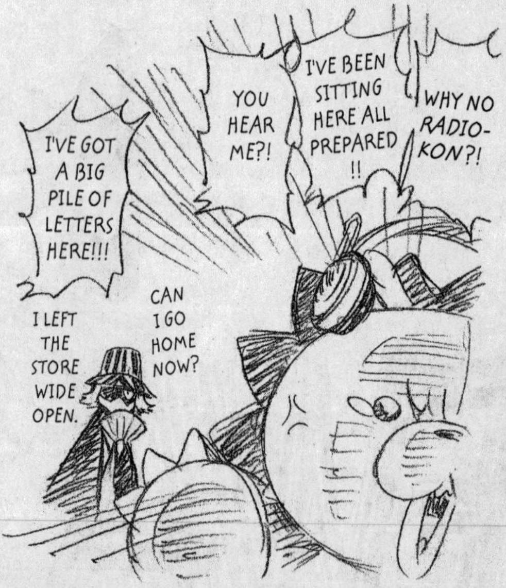
WHY NO RADIO-KON?!
I'VE BEEN SITTING HERE ALL PREPARED !!
YOU HEAR ME?!
I'VE GOT A BIG PILE OF LETTERS HERE!!!
CAN I GO HOME NOW?
I LEFT THE STORE WIDE OPEN.

The first ever *Bleach* game has been released (it's been out for a while) for the world's most anticipated console, the PSP (PlayStation Portable)! I don't know what to say except that it's really cutting-edge. This game is every boy's dream—a fighting game! Naturally, the first time you play, you've got to be Ichigo. But on my very first go, I got my butt kicked by Orihime! C'mon, Ichigo, you can do better than that.

-Tite Kubo, 2005

Red like blood
White like bone
Red like solitude
White like silence
Red like the senses of a beast
White like the heart of a god
Red like molten hatred
White like chilling cries of pain
Red like the shadows that feed on the night
Like a sigh piercing the moon
It shines white and scatters red

BLEACH17

ROSA RUBICUNDIOR, LILIO CANDIDIOR

STARS AND

柊木白哉

Byakuya Kuchiki

Rukia Kuchiki

朽木ルキア

Renji Abarai

阿散井恋次

plot

As Rukia's date with death looms ever nearer, Ichigo struggles desperately to achieve Bankai. Meanwhile, Orihime and the others, lacking a leader, enlist the aid of the fearsome Kenpachi Zaraki. And Renji, fearing that Ichigo will be too late to save Rukia, goes to save her himself, only to be intercepted by the deadly Byakuya Kuchiki!

BLEACH ALL

東仙要

Kaname Tôsen

市丸ギン

Gin Ichimaru

Kenpachi Zaraki

更木剣八

STORIES

BLEACH17

ROSA RUBICUNDIOR, LILIO CANDIDIOR

Contents

140. Bite at the Moon

I WAS AFRAID...

PRETENDING TO CHASE...
PRETENDING TO SHARPEN MY FANGS...

BUT IN TRUTH, I WAS AFRAID...

...TO EVEN STEP ON YOUR SHADOW.

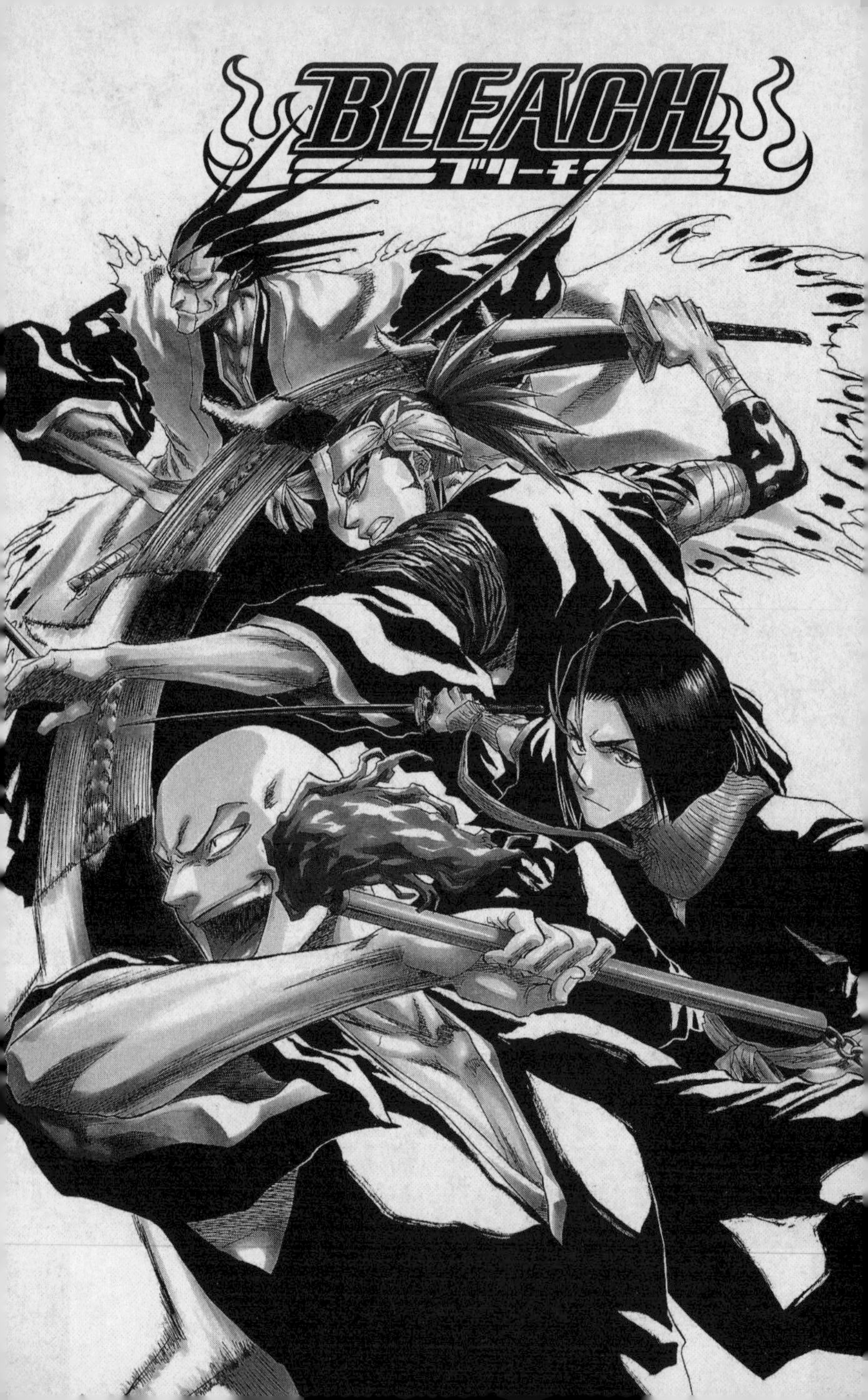
BLEACH
ブリーチ

140. Bite at the Moon

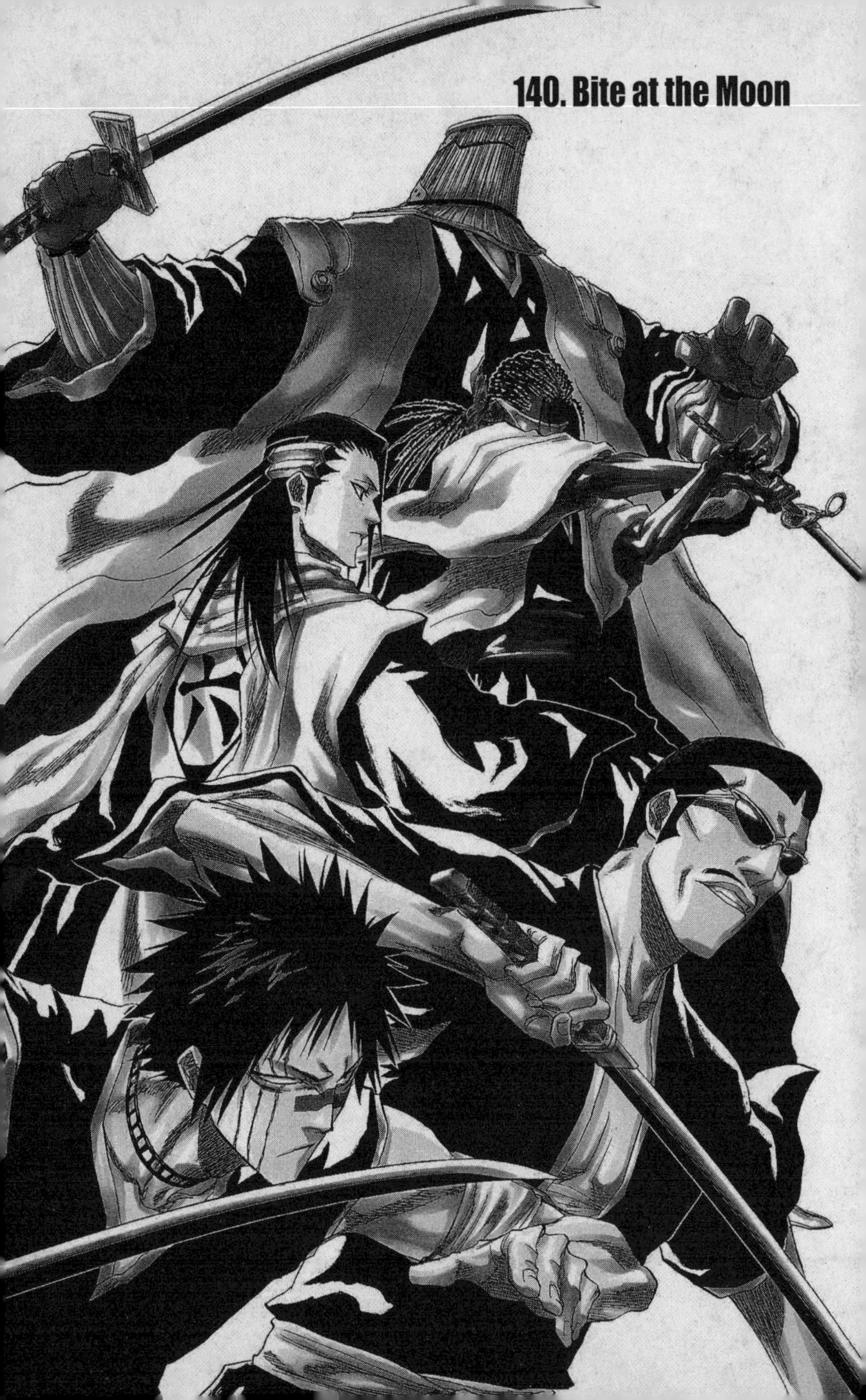

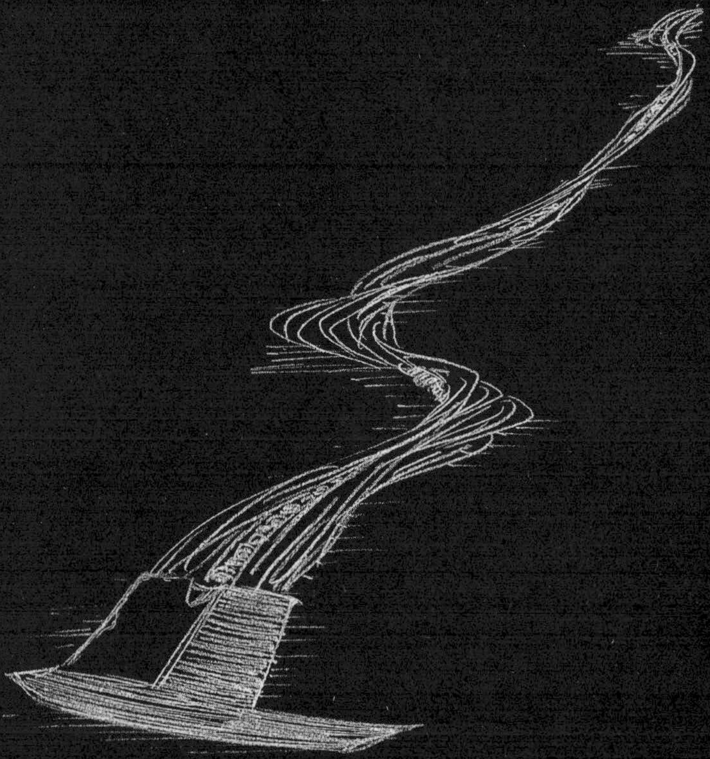

BLEACH
ブリーチ

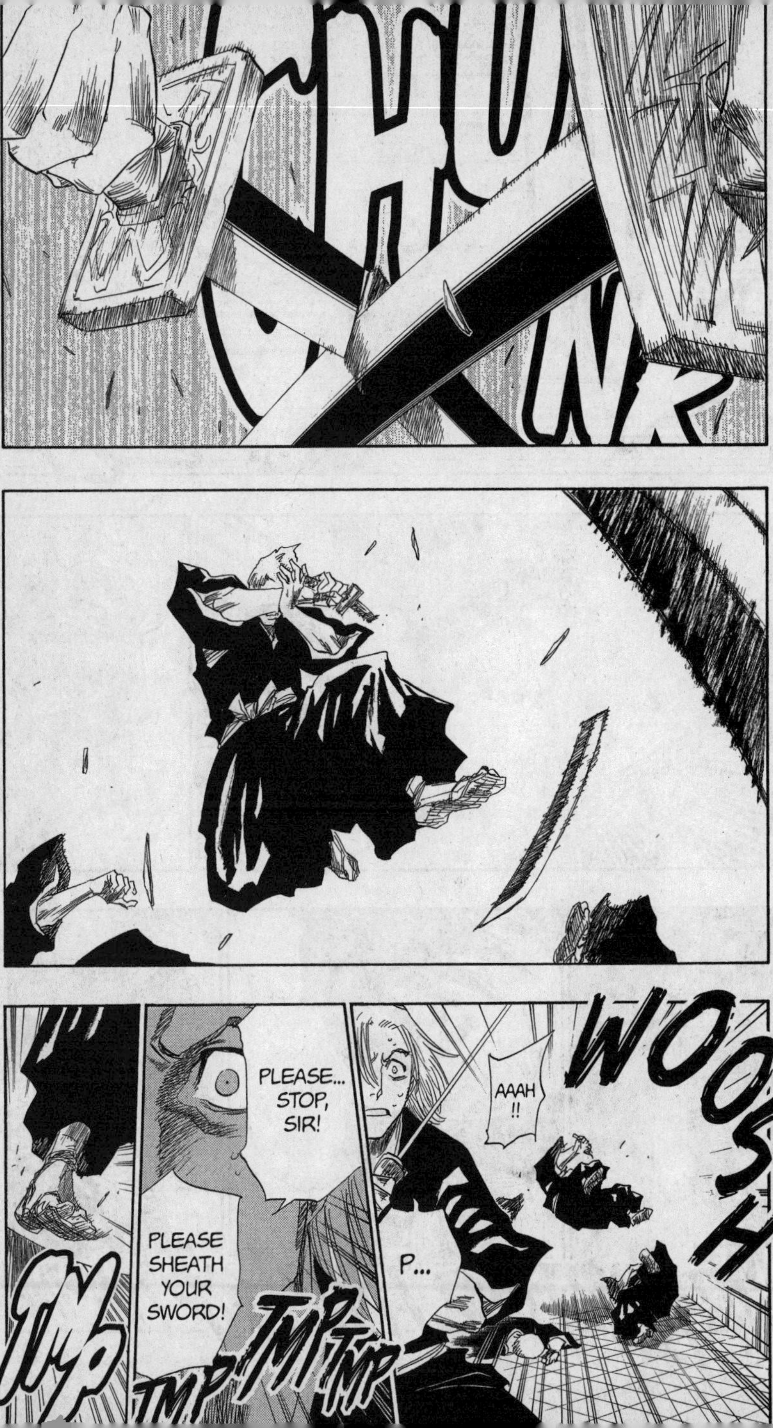
WOOSH
AAAH !!
P...
TMP TMP
PLEASE... STOP, SIR!
PLEASE SHEATH YOUR SWORD!
TMP
TMP

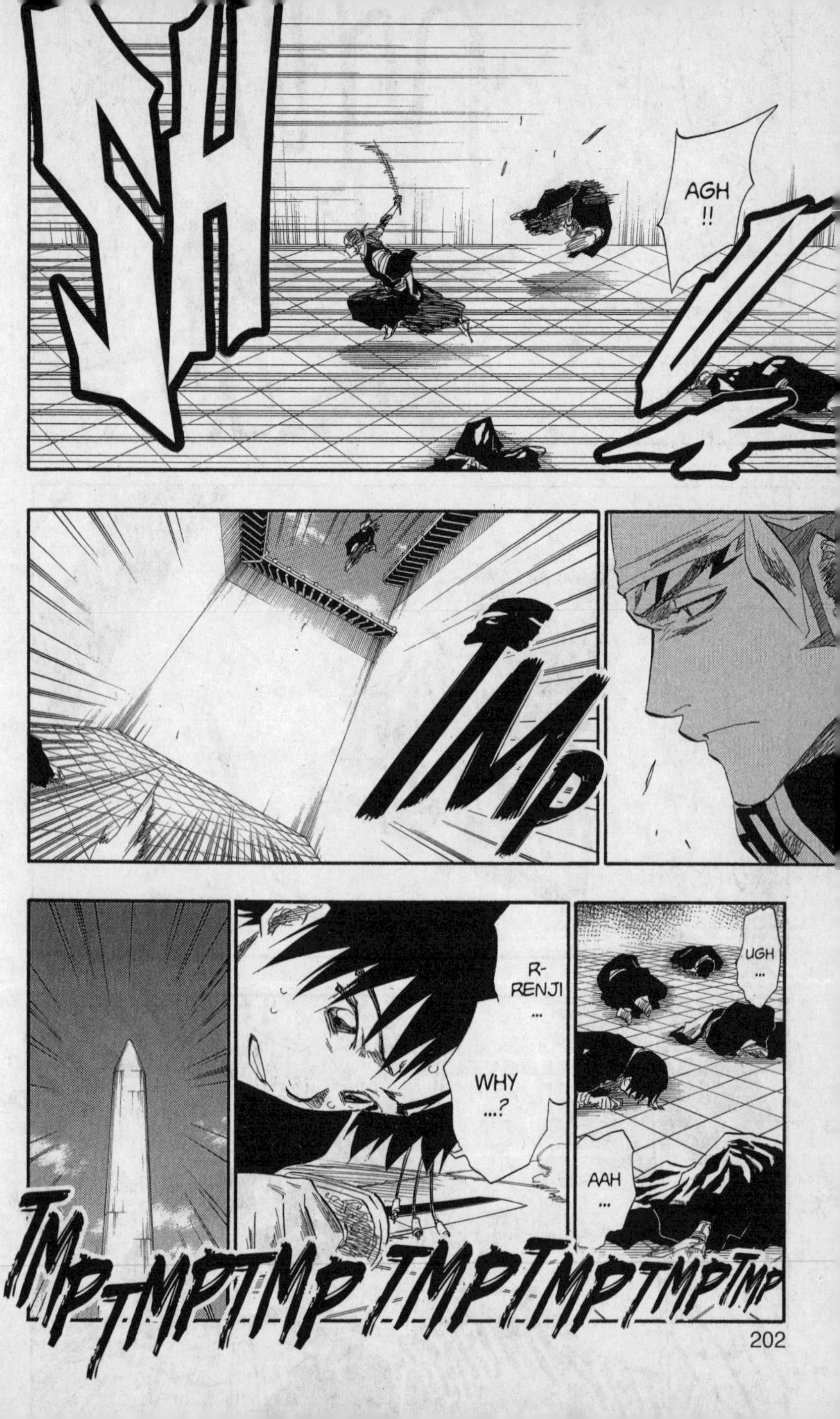
AGH !!
SH
TMP
UGH ...
AAH ...
R-RENJI ...
WHY ...?
TMPTMPTMP TMPTMPTMPTMP

READ THIS WAY

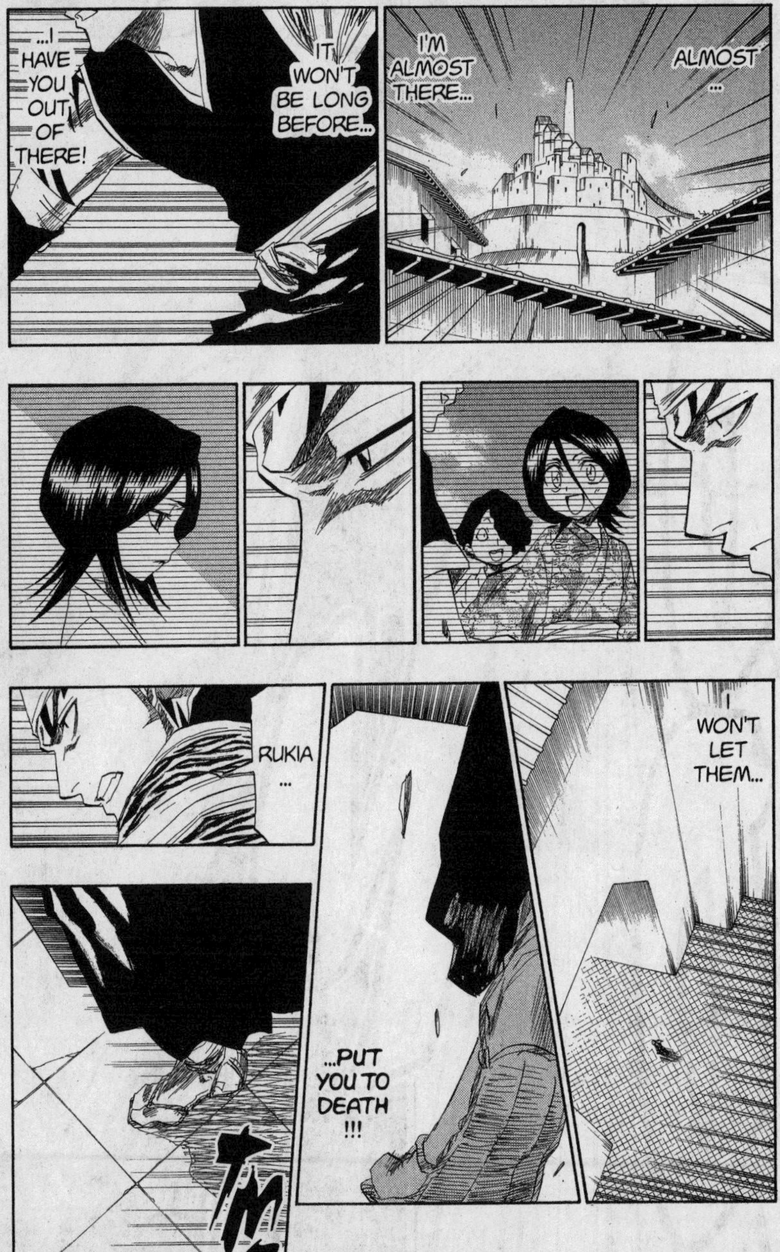
ALMOST ...
I'M ALMOST THERE...
IT WON'T BE LONG BEFORE...
...I HAVE YOU OUT OF THERE!
I WON'T LET THEM...
...PUT YOU TO DEATH !!!
RUKIA ...
TMP

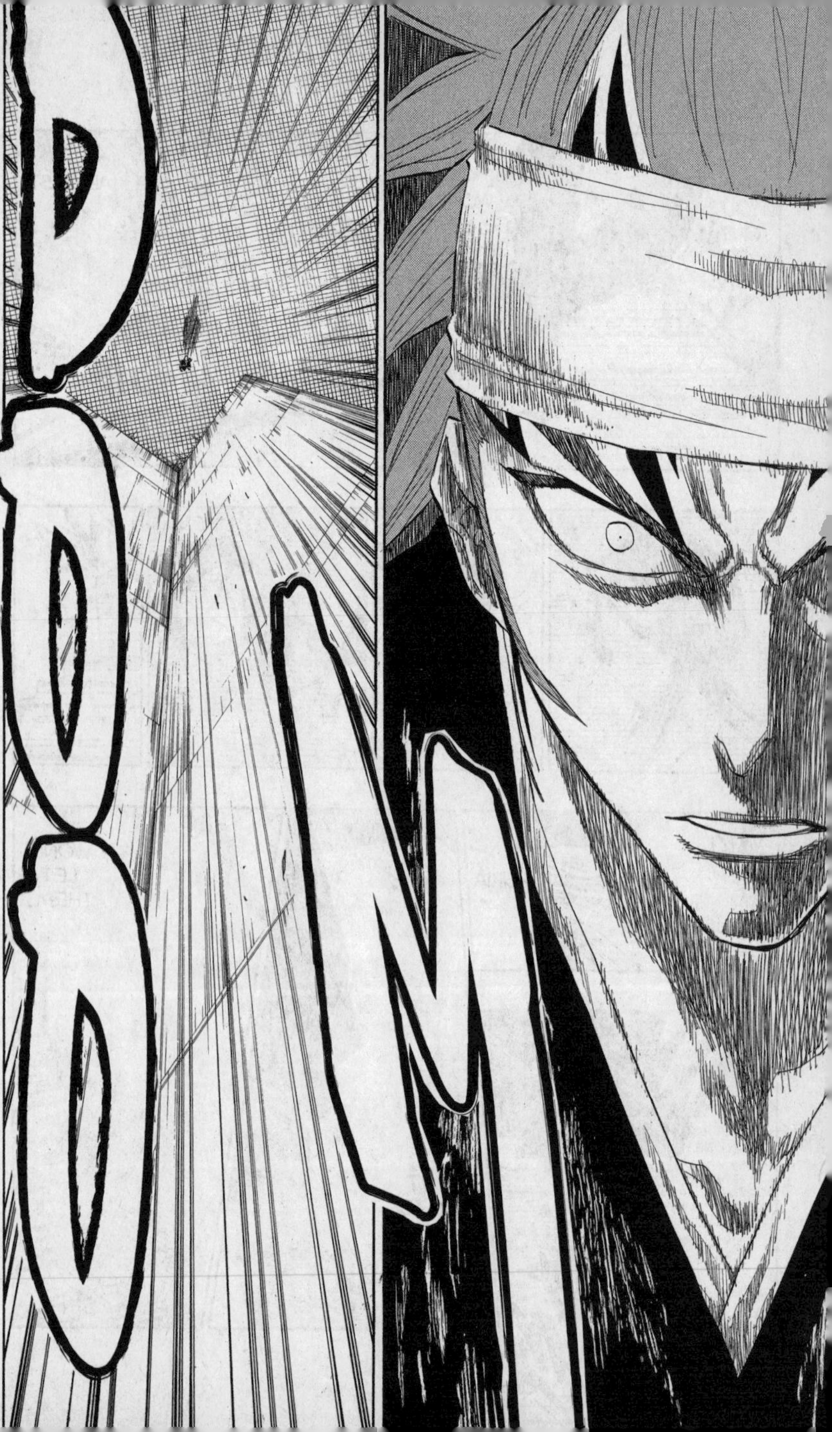
DOOM

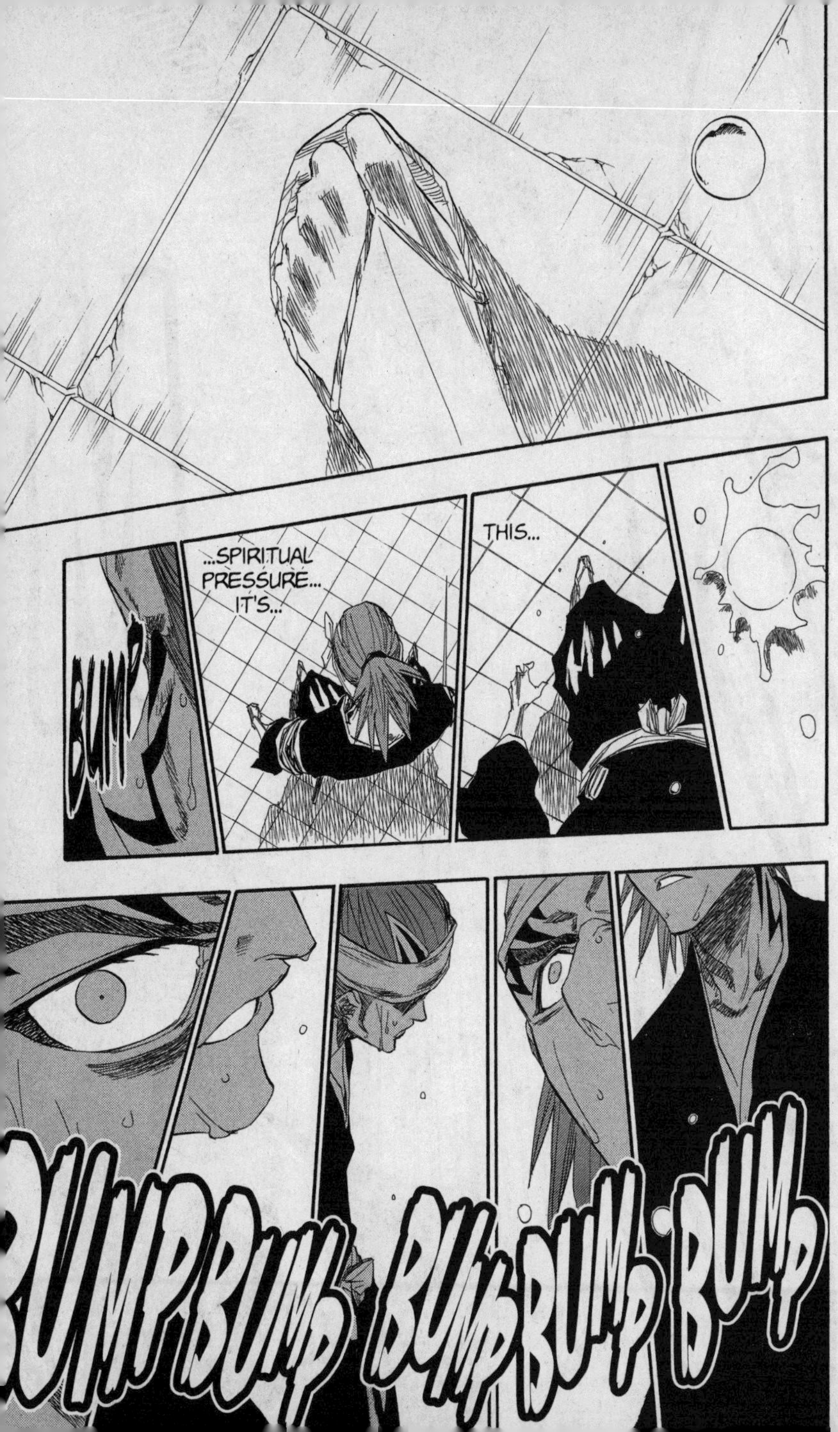
THIS...
...SPIRITUAL PRESSURE... IT'S...
BUMP
BUMP BUMP BUMP BUMP BUMP

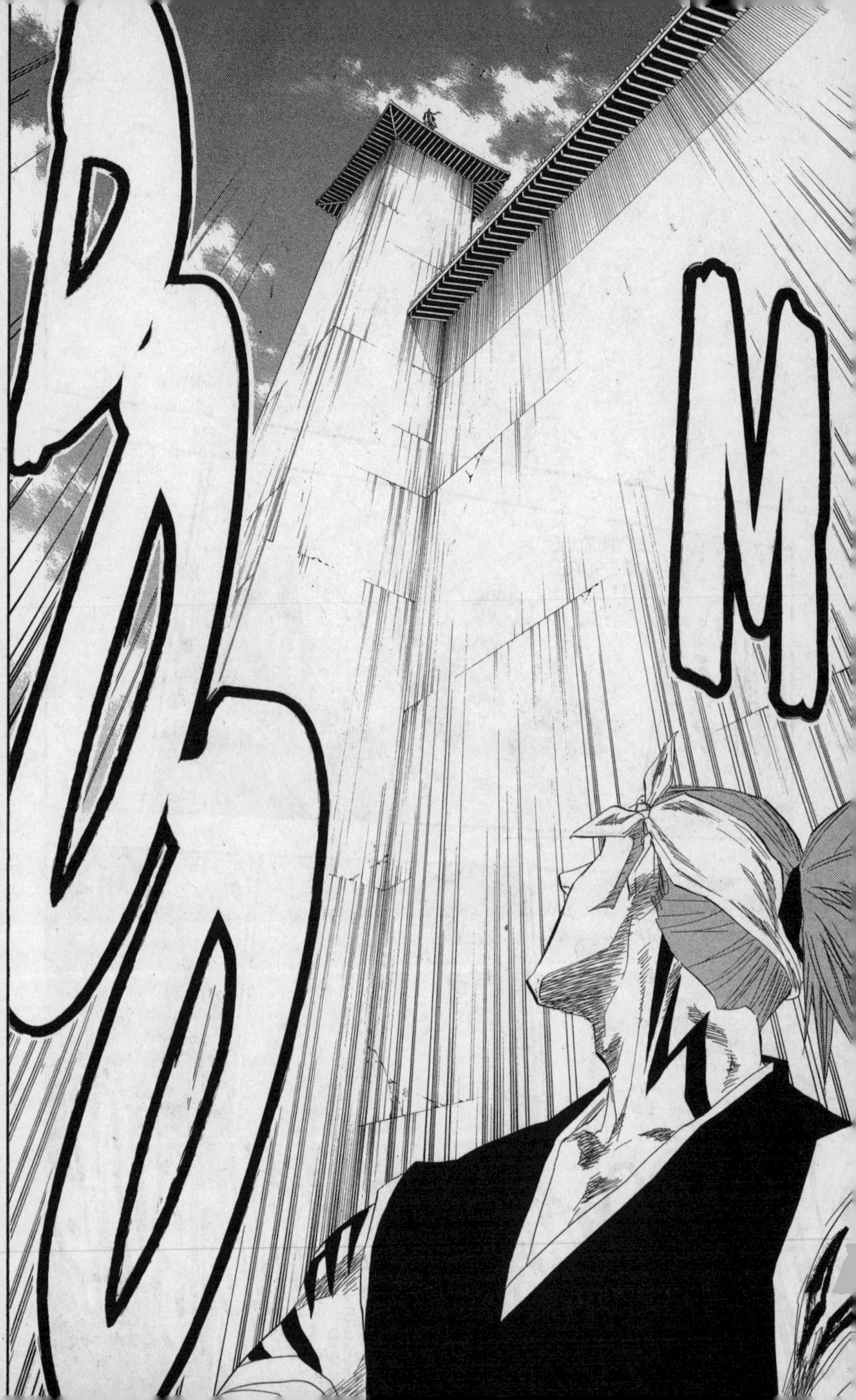
M

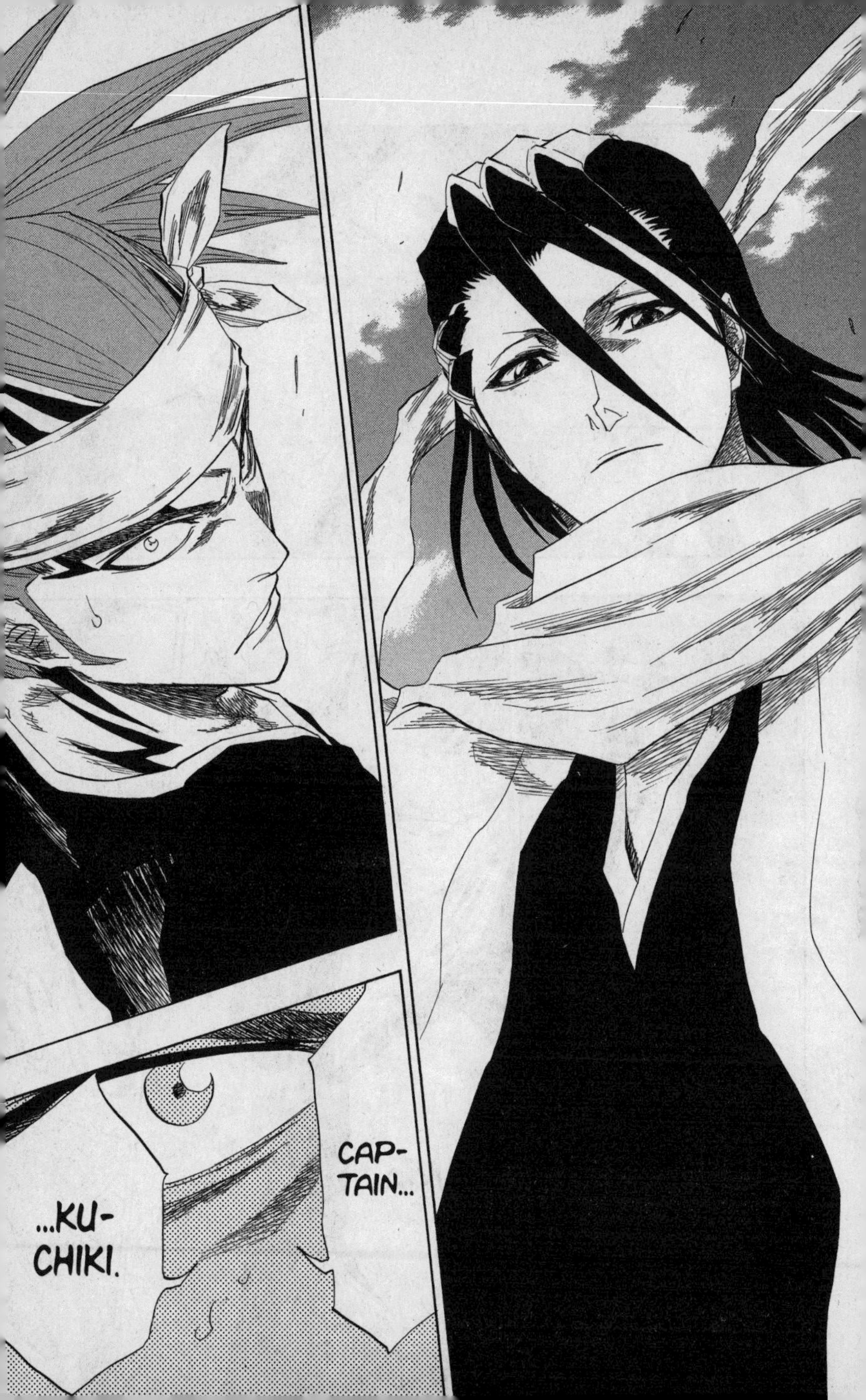
CAP-
TAIN...
...KU-
CHIKI.

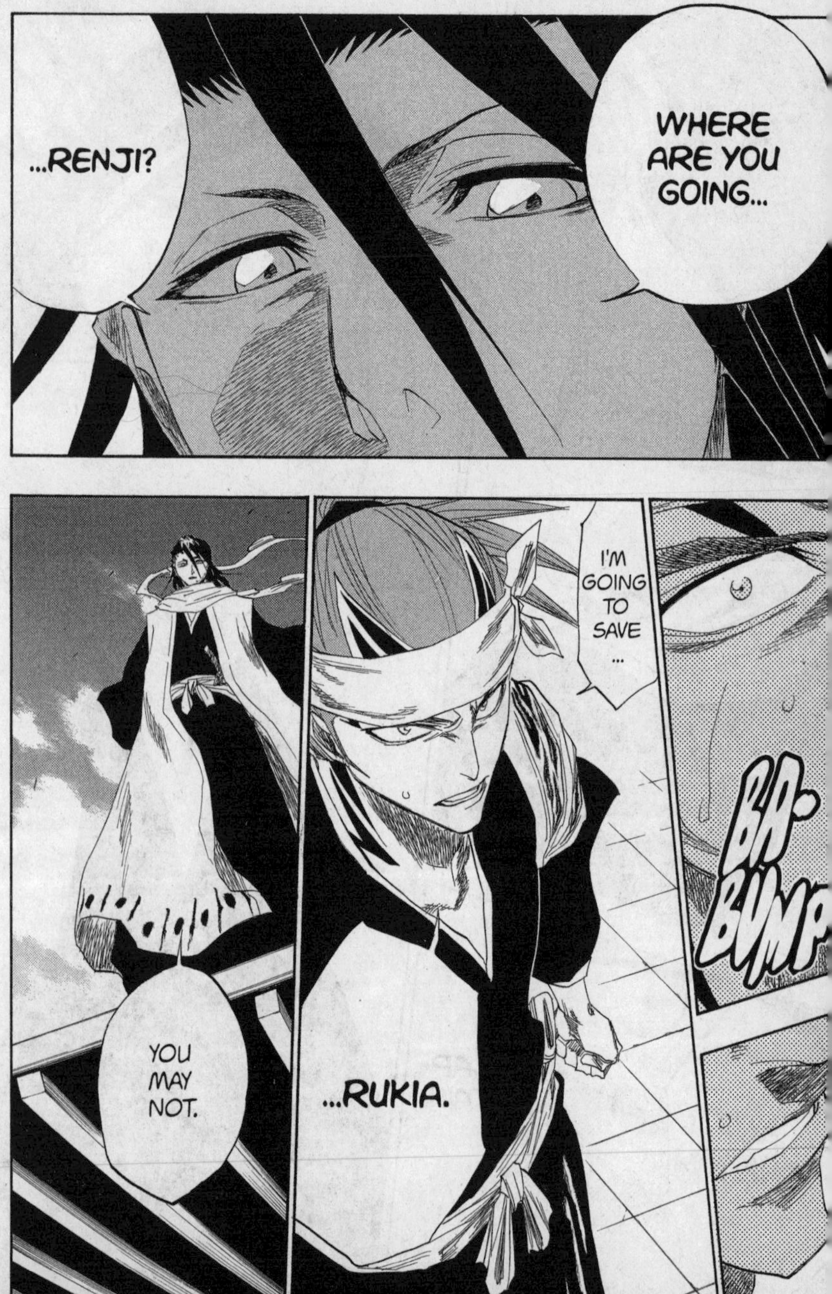
WHERE ARE YOU GOING...
...RENJI?
BA-BUMP
I'M GOING TO SAVE ...
...RUKIA.
YOU MAY NOT.

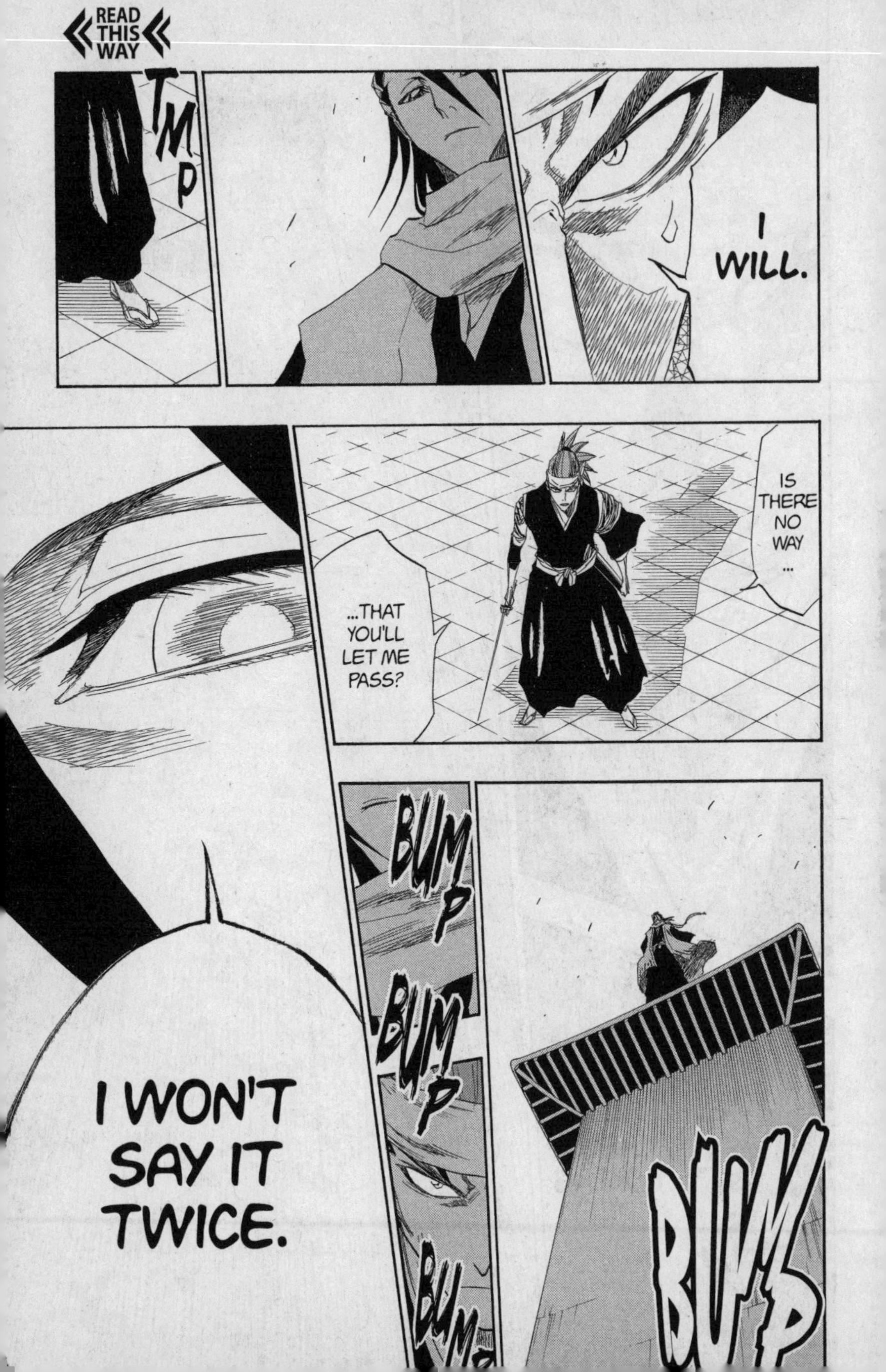
READ THIS WAY
I WILL.
TMP
IS THERE NO WAY ...
...THAT YOU'LL LET ME PASS?
I WON'T SAY IT TWICE.
BUMP
BUMP
BUMP
BUMP

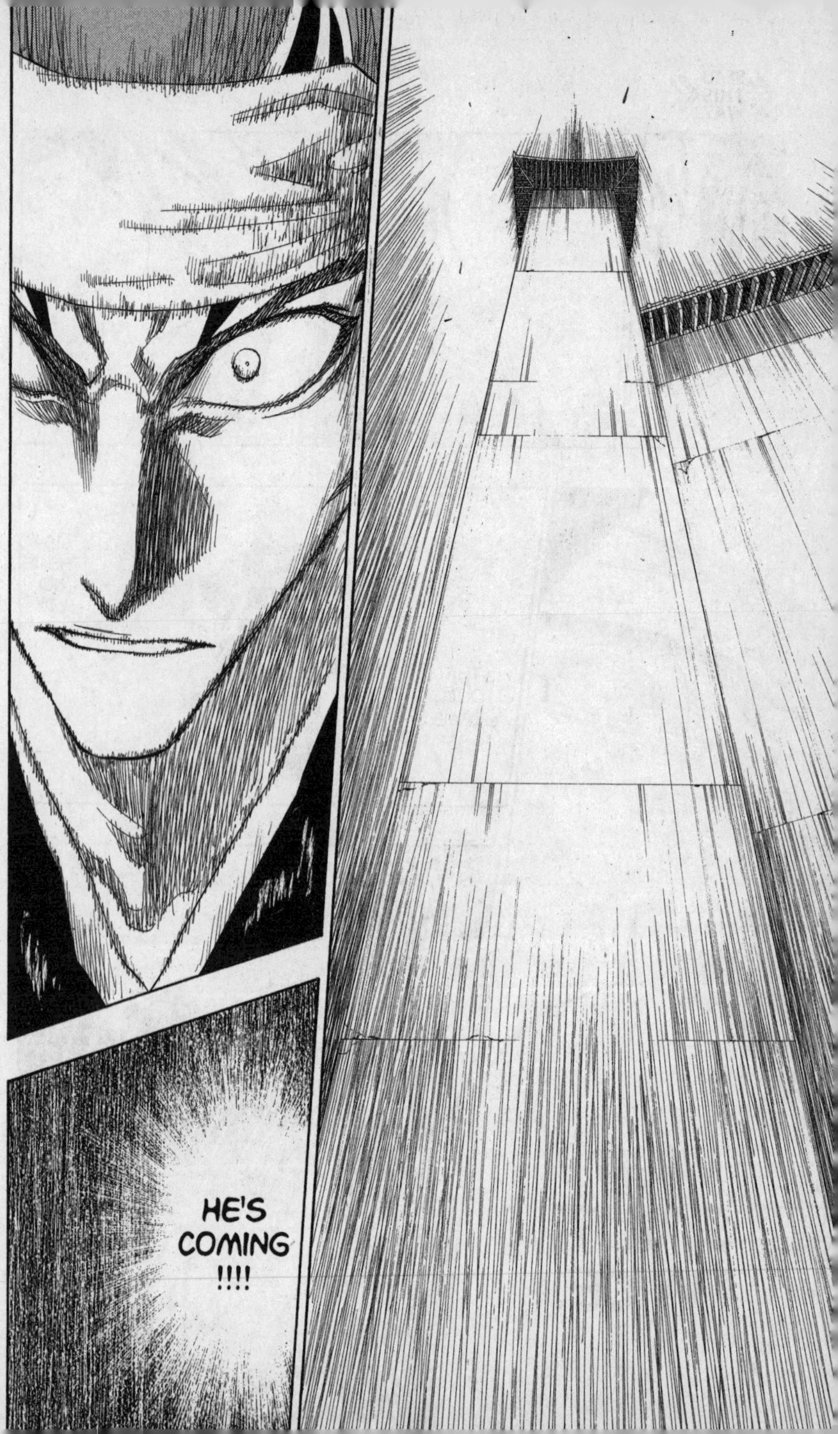
HE'S COMING !!!!

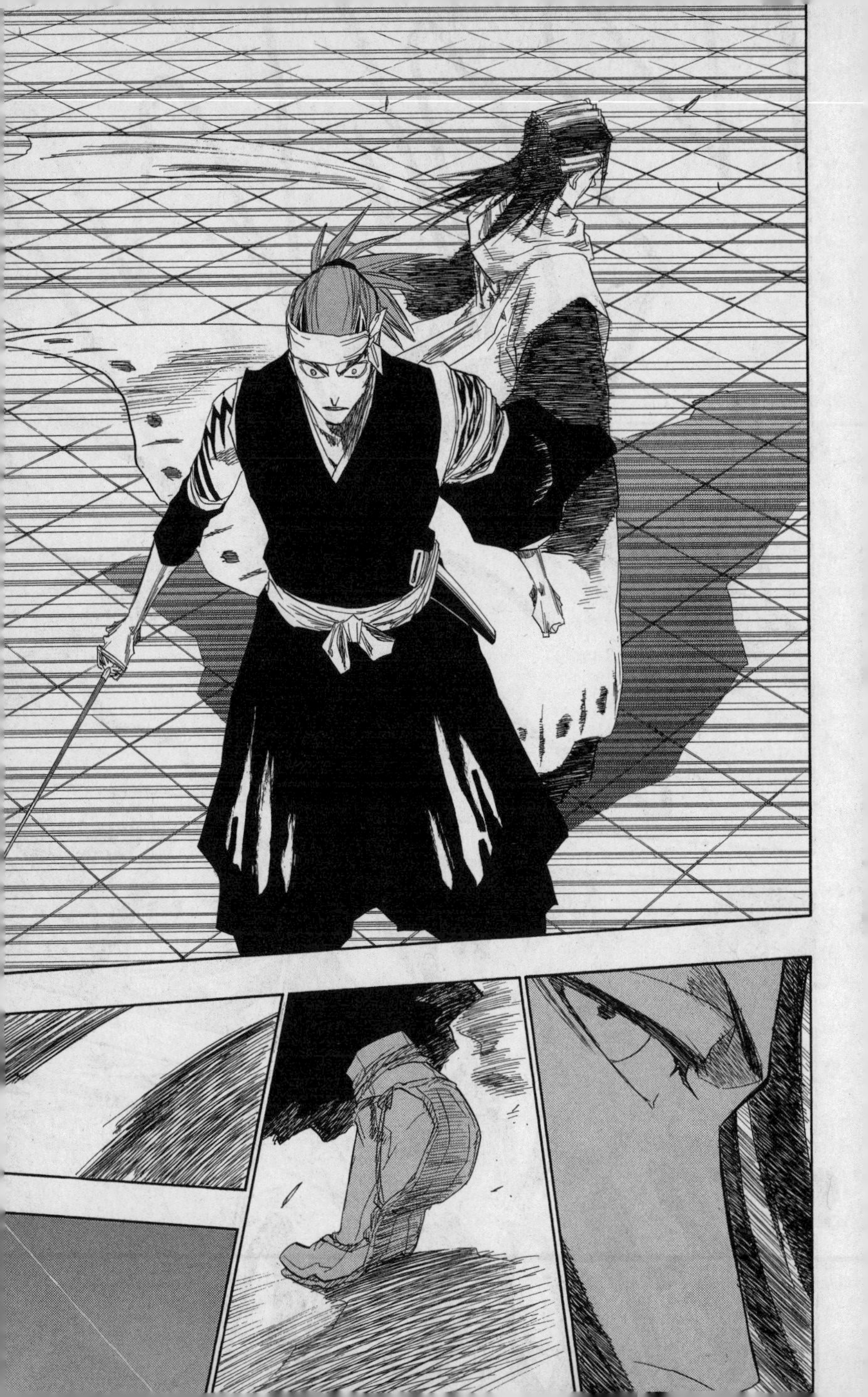

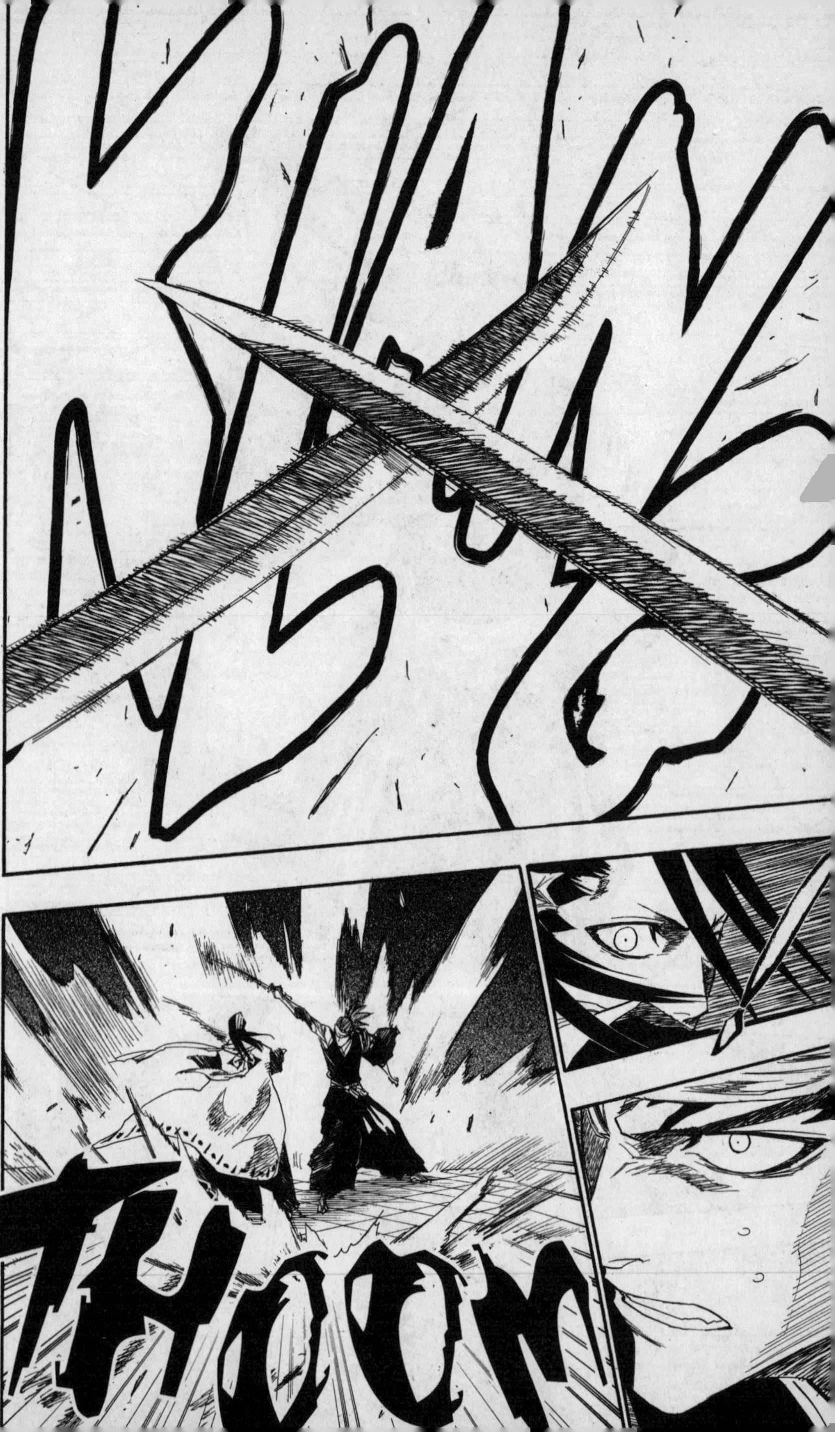
THOOM

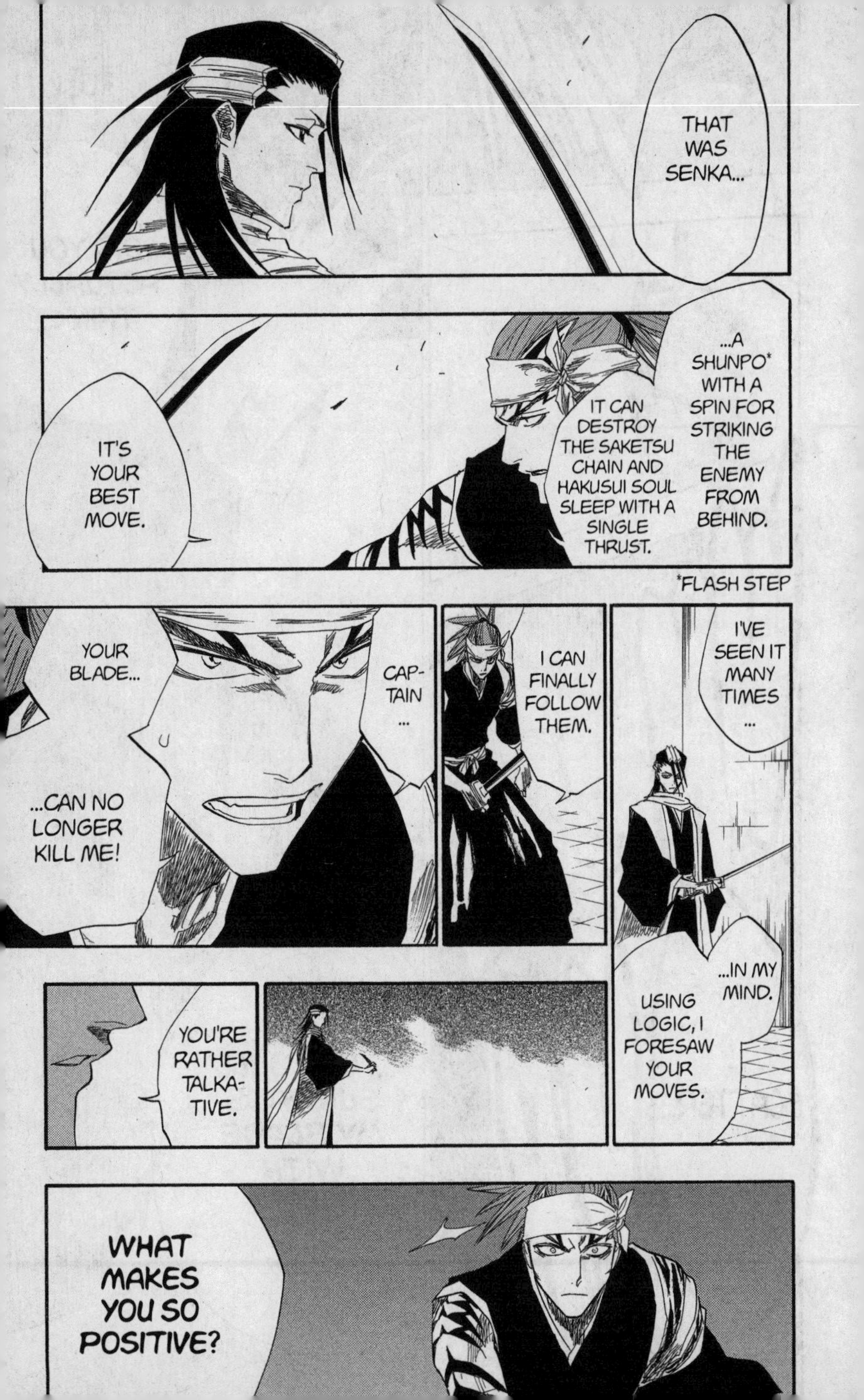
THAT WAS SENKA...
...A SHUNPO* WITH A SPIN FOR STRIKING THE ENEMY FROM BEHIND.
IT CAN DESTROY THE SAKETSU CHAIN AND HAKUSUI SOUL SLEEP WITH A SINGLE THRUST.
IT'S YOUR BEST MOVE.
*FLASH STEP
I'VE SEEN IT MANY TIMES...
...IN MY MIND.
USING LOGIC, I FORESAW YOUR MOVES.
I CAN FINALLY FOLLOW THEM.
CAPTAIN...
YOUR BLADE...
...CAN NO LONGER KILL ME!
YOU'RE RATHER TALKATIVE.
WHAT MAKES YOU SO POSITIVE?

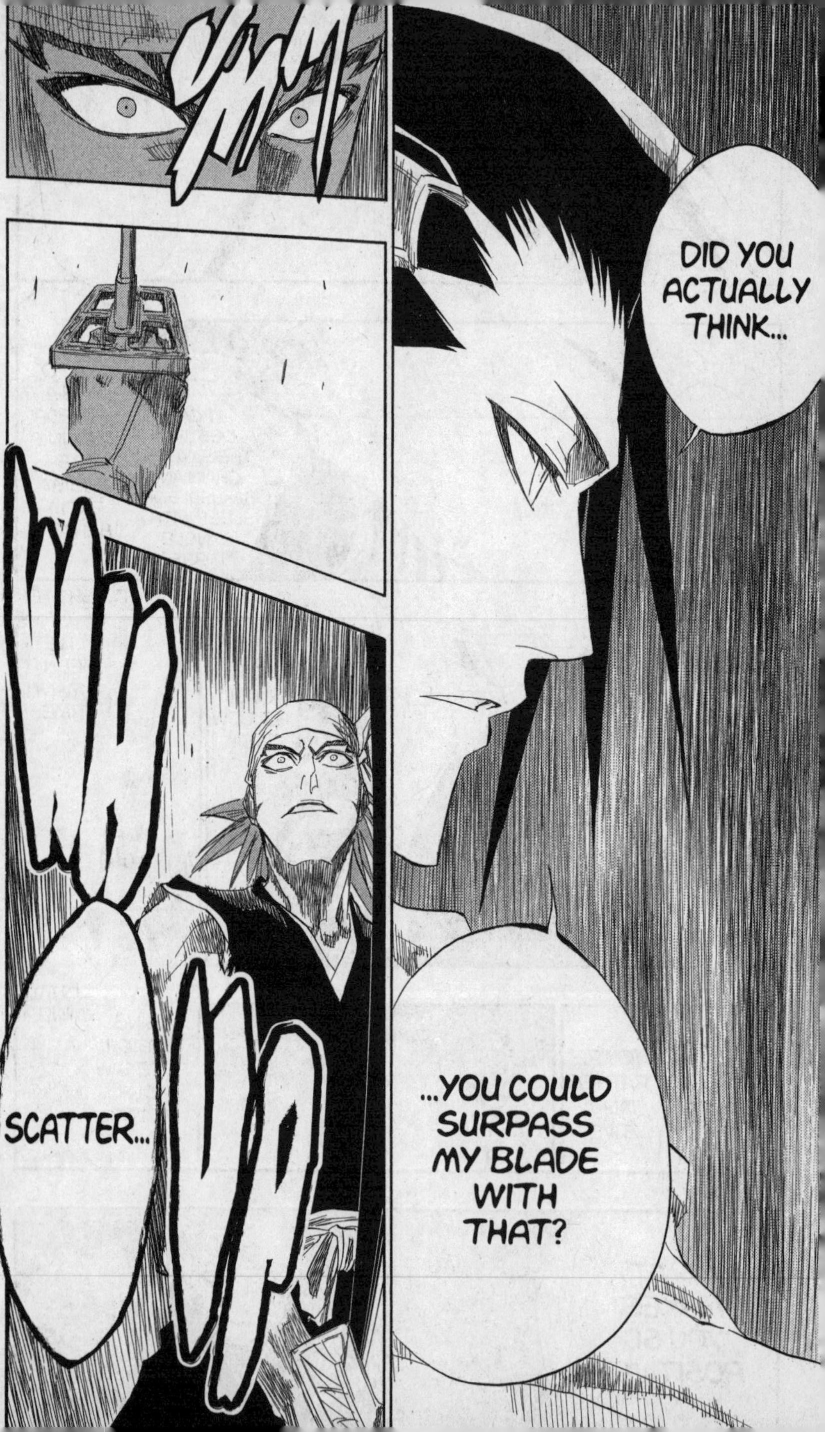
DID YOU ACTUALLY THINK...
...YOU COULD SURPASS MY BLADE WITH THAT?
SCATTER...

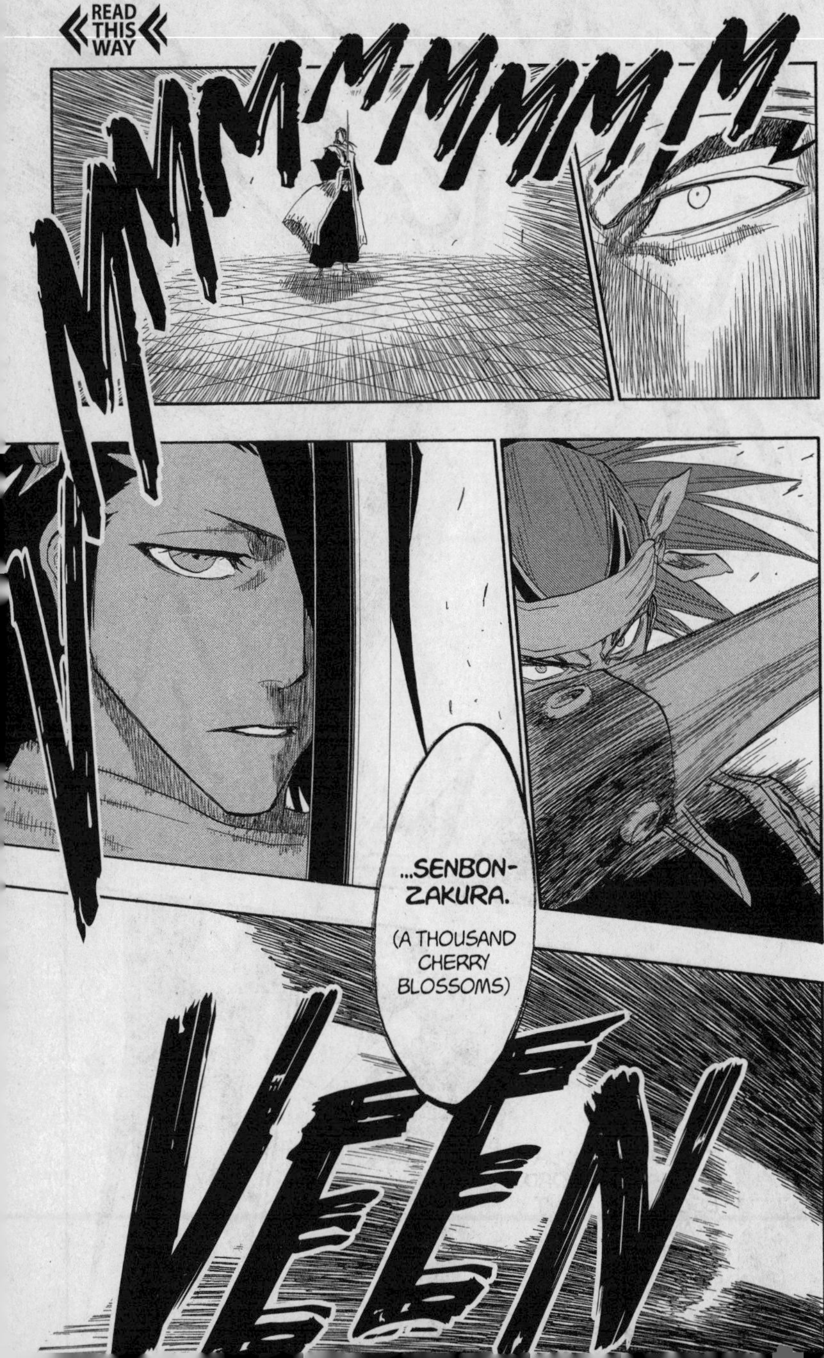
READ THIS WAY
MMMMMMMMM
...SENBON-ZAKURA.
(A THOUSAND CHERRY BLOSSOMS)
VEEN

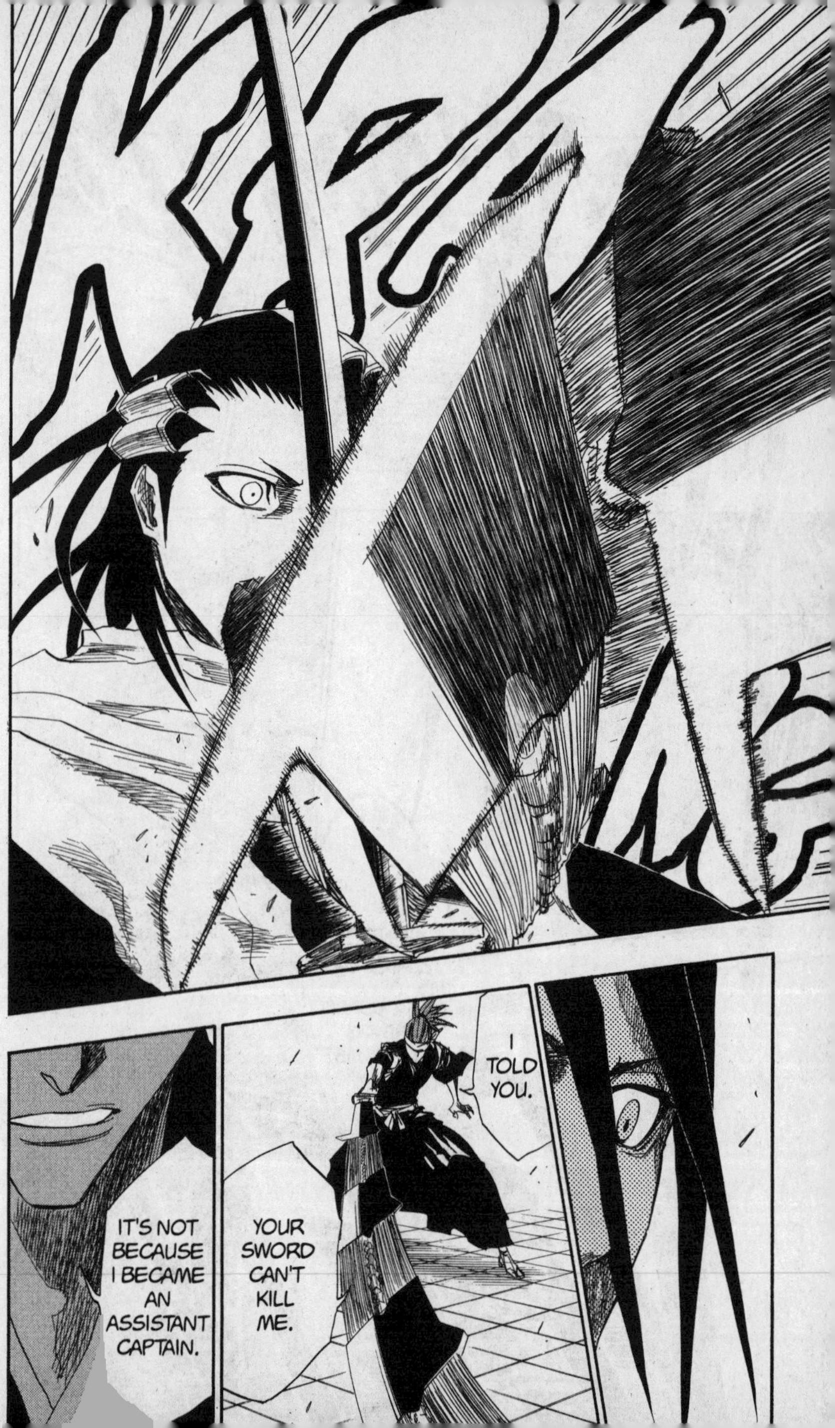
I TOLD YOU.
YOUR SWORD CAN'T KILL ME.
IT'S NOT BECAUSE I BECAME AN ASSISTANT CAPTAIN.

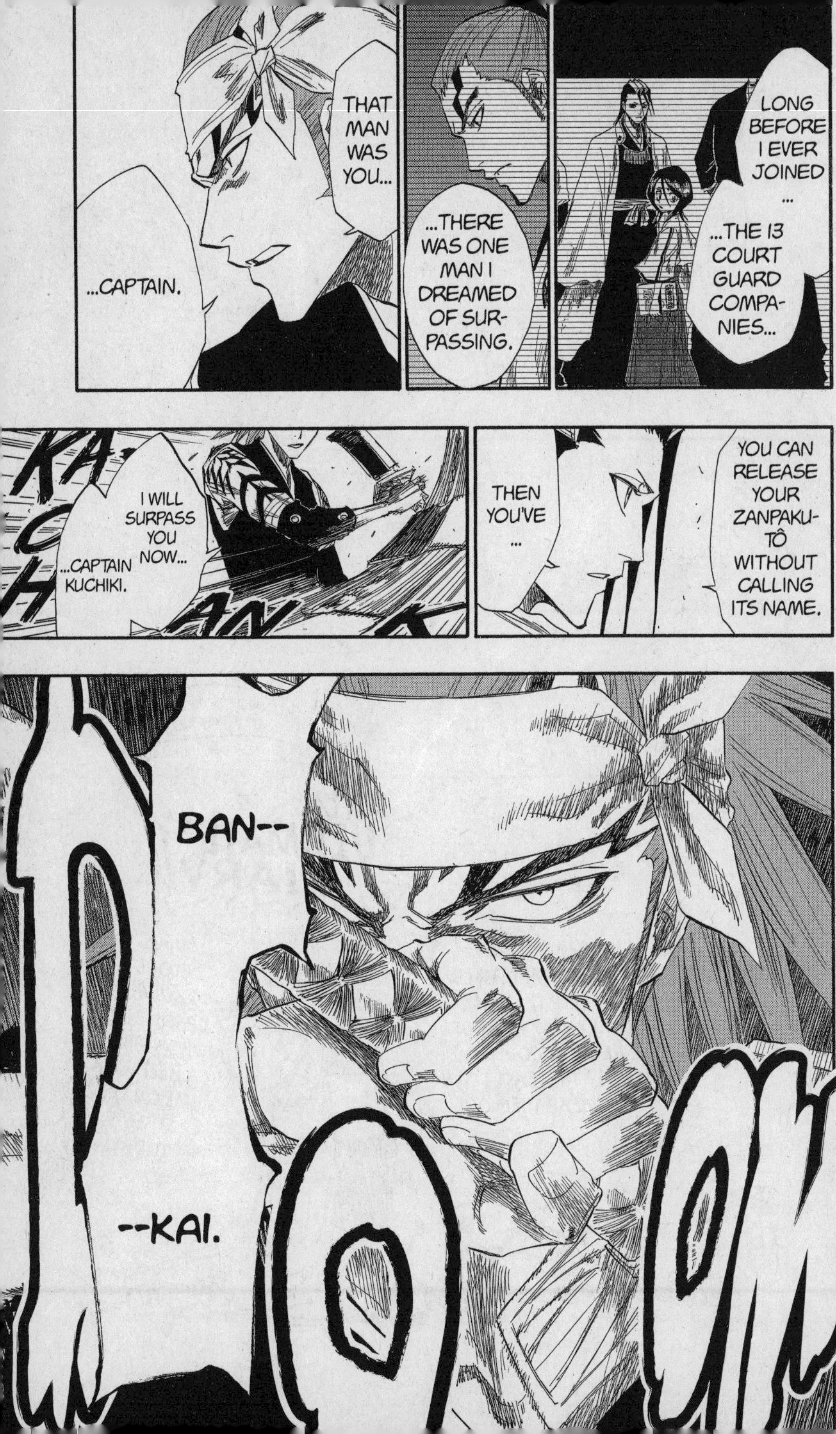
LONG BEFORE I EVER JOINED ...
...THE 13 COURT GUARD COMPANIES...
...THERE WAS ONE MAN I DREAMED OF SURPASSING.
THAT MAN WAS YOU...
...CAPTAIN.
YOU CAN RELEASE YOUR ZANPAKU-TÔ WITHOUT CALLING ITS NAME.
THEN YOU'VE ...
I WILL SURPASS YOU NOW...
...CAPTAIN KUCHIKI.
BAN--
--KAI.

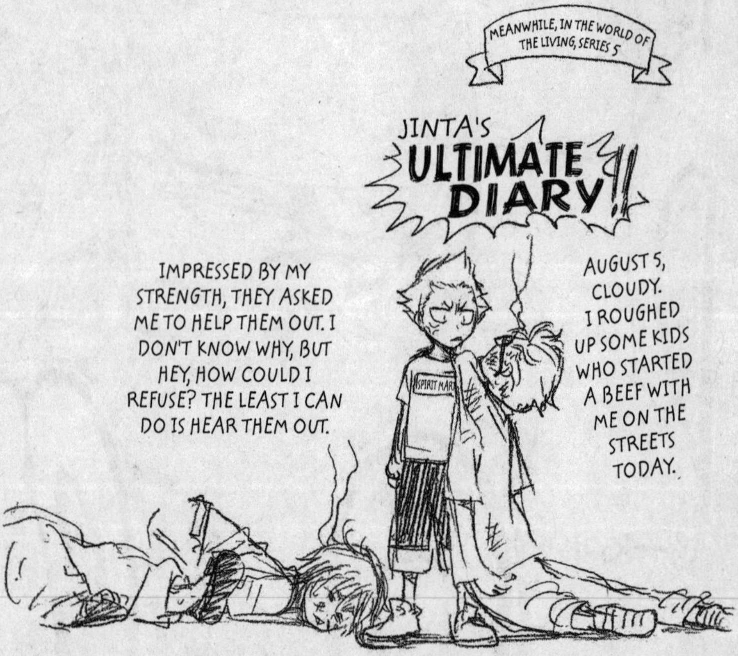
MEANWHILE, IN THE WORLD OF THE LIVING, SERIES 5
JINTA'S ULTIMATE DIARY!!
AUGUST 5, CLOUDY. I ROUGHED UP SOME KIDS WHO STARTED A BEEF WITH ME ON THE STREETS TODAY.
IMPRESSED BY MY STRENGTH, THEY ASKED ME TO HELP THEM OUT. I DON'T KNOW WHY, BUT HEY, HOW COULD I REFUSE? THE LEAST I CAN DO IS HEAR THEM OUT.
SPIRIT MART

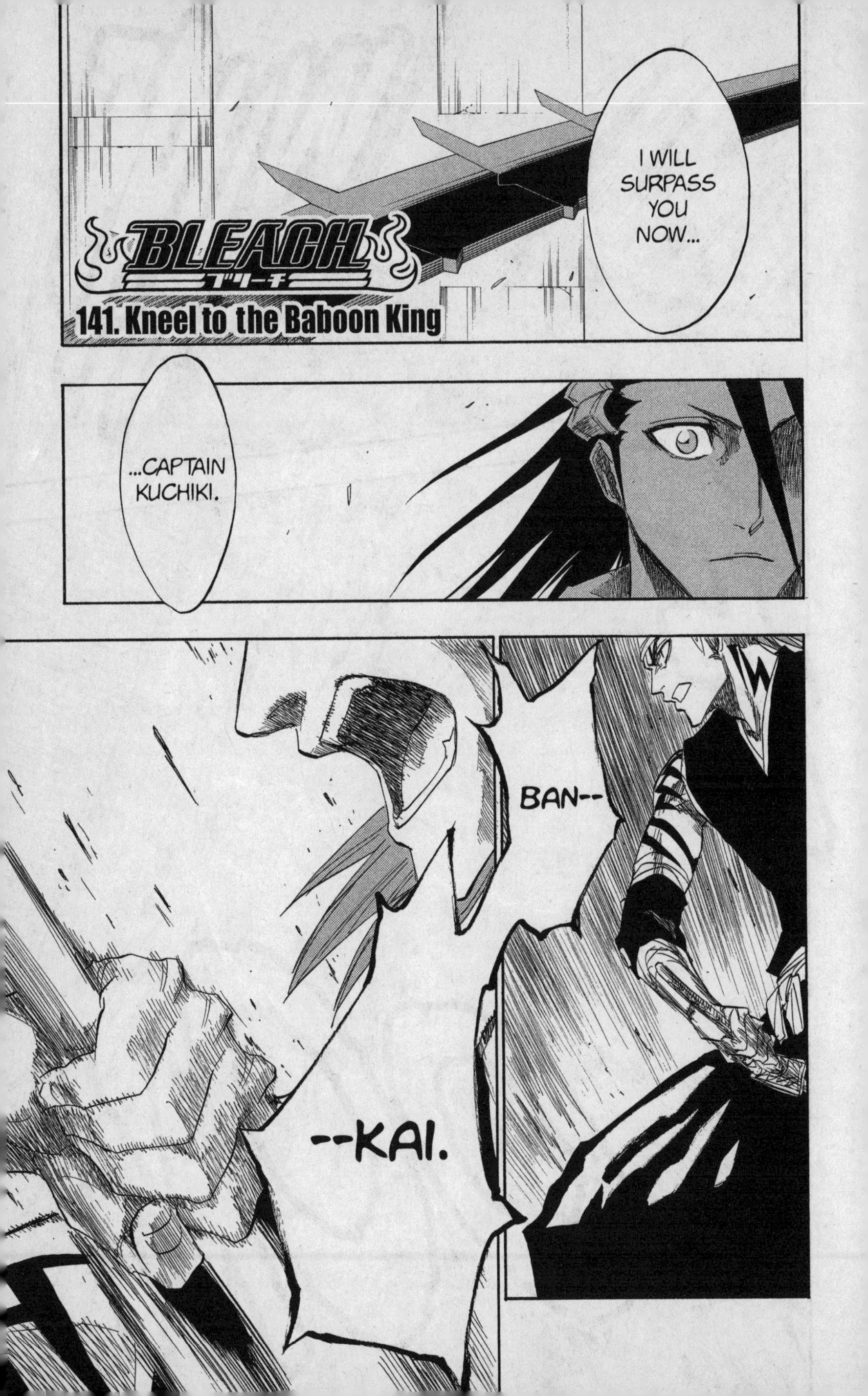
BLEACH
ブリーチ
141. Kneel to the Baboon King
I WILL SURPASS YOU NOW...
...CAPTAIN KUCHIKI.
BAN--
--KAI.

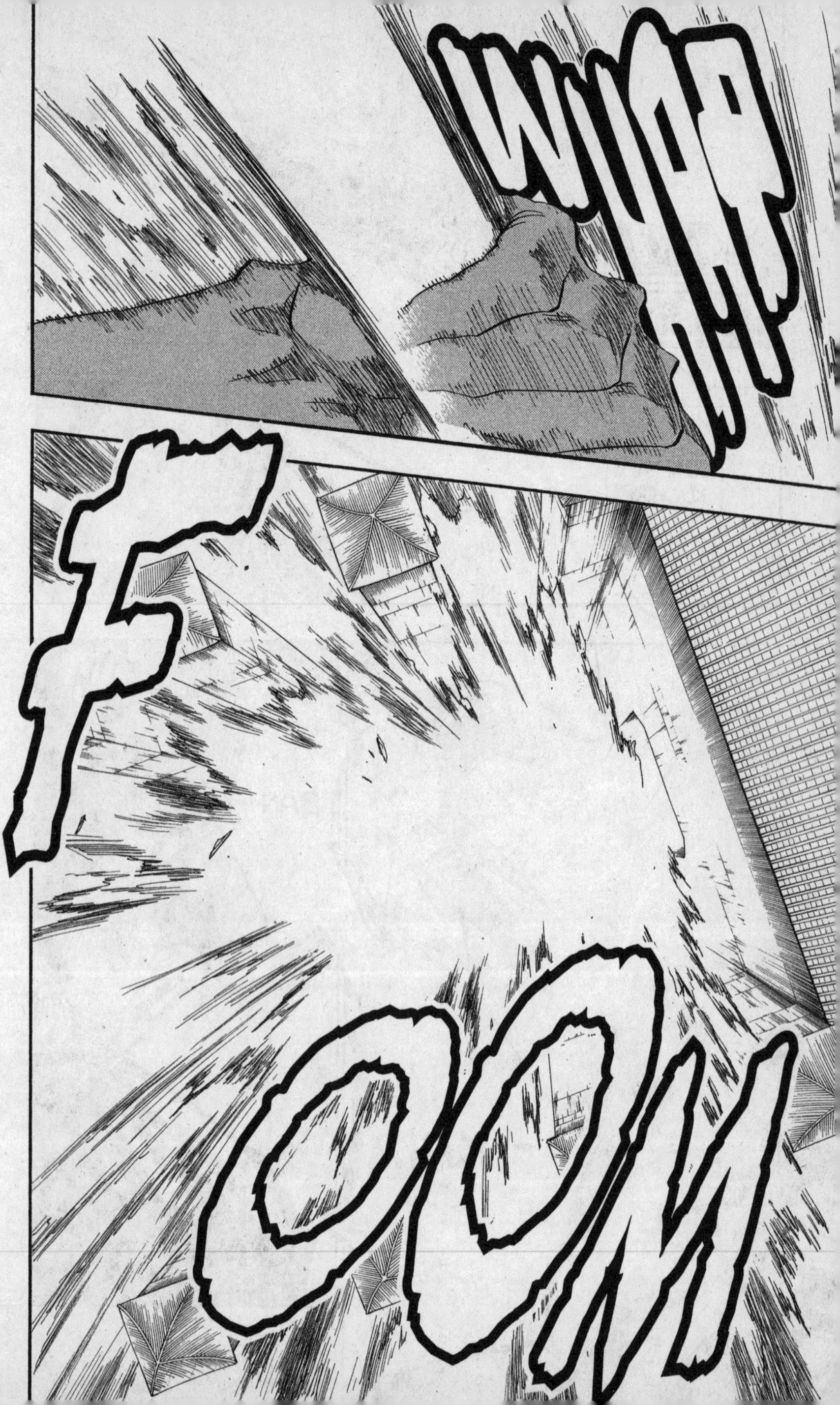
WHAP
FOOM

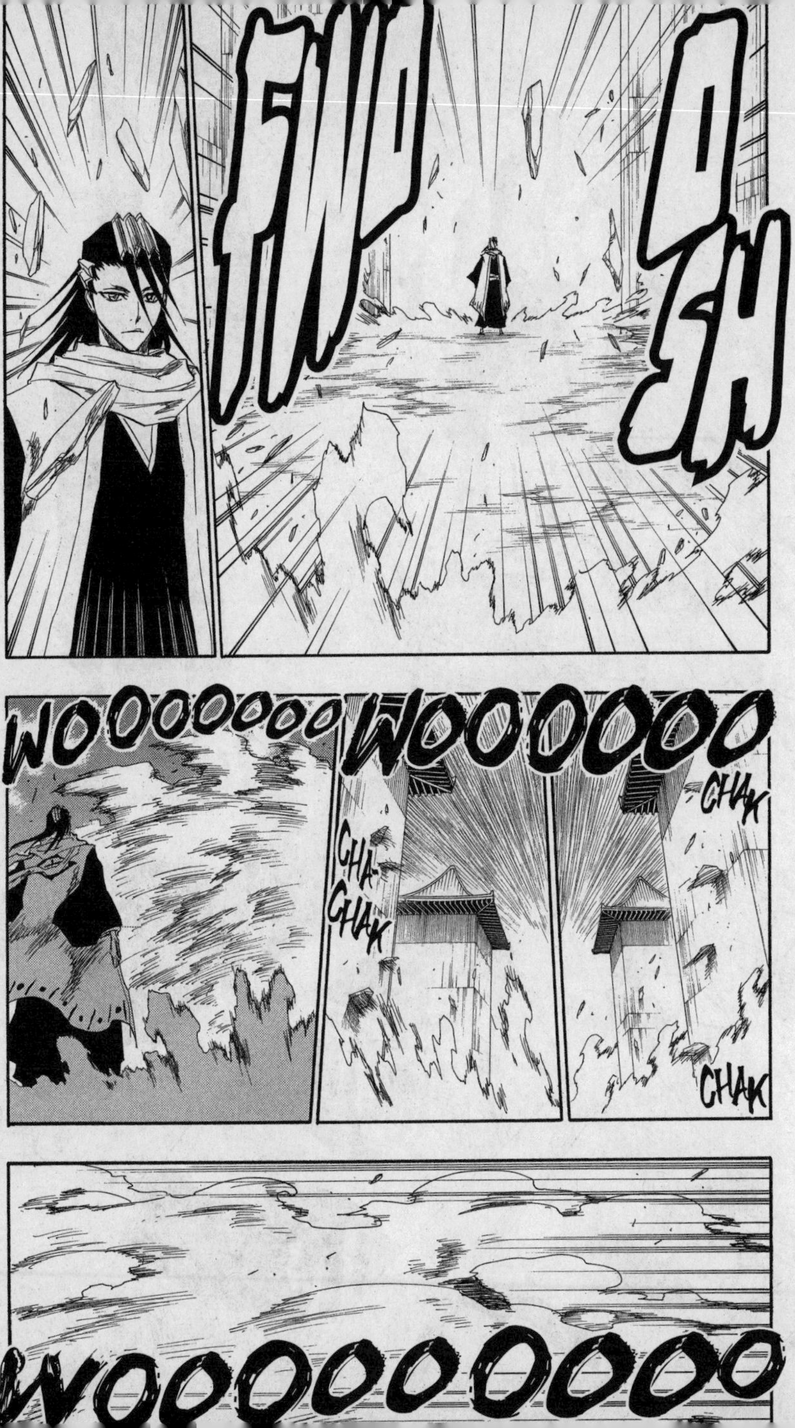
FWOOSH
WOOOOOOO
CHAK
CHAK
CHA CHAK
WOOOOOOO
WOOOOOOOOOOO

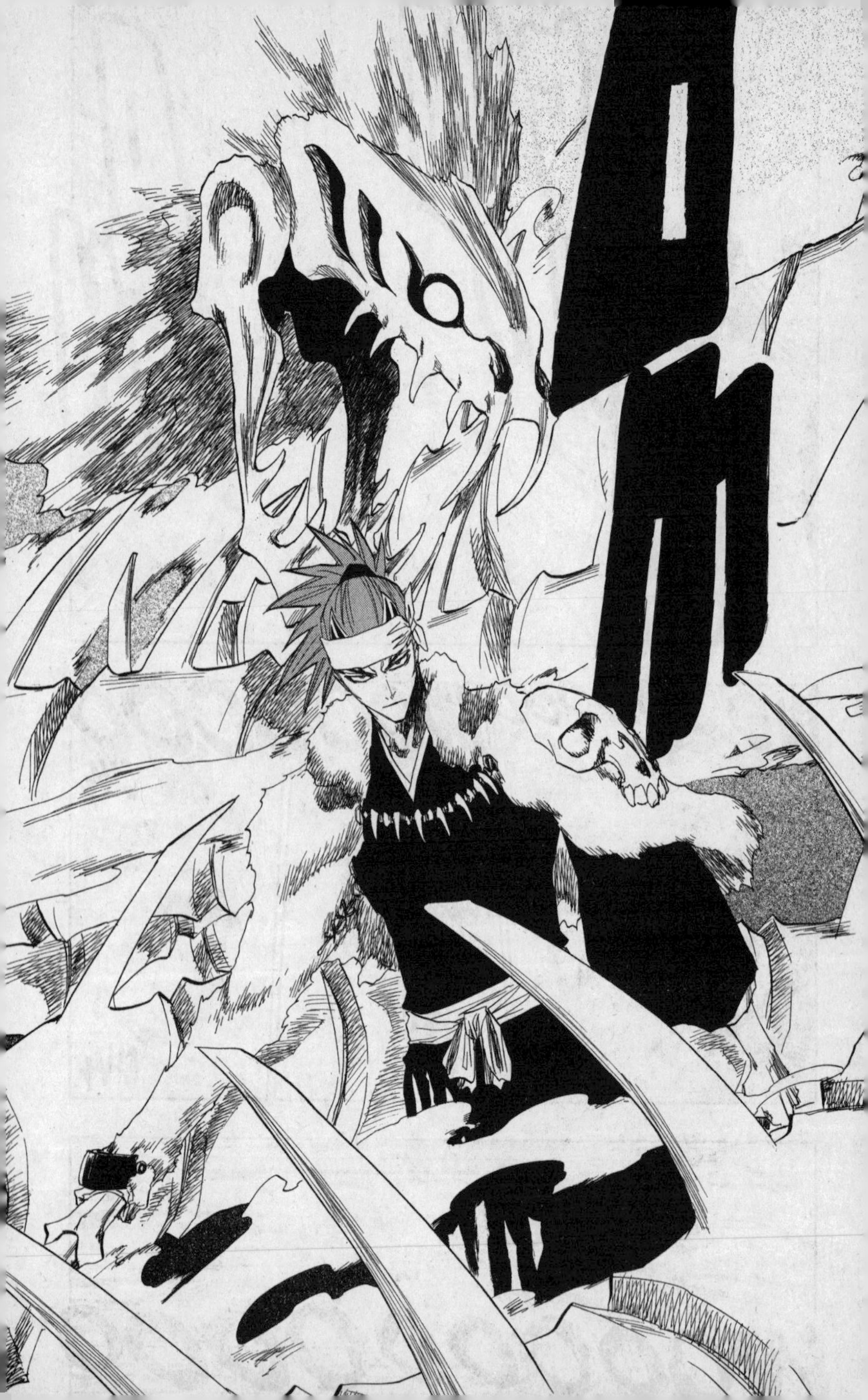

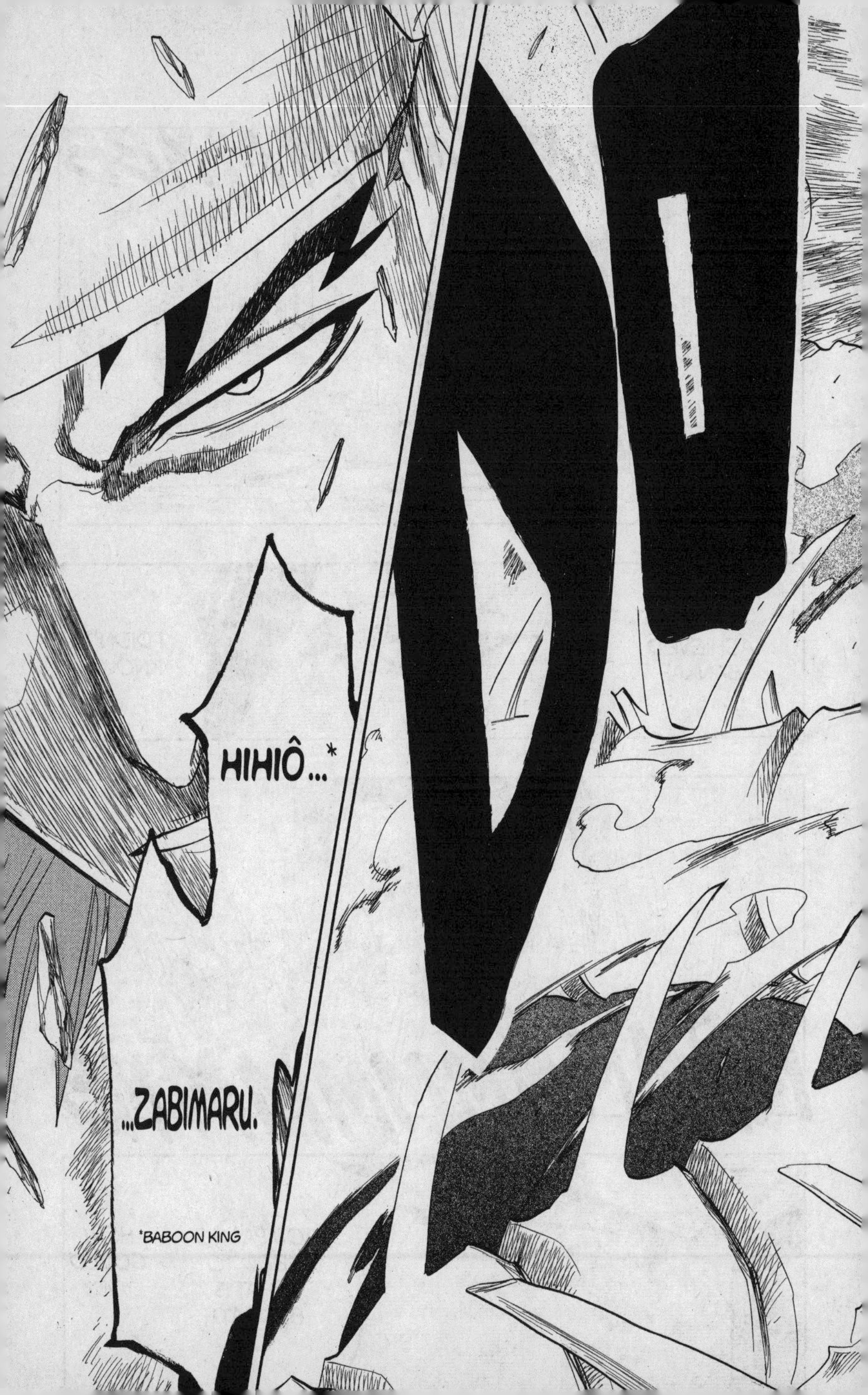
HIHIÔ...*
...ZABIMARU.
*BABOON KING

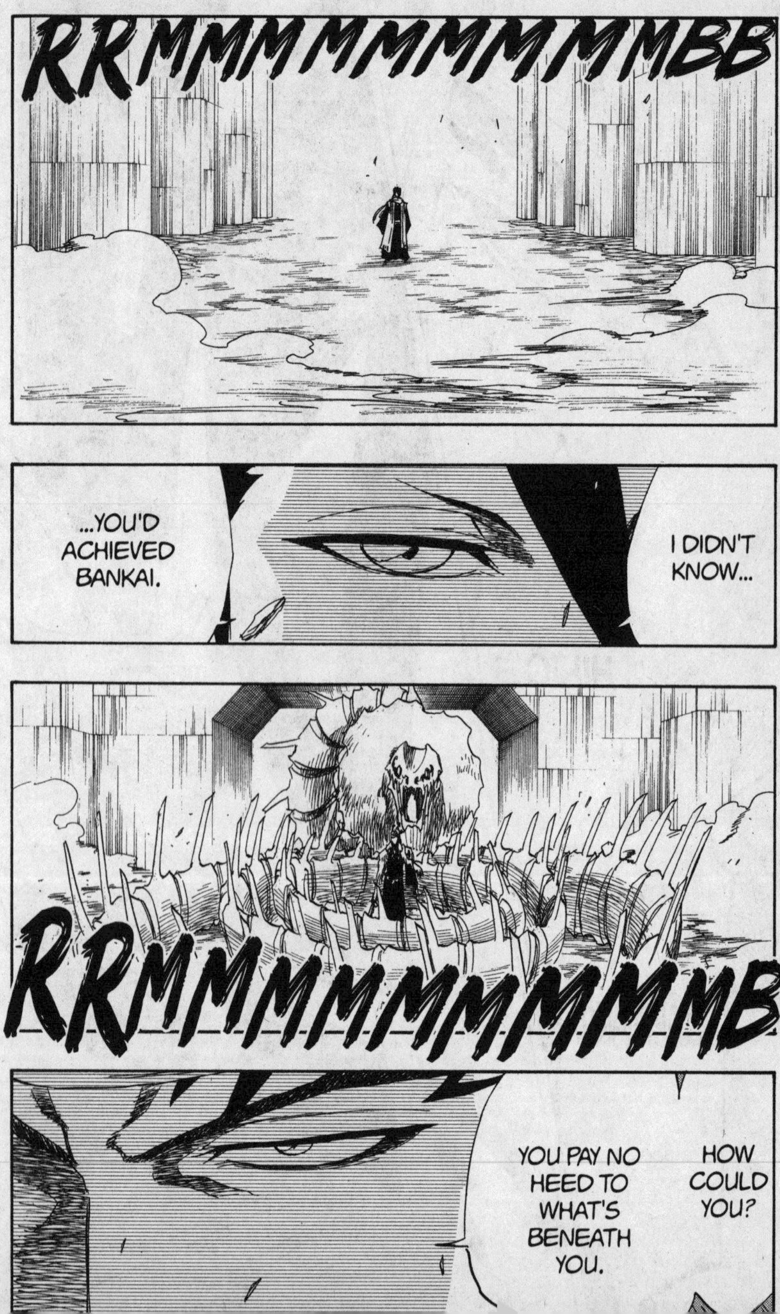
RRMMMMMMMMMMBB
I DIDN'T KNOW...
...YOU'D ACHIEVED BANKAI.
RRMMMMMMMMMMB
HOW COULD YOU?
YOU PAY NO HEED TO WHAT'S BENEATH YOU.

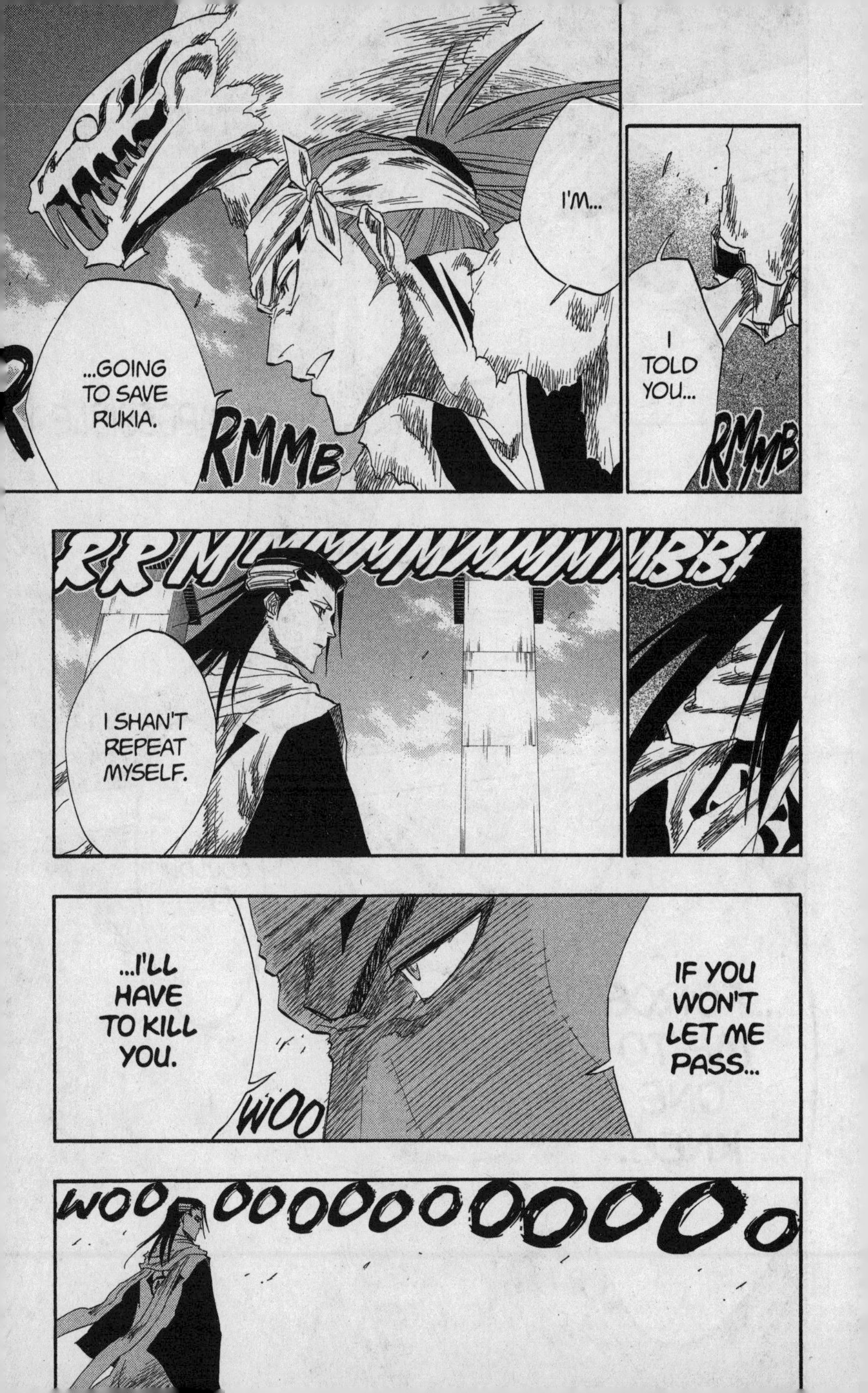
I TOLD YOU...
RMMB
I'M...
...GOING TO SAVE RUKIA.
RMMB
RRMMMMMMMMMMMBB!
I SHAN'T REPEAT MYSELF.
IF YOU WON'T LET ME PASS...
...I'LL HAVE TO KILL YOU.
WOO
WOO OOOOOOOOOOOOO

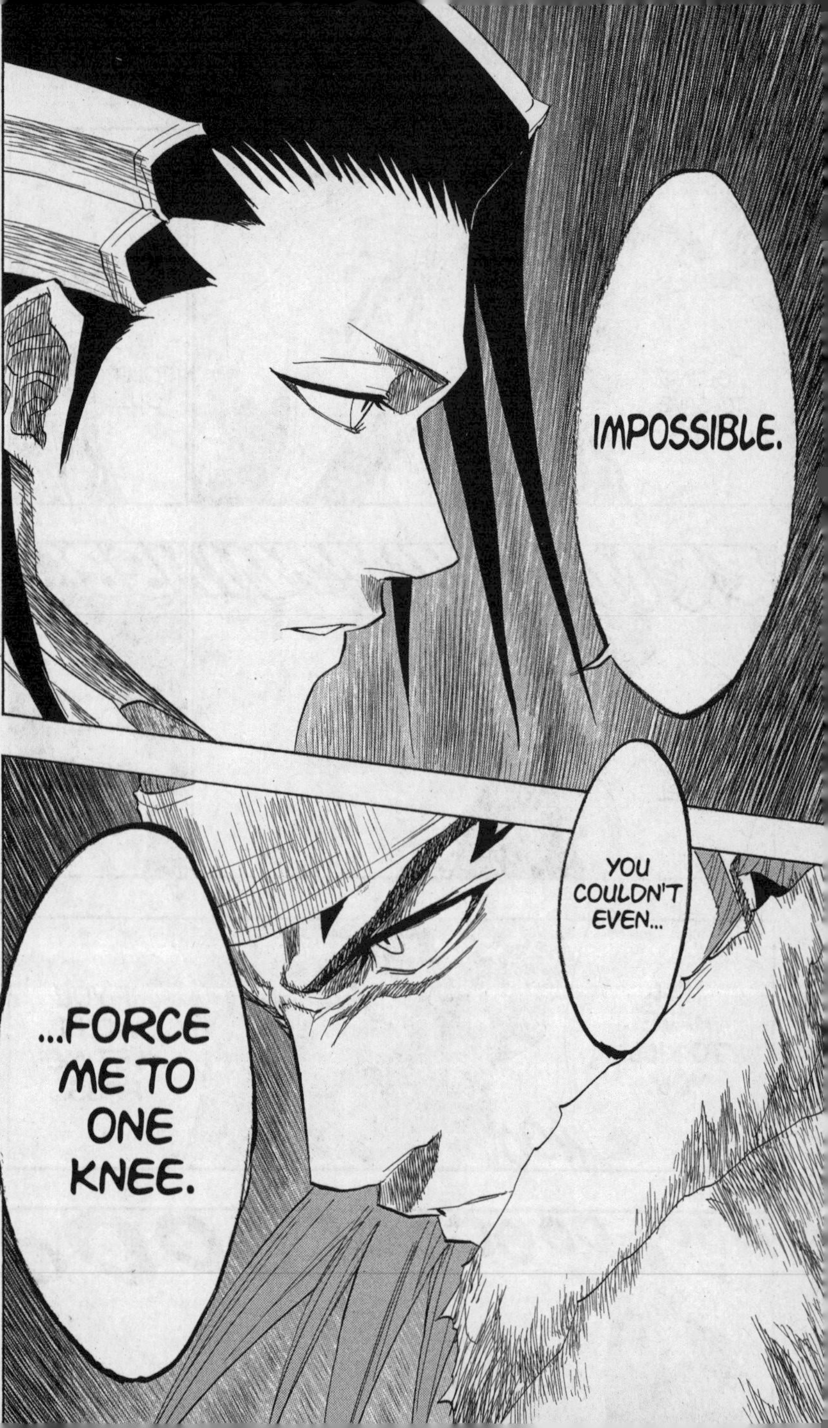
IMPOSSIBLE.
YOU COULDN'T EVEN...
...FORCE ME TO ONE KNEE.

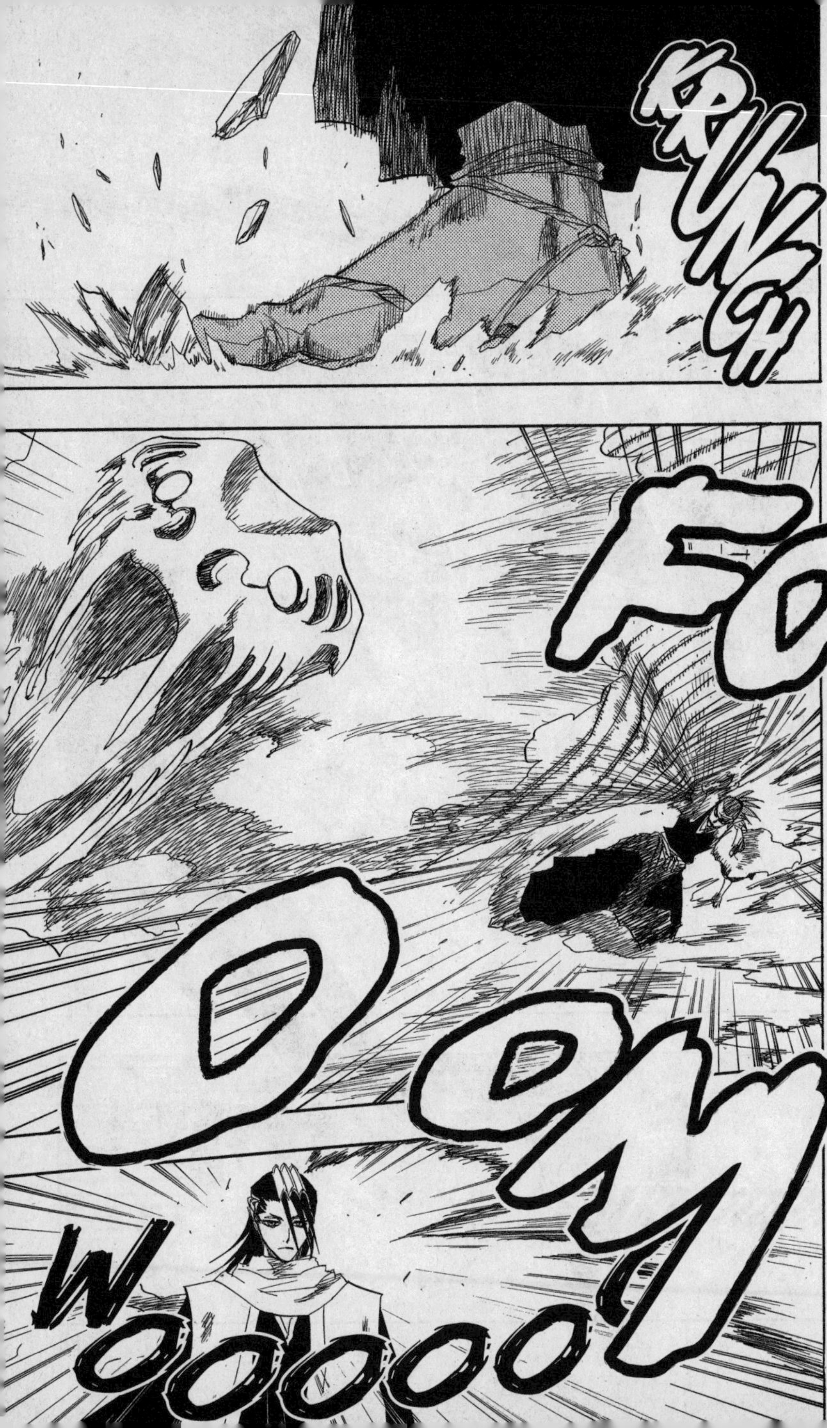
KRUNCH
FOOOM
WOOOOO

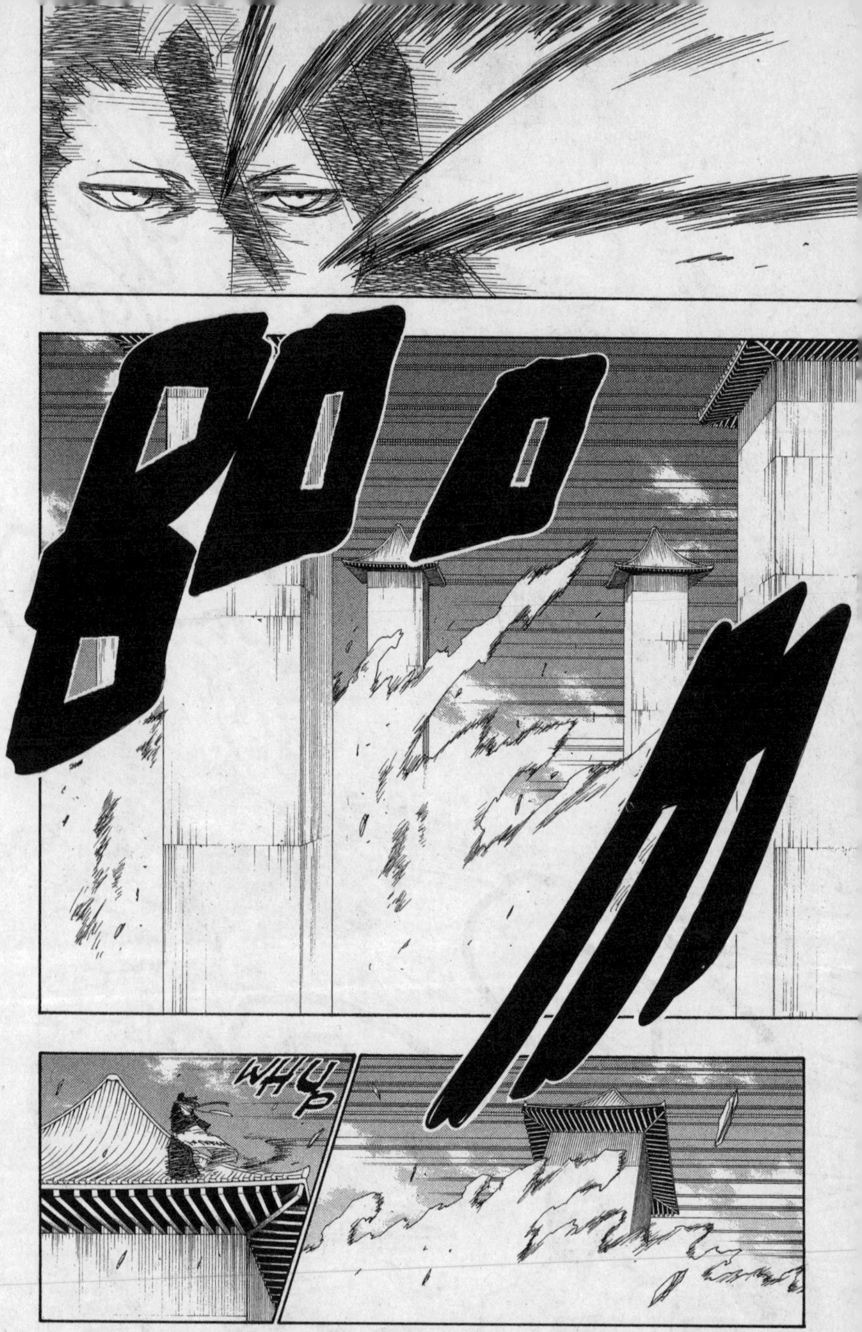
BOOM
WHUP

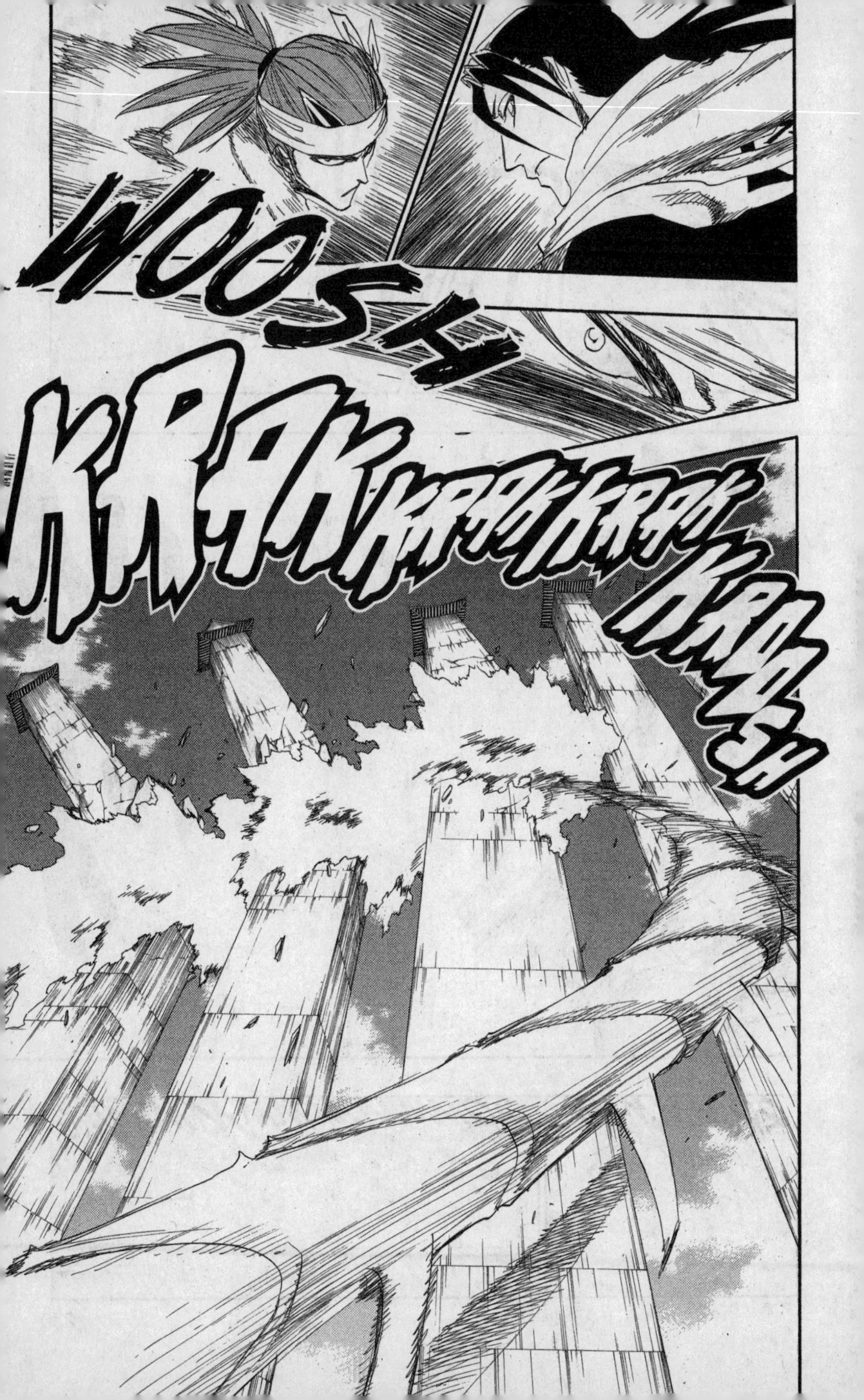
WOOSH
KRAKKRAKKRAKKRAK KRASH

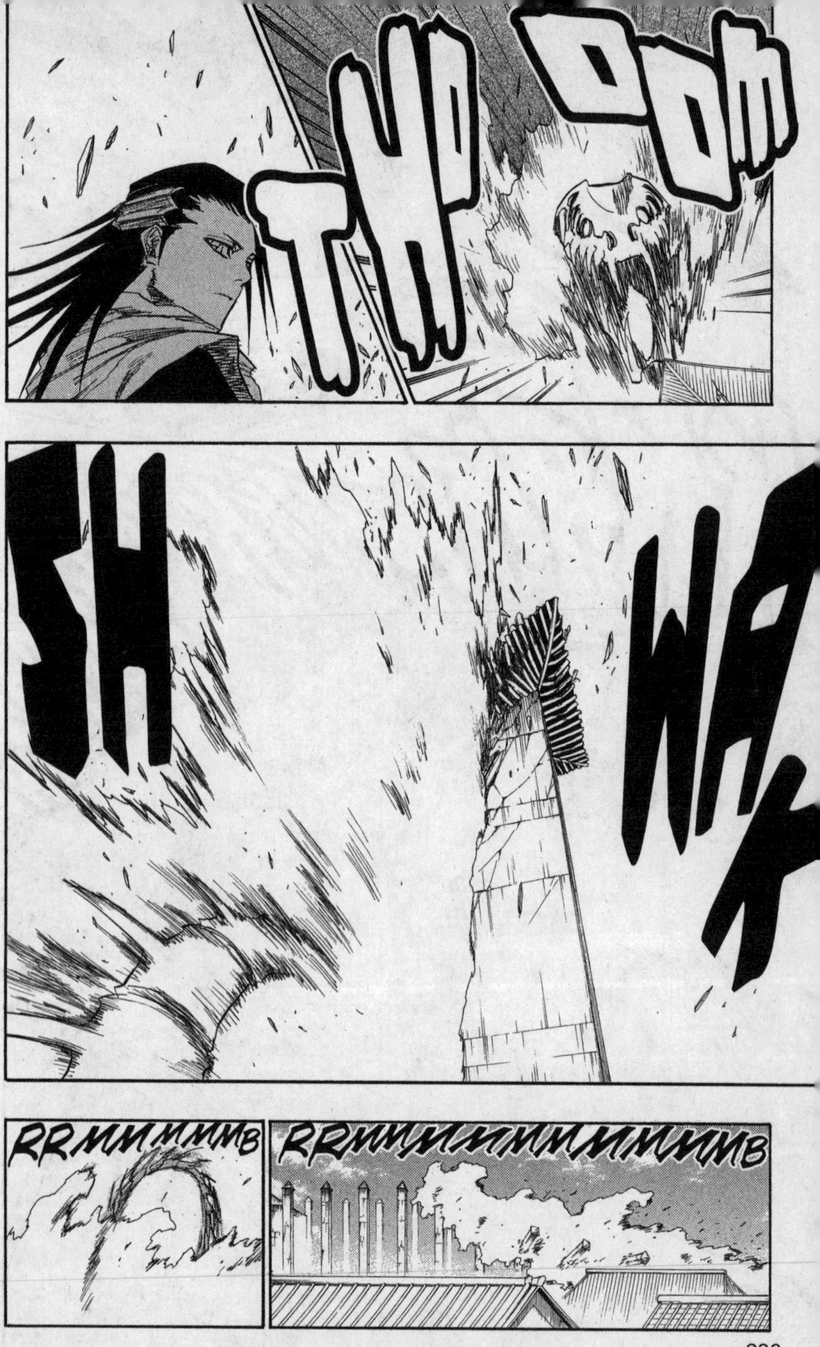
THOOOM
SHWA
RRMMMMMB
RRMMMMMMMMMMMB

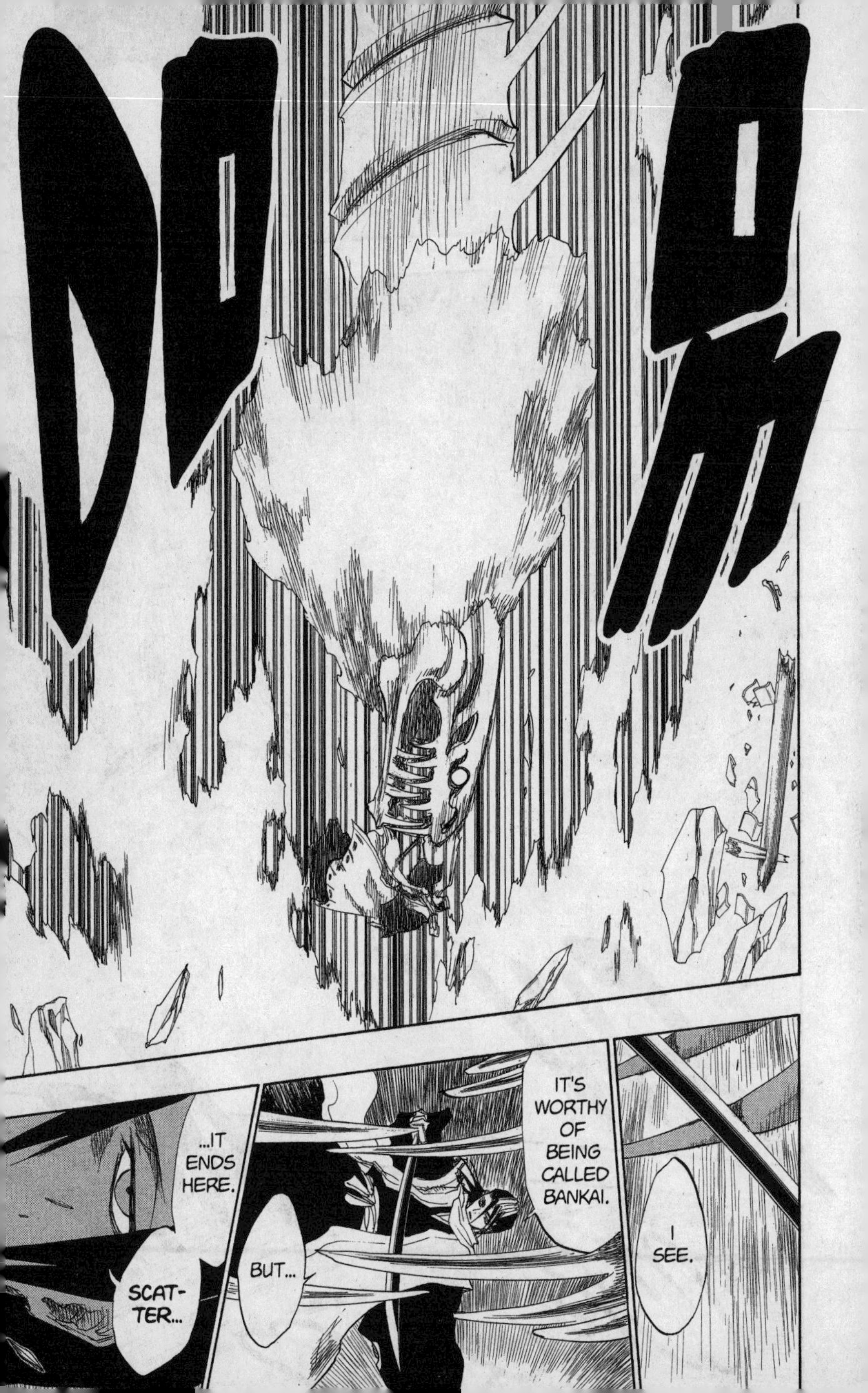
I SEE.
IT'S WORTHY OF BEING CALLED BANKAI.
BUT...
...IT ENDS HERE.
SCAT-TER...

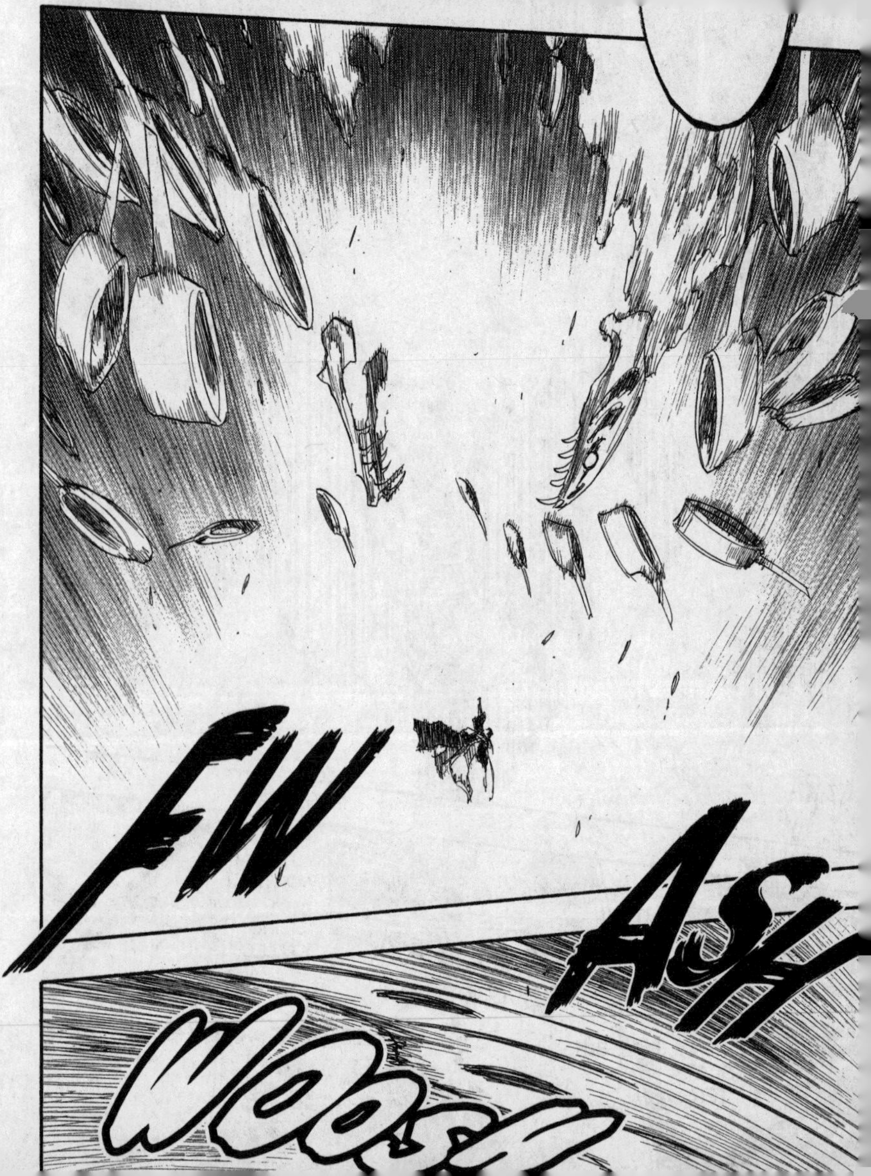
FWASH
WOOSH

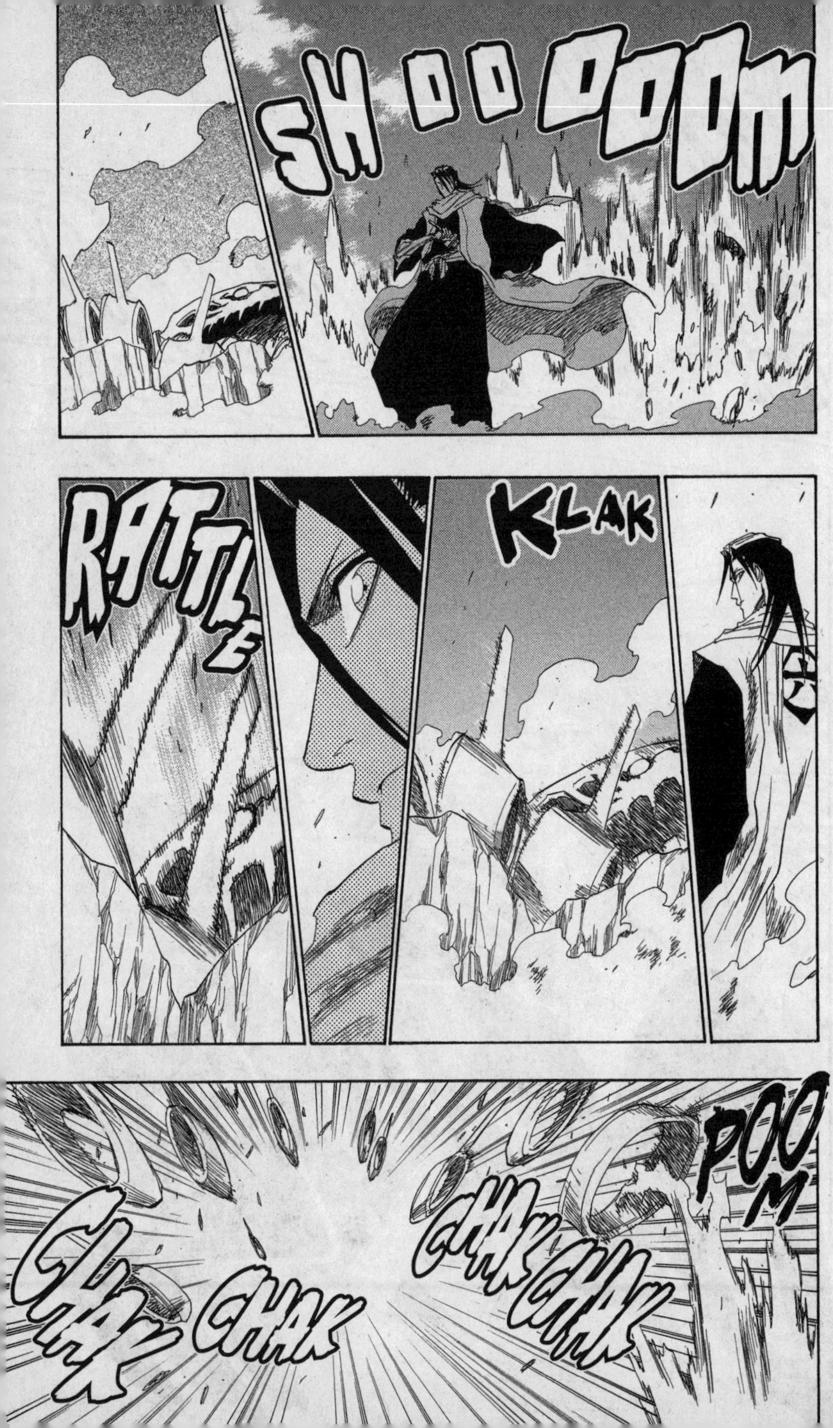
SHOOOOOM
KLAK
RATTLE
POOM
CHAK CHAK
CHAK
CHAK

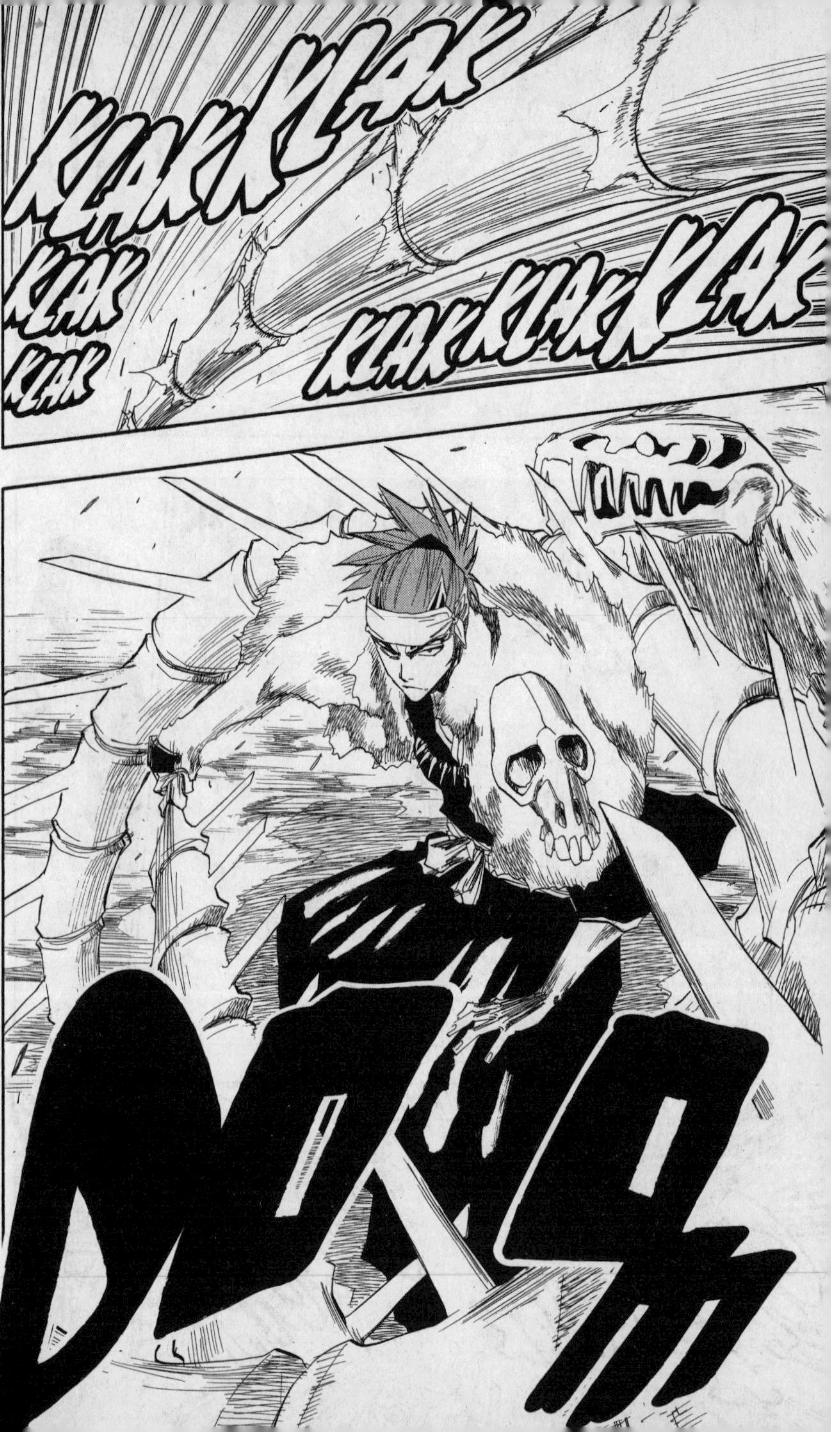
KLAK KLAK
KLAK KLAK KLAK
KLAK
KLAK

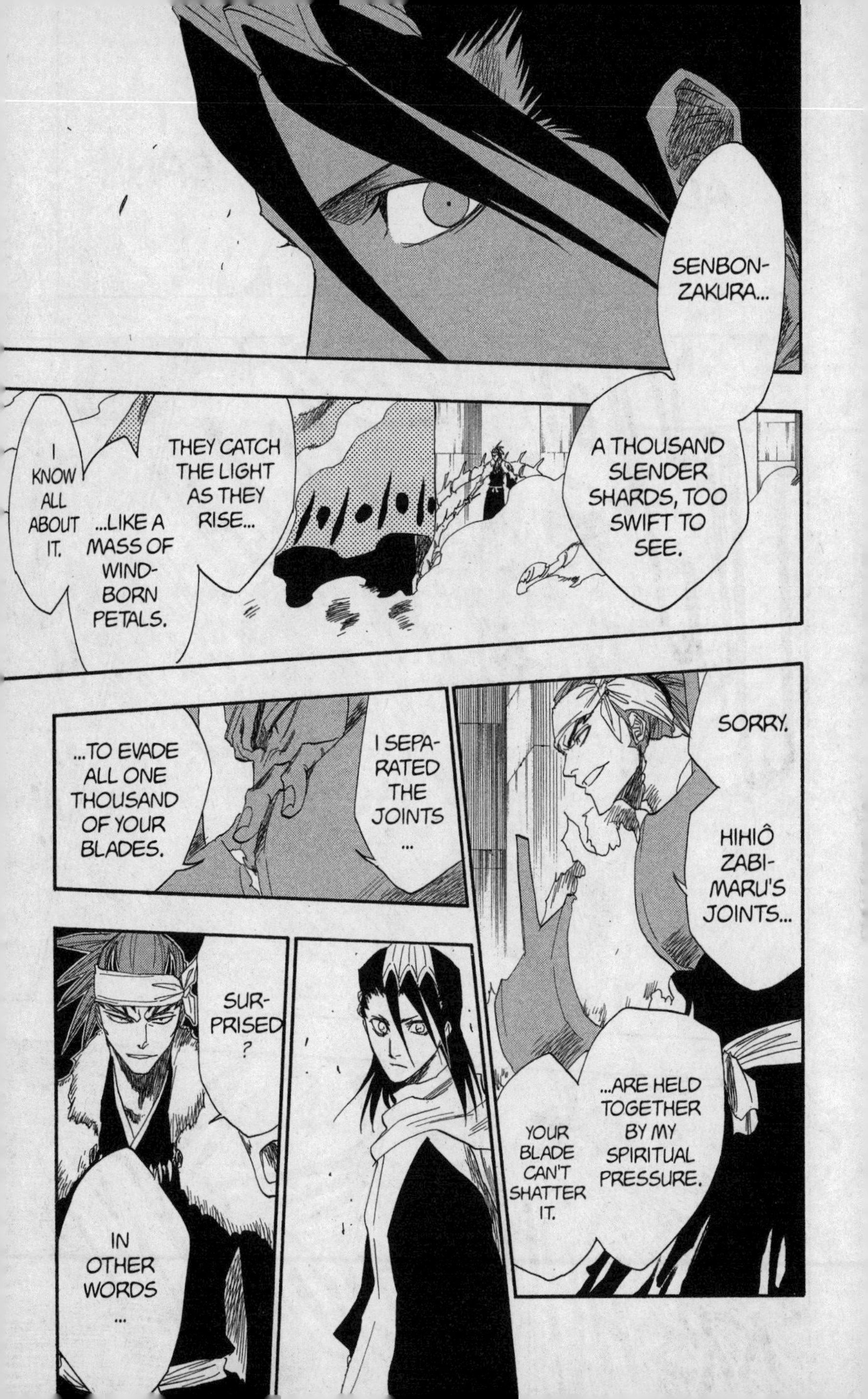

SENBON-ZAKURA...
A THOUSAND SLENDER SHARDS, TOO SWIFT TO SEE.
THEY CATCH THE LIGHT AS THEY RISE...
...LIKE A MASS OF WIND-BORN PETALS.
I KNOW ALL ABOUT IT.
SORRY.
HIHIÔ ZABI-MARU'S JOINTS...
...ARE HELD TOGETHER BY MY SPIRITUAL PRESSURE.
YOUR BLADE CAN'T SHATTER IT.
I SEPA-RATED THE JOINTS...
...TO EVADE ALL ONE THOUSAND OF YOUR BLADES.
SUR-PRISED?
IN OTHER WORDS...

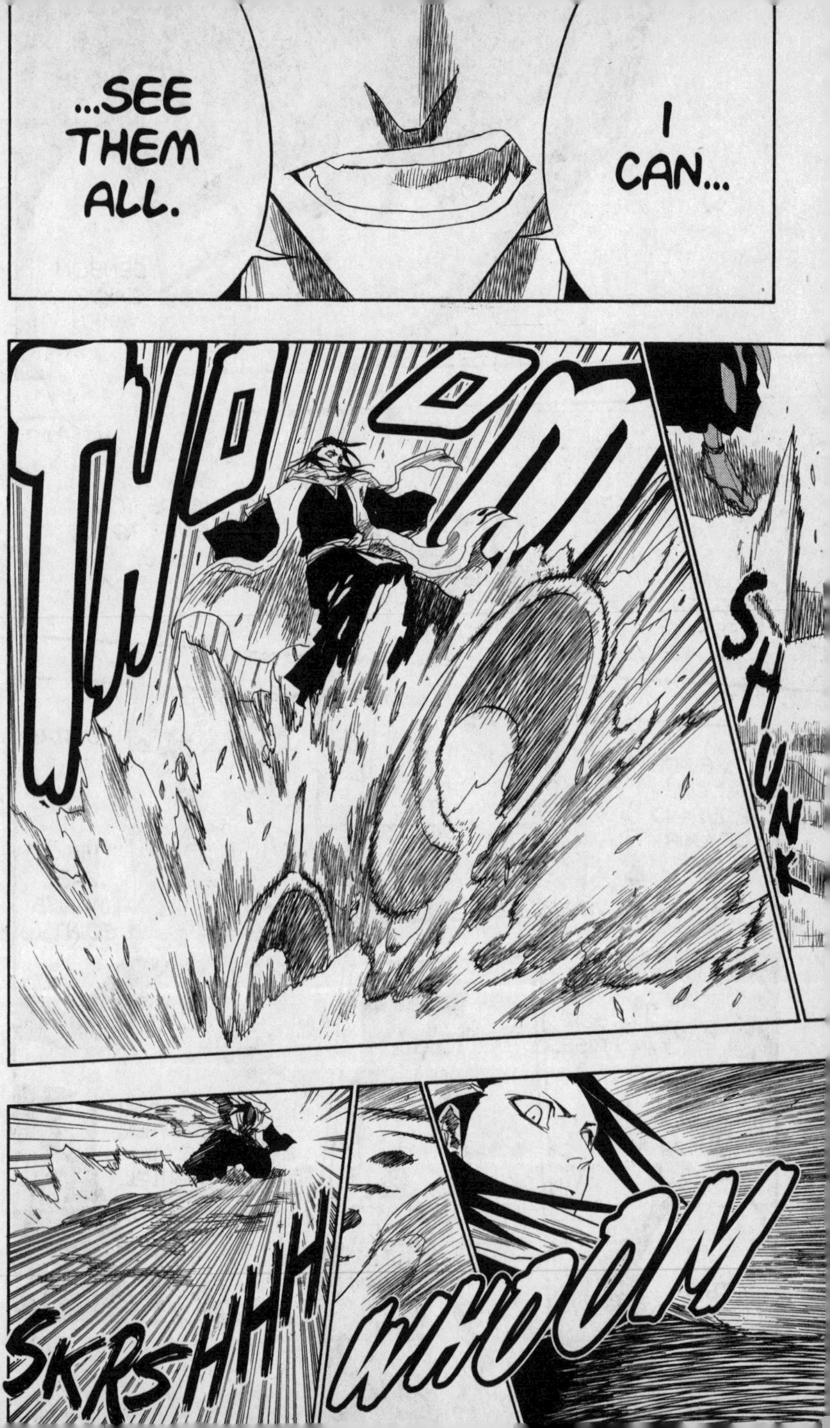
I CAN...
...SEE THEM ALL.
SHUNK
THOOM
WHOOM
SKRSHHH

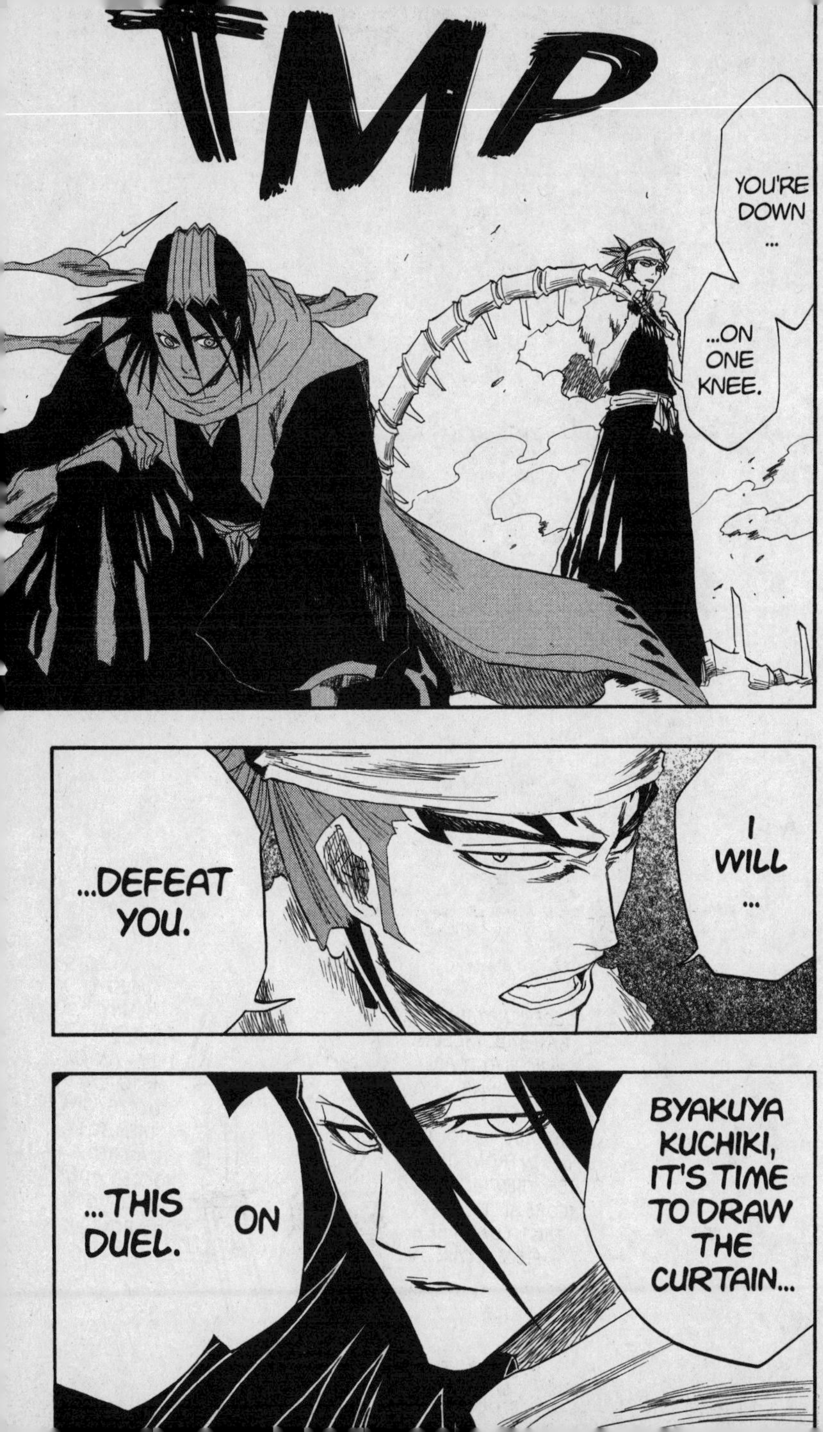
TMP
YOU'RE DOWN ...
...ON ONE KNEE.
I WILL ...
...DEFEAT YOU.
BYAKUYA KUCHIKI, IT'S TIME TO DRAW THE CURTAIN...
ON
...THIS DUEL.

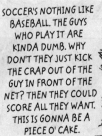

AUGUST 9, RAINY. TURNS OUT THEY WANTED ME TO PLAY SOCCER FOR THEM. SO I WATCHED A SOCCER VIDEO THEY GAVE ME TO BONE UP.

SOCCER'S NOTHING LIKE BASEBALL. THE GUYS WHO PLAY IT ARE KINDA DUMB. WHY DON'T THEY JUST KICK THE CRAP OUT OF THE GUY IN FRONT OF THE NET? THEN THEY COULD SCORE ALL THEY WANT. THIS IS GONNA BE A PIECE O' CAKE.

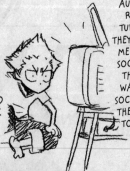

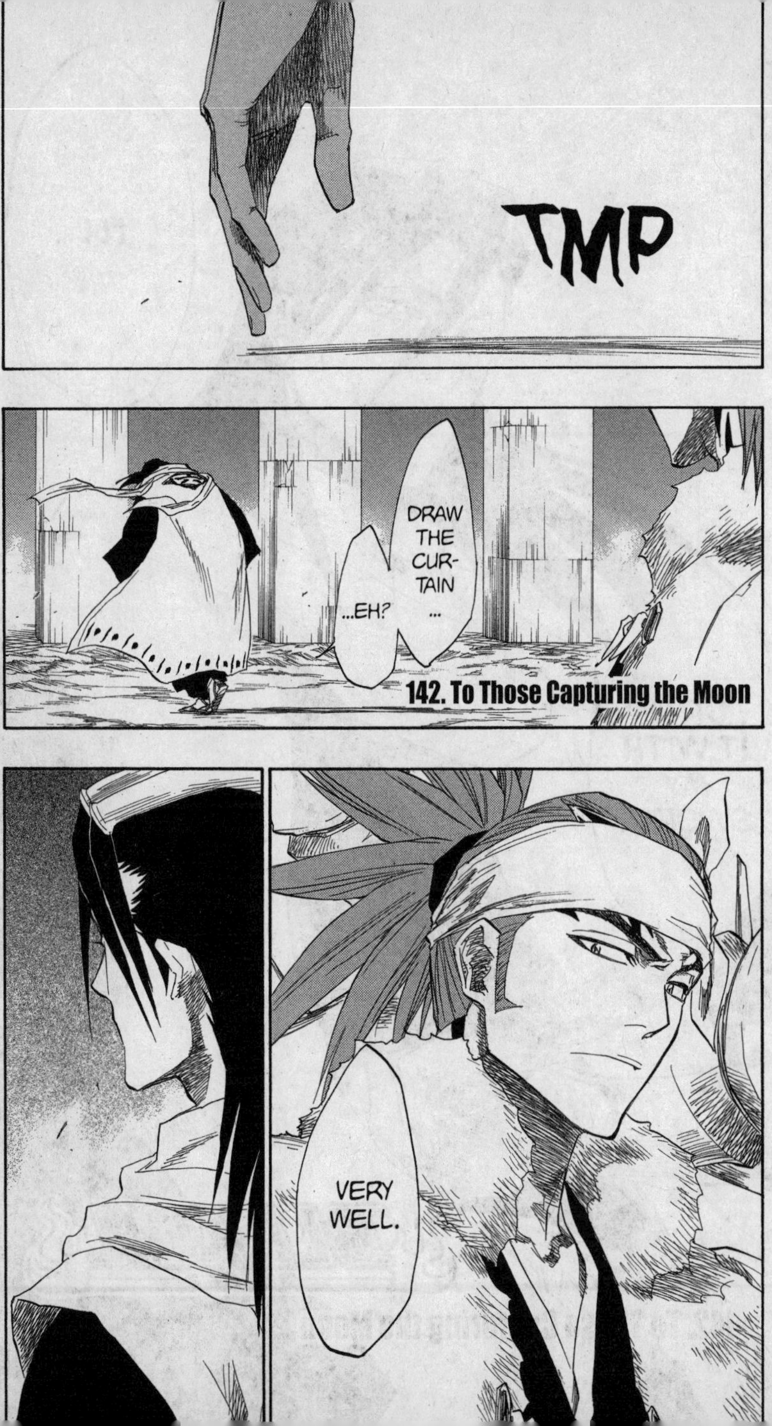
TMP
DRAW THE CURTAIN...
...EH?
142. To Those Capturing the Moon
VERY WELL.

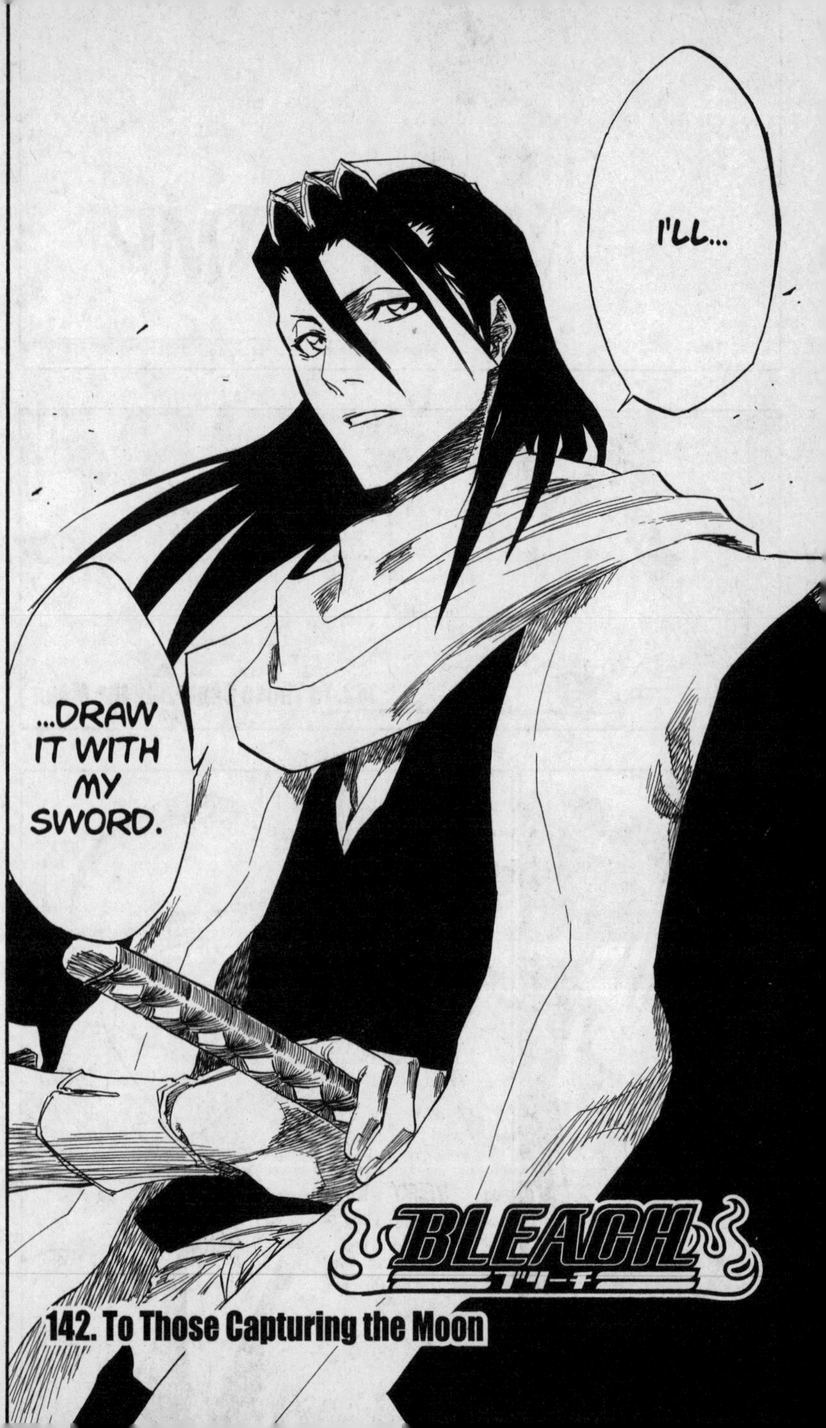
I'LL...
...DRAW IT WITH MY SWORD.
BLEACH
ブリーチ
142. To Those Capturing the Moon

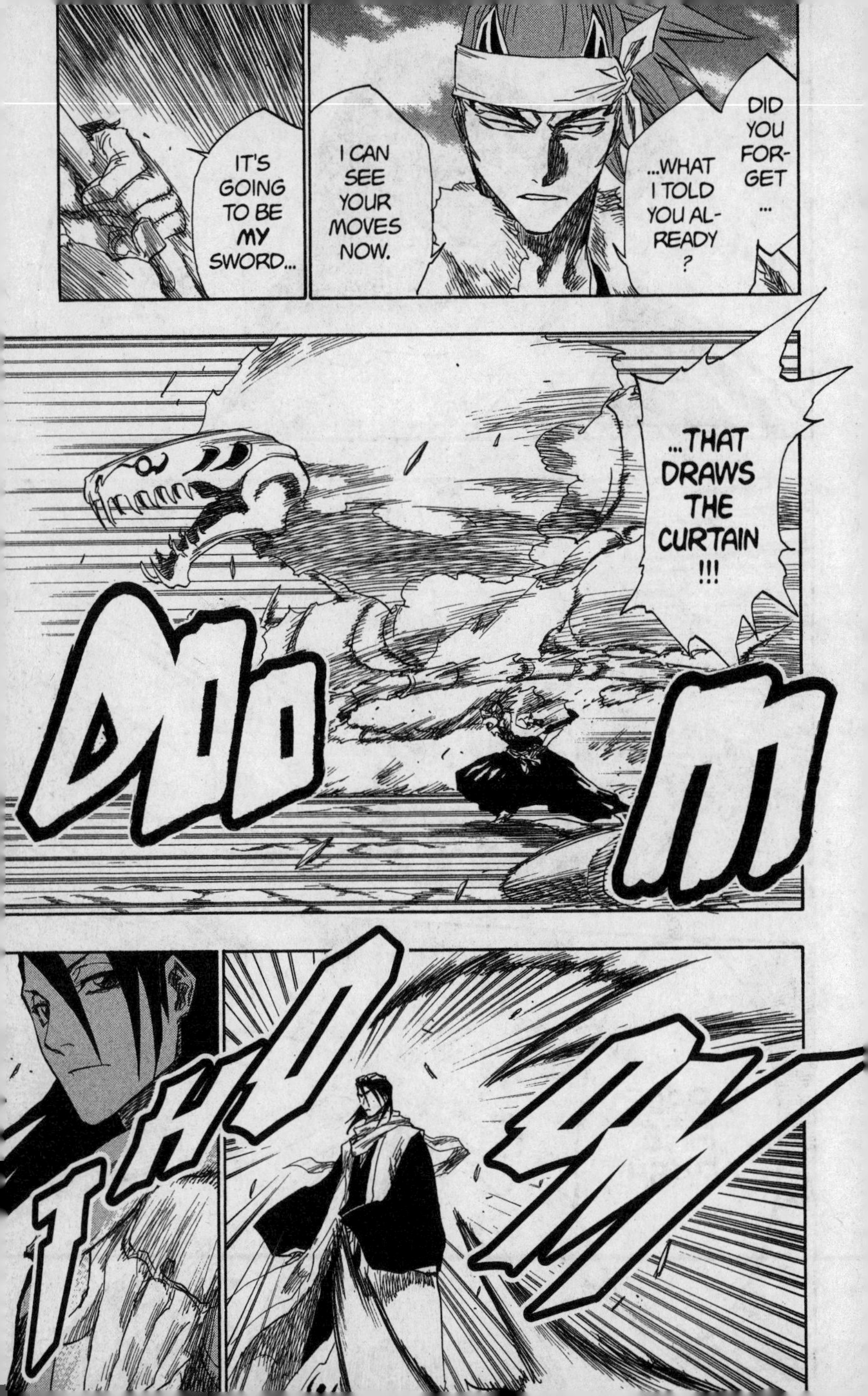
DID YOU FOR-GET...
...WHAT I TOLD YOU AL-READY?
I CAN SEE YOUR MOVES NOW.
IT'S GOING TO BE MY SWORD...
...THAT DRAWS THE CURTAIN!!!
DOOM

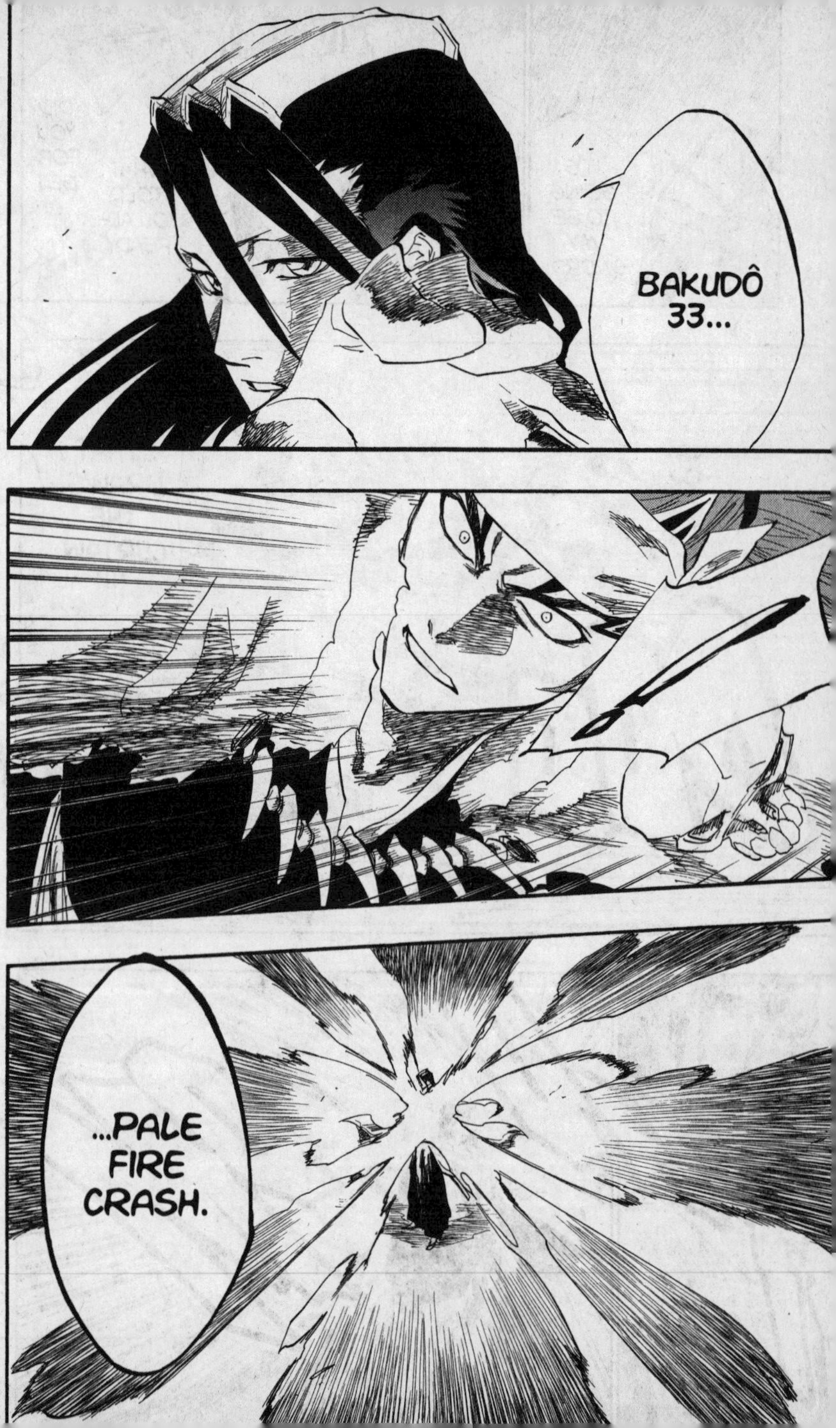
BAKUDÔ 33...
...PALE FIRE CRASH.

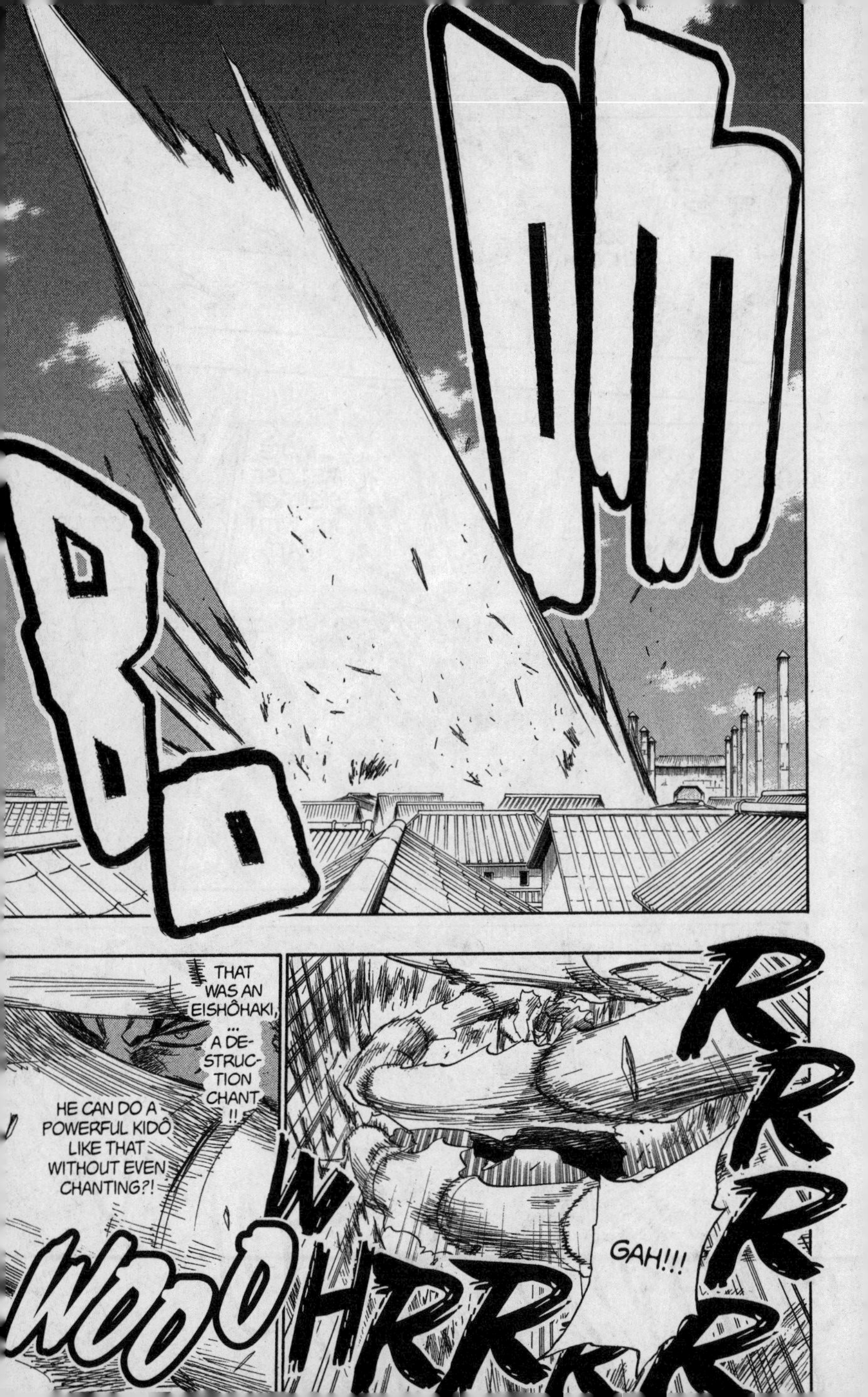

GAH!!!
THAT WAS AN EISHÔHAKI ... A DESTRUCTION CHANT!!
HE CAN DO A POWERFUL KIDÔ LIKE THAT WITHOUT EVEN CHANTING?!

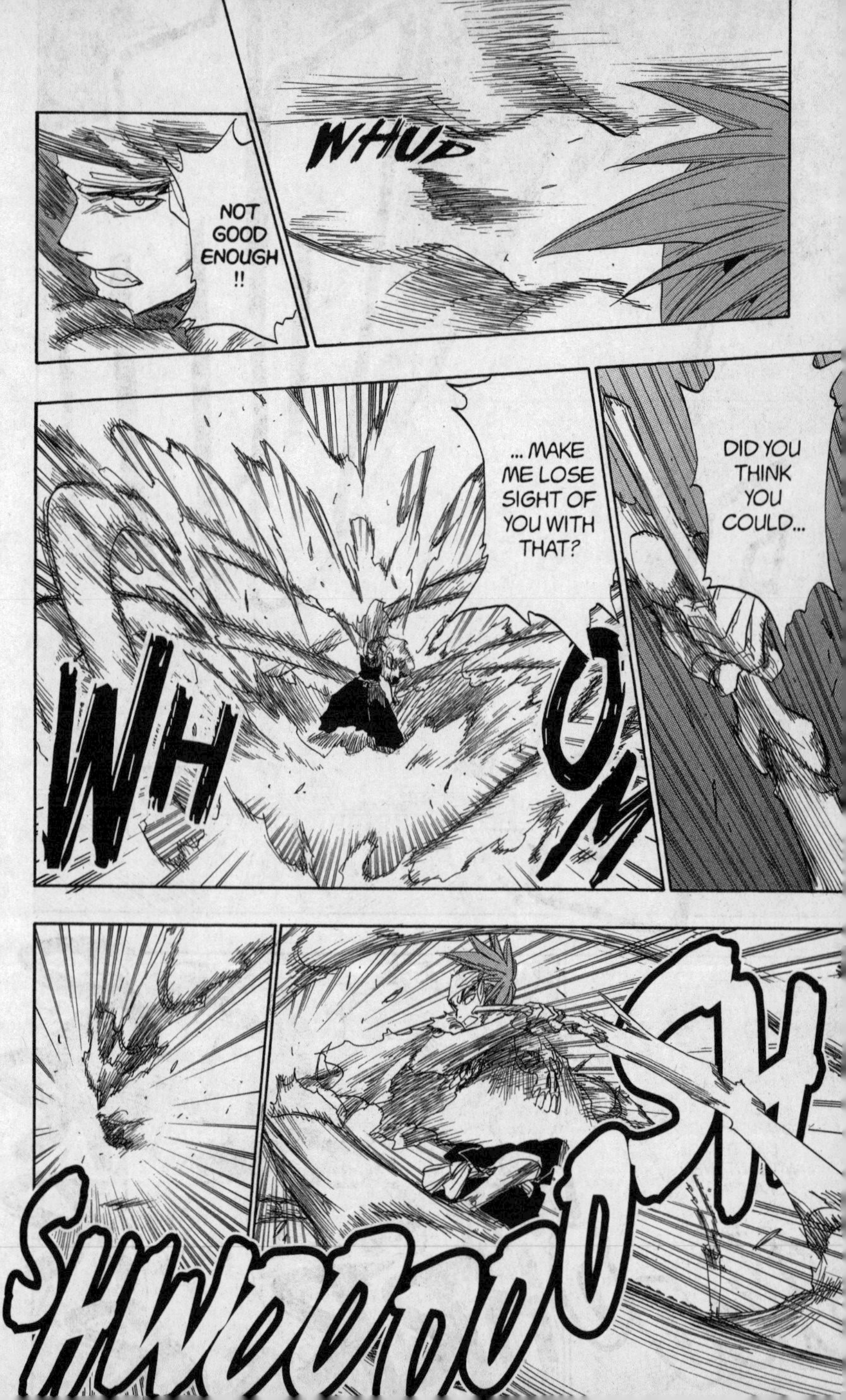
WHUD
NOT GOOD ENOUGH !!
DID YOU THINK YOU COULD...
...MAKE ME LOSE SIGHT OF YOU WITH THAT?
WHOM
SHUOOOOSH

READ THIS WAY

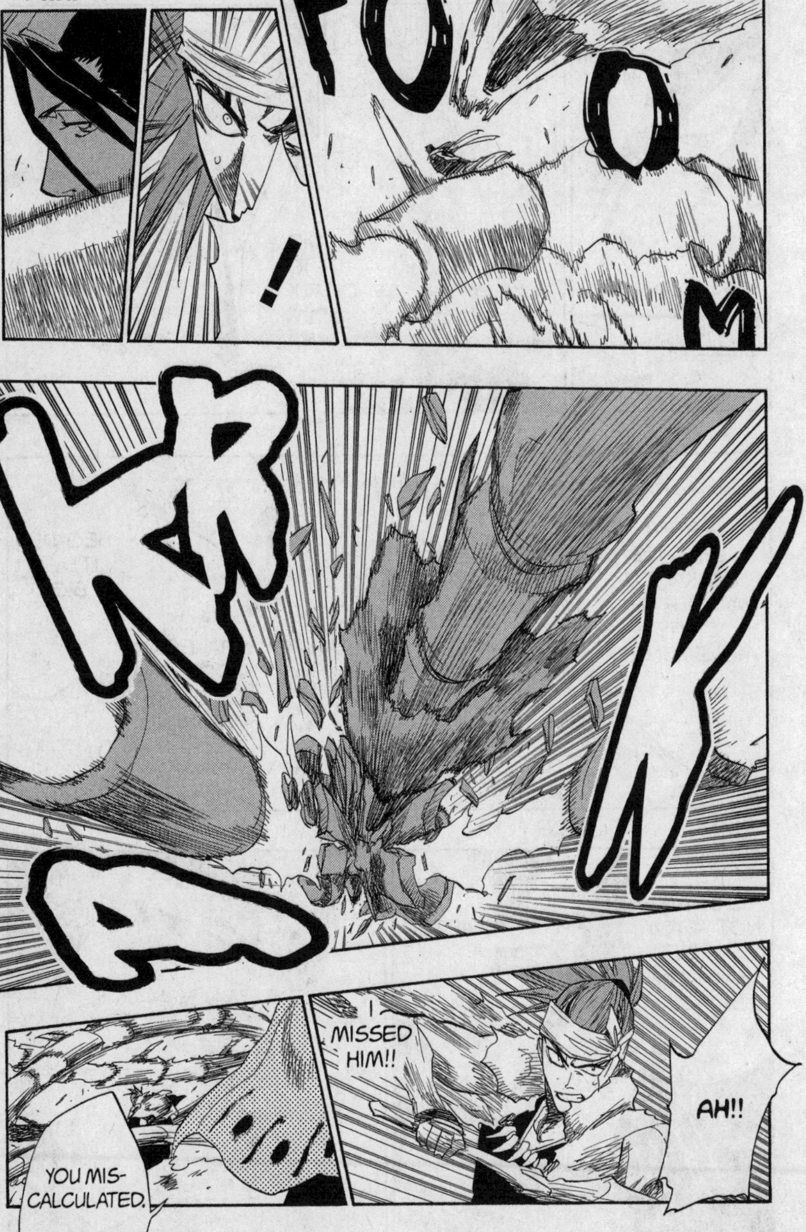
FOOOM
!
KRAK
AH!!
I MISSED HIM!!
YOU MIS-CALCULATED.

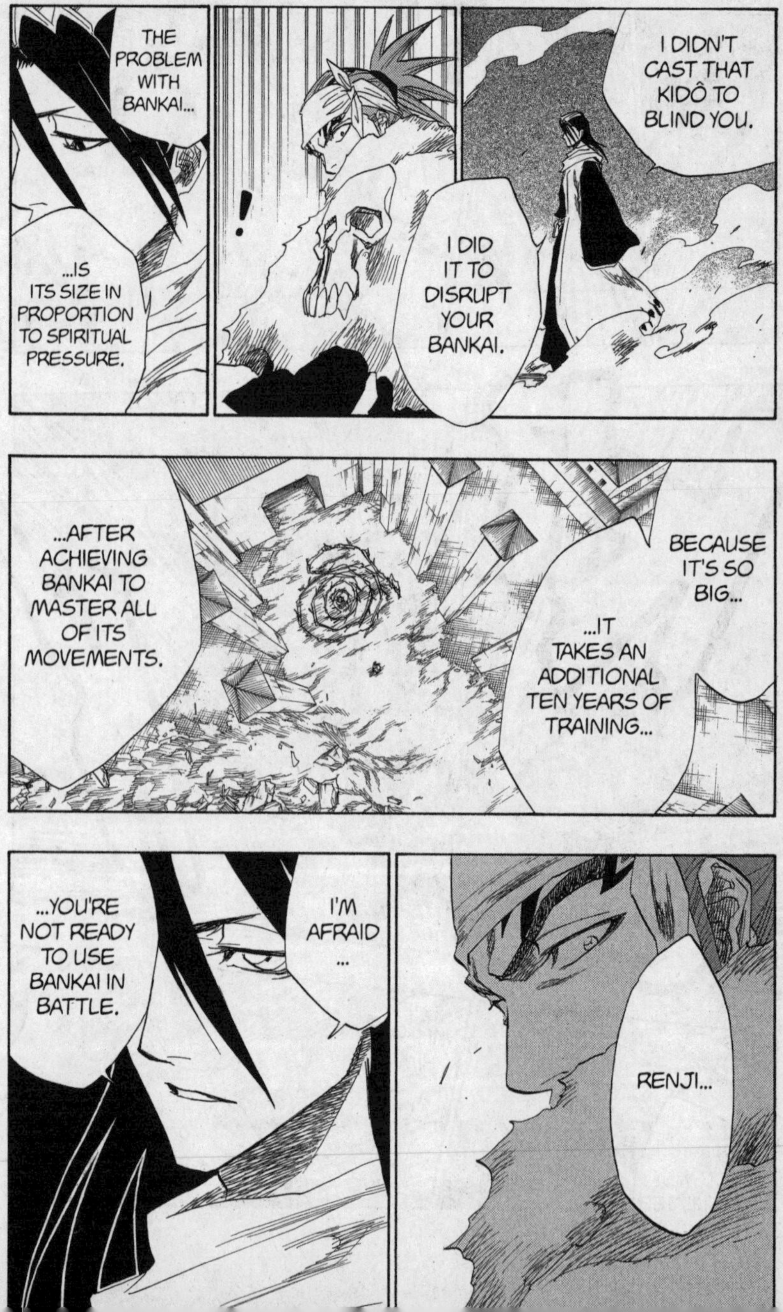
I DIDN'T CAST THAT KIDÔ TO BLIND YOU.
!
I DID IT TO DISRUPT YOUR BANKAI.
THE PROBLEM WITH BANKAI...
...IS ITS SIZE IN PROPORTION TO SPIRITUAL PRESSURE.
BECAUSE IT'S SO BIG...
...IT TAKES AN ADDITIONAL TEN YEARS OF TRAINING...
...AFTER ACHIEVING BANKAI TO MASTER ALL OF ITS MOVEMENTS.
RENJI...
I'M AFRAID ...
...YOU'RE NOT READY TO USE BANKAI IN BATTLE.

READ THIS WAY

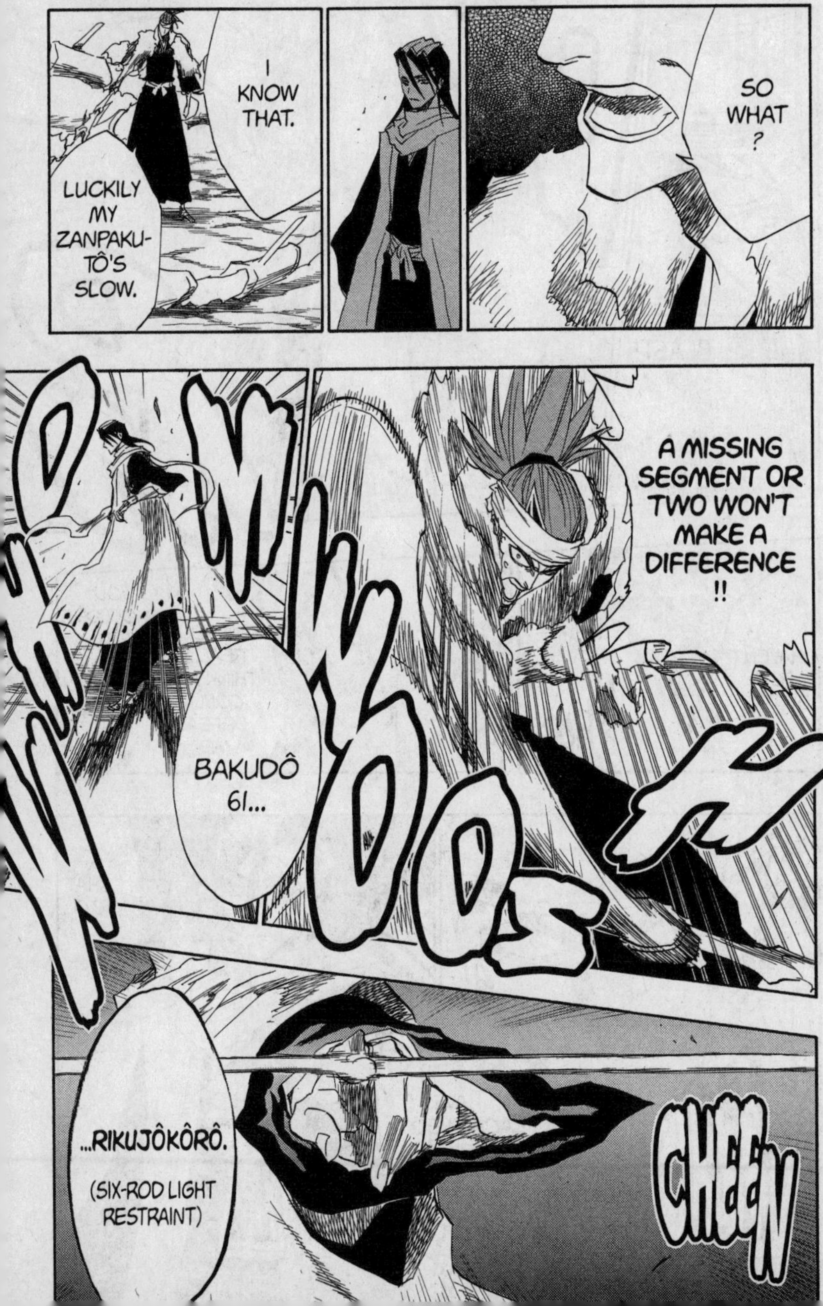

SO WHAT?
I KNOW THAT.
LUCKILY MY ZANPAKU-TÔ'S SLOW.
A MISSING SEGMENT OR TWO WON'T MAKE A DIFFERENCE!!
BAKUDÔ 61...
...RIKUJÔKÔRÔ.
(SIX-ROD LIGHT RESTRAINT)
CHEEN

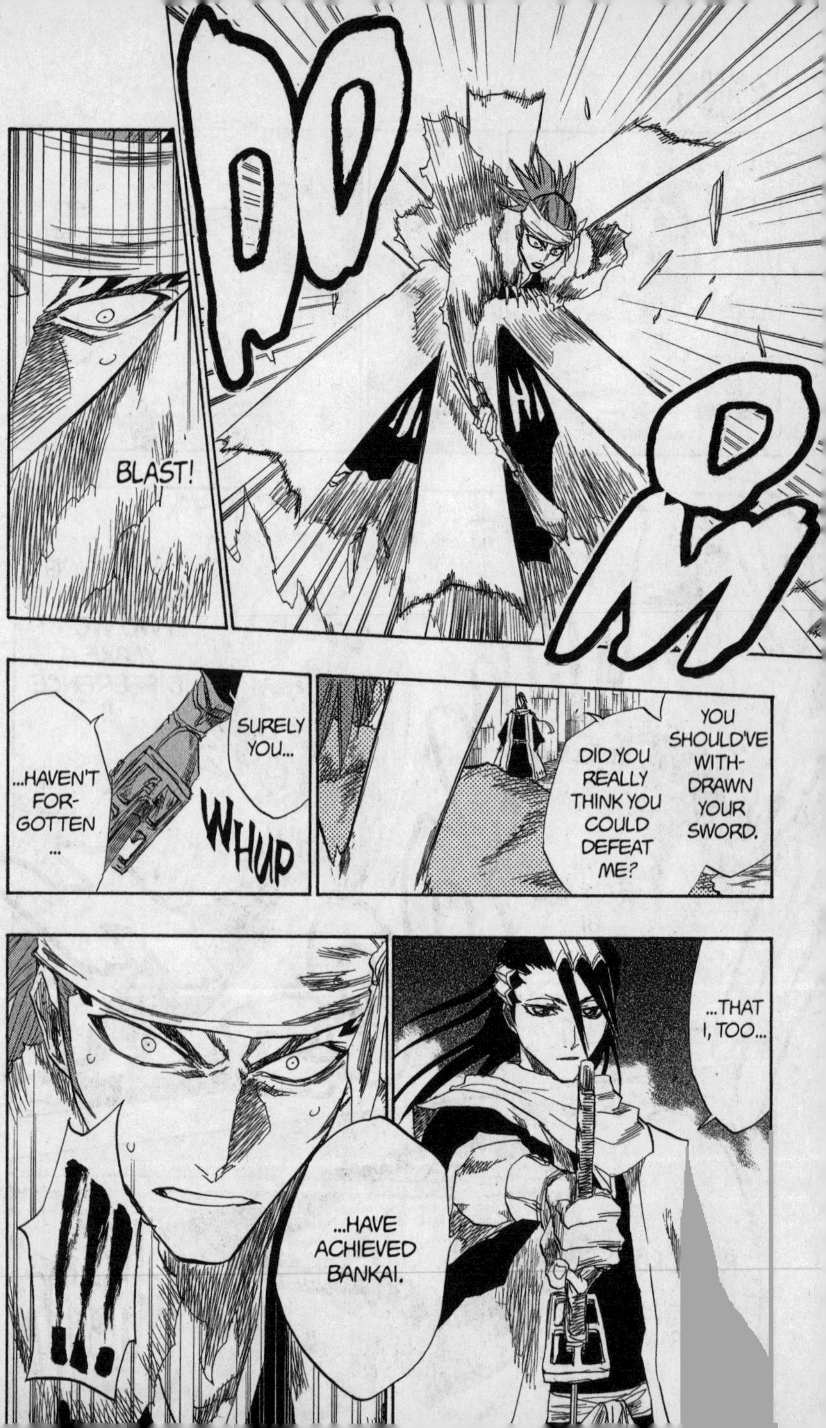
DOOM
BLAST!
YOU SHOULD'VE WITH- DRAWN YOUR SWORD.
DID YOU REALLY THINK YOU COULD DEFEAT ME?
SURELY YOU...
WHUP
...HAVEN'T FOR- GOTTEN ...
...THAT I, TOO...
...HAVE ACHIEVED BANKAI.
!!!

BANKAI.

V E E E N

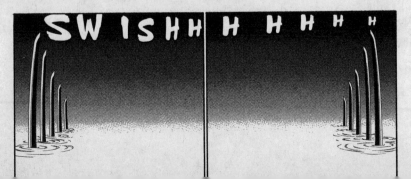

SWISHH H H H H H

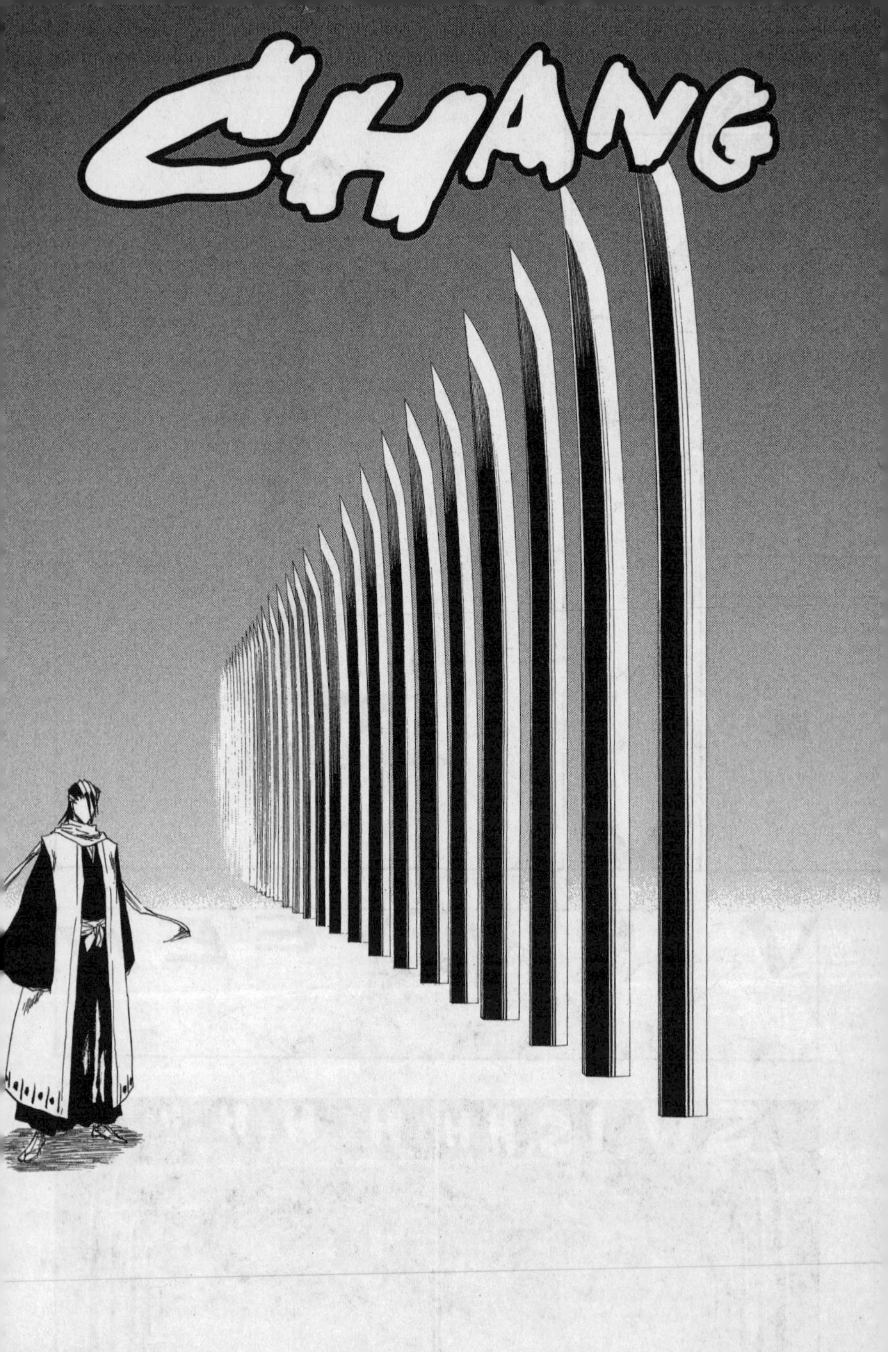
CHANG

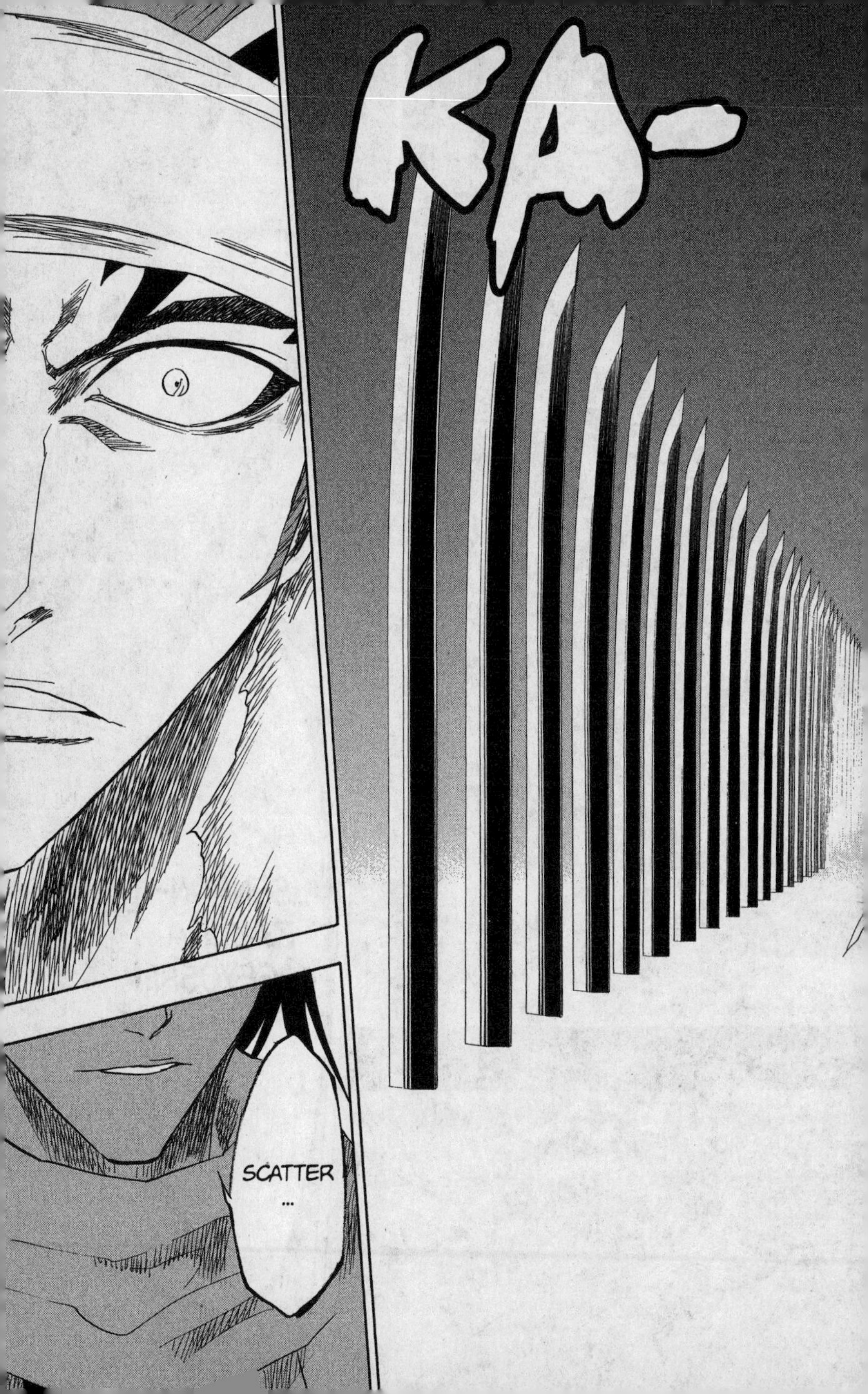
KA-
SCATTER
...

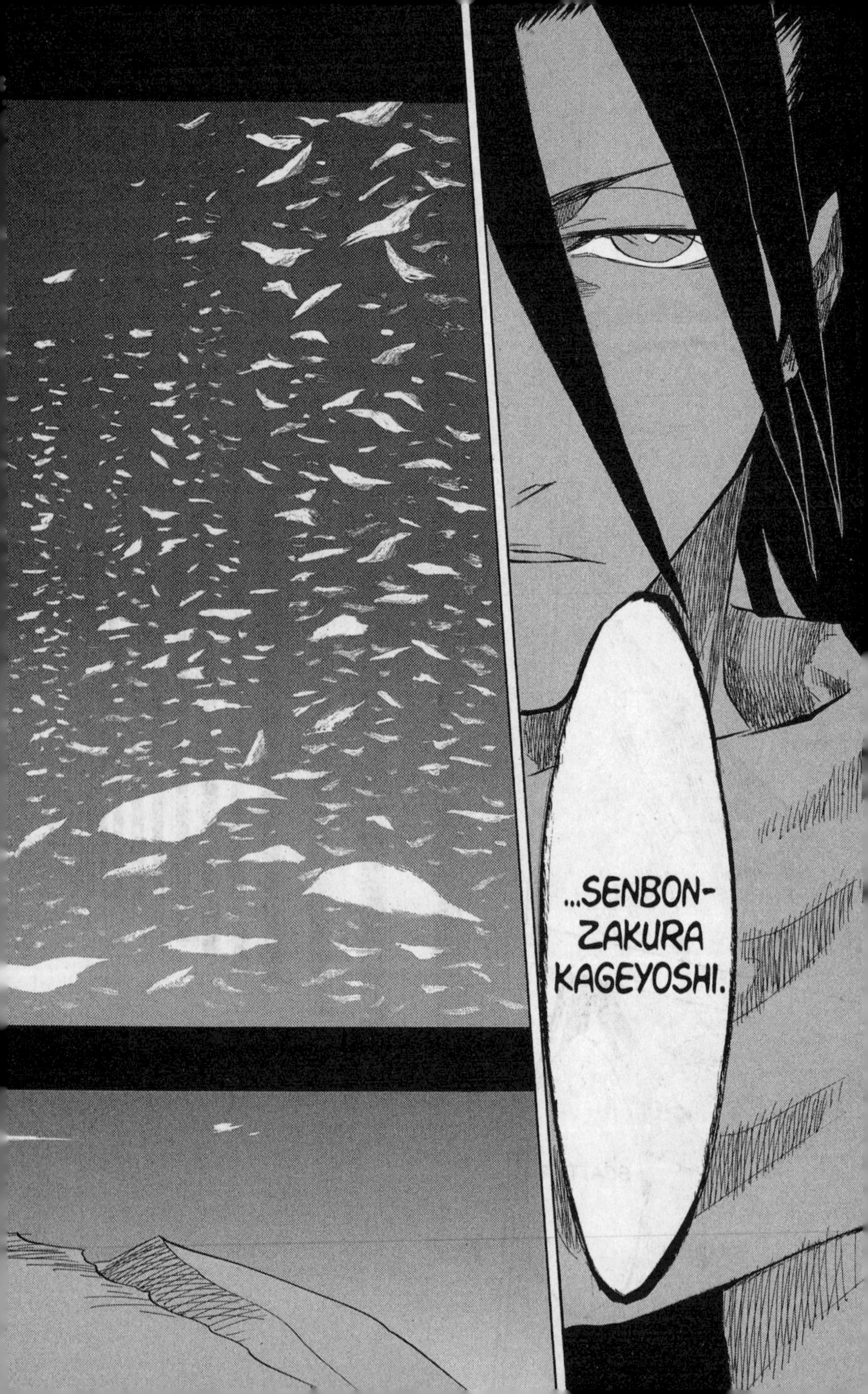
...SENBON-ZAKURA KAGEYOSHI.

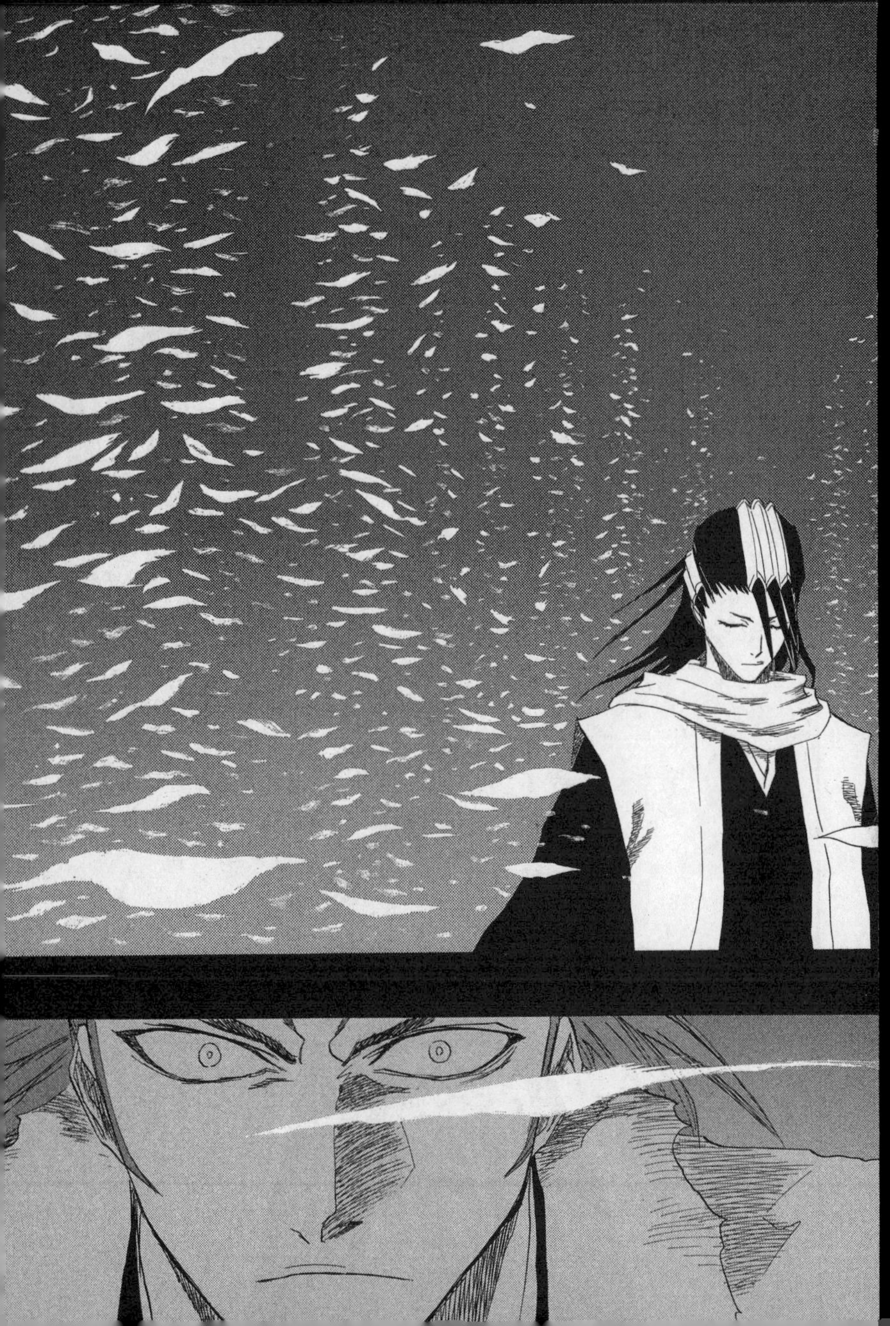

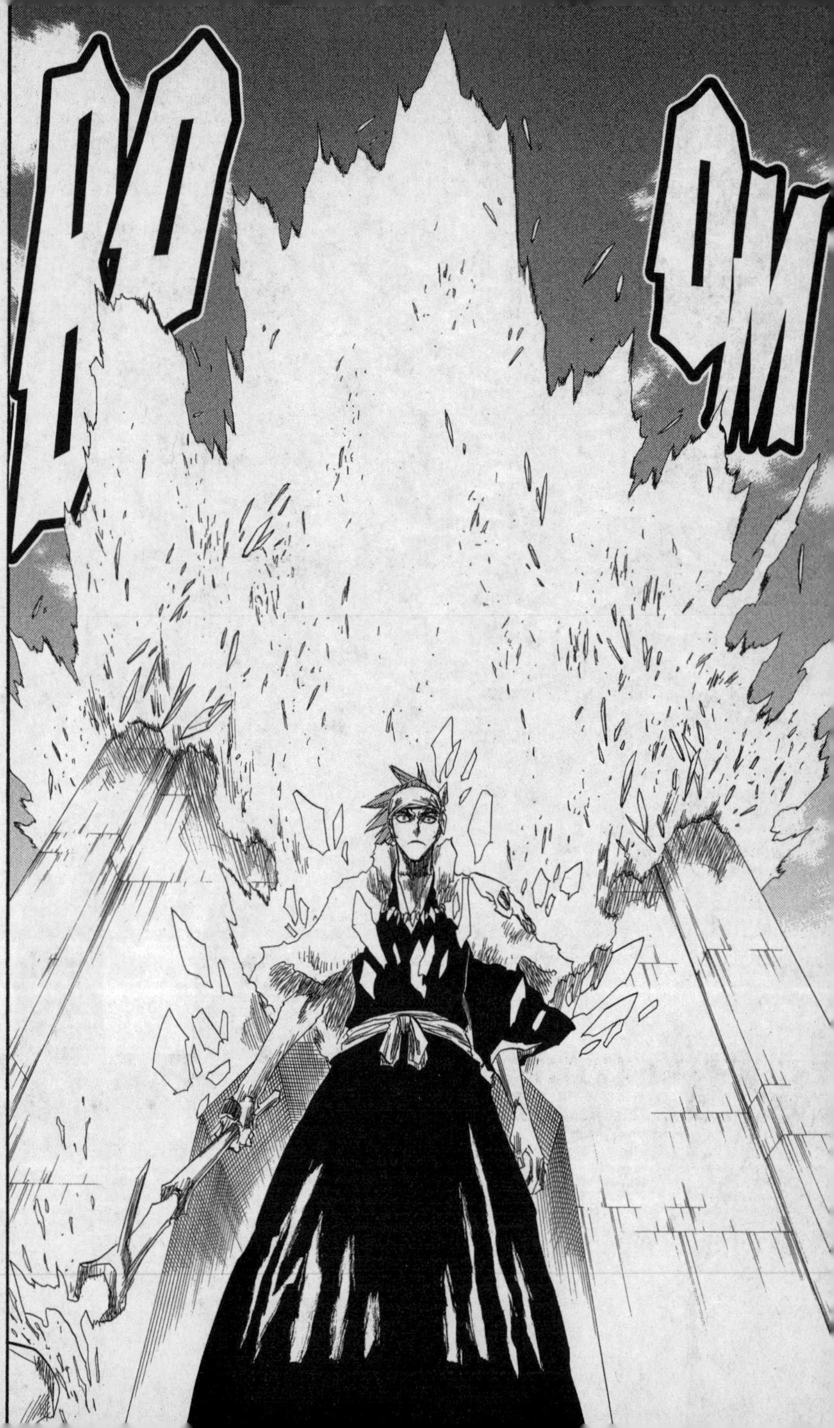
BOOM

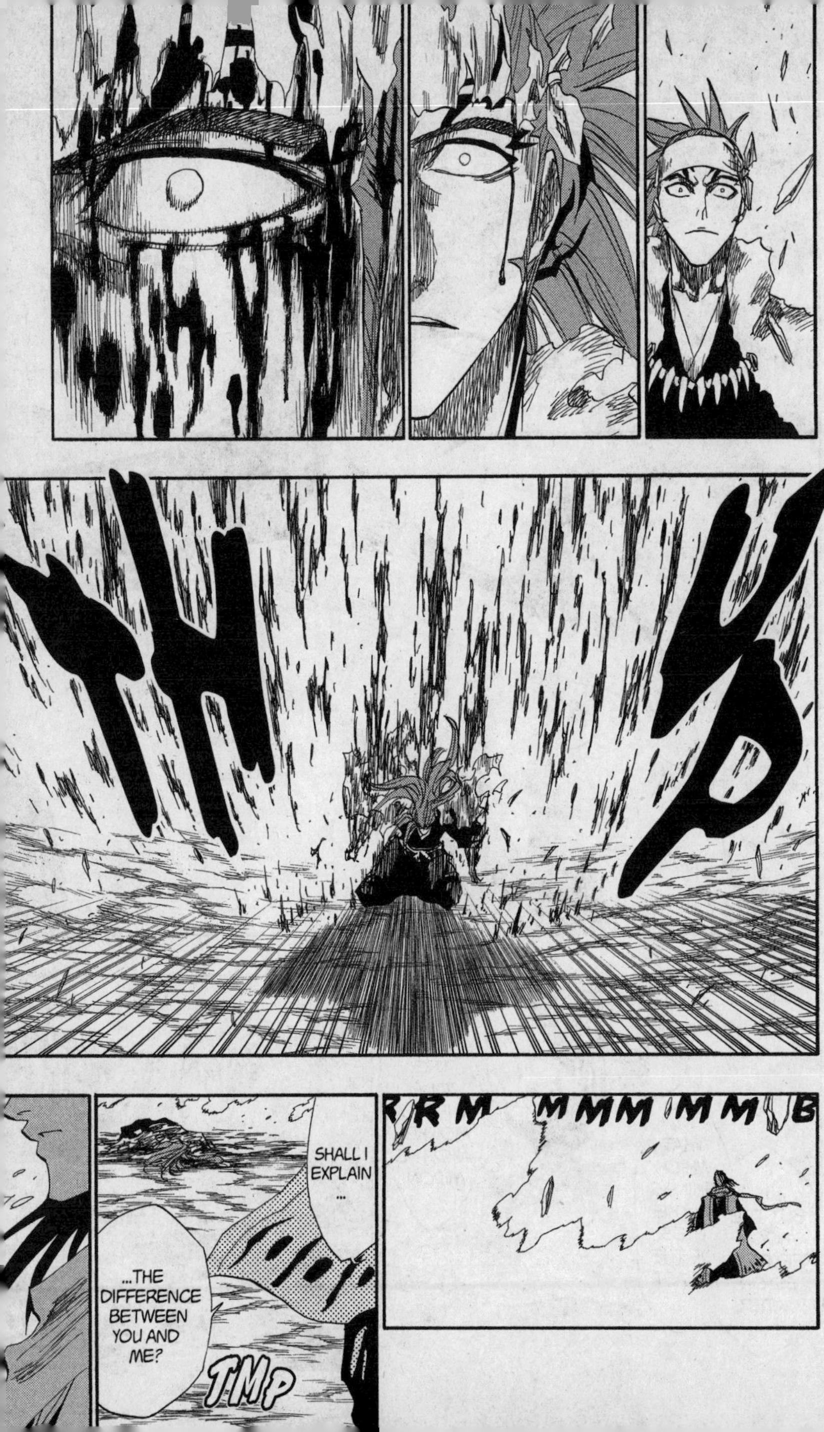
RRM MMM MMM B
SHALL I EXPLAIN ...
...THE DIFFERENCE BETWEEN YOU AND ME?
TMP

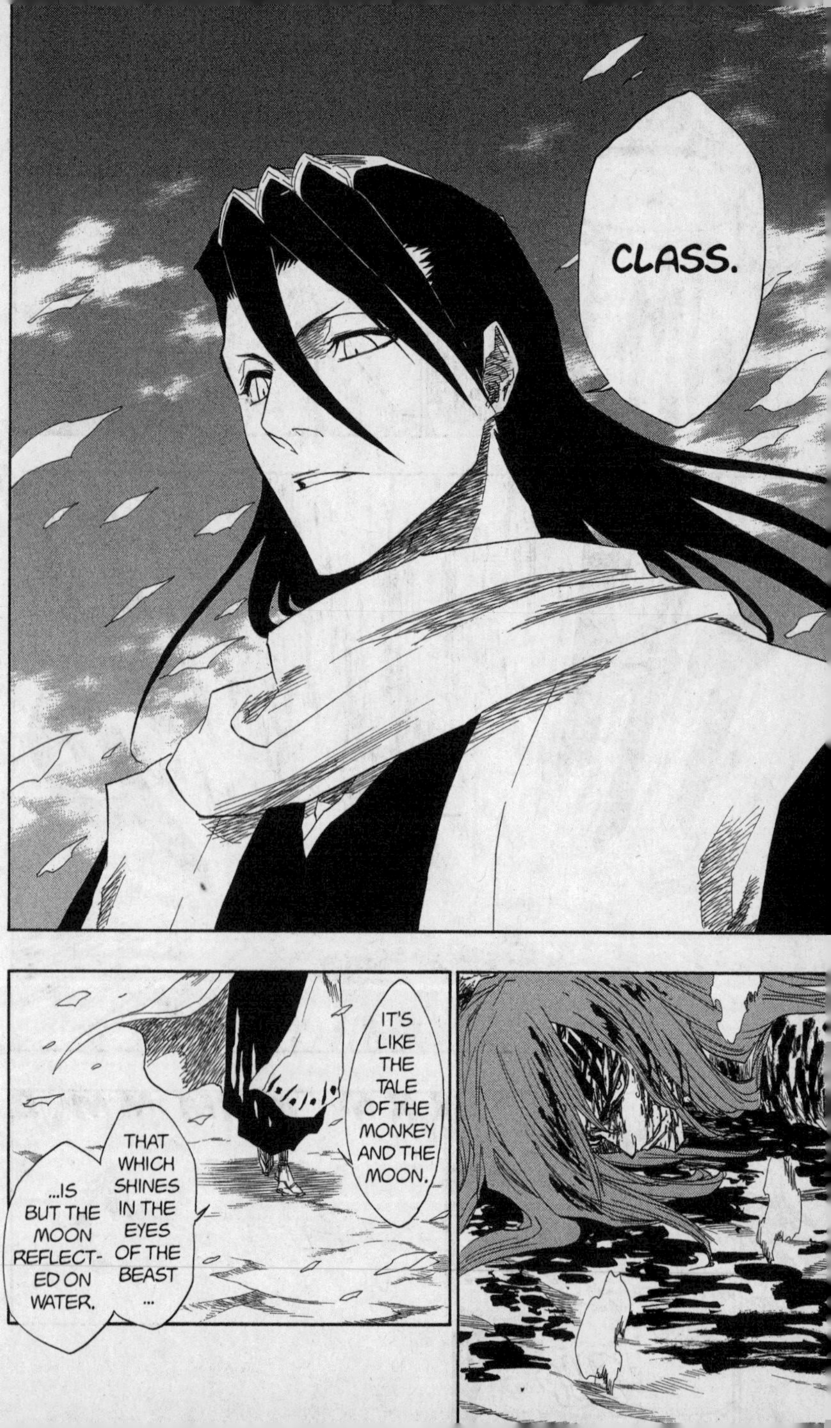
CLASS.
IT'S LIKE THE TALE OF THE MONKEY AND THE MOON.
THAT WHICH SHINES IN THE EYES OF THE BEAST...
...IS BUT THE MOON REFLECT-ED ON WATER.

READ THIS WAY

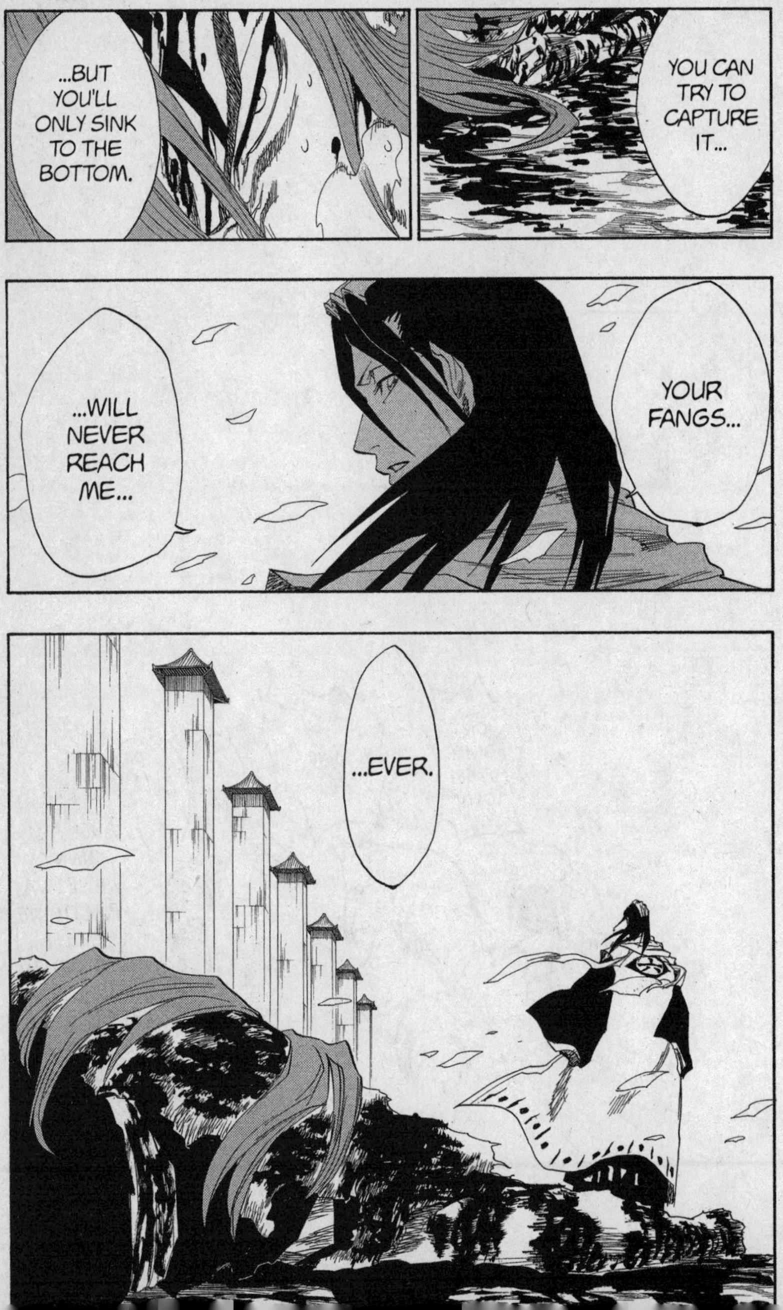
YOU CAN TRY TO CAPTURE IT...
...BUT YOU'LL ONLY SINK TO THE BOTTOM.
YOUR FANGS...
...WILL NEVER REACH ME...
...EVER.

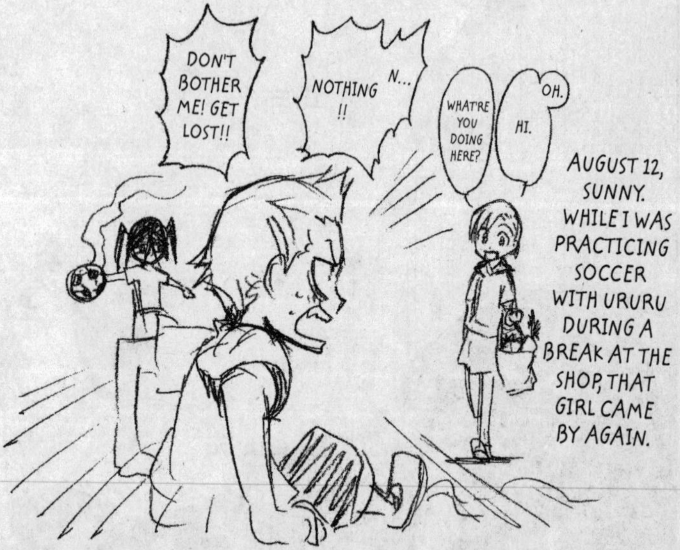
AUGUST 12, SUNNY. WHILE I WAS PRACTICING SOCCER WITH URURU DURING A BREAK AT THE SHOP, THAT GIRL CAME BY AGAIN.
OH.
HI.
WHAT'RE YOU DOING HERE?
N...
NOTHING!!
DON'T BOTHER ME! GET LOST!!

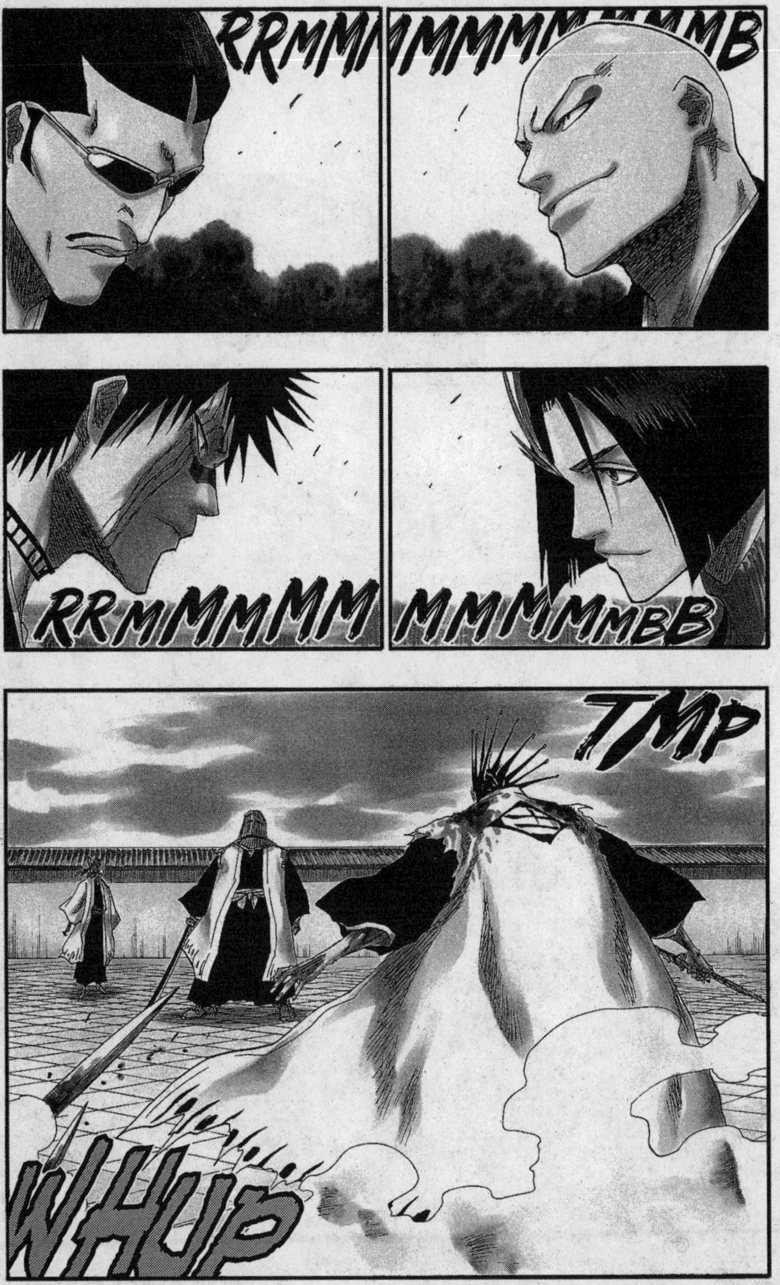
RRMMMMMMMMMMMB
RRMMMMMM
MMMMMBB
TMP
WHUP

143. Blazing Souls

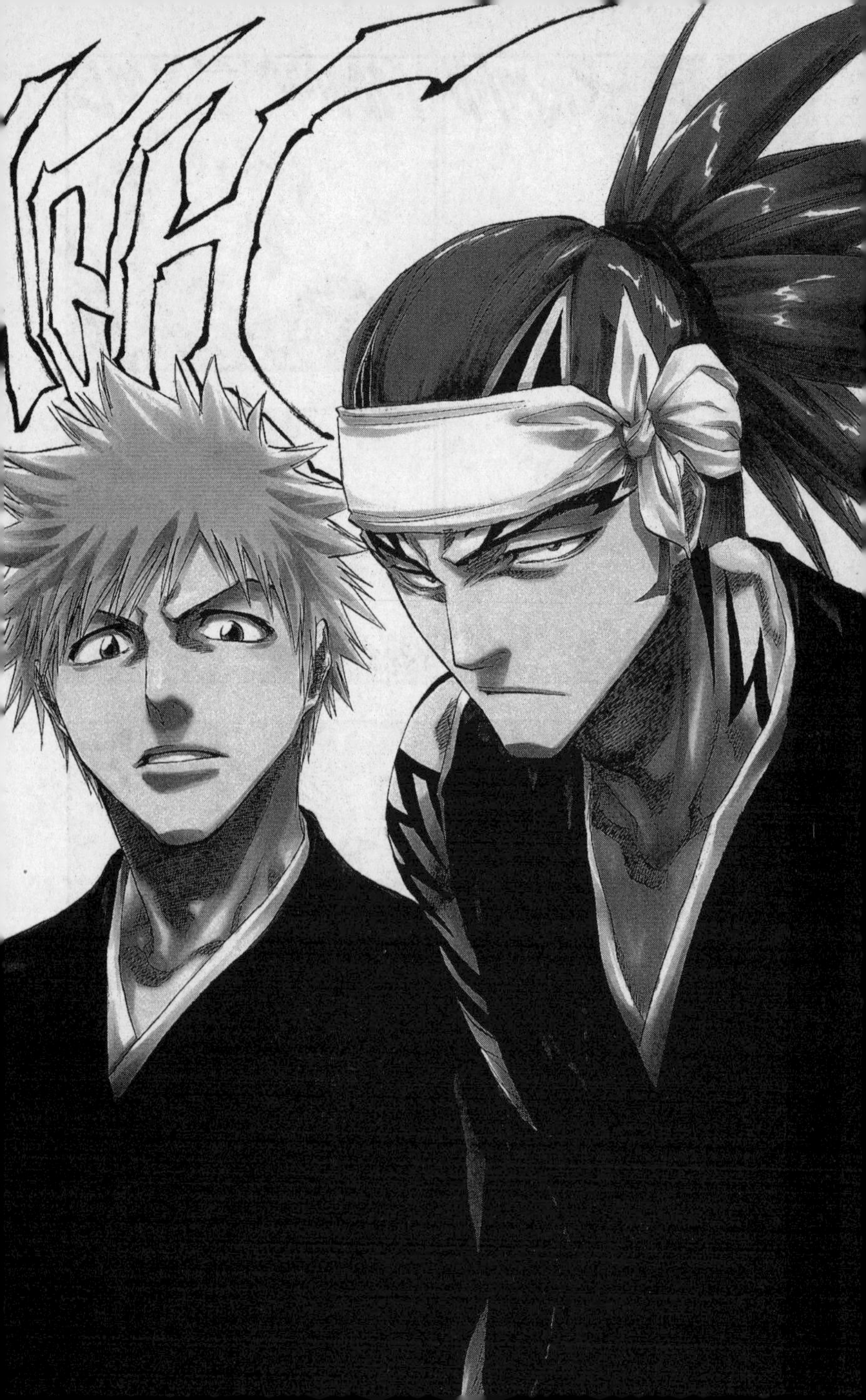

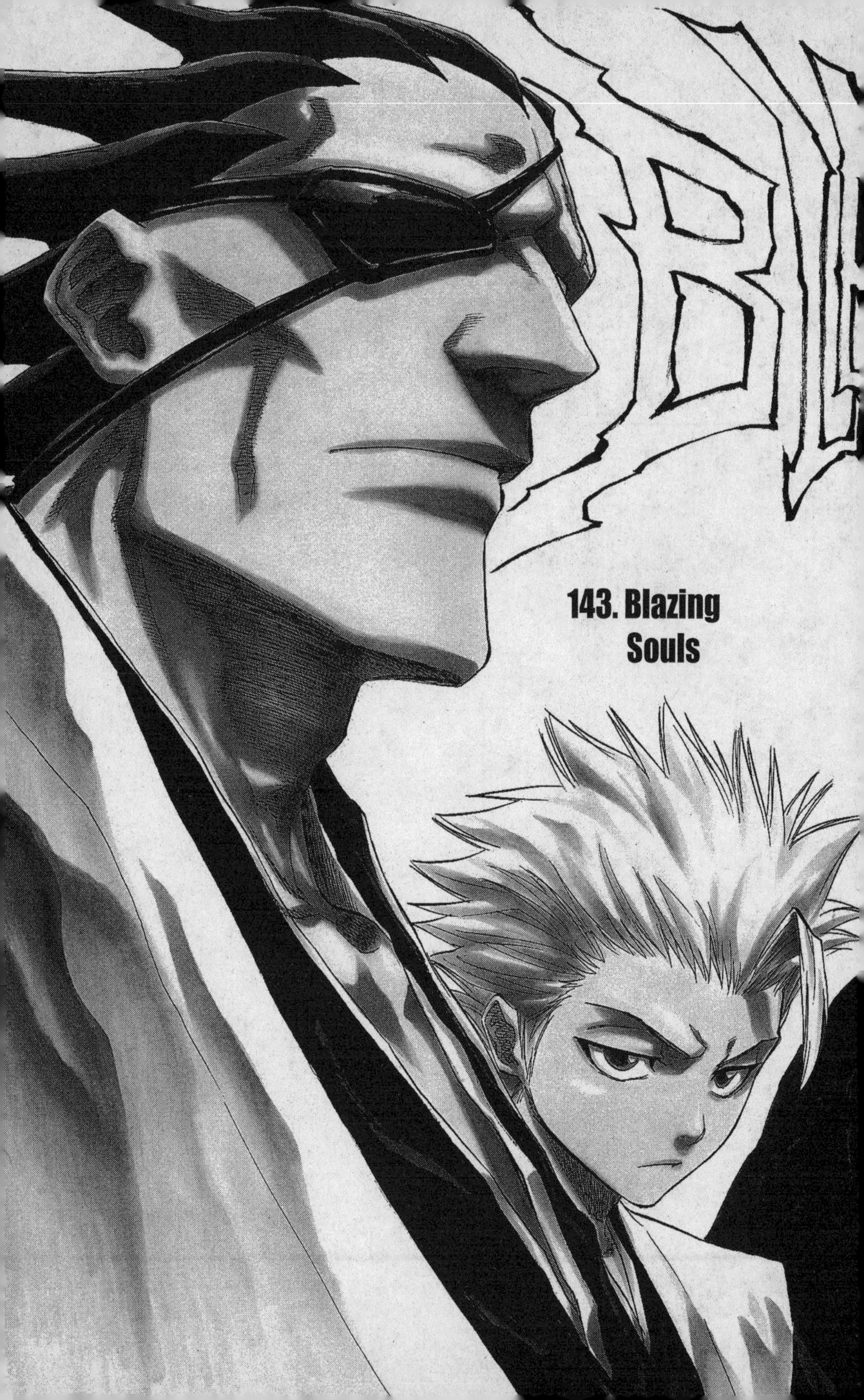
143. Blazing
Souls

BLEACH
ブリーチ

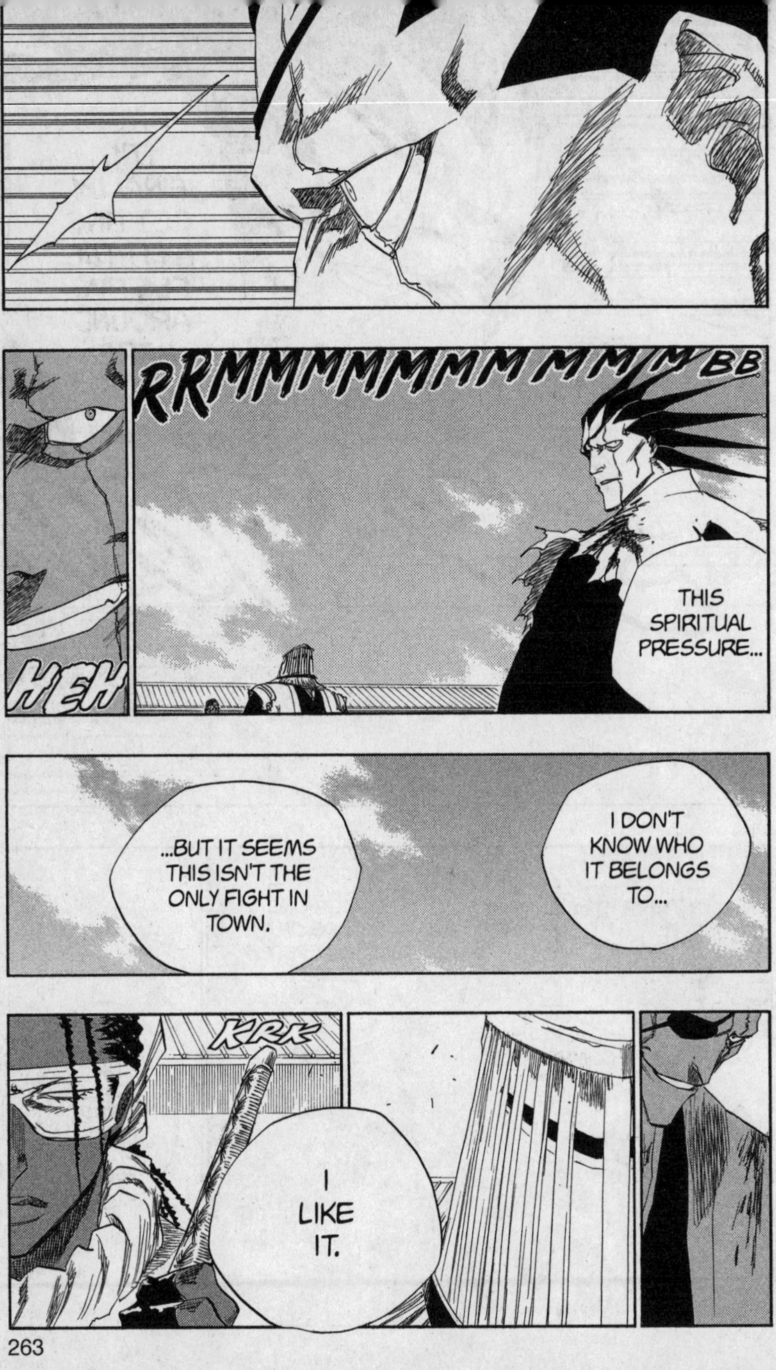
RRMMMMMMMMMMMMMBB
THIS SPIRITUAL PRESSURE...
HEH
I DON'T KNOW WHO IT BELONGS TO...
...BUT IT SEEMS THIS ISN'T THE ONLY FIGHT IN TOWN.
KRK
I LIKE IT.

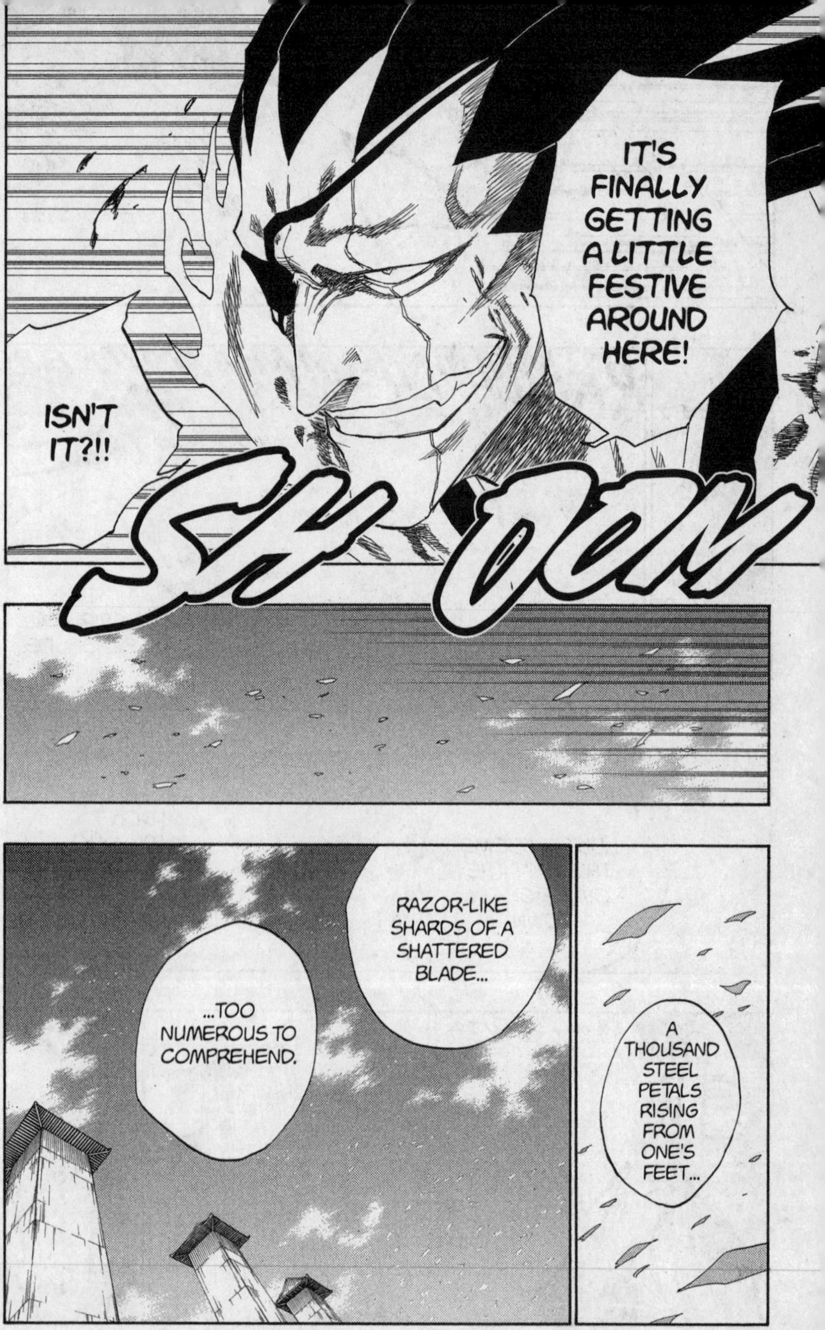
IT'S FINALLY GETTING A LITTLE FESTIVE AROUND HERE!
ISN'T IT?!!
SH OOM
A THOUSAND STEEL PETALS RISING FROM ONE'S FEET...
RAZOR-LIKE SHARDS OF A SHATTERED BLADE...
...TOO NUMEROUS TO COMPREHEND.

READ THIS WAY

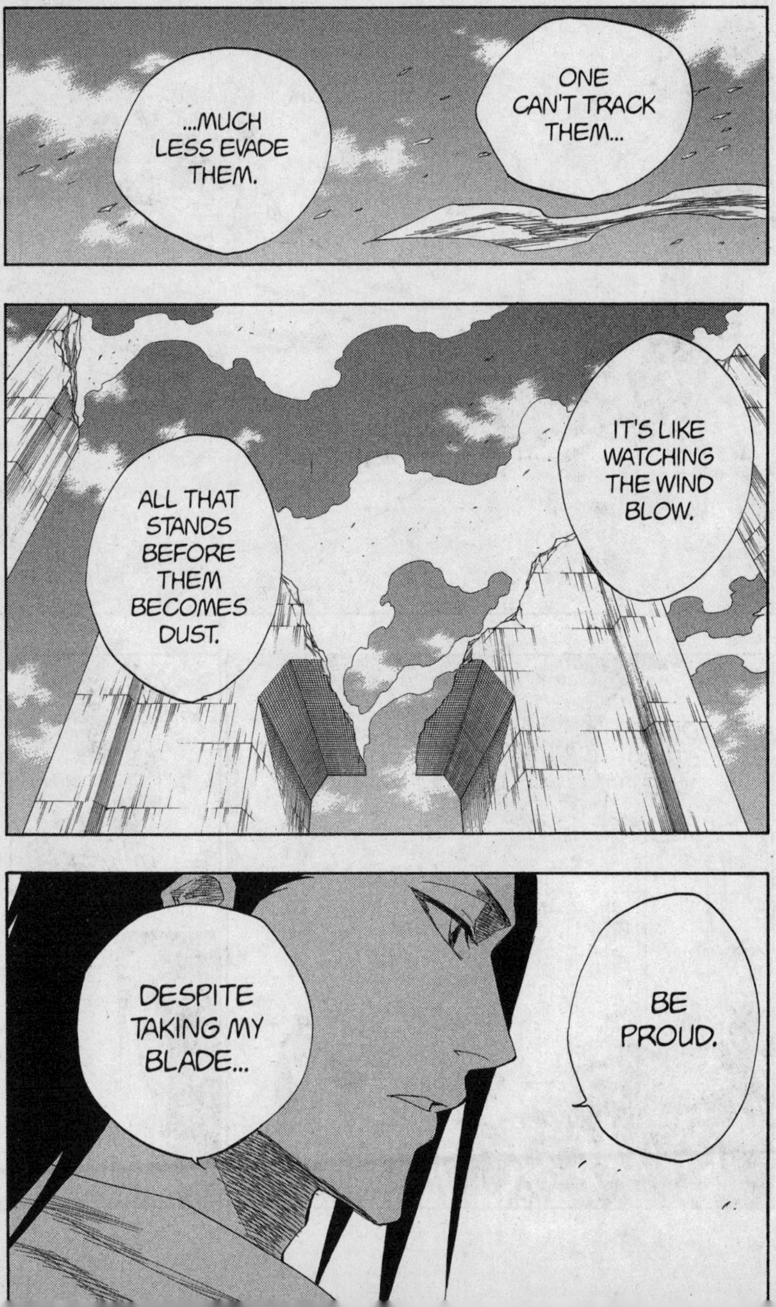
ONE CAN'T TRACK THEM...
...MUCH LESS EVADE THEM.
IT'S LIKE WATCHING THE WIND BLOW.
ALL THAT STANDS BEFORE THEM BECOMES DUST.
BE PROUD.
DESPITE TAKING MY BLADE...

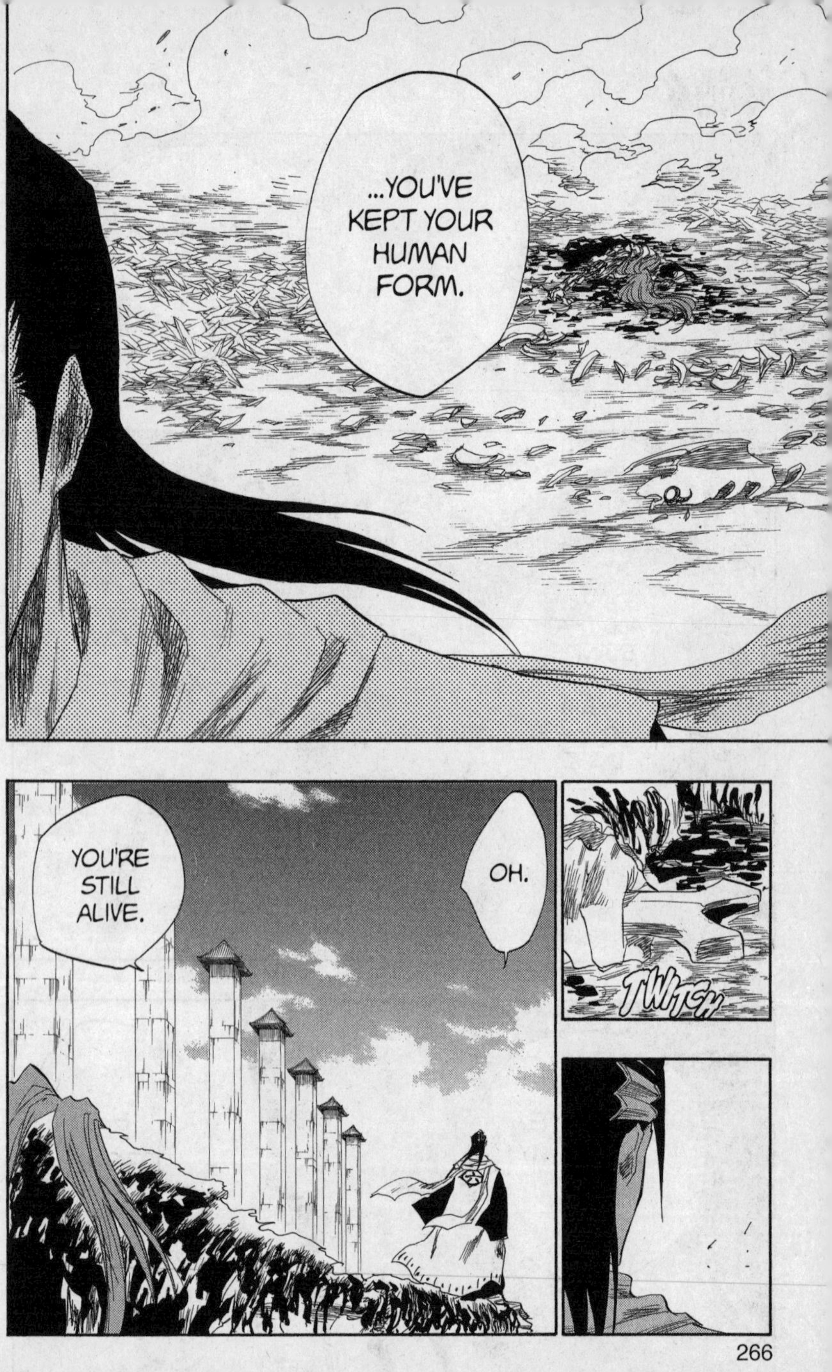
...YOU'VE KEPT YOUR HUMAN FORM.
TWITCH
OH.
YOU'RE STILL ALIVE.

READ THIS WAY

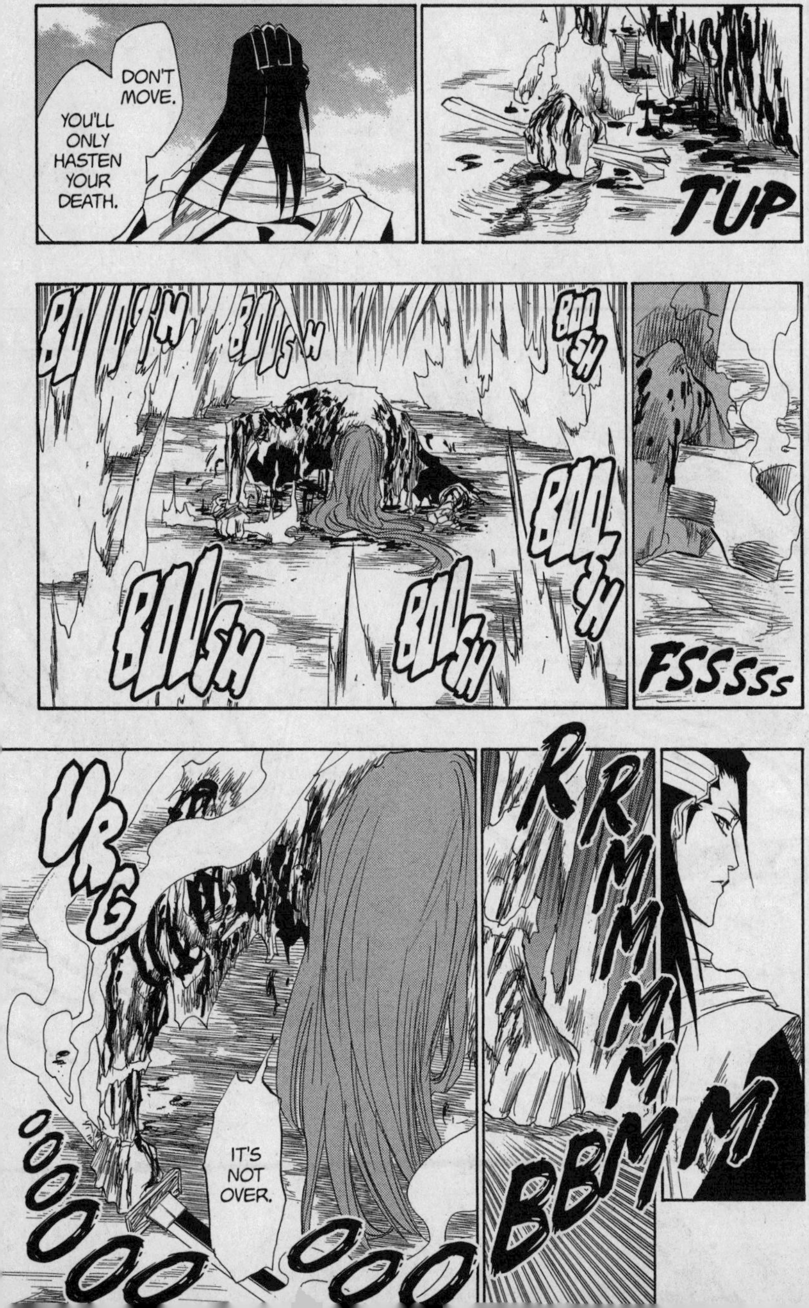
TUP
DON'T MOVE.
YOU'LL ONLY HASTEN YOUR DEATH.
FSSSSS
BOOSH
BOOSH
BOOSH
BOOSH
BOOSH
BOOSH
RRMMMMMBBMM
URG
IT'S NOT OVER.
OOOOOOO-OOOO

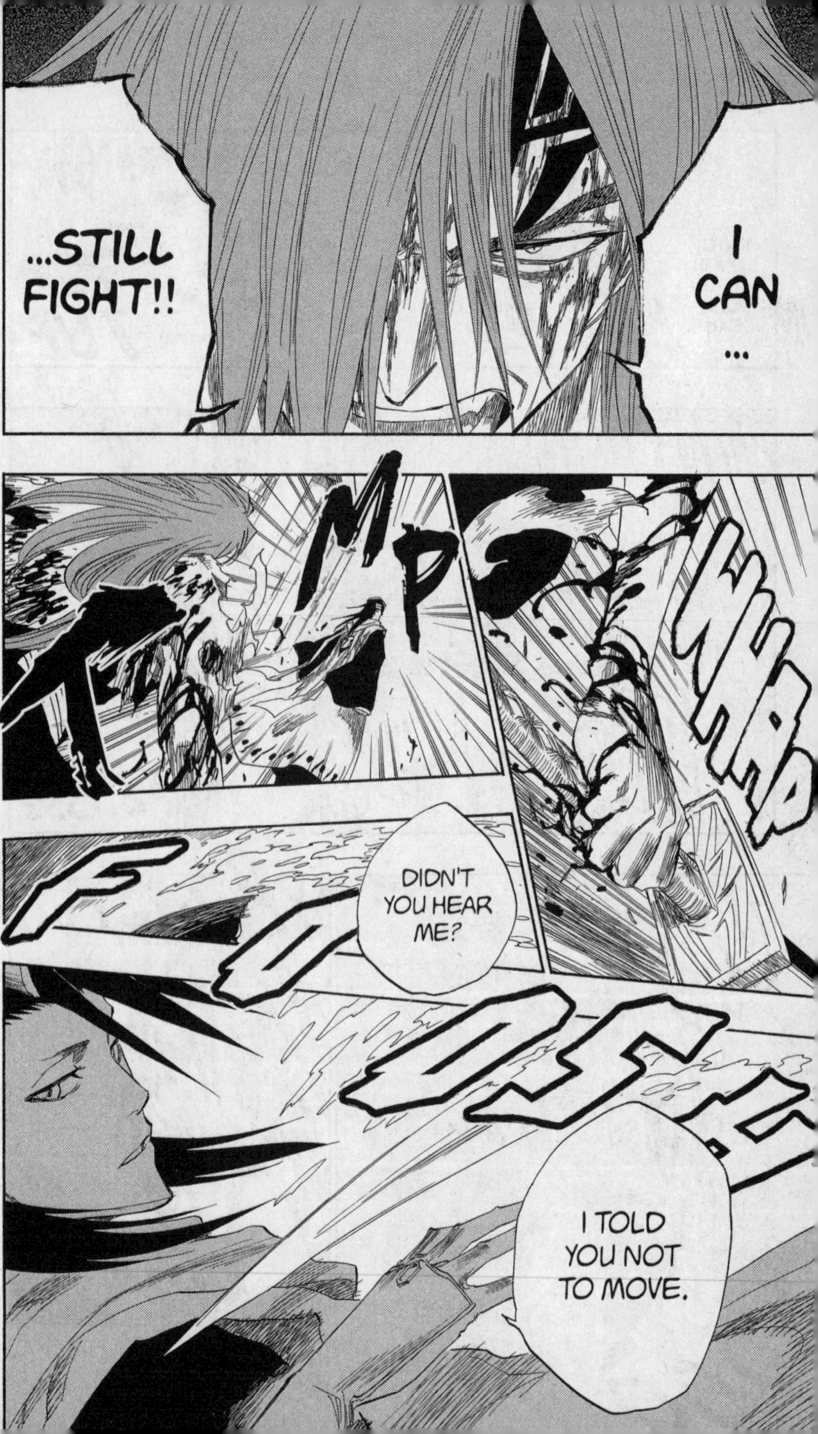
I CAN...
...STILL FIGHT!!
WHAP
DIDN'T YOU HEAR ME?
I TOLD YOU NOT TO MOVE.

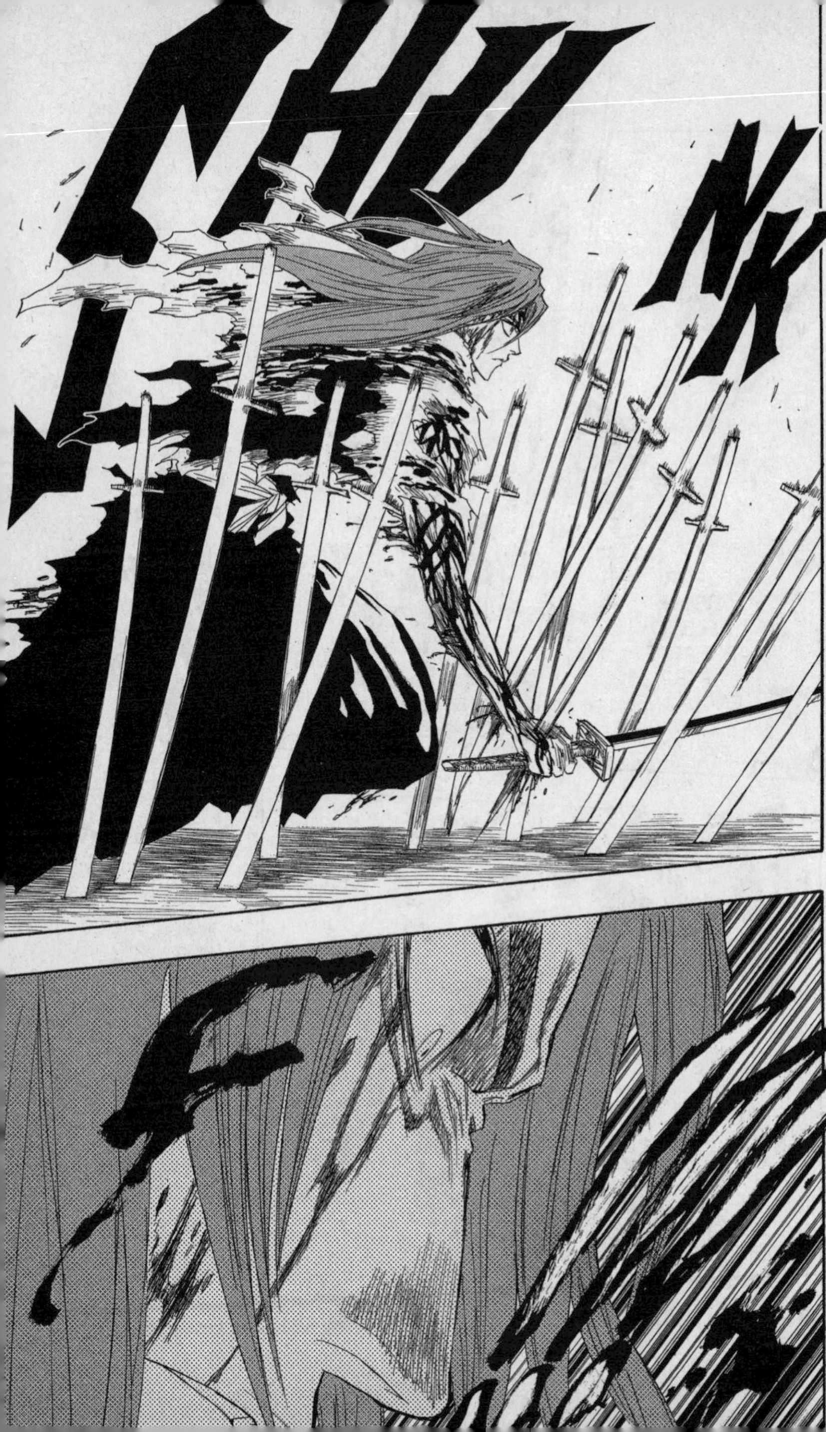
CHUNK

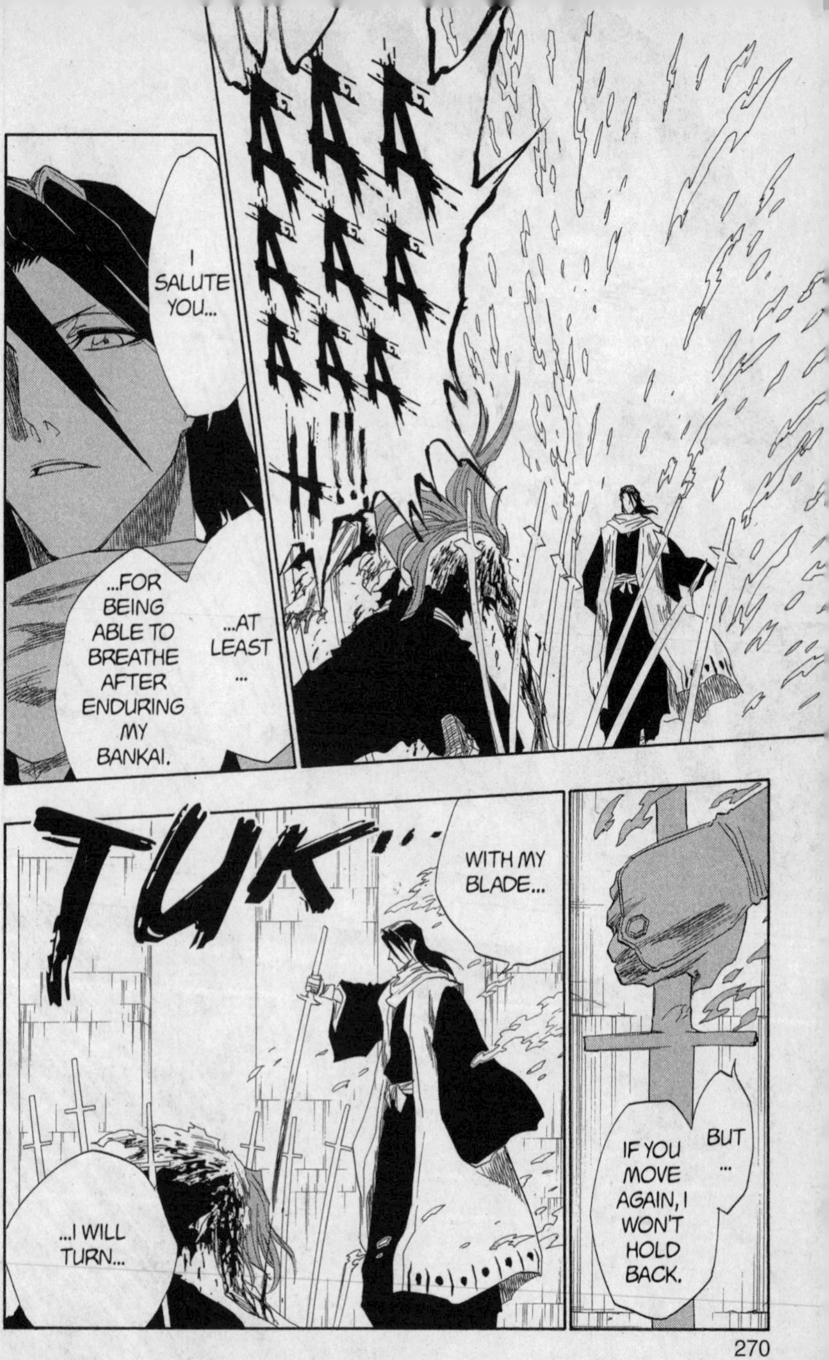
AAAAAAAAAH!!!
I SALUTE YOU...
...AT LEAST...
...FOR BEING ABLE TO BREATHE AFTER ENDURING MY BANKAI.
BUT...
IF YOU MOVE AGAIN, I WON'T HOLD BACK.
TUK...
WITH MY BLADE...
...I WILL TURN...

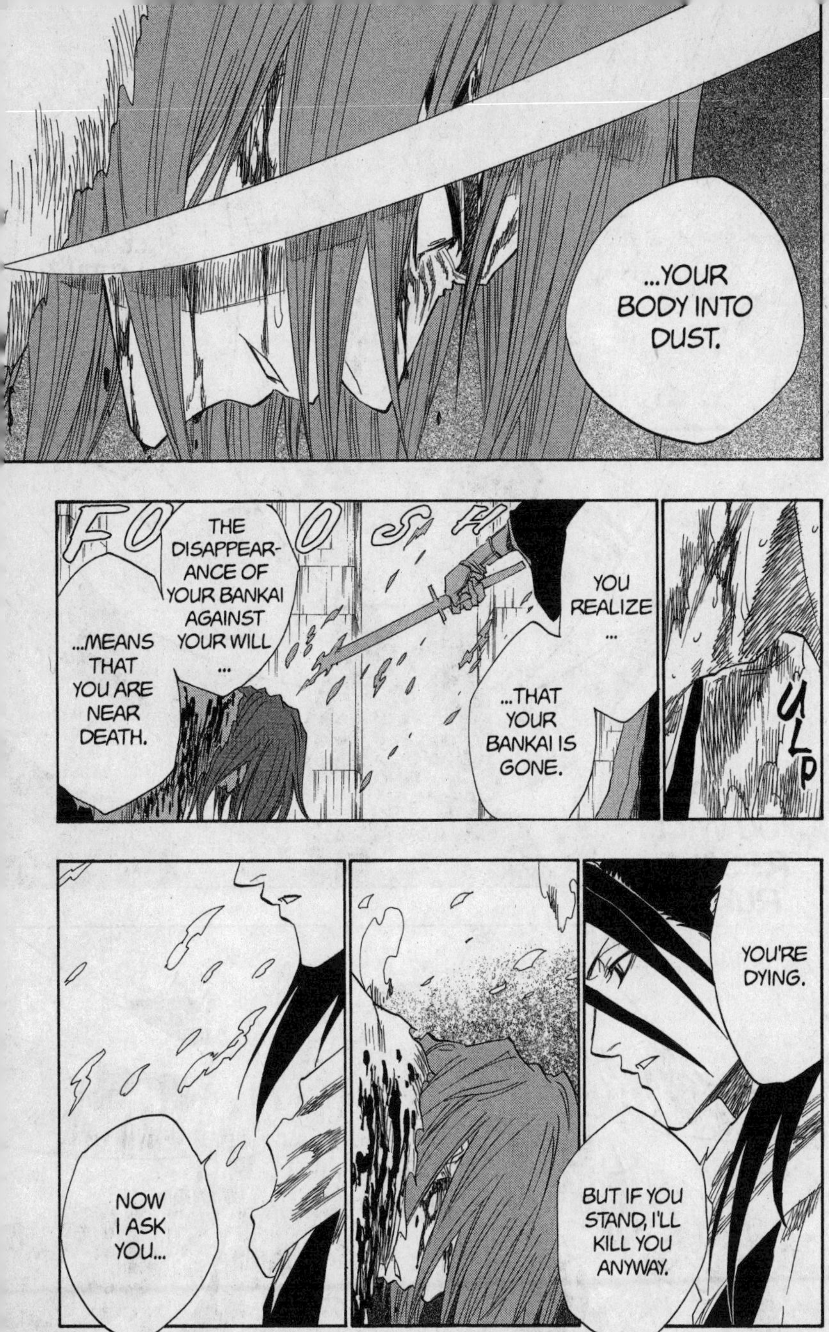
...YOUR BODY INTO DUST.
ULP
FOOSH
YOU REALIZE ...
...THAT YOUR BANKAI IS GONE.
THE DISAPPEARANCE OF YOUR BANKAI AGAINST YOUR WILL ...
...MEANS THAT YOU ARE NEAR DEATH.
YOU'RE DYING.
BUT IF YOU STAND, I'LL KILL YOU ANYWAY.
NOW I ASK YOU...

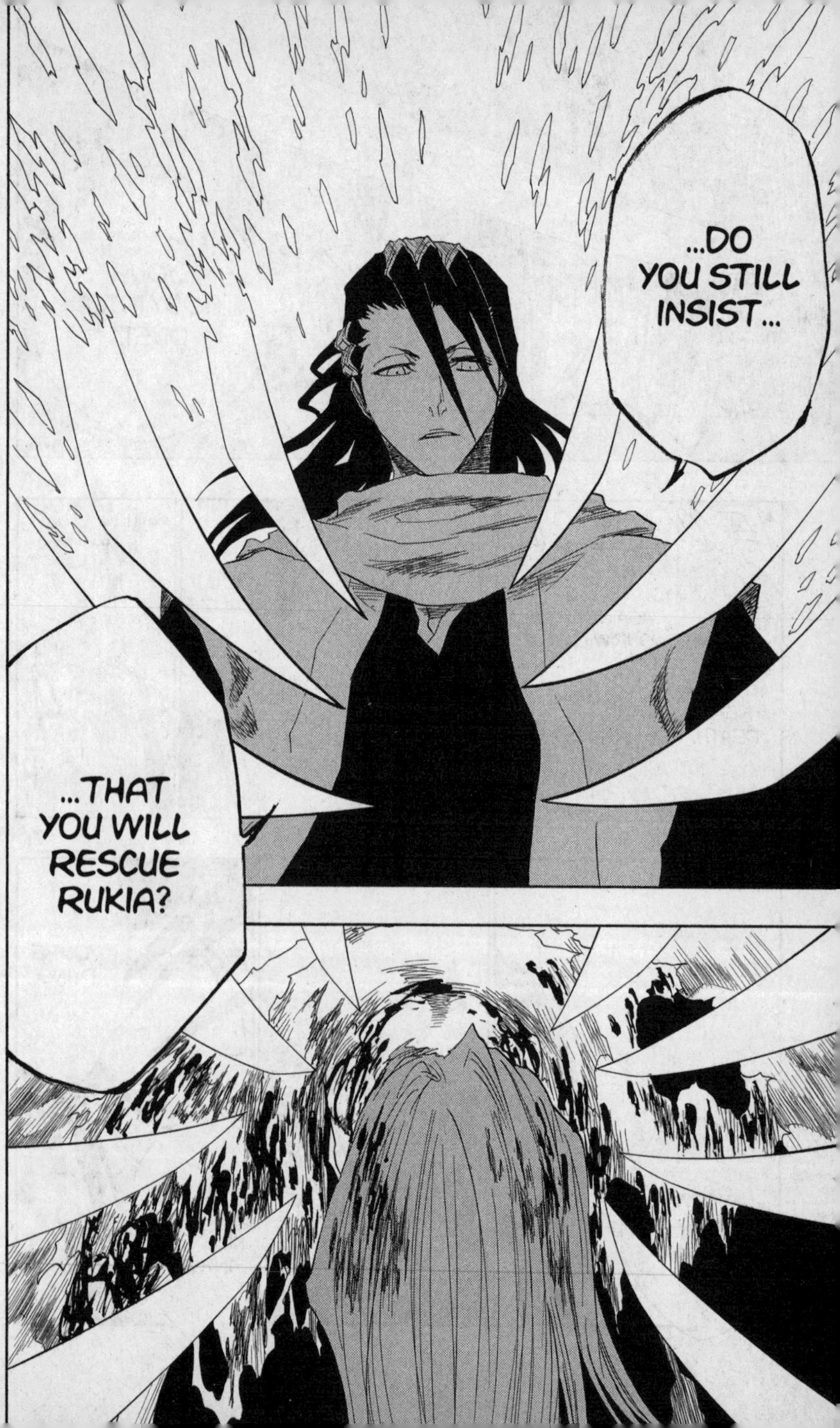
...DO YOU STILL INSIST...
...THAT YOU WILL RESCUE RUKIA?

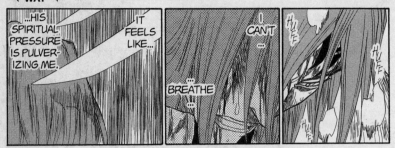

...HIS SPIRITUAL PRESSURE IS PULVERIZING ME.

IT FEELS LIKE...

...BREATHE...

I CAN'T ...

HUFF

HUFF

HUFF

HE WAS FAR BEYOND MY REACH.

BLAST ...

I CAN'T EVEN ...

I HAD NO CHANCE ...

...MOVE A FINGER.

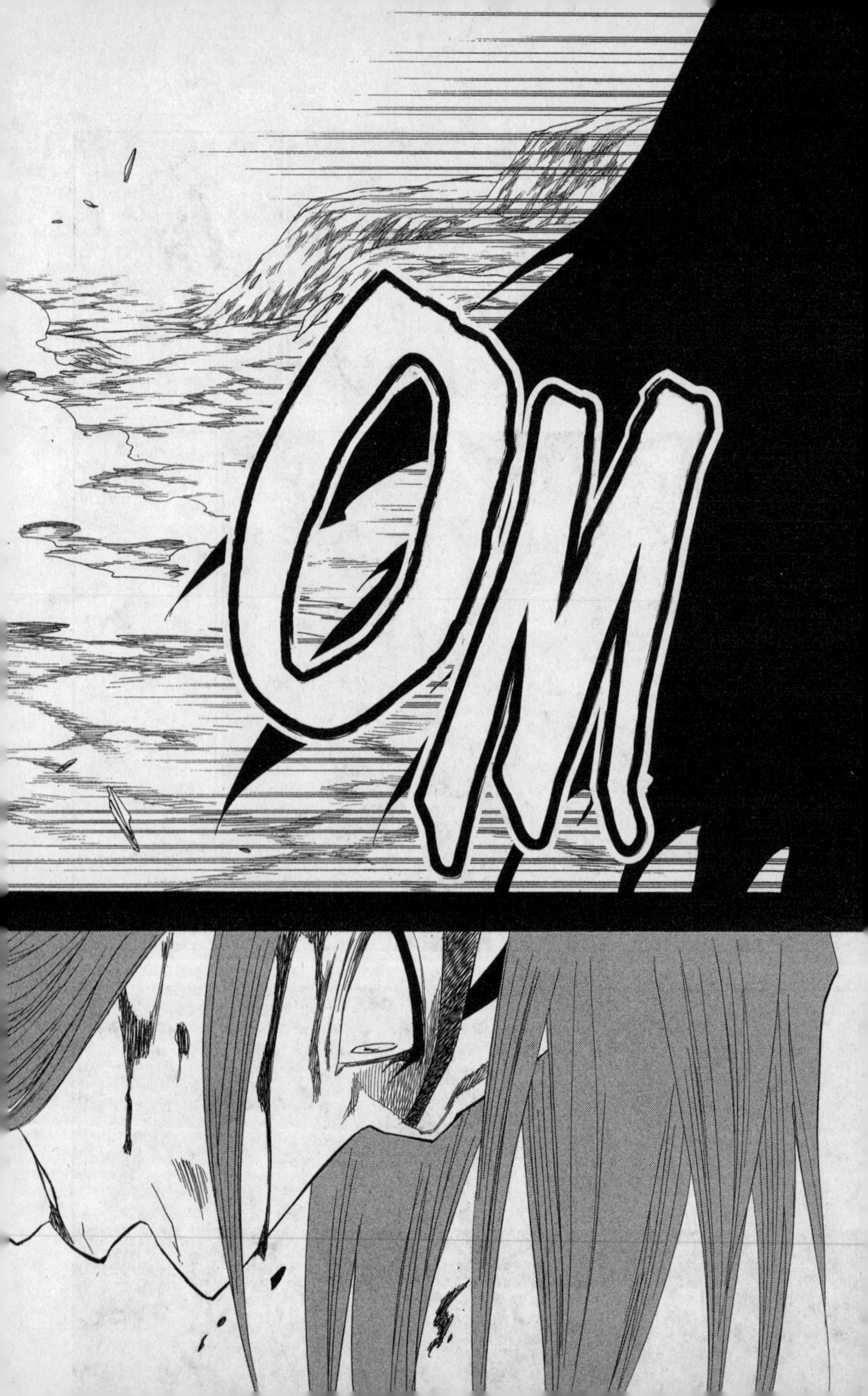
OM

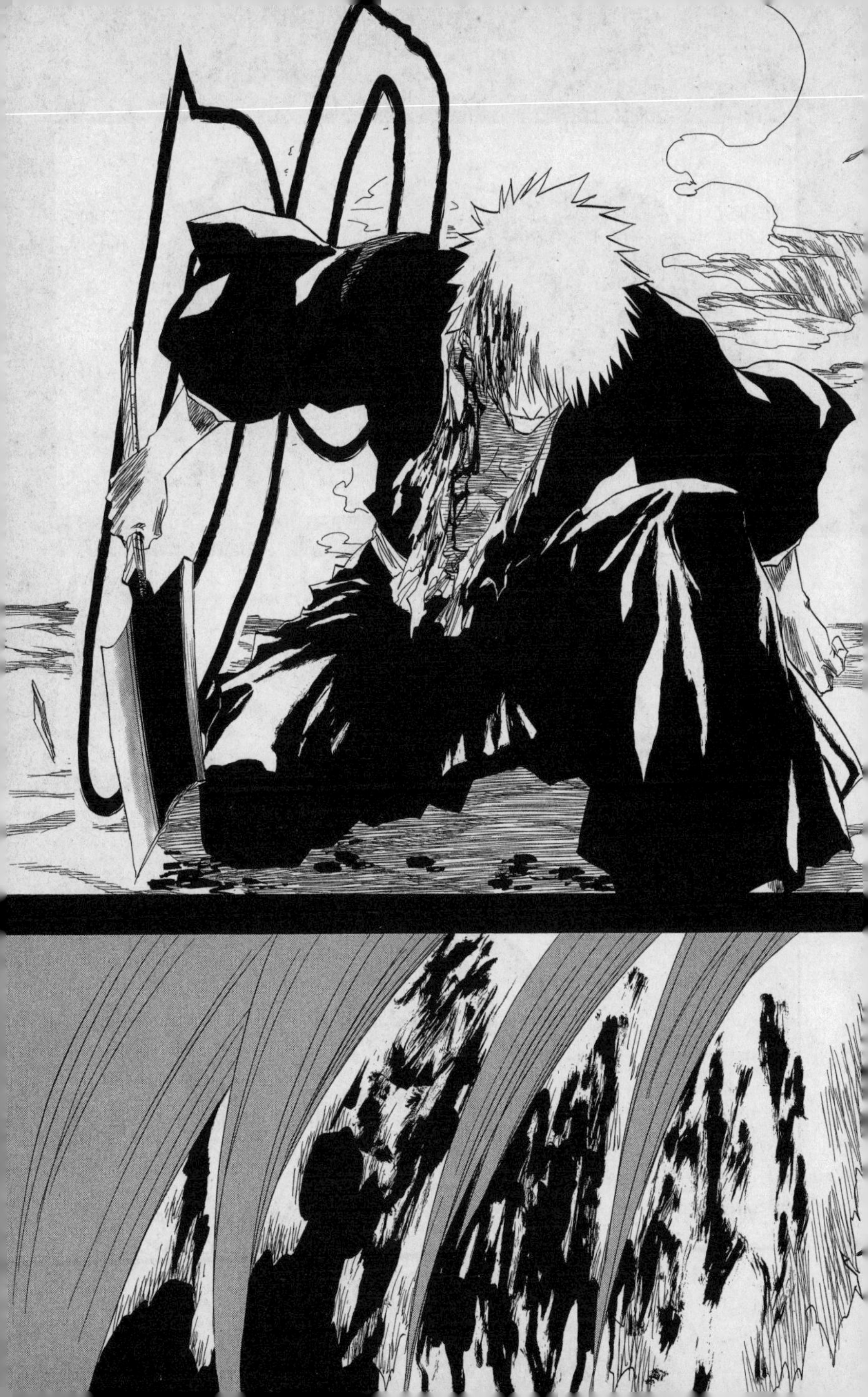

...ICHIGO ?!

GETTING UP AGAIN...

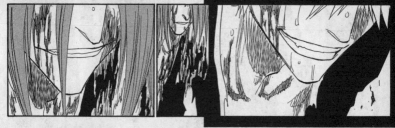

WOOO

WHAT?

OF COURSE.

READ THIS WAY

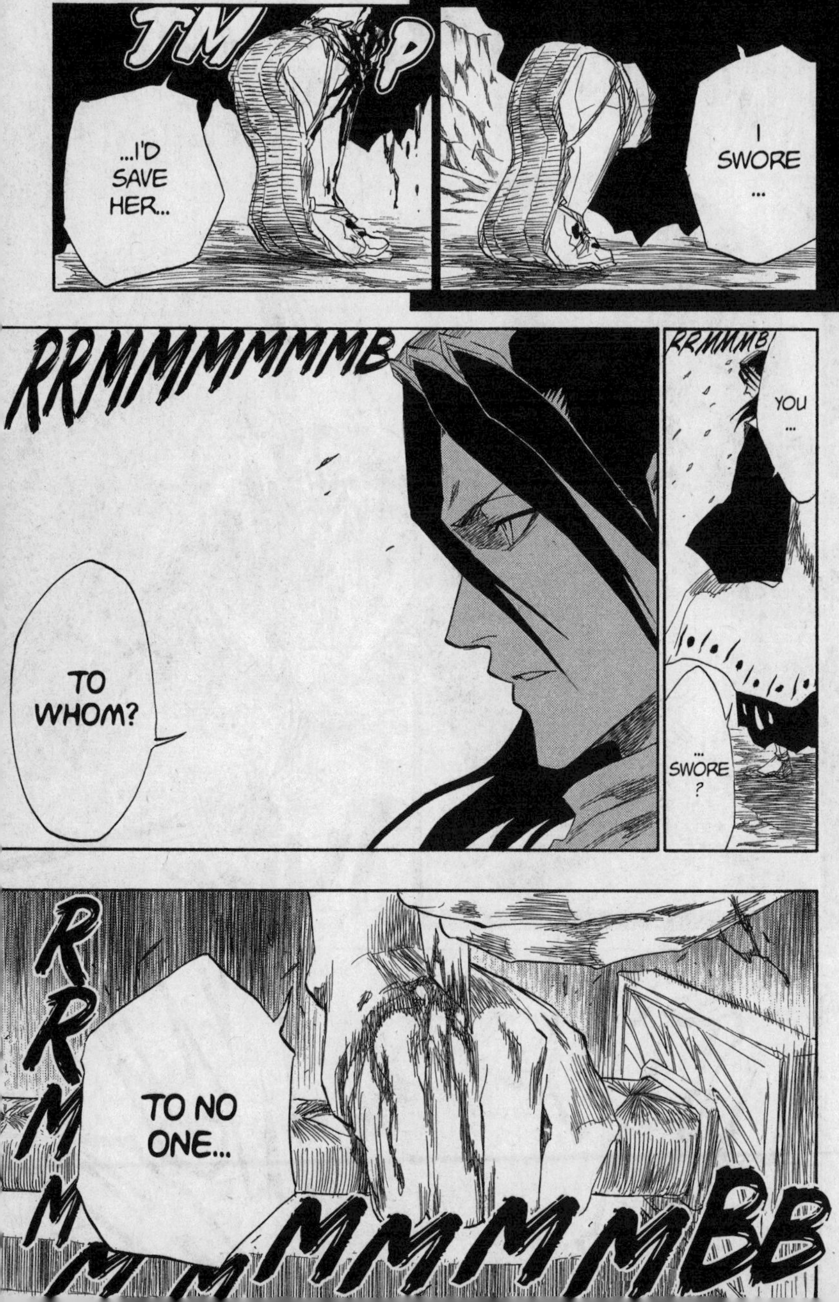
I SWORE ...
TMP
...I'D SAVE HER...
RRMMMB
YOU ...
... SWORE ?
RRMMMMMMMB
TO WHOM?
RRMMM
TO NO ONE...
MMMMMBB

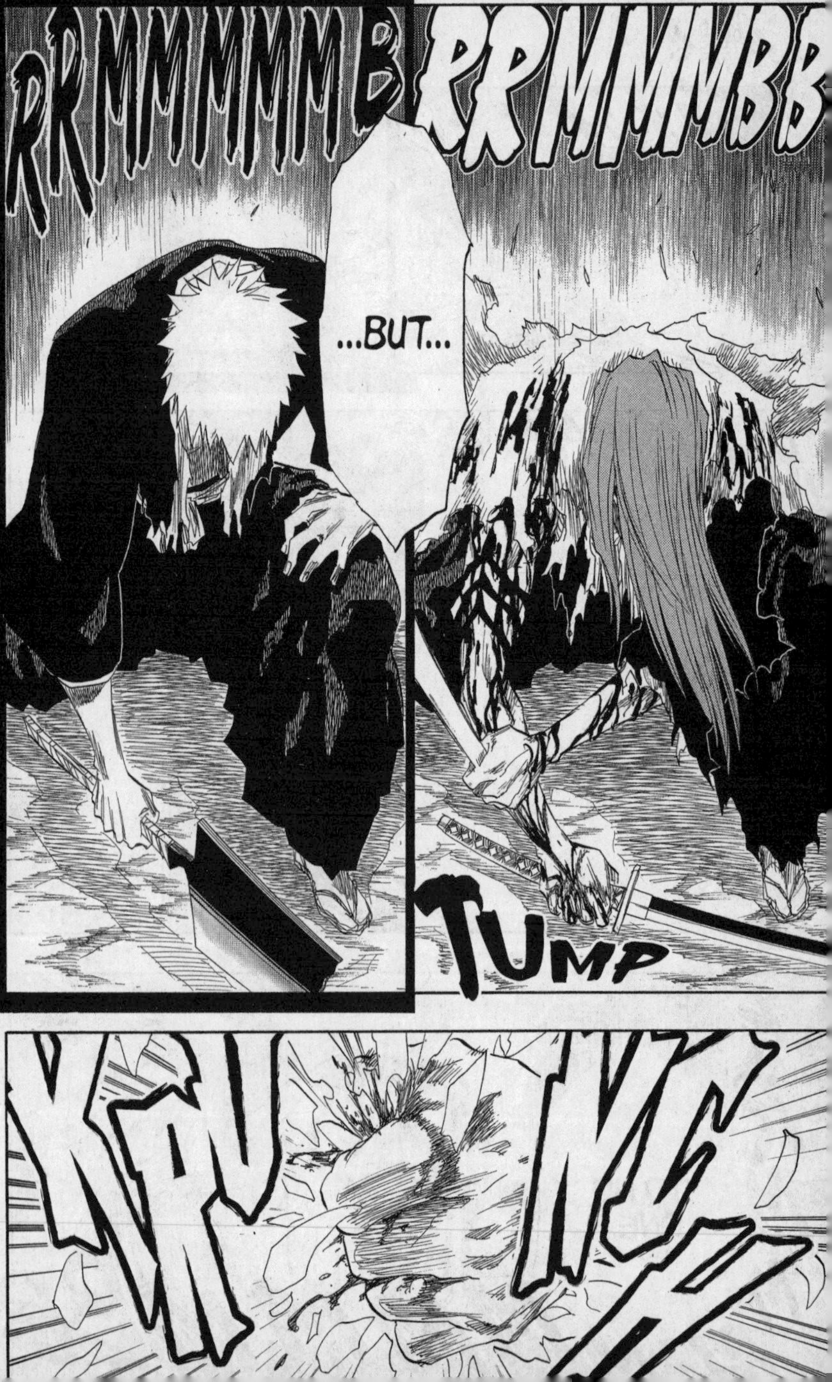
RRMMMBB
TUMP
RRMMMMMB
...BUT...

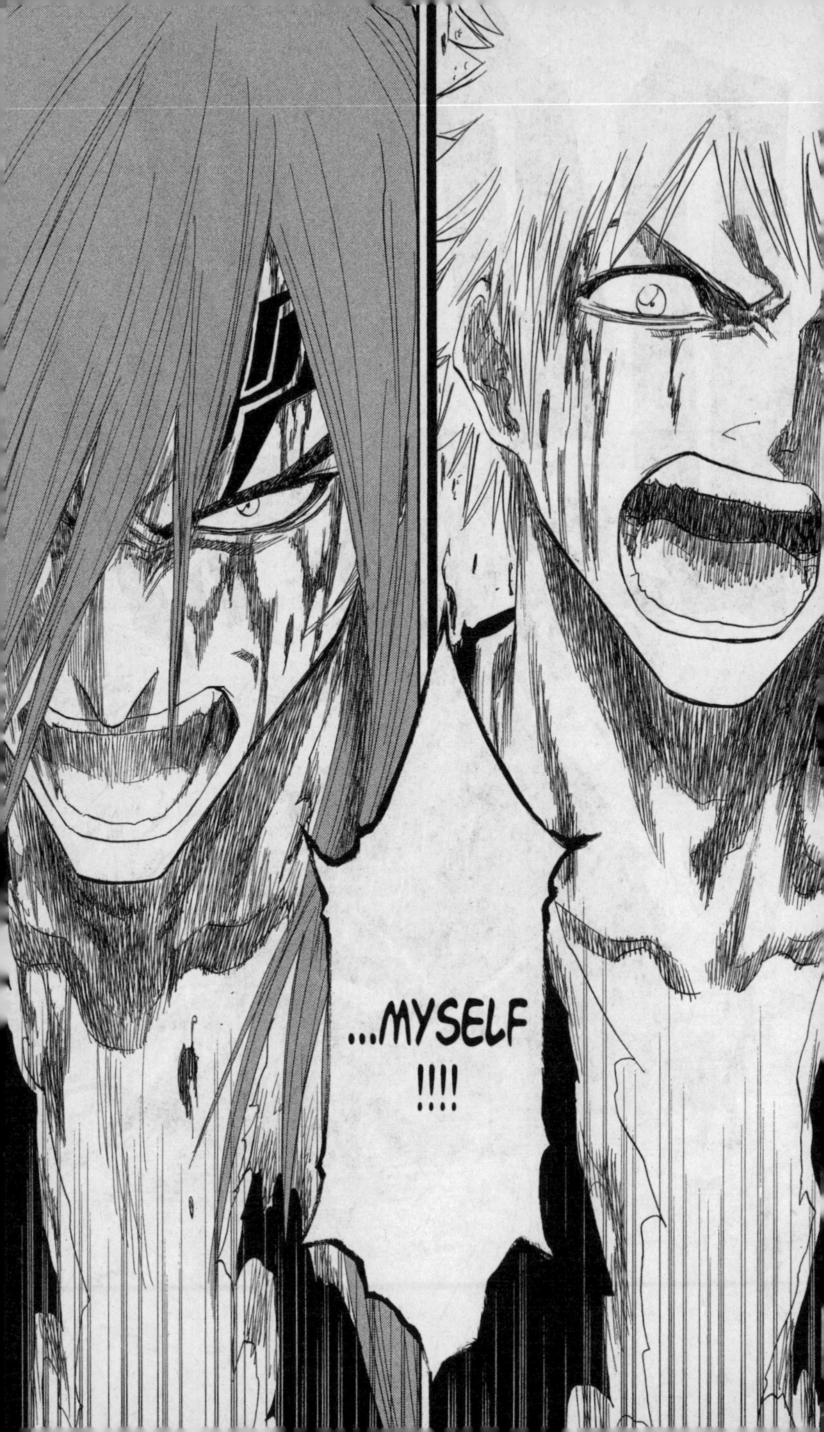
...MYSELF
!!!!

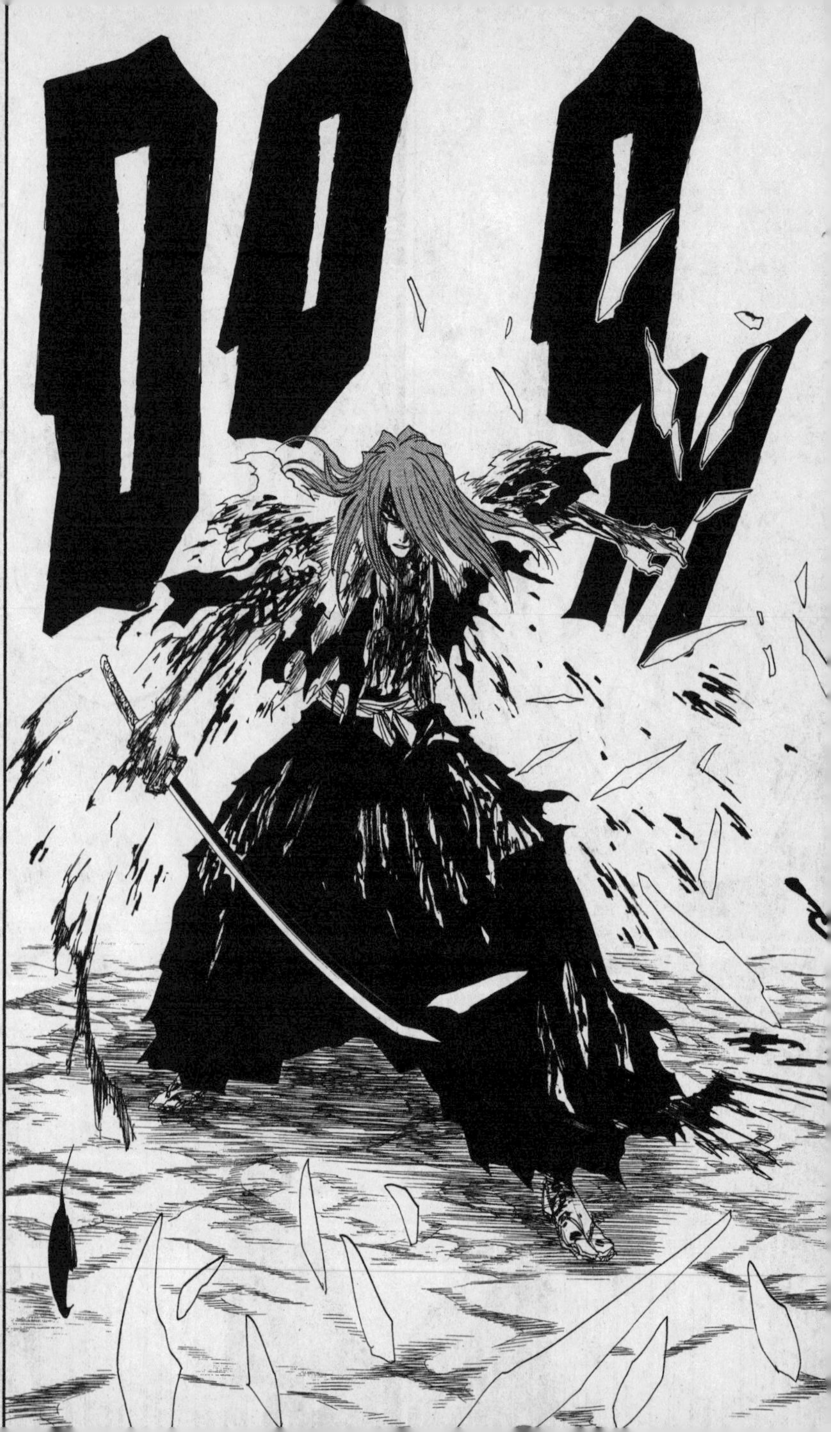
DOOM

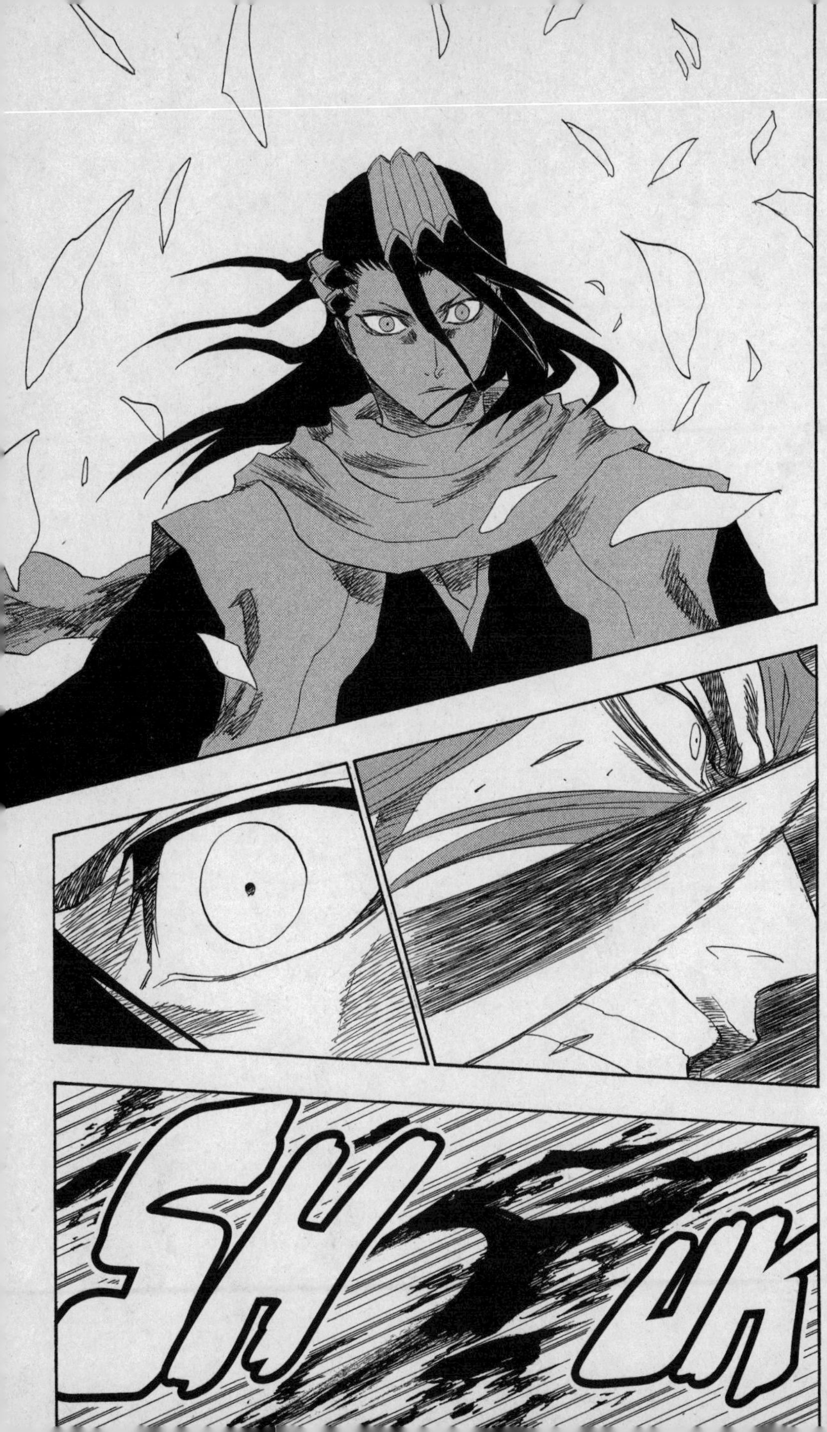

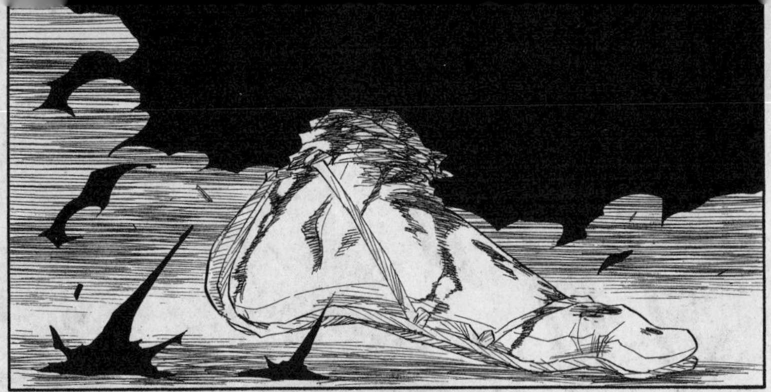

144. Rosa Rubicundior, Lilio Candidior*

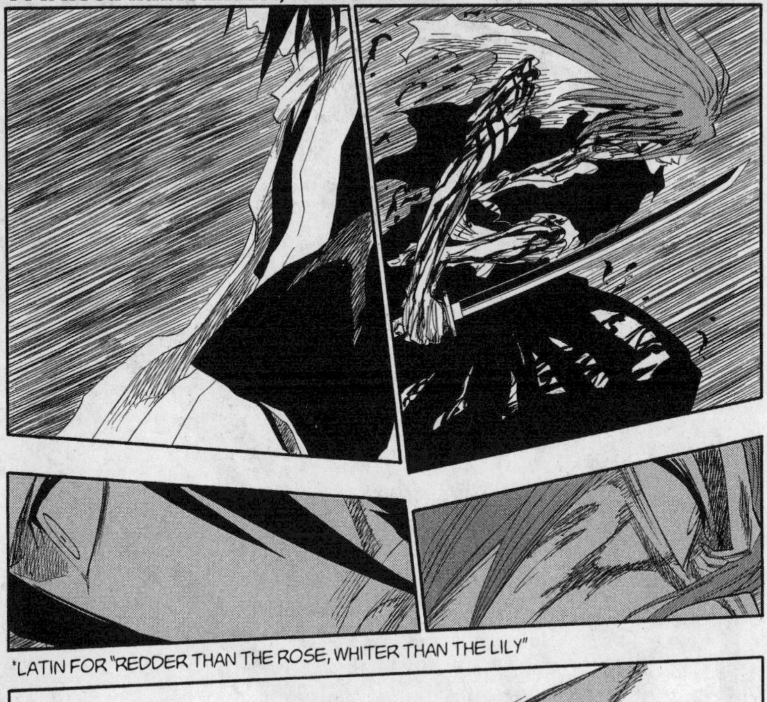

*LATIN FOR "REDDER THAN THE ROSE, WHITER THAN THE LILY"

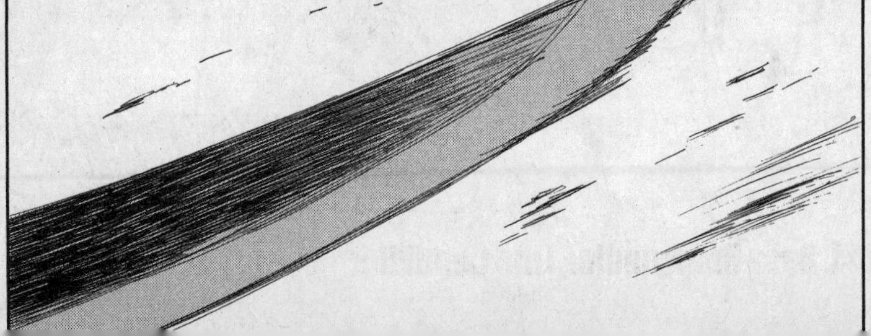

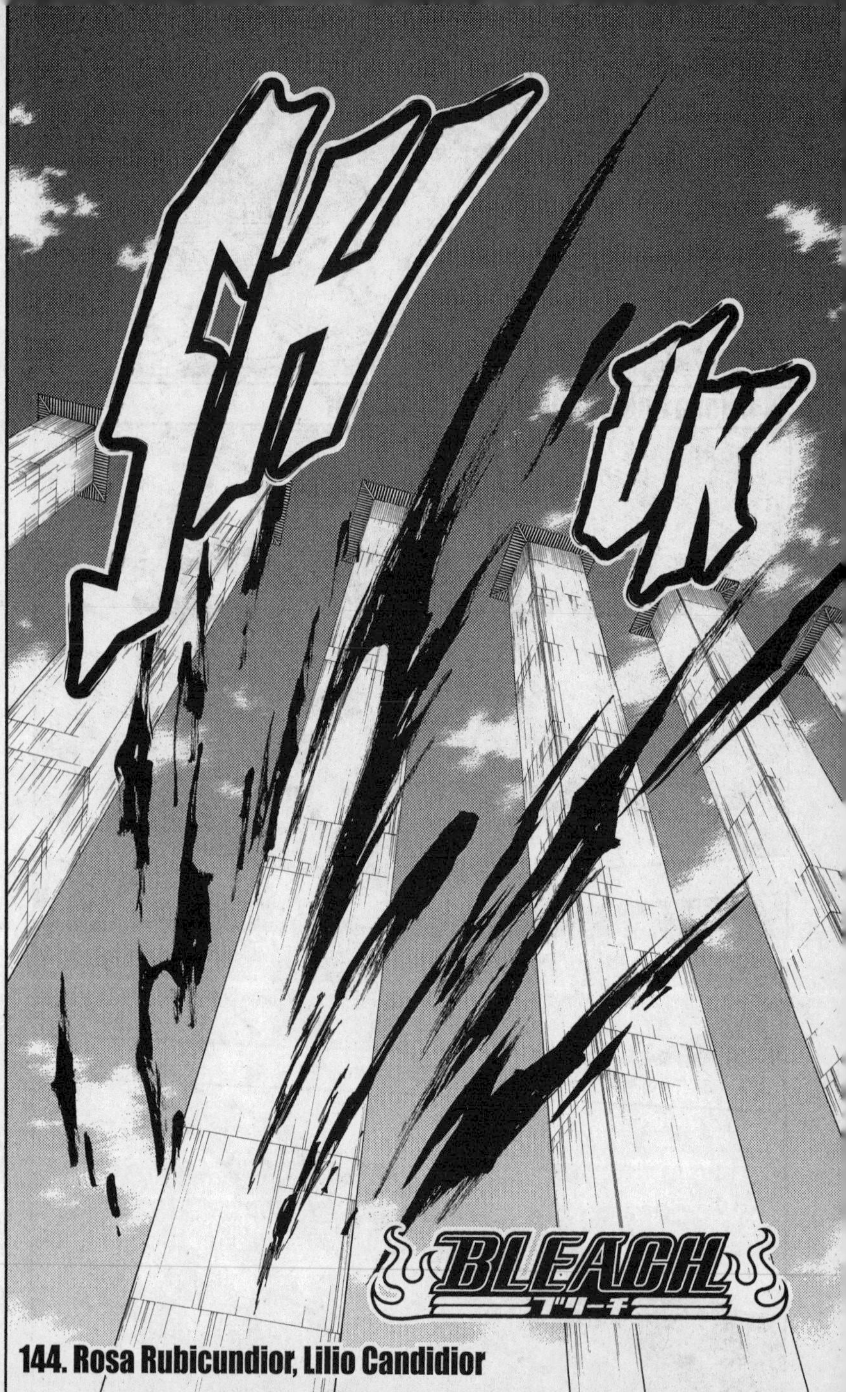
SHUK
BLEACH
ブリーチ

144. Rosa Rubicundior, Lilio Candidior

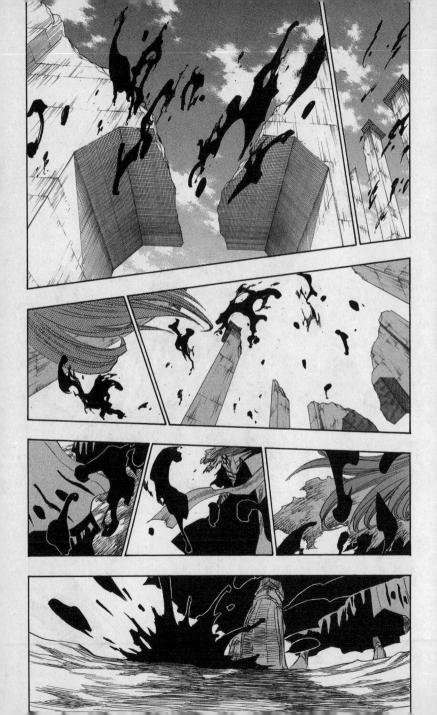

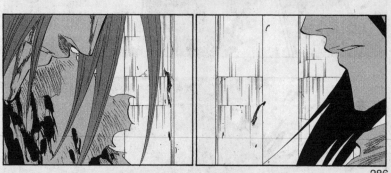

READ THIS WAY

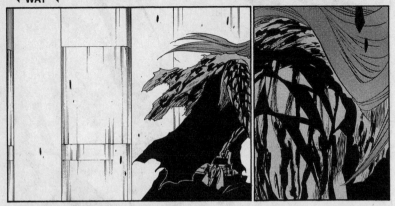

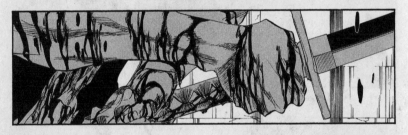

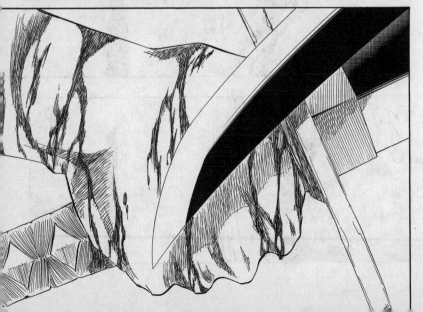

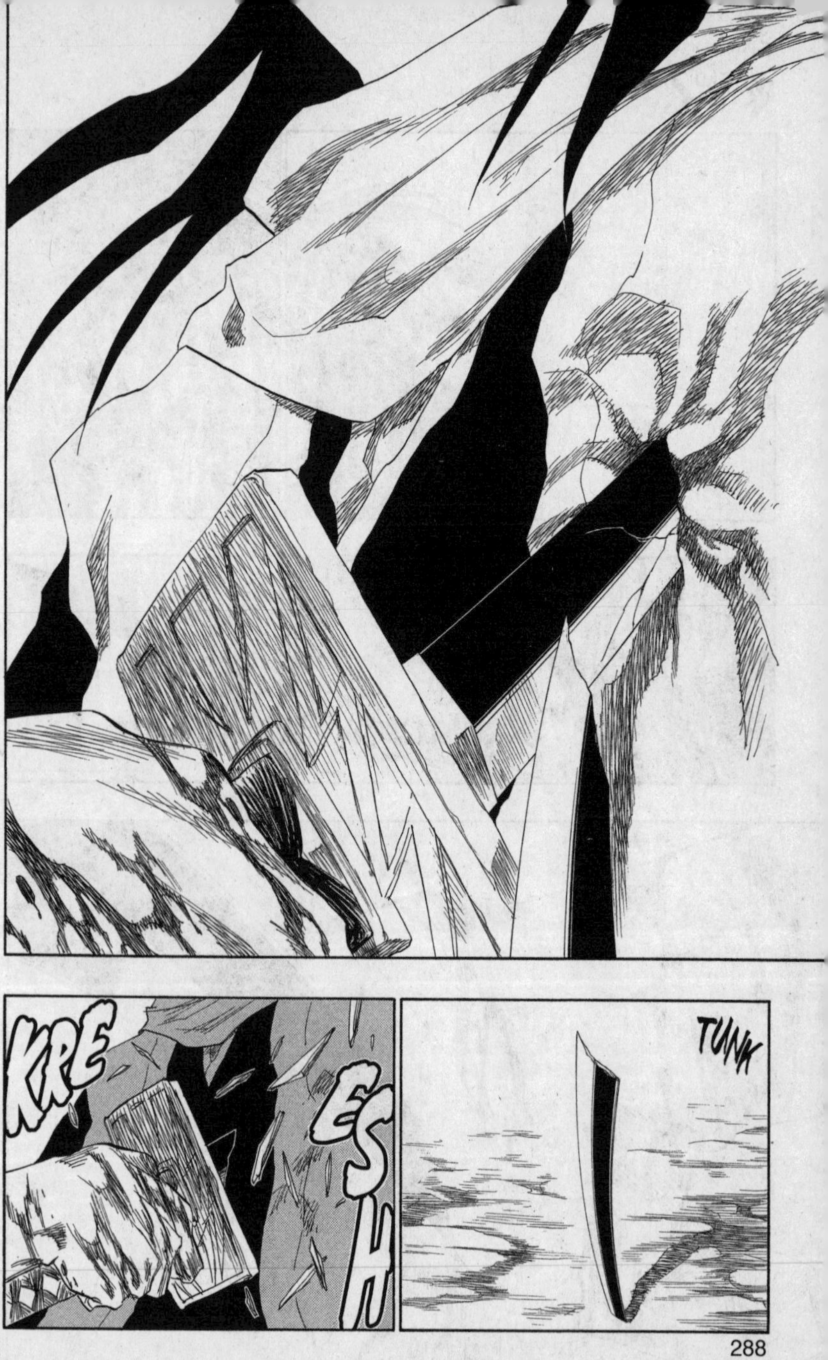
TUNK
KRE
ESH

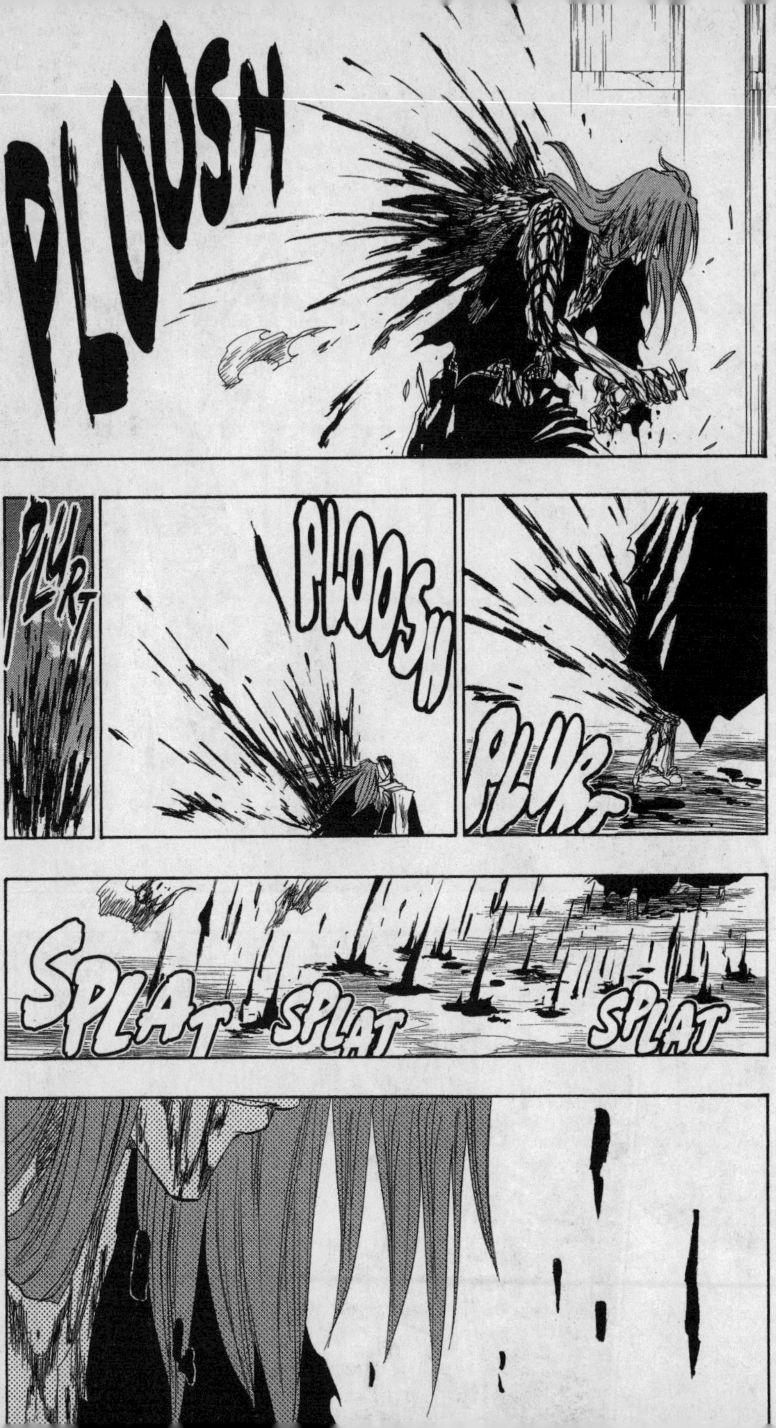
PLOOSH
PLURT
PLOOSH
PLURT
SPLAT
SPLAT
SPLAT

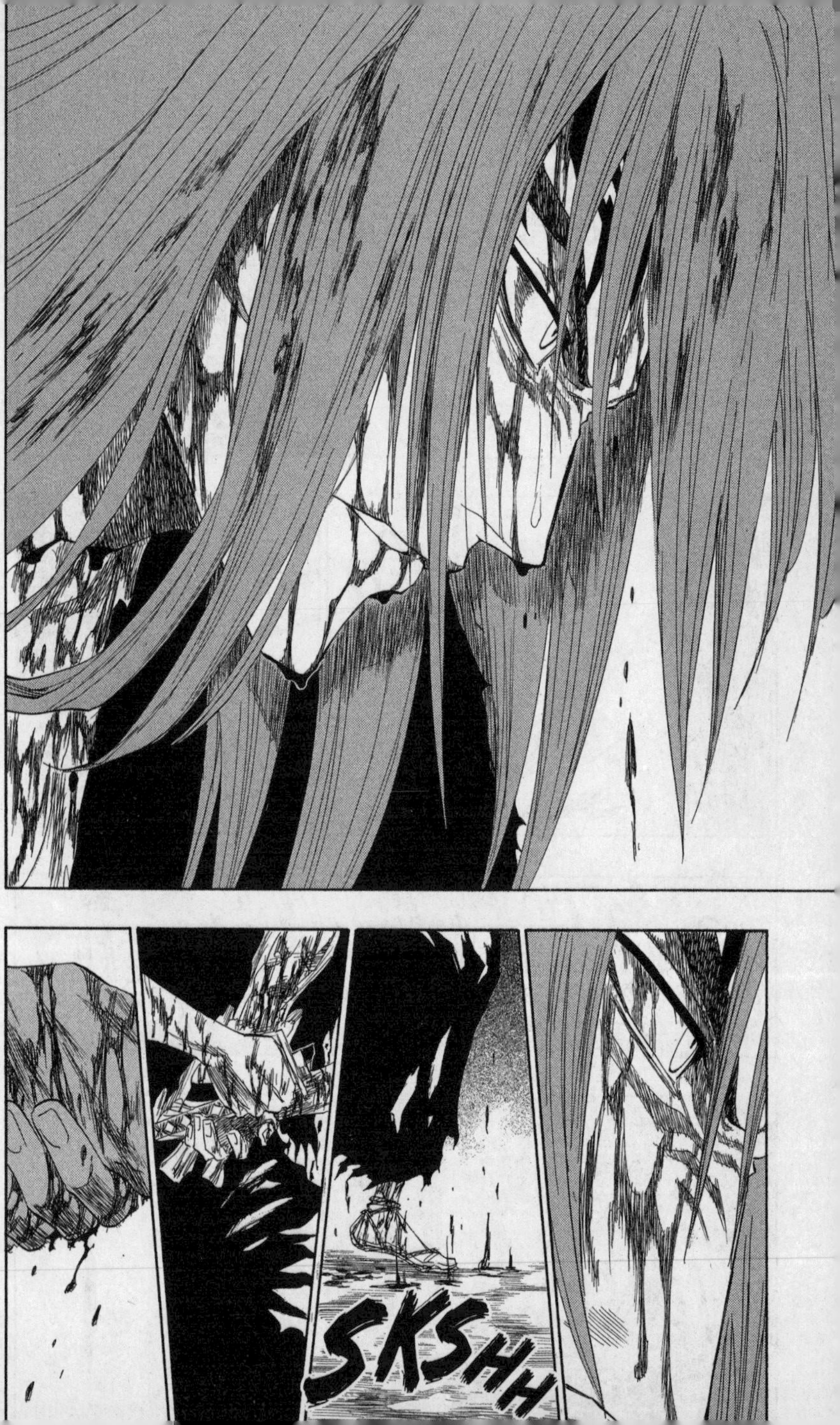
SKSHH

READ THIS WAY

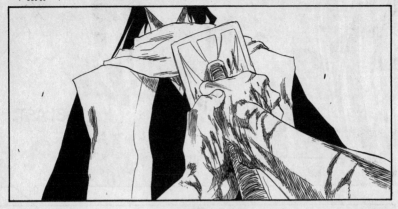

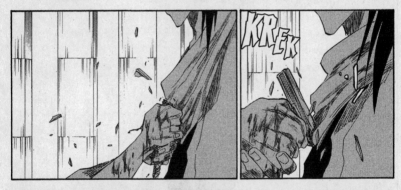

KREK

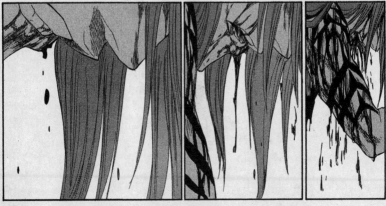

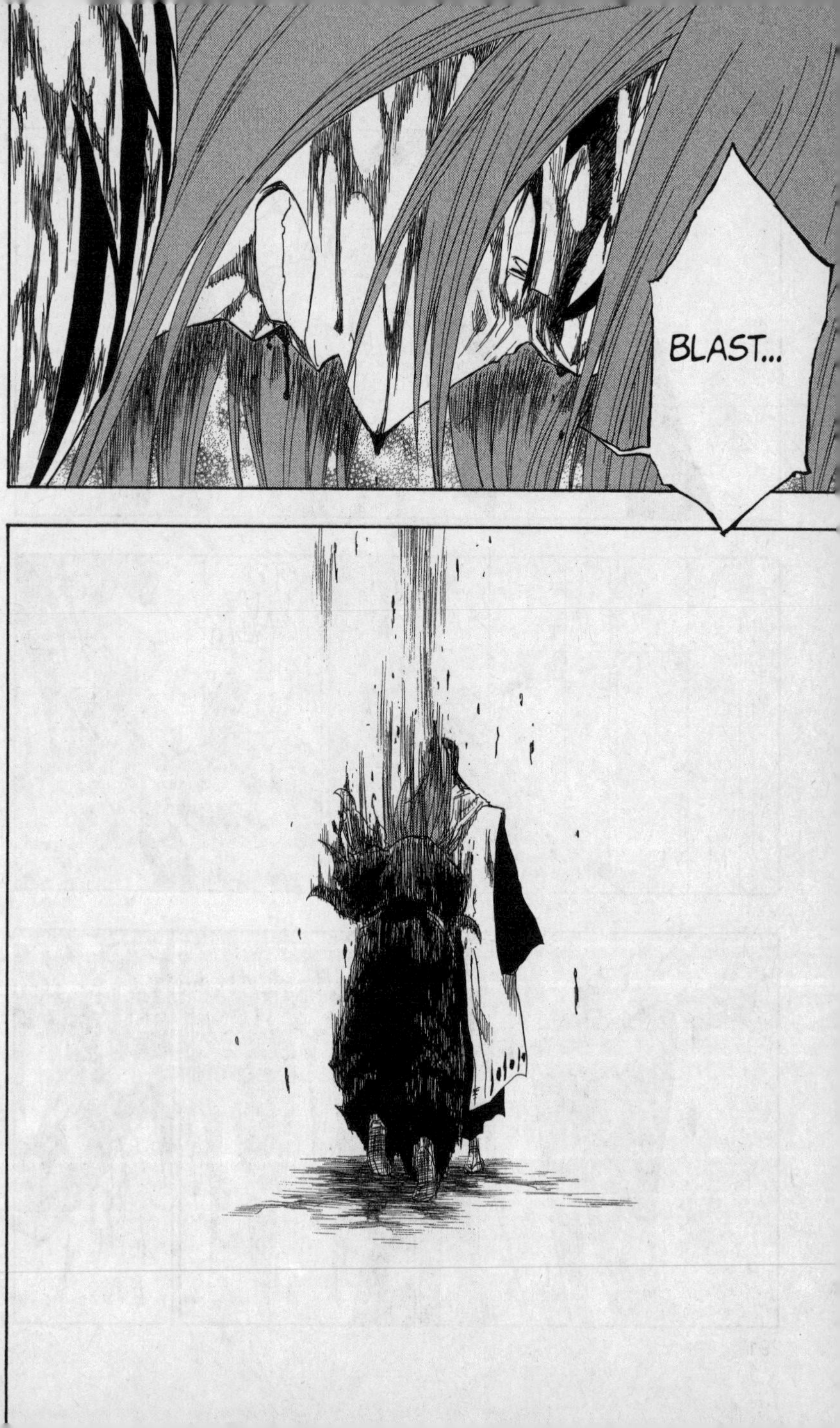
BLAST...

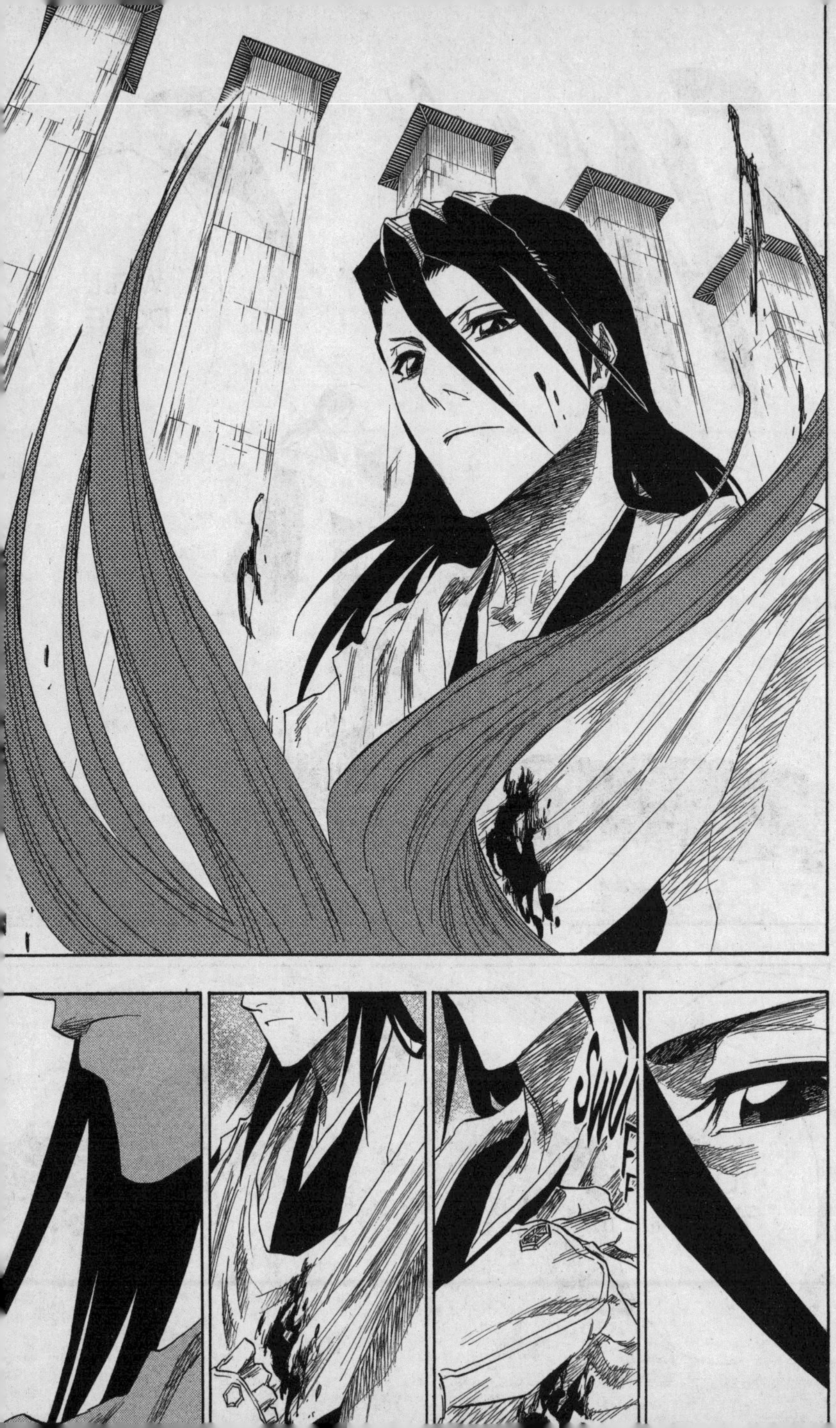
SWUFF

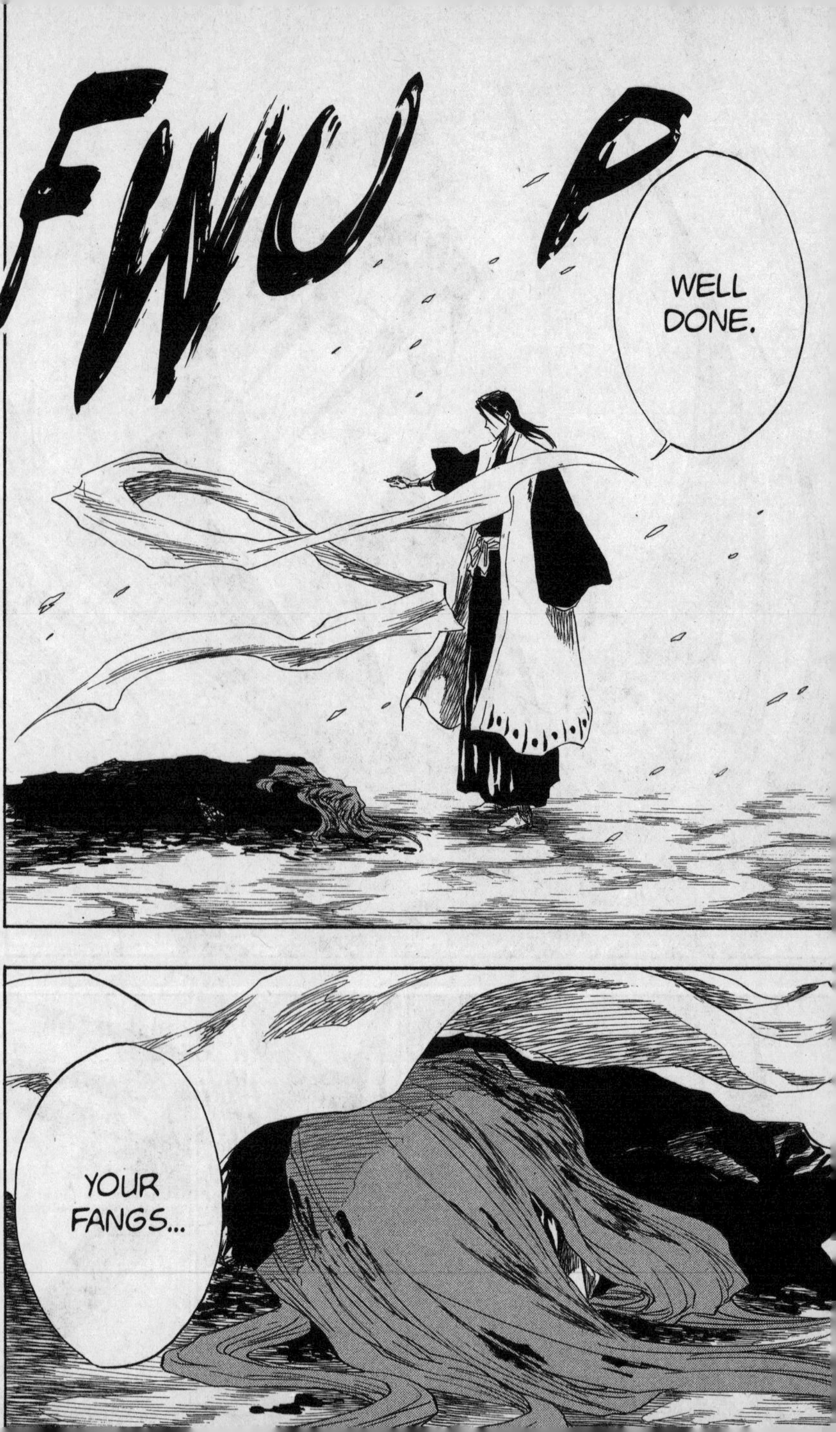
FWUP
WELL DONE.
YOUR FANGS...

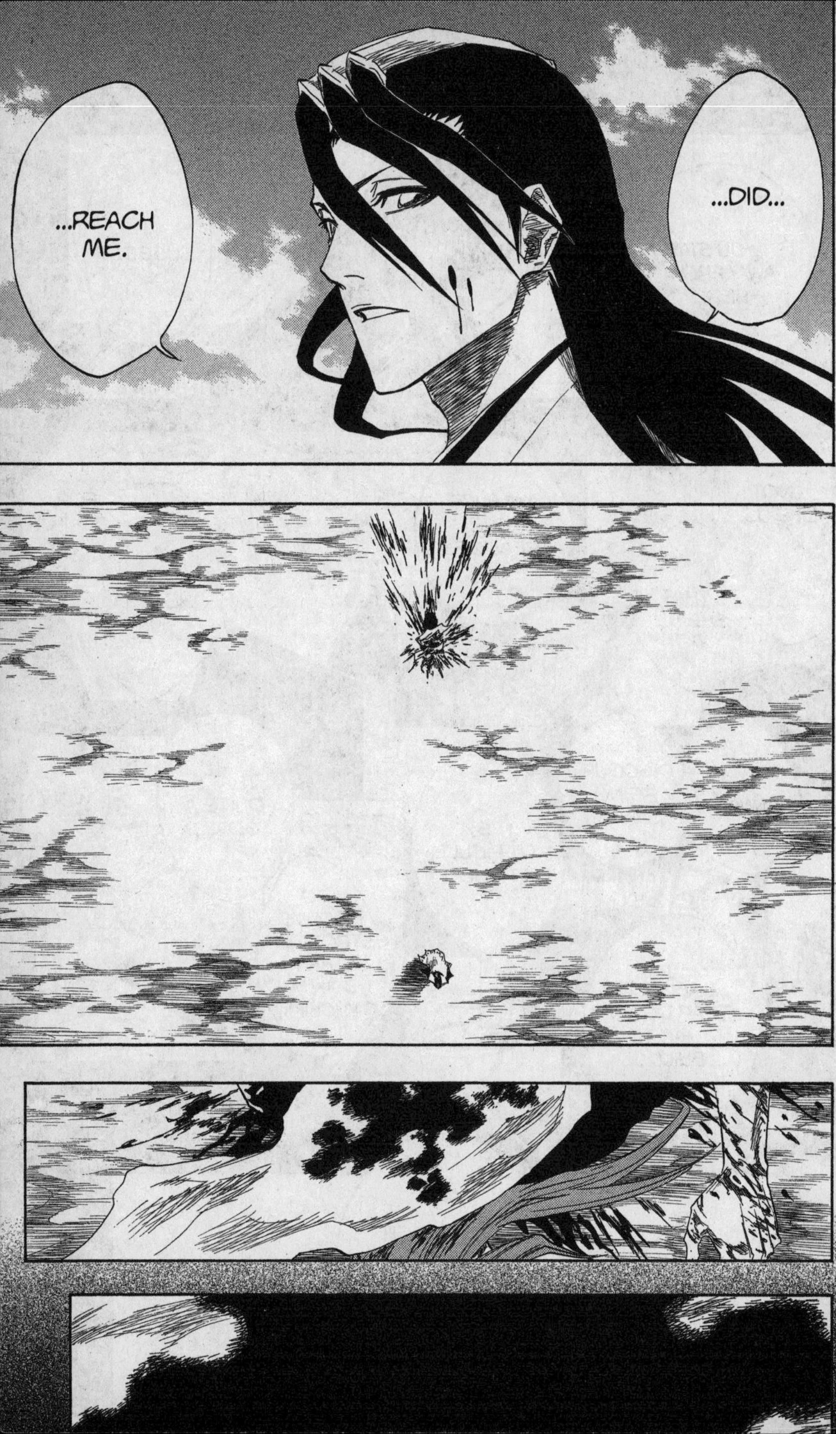
...DID...
...REACH ME.

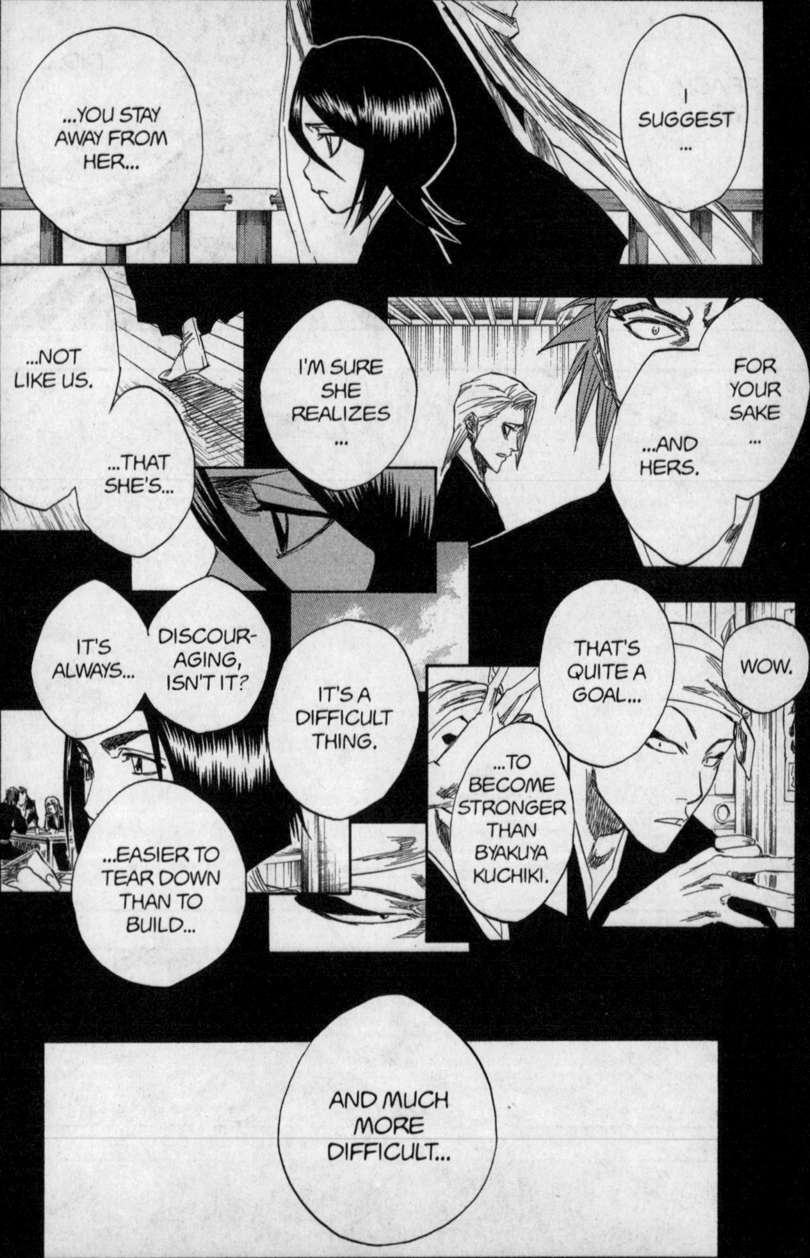
I SUGGEST ...
...YOU STAY AWAY FROM HER...
FOR YOUR SAKE ...
...AND HERS.
I'M SURE SHE REALIZES ...
...THAT SHE'S...
...NOT LIKE US.
WOW.
THAT'S QUITE A GOAL...
...TO BECOME STRONGER THAN BYAKUYA KUCHIKI.
IT'S A DIFFICULT THING.
DISCOUR-AGING, ISN'T IT?
IT'S ALWAYS...
...EASIER TO TEAR DOWN THAN TO BUILD...
AND MUCH MORE DIFFICULT...

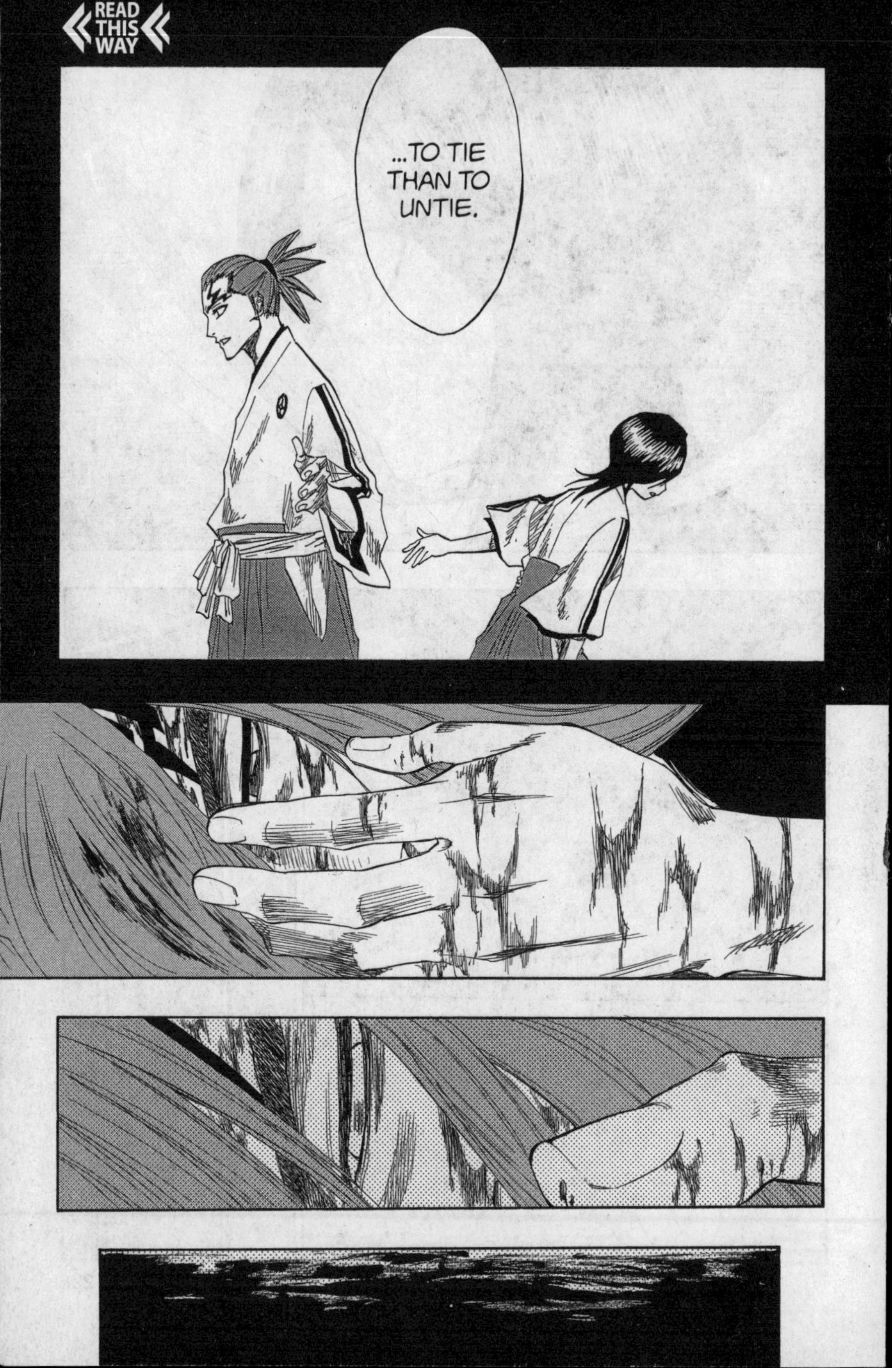
READ THIS WAY
...TO TIE THAN TO UNTIE.

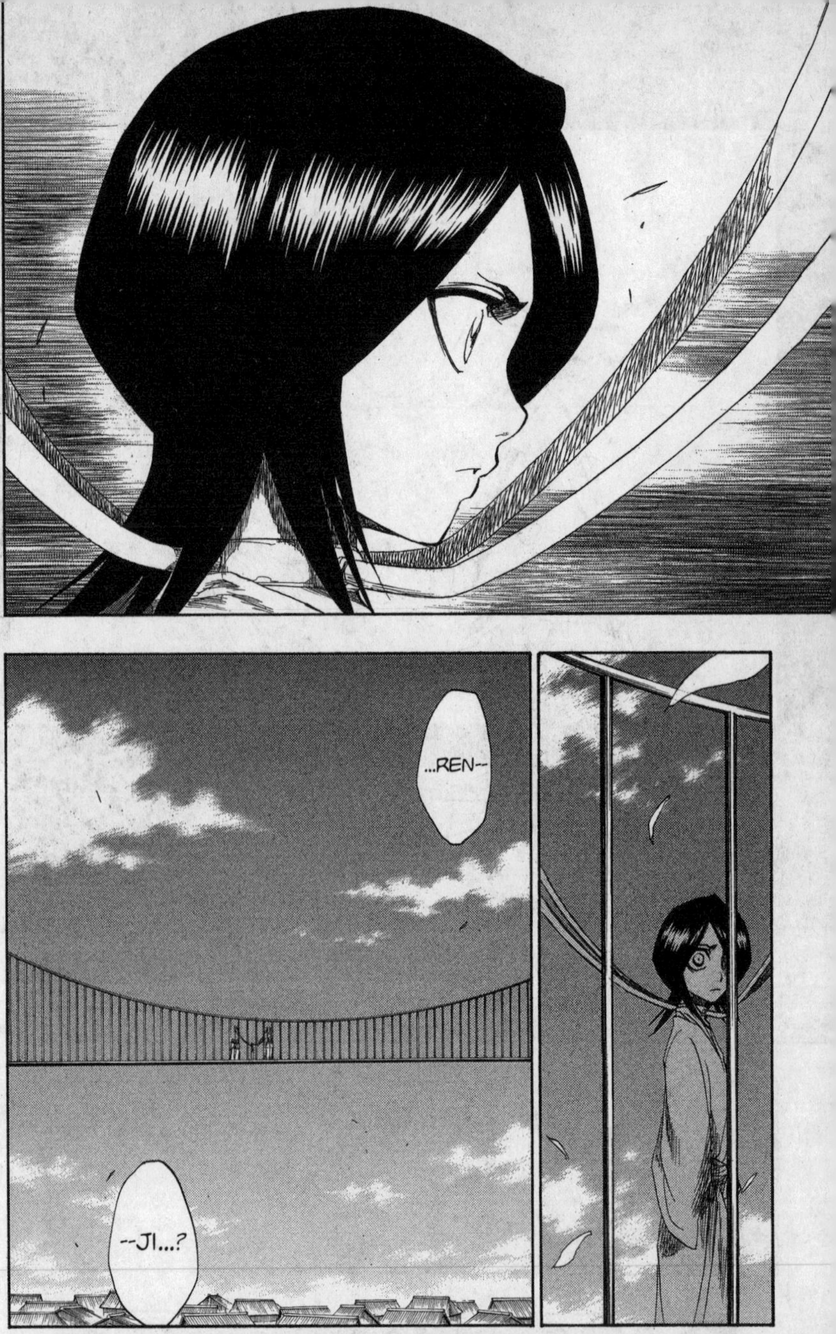
...REN--
--JI...?

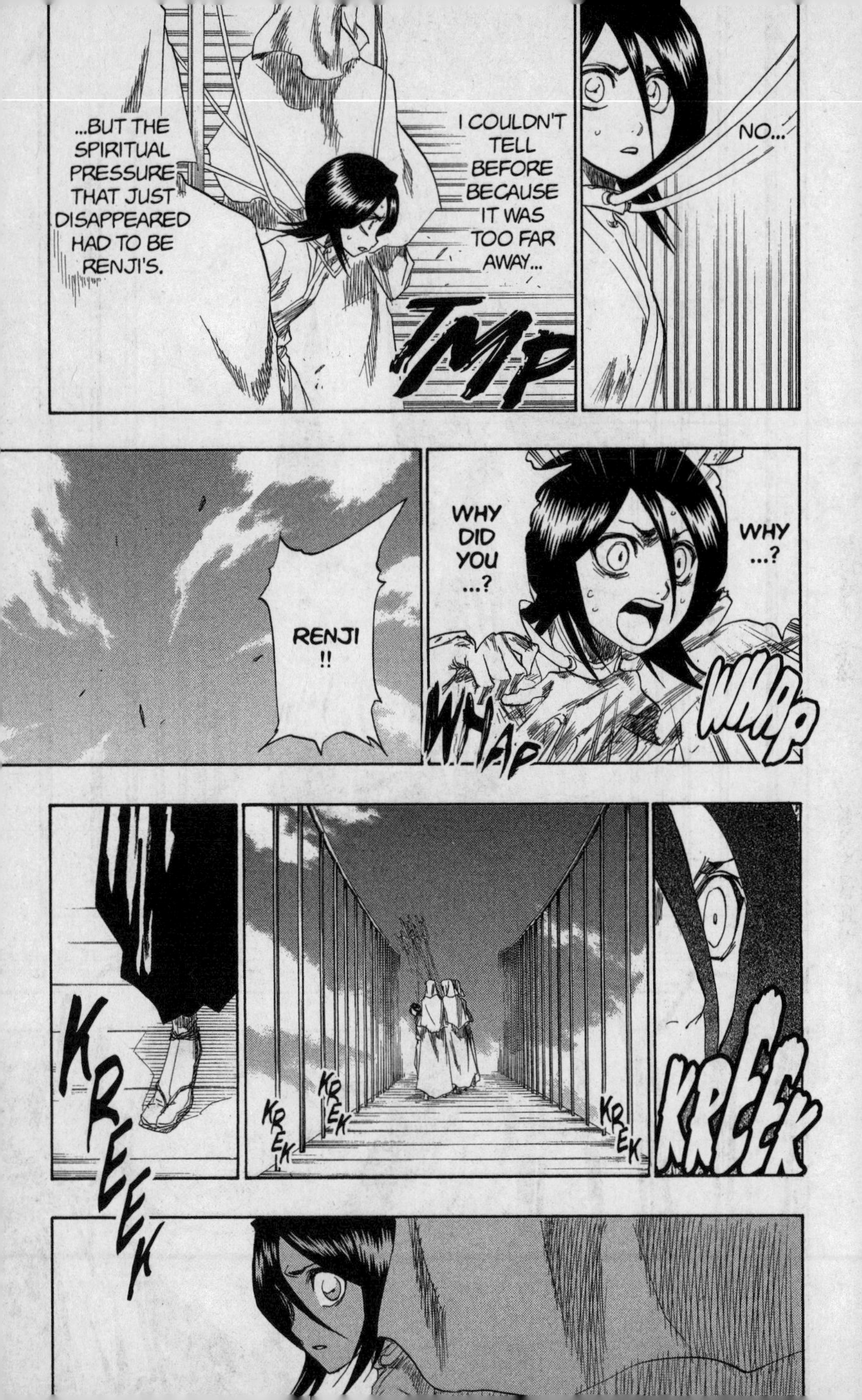
NO...
I COULDN'T TELL BEFORE BECAUSE IT WAS TOO FAR AWAY...
...BUT THE SPIRITUAL PRESSURE THAT JUST DISAPPEARED HAD TO BE RENJI'S.
TMP
WHY ...?
WHY DID YOU ...?
WHAP
WHAP
RENJI !!
KREEK
KREK
KREK
KREK
KREEEK

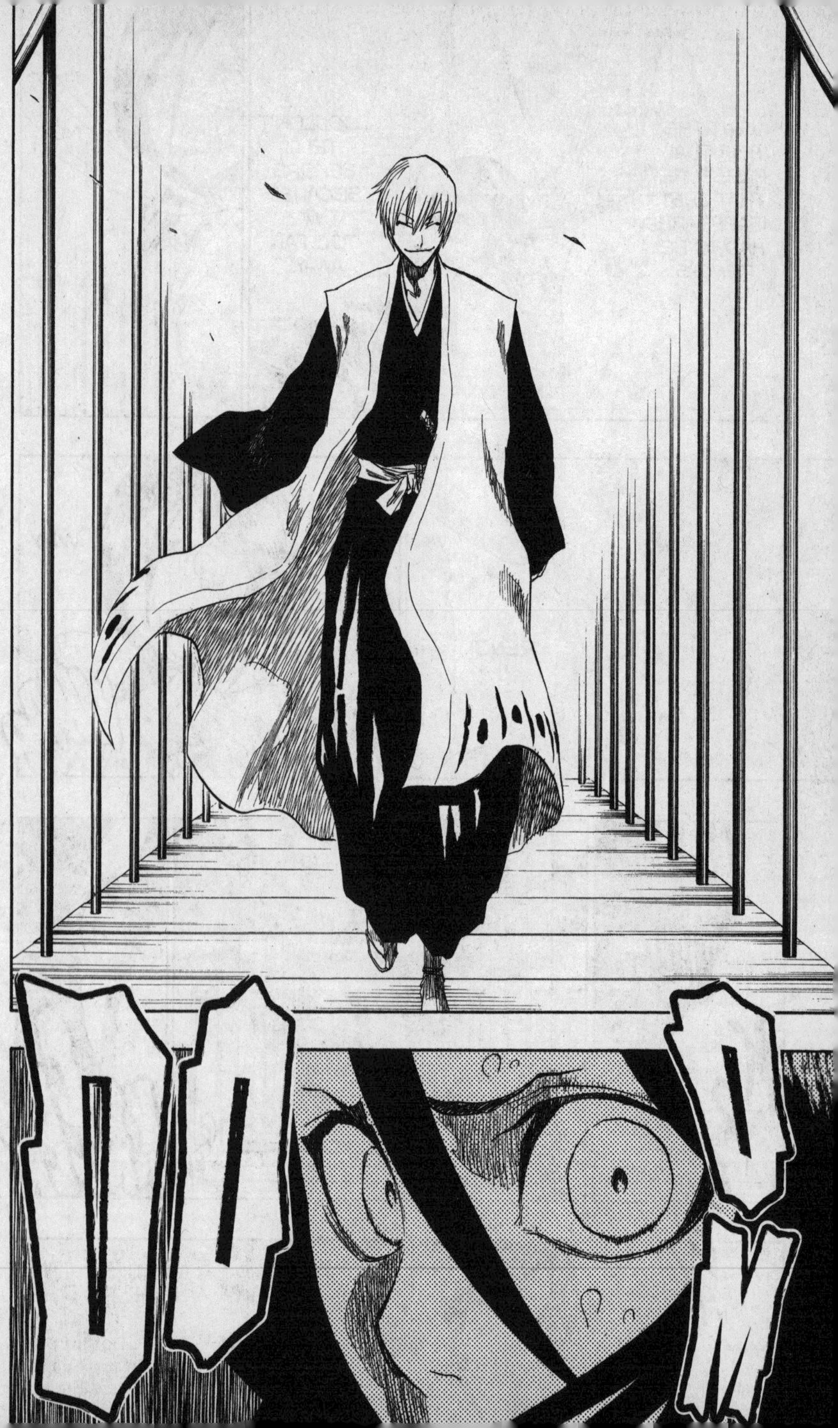
DOOM

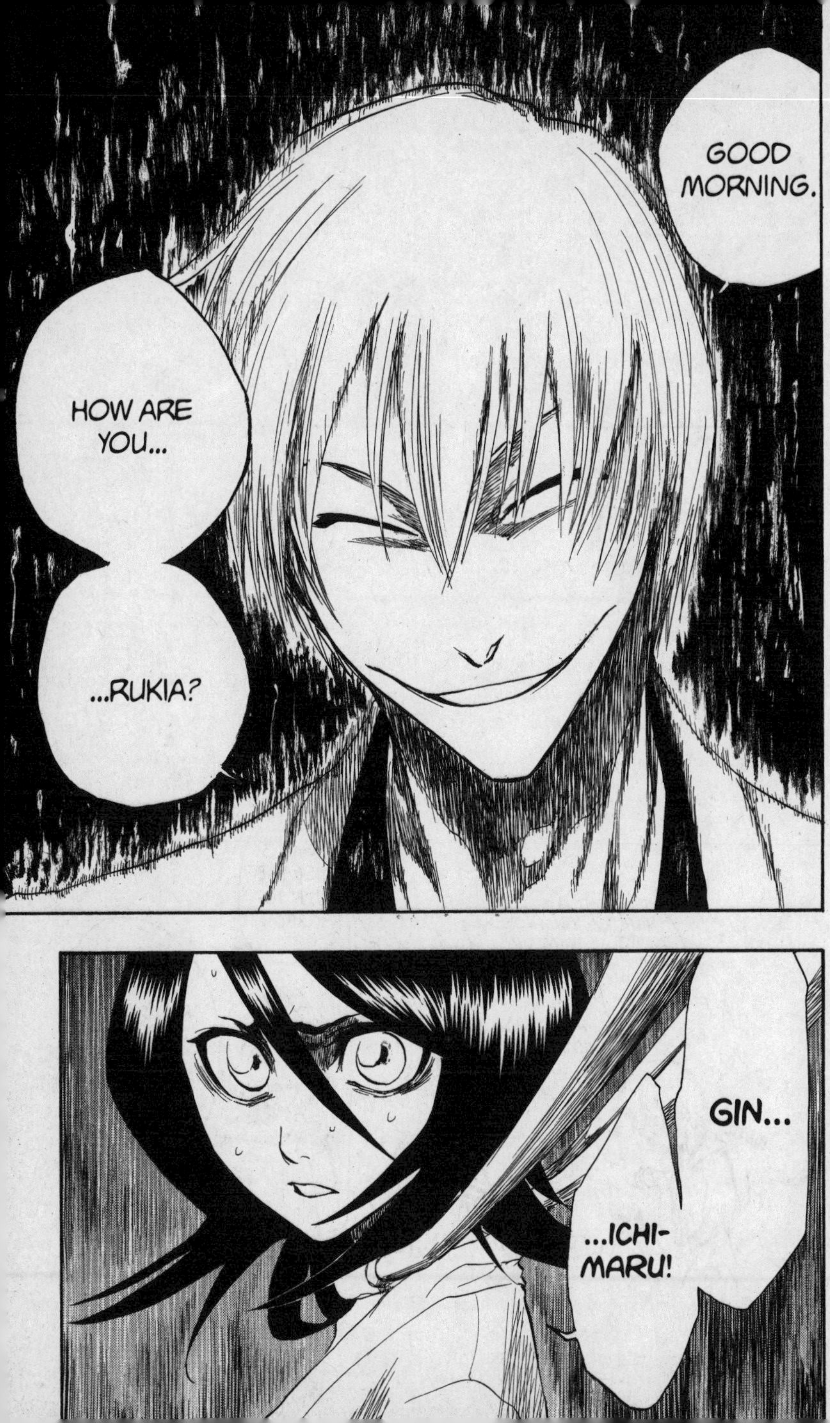
GOOD MORNING.
HOW ARE YOU...
...RUKIA?
GIN...
...ICHI-MARU!

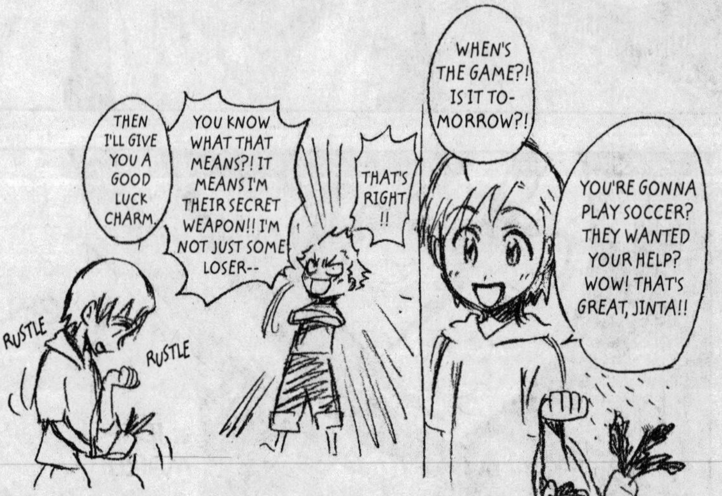
YOU'RE GONNA PLAY SOCCER? THEY WANTED YOUR HELP? WOW! THAT'S GREAT, JINTA!!
WHEN'S THE GAME?! IS IT TO-MORROW?!
THAT'S RIGHT!!
YOU KNOW WHAT THAT MEANS?! IT MEANS I'M THEIR SECRET WEAPON!! I'M NOT JUST SOME LOSER--
THEN I'LL GIVE YOU A GOOD LUCK CHARM.
RUSTLE
RUSTLE

READ THIS WAY

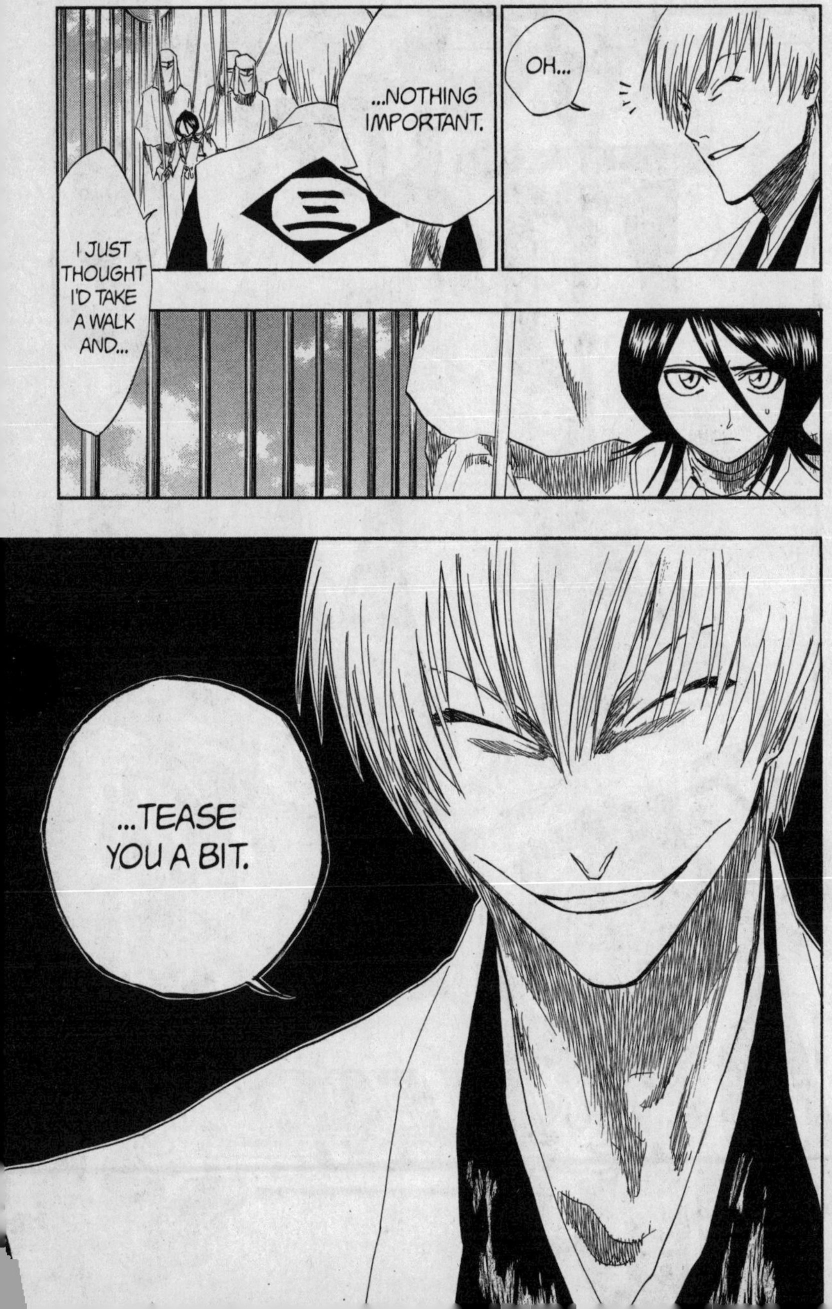

OH...
...NOTHING IMPORTANT.
I JUST THOUGHT I'D TAKE A WALK AND...
...TEASE YOU A BIT.

145. Shaken

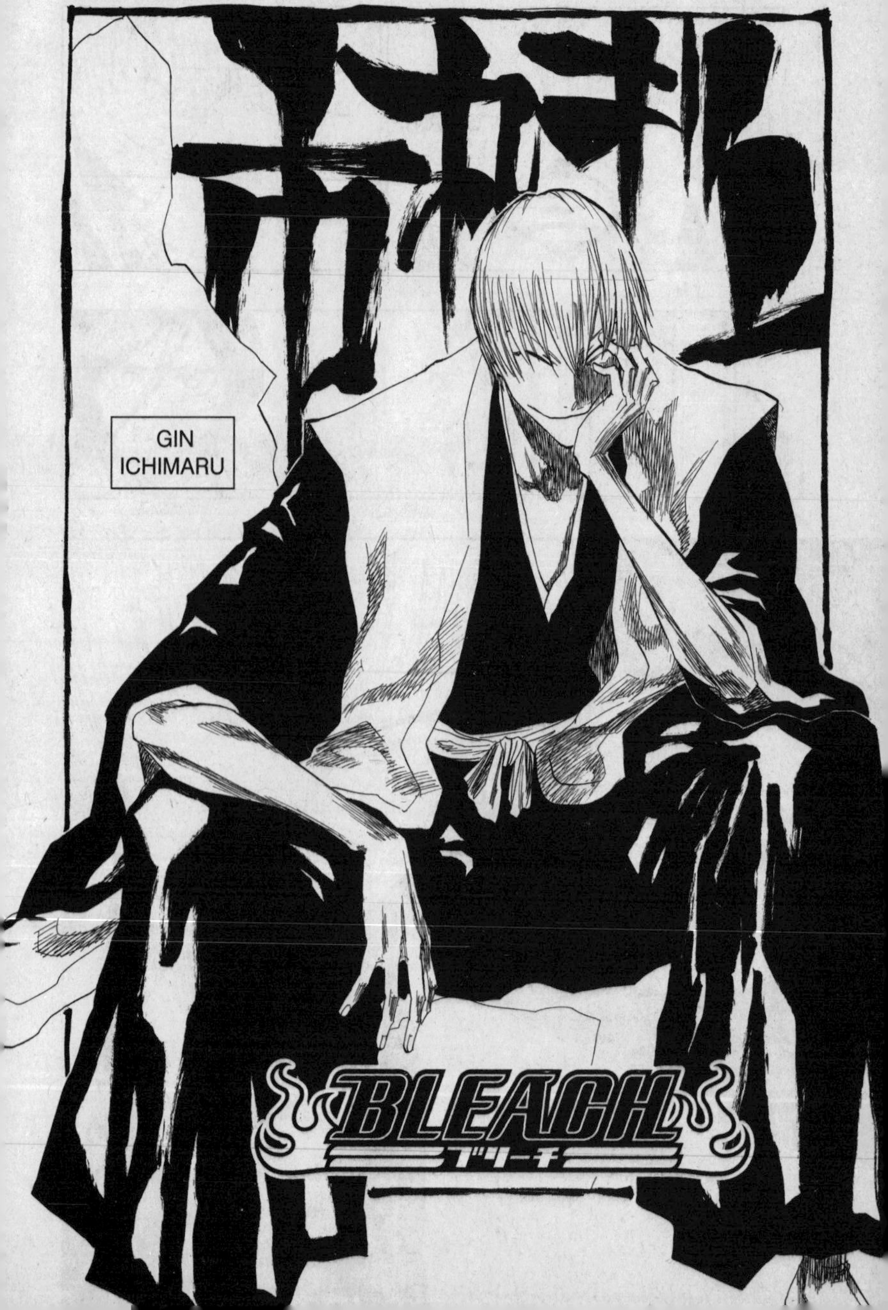
GIN
ICHIMARU
BLEACH
ブリーチ

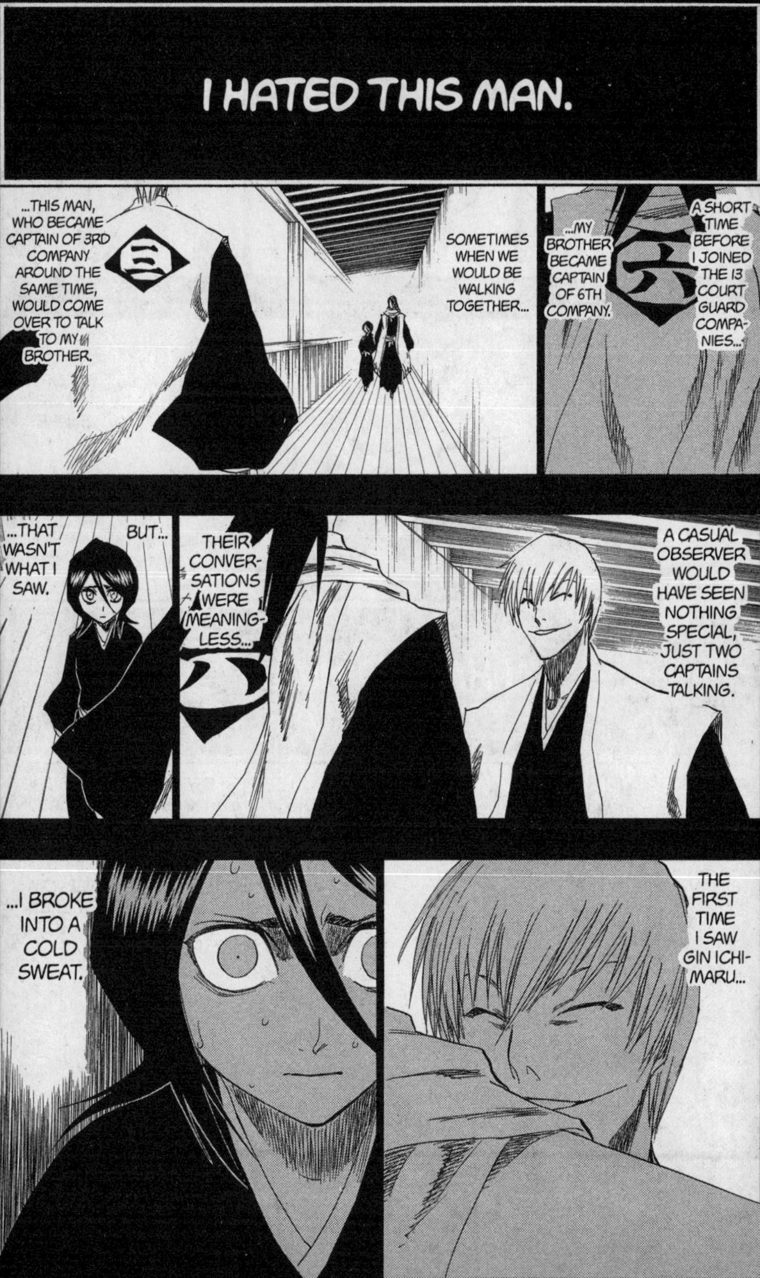
I HATED THIS MAN.
A SHORT TIME BEFORE I JOINED THE 13 COURT GUARD COMPANIES...
...MY BROTHER BECAME CAPTAIN OF 6TH COMPANY.
SOMETIMES WHEN WE WOULD BE WALKING TOGETHER...
...THIS MAN, WHO BECAME CAPTAIN OF 3RD COMPANY AROUND THE SAME TIME, WOULD COME OVER TO TALK TO MY BROTHER.
A CASUAL OBSERVER WOULD HAVE SEEN NOTHING SPECIAL, JUST TWO CAPTAINS TALKING.
THEIR CONVER-SATIONS WERE MEANING-LESS...
BUT...
...THAT WASN'T WHAT I SAW.
THE FIRST TIME I SAW GIN ICHI-MARU...
...I BROKE INTO A COLD SWEAT.

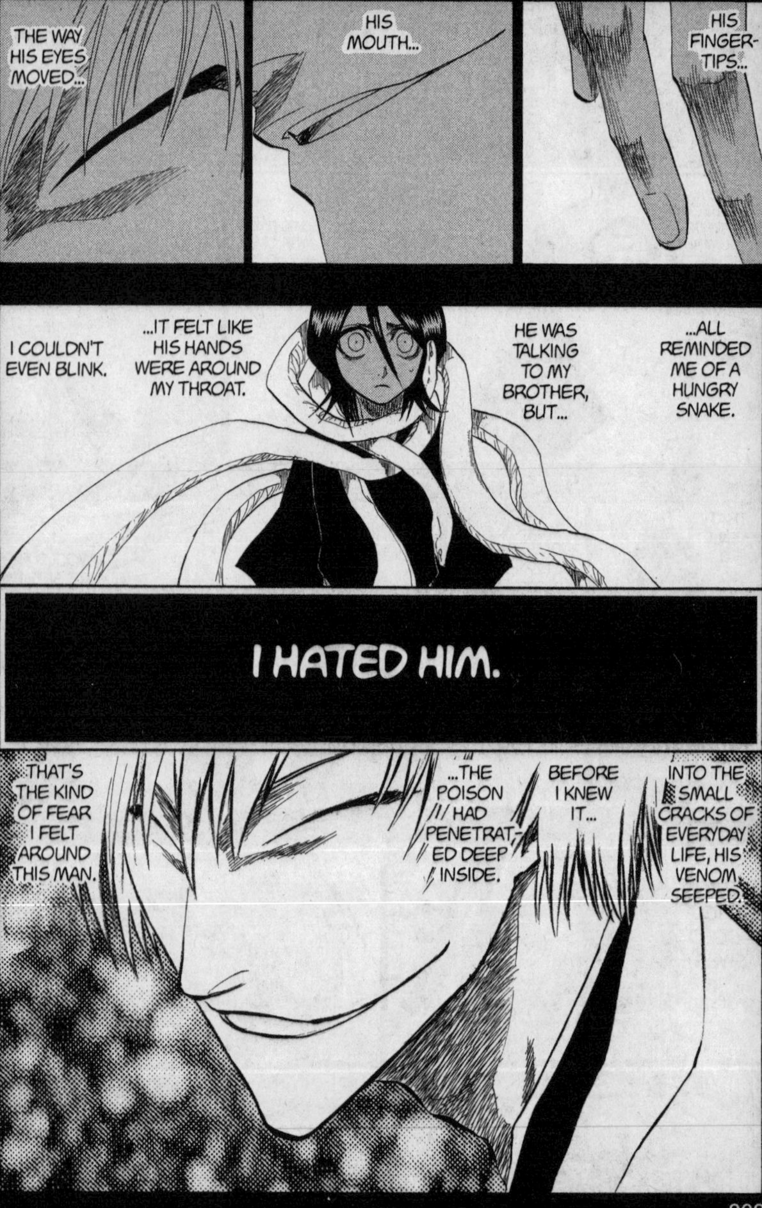
HIS FINGER-TIPS...
HIS MOUTH...
THE WAY HIS EYES MOVED...
...ALL REMINDED ME OF A HUNGRY SNAKE.
HE WAS TALKING TO MY BROTHER, BUT...
...IT FELT LIKE HIS HANDS WERE AROUND MY THROAT.
I COULDN'T EVEN BLINK.
I HATED HIM.
INTO THE SMALL CRACKS OF EVERYDAY LIFE, HIS VENOM SEEPED.
BEFORE I KNEW IT...
...THE POISON HAD PENETRAT-ED DEEP INSIDE.
THAT'S THE KIND OF FEAR I FELT AROUND THIS MAN.

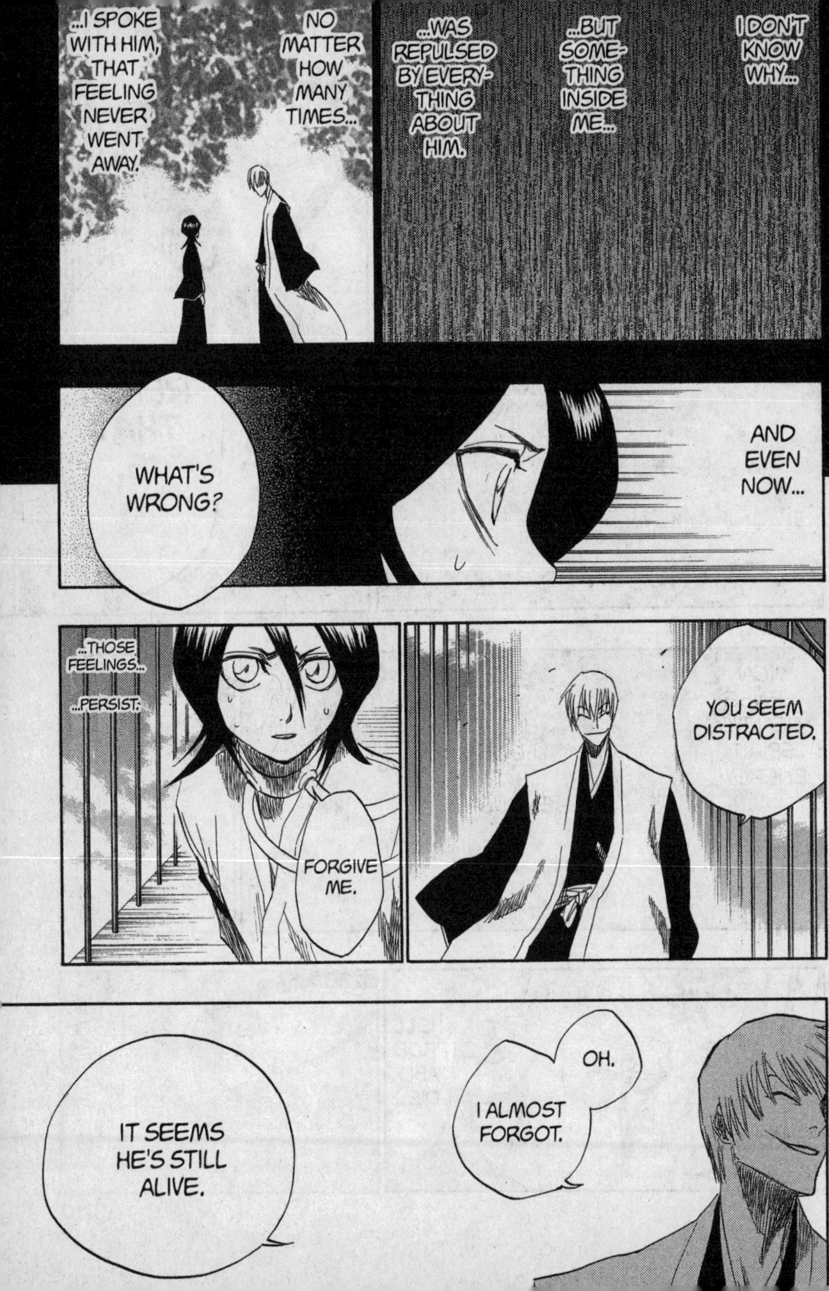
I DON'T KNOW WHY...
...BUT SOMETHING INSIDE ME...
...WAS REPULSED BY EVERYTHING ABOUT HIM.
NO MATTER HOW MANY TIMES...
...I SPOKE WITH HIM, THAT FEELING NEVER WENT AWAY.
AND EVEN NOW...
WHAT'S WRONG?
YOU SEEM DISTRACTED.
...THOSE FEELINGS...
...PERSIST.
FORGIVE ME.
OH.
I ALMOST FORGOT.
IT SEEMS HE'S STILL ALIVE.

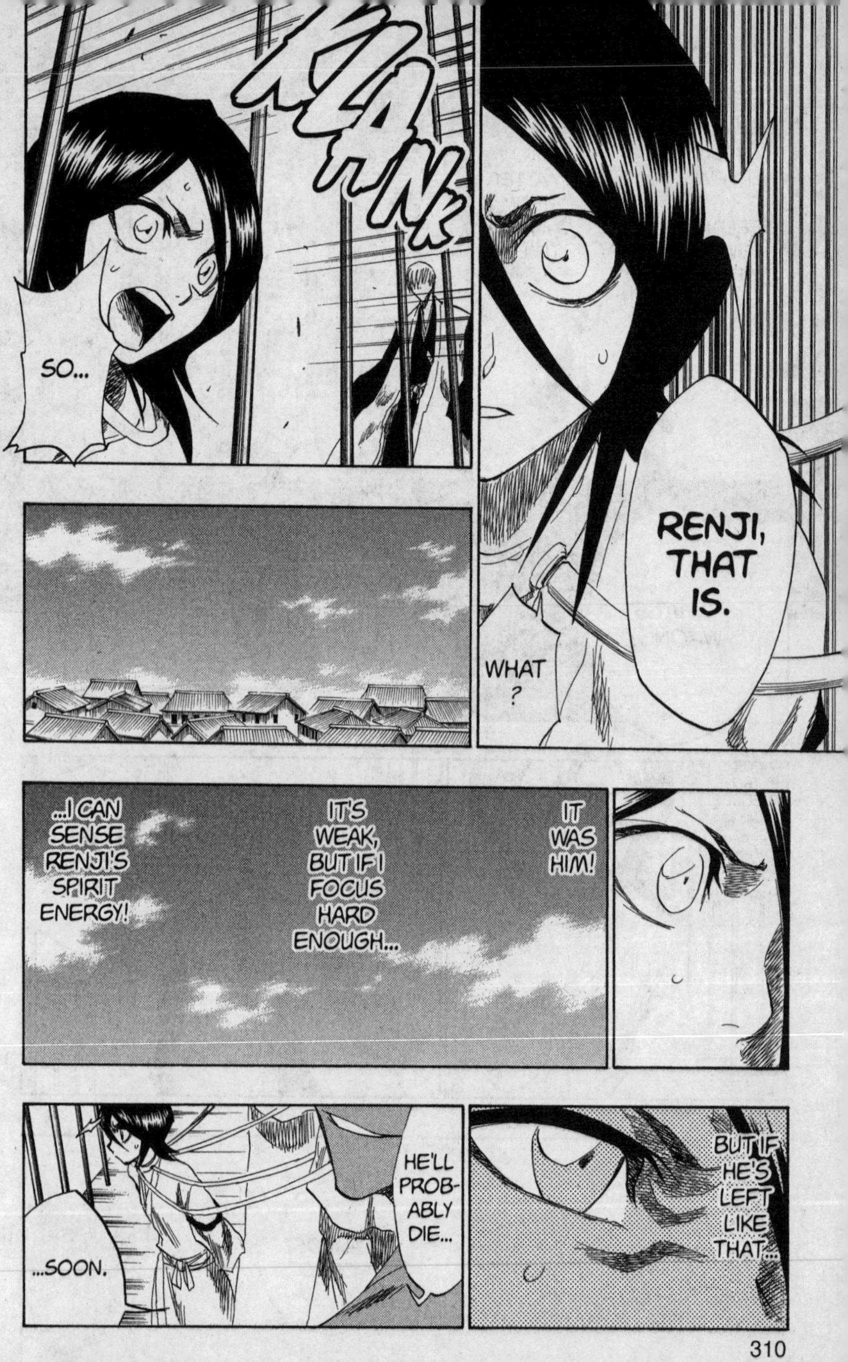
RENJI, THAT IS.
WHAT ?
KLANK
SO...
IT WAS HIM!
IT'S WEAK, BUT IF I FOCUS HARD ENOUGH...
...I CAN SENSE RENJI'S SPIRIT ENERGY!
BUT IF HE'S LEFT LIKE THAT...
HE'LL PROBABLY DIE...
...SOON.

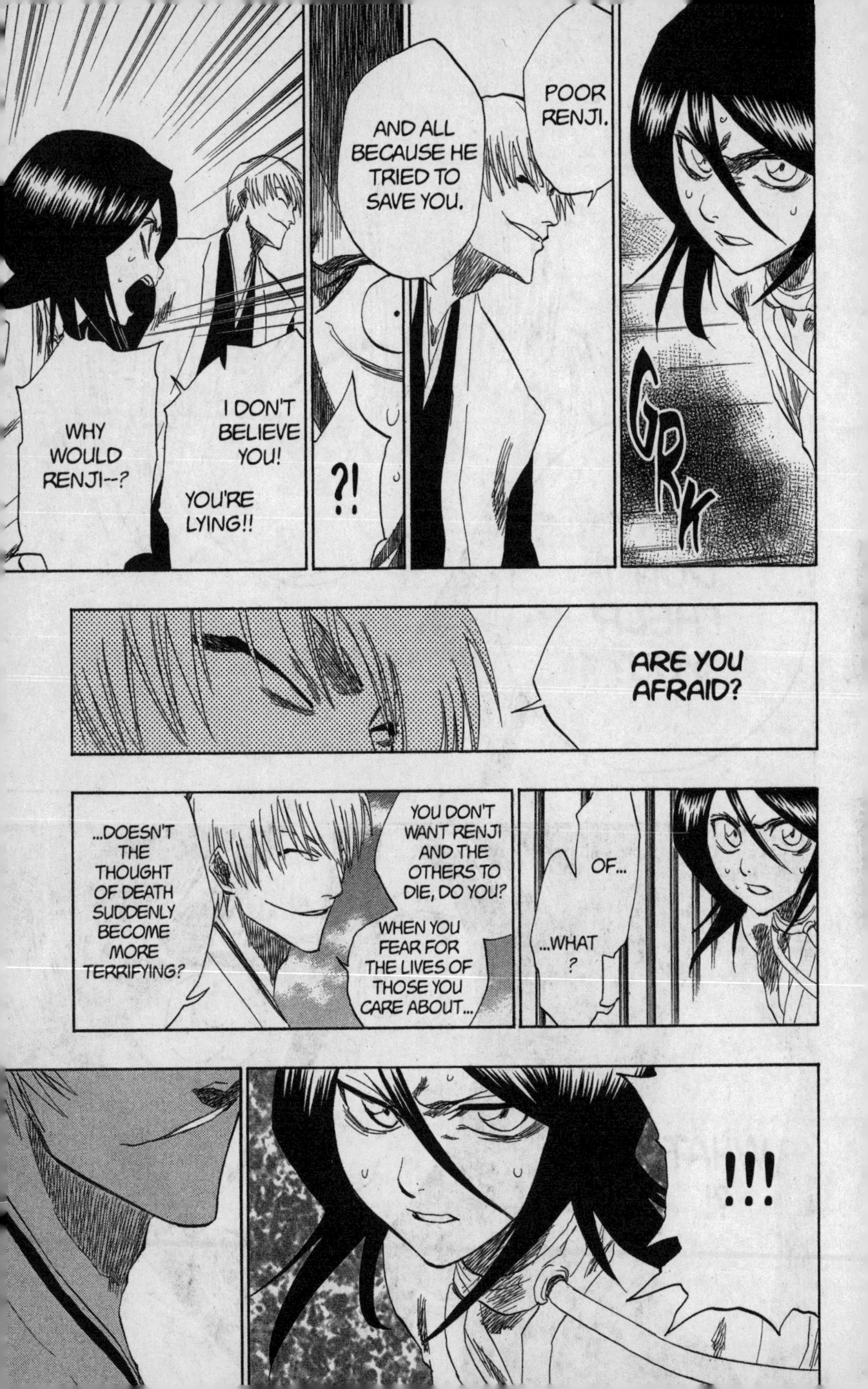
POOR RENJI.
GRK
AND ALL BECAUSE HE TRIED TO SAVE YOU.
?!
WHY WOULD RENJI--?
I DON'T BELIEVE YOU!
YOU'RE LYING!!
ARE YOU AFRAID?
OF...
...WHAT?
YOU DON'T WANT RENJI AND THE OTHERS TO DIE, DO YOU?
WHEN YOU FEAR FOR THE LIVES OF THOSE YOU CARE ABOUT...
...DOESN'T THE THOUGHT OF DEATH SUDDENLY BECOME MORE TERRIFYING?
!!!

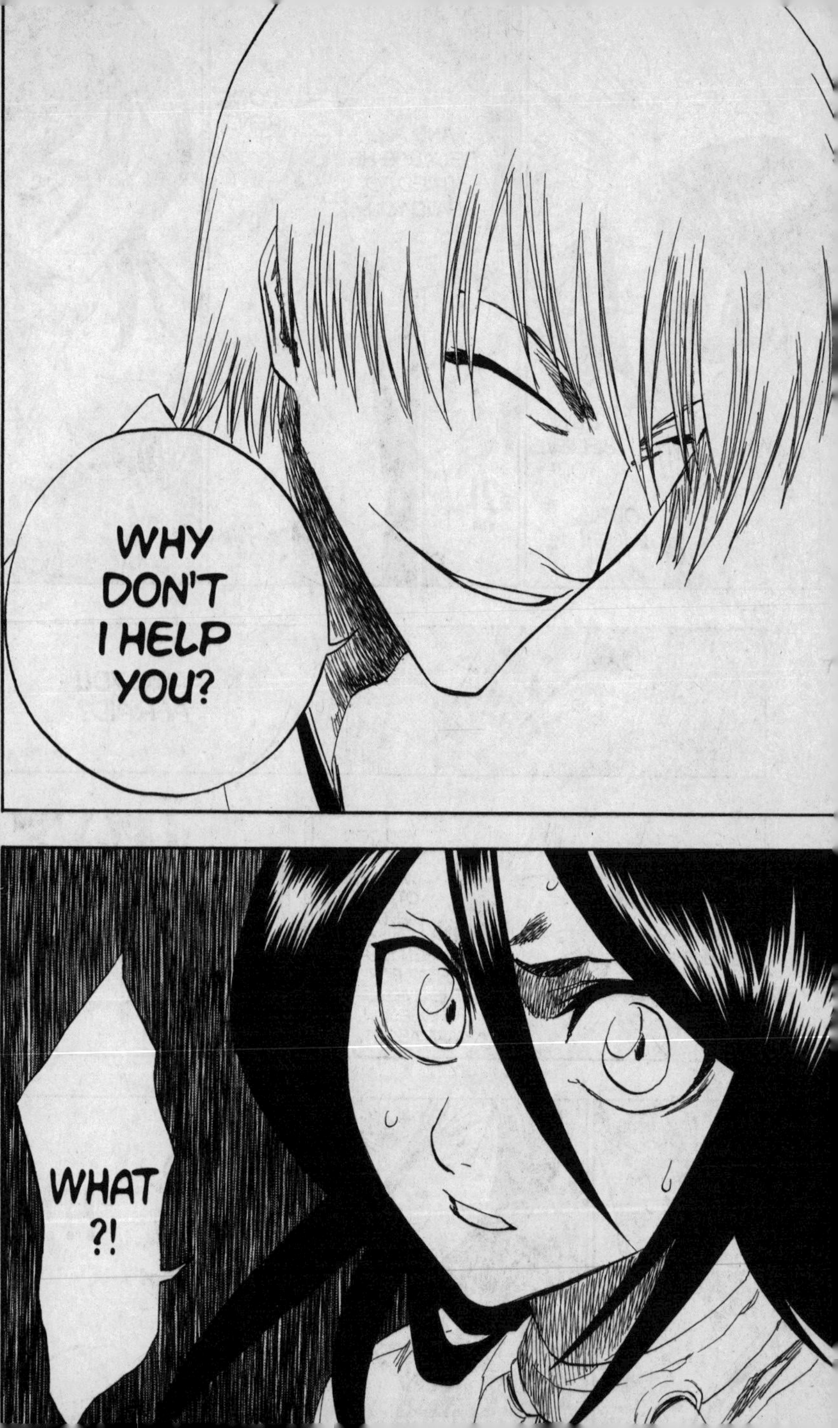
WHY DON'T I HELP YOU?
WHAT ?!

READ THIS WAY

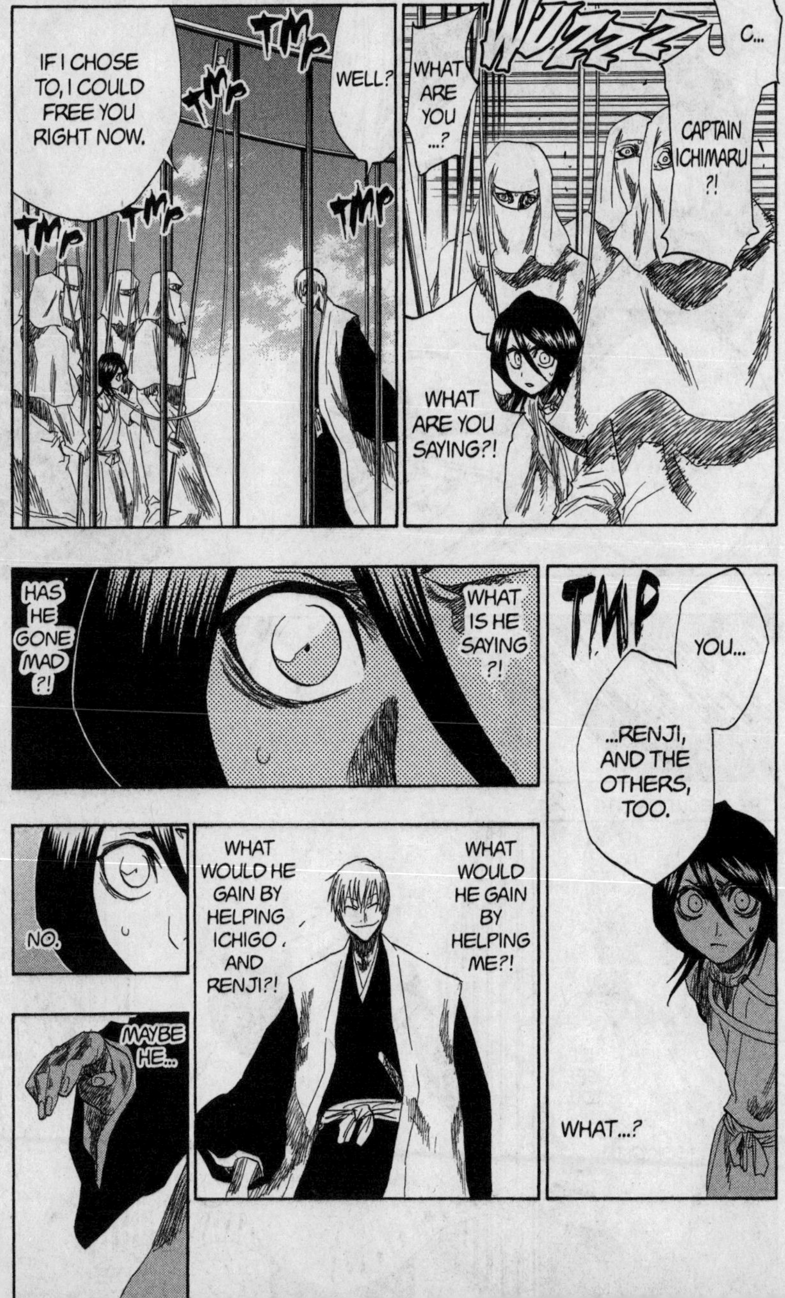
C...
CAPTAIN ICHIMARU?!
WUZZZ
WHAT ARE YOU ...?
WHAT ARE YOU SAYING?!
WELL?
TMP
TMP
TMP
IF I CHOSE TO, I COULD FREE YOU RIGHT NOW.
TMP
TMP
TMP
YOU...
...RENJI, AND THE OTHERS, TOO.
WHAT...?
WHAT IS HE SAYING?!
HAS HE GONE MAD?!
WHAT WOULD HE GAIN BY HELPING ME?!
WHAT WOULD HE GAIN BY HELPING ICHIGO AND RENJI?!
NO.
MAYBE HE...

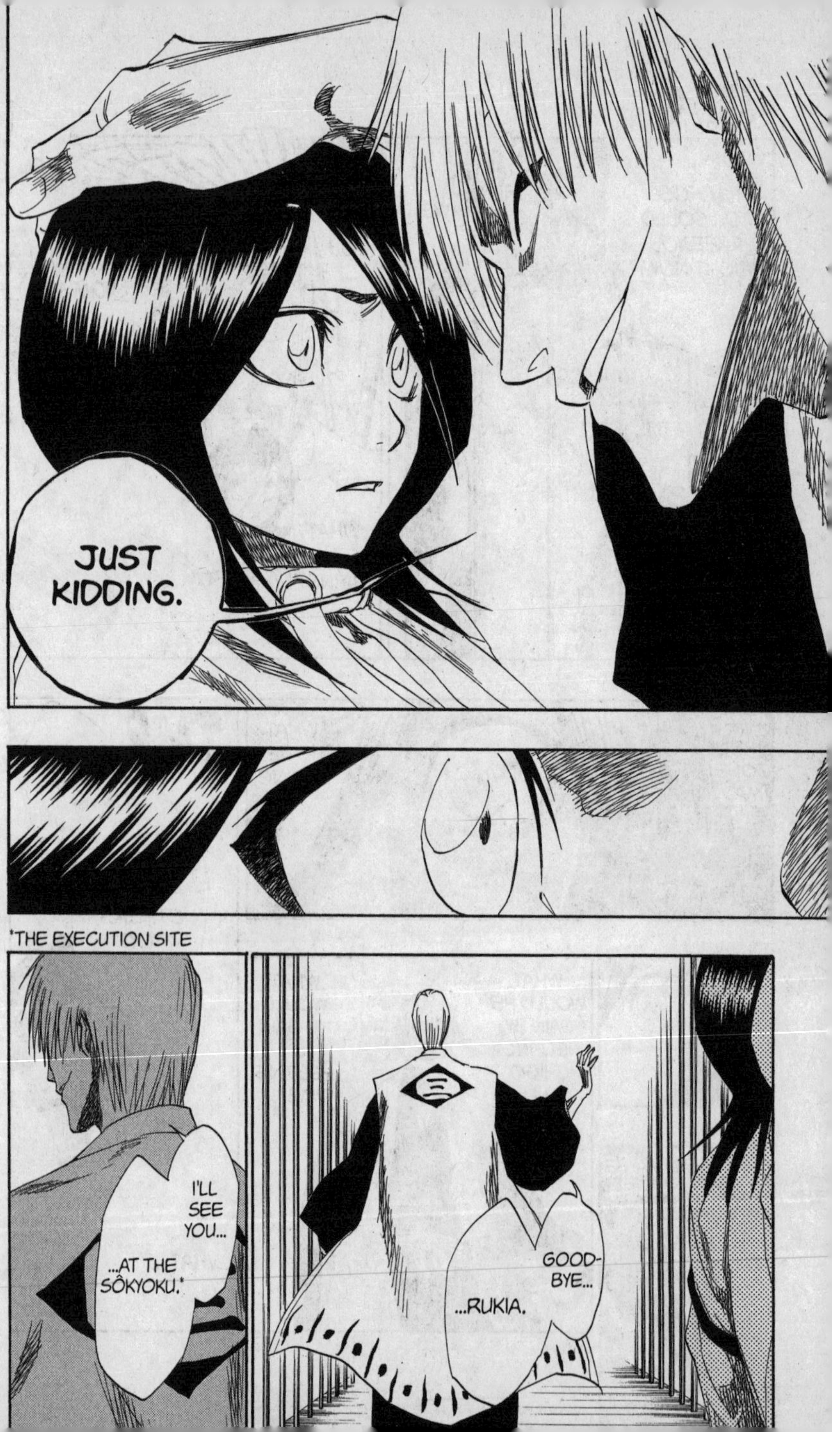
JUST KIDDING.
GOOD-BYE...
...RUKIA.
I'LL SEE YOU...
...AT THE SÔKYOKU.*

*THE EXECUTION SITE

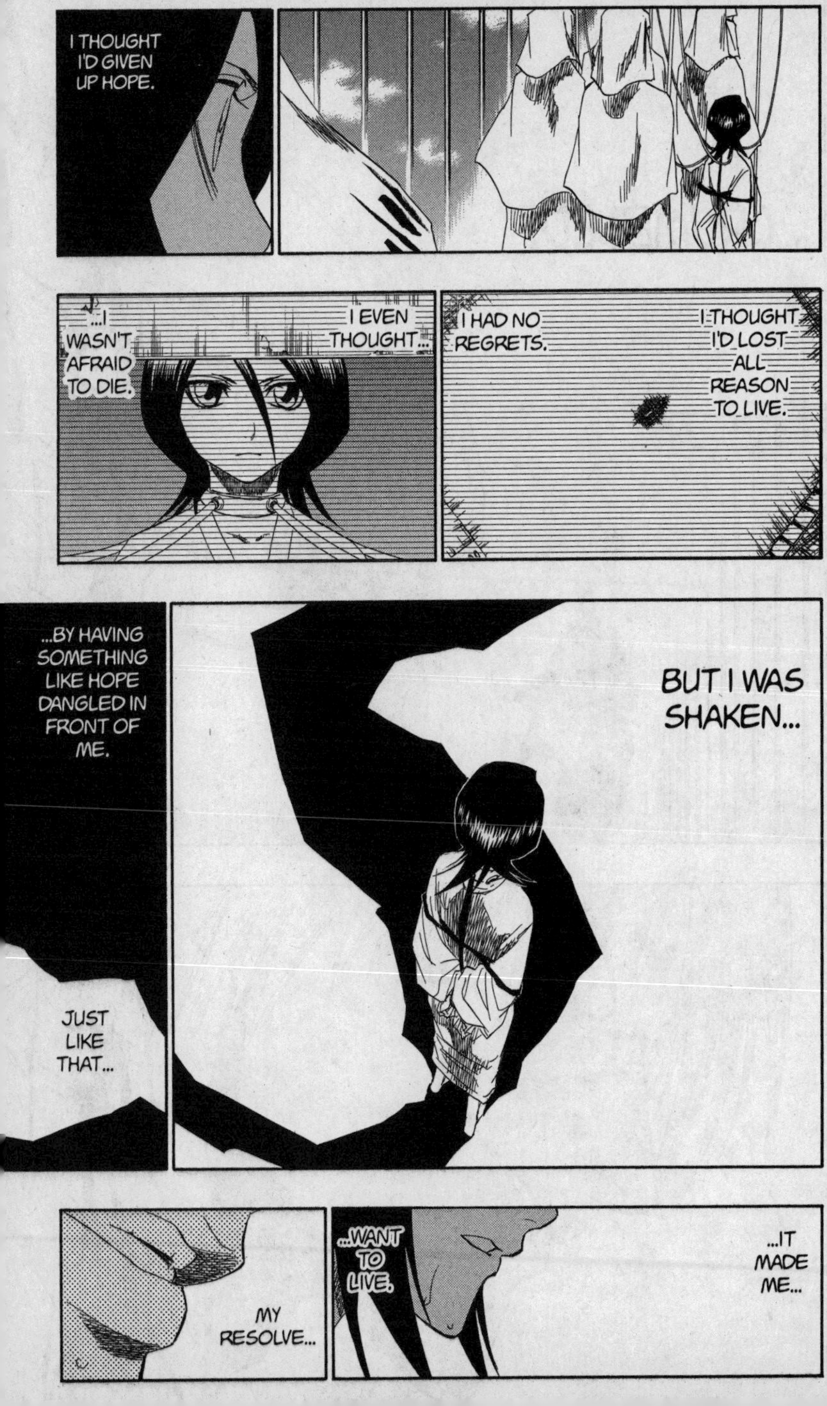

I THOUGHT I'D GIVEN UP HOPE.
I THOUGHT I'D LOST ALL REASON TO LIVE.
I HAD NO REGRETS.
I EVEN THOUGHT...
...I WASN'T AFRAID TO DIE.
BUT I WAS SHAKEN...
...BY HAVING SOMETHING LIKE HOPE DANGLED IN FRONT OF ME.
JUST LIKE THAT...
...IT MADE ME...
...WANT TO LIVE.
MY RESOLVE...

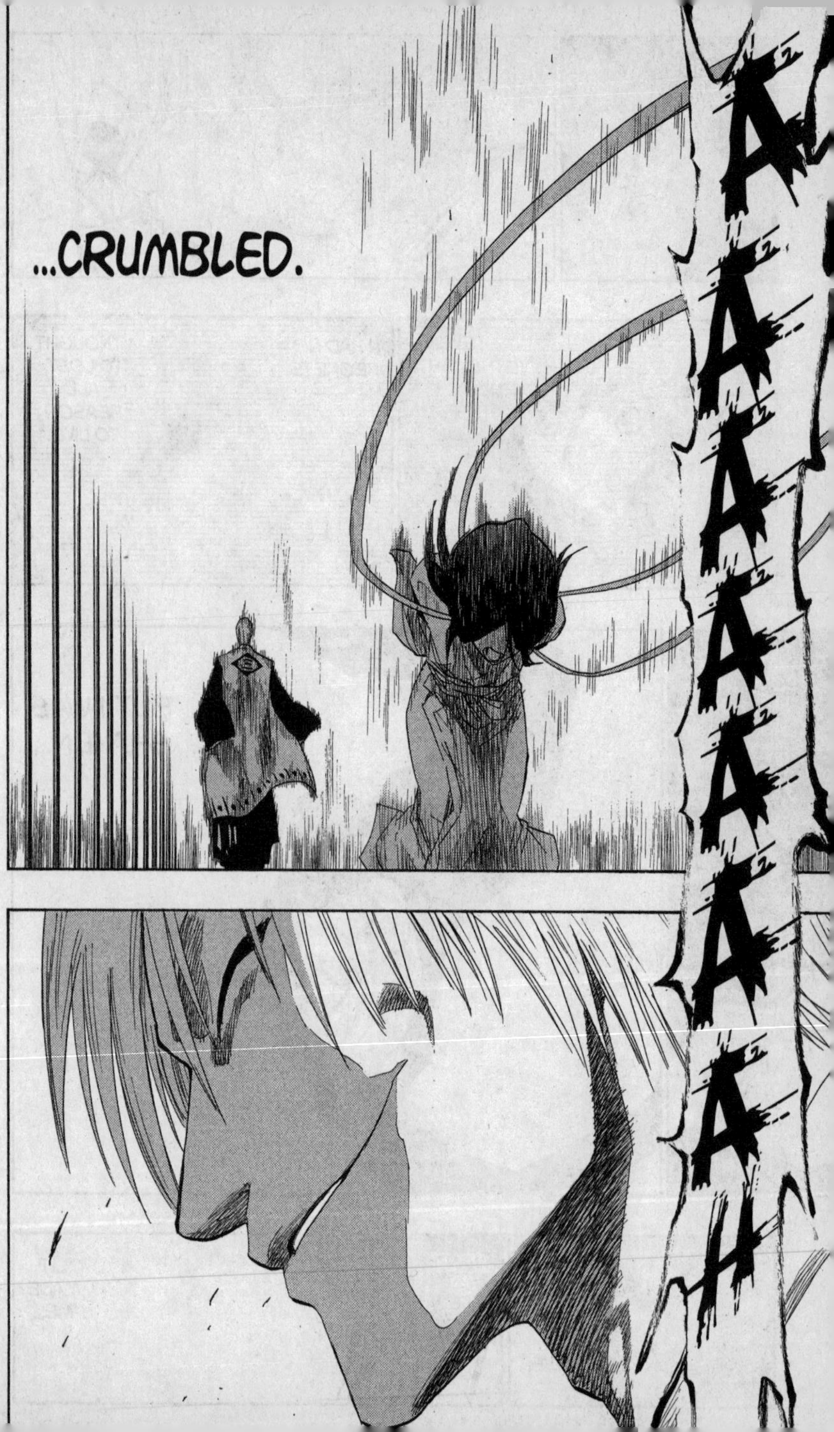
...CRUMBLED.
AAAAAAAH

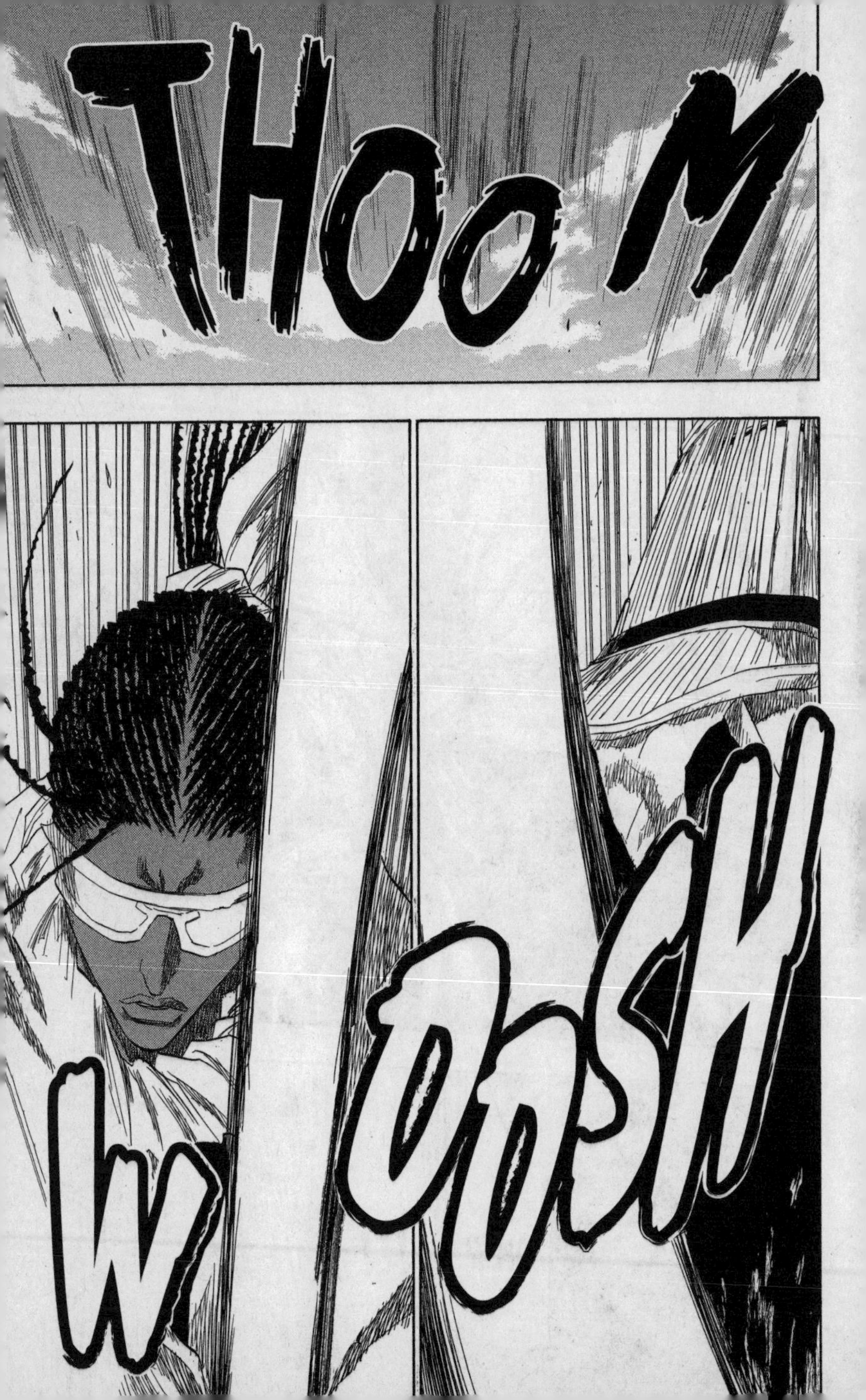
THOOM
WHOOSH

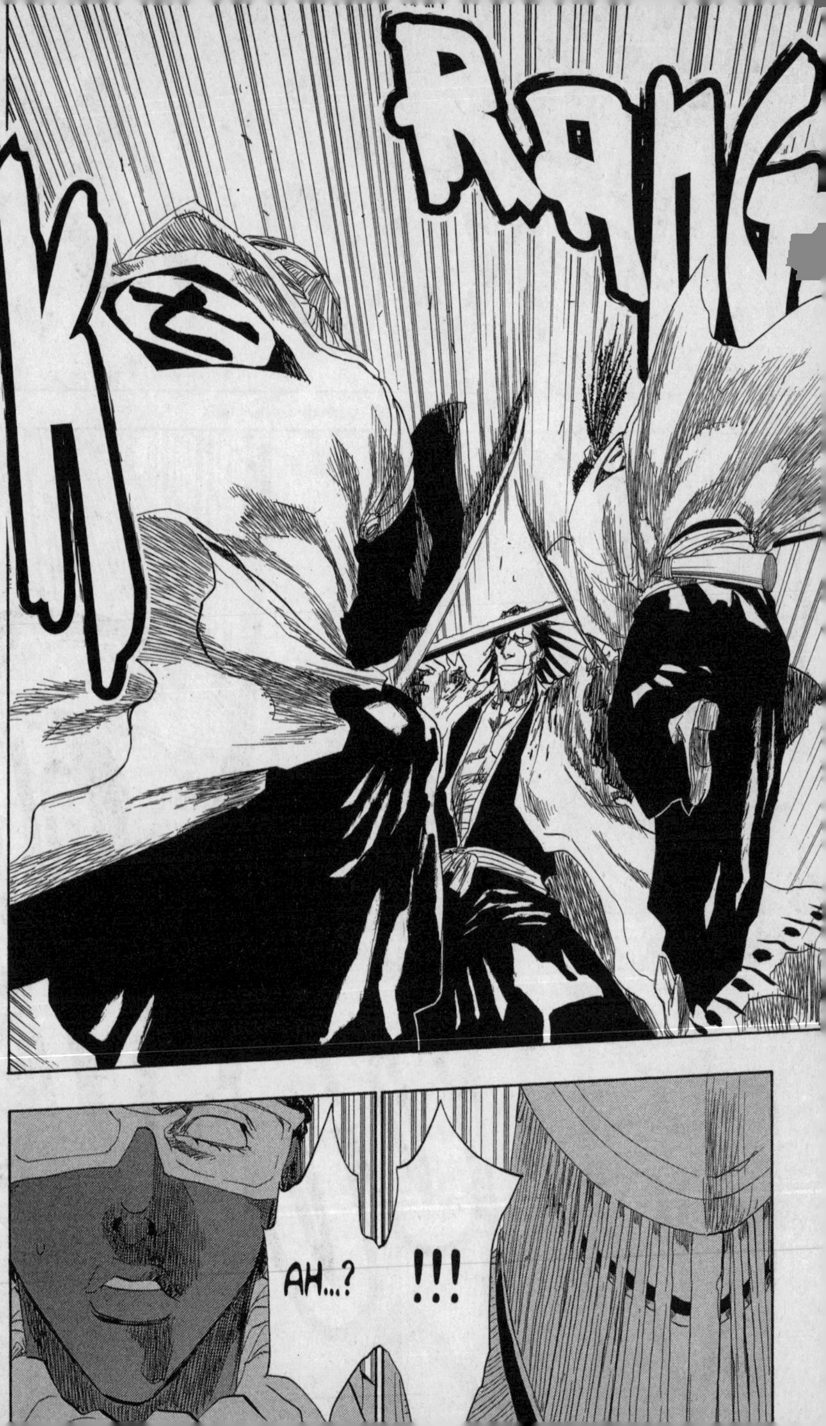
!!!
AH...?

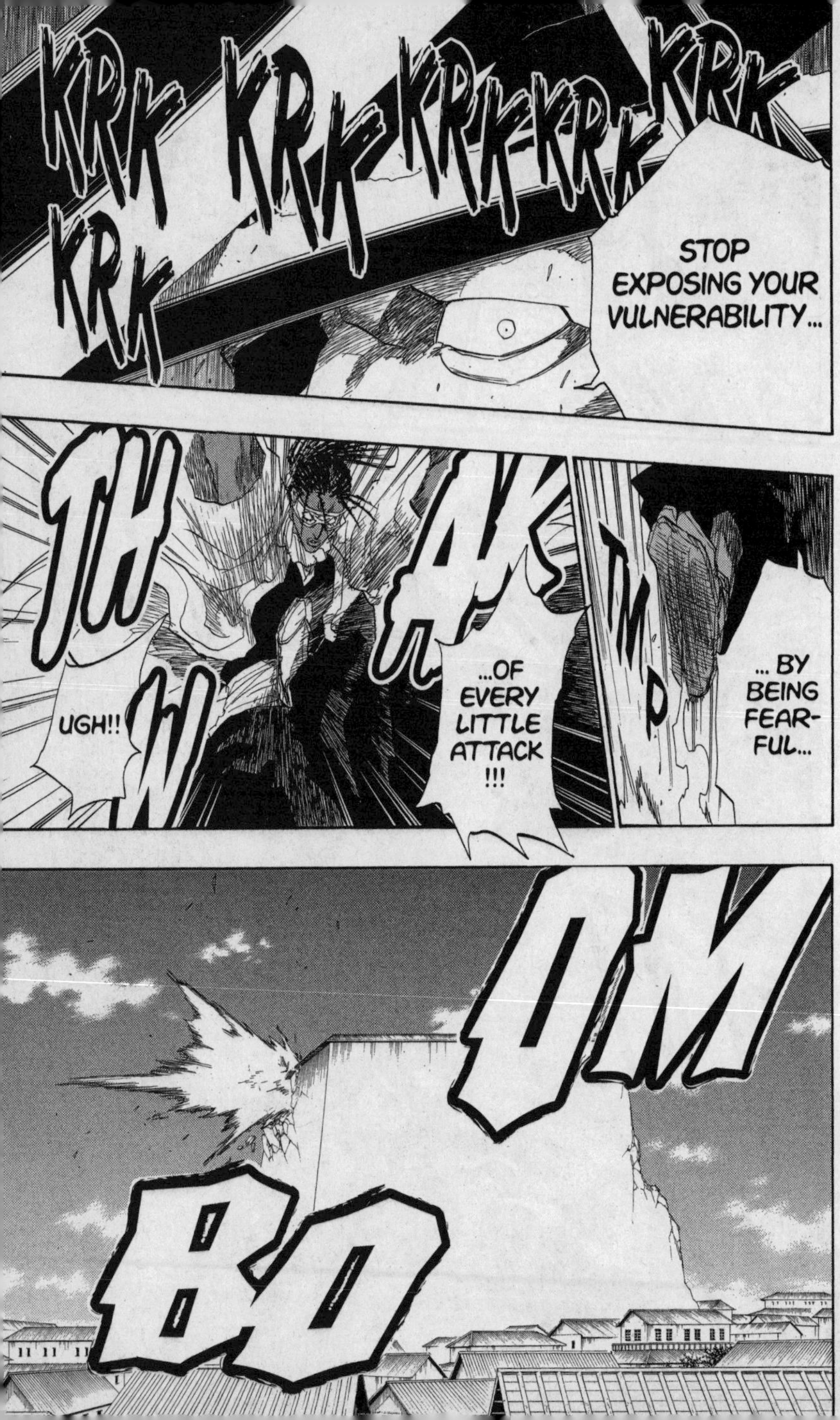
KRK KRK KRK KRK KRK KRK
STOP EXPOSING YOUR VULNERABILITY...
TMP
... BY BEING FEAR-FUL...
...OF EVERY LITTLE ATTACK!!!
THWAK
UGH!!
BOOM

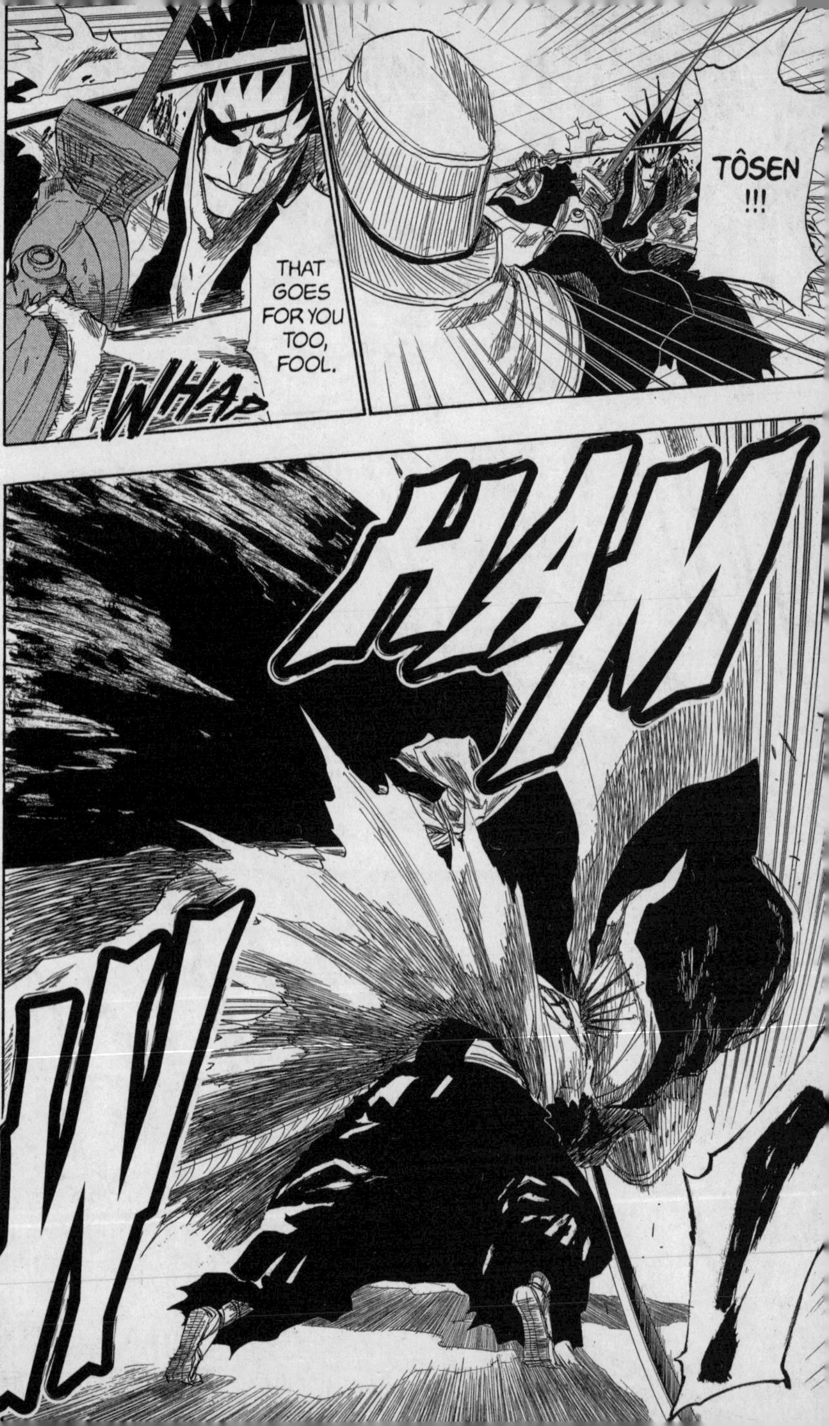
TÔSEN !!!
THAT GOES FOR YOU TOO, FOOL.
WHAP
WHAM!

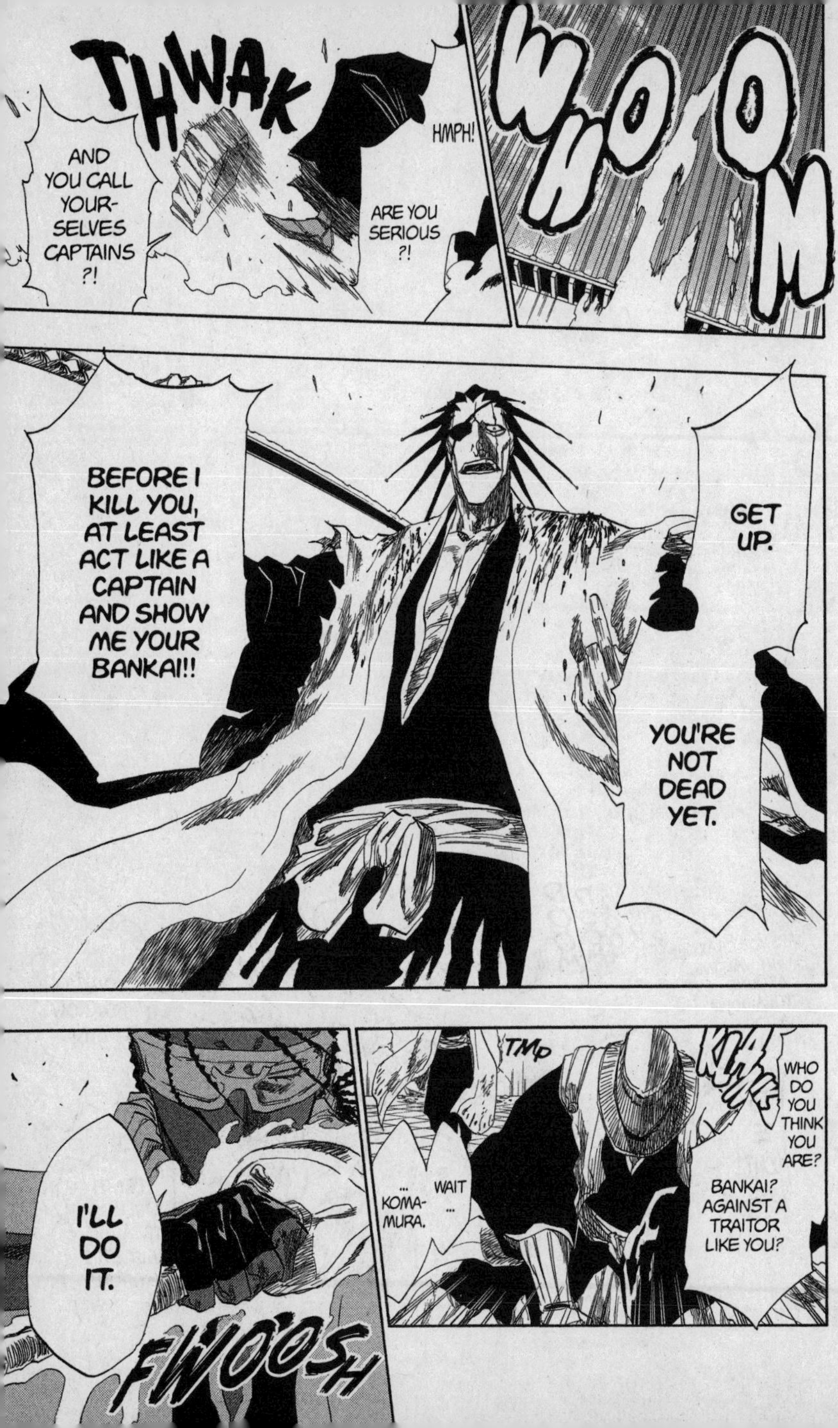
WHOOOM
HMPH!
THWAK
ARE YOU SERIOUS ?!
AND YOU CALL YOUR-SELVES CAPTAINS ?!
GET UP.
YOU'RE NOT DEAD YET.
BEFORE I KILL YOU, AT LEAST ACT LIKE A CAPTAIN AND SHOW ME YOUR BANKAI!!
KLANK
TMP
WHO DO YOU THINK YOU ARE?
BANKAI? AGAINST A TRAITOR LIKE YOU?
WAIT ...
... KOMA-MURA.
I'LL DO IT.
FWOOSH

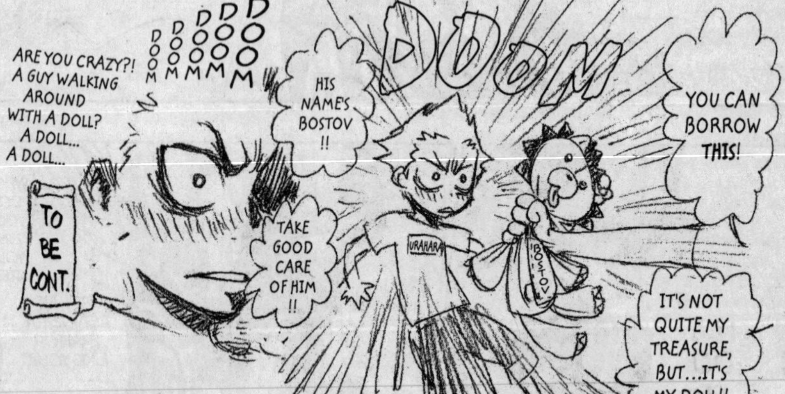

YOU CAN BORROW THIS!
IT'S NOT QUITE MY TREASURE, BUT...IT'S MY DOLL!!
DOOM
HIS NAME'S BOSTOV!!
TAKE GOOD CARE OF HIM!!
URAHARA
BOSTOV
DOOOM
DOOOM
DOOOM
DOOM
DOOM
ARE YOU CRAZY?! A GUY WALKING AROUND WITH A DOLL? A DOLL... A DOLL...
TO BE CONT.

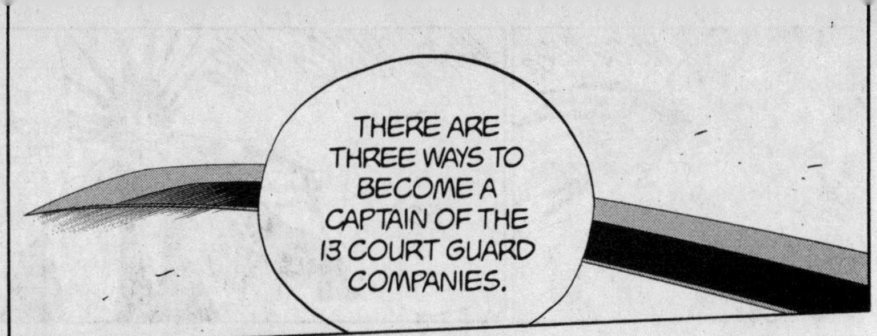
THERE ARE THREE WAYS TO BECOME A CAPTAIN OF THE 13 COURT GUARD COMPANIES.

146. Demon Loves the Dark

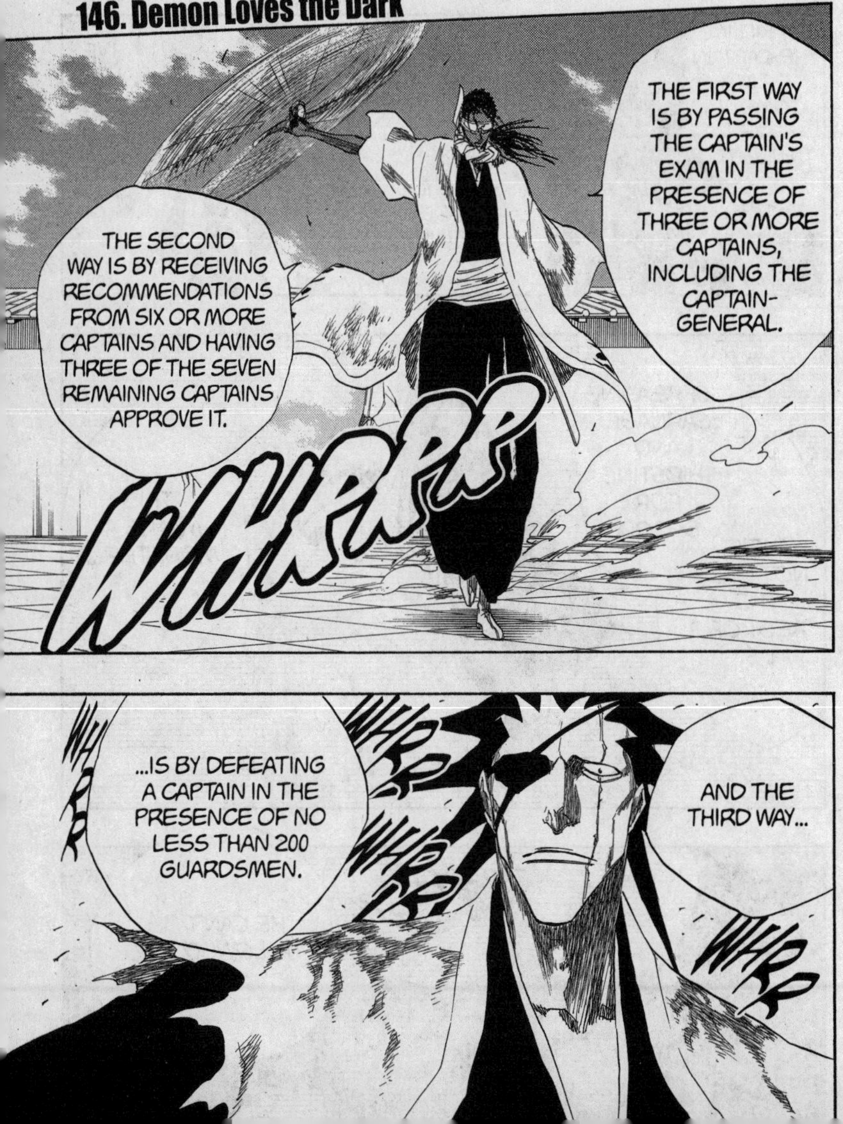
THE FIRST WAY IS BY PASSING THE CAPTAIN'S EXAM IN THE PRESENCE OF THREE OR MORE CAPTAINS, INCLUDING THE CAPTAIN-GENERAL.
THE SECOND WAY IS BY RECEIVING RECOMMENDATIONS FROM SIX OR MORE CAPTAINS AND HAVING THREE OF THE SEVEN REMAINING CAPTAINS APPROVE IT.
WHRRR
AND THE THIRD WAY...
WHRR
WHRR
WHRR
...IS BY DEFEATING A CAPTAIN IN THE PRESENCE OF NO LESS THAN 200 GUARDSMEN.
WHRR

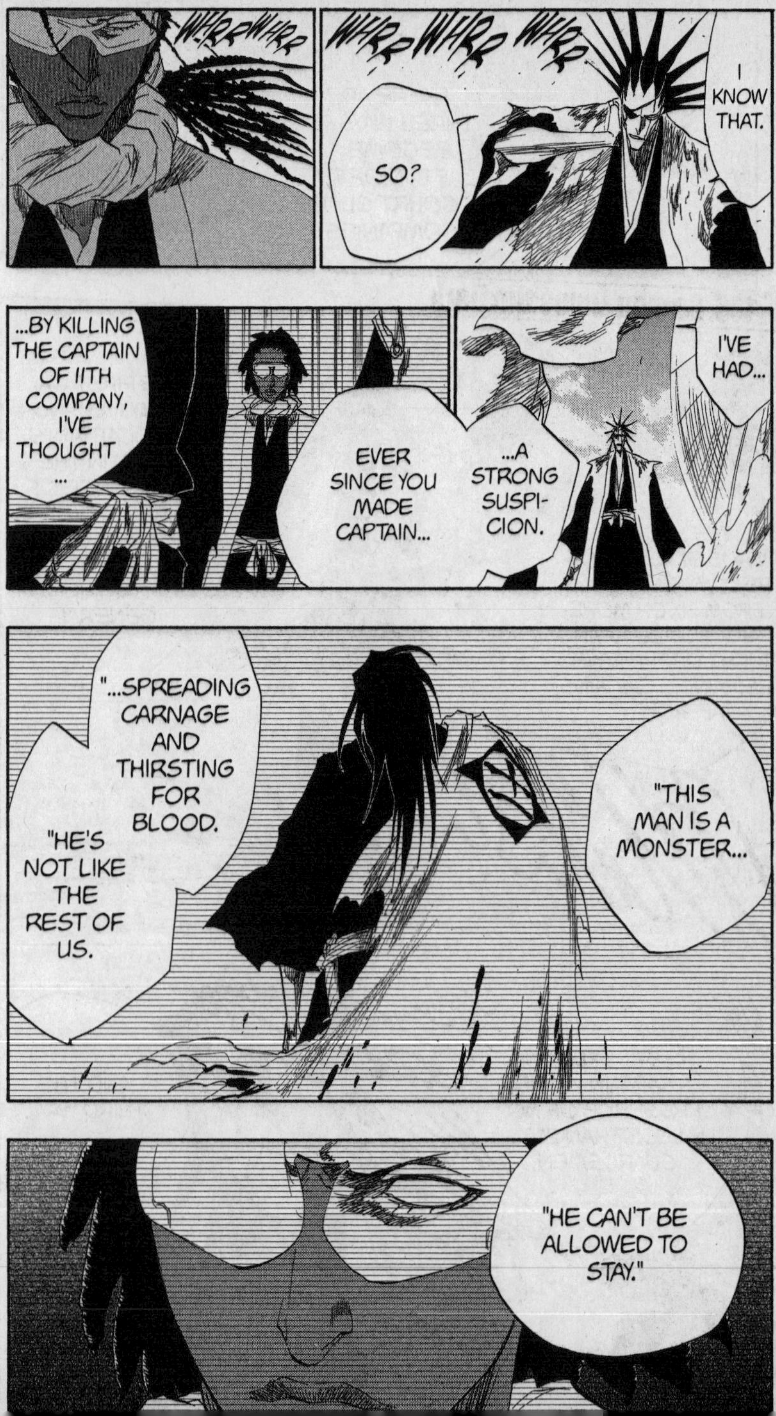
WHRR WHRR WHRR
I KNOW THAT.
SO?
WHRR WHRR
I'VE HAD...
...A STRONG SUSPICION.
EVER SINCE YOU MADE CAPTAIN...
...BY KILLING THE CAPTAIN OF 11TH COMPANY, I'VE THOUGHT ...
"THIS MAN IS A MONSTER...
"...SPREADING CARNAGE AND THIRSTING FOR BLOOD.
"HE'S NOT LIKE THE REST OF US.
"HE CAN'T BE ALLOWED TO STAY."

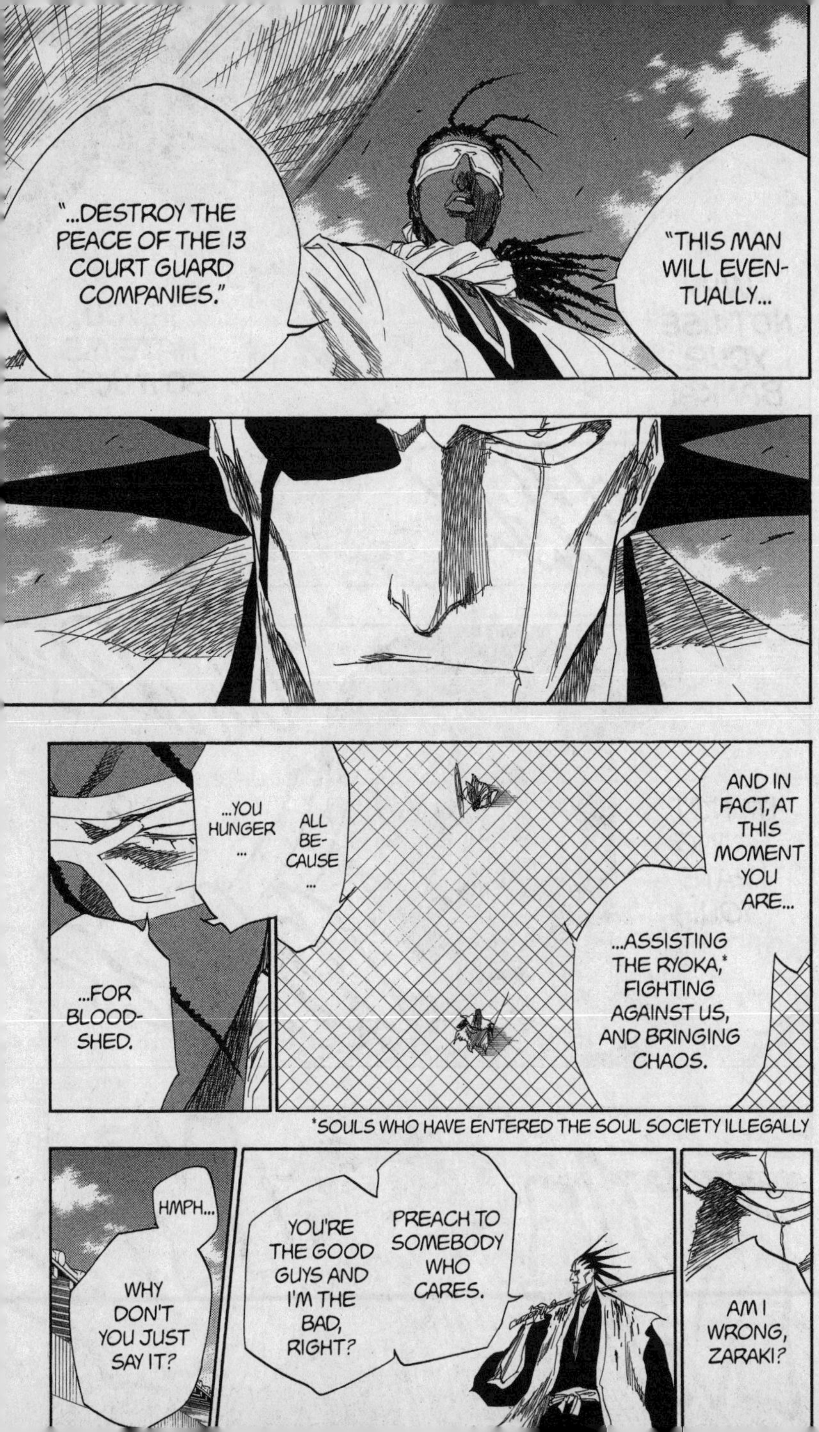
"THIS MAN WILL EVENTUALLY...
"...DESTROY THE PEACE OF THE 13 COURT GUARD COMPANIES."
AND IN FACT, AT THIS MOMENT YOU ARE...
...ASSISTING THE RYOKA,* FIGHTING AGAINST US, AND BRINGING CHAOS.
ALL BECAUSE ...
...YOU HUNGER ...
...FOR BLOODSHED.
AM I WRONG, ZARAKI?
PREACH TO SOMEBODY WHO CARES.
YOU'RE THE GOOD GUYS AND I'M THE BAD, RIGHT?
HMPH...
WHY DON'T YOU JUST SAY IT?

*SOULS WHO HAVE ENTERED THE SOUL SOCIETY ILLEGALLY

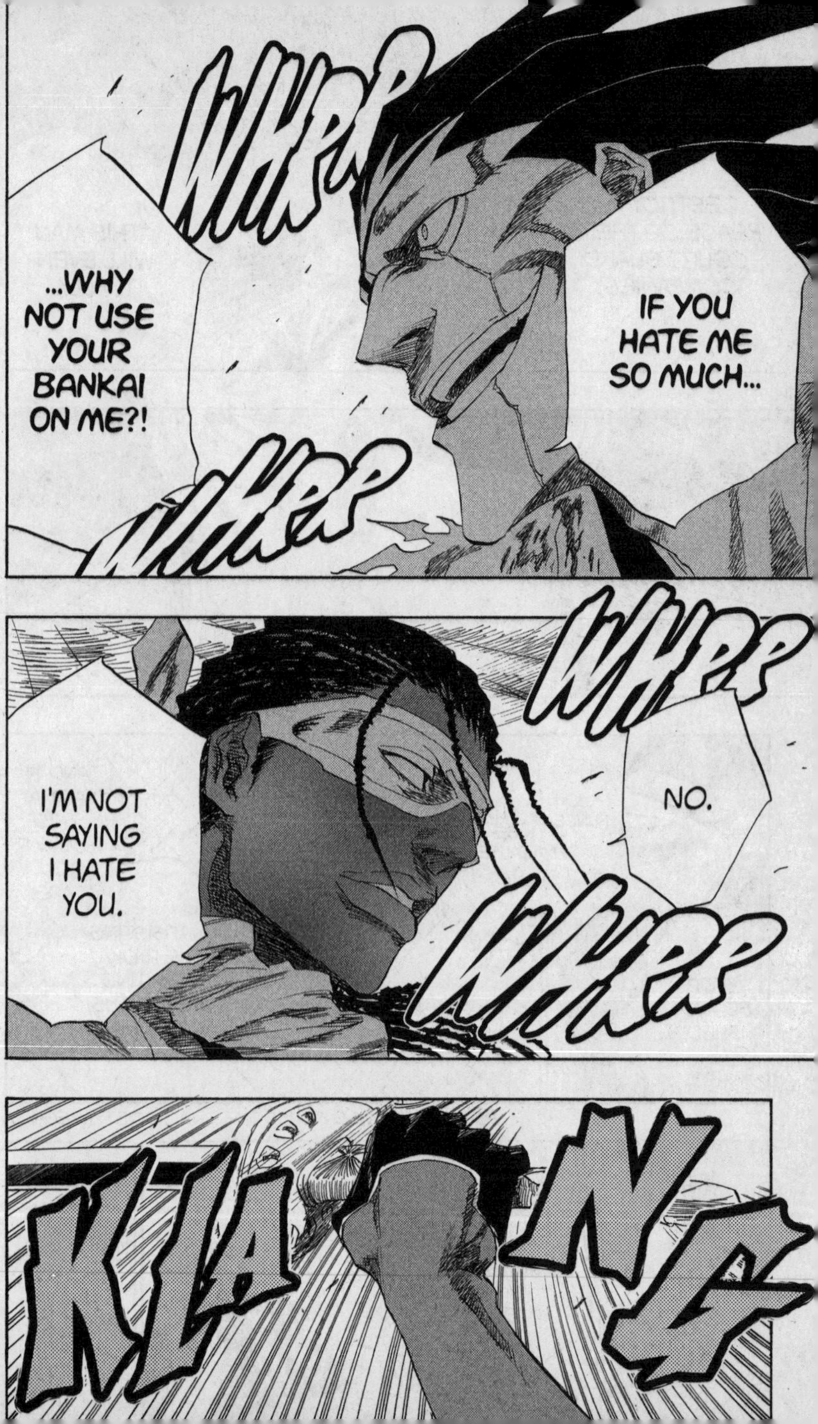
WHPP
IF YOU HATE ME SO MUCH...
...WHY NOT USE YOUR BANKAI ON ME?!
WHPP
WHPP
NO.
I'M NOT SAYING I HATE YOU.
WHPP
KLANG

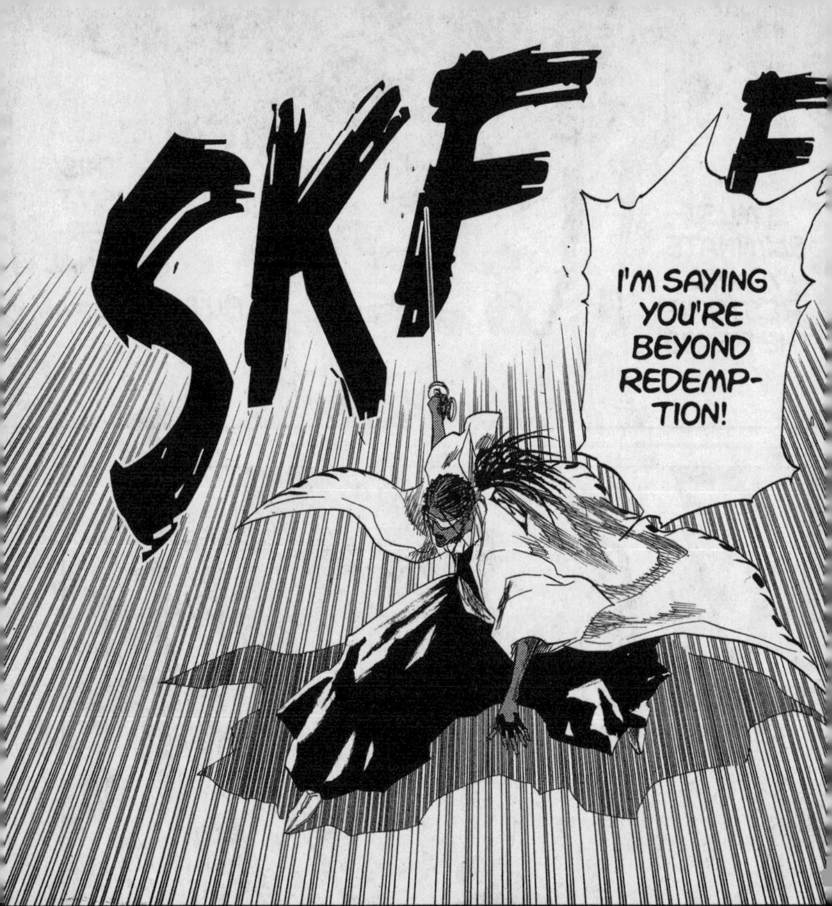
I'M SAYING YOU'RE BEYOND REDEMPTION!
SKF

146. Demon Loves the Dark

BLEACH -ブリーチ-

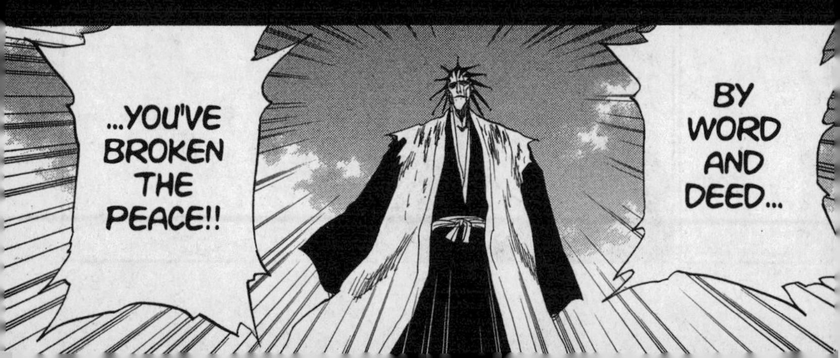
BY WORD AND DEED...
...YOU'VE BROKEN THE PEACE!!

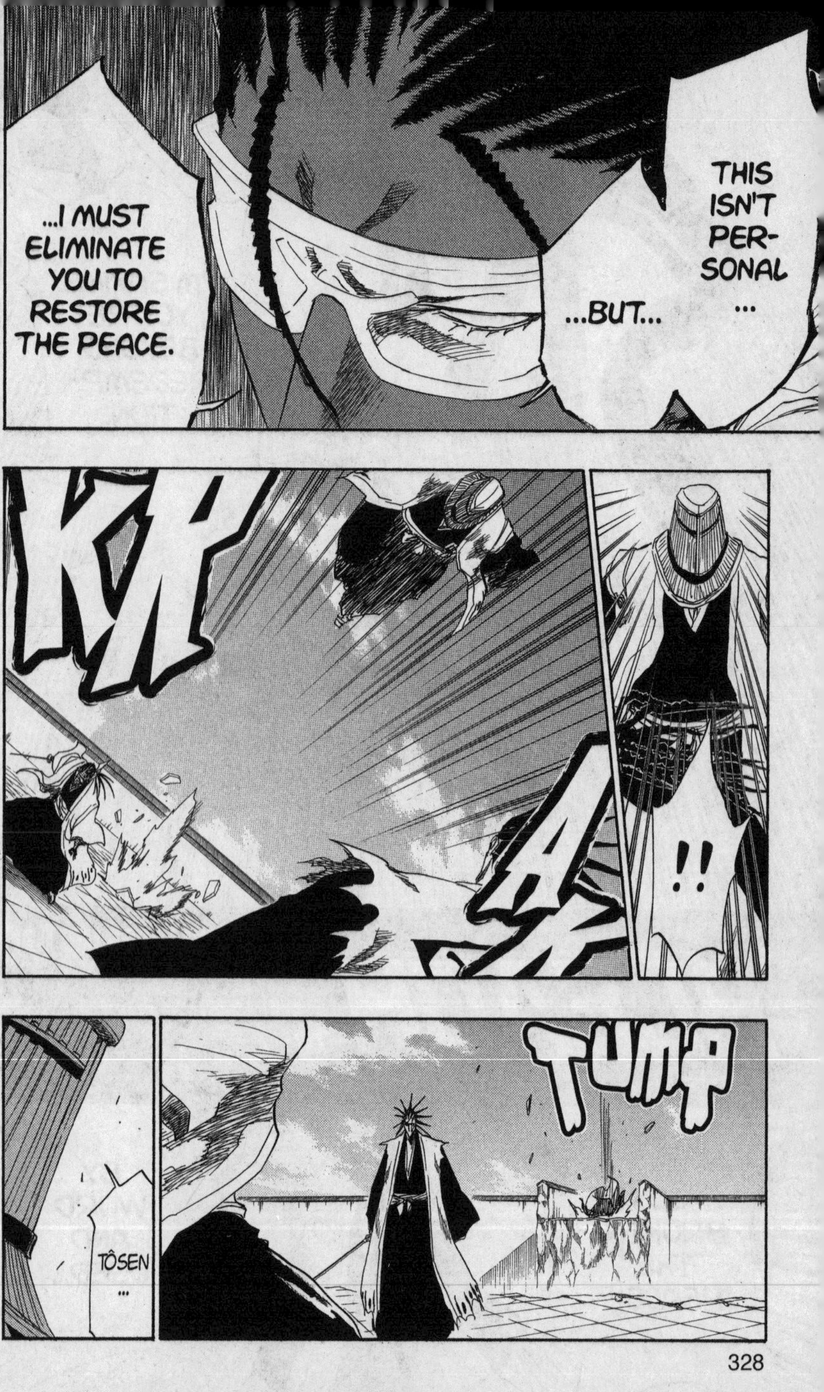
THIS ISN'T PER-SONAL ...
...BUT...
...I MUST ELIMINATE YOU TO RESTORE THE PEACE.
!!
TUMP
TÔSEN ...

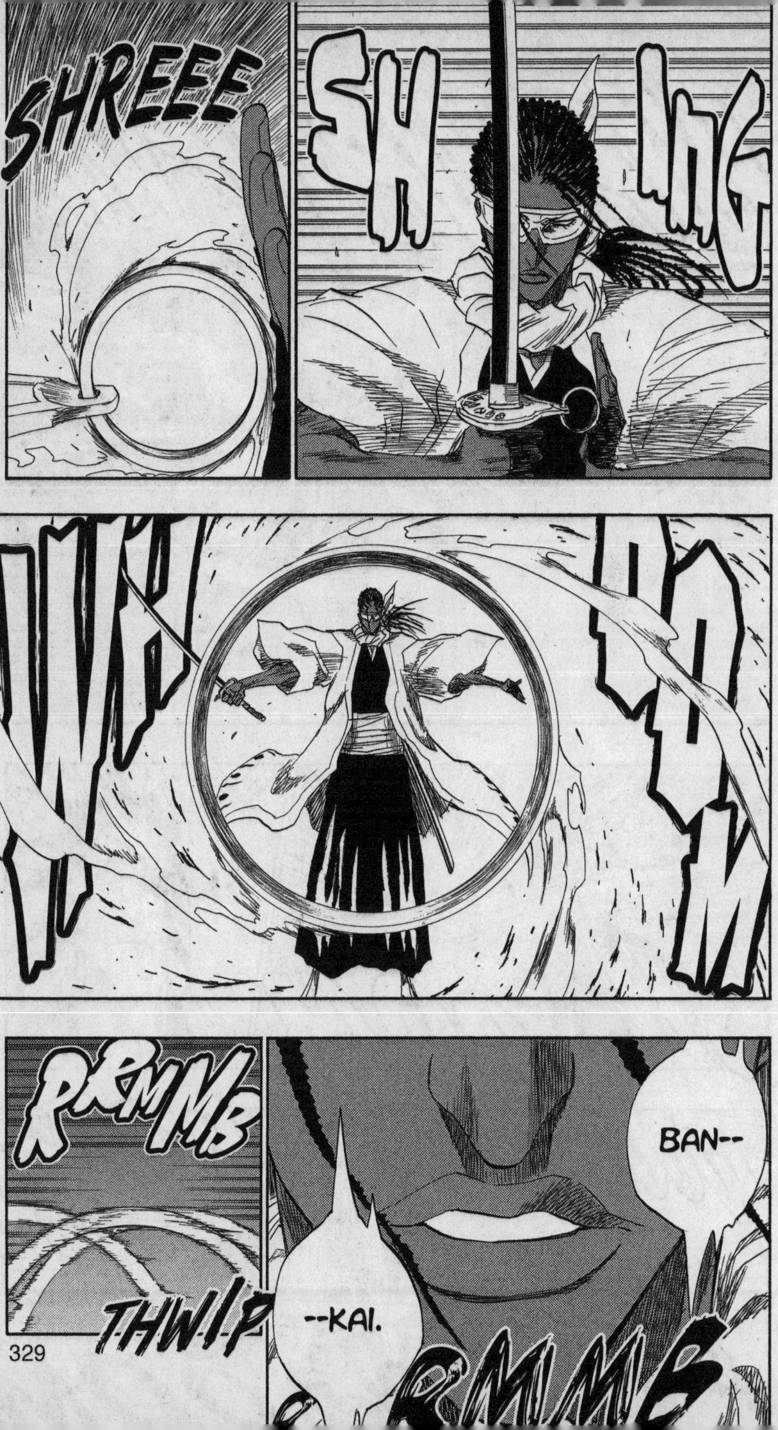
SHING
SHREEE
BAN--
--KAI.
RMMB
RMMB
THWIP

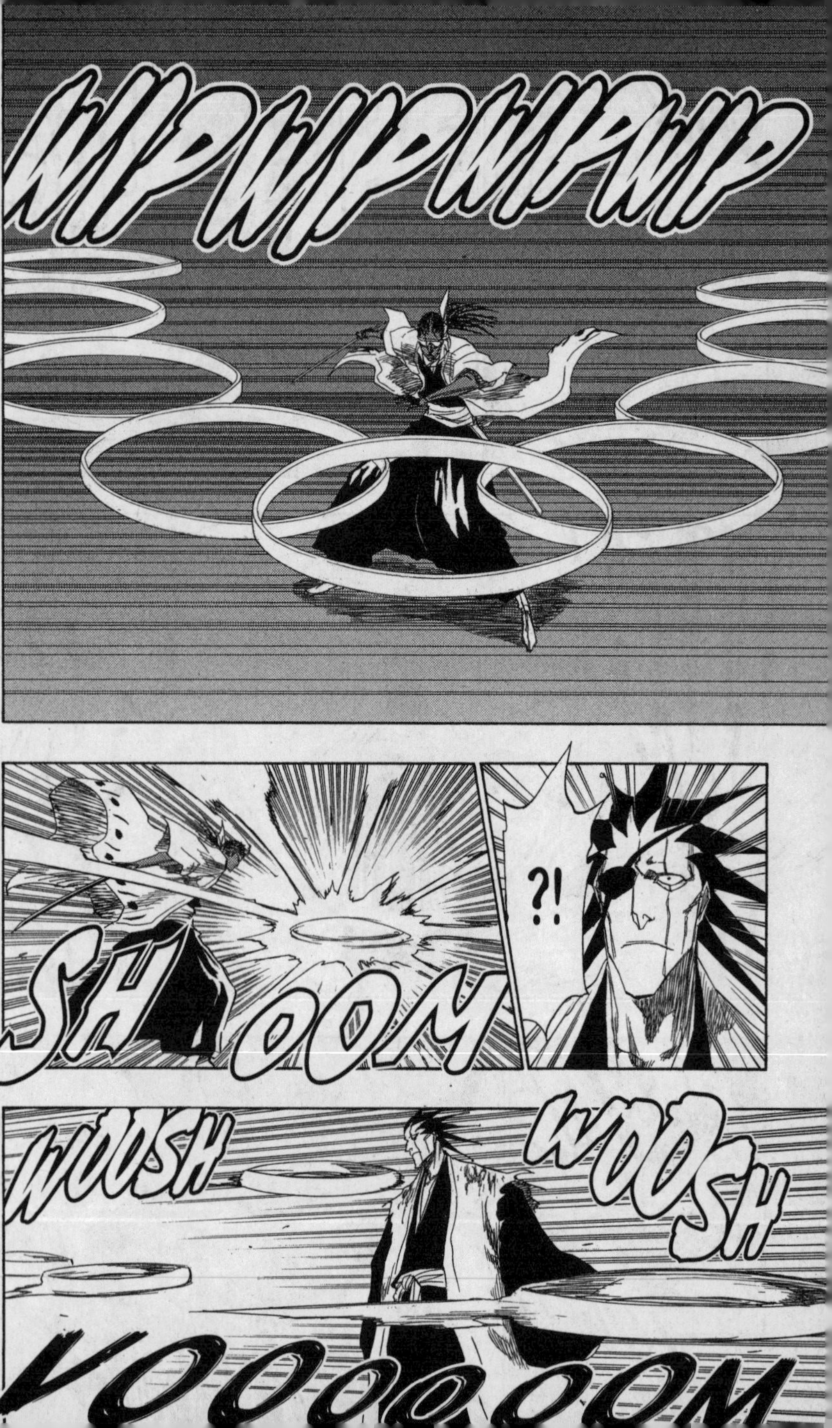

WHIPWHIPWHIPWHIP
?!
SHOOM
WOOSH
WOOSH
VOOOOOOM

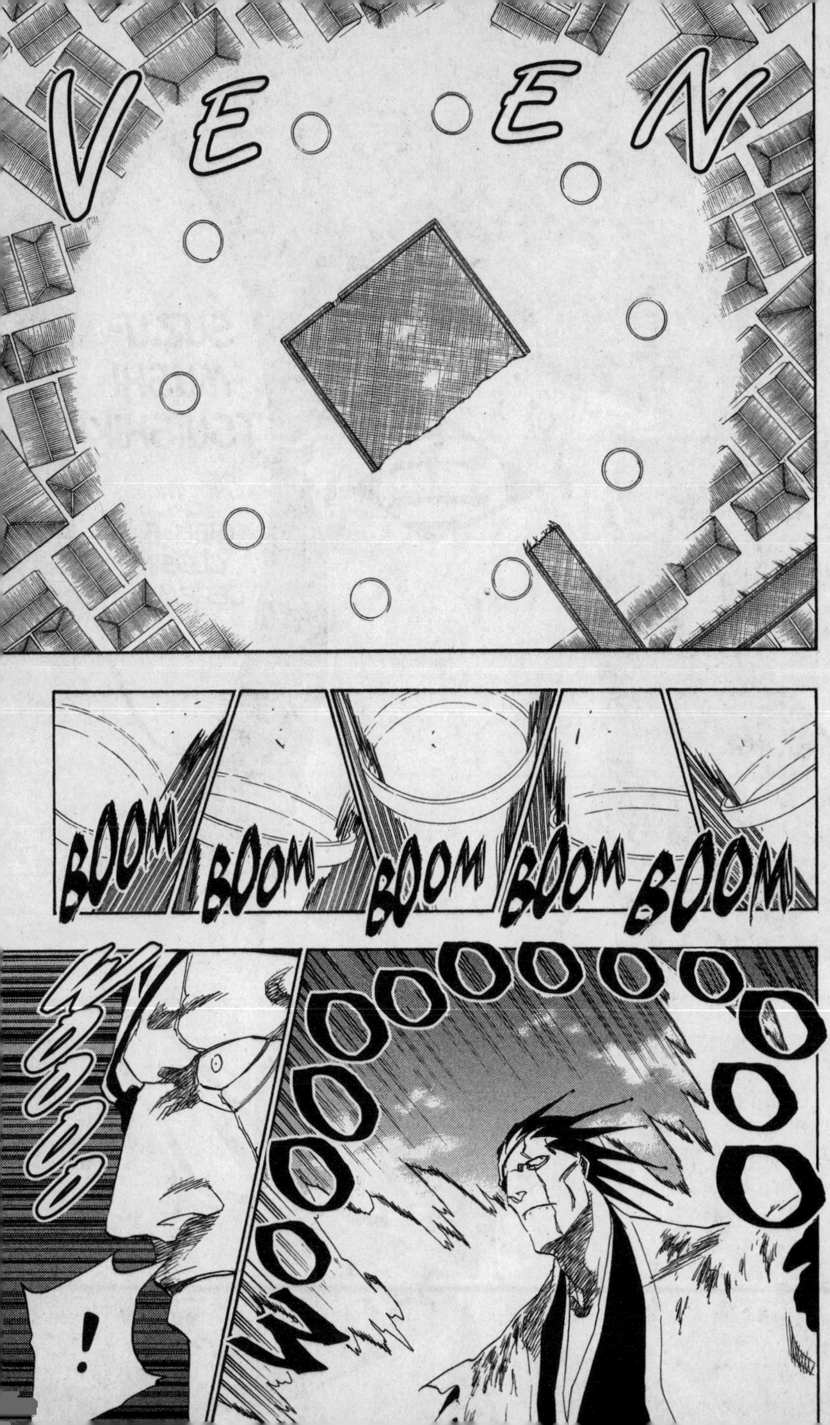
V E E N
BOOM BOOM BOOM BOOM BOOM
!

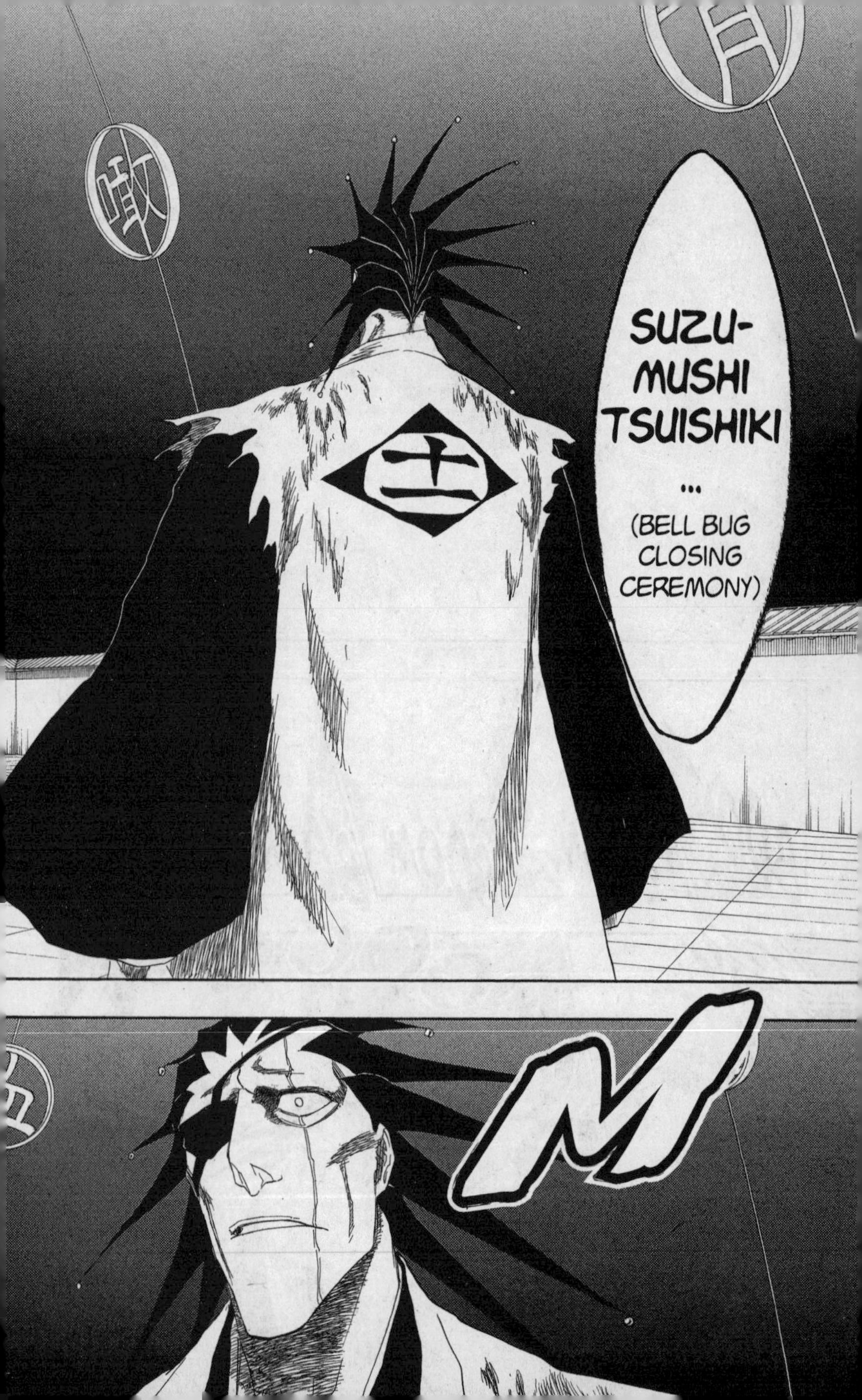
SUZU-MUSHI TSUISHIKI ... (BELL BUG CLOSING CEREMONY)
M

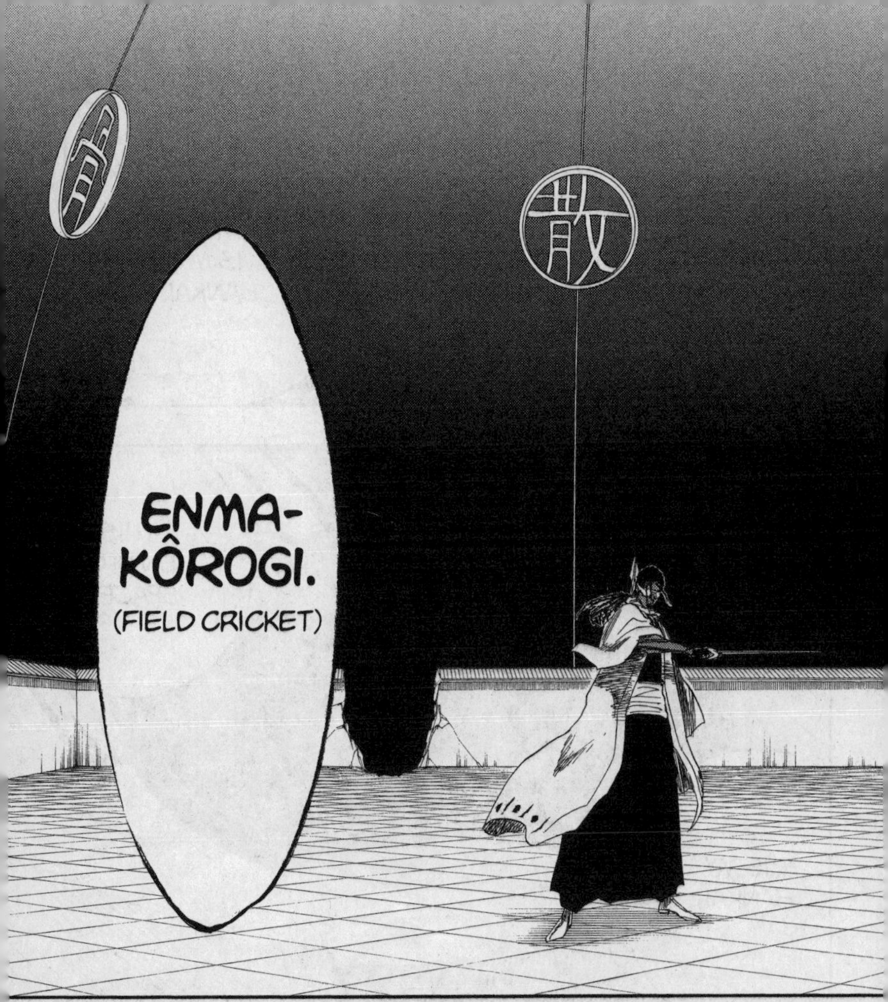
ENMA-
KÔROGI.
(FIELD CRICKET)

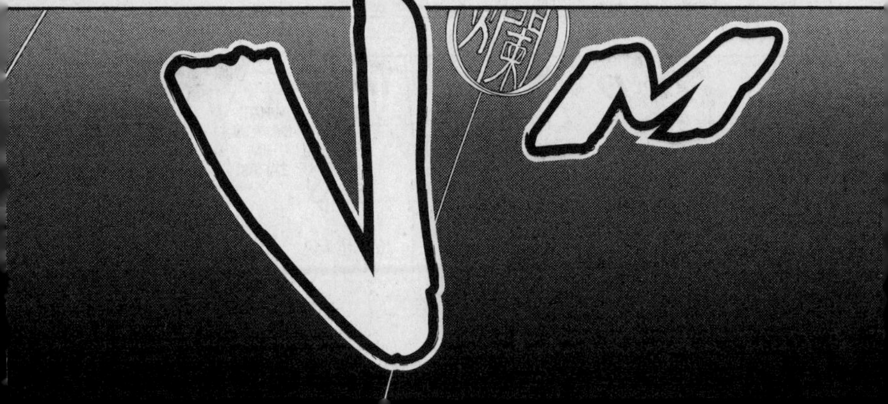
VM

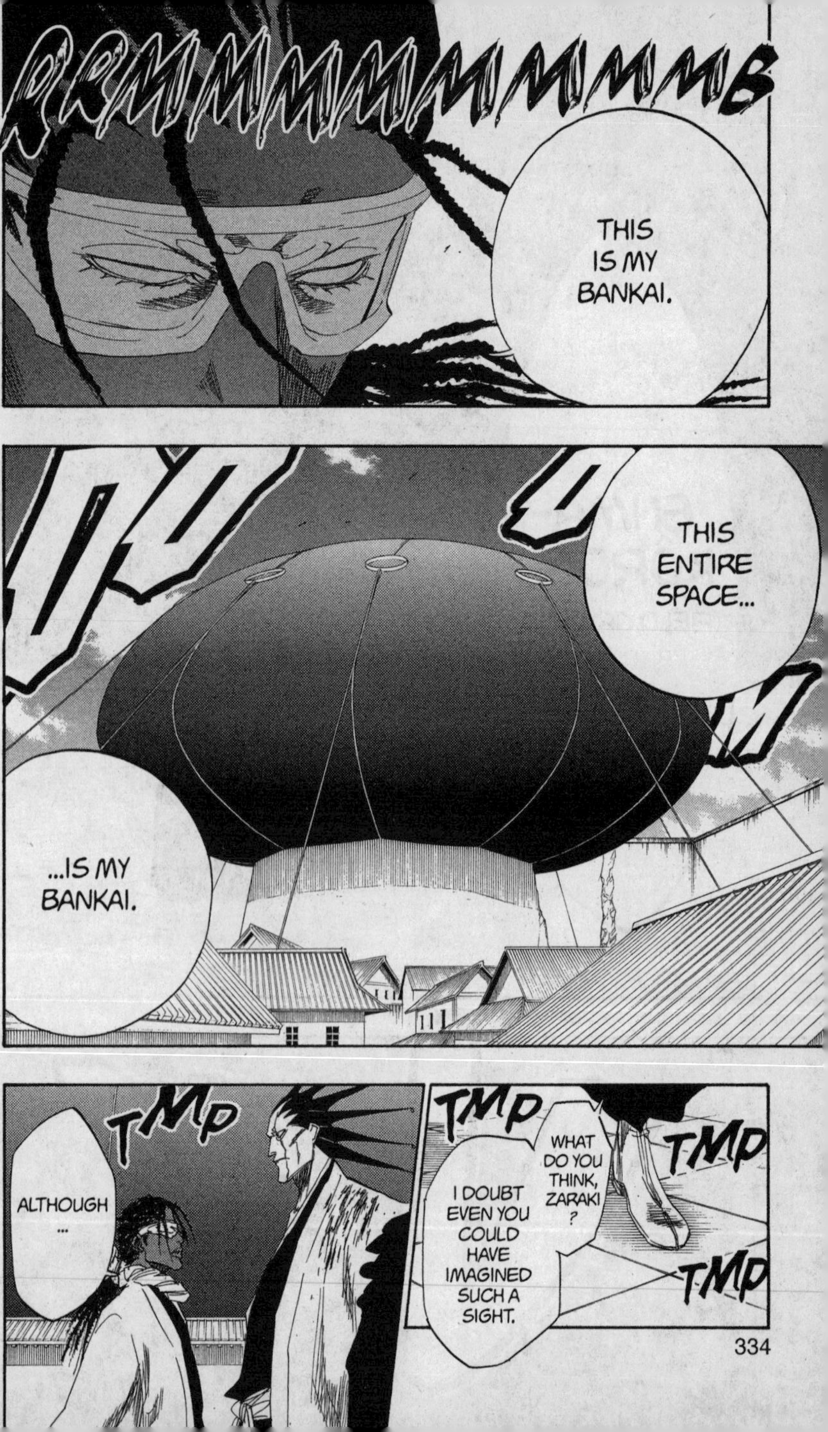
THIS IS MY BANKAI.
THIS ENTIRE SPACE...
...IS MY BANKAI.
TMP
WHAT DO YOU THINK, ZARAKI?
TMP
I DOUBT EVEN YOU COULD HAVE IMAGINED SUCH A SIGHT.
TMP
TMP
ALTHOUGH ...

...YOU PROBABLY...

...CAN'T SEE ANYTHING NOW.

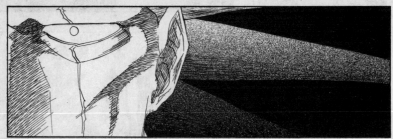

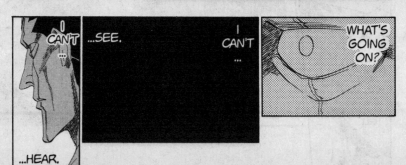

I CAN'T ...

...SEE.

I CAN'T ...

...HEAR.

WHAT'S GOING ON?

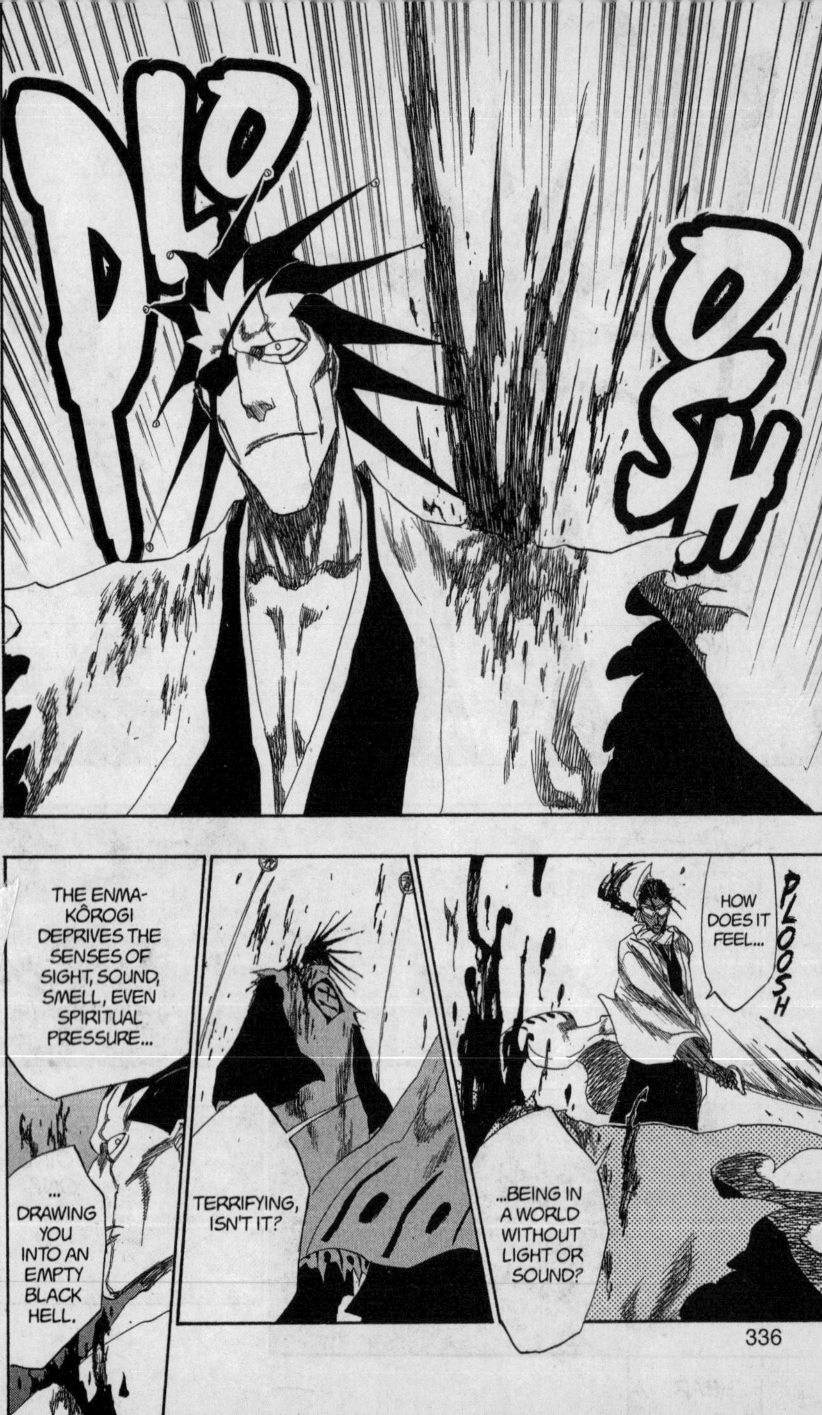
DOOSH
PLOOSH
HOW DOES IT FEEL...
...BEING IN A WORLD WITHOUT LIGHT OR SOUND?
TERRIFYING, ISN'T IT?
THE ENMA-KÔROGI DEPRIVES THE SENSES OF SIGHT, SOUND, SMELL, EVEN SPIRITUAL PRESSURE...
...DRAWING YOU INTO AN EMPTY BLACK HELL.

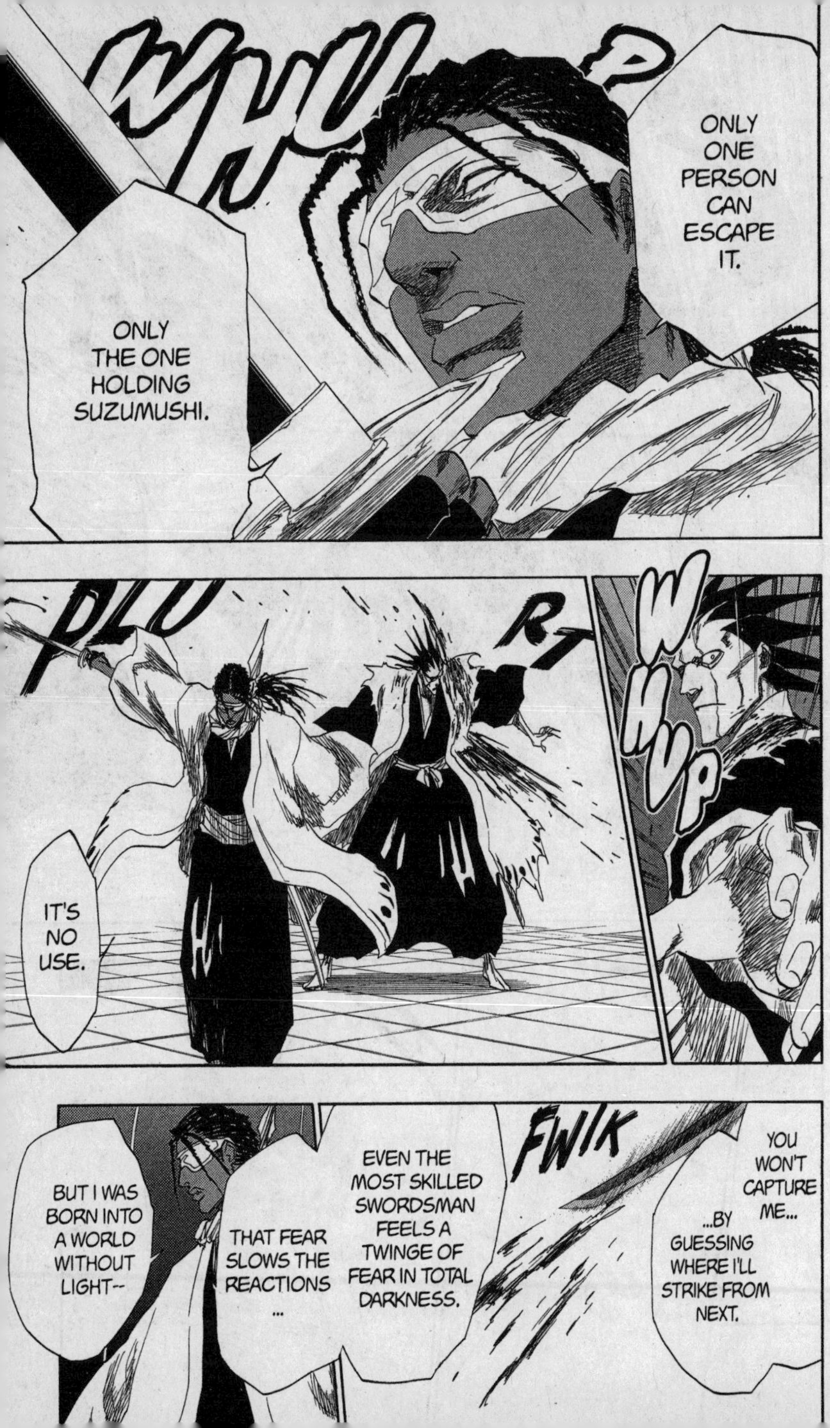
ONLY ONE PERSON CAN ESCAPE IT.
ONLY THE ONE HOLDING SUZUMUSHI.
WHUP
IT'S NO USE.
YOU WON'T CAPTURE ME...
...BY GUESSING WHERE I'LL STRIKE FROM NEXT.
FWIK
EVEN THE MOST SKILLED SWORDSMAN FEELS A TWINGE OF FEAR IN TOTAL DARKNESS.
THAT FEAR SLOWS THE REACTIONS ...
BUT I WAS BORN INTO A WORLD WITHOUT LIGHT--

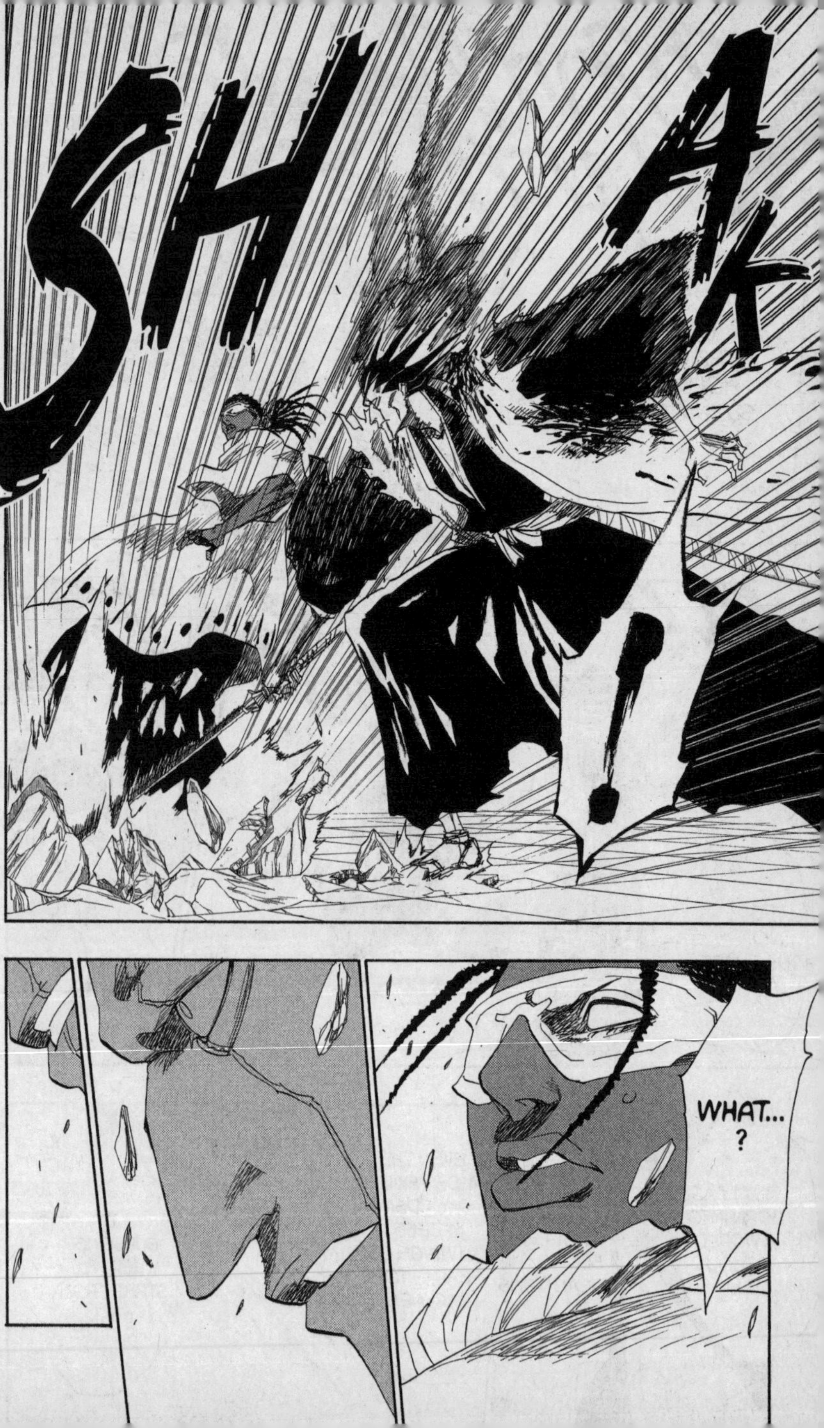
SHAK
!
WHAT...
?

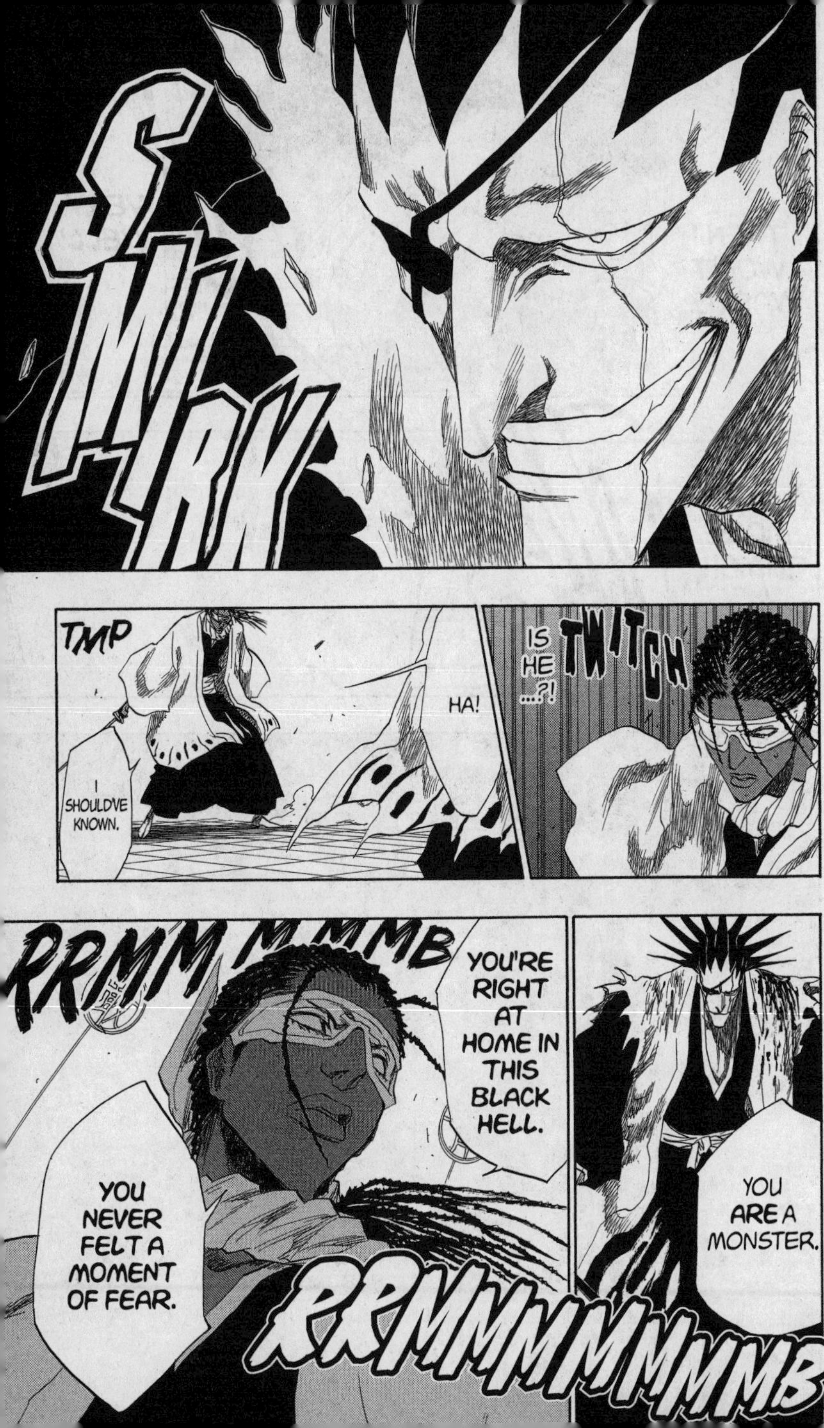
SMIRK
TWITCH
IS HE ...?!
HA!
TMP
I SHOULD'VE KNOWN.
YOU ARE A MONSTER.
RRMMMMMMB
YOU'RE RIGHT AT HOME IN THIS BLACK HELL.
YOU NEVER FELT A MOMENT OF FEAR.
RRMMMMMMMMMB

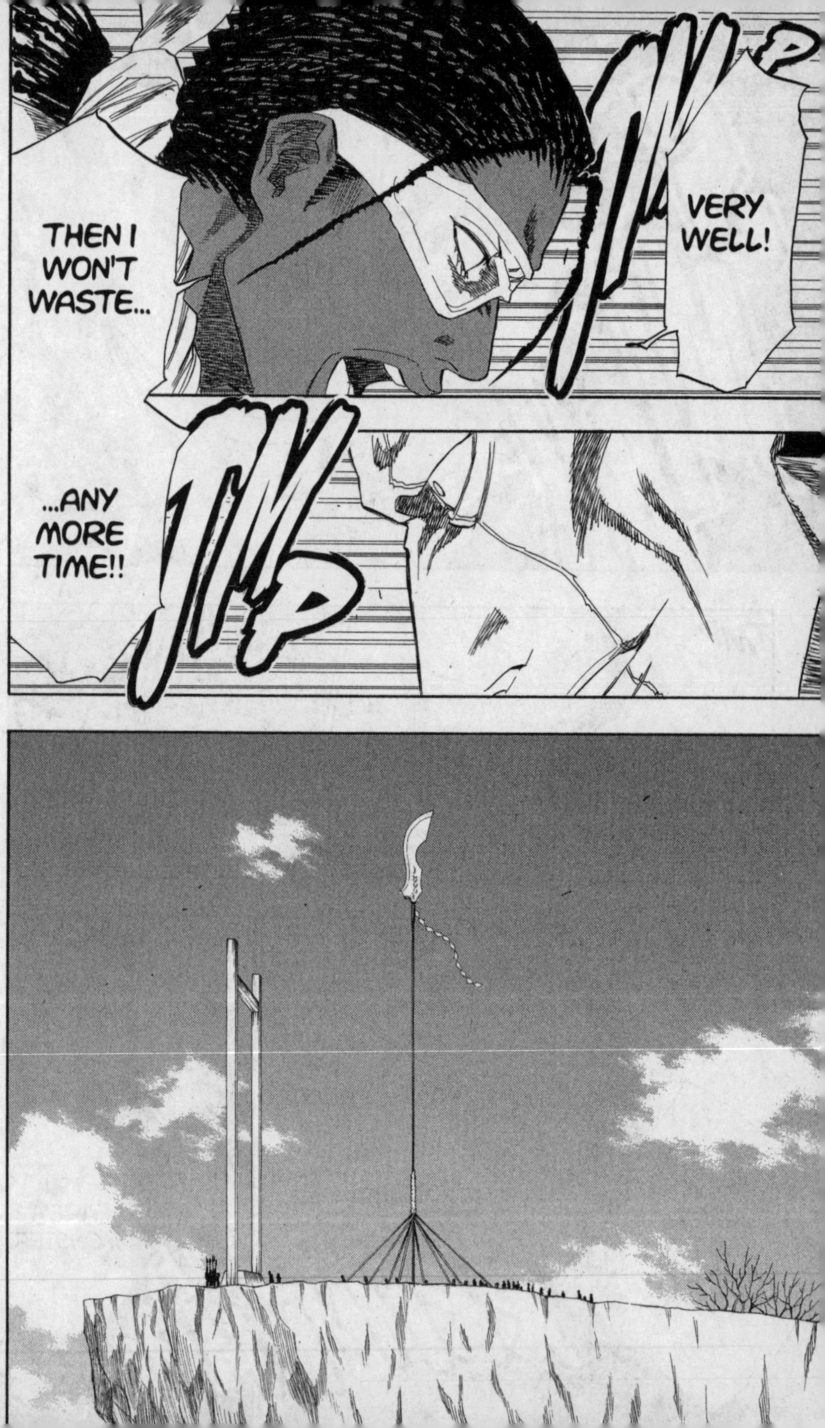
VERY WELL!
THEN I WON'T WASTE...
...ANY MORE TIME!!

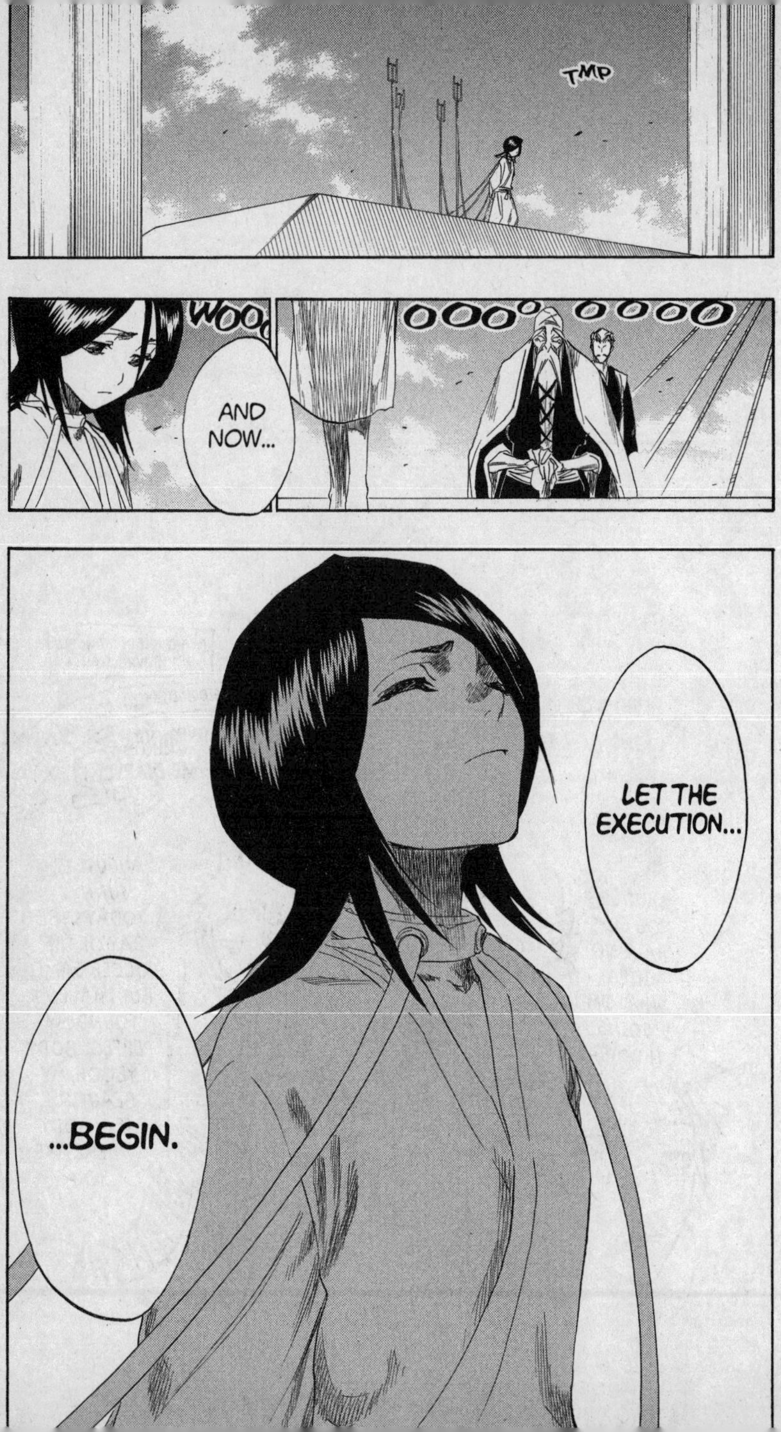
TMP
OOOOOOOO
WOOO
AND NOW...
LET THE EXECUTION...
...BEGIN.

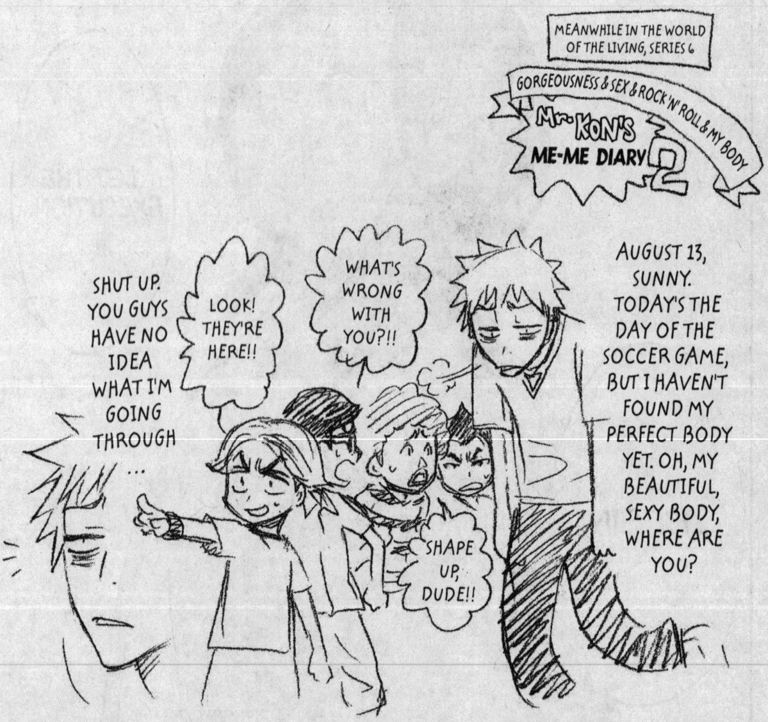
MEANWHILE IN THE WORLD OF THE LIVING, SERIES 6
GORGEOUSNESS & SEX & ROCK 'N' ROLL & MY BODY
Mr. KON'S ME-ME DIARY 2
AUGUST 13, SUNNY. TODAY'S THE DAY OF THE SOCCER GAME, BUT I HAVEN'T FOUND MY PERFECT BODY YET. OH, MY BEAUTIFUL, SEXY BODY, WHERE ARE YOU?
WHAT'S WRONG WITH YOU?!!
SHAPE UP, DUDE!!
LOOK! THEY'RE HERE!!
SHUT UP. YOU GUYS HAVE NO IDEA WHAT I'M GOING THROUGH ...

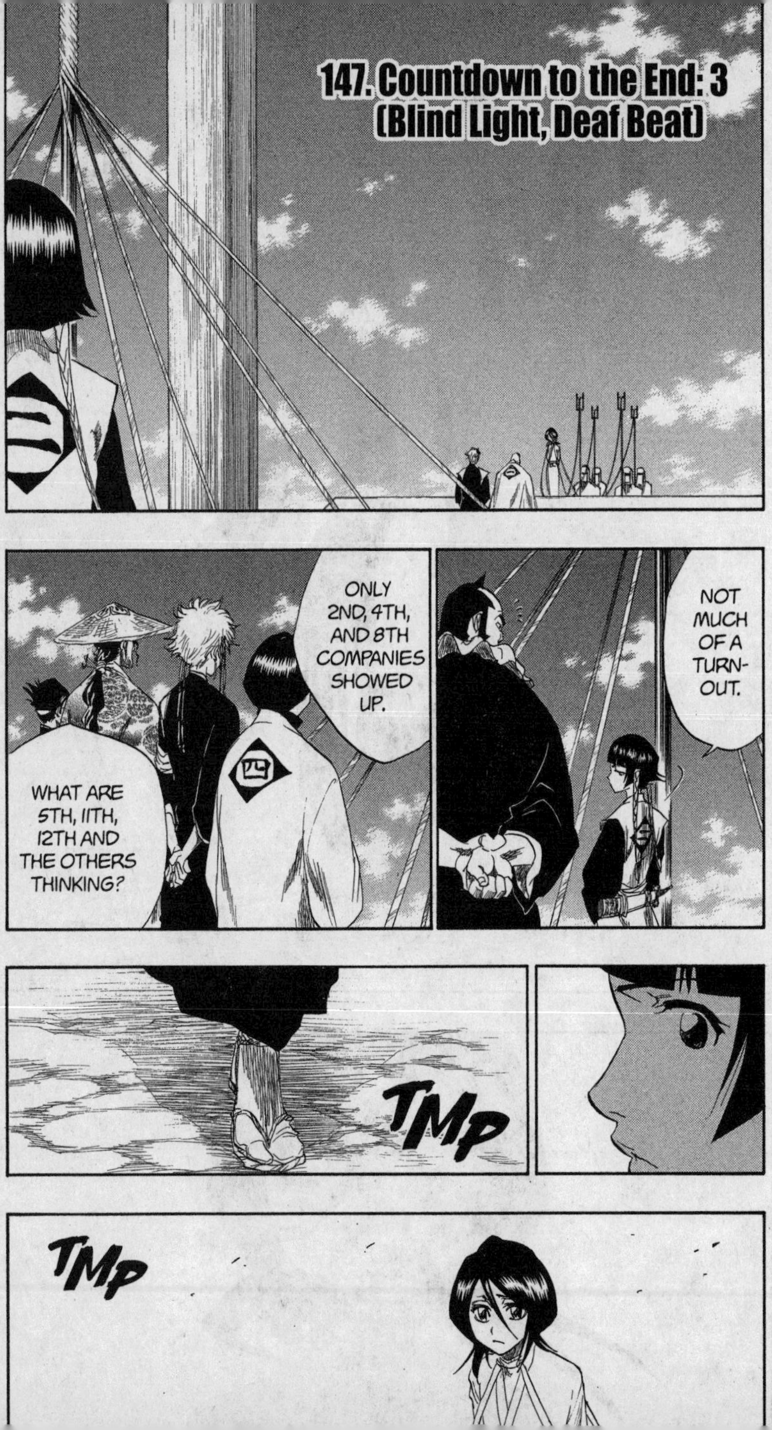
147. Countdown to the End: 3
(Blind Light, Deaf Beat)
NOT MUCH OF A TURN-OUT.
ONLY 2ND, 4TH, AND 8TH COMPANIES SHOWED UP.
WHAT ARE 5TH, 11TH, 12TH AND THE OTHERS THINKING?
TMP
TMP

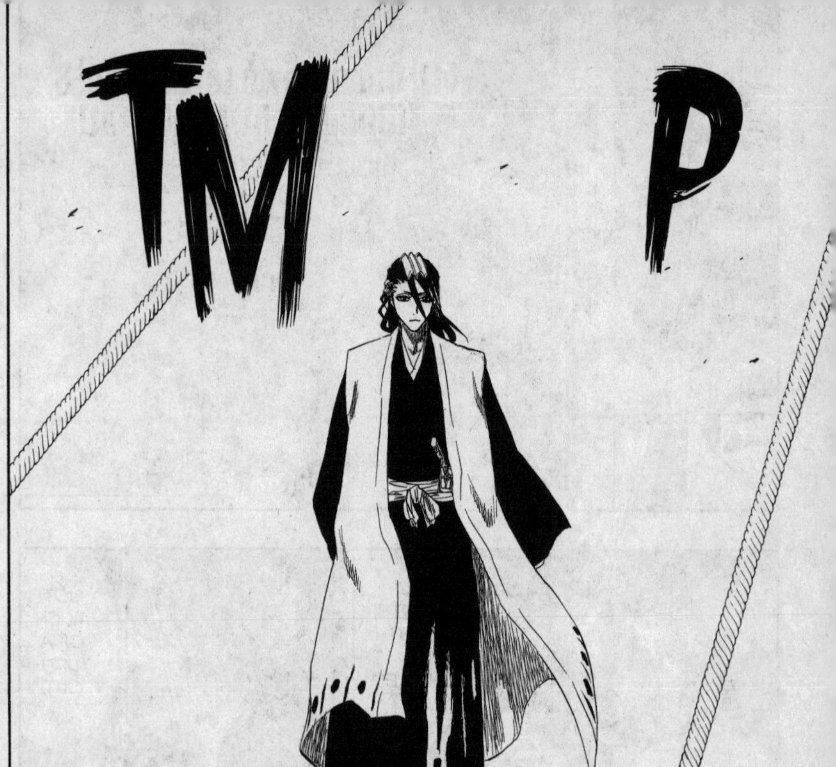
TMP
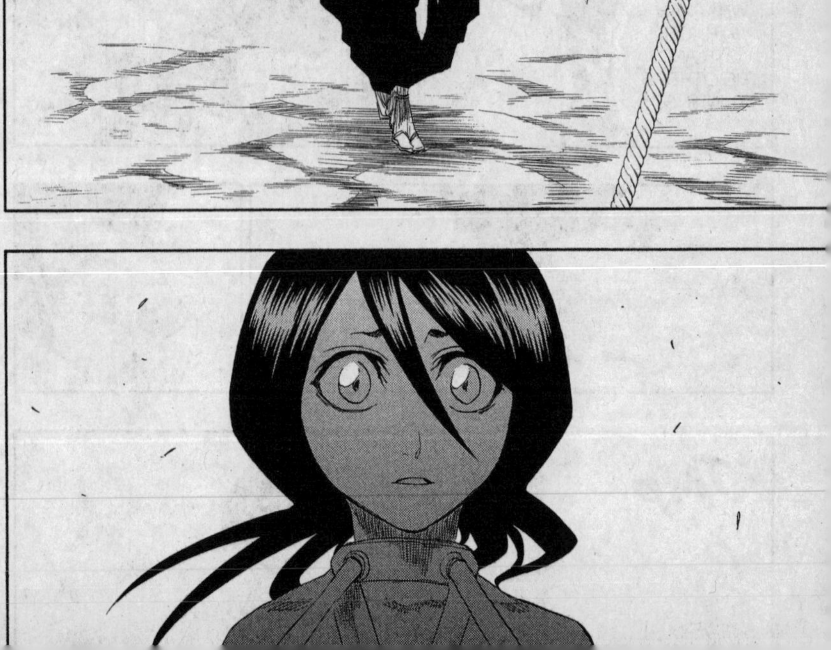

BYA--

B...

TMP

--KUYA...

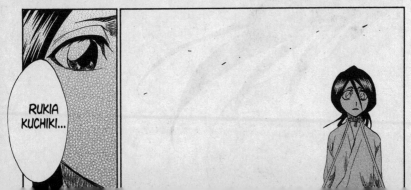

RUKIA
KUCHIKI...

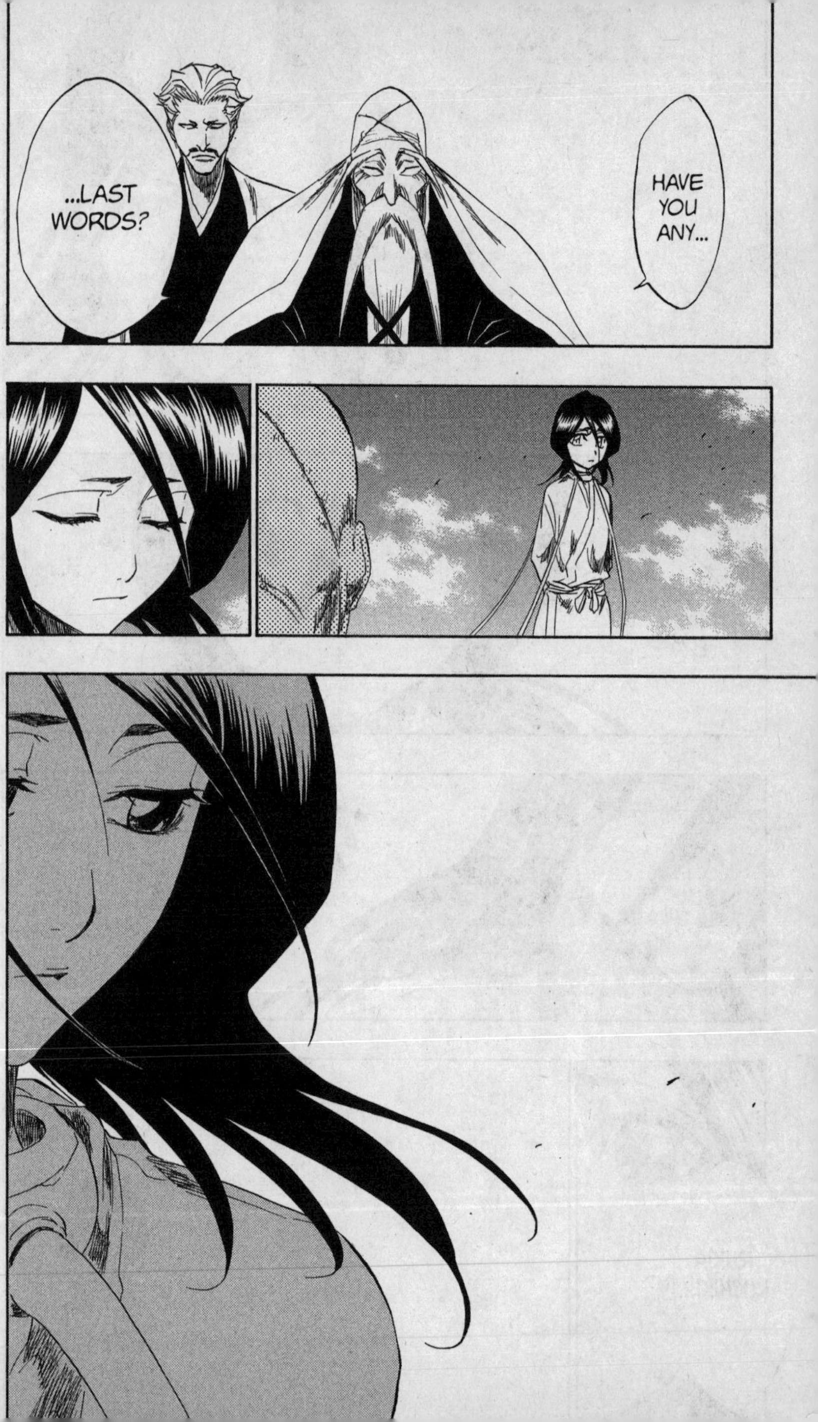
HAVE YOU ANY...
...LAST WORDS?

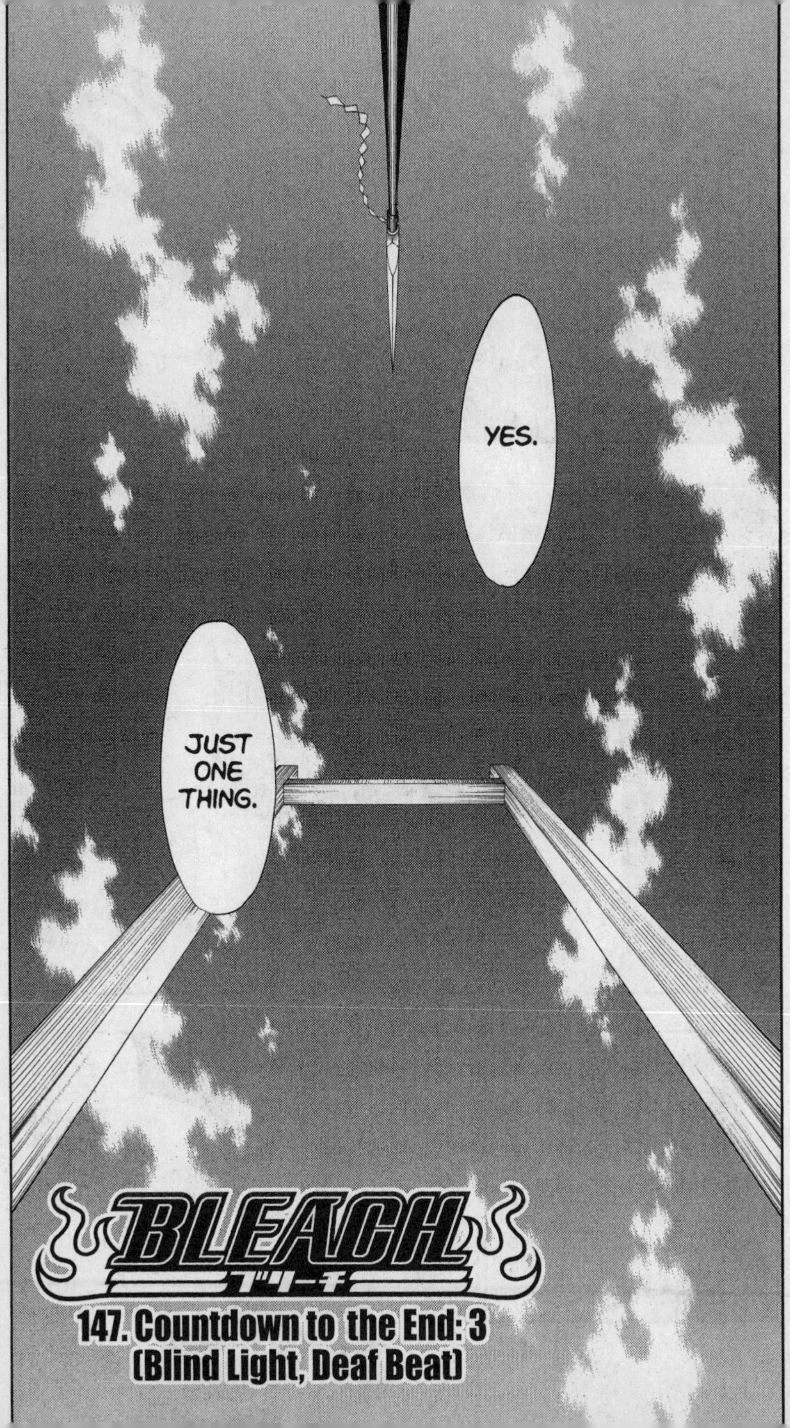
YES.
JUST ONE THING.
BLEACH
ブリーチ
147. Countdown to the End: 3
(Blind Light, Deaf Beat)

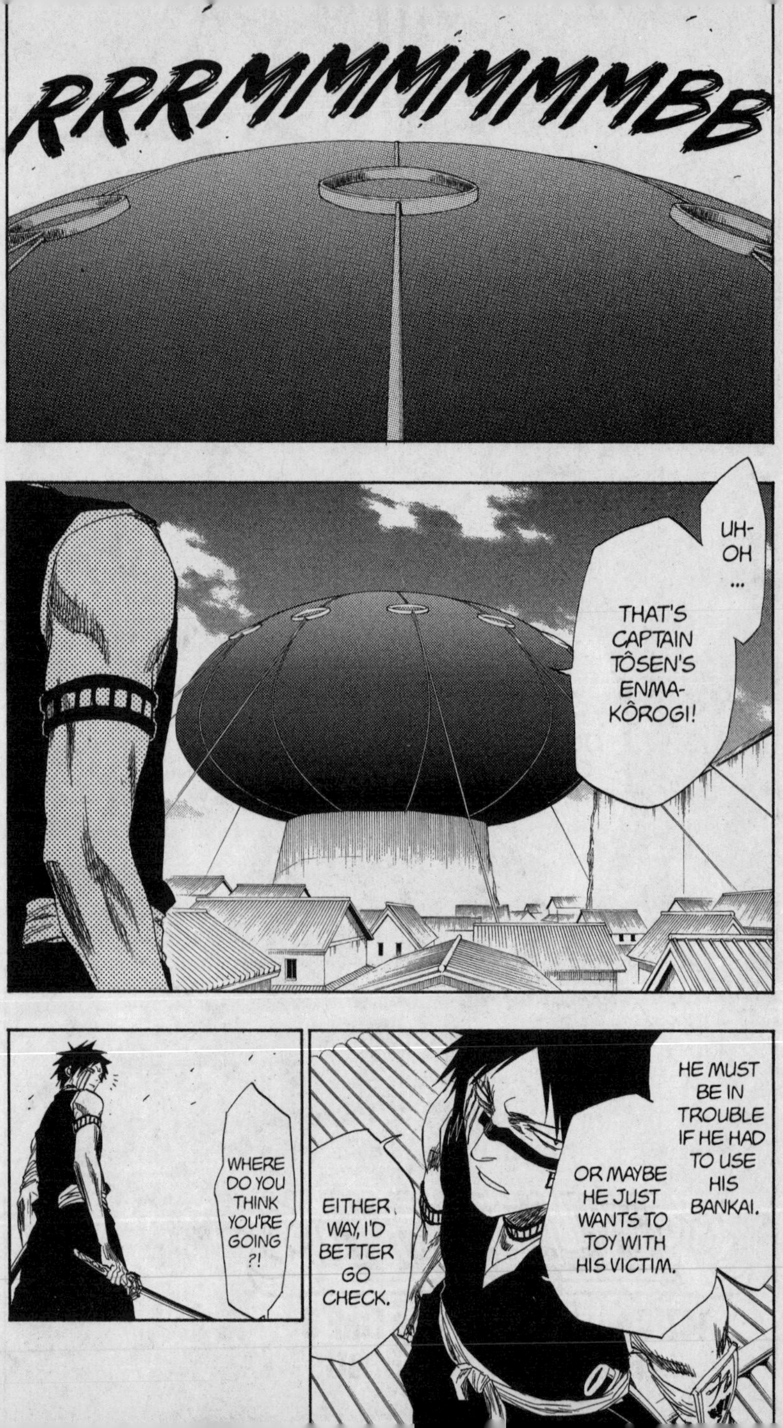
RRRMMMMMMMBB
UH-OH ...
THAT'S CAPTAIN TÔSEN'S ENMA-KÔROGI!
HE MUST BE IN TROUBLE IF HE HAD TO USE HIS BANKAI.
OR MAYBE HE JUST WANTS TO TOY WITH HIS VICTIM.
EITHER WAY, I'D BETTER GO CHECK.
WHERE DO YOU THINK YOU'RE GOING ?!

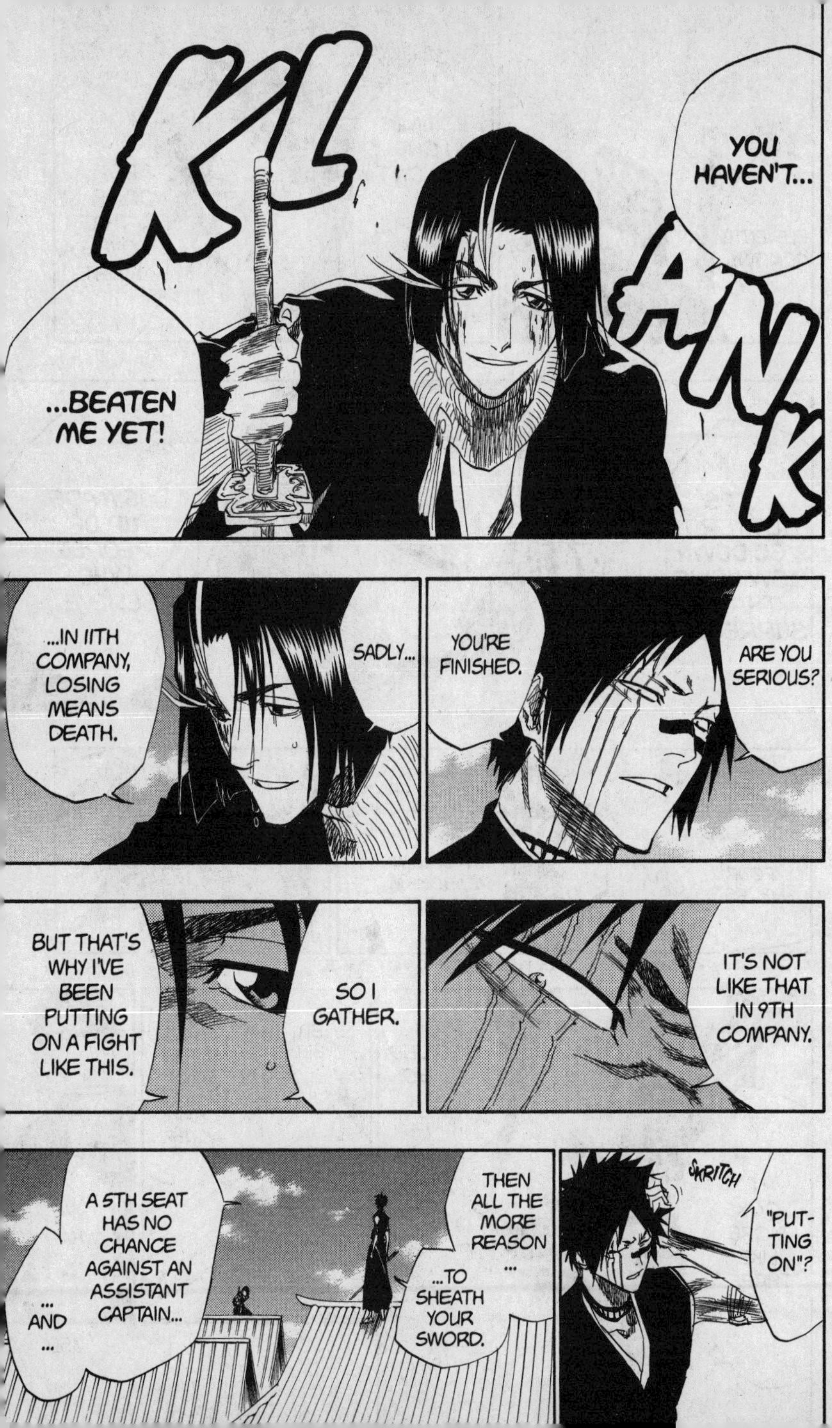
YOU HAVEN'T...
KLANK
...BEATEN ME YET!
ARE YOU SERIOUS?
YOU'RE FINISHED.
SADLY...
...IN 11TH COMPANY, LOSING MEANS DEATH.
IT'S NOT LIKE THAT IN 9TH COMPANY.
SO I GATHER.
BUT THAT'S WHY I'VE BEEN PUTTING ON A FIGHT LIKE THIS.
SKRITCH
"PUT-TING ON"?
THEN ALL THE MORE REASON ...
...TO SHEATH YOUR SWORD.
A 5TH SEAT HAS NO CHANCE AGAINST AN ASSISTANT CAPTAIN...
... AND ...

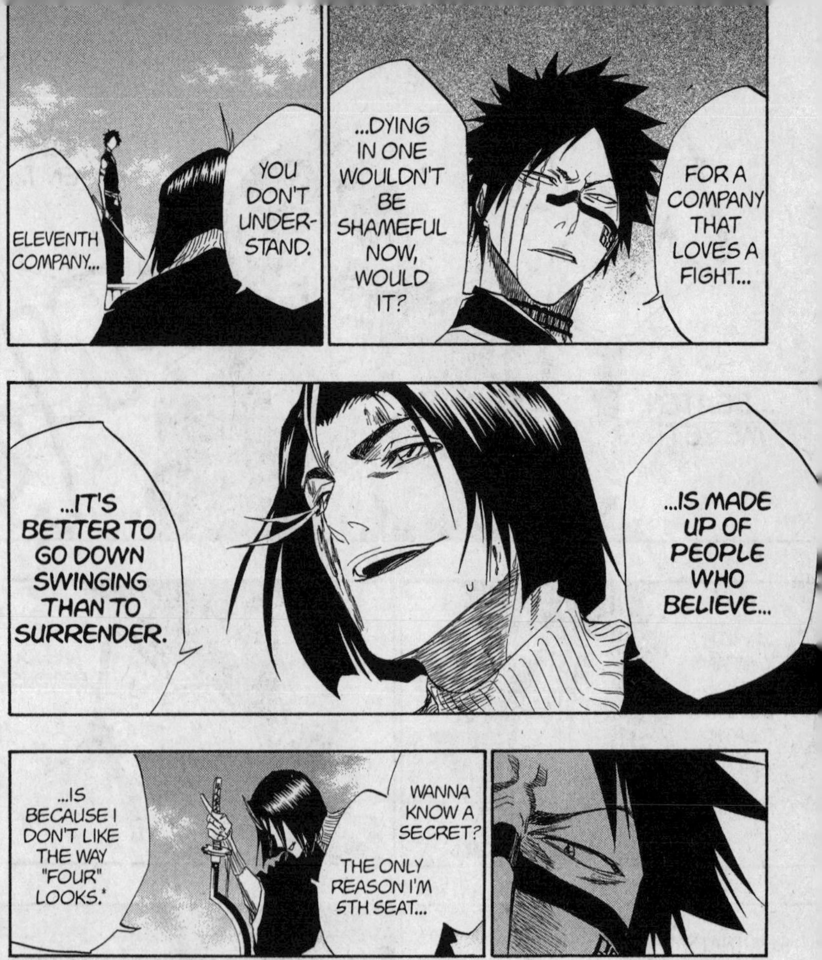
FOR A COMPANY THAT LOVES A FIGHT...
...DYING IN ONE WOULDN'T BE SHAMEFUL NOW, WOULD IT?
YOU DON'T UNDER-STAND.
ELEVENTH COMPANY...
...IS MADE UP OF PEOPLE WHO BELIEVE...
...IT'S BETTER TO GO DOWN SWINGING THAN TO SURRENDER.
WANNA KNOW A SECRET?
THE ONLY REASON I'M 5TH SEAT...
...IS BECAUSE I DON'T LIKE THE WAY "FOUR" LOOKS.*

*IN JAPANESE KANJI CHARACTERS, THREE IS 三, FOUR IS 四 AND FIVE IS 五.

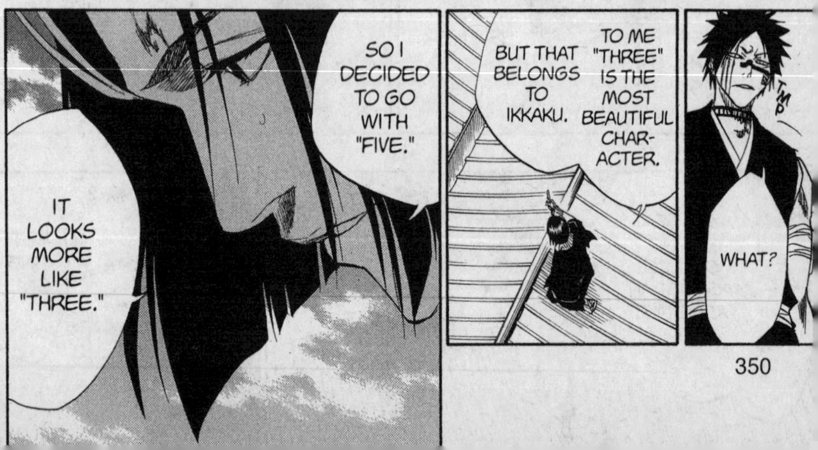
TMP
WHAT?
TO ME "THREE" IS THE MOST BEAUTIFUL CHAR-ACTER.
BUT THAT BELONGS TO IKKAKU.
SO I DECIDED TO GO WITH "FIVE."
IT LOOKS MORE LIKE "THREE."

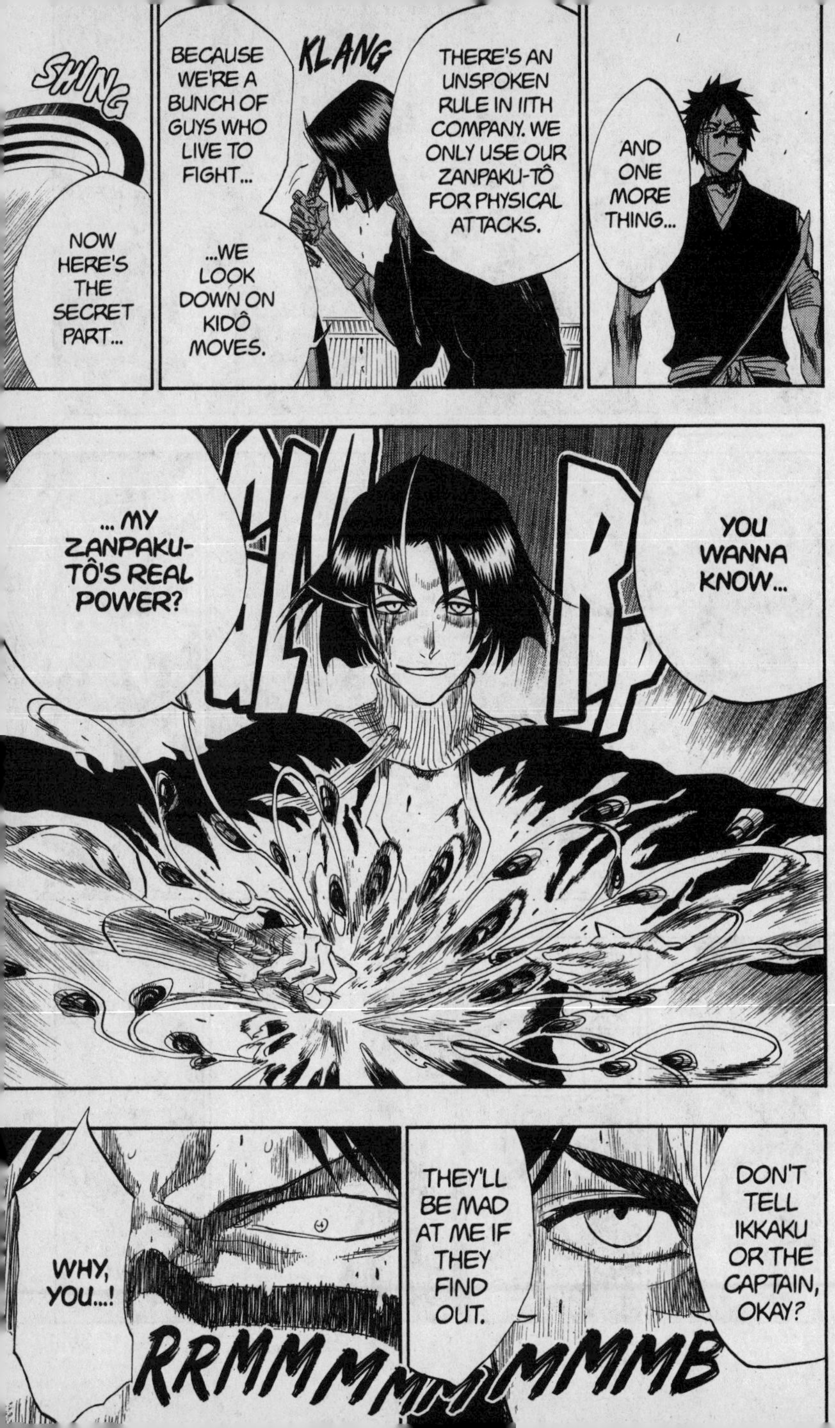
AND ONE MORE THING...
THERE'S AN UNSPOKEN RULE IN 11TH COMPANY. WE ONLY USE OUR ZANPAKU-TÔ FOR PHYSICAL ATTACKS.
KLANG
BECAUSE WE'RE A BUNCH OF GUYS WHO LIVE TO FIGHT...
...WE LOOK DOWN ON KIDÔ MOVES.
SHING
NOW HERE'S THE SECRET PART...
YOU WANNA KNOW...
... MY ZANPAKU-TÔ'S REAL POWER?
DON'T TELL IKKAKU OR THE CAPTAIN, OKAY?
THEY'LL BE MAD AT ME IF THEY FIND OUT.
WHY, YOU...!
RRMMMMMMMMMMB

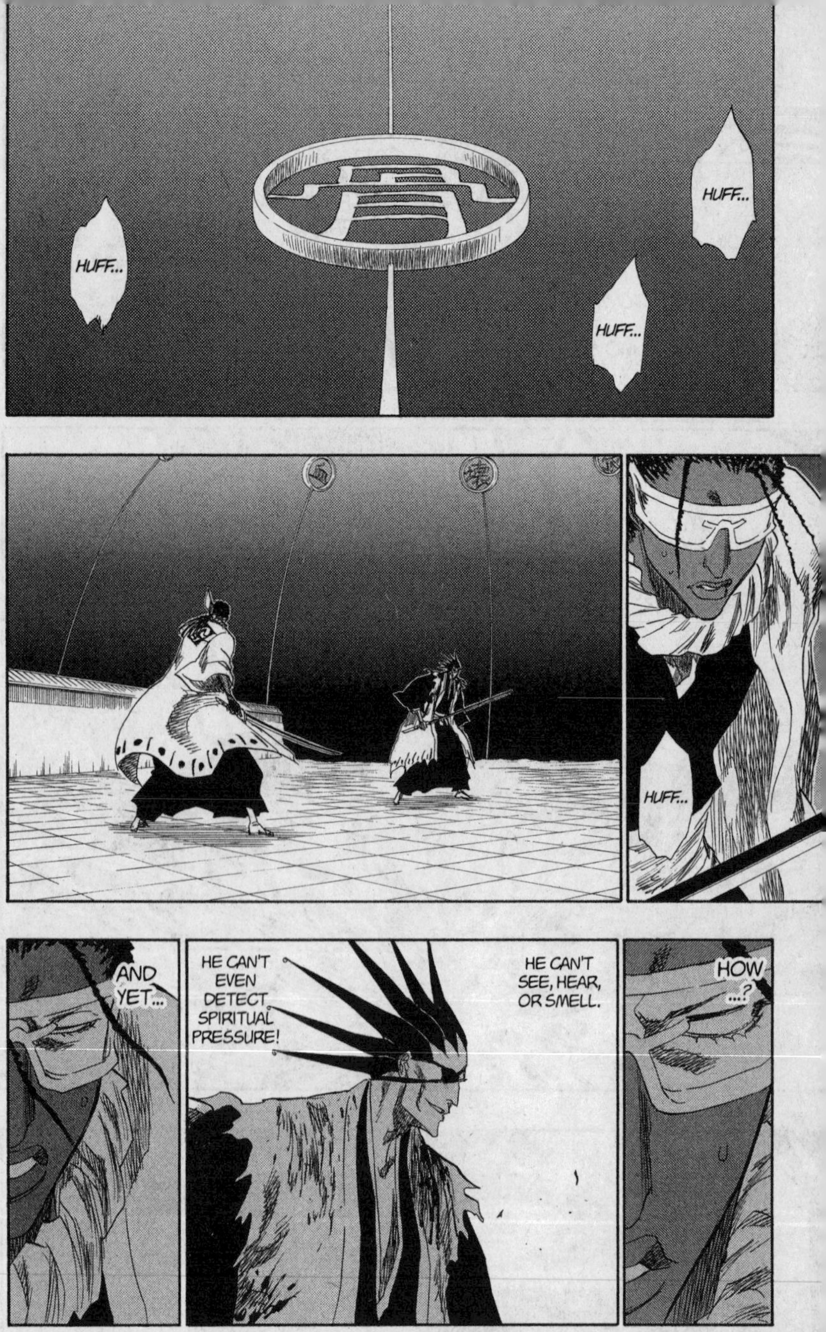
HUFF...
HUFF...
HUFF...
HUFF...
HOW ...?
HE CAN'T SEE, HEAR, OR SMELL.
HE CAN'T EVEN DETECT SPIRITUAL PRESSURE!
AND YET...

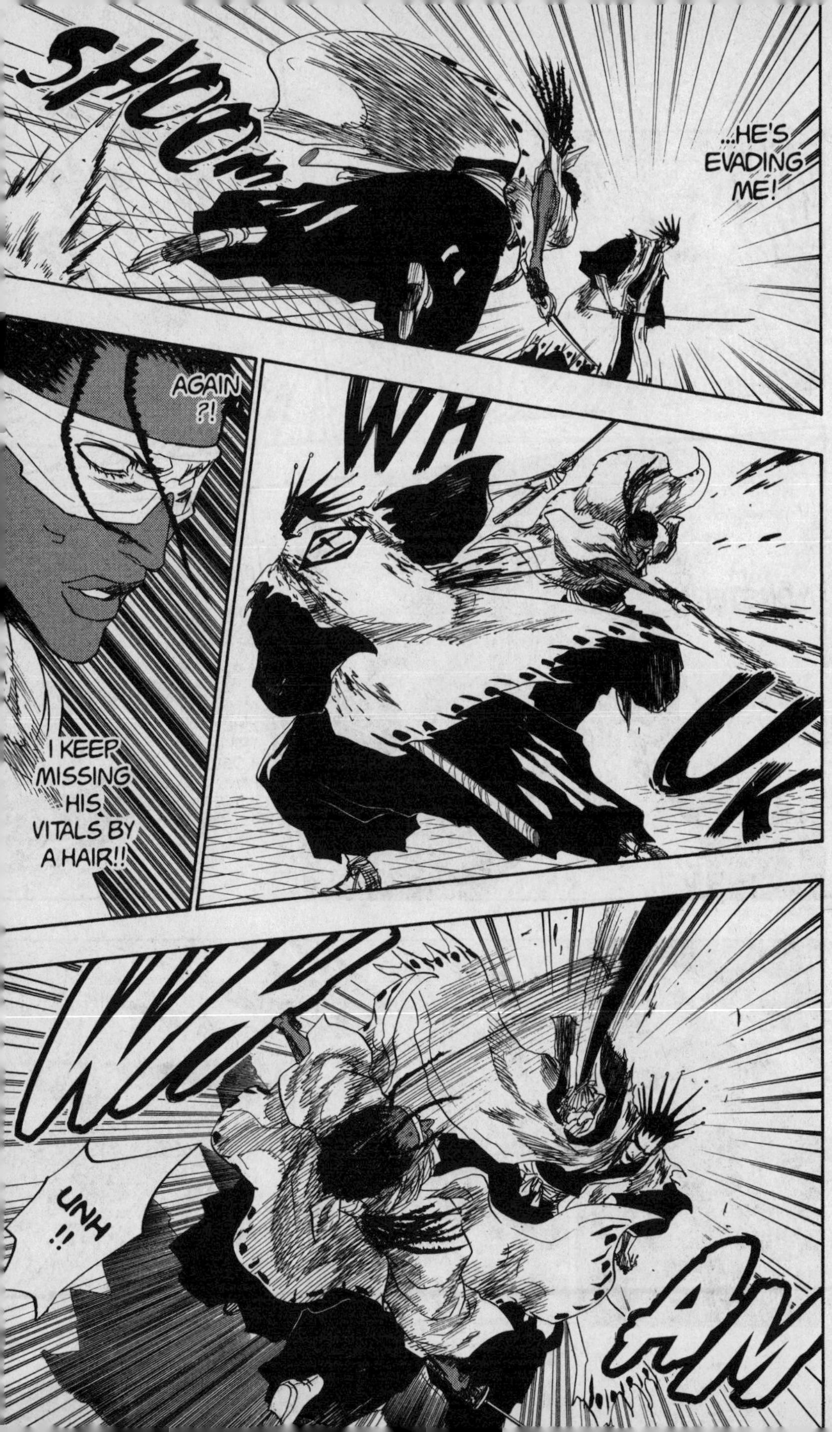
...HE'S EVADING ME!
SHOOM
WH
UK
AGAIN ?!
I KEEP MISSING HIS VITALS BY A HAIR!!
UNH !!

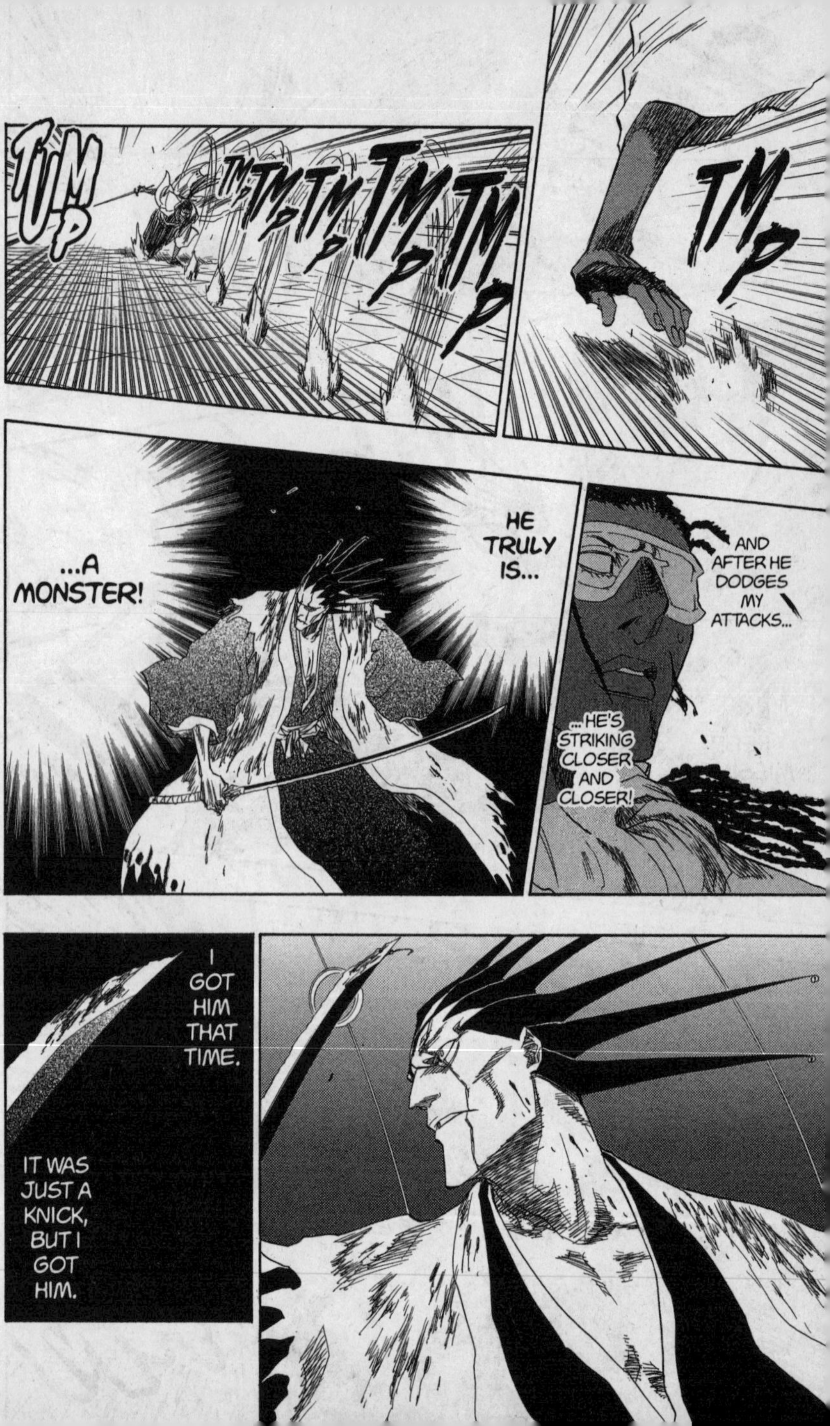
TMP
TUMP
TMP TMP TMP TMP TMP TMP
AND AFTER HE DODGES MY ATTACKS...
...HE'S STRIKING CLOSER AND CLOSER!
HE TRULY IS...
...A MONSTER!
I GOT HIM THAT TIME.
IT WAS JUST A KNICK, BUT I GOT HIM.

READ THIS WAY

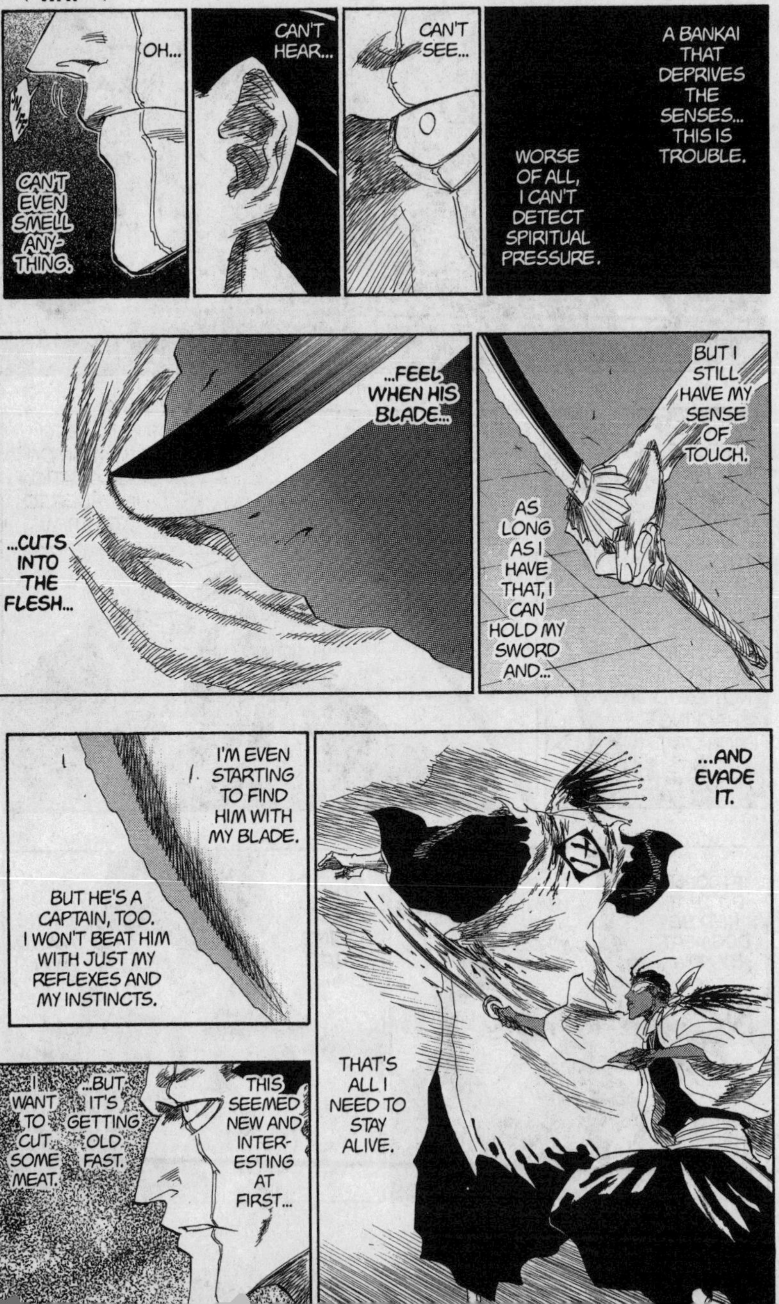
A BANKAI THAT DEPRIVES THE SENSES... THIS IS TROUBLE.
WORSE OF ALL, I CAN'T DETECT SPIRITUAL PRESSURE.
CAN'T SEE...
CAN'T HEAR...
OH...
CAN'T EVEN SMELL ANYTHING.
BUT I STILL HAVE MY SENSE OF TOUCH.
AS LONG AS I HAVE THAT, I CAN HOLD MY SWORD AND...
...FEEL WHEN HIS BLADE...
...CUTS INTO THE FLESH...
...AND EVADE IT.
THAT'S ALL I NEED TO STAY ALIVE.
I'M EVEN STARTING TO FIND HIM WITH MY BLADE.
BUT HE'S A CAPTAIN, TOO. I WON'T BEAT HIM WITH JUST MY REFLEXES AND MY INSTINCTS.
THIS SEEMED NEW AND INTERESTING AT FIRST...
...BUT IT'S GETTING OLD FAST.
I WANT TO CUT SOME MEAT.

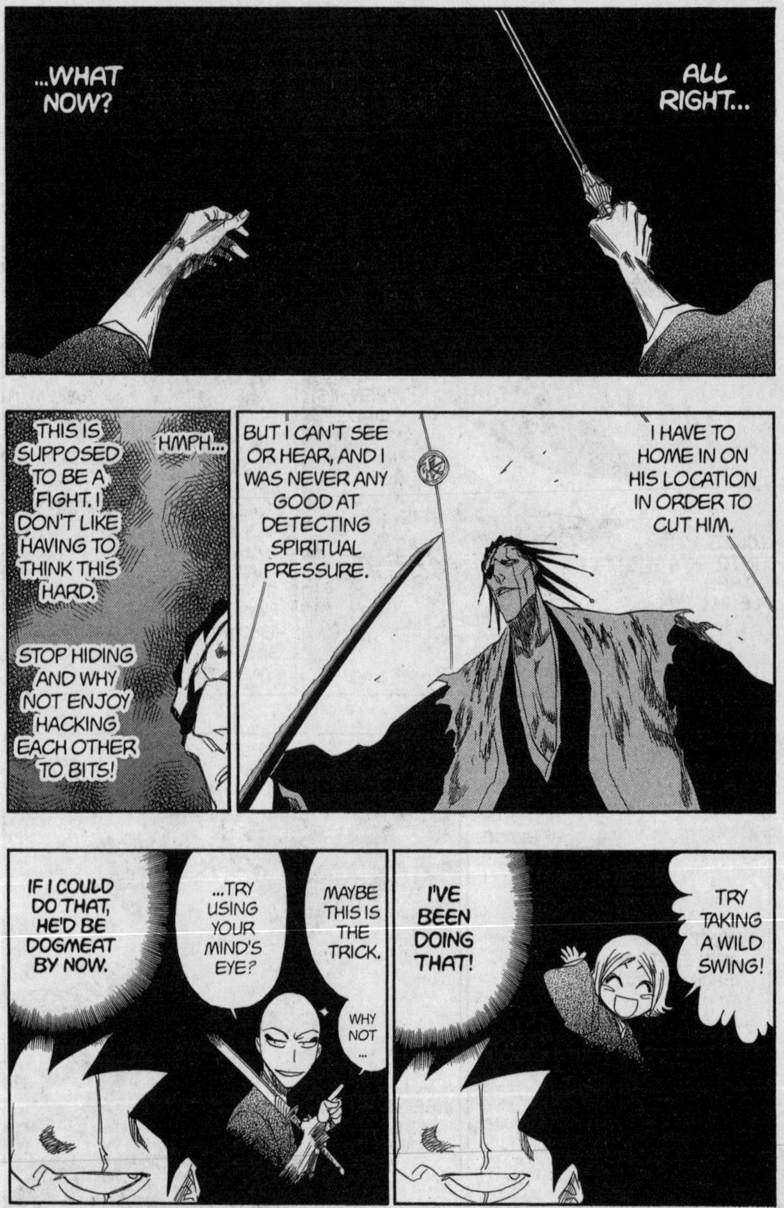
ALL RIGHT...
...WHAT NOW?
I HAVE TO HOME IN ON HIS LOCATION IN ORDER TO CUT HIM.
BUT I CAN'T SEE OR HEAR, AND I WAS NEVER ANY GOOD AT DETECTING SPIRITUAL PRESSURE.
HMPH...
THIS IS SUPPOSED TO BE A FIGHT. I DON'T LIKE HAVING TO THINK THIS HARD.
STOP HIDING AND WHY NOT ENJOY HACKING EACH OTHER TO BITS!
TRY TAKING A WILD SWING!
I'VE BEEN DOING THAT!
MAYBE THIS IS THE TRICK.
WHY NOT ...
...TRY USING YOUR MIND'S EYE?
IF I COULD DO THAT, HE'D BE DOGMEAT BY NOW.

READ THIS WAY

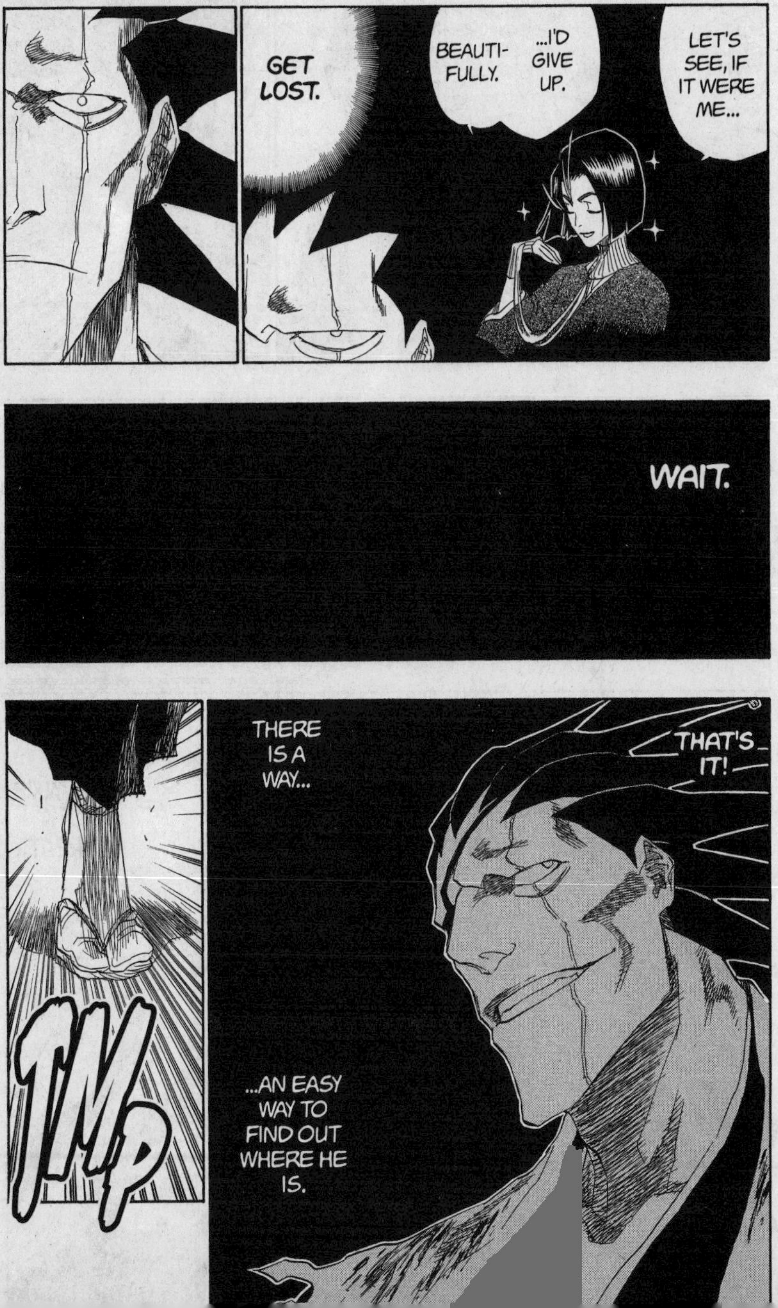

LET'S SEE, IF IT WERE ME...
...I'D GIVE UP.
BEAUTI-FULLY.
GET LOST.
WAIT.
THAT'S IT!
THERE IS A WAY...
...AN EASY WAY TO FIND OUT WHERE HE IS.
TMP

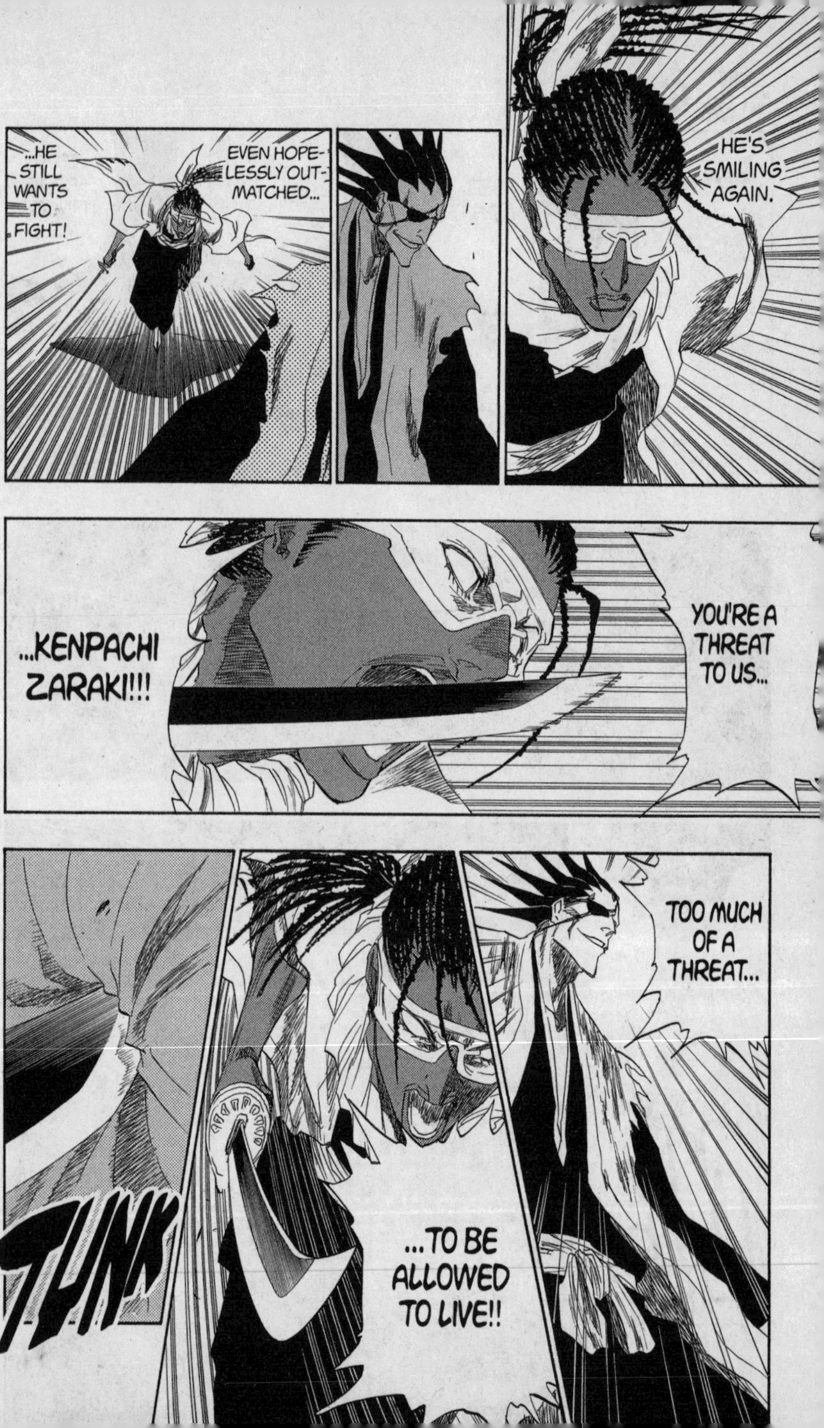
HE'S SMILING AGAIN.
EVEN HOPE-LESSLY OUT-MATCHED...
...HE STILL WANTS TO FIGHT!
YOU'RE A THREAT TO US...
...KENPACHI ZARAKI!!!
TOO MUCH OF A THREAT...
...TO BE ALLOWED TO LIVE!!
THNK

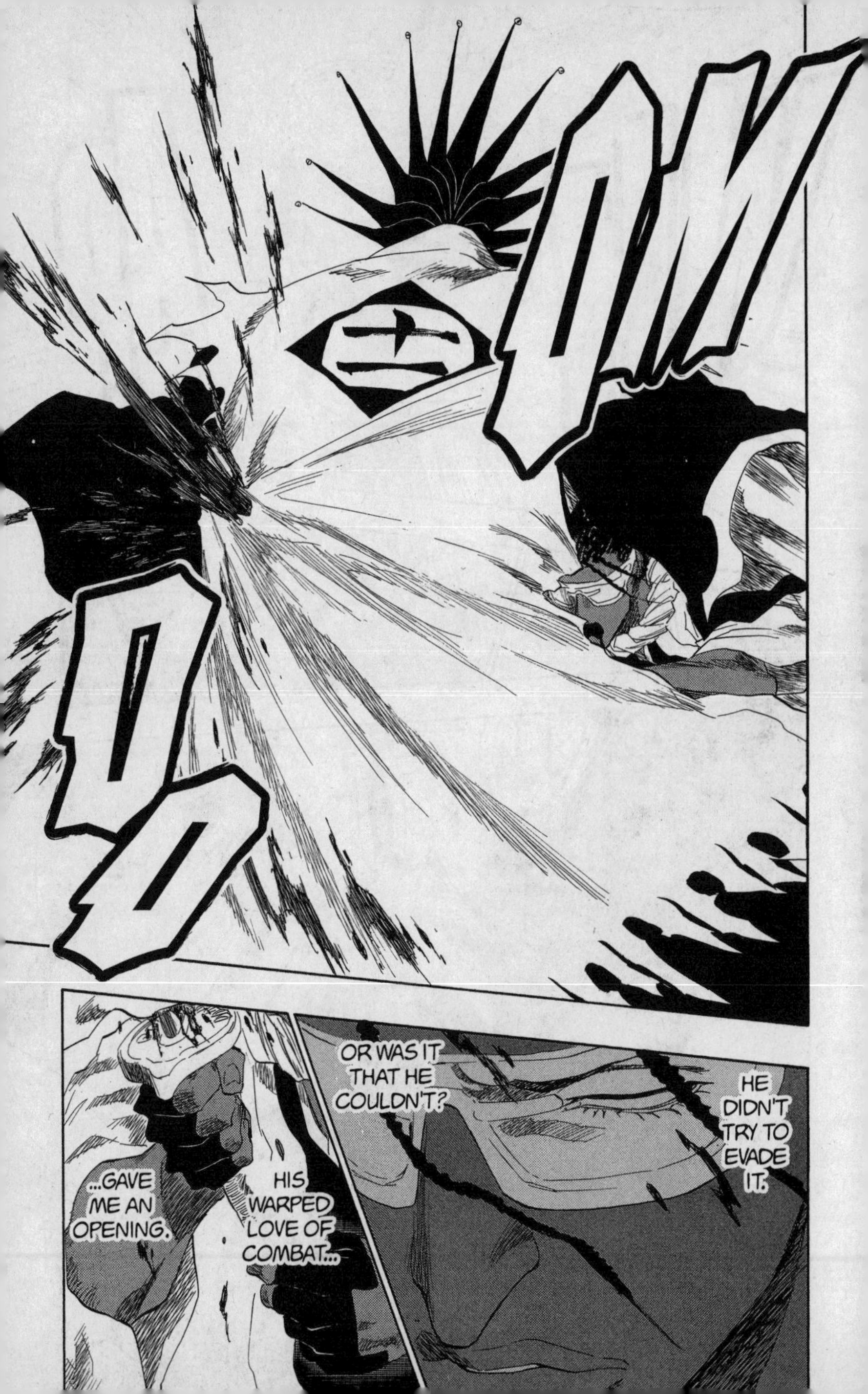
HE DIDN'T TRY TO EVADE IT.
OR WAS IT THAT HE COULDN'T?
HIS WARPED LOVE OF COMBAT...
...GAVE ME AN OPENING.

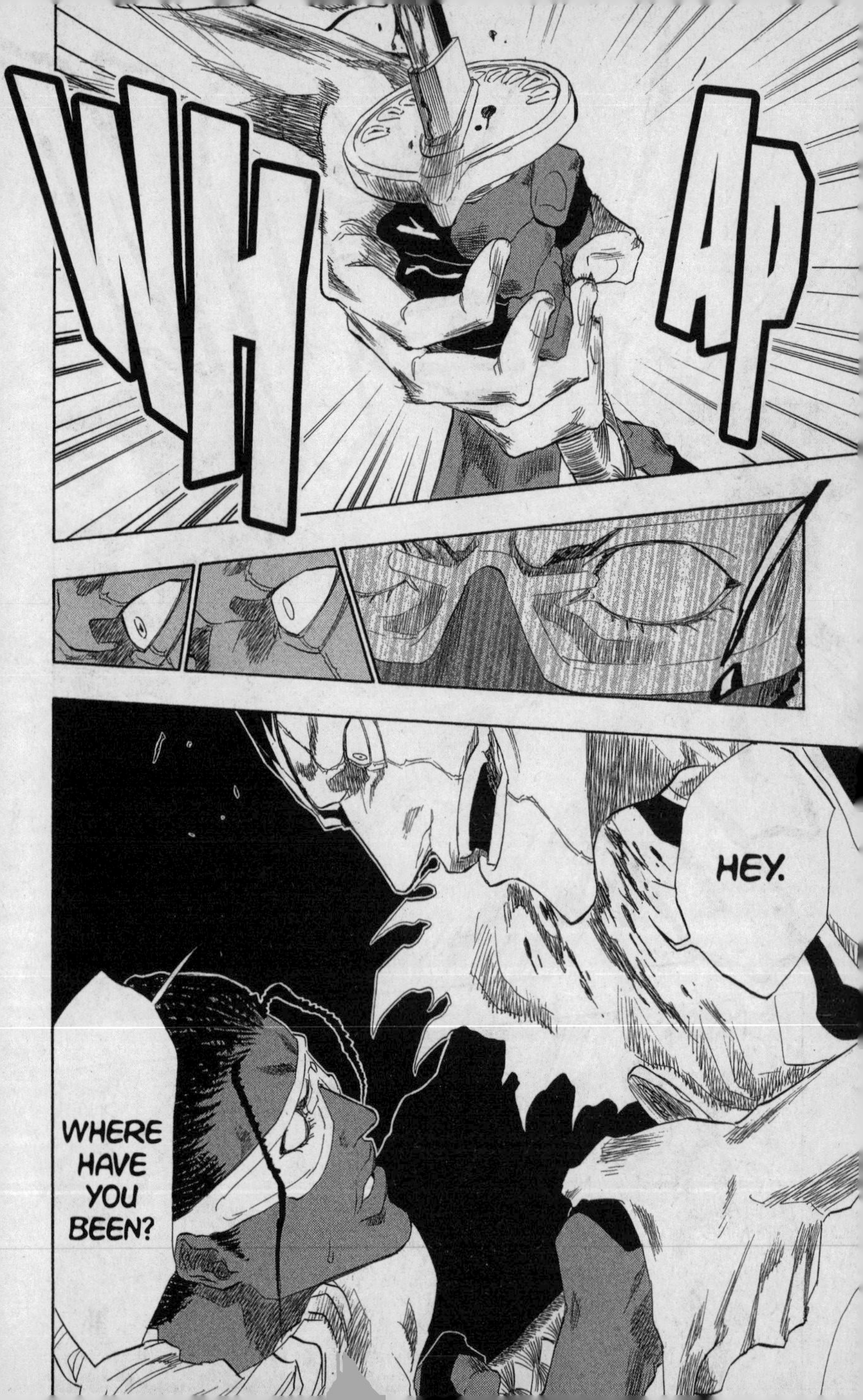
WHAP
HEY.
WHERE HAVE YOU BEEN?

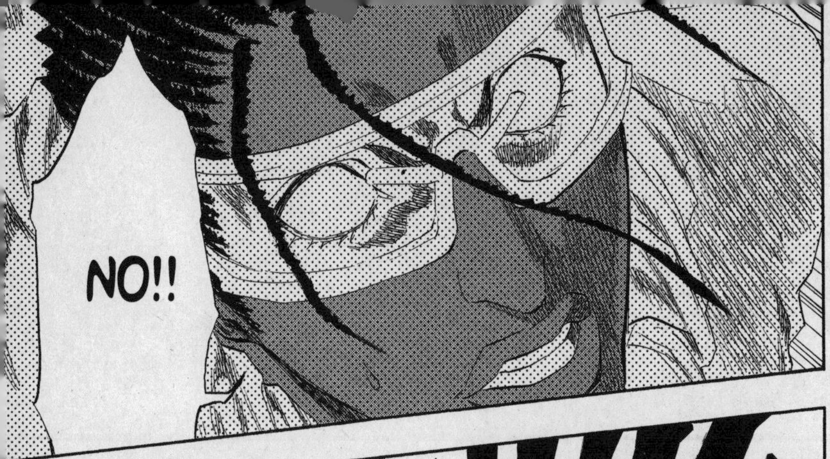
NO!!
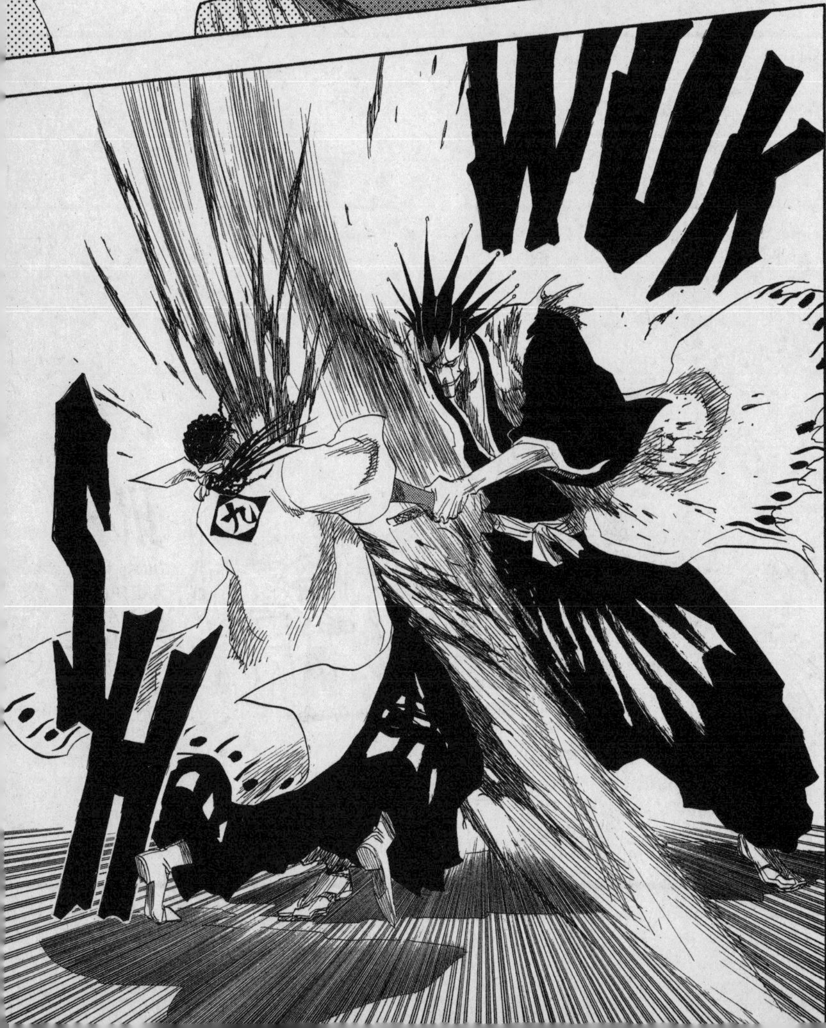
WUK
SH

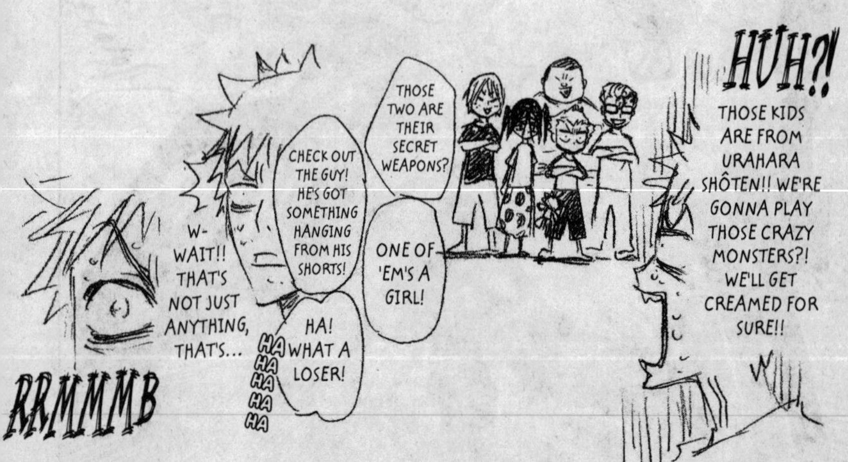
HUH?!
THOSE KIDS ARE FROM URAHARA SHÔTEN!! WE'RE GONNA PLAY THOSE CRAZY MONSTERS?! WE'LL GET CREAMED FOR SURE!!
THOSE TWO ARE THEIR SECRET WEAPONS?
CHECK OUT THE GUY! HE'S GOT SOMETHING HANGING FROM HIS SHORTS!
ONE OF 'EM'S A GIRL!
HA! WHAT A LOSER!
HA HA HA HA HA
W-WAIT!! THAT'S NOT JUST ANYTHING, THAT'S...
RRMMMB

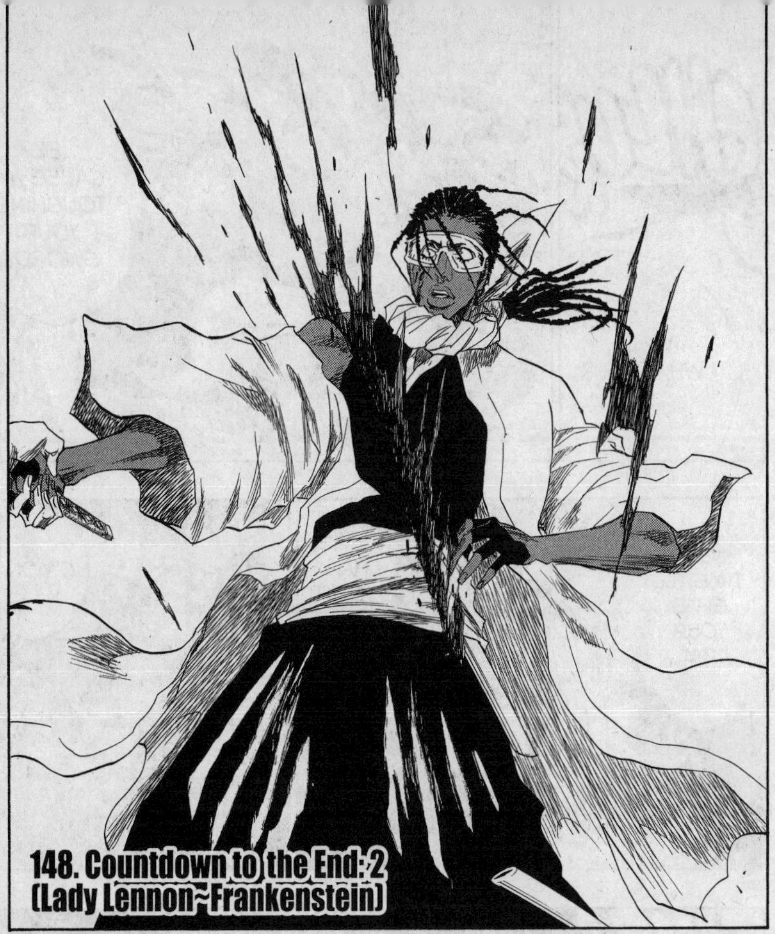

148. Countdown to the End: 2 (Lady Lennon~Frankenstein)

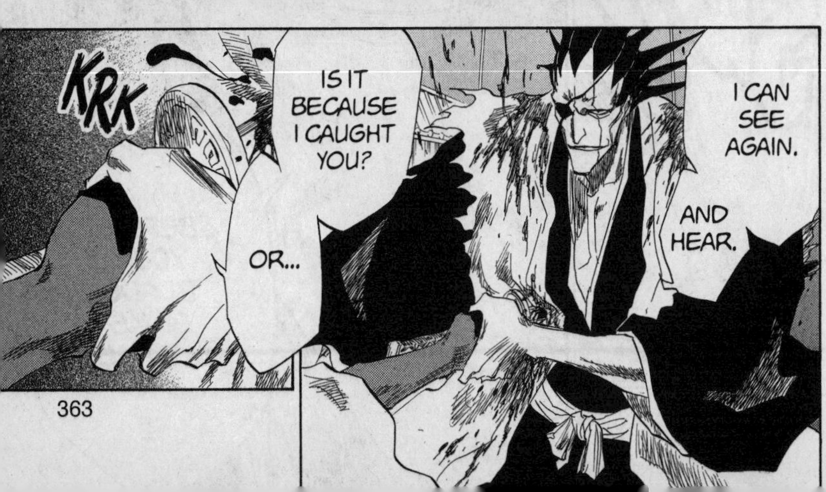
I CAN SEE AGAIN.
AND HEAR.
IS IT BECAUSE I CAUGHT YOU?
OR...
KRK

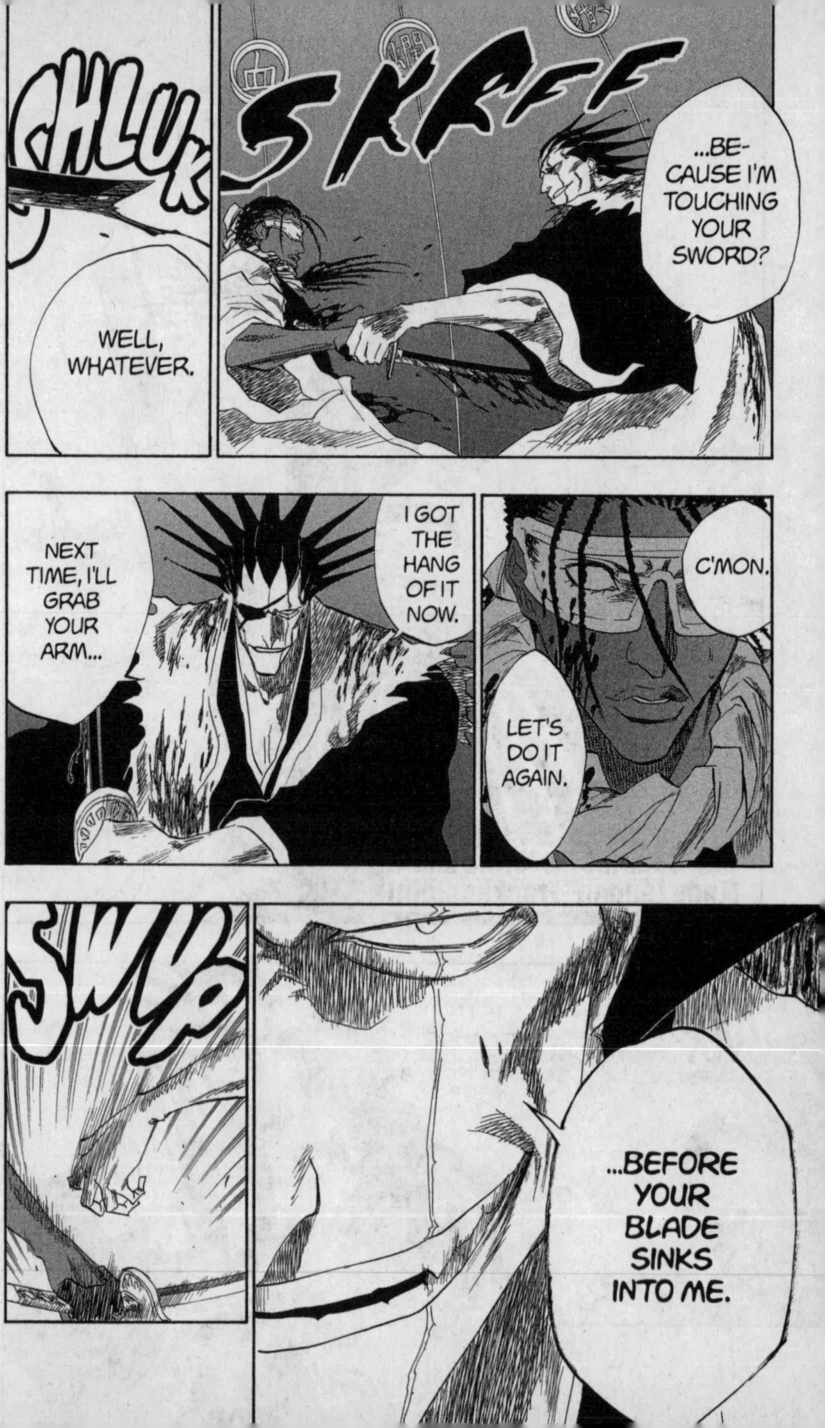
SKRFF
...BE-CAUSE I'M TOUCHING YOUR SWORD?
CHLUK
WELL, WHATEVER.
C'MON.
LET'S DO IT AGAIN.
I GOT THE HANG OF IT NOW.
NEXT TIME, I'LL GRAB YOUR ARM...
...BEFORE YOUR BLADE SINKS INTO ME.
SWIP

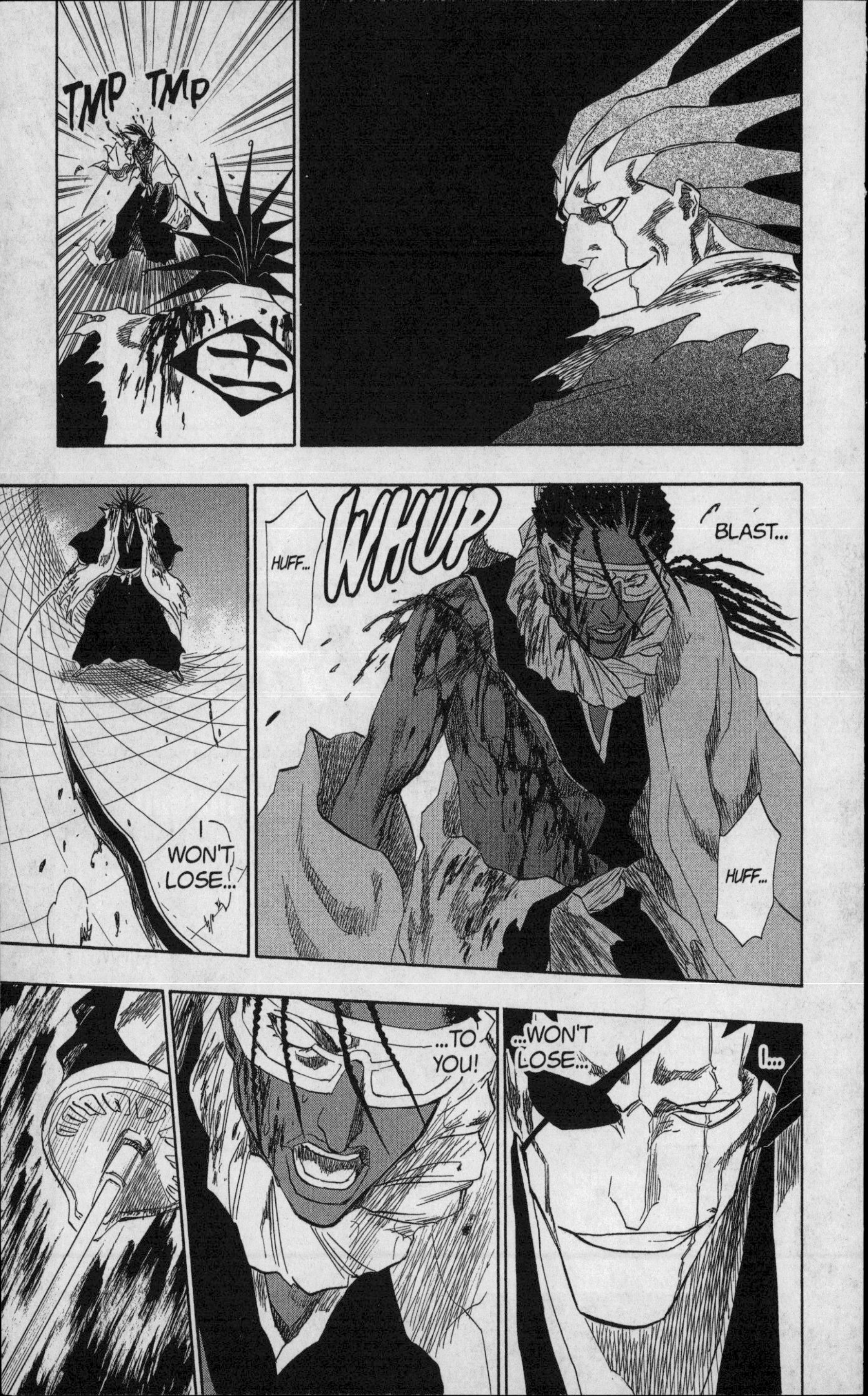
TMP TMP
BLAST...
WHUP
HUFF...
HUFF...
I WON'T LOSE...
I...
...WON'T LOSE...
...TO YOU!

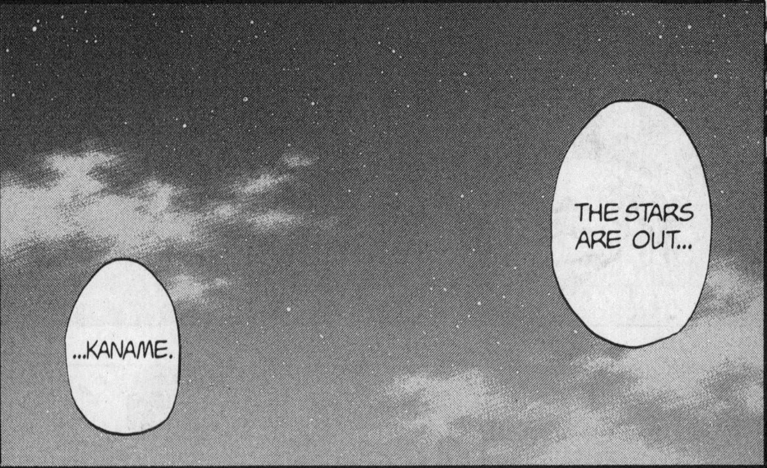
THE STARS ARE OUT...
...KANAME.

BLEACH

—ブリーチ—

148. Countdown to the End: 2
(Lady Lennon~Frankenstein)

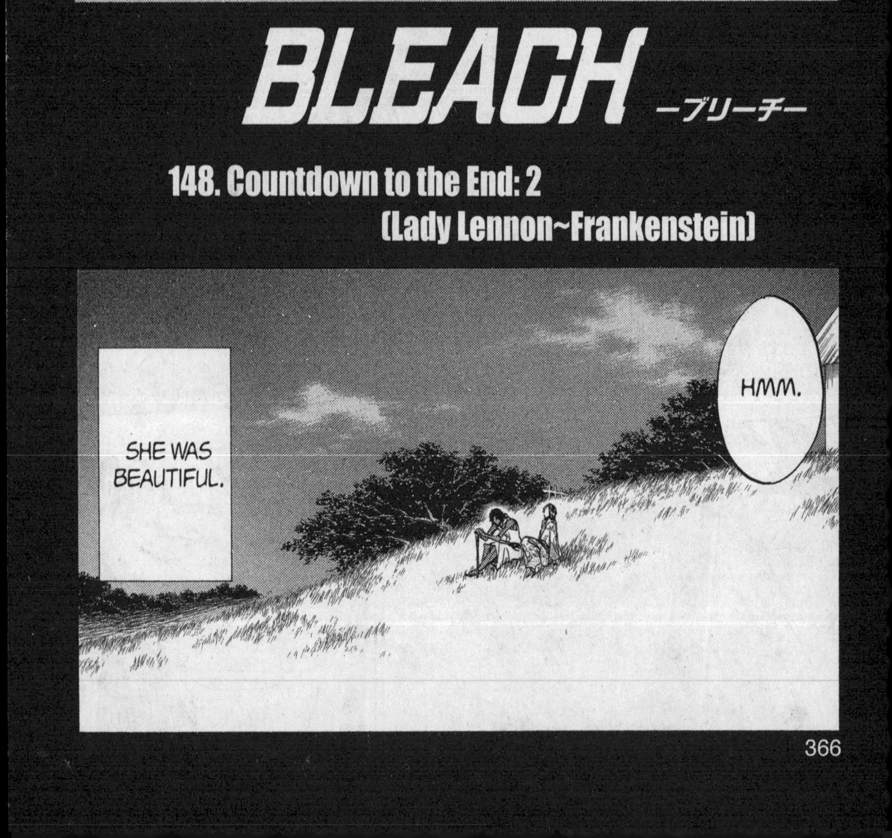
HMM.
SHE WAS BEAUTIFUL.

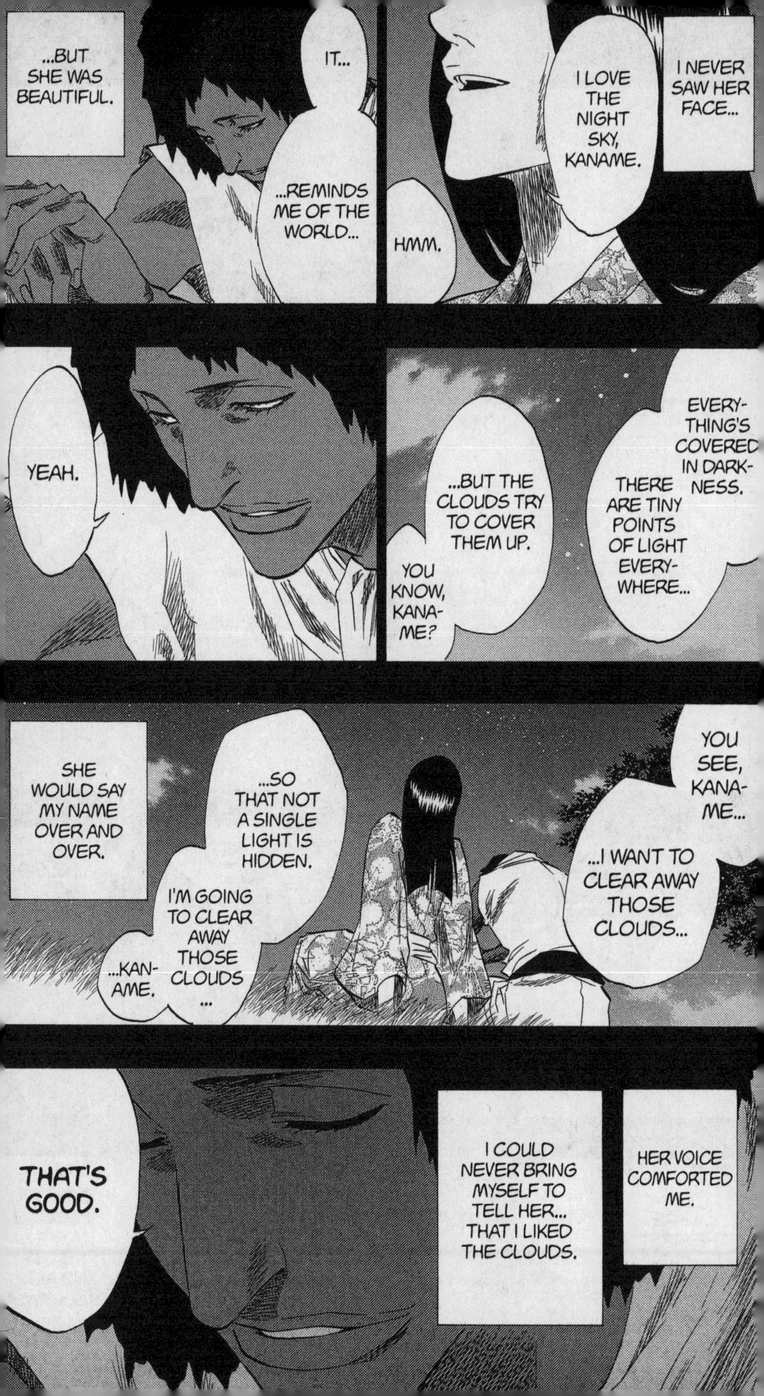
I NEVER SAW HER FACE...
I LOVE THE NIGHT SKY, KANAME.
HMM.
IT...
...REMINDS ME OF THE WORLD...
...BUT SHE WAS BEAUTIFUL.
EVERY-THING'S COVERED IN DARK-NESS.
THERE ARE TINY POINTS OF LIGHT EVERY-WHERE...
...BUT THE CLOUDS TRY TO COVER THEM UP.
YOU KNOW, KANA-ME?
YEAH.
YOU SEE, KANA-ME...
...I WANT TO CLEAR AWAY THOSE CLOUDS...
...SO THAT NOT A SINGLE LIGHT IS HIDDEN.
I'M GOING TO CLEAR AWAY THOSE CLOUDS ...
...KAN-AME.
SHE WOULD SAY MY NAME OVER AND OVER.
HER VOICE COMFORTED ME.
I COULD NEVER BRING MYSELF TO TELL HER... THAT I LIKED THE CLOUDS.
THAT'S GOOD.

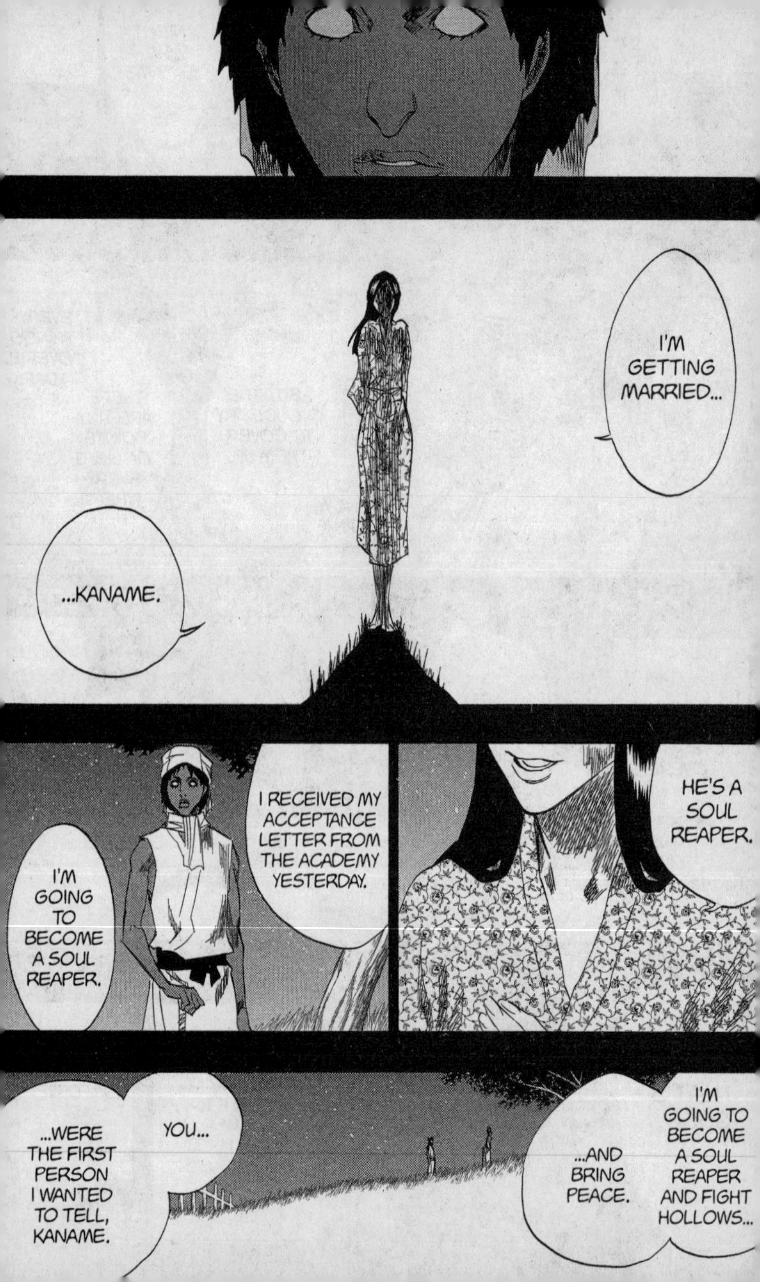
I'M GETTING MARRIED...
...KANAME.
HE'S A SOUL REAPER.
I RECEIVED MY ACCEPTANCE LETTER FROM THE ACADEMY YESTERDAY.
I'M GOING TO BECOME A SOUL REAPER.
I'M GOING TO BECOME A SOUL REAPER AND FIGHT HOLLOWS...
...AND BRING PEACE.
YOU...
...WERE THE FIRST PERSON I WANTED TO TELL, KANAME.

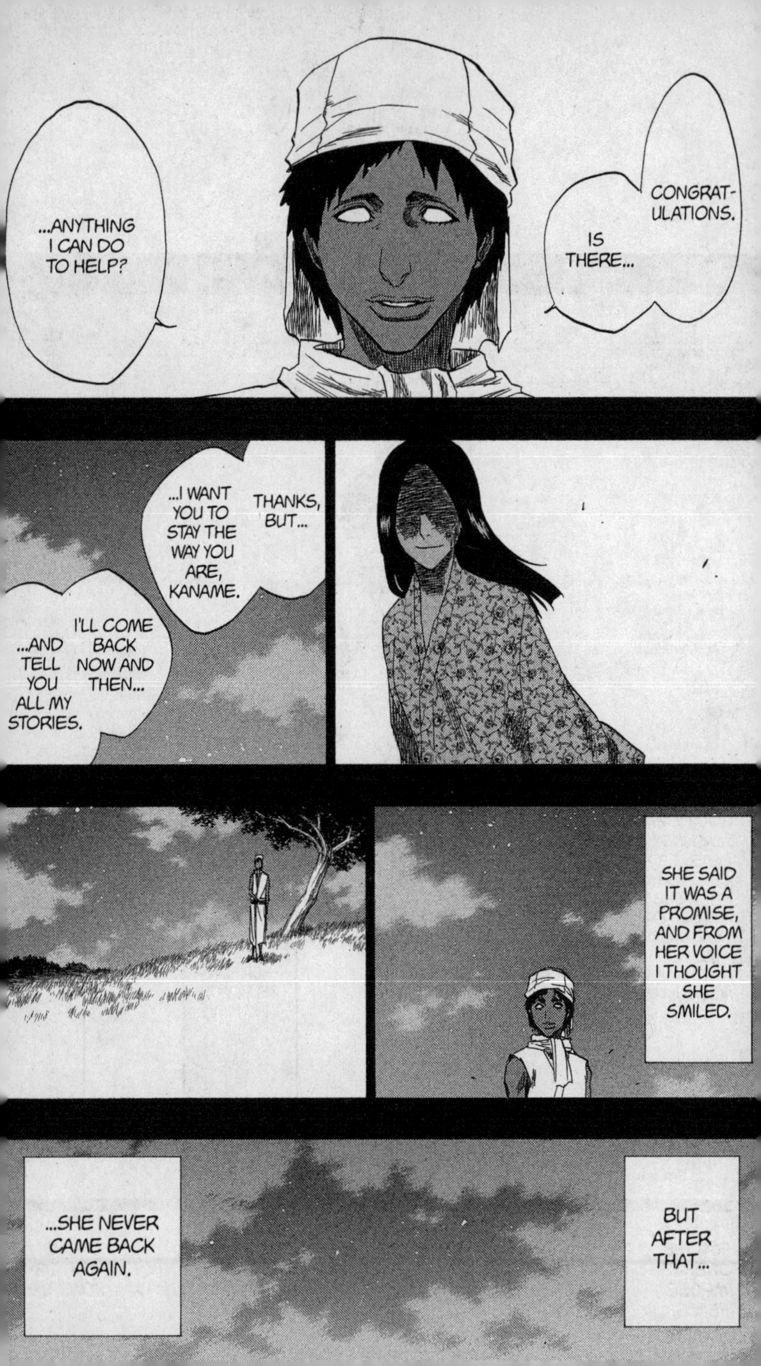
CONGRATULATIONS.
IS THERE...
...ANYTHING I CAN DO TO HELP?
THANKS, BUT...
...I WANT YOU TO STAY THE WAY YOU ARE, KANAME.
I'LL COME BACK NOW AND THEN...
...AND TELL YOU ALL MY STORIES.
SHE SAID IT WAS A PROMISE, AND FROM HER VOICE I THOUGHT SHE SMILED.
BUT AFTER THAT...
...SHE NEVER CAME BACK AGAIN.

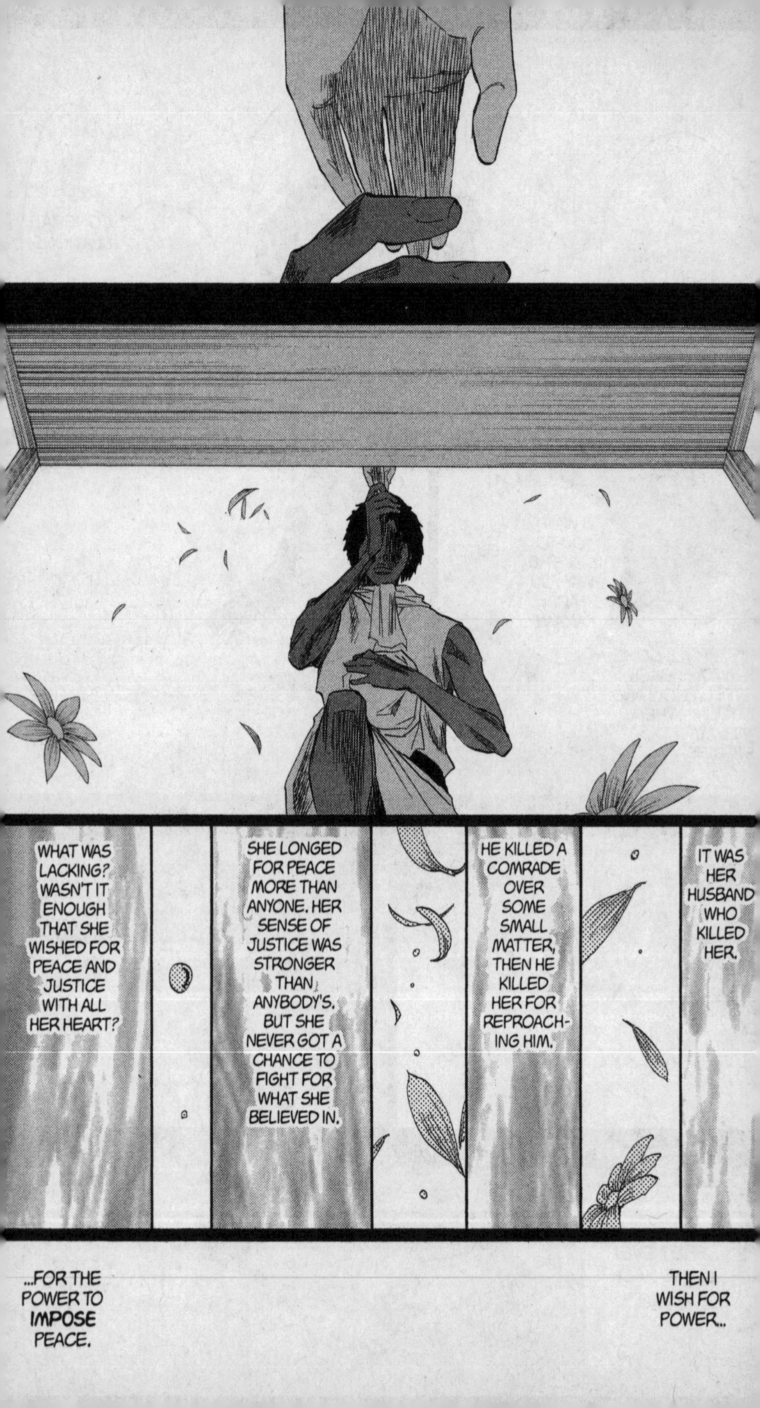
IT WAS HER HUSBAND WHO KILLED HER.
HE KILLED A COMRADE OVER SOME SMALL MATTER, THEN HE KILLED HER FOR REPROACHING HIM.
SHE LONGED FOR PEACE MORE THAN ANYONE. HER SENSE OF JUSTICE WAS STRONGER THAN ANYBODY'S. BUT SHE NEVER GOT A CHANCE TO FIGHT FOR WHAT SHE BELIEVED IN.
WHAT WAS LACKING? WASN'T IT ENOUGH THAT SHE WISHED FOR PEACE AND JUSTICE WITH ALL HER HEART?
THEN I WISH FOR POWER...
...FOR THE POWER TO **IMPOSE** PEACE.

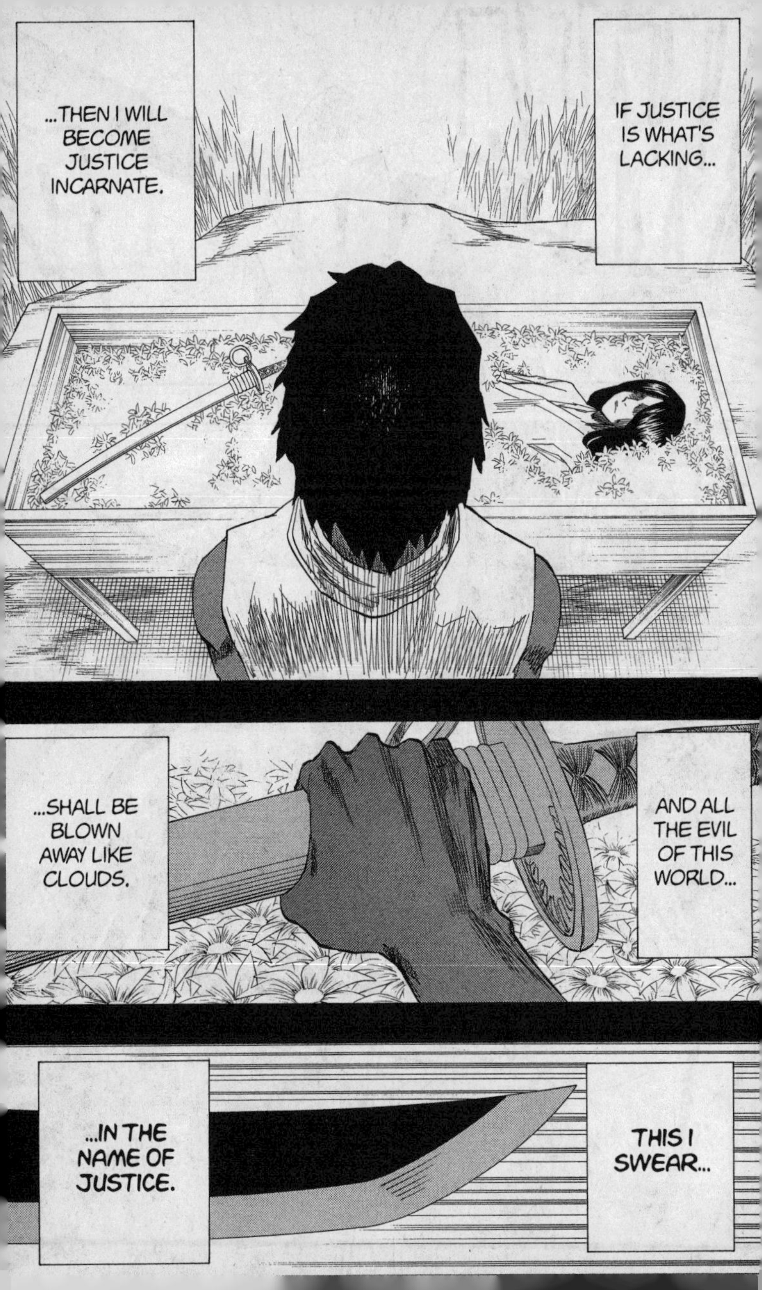
IF JUSTICE IS WHAT'S LACKING...
...THEN I WILL BECOME JUSTICE INCARNATE.
AND ALL THE EVIL OF THIS WORLD...
...SHALL BE BLOWN AWAY LIKE CLOUDS.
THIS I SWEAR...
...IN THE NAME OF JUSTICE.

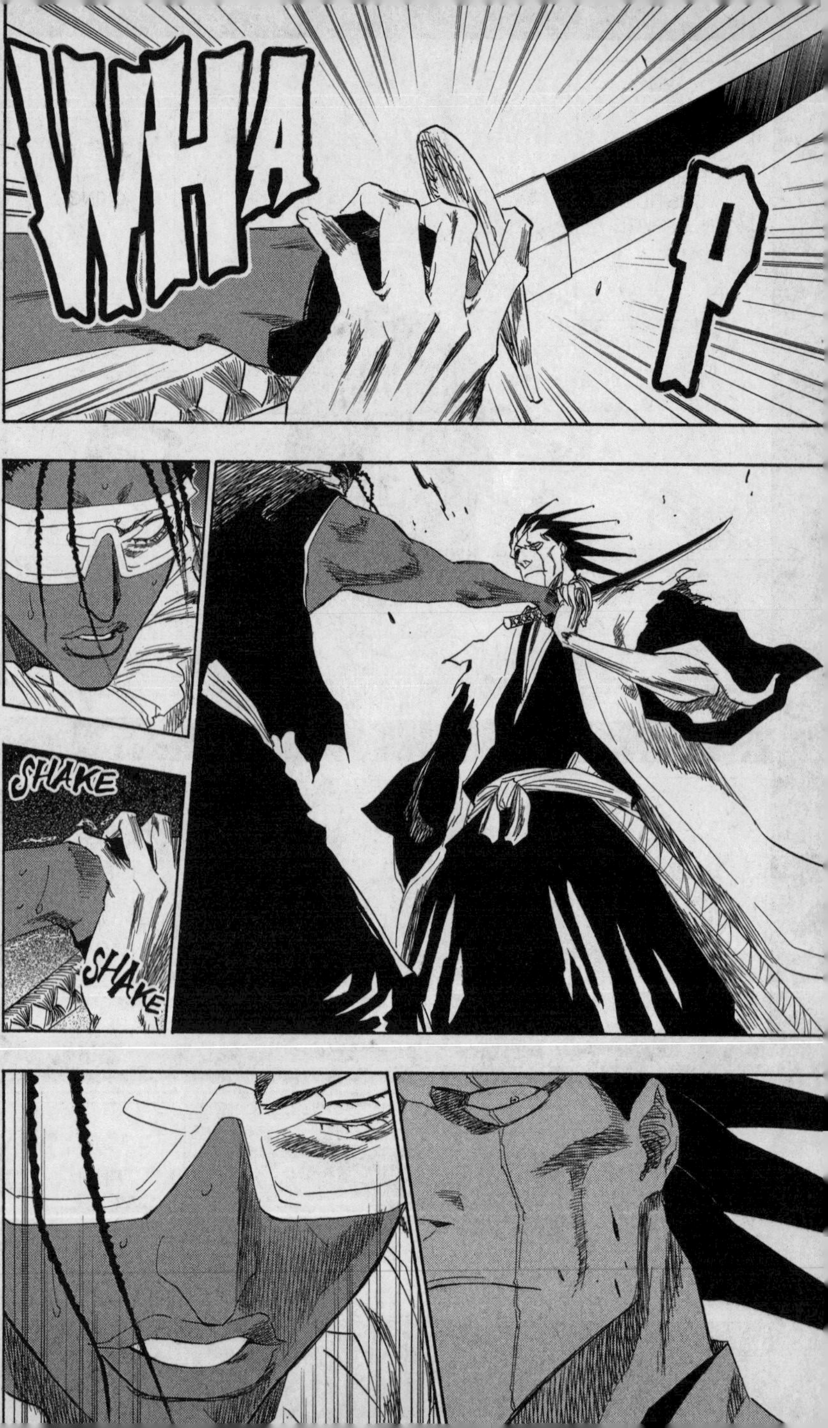
WHAP
SHAKE
SHAKE

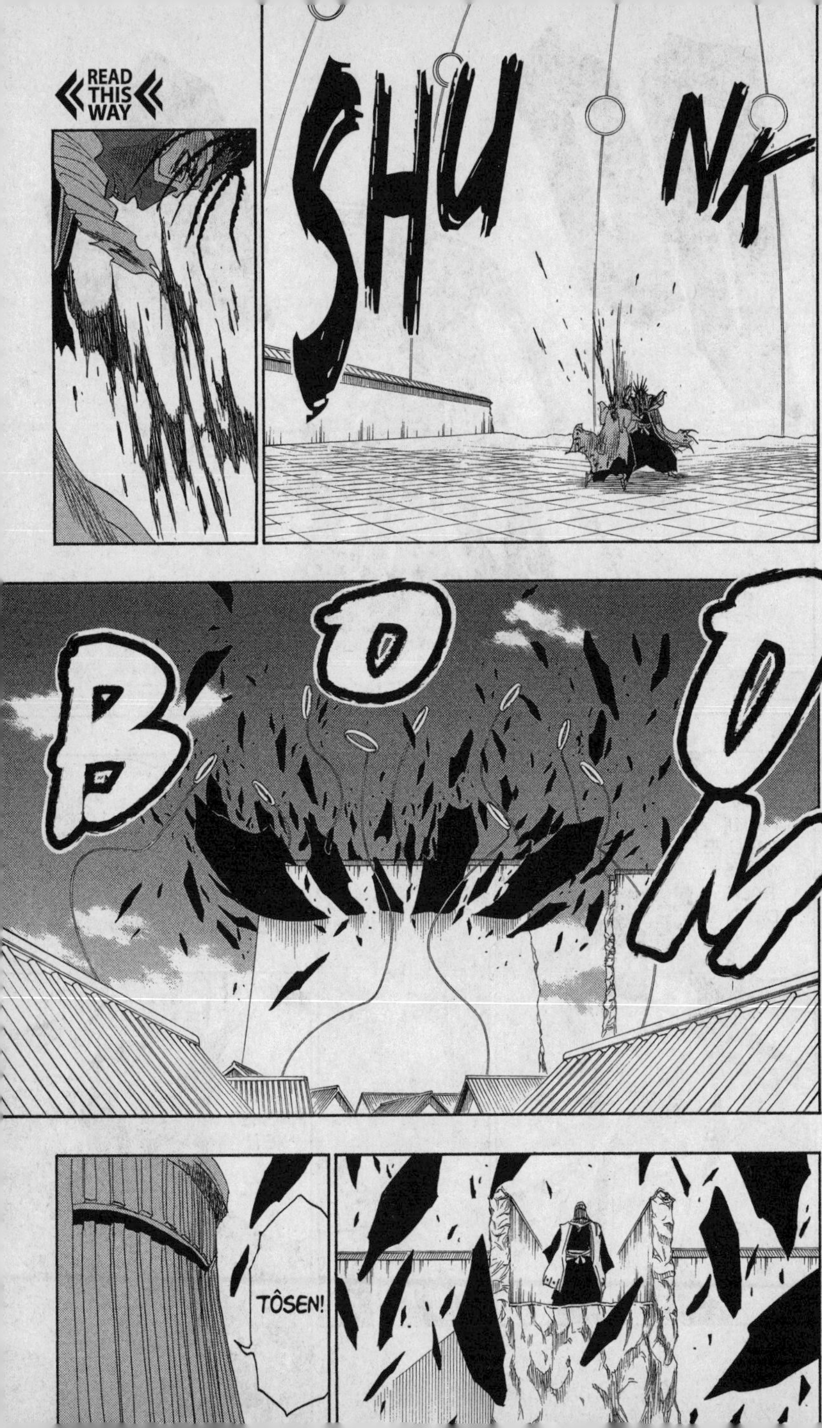
READ THIS WAY
SHUNK
BOOM
TÔSEN!

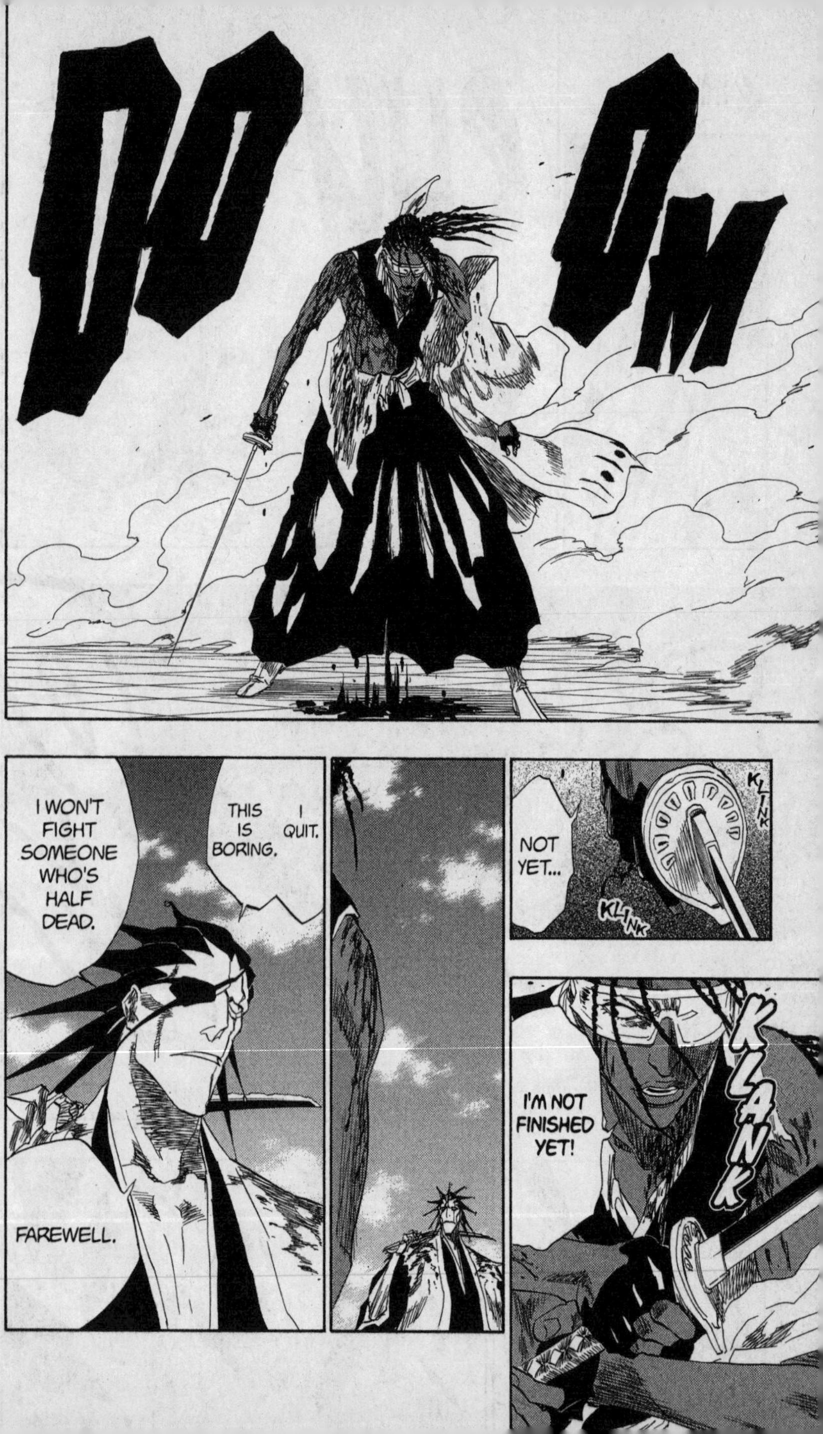
DO OM
NOT YET...
KLINK
KLINK
I'M NOT FINISHED YET!
KLANK
THIS IS BORING. I QUIT.
I WON'T FIGHT SOMEONE WHO'S HALF DEAD.
FAREWELL.

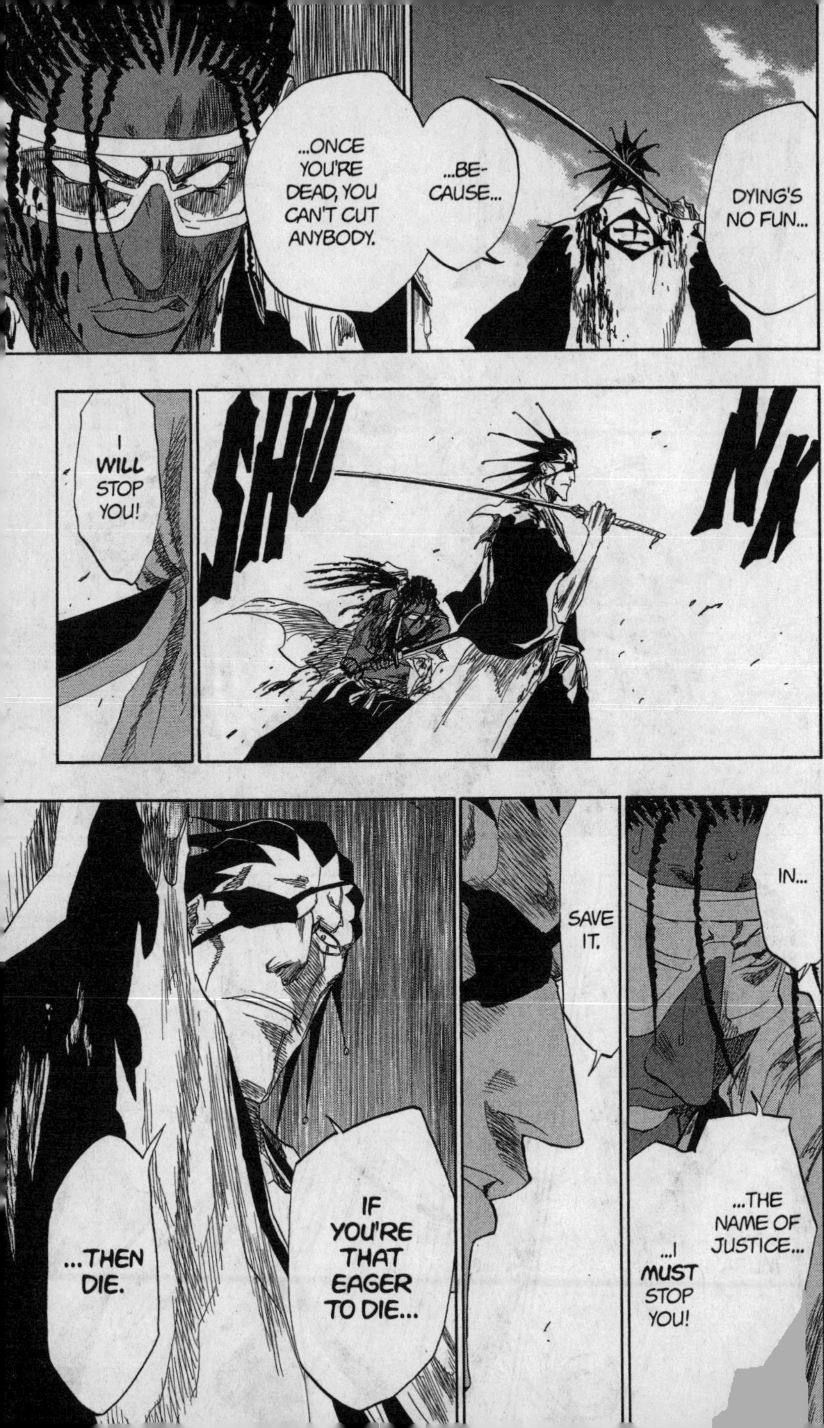
DYING'S NO FUN...
...BE-CAUSE...
...ONCE YOU'RE DEAD, YOU CAN'T CUT ANYBODY.
SHUNK
I WILL STOP YOU!
IN...
...THE NAME OF JUSTICE...
...I MUST STOP YOU!
SAVE IT.
IF YOU'RE THAT EAGER TO DIE...
...THEN DIE.

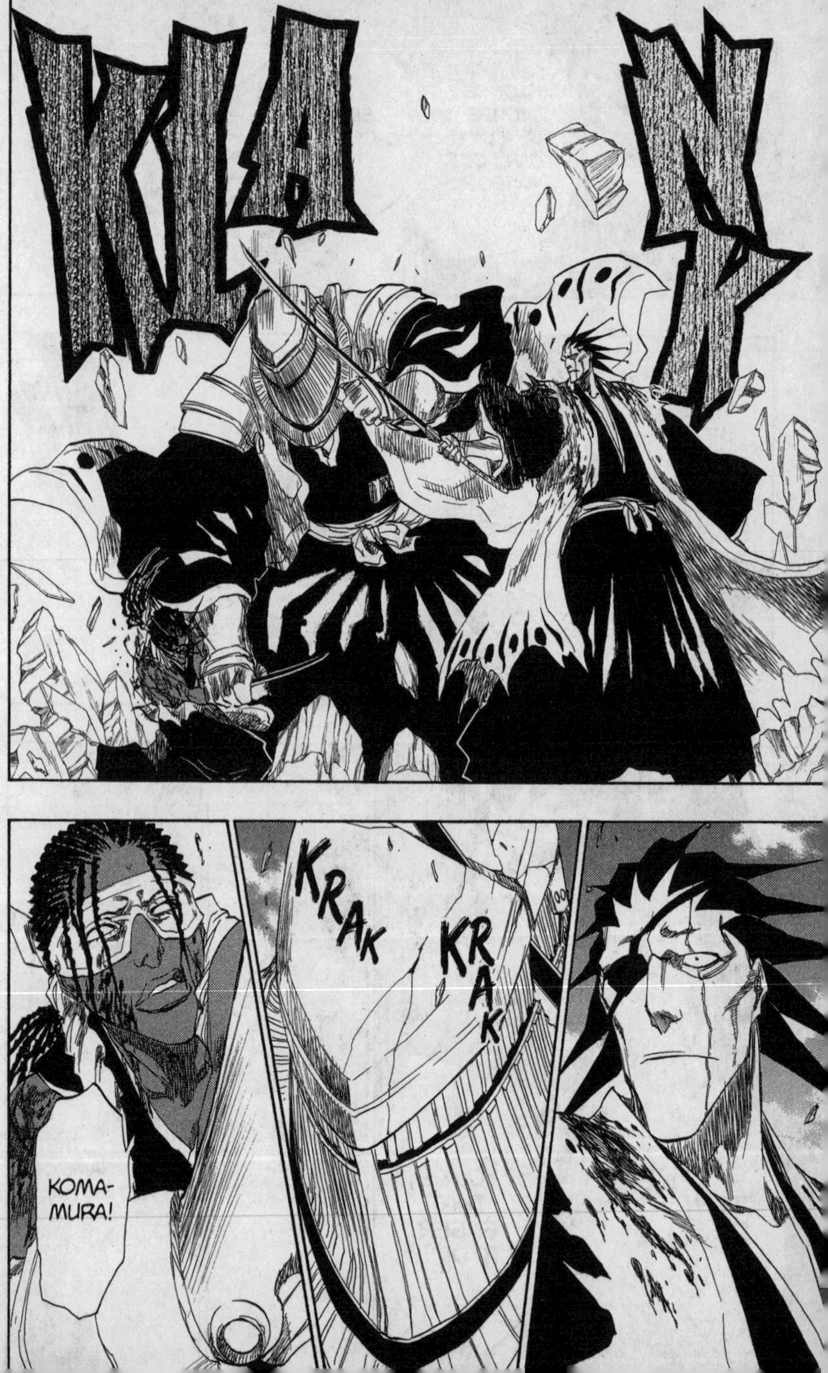
KLANK
KRAK KRAK
KOMA-
MURA!

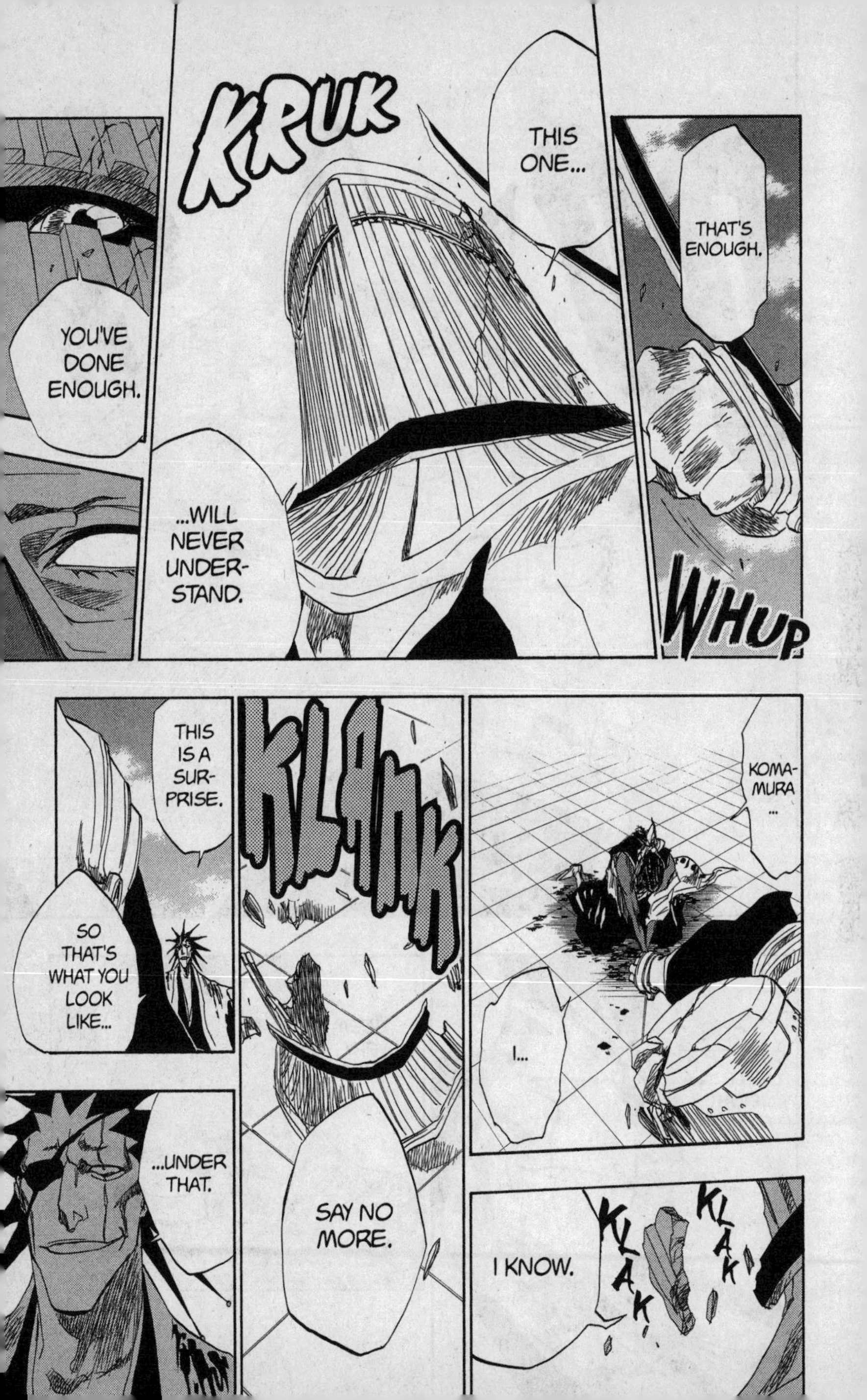
THAT'S ENOUGH.
WHUP
KRUK
THIS ONE...
...WILL NEVER UNDER-STAND.
YOU'VE DONE ENOUGH.
KOMA-MURA ...
I...
I KNOW.
KLAK
KLAK
KLANK
SAY NO MORE.
THIS IS A SUR-PRISE.
SO THAT'S WHAT YOU LOOK LIKE...
...UNDER THAT.

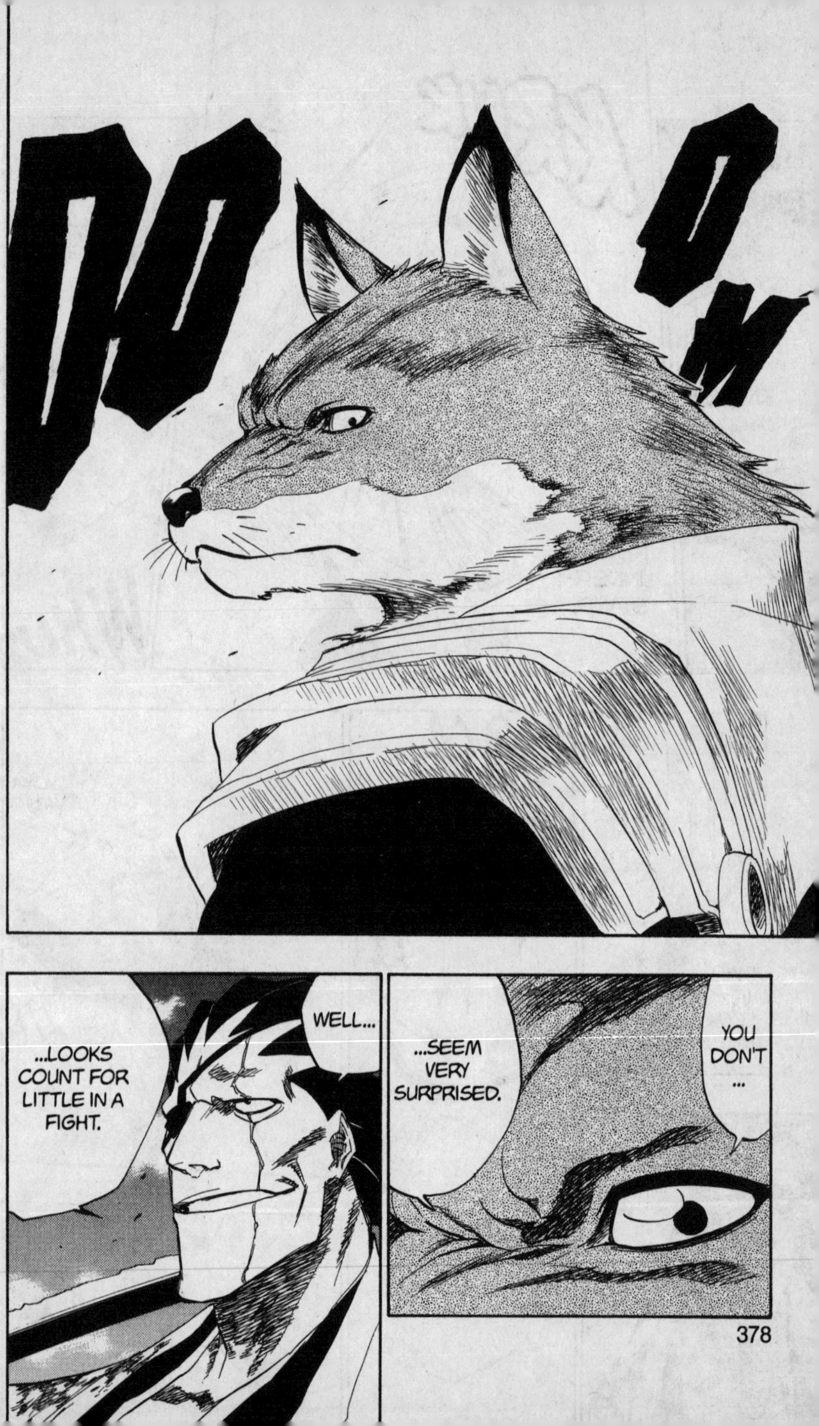
DOOM
YOU DON'T ...
...SEEM VERY SURPRISED.
WELL...
...LOOKS COUNT FOR LITTLE IN A FIGHT.

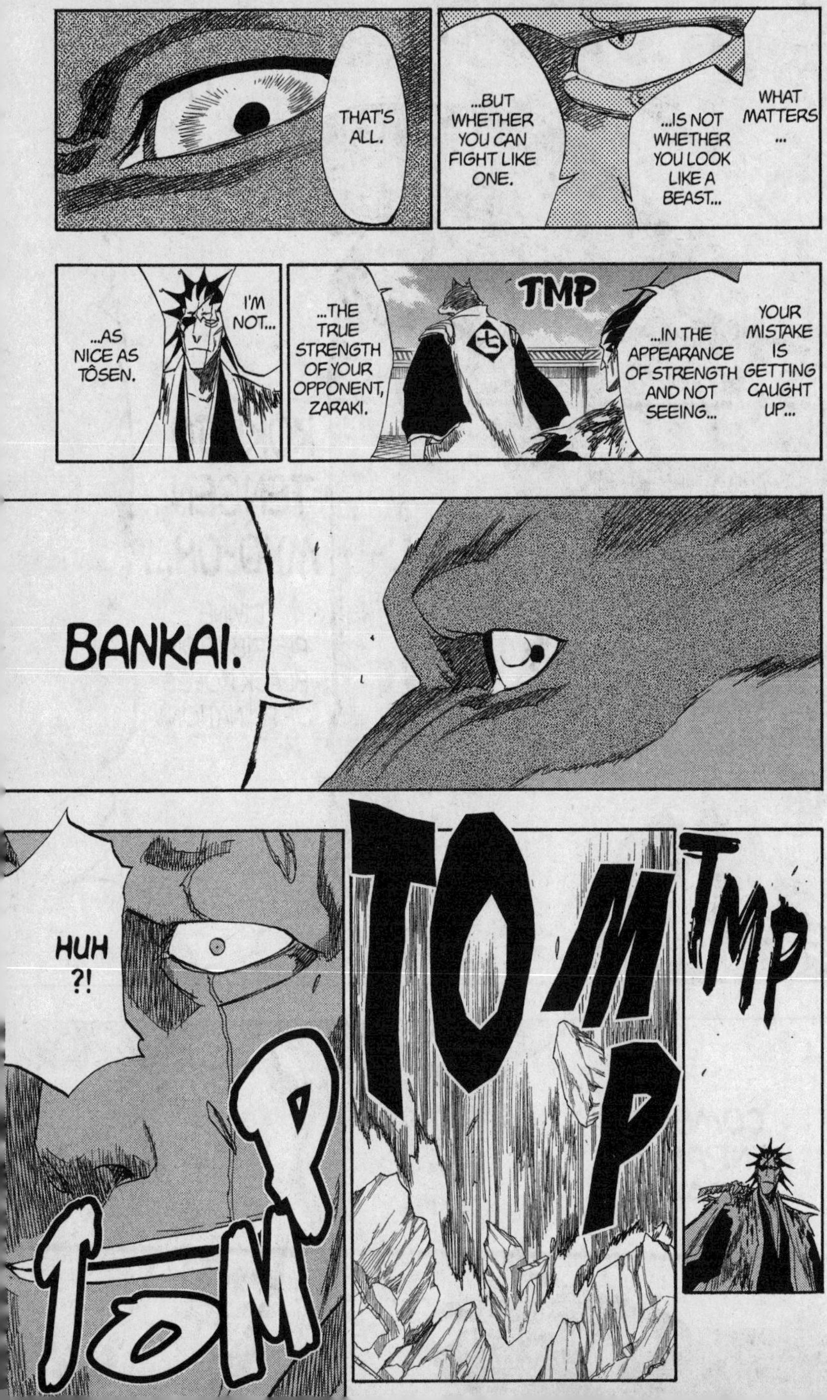
WHAT MATTERS ...
...IS NOT WHETHER YOU LOOK LIKE A BEAST...
...BUT WHETHER YOU CAN FIGHT LIKE ONE.
THAT'S ALL.
TMP
YOUR MISTAKE IS GETTING CAUGHT UP...
...IN THE APPEARANCE OF STRENGTH AND NOT SEEING...
...THE TRUE STRENGTH OF YOUR OPPONENT, ZARAKI.
I'M NOT...
...AS NICE AS TÔSEN.
BANKAI.
TMP
TOMP
HUH ?!
TOMP

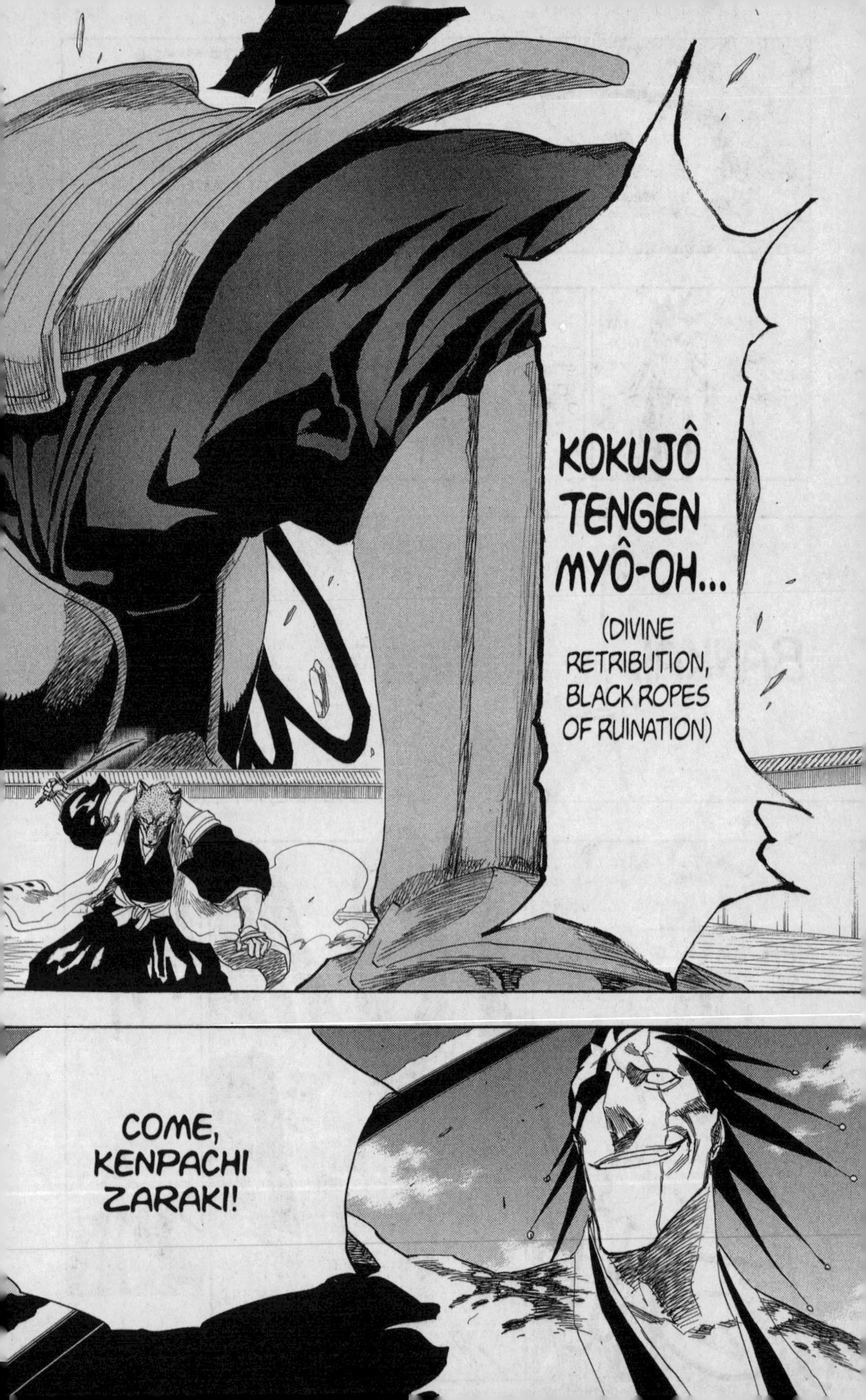
KOKUJÔ TENGEN MYÔ-OH...
(DIVINE RETRIBUTION, BLACK ROPES OF RUINATION)
COME, KENPACHI ZARAKI!

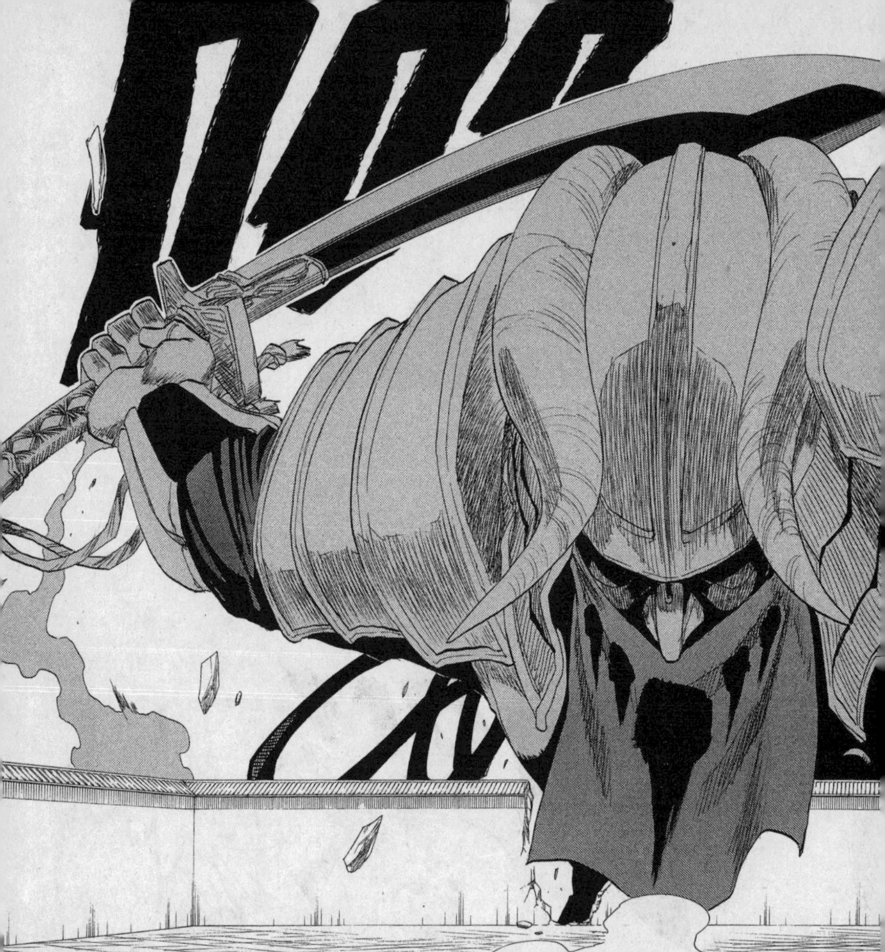

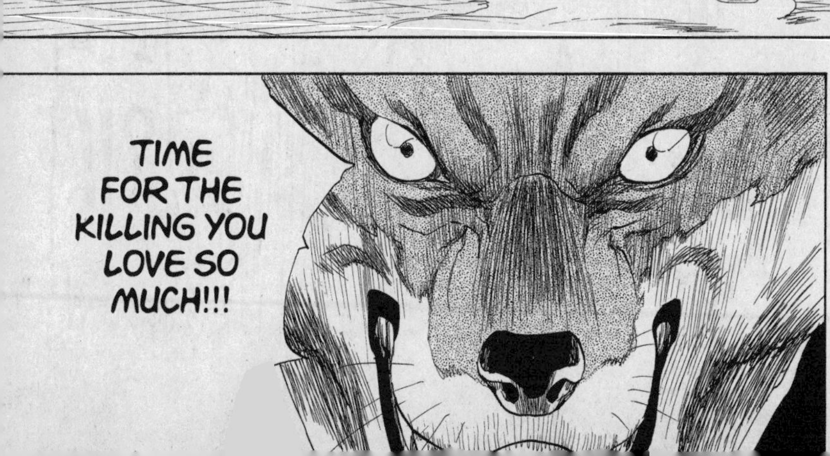
TIME FOR THE KILLING YOU LOVE SO MUCH!!!

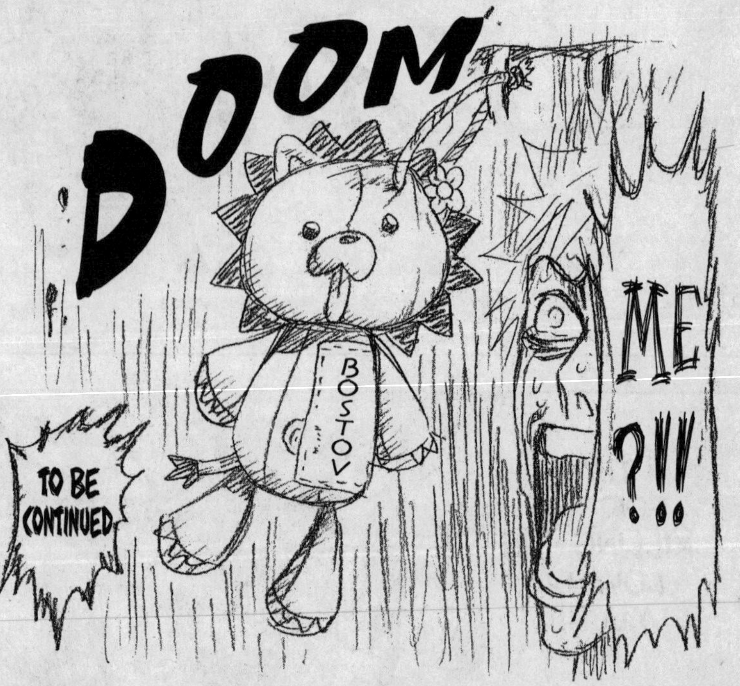
DOOM
ME?!!
BOSTOV
TO BE CONTINUED

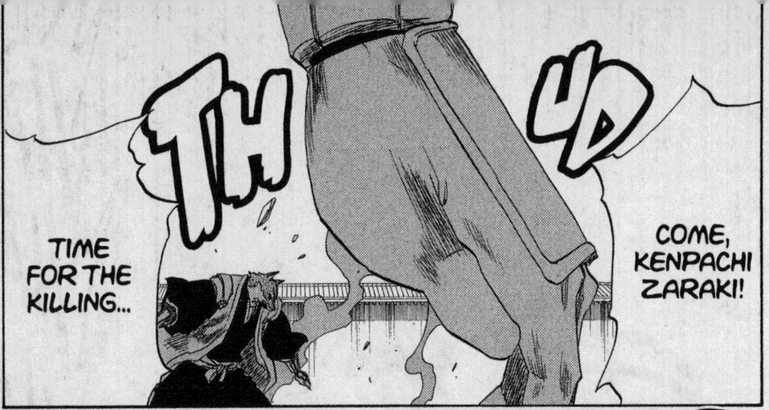
THUD
COME, KENPACHI ZARAKI!
TIME FOR THE KILLING...

149. COUNTDOWN TO THE END: 1 (ONLY MERCIFULLY)

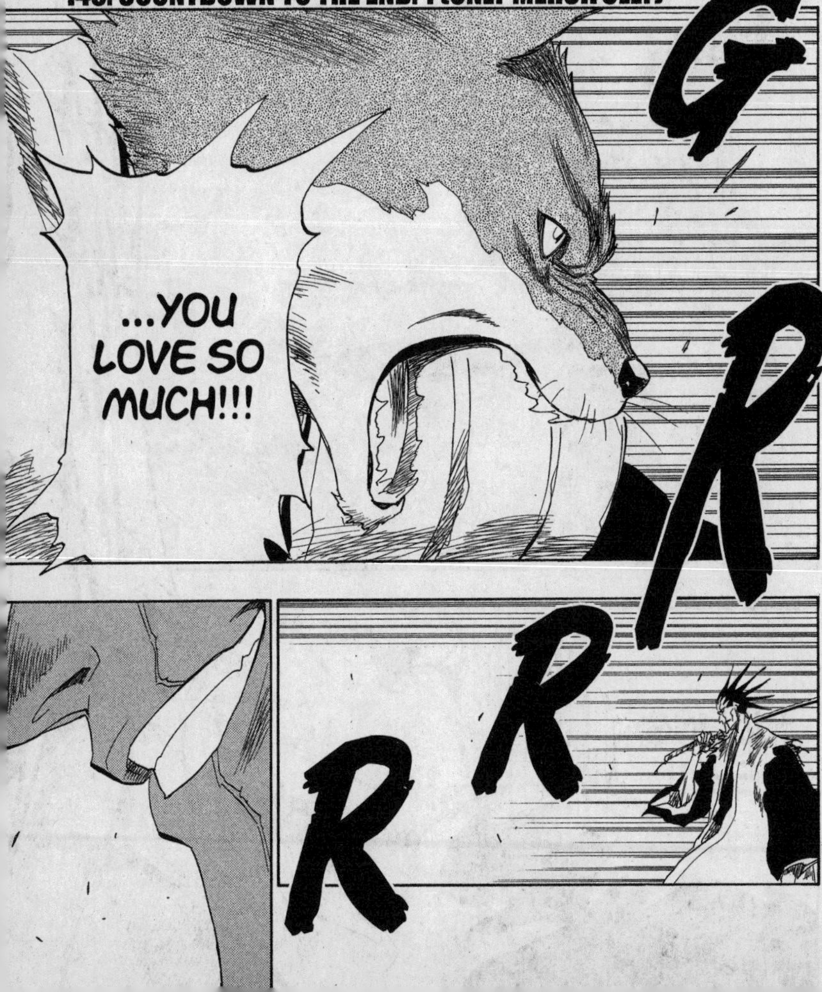
GRRRR
...YOU LOVE SO MUCH!!!

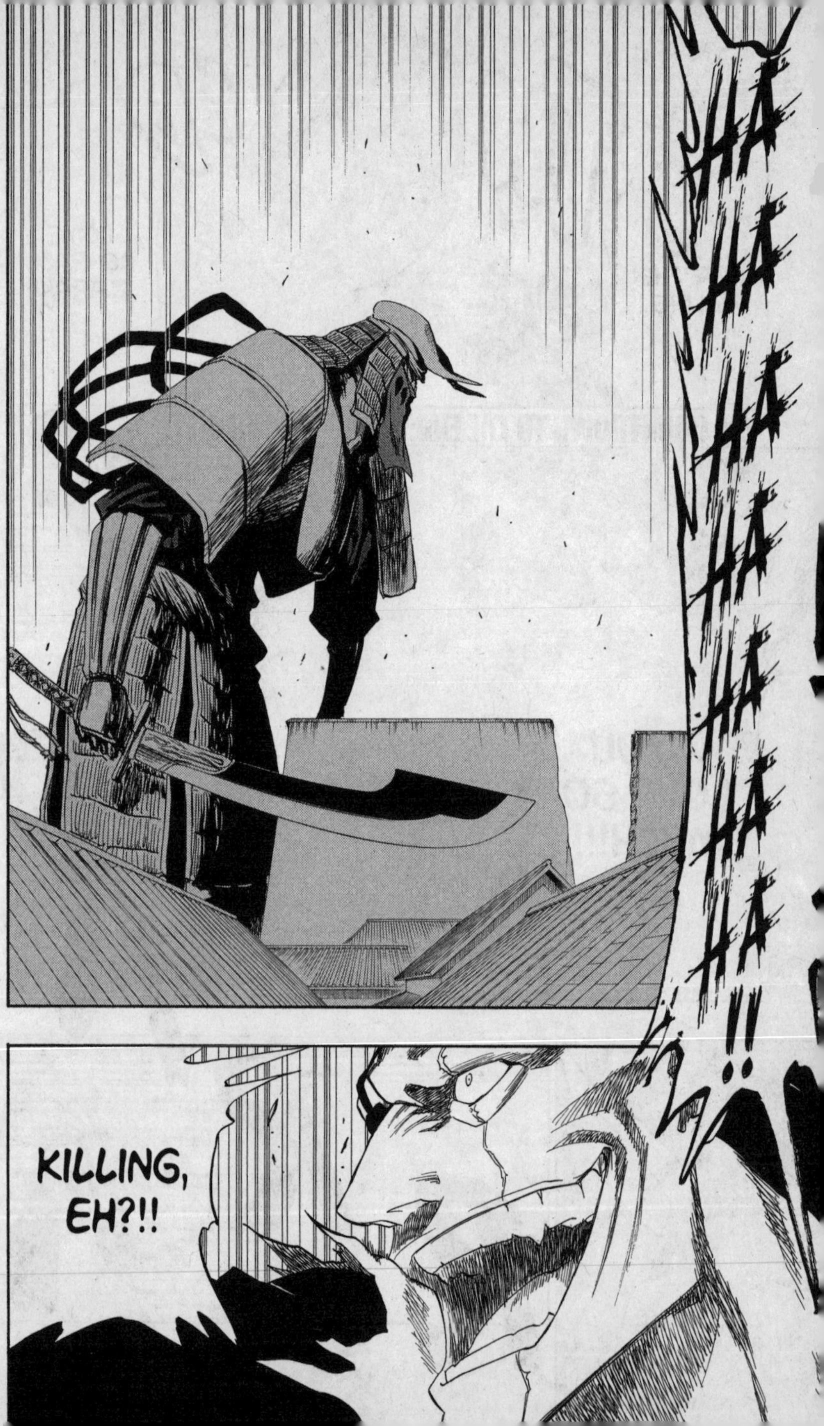
HA HA HA HA HA HA HA HA HA HA!!
KILLING, EH?!!

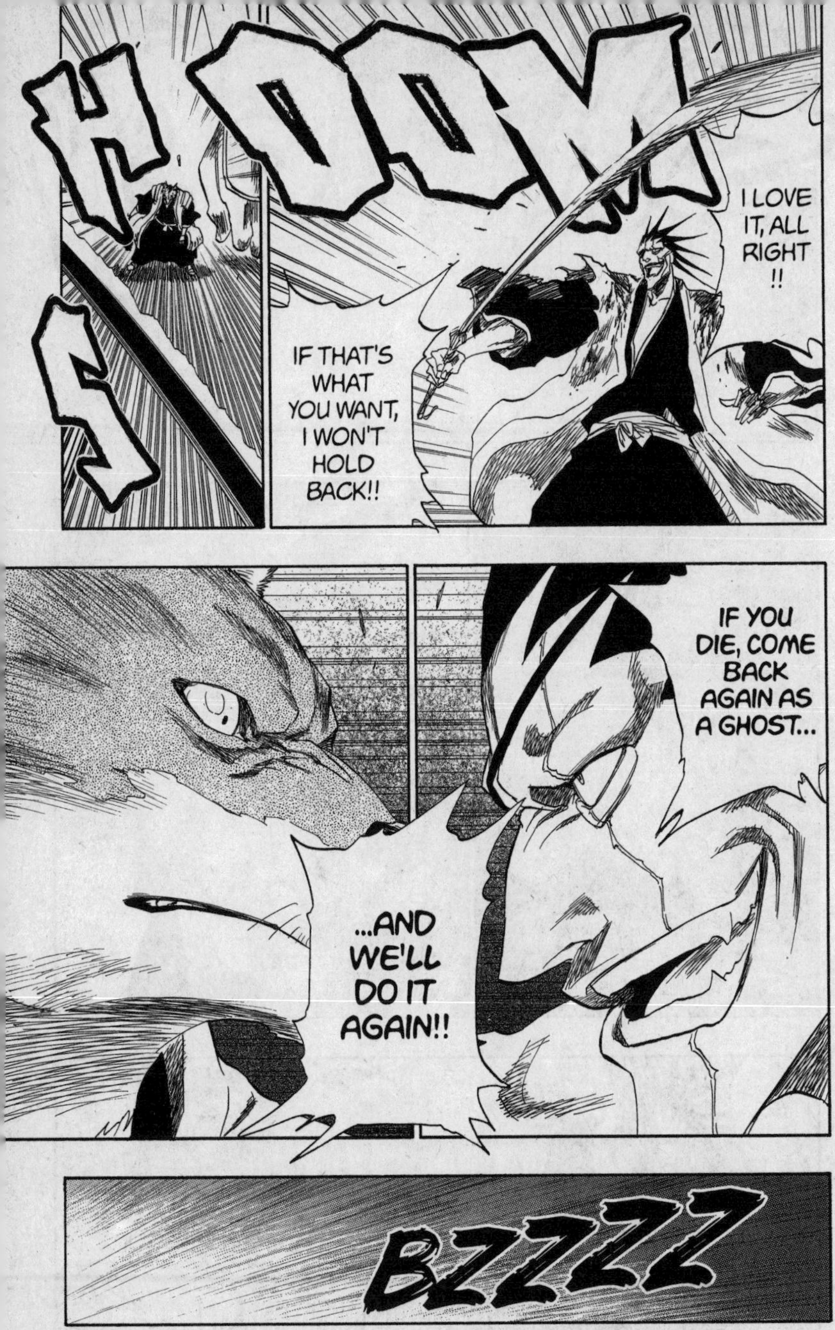
I LOVE IT, ALL RIGHT!!
IF THAT'S WHAT YOU WANT, I WON'T HOLD BACK!!
SHOOM
IF YOU DIE, COME BACK AGAIN AS A GHOST...
...AND WE'LL DO IT AGAIN!!
BZZZZ

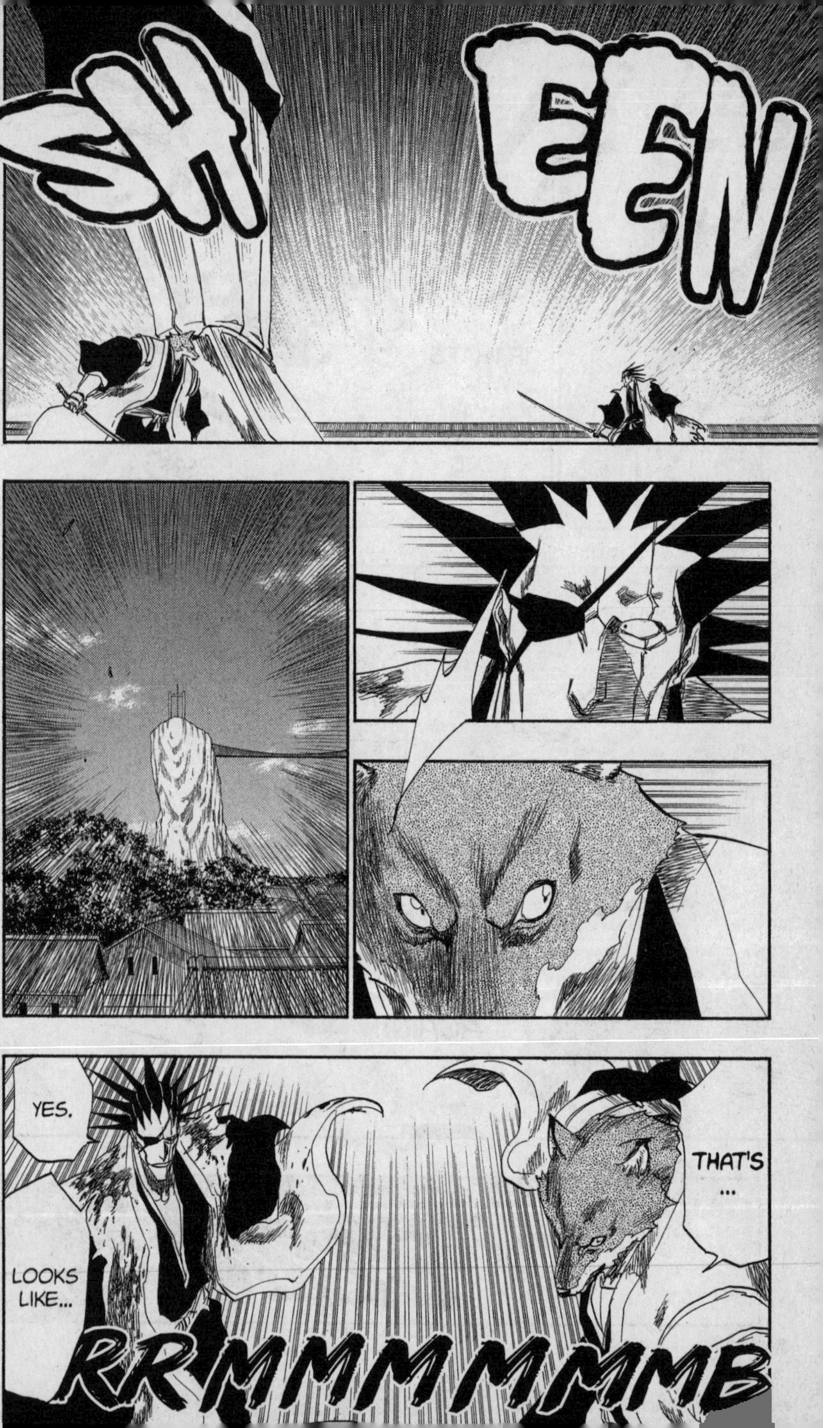
SH EEN
THAT'S ...
YES.
LOOKS LIKE...
RRMMMMMMMB

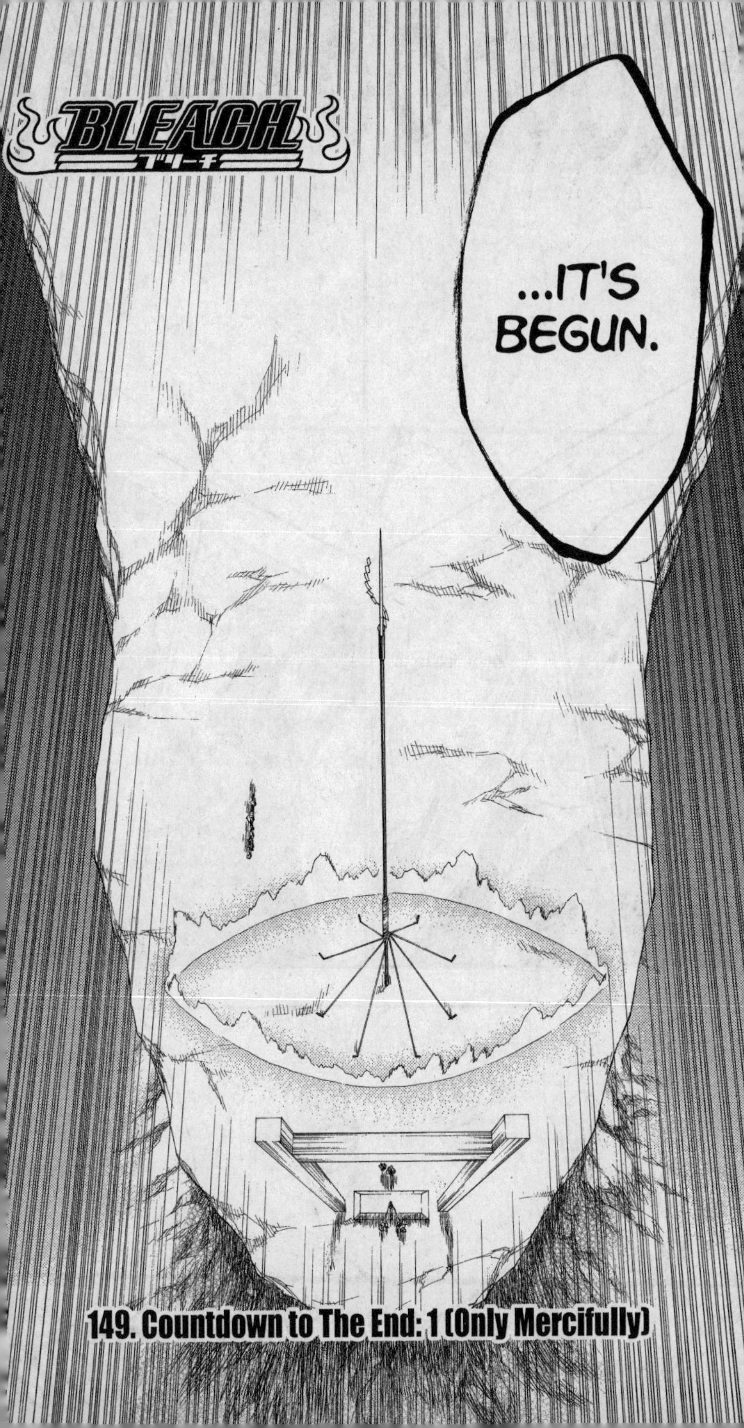
BLEACH
ブリーチ
...IT'S BEGUN.
149. Countdown to The End: 1 (Only Mercifully)

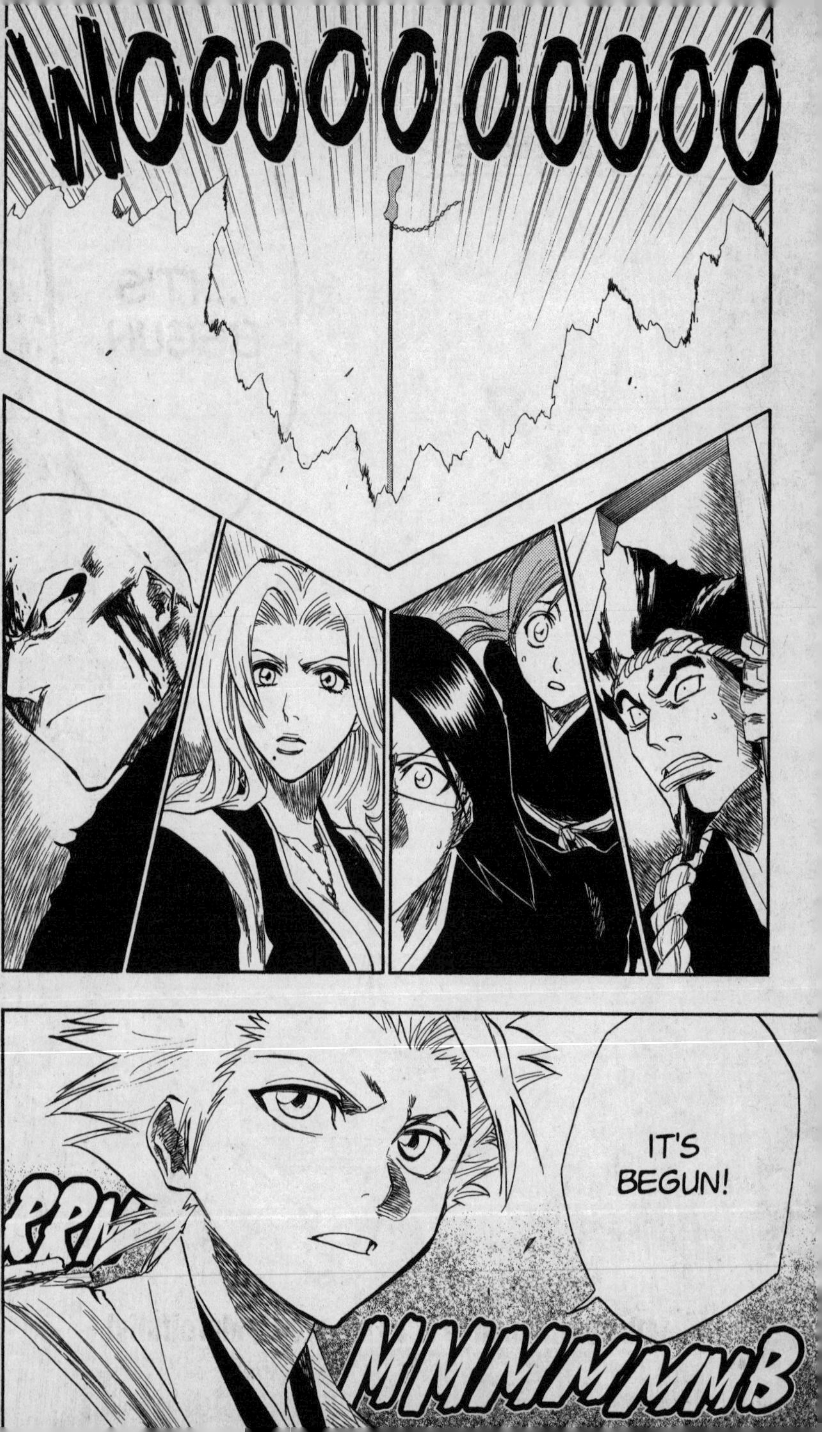
WOOOOO OOOOOO
IT'S BEGUN!
MMMMMMB

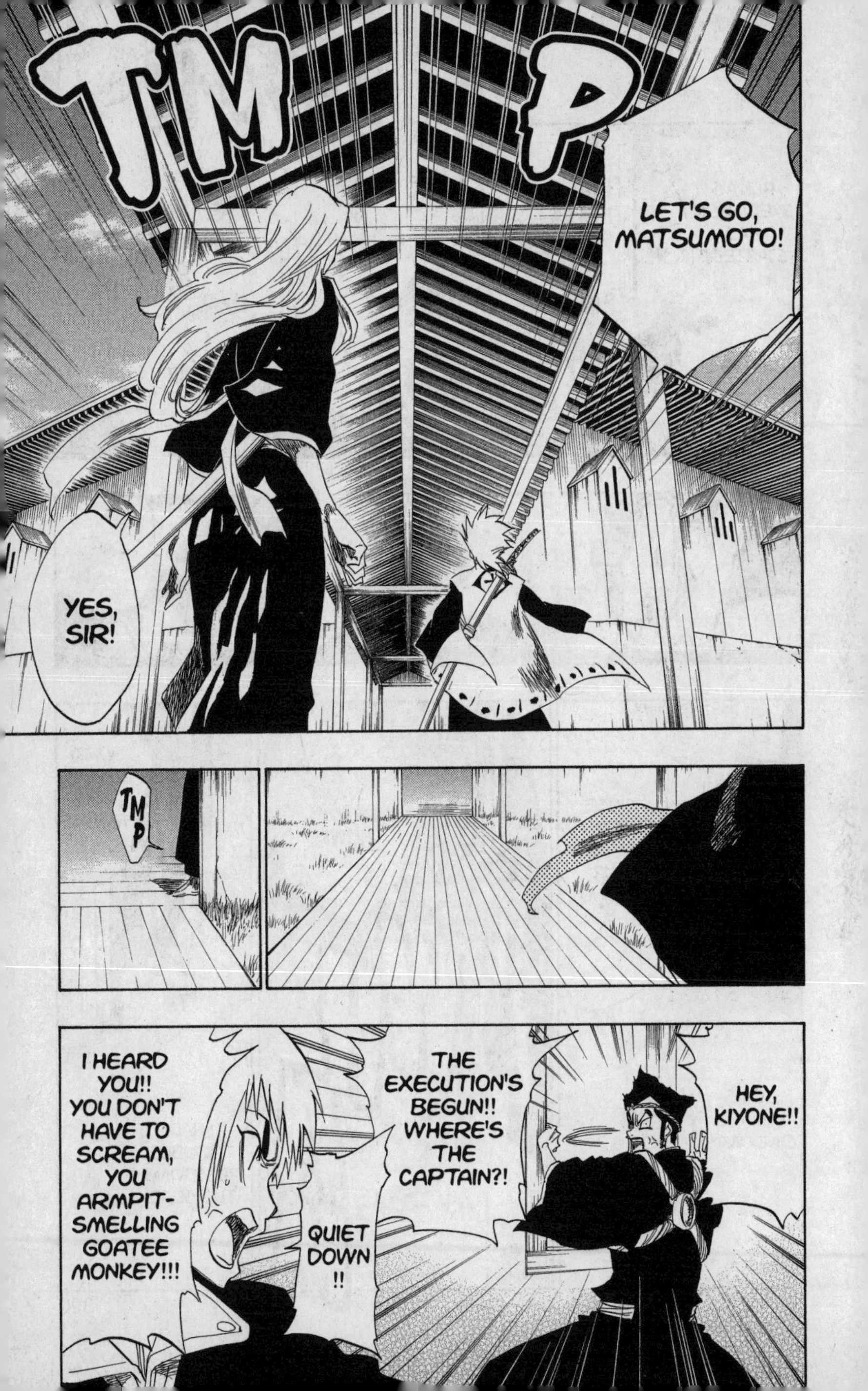
TMP
LET'S GO, MATSUMOTO!
YES, SIR!
TMP
HEY, KIYONE!!
THE EXECUTION'S BEGUN!! WHERE'S THE CAPTAIN?!
I HEARD YOU!! YOU DON'T HAVE TO SCREAM, YOU ARMPIT-SMELLING GOATEE MONKEY!!!
QUIET DOWN!!

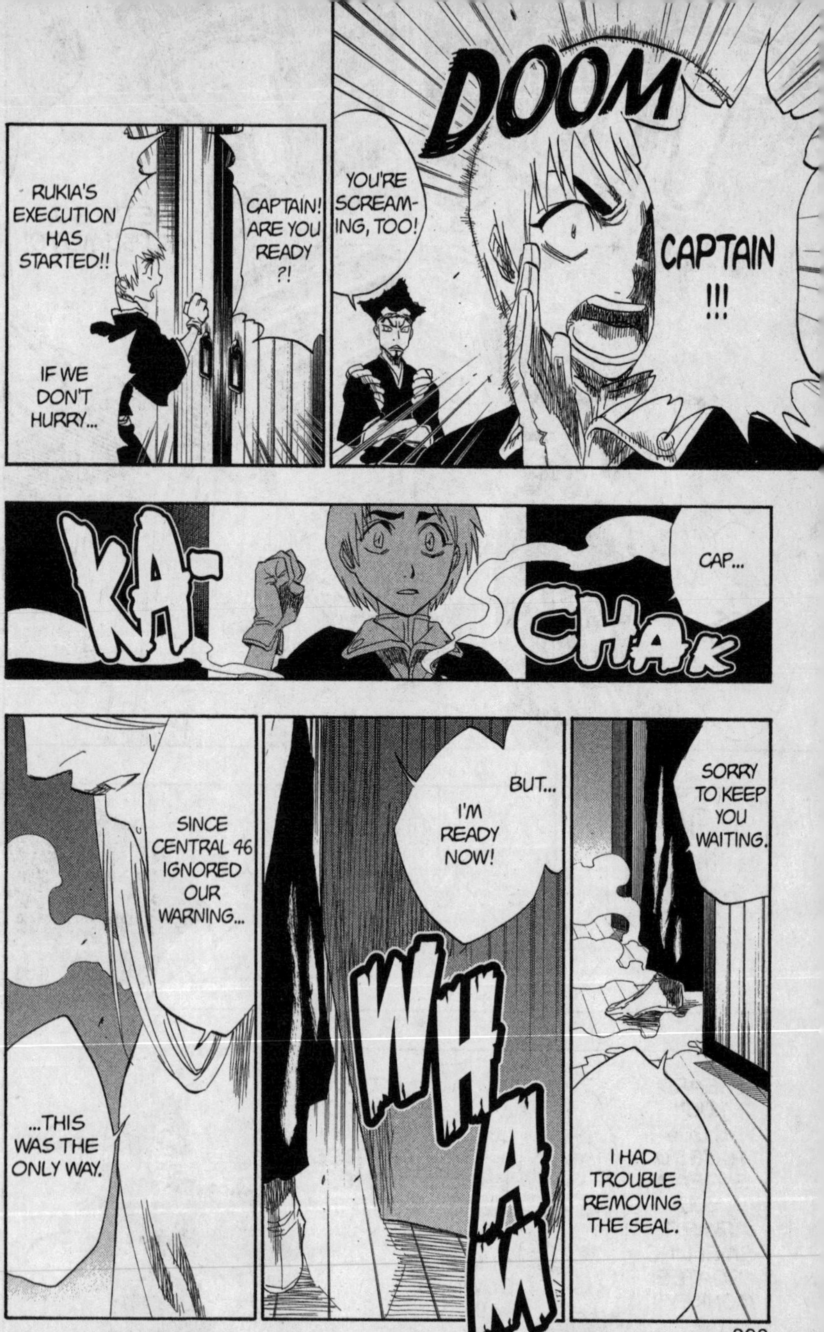
DOOM
CAPTAIN !!!
YOU'RE SCREAMING, TOO!
CAPTAIN! ARE YOU READY ?!
RUKIA'S EXECUTION HAS STARTED!!
IF WE DON'T HURRY...
CAP...
KA-CHAK
SORRY TO KEEP YOU WAITING.
I HAD TROUBLE REMOVING THE SEAL.
BUT...
I'M READY NOW!
WHAM
SINCE CENTRAL 46 IGNORED OUR WARNING...
...THIS WAS THE ONLY WAY.

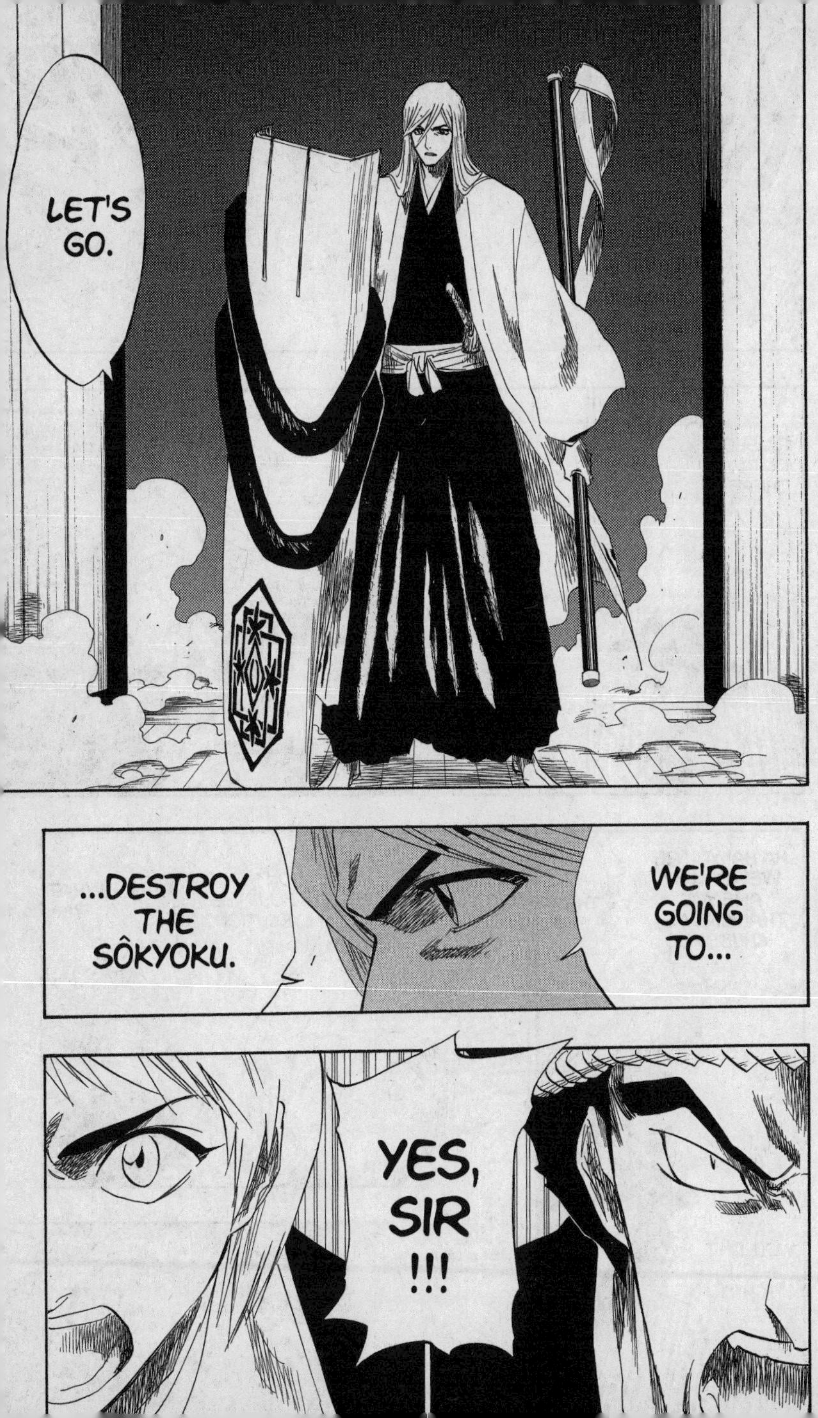
LET'S GO.
WE'RE GOING TO...
...DESTROY THE SÔKYOKU.
YES, SIR !!!

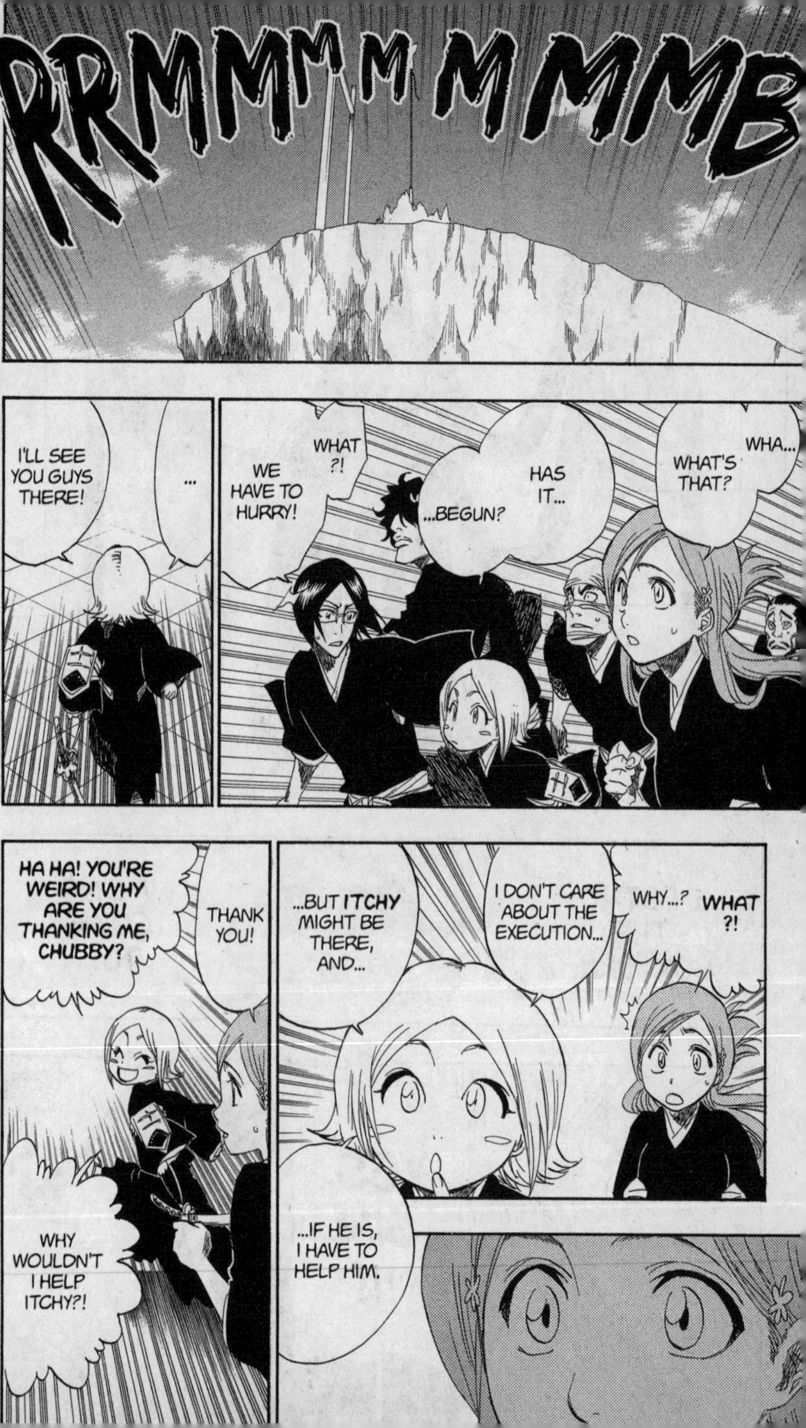
RRMMMMMMMMB
WHA...
WHAT'S THAT?
HAS IT...
...BEGUN?
WHAT ?!
WE HAVE TO HURRY!
...
I'LL SEE YOU GUYS THERE!
WHAT ?!
WHY...?
I DON'T CARE ABOUT THE EXECUTION...
...BUT ITCHY MIGHT BE THERE, AND...
...IF HE IS, I HAVE TO HELP HIM.
THANK YOU!
HA HA! YOU'RE WEIRD! WHY ARE YOU THANKING ME, CHUBBY?
WHY WOULDN'T I HELP ITCHY?!

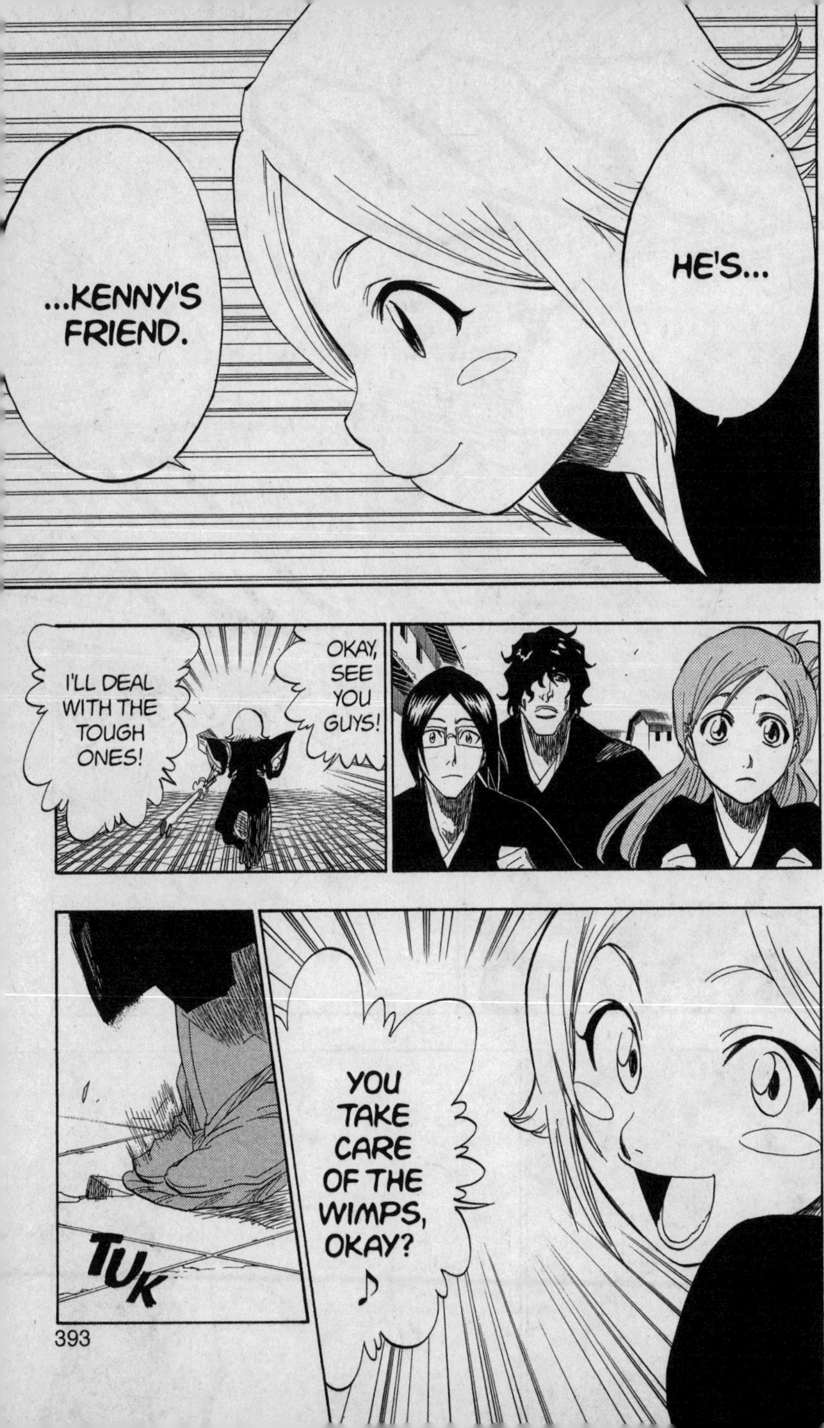
HE'S...
...KENNY'S FRIEND.
OKAY, SEE YOU GUYS!
I'LL DEAL WITH THE TOUGH ONES!
YOU TAKE CARE OF THE WIMPS, OKAY? ♪
TUK

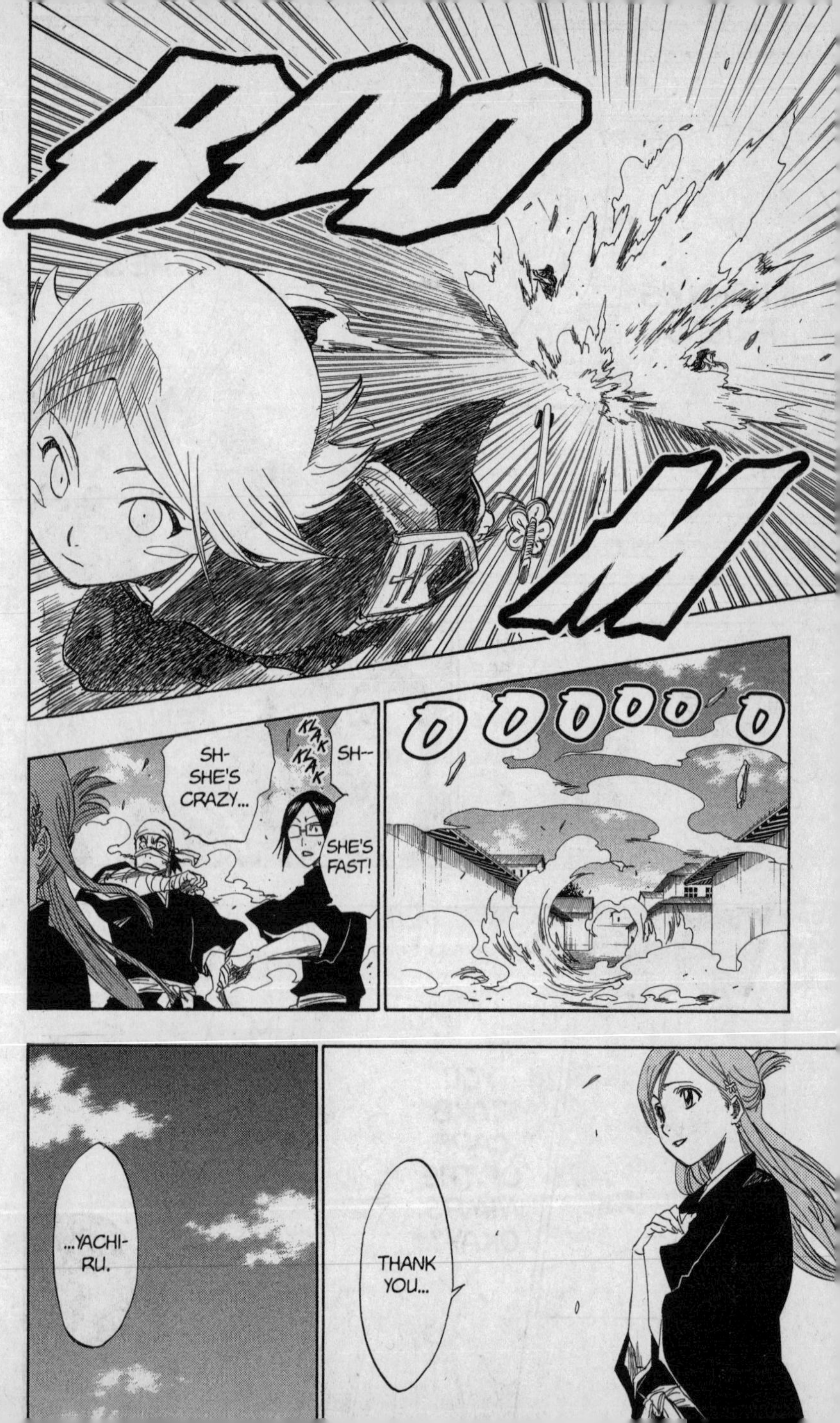
BOOM
DOOOOOO
SH--
KLAK KLAK KLAK
SHE'S FAST!
SH- SHE'S CRAZY...
THANK YOU...
...YACHI-RU.

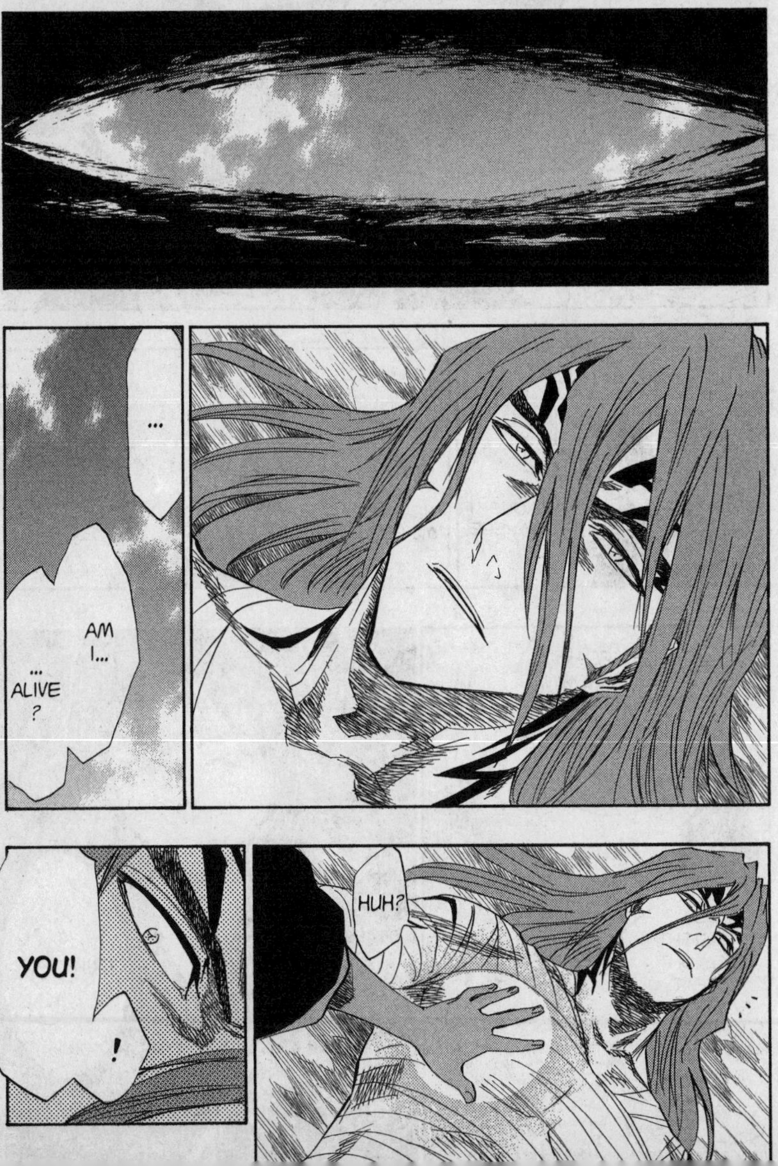
...
AM I... ...ALIVE?
HUH?
...
YOU!
!

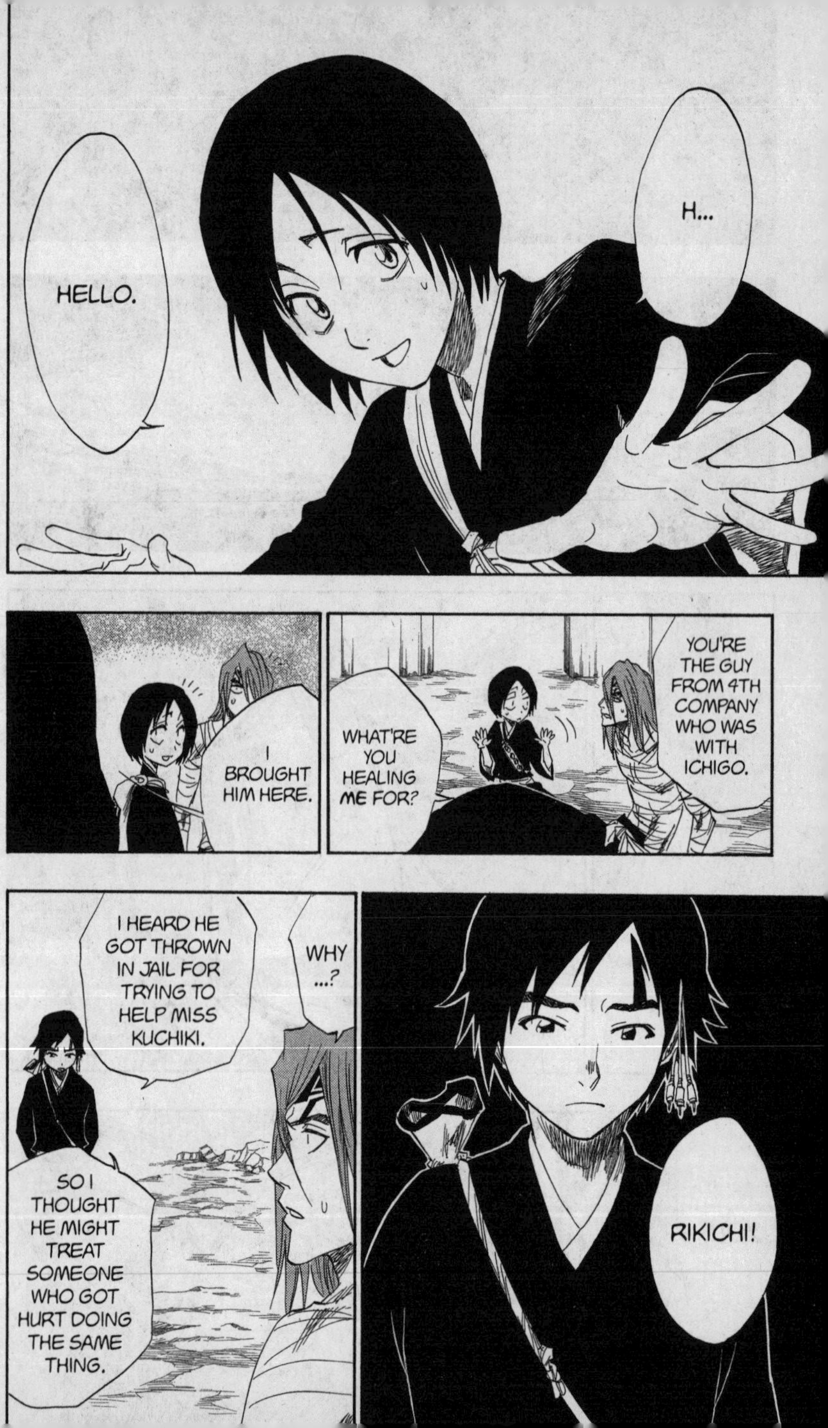
H...
HELLO.
YOU'RE THE GUY FROM 4TH COMPANY WHO WAS WITH ICHIGO.
WHAT'RE YOU HEALING ME FOR?
I BROUGHT HIM HERE.
RIKICHI!
WHY...?
I HEARD HE GOT THROWN IN JAIL FOR TRYING TO HELP MISS KUCHIKI.
SO I THOUGHT HE MIGHT TREAT SOMEONE WHO GOT HURT DOING THE SAME THING.

READ THIS WAY

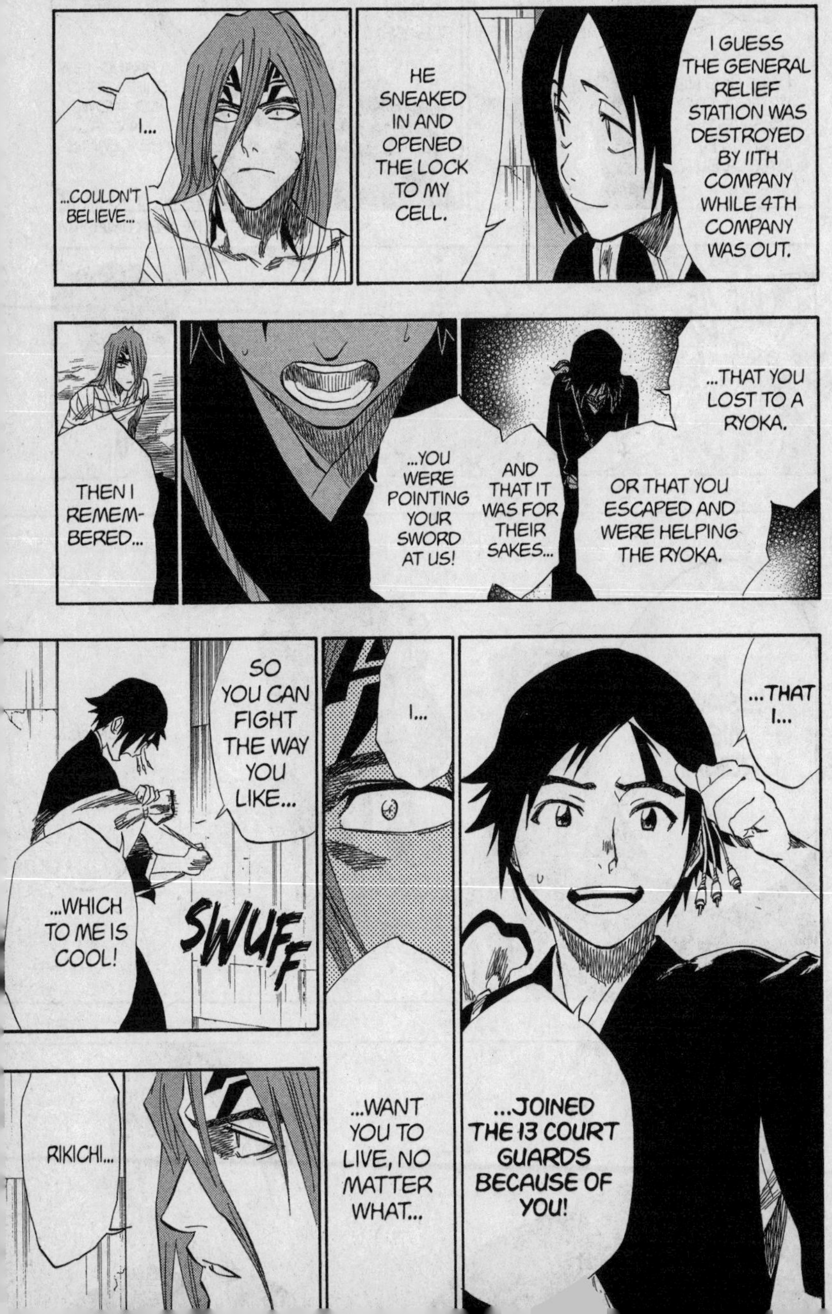
I GUESS THE GENERAL RELIEF STATION WAS DESTROYED BY 11TH COMPANY WHILE 4TH COMPANY WAS OUT.
HE SNEAKED IN AND OPENED THE LOCK TO MY CELL.
I...
...COULDN'T BELIEVE...
...THAT YOU LOST TO A RYOKA.
OR THAT YOU ESCAPED AND WERE HELPING THE RYOKA.
AND THAT IT WAS FOR THEIR SAKES...
...YOU WERE POINTING YOUR SWORD AT US!
THEN I REMEMBERED...
...THAT I...
...JOINED THE 13 COURT GUARDS BECAUSE OF YOU!
I...
...WANT YOU TO LIVE, NO MATTER WHAT...
SO YOU CAN FIGHT THE WAY YOU LIKE...
...WHICH TO ME IS COOL!
SWUFF
RIKICHI...

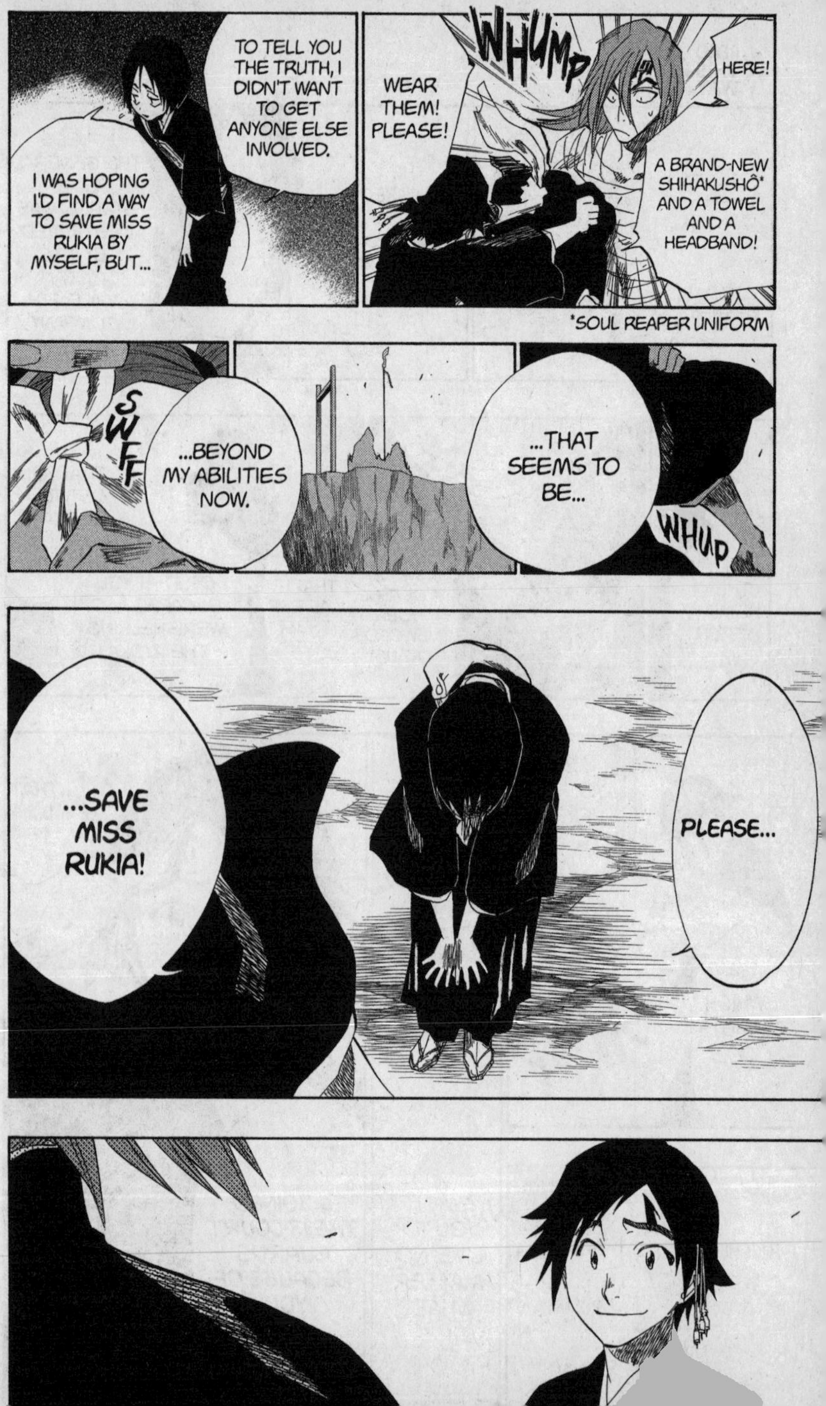
WHUMP
HERE!
A BRAND-NEW SHIHAKUSHÔ* AND A TOWEL AND A HEADBAND!
WEAR THEM! PLEASE!
TO TELL YOU THE TRUTH, I DIDN'T WANT TO GET ANYONE ELSE INVOLVED.
I WAS HOPING I'D FIND A WAY TO SAVE MISS RUKIA BY MYSELF, BUT...
*SOUL REAPER UNIFORM
WHUP
...THAT SEEMS TO BE...
...BEYOND MY ABILITIES NOW.
SWFF
PLEASE...
...SAVE MISS RUKIA!

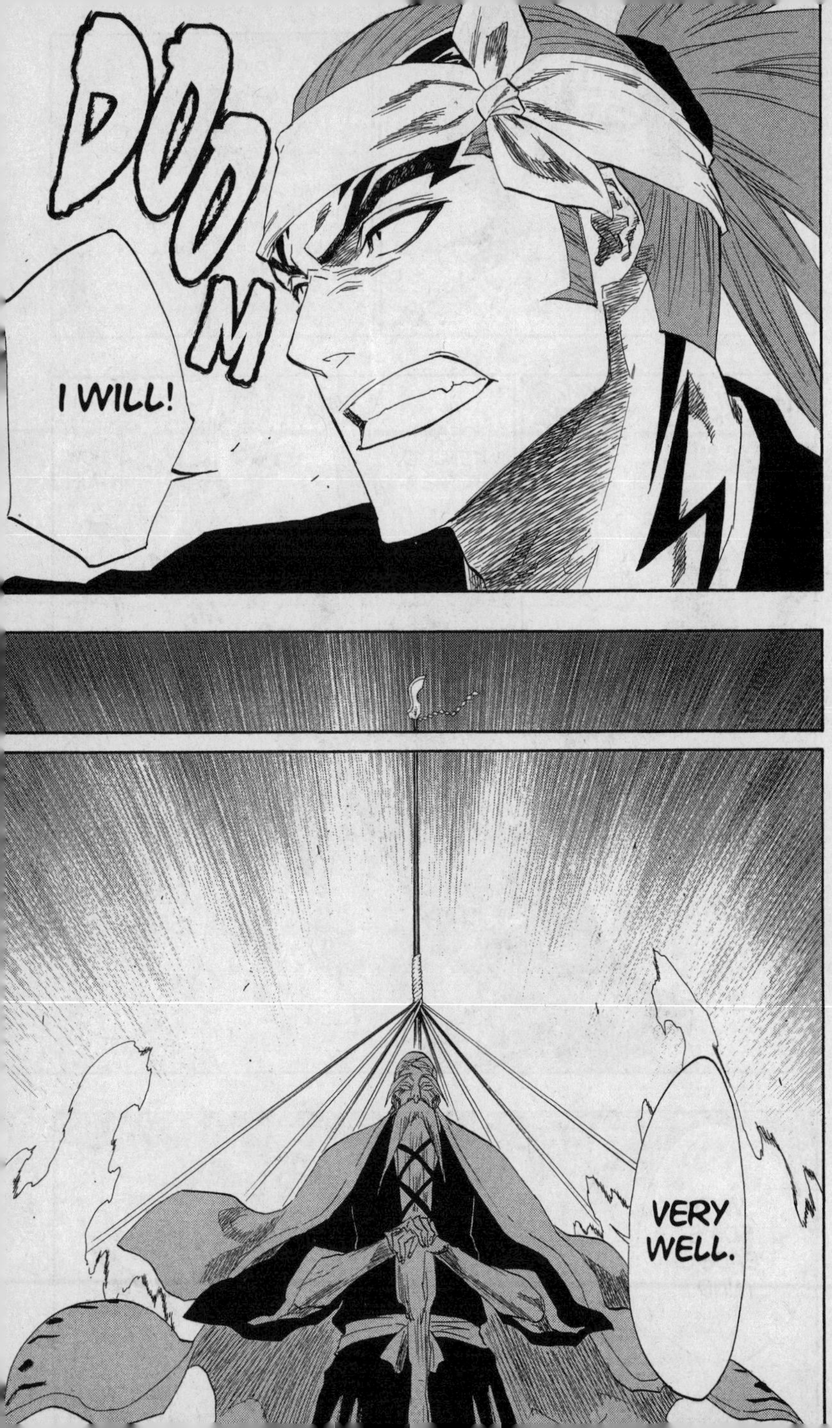
DOOM
I WILL!
VERY WELL.

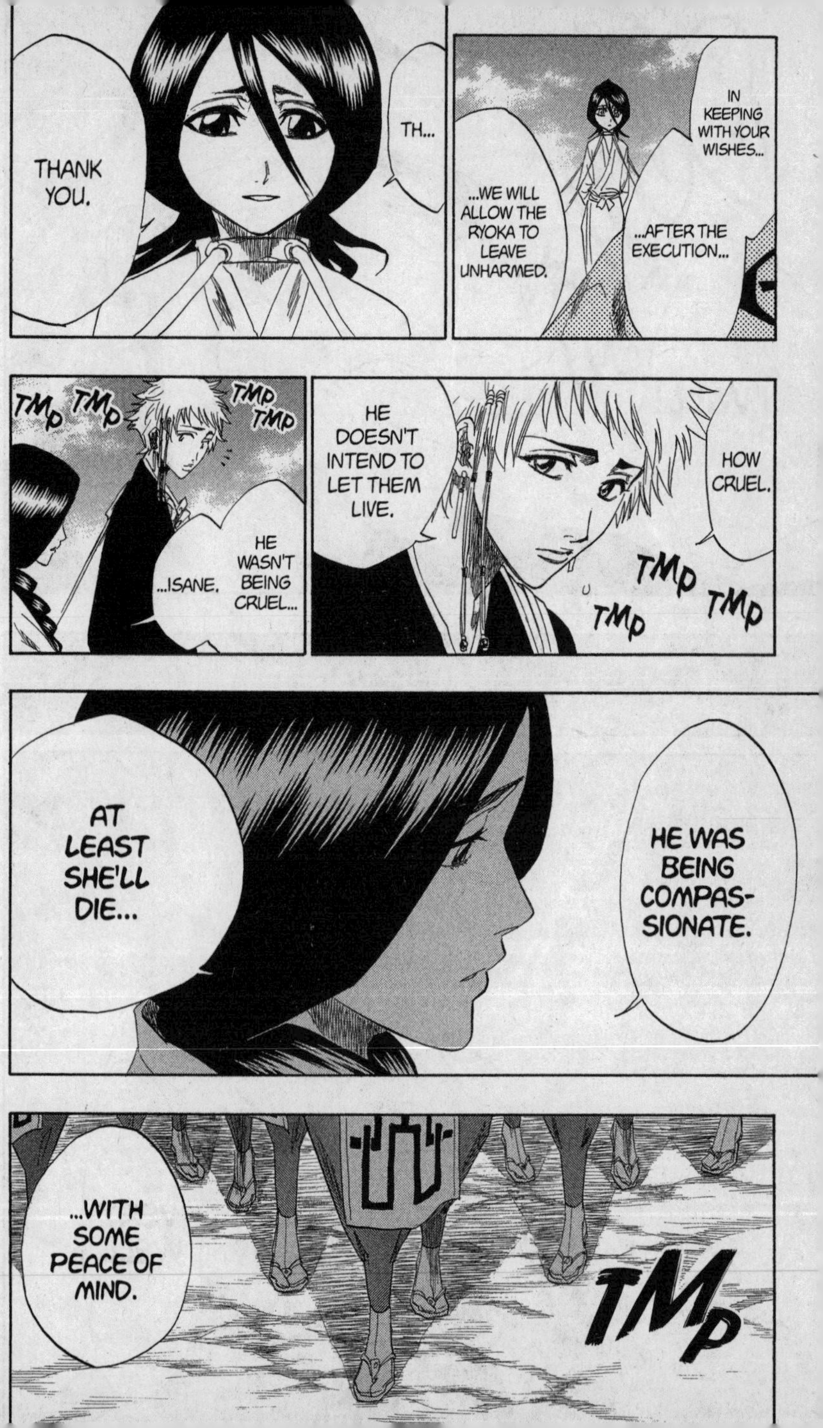
IN KEEPING WITH YOUR WISHES...
...AFTER THE EXECUTION...
...WE WILL ALLOW THE RYOKA TO LEAVE UNHARMED.
TH...
THANK YOU.
HOW CRUEL.
TMP TMP TMP
HE DOESN'T INTEND TO LET THEM LIVE.
TMP TMP TMP TMP
HE WASN'T BEING CRUEL...
...ISANE.
HE WAS BEING COMPAS-SIONATE.
AT LEAST SHE'LL DIE...
TMP
...WITH SOME PEACE OF MIND.

...WORRY.

AT LEAST SHE WON'T...

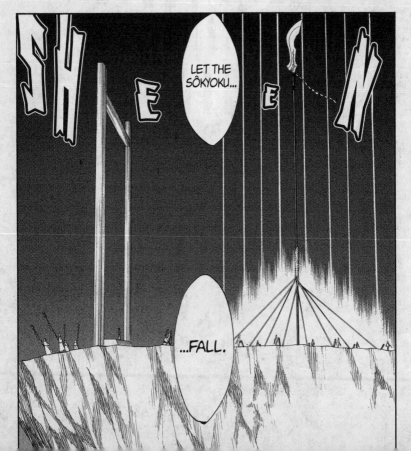

LET THE SÔKYOKU...

...FALL.

CONTI
NUED
IN
BLEACH
18

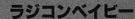

ラジコンベイビー

RADIO-KON★BABY!!

OPENING THEME MUSIC: "WE ARE RADIO-KON BABY!!"

★4★

YO! HOW YOU FOOLS DOING ?!

IT'S BEEN TOO LONG! WAY TOO LONG!! YOU KNOW HOW LONG IT'S BEEN?! FIFTEEN MONTHS!! ONE YEAR AND THREE MONTHS!!! WHAT THE HECK'S A YEAR?! IT'S BEEN SO LONG, OUR LAST TAPING'S JUST A FOND MEMORY!!

SO TODAY, TO WORK OUT ALL THE FRUSTRATION THAT'S BUILT UP OVER THE LAST YEAR, I'M GONNA BE READING SOME OF YOUR LETTERS. THAT MEANS THERE WON'T BE MUCH TIME FOR CHITCHAT!! ALL RIGHT THEN, HERE'S "RADIO-KON 4"!! OUR GUEST IS... AW!! I KINDA HATE THIS GUY... KISUKE URAHARA!! SAY HELLO!!

HELLO. ♡

THANK YOU FOR YOUR PATIENCE, LADIES AND GENTLEMEN.♡ THIS IS URAHARA SHÔTEN'S SLIGHTLY SHADY BUT HANDSOME MANAGER, KISUKE URA--

Q DOES MR. URAHARA WEAR A TOUPEE? TAKASHI YAMASHITA--YAMAGUCHI

WOW, THAT WAS ABRUPT. C'MON, I WAITED A LONG TIME FOR THIS, SO GIVE ME TIME TO TALK. EVEN THAT QUESTION WAS TOO SHORT.

THAT'S WHY I SAID THERE WOULDN'T BE MUCH CHITCHAT! NOW ANSWER THE QUESTION!

IT'S A TOUPEE.

ALL RIGHT! WHAT'S NEXT?

HUH ?!

NOT REALLY.

...

Q THE OTHER DAY IN P.E., WE HAD TO RUN A 50-METER DASH. I SAID, "TAKE THE POWER OF JUSTICE! THE ARMOR AND HEAD-BAND OF JUSTICE!!"

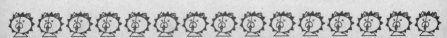

THEN I PUT MY HEADBAND ON. I RAN .75 SECONDS FASTER THAN I EVER HAVE BEFORE. WAS THAT SOME KIND OF MAGIC, OR DID I JUST HAVE A GOOD DAY? TSUBASA YAMAMOTO--TOYAMA

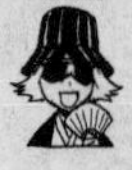

IT WAS 100 PERCENT MAGIC.

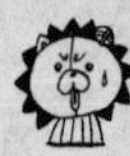

DUDE, ARE YOU GONNA ANSWER THESE QUESTIONS SERIOUSLY, OR NOT?

Q MR. URAHARA! I LOVE YOU!! MARRY ME!! AYAKA--WAKAYAMA

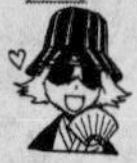

OKAY. ♡

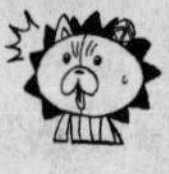

HEY! DON'T BE TAKING QUESTIONS WHEN I'M TALKING!!

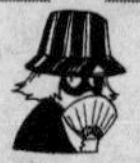

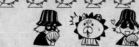

BUT YOU SAID YOU WEREN'T GOING TO TALK MUCH.

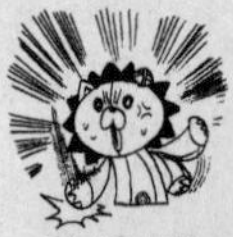

SHUT UP!! I GET TO TALK AS MUCH AS I WANT!! I'M THE HOST HERE!

Q THERE WAS A SCENE IN VOLUME TWO WHERE YOU HUGGED URURU! I'M JEALOUS. WOULD YOU HUG ME, TOO? MAKIKO NAKAMURA--HOKKAIDO

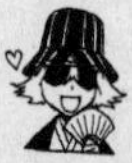

SURE! ♡

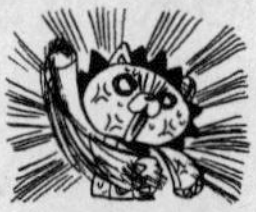

HEY!! DON'T CUT ME OFF LIKE THAT!! AND THAT QUESTION TICKS ME OFF, TOO!!

Q AT THE END OF ICHIGO'S TRAINING, THE HAT THAT YOU WORE (AND THAT ICHIGO CUT) WAS FIXED. WHO FIXED IT? OR DO YOU KEEP SPARES, LIKE URYÛ? TANAKA--NAGANO

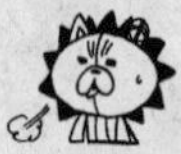

SO WE FINALLY ARRIVE AT THIS, THE MOST COMMONLY ASKED QUESTION. WELL? WHAT'S THE DEAL?

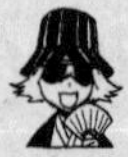

I HAVE A LOT OF THOSE HATS, MAYBE A HUNDRED OF THEM. BY THE WAY, I HAVE A LOT OF IDENTICAL ROBES AND CLOGS AND *JINBEI* (SUMMER CASUAL WEAR) TOO. ♪

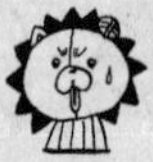

WOW... IF I WERE A DRAWER AND HAD A BUNCH OF IDENTICAL THINGS STUFFED INTO ME, I'D GO NUTS.

Q WHAT KIND OF PEOPLE SHOP AT URAHARA SHÔTEN AND WHAT DO THEY BUY? JUN KAMATA--FUKUSHIMA

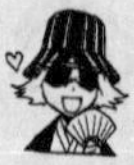

EVERYONE FROM LITTLE GIRLS TO HOUSEWIVES WITH TOO MUCH TIME ON THEIR HANDS SHOPS THERE. THEY BUY THINGS THAT I CAN'T EVEN MENTION IN MIXED COMPANY.

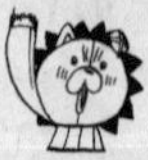

ARE YOU SERIOUS?! I TOTALLY WANNA GO THERE!!!

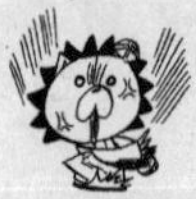

NO!! WHAT THE HECK?! YOU'VE ONLY ANSWERED ONE QUESTION SERIOUSLY SO FAR!!

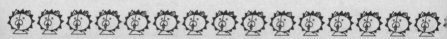

   Q

| HMM... AND? | WELL, YORUICHI AND I ARE VERY CLOSE. I REALLY CAN'T SAY ANY MORE. | **WHAT?! THAT'S INEXCUSABLE!!** | NAKED? OF COURSE! | JUST ANSWER THE QUESTION! | THAT'S A FUNNY NAME YOU HAVE... | HAVE YOU SEEN MS. YORUICHI NAKED? SAKI KENMA--OKAYAMA | I'VE BEEN ANSWERING THEM AS HONESTLY AS I CAN. | YOU TRYING TO RUIN MY SHOW?! |

→ Innocent Bystander

N-N-NOOO OOOO OOOO OO...

DON'T BE SHY. "BEYOND NAKED," HUH? LET'S START BY CHECKING OUT YOUR BONES.

AW, C'MON, YORUICHI. NOT HERE...

I SEE. I DIDN'T KNOW WE WERE SO INTIMATE. WOULD YOU CARE TO ELABORATE?

HMM...

I'VE SEEN PARTS OF HER BEYOND NAKED!!

NOW ACCEPTING LETTERS!!

ANY QUESTION IS OKAY!!
WE'RE ACCEPTING SUGGESTIONS FOR ENDING THEME MUSIC AS WELL AS QUESTIONS!! WRITE DOWN THE TITLE OF A SONG OR THE NAME OF AN ARTIST THAT INCLUDES THE WORD "LION," AND STUFF IT IN THE NEAREST MAILBOX!! OUR NEXT GUEST WILL BE HANATARO YAMADA (CONFIRMED)!! INCLUDE YOUR QUESTION, NAME, ADDRESS, AGE, AND TELEPHONE NUMBER AND SEND TO THE ADDRESS BELOW!!
**SHONEN JUMP C/O VIZ MEDIA, LLC
P.O. BOX 77010, SAN FRANCISCO, CA 94107
ATTN: "BLEACH" RADIO-KON BABY!!**

SINGLE: "GOODNIGHT RADIO-KON BABY!" ENDING THEME MUSIC: "CAN YOU FEEL THE LOVE TONIGHT" FROM *THE LION KING*, REQUESTED BY KANAGAWA (WHO LOVES CAPTAIN AIZEN)

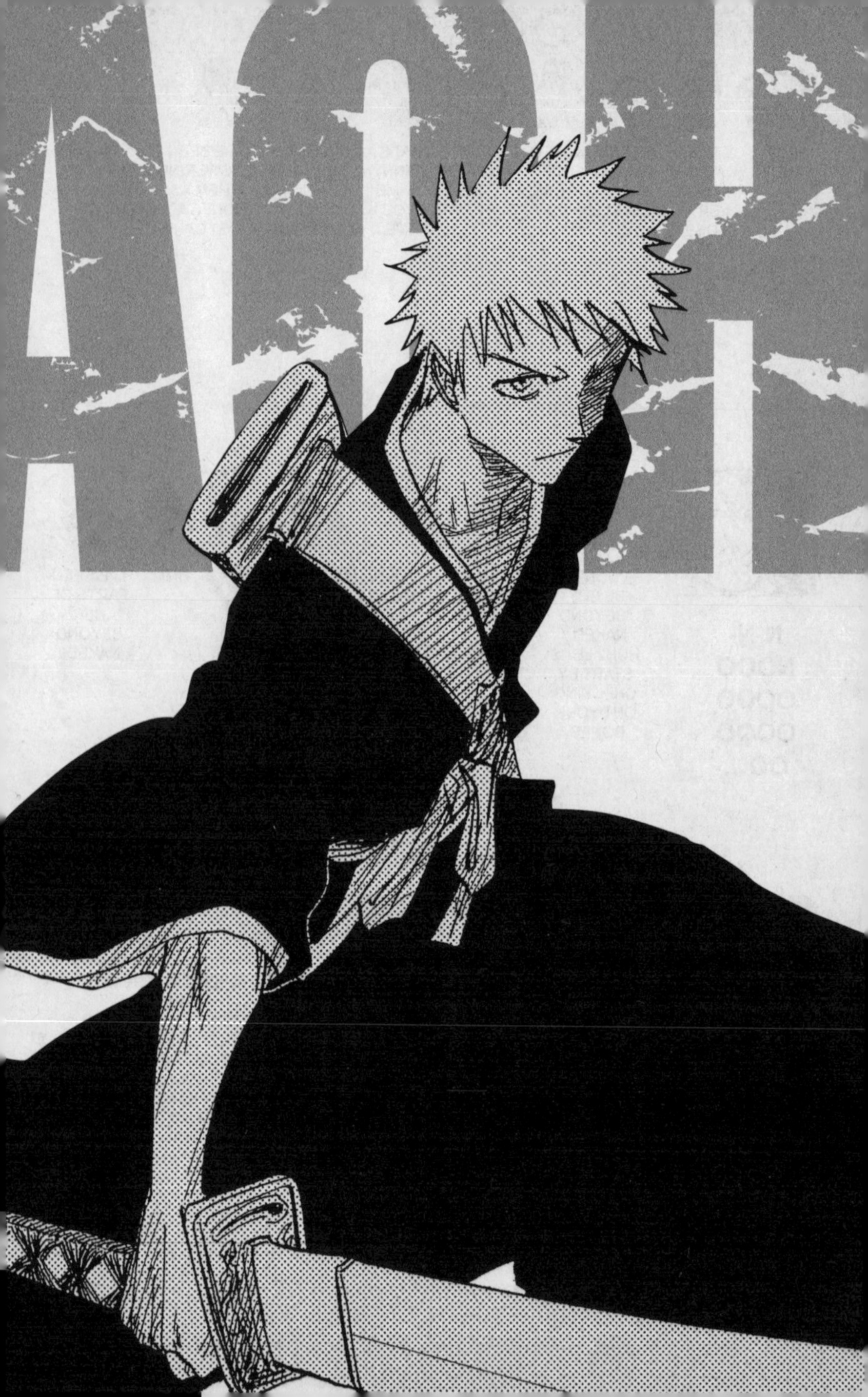

FIRST GRANDCHILD

初孫

FIRSTLING!

A NEVER BEFORE SEEN

Chapters 150 and 151 in this volume were
featured on the cover of *Weekly Shonen Jump*
and printed in color for two straight weeks.
According to the editor in chief, it was a
first for the magazine. I'm thankful.
Firsts are always nice. I love them.

-Tite Kubo, 2005

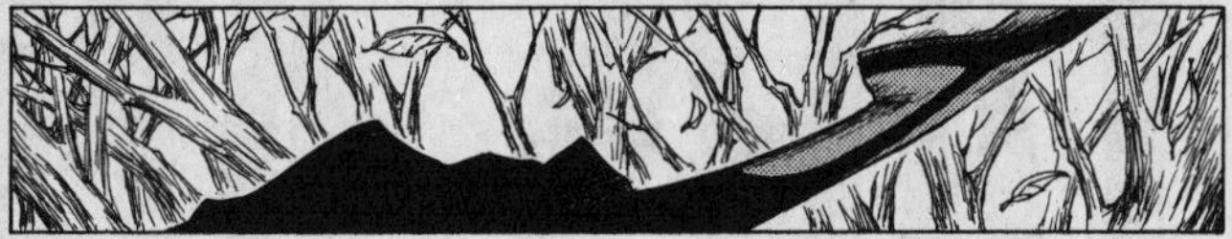

Your shadow, quietly
Like a vagrant poison needle,
Stitches my footsteps.

Your radiance, lithely
Like lightning striking a water tower,
Cuts down the source of my life.

BLEACH 18
THE DEATHBERRY RETURNS

Shonen Jump Manga

STARS AND

浮竹十四郎

Jûshirô Ukitake

Shunsui Kyôraku

京楽春水

Ichigo Kurosaki

黒崎一護

plot

As Rukia's date with death looms ever nearer, Ichigo struggles desperately to achieve Bankai. Meanwhile, Orihime and the others, lacking a leader, enlist the aid of the fearsome Kenpachi Zaraki. And Renji, fearing that Ichigo will be too late to save Rukia, goes to save her himself, only to be intercepted by the deadly Byakuya Kuchiki!

BLEACH ALL

砕蜂

Soi Fon

山本元柳斎重國

**Shigekuni Genryûsai
Yamamoto**

Yoruichi Shihôin

四楓院夜一

STORIES

BLEACH18

THE DEATHBERRY RETURNS

Contents

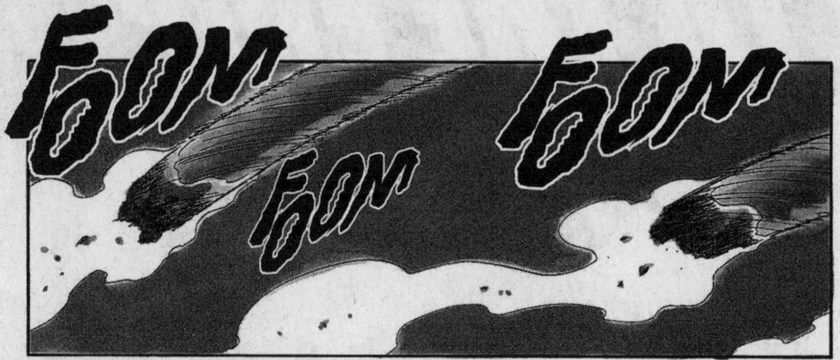
BOM
BOM
BOM

150. Countdown to the End: 0

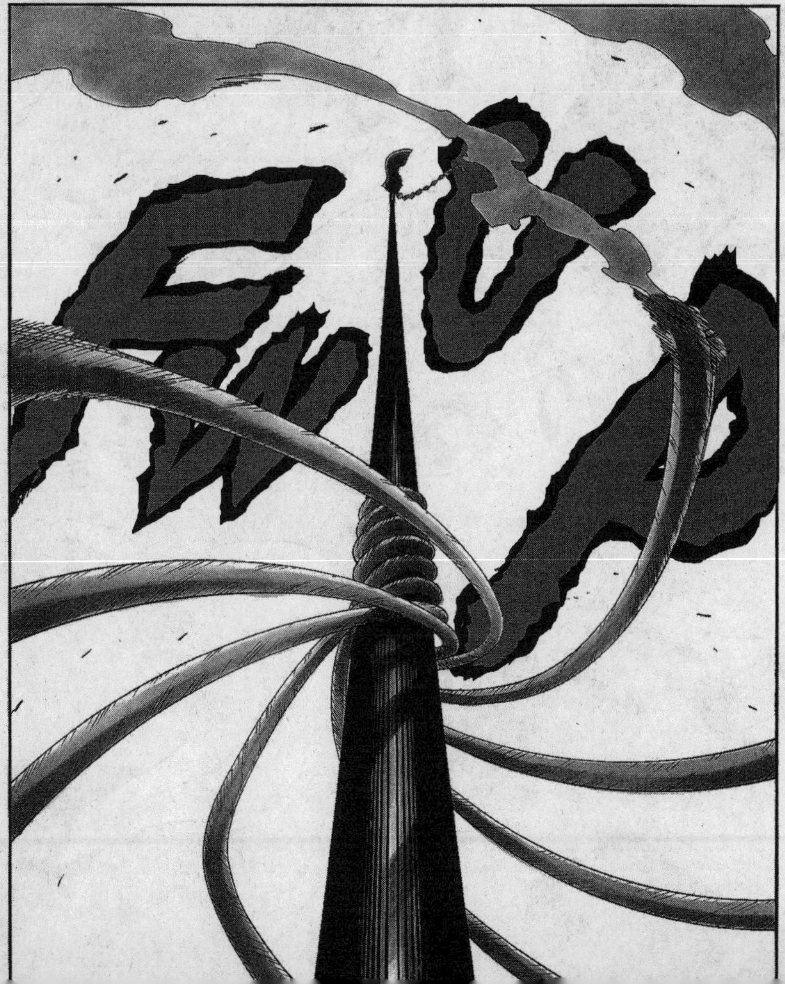

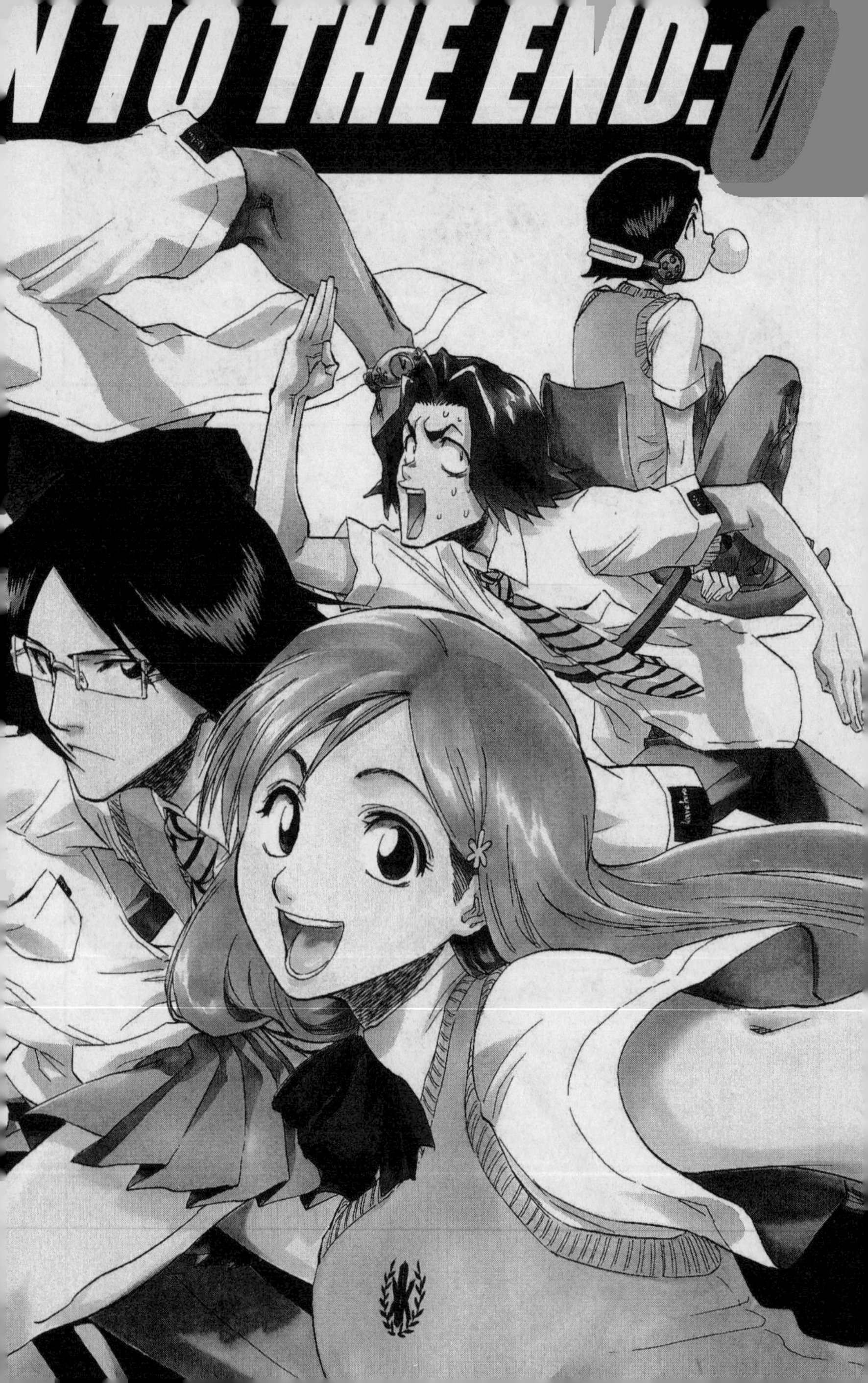
N TO THE END: 0

150.COUNTDOW

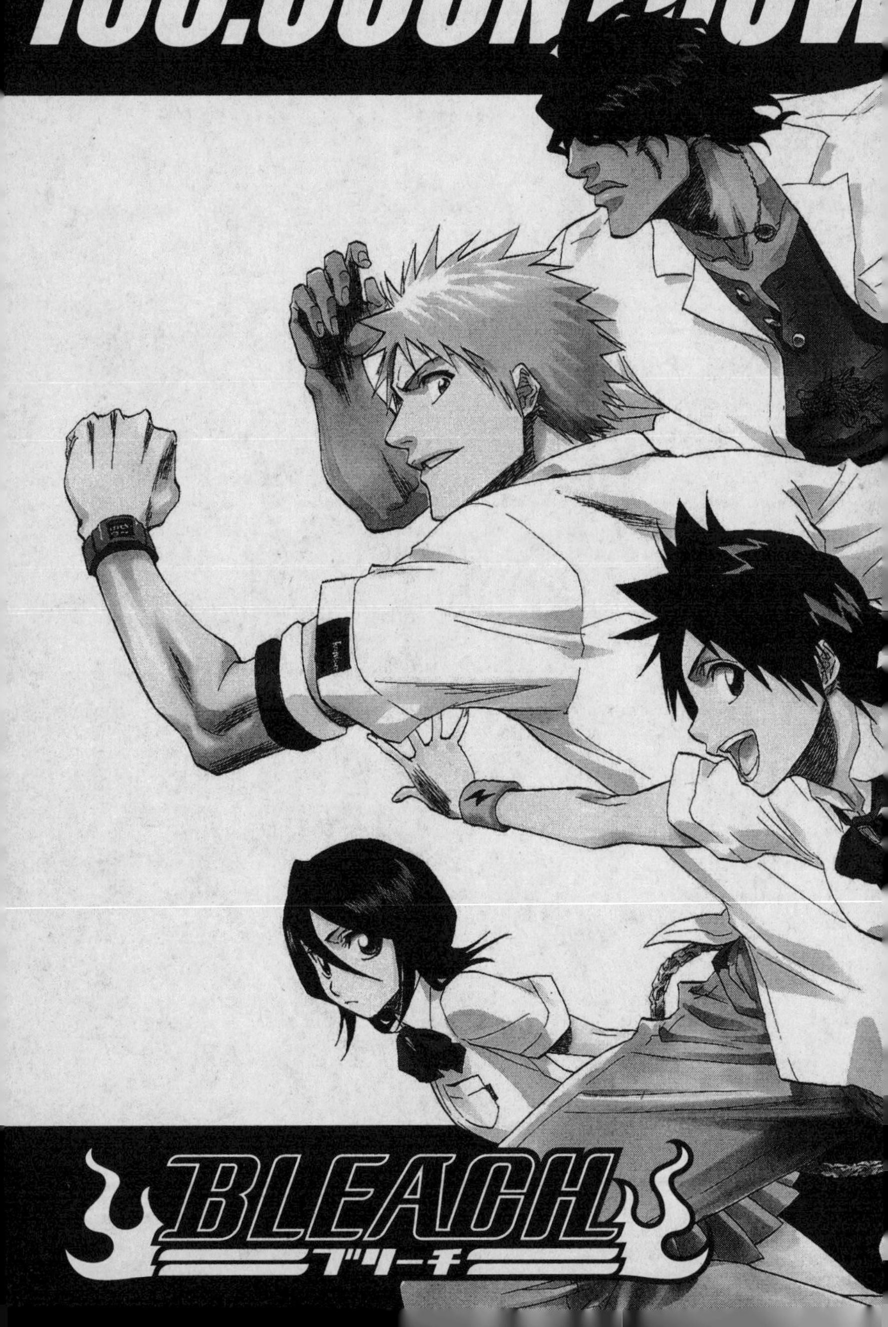
BLEACH
ブリーチ

BLEACH
ブリーチ

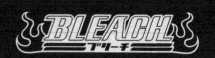

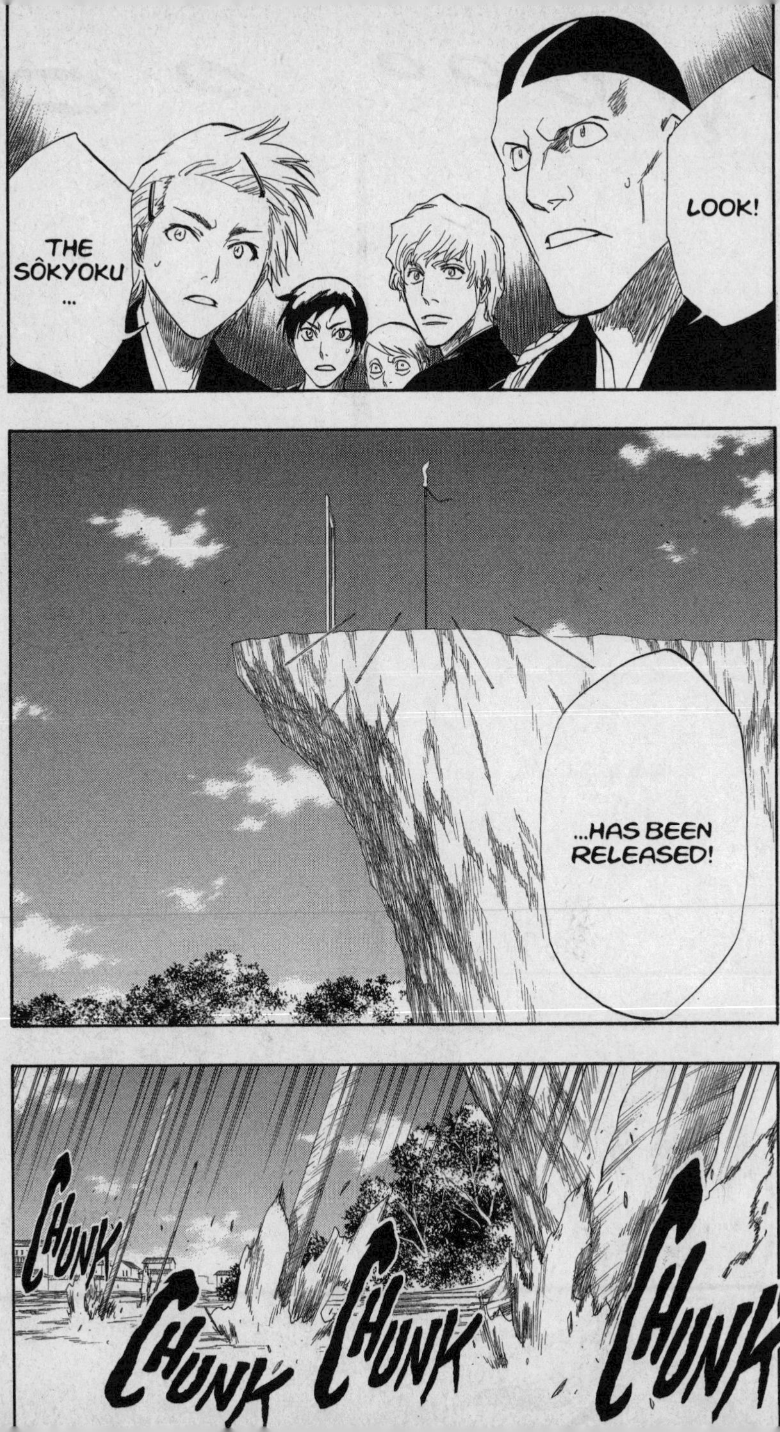
LOOK!
THE SÔKYOKU ...
...HAS BEEN RELEASED!
CHUNK
CHUNK
CHUNK
CHUNK

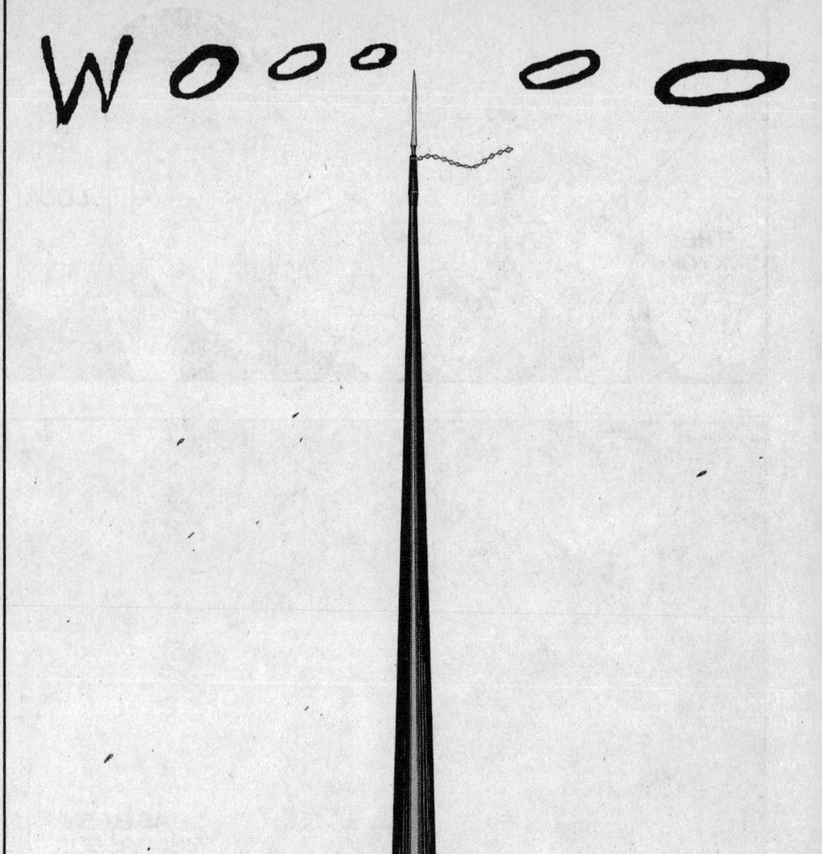
WOOOOOO
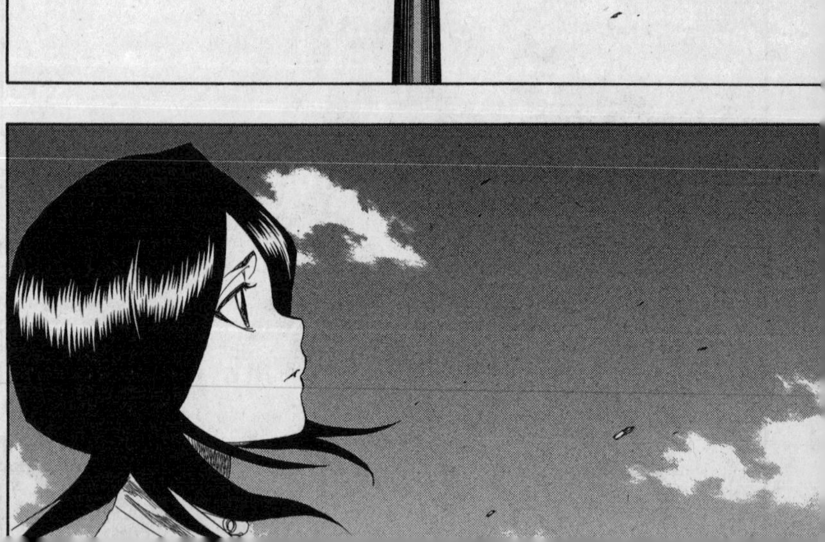

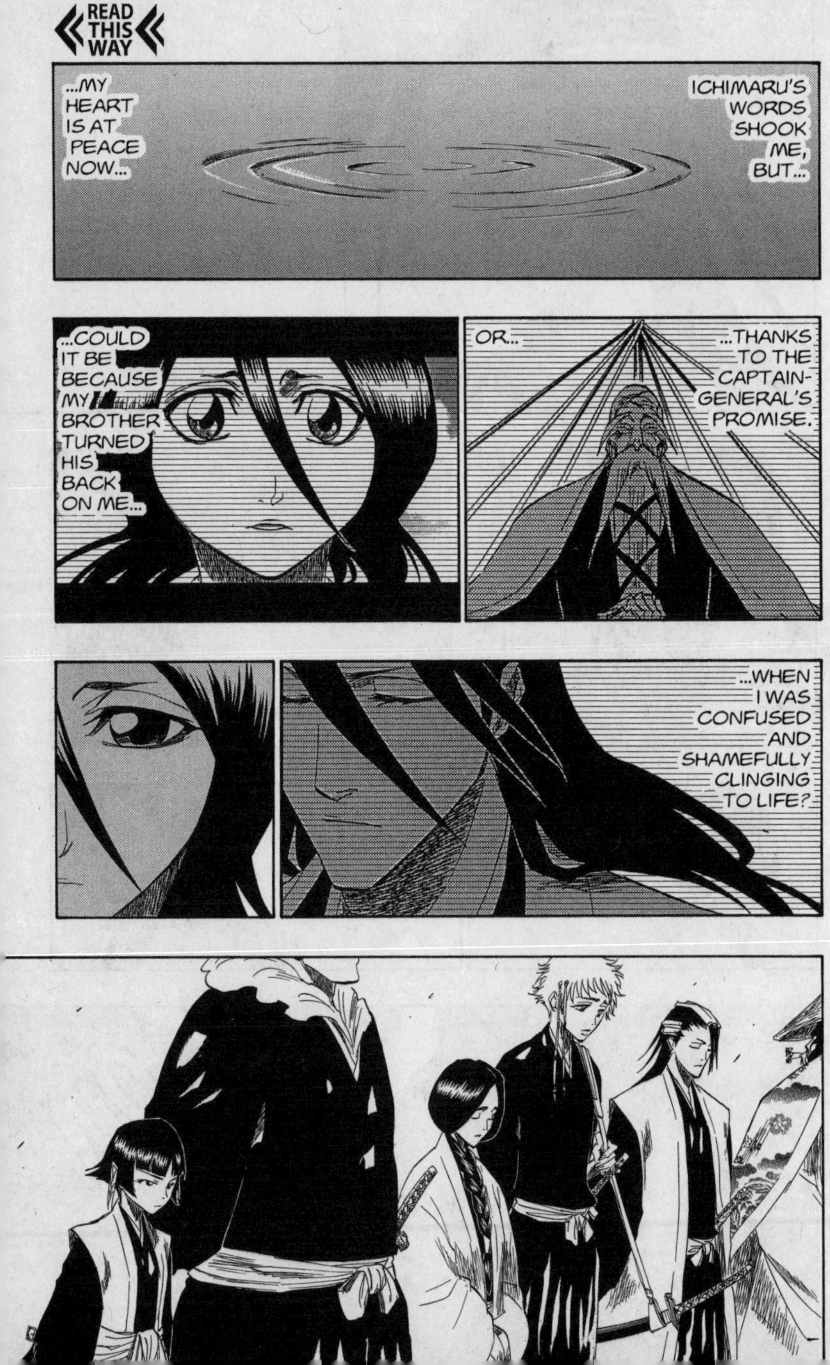
READ THIS WAY
ICHIMARU'S WORDS SHOOK ME, BUT...
...MY HEART IS AT PEACE NOW...
OR...
...THANKS TO THE CAPTAIN-GENERAL'S PROMISE.
...COULD IT BE BECAUSE MY BROTHER TURNED HIS BACK ON ME...
...WHEN I WAS CONFUSED AND SHAMEFULLY CLINGING TO LIFE?

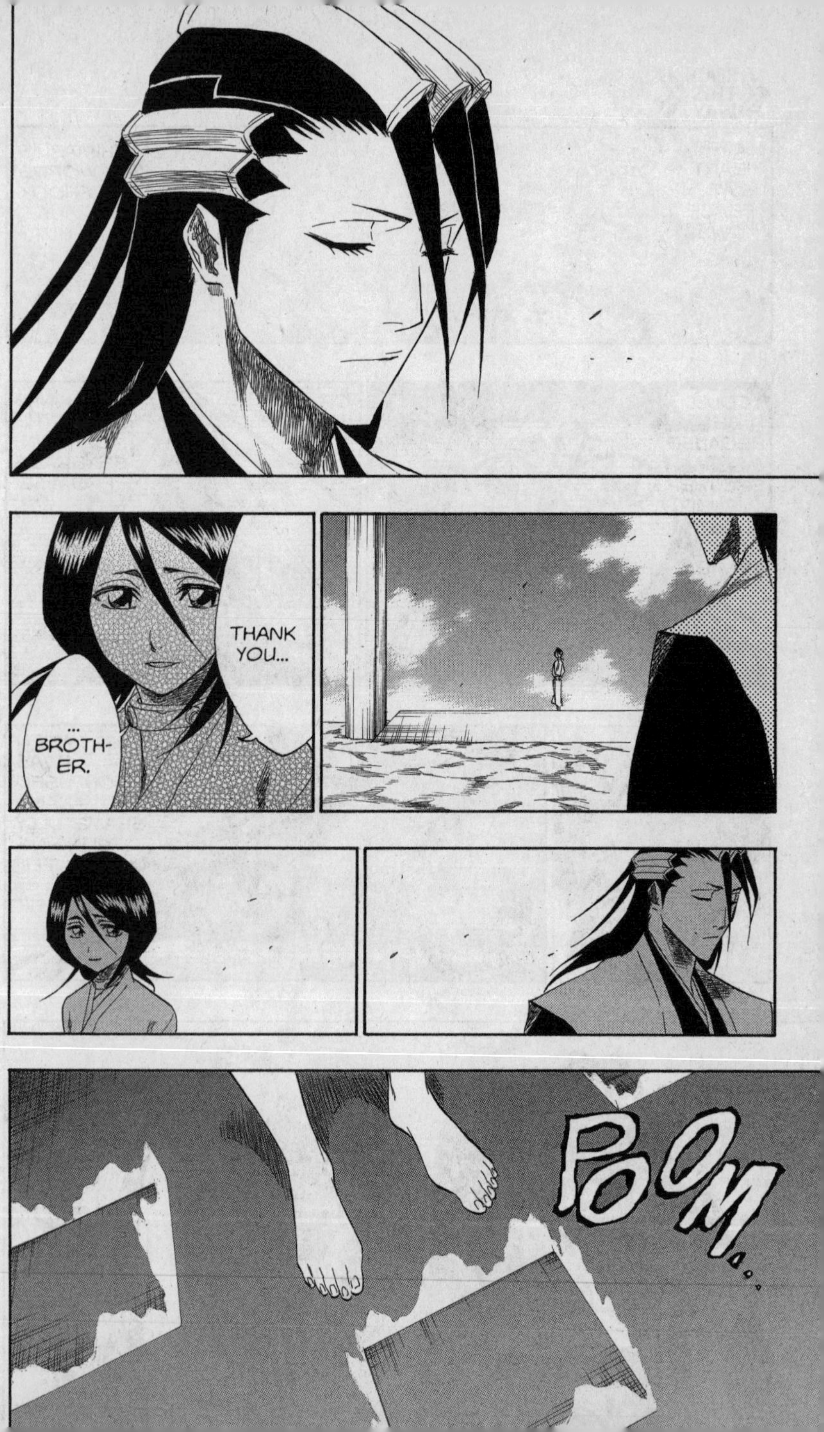
THANK YOU...
... BROTH-ER.
POOM...

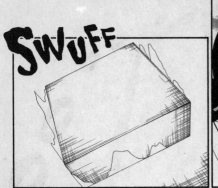

SWUFF

SWUFF

SWUFF

WH

OOM

!

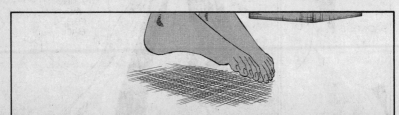

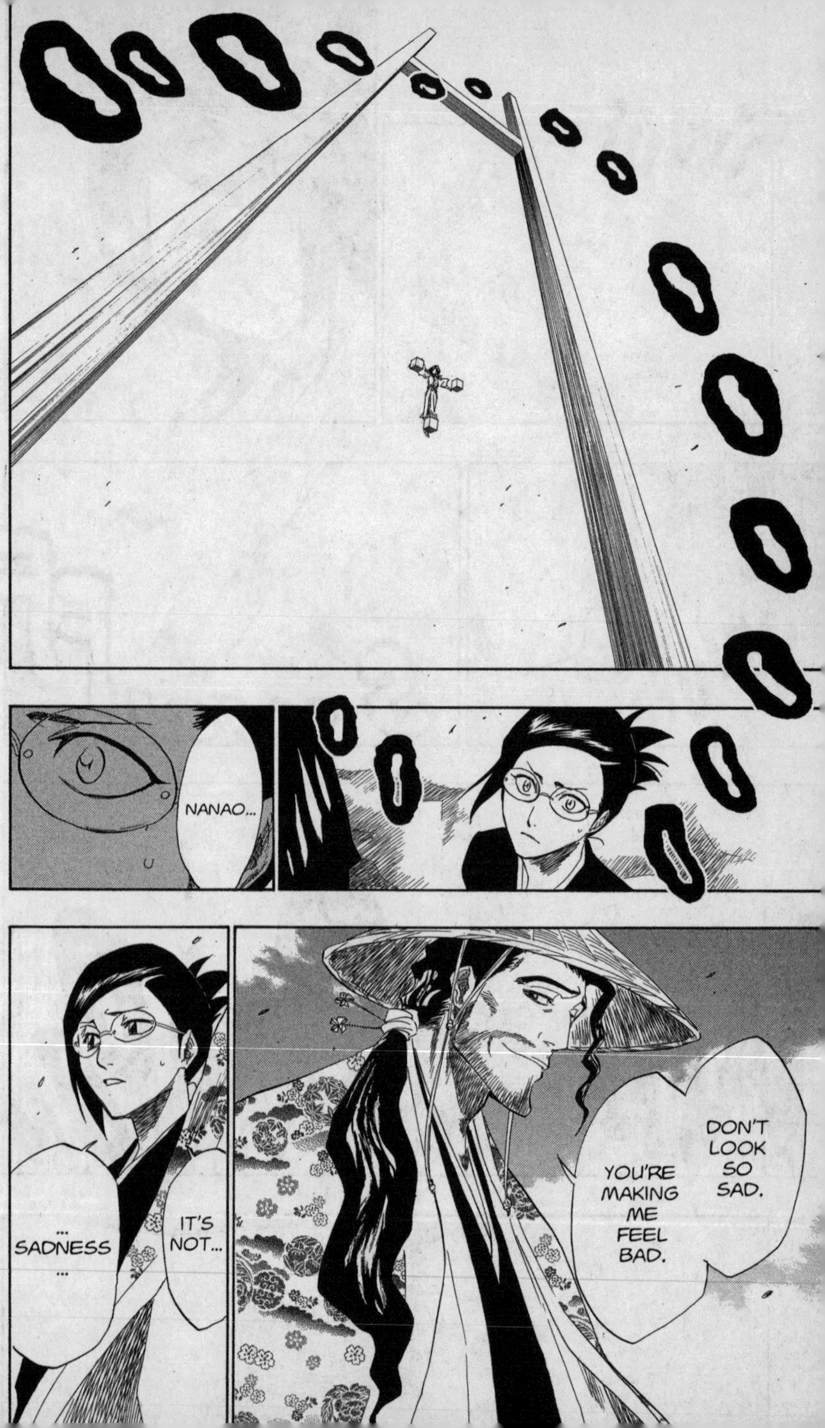
NANAO...
DON'T LOOK SO SAD.
YOU'RE MAKING ME FEEL BAD.
IT'S NOT...
...SADNESS...

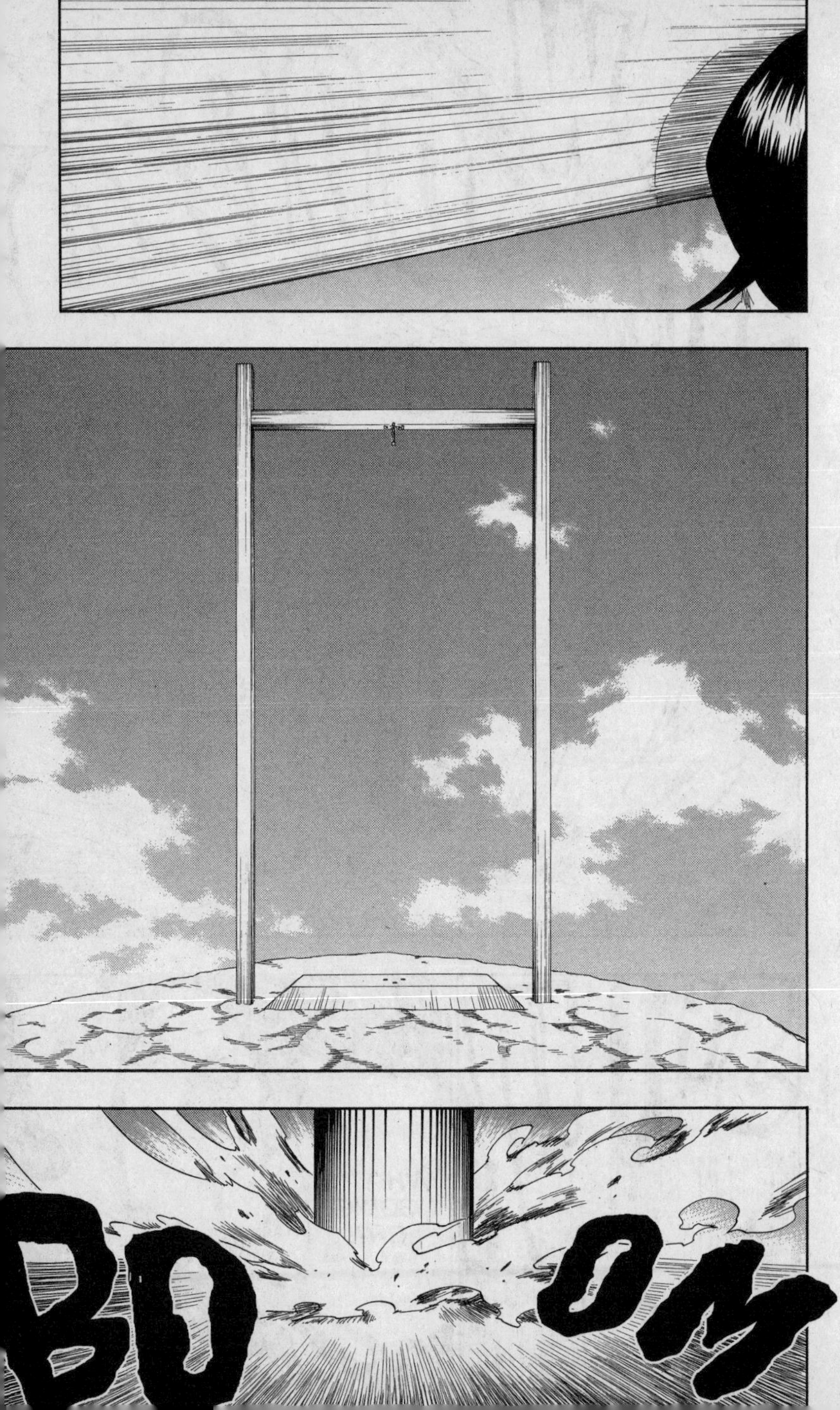
BOOM

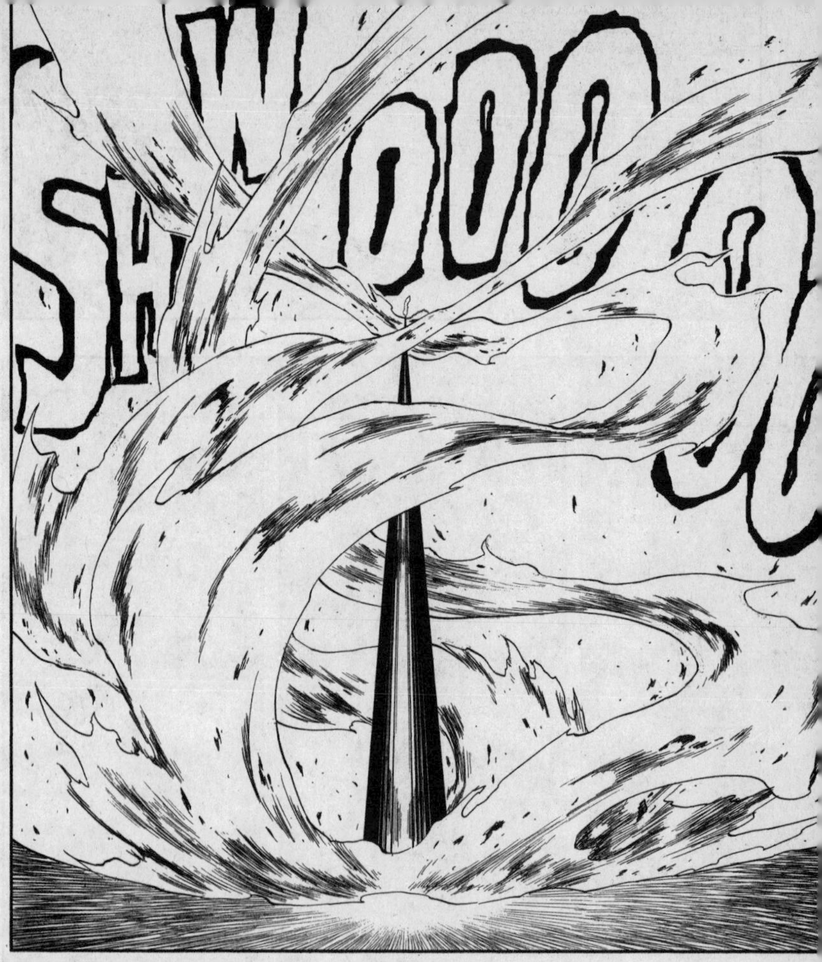

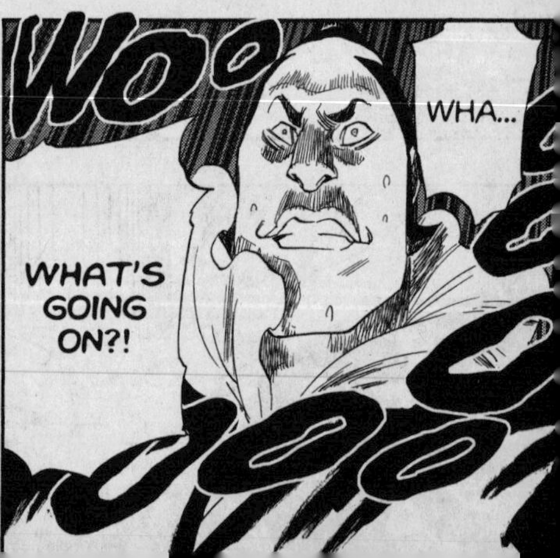
WHA...
WHAT'S GOING ON?!

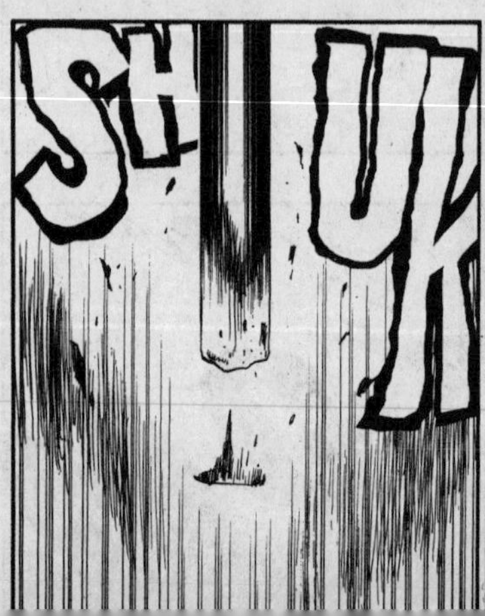
SHUK

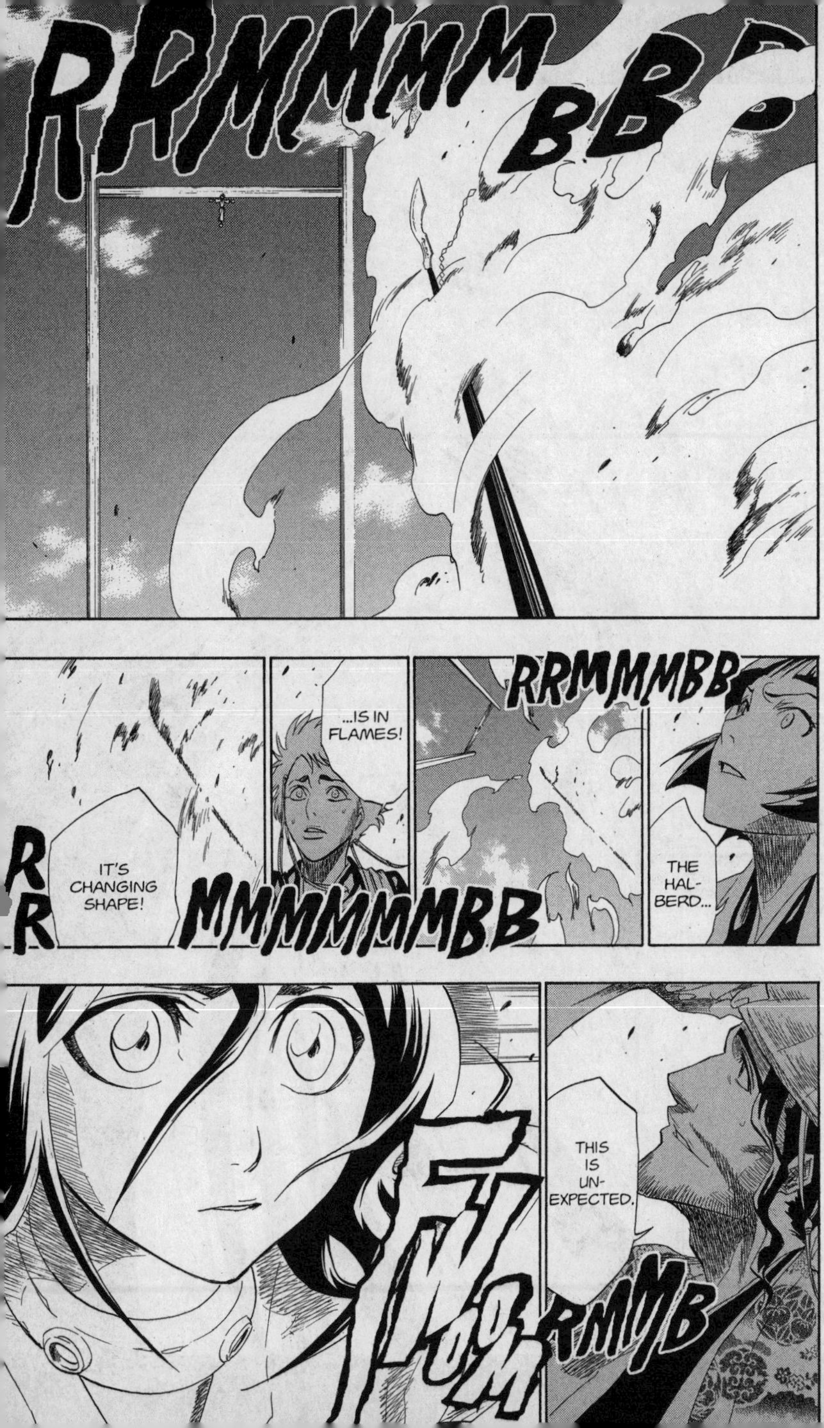
RRMMMMMBBB
RRMMMBB
THE HAL-BERD...
...IS IN FLAMES!
IT'S CHANGING SHAPE!
RRMMMMMMMBB
THIS IS UN-EXPECTED.
RMMMB

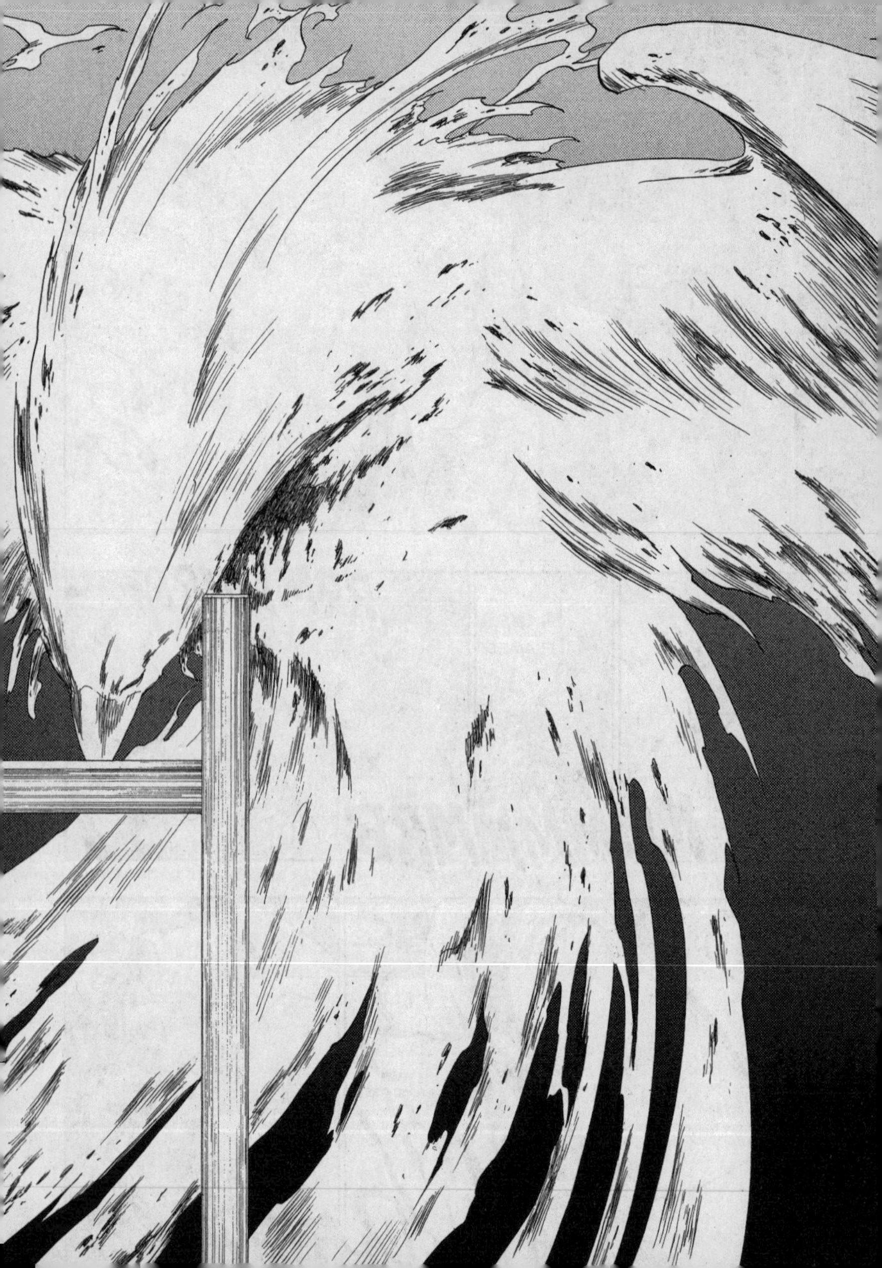

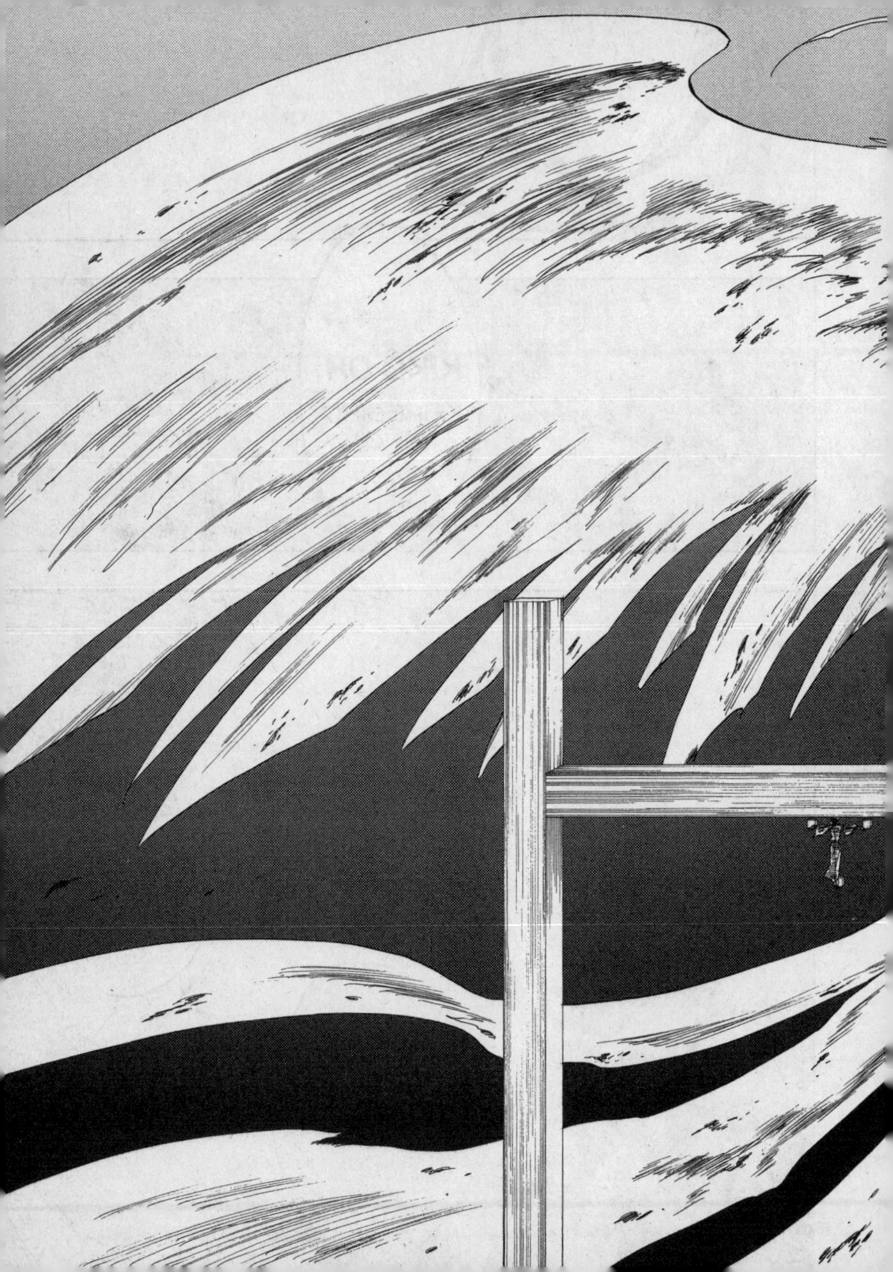

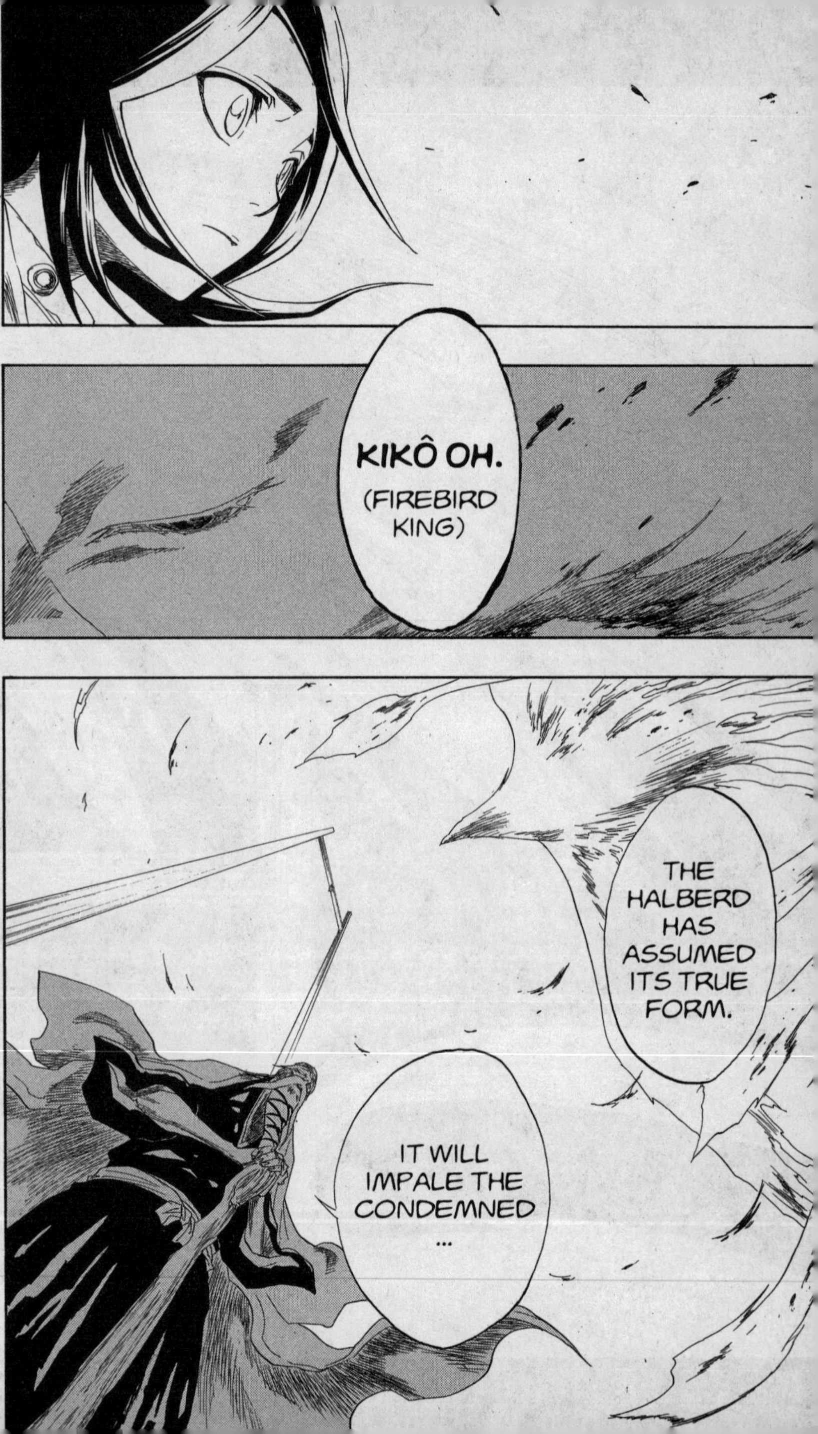
KIKÔ OH.
(FIREBIRD KING)
THE HALBERD HAS ASSUMED ITS TRUE FORM.
IT WILL IMPALE THE CONDEMNED ...

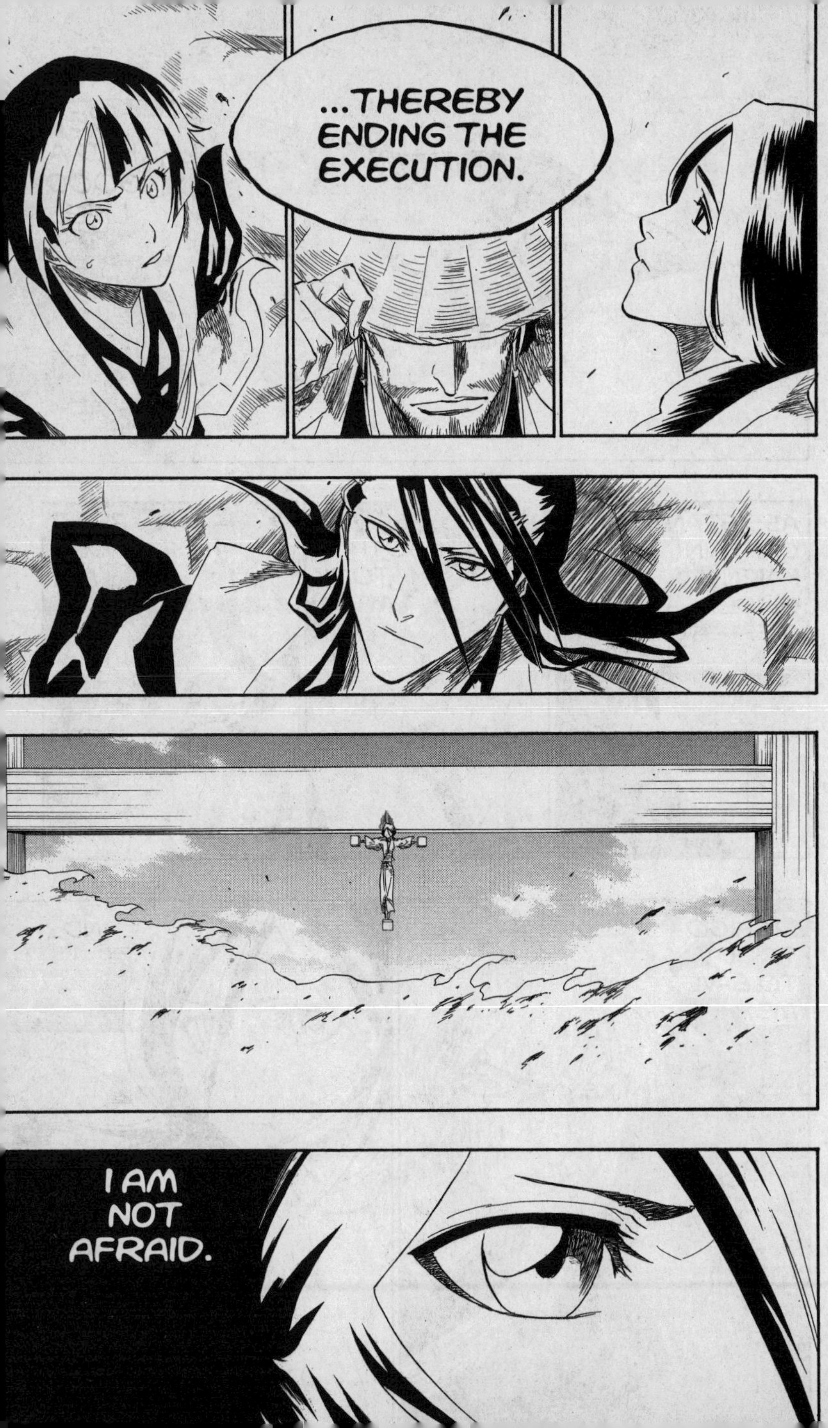
...THEREBY ENDING THE EXECUTION.
I AM NOT AFRAID.

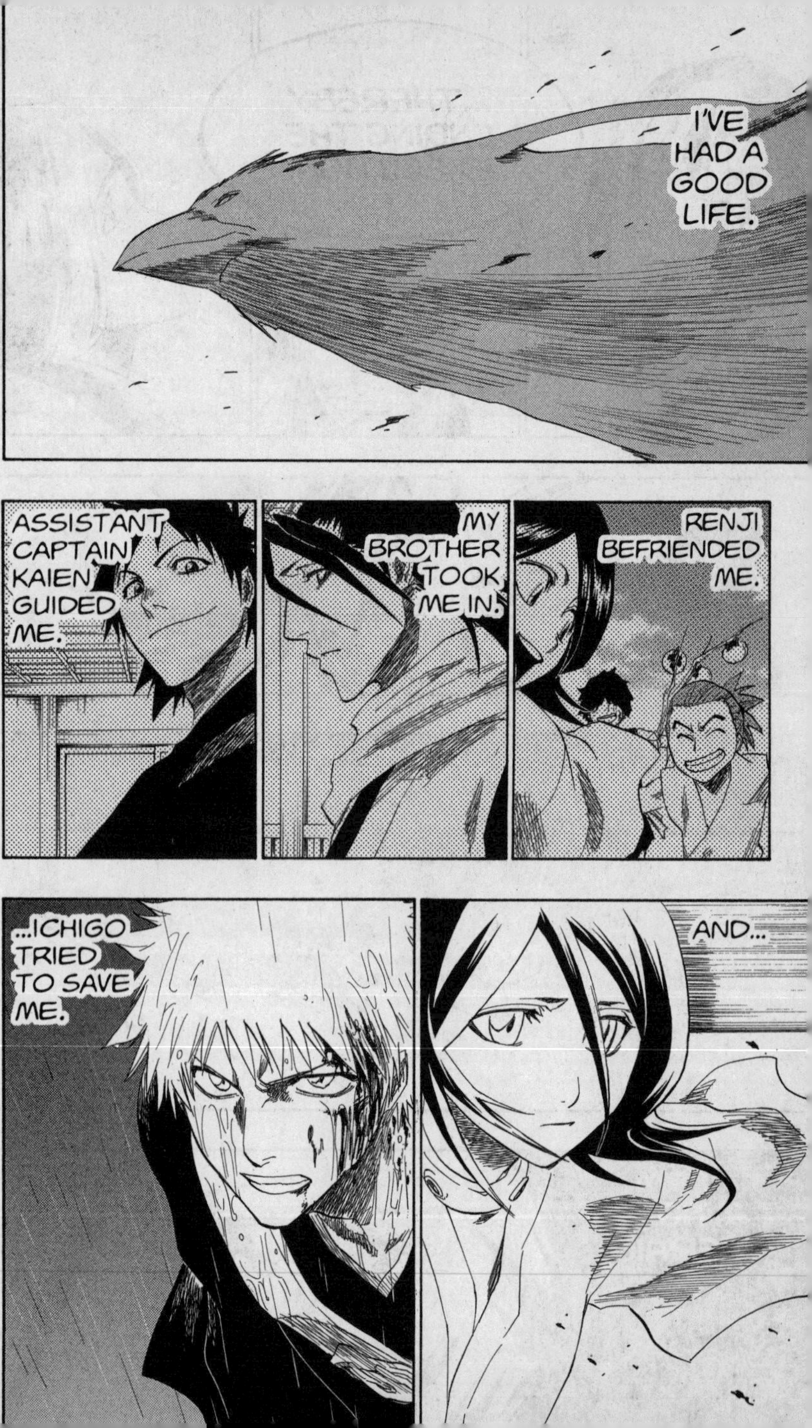
I'VE HAD A GOOD LIFE.
RENJI BEFRIENDED ME.
MY BROTHER TOOK ME IN.
ASSISTANT CAPTAIN KAIEN GUIDED ME.
AND...
...ICHIGO TRIED TO SAVE ME.

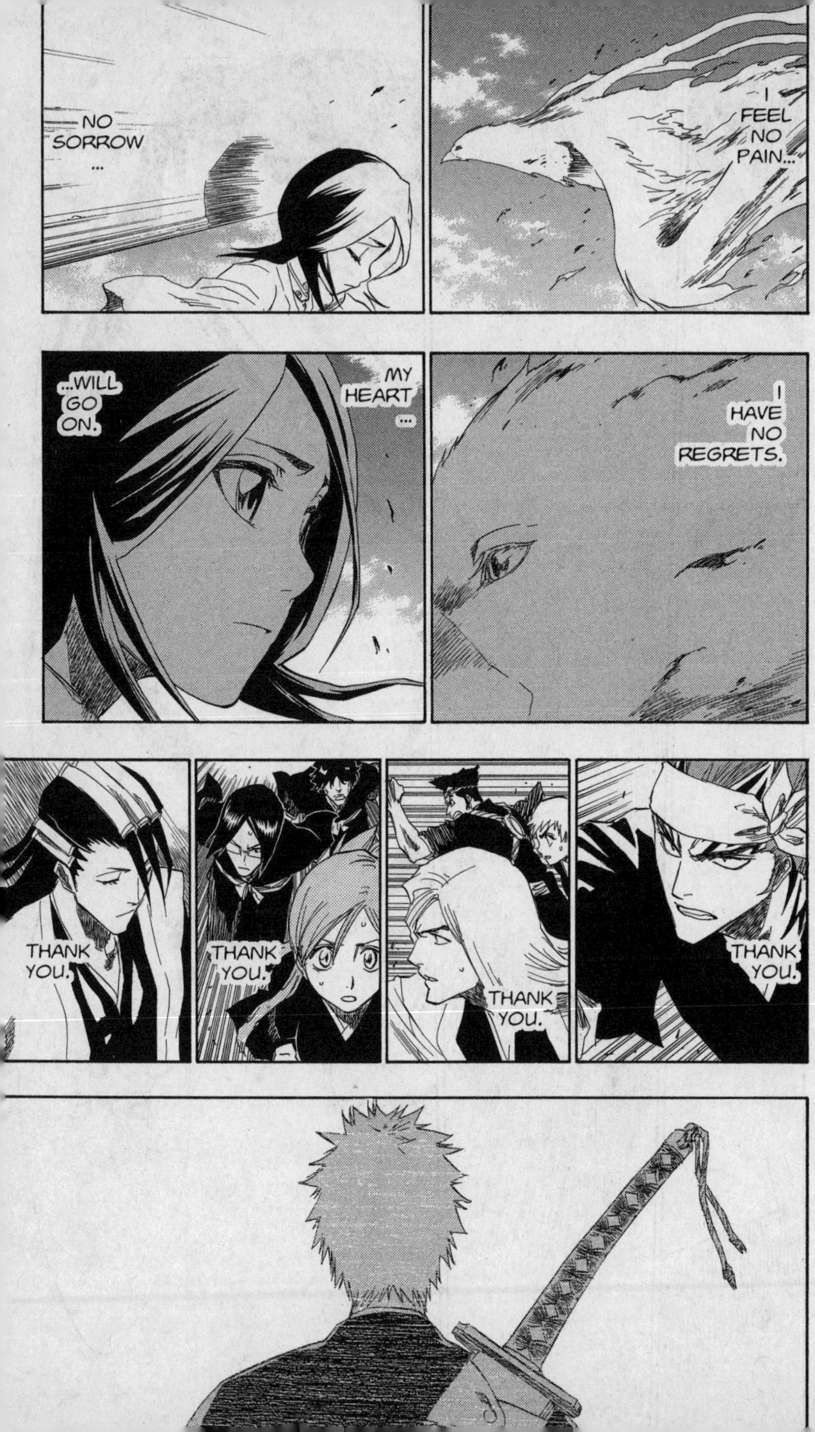
I FEEL NO PAIN...
NO SORROW ...
I HAVE NO REGRETS.
MY HEART ...
...WILL GO ON.
THANK YOU.
THANK YOU.
THANK YOU.
THANK YOU.

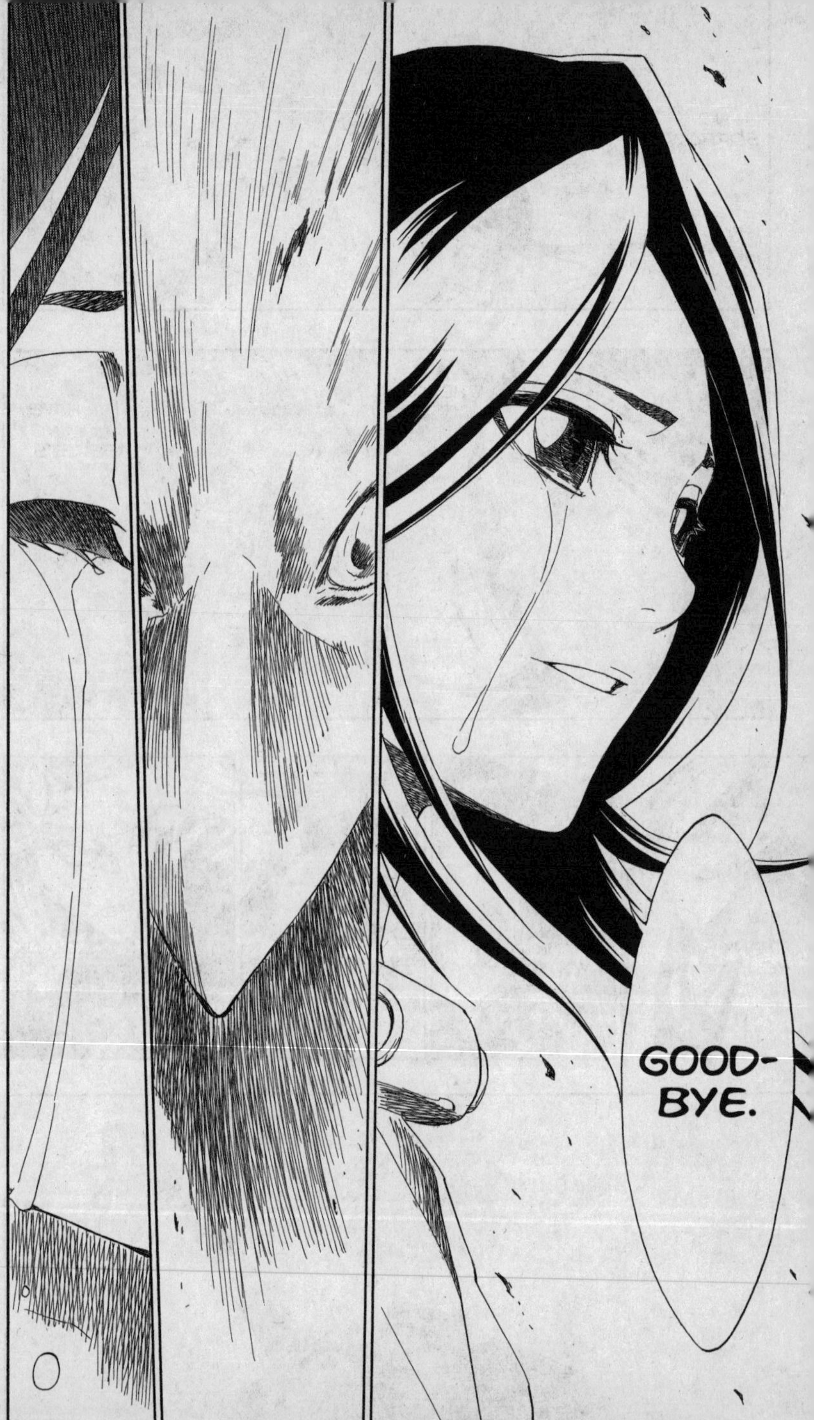
GOOD-BYE.

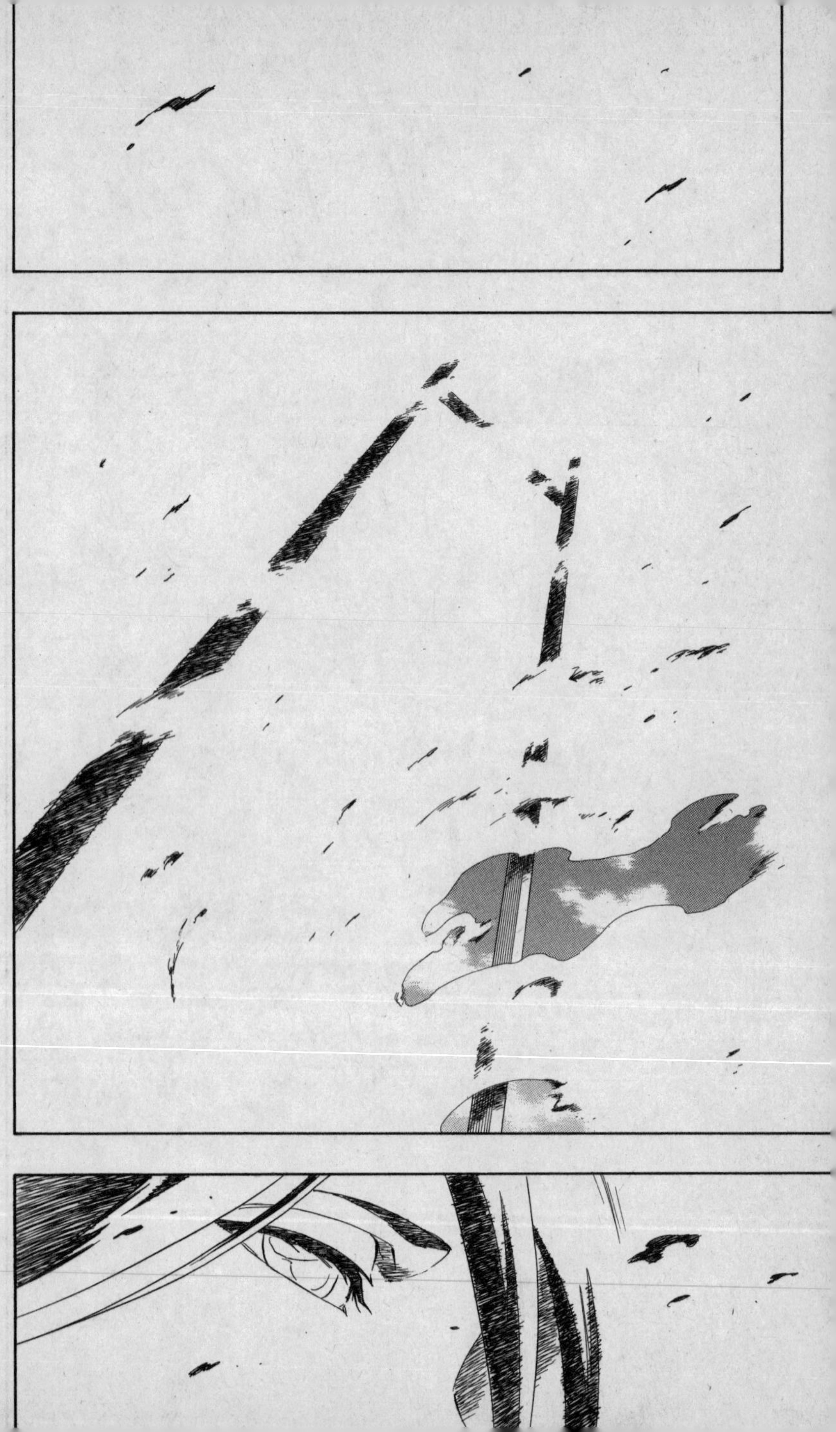

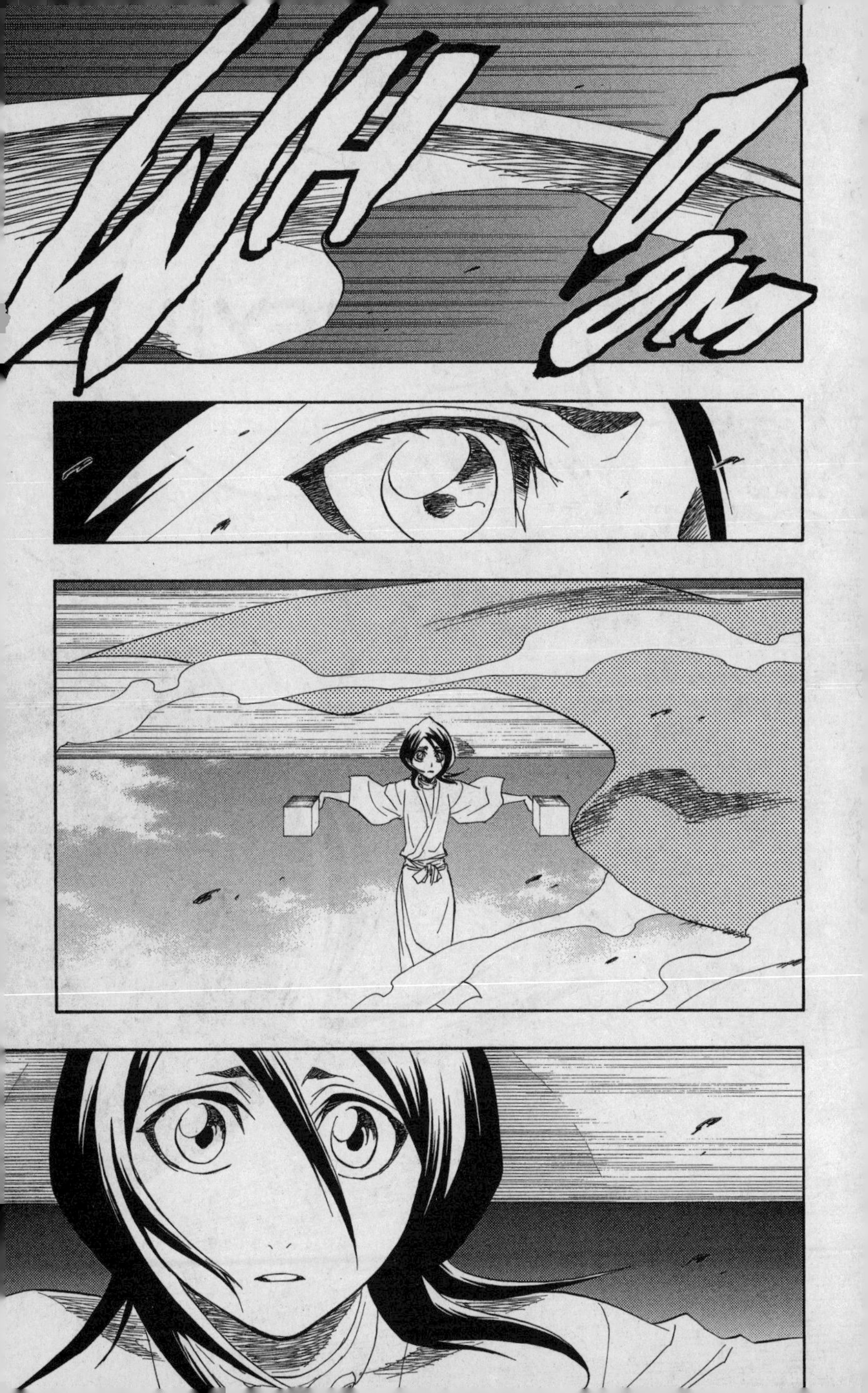
WHOOM

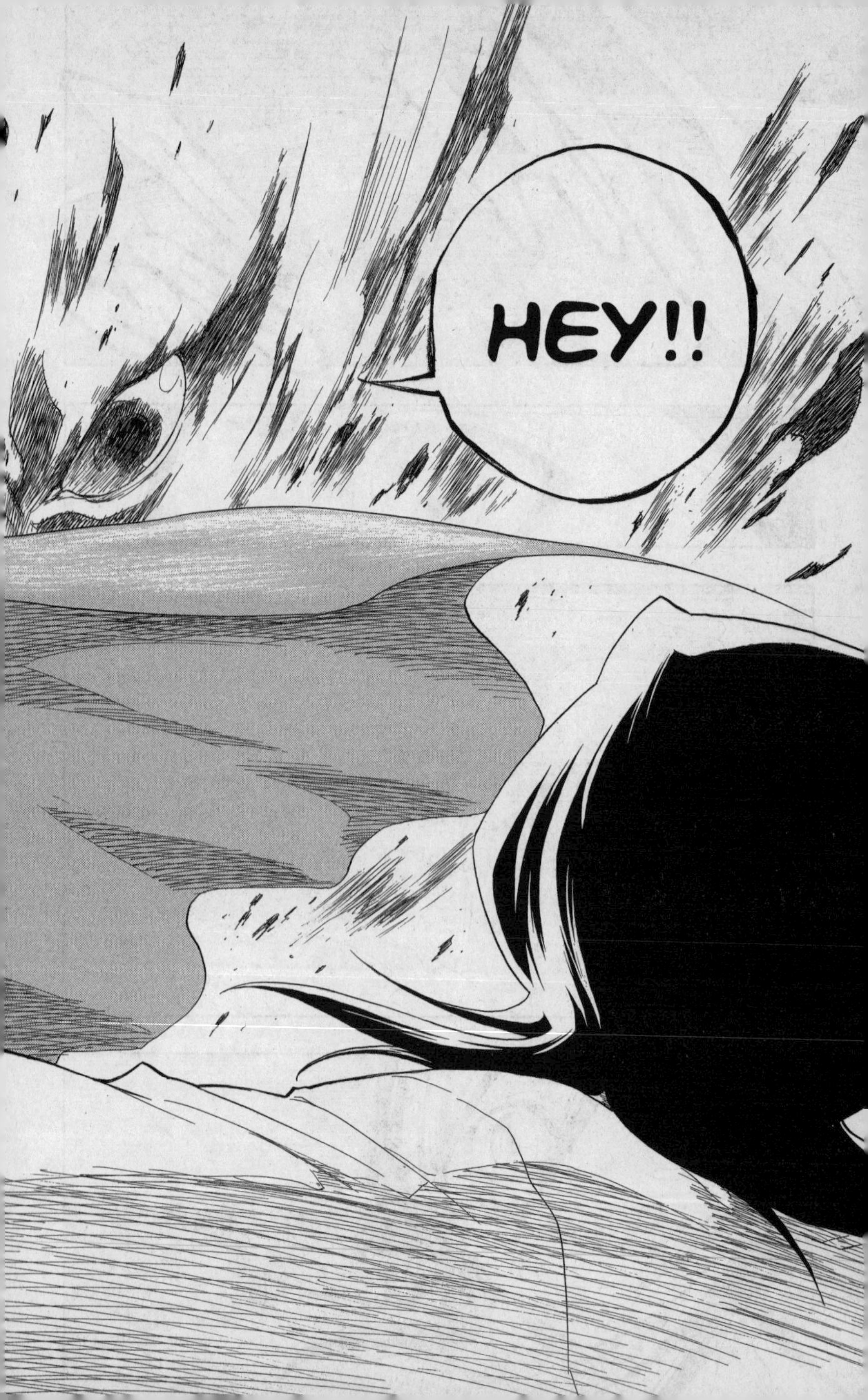
HEY!!

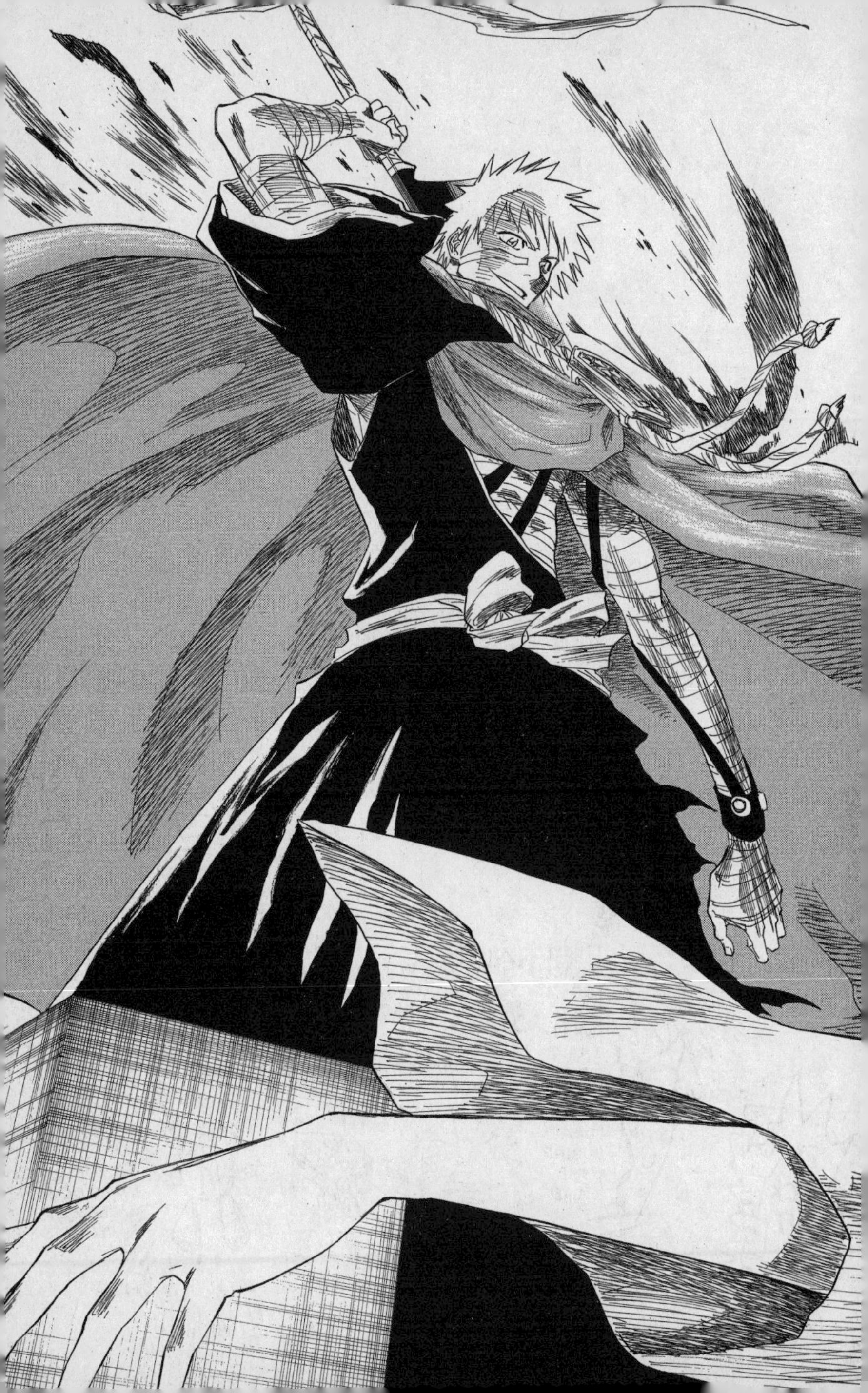

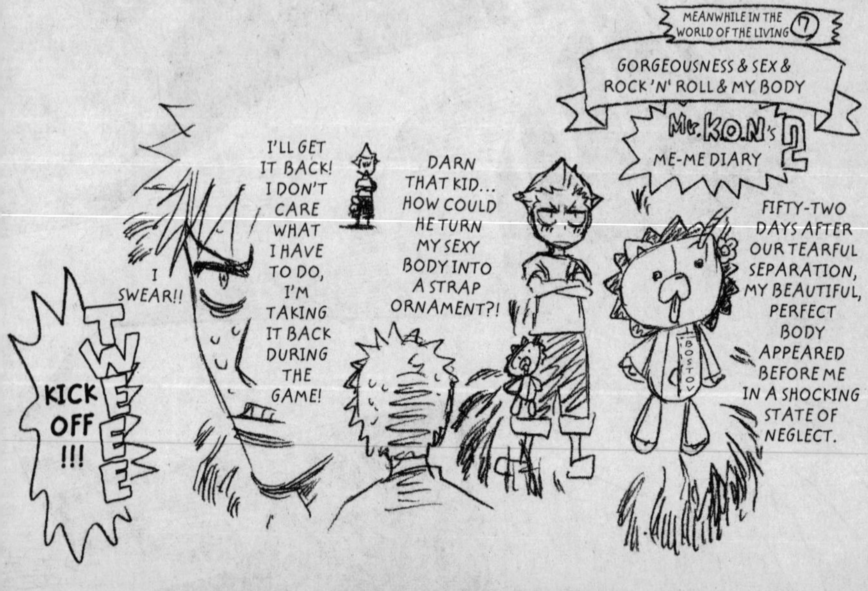
MEANWHILE IN THE WORLD OF THE LIVING 7
GORGEOUSNESS & SEX & ROCK 'N' ROLL & MY BODY
Mr. K.O.N's ME-ME DIARY 2
FIFTY-TWO DAYS AFTER OUR TEARFUL SEPARATION, MY BEAUTIFUL, PERFECT BODY APPEARED BEFORE ME IN A SHOCKING STATE OF NEGLECT.
BOSTOV
DARN THAT KID... HOW COULD HE TURN MY SEXY BODY INTO A STRAP ORNAMENT?!
I'LL GET IT BACK! I DON'T CARE WHAT I HAVE TO DO, I'M TAKING IT BACK DURING THE GAME!
I SWEAR!!
TWEEE
KICK OFF!!!

151. Deathberry Returns

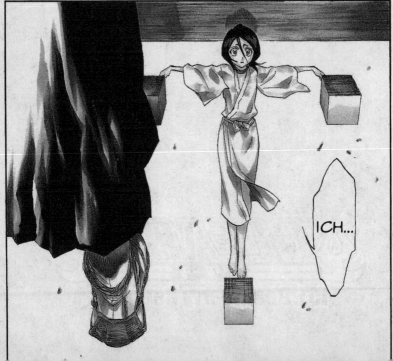

ICH...

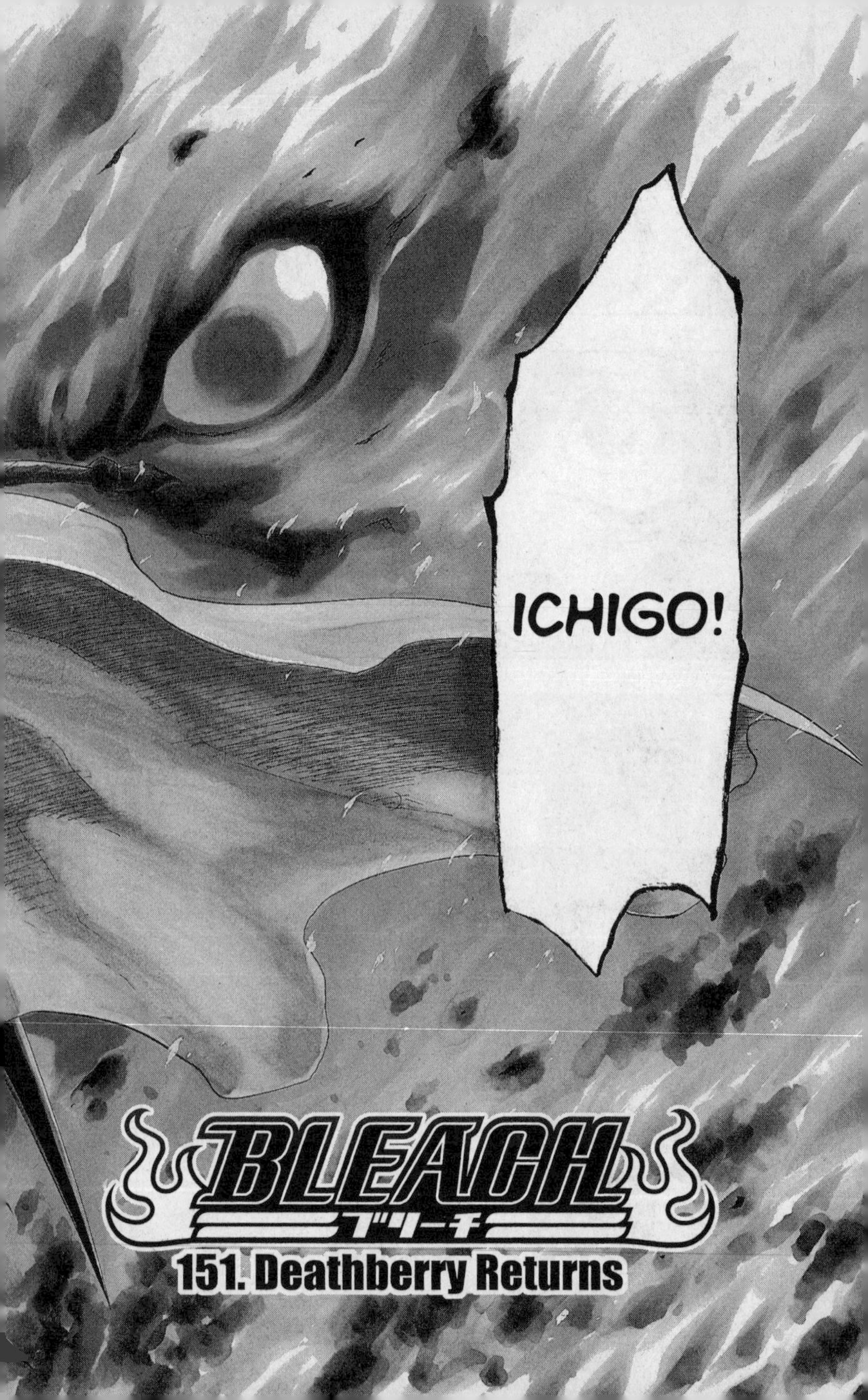
ICHIGO!
BLEACH
ブリーチ
151. Deathberry Returns

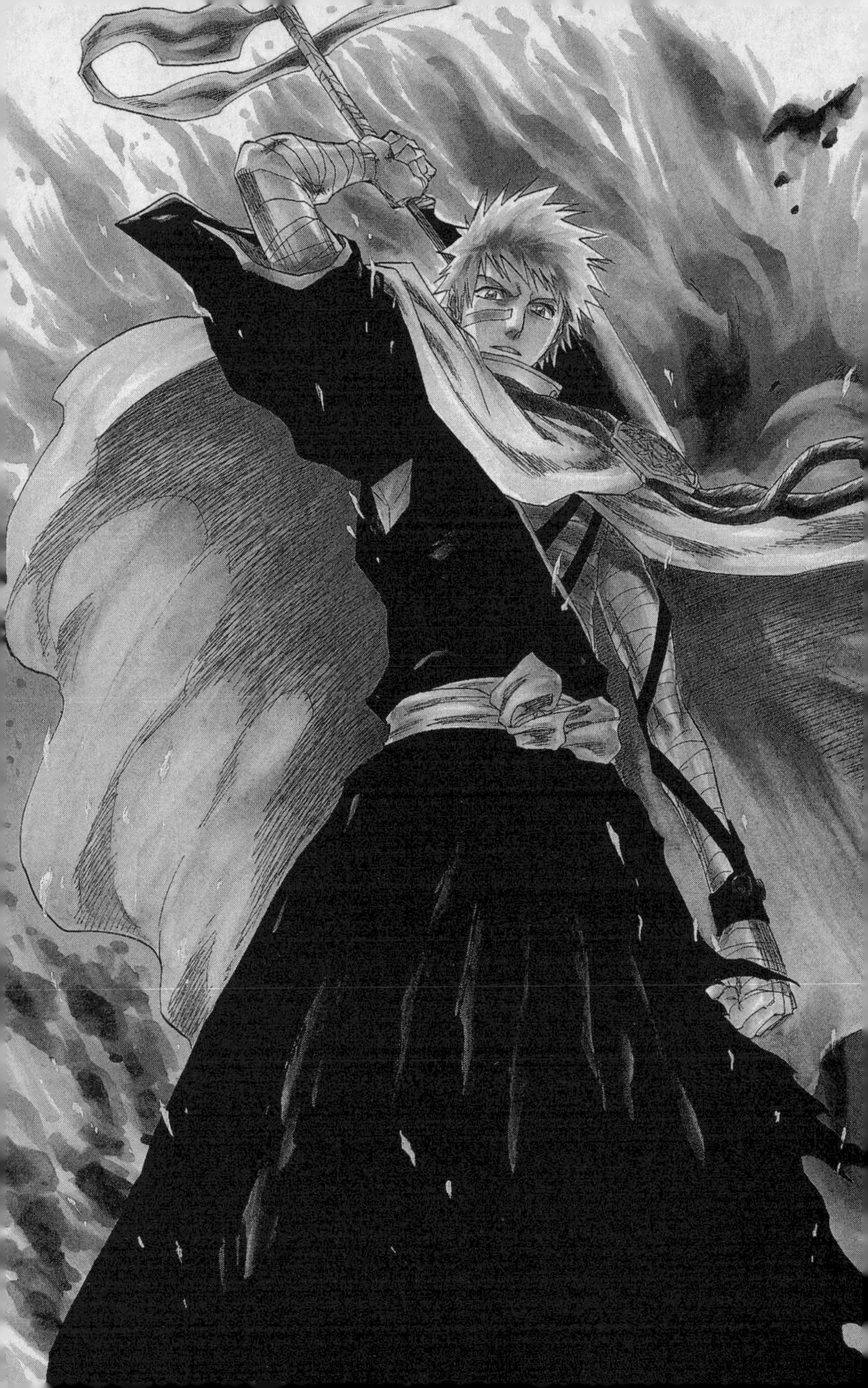

BLEACH
ブリーチ

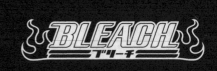

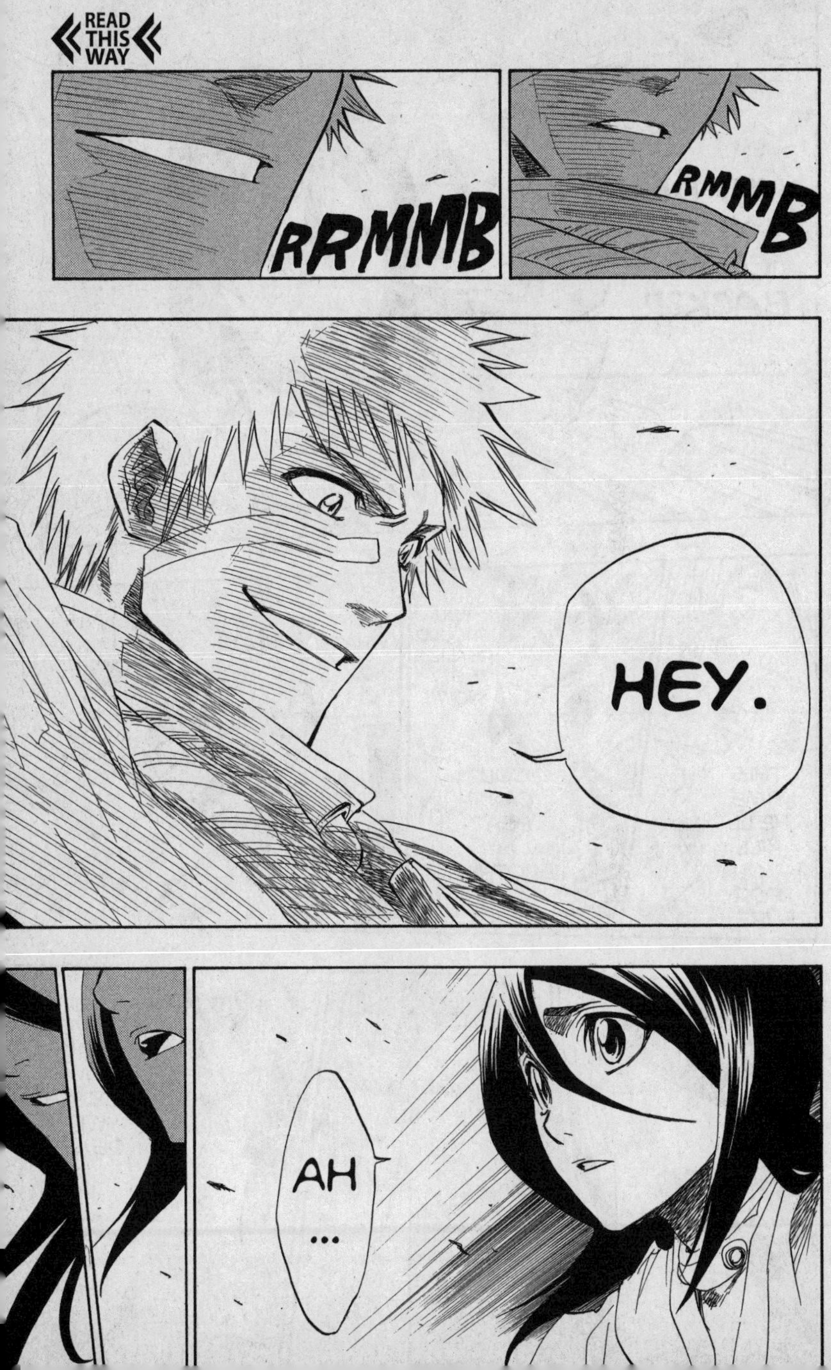
READ THIS WAY
RMMB
RRMMB
HEY.
AH
...

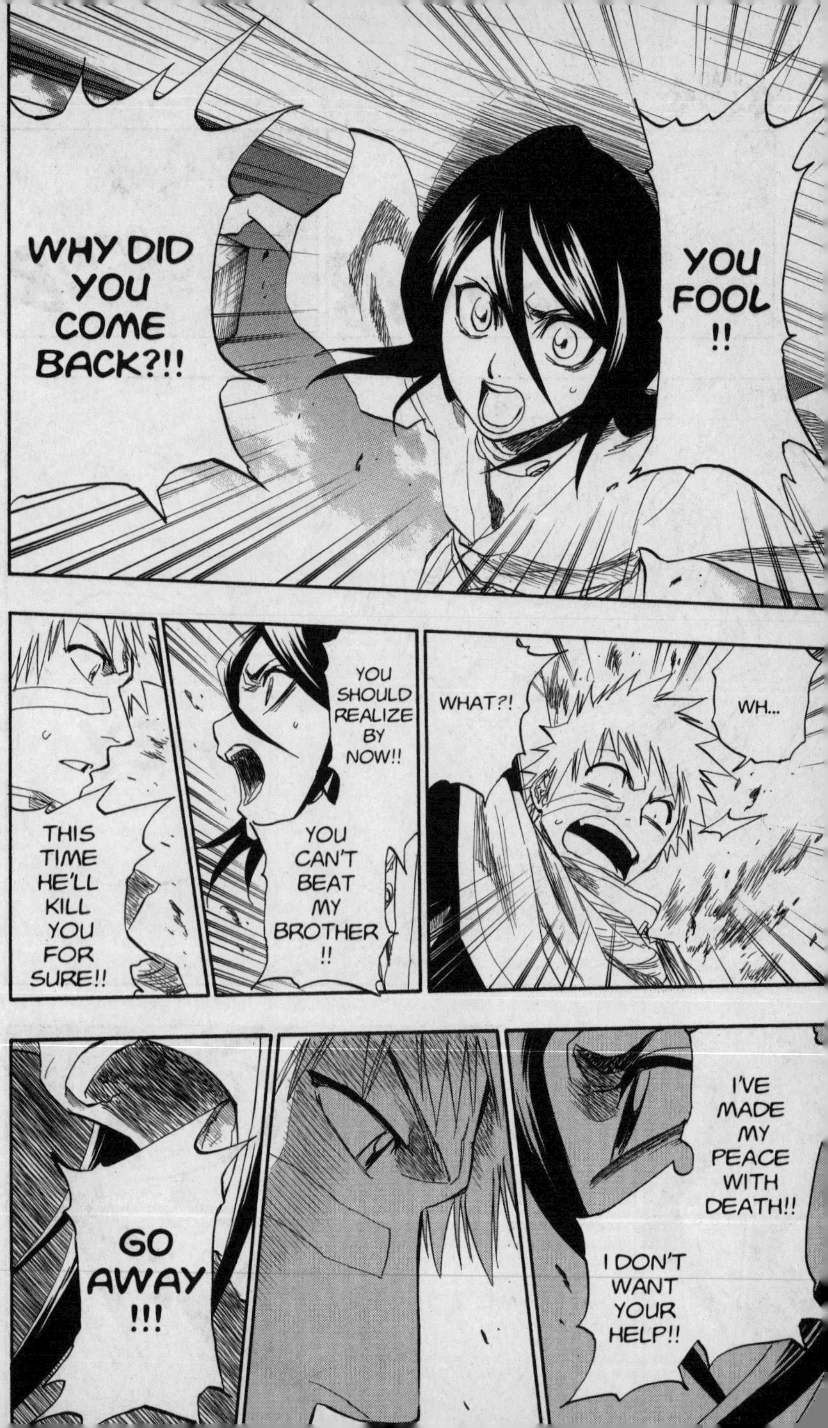
YOU FOOL!!
WHY DID YOU COME BACK?!!
WH...
WHAT?!
YOU SHOULD REALIZE BY NOW!!
YOU CAN'T BEAT MY BROTHER!!
THIS TIME HE'LL KILL YOU FOR SURE!!
I'VE MADE MY PEACE WITH DEATH!!
I DON'T WANT YOUR HELP!!
GO AWAY!!!

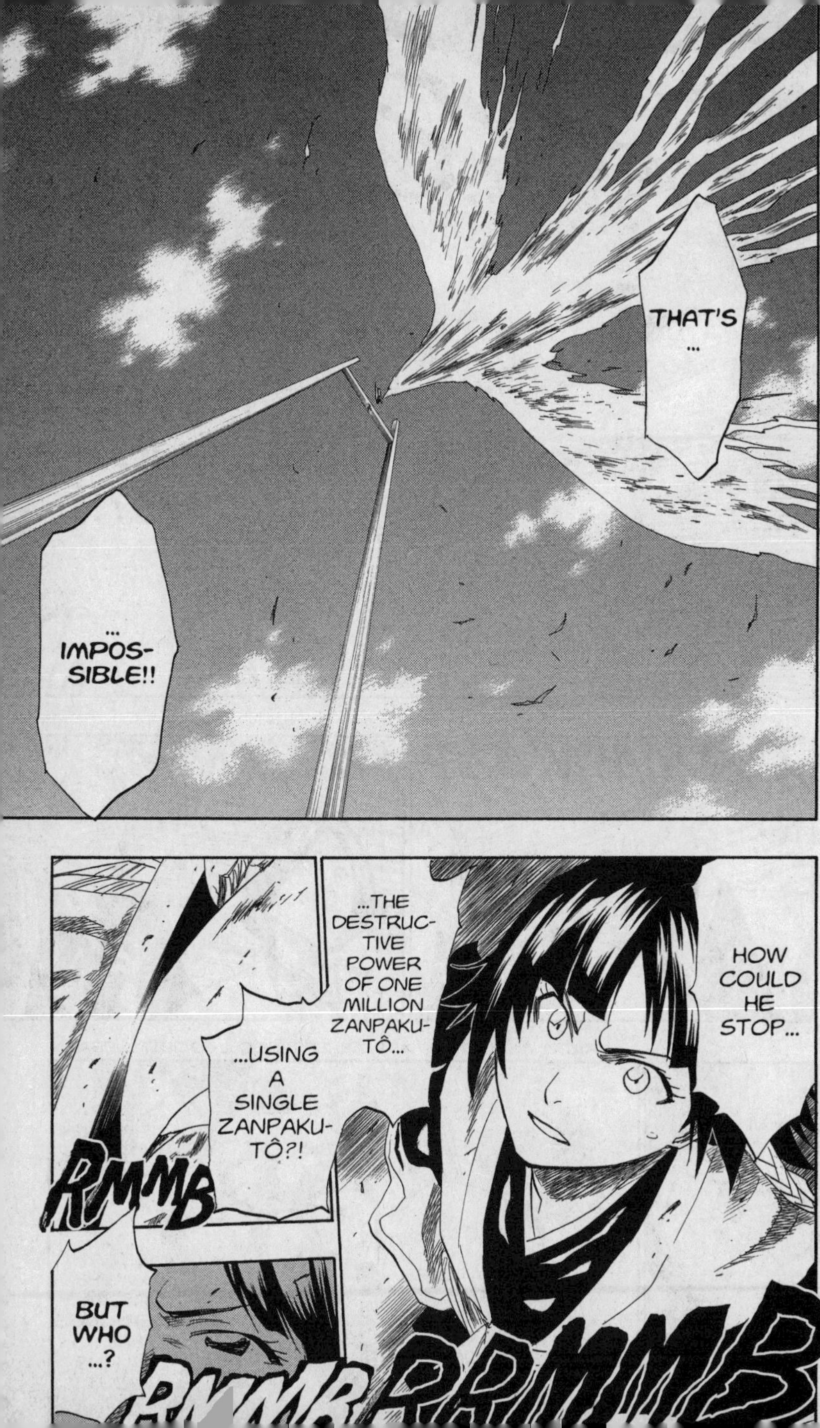
THAT'S ...
... IMPOSSIBLE!!
HOW COULD HE STOP...
...THE DESTRUCTIVE POWER OF ONE MILLION ZANPAKUTÔ...
...USING A SINGLE ZANPAKUTÔ?!
RMMB
RMMMB
RMMB
BUT WHO ...?

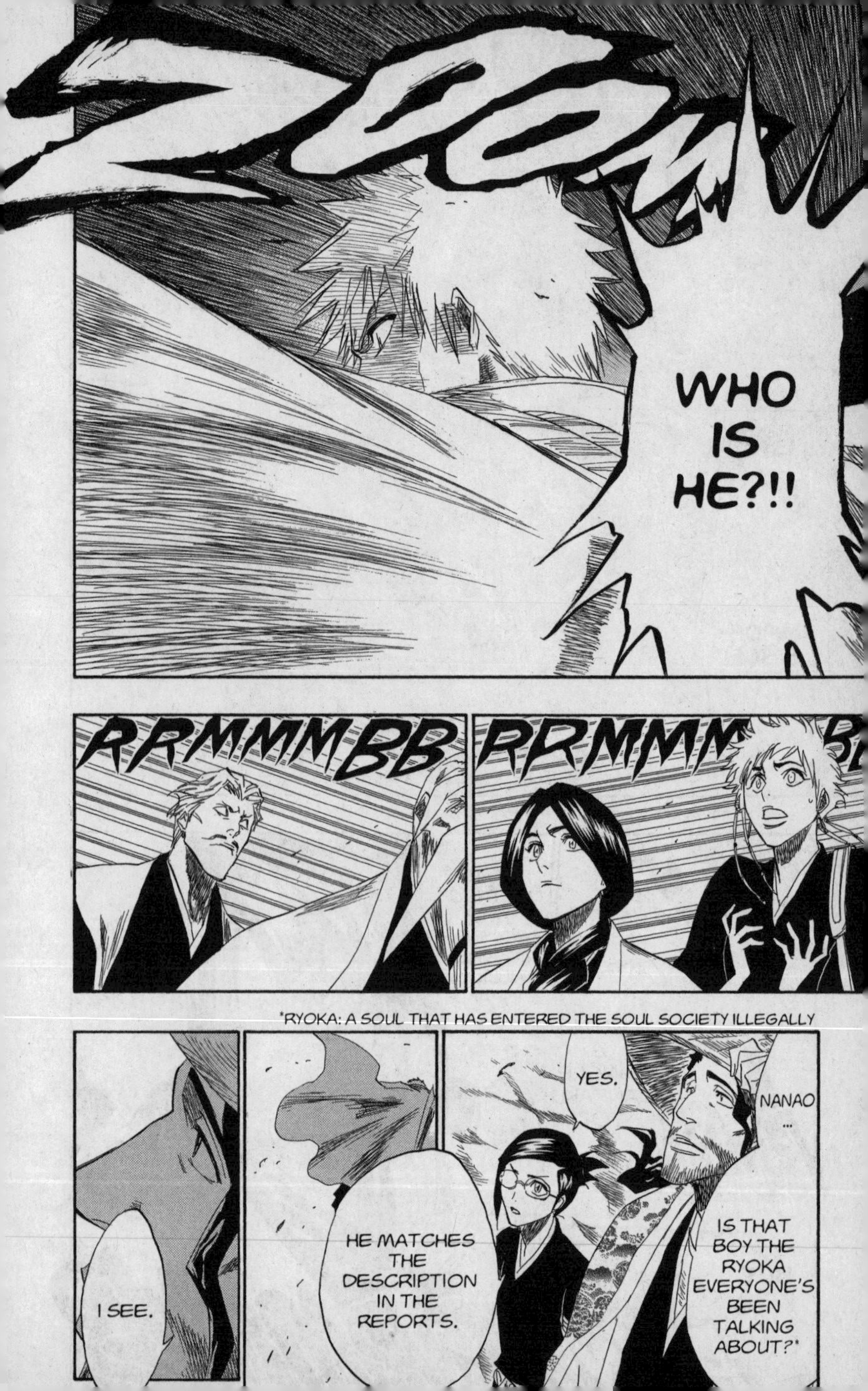
WHO IS HE?!!
RRMMM
RRMMMBB
NANAO...
IS THAT BOY THE RYOKA EVERYONE'S BEEN TALKING ABOUT?*
YES.
HE MATCHES THE DESCRIPTION IN THE REPORTS.
I SEE.

*RYOKA: A SOUL THAT HAS ENTERED THE SOUL SOCIETY ILLEGALLY

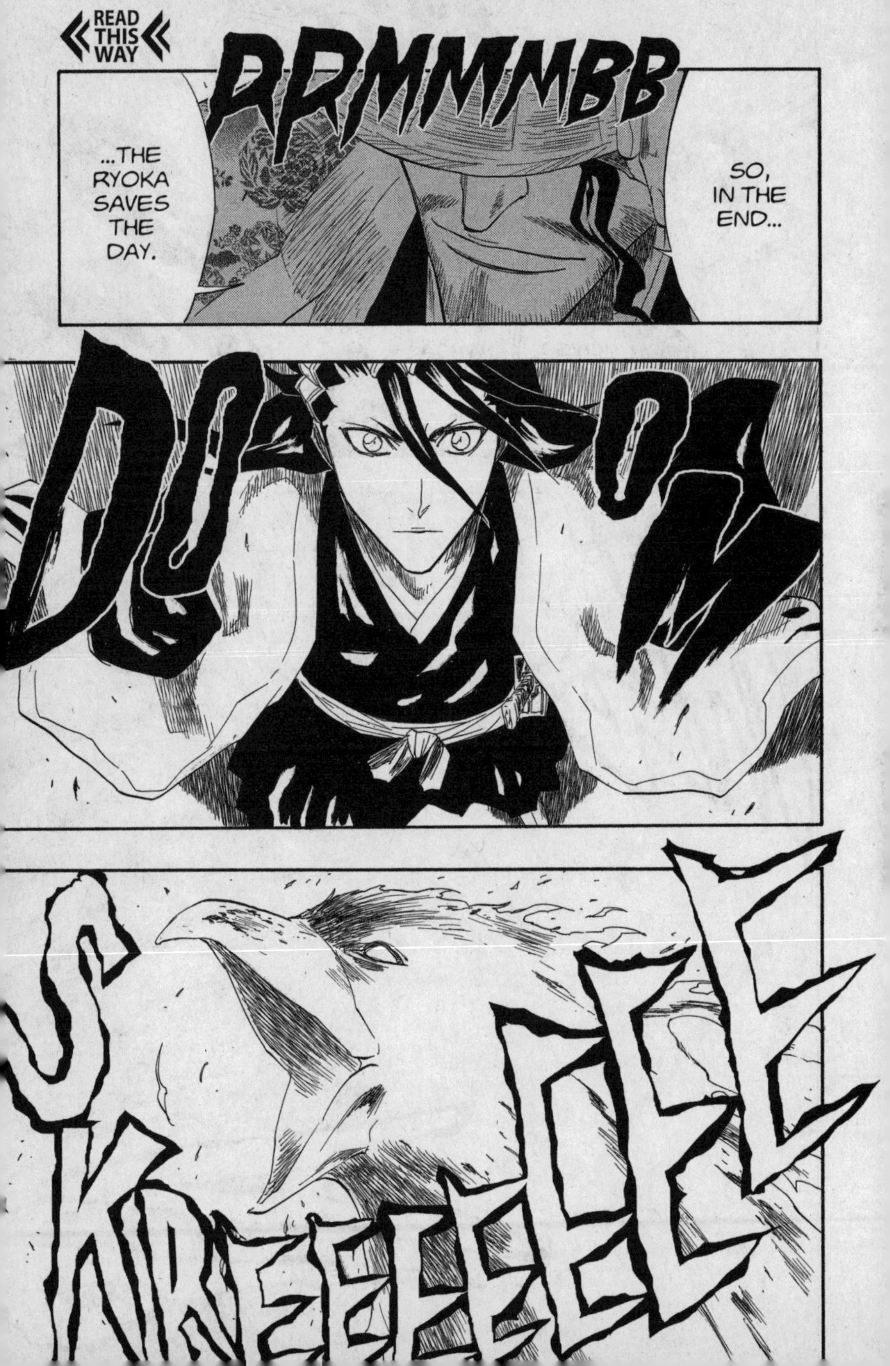
READ THIS WAY
RRMMMBB
SO, IN THE END...
...THE RYOKA SAVES THE DAY.
DOOM
SKREEEEEEEE

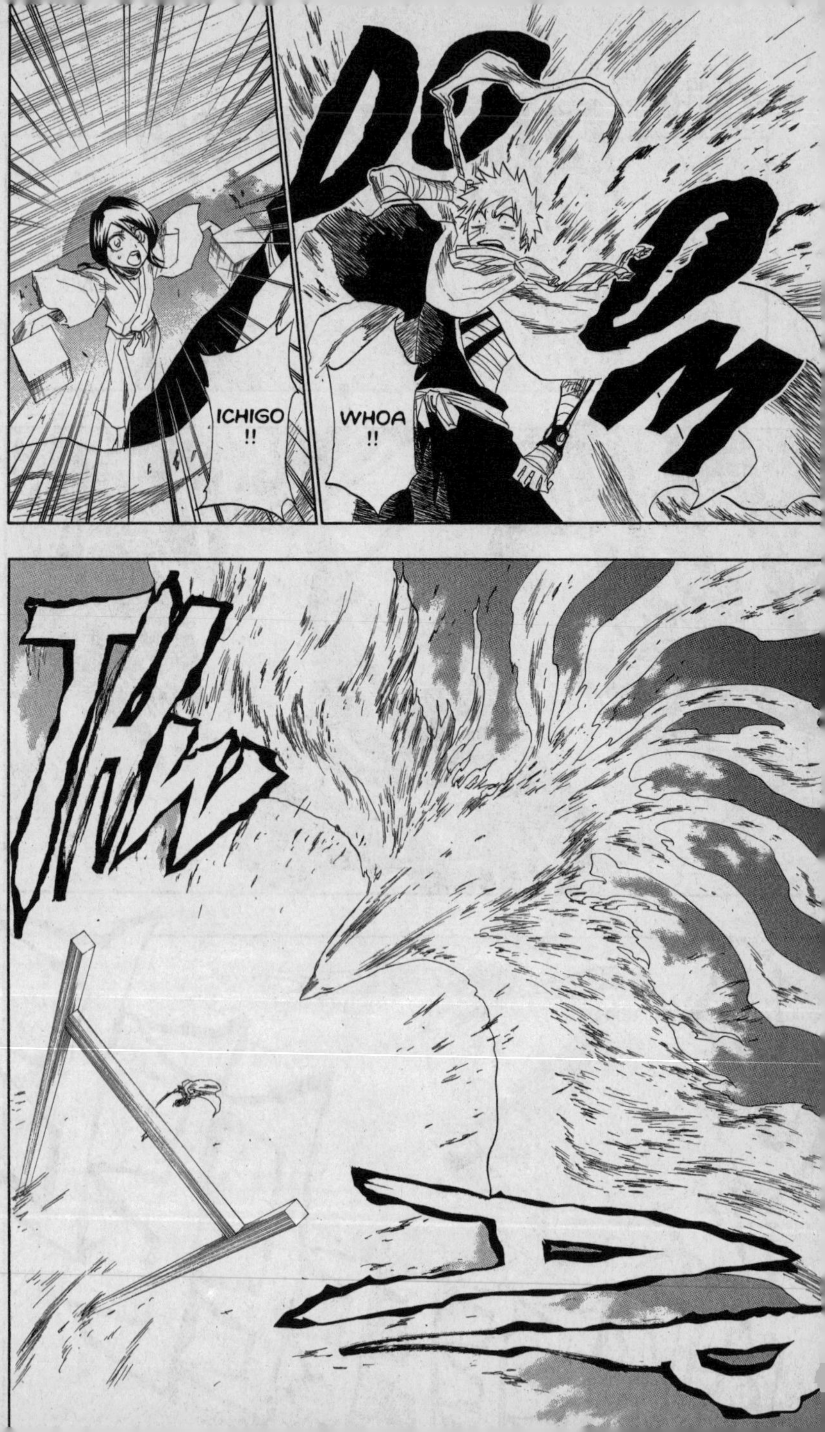
DOOM
WHOA !!
ICHIGO !!

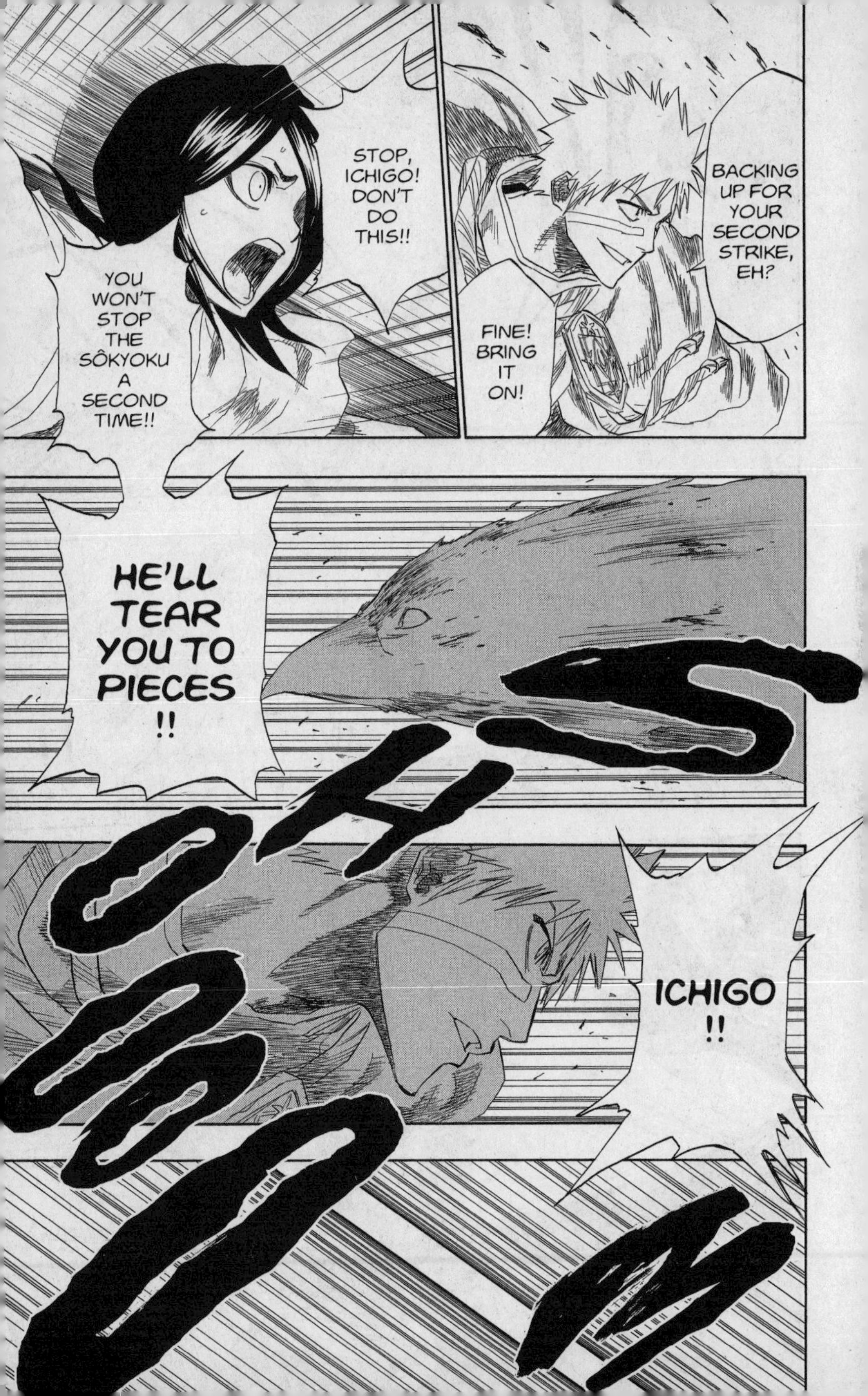
BACKING UP FOR YOUR SECOND STRIKE, EH?
FINE! BRING IT ON!
STOP, ICHIGO! DON'T DO THIS!!
YOU WON'T STOP THE SÔKYOKU A SECOND TIME!!
HE'LL TEAR YOU TO PIECES!!
ICHIGO!!

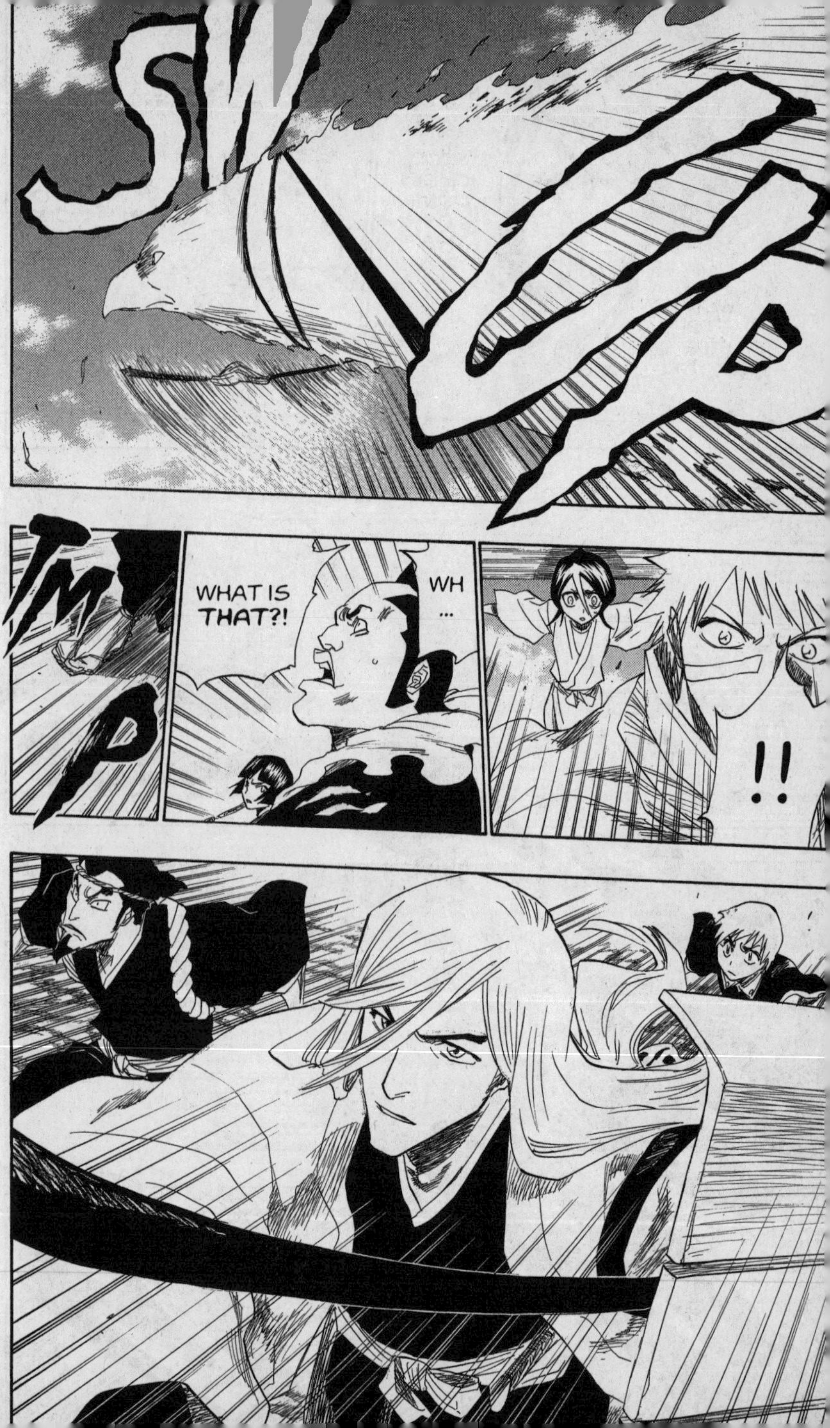
SWOP
!!
WH ...
WHAT IS THAT?!
TMP

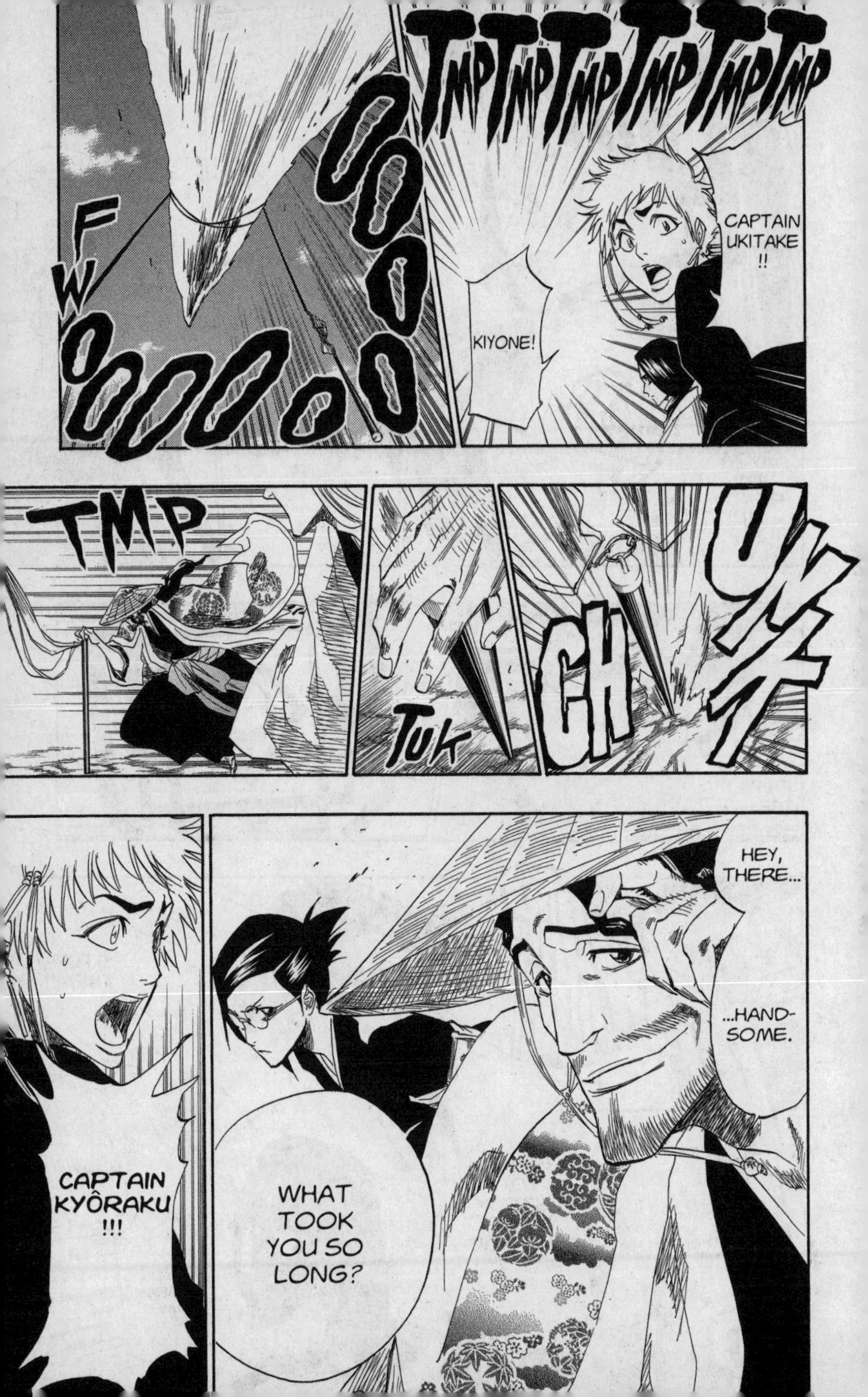
TMPTMPTMPTMPTMPTMP
CAPTAIN UKITAKE!!
KIYONE!
FWOOOOOOOOOO
UNK
CH
TUK
TMP
HEY, THERE...
...HANDSOME.
WHAT TOOK YOU SO LONG?
CAPTAIN KYÔRAKU!!!

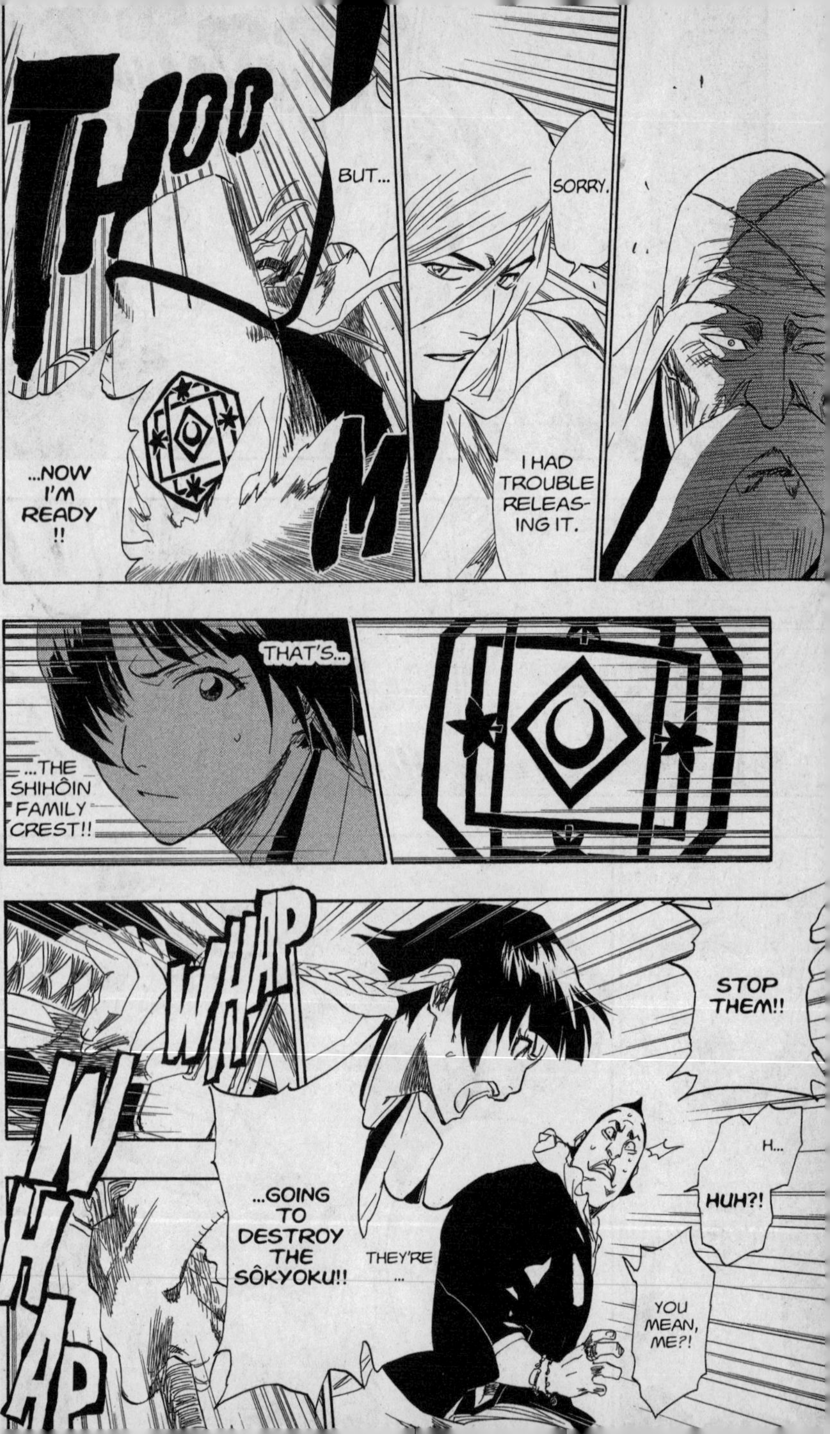
SORRY.
I HAD TROUBLE RELEASING IT.
BUT...
THOOM
...NOW I'M READY!!
THAT'S...
...THE SHIHÔIN FAMILY CREST!!
STOP THEM!!
WHAP
H...
HUH?!
YOU MEAN, ME?!
THEY'RE ...
...GOING TO DESTROY THE SÔKYOKU!!
WHHAP

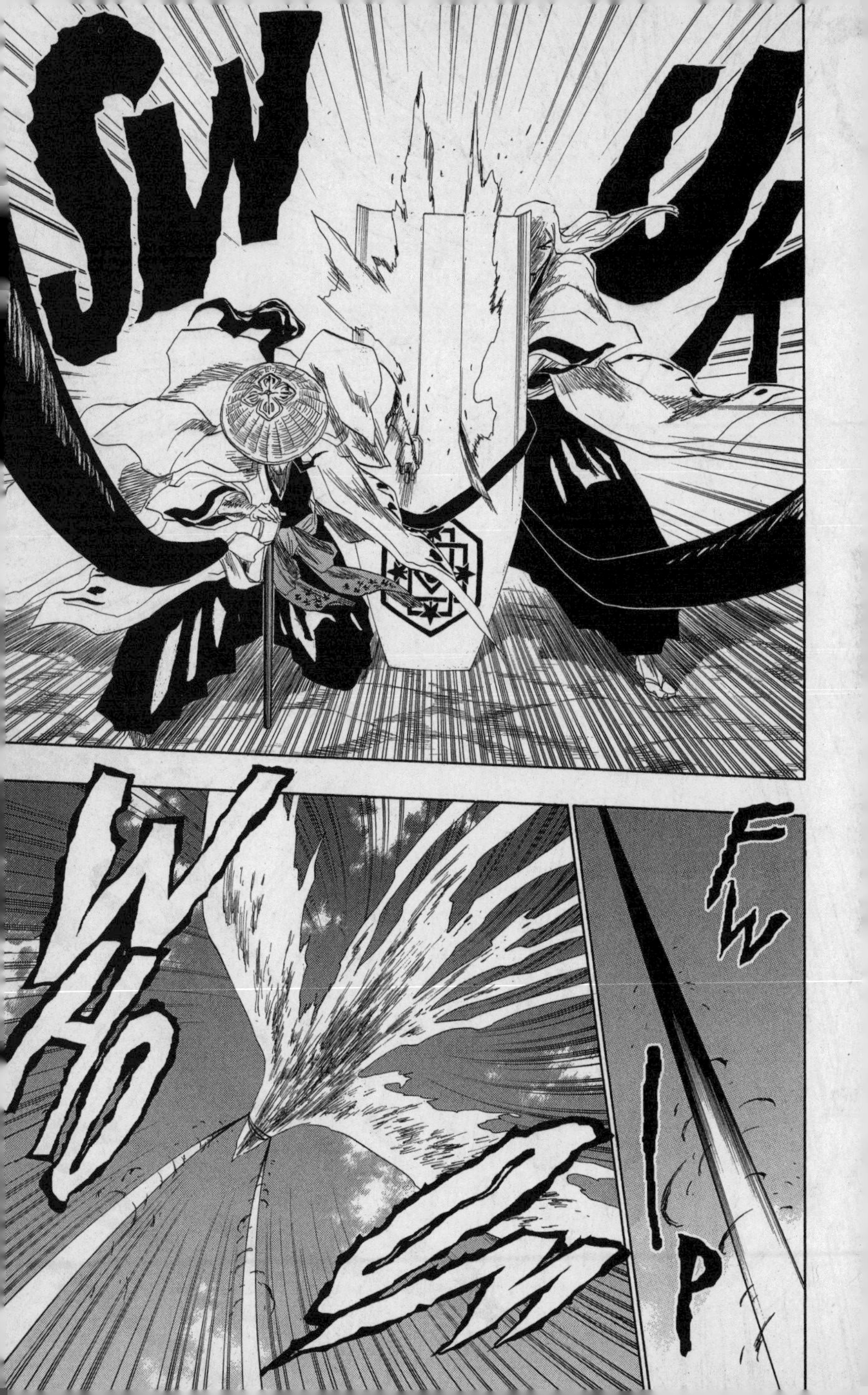
SW
FWIP
WHO

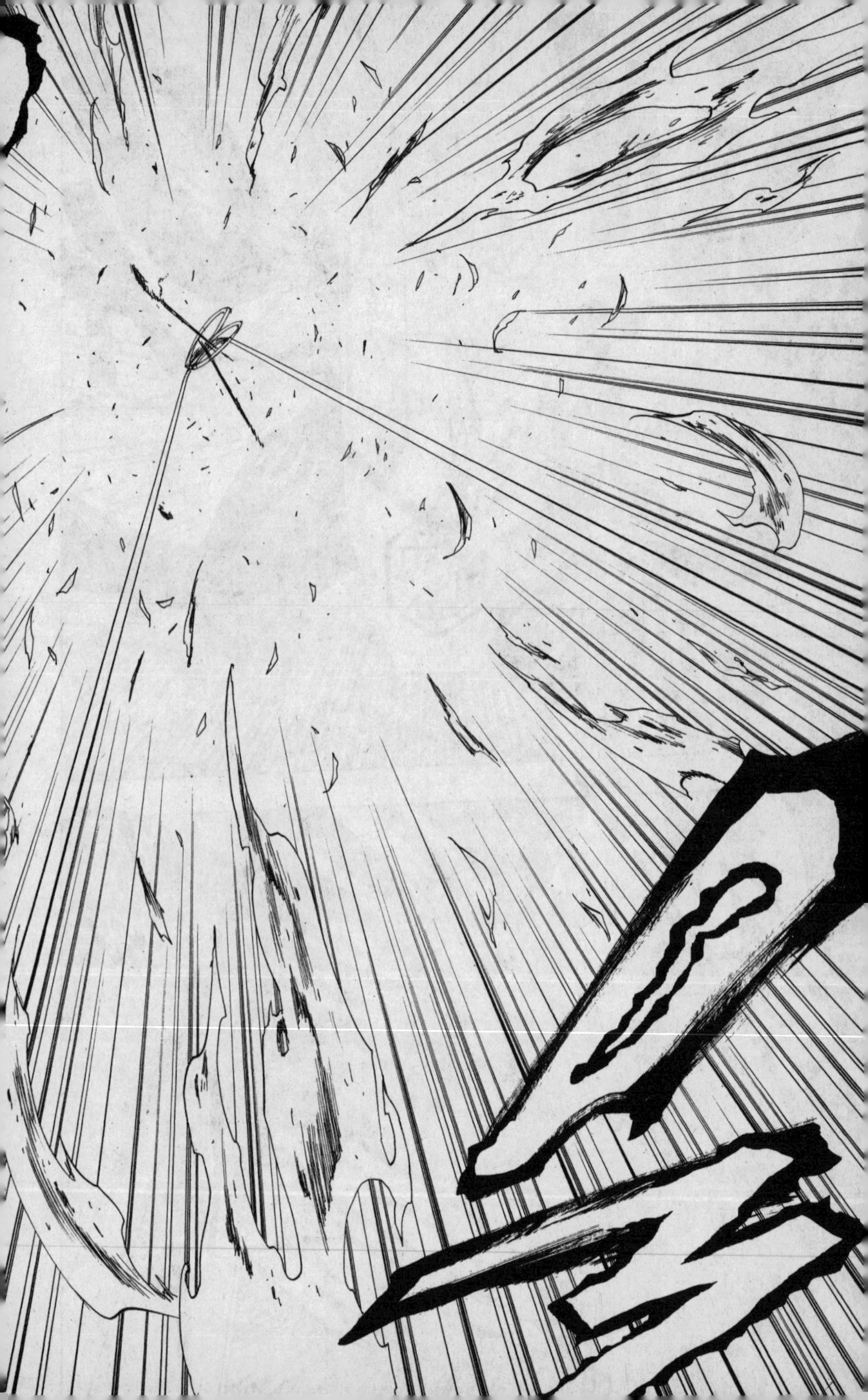

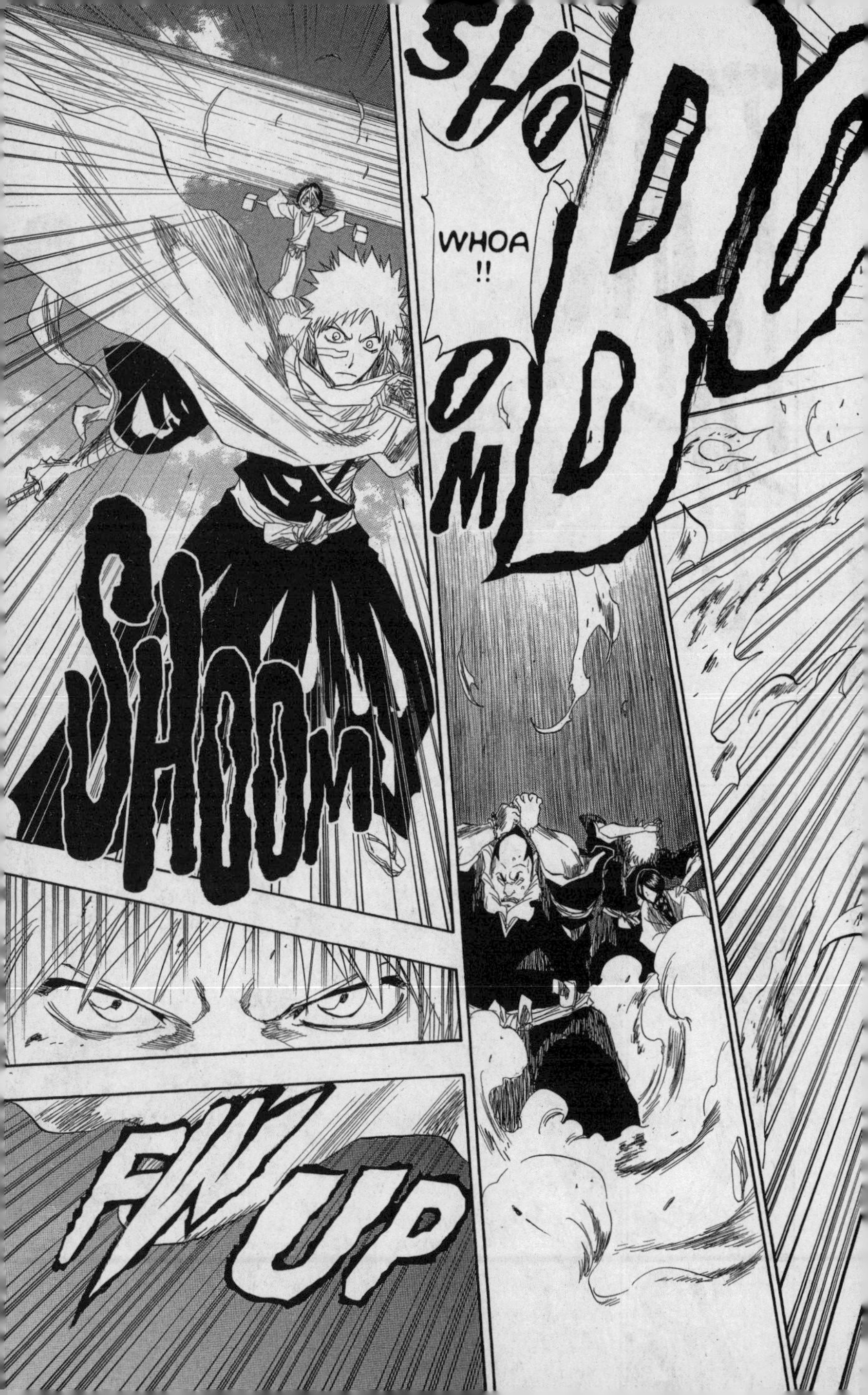
SHOOOM
WHOA !!
DOOOM
SHOOM
FWUP

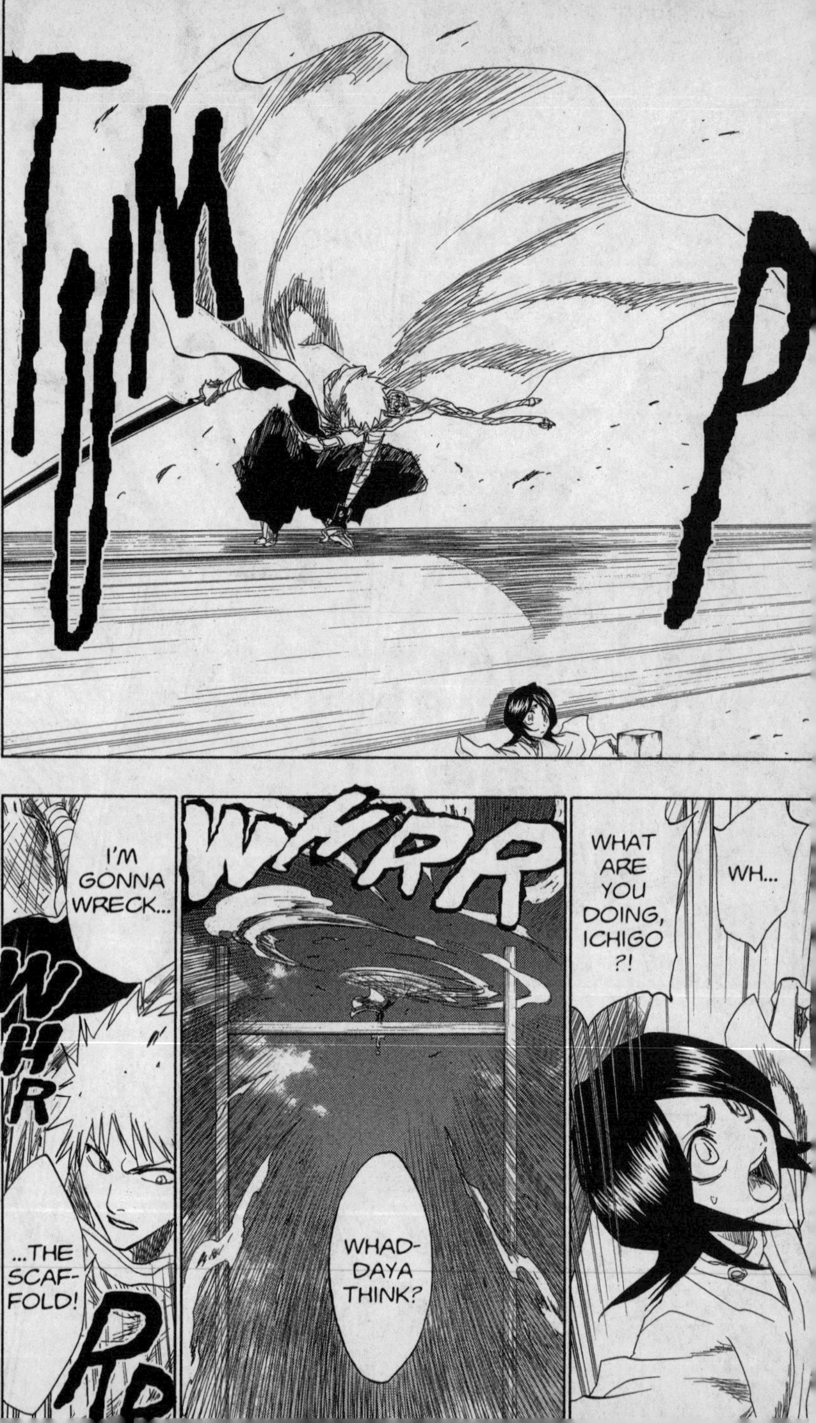
TUMP
WH...
WHAT ARE YOU DOING, ICHIGO?!
WHRR
WHAD-DAYA THINK?
I'M GONNA WRECK...
WHR
...THE SCAF-FOLD!
RR

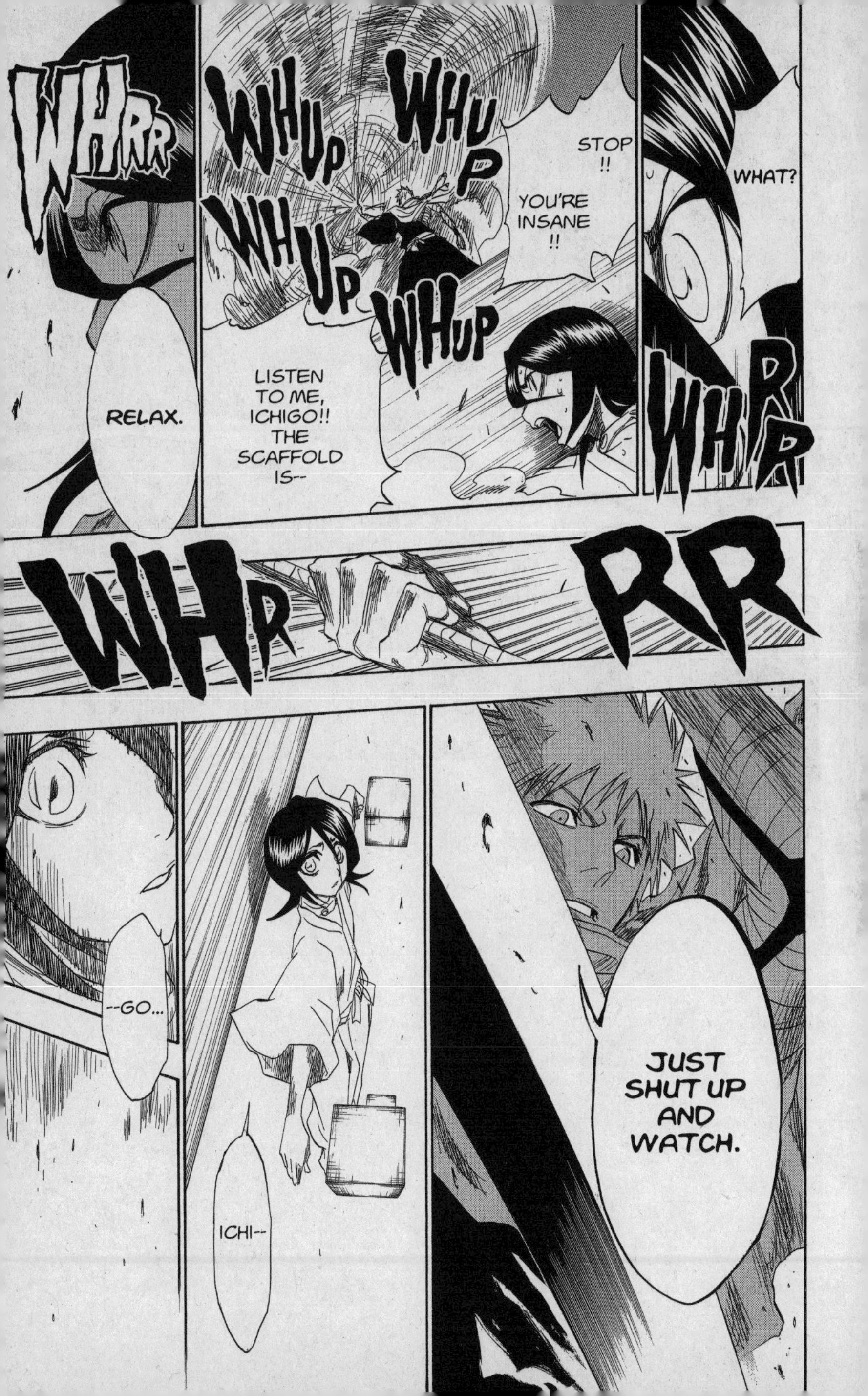
WHAT?
WHRR
WHUP
STOP!!
YOU'RE INSANE!!
WHUP
WHUP
WHUP
WHUP
LISTEN TO ME, ICHIGO!! THE SCAFFOLD IS--
WHRR
RELAX.
WHRRR
JUST SHUT UP AND WATCH.
ICHI--
--GO...

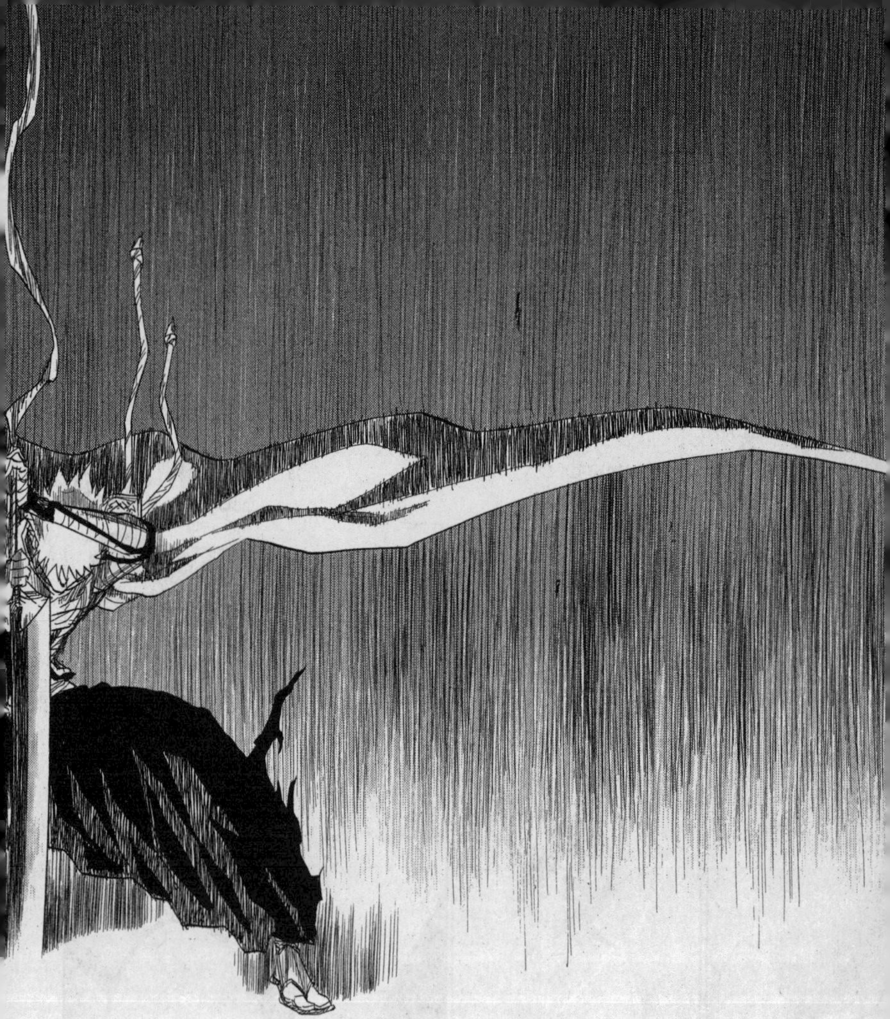

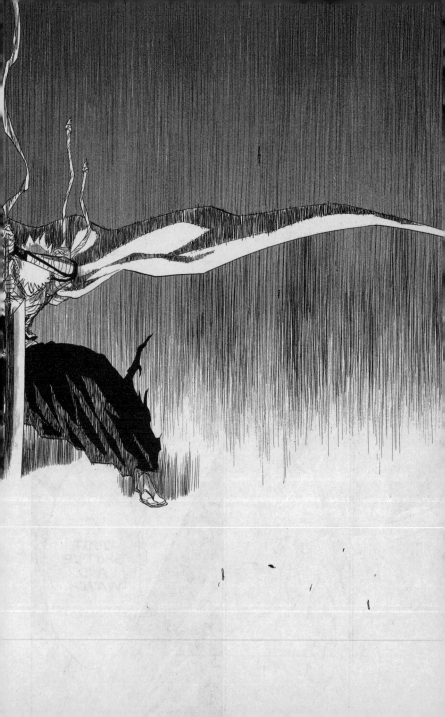

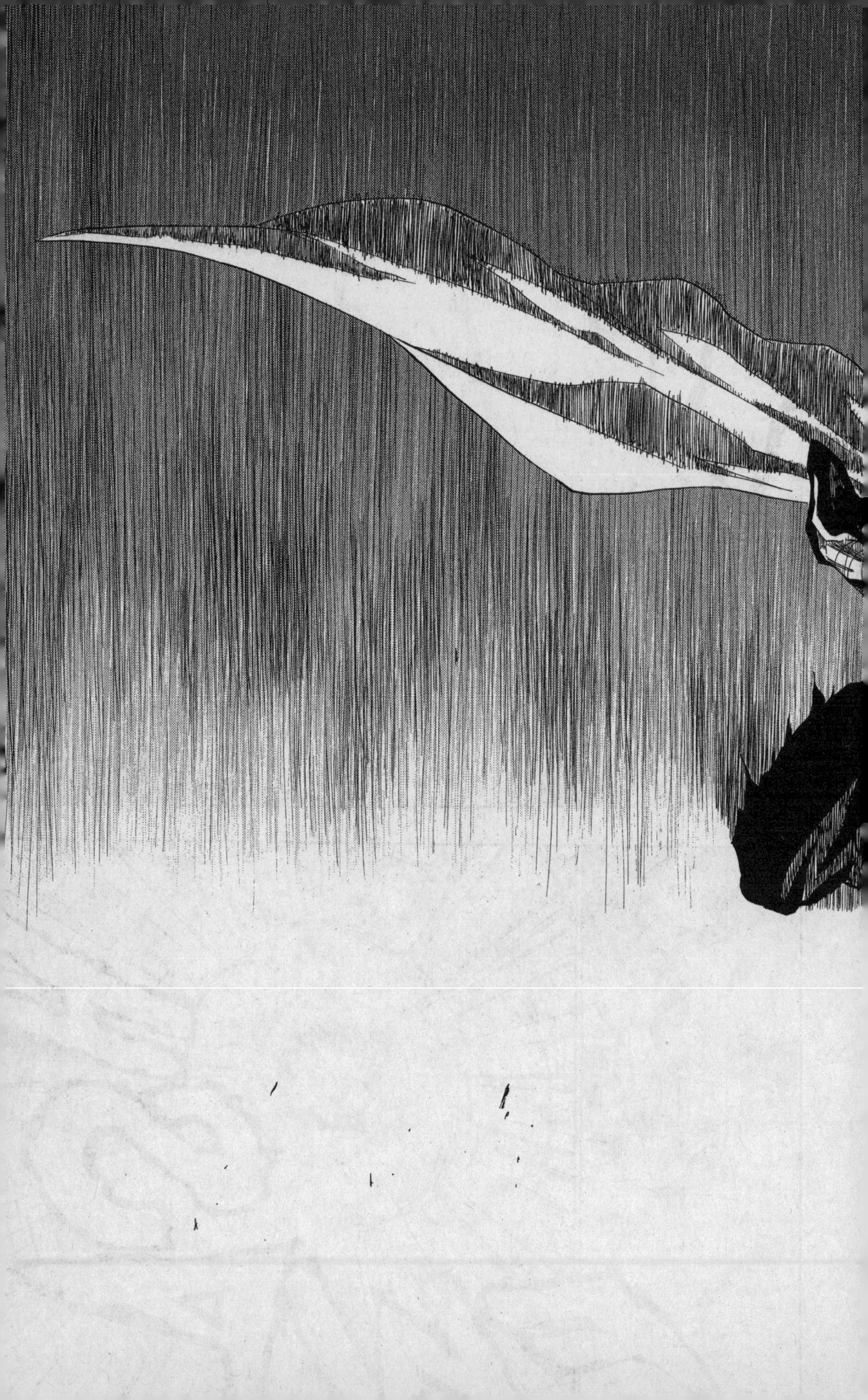

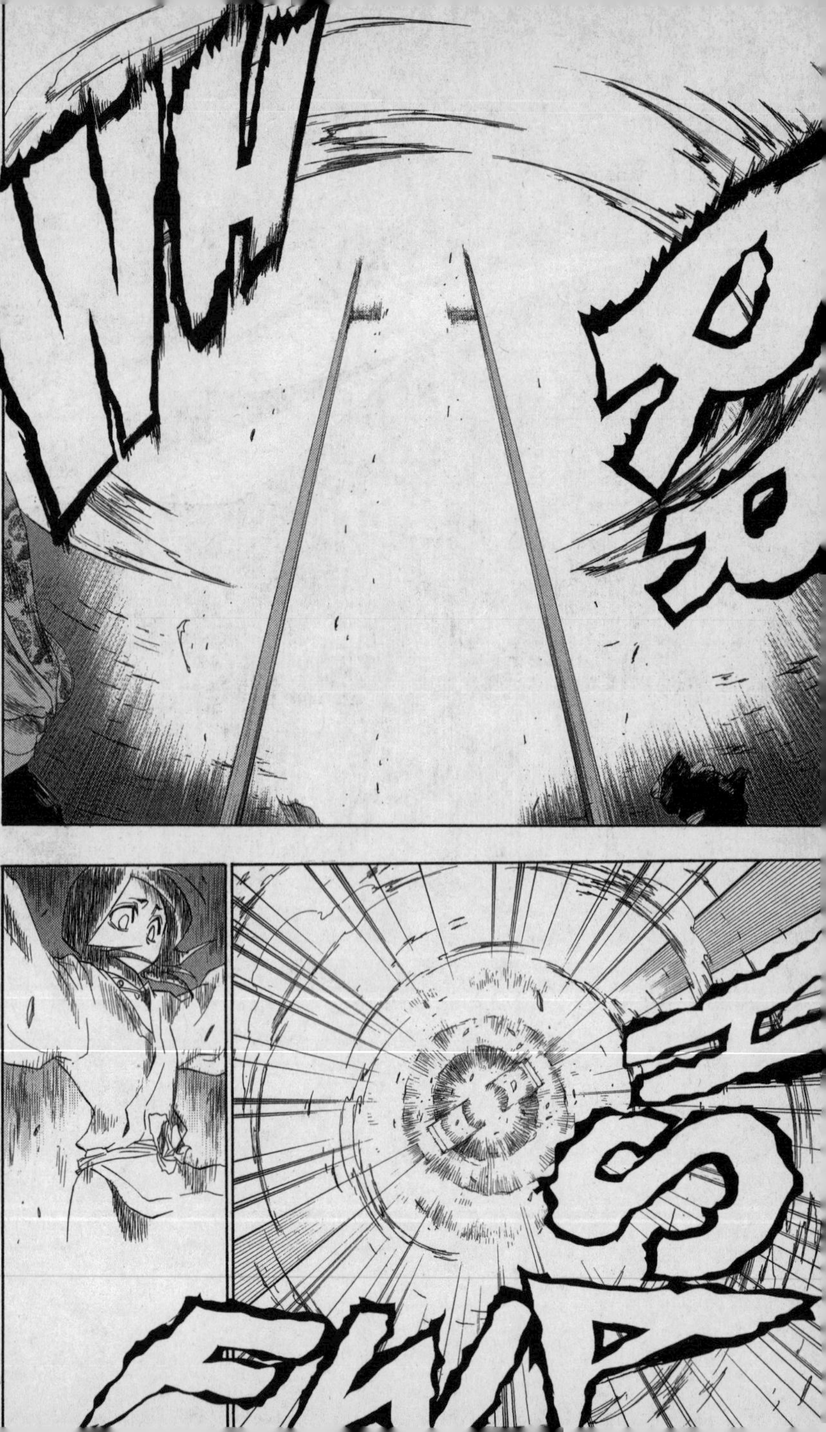

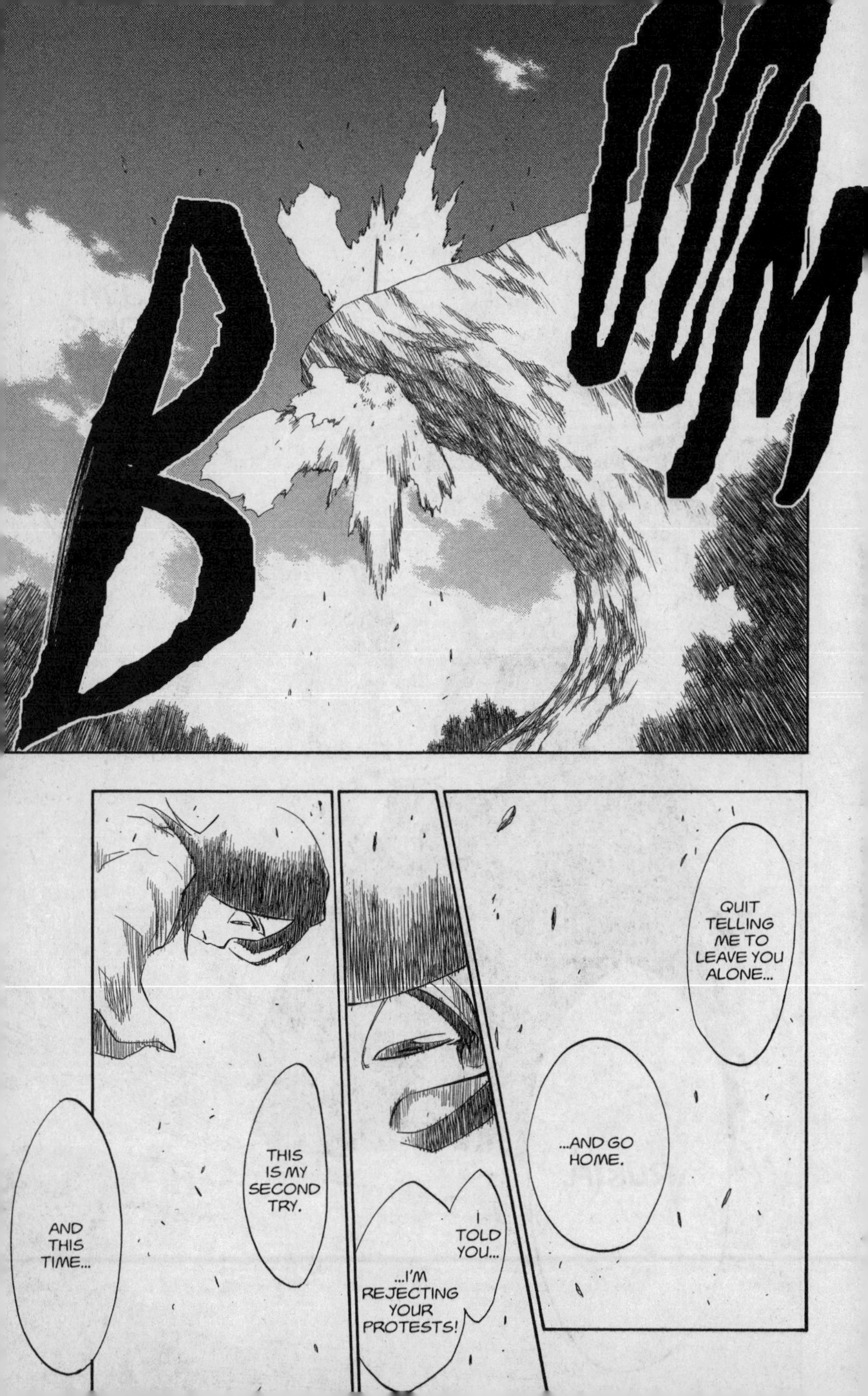
BOOM
QUIT TELLING ME TO LEAVE YOU ALONE...
...AND GO HOME.
I TOLD YOU...
...I'M REJECTING YOUR PROTESTS!
THIS IS MY SECOND TRY.
AND THIS TIME...

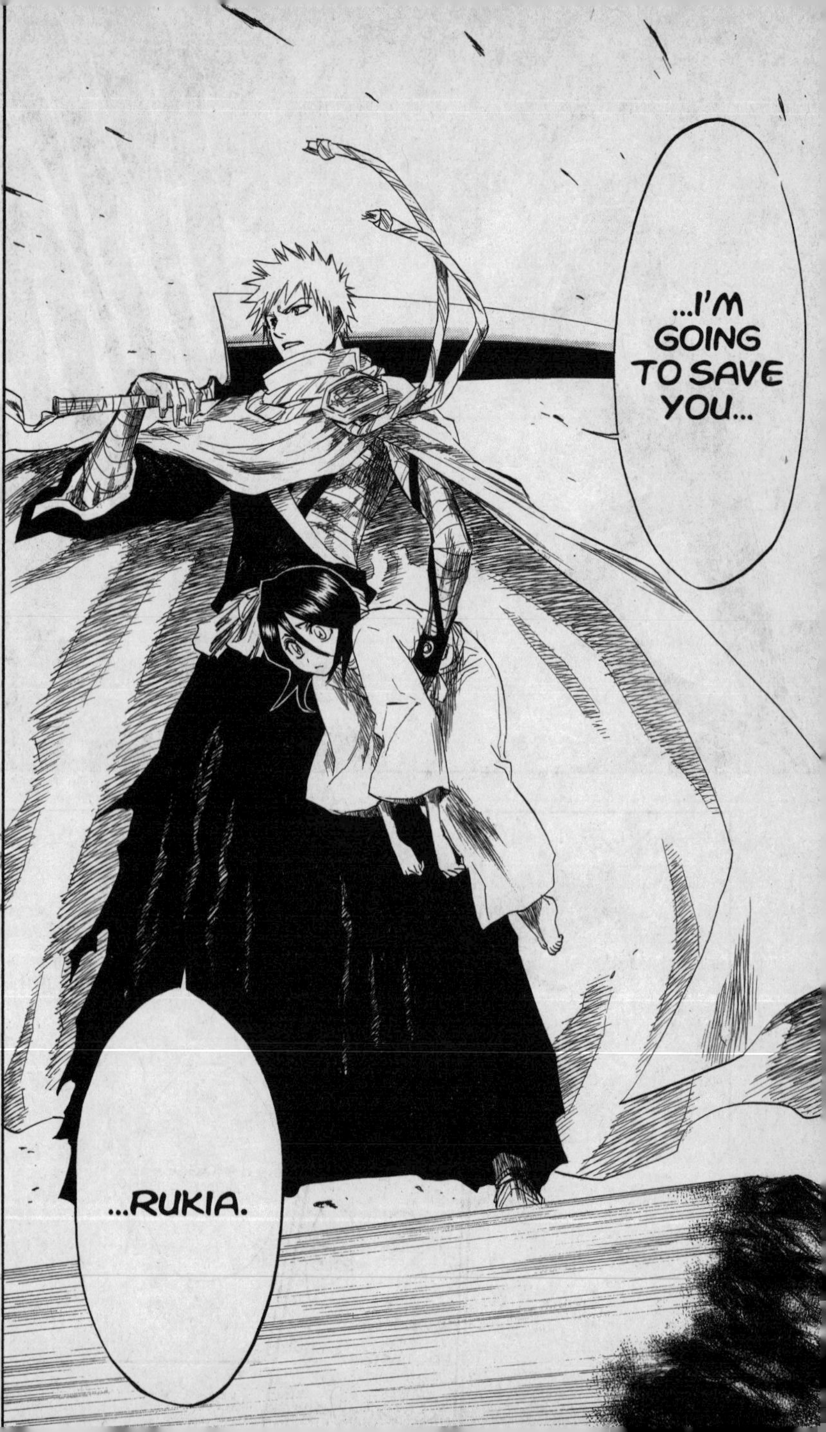
...I'M GOING TO SAVE YOU...
...RUKIA.

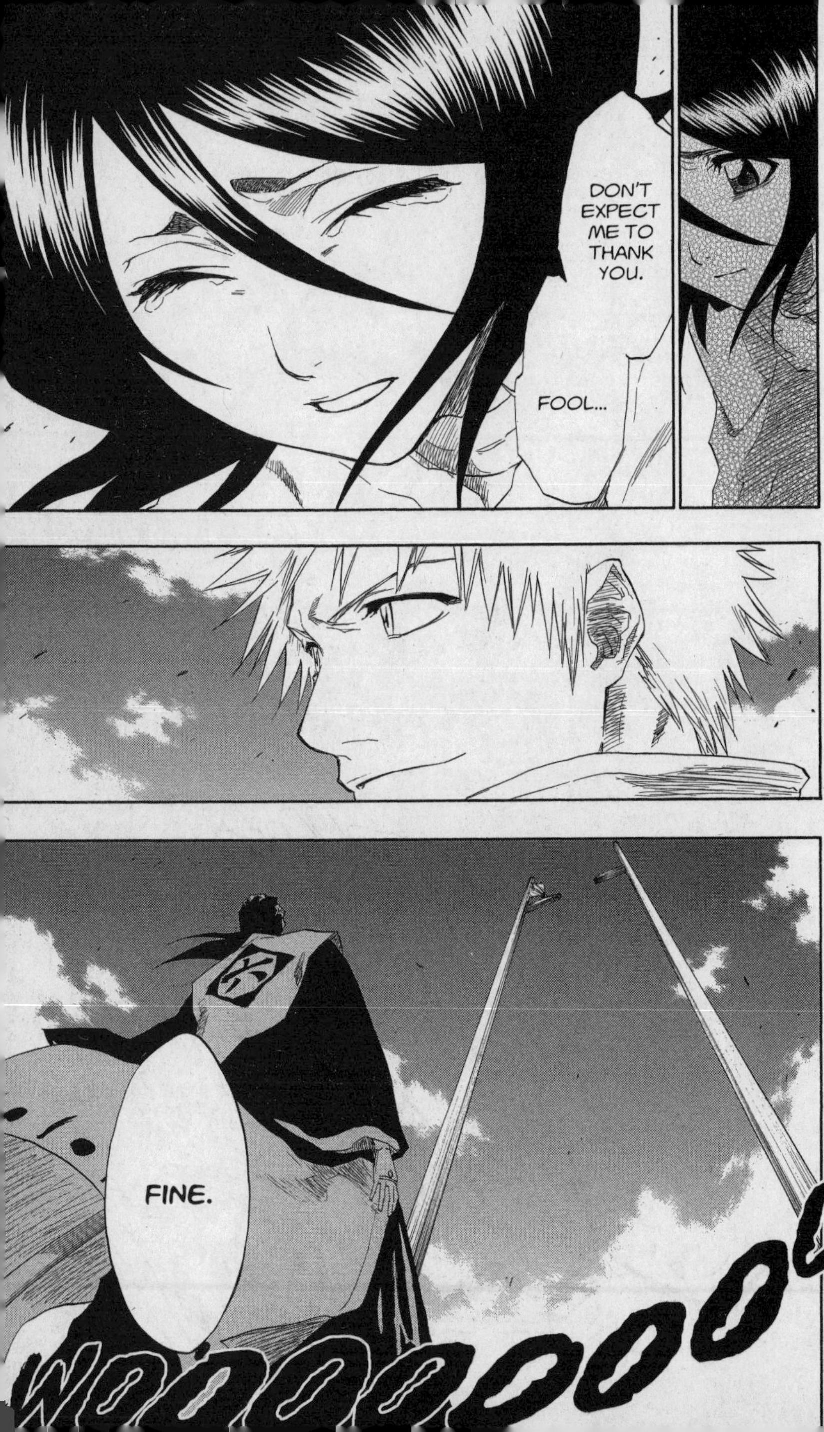
DON'T EXPECT ME TO THANK YOU.
FOOL...
FINE.
WOOOOOOOOOOOO

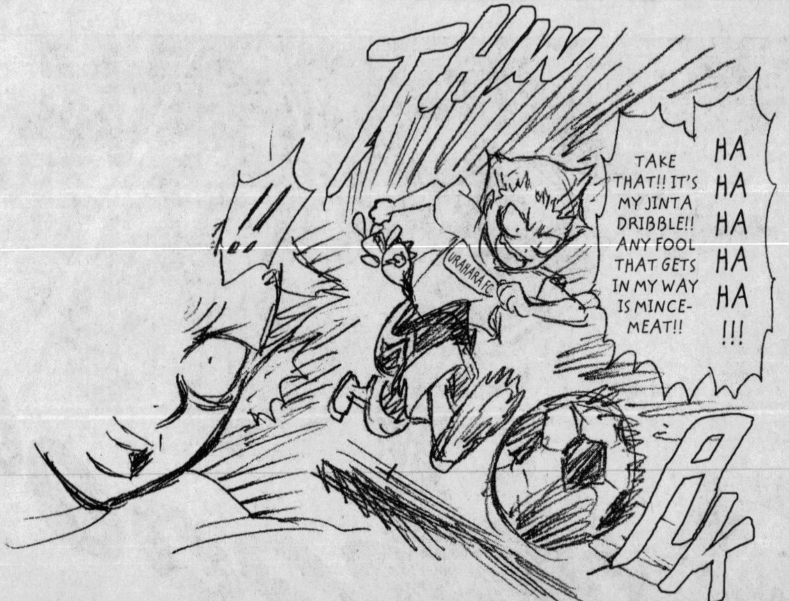
HA HA HA HA HA !!!
TAKE THAT!! IT'S MY JINTA DRIBBLE!! ANY FOOL THAT GETS IN MY WAY IS MINCE-MEAT!!
THWAK
URAHARA FC
!!

152. The Speed Phantom

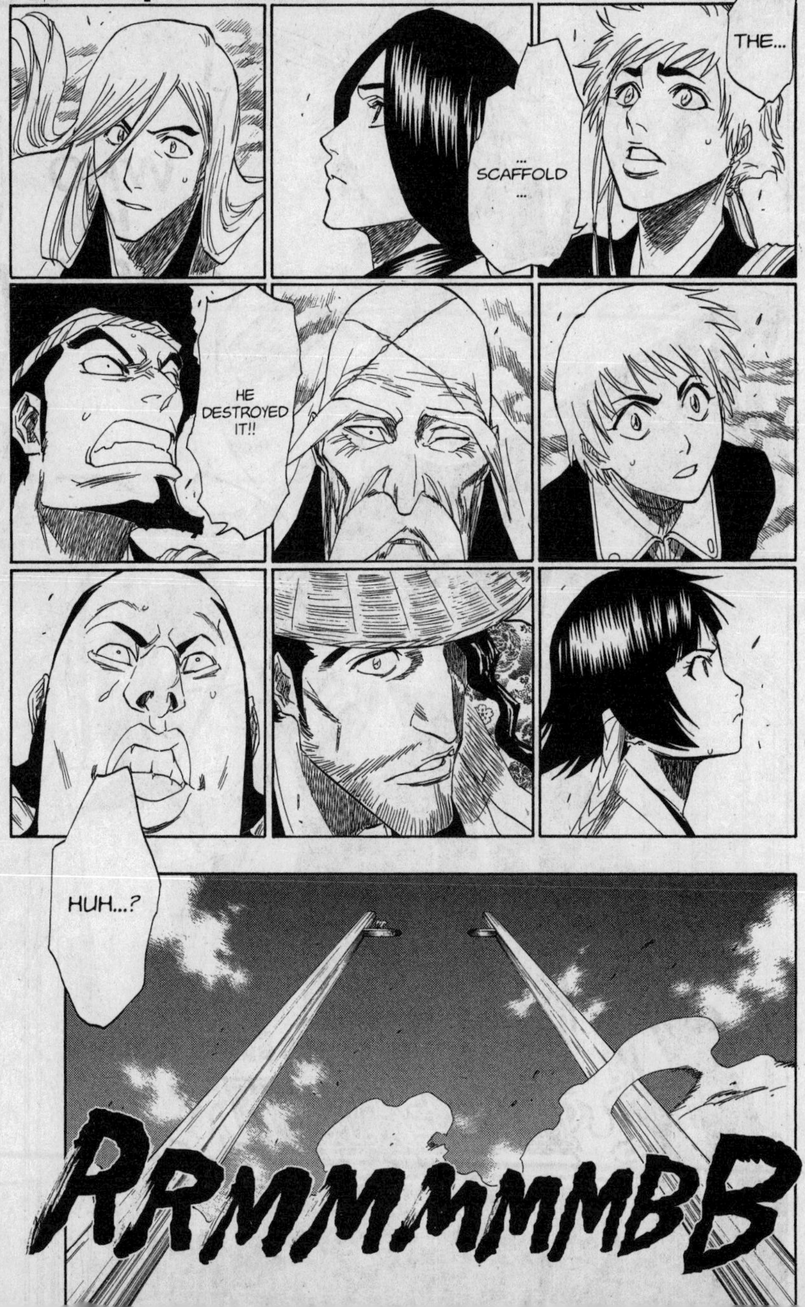
THE...
... SCAFFOLD ...
HE DESTROYED IT!!
HUH...?
RRMMMMMMBB

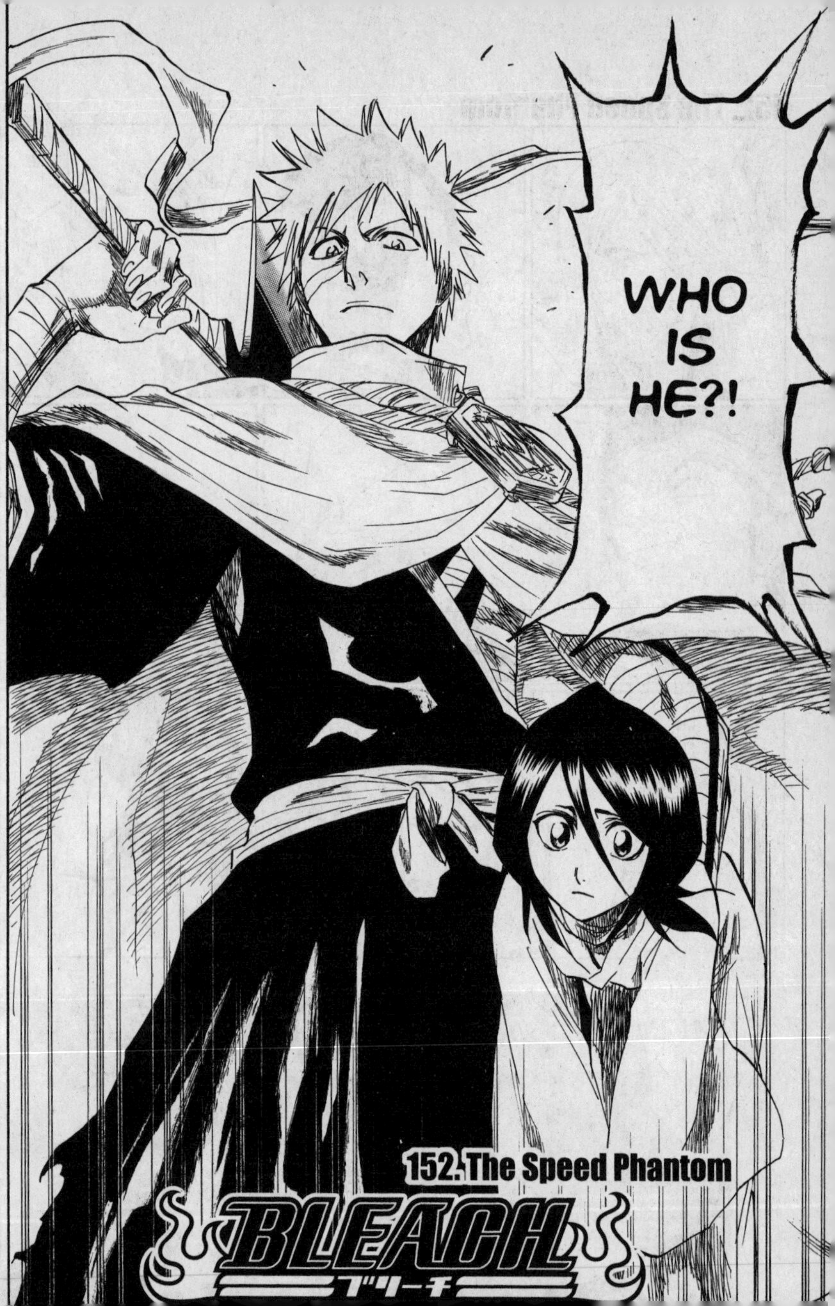
WHO IS HE?!
152. The Speed Phantom
BLEACH
ブリーチ

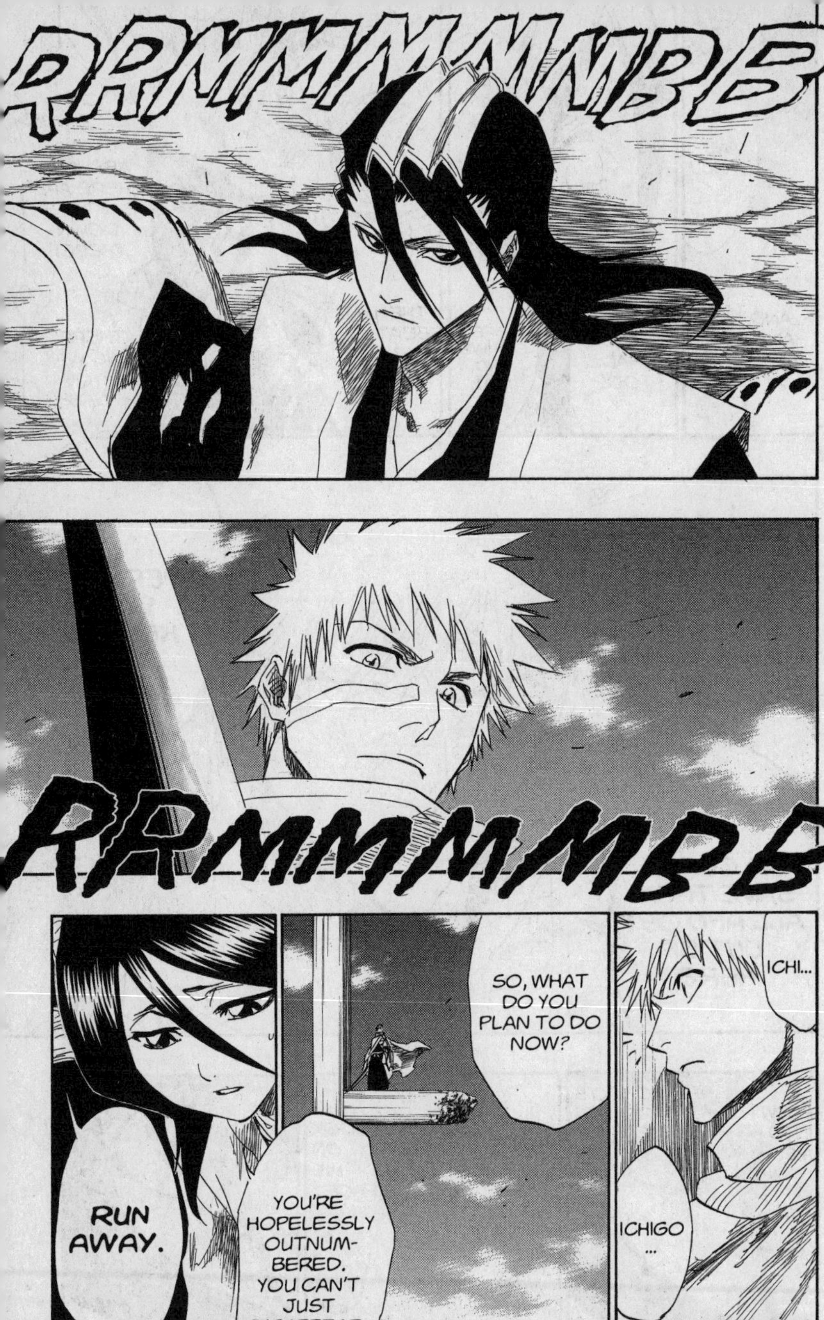
RRMMMMMBB
RRMMMMBB
ICHI...
ICHIGO ...
SO, WHAT DO YOU PLAN TO DO NOW?
YOU'RE HOPELESSLY OUTNUM- BERED. YOU CAN'T JUST DISAPPEAR.
RUN AWAY.

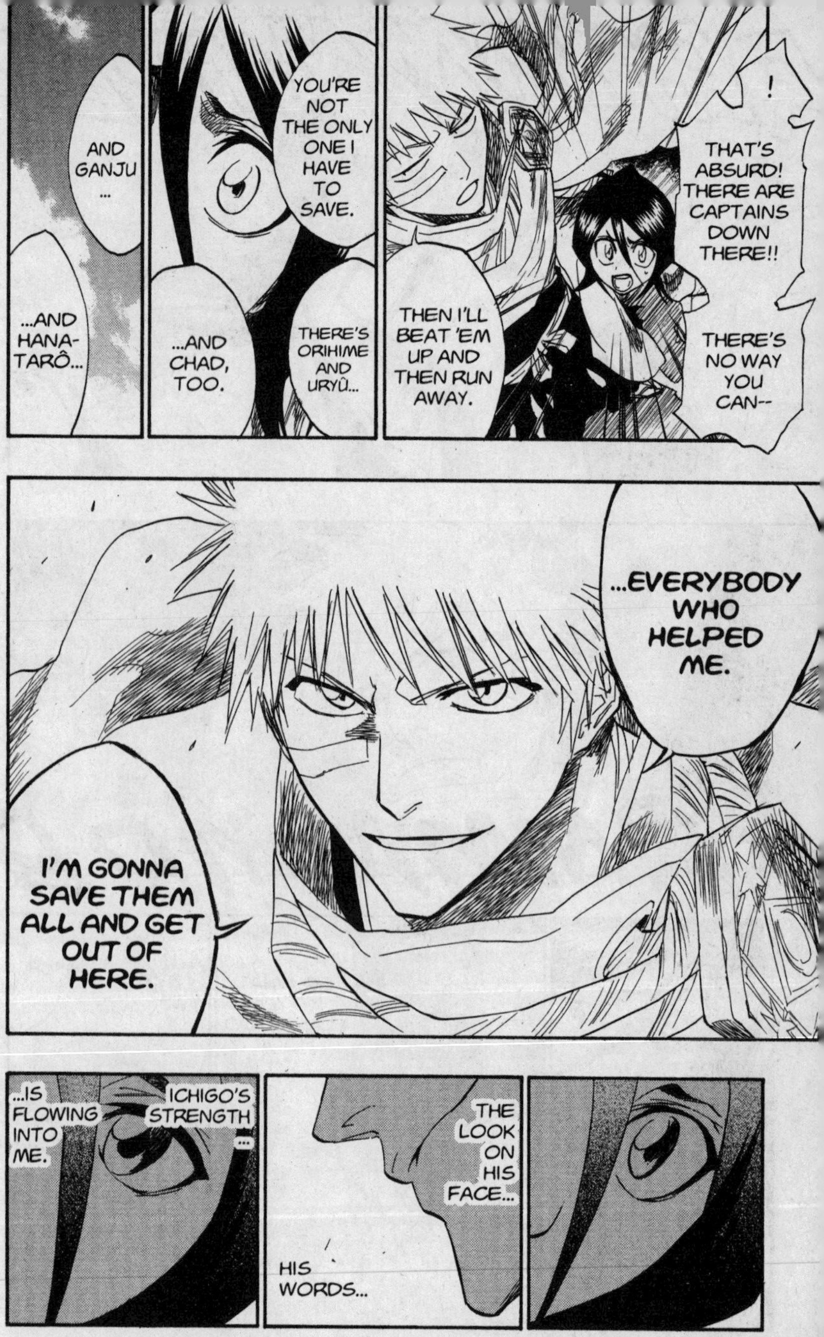
!
THAT'S ABSURD! THERE ARE CAPTAINS DOWN THERE!!
THERE'S NO WAY YOU CAN--
THEN I'LL BEAT 'EM UP AND THEN RUN AWAY.
YOU'RE NOT THE ONLY ONE I HAVE TO SAVE.
THERE'S ORIHIME AND URYÛ...
...AND CHAD, TOO.
AND GANJU ...
...AND HANATARÔ...
...EVERYBODY WHO HELPED ME.
I'M GONNA SAVE THEM ALL AND GET OUT OF HERE.
THE LOOK ON HIS FACE...
HIS WORDS...
ICHIGO'S STRENGTH ...
...IS FLOWING INTO ME.

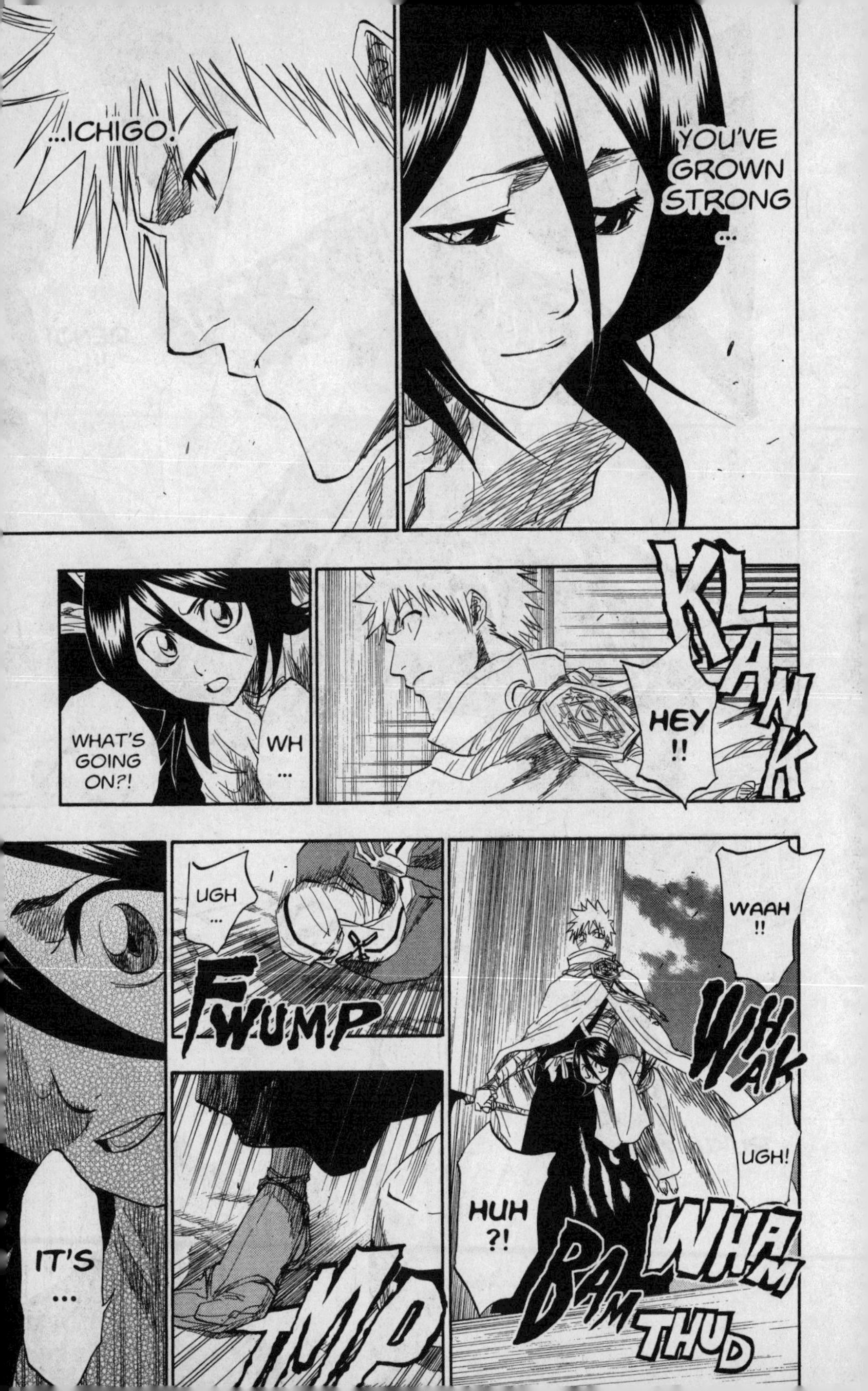
YOU'VE GROWN STRONG ...
...ICHIGO!
KLANK
HEY !!
WH ...
WHAT'S GOING ON?!
WAAH !!
WHAK
UGH!
WHAM
HUH ?!
BAM
THUD
UGH ...
FWUMP
TMP
IT'S ...

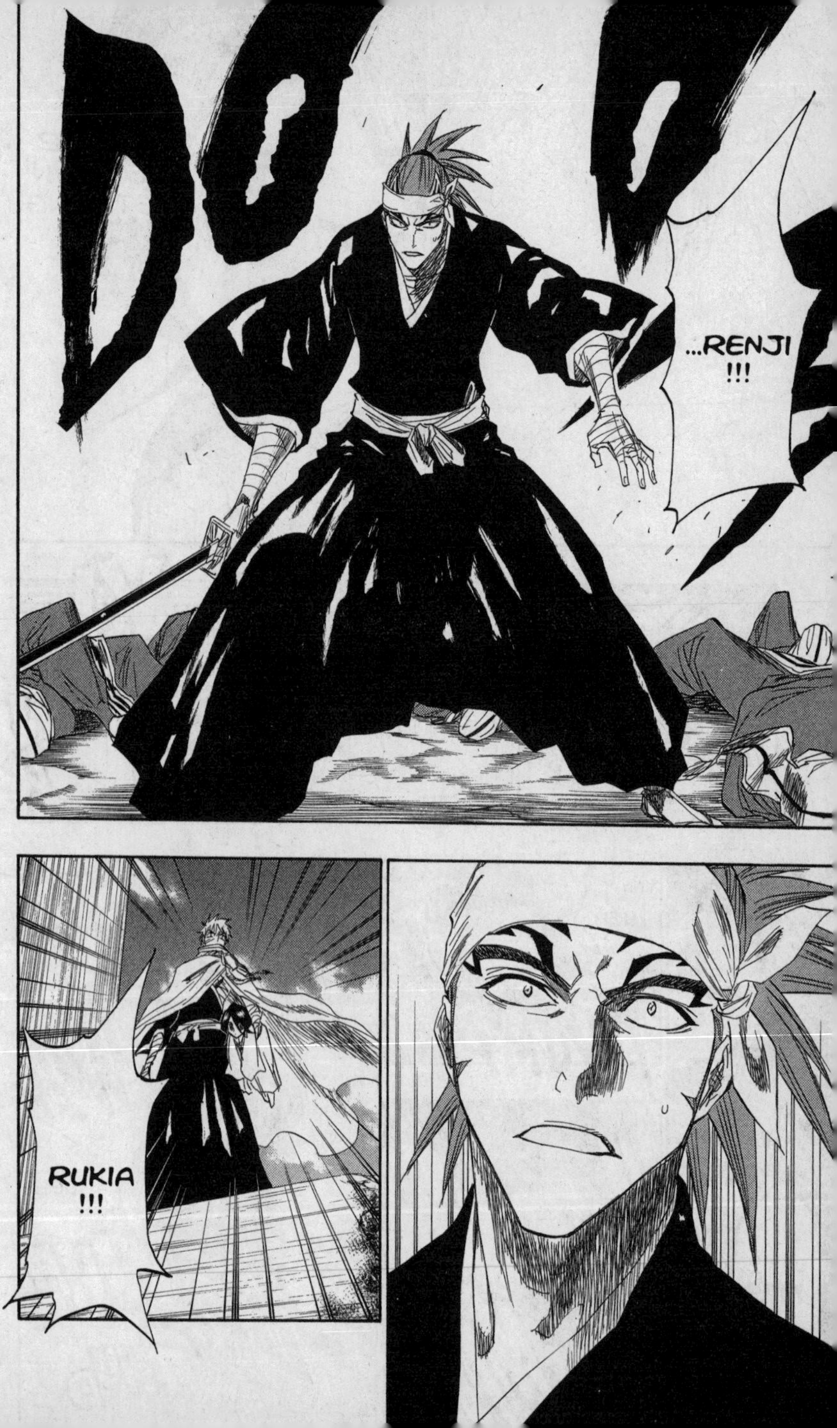
DO
...RENJI !!!
RUKIA !!!

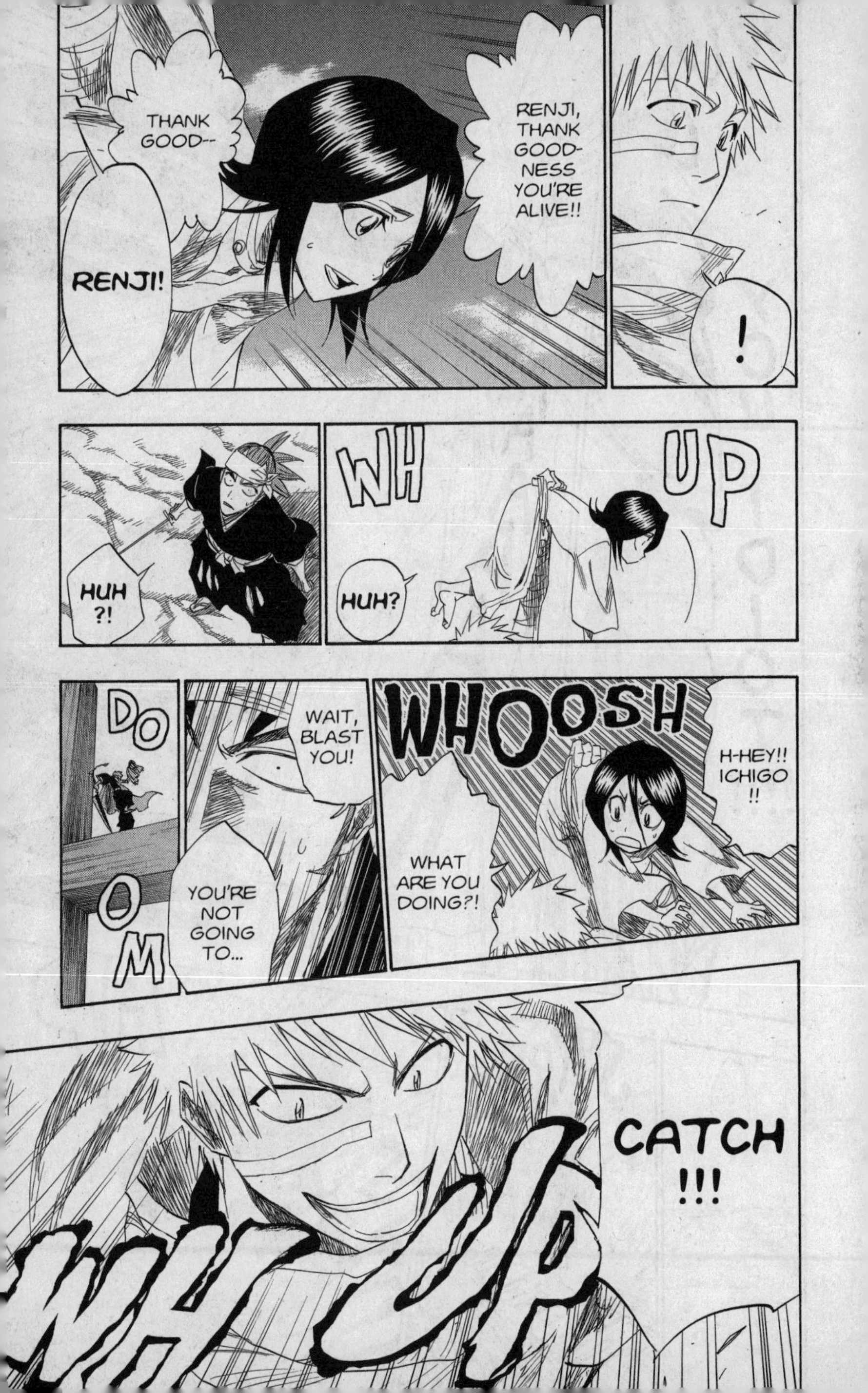
!
RENJI, THANK GOODNESS YOU'RE ALIVE!!
THANK GOOD--
RENJI!
WHUP
HUH?
HUH ?!
H-HEY!! ICHIGO !!
WHOOSH
WHAT ARE YOU DOING?!
WAIT, BLAST YOU!
YOU'RE NOT GOING TO...
DOOM
CATCH !!!
WHUP

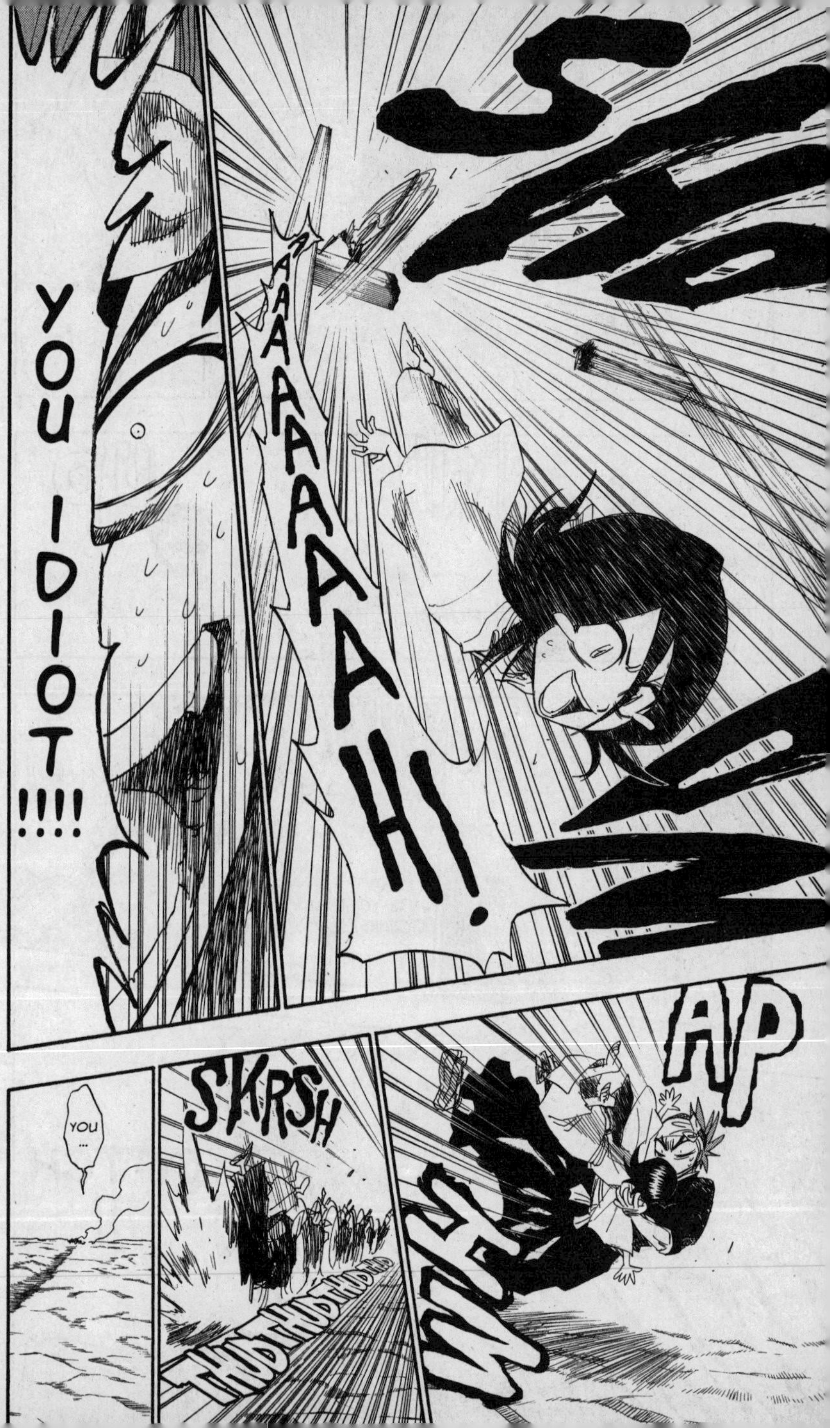
AAAAAAAAAH!
YOU IDIOT!!!!
AP
SKRSH
THUD THUD THUD
YOU ...

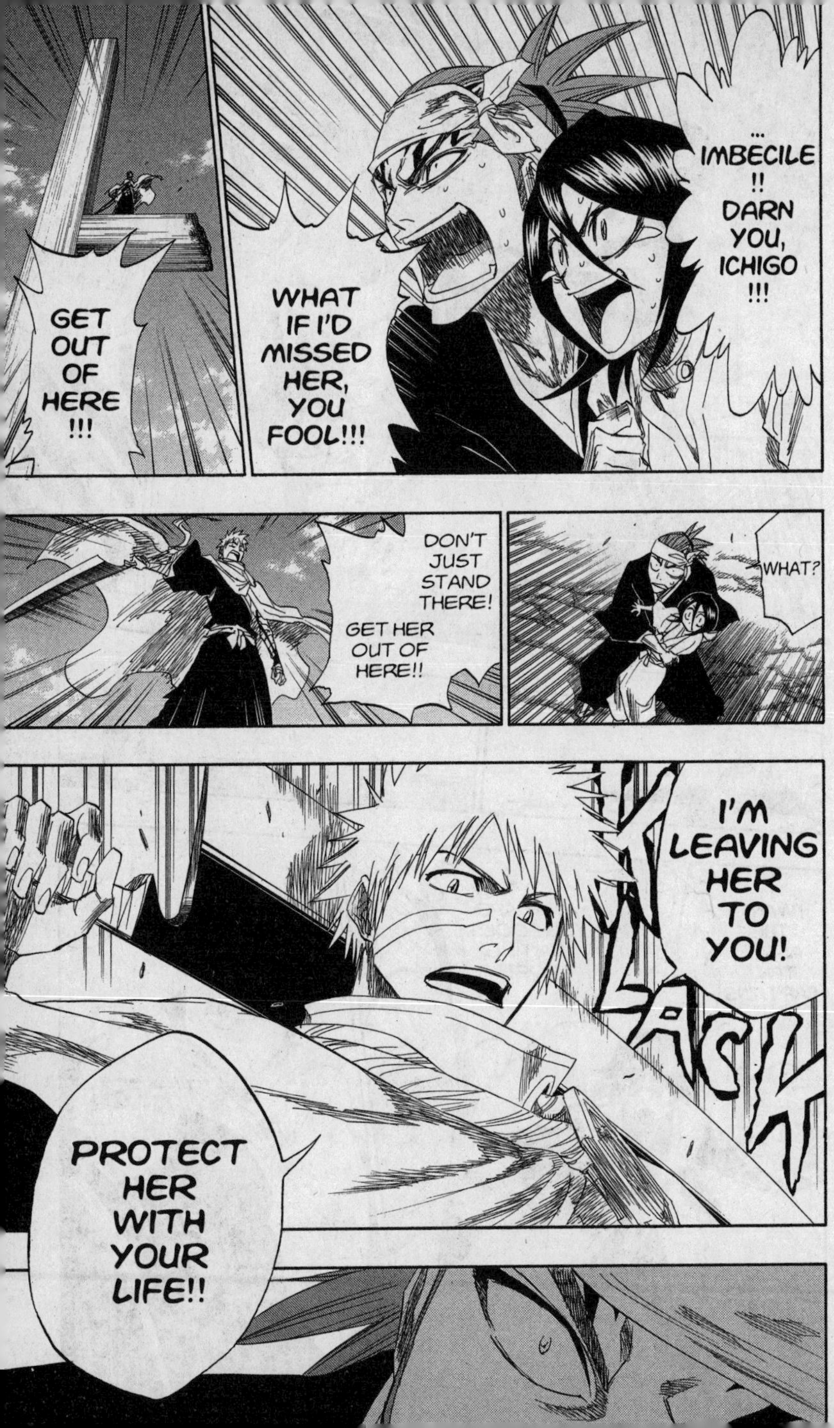
... IMBECILE!! DARN YOU, ICHIGO!!!
WHAT IF I'D MISSED HER, YOU FOOL!!!
GET OUT OF HERE!!!
WHAT?
DON'T JUST STAND THERE!
GET HER OUT OF HERE!!
I'M LEAVING HER TO YOU!
PROTECT HER WITH YOUR LIFE!!

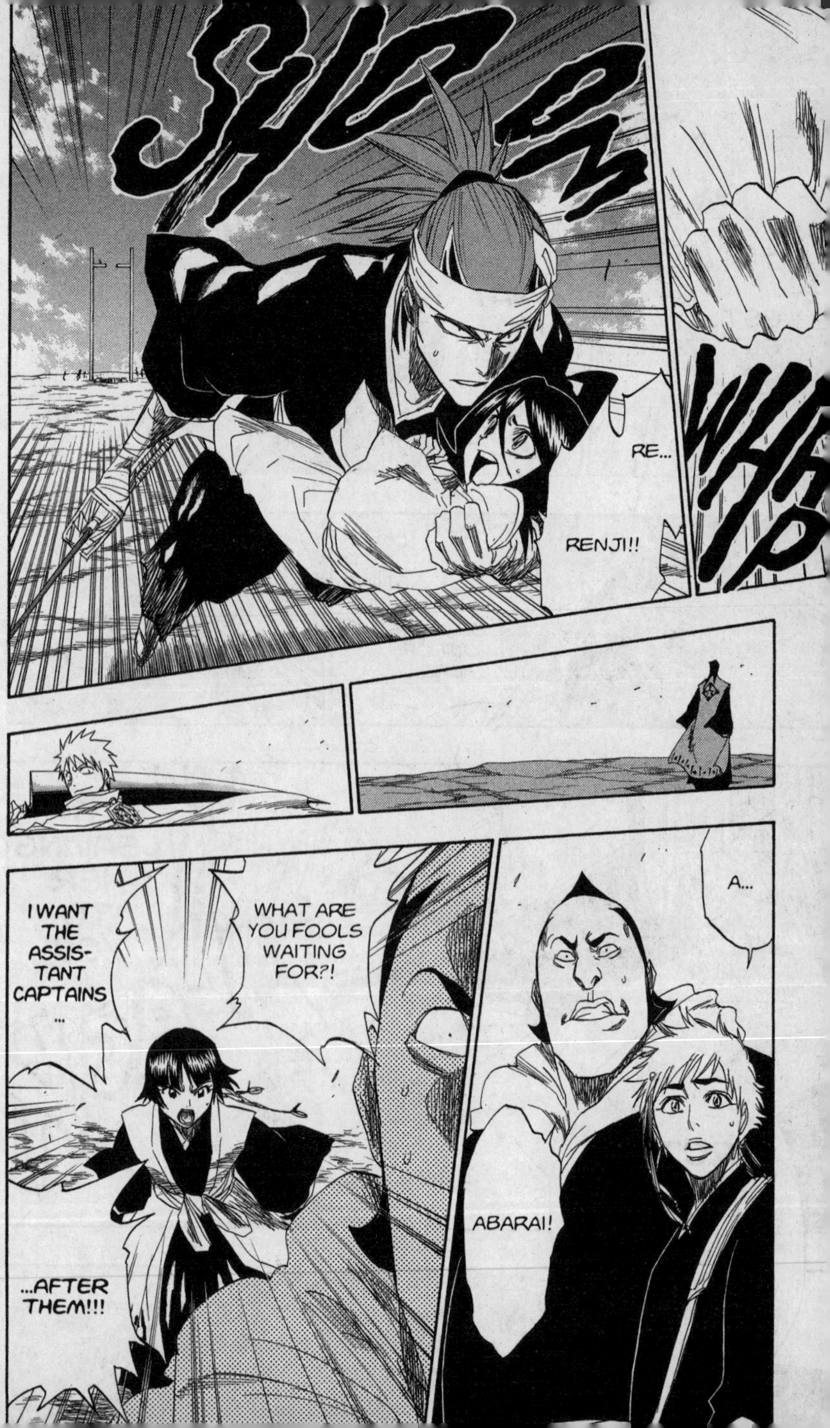
WHIP
SHUN
RE...
RENJI!!
A...
ABARAI!
WHAT ARE YOU FOOLS WAITING FOR?!
I WANT THE ASSISTANT CAPTAINS...
...AFTER THEM!!!

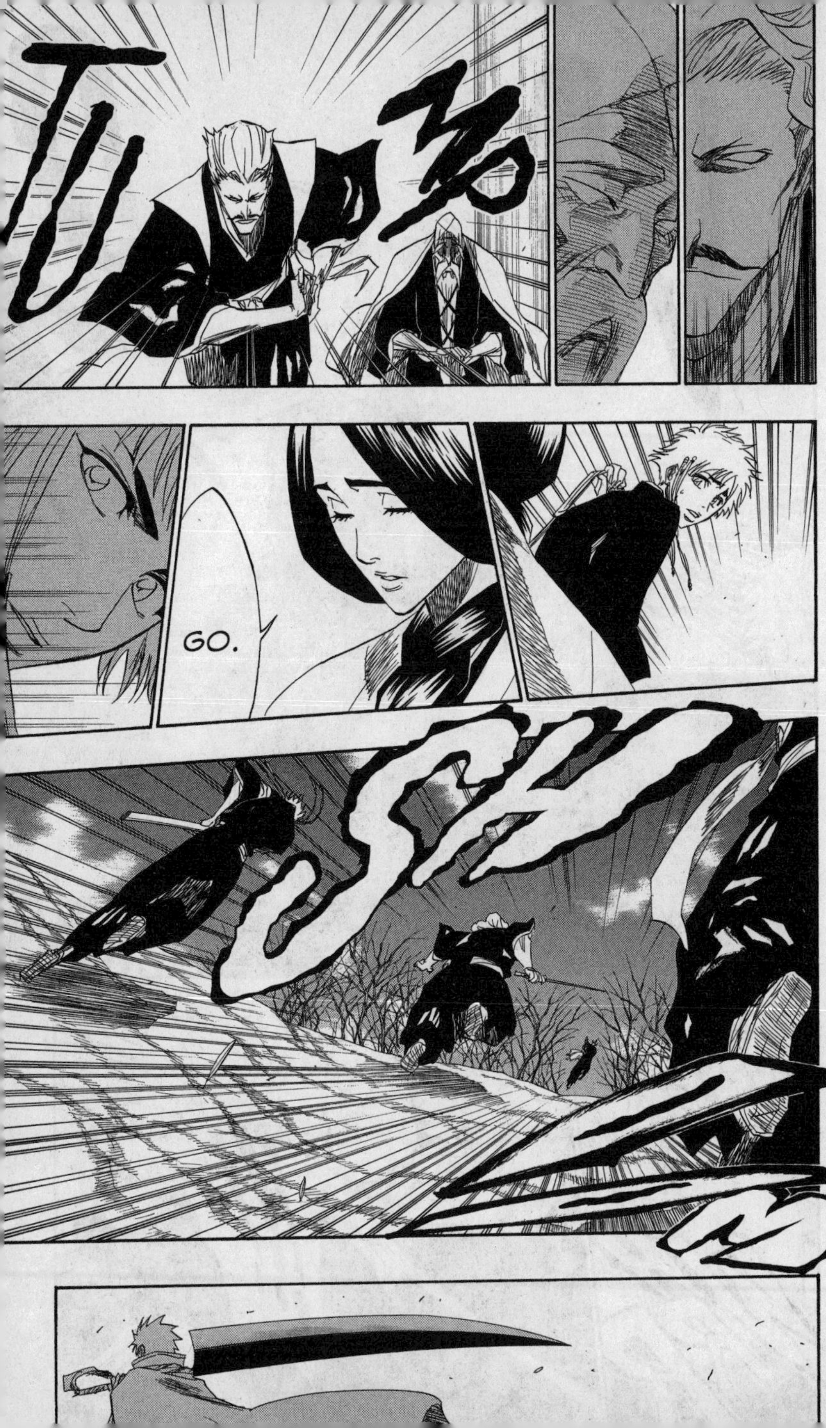
GO.

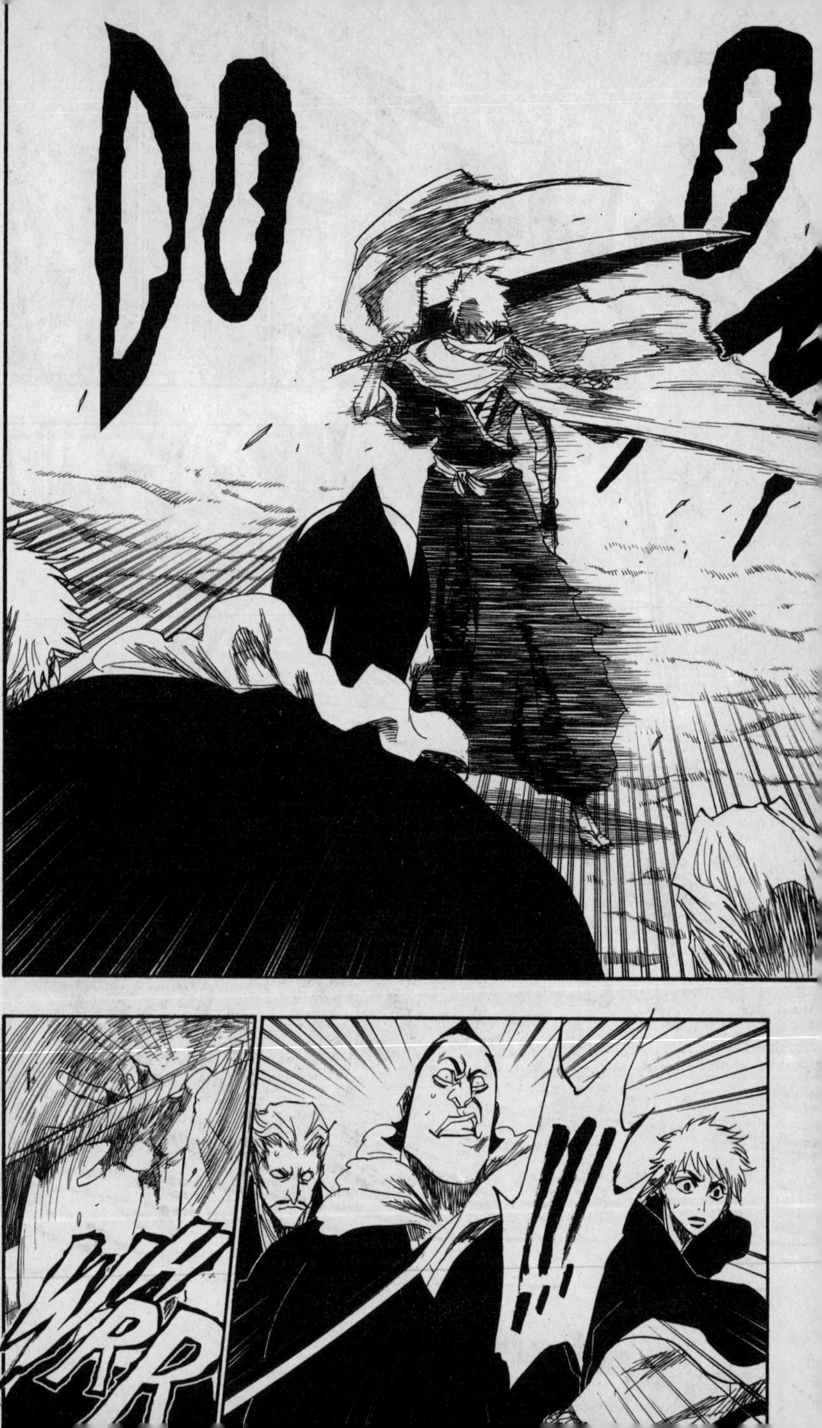
DOON
!!
WHRR

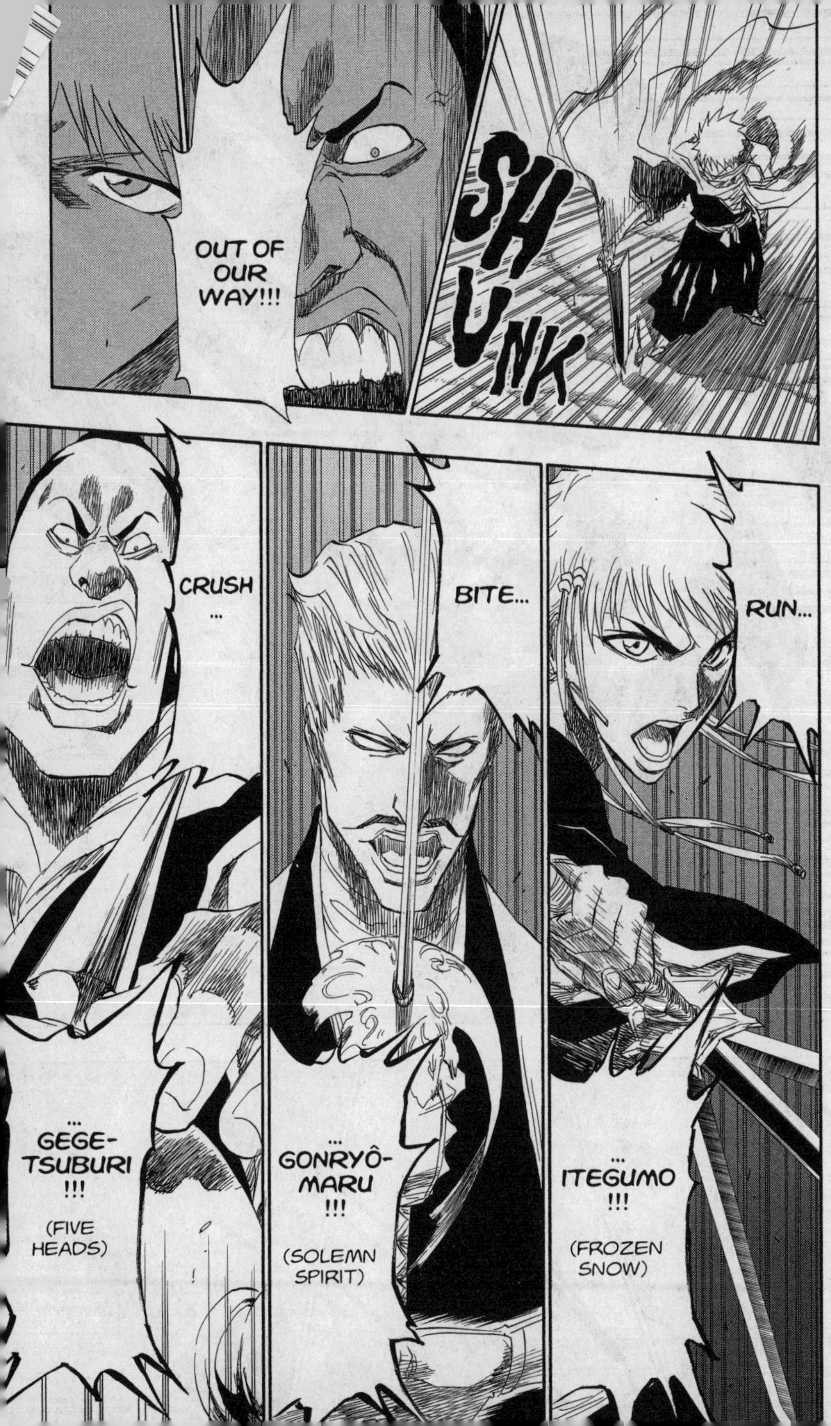
SHUNK
OUT OF OUR WAY!!!
RUN...
...ITEGUMO!!!
(FROZEN SNOW)
BITE...
...GONRYÔ-MARU!!!
(SOLEMN SPIRIT)
CRUSH...
...GEGE-TSUBURI!!!
(FIVE HEADS)

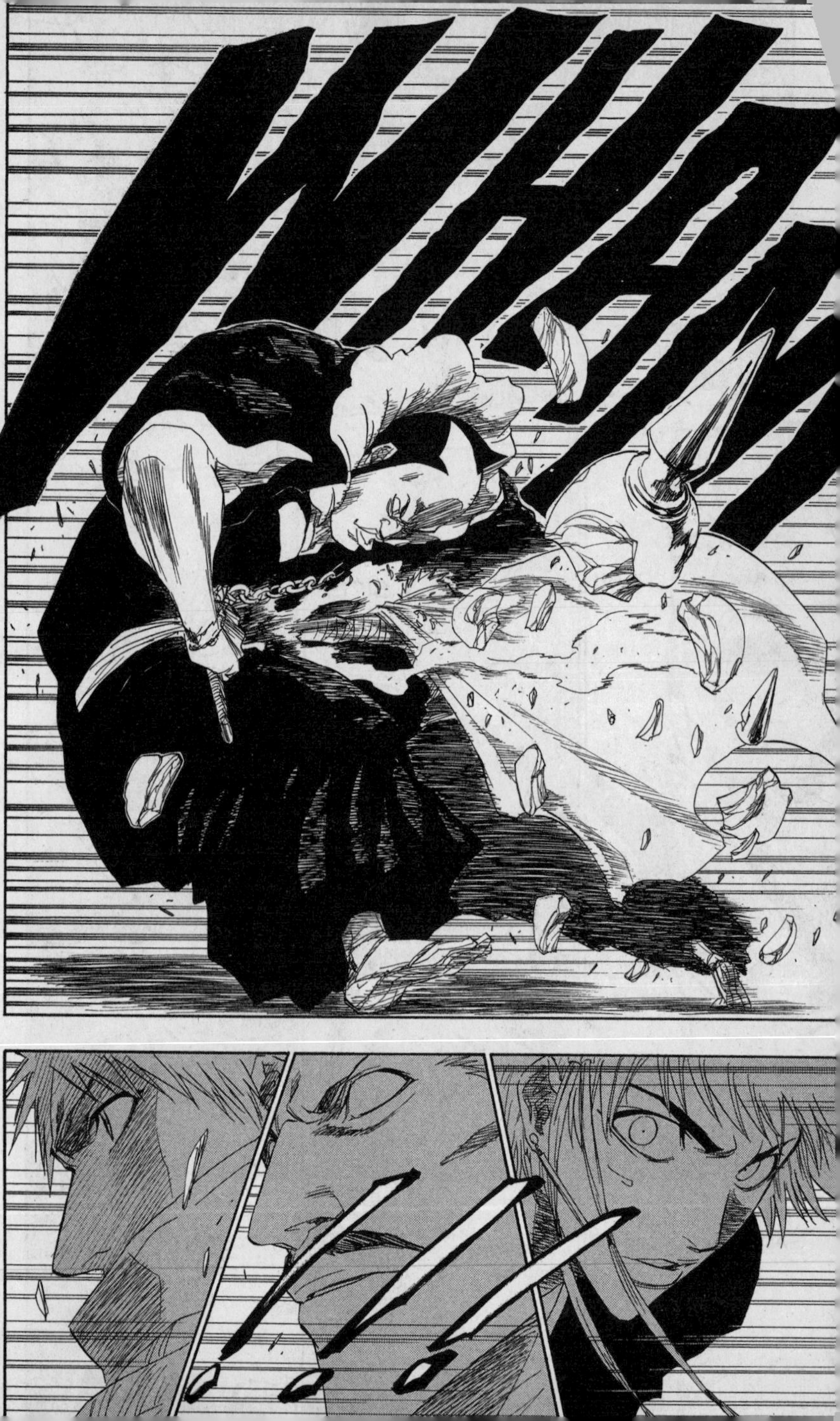
WHAM

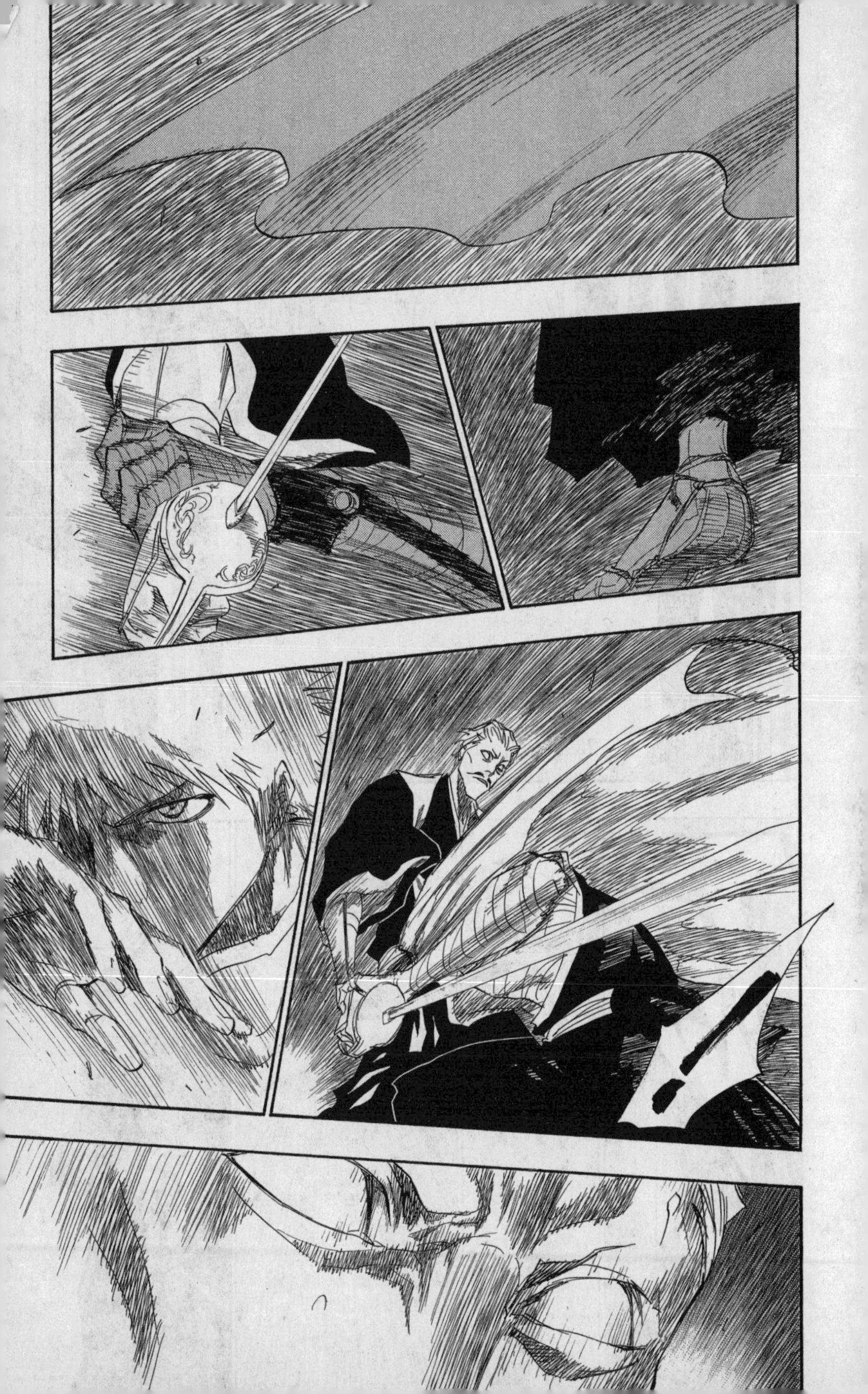

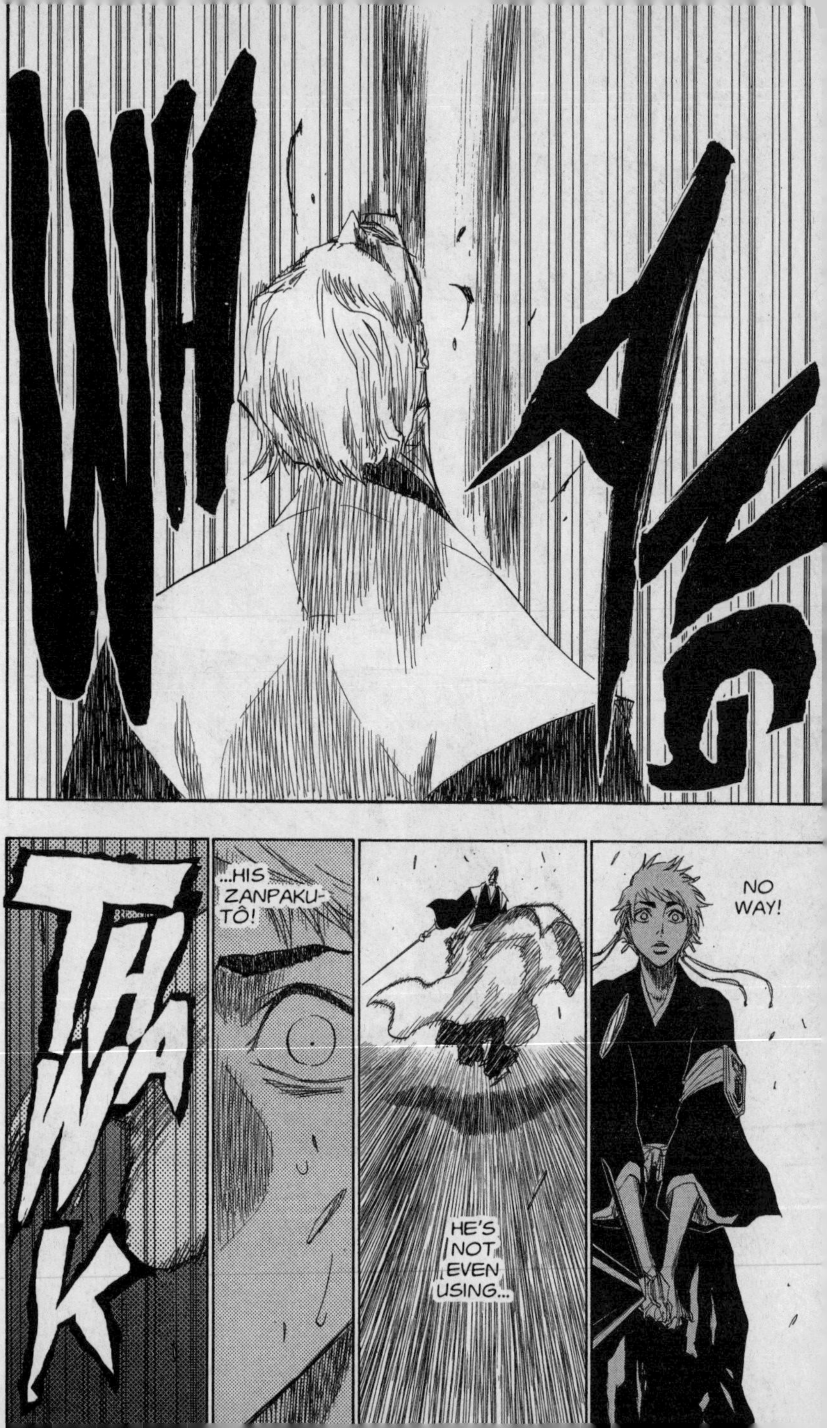
WHANG
NO WAY!
HE'S NOT EVEN USING...
...HIS ZANPAKU-TÔ!
THWAK

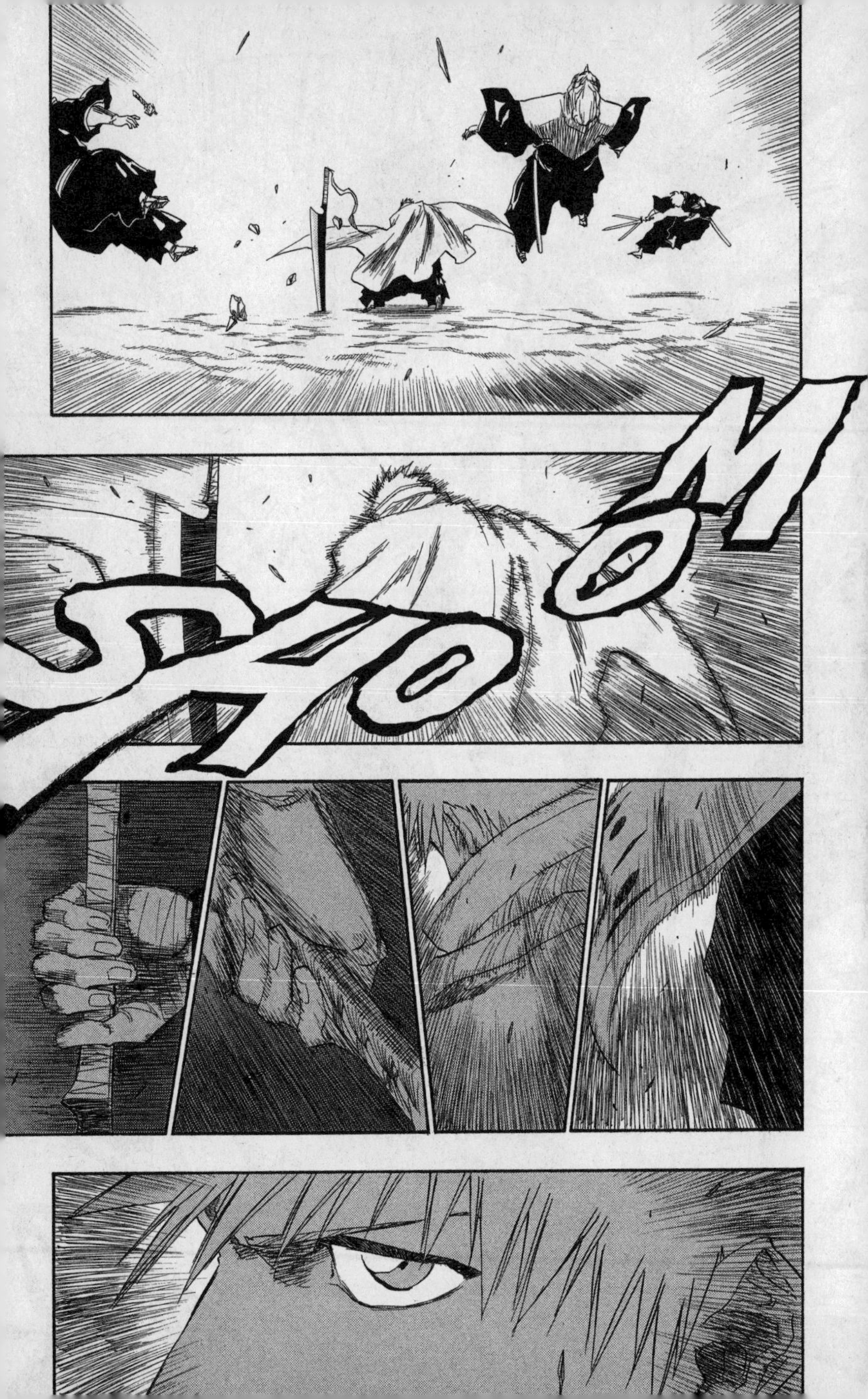
STOOM

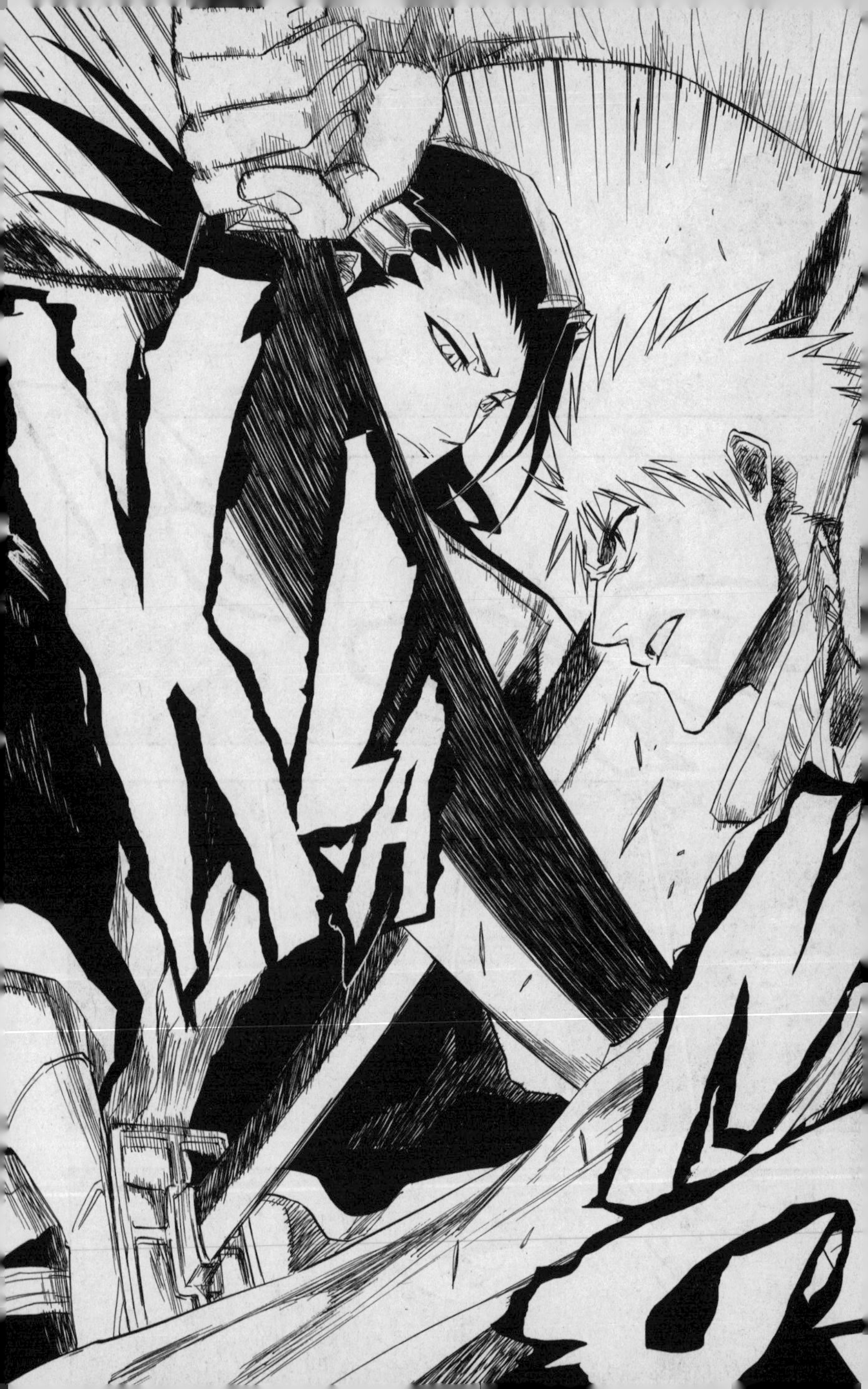

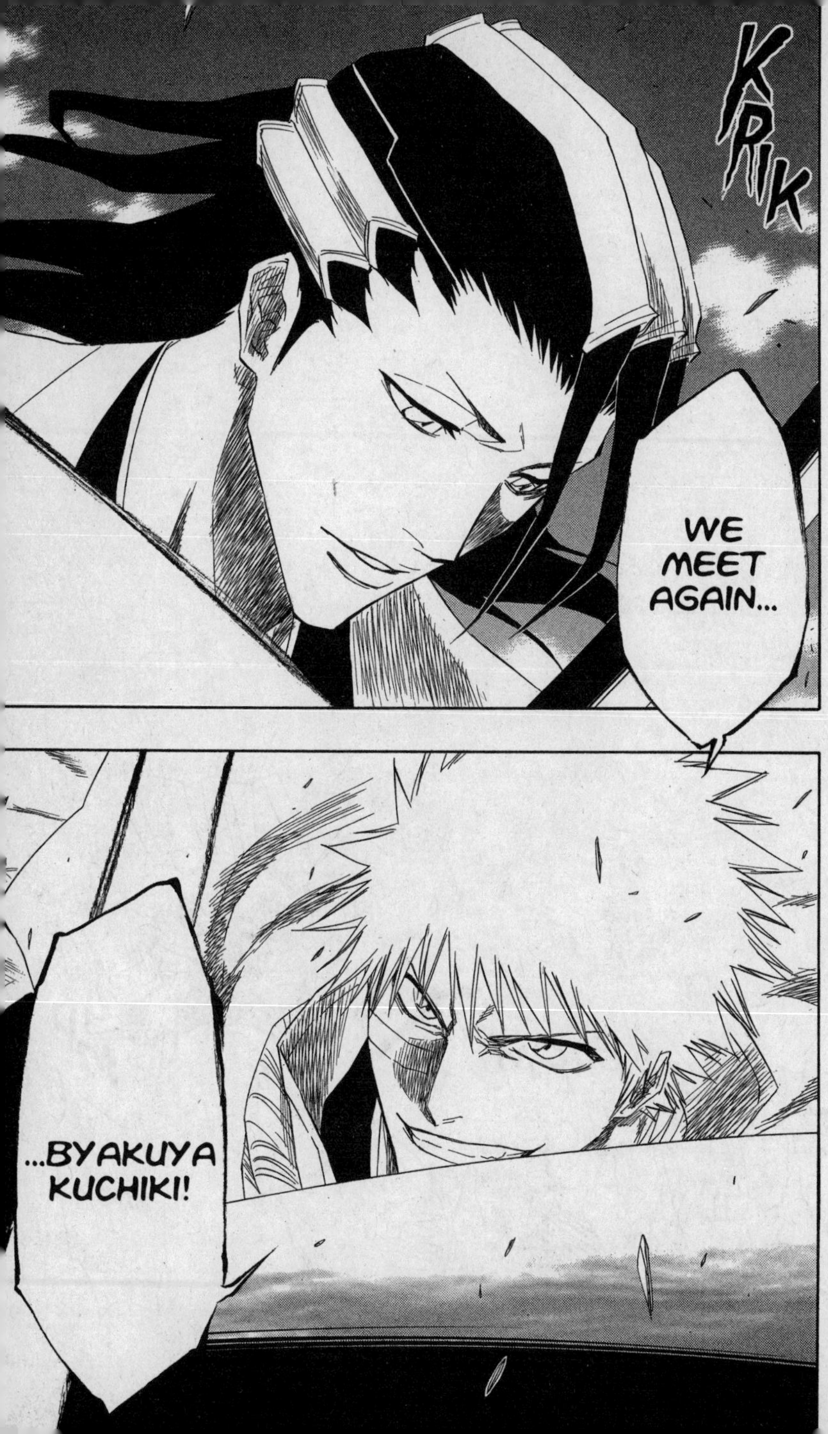
KRIK
WE MEET AGAIN...
...BYAKUYA KUCHIKI!

KILL!
TUMP
WHOA!!
BOOM
WHAT'RE THEY DOING?!
THAT'S A RED CARD!
WHAT?! IT'S NOT A FOUL?!
WAIT, YOU'RE THE REF?!

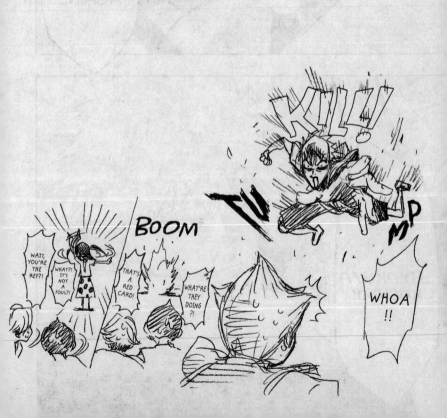

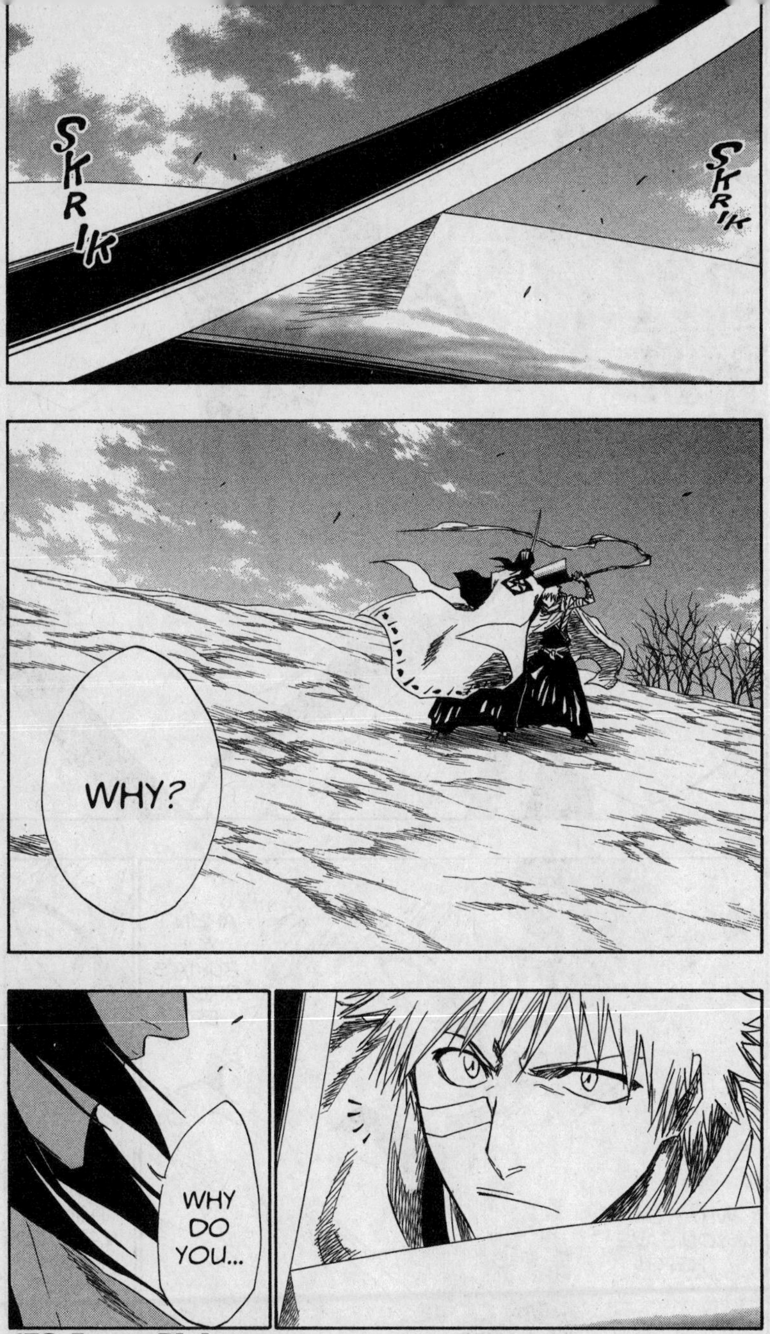
SKRIK
SKRIK
WHY?
WHY DO YOU...

153. Empty Dialogue

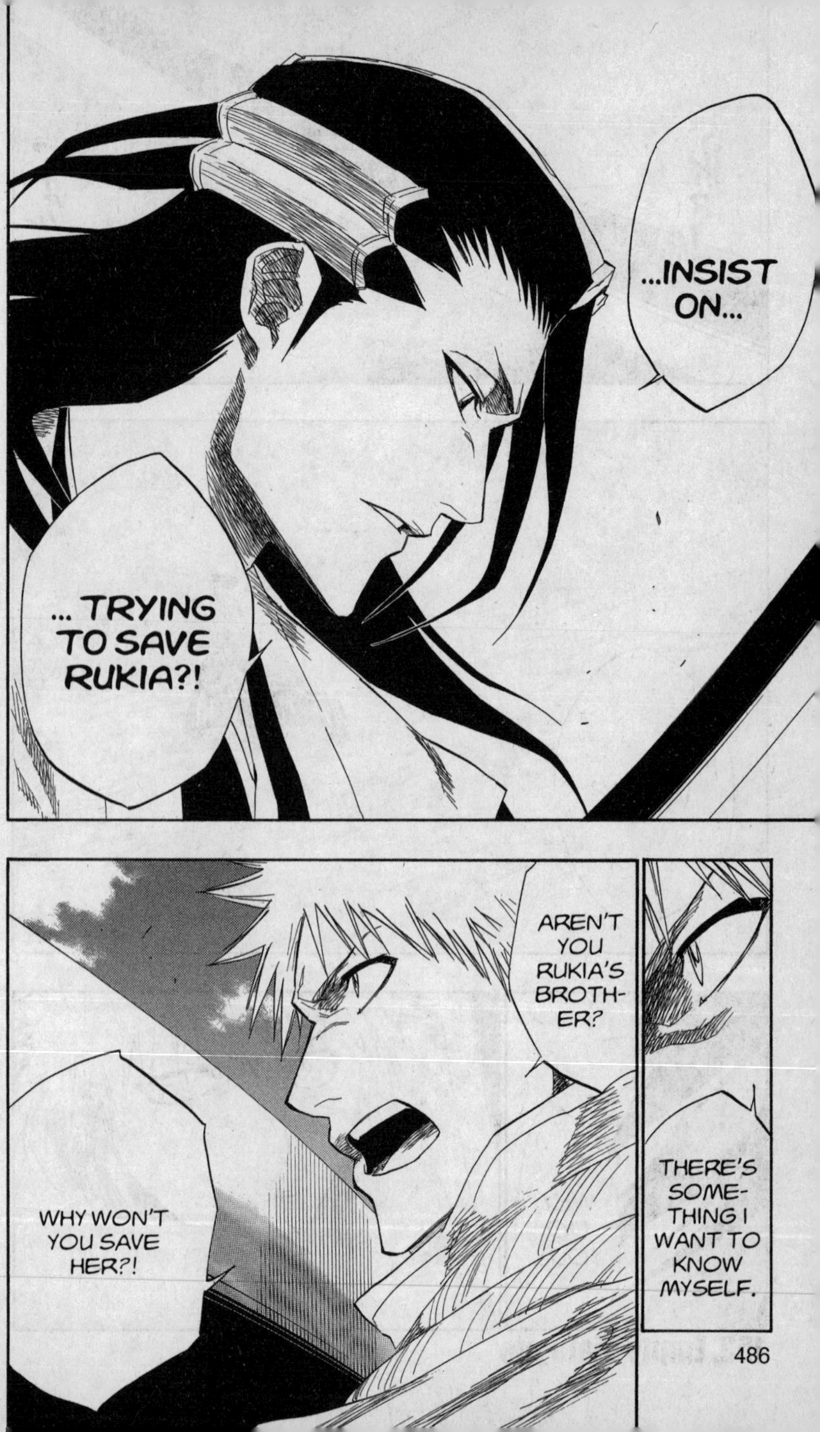
...INSIST ON...
... TRYING TO SAVE RUKIA?!
THERE'S SOMETHING I WANT TO KNOW MYSELF.
AREN'T YOU RUKIA'S BROTHER?
WHY WON'T YOU SAVE HER?!

READ THIS WAY

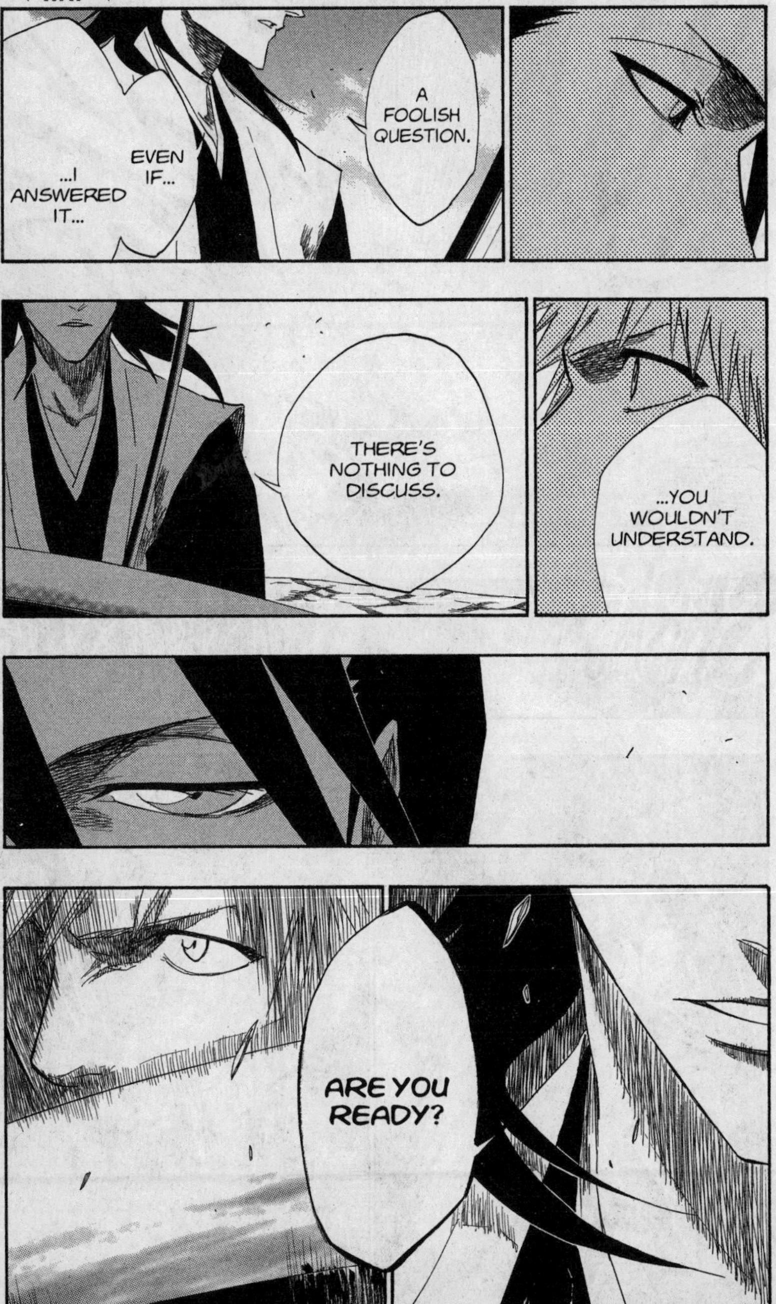
A FOOLISH QUESTION.
EVEN IF...
...I ANSWERED IT...
...YOU WOULDN'T UNDERSTAND.
THERE'S NOTHING TO DISCUSS.
ARE YOU READY?

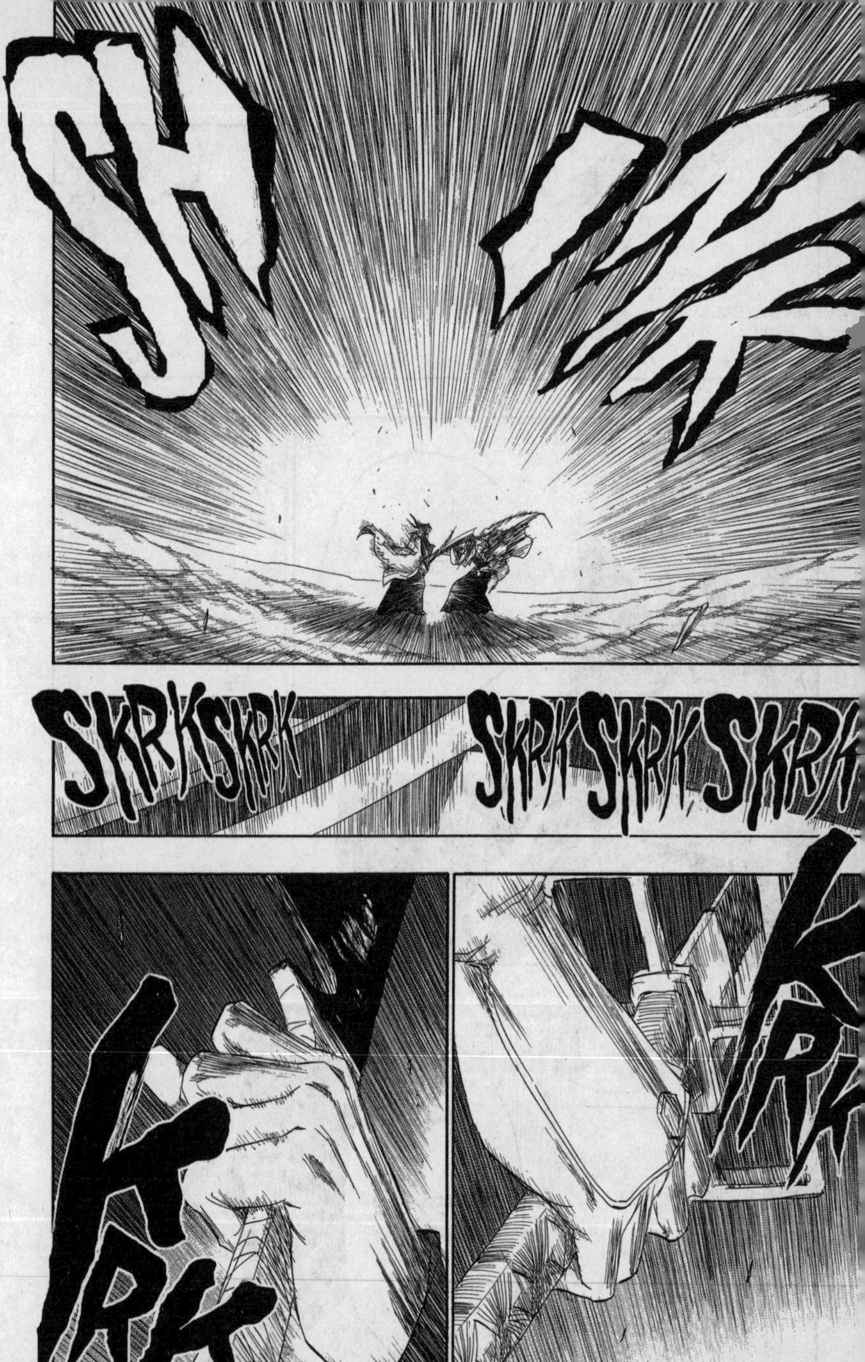
SH
SKRK SKRK SKRK
SKRKSKRK
KRK
KRK

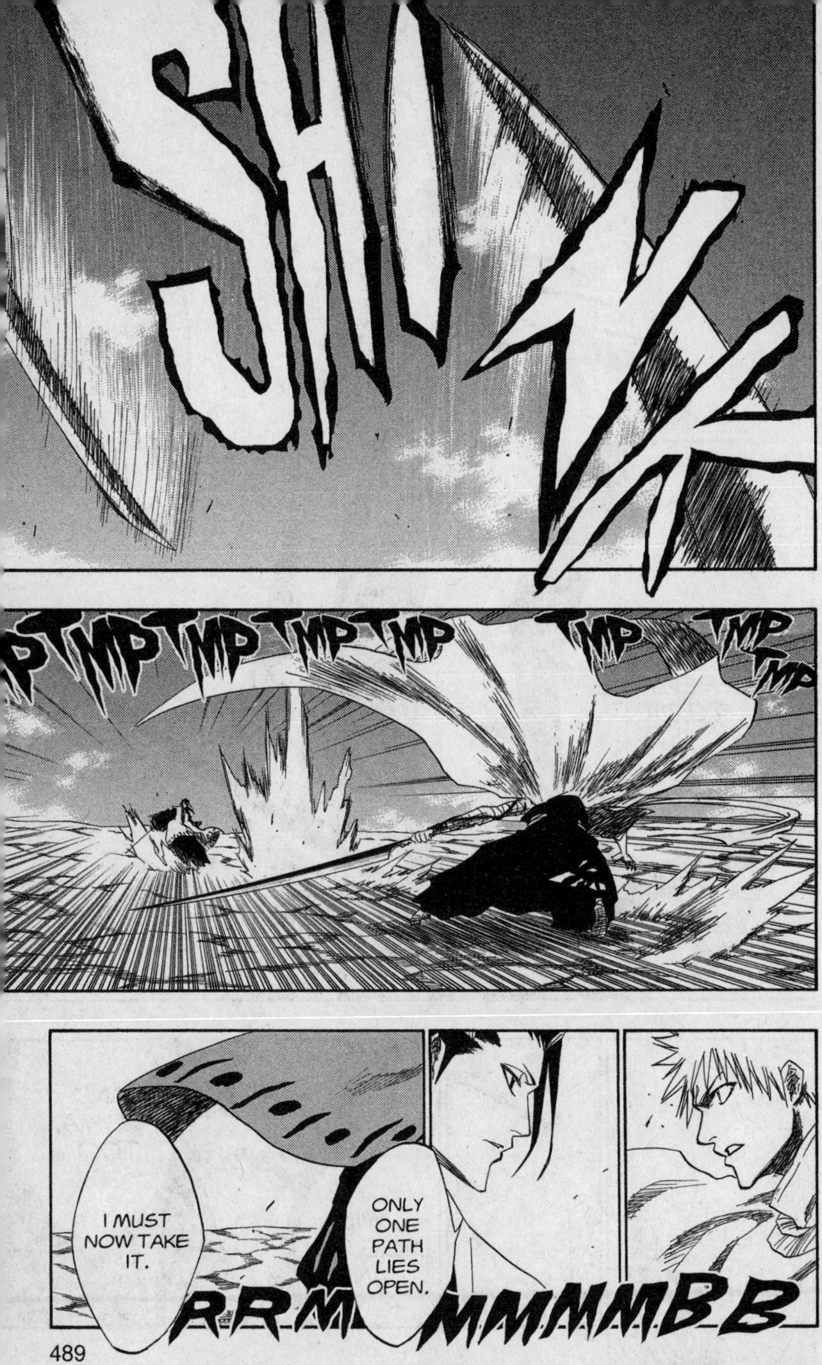
SHUNK
TMP TMP TMP TMP TMP TMP TMP
ONLY ONE PATH LIES OPEN.
I MUST NOW TAKE IT.
RRMMMMMMBB

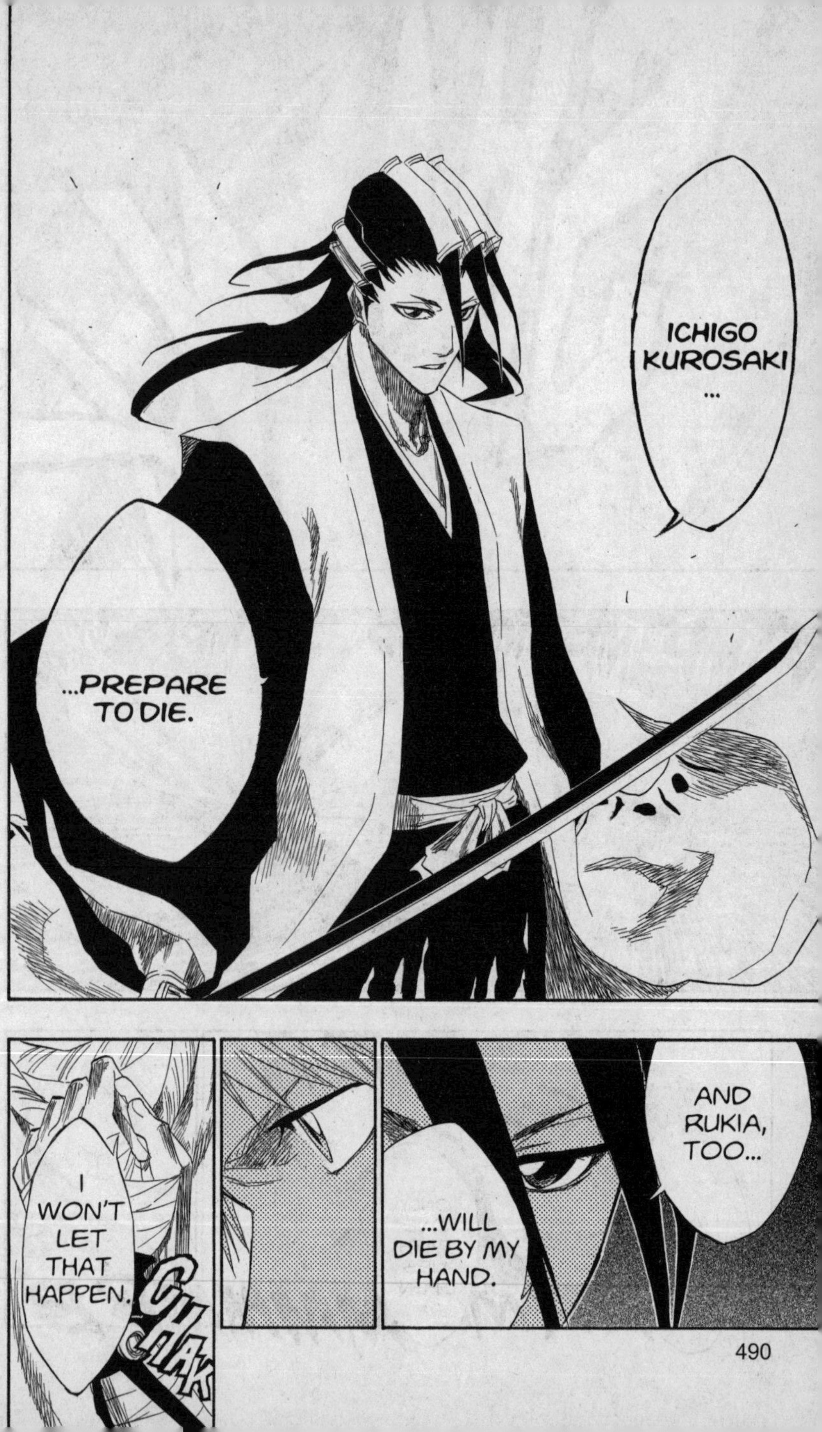
ICHIGO KUROSAKI ...
...PREPARE TO DIE.
AND RUKIA, TOO...
...WILL DIE BY MY HAND.
I WON'T LET THAT HAPPEN.
CHAK

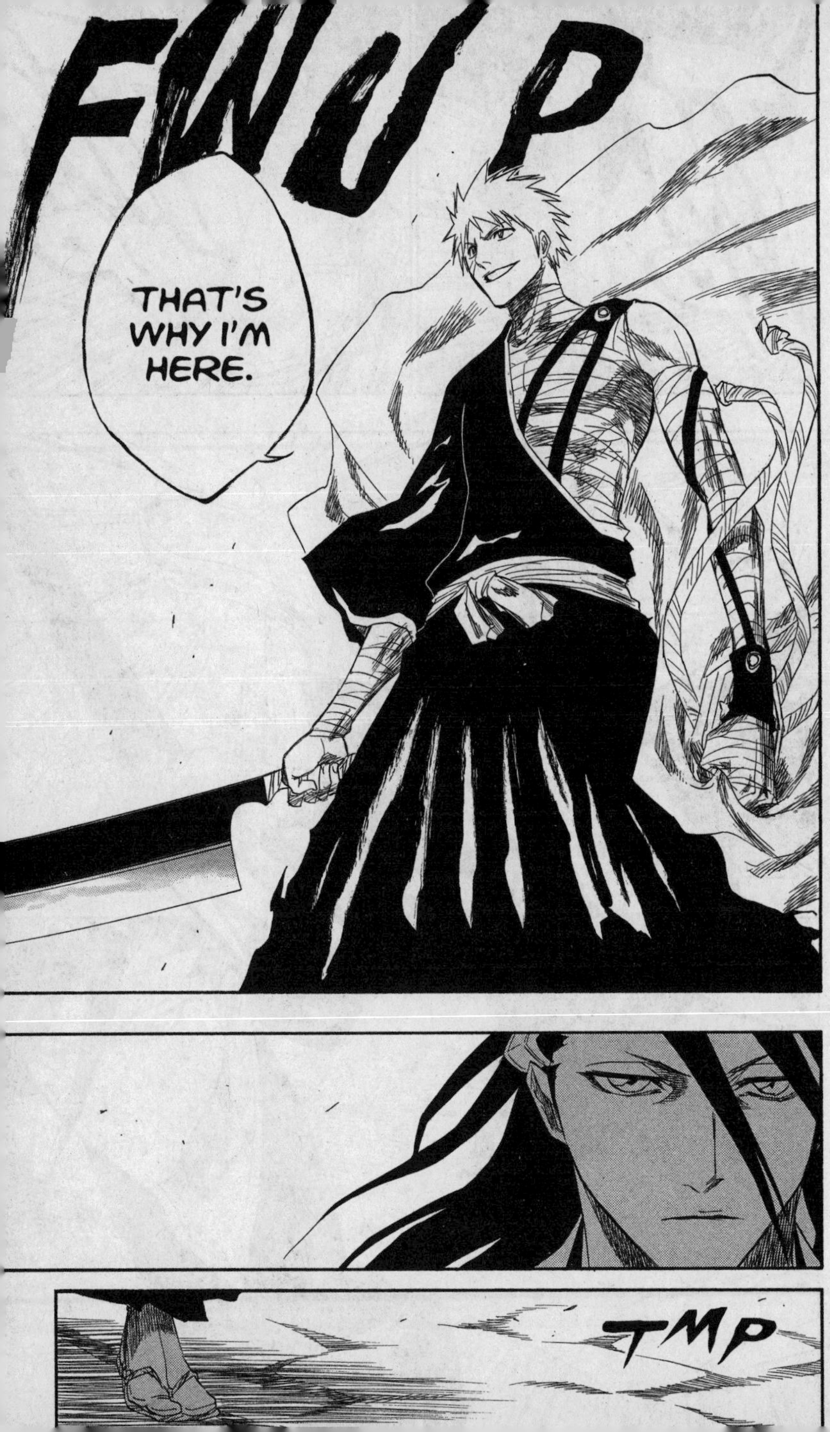
FWUP
THAT'S WHY I'M HERE.
TMP

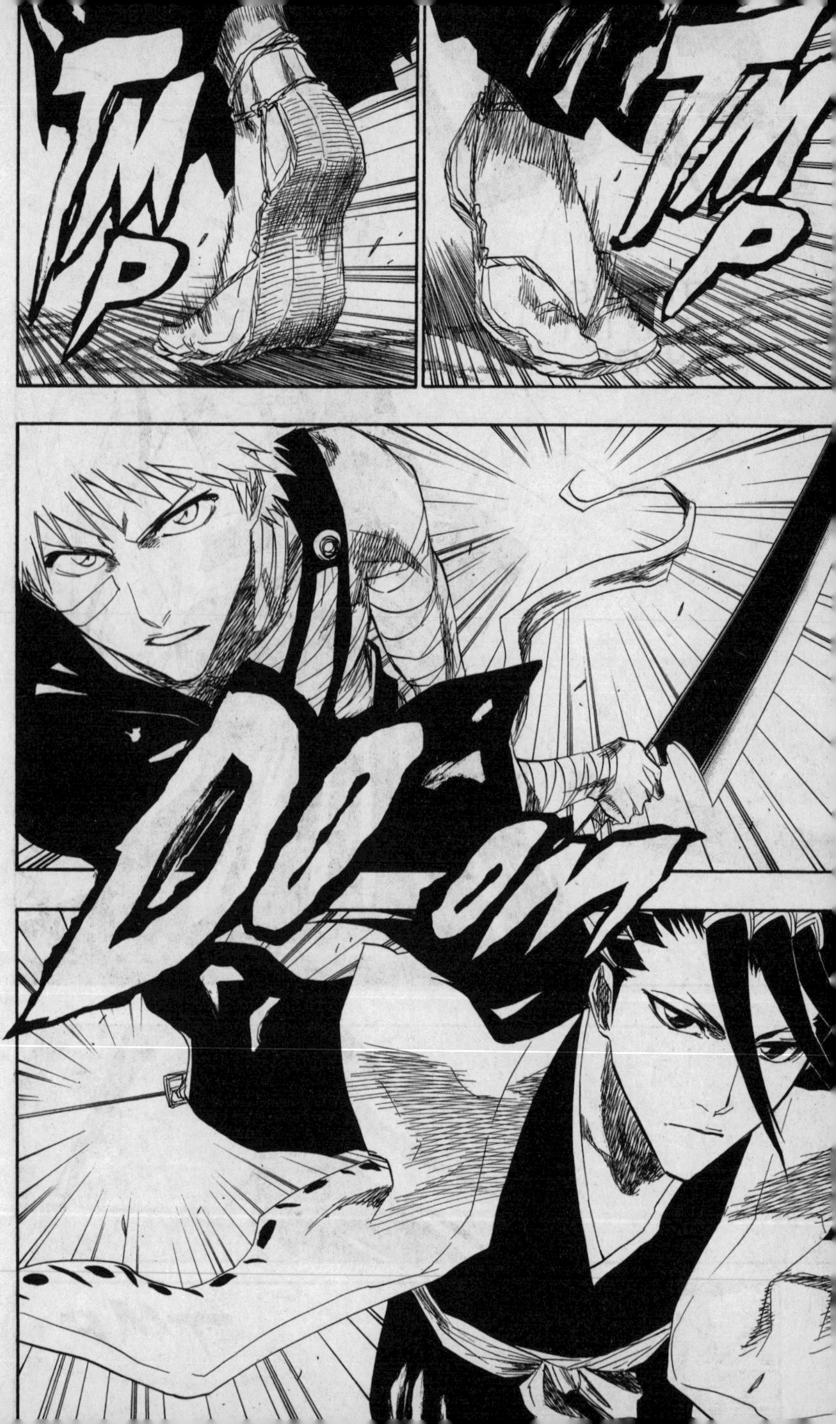

TMP
TMP
DO-OM

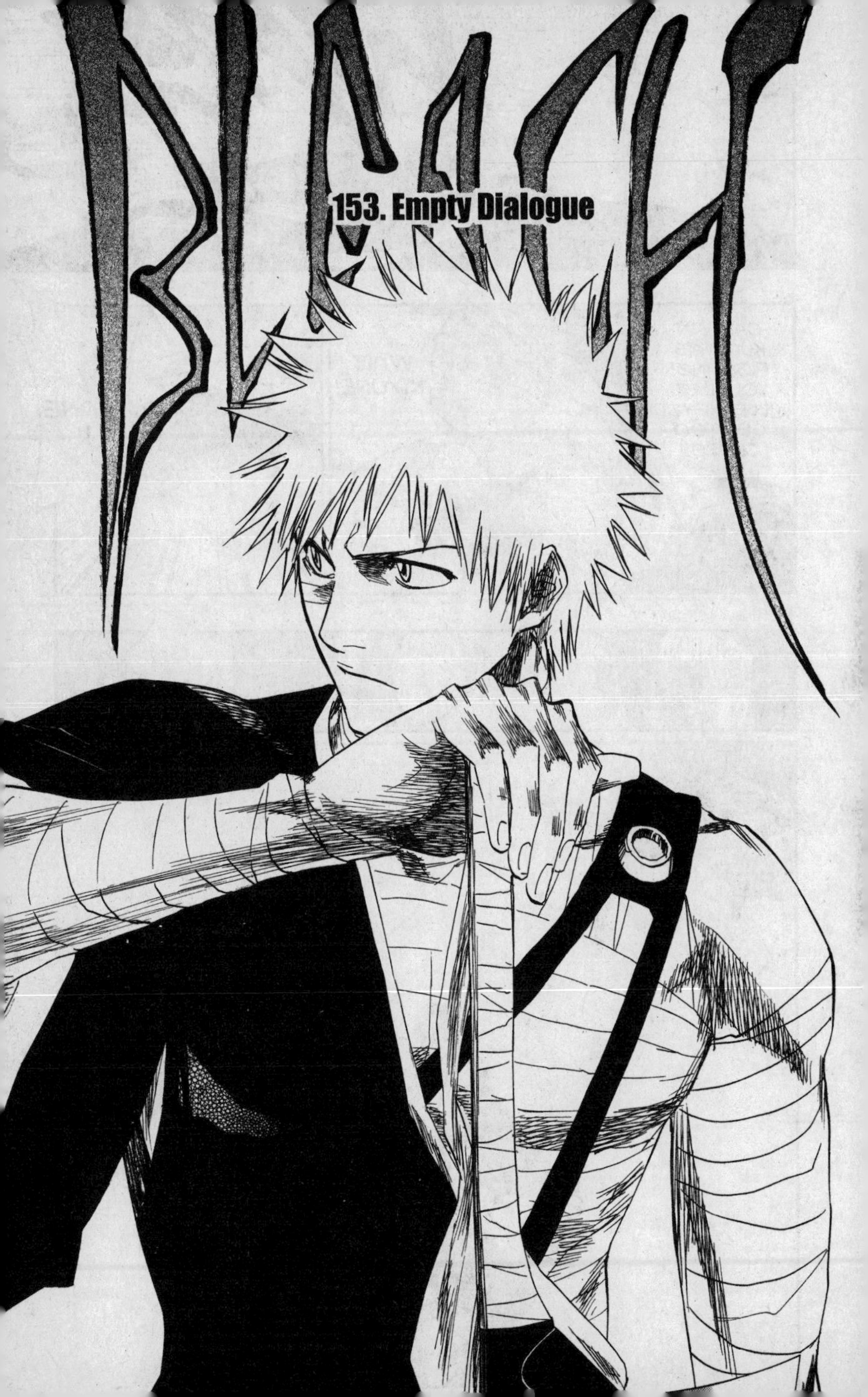
BLEACH
153. Empty Dialogue

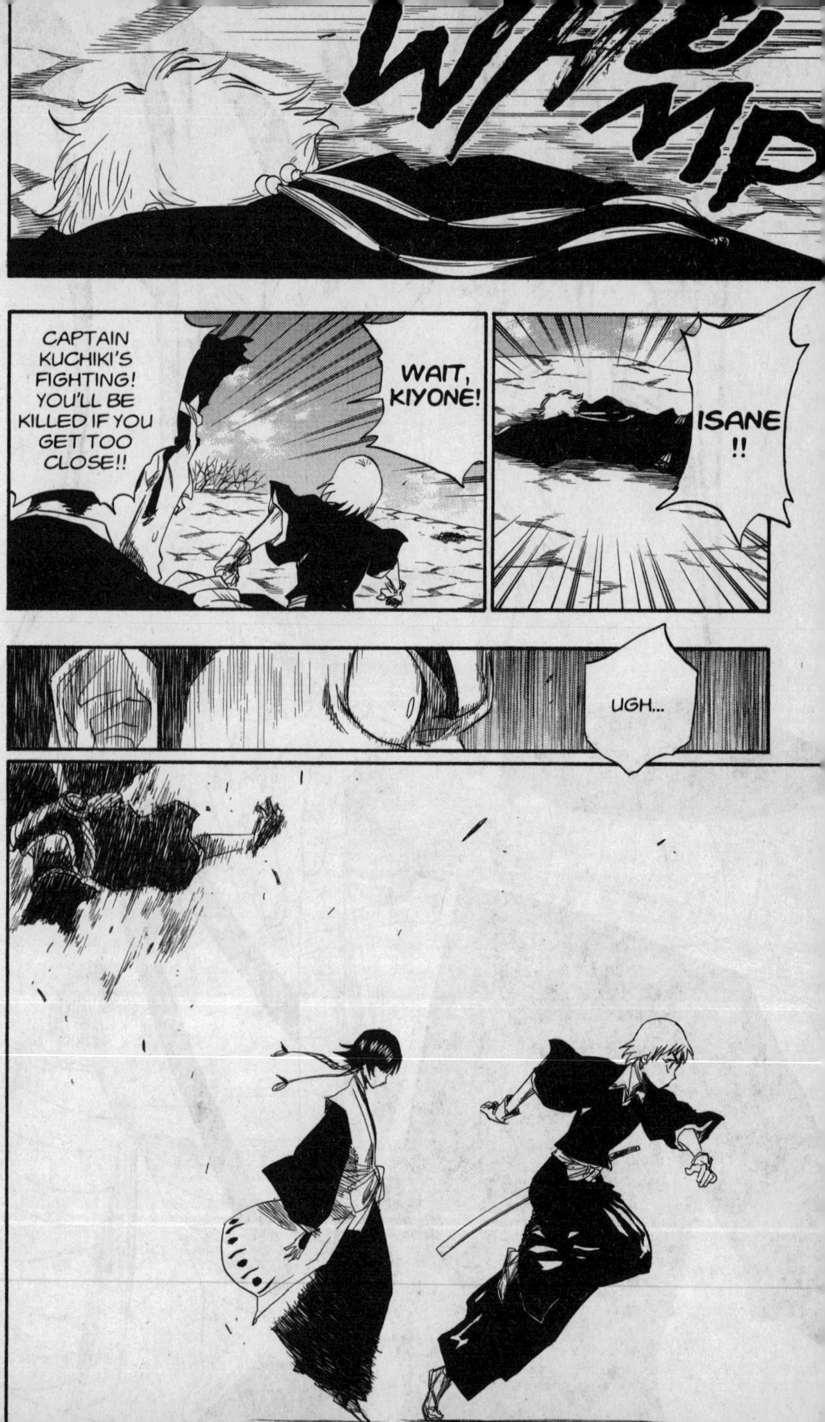
WHUMP
ISANE!!
WAIT, KIYONE!
CAPTAIN KUCHIKI'S FIGHTING! YOU'LL BE KILLED IF YOU GET TOO CLOSE!!
UGH...

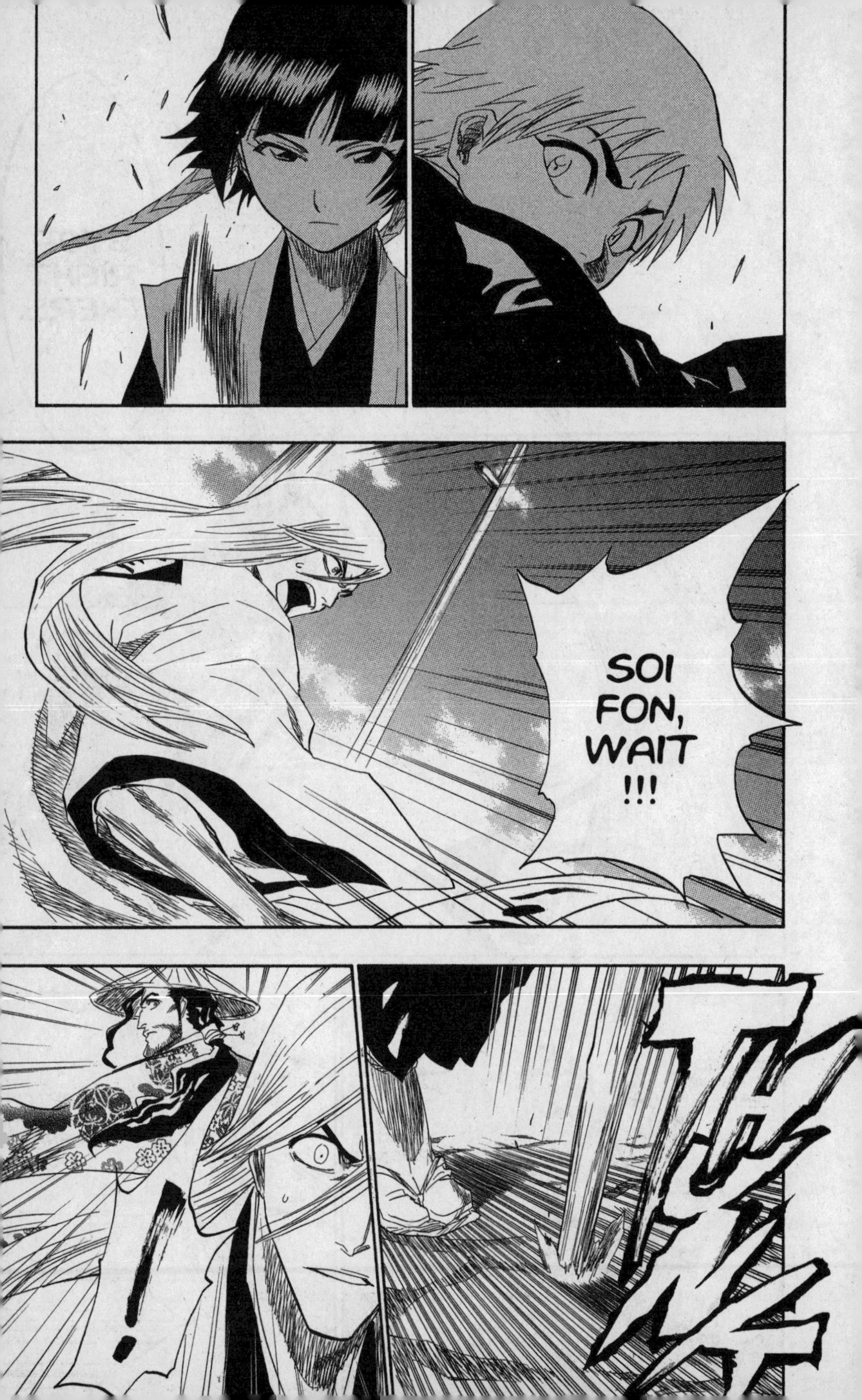
SOI FON, WAIT !!!
!

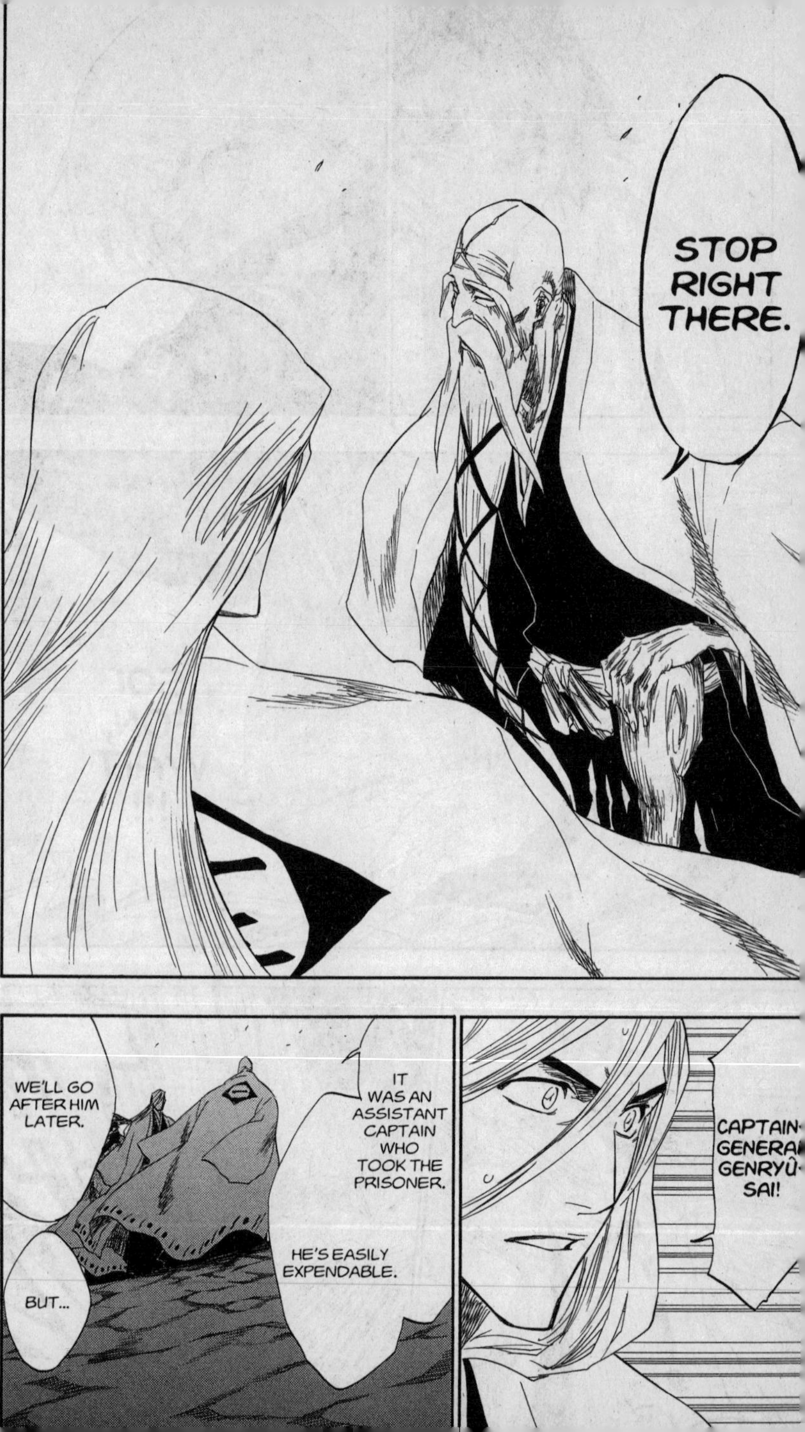
STOP RIGHT THERE.
CAPTAIN-GENERA GENRYÛ-SAI!
IT WAS AN ASSISTANT CAPTAIN WHO TOOK THE PRISONER.
HE'S EASILY EXPENDABLE.
WE'LL GO AFTER HIM LATER.
BUT...

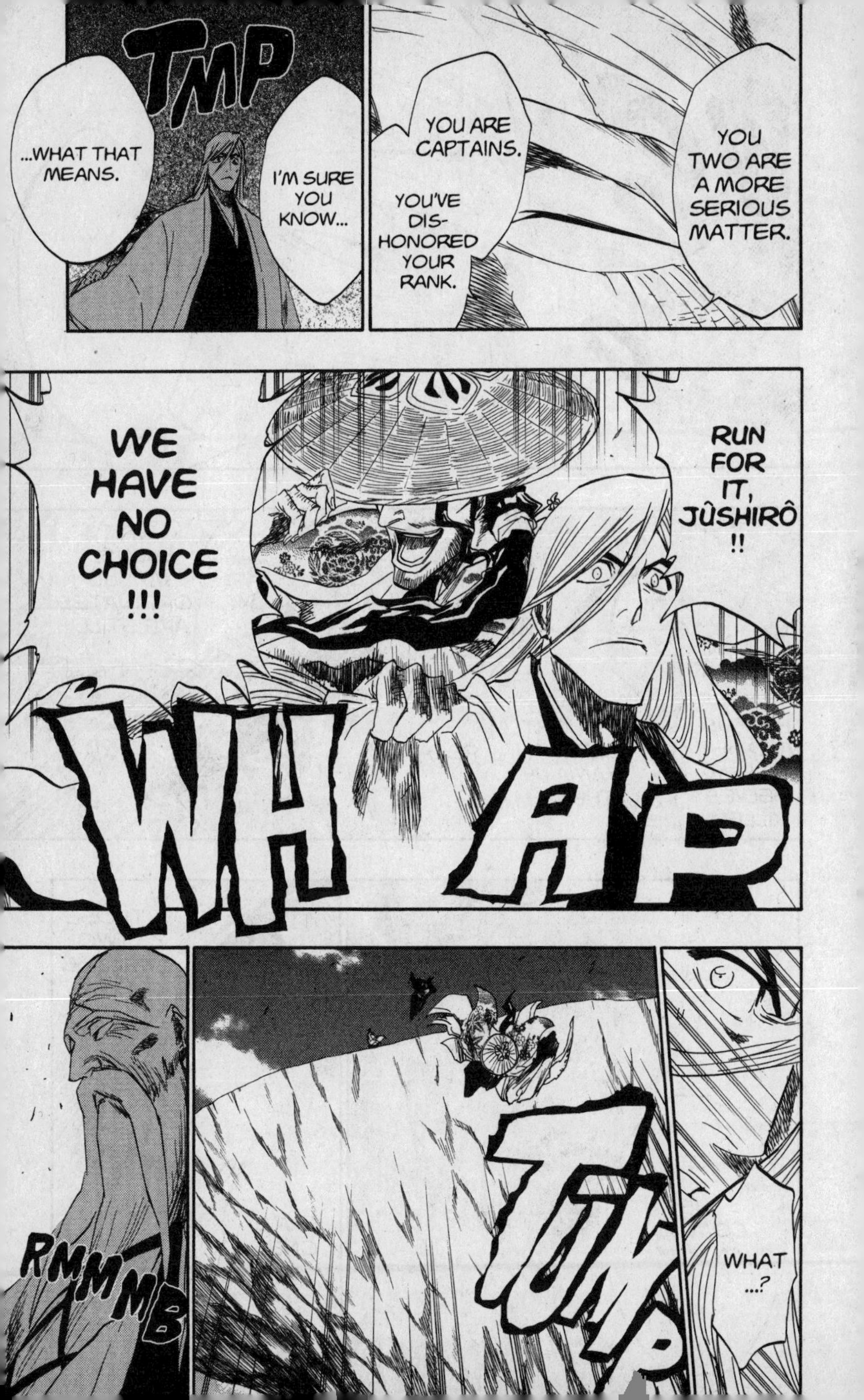
YOU TWO ARE A MORE SERIOUS MATTER.
YOU ARE CAPTAINS.
YOU'VE DIS-HONORED YOUR RANK.
TMP
I'M SURE YOU KNOW...
...WHAT THAT MEANS.
RUN FOR IT, JÛSHIRÔ!!
WE HAVE NO CHOICE!!!
WHAP
WHAT...?
TOMP
RMMMB

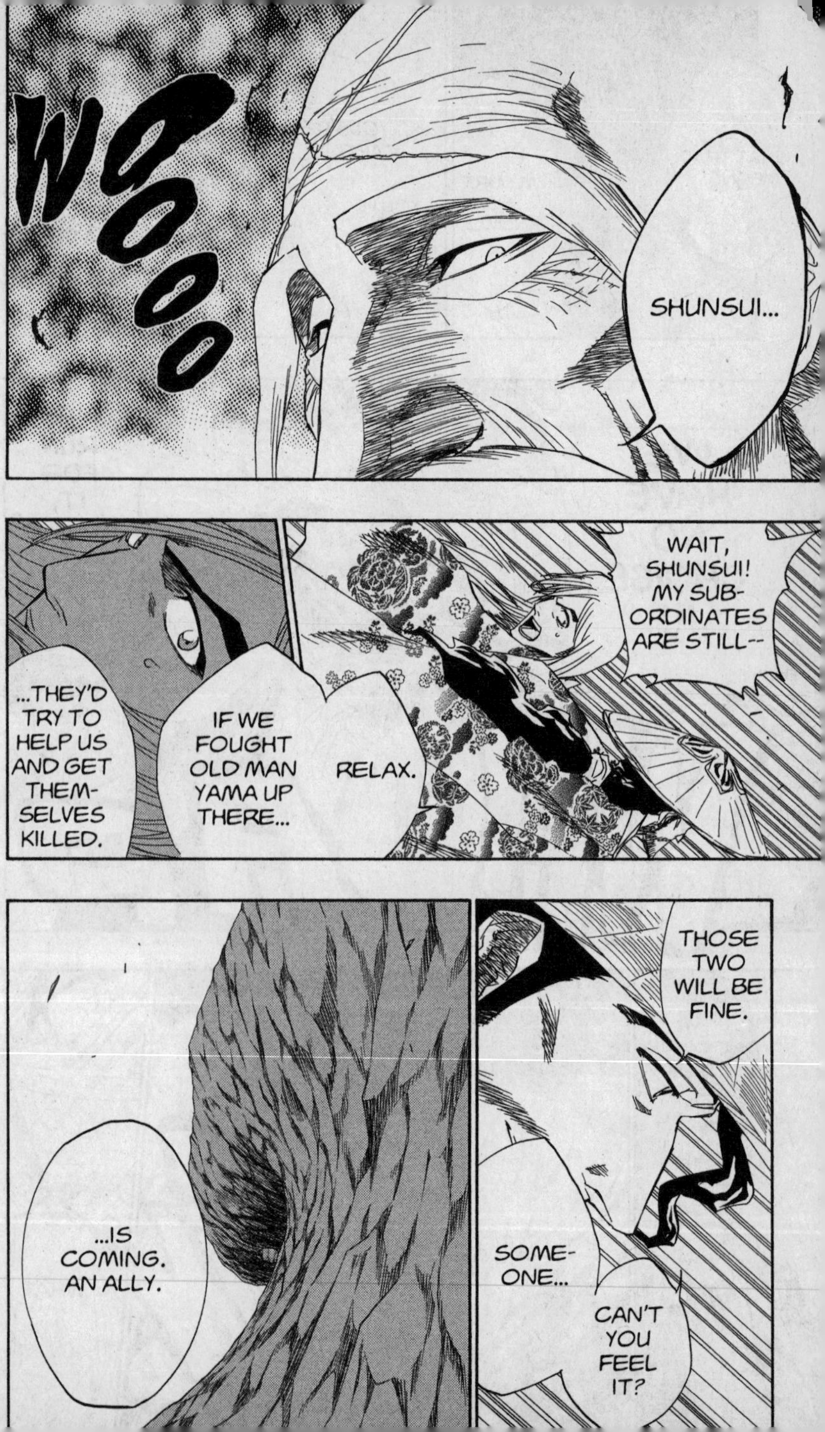
SHUNSUI...
WOOOOO
WAIT, SHUNSUI! MY SUB-ORDINATES ARE STILL--
RELAX.
IF WE FOUGHT OLD MAN YAMA UP THERE...
...THEY'D TRY TO HELP US AND GET THEM-SELVES KILLED.
THOSE TWO WILL BE FINE.
SOME-ONE...
CAN'T YOU FEEL IT?
...IS COMING. AN ALLY.

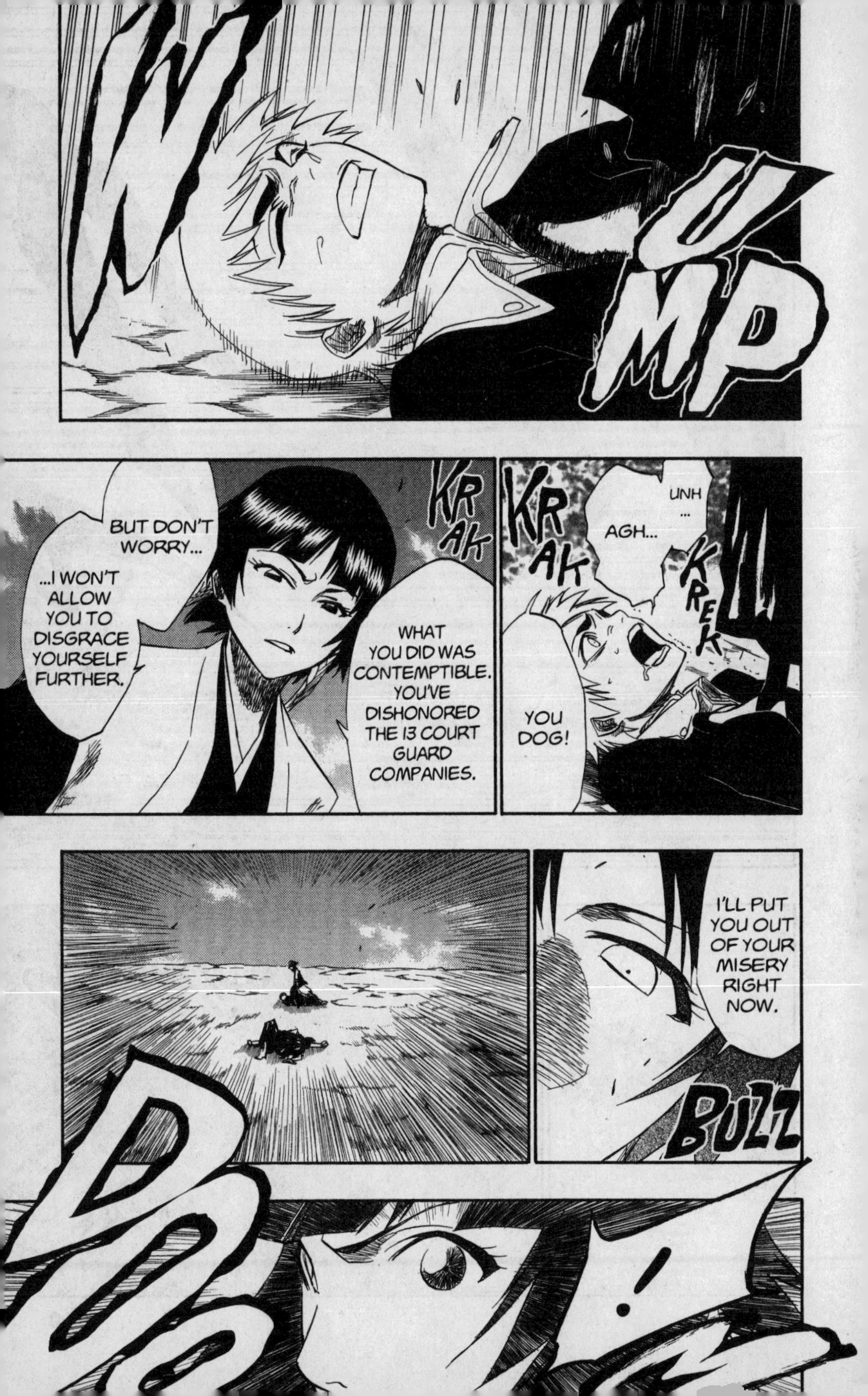
WUMP
UNH...
KREK
KRAK
AGH...
YOU DOG!
KRAK
WHAT YOU DID WAS CONTEMPTIBLE. YOU'VE DISHONORED THE 13 COURT GUARD COMPANIES.
BUT DON'T WORRY...
...I WON'T ALLOW YOU TO DISGRACE YOURSELF FURTHER.
I'LL PUT YOU OUT OF YOUR MISERY RIGHT NOW.
BUZZ

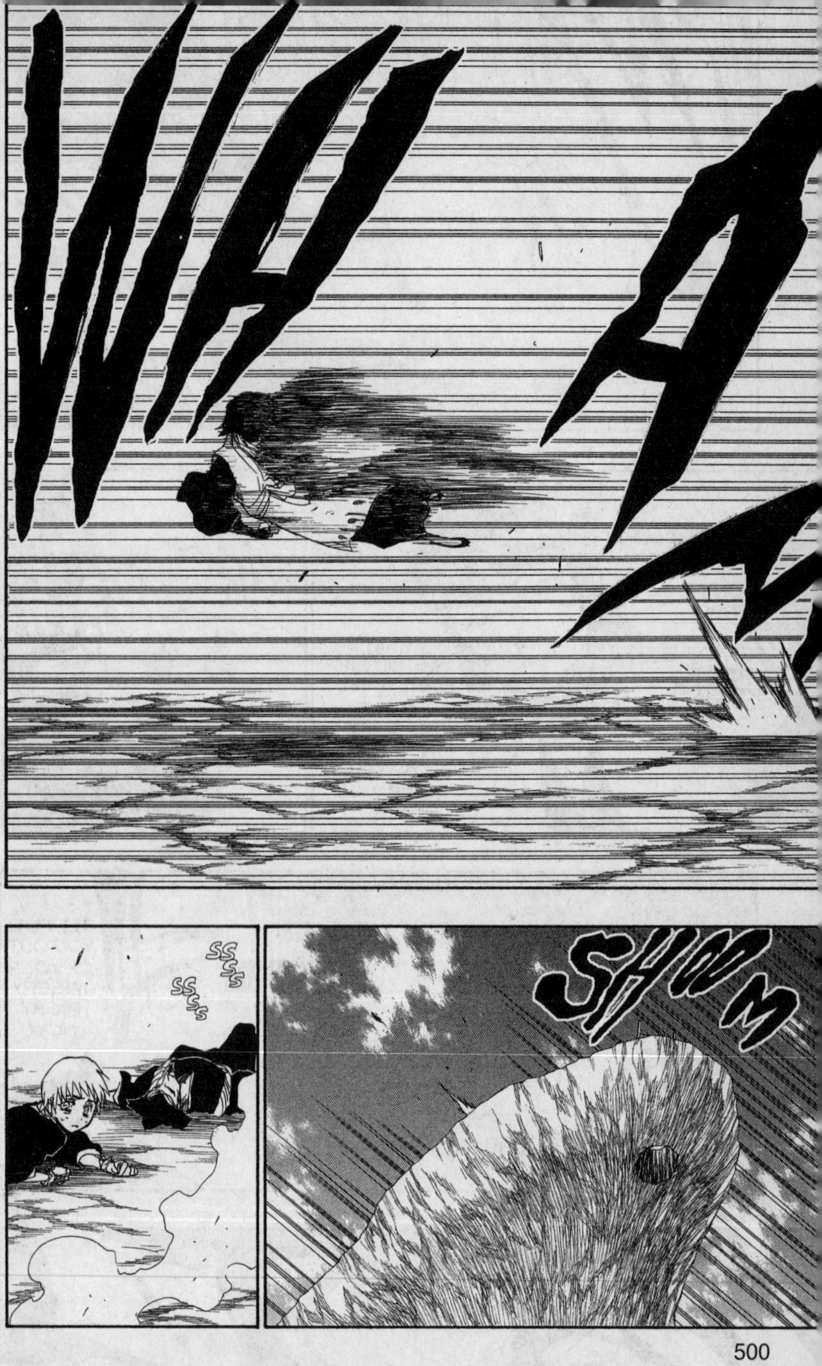
WHAM
SHOOM
SSSS
SSSS

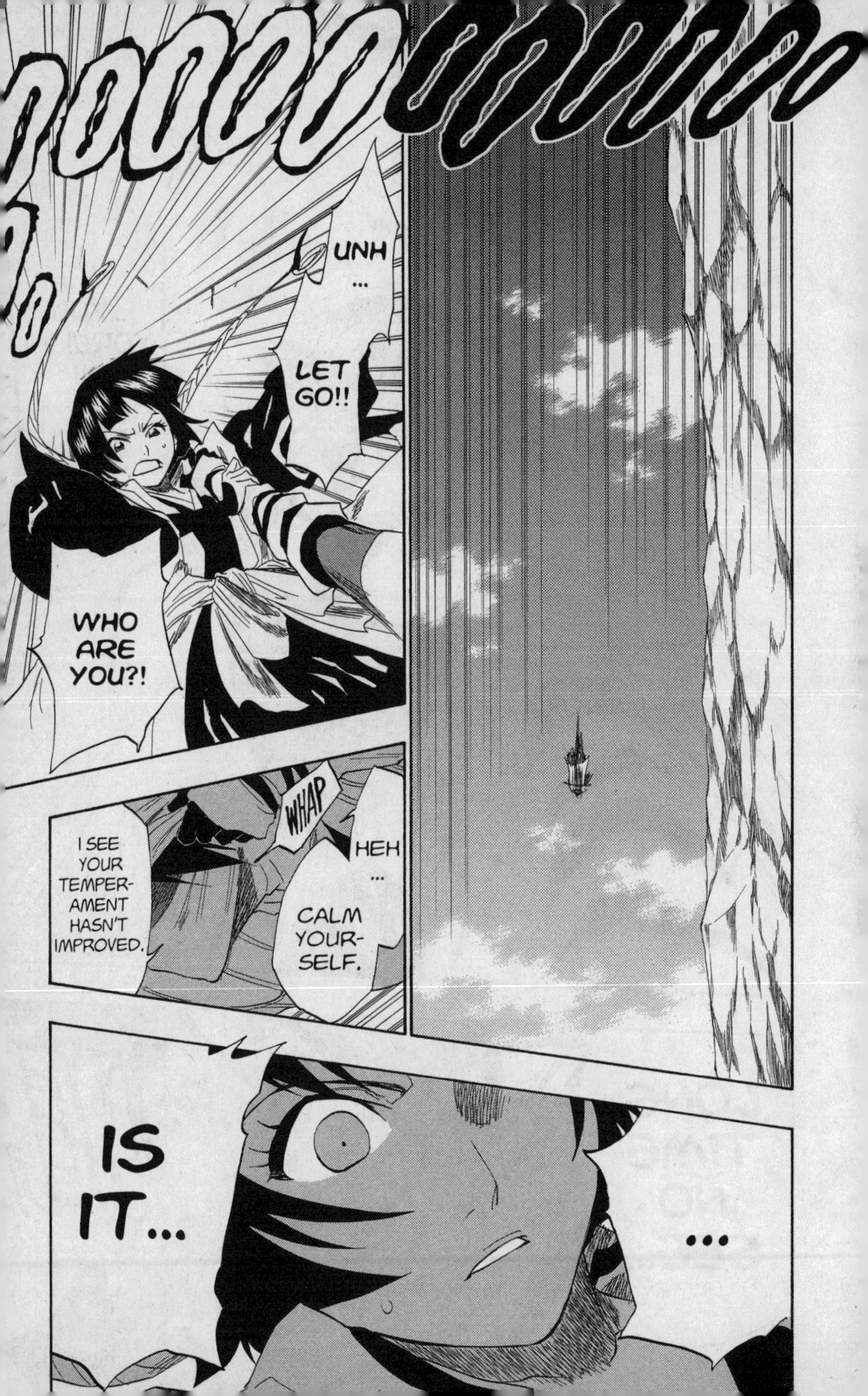
UNH ...
LET GO!!
WHO ARE YOU?!
WHAP
HEH ...
CALM YOURSELF.
I SEE YOUR TEMPERAMENT HASN'T IMPROVED.
...
IS IT...

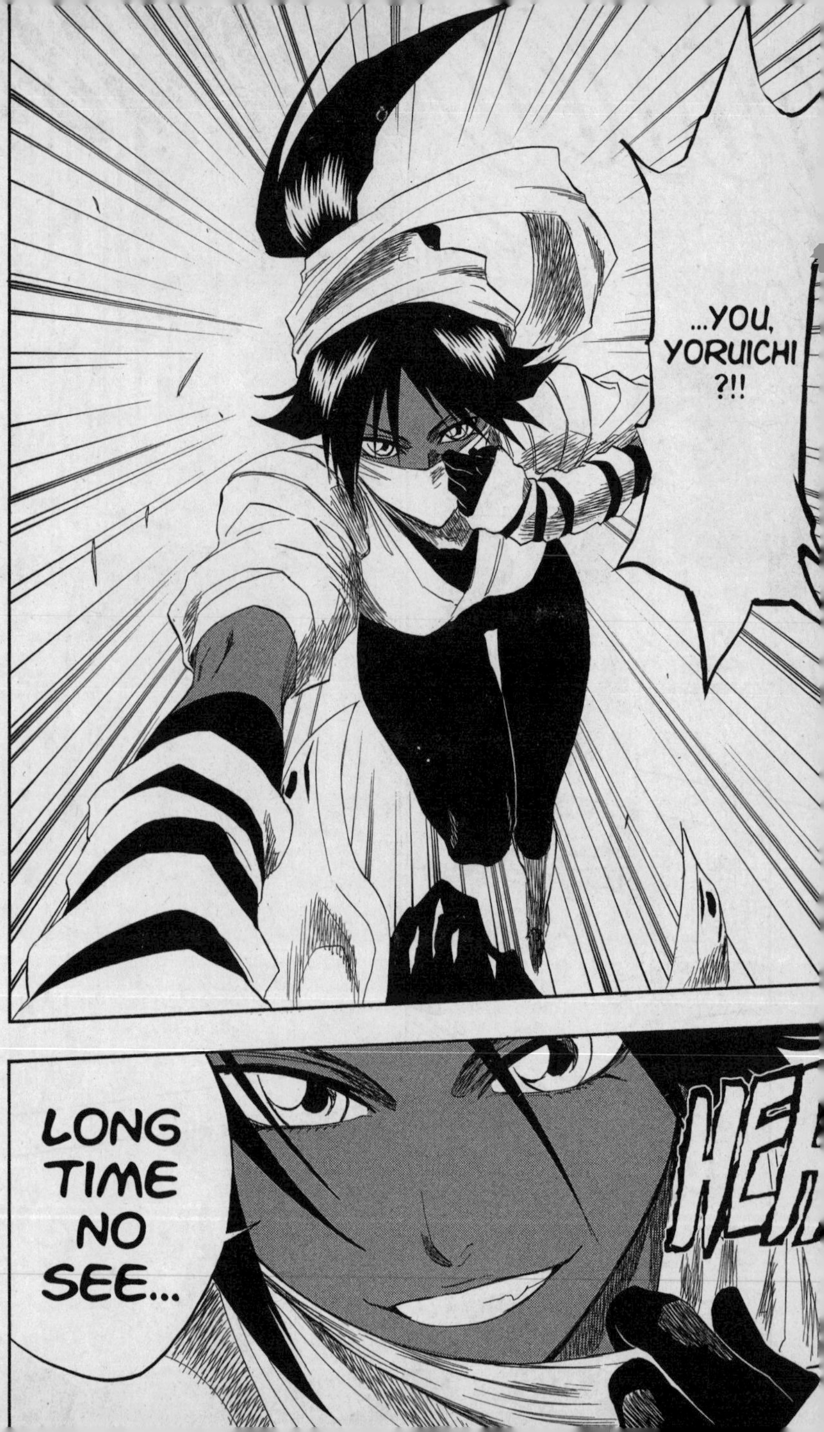
...YOU, YORUICHI ?!!
LONG TIME NO SEE...

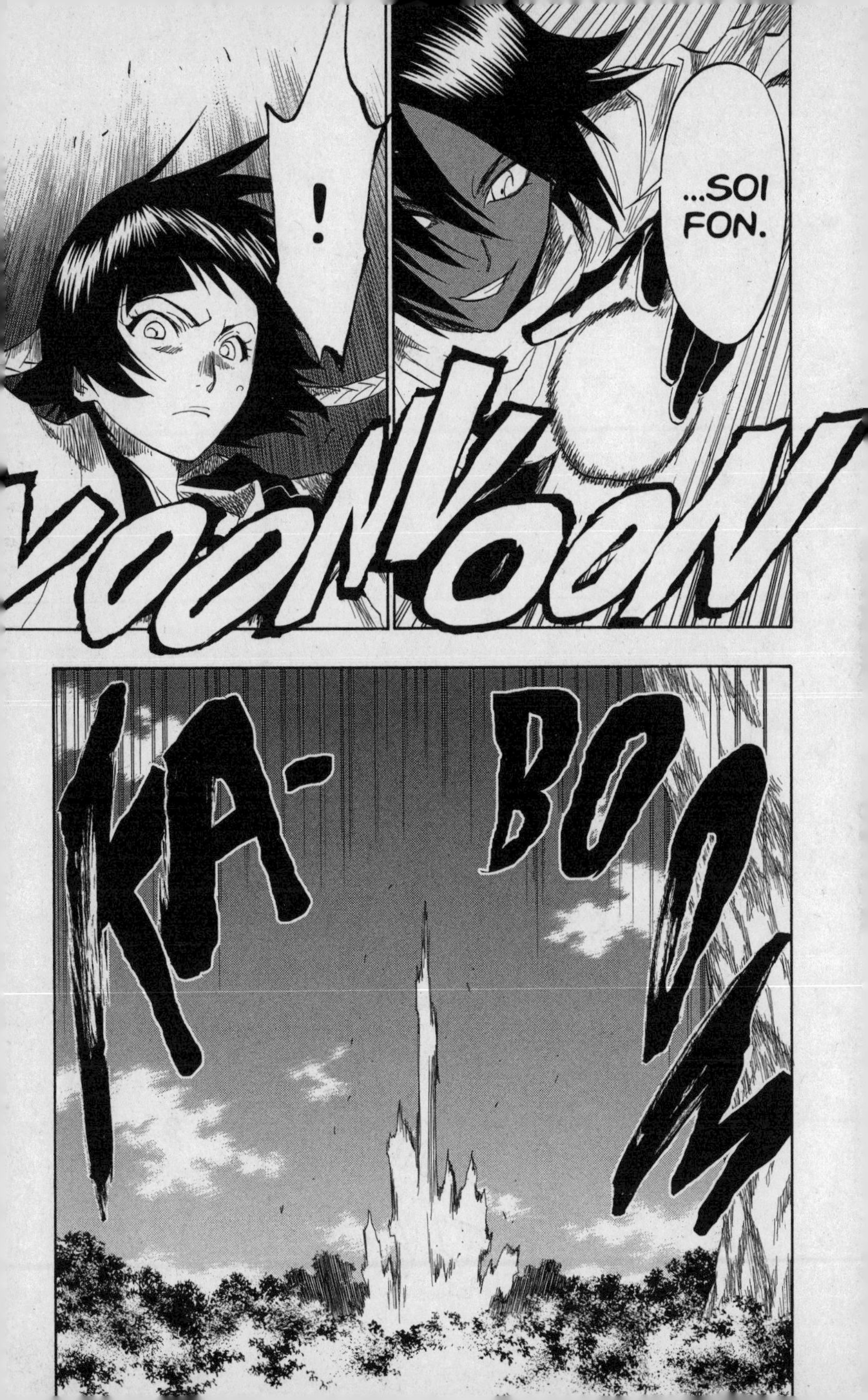
...SOI FON.
!
VOOM
VOOM
KA-BOOM

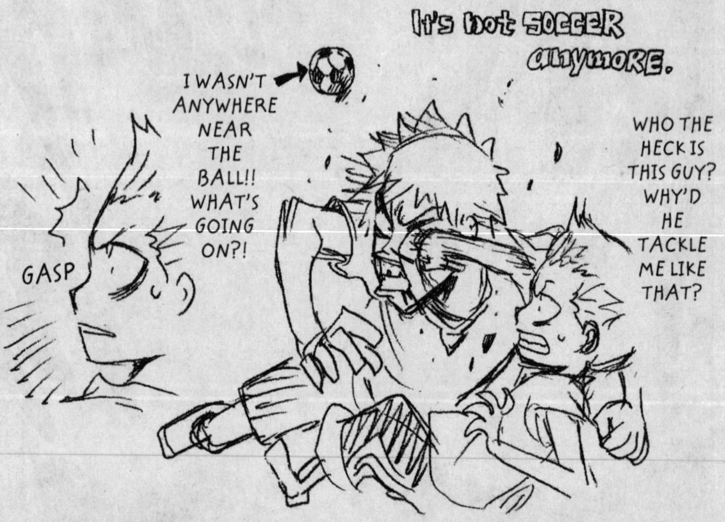
It's not SOCCER anymore.
WHO THE HECK IS THIS GUY? WHY'D HE TACKLE ME LIKE THAT?
I WASN'T ANYWHERE NEAR THE BALL!! WHAT'S GOING ON?!
GASP

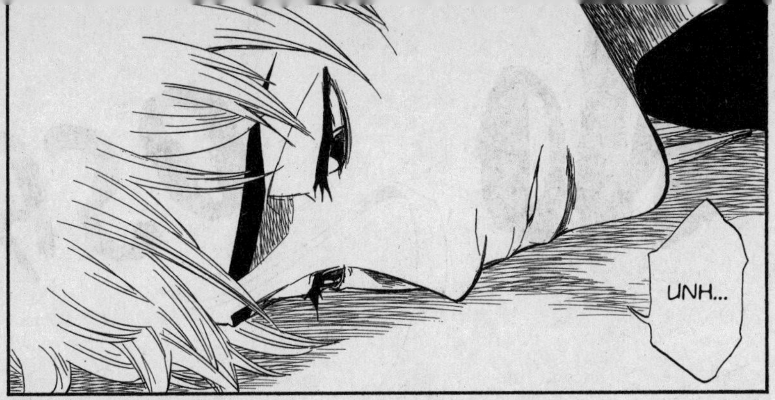
UNH...

154. "Flash Master"

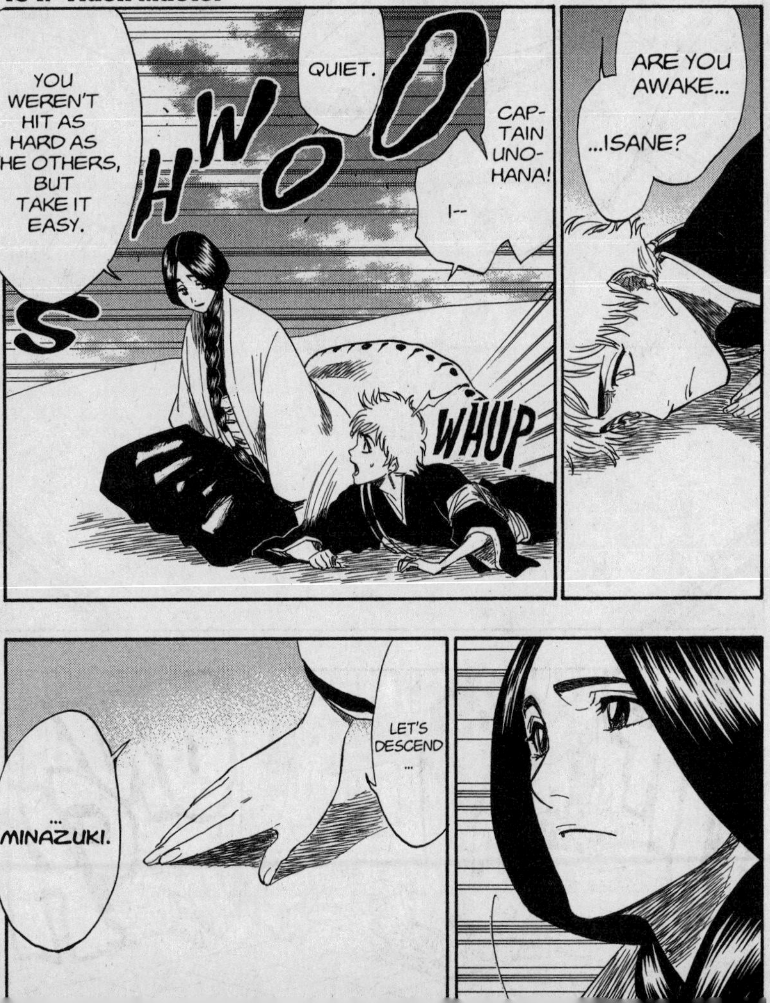
ARE YOU AWAKE...
...ISANE?
CAP-TAIN UNO-HANA!
I--
QUIET.
SHWOO
YOU WEREN'T HIT AS HARD AS THE OTHERS, BUT TAKE IT EASY.
WHUP
LET'S DESCEND...
...MINAZUKI.

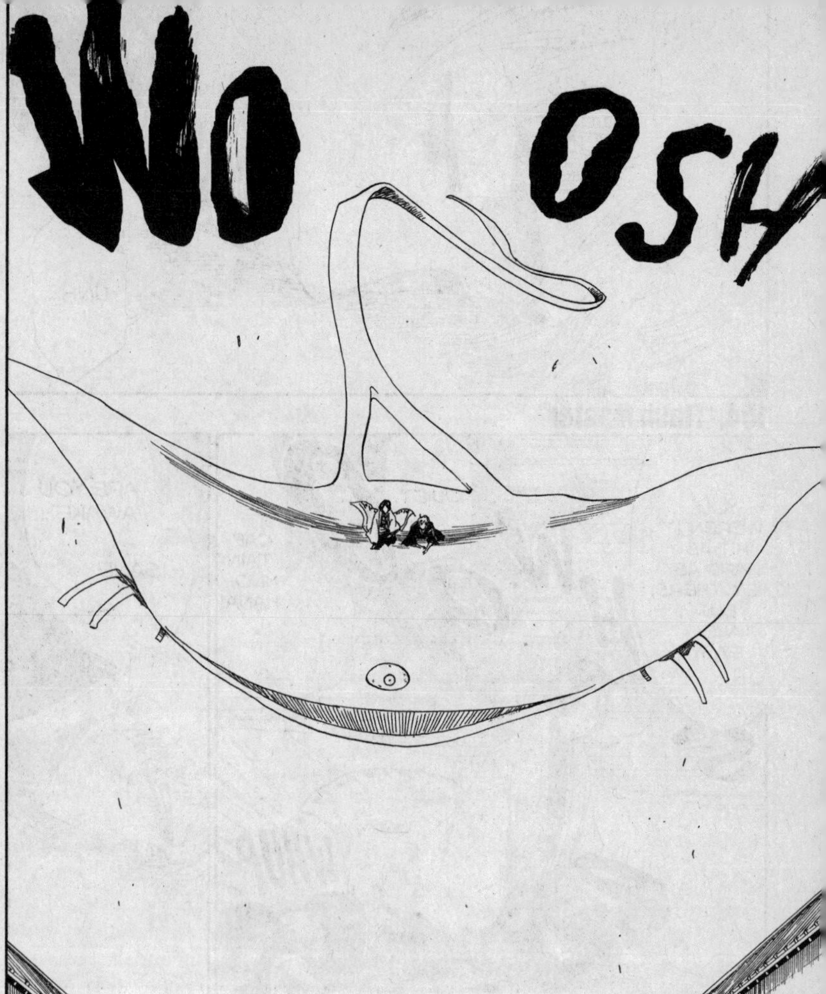
WOOSH
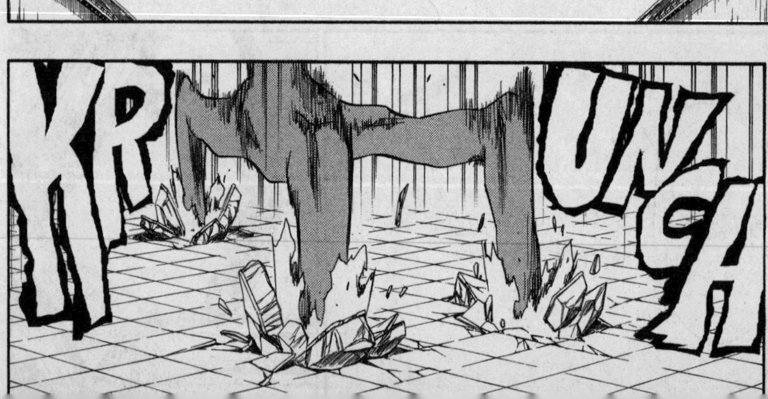
KRUNCH

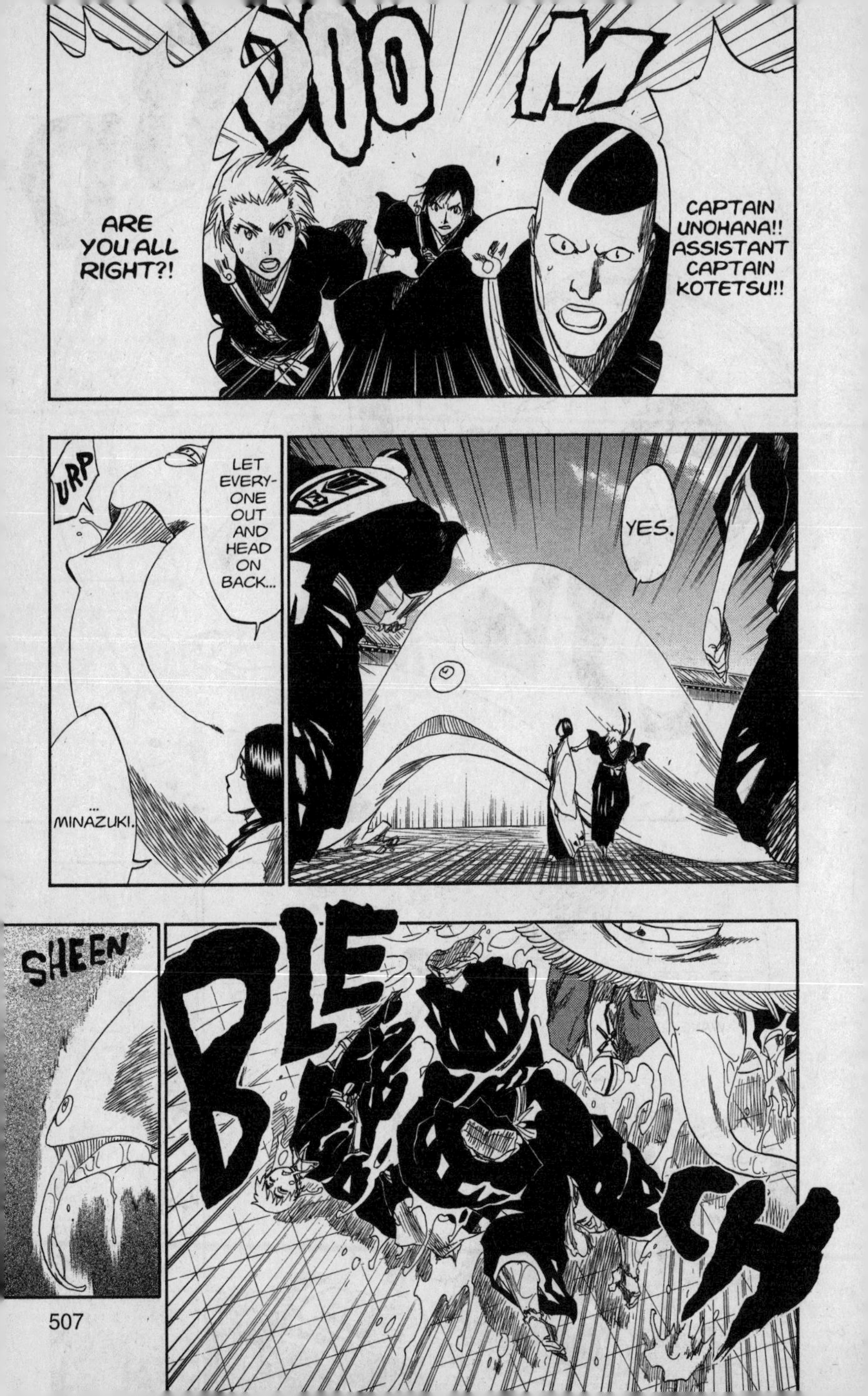
BOOM
CAPTAIN UNOHANA!! ASSISTANT CAPTAIN KOTETSU!!
ARE YOU ALL RIGHT?!
YES.
LET EVERYONE OUT AND HEAD ON BACK...
URP
... MINAZUKI.
SHEEN

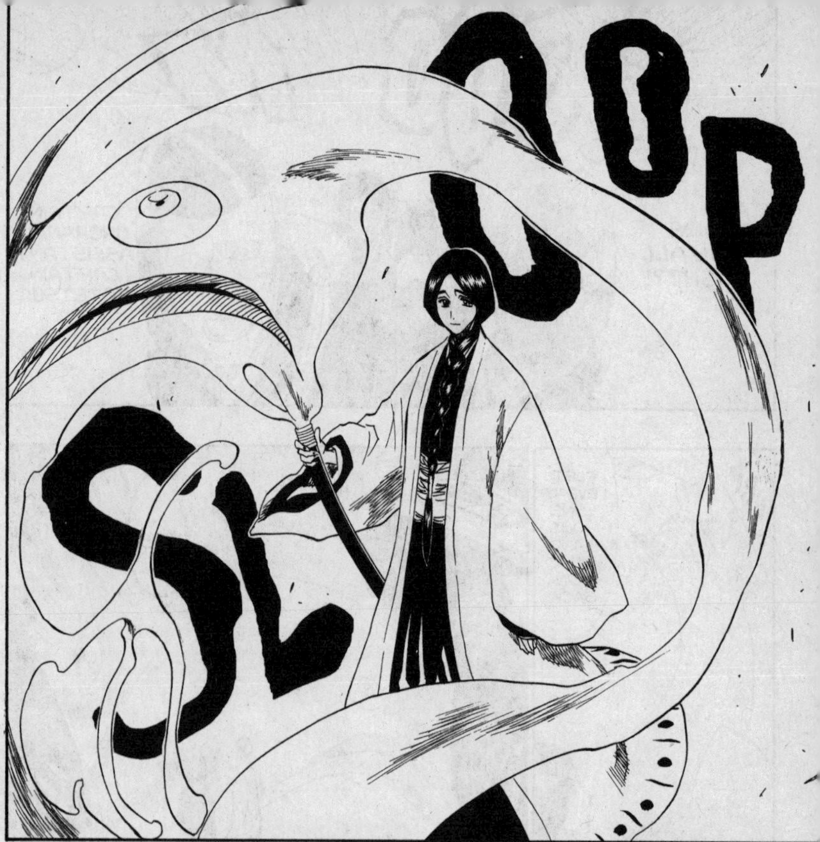
SLOOP

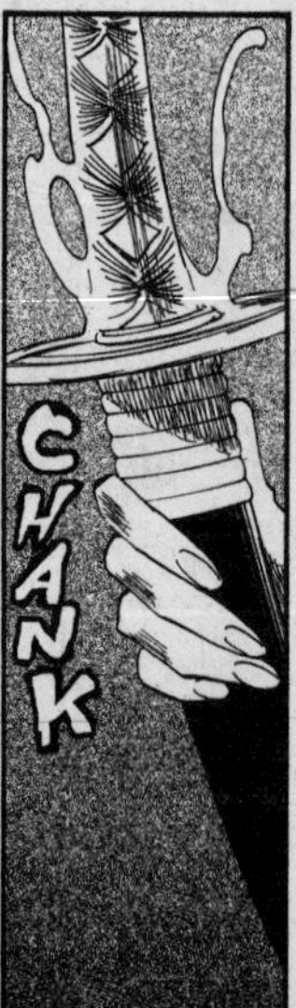
CHANK

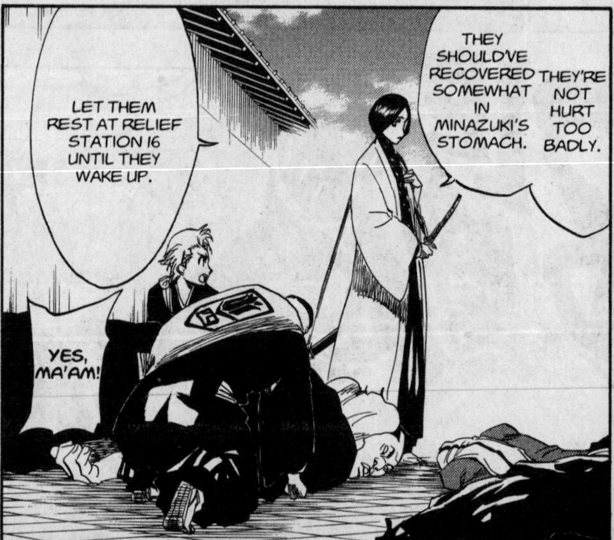
THEY'RE NOT HURT TOO BADLY.
THEY SHOULD'VE RECOVERED SOMEWHAT IN MINAZUKI'S STOMACH.
LET THEM REST AT RELIEF STATION 16 UNTIL THEY WAKE UP.
YES, MA'AM!

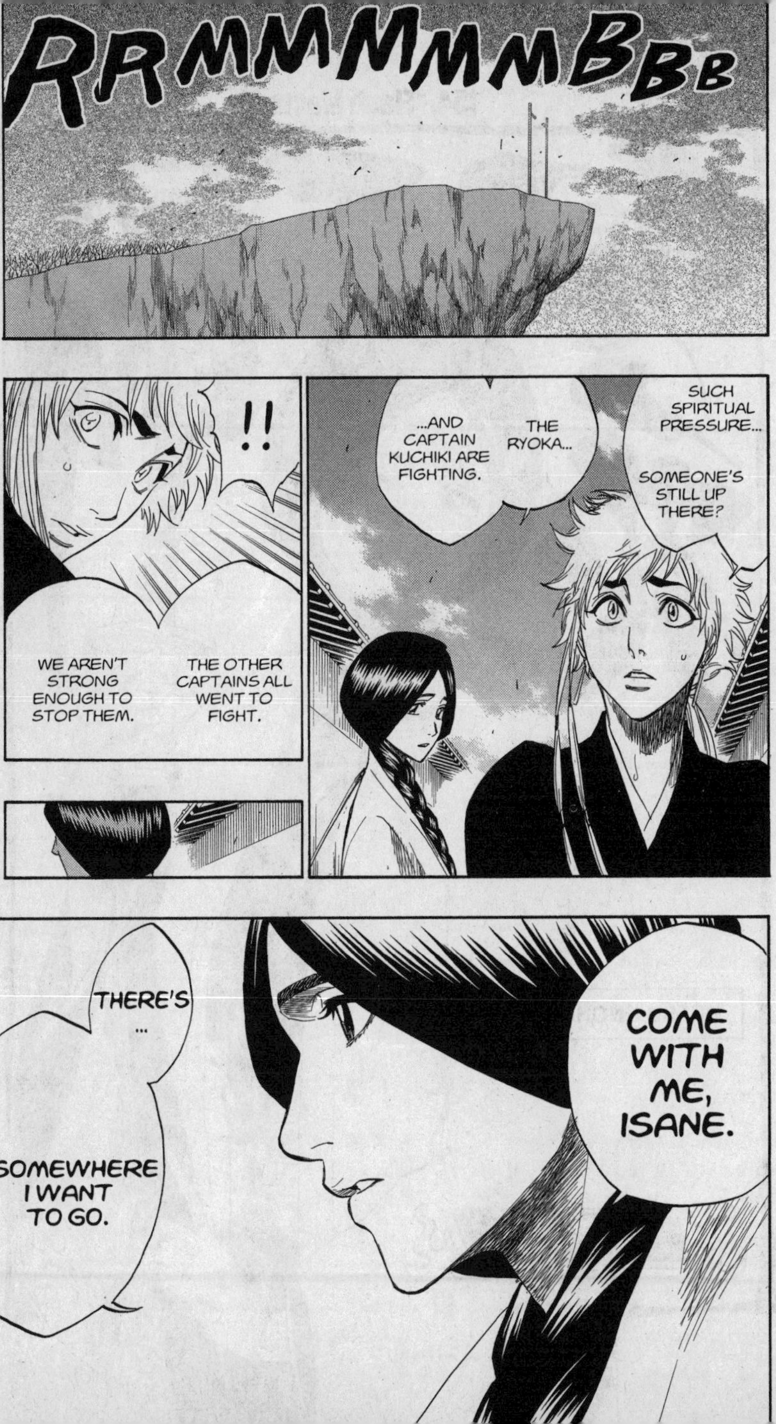
RRMMMMMBBB
SUCH SPIRITUAL PRESSURE...
SOMEONE'S STILL UP THERE?
THE RYOKA...
...AND CAPTAIN KUCHIKI ARE FIGHTING.
!!
THE OTHER CAPTAINS ALL WENT TO FIGHT.
WE AREN'T STRONG ENOUGH TO STOP THEM.
COME WITH ME, ISANE.
THERE'S ...
...SOMEWHERE I WANT TO GO.

154. "Flash Master"

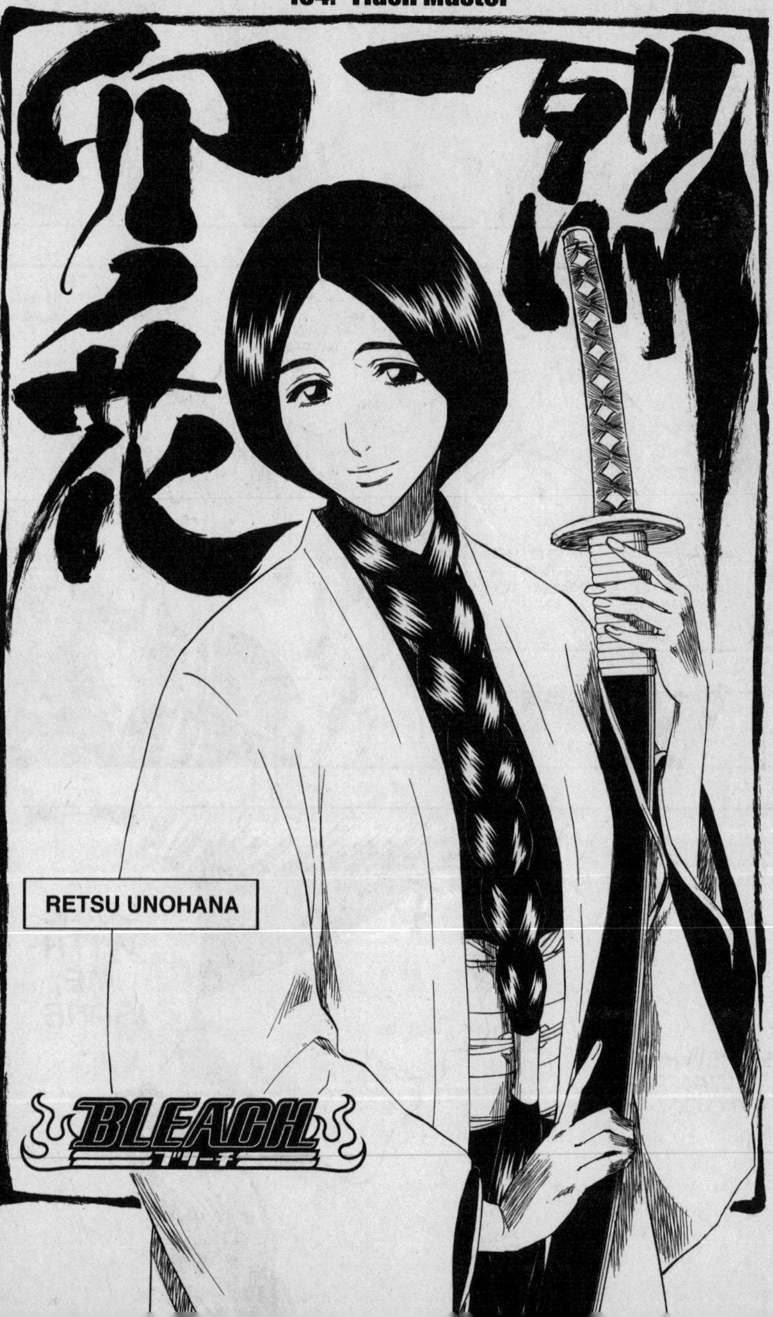
RETSU UNOHANA
BLEACH
ブリーチ

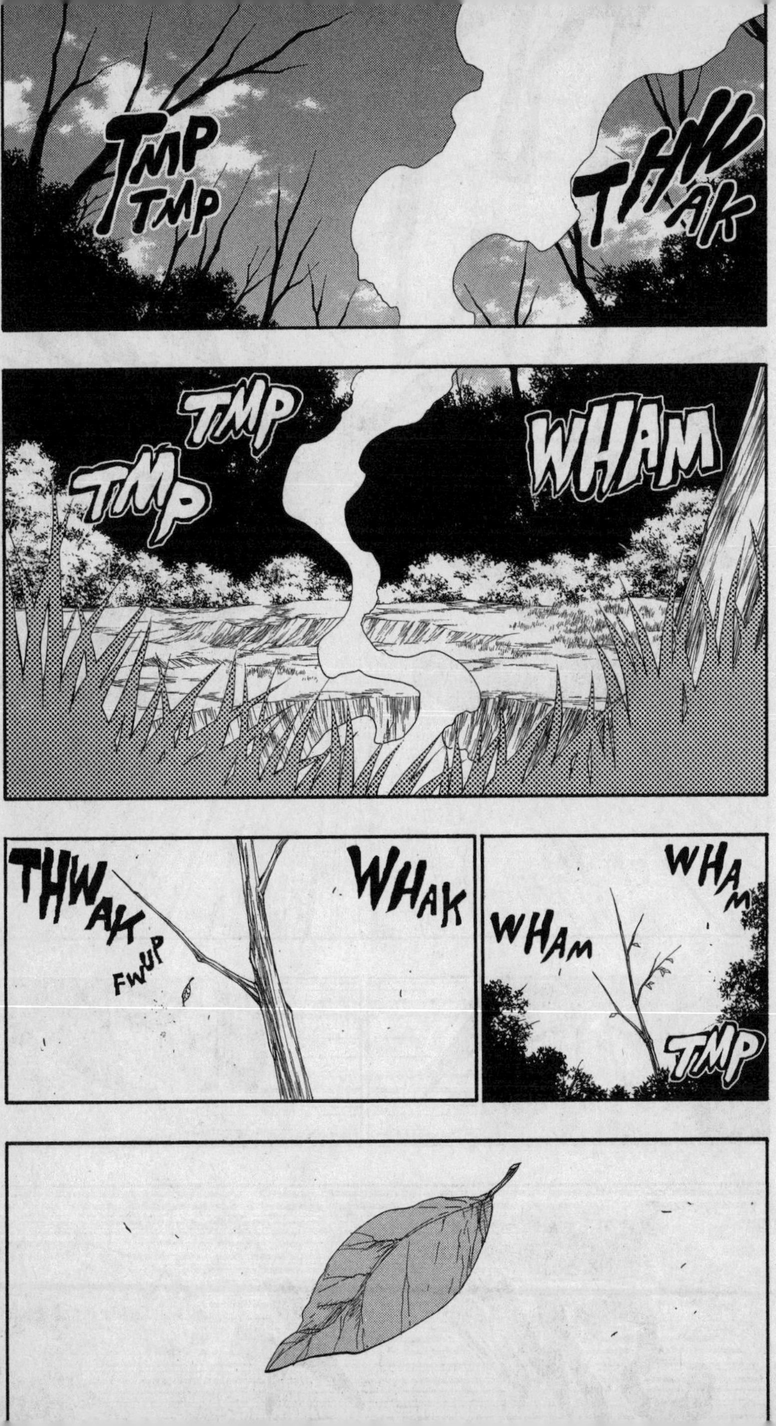
THWAK
TMP TMP
WHAM
TMP TMP
WHAM
WHAM
TMP
WHAK
THWAK
FWUP

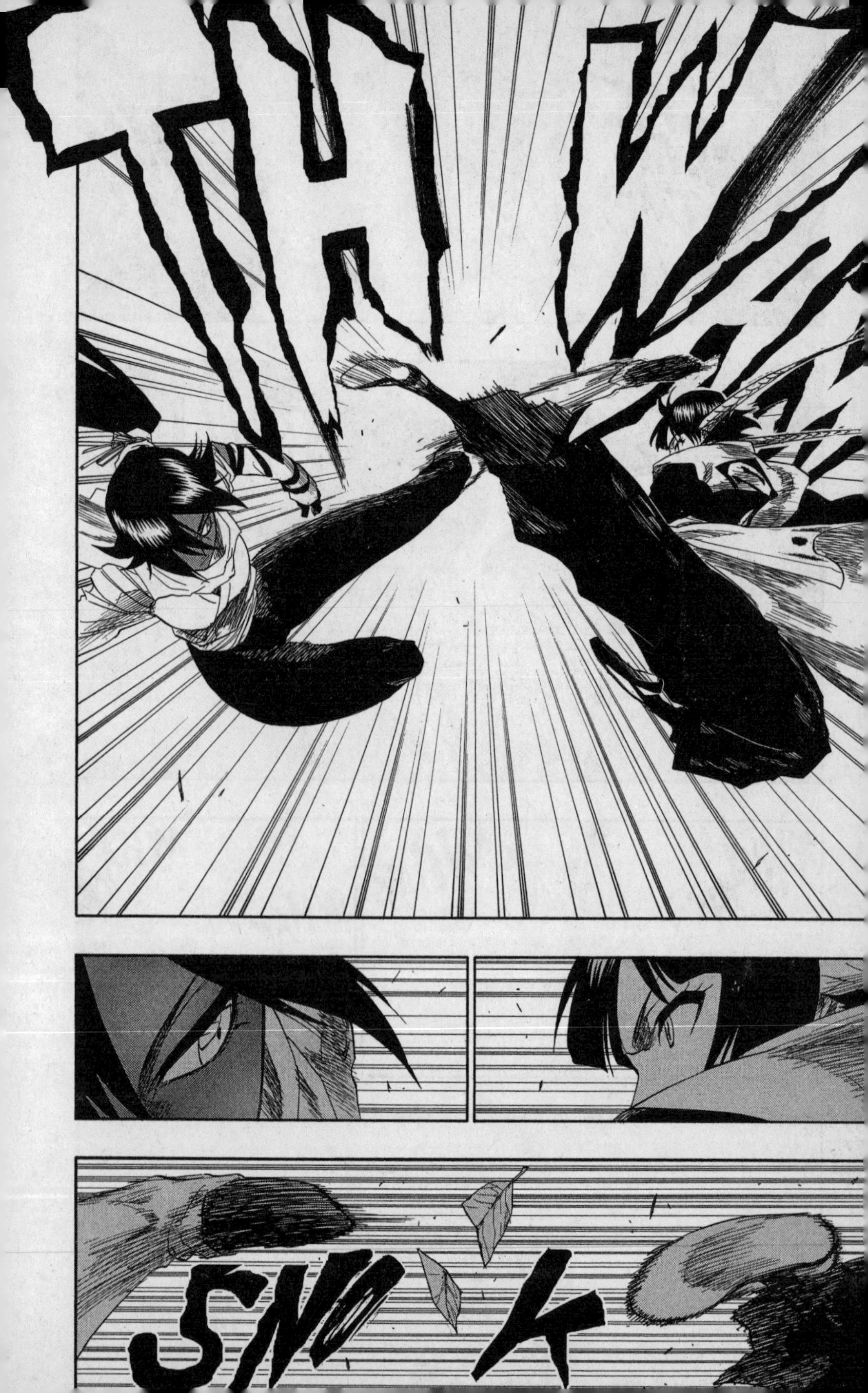
THWAM
SNOK

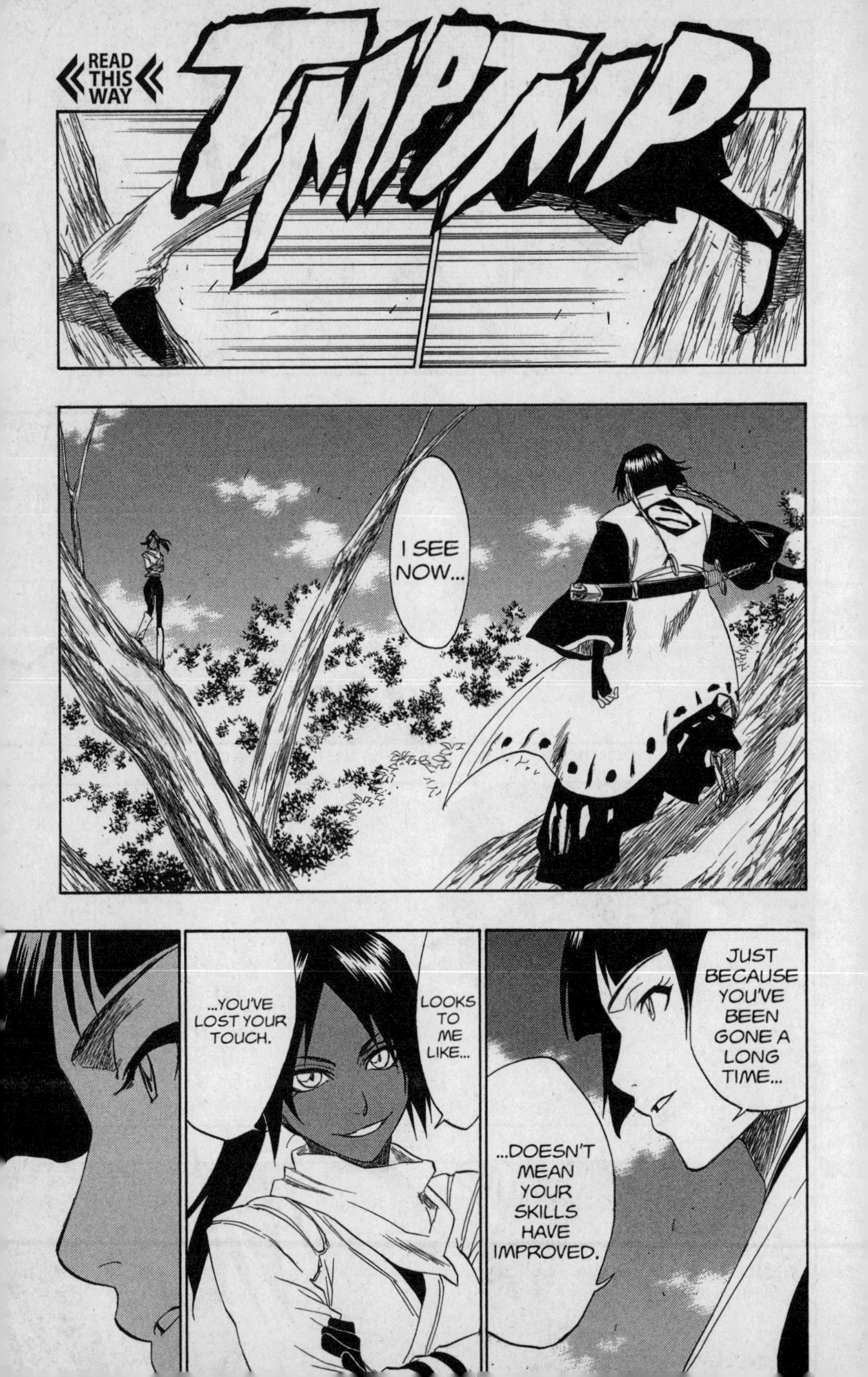
READ THIS WAY
TMP TMP
I SEE NOW...
JUST BECAUSE YOU'VE BEEN GONE A LONG TIME...
...DOESN'T MEAN YOUR SKILLS HAVE IMPROVED.
LOOKS TO ME LIKE...
...YOU'VE LOST YOUR TOUCH.

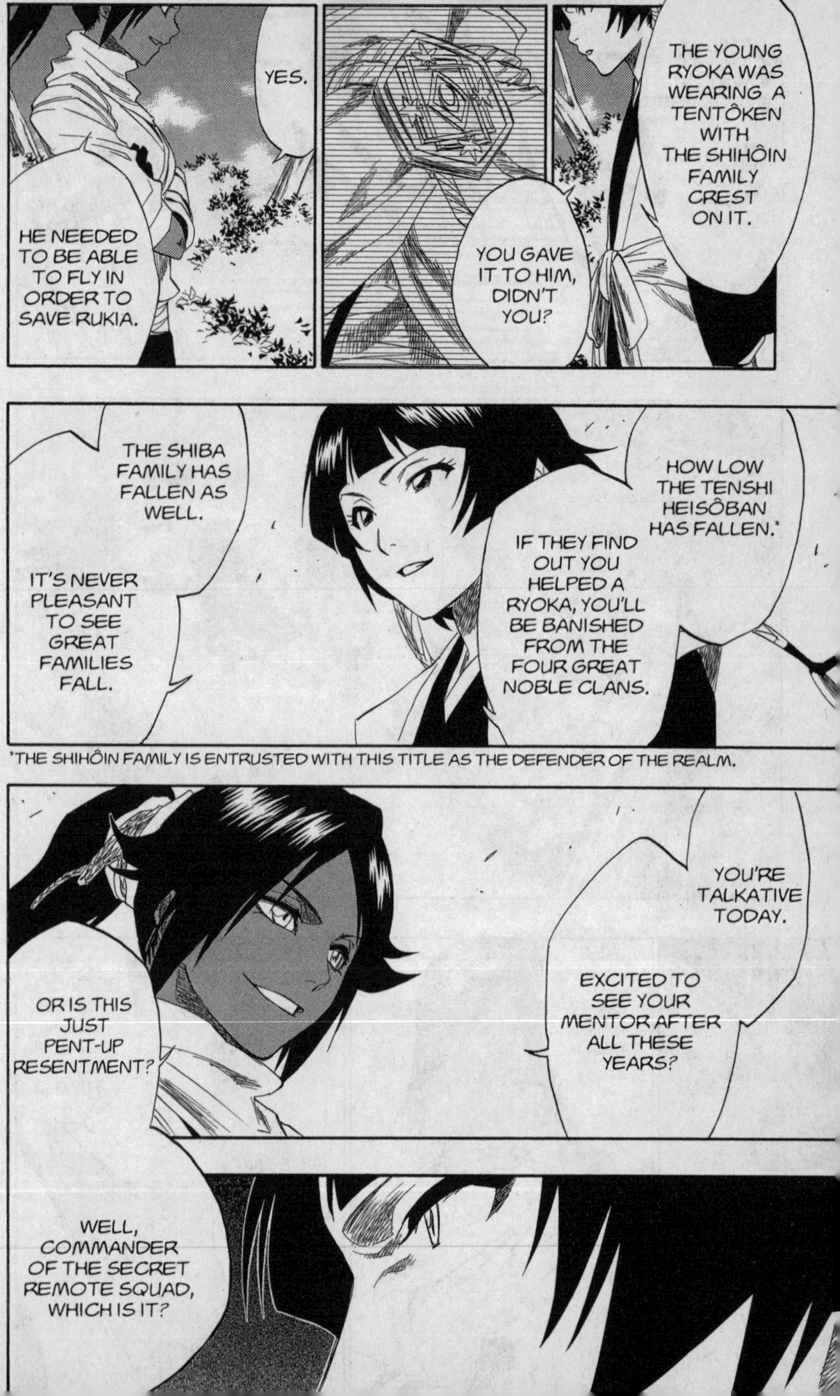
THE YOUNG RYOKA WAS WEARING A TENTÔKEN WITH THE SHIHÔIN FAMILY CREST ON IT.
YOU GAVE IT TO HIM, DIDN'T YOU?
YES.
HE NEEDED TO BE ABLE TO FLY IN ORDER TO SAVE RUKIA.
HOW LOW THE TENSHI HEISÔBAN HAS FALLEN.*
IF THEY FIND OUT YOU HELPED A RYOKA, YOU'LL BE BANISHED FROM THE FOUR GREAT NOBLE CLANS.
THE SHIBA FAMILY HAS FALLEN AS WELL.
IT'S NEVER PLEASANT TO SEE GREAT FAMILIES FALL.
YOU'RE TALKATIVE TODAY.
EXCITED TO SEE YOUR MENTOR AFTER ALL THESE YEARS?
OR IS THIS JUST PENT-UP RESENTMENT?
WELL, COMMANDER OF THE SECRET REMOTE SQUAD, WHICH IS IT?

*THE SHIHÔIN FAMILY IS ENTRUSTED WITH THIS TITLE AS THE DEFENDER OF THE REALM.

READ THIS WAY

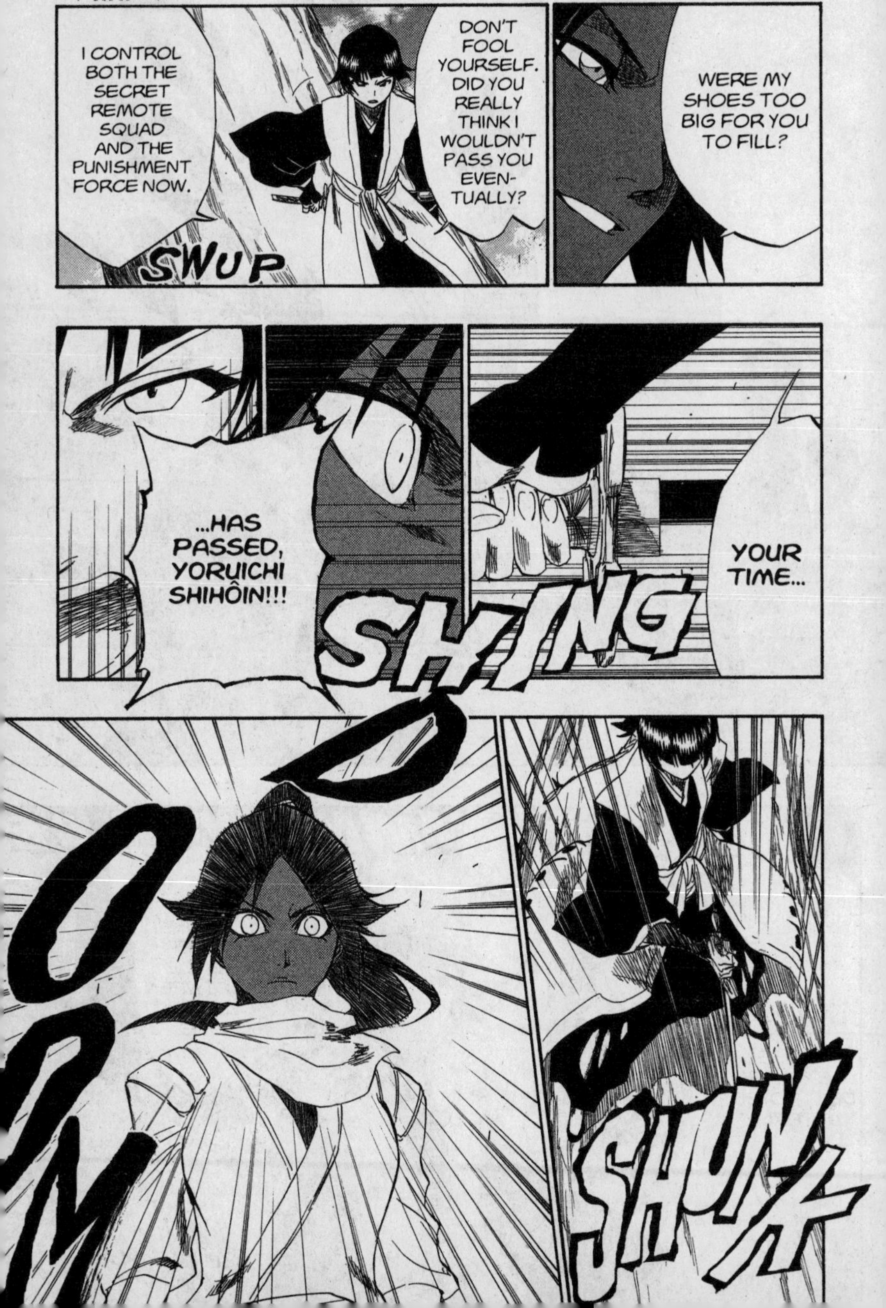
WERE MY SHOES TOO BIG FOR YOU TO FILL?
DON'T FOOL YOURSELF. DID YOU REALLY THINK I WOULDN'T PASS YOU EVEN-TUALLY?
I CONTROL BOTH THE SECRET REMOTE SQUAD AND THE PUNISHMENT FORCE NOW.
SWUP
YOUR TIME...
SHING
...HAS PASSED, YORUICHI SHIHÔIN!!!

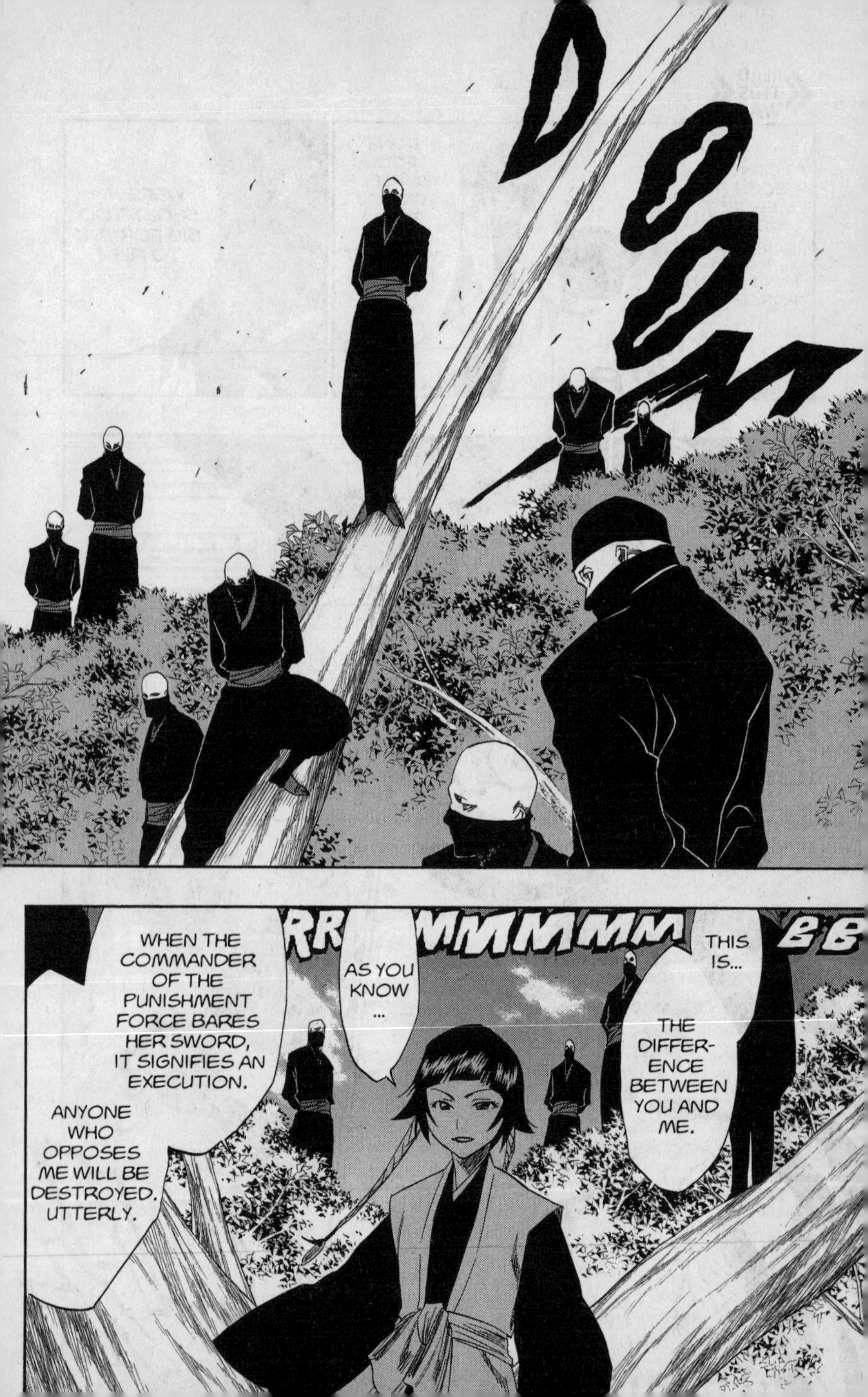
DOOM
RRMMMMMMMBB
THIS IS...
THE DIFFERENCE BETWEEN YOU AND ME.
AS YOU KNOW ...
WHEN THE COMMANDER OF THE PUNISHMENT FORCE BARES HER SWORD, IT SIGNIFIES AN EXECUTION.
ANYONE WHO OPPOSES ME WILL BE DESTROYED. UTTERLY.

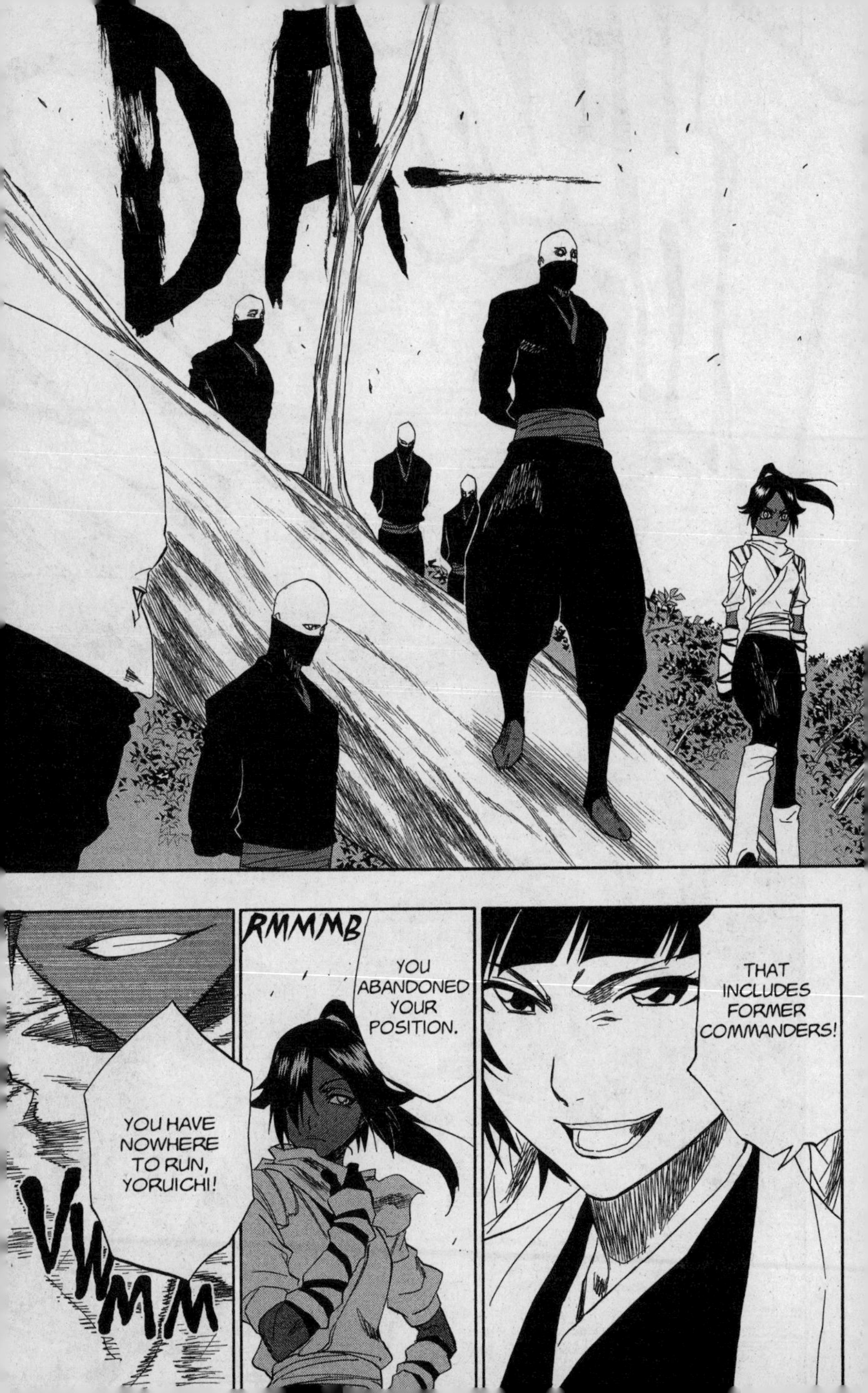
DA
THAT INCLUDES FORMER COMMANDERS!
RMMMB
YOU ABANDONED YOUR POSITION.
YOU HAVE NOWHERE TO RUN, YORUICHI!
VWMM

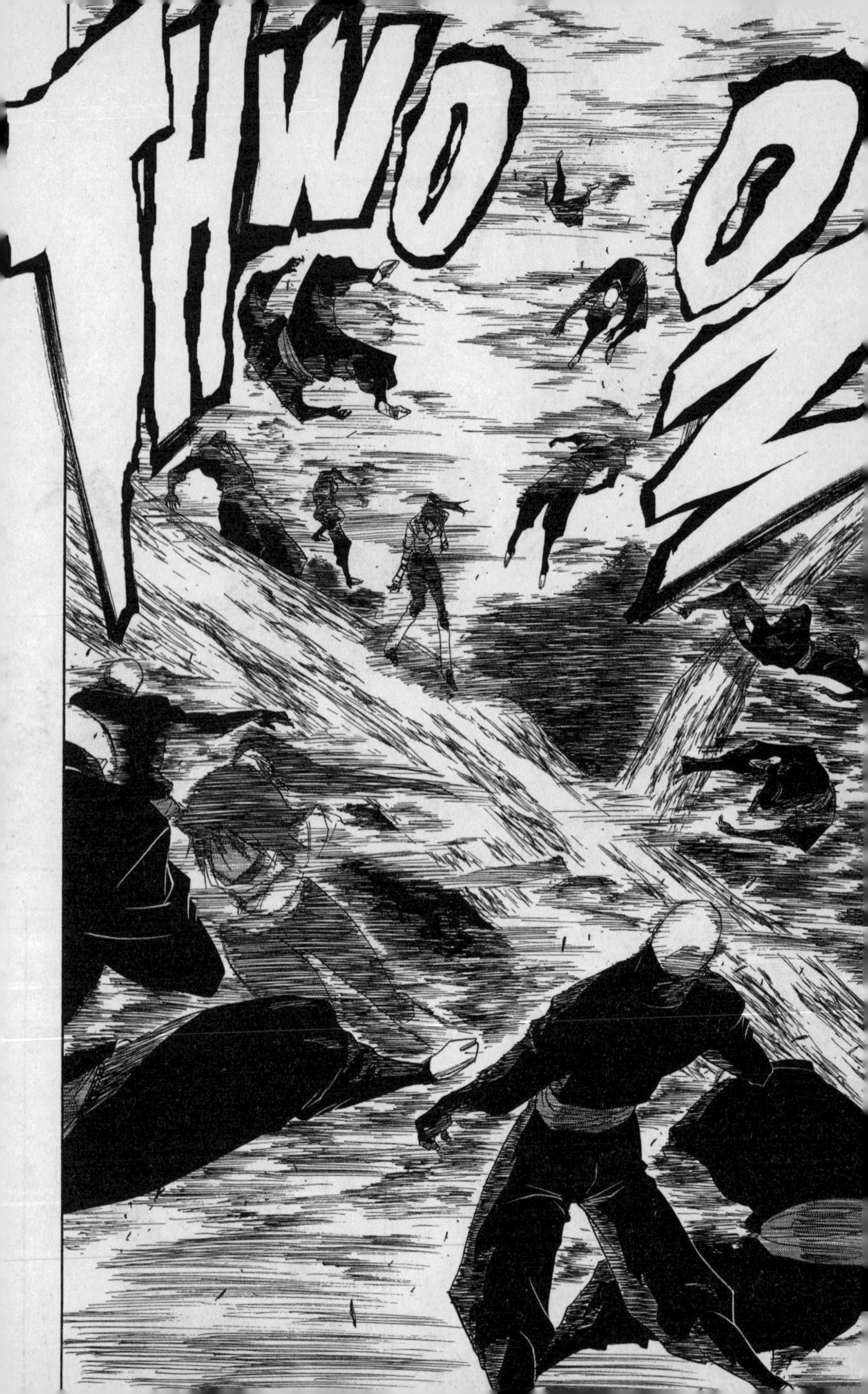
THWOOM

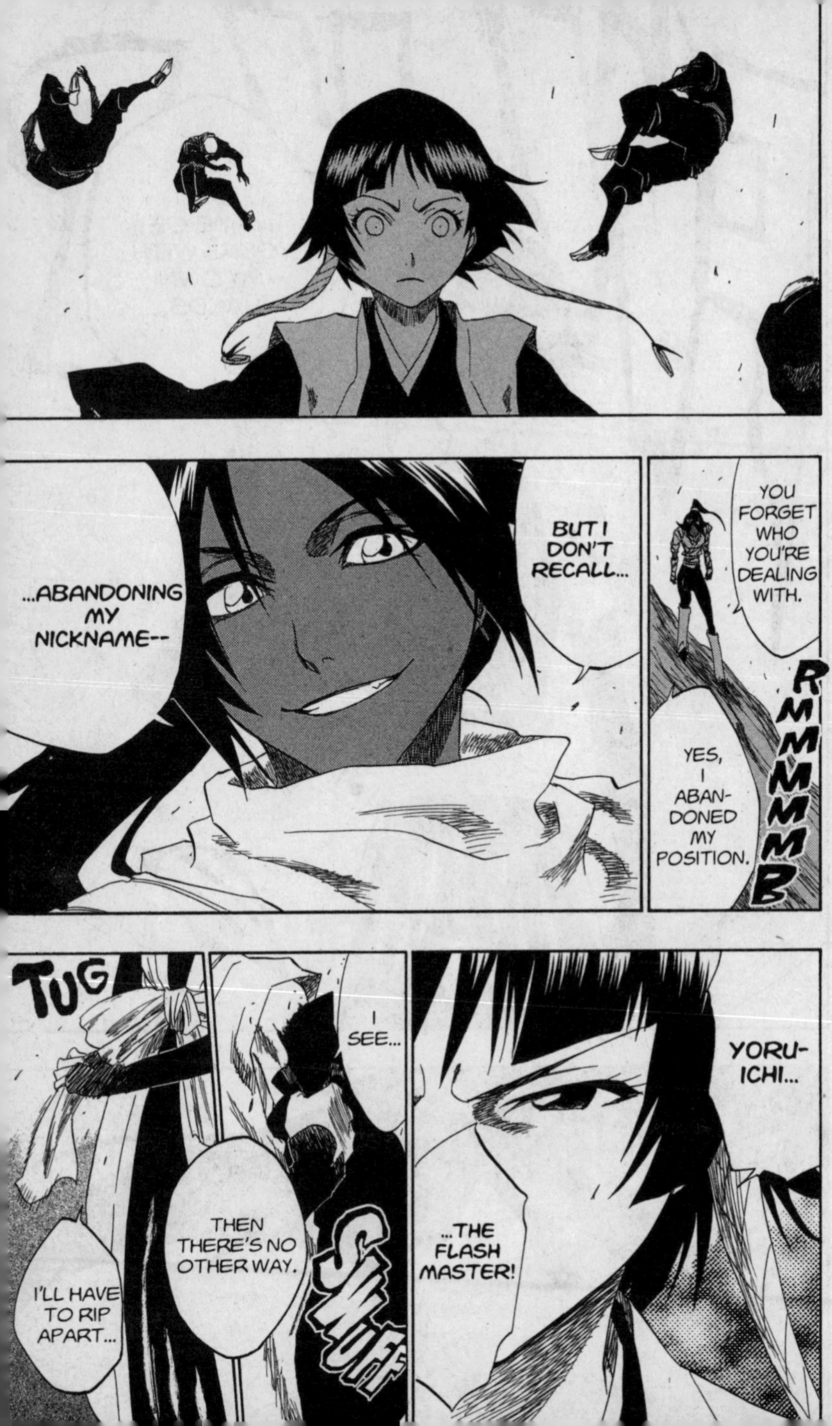
YOU FORGET WHO YOU'RE DEALING WITH.
YES, I ABAN-DONED MY POSITION.
RMMMMMB
BUT I DON'T RECALL...
...ABANDONING MY NICKNAME--
YORU-ICHI...
...THE FLASH MASTER!
I SEE...
THEN THERE'S NO OTHER WAY.
SHUFF
TUG
I'LL HAVE TO RIP APART...

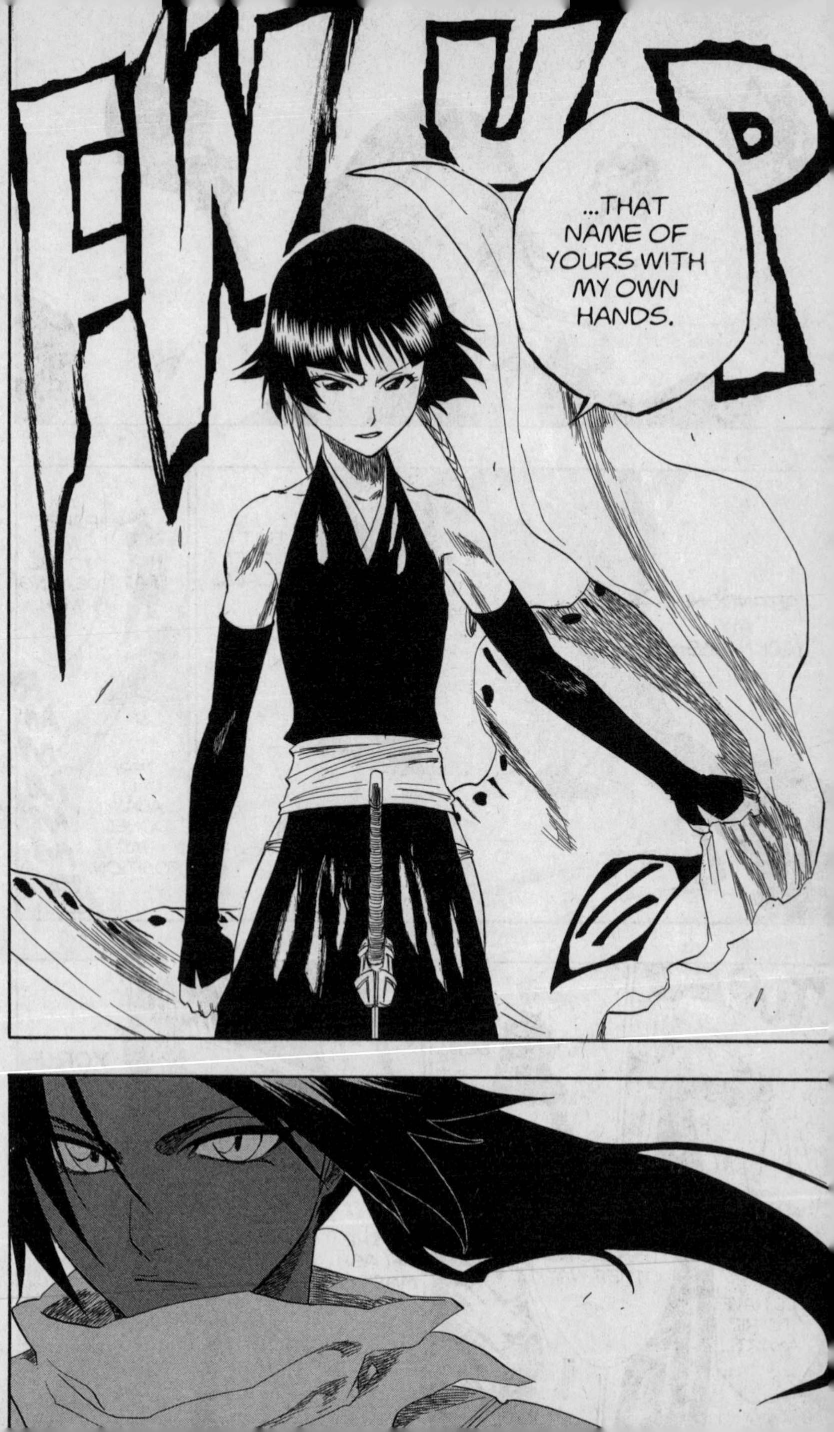
...THAT NAME OF YOURS WITH MY OWN HANDS.

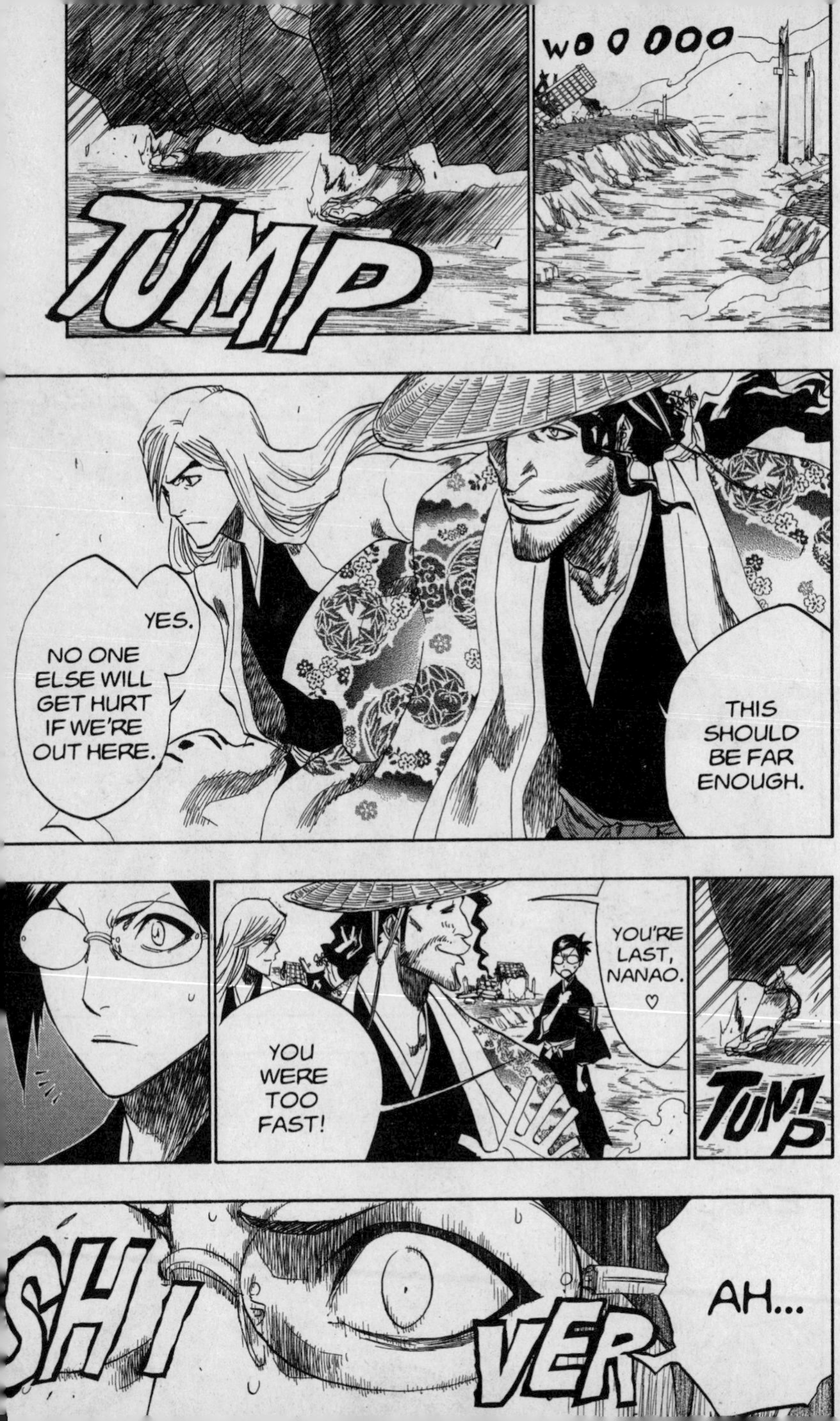
WO O OOO
TUMP
THIS SHOULD BE FAR ENOUGH.
YES.
NO ONE ELSE WILL GET HURT IF WE'RE OUT HERE.
TUMP
YOU'RE LAST, NANAO. ♡
YOU WERE TOO FAST!
AH...
SHIVER

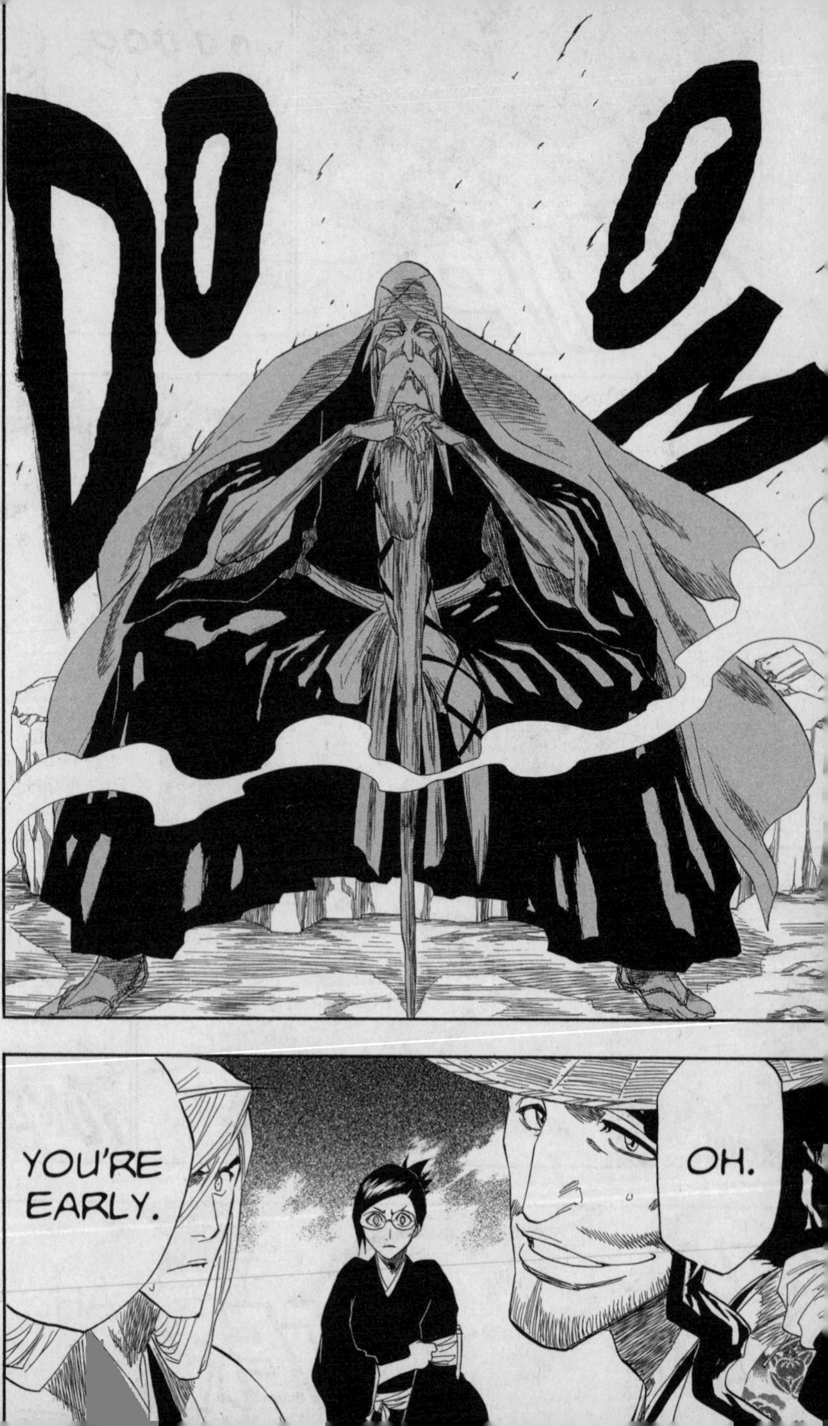
DOOM
OH.
YOU'RE EARLY.

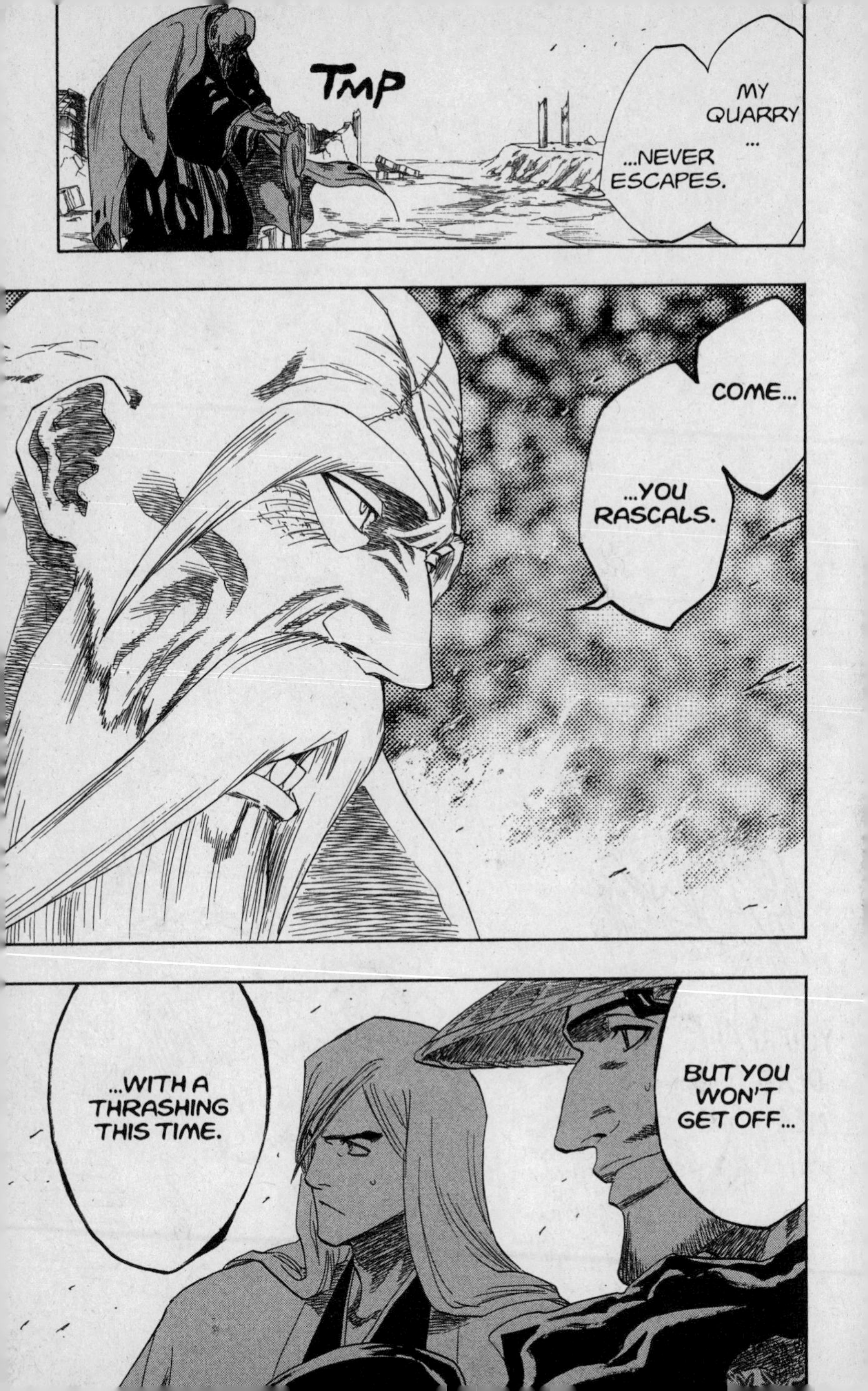
MY QUARRY ...
...NEVER ESCAPES.
TMP
COME...
...YOU RASCALS.
BUT YOU WON'T GET OFF...
...WITH A THRASHING THIS TIME.

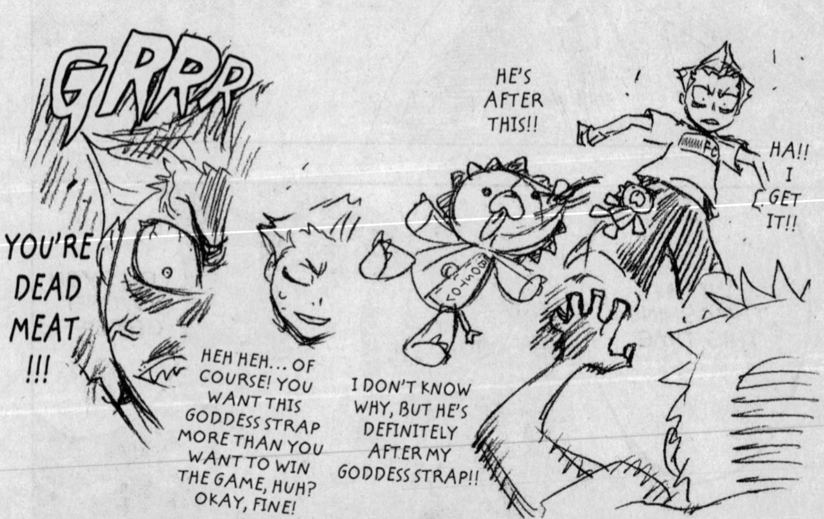
HA!! I GET IT!!
HE'S AFTER THIS!!
I DON'T KNOW WHY, BUT HE'S DEFINITELY AFTER MY GODDESS STRAP!!
HEH HEH... OF COURSE! YOU WANT THIS GODDESS STRAP MORE THAN YOU WANT TO WIN THE GAME, HUH? OKAY, FINE!
GRRR
YOU'RE DEAD MEAT!!!

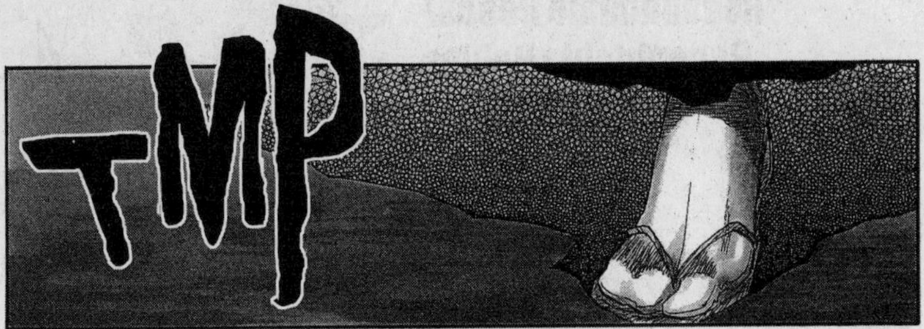
TMP

155: Redoundable Deeds/Redoubtable Babies

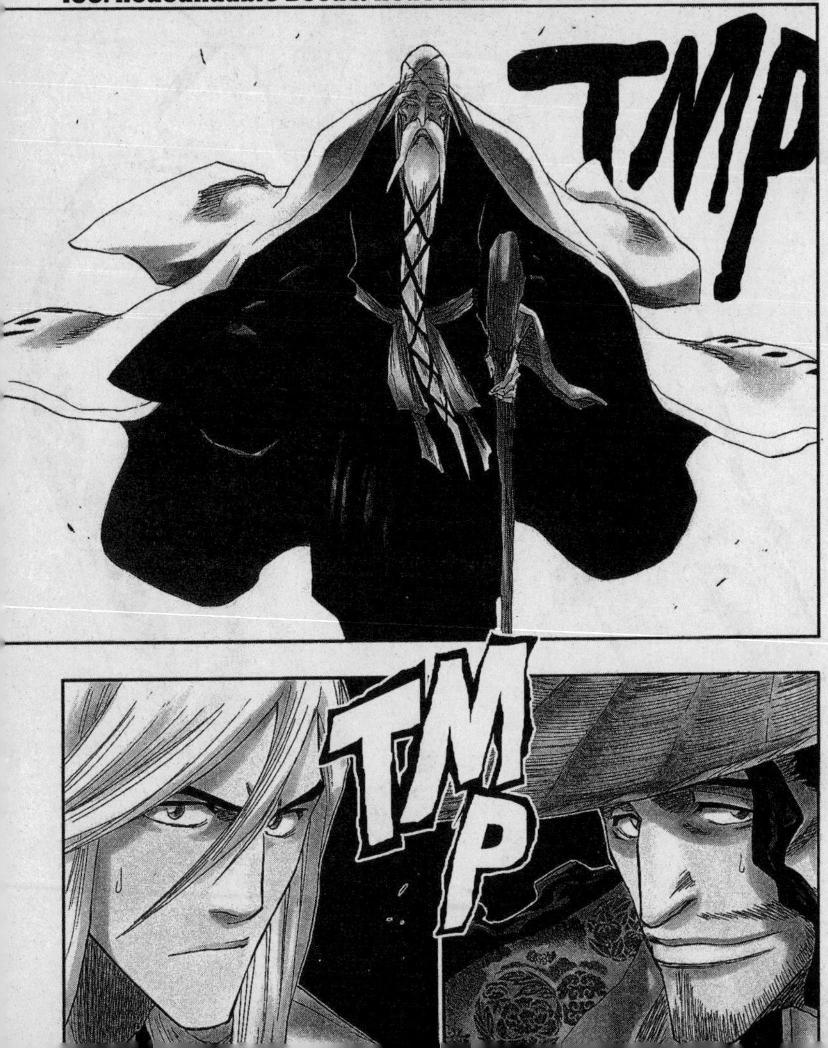
TMP
TMP

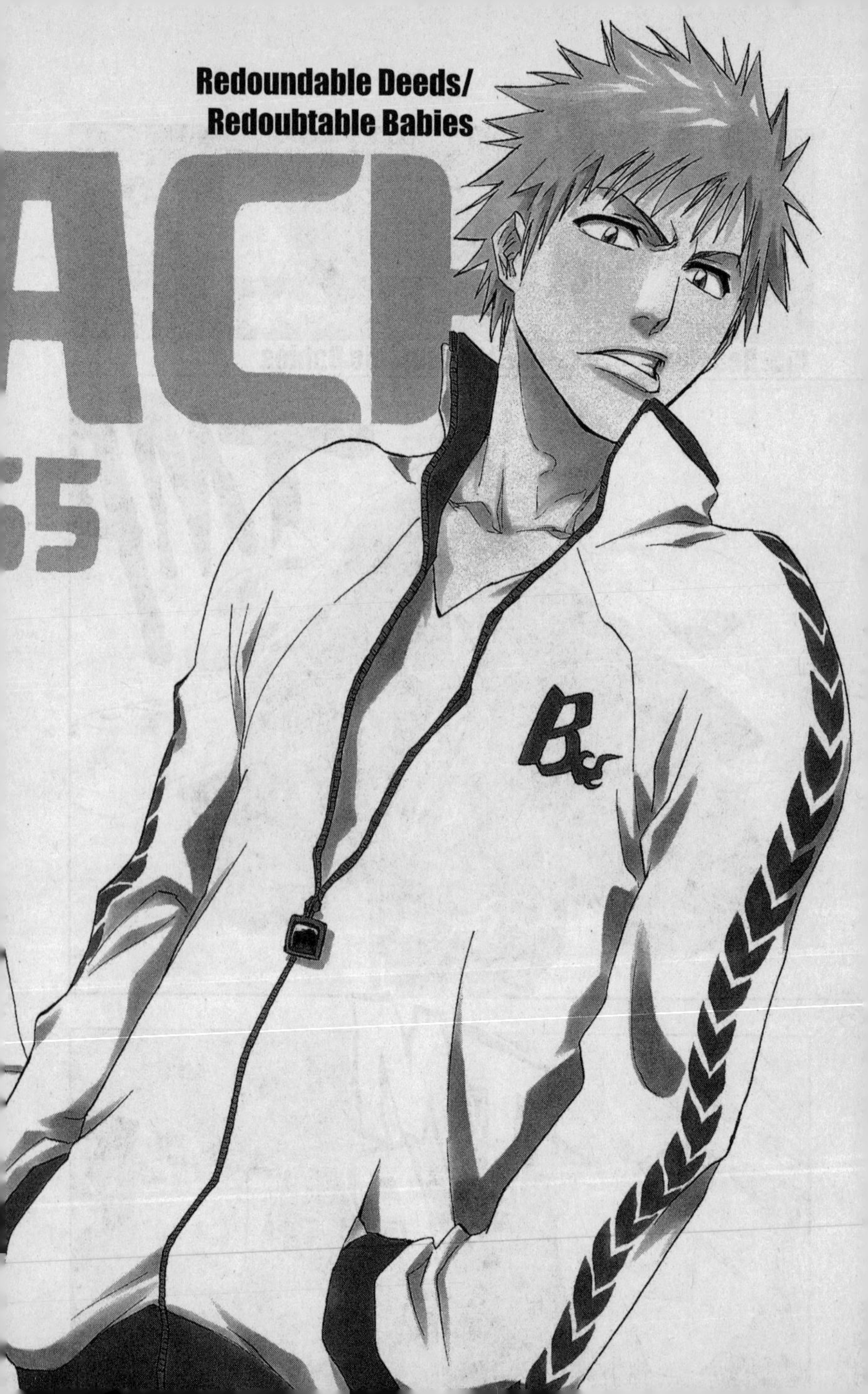
Redoundable Deeds/
Redoubtable Babies

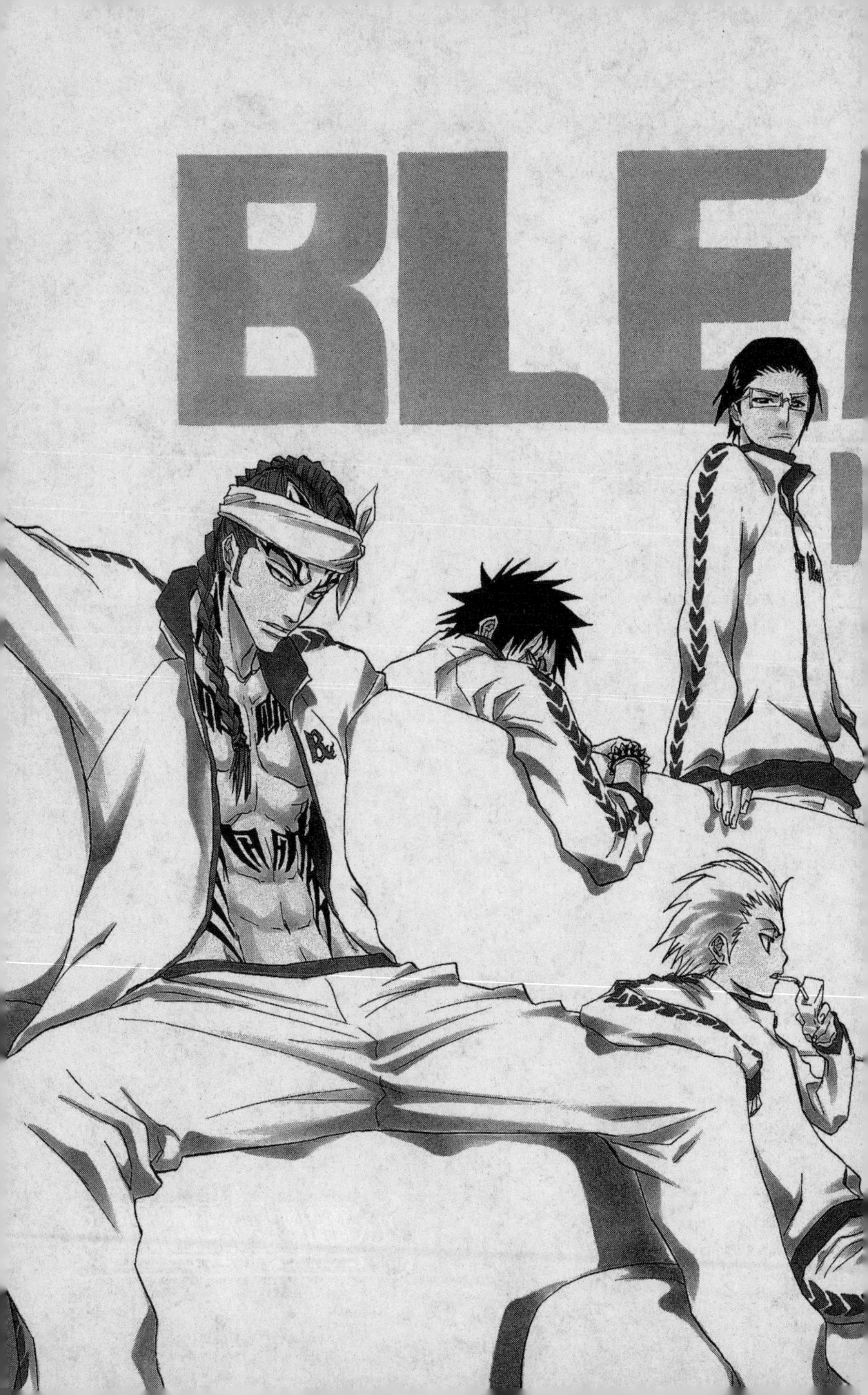
BLE

BLEACH
ブリーチ

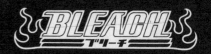

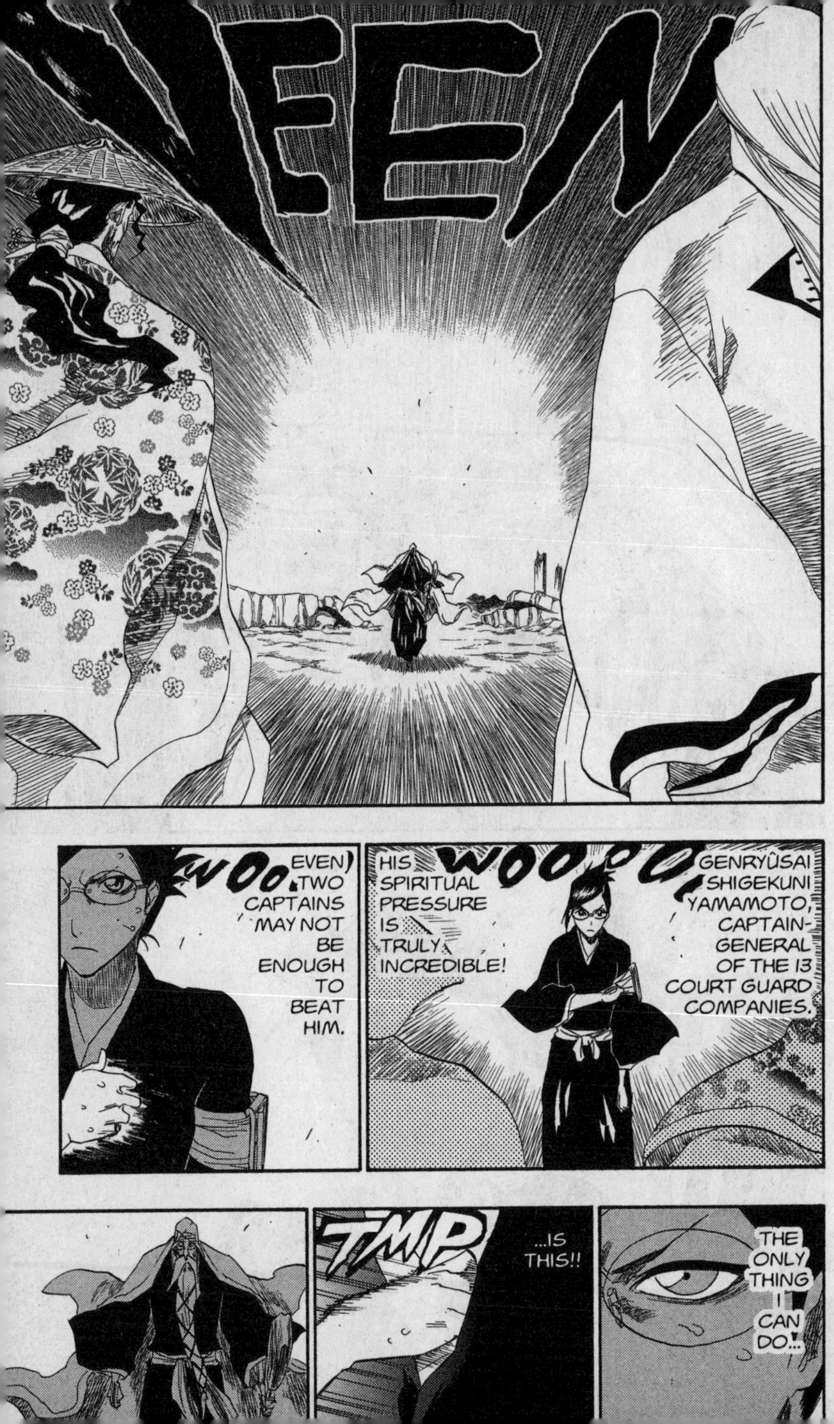
GENRYÛSAI SHIGEKUNI YAMAMOTO, CAPTAIN-GENERAL OF THE 13 COURT GUARD COMPANIES.
HIS SPIRITUAL PRESSURE IS TRULY INCREDIBLE!
EVEN TWO CAPTAINS MAY NOT BE ENOUGH TO BEAT HIM.
THE ONLY THING I CAN DO...
...IS THIS!!
TMP

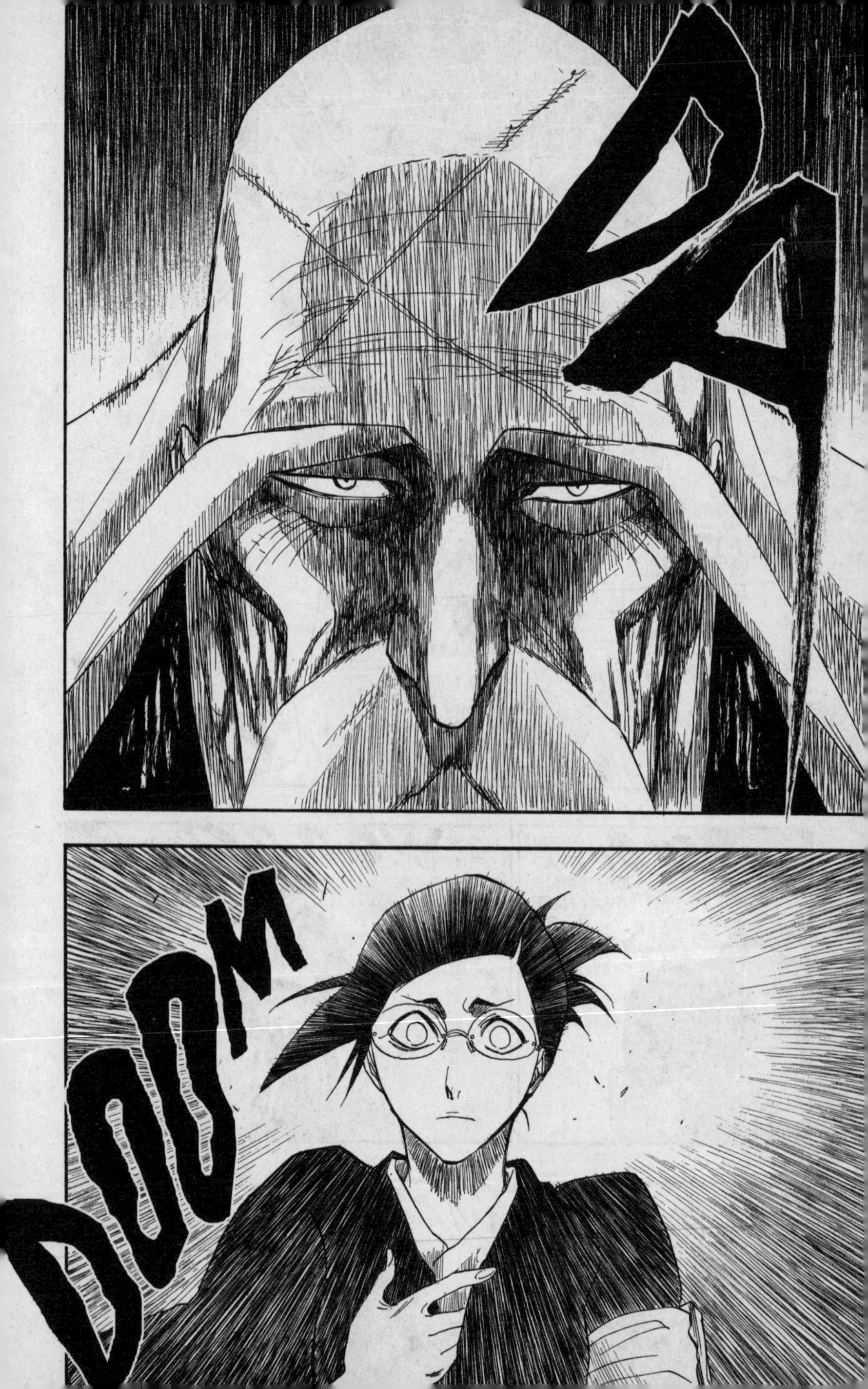
DOOM

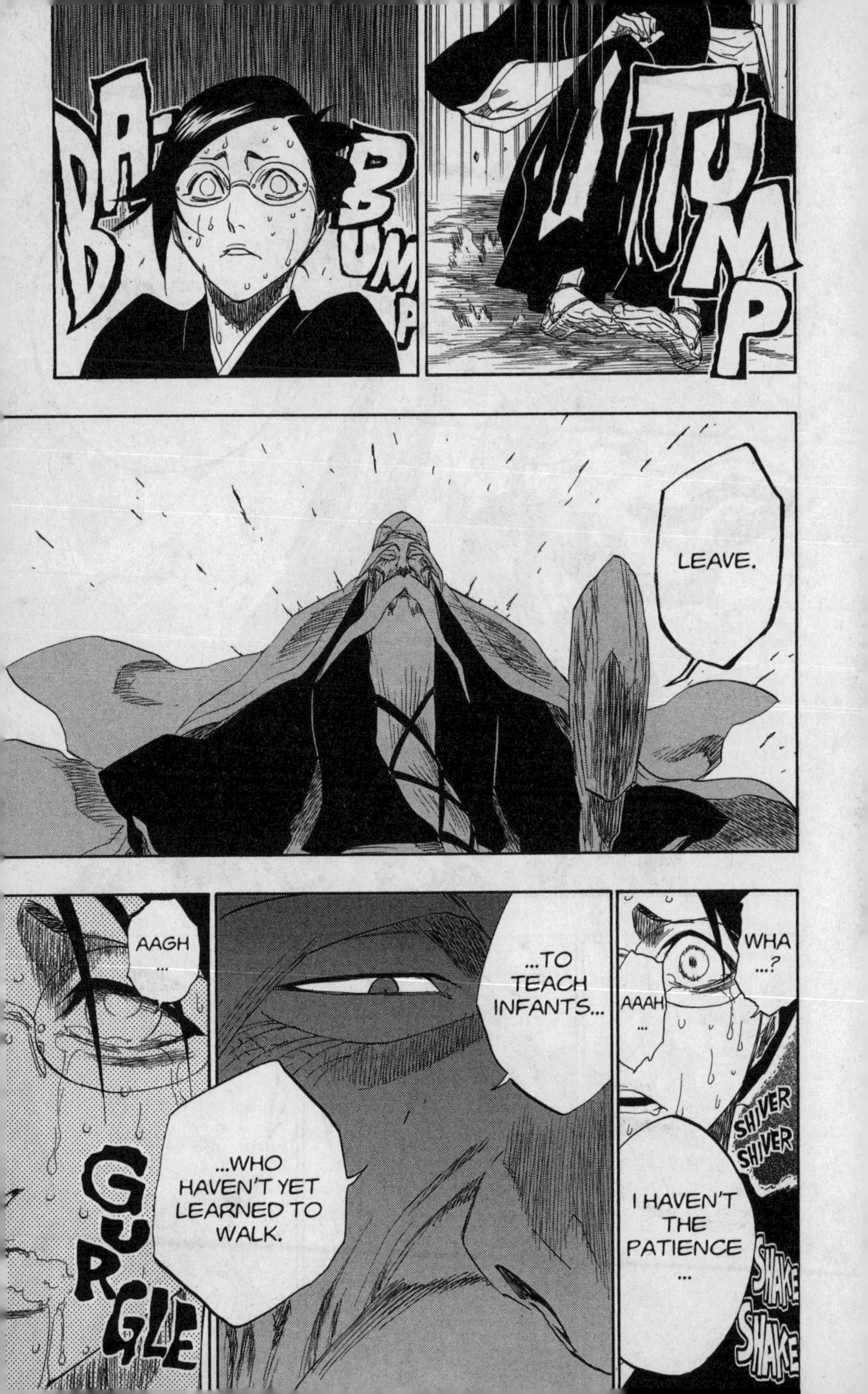
TUMP
BUMP
LEAVE.
WHA ...?
AAAH ...
SHIVER SHIVER
I HAVEN'T THE PATIENCE ...
SHAKE SHAKE
...TO TEACH INFANTS...
...WHO HAVEN'T YET LEARNED TO WALK.
AAGH ...
GURGLE

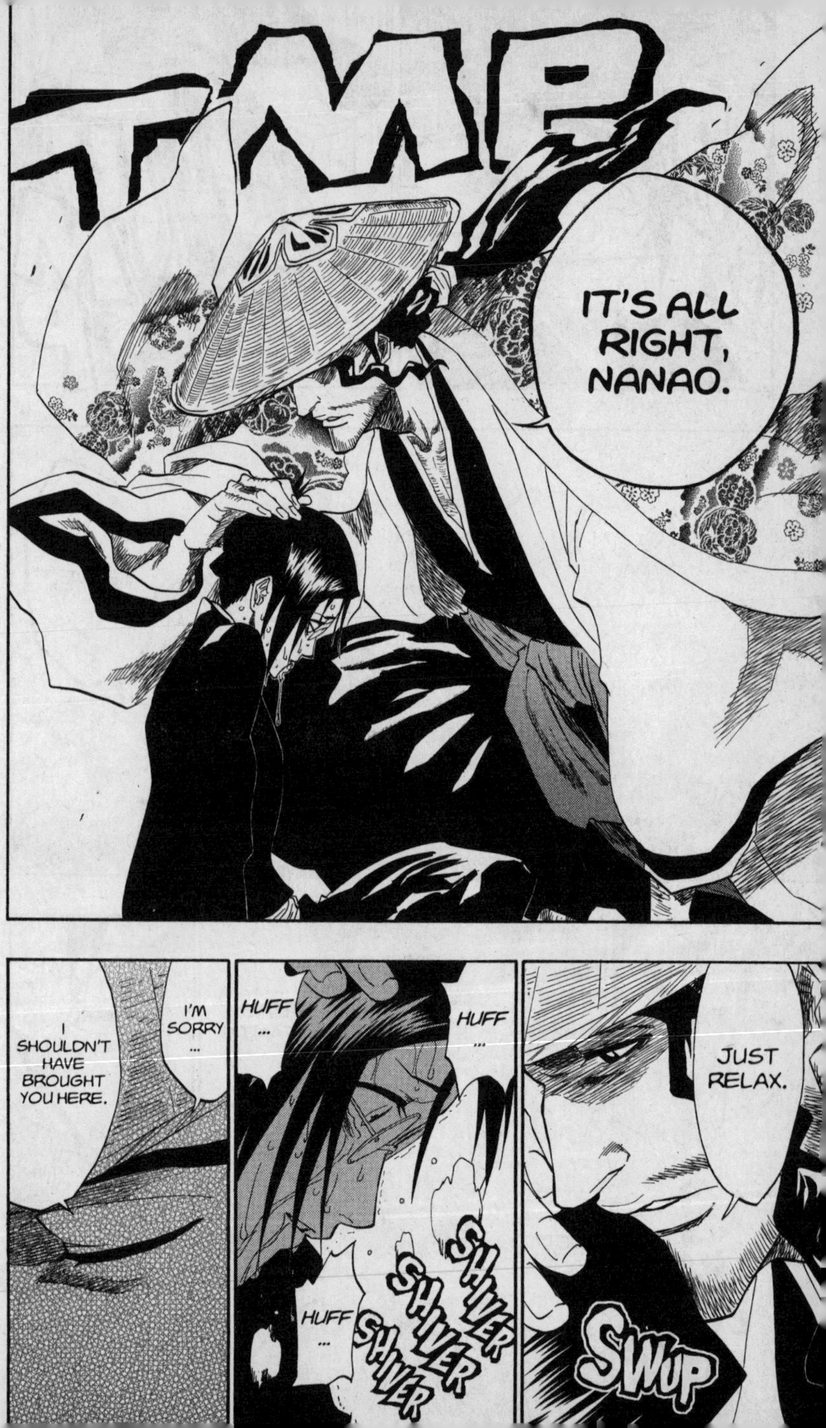
TMP
IT'S ALL RIGHT, NANAO.
JUST RELAX.
SWUP
HUFF ...
HUFF ...
SHIVER SHIVER SHIVER
HUFF ...
I'M SORRY ...
I SHOULDN'T HAVE BROUGHT YOU HERE.

READ THIS WAY

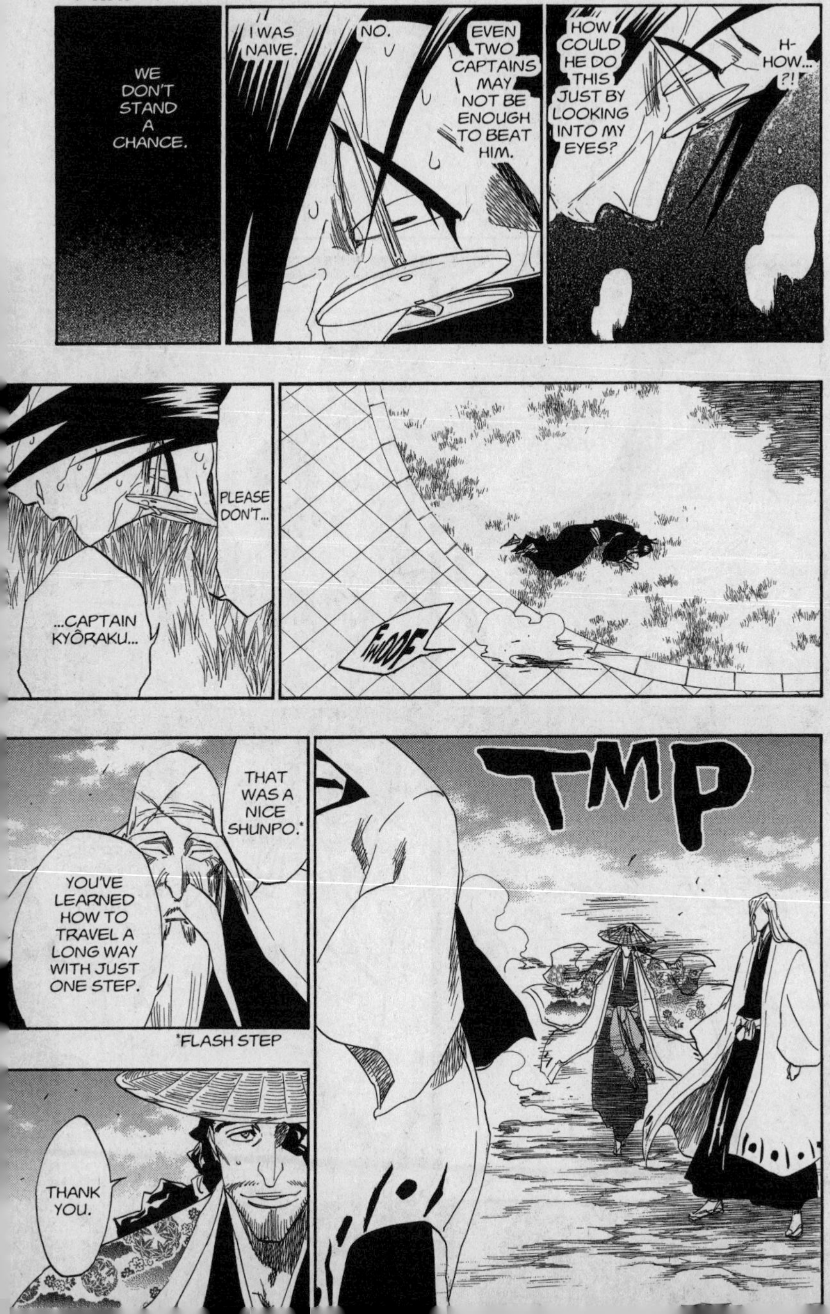
H-HOW...?!
HOW COULD HE DO THIS JUST BY LOOKING INTO MY EYES?
EVEN TWO CAPTAINS MAY NOT BE ENOUGH TO BEAT HIM.
NO.
I WAS NAIVE.
WE DON'T STAND A CHANCE.
FWOOF
PLEASE DON'T...
...CAPTAIN KYÔRAKU...
TMP
THAT WAS A NICE SHUNPO.*
YOU'VE LEARNED HOW TO TRAVEL A LONG WAY WITH JUST ONE STEP.
*FLASH STEP
THANK YOU.

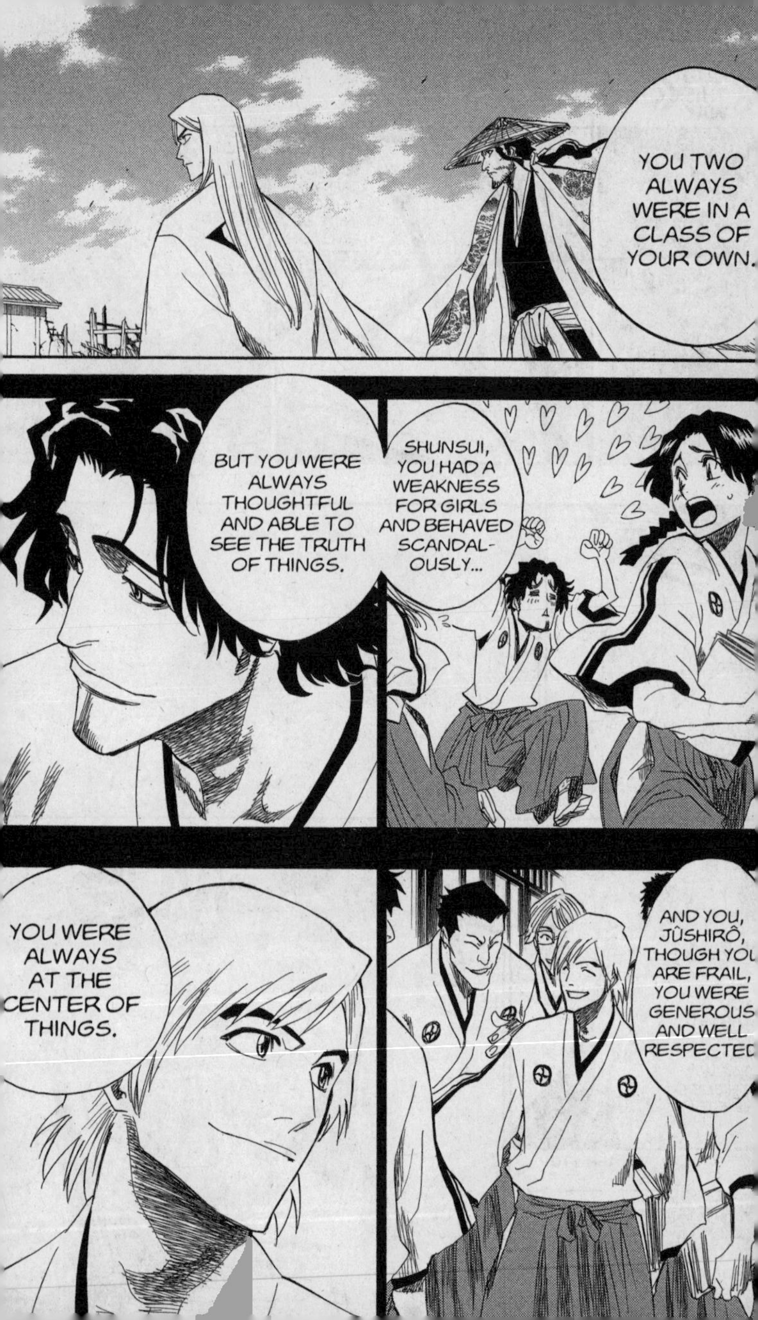
YOU TWO ALWAYS WERE IN A CLASS OF YOUR OWN.
SHUNSUI, YOU HAD A WEAKNESS FOR GIRLS AND BEHAVED SCANDAL-OUSLY...
BUT YOU WERE ALWAYS THOUGHTFUL AND ABLE TO SEE THE TRUTH OF THINGS.
AND YOU, JÛSHIRÔ, THOUGH YOU ARE FRAIL, YOU WERE GENEROUS AND WELL RESPECTED
YOU WERE ALWAYS AT THE CENTER OF THINGS.

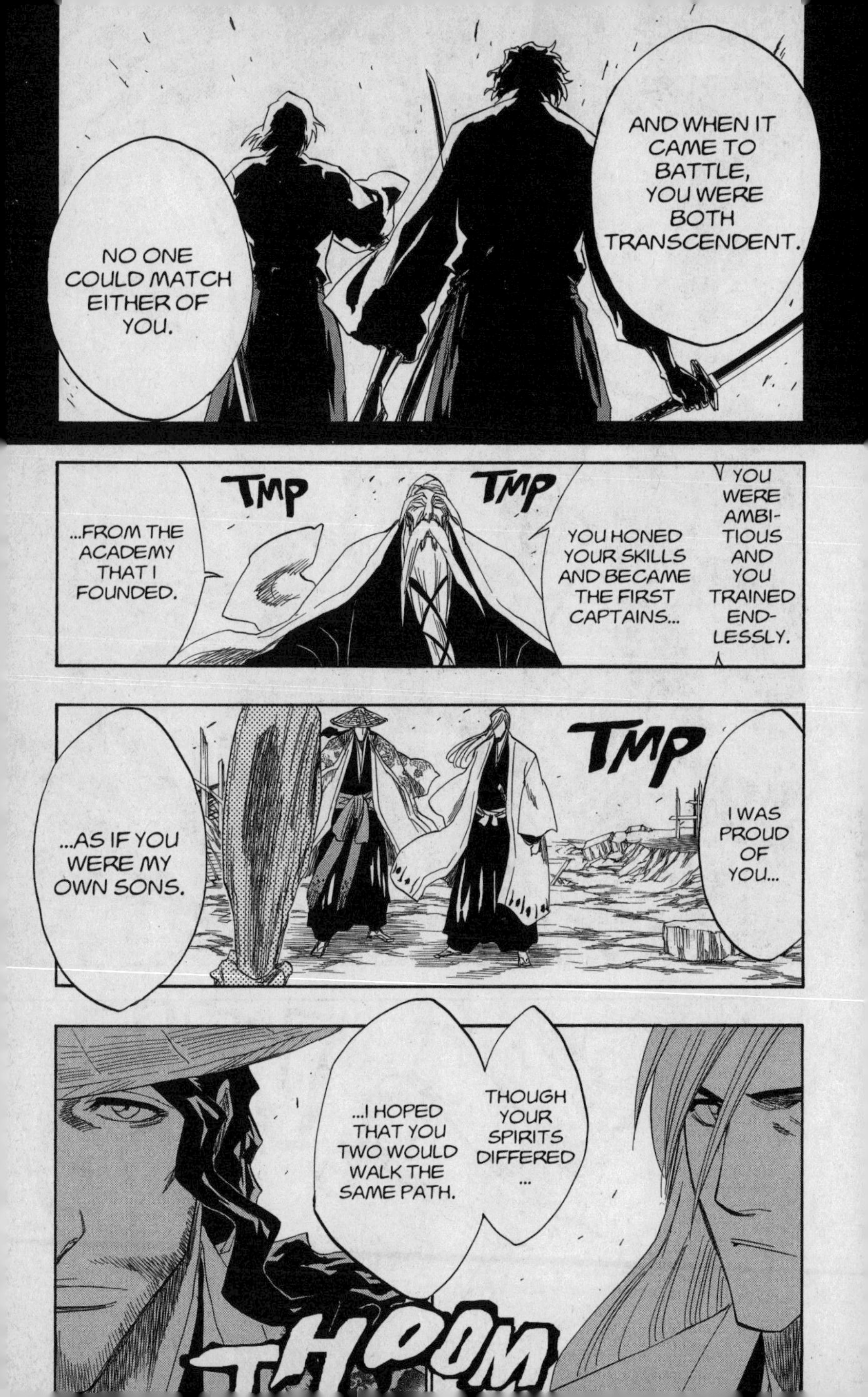
AND WHEN IT CAME TO BATTLE, YOU WERE BOTH TRANSCENDENT.
NO ONE COULD MATCH EITHER OF YOU.
YOU WERE AMBITIOUS AND YOU TRAINED ENDLESSLY.
TMP
YOU HONED YOUR SKILLS AND BECAME THE FIRST CAPTAINS...
TMP
...FROM THE ACADEMY THAT I FOUNDED.
I WAS PROUD OF YOU...
TMP
...AS IF YOU WERE MY OWN SONS.
THOUGH YOUR SPIRITS DIFFERED...
...I HOPED THAT YOU TWO WOULD WALK THE SAME PATH.
THOOM

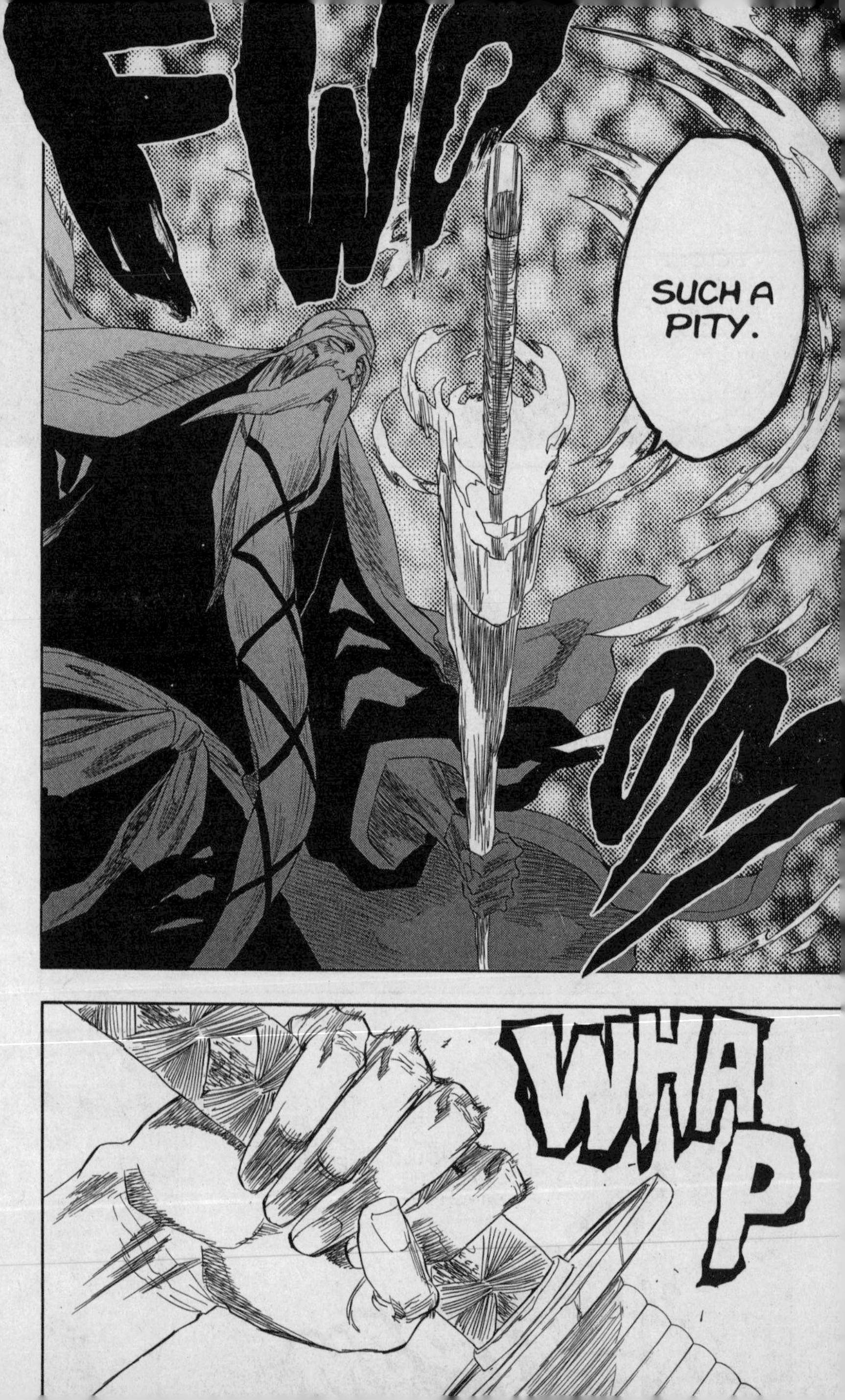
SUCH A PITY.
WHAP

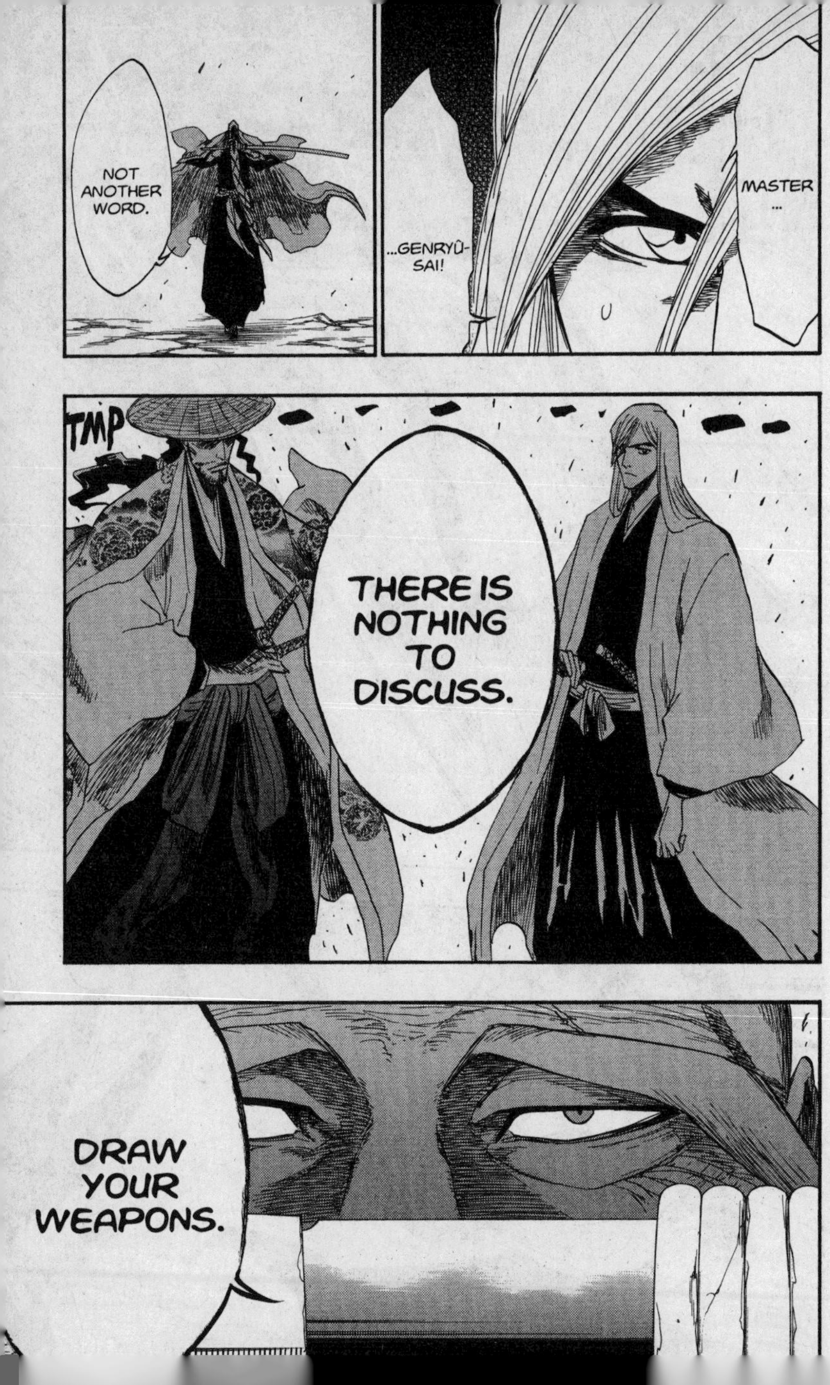
MASTER ...
...GENRYÛ-SAI!
NOT ANOTHER WORD.
TMP
THERE IS NOTHING TO DISCUSS.
DRAW YOUR WEAPONS.

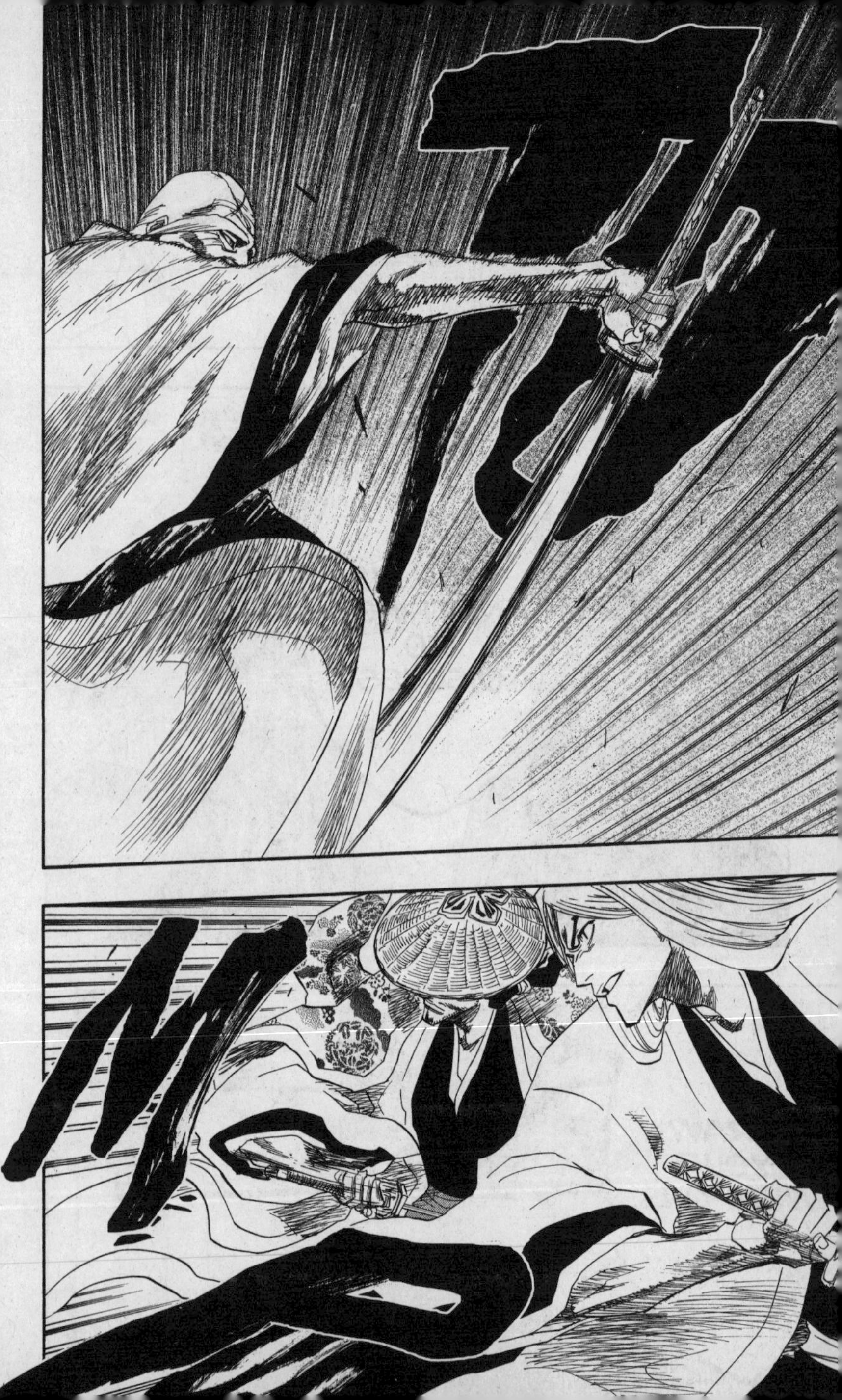

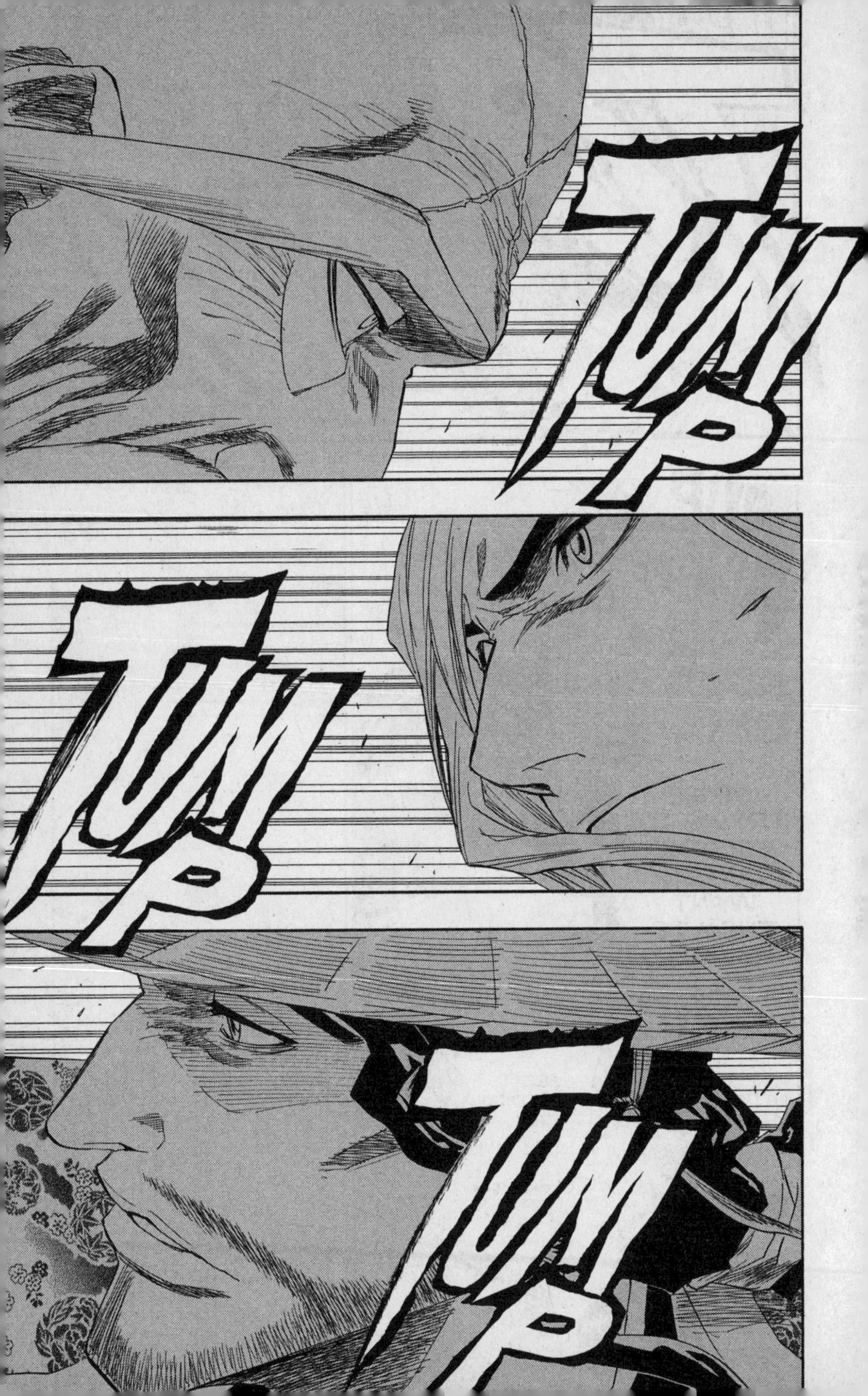
TUMP
TUMP
TUMP

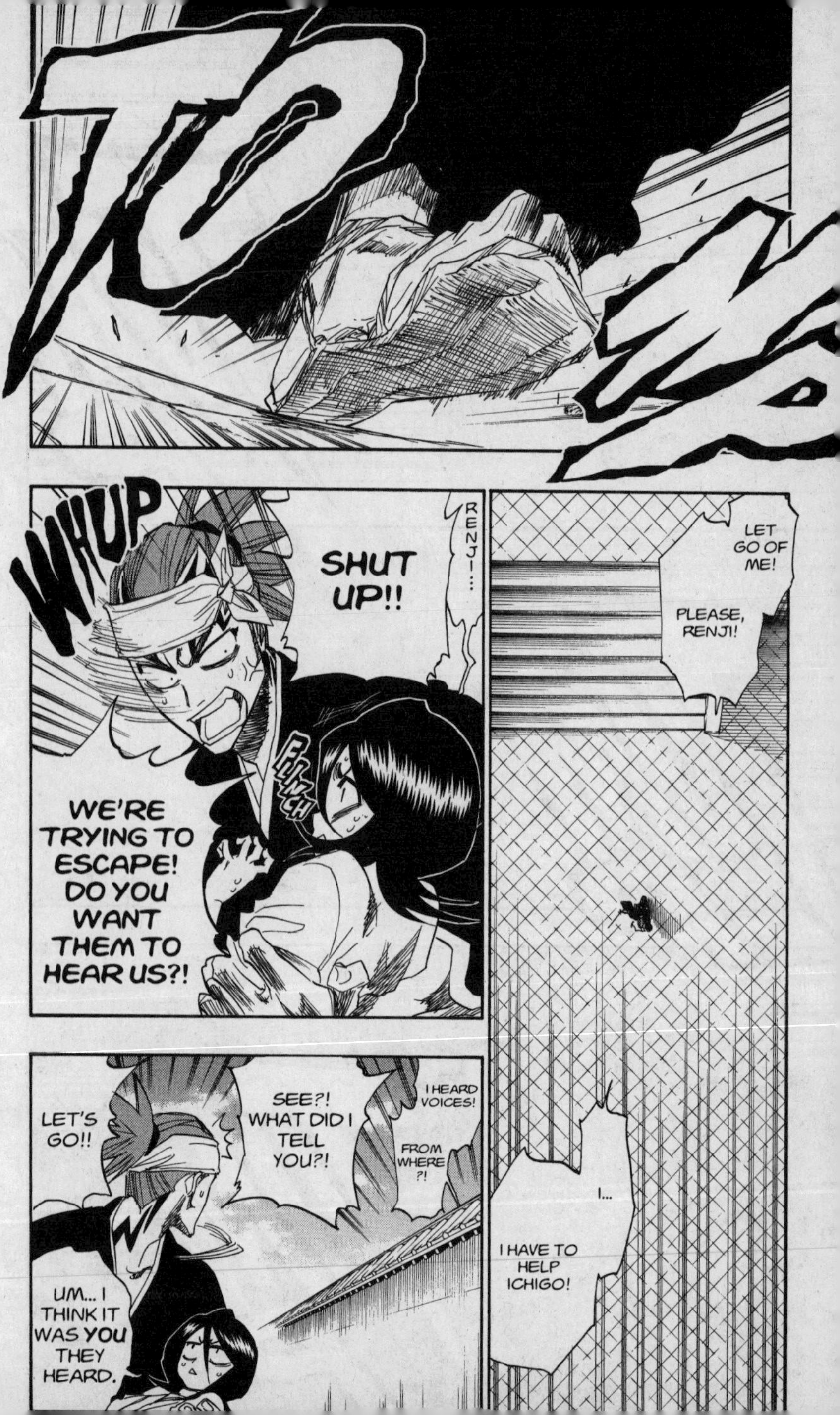
LET GO OF ME!
PLEASE, RENJI!
I...
I HAVE TO HELP ICHIGO!
RENJI...
SHUT UP!!
WHUP
FLINCH
WE'RE TRYING TO ESCAPE! DO YOU WANT THEM TO HEAR US?!
I HEARD VOICES!
FROM WHERE?!
SEE?! WHAT DID I TELL YOU?!
LET'S GO!!
UM... I THINK IT WAS YOU THEY HEARD.

...ICHIGO.

THAT JERK...

REPAY
...
...ME?

HE SAID HE WANTED TO REPAY YOU.

HE SAID, "RUKIA...

RUKIA SAVED MY LIFE.

YEAH.

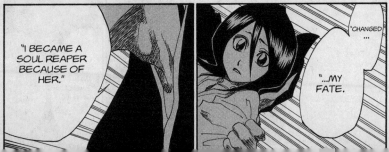

"I BECAME A SOUL REAPER BECAUSE OF HER."

"CHANGED
...

...MY FATE.

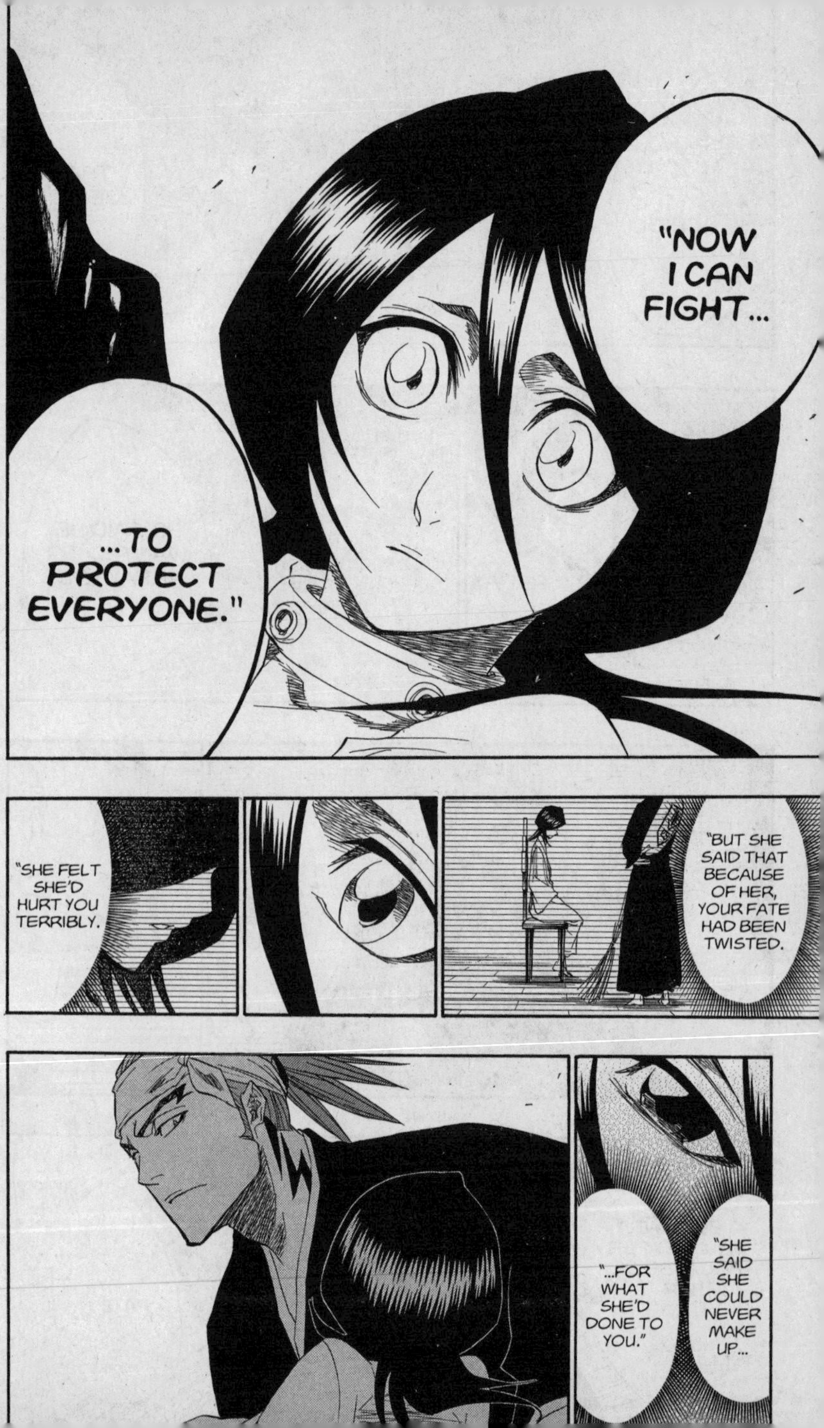
"NOW I CAN FIGHT...
...TO PROTECT EVERYONE."
"BUT SHE SAID THAT BECAUSE OF HER, YOUR FATE HAD BEEN TWISTED.
"SHE FELT SHE'D HURT YOU TERRIBLY.
"SHE SAID SHE COULD NEVER MAKE UP...
"...FOR WHAT SHE'D DONE TO YOU."

READ THIS WAY

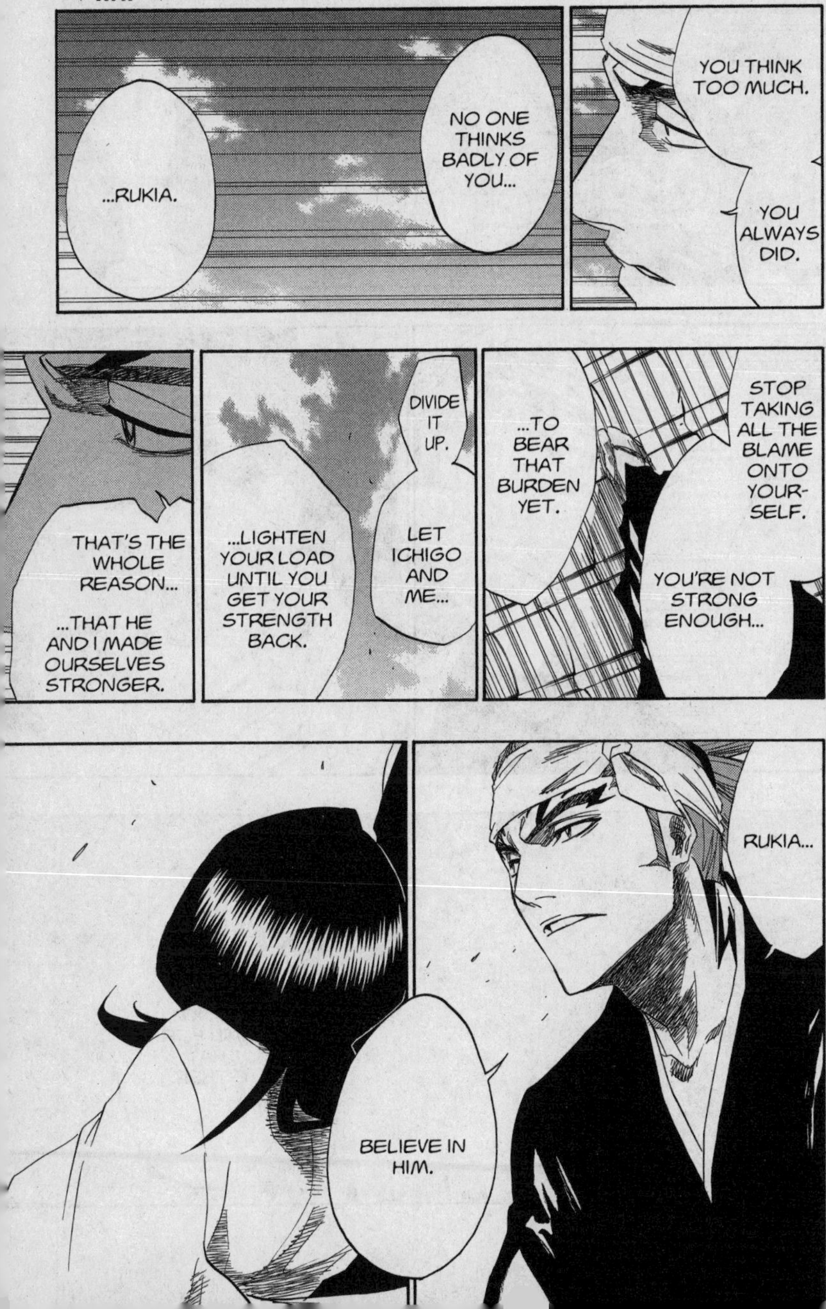
YOU THINK TOO MUCH.
YOU ALWAYS DID.
NO ONE THINKS BADLY OF YOU...
...RUKIA.
STOP TAKING ALL THE BLAME ONTO YOUR-SELF.
YOU'RE NOT STRONG ENOUGH...
...TO BEAR THAT BURDEN YET.
DIVIDE IT UP.
LET ICHIGO AND ME...
...LIGHTEN YOUR LOAD UNTIL YOU GET YOUR STRENGTH BACK.
THAT'S THE WHOLE REASON...
...THAT HE AND I MADE OURSELVES STRONGER.
RUKIA...
BELIEVE IN HIM.

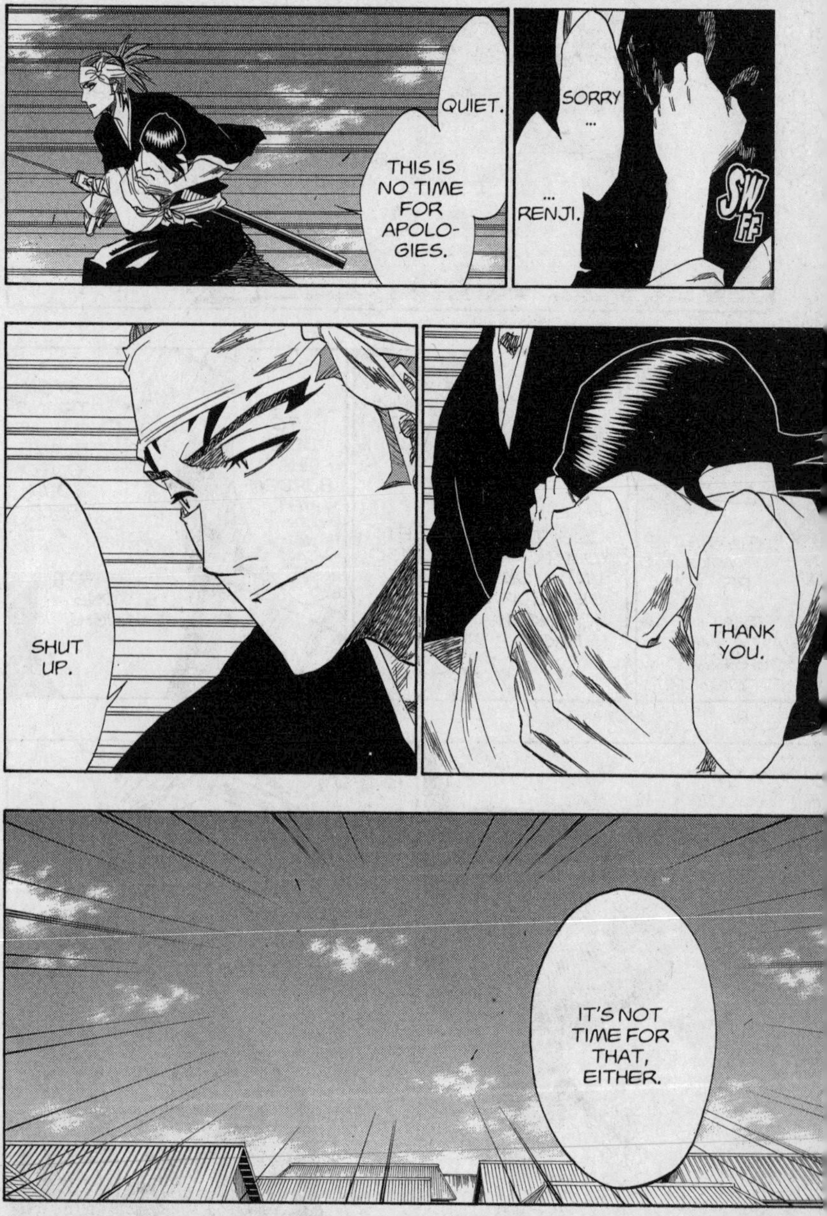
SORRY ...
... RENJI.
SWFF
QUIET.
THIS IS NO TIME FOR APOLOGIES.
THANK YOU.
SHUT UP.
IT'S NOT TIME FOR THAT, EITHER.

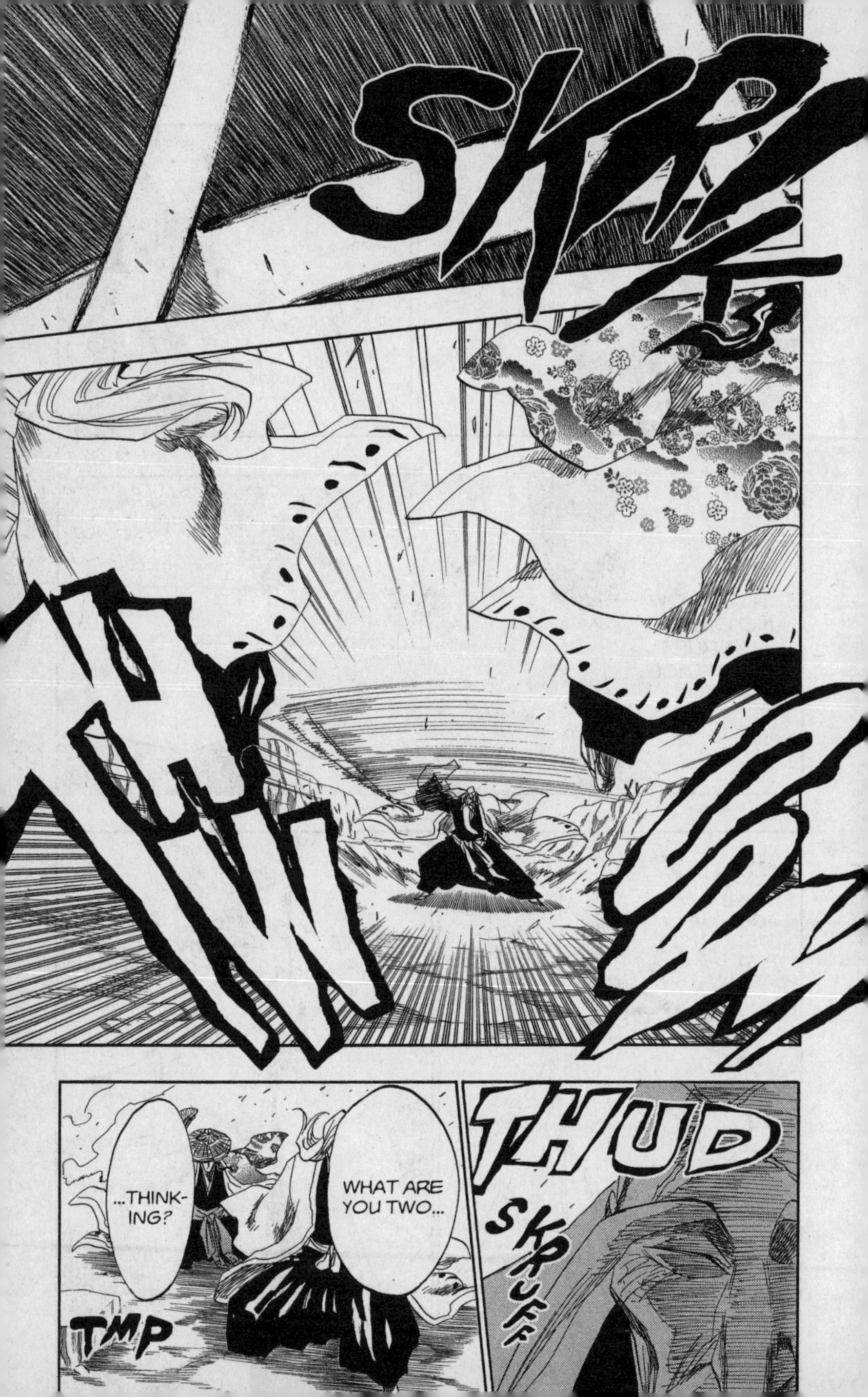
THUD
SKRUFF
WHAT ARE YOU TWO...
...THINKING?
TMP

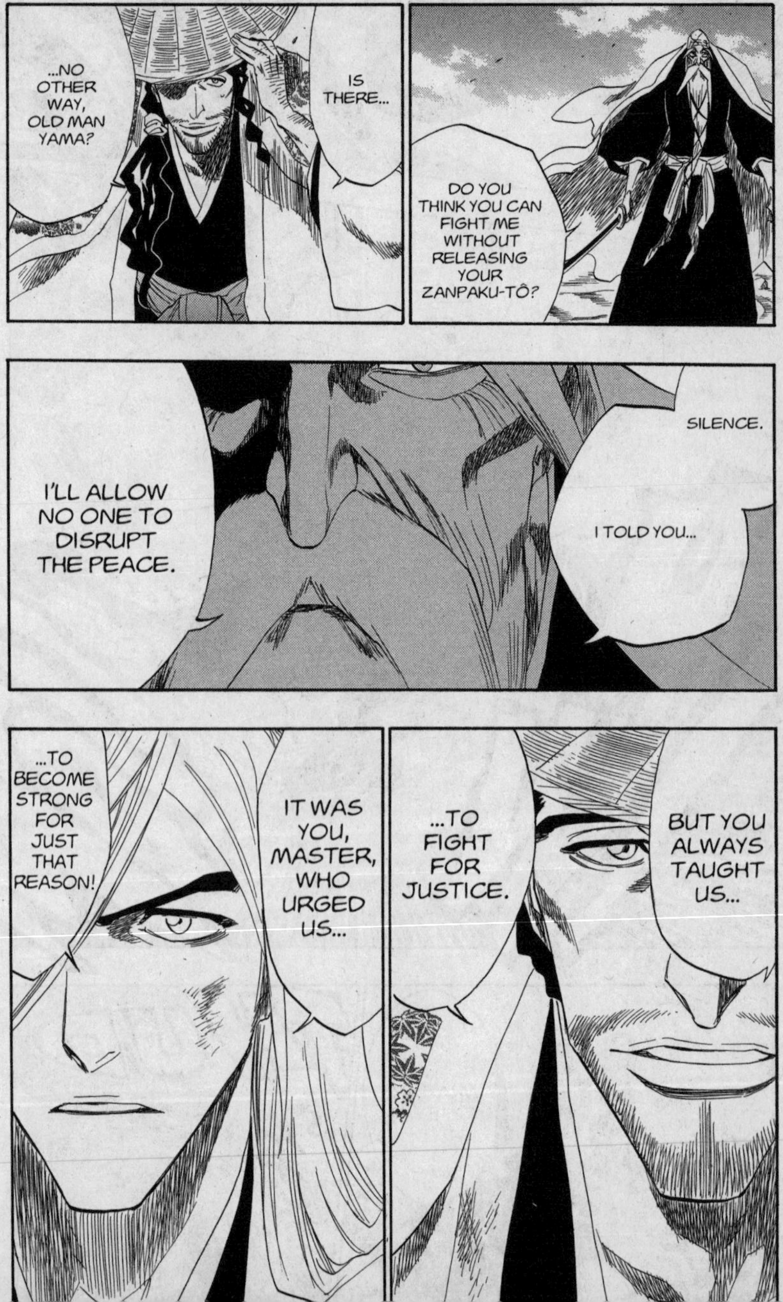
DO YOU THINK YOU CAN FIGHT ME WITHOUT RELEASING YOUR ZANPAKU-TÔ?
IS THERE...
...NO OTHER WAY, OLD MAN YAMA?
SILENCE.
I TOLD YOU...
I'LL ALLOW NO ONE TO DISRUPT THE PEACE.
BUT YOU ALWAYS TAUGHT US...
...TO FIGHT FOR JUSTICE.
IT WAS YOU, MASTER, WHO URGED US...
...TO BECOME STRONG FOR JUST THAT REASON!

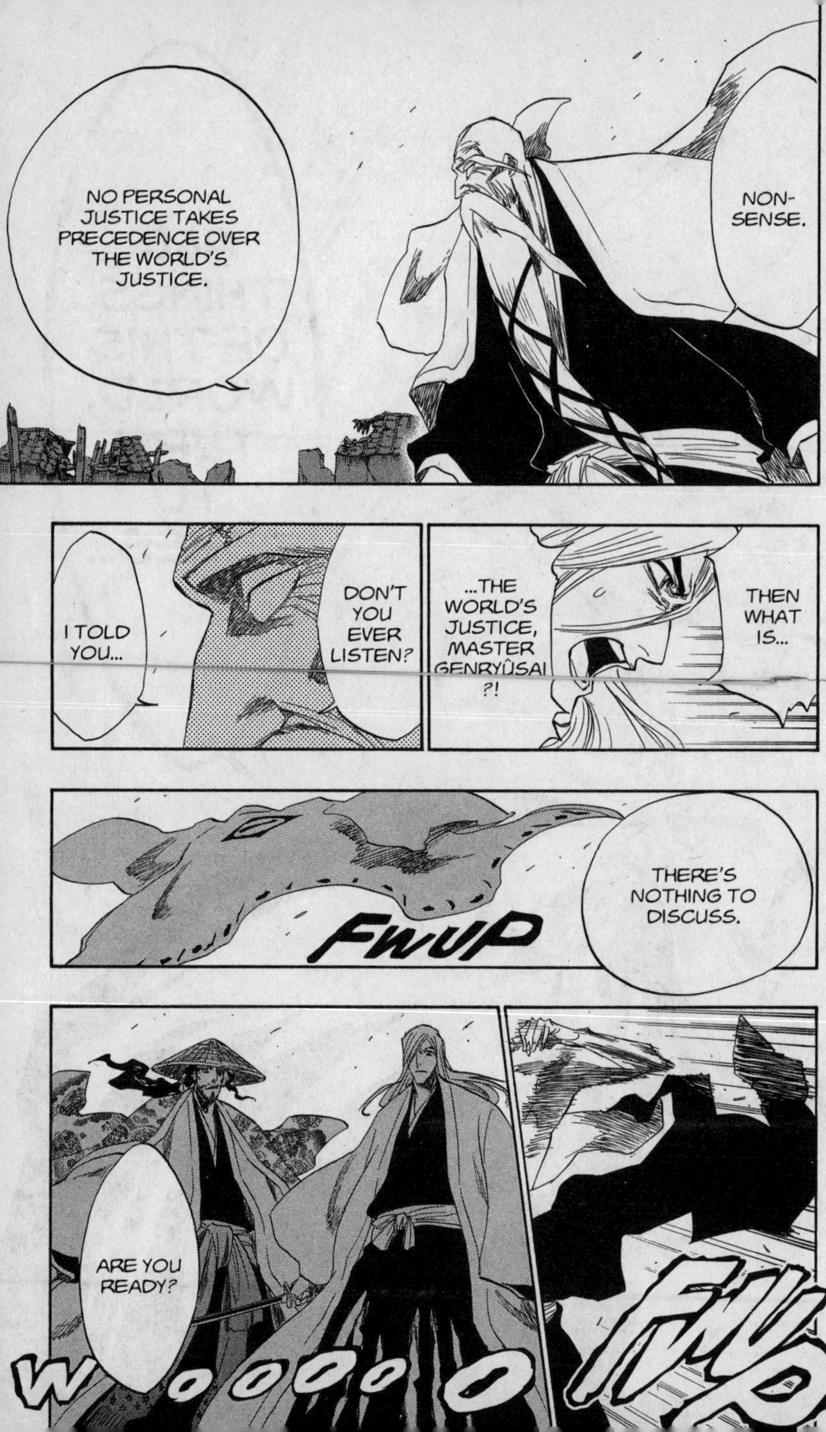
NON-SENSE.
NO PERSONAL JUSTICE TAKES PRECEDENCE OVER THE WORLD'S JUSTICE.
THEN WHAT IS...
...THE WORLD'S JUSTICE, MASTER GENRYÛSAI ?!
DON'T YOU EVER LISTEN?
I TOLD YOU...
THERE'S NOTHING TO DISCUSS.
FWUP
FWUP
ARE YOU READY?
WOOOOO

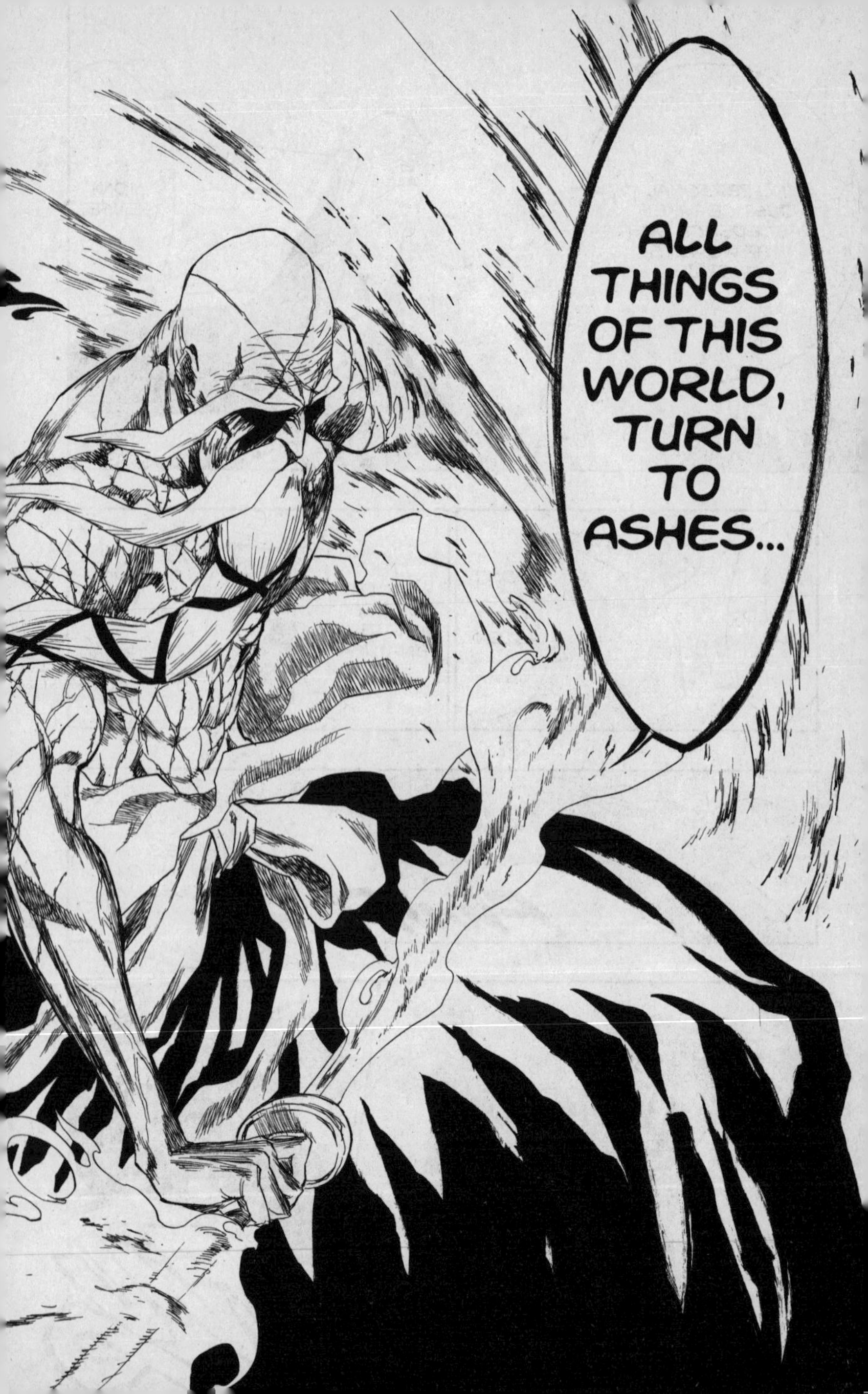
ALL THINGS OF THIS WORLD, TURN TO ASHES...

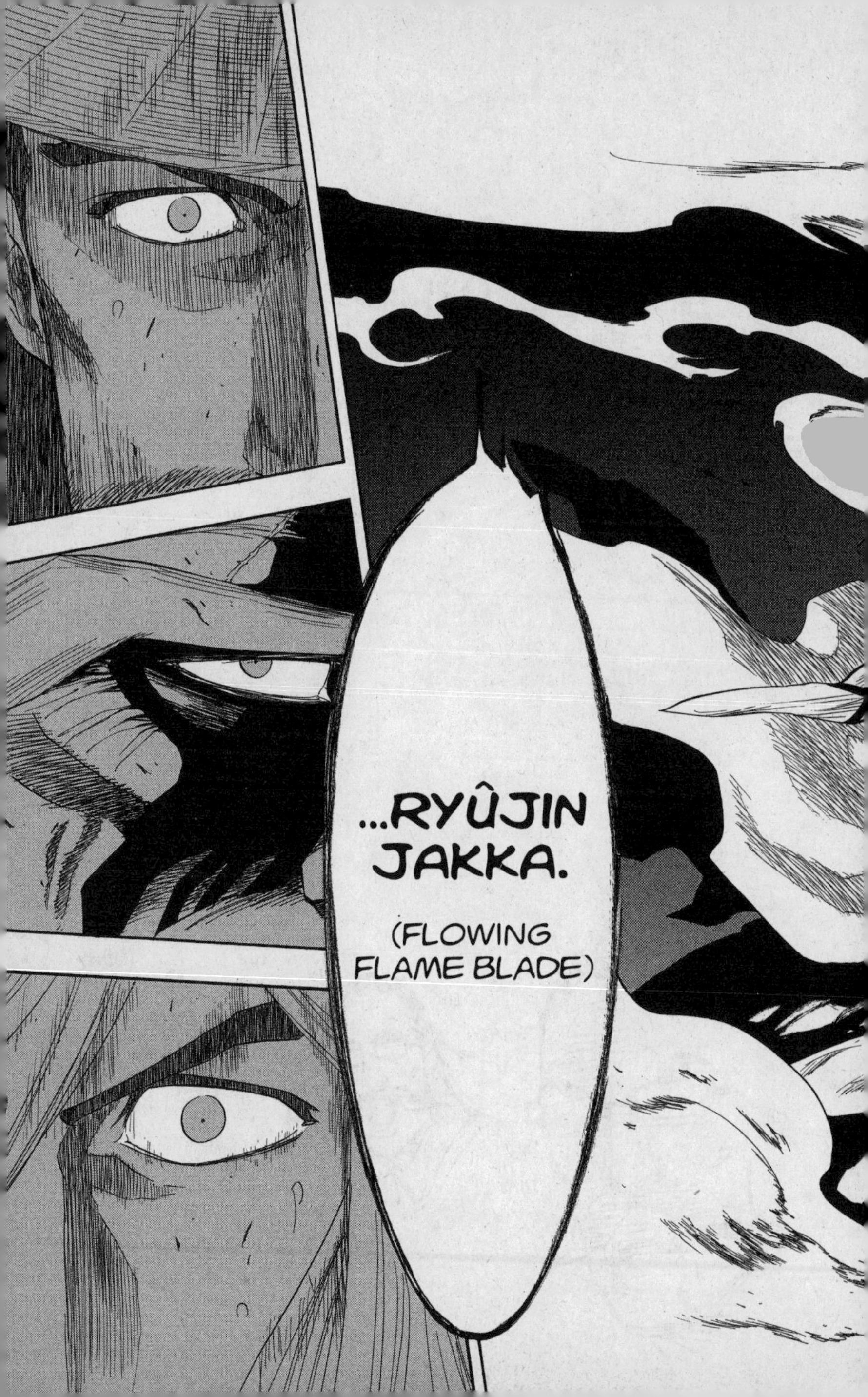
...RYÛJIN JAKKA.
(FLOWING FLAME BLADE)

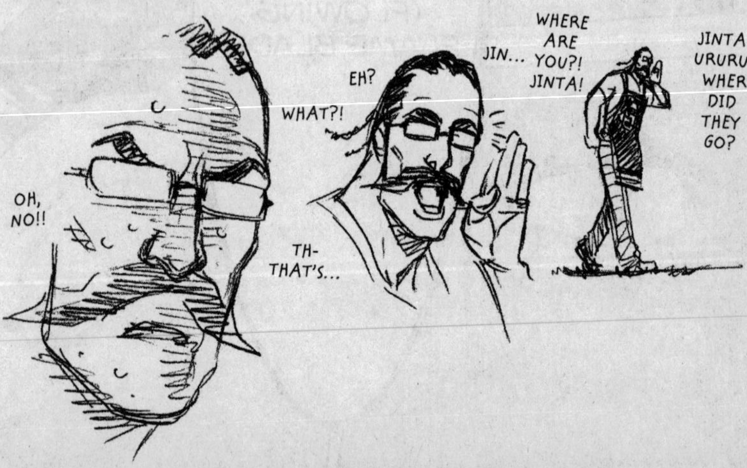
JINTA! URURU! WHERE DID THEY GO?
JIN...
WHERE ARE YOU?! JINTA!
EH?
WHAT?!
TH- THAT'S...
OH, NO!!

156. Welcome to Purgatory

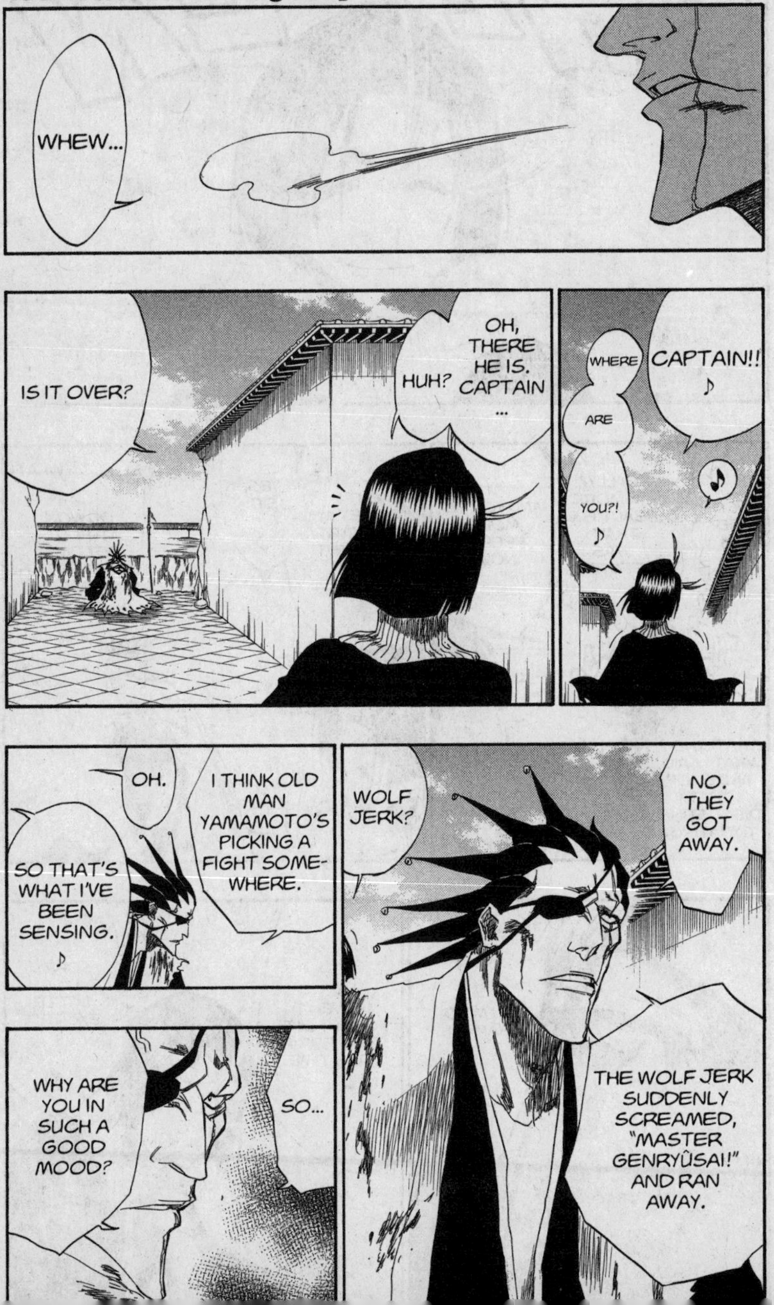
WHEW...
CAPTAIN!! ♪
WHERE ARE YOU?! ♪
OH, THERE HE IS. CAPTAIN...
HUH?
IS IT OVER?
NO. THEY GOT AWAY.
WOLF JERK?
THE WOLF JERK SUDDENLY SCREAMED, "MASTER GENRYÛSAI!" AND RAN AWAY.
I THINK OLD MAN YAMAMOTO'S PICKING A FIGHT SOME-WHERE.
OH.
SO THAT'S WHAT I'VE BEEN SENSING. ♪
SO...
WHY ARE YOU IN SUCH A GOOD MOOD?

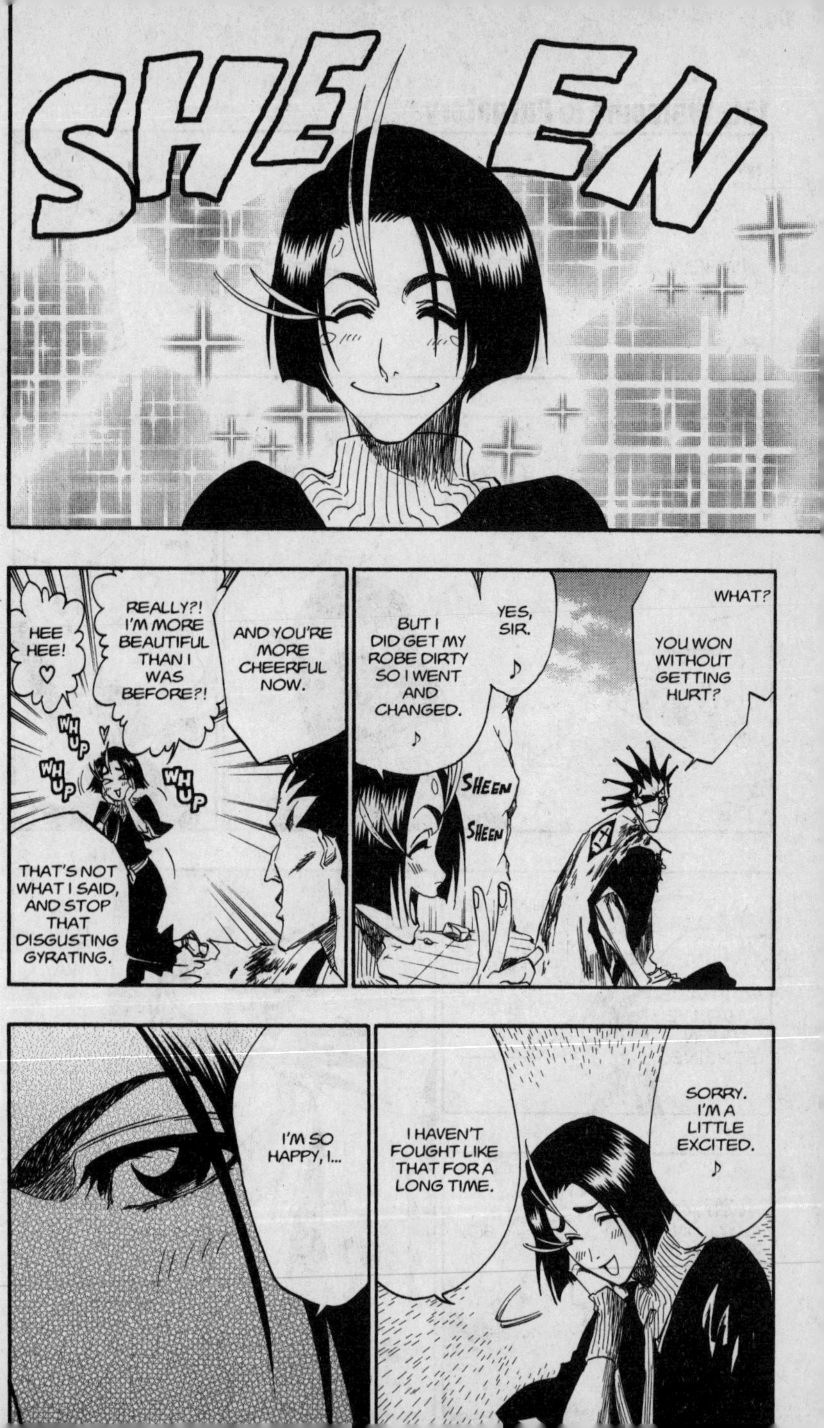
SHE EN
WHAT?
YOU WON WITHOUT GETTING HURT?
YES, SIR. ♪
BUT I DID GET MY ROBE DIRTY SO I WENT AND CHANGED. ♪
SHEEN
SHEEN
AND YOU'RE MORE CHEERFUL NOW.
REALLY?! I'M MORE BEAUTIFUL THAN I WAS BEFORE?!
HEE HEE! ♡
WHUP
WHUP
WHUP
THAT'S NOT WHAT I SAID, AND STOP THAT DISGUSTING GYRATING.
SORRY. I'M A LITTLE EXCITED. ♪
I HAVEN'T FOUGHT LIKE THAT FOR A LONG TIME.
I'M SO HAPPY, I...

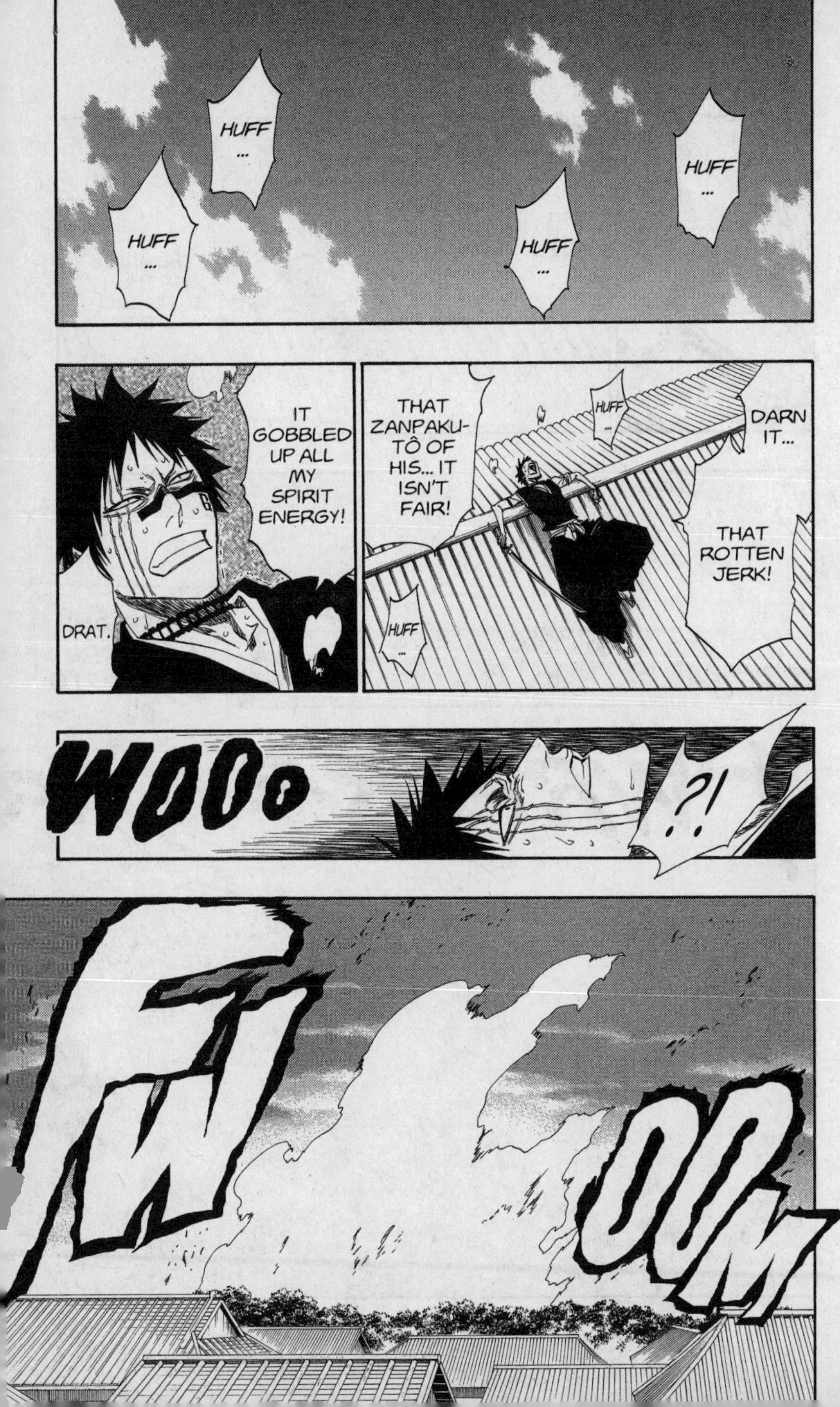
HUFF...
HUFF...
HUFF...
HUFF...
HUFF...
DARN IT...
THAT ROTTEN JERK!
THAT ZANPAKU-TÔ OF HIS... IT ISN'T FAIR!
HUFF...
IT GOBBLED UP ALL MY SPIRIT ENERGY!
DRAT.
?!
WOOo
FWOOM

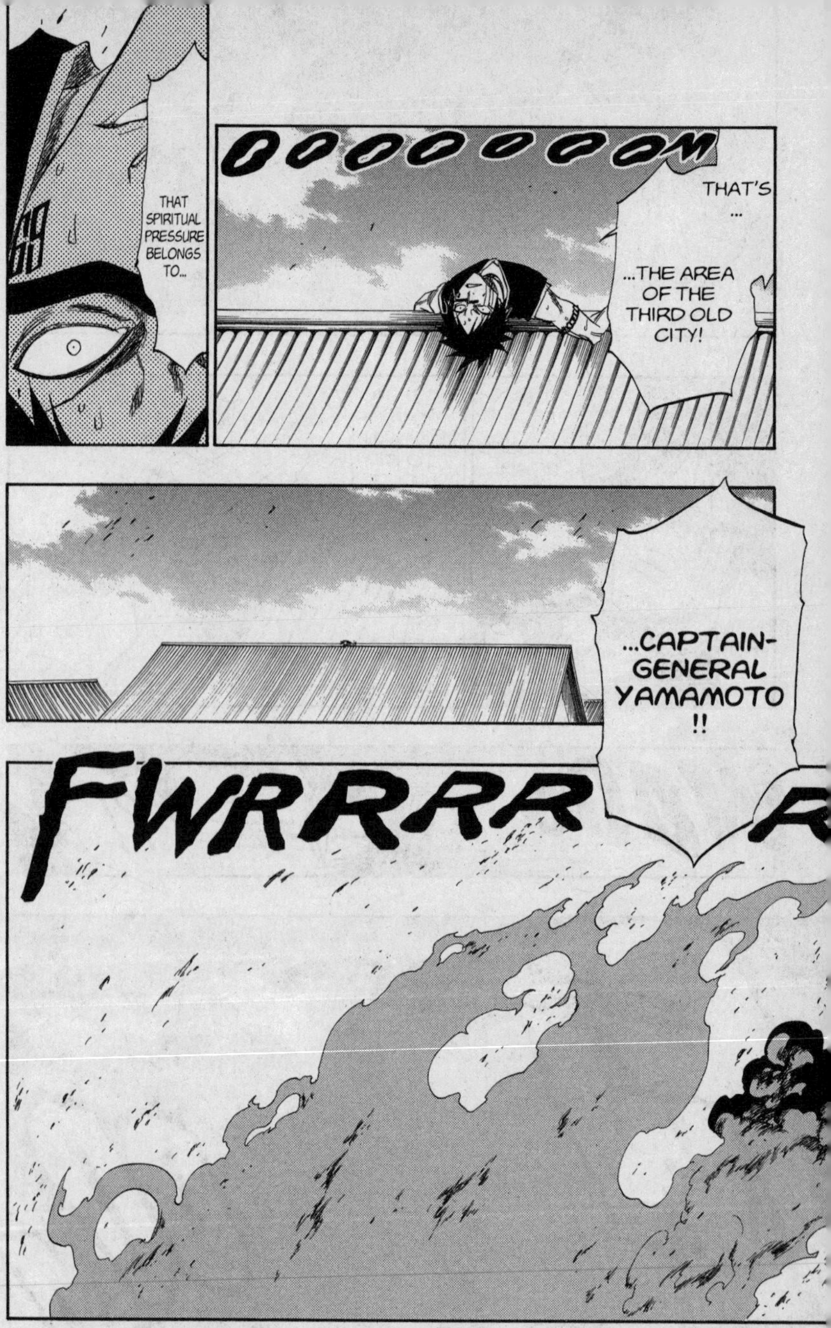
OOOOOOOM
THAT'S...
...THE AREA OF THE THIRD OLD CITY!
THAT SPIRITUAL PRESSURE BELONGS TO...
...CAPTAIN-GENERAL YAMAMOTO!!
FWRRRRR

156. Welcome to Purgatory

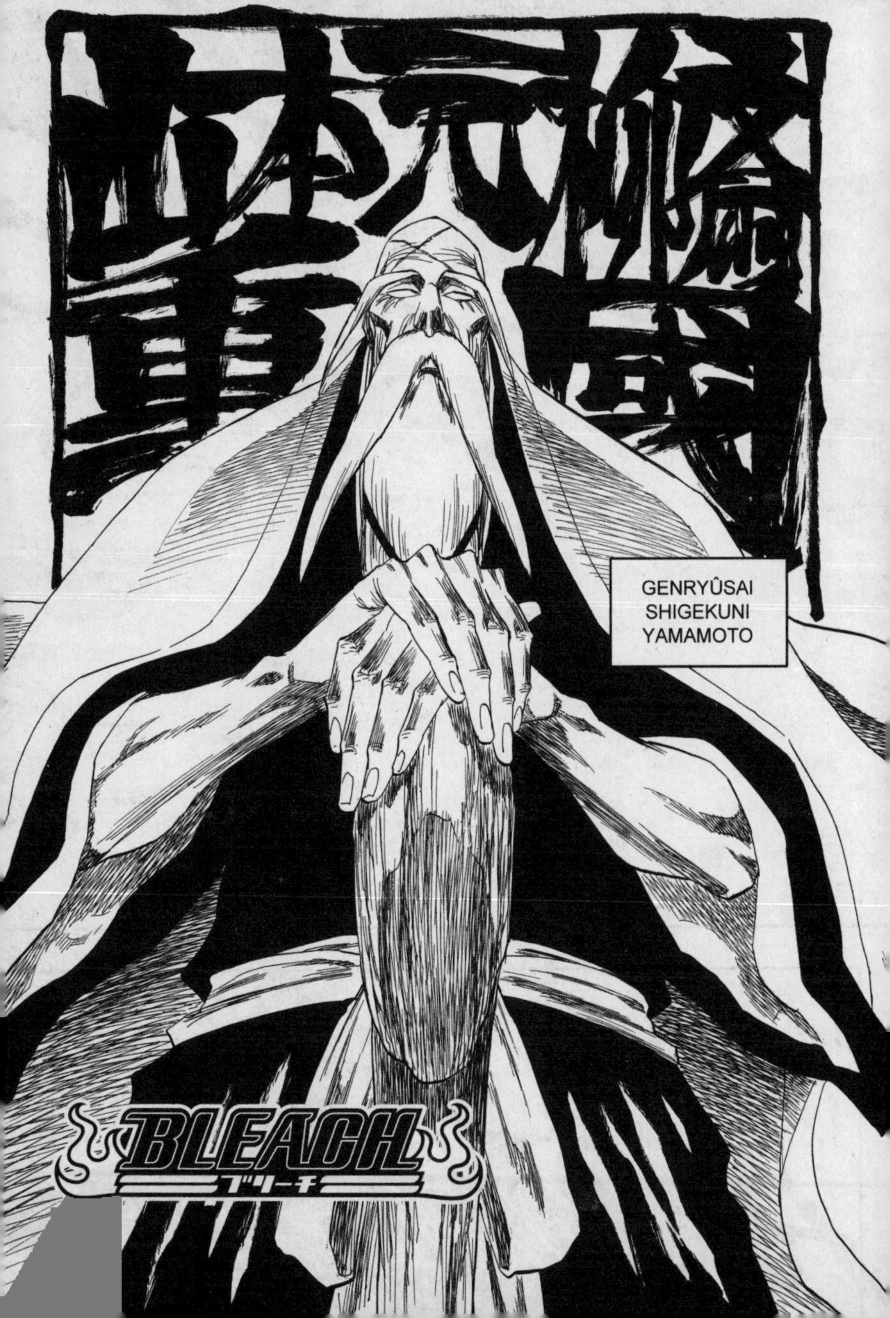
GENRYÛSAI
SHIGEKUNI
YAMAMOTO

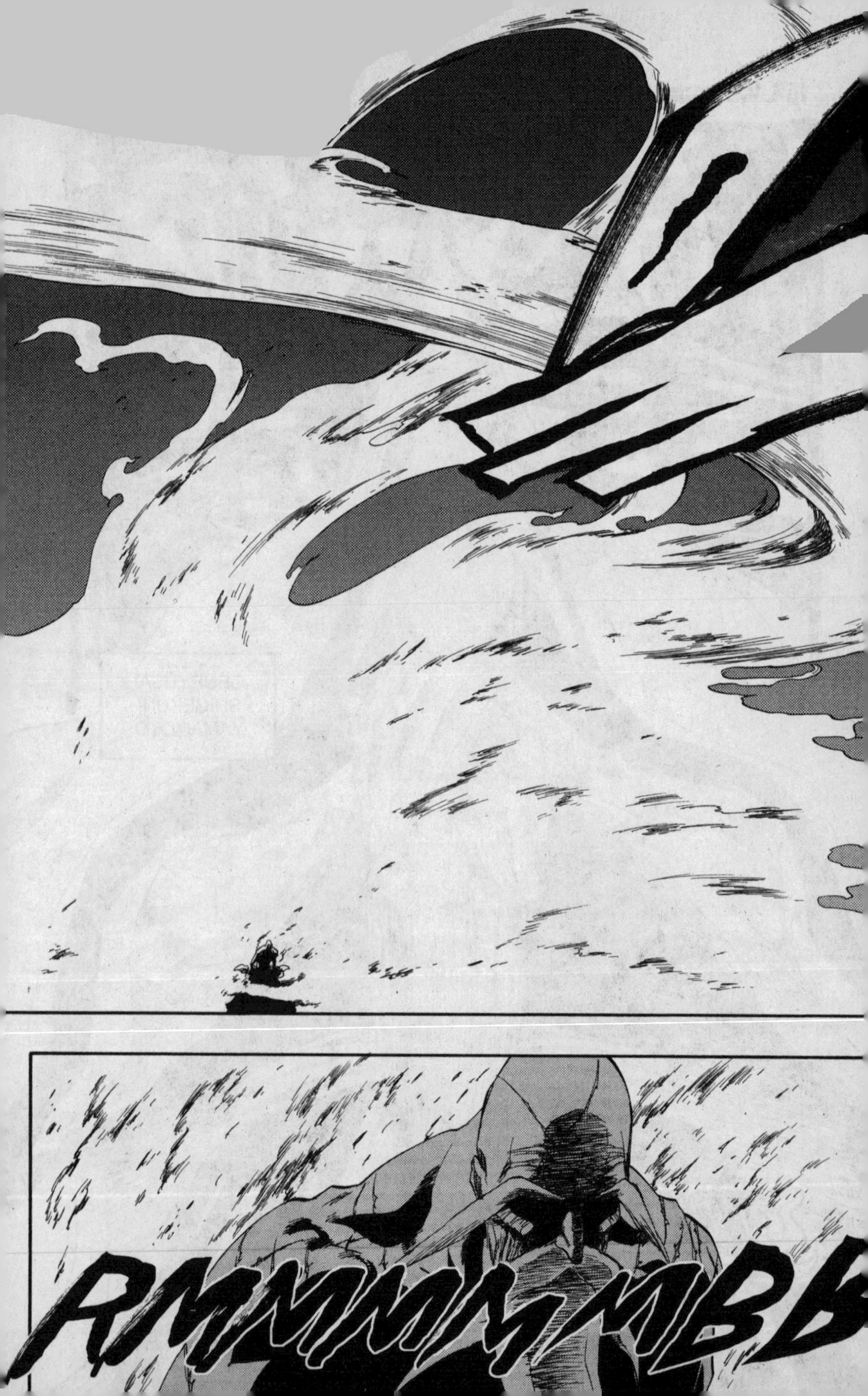
RMMMMMBB

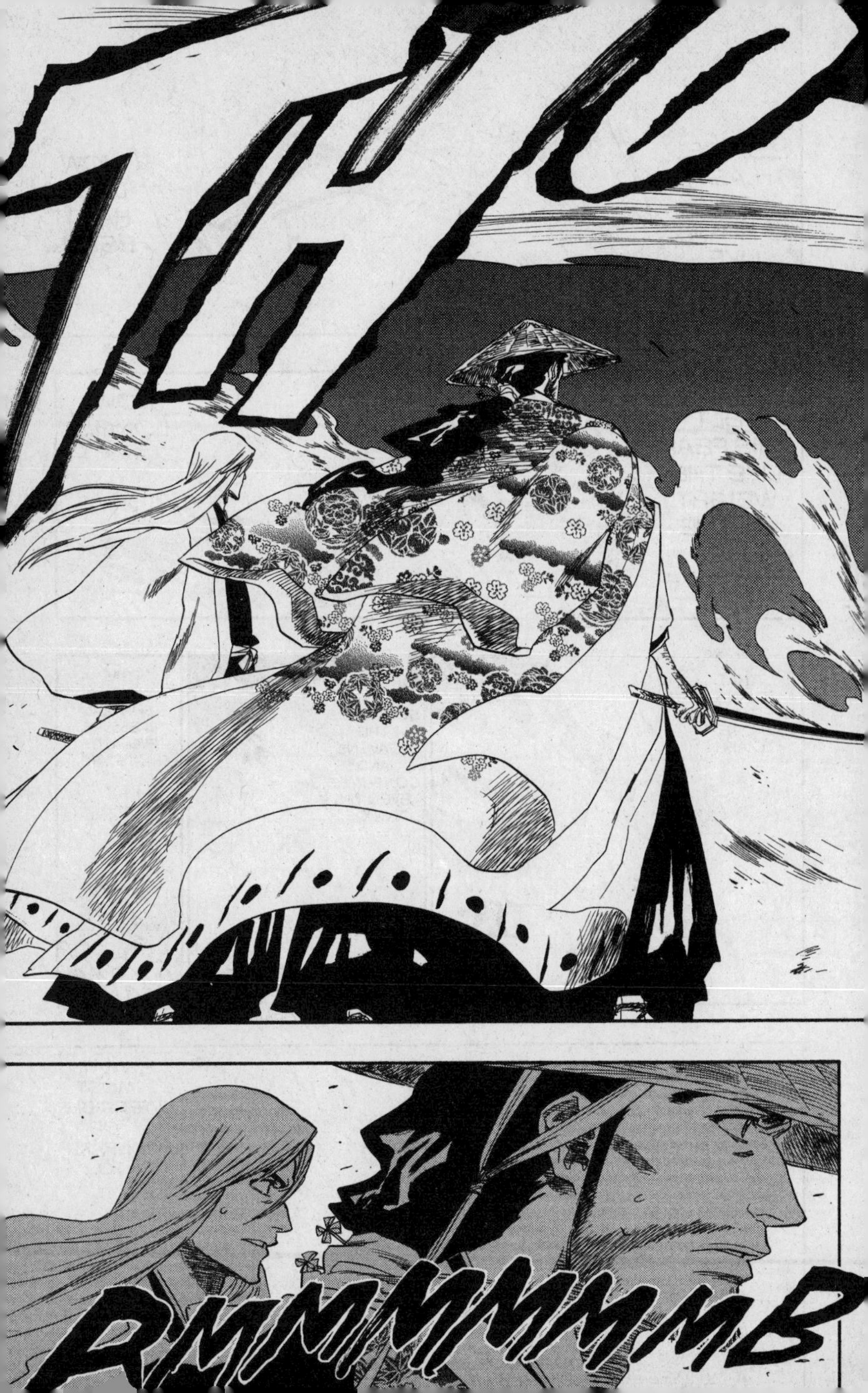
RMMMMMMMB

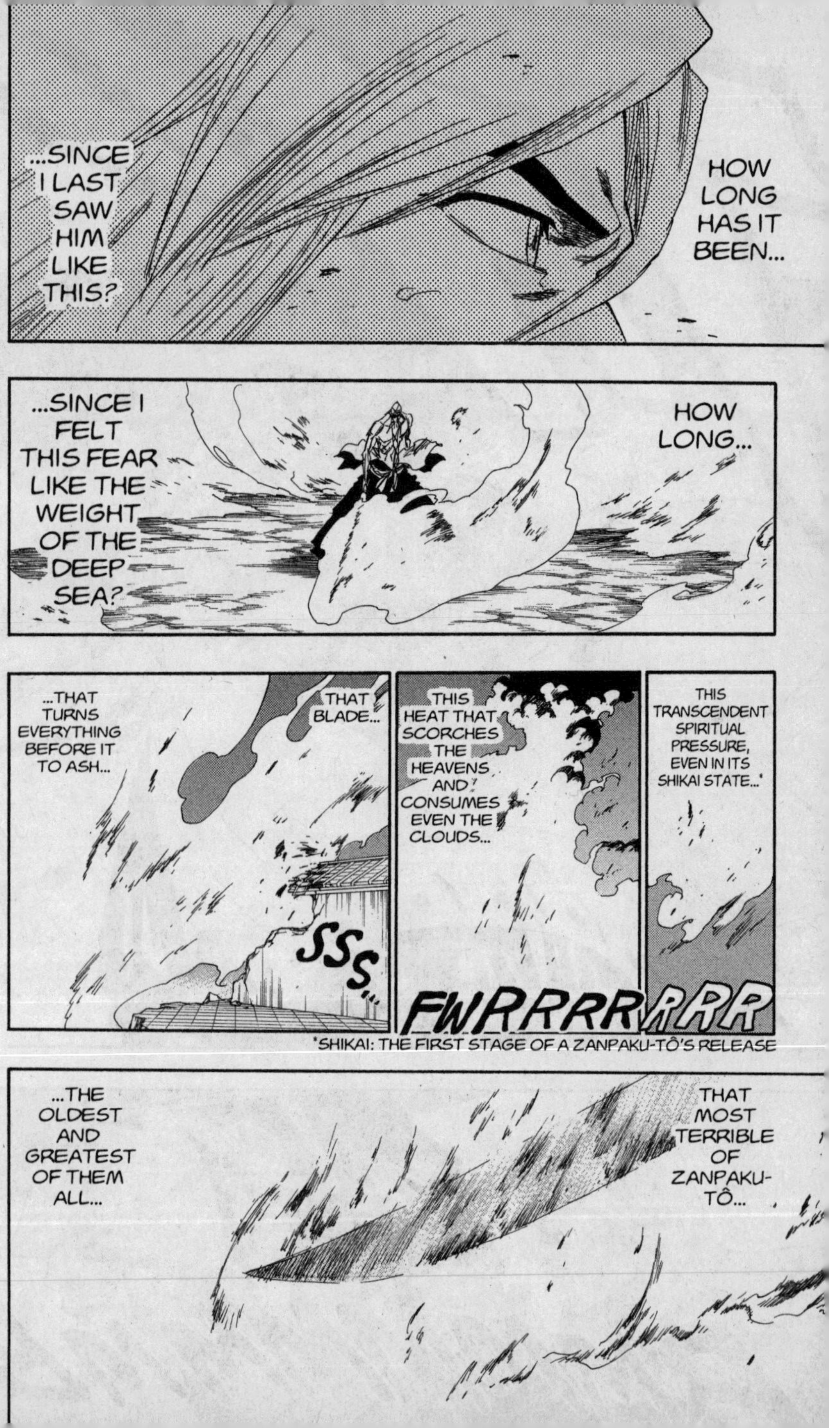
HOW LONG HAS IT BEEN...
...SINCE I LAST SAW HIM LIKE THIS?
HOW LONG...
...SINCE I FELT THIS FEAR LIKE THE WEIGHT OF THE DEEP SEA?
THIS TRANSCENDENT SPIRITUAL PRESSURE, EVEN IN ITS SHIKAI STATE...*
THIS HEAT THAT SCORCHES THE HEAVENS AND CONSUMES EVEN THE CLOUDS...
FWRRRRRRR
THAT BLADE...
...THAT TURNS EVERYTHING BEFORE IT TO ASH...
SSS...
THAT MOST TERRIBLE OF ZANPAKU-TÔ...
...THE OLDEST AND GREATEST OF THEM ALL...

*SHIKAI: THE FIRST STAGE OF A ZANPAKU-TÔ'S RELEASE

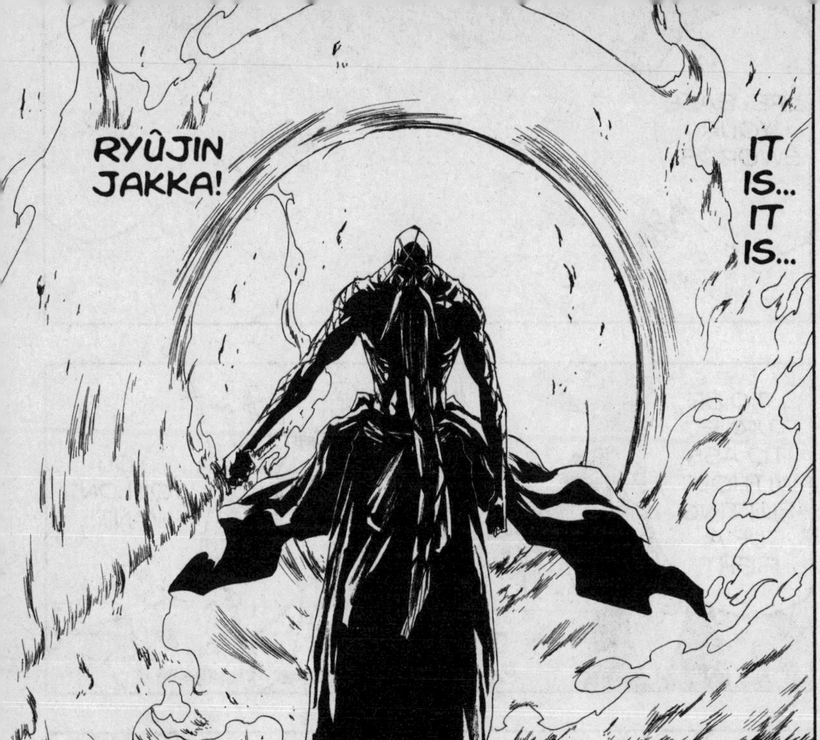
IT IS... IT IS...
RYÛJIN JAKKA!
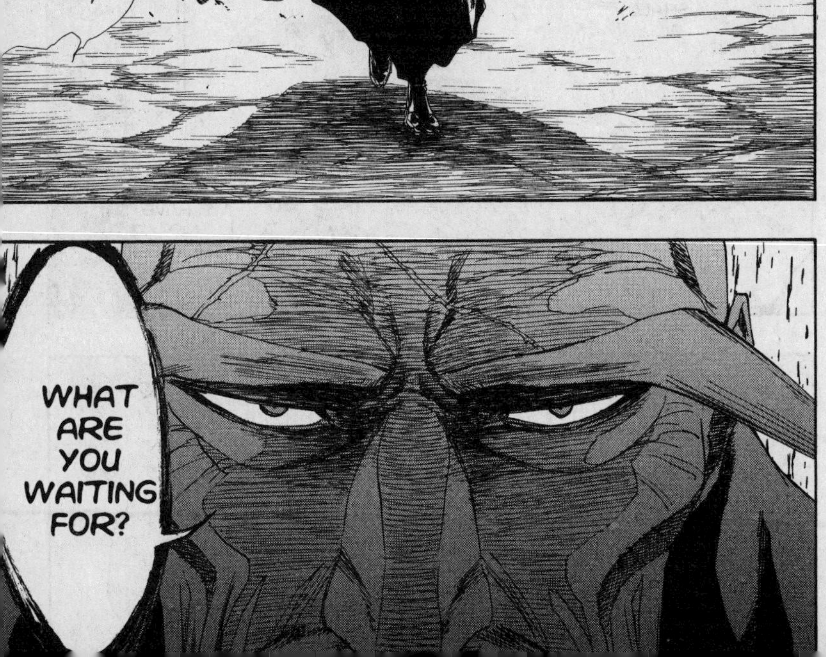
WHAT ARE YOU WAITING FOR?

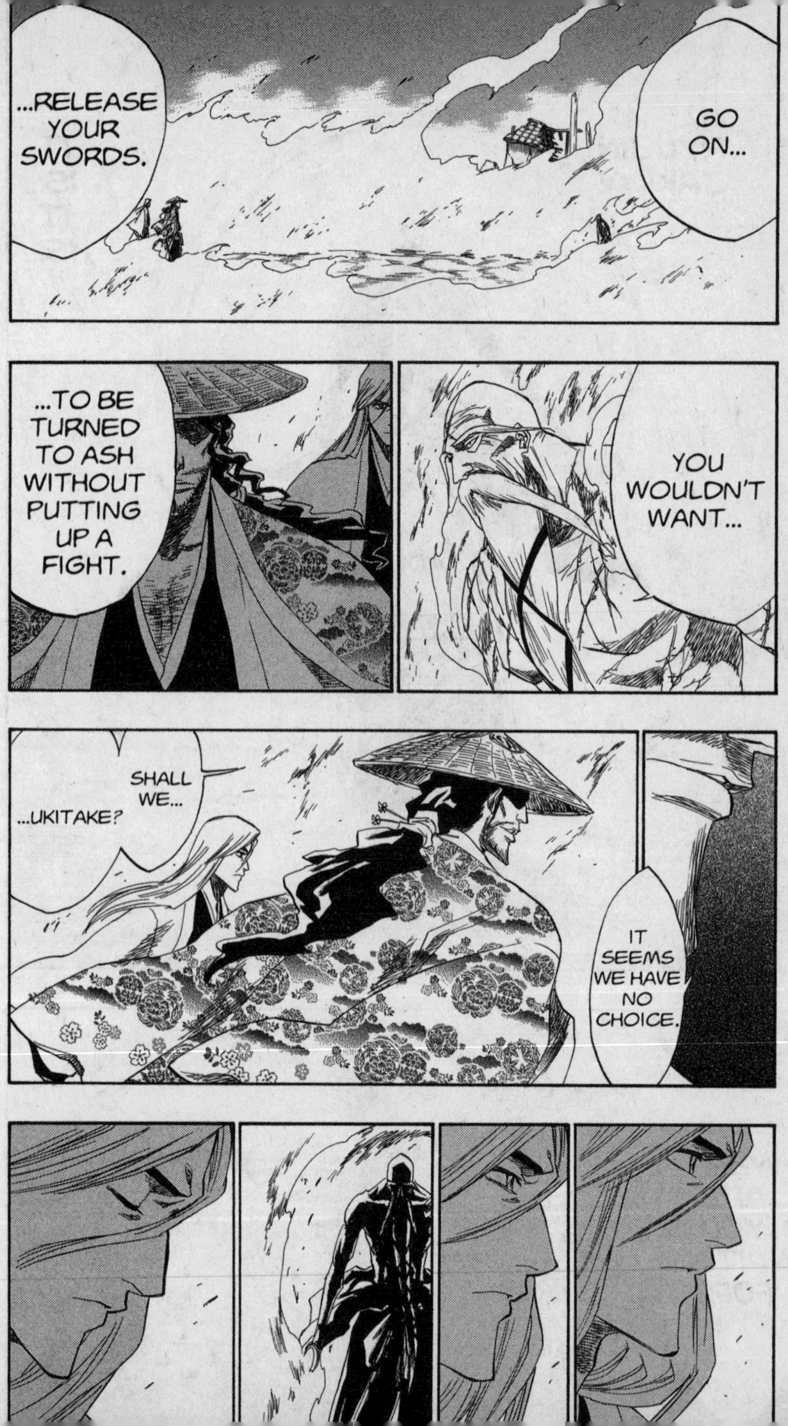
GO ON...
...RELEASE YOUR SWORDS.
YOU WOULDN'T WANT...
...TO BE TURNED TO ASH WITHOUT PUTTING UP A FIGHT.
IT SEEMS WE HAVE NO CHOICE.
SHALL WE...
...UKITAKE?

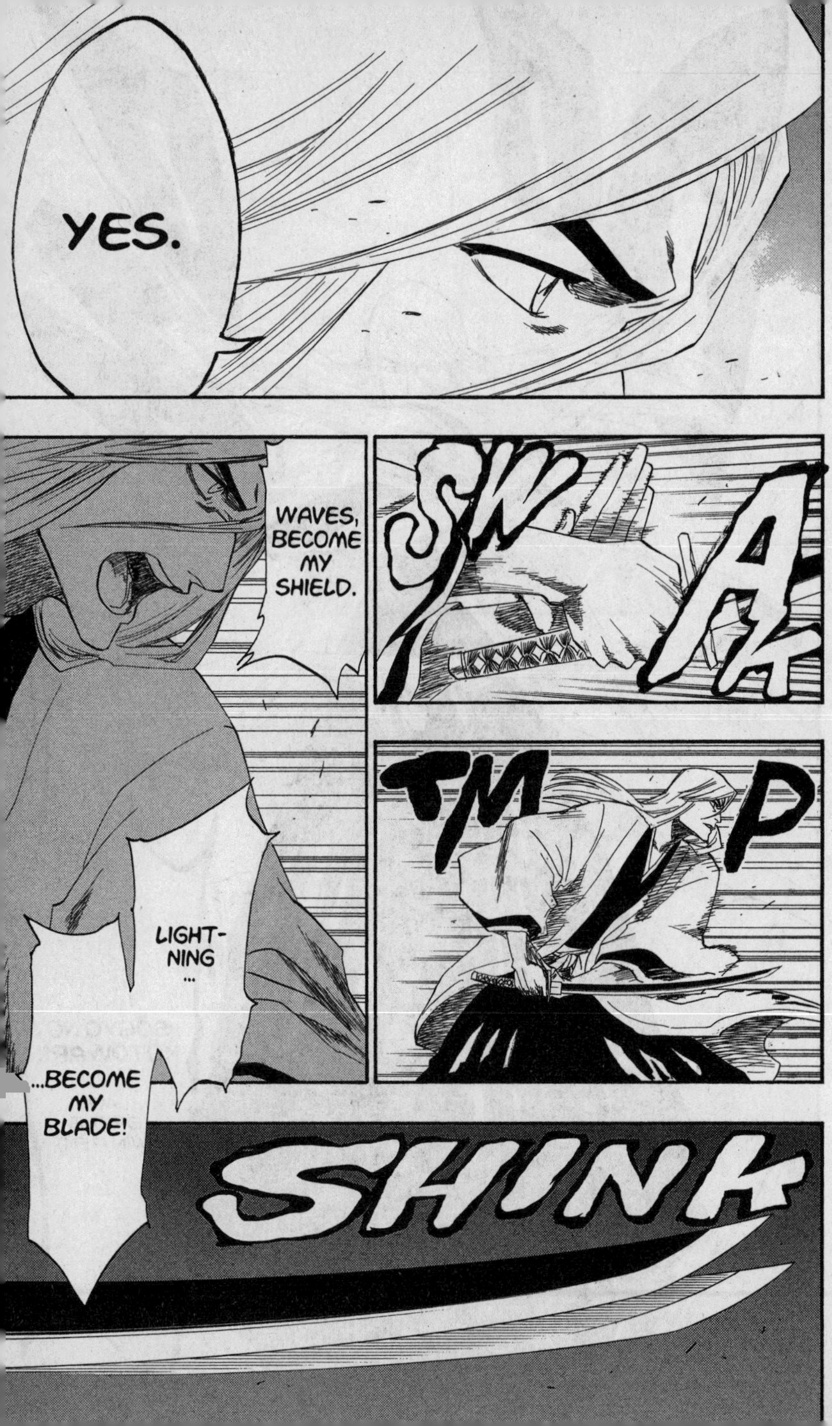
YES.
SWAK
TMP
WAVES, BECOME MY SHIELD.
LIGHTNING...
...BECOME MY BLADE!
SHINK

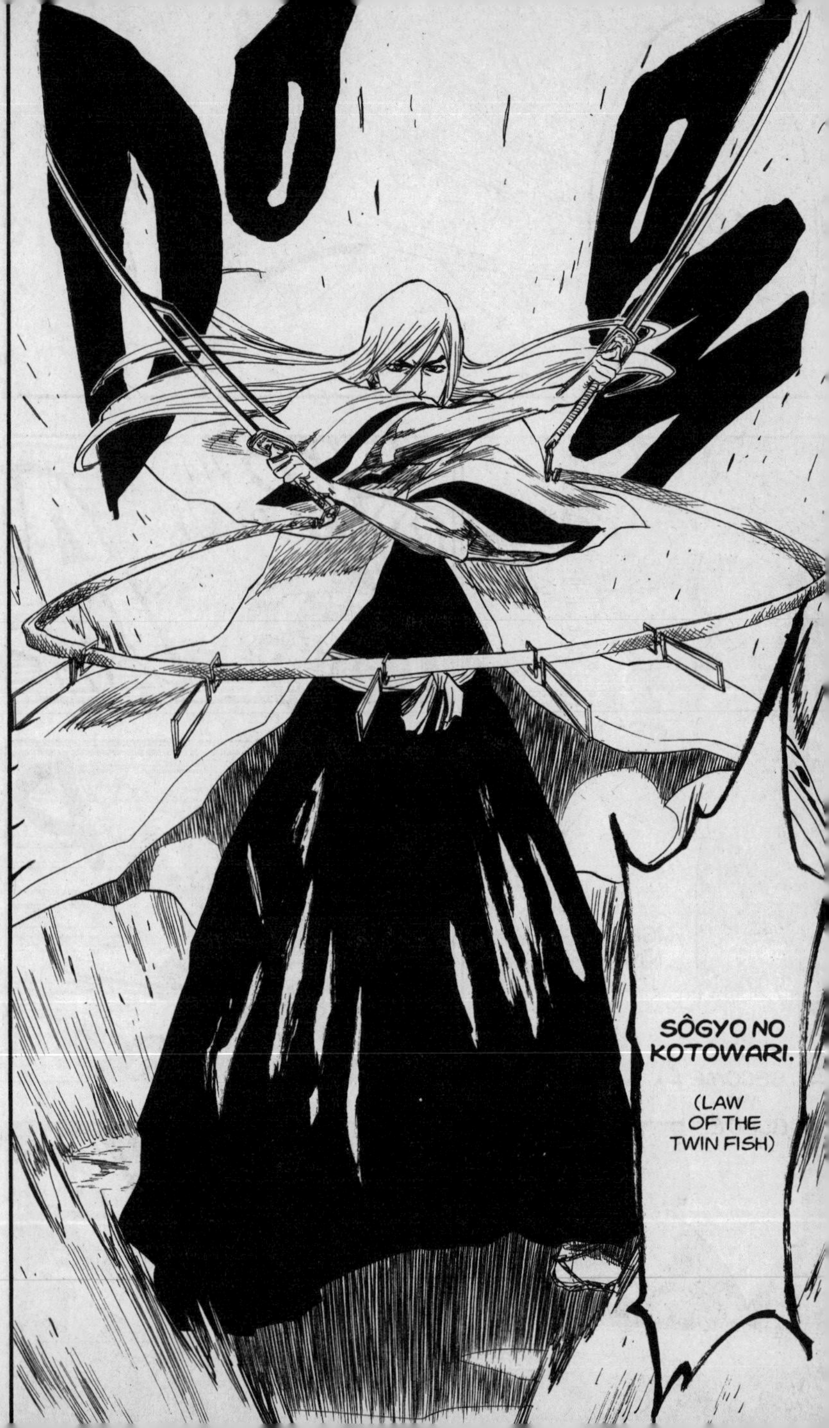
DOOM
SÔGYO NO KOTOWARI.
(LAW OF THE TWIN FISH)

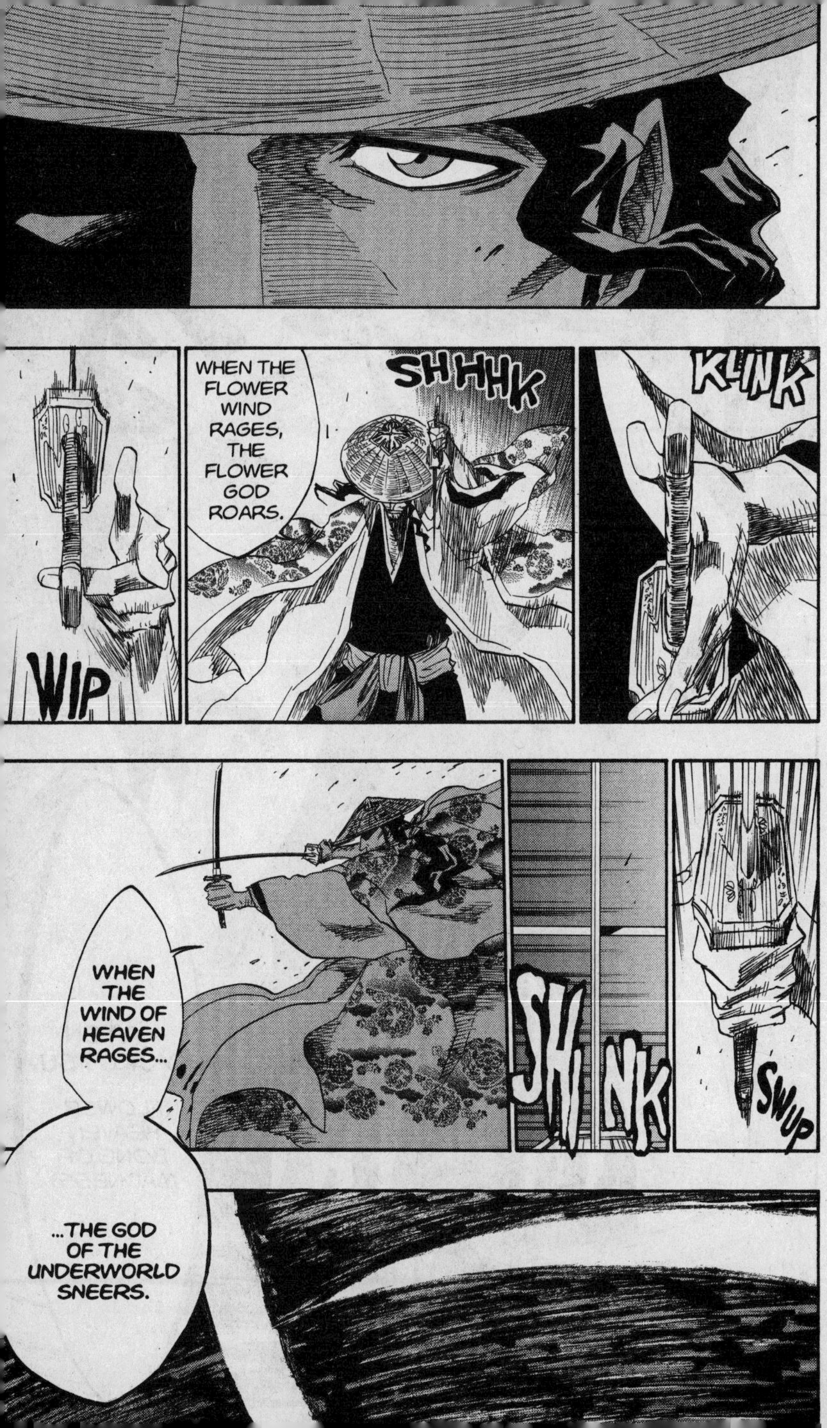
KLINK
SHHHK
WHEN THE FLOWER WIND RAGES, THE FLOWER GOD ROARS.
WIP
SWUP
SHINK
WHEN THE WIND OF HEAVEN RAGES...
...THE GOD OF THE UNDERWORLD SNEERS.

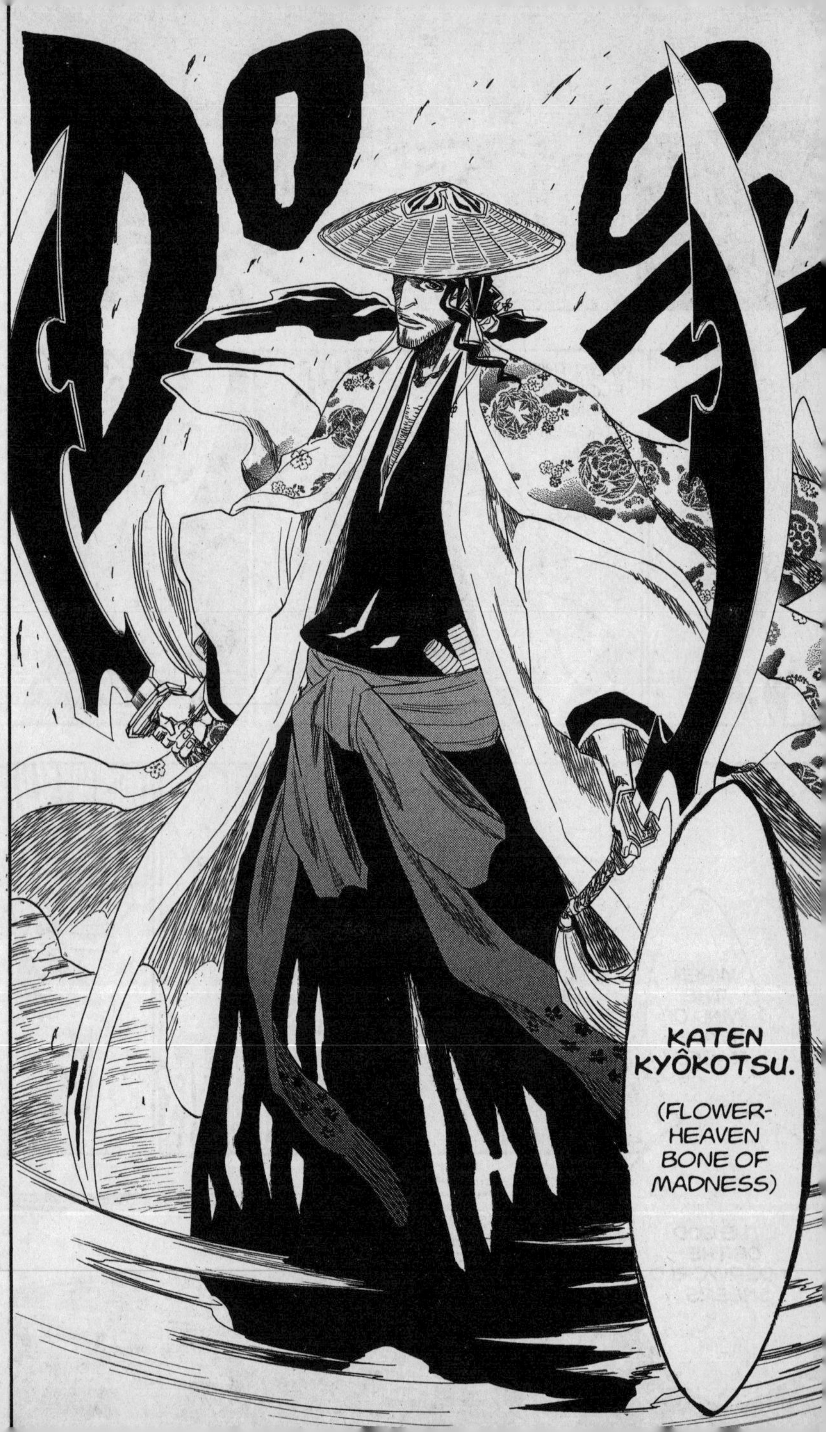
DOG
KATEN KYÔKOTSU.
(FLOWER-HEAVEN BONE OF MADNESS)

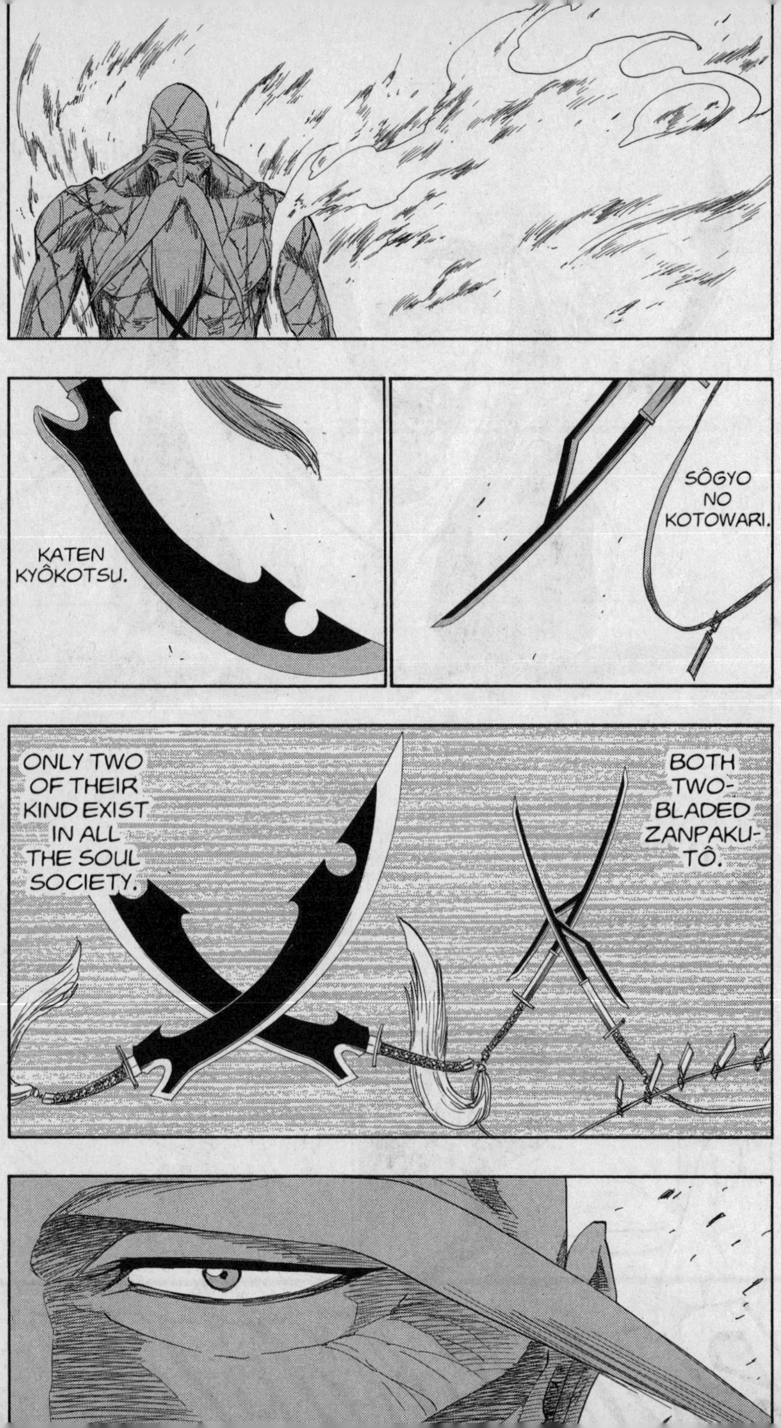
SÔGYO NO KOTOWARI.
KATEN KYÔKOTSU.
BOTH TWO-BLADED ZANPAKU-TÔ.
ONLY TWO OF THEIR KIND EXIST IN ALL THE SOUL SOCIETY.

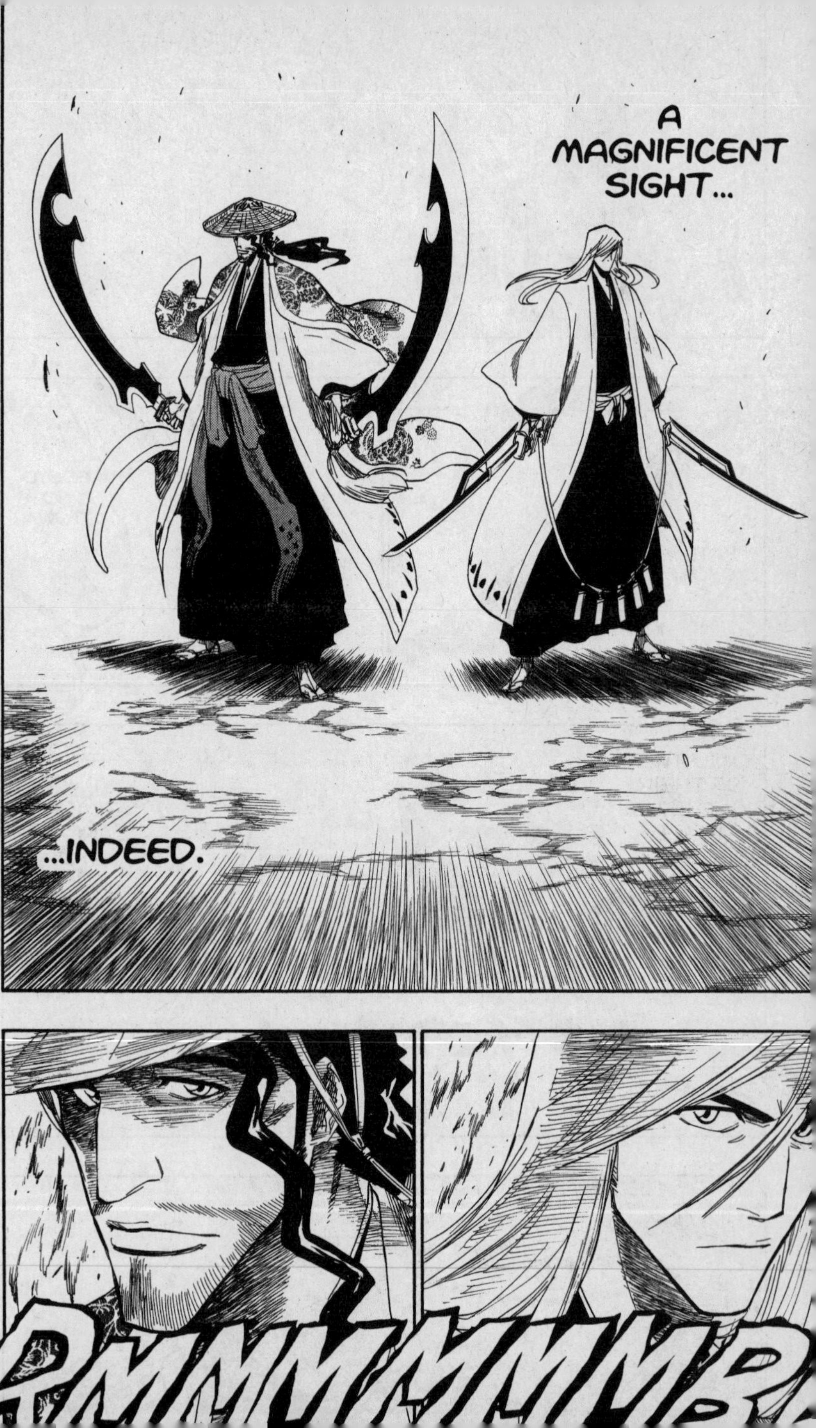
A MAGNIFICENT SIGHT...
...INDEED.
RMMMMMM

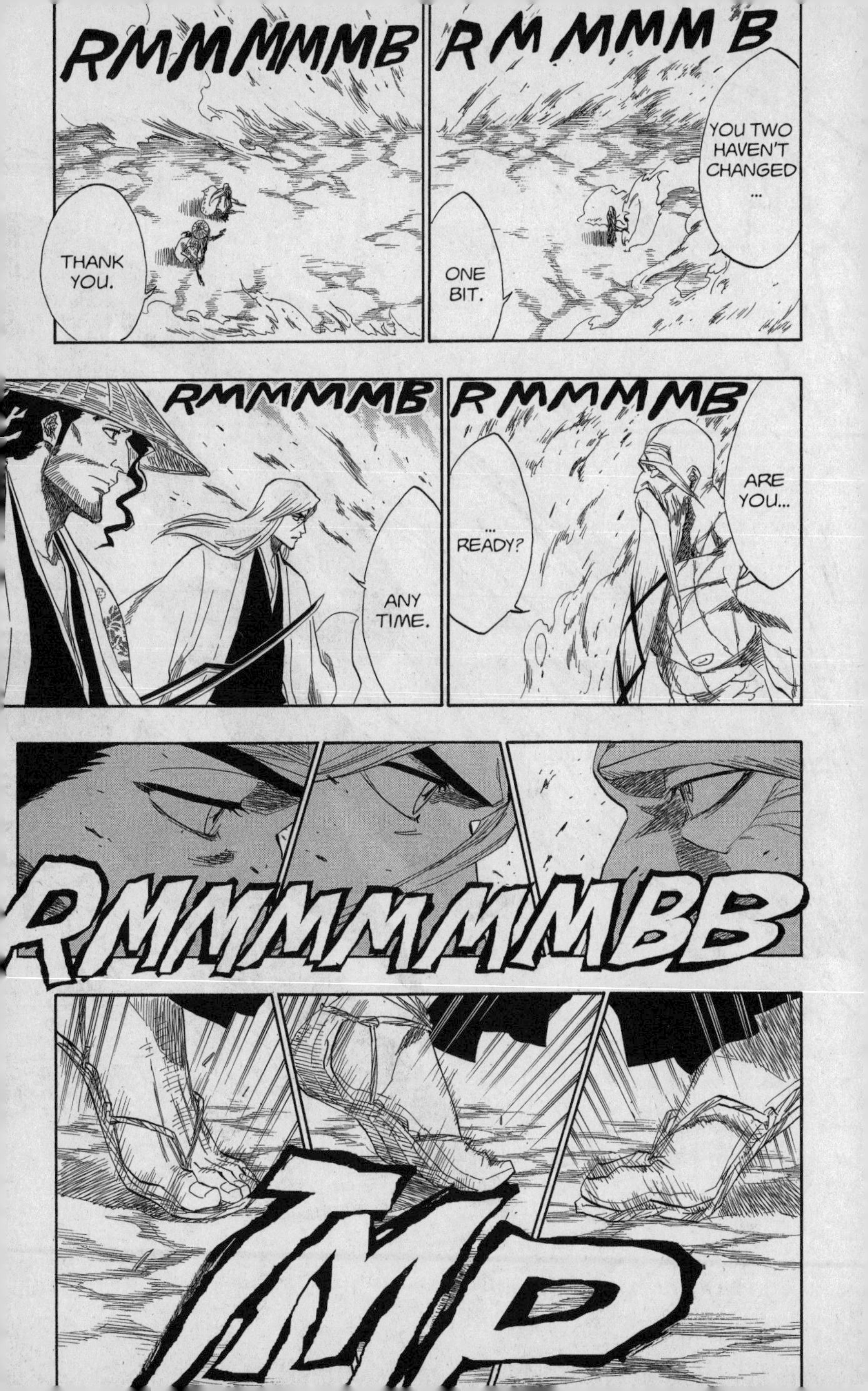
RMMMMB
YOU TWO HAVEN'T CHANGED ...
ONE BIT.
RMMMMMB
THANK YOU.
RMMMMMB
ARE YOU...
... READY?
RMMMMB
ANY TIME.
RMMMMMMMBB
TMP

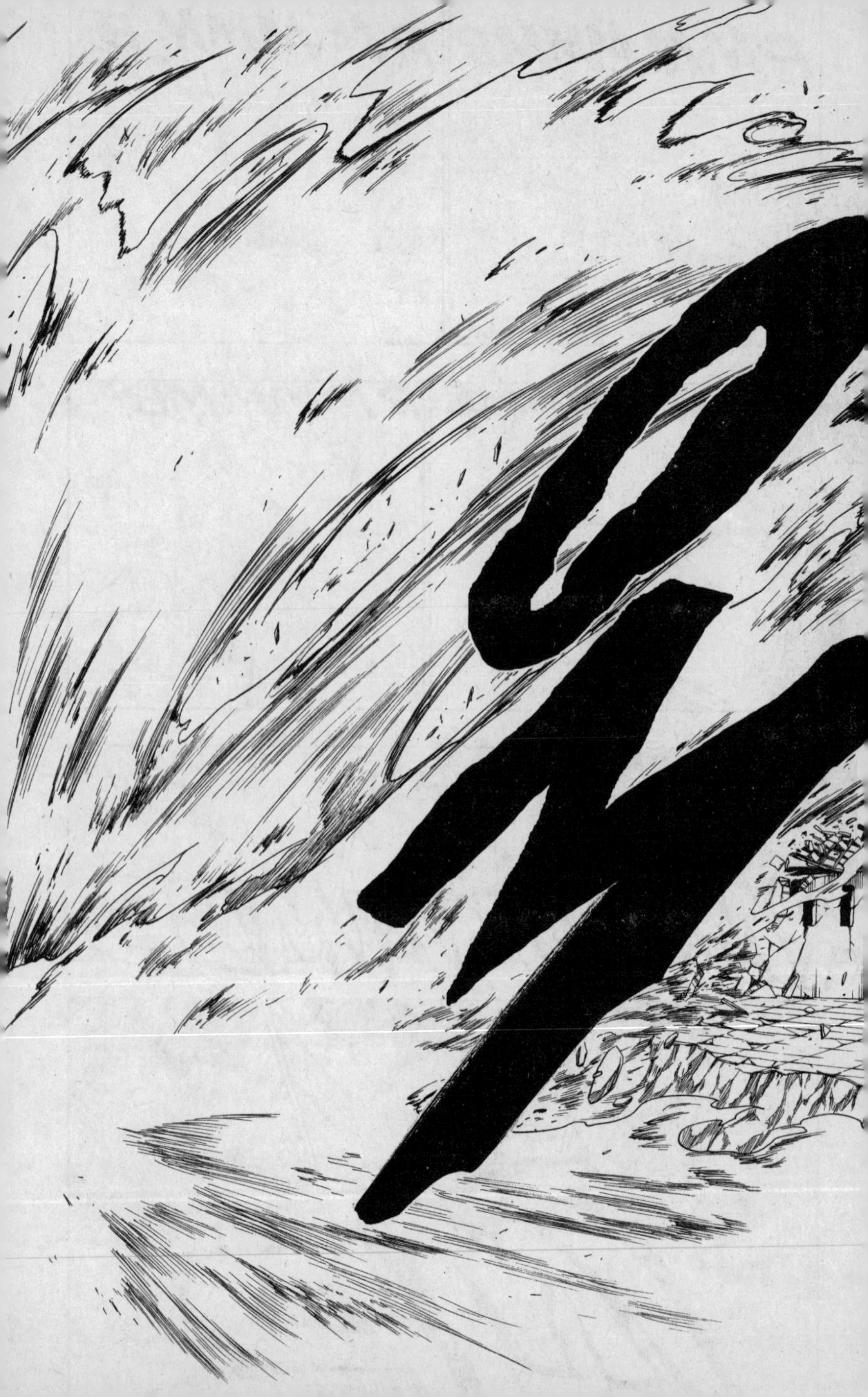

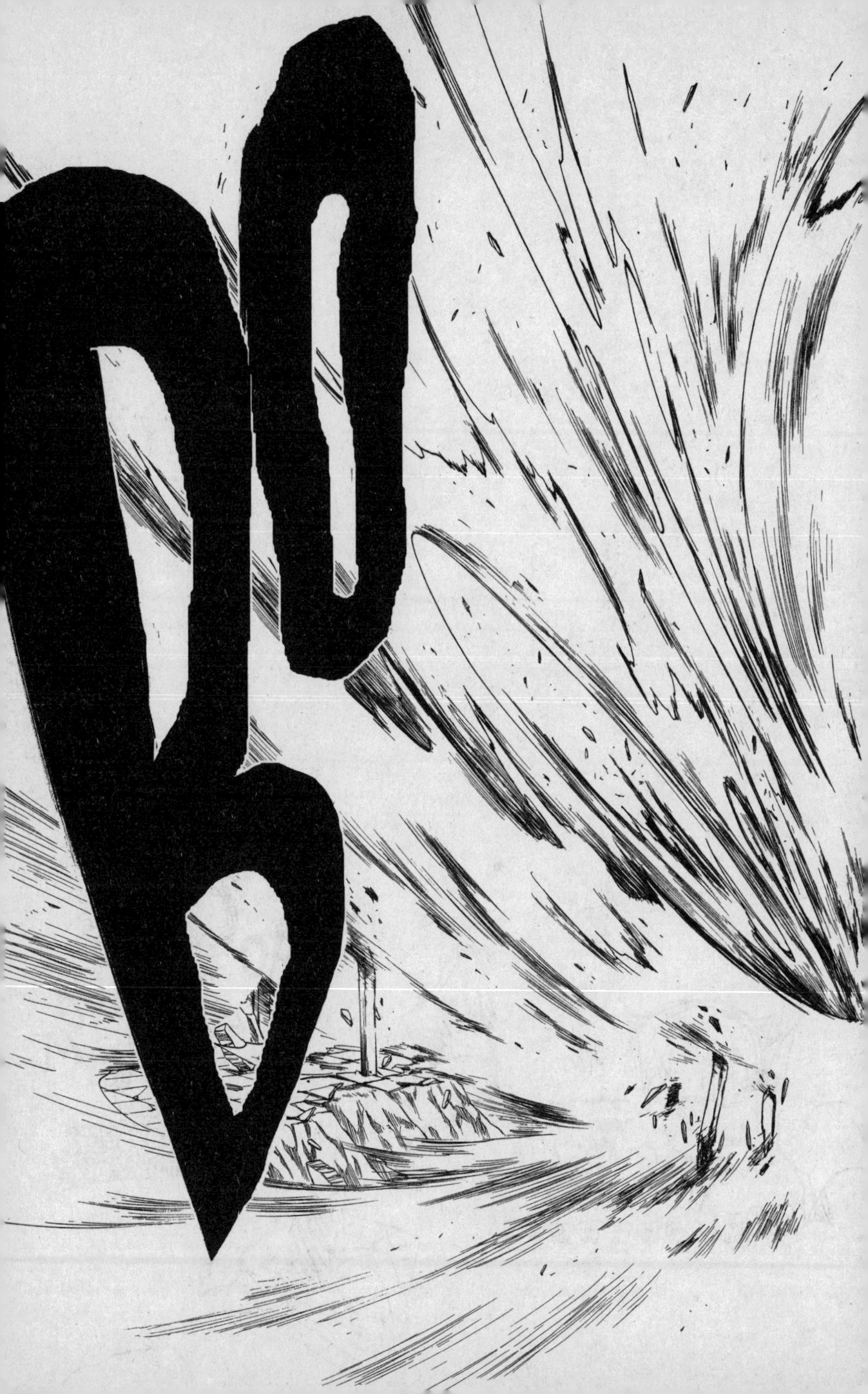

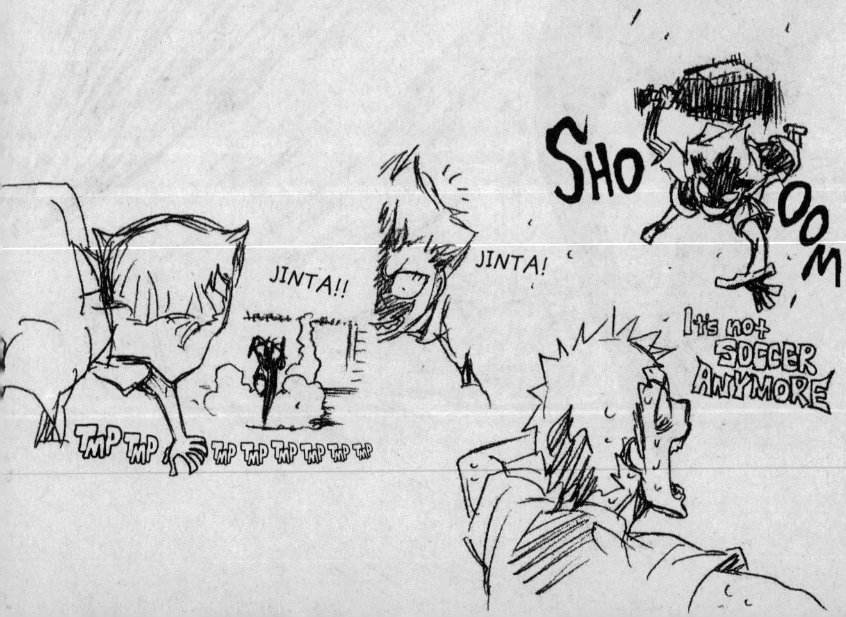
SHOOOM
It's not SOCCER ANYMORE
JINTA!
JINTA!!
TMP TMP
TMP TMP TMP TMP TMP TMP

157. Cat and Hornet

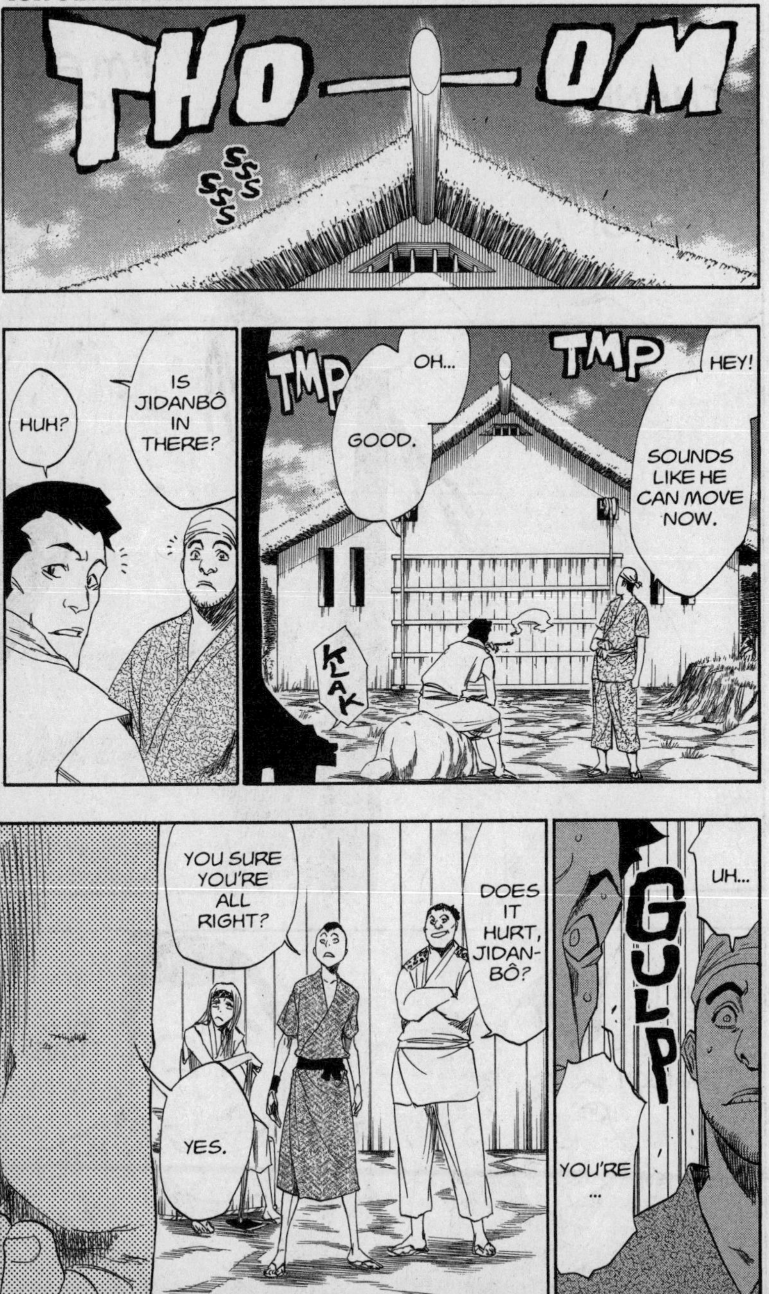
THO—OM
SSS SSS
TMP
HEY!
SOUNDS LIKE HE CAN MOVE NOW.
OH... GOOD.
TMP
KLAK
IS JIDANBÔ IN THERE?
HUH?
UH...
GULP
YOU'RE ...
DOES IT HURT, JIDANBÔ?
YOU SURE YOU'RE ALL RIGHT?
YES.

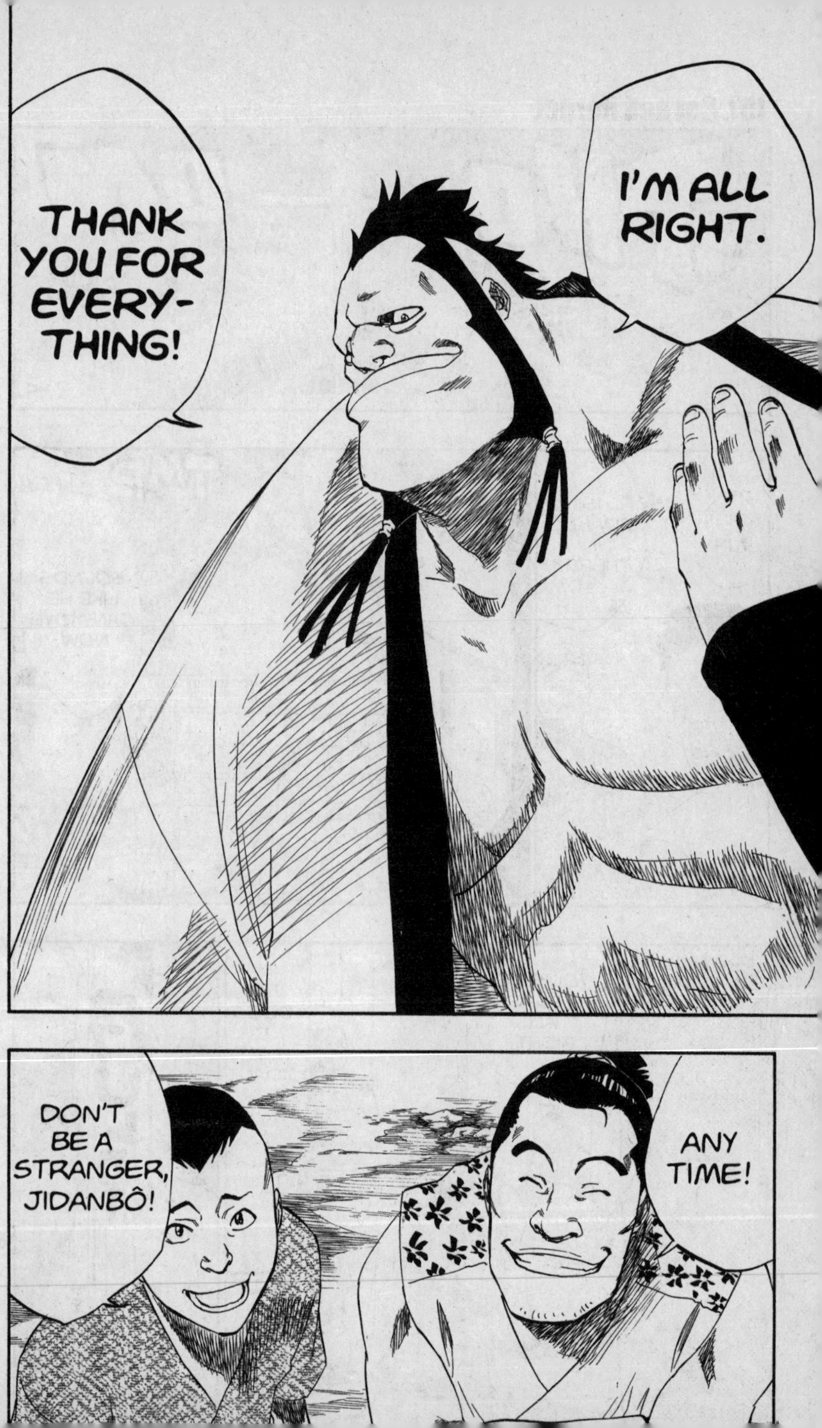
I'M ALL RIGHT.
THANK YOU FOR EVERY-THING!
ANY TIME!
DON'T BE A STRANGER, JIDANBÔ!

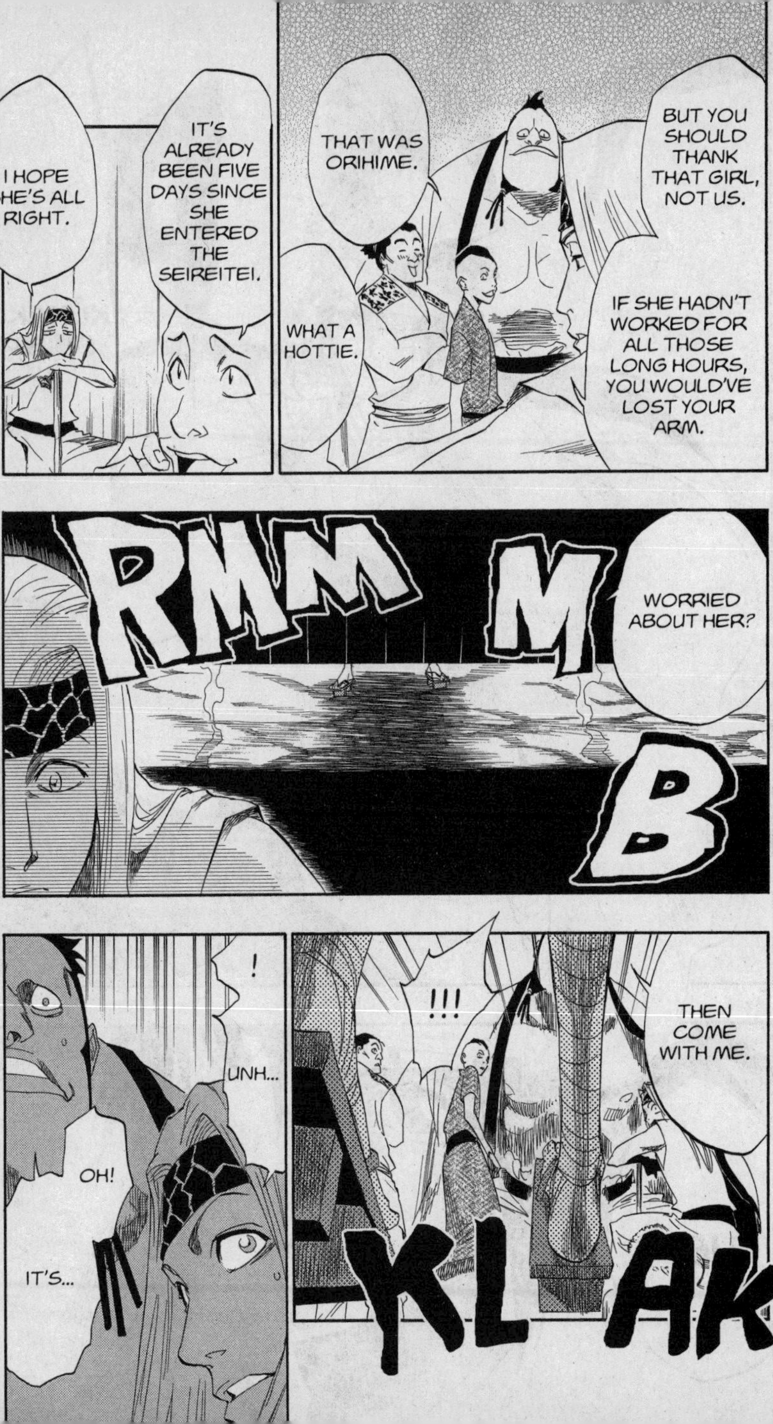
BUT YOU SHOULD THANK THAT GIRL, NOT US.
THAT WAS ORIHIME.
IF SHE HADN'T WORKED FOR ALL THOSE LONG HOURS, YOU WOULD'VE LOST YOUR ARM.
WHAT A HOTTIE.
IT'S ALREADY BEEN FIVE DAYS SINCE SHE ENTERED THE SEIREITEI.
I HOPE SHE'S ALL RIGHT.
WORRIED ABOUT HER?
RMMMB
THEN COME WITH ME.
!!!
KLAK
!
UNH...
OH!
IT'S...

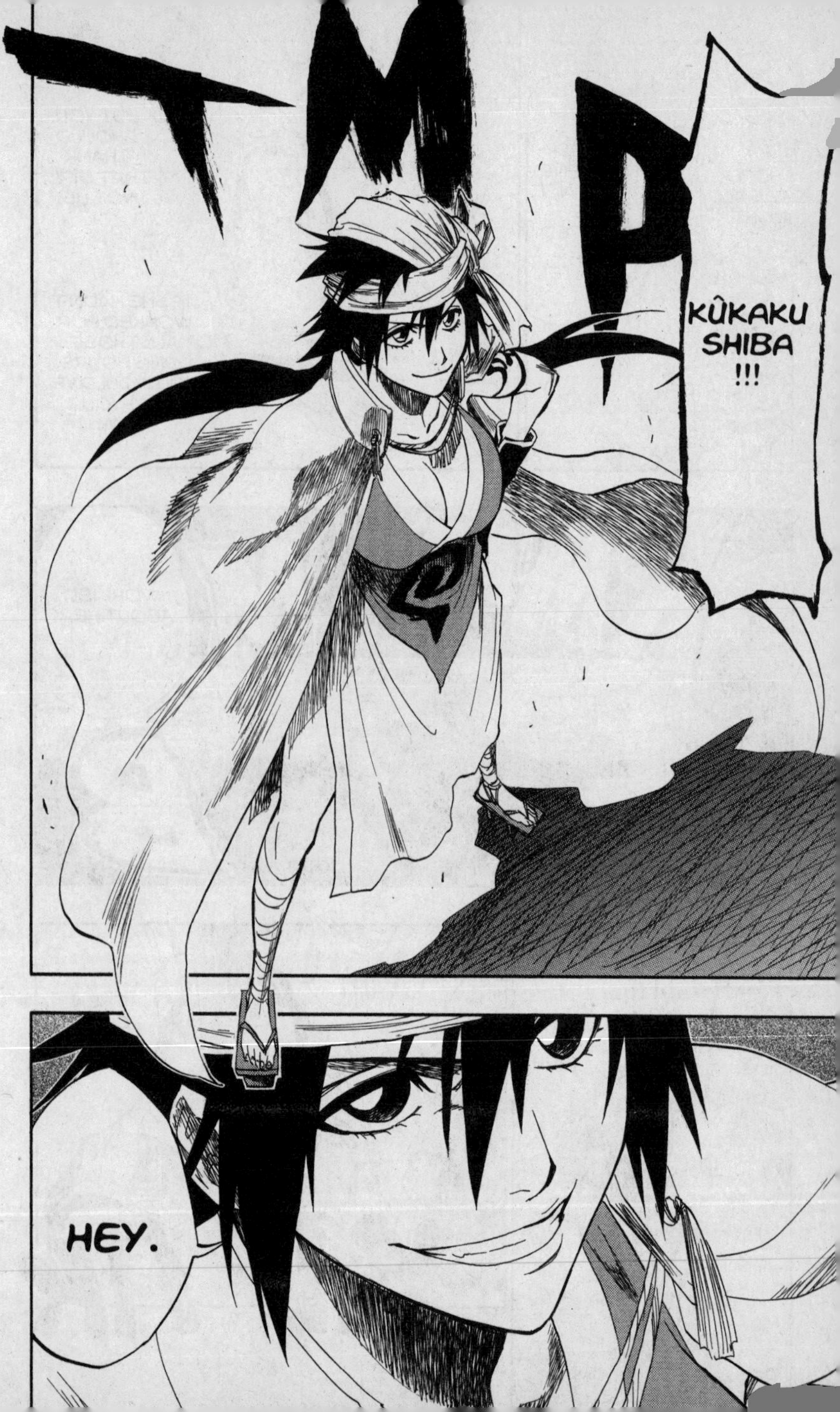
TMP
KÛKAKU SHIBA !!!
HEY.

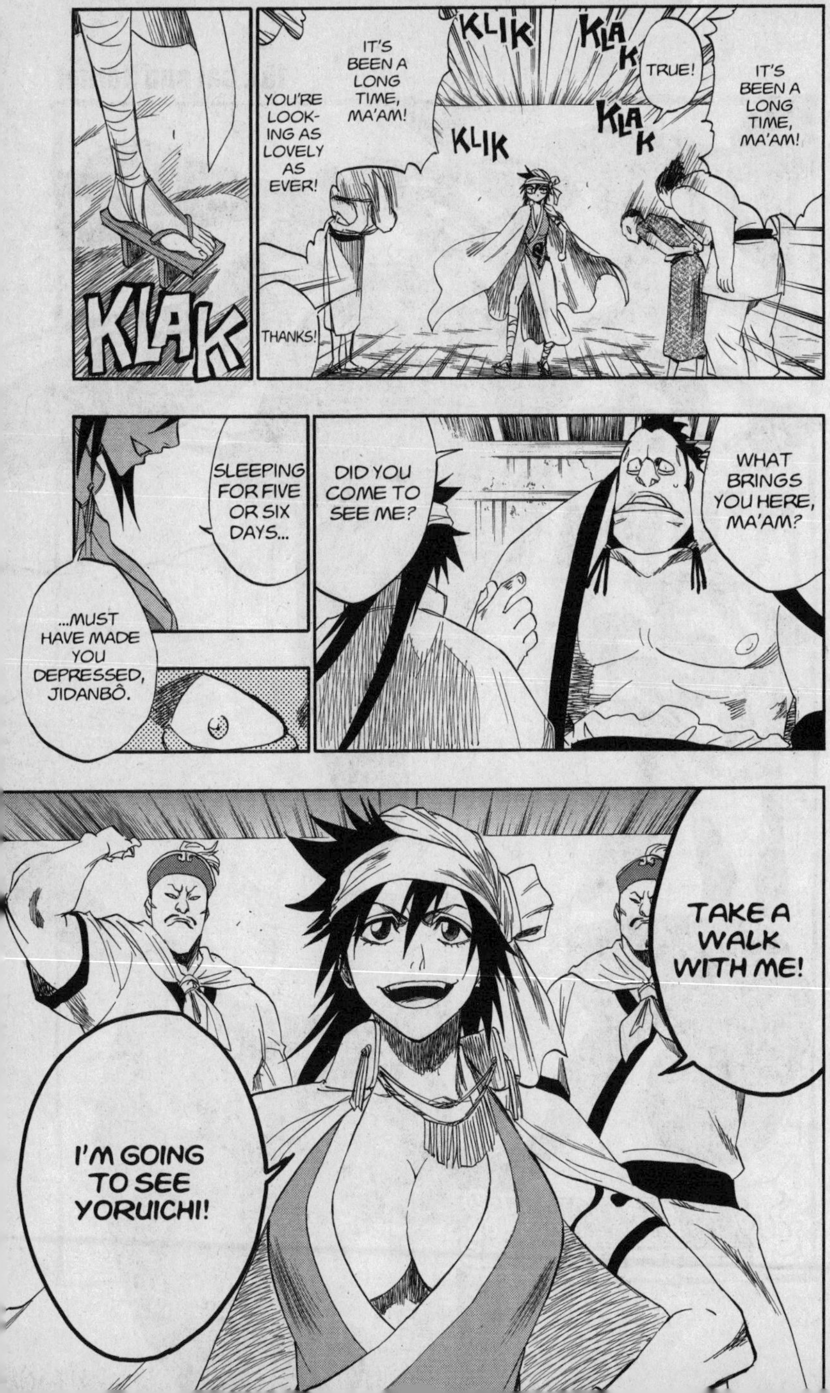
IT'S BEEN A LONG TIME, MA'AM!
TRUE!
KLAK
KLIK
KLAK
IT'S BEEN A LONG TIME, MA'AM!
YOU'RE LOOKING AS LOVELY AS EVER!
KLIK
THANKS!
KLAK
WHAT BRINGS YOU HERE, MA'AM?
DID YOU COME TO SEE ME?
SLEEPING FOR FIVE OR SIX DAYS...
...MUST HAVE MADE YOU DEPRESSED, JIDANBÔ.
TAKE A WALK WITH ME!
I'M GOING TO SEE YORUICHI!

157. Cat and Hornet

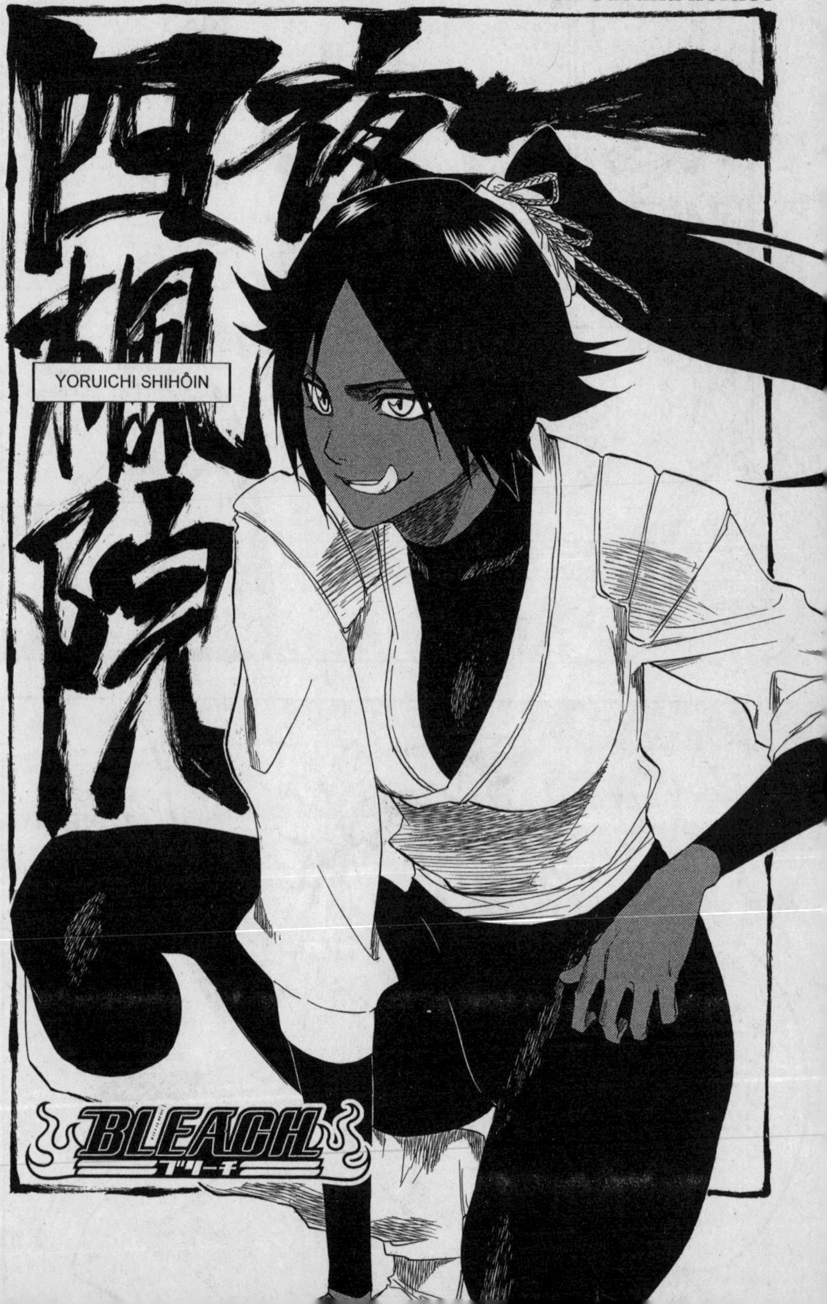
YORUICHI SHIHÔIN
BLEACH
ブリーチ

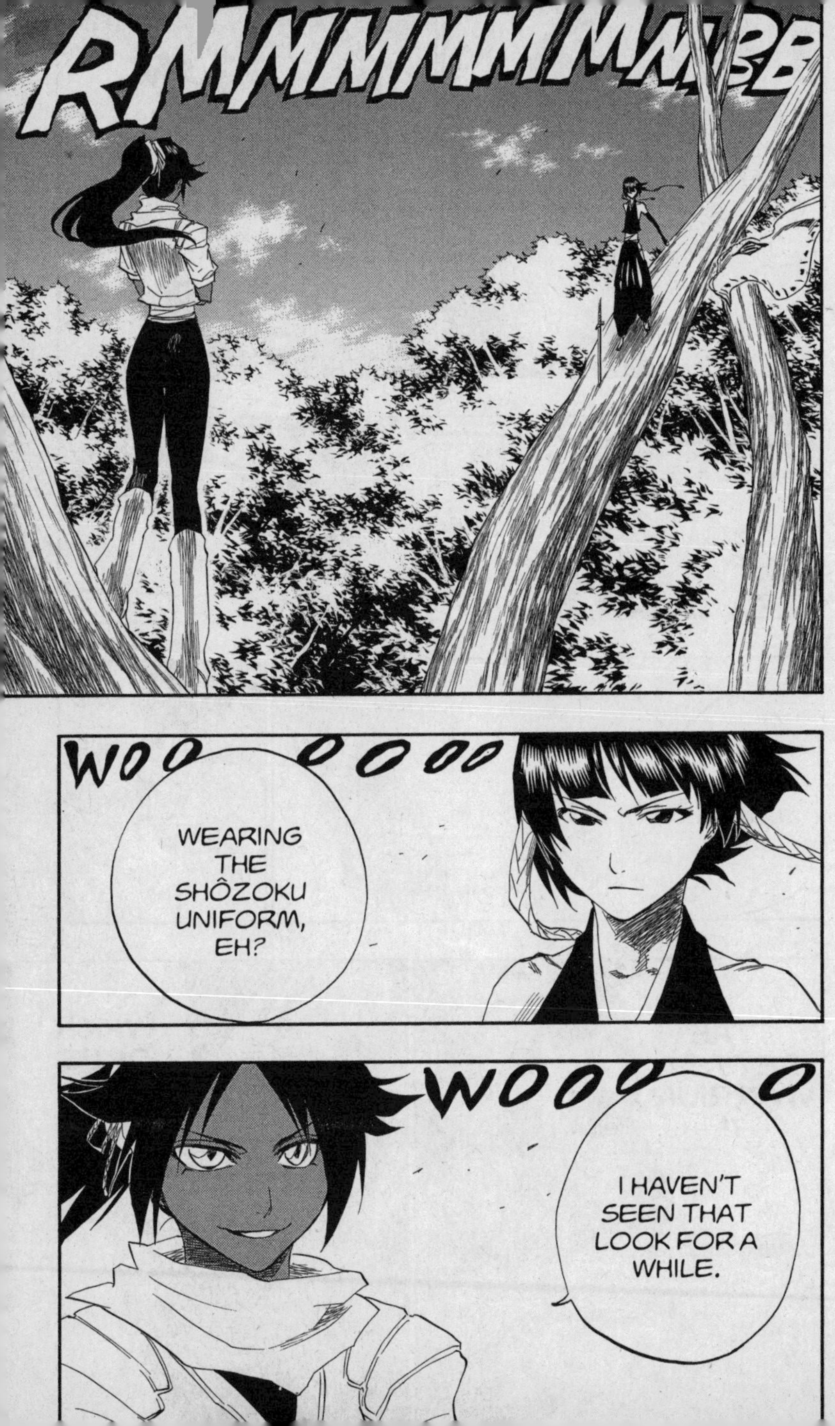
RMMMMMMMBB
WOO OOOO
WEARING THE SHÔZOKU UNIFORM, EH?
WOOO O
I HAVEN'T SEEN THAT LOOK FOR A WHILE.

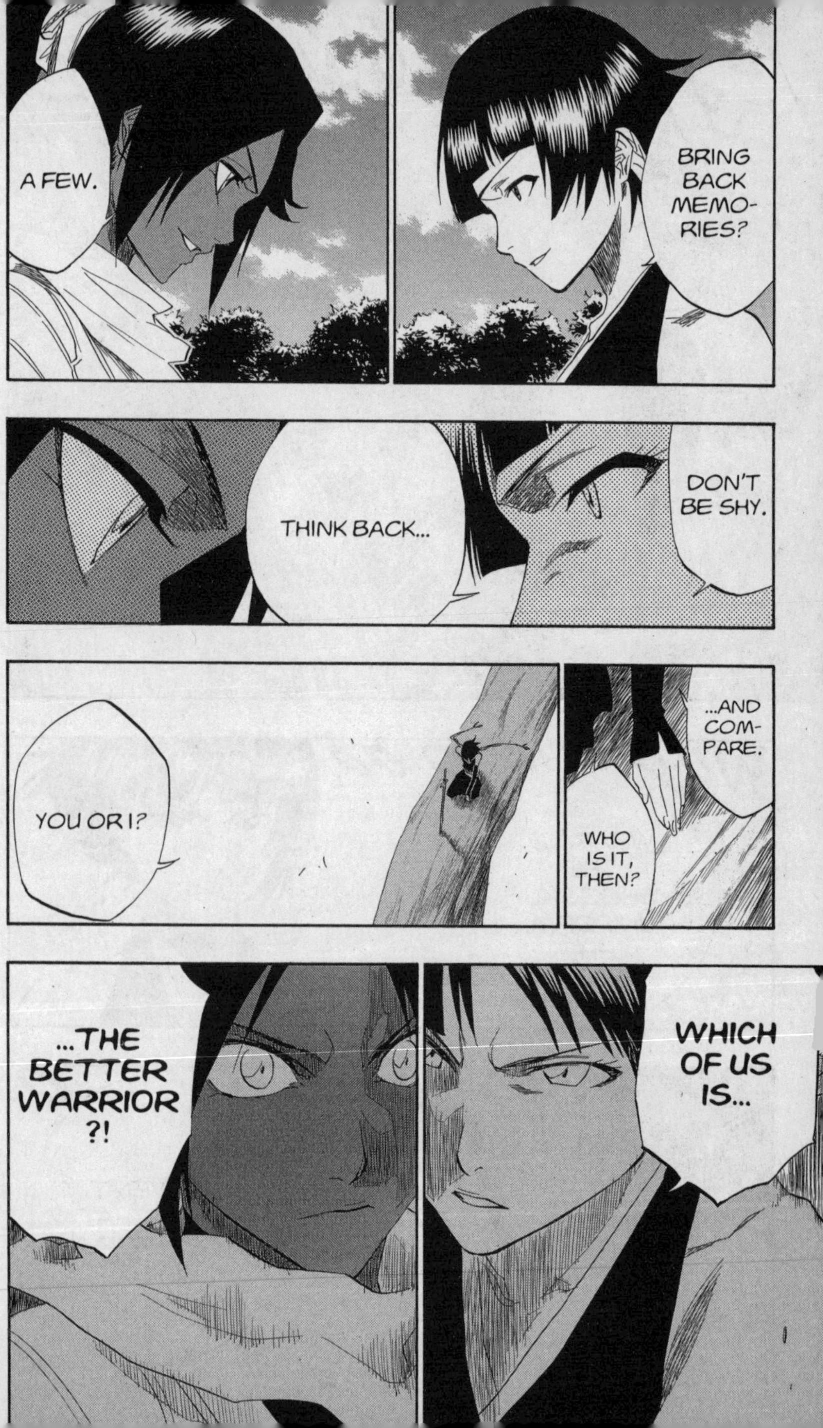
BRING BACK MEMO-RIES?
A FEW.
DON'T BE SHY.
THINK BACK...
...AND COM-PARE.
WHO IS IT, THEN?
YOU OR I?
WHICH OF US IS...
...THE BETTER WARRIOR ?!

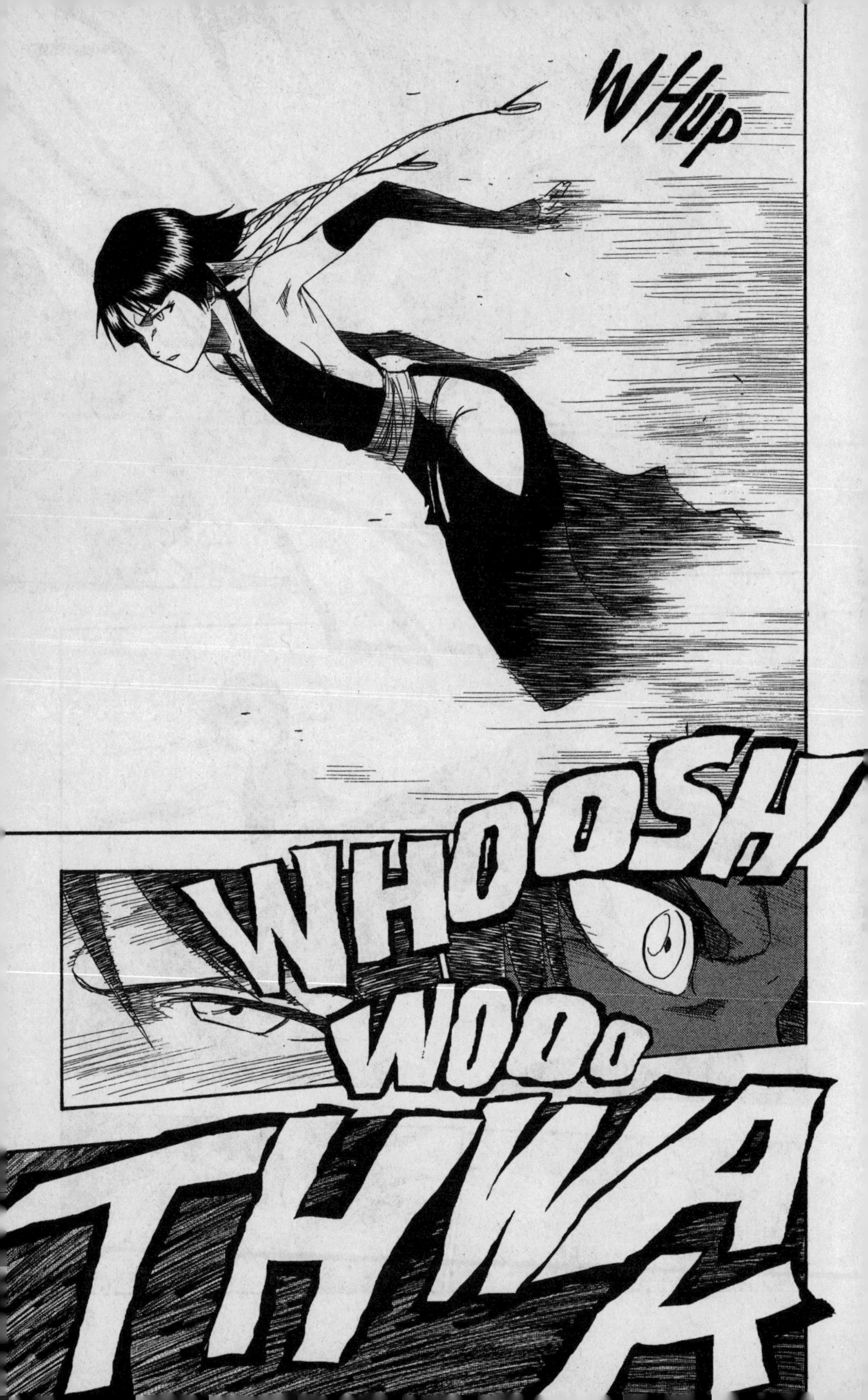
WHUP
WHOOSH
WOOO
THWA

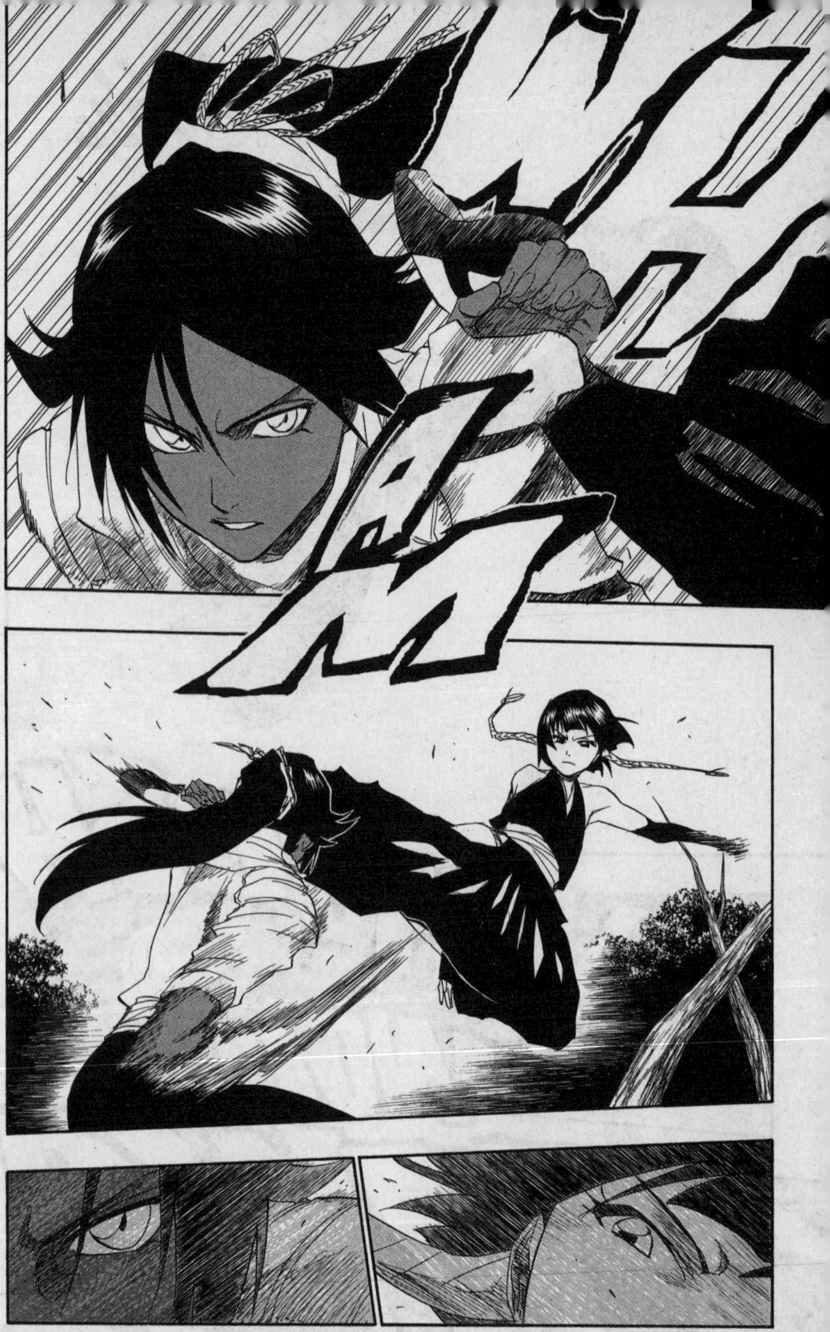

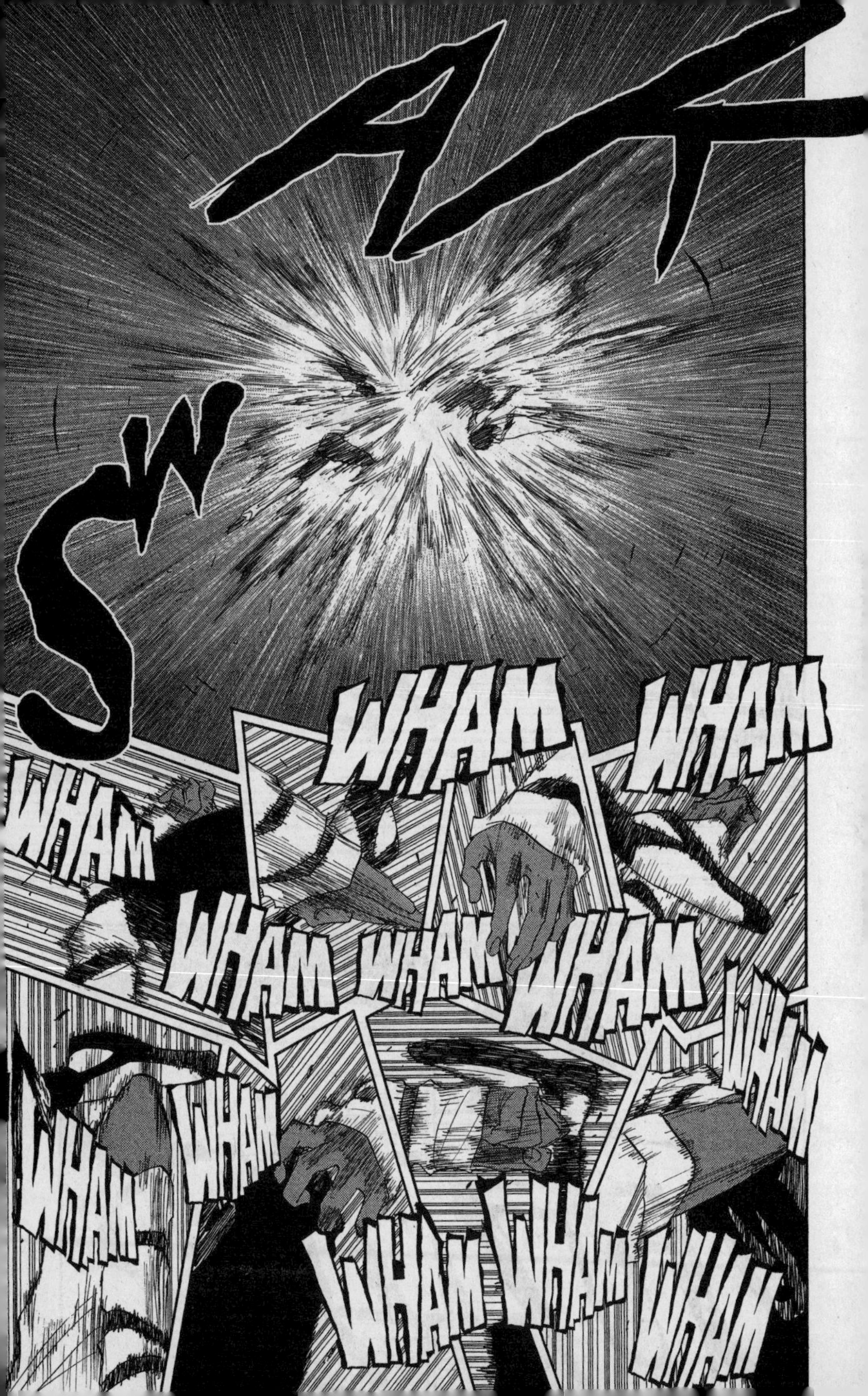
SWAT
WHAM
WHAM
WHAM
WHAM
WHAM
WHAM
WHAM
WHAM
WHAM
WHAM
WHAM
WHAM

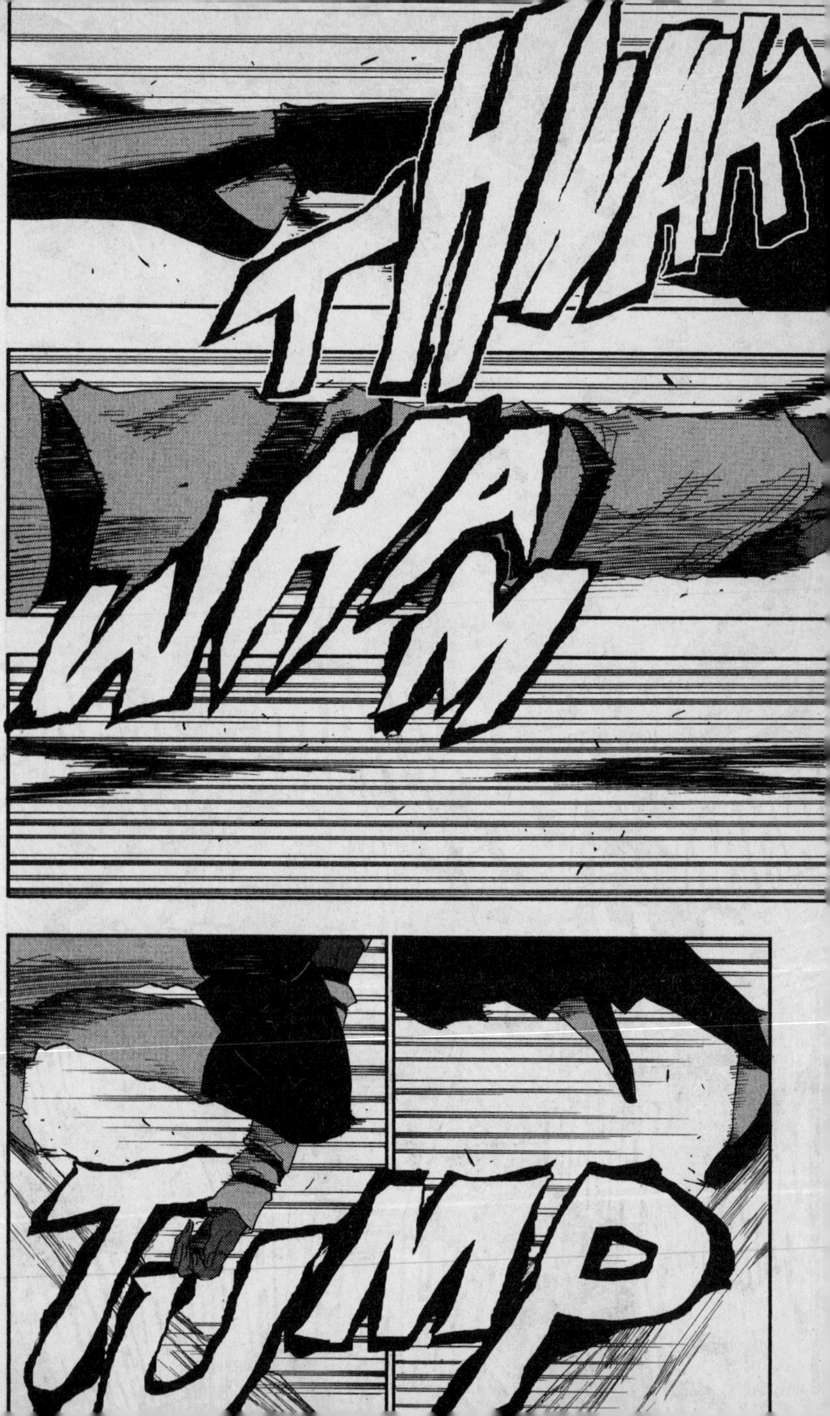
THWAK
WHAM
TUMP

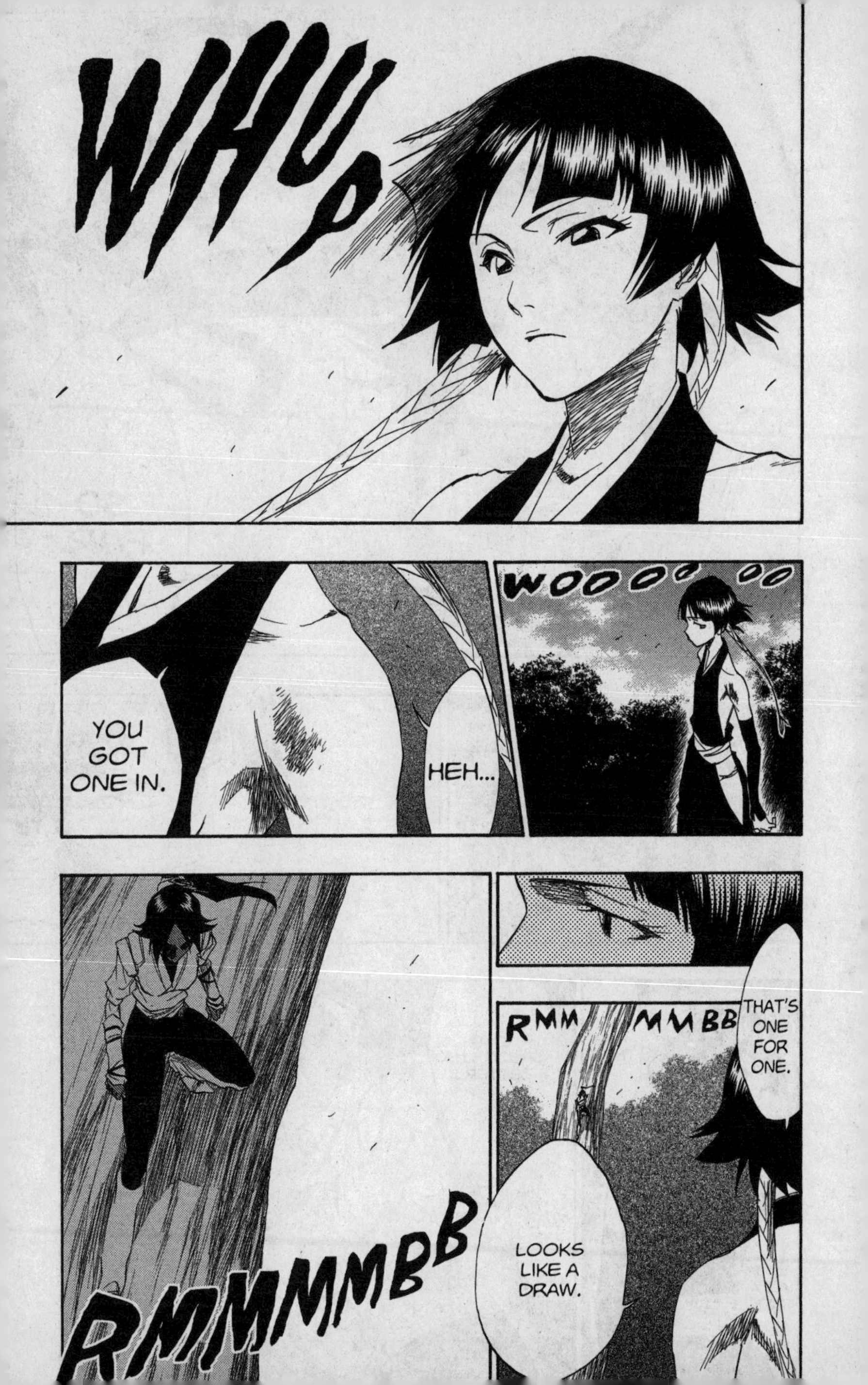
WHUP
WOOOOOO
HEH...
YOU GOT ONE IN.
THAT'S ONE FOR ONE.
RMMMMMBB
LOOKS LIKE A DRAW.
RMMMMMBB

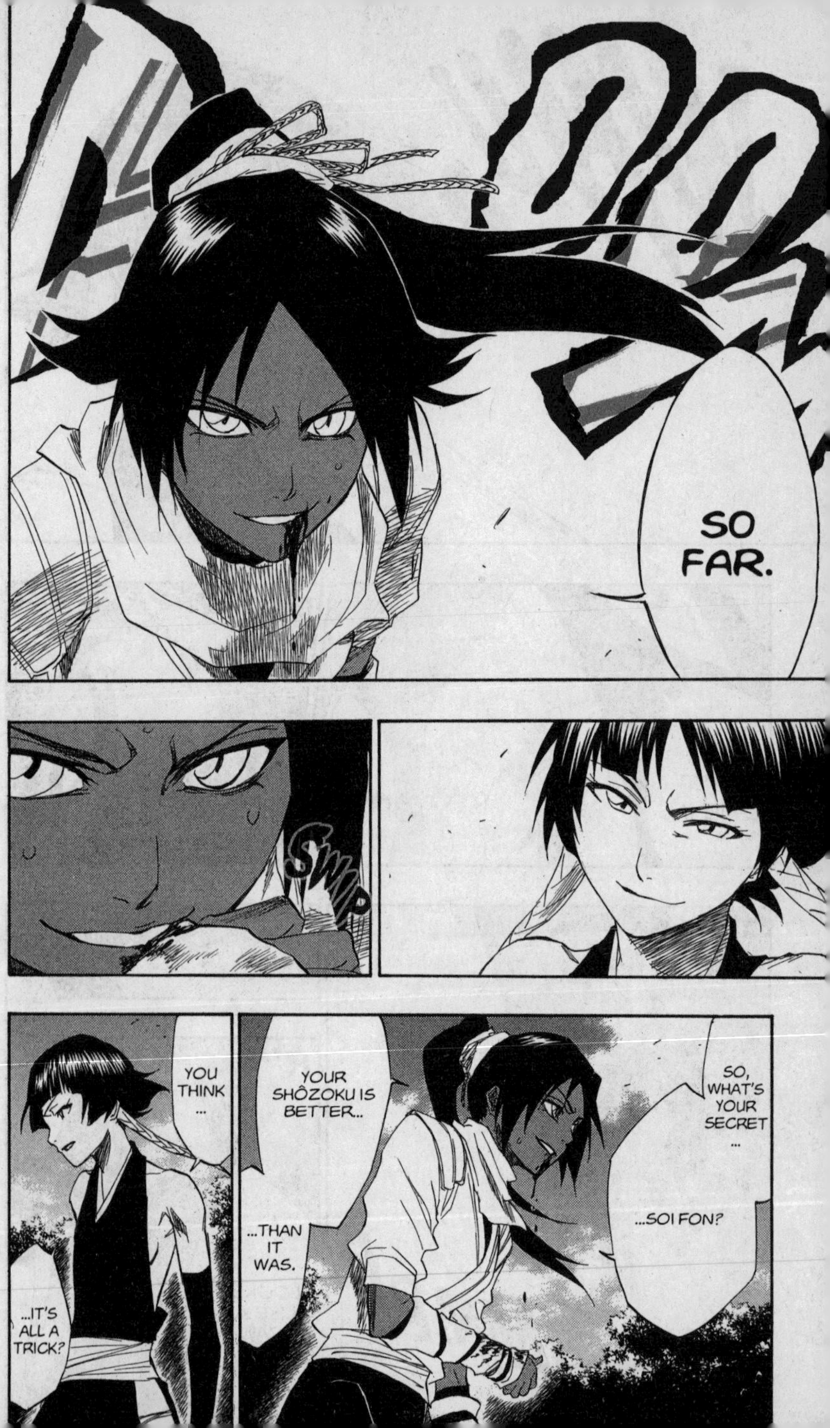
SO FAR.
SO, WHAT'S YOUR SECRET ...
...SOI FON?
YOUR SHÔZOKU IS BETTER...
...THAN IT WAS.
YOU THINK ...
...IT'S ALL A TRICK?

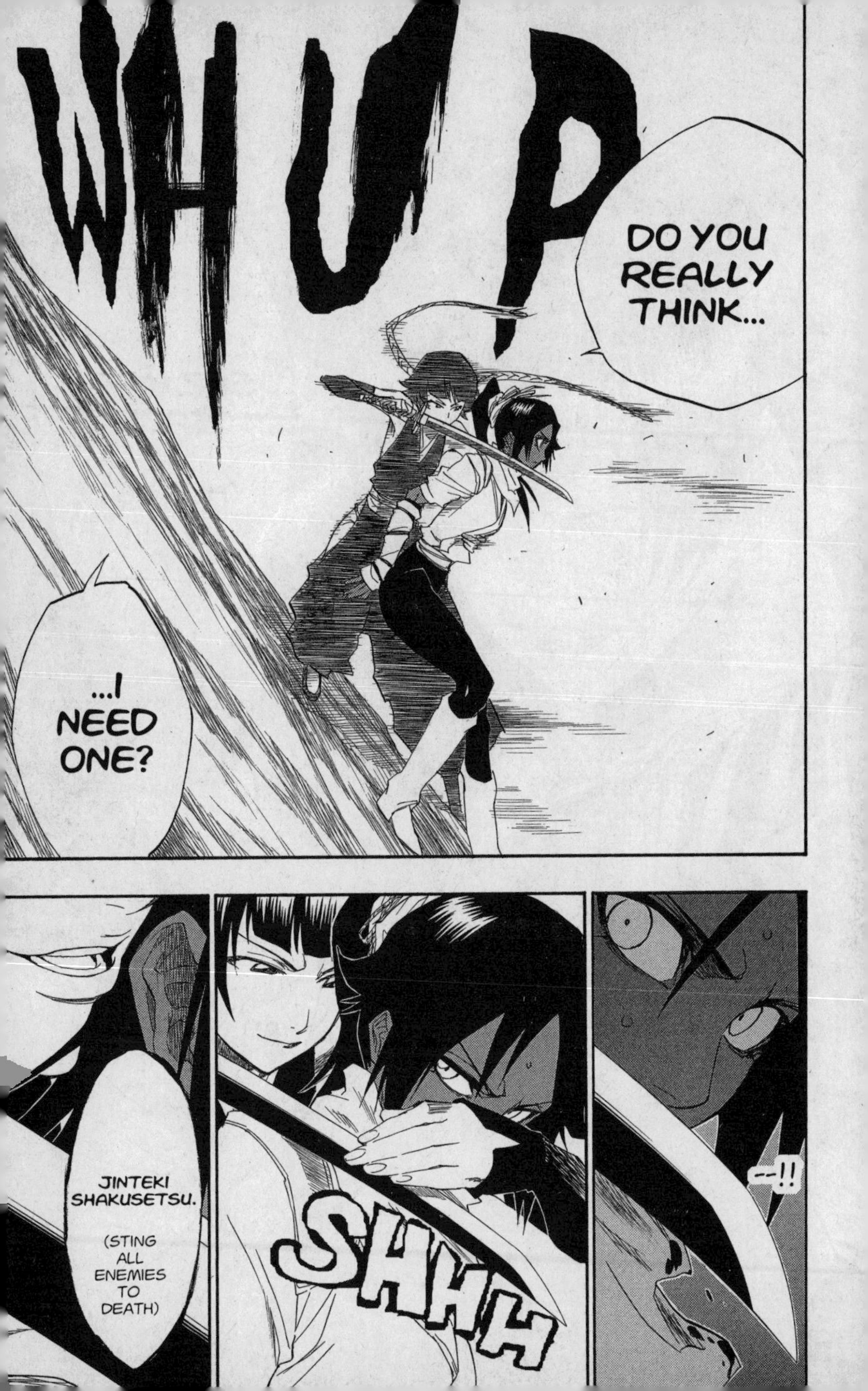
WHUP
DO YOU REALLY THINK...
...I NEED ONE?
--!!
SHHH
JINTEKI SHAKUSETSU.
(STING ALL ENEMIES TO DEATH)

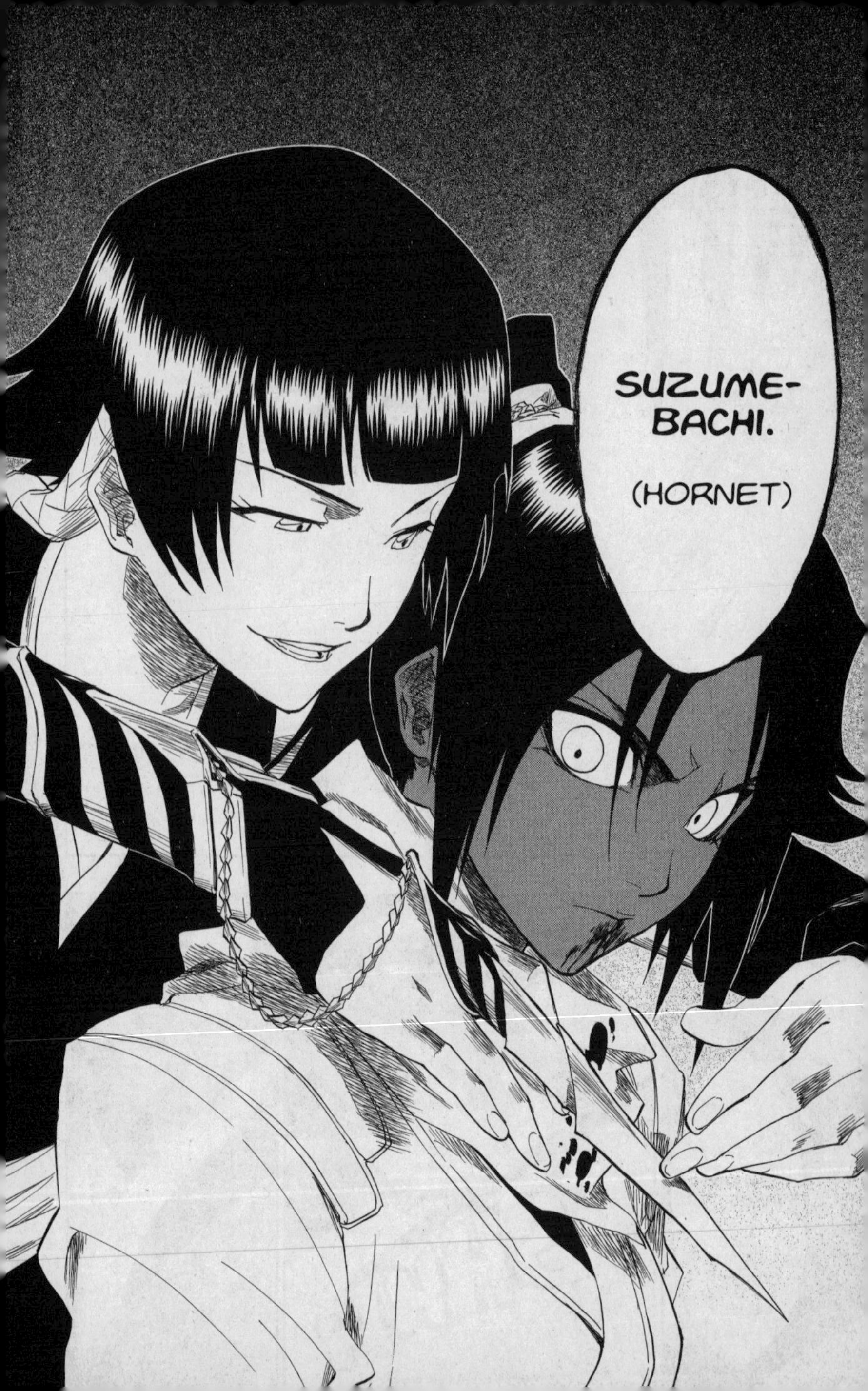
SUZUME-
BACHI.
(HORNET)

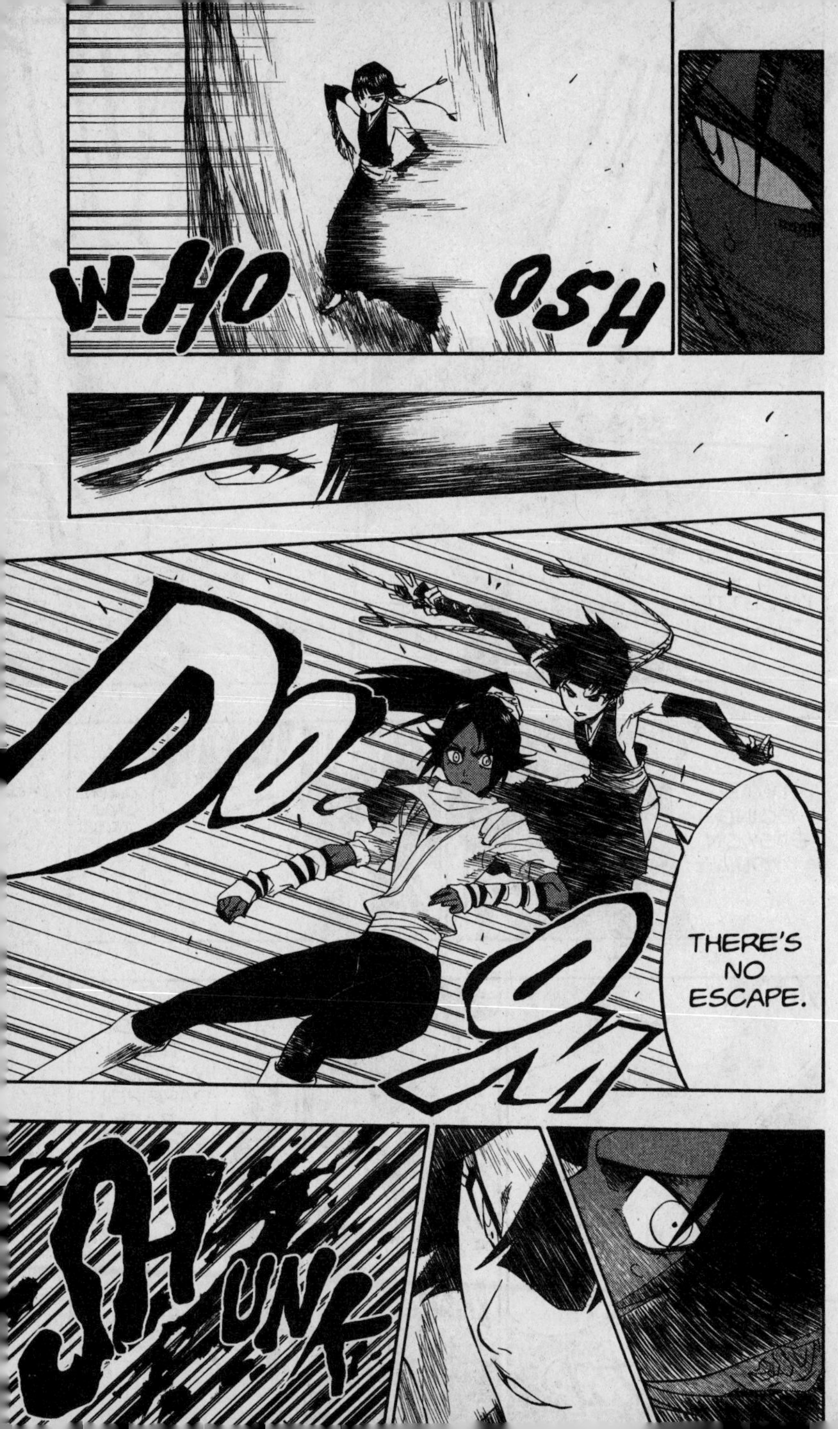
WHOOSH
DOOM
THERE'S NO ESCAPE.
SHUNK

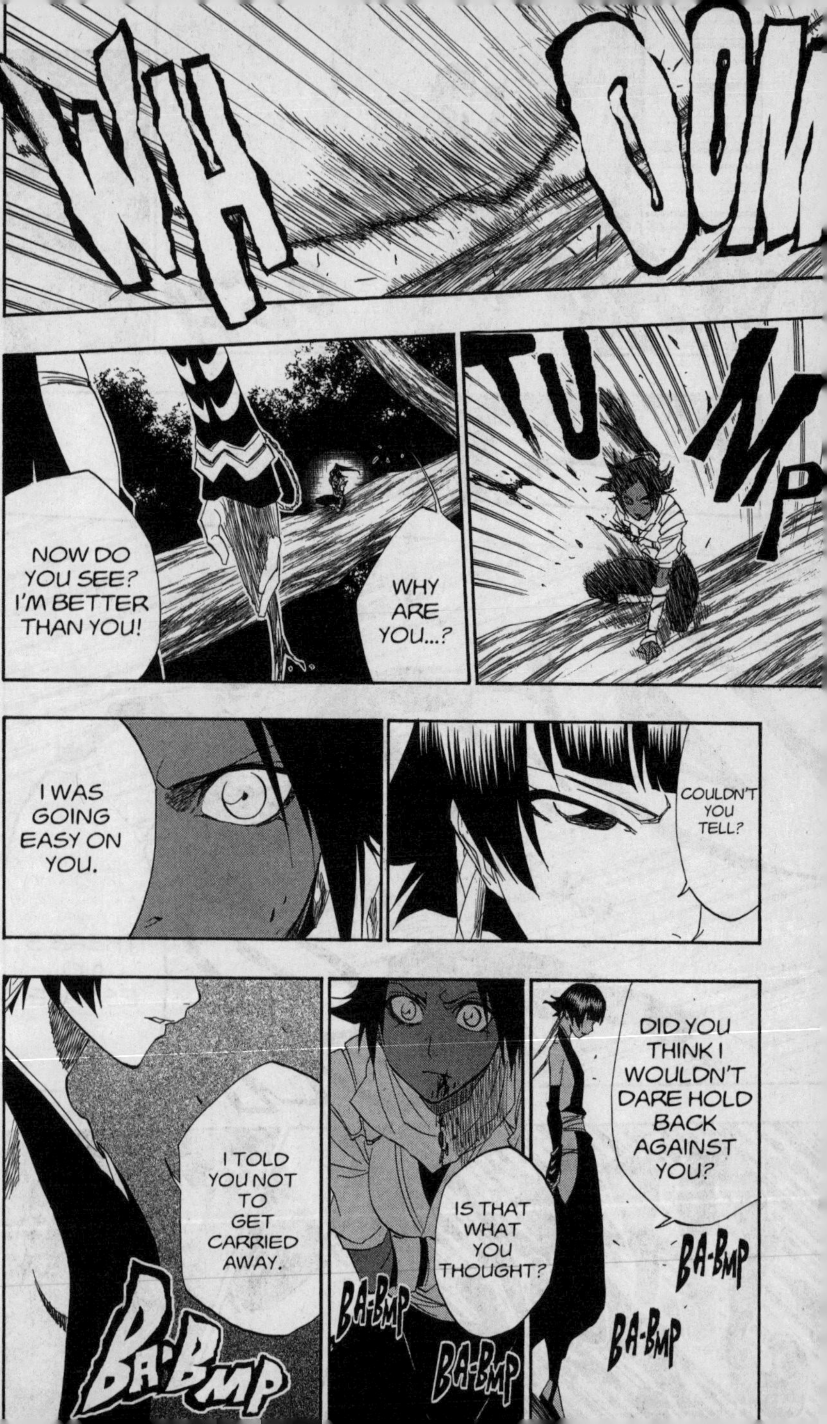
WHA OOM
TUMP
WHY ARE YOU...?
NOW DO YOU SEE? I'M BETTER THAN YOU!
COULDN'T YOU TELL?
I WAS GOING EASY ON YOU.
DID YOU THINK I WOULDN'T DARE HOLD BACK AGAINST YOU?
BA-BMP
BA-BMP
IS THAT WHAT YOU THOUGHT?
BA-BMP
BA-BMP
I TOLD YOU NOT TO GET CARRIED AWAY.
BA-BMP

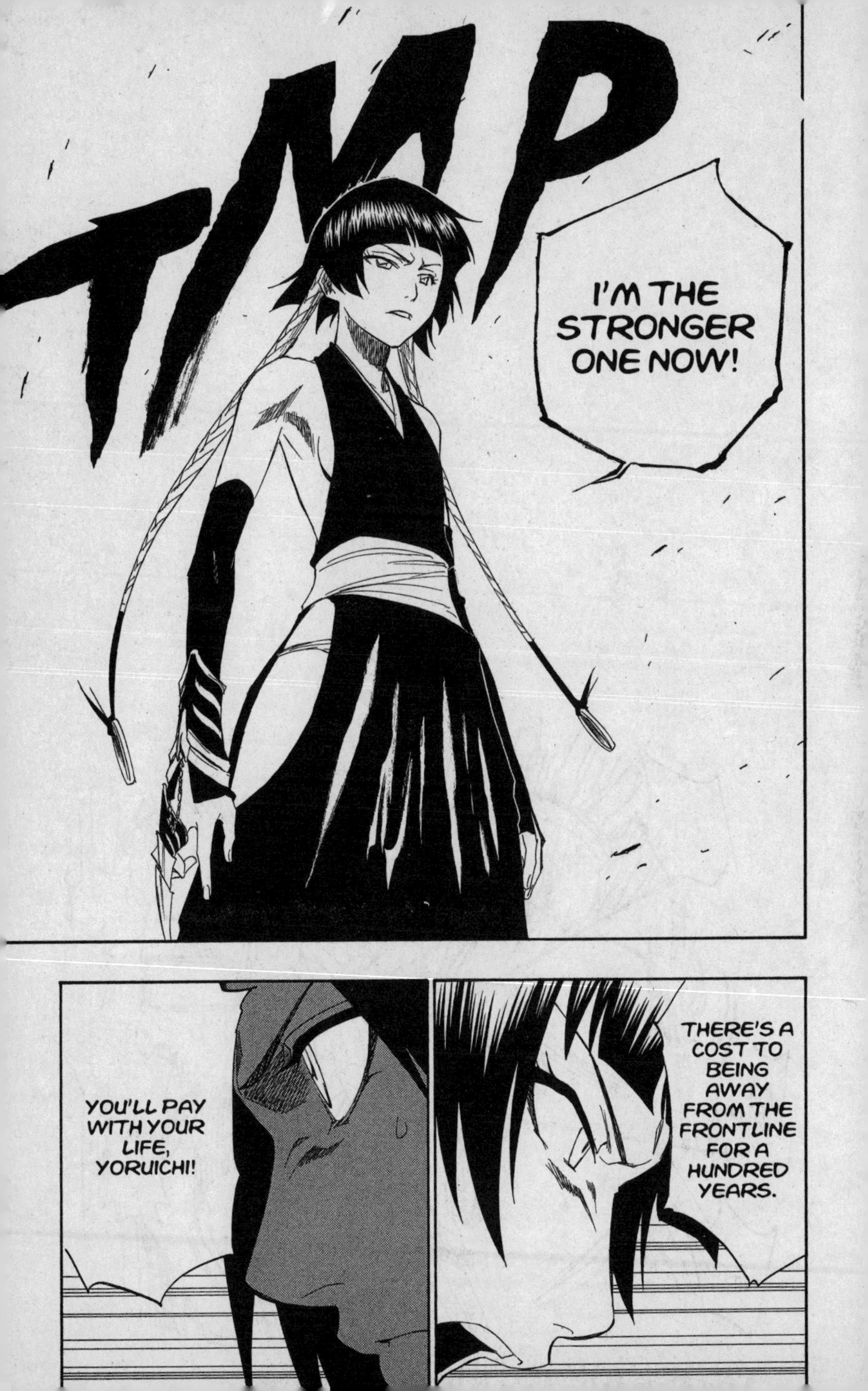
TMP
I'M THE STRONGER ONE NOW!
THERE'S A COST TO BEING AWAY FROM THE FRONTLINE FOR A HUNDRED YEARS.
YOU'LL PAY WITH YOUR LIFE, YORUICHI!

JINTA!!
I FORBID IT!!
DON'T USE YOUR INVINCIBLE IRON CLUB...
...ON A NORMAL PERSON!
I...
FOR-BID
IT!!

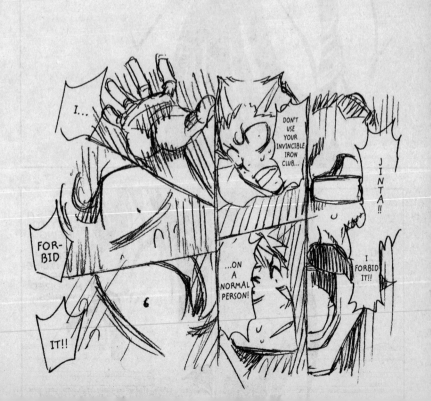

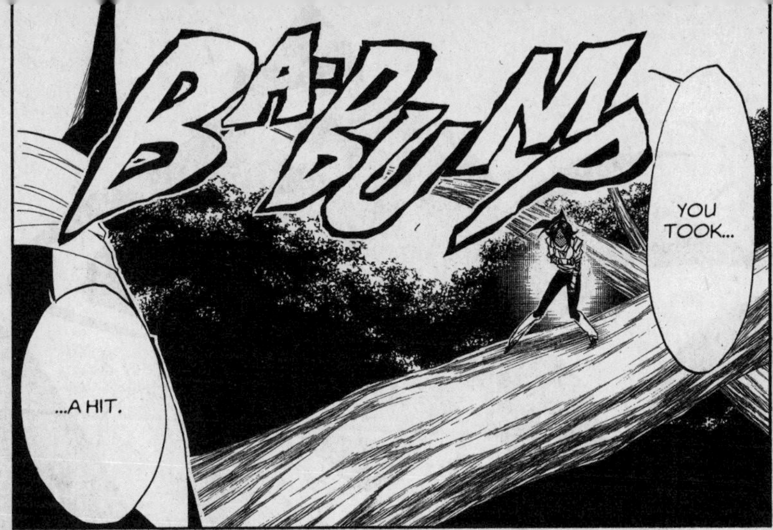
BA-DUMP
YOU TOOK...
...A HIT.

158. Sky Leopardess

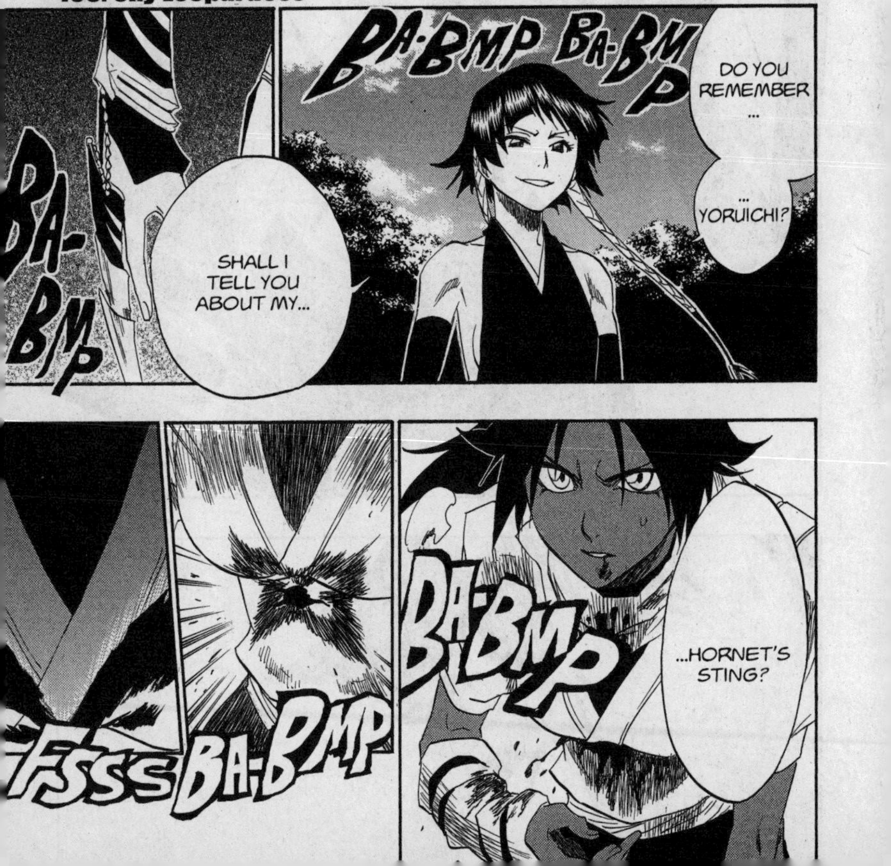
BA-BMP BA-BMP
DO YOU REMEMBER ...
... YORUICHI?
SHALL I TELL YOU ABOUT MY...
BA-BMP
BA-BMP
...HORNET'S STING?
FSSS BA-BMP

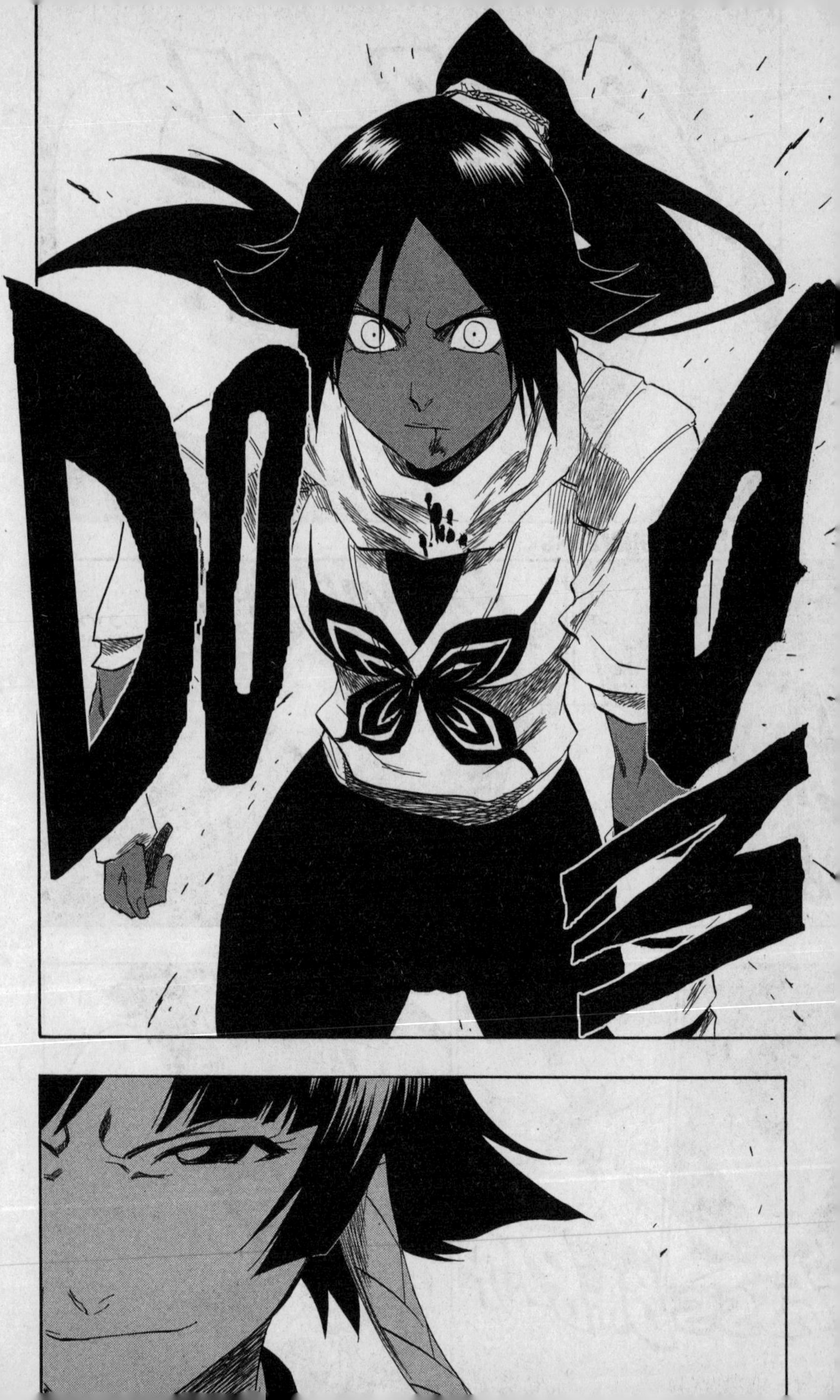
DOOM

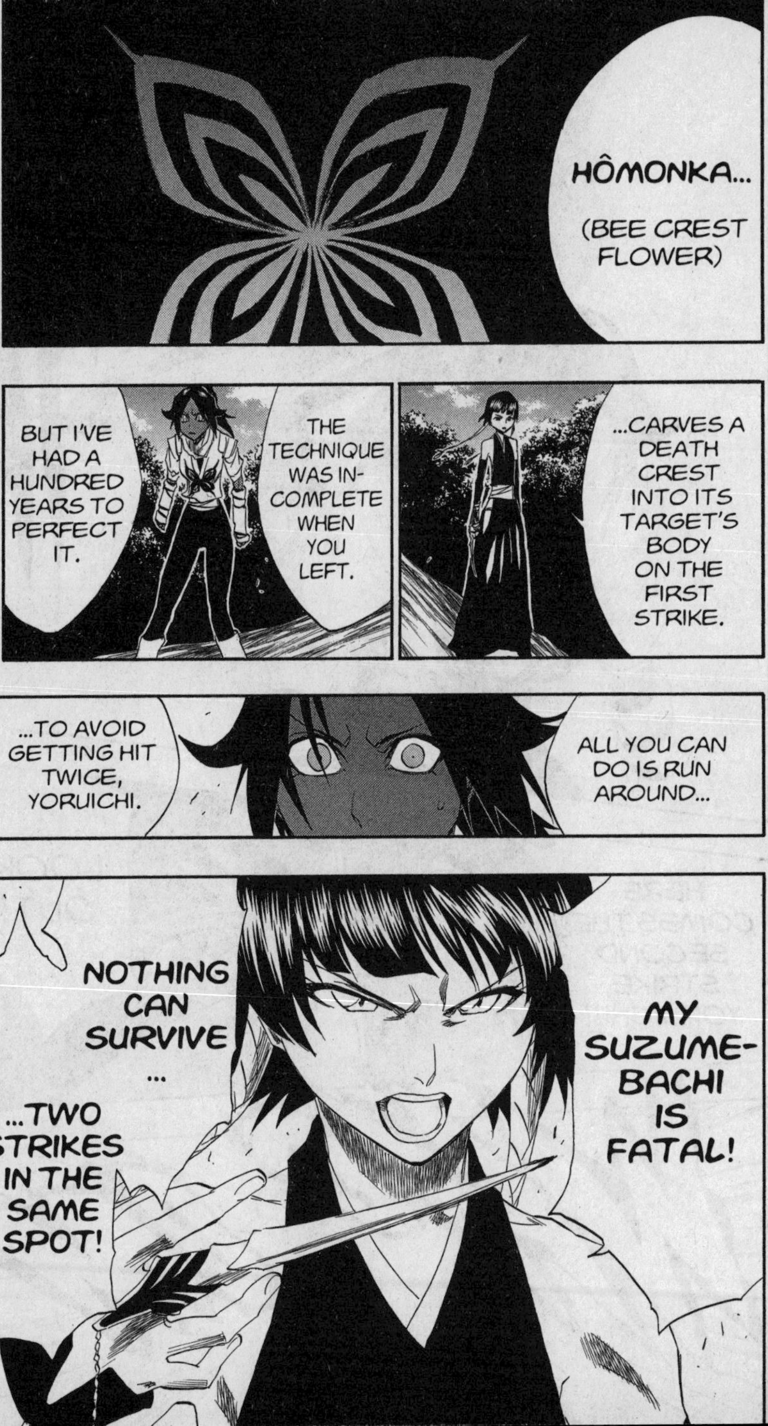
HÔMONKA...
(BEE CREST FLOWER)
...CARVES A DEATH CREST INTO ITS TARGET'S BODY ON THE FIRST STRIKE.
THE TECHNIQUE WAS IN-COMPLETE WHEN YOU LEFT.
BUT I'VE HAD A HUNDRED YEARS TO PERFECT IT.
ALL YOU CAN DO IS RUN AROUND...
...TO AVOID GETTING HIT TWICE, YORUICHI.
MY SUZUME-BACHI IS FATAL!
NOTHING CAN SURVIVE ...
...TWO STRIKES IN THE SAME SPOT!

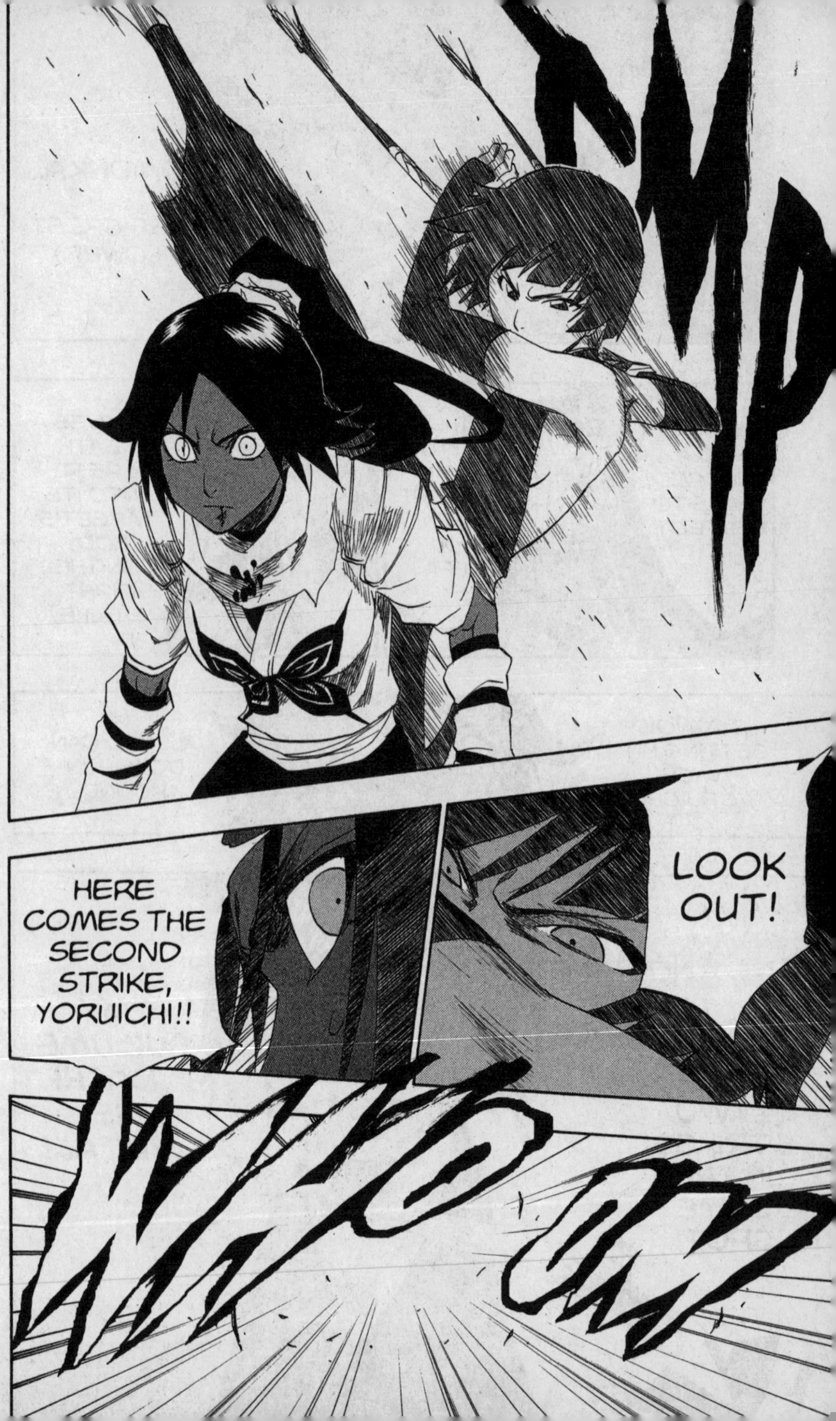
LOOK OUT!
HERE COMES THE SECOND STRIKE, YORUICHI!!

158: Sky Leopardess

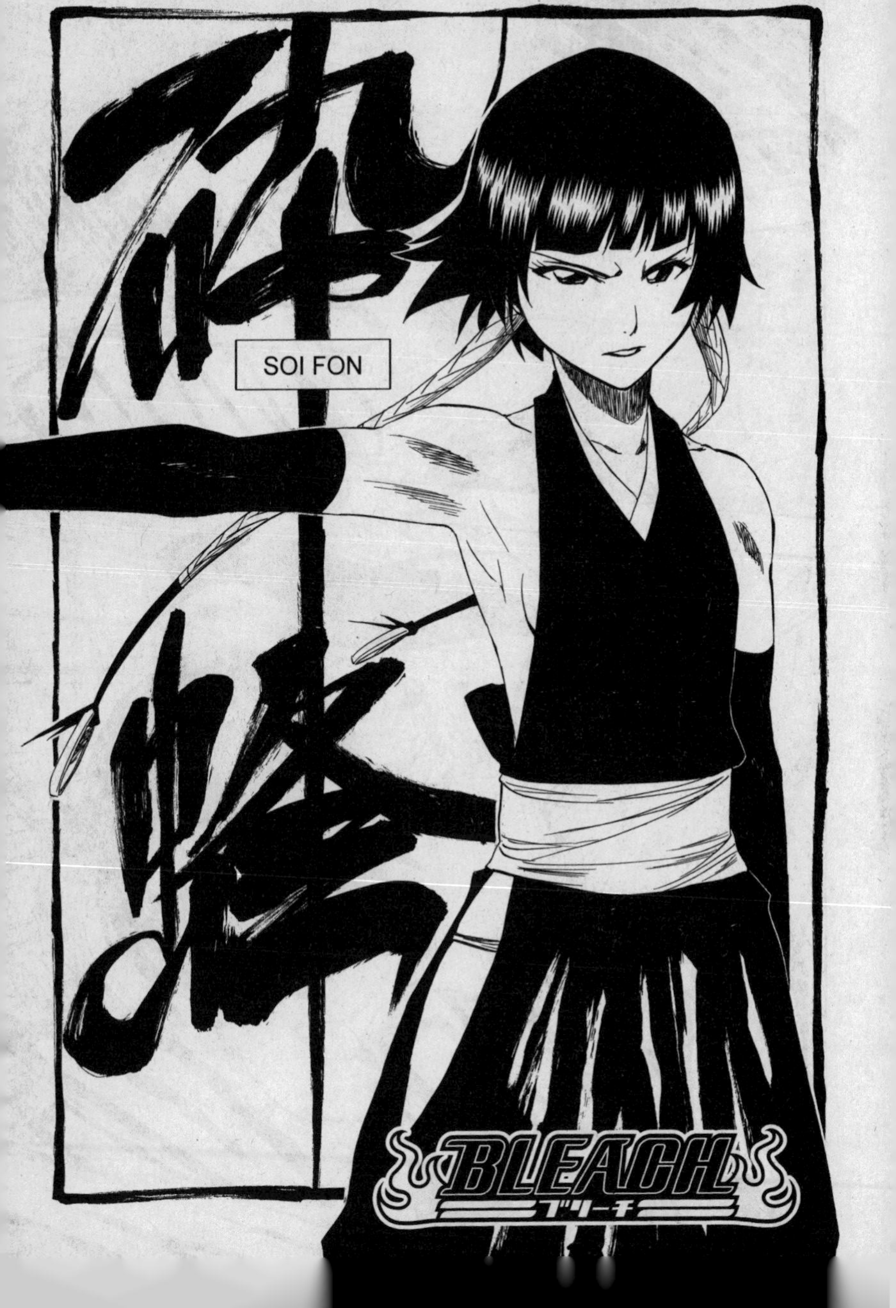
SOI FON
BLEACH
ブリーチ

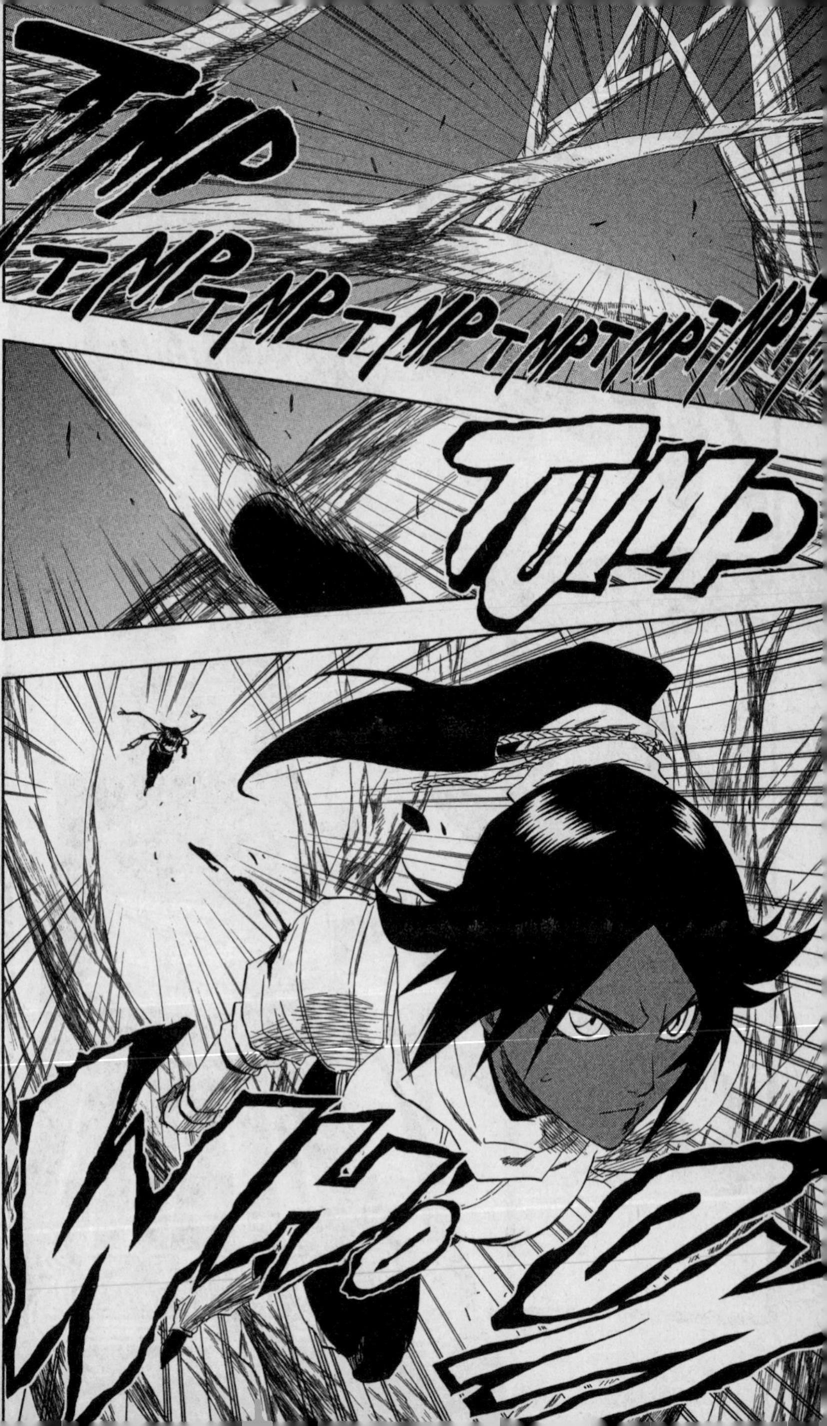
TMP
TMP TMP TMP TMP

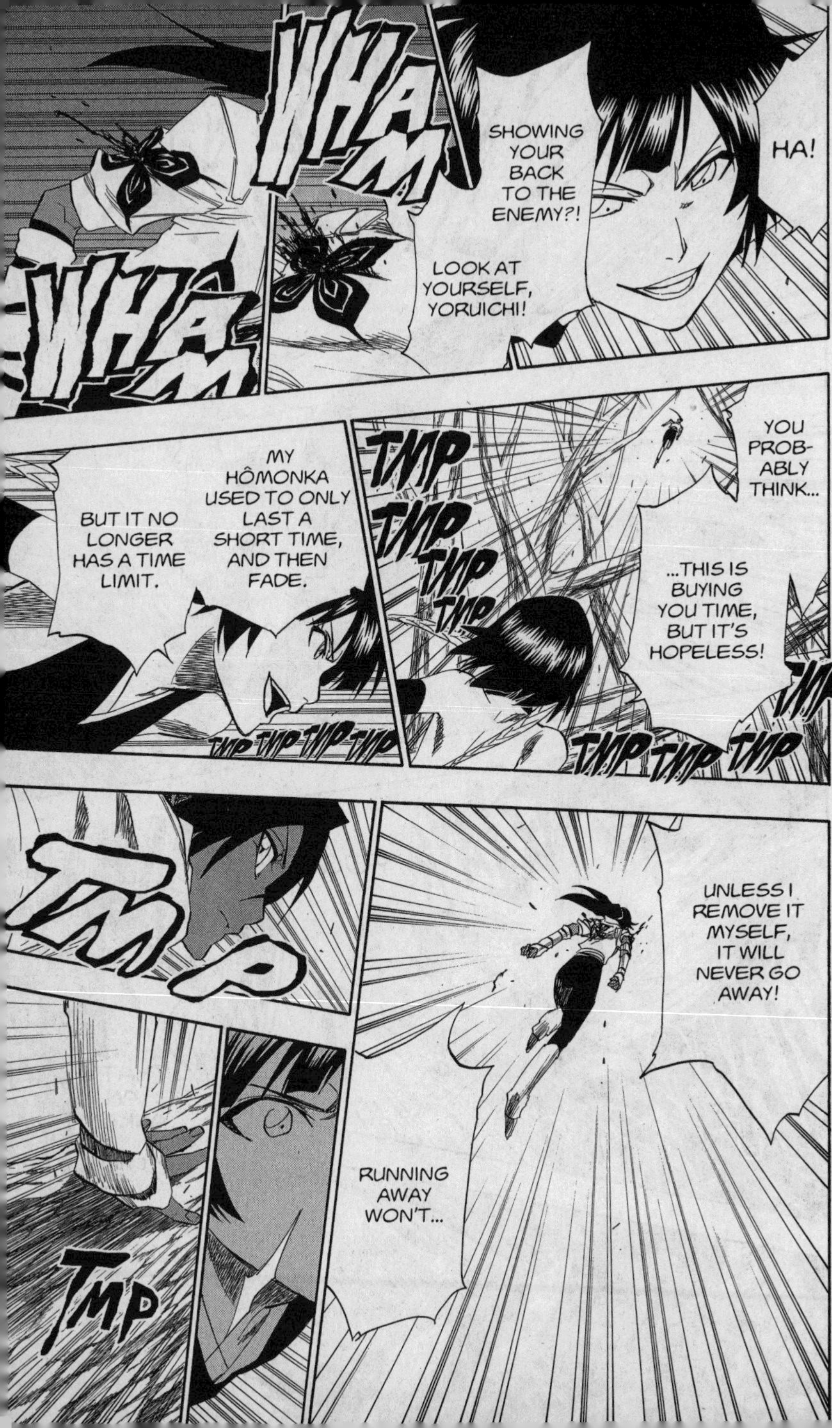
HA!
SHOWING YOUR BACK TO THE ENEMY?!
LOOK AT YOURSELF, YORUICHI!
WHAM
WHAM
YOU PROBABLY THINK...
...THIS IS BUYING YOU TIME, BUT IT'S HOPELESS!
TMP TMP TMP
TMP TMP TMP TMP
MY HÔMONKA USED TO ONLY LAST A SHORT TIME, AND THEN FADE.
BUT IT NO LONGER HAS A TIME LIMIT.
TMP TMP TMP TMP
UNLESS I REMOVE IT MYSELF, IT WILL NEVER GO AWAY!
RUNNING AWAY WON'T...
TMP
TMP

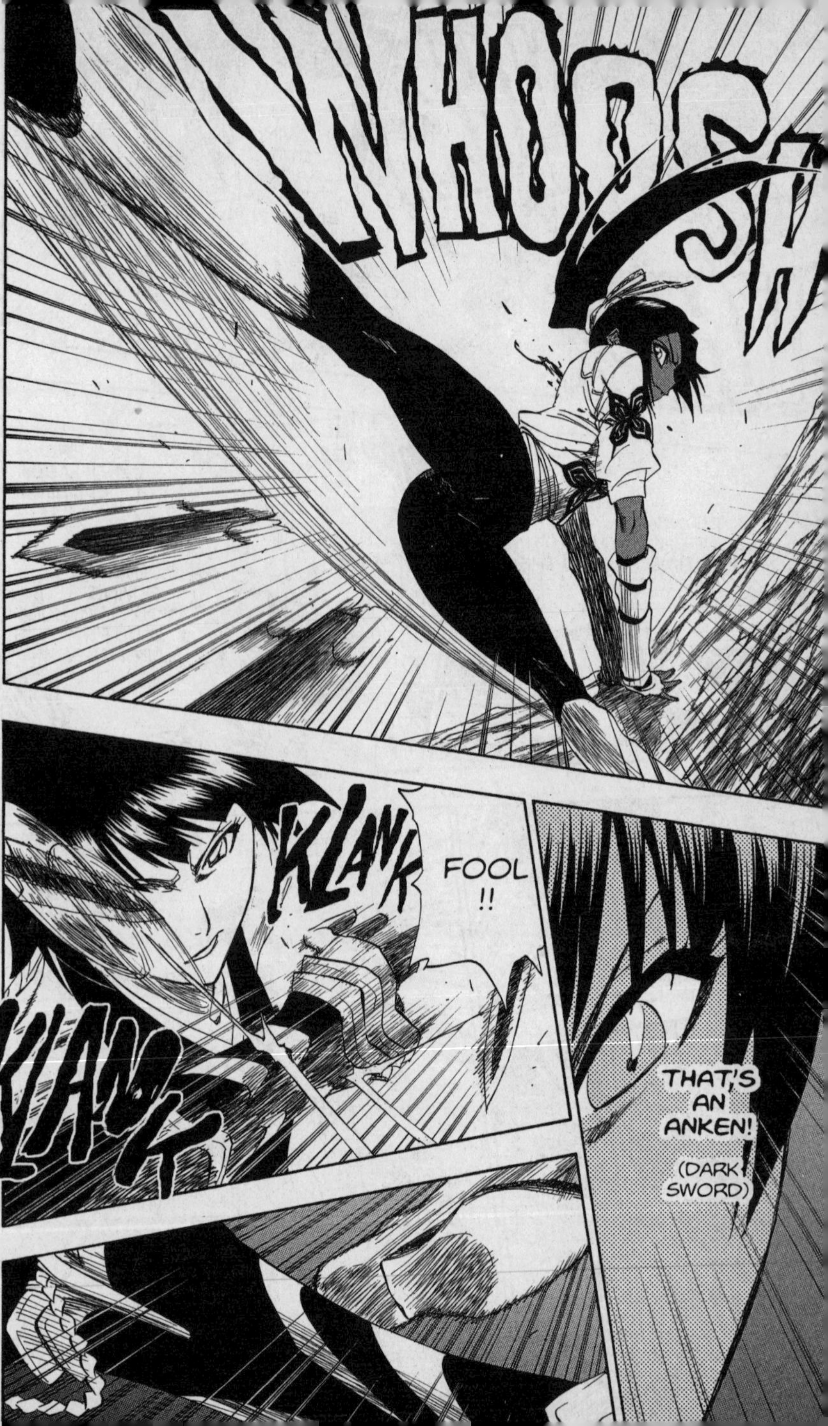
WHOOSH
THAT'S AN ANKEN!
(DARK SWORD)
KLANK
FOOL!!
KLANK

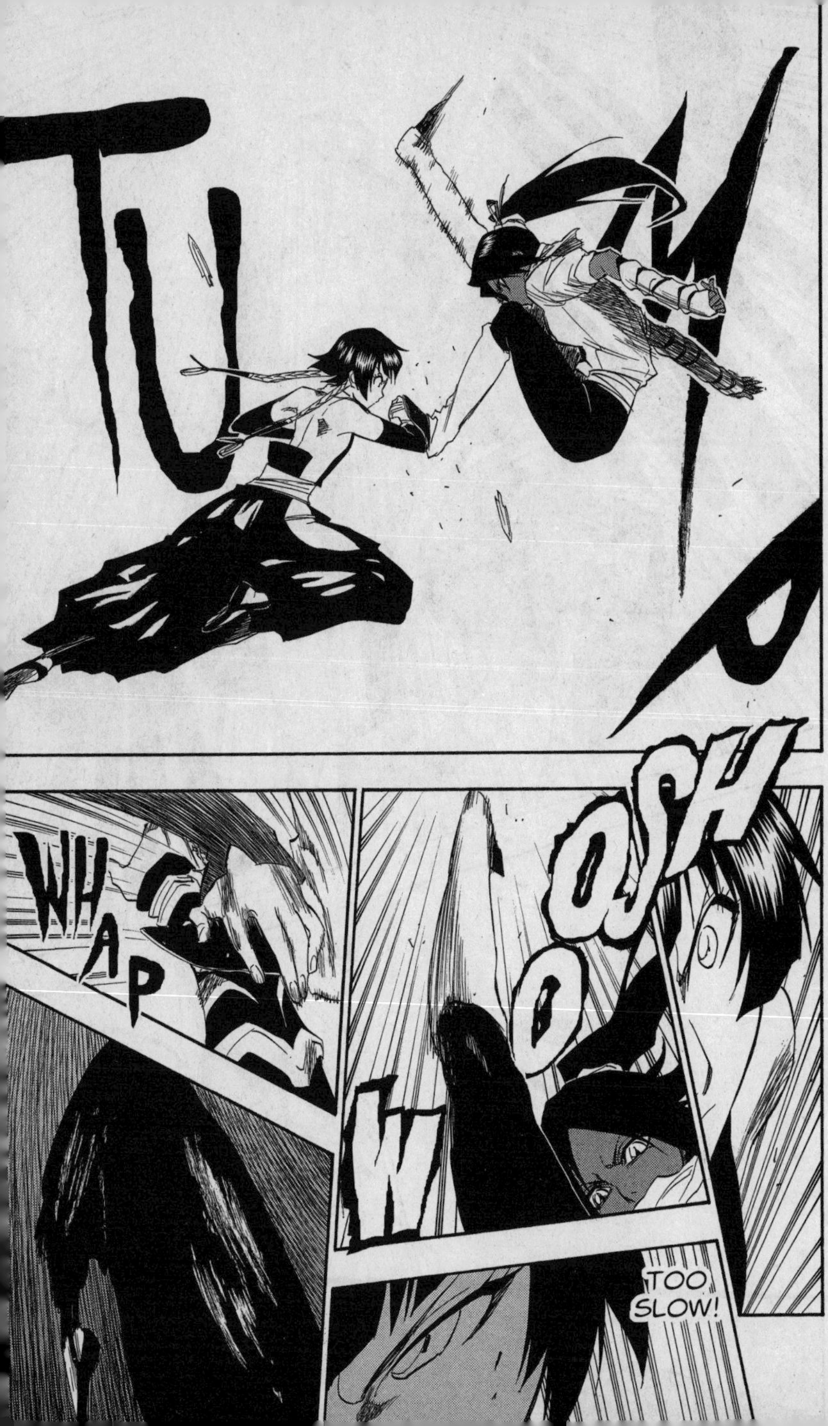
TUMP
WHOOSH
TOO SLOW!
WHAP

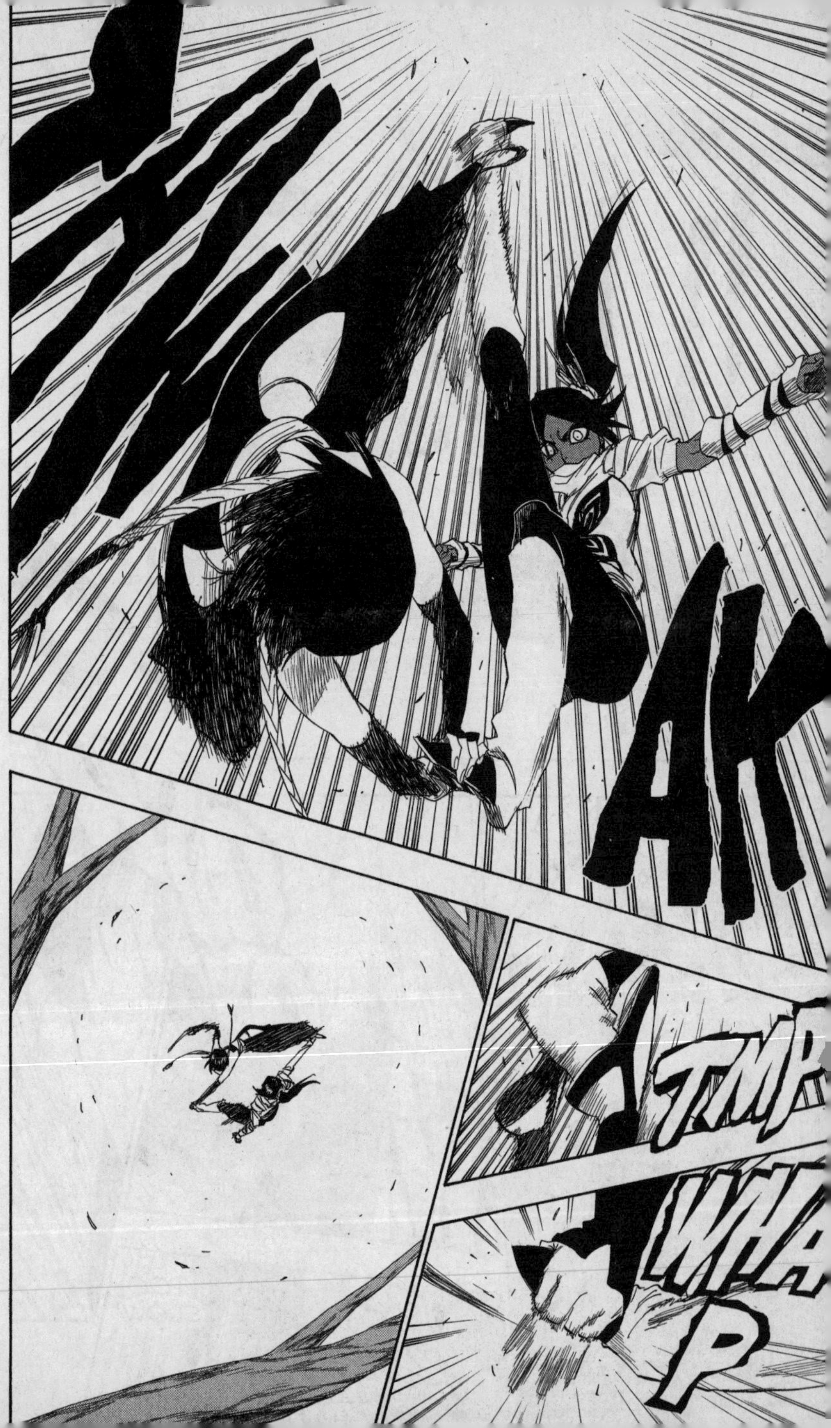
TMP
WHAP

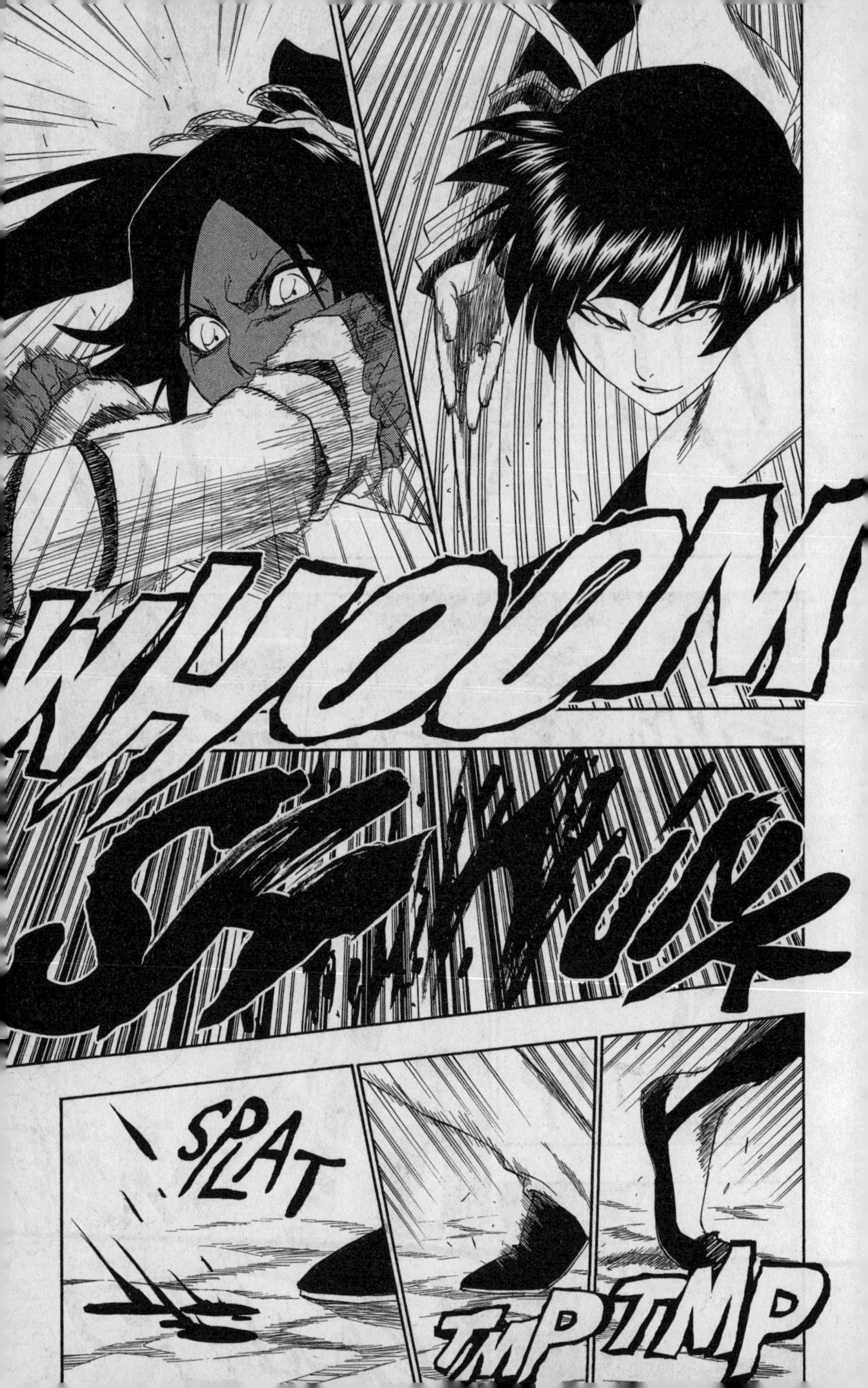
WHOOM
SHUNK
TMP TMP
SPLAT

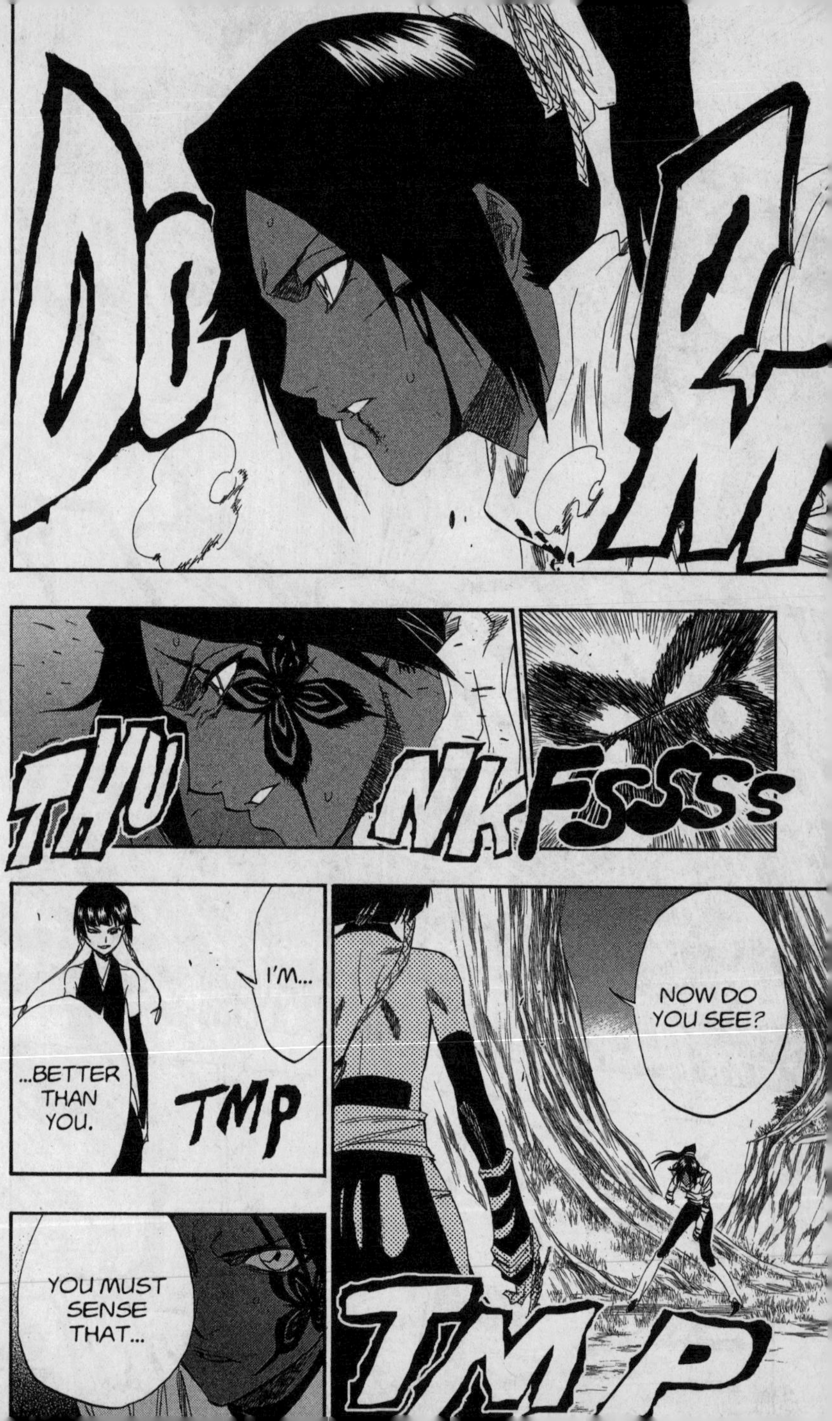
DOOM
FSSSSs
THUNK
NOW DO YOU SEE?
TMP
I'M...
...BETTER THAN YOU.
TMP
YOU MUST SENSE THAT...

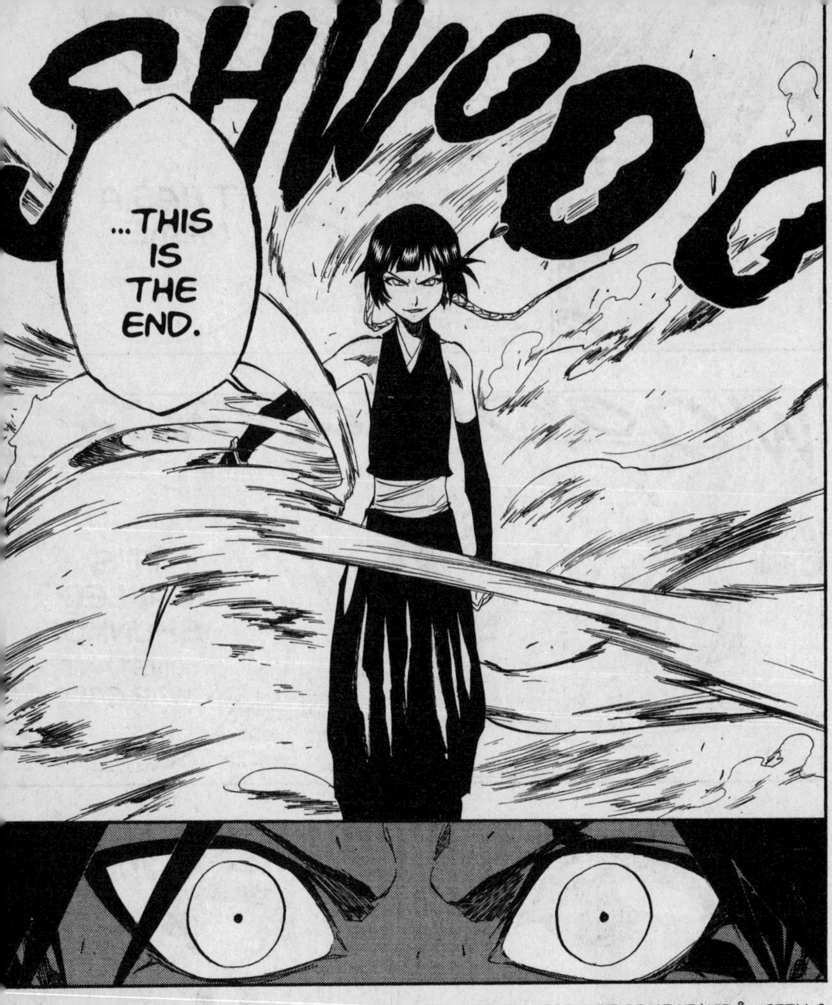
SHWOOOG
...THIS IS THE END.

*HAKUDA = WHITE STRIKE, A FORM OF COMBAT / KIDÔ = SPELLS

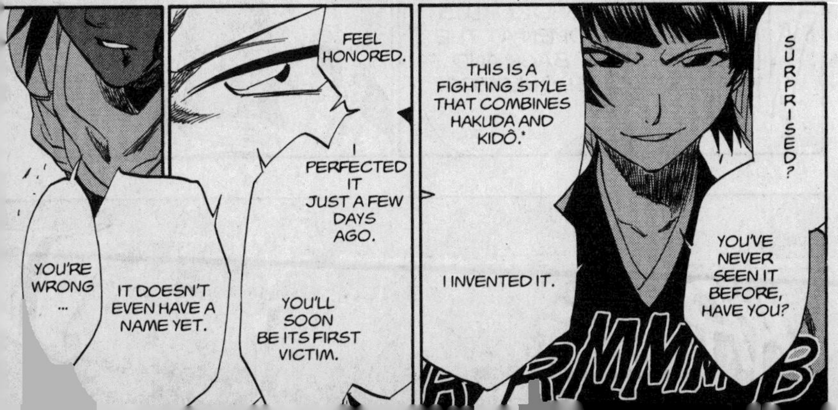
SURPRISED?
YOU'VE NEVER SEEN IT BEFORE, HAVE YOU?
THIS IS A FIGHTING STYLE THAT COMBINES HAKUDA AND KIDÔ.*
I INVENTED IT.
RMMMMB
FEEL HONORED.
I PERFECTED IT JUST A FEW DAYS AGO.
YOU'LL SOON BE ITS FIRST VICTIM.
IT DOESN'T EVEN HAVE A NAME YET.
YOU'RE WRONG ...

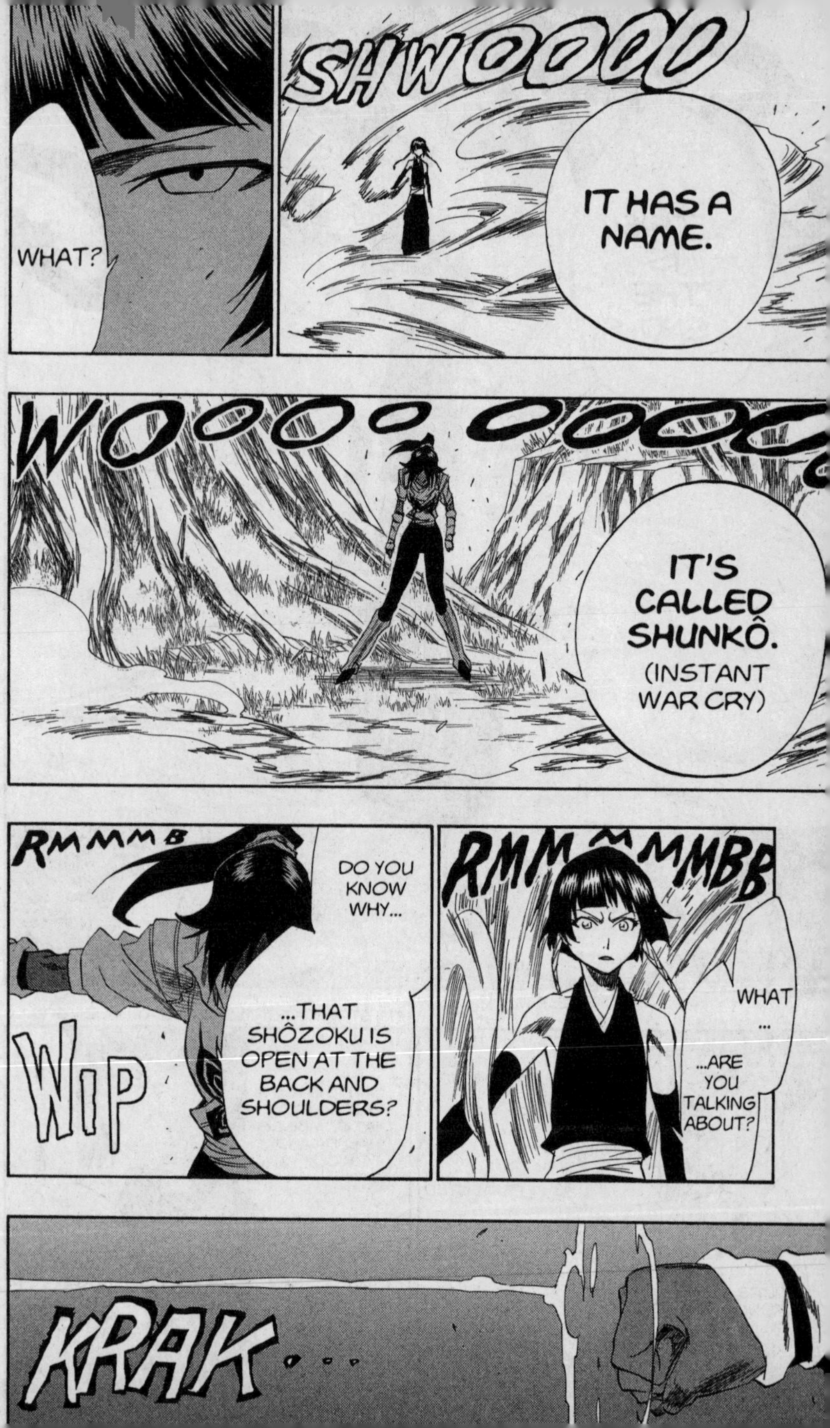
SHWOOOOO
IT HAS A NAME.
WHAT?
WOOOO OOOOO
IT'S CALLED SHUNKÔ. (INSTANT WAR CRY)
RMMMMMBB
WHAT ...
...ARE YOU TALKING ABOUT?
RMMMB
DO YOU KNOW WHY...
...THAT SHÔZOKU IS OPEN AT THE BACK AND SHOULDERS?
WIP
KRAK...

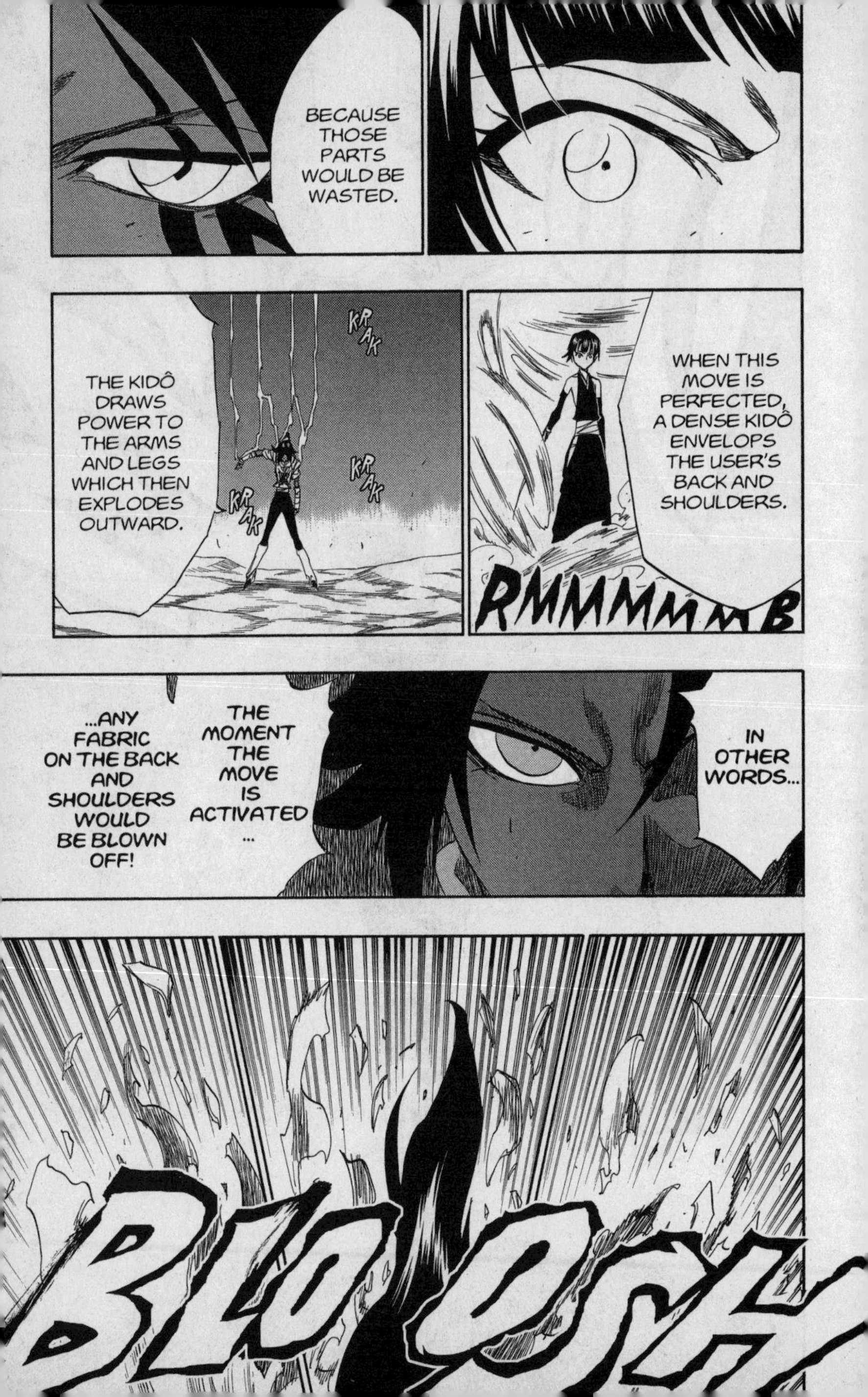
BECAUSE THOSE PARTS WOULD BE WASTED.
WHEN THIS MOVE IS PERFECTED, A DENSE KIDÔ ENVELOPS THE USER'S BACK AND SHOULDERS.
RMMMMMB
KRAK
KRAK
THE KIDÔ DRAWS POWER TO THE ARMS AND LEGS WHICH THEN EXPLODES OUTWARD.
KRAK
IN OTHER WORDS...
THE MOMENT THE MOVE IS ACTIVATED...
...ANY FABRIC ON THE BACK AND SHOULDERS WOULD BE BLOWN OFF!
BLOOSH

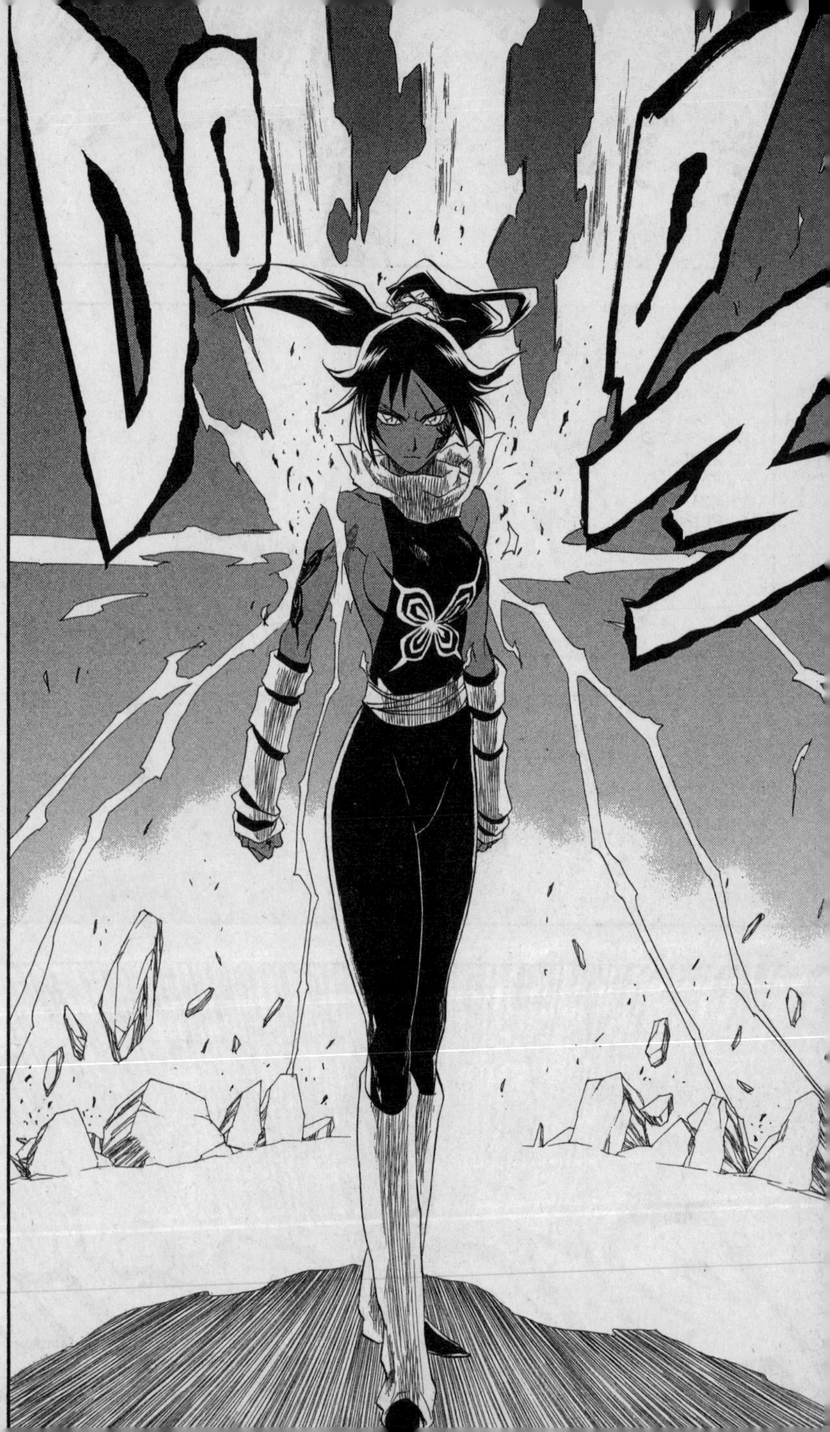
DOOM

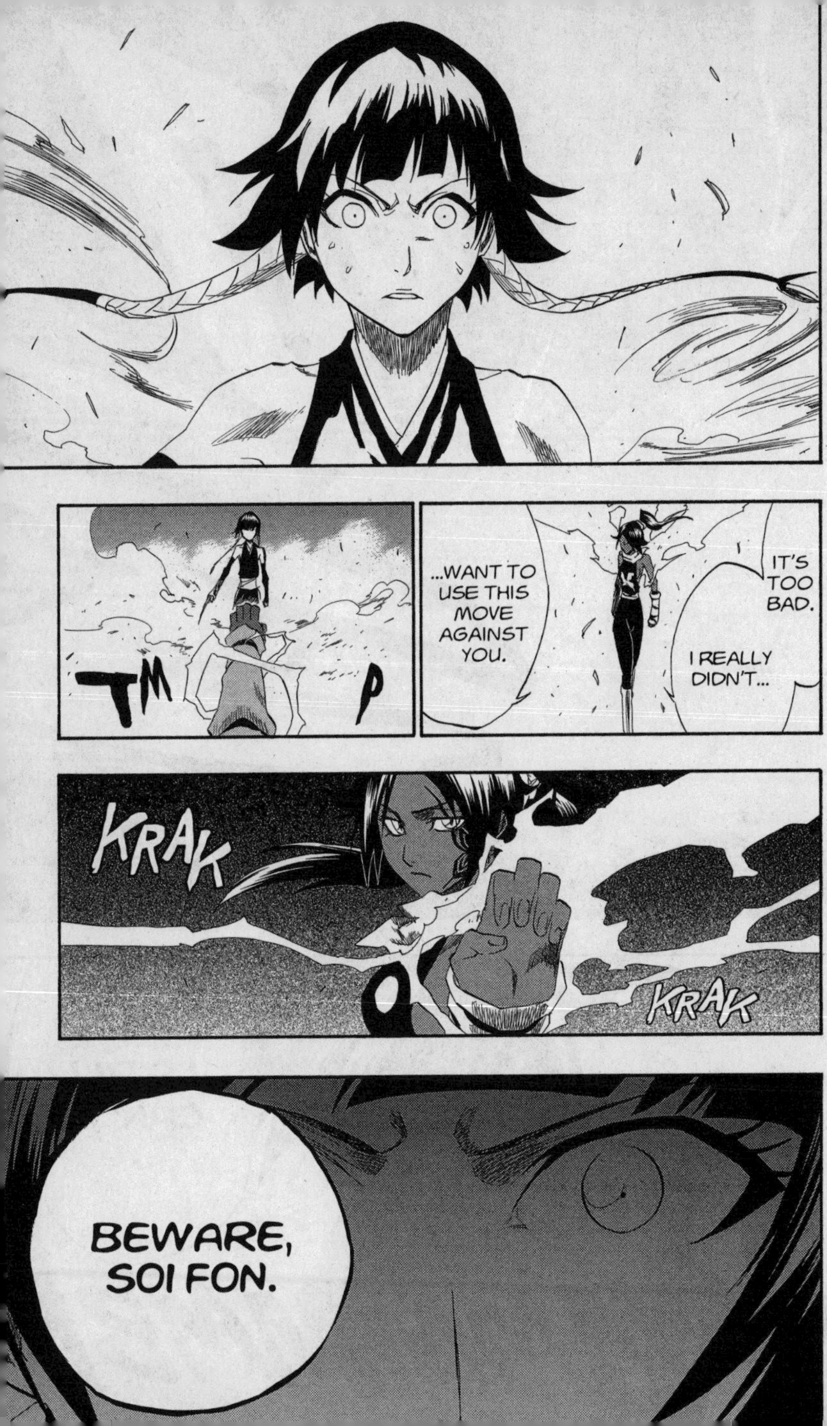
IT'S TOO BAD.
I REALLY DIDN'T...
...WANT TO USE THIS MOVE AGAINST YOU.
TMP
KRAK
KRAK
BEWARE, SOI FON.

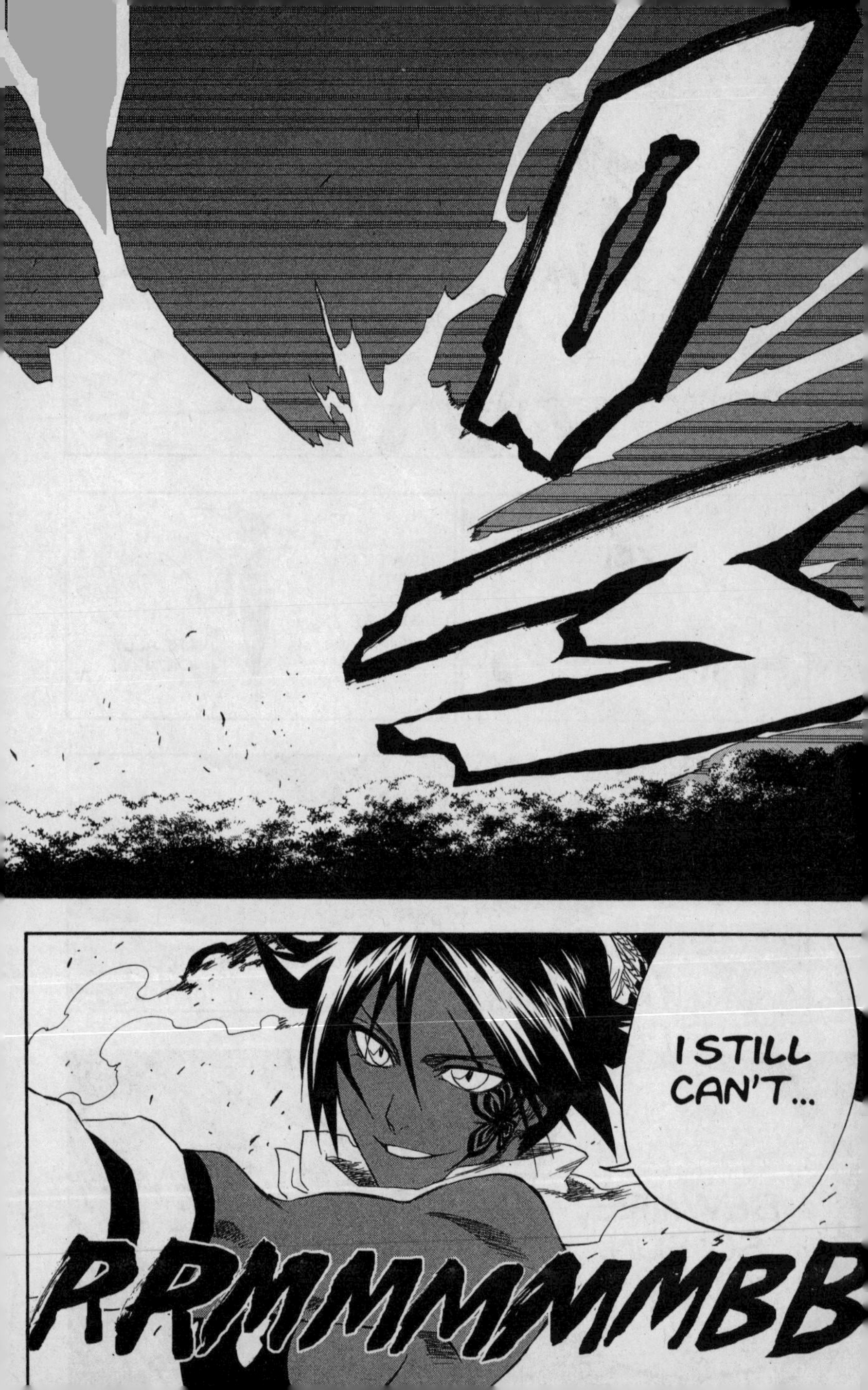
I STILL CAN'T...
RRMMMMMBB

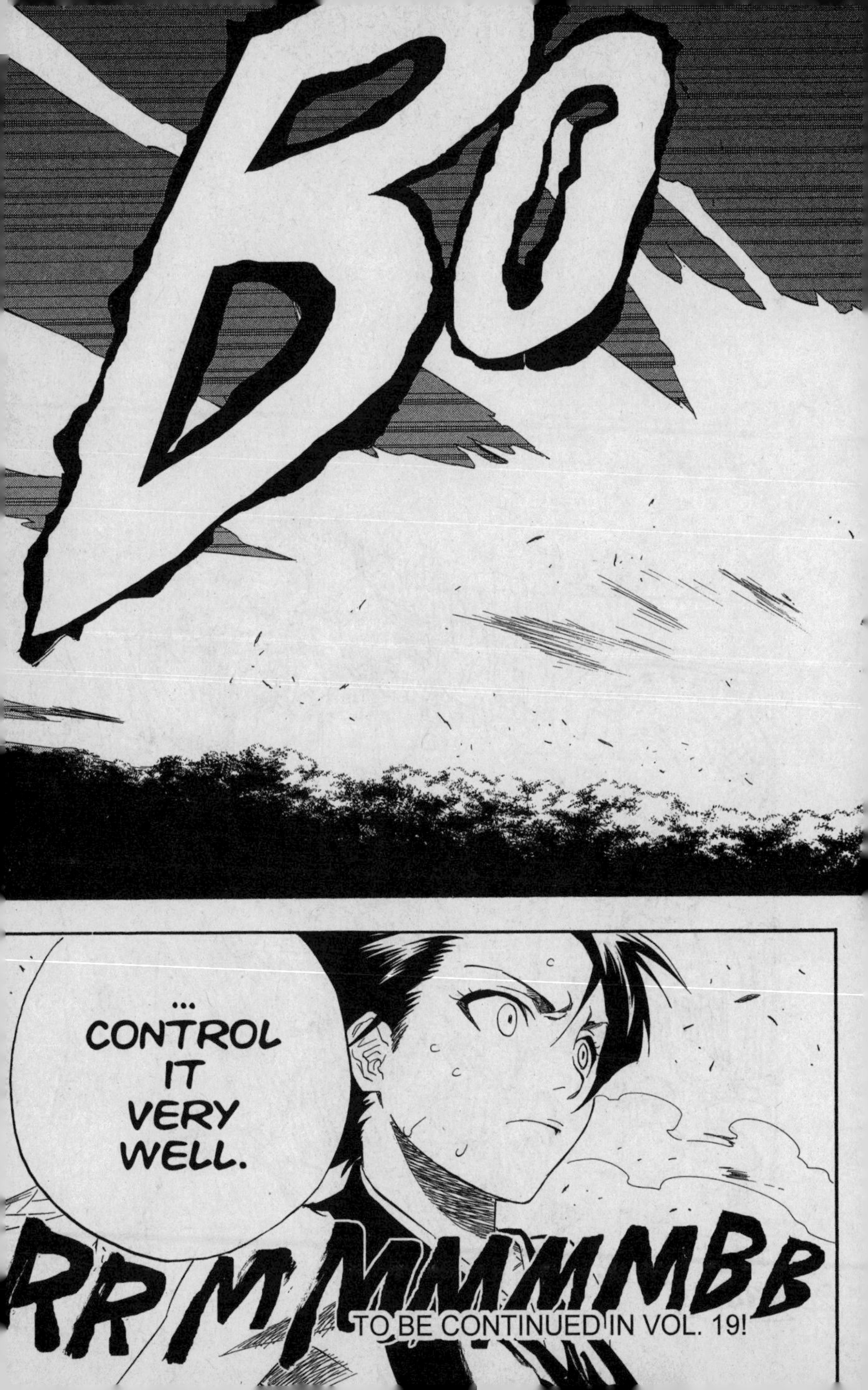
BOOM
... CONTROL IT VERY WELL.
RRMMMMMMBB
TO BE CONTINUED IN VOL. 19!

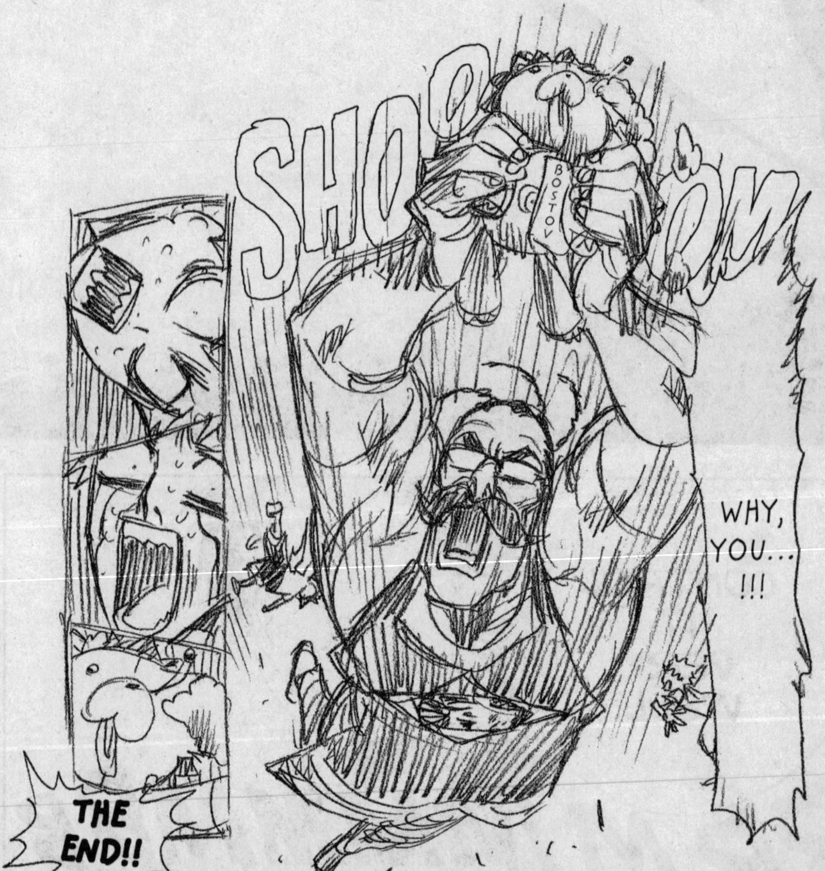
SHOOOM
BOSTOV
WHY, YOU... !!!
THE END!!

★ ★ ★ here is the data of **BLEACH!!**

13 COURT GUARD COMPANIES	浮竹十四郎	CAPTAIN JÛSHIRÔ UKITAKE 13TH COMPANY

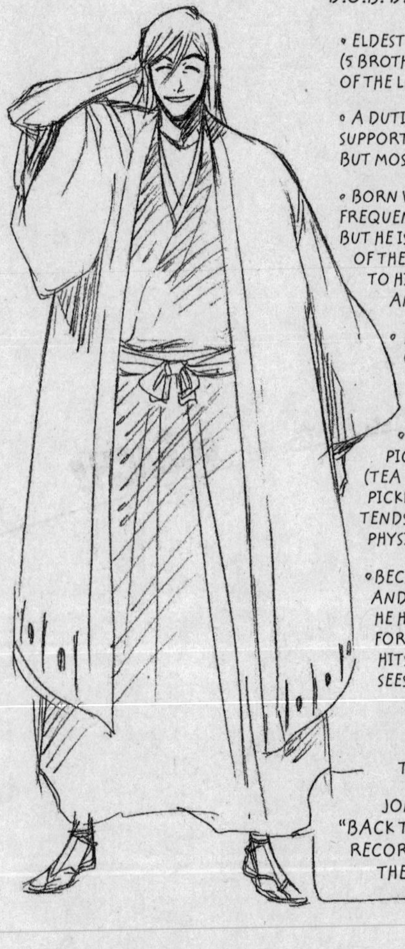

187 CM
72 KG
D.O.B. DECEMBER 21

- ELDEST OF EIGHT CHILDREN (5 BROTHERS, 2 SISTERS). HIS FAMILY IS OF THE LESSER NOBILITY.
- A DUTIFUL SON, HE NOT ONLY SUPPORTS HIS PARENTS AND SIBLINGS, BUT MOST OF HIS RELATIVES AS WELL.
- BORN WITH A LUNG AILMENT THAT FREQUENTLY INCAPACITATES HIM, BUT HE IS WELL LIKED BY THE MEMBERS OF THE OTHER COMPANIES DUE TO HIS AFFABLE PERSONALITY AND IMPRESSIVE SKILLS.
- HAS GRAY HAIR. HIS HAIR WENT GRAY OVER THE COURSE OF THREE DAYS DURING ONE OF HIS SICK SPELLS.
- HIS FAVORITE FOOD IS PICKLED *UME OCHAZUKE* (TEA POURED OVER RICE WITH PICKLED JAPANESE APRICOTS). TENDS TO EAT EVERYTHING, BUT IS PHYSICALLY FRAGILE.
- BECAUSE THE NAMES JÛSHIRÔ AND TÔSHIRÔ SOUND SIMILAR, HE HAS A ONE-SIDED AFFECTION FOR TÔSHIRÔ HITSUGAYA. OFFERS HITSUGAYA FOOD EVERY TIME HE SEES HIM.

THEME SONG

JONATHAN CAIN
"BACK TO THE INNOCENCE"
RECORDED ON "BACK TO THE INNOCENCE"

13 COURT GUARD COMPANIES	京楽春水	CAPTAIN SHUNSUI KYÔRAKU 8TH COMPANY

192 CM
87 KG
D.O.B. JULY 11

- FAVORITE FOOD: TOKKURI SAICHÛ (A WAFER WITH BEAN JAM FILLING) FROM KURIYA, THE SEIREITEI'S POPULAR CONFECTIONERY SHOP. TENDS TO EAT IT WHEN NANAO IS IN A BAD MOOD AND WON'T LET HIM DRINK.
- HE'S GOOD DRINKING BUDDIES WITH RANGIKU.

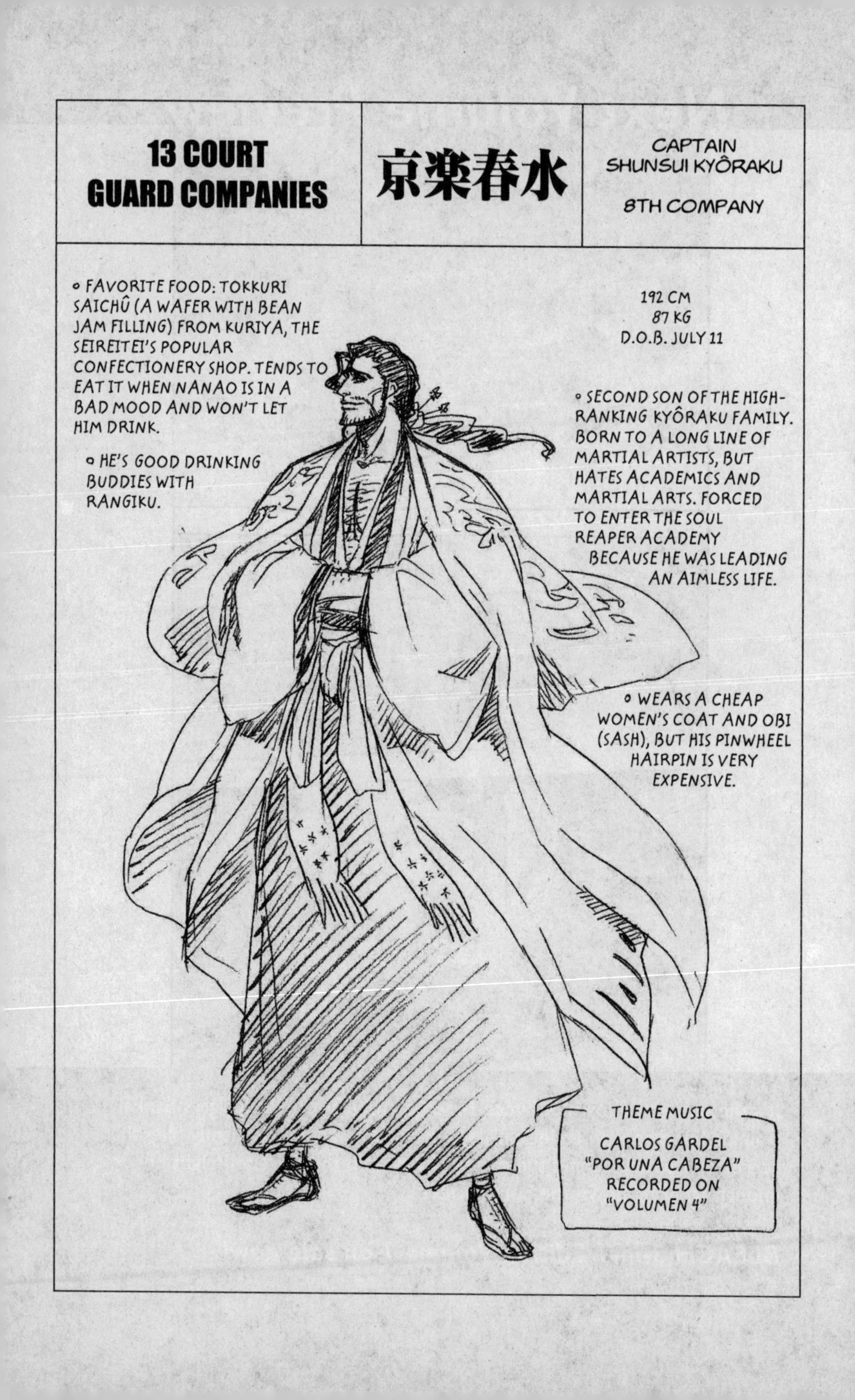

- SECOND SON OF THE HIGH-RANKING KYÔRAKU FAMILY. BORN TO A LONG LINE OF MARTIAL ARTISTS, BUT HATES ACADEMICS AND MARTIAL ARTS. FORCED TO ENTER THE SOUL REAPER ACADEMY BECAUSE HE WAS LEADING AN AIMLESS LIFE.
- WEARS A CHEAP WOMEN'S COAT AND OBI (SASH), BUT HIS PINWHEEL HAIRPIN IS VERY EXPENSIVE.

THEME MUSIC

CARLOS GARDEL
"POR UNA CABEZA"
RECORDED ON
"VOLUMEN 4"

Next Volume Preview

It's the final showdown between Byakuya and Ichigo! Has Ichigo's bankai training been enough to let him face Byakuya as an equal? Meanwhile, the secret conspiracy behind the recent troubles in the Seireitei might be enough to bring down the Soul Society!!

BLEACH 3-in-1 Edition Volume 7 on sale now!

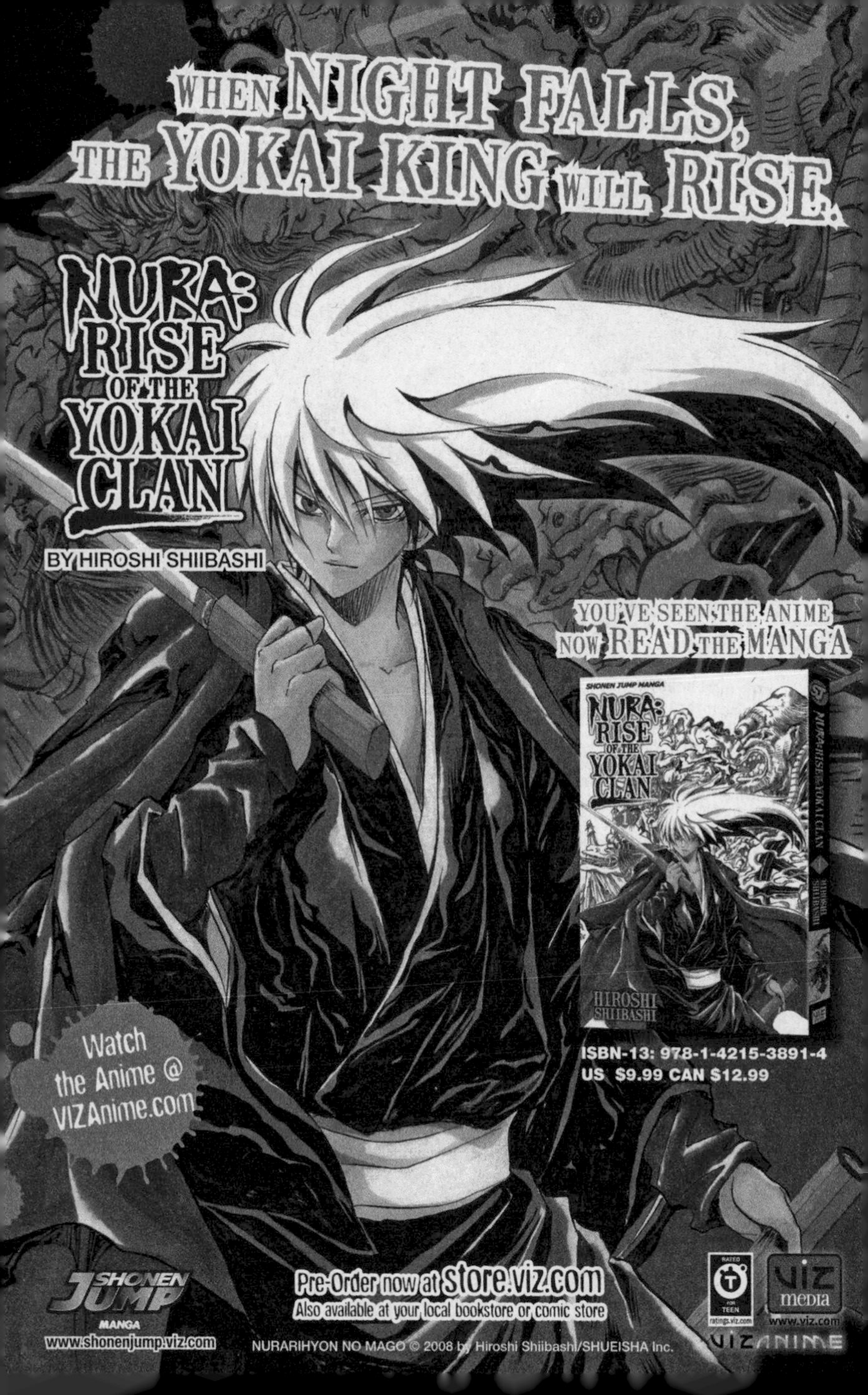

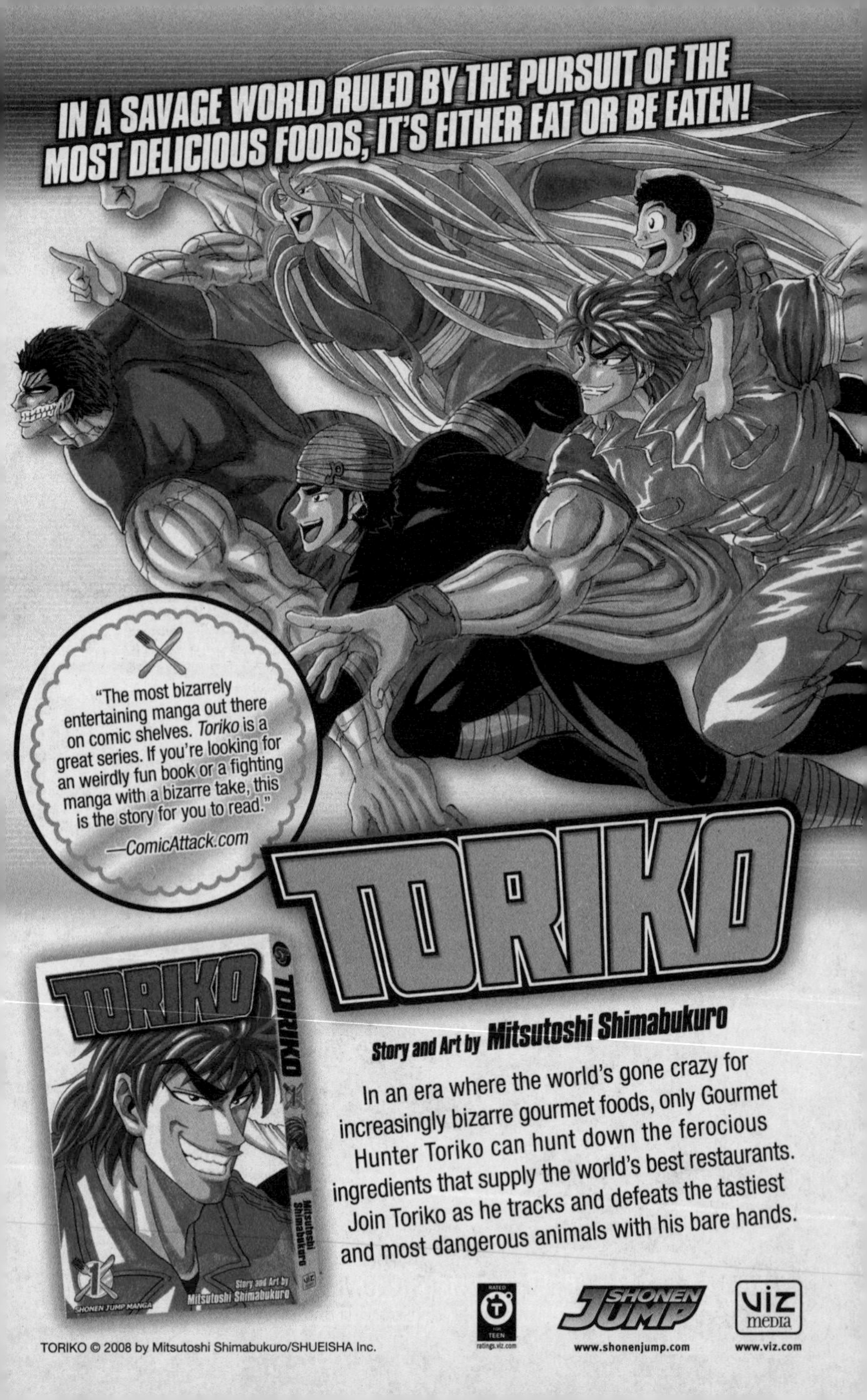
IN A SAVAGE WORLD RULED BY THE PURSUIT OF THE MOST DELICIOUS FOODS, IT'S EITHER EAT OR BE EATEN!
"The most bizarrely entertaining manga out there on comic shelves. Toriko is a great series. If you're looking for an weirdly fun book or a fighting manga with a bizarre take, this is the story for you to read."
—ComicAttack.com
TORIKO
TORIKO
TORIKO
Mitsutoshi Shimabukuro
Story and Art by
Mitsutoshi Shimabukuro
SHONEN JUMP MANGA
Story and Art by Mitsutoshi Shimabukuro
In an era where the world's gone crazy for increasingly bizarre gourmet foods, only Gourmet Hunter Toriko can hunt down the ferocious ingredients that supply the world's best restaurants. Join Toriko as he tracks and defeats the tastiest and most dangerous animals with his bare hands.
RATED T TEEN
ratings.viz.com
SHONEN JUMP
www.shonenjump.com
VIZ media
www.viz.com
TORIKO © 2008 by Mitsutoshi Shimabukuro/SHUEISHA Inc.

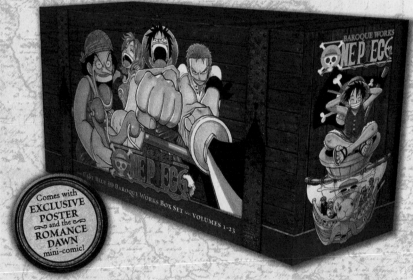

THE ACTION-PACKED SUPERHERO COMEDY ABOUT ONE MAN'S AMBITION TO BE A HERO FOR FUN!

ONE-PUNCH MAN

STORY BY
ONE

ART BY
YUSUKE MURATA

Nothing about Saitama passes the eyeball test when it comes to superheroes, from his lifeless expression to his bald head to his unimpressive physique. However, this average-looking guy has a not-so-average problem—he just can't seem to find an opponent strong enough to take on!

Can he finally find an opponent who can go toe-to-toe with him and give his life some meaning? Or is he doomed to a life of superpowered boredom?

www.viz.com

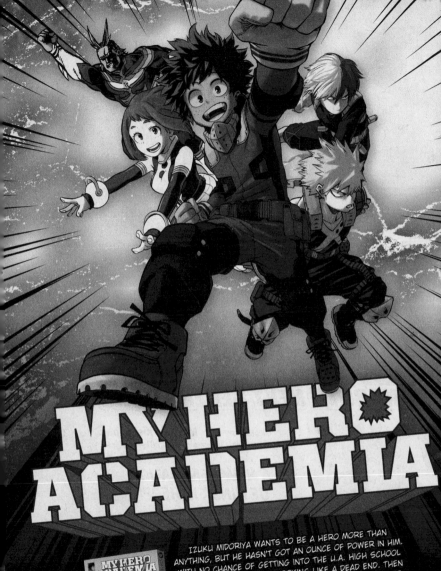

MY HERO ACADEMIA

IZUKU MIDORIYA WANTS TO BE A HERO MORE THAN ANYTHING, BUT HE HASN'T GOT AN OUNCE OF POWER IN HIM. WITH NO CHANCE OF GETTING INTO THE U.A. HIGH SCHOOL FOR HEROES, HIS LIFE IS LOOKING LIKE A DEAD END. THEN AN ENCOUNTER WITH ALL MIGHT, THE GREATEST HERO OF ALL, GIVES HIM A CHANCE TO CHANGE HIS DESTINY...

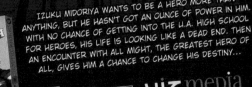

www.viz.com

BOKU NO HERO ACADEMIA © 2014 by Kohei Horikoshi/SHUEISHA Inc.

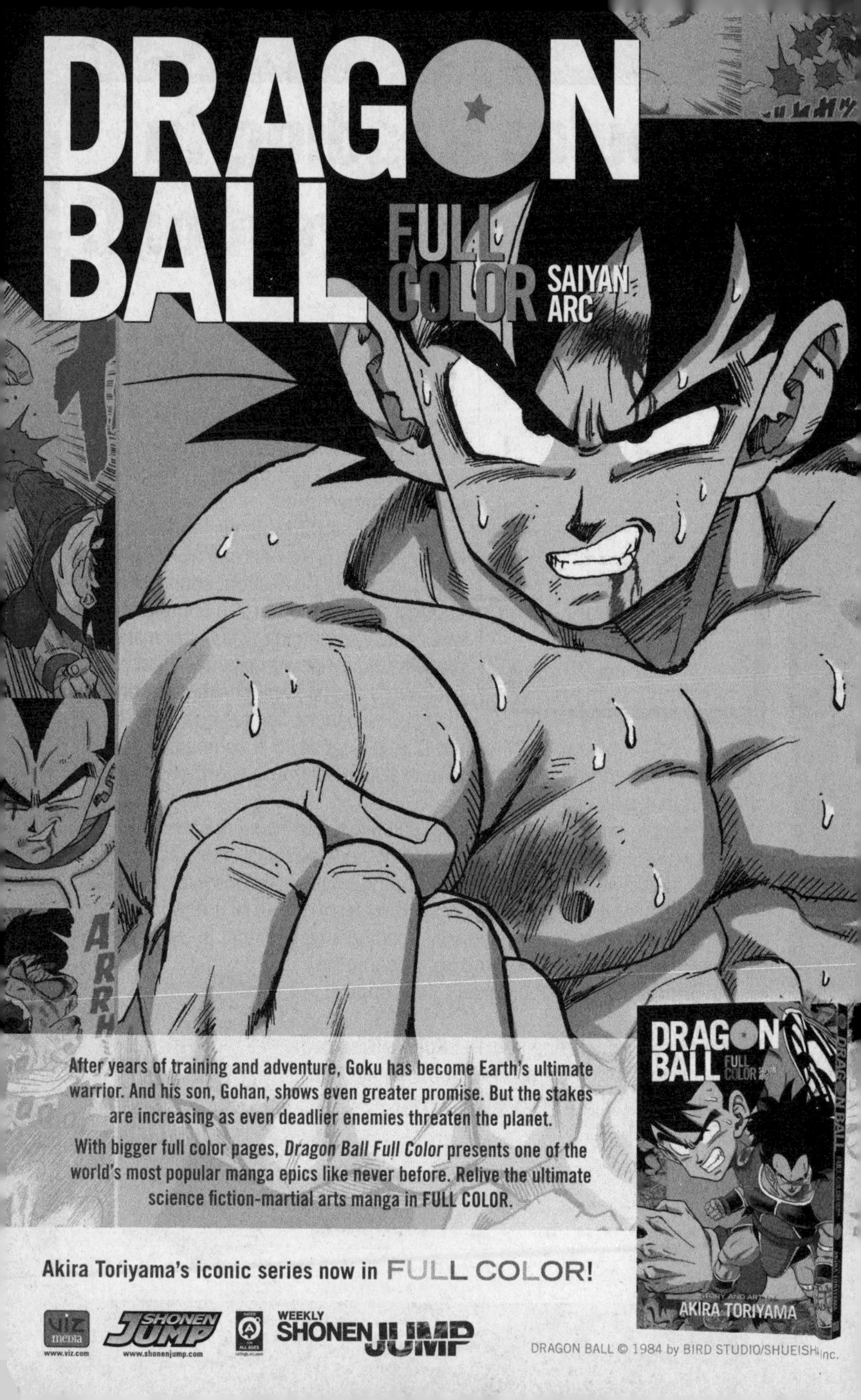

DRAGON BALL

FULL COLOR
SAIYAN ARC

After years of training and adventure, Goku has become Earth's ultimate warrior. And his son, Gohan, shows even greater promise. But the stakes are increasing as even deadlier enemies threaten the planet.

With bigger full color pages, *Dragon Ball Full Color* presents one of the world's most popular manga epics like never before. Relive the ultimate science fiction-martial arts manga in FULL COLOR.

DRAGON BALL FULL COLOR

STORY AND ART BY
AKIRA TORIYAMA

Akira Toriyama's iconic series now in FULL COLOR!

You're Reading in the Wrong Direction!!

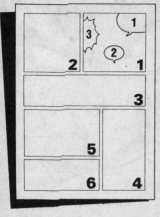

Whoops! Guess what? You're starting at the wrong end of the comic!

…It's true! In keeping with the original Japanese format, **Bleach** is meant to be read from right to left, starting in the upper-right corner.

Unlike English, which is read from left to right, Japanese is read from right to left, meaning that action, sound effects and word-balloon order are completely reversed… something which can make readers unfamiliar with Japanese feel pretty backwards themselves. For this reason, manga or Japanese comics published in the U.S. in English have sometimes been published "flopped"—that is, printed in exact reverse order, as though seen from the other side of a mirror.

By flopping pages, U.S. publishers can avoid confusing readers, but the compromise is not without its downside. For one thing, a character in a flopped manga series who once wore in the original Japanese version a T-shirt emblazoned with "M A Y" (as in "the merry month of") now wears one which reads "Y A M"! Additionally, many manga creators in Japan are themselves unhappy with the process, as some feel the mirror-imaging of their art skews their original intentions.

We are proud to bring you Tite Kubo's **Bleach** in the original unflopped format. For now, though, turn to the other side of the book and let the adventure begin…!

—Editor